Secrets
of the
Steelpan

Secrets of the Steelpan

Unlocking the Secrets of the Science, Technology, Tuning and Operation of the Steelpan

Dr. Anthony Achong

Copyright © 2013 by Dr. Anthony Achong.

Library of Congress Control Number: 2013907942
ISBN: Softcover   978-1-4836-3484-5
               Ebook   978-1-4836-3485-2

All rights reserved. No part of this book may be reproduced or transmitted in any form or by any means, electronic or mechanical, including photocopying, recording, or by any information storage and retrieval system, without permission in writing from the copyright owner.

This book was printed in the United States of America.

Rev. date: 10/24/2013

To order additional copies of this book, contact:
Xlibris LLC
1-888-795-4274
www.Xlibris.com
Orders@Xlibris.com
133826

I dedicate this book to my wife, Dermarie
my children Tricia, Travis, Carlon, Ria
and my grandchildren
Zachary and Rhianon

CONTENTS

CHAPTER 1 33

Introduction 33

1.1 The Steelpan
1.2 A Brief History of the Author's Early Work
1.3 Naked Rhythm and a Short Imaginative History on the Pan and its Frequency Range as I see it!
1.4 Finding the Answers
1.5 Persons who Share a Deep Dedication to Pan
1.6 Naming the Instruments by Type and a Glimpse at its Beginning
1.7 On the Shoulders of Giants — Men who saw "Gems in the Steel"

CHAPTER 2 52

The Rawform — Preparation and Treatment 52

2.1 The Rawform
2.2 The Seams or Chimes
2.3 Steel Gauges
2.4 General Properties of low-carbon steel and stainless steel
2.5 Sinking: Indenting the Pan Face by Hammer Peening
2.6 Obliquity
2.7 Pan Making Process Control Schedule
2.8 Saturation
2.9 Residual Stress
2.10 Load Analysis of the Chime
2.10.1 Load Analysis of the Chime before Sinking
2.10.2 Compatibility
2.10.3 Equilibrium
3.10.4 Constitutive Laws
2.10.5 Load Analysis of the Chime after Sinking

2.10.6 Compatibility
2.10.7 Equilibrium
2.10.8 Constitutive Laws
2.10.9 Extension of the Equations to the Triple-Seamed Chime
2.11 Chime Rotation and Welded Chimes
2.12 Role of the Skirt in Maintaining Static and Dimensional Stability
2.13 Simple Experiments using Homemade Mini-Pans — Tin-Can experiments on a shoestring budget
2.14 Pan face with Cutout
2.15 Additional Degrees of Freedom: New modes with Cutout
2.16 Stress Loading on the Pan Assembly
2.17 Guidelines for Buckling Avoidance
2.18 Stress Corrosion Cracking (SCC)
2.19 Some Sections of the Pan Subjected to High Localized Stresses
2.20 Mechanical Failure
2.21 Control of SCC
2.22 A Brief Descriptive Introduction to Crystalline Structure and some Rudiments of Metallurgy
2.22.1. Crystal Structure
2.22.2. The Importance of Dislocations to Pan Making and Note Dynamics
2.23 Low Temperature Stress Relief Anneal — Burning
2.23.1 Eutectoid Reaction in Carbon Steel
2.23.2 Annealing
2.23.3 Low-Temperature Stress-Relief-Anneal for the Steelpan
2.24 Chroming
2.24.1 Effects of Coating on the material properties of notes
2.24.2 Negative effect of Chroming on Tonality
2.25 Powder Coating and some Negative Effects on Tonality
2.26 Nitriding

CHAPTER 3 107

Non-Linear Dynamical and Statical Analysis of Elastic Shell Structures on the Steelpan... 107

3.1 Introduction
3.2.1 Note Preparation and Dynamic Behaviour
3.2.2 Boundary Conditions, Internal Stresses and Advanced Tuning
3.3 Observations
3.4 Non-Linear Analysis
3.4.1 The Basic Shell Structure
3.4.2 Non-linear Shallow Shell Theory
3.5 Forced Oscillations and Stick Impacts
3.6 Internal Damping
3.7 Compressive and Thermal Stresses
3.7.1 Compressive in-plane Loading
3.7.2 Uniform Temperature Change

3.8 The Shape Function
3.9 Modified Dynamical Equations
3.10 Statical and Dynamical States
3.10.1 MDOF Solution of the Non-Linear Equations
3.10.2 General Solution Procedure
3.10.3 Definition of Functionals
3.10.4 The Static State
3.10.5 Static Force Distribution
3.10.6 The Shape Function, $Q(x)$
3.11 The Pan Jumbie
3.11.1 Discussion on the Static State
3.11.2 Case 1: Zero Compressive and Thermal Stresses
3.11.3 Case 2: Non-Zero Compressive and Thermal Stresses
3.12 The Dynamical State in MDOF Representation
3.12.1 The General Dynamical Equations
3.12.2 Quadratic Coupling Coefficients
3.12.2.1 Square-Term Coefficients
3.12.2.2 Cross-Term Coefficients
3.12.3 Cubic Coupling Coefficients
3.12 4 Small-displacement Modal Frequencies
3.13 Tuning the Pan with a Blowtorch
3.14 The History of a Note
3.15 Buckling
3.16 Ellipsoidal Notes

CHAPTER 4 151

The Steelpan as a System of Non-Linear Mode-Localized Oscillators: Theory, Simulations and Experiments 151

4.1 Mode Localization
4.2 Non-Linearities in other Musical Instruments
4.3 Scope of the Section
4.4 Time-Domain Analysis
4.4.1 Impact Phase
4.4.2 Free Vibration Phase
4.4.3 The 3-DOF Note —Key-note, Octave and Twelfth
4.5 Parametric Excitations and Internal Resonances
4.6 Multi Time-scale Analysis Applied to the Free Phase
4.7 Solution for 4-DOF Notes — Key-note, Octave, Twelfth and Second octave
4.7.1 Single Note with Quadratic and Cubic Non-linearities: Free Vibration
4.8 Signal Processing
4.8.1 Short Time Fourier Transform
4.8.2 STFT of Velocity and Displacement

4.9 Experimental and Computational Methods
4.10 Results and Discussion
4.10.1 Numerical and Experimental Results
4.10.2 B_4 Note
4.10.3 $F_4^{\#}$ Note
4.10.4 E_4^{b} Note
4.11 Effects of Stick Impact on Tonal Structure
4.12 Area of Confinement

CHAPTER 5 183

The Steelpan as a System of Non-Linear Mode-Localized Oscillators: Coupled Sub-Systems, Simulations and Experiments 183

5.1 Introduction
5.2 Theoretical Development
5.2.1 The Combinatorics and Fundamental Properties of the System
5.2.2 The Internote as a network of Linear Mechanical Filters
5.2.3 The Dynamics of the System
5.3 The Multi Time-scale Procedure
5.3.1 Theory
5.3.2 Case 1: Note-Note Interaction
5.3.2.1 Marshall Pairs
5.3.2.2 Solvability Equations
5.3.3 Case 2: Note-Skirt Interactions
5.4 Energy Exchanges between Domains
5.4.1 Note-Note Exchanges between Marshall Pairs
5.4.2 Note-Skirt Exchanges
5.5 Experimental and Computational Methods
5.5.1 General Procedure
5.5.2 Experimentally and Theoretically generated Tonal Structures
5.5.2.1 Note-Note coupling of a $\{E_4 ; E_5\}$ Pair: Playing the E_4 Note
5.5.2.2 Note-Note coupling of a $\{E_4 ; E_5\}$ Pair: Playing the E_5 Note
5.5.3 Note-Note Coupling on a Pair of A_4 and A_5 Tenor Notes
5.5.4 Note-Skirt Interaction on the Bass D_3
5.5.4.1 Forte Level
5.5.4.2 Piano Level
5.5.5 Note-Skirt Coupling on the $F_3^{\#}$ Note of a Double-Second Steelpan
5.6 Modal Frequencies on a Clamped-Free Cylindrical Skirt
5.7 Statistical Study of Coincidences
5.8 Partially Opened Skirts
5.9 Chapter Summary

CHAPTER 6 227

The Steelpan as a System of Non-linear Mode-Localized
Oscillators: the Inverse Problem — Parameter Estimation 227

6.1 Introduction
6.2. Theoretical Development
6.2.1. Phase Flow
6.2.2. Frequency-Amplitude Relation
6.3. Solution to the Inverse Problem
6.3.1. Observation Data
6.3.2. Inverse Parameter Value Problem.
6.3.3. The Mirror Functions and a New Signal Processing Technique
6.3.4. Minimization and Discretization
6.4. Simulation
6.5 Example Applications
6.5.1 General Remarks
6.5.2. The $F_4^{\#}$ Note on a Tenor Pan
6.5.3 $F_4^{\#}$ Simulation
6.5.4 The E_4^b Note
6.5.5 E_4^b Simulation
6.5.6 Optimizing the STFT
6.5.7 The Damping Coefficients
6.6 Comparison of Note Dynamics
6.7 Equal Damping and Summary of Analytical Technique
6.8 Confirmation of the Mode-Localization or Mode
    Confinement Phenomenon

CHAPTER 7 248

Parametric Excitations 248

7.1 Theoretical Basis
7.2 SDOF Solutions
7.3 Restoring Forces
7.4 Frequency-Amplitude Dependence
7.5 Drift
7.6 Parametric Excitations with a^n and $a_m a_n$ Amplitude
    Dependencies. Heterodyning
7.6.1 Parametric Excitations
7.6.2 Double Peaks in Pan Spectra
7.6.3 Combination Frequencies: Heterodyning
7.6.4 Further Checks and Confirmation
7.6.5 No Evidence for Frequency Splitting
7.7 Chapter Summary

CHAPTER 8 258

The SDOF Model of steelpan notes; Quality Factor, Hardening and Softening effects, Potential Wells and Frequency Shifts 258

    8.1 Introduction
    8.2 The Static State of the Note as a SDOF System
    8.3 Dynamical Equations
    8.3.1 Case I: Zero Compressive/Thermal Stress
    8.3.2 Case II: Non-zero Compressive/Thermal Stress
    8.4 Solving the SDOF Equation for the Coupling Parameters
    8.5 Buckling (Flapping) Analysis and the State of the Note at Rest
    8.5.1 Flapping Analysis
    8.5.2 Static State of the Note
    8.6. Note Deformation under Thermal/Compressive Stresses
    8.7 Frequency Shifts: Why is the bass pan more greatly affected by temperature and residual stress?
    8.8 Applying the Method to Small and Large Stress Changes
    8.8.1 Small Changes in Temperature and Compressive Stress
    8.8.2 The Method for Large Stress Changes
    8.9 Use of other Materials — Brass and Aluminum
    8.10 Potential Energy, Internal Forces, Note Geometries, Potential Wells
    8.10.1 Potential Energy
    8.10.2 Linear and Non-linear Internal Forces
    8.11 Response of the Note to External Excitation
    8.11.1 Linear Frequency Response
    8.11.2 The Transient Term
    8.11.3 The Steady State Term
    8.11.4 Power Relations and the Resonance Curve
    8.11.5 The Quality Factor, Q and Frequency Bandwidth, B
    8.11.6 Non-Linear Frequency, Hardening and Softening Springs
    8.12 Note Geometries, Potential Wells and Critical Points
    8.12.1 Critical Points and their Properties
    8.12.2 Potential Energy Function and Potential Wells
    8.12.3 Conditions for the existence of a Secondary Well and the Stability of Steelpan Notes
    8.13 Conditions on the Forces related to the Tonic and the Octave
    8.14 Numerical Computations
    8.15 Modeling Real Notes
    8.15.1 Shaping Functions and Note Shapes
    8.15.2 Parameters for the Modeled Potential Wells
    8.15.3 The Quiescent State
    8.15.4 Some Remarks on the Compressive Stresses

8.16 Modeled Notes
8.17 Comparison with the Euler Load on a Strip of Note Material
8.18 The Pre-stressed State, Mechanical Bias and De-localization
8.18.1 The Pre-stressed State
8.18.2 Mechanical Bias and De-localization
8.19 Effects of Hammer Marks and Small Indentations or Humps
8.20 The Frequency Characteristics of Modeled Notes
8.20.1 Small Amplitude Frequencies of Steel and Brass Notes: Curvature Effects
8.20.2 Spherical Form
8.20.3 Shaping Function $q(x) = 0.5\ k(1 + \cos(\pi (x-1))$
8.20.3.1 Observations: Quiescent State and System Stability
8.20.3.2 Effects due to Thermal/Compressive Stresses
8.20.4 Shaping Function $q(x) = k\ (1 - 2.4x^2 + 1.4x^3)$
8.20.4.1 Temperature Effects
8.20.4.2 Observation
8.21. More Shapes and more Results
8.22 Can the Note Frequency be made Amplitude Independent?
8.23 Special comments on Nipple Shaped Notes: The Pang

CHAPTER 9 353

Thermal and Compressive Stresses: Damping: Microstructural Control and Engineering Designs 353

9.1 Introduction
9.1.1 The Tuning Temperature
9.2 Dependence of Frequency on In-plane Stress
9.3 Dependence of Young's Modulus and Poisson's Ratio on Temperature
9.4 Including the Effects due to Direct Linear Expansion/Contraction (Scaling) of the Note
9.5. Experimental Observations
9.5.1 Thermal Effects on Frequency Spectra
9.5.1.1 The Tenor
9.5.1.2 The Bass
9.5.1.3 The Cello
9.5.1.4 General Observations
9.6 Dependence of Q-Factor, Mechanical Resistance and Damping Capacity on Temperature
9.6.1 Experimental Results
9.7 Damping Mechanisms
9.7.1 General Methods of Energy Dissipation
9.7.2 Magnetomechanical Damping (MMD)
9.8 Microstructural Control
9.9 The Vibrating Note at Elevated Temperatures

9.10 The Transition Period between First and Second Tuning
9.11 Engineering Designs
9.11.1 General design considerations
9.11.2 Notes Designed with Low Mechanical Bias
9.11.3 Intensity (Loudness) Problems with the Bass Notes and the "Wobbly Effect"
9.11.4 Notes Designed with High Mechanical Bias

CHAPTER 10 395

Mode Locking on the Non-Linear Notes of the Steelpan 395

10.1 Introduction
10.2. Modal Equations
10.3 Growth and Decay of Modal Amplitudes
10.4 Mode Locking
10.5 The Lock or Synchronous Mode
10.6 Analysis of Real and Simulated $F^{\#}_4$ and E_4 Notes
10.7 Mode Locking on the Pung Tone

CHAPTER 11 405

Vibrational Analyses of Mass Loaded Plates and Shallow Shells by the Receptance Method with Application to the Steelpan 405

11.1 Introduction
11.2. Receptance Method Applied to the Mass-Loading Problem
11.2.1 The Mass-Loaded Plate
11.3.1 The Elliptical Plate
11.3.2 Thin, Shallow Shells
11.3.3 The Powder-Coated Note
11.4 Approximate Mode Shape Determination
11.4.1 Fundamental Mode
11.4.2 Generalizing to Higher Modes
11.5 Experimental Data on the Steelpan
11.6 Chapter Summary

CHAPTER 12 422

Acoustics of the Steelpan 422

12.1 The Air Column semi-enclosed by the Skirt and Pan Face
12.2 Acoustic Terms and Standards of Reference
12.3 Sound Pressure and Sound Pressure Level (SPL)
12.4 Sound Intensity and Sound Intensity Level
12.5 Loudness

12.6 Bass Loss Problem
12.7 Total SPL for a number of Incoherent Sources
12.8 Measurement of Sound Level
12.9 Acoustical Radiation from the Steelpan
12.10 Acoustical Radiation from a Single Note
12.11 Acoustical Pressure at a remote point in the
     air medium—the Far Field
12.11.1 The Flat Radiator Embedded in a Rigid Surface
    (the Infinite Baffle)
12.11.2 The Model Note Embedded in a Rigid Surface radiating
    in Free Air
12.11.3 The Transition from Near Field to Far Field
12.11.4 Radiation Patterns for the Vibrating Note
12.11.5 Effects of Mode Shape on the Radiation Pattern —
    Shaded Source and the Absence of Minor Lobes
12.12 Effects of Finite Pan Face and Bottom Radiation;
     the Hass Effect or Precedence Effect
12.13 Mechanical Impedance of the Radiating Mass Loaded Note
12.14 Acoustic Power Output and Acoustic Efficiency
12.15 Acoustical Reaction Force and Acoustic Impedance in Free Air
12.16 Note Response to Continuous External Excitation
12.17 Transmission Losses across Note Boundaries
12.18 Equivalent Electrical Circuit
12.19 Some Numerical Examples on Model Notes
12.20 Acoustic Radiation Efficiency
12.20.1 Uncoated Notes
12.20.2 Paint-Coated (Powder-Coated) Notes
12.20.3 Chrome-Plated or Nickel-Plated Notes
12.20.4 Acoustic Efficiency of Notes
12.21 A Few Hints on Selecting Coating Formulation and Note Material
12.22 Using Horns or other Attachments to modify the
     Radiation Characteristics

CHAPTER 13 483

Stick-Note Impact — Impact Phase 483

13.1 Introduction
13.2 Rubber Compositions, Stick Aging and Tip Material Properties
13.3 Protective Chemicals
13.4 Impact Abrasion
13.5 Basic Stick-Note Interaction
13.5.1 General Remarks
13.5.2 Time-History of a Sounding Tone — the Two Phases
13.6 Static Analysis of the Stick
13.6.1 Stick Non-Linearity
13.6.2 Hysteresis

13.6.3 Measurement Methods
13.6.4 The P-index in Static Deformation
13.7 Statical Analysis of the Stick-Note System
13.7.1 Model Stick
13.7.2 The p-index in Compression and Restitution
13.8 Dynamical Analysis of the Stick-Note System
13.8.1 Analysis of the Linearized Form
13.8.2 Analysis of the Non-linear Form
13.9 Stick-Note Impact Dynamics
13.9.1 Origin of the Contact Force
13.9.2 The Stick-Note Model in the SDOF Representation
13.9.3 Impact Phase: SDOF (Single-mode)
13.9.3.1 Without Stick Memory Non-Linearity — No Hysteresis
13.9.3.2 With Stick Memory Non-linearity — Hysteresis
13.9.4 Free Vibration Phase: SDOF (Single-Mode)
13.9.5 Modeling the Hand Action in solving the Stick-Note Dynamic Equations
13.9.6 Soft-Stick Hard-Note Approximation
13.10 Examples of Modeled Stick-Note Impacts
13.11 Notes Impacted with Negligible Hand Action ($F_H = 0$)
13.11.1 The Reduced Equation
13.11.2 Contact Force in the Linearized Model
13.11.3 Non-linear Form for F_{max} with No Losses
13.11.4 Aging and Impact Force
13.11.5 Contact Times
13.11.6 Effects associated with Stick Dissipation
13.11.7 Initial Contact Force
13.11.8 Contact-width
13.11.9 Limits on the Linear Approximation
13.11.10 Non-linear Treatment of Contact Time
13.11.10.1 General Solution of the Tip Displacement-Time Problem
13.11.10.2 Case 1: Displacement Profile
13.11.10.3 Case 2: Contact Time from "make" to "break", without Hysteresis
13.11.10.4 Case 3: Contact Time at ½-Maximum Points, without Hysteresis
13.11.10.5 Case 4: Contact Time from "make" to "break", with Hysteresis
13.11.10.6 Case 5: Contact Time at ½-Maximum Points, with Hysteresis
13.12 Scattering of Stress Waves in the Stick Tip and Shank
13.12.1 A Simplified Model
13.12.2. Refraction and Reflection
13.12.3 Effective Tip Size Reduction
13.12.4 Optimum Design Criterion
13.12.5 Design Examples
13.12.6 Recommendations

13.13 The Coefficient of Restitution (COR) of Stick Tips
13.13.1 What is the COR?
13.13.2 The COR Equation by Energy Balance
13.13.2.1 General Nature of the approach
13.13.2.2 Hysteretic Losses
13.13.2.3 Mechanical Work
13.13.2.4 Shank Absorption
13.13.2.5 Energy-Balance Equation
13.14 Wrapped Sticks
13.14.1 Basic Ideas on the Wrapped Stick
13.14.2 Single Layer Stretch-Fitted or Force-Fitted Tip
13.14.3 The Basic Multi-layer Wrap
13.14.4 Hitting a Local Hump or Depression on the Note
13.14.5 The Crisscross Wrap
13.14.6. Feel and Responsiveness
13.14.7 Wrapped Stick with a Felt or other Lossy Overlay
13.15 Contact Force Analysis of the Wrapped Stick
13.15.1 Introduction
13.15.2 The Contact Area
13.15.3 Pressure Distribution
13.15.4 General Impact Dynamics with Pre-Stress and
   Hand Action Included
13.15.5 Details of the Hand Action and Stick Retrieval— Advanced
   and Delayed Stick Retrieval
13.15.6 Solutions of the Integral $\int f_H dw$; Advanced Retrieval and
   Delayed Retrieval
13.15.7 The Compression and Restitution Formulas
13.15.8 The Stick Compression Formula
13.15.9 The Stick Restitution Formula
13.15.10 Inclusion of Absorption Mats for Experimental purposes
13.16 Solutions for the Stick Compression Formula
13.16.1 Solution Methods
13.16.2 Impact Force
13.16.3 Effective and Dynamic Tip Stiffness
13.16.4 A Softening Effect Discovered on the Wrapped Sticks
13.16.5 Contact Time for Normal and Wrapped Tips no Hysteresis
   with $r_{ms} = 0$ and $E_{SA} = 0$
13.16.6 Contact Time for Normal and Wrapped Tips with Hysteresis,
   for $r_{ms} = 0$ and $E_{SA} = 0$
13.17 Numerical Modeling of Stick-Note Impacts
13.17.1 Numerical Solutions Using Closed-form Equations
13.17.2 Numerical Solutions Using the General ODE
13.17.2.1 Hand Action on the Tenor
13.17.2.2 Numerical Modeling of Stick-Note impacts on the Tenor
13.17.2.3 Excitation of the Marginal Notes: Effective Tip
   Radius Reduction

13.17.2.4 Numerical Modeling of Stick-Note impacts on the Guitar and Cello Pans
13.17.2.5 Numerical Modeling of Stick-Note impacts on the Bass Pan
13.18 General COR Formula for all Sticks
13.18.1 Energy Balance Method and Velocity Method
13.18.2 Comparison of Methods
13.18.3 Equivalence of the Two COR Equations
13.19 Dependence of COR on Elastic Modulus, Pre-stress and Impact Velocity — Effect on the "Nuances of Touch".
13.20 The Inclusion of Mechanical Resistance, Residual Compression, Shank Absorption and Lossy Overlay
13.21 Experimental Determination of COR
13.21.1 My 'Swinging Stick Method' and the Swinging Stick COR Formula
13.21.2 Approximate formula and Simple Stick Tip COR Meter
13.21.3 COR Values for an Assortment of Tips
13.22 Tactile Feedback and Impact Force
13.22.1 Feedback — Tactile, Auditory and Visual
13.22.2 Impact Force and Hand Control
13.22.3 Simple Formula Combining Rebound Angle and Contact Force Ratio
13.23 Contact Pressure Distribution in Impact Dynamics
13.23.1 Condition for use of the Statical Contact Pressure Distribution Formula
13.23.2 Time-dependent Contact Pressure Distribution
13.24 MDOF Analysis of the Stick-Note Contact Phase
13.24.1 Generalization of the Pressure Distribution Function
13.24.2 A Quick Comparison between SDOF and MDOF
13.24.3 Modal Equivalent Mass
13.24.4 The Impact Equations in the MDOF Representation
13.24.5 The Stick-Note Impact Function describing the 'Player's Action'
13.24.6 Mode Emphasis and De-emphasis by Control of the Impact Point — The Panist making use of the Stick-Note Impact Function
13.24.7 Assigning values to the Impact Function $S(m,r,\phi)$
13.25 Spectral Distribution of the Contact Force — the Primary Forces generated by Impact
13.25.1 General Aspects of the Problem
13.25.2 The Fourier Transform
13.25.3 Application to the Impact Problem
13.25.4 Improved Formulation and Dead Sticks
13.25.5 Forces due to Mechanical Resistance
13.26 Effect of Hand Action F_H on the Contact Force Spectrum

13.27 Contact Force Produced by the ½-Sine Force Function
13.27.1 General Application to the Impacts on all Pans
13.27.2 The Tenor
13.27.3 Dead Stick versus Good Stick on the Tenor
13.27.4 Marginal Notes and the Marginal Zone
13.27.5 The Cello
13.27.6 Marginal Notes; the Cello and its Accent
13.27.7 The Bass
13.27.8 Marginal Notes—Bass
13.27.9 Playing the Tenor with a Bass Stick
13.27.10 The Unused Region of the Contact Force Spectrum below the Bass Note Frequencies
13.27.11 Summary of Frequency Band-limiting on all Pans
13.27.12 Extending the Musical Range of Steelpans
13.28 Stick Contact Noise and Tip Mechanical Resistance
13.28.1 Origin of the Stick Contact Noise
13.28.2 Stick Contact Noise (SCN) or Stick-Note Clap (SNC)
13.28.3 Some Physical Considerations —The Tenor Stick Example
13.28.4 Solution to the Stick-Note Clap Problem
13.29 Dynamical Equations for the Two Types of Vibrations Produced by Stick-Note Contact
13.29.1 The Major Sound —Engineering Formulas
13.29.2 The Minor Sound — Stick-Note Clap
13.29.3 Effect of note material losses
13.30 Contact-Width Wavelength Band-Limiting
13.30.1 The Basic Nature of Wavelength Band-Limiting
13.30.2 The Generalized Wavelength of a Spatially Periodic Function
13.30.3 Generalized Wavelength on the Note Surface
13.31 The Condition for Suppressing Unwanted High Frequency Modes
13.32 The Spatial and Temporal Conditions for Initial Mode Excitation and Choice of Sticks
13.32.1 The Guiding Principles
13.32.2 Use of Other Objects for Note Impacts
13.32.3 The Very Lossy, Dead Stick
13.33 Why is Band-Limiting Essential on the Steelpan?
13.34 Playing the Roll — The Tremolando
13.35 Strumming
13.36 Playing Notes with Sympathetic Interaction
13.37 A Standard Measure for Tip Compression (TC)
13.37.1 The Classification of Sticks
13.37.2 Matching a Pair of Sticks
13.37.3 The Measure
13.37.4 Application of TC Values

CHAPTER 14 789

INSIDE PAN TUNING — FREQUENCY RANGE, METHODS
OF TUNING, PRINCIPLES OF STEELPAN OPERATION,
Tuning Scenarios and the Tonal Structure of Steelpan Notes 789

14.1 Introduction
14.2 Definitions I
14.3 Definitions II
14.3.1 Pythagorean Intonation
14.3.2 Just Intonation
14.3.3 Equal Temperament
14.3.4 The Fifth and Third above the Octave
14.4 The Frequency Range of Pans
14.5 Standard Note Layout on the Pan
14.6 Musical Range and the Distribution of Notes: Singles, Pairs and Triples on the Standard Pans
14.7 Musical Range and the Distribution of Notes: Singles, Pairs and Triples on the Invaders C-Pan Tenor
14.8 Going beyond $E^b{}_7$ — Dream or Reality
14.9 More on the Singles, Pairs and Triples
14.10 Note Distributions and Space Limitations
4.10.1 Note Distribution on the Standard Tenor and the Invaders C-Pan Tenor
14.10.2 Space Limitations on the Low "C" Tenor
14.11 Mechanical Filters on the Pan face — The Network or Plexus Concept
14.11.1 Filter Definition
14.11.2 The Filter Networks on the Pan
14.11.3 Extending the Concepts to the Stick-Note Impact
14.12 Unlocking the Secret behind the Process of Blocking
14.12.1 Setting the Characteristic Impedance of the Internote in the Neighborhood of the Note
14.12.2 Employing Grooves
14.12.3 Employing Bore Holes
14.12.4 Effect of Bore Holes and Grooves on Note-Note Coupling
14.12.5 Impedance Requirement for Blocking on the Internote — The Blocking Condition
14.12.6 Mass Loading on the Internote — not recommended. Mass Loading acceptable on the Skirt
14.12.7 Blocking Problems on Completely Press-formed Pan Face plus Notes
14.13 Vibration Processes at the Chime
14.14 Note Placements and Note-Note Coupling across the pan face
14.14.1 Transmission across the Pan face
14.14.2 "Hiding" as a Mechanism for Isolating Notes
14.15 More on Blocking

14.16 Return to the Tenors — Note Placement Rule
14.17 On New Pan Types
14.18 The Development of Tones that Define the Pan
14.19 Gradation of Tones
14.19.1 Introduction
14.19.2 Energy Loss and Detuning
14.19.3 Detuning Parameters
14.19.4 Summary of Factors that Determine Pitch and Timbre
14.19.5 Pitch Setting Rules: Stretching and Compressing the Octave and Twelfth on Single Notes
14.20 Experimental and Simulation Results
14.20.1 Sample Note and its Simulation
14.20.2 The Sampled $E_4^{\flat}$ on a Real Pan and its Simulation
14.20.3 Varying the magnitude of the detuning parameter
14.21 The Image Note
14.21.1 Note and Image, Example 1 — AM and FM Profiles
14.21.2 Note and Image, Example 2 — With Trill and Pitch Glides or Glissando
14.22 Definition and Tuning Possibilities with the Image Note
14.22.1 Definition
14.22.2 Tuning Possibilities
14.22.3 A New Pan Combination — The Tenor-Pair
14.24 The "Pung tone"
14.24.1 Introduction
14.24.2 A Typical Pung Tone on a Real Pan and some Simulations
14.24.3 Definition of the Pung Tone
14.25 The Fundamental Law of the Steelpan, the Steelpan Law of Ratios and the $5/4^{ths}$-Law — the Wonderful Magic of Pan Tuning
14.25.1 The Identity of the True Note and The Fundamental law of the Steelpan
14.25.2 Introducing the Five-Fourths $5/4^{ths}$- Law of the Steelpan
14.25.3 Following a Path consistent with the actions of the Good Pan Maker
14.25.4 A Simple Rotation Device for Deriving the $5/4^{ths}$-Law — Symmetry Considerations
14.25.5 Setting up a Perturbational Framework that solves the Problem
14.25.6 The Steelpan Law of Ratios
14.25.7 Our Goal — The $5/4^{ths}$-Law
14.25.8 The Connection between the $5/4^{ths}$-Law and Mode-Localization or Mode Confinement — the Theory of the Pan in a Nutshell
14.25.9 Some Important Questions and Comments
14.26 Using the Third on the Bass Notes
14.26.1 The $9/8^{ths}$-Rule
14.26.2 Benefits of using the Third on the Bass
14.27 Marking and Forming the Notes

14.27.1 Non-Ellipsoidal (Ovoid) Note Shapes
14.27.2 Ellipsoidal Note Shapes on Elliptical Planforms
14.28 Tuning the Key-note, Octave and Fifth or Third;
Using the Pan Maker's Formula
14.29 Energy Exchanges, Frequency Pulling, Reflected Impedances and Modulations — another Journey into the Deep Mysteries of the Pan.
14.29.1 Energy Exchanges
14.29.2 Frequency Pulling and Reflected (or Coupled) Impedances
14.29.3 Further Insight on the Frequency and Amplitude Modulations
14.30 Typical Tuning Scenarios in Musical Space: The Amplitude and Frequency Profiles of the Pan
14.30.1 Typical Tuning Scenarios
14.30.2 Musical Space and Flavor
14.30.3 A 'Busy Note' — Good AM and FM
14.31 Four Types of Note Settings
14.32 Setting the Timbre by altering the α-parameters
14.33 Tuning to Produce Strong Octave and Twelfth
14.34 Tuning by Altering the Compressive Stresses
14.35 Setting the Boundary Conditions — The Spring Supports
14.36 Forming and Tuning Grooveless Notes
14.37 Forming and Tuning the Low-End Pans
14.38 Tuning Marshall Pairs on the Tenor and Medium Range Pans: Weak and Strong Marshall Pairs
14.39 Tuning the Triples (Whole Notes) on the Three Cello
14.40 Tuning weak Marshall Pairs on the Bass
14.41 Summary of Tuning Rules and Practice: Single Notes and Marshall Pairs
14.42 Specifications for the Tuned State of a Note
14.43 Notes of Quality for a "Competition Grade" Pan
14.43.1 Complex Tuning and Advanced Tuning
14.43.2 Maximizing the Accuracy of Partials and Attaining Quality
14.44 Excitation of the Steelpan by an External Agency and the role played by Blocking
14.45 Voicing
14.45.1 Symptoms of a Pan-Stick Combination in need of Voicing
14.45.2 Voicing the Sticks
14.45.3 Accent
14.46 Balancing
14.46.1 Definition I, for the Individual Pan
14.46.2 Definition II for the Steel Orchestra
14.47 Blending
14.48 Detailing

CHAPTER 15 1021

The Chorus Effect in Steel Orchestras 1021

15.1 Introduction
15.2 The Parameters
15.2.1 Number of Sections N_s
15.2.2 Number (N_v) of Voices in a Section
15.2.3 Maximum detuning
15.2.4 AM and FM Modulations
15.2.5 Tremolo, Trill (and Vibrato)
15.2.6 Spread in Delay Time (milliseconds, ms)
15.2.7 Spectral magnitude of key-note and partials

CHAPTER 16 1033

Harshness Produced by Orchestral Steelpan Tones 1033

16.1 Introduction
16.2 The Human Auditory System – The Ear
16.3. Steelpan Spectra
16.4. Combination Tones and Aural Harmonics
16.5. Chapter Summary

CHAPTER 17 1041

The G-Pan — My Critical View in Defense of the Steelpan 1041

17.1 The G-Pan Patent Abstract
17.2 Preamble
17.3 On Patents
17.4 Traditional Prior Art
17.5 My Critical View
17.6 Musical Range—Stick-Note Problem
17.7 G-Pan Note Covers
17.8 Coupling on the Pan Face
17.9 Tuning, Blending and the Gradation of Tone
17.10 Orchestral use of the G-Pan
17.11 Some Major Technical Errors and Difficulties
17.12 Resonators and the non-existent 'Plague' reported in the patent
17.13 The Confusion
17.14 What is a Drum?
17.15 The Correct Historical Setting of the Steelpan
17.16 My Further Views
17.17 Claims on the use of Tension — while Compressive Stress is totally ignored
17.18 Ring of Bolts and All That

17.19 The Ubiquitous Pan Jumbie — Structural Engineering in Traditional Art
17.20 The Pan Jumbie and Non-local Effects on the Pan Face
17.21 Removing the Skirt is Folly
17.22 A Host of Pan Jumbies
17.23 A Victim of its Own Complexity

CHAPTER 18 1119

EXOTIC EFFECTS ON THE STEELPAN — Jump Phenomenon, Hopf Bifurcation and Chaos 1119

18.1 Excitation of the Non-Linear Steelpan Note System
18.2 System Equations
18.2.1 Analysis of 2-Mode Systems (with 2:1 Resonances)
18.3 Steady-State Periodic Orbits
18.4 Bifurcation
18.5 Linear Stability Analysis
18.6 Numerical Results: Jump and Hopf Instabilities
18.7 Real Pan Results
18.8 Results from Electronic Simulations
18.9 The Experimental Results
18.9.1 2-Mode system: Hopf Bifurcation and Jump Phenomena
18.10 Chaos
18.10.1 Analytical Methods
18.10.2 Definitions
18.11 Route to Chaos
18.12 Chaotic Behaviour of the 2-Mode System
18.13 Simulated Partially Tuned Note (Single Mode — Simple Tuning)
18.13.1 Numerical Experiments and Results
18.13.2 Experimental Results for the Electronically Simulated Partially Tuned Note

PREFACE

Inspiration and Purpose

The mathematical and physical sciences (mathematics and physics) are especially distinguished by the rigor of their operations; I can therefore find no better setting for the Science of the Steelpan, the National Instrument of my homeland, Trinidad and Tobago. The special status of the Steelpan demands that the best of rigor be applied to its analysis. As you read this book, don't be offended by the mathematical insertions, pass over them if they are 'too hard' because there is something about the pan for everyone on each line. I have tried to give a good balance between the musical and the mathematical aspects. Perhaps there are, hopefully in the minority, some players and pan makers who may settle for a less than perfect steelpan. But the pan maker who goes about his task with earnest, corrects his errors, and with dedication, hammer peens, stress relieves and finely tunes his pans is richly rewarded with a finished instrument that will find high appreciation from the top musicians. Such an instrument emphasizes those subtleties sought after by the loftiest of musicians. So too, in unlocking those secrets held close to the chest of the master pan makers, the physicists/mathematician must go to great analytical depths to find answers to questions on the steelpan. If steelpans were simple instruments this book would have been much shorter and my task would have been long completed.

To those who may view the scientific rigor of this book as 'overkill,' I offer no apologies inasmuch as makers of this instrument demand no excuses for their musical and practical brilliance in producing these fine instruments. Whether in the execution of a masterful piece of music or in the analysis of the musical instrument producing this music, there is never any 'overkill' when dealing with the steelpan! The people of Trinidad and Tobago highly prize their National Instrument; being one of them, and having immersed myself so deeply into this instrument, I know and understand the feeling of delight when the *'inner lights'* of *'The Pan'* are revealed! In my life's work, as revealed in this book, I have forced 'The Pan' to reveal its deepest secrets. Even while just a little boy, I held the vision that 'The Pan' is an *'Instrument of Praise.'* I hold that vision today and it has been my *'guiding light*!'

For there it all began in the early 1950s as a little boy, standing bare-footed in short pants, my face at the level of the instrument mounted on stands, listening to the sounds of a *'Ping Pong'* played by my elder sister Andrea, on the front yard of our home at 32 Drayton Street, San Fernando, Trinidad, staring at the raised notes on the metal pan face and wondering *'how does it work?'*

So as you set about to read this book, remember, that steelpans offer an interesting challenge to physicists like myself because musicians are sensitive to quite subtle effects in instrument performance. In fact the musical tones, technically, *the acoustical radiation, which is all that this musical instrument really is about, plays a minor role in the dynamics of the notes.* This may come as a surprise, even mind-boggling, but it is true. But I must speak truly of this instrument; for while the acoustical energy produced by a sounding note is just a small fraction of the total vibrational energy, which allows for the above remark, the complexity and subtlety of its tones are very clearly expressed.

> *For while The Pan is relatively muted it is not tone deaf and we are its ears! The listener must attune his ears to gain full appreciation of the marvelous beauty of the Sound of Pan!*

In order to fully explain the features of this musical instrument that are important to players and pan makers, physical measurements must be made with high precision and theoretical analyses must include high order effects which are sometimes deeply mathematical. That's the nature of this Pan instrument so *don't blame me*!

This book is a response to a call made by the instrument itself, a call uttered by the wonderful tones of her voice — I couldn't help but give her an answer!

During the preparation of the manuscripts I recall saying to myself on seeing that Chapter 13 on stick-note impacts was approaching sixty pages, 'Why am I spending so much time here for an event that lasts just a few milliseconds at most?' But the *'pan magnet'* (not the *'Pan Jumbie'* which we shall meet later), kept me writing, putting on record all that I knew about the pan, the sticks and the action of the player, not wanting to leave anything out.

Who would have thought that it is possible to not only write down equations that describe how the pan works but also equations that say what you can and cannot do with just a rubber-tipped stick in your hand? And who would have thought that the art of playing the pan could be captured in a set of mathematical formulas that describe the action of the player and the response of the instrument? **But the real results of the player's action, delivered live, in the warmth of the music, will always exceed anything that anyone can put down on paper!**

For reading these pages I will reward you with some little secrets that may help you to understand the construction of this book and to learn something about the author that only readers of this book should know. As I grew up, I supplemented my school education with much more extensive learning outside of the classroom. At age nine, I was severely injured in an accidental fall and hospitalized for six weeks. While bedridden, my father brought me copies of his AIEE/IRE (IEEE) journals because he knew I loved to read them. I developed a love for engineering and the sciences through the reading of these journals. As a young boy, I dreamt about the contents of this book by day and by night. But in later years my other dreams and interests in physics and mathematics occupied my thoughts to the point where for many years I worked out, only in my mind, many of the equations that appear in this book. I quickly learnt that I could solve problems better in my mind than on paper! After years of thought, the physics of the pan became so fundamental in my mind that as I closely watched and listened to pans being played in the local 'pan yard' I would explain to myself immediately how each tone was generated even the non-musical ones. Because I took so much of my knowledge as merely '*physics common-sense,*' it is possible for me to omit some of my pan discoveries from this publication. But these omissions are only of the explicit kind. Implicitly they are contained in the writings of this book or in my other publications because they guide my thoughts. But don't draw the conclusion that I take things for granted on matters concerning the pan, certainly not.

To help you understand why I have analytically taken the pan and sticks apart, dissected them and forced them to reveal their secrets, I give the same reason why at five, on our verandah overlooking Drayton Street, I completely dismantled my parents 'box' camera, an Eastman Kodak, Brownie. I also give you further bits of information; just three bits. Firstly, I did these things out of *pure curiosity*! I had to find out what went on in that black box — the Brownie camera! I knew it produced 'pictures' but how? Secondly, I dislike having to solve the same problem twice unless by a second method. This is why I offer you, the reader, alternative solutions to some of the more difficult equations in this book. The added benefit is that it gives you a better understanding of my techniques. In my student years, if my examiners were aware of this 'dislike' it would have been somewhat unpleasant for me. In any event I would have devised an original solution to the problem set before me as I often did in my O-Level, A-Level and university examinations. The fact is that in my student and professional life I never liked to follow a textbook! I prefer to work things out myself! Thirdly, as a self-taught student of A-Level physics, pure mathematics and applied mathematics, and later a Secondary School Teacher and University Lecturer, I feared being asked a question I could not answer. For my A-Levels, completed in $1\frac{1}{2}$ years of intense study, I went far beyond the requirements of the London A-Level syllabuses, developing as I went along, techniques that I could use in problem solving. Being self-taught, after I had exhausted all the questions in mathematics and physics in my textbooks and those available at the San Fernando, Carnegie Free Library, I had to prepare examination questions to test myself (!). The rate at which I devoured those questions (over 5000 in 1½ years) forced me to use brown paper grocery bags to write my solutions! My father also brought me rolls of used graph paper from his workplace. To be sure of what I was doing I needed some way of deciding when a question I set myself contained sufficient information to make a solution possible. Using a nice logical procedure that I developed, I worked out a simple logarithmic formula that did the job. I was elated but contained my joy. I did all my expressions of joy at Church!

Those teenage years were rewarding because they allowed me the opportunity to discover some other marvelous things before I sat my A-Level examinations. Among them, and by using the mathematical notion of *congruence* (an advanced mathematical method in Modular Arithmetic, credited to 'the shrewdest of men' Leonhard Euler (1707-1783) and to the 'prince of mathematicians' Carl Friedrich Gauss, 1777-1855), that was certainly not on the syllabus, I produced extensions for Wilson's Theorem (on prime numbers) and one of Euler's theorems, both in the *Theory of Numbers*. In my youthful enthusiasm I did not care about publishing these results but much later I published the former but the single manuscript for the latter was among items 'lost' during shipment (in fact the box containing the manuscript 'disappeared' at the port, a common occurrence at sea ports I believe). Sadly, my dislike for repeating a solution took its toll. I have no regrets. But my first transistorized power amplifier built around age thirteen was among the lost items — that one, I surely missed!

I received my early scientific tutelage, particularly in radio electronics (tube radios that is), from my father, Anthony Zachariah Cosma Achong, and learned the importance of good arithmetic from my mother, Louise Achong, a good math teacher and first-rate seamstress, skills she carried all her adult life. It would therefore have pleased them both to know that in my analyses of the steelpan, I chose the scientific and mathematical approach to demonstrate the arguments that expose the subtle workings of the steelpan. I could have chosen to simply request that the reader take the results on trust but, for this wonderful instrument, my approach gives to the reader, examples of the way mathematicians obtain their results. These techniques can be used by readers to further their own work on the instrument.

I grew up in a home full of musical instruments and pulsing with the sound of music. At an early age my mother tried to convince me that I should take music and piano lessons like my older siblings. But after seeing that the music teacher would tap you on your knuckles with a ruler if you raised your knuckles too high on the keyboard I decided against it! If my mother were alive today she would have been pleased with this book. In fact as she herself had reminded me, the Ping Pong that held my attention on the front yard of 32 Drayton Street was one of the instruments belonging to the steelband, *Silver Lining,* which was founded in our home in the early 1950s but moved to a nearby location about 100 yards (meters) away when the space which the band occupied was needed for a woodworking shop. I thank Mr. J. J. Connell, the master joiner in the woodworking shop, for rescuing me after my 'first fall' from the balcony at 32 Drayton St.

Years later, after I was awarded a post-graduate scholarship to pursue a Masters Degree in mathematics, I learnt from my assigned supervisor that according to university stipulations, having pursued my first degree in Special Physics, I would be required to take a one year program in mathematics and sit a qualifying examination. With my excellent mathematics record, the basis for my scholarship, (math professor Campbell held that I was his best ever student) I felt this to be a waste of time since, for me, the qualifying exam would only test what I already knew (I went on to demonstrate this on the spot to my supervisor). The stipulation held sway, so I switched back to physics. Having built and operated a Raman Spectrometer for my B.Sc. final year project, I proposed as my post-graduate research project, the building of the first-ever Raman Laser. I proved theoretically to the physics department that my proposal was physically feasible despite it being entirely novel. However the department had doubts. (Today, Raman Lasers can be found in any good optical research laboratory.) I therefore switched to Astronomy where I did my Ph.D. In fact on the day I graduated, Professor Orb, Head of the mathematics department thought that I was receiving my Ph.D. in mathematics! I never left the subject! My own post-graduate (M.Phil. and Ph.D.) students did work in Astronomy, Materials Science and Medical Physics while I continued my exploits and publications in other areas which included Electronics, Particles and Fields and the Steelpan (obviously). I honor my father by keeping Electronics my passionate hobby.

So enjoy yourself as you read this book for it is true to say that I found greater enjoyment writing this book than I found in completing it. I could have written more than eighteen chapters but as my grandson Zachary (then 9 years old) said to me one day, *'Grandpa! When are you going to finish this book? Would I have to finish it for you?'* I got the message! Zachary has spent his entire life seeing me daily on my computer writing about The Pan! There is always more to write about this wonderful instrument, but on my grandson's urging, I close the computer files on this book so that you can open the pages to read them while I open a new file on a topic that just came to my mind — 'Thematics in the Performing Steelpan Orchestra.' I am tempted to tell you what it is all about but I leave it to your imagination! Ok, just a hint; think of *'Pan Ramajay.'* How do you analyze that? Think of what we share as a group when we sit together to listen to a steel orchestra performing classical music and calypso music. Are there differences? What goes on within the orchestra to produce these differences? You cannot simply search through the music sheets for all the answers, certainly not the major ones! If the answers were all there you wouldn't need a steelband! You could easily stay at home and read the sheets! Certainly …

A. Achong

CHAPTER 1

Introduction

1.1 The Steelpan

The Steelpan or Pan is a musical instrument of the percussion family, with rigid vibrators (Achong 1996a, Blades 1975 and Fletcher and Rossing 1991).

Musical categorization: The Steelpan is a percussion instrument in the idiophone class under the category shells.

Definition of idiophone: an idiophone is an instrument that produces sound from the substance of the instrument itself when struck, shaken, scraped or rubbed without the use of strings or membranes. Most percussion instruments that are not drums are idiophones. Examples are bells, cymbals, rattles, steelpans and xylophones.

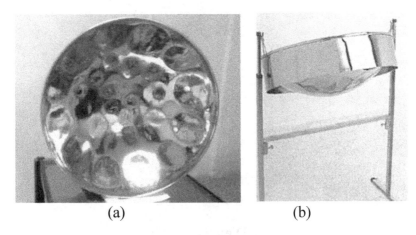

Fig. 1.1. Chrome-plated tenor pan photographed by the author (May, 2011). Distorted images of the author appear on some of the notes in panel (a). The pan mounted in the playing position is shown in panel (b).

The steelpan comes in a variety of musical ranges from the bass (G_1(48.999 Hz) to G_3(196.00 Hz)), which may consist of up to nine pans in a set, to the single tenor (D_4 (293.66 Hz) to F_6 (1396.9 Hz)). This instrument is constructed from cylindrical steel drums having one end open, by indenting the circular plate on the closed end to form the concave pan face (see Figure 1.1). On a special note, just as my personality is embedded in the pages of this book, my images (by reflection) are smeared over the notes of the pan in Figure 1.1 (a) — yes, I am there, but the pan dominates the picture as it ought. On the pan face, the slightly domed areas are the 'notes,' arranged circumferentially or set in the central region. The shaping and tuning of the instrument is done by hammer peening. The elastic parameters and residual stresses vary across the pan face because of the variations in the hammer impacts made by the pan maker during the peening process. The tempering process that follows the initial shaping, reduces these inhomogeneities as well as the magnitude of these induced stresses, and presents a more mechanically homogeneous surface for the notes on the instrument.

The notes, together with the rest of the pan face and the cylindrical 'skirt,' form a complex composite shell structure. This complexity exists not only in terms of the geometrical structure but also in the stress distribution over the entire pan.

For the bass, the skirt length measures the full length of the original steel drum rawform. The tenor steelpan with its shorter skirt length has as many as 28 notes arranged on the pan face while the bass may have as few as two notes on each pan. The notes are played with soft rubber-tipped sticks. On the 'bore' pan, small holes are drilled along the traditional boundary of each note to produce a brilliant and more expressive tone. The 'normal' pans do not contain this feature.

Fig. 1.2. A section of the Invaders Steel Orchestra in an outdoor setting showing an array of excellent pans tuned by Master Tuner Bertrand 'Birch' Kellman. The Four Cello featured in the foreground is played by the very talented panist Desiree Myers.

The picture in Figure 1.2 captures an assortment of beautifully crafted and exceptionally tuned steelpans found in the Invaders Steel Orchestra of Trinidad. These instruments were tuned by the skillful Bertrand 'Birch' Kellman. Dominating this picture, in almost 'golden' appearance is a Four Cello which, when played by the accomplished panist Desiree Myers, produces splashes of color that are truly golden.

Figure 1.3 shows a Herman Guppy production, as beautiful in tone as it is in craftsmanship. The notes on this Double Second are powerful for their size — an indication of good preparation, careful blocking and excellent tuning. Shown in Figures 1.4 and 1.5 are two steel orchestras performing outdoors in Pan Trinbago's 'Pan in the Countryside, 2011.'

Fig. 1.3. This Double Second tuned by the accomplished Master Tuner Herman Guppy belongs to the TTEC Tropical Angel Harps Steel Orchestra with Phillip Morris as resident tuner.

Fig. 1.4. The St. Margaret's Boys AC Steel Orchestra 'with a girl.' Pans tuned by Jimmy Phillips. This band contains a number of talented young players and an array of good instruments that form a well balanced band. See Section 13.26 for a short but interesting comment.

Fig. 1.5. The Tamana Pioneers Steel Orchestra with pans tuned by Herman Guppy. This band contains some gifted young players such as the tenor panist to the front left and the bass panist on the right. This is an excellent sounding band with good tonality and balance.

1.2 A Brief History of the Author's Early Work

Although as a youth the steelpan occupied my thoughts and I developed the concept of *'shape vibration'* (that's what I first called it) at an early age, I carried out much of the theoretical work on the physics of the steelpan in the 1980s but I did not begin to publish this work until my seminal paper of 1992 (Achong 1992). As I gazed in wonder at the dome shaped structures of the notes on the steelpan and the thought of 'shape vibration' entered my mind, little did I know that it was the beginning of the correct path to a full understanding of the steelpan! It took a while and years passed before I discovered in 1986 the *non-linear mode confinement* which lies at the heart of steelpan note dynamics. This discovery came as I puzzled over the curious appearance on some of my early computer displays of note surface velocity versus time envelopes. At that time I still relied on my Commodore 64 computer (I preferred it to my home-built 'IBM compatible'; hopefully readers remember these devices, if only by name!). Do not underestimate the 1 MHz C64 computer with its 64 Kilobyte of memory — no match you say for today's 3 GHz, 4 Gigabyte computers with over a Terabyte of hard drive memory! I did marvelous things with the C64, even calculated the first 255 digits of pi (π) using this C64 machine which I still keep in working order: (I have a couple of them, with Z80 co-processors and floppy drives — the only drives you will find with built-in processors)!

Perhaps it was fortuitous that I was using the C64 and not one of today's fast and powerful systems with all the fancy, easy-to-use plotting software like those that I used in plotting the graphs in this book. It was during that struggle, using *Basic* and M*achine Language routines*, to get good plots on-screen and on hard-copy printout that I noticed the tell-tale features of *non-linear modal coupling* in the vibrational modes of the pan notes. Sitting before the computer monitor, I had to wait for the plots of note surface velocity amplitudes to slowly develop on the monitor screen on this slow (by today's standards) machine. As I watched the plots grow across the screen my eyes followed the up-and-down movements (modulations) on the velocity envelopes. What I saw, for the first time, on October 12, 1986 was truly startling!

- *The two modes, key-note and octave, were exchanging energy between themselves!* They were coupled!
- It was quite clear to me that since these two modes, key-note and octave were vibrating at different frequencies the coupling mechanism must necessarily be *non-linear*.
- *If the keynote and the octave on a note are coupled by energy exchanges then, I reasoned, they must 'stay together!'*
- I further reasoned that in order to do this, these two modes must be **confined to a well defined area within the traditional note. This *confinement* therefore made it possible for a number of notes to be placed on the same pan face!**
- So there it was — **the underlying operating principle of the steelpan** revealed for the first time on October 12, 1986!
- Did I shout *eureka*? No: I jumped up and thanked my Lord and Maker! Yet I was in no rush to publish. When you find something precious or valuable you like to look at it, turn it around, squeeze it, or whatever, before you show it to someone else! It's natural!

Because I owe so much to the C64 I think it fitting for me to let readers know that all the computations in the paper, Achong (1995), including the minimizations, were carried out on the C64! Before I leave this trusty computing machine I should also let readers know that my early modeling of the steelpan notes with all the non-linearities and the Bessel functions for mode shapes ran on the C64 (with its 5¼ inch floppy drive for 'mass storage'!) at the snail's pace of *one simulation per day* (literally 24 hours for the C64 to print out the results)! Waiting 24 hours was never a 'hand-wringing' ordeal instead it was a day of great expectation. Today my computer can do these things in a flash! I leave it to the readers to decide which gave me the greater pleasure.

In my life as a physicist I have learnt the necessity for caution when making public announcements on any new discovery. Therefore, it was very natural for me to await my subsequent development of the theoretical and mathematical aspects of the pan dynamics before I 'went public.' There were no existing theory of the steelpan at that time but I understood quite clearly that I couldn't disclose my findings to the pan makers until I could relate my scientific methods to the methods and practices of the pan artisans. The two methods complement each other to the point where it is true to say that the beautiful mathematical structure of pan dynamics is matched by the profoundly beautiful sounds of pan music.

But why, my readers may ask, did I not publish my discovery of mode confinement on the steelpan first? Why did I not make full mention of it in my seminal paper of 1992? And why was its full publication preceded by the papers of 1995 and 1996a? Did I withhold publication of the discovery for 10 years simply to 'look at it, turn it around, and squeeze it or whatever'? This is not the only instance in which I withheld publication of my work for a period spanning many years! This book is about unlocking the secrets of the steelpan so I must share this little secret with my readers. Back then (1986 to 1992) I knew that the work I had done on the steelpan would require publication in the best journal available that deals with sound and vibration and that the papers would be 'unusually mathematical' for a musical instrument. I also knew that I was walking along a lonely road on the *Physics of the Steelpan*! I comforted myself with the understanding that as long as the path remained lonely, I could hold on to my newly found 'secret.' Therefore, when the thoughts of publishing entered my mind, I adopted the strategy of drawing the attention of the best researchers in sound and vibration to my work before I laid out my findings on the Pan. I thought that by having some critical 'onlookers' as I did my 'walk' through the physics, the journey could be made more worthwhile! I therefore looked for a current problem on the vibration of plates that was still awaiting a full solution. I tackled the problem of vibrating elliptical plates on elastic supports and I made it more difficult by attaching point and ring mass loading to the plates. That was my 1995 paper in the *Journal of Sound and Vibration* which was submitted for publication in June 1993. This received much attention and a supporting *Letter to the Editor*. In those days it took about two years (sometimes more) after submission for a paper to appear in print! Next, I had to introduce the steelpan so in 1994 I wrote another paper (Achong 1996a) on mass loaded plates and shells with application to the steelpan. This was immediately followed by a sequel of three papers strictly on the non-linear nature of the steelpan dynamics and mode confinement. I should mention that my paper *'Mode locking on the non-linear notes of the steelpan'* was completely written in *one day* but published, unmodified, except for updated referencing, seven years later in 2003!

- *The incubation of a scientific idea is a very important aspect of scientific research; Secrecy is another.*

During the years 1986 to 1993 I also found that the areas of mode confinement formed dynamically within the traditional notes were really ellipsoidal shells on the surface of the notes. I therefore set about working on the theory of non-linear vibration of these ellipsoidal shells. This kind of thing is hard to do in full generality but I stuck to my habit of doing all the work by myself without looking for previous publications in the field. I prefer to think about what I have to do rather than what others have done. Some readers may consider this approach as a waste of time since you can get along faster by making use of previously published results. Things are a bit different with me! I prefer to work things out myself, then when I am ready to publish, scoop up all the available literature that bear some relation to my work. This method has paid off for me since my satisfaction comes mainly from *doing* the research; *to me, publication is secondary.*

- *The well known adage 'publish or perish' is to me, more like a 'schoolmaster's whip' than a source of motivation.*

To be sure, my approach opened up the window for me to discover and to rediscover a number of mathematical techniques and methods. In fact I wrote a paper (unpublished) on one of these methods, only to discover afterwards on searching the literature that the method was first formulated in 1945 but lay dormant for many years. Today the method is well known and much used, I refer to the analytical method of 'Wavelet Analysis' which I rediscovered in my attempts to 'speed up' my computations on that 'not to be forgotten' C64. In fact I had given my method exactly the same name and did so not by coincidence but because of the graphical form of my sampling function. I found that I could greatly reduce computation time in my spectral analysis of steelpan tones by storing as a 'look-up table' a sampling function in the form of a wavelet which I expanded or contracted to vary the analyzing frequency. I saw this as a neat idea. After it became clear to me that it was just a rediscovery, I switched to the Short Time Fourier Transform method instead. I don't consider that a waste of time!

The requirement on referencing is however very important because having found a solution for the non-linear vibration problem on the ellipsoidal shells the full solution turned out to be so long and, as expected, did not yield closed-form solutions except in reduced form as the ellipsoid approached the shape of a spheroid, that on presenting the Achong 1999 paper for publication in 1998, I used the work done by Connor (1962) and Grossman et al. (1969) on spherical shells as the basis. I used my own work as a guide in formulating a workable adaptation of the spherical shell results to the deformed shell. I was driven by this approach because I felt my work, being so mathematical was moving too far away from the pan makers and tuners to whom I must finally present my findings. I decided that by going from the spherical shell to the deformed shell I could include the tuning process of *shaping the notes*, giving the pan tuner some (implicit) role to play in the paper. It worked! I have maintained this approach in the present book. My original unpublished work on the ellipsoidal notes later guided me to the $5/4^{ths}$ *Law* on steelpans that you will read about later.

The very observant reader of my publications during the period, 1996 to 1999 will notice that the theory, on which the 1996 to 1998 papers were based, appeared in 1999! This reverse order I found necessary because the steelpan, while recognized worldwide today, was not well known among researchers in the field of sound and vibration. I first used a somewhat 'generic' approach for the non-linear behavior of the instrument in order to focus on the musical instrument itself. The 1999 paper then served to inform readers of those papers, on the secure analytical foundation on which the pan note dynamics rest. In this book I have reversed the order!

My first pan was a 'discard!' I am not ashamed to admit this fact, for I know of no pan maker who began his career with a good *'Competition Grade'* pan (more about that classification later). Having a 'discard' meant that I had to tune this pan myself! What a good opportunity to learn the trade! Some of my tests on that first pan destroyed some of the notes with holes and entire notes cut out to prove basic principles — a necessary price to pay for discovery. My computer room became my *Steelpan Research Laboratory* (the former President of Pan Trinbago, Owen Serrette, found out about my laboratory and at a Pan Trinbago Meeting in Curepe, Trinidad, he told me, 'You can't hide!'). Later, my webpage carried the name — *stelpanresearch.com* (don't try it on the internet it is temporarily closed at the time of writing). In former years, visitors to my webpage could play my *'web pan'* — the first playable online pan with authentic pan tones. It's a long story, too long for these pages.

I must admit that initially I began to document my work in book form as I felt no compelling reason to publish the work as research papers! Over the years however, I have published a wealth of information on the steelpan, detailing the theory of operation of the instrument and the dynamics of the vibrating note subjected to stick impacts. Useful information for the Pan Maker can be obtained from my special publication *The Pan Makers' Handbook* (1999a), A. Achong, *distributed by* Pan Trinbago. A good reference source is *The Proceedings of the International Conference on the Science and Technology of the Steelpan (ICSTS 2000)*, A. Achong, (Ed.), Trinidad and Tobago Government Printery (*distributed by* NIHERST). In my opinion however, I believe that my Lectures and Seminars on the Steelpan were more interesting and informative than my writings and I gave many of those publicly (as I always told my university physics students, my lectures are far better than my lecture notes!). I say this because the direct interaction stimulated me to transfer to the audience or class much more of what I knew and it gave me more lasting joy. I recall the satisfaction that I saw on the faces of tuners and pan makers and most of all I thank my audiences for the 'nods of appreciation' that I received especially from the older, more experienced members of the audience. Whenever I saw the 'nod' I knew that I had reached deeply into the mind and thoughts of the listener — like sweet music!

In all my writings on the Steelpan I have tried to state the final results of the analyses in a manner that can be directly related to what the pan maker, tuner or player does. Sometimes this was done at the expense of greater generality. For example when a note is being tuned, no tuner purposely shapes the note first into the form of a spherical cap then distorts it into an ellipsoid or some other final shape. But among the millions of notes that pan makers have tuned, it is just possible that a note was tuned that way! Yet, for simplicity in explaining the shaping process and in order to preserve, in an explicit form, some clearly obvious geometrical aspects of the note such as the rise of the 'dome', I chose this procedure for my analyses. Mathematically, and practically, it does not matter what shape the note started out with, it is the final form that matters provided that in shaping the note the proper boundary conditions and material properties are set. ***There is no unique 'must use' 3-dimensional note shape known only to the pan maker!*** This is one of the now *'unlocked secrets'* of pan tuning that I am disclosing here. I have seen a patent application that relied on copies of the shapes of notes tuned by well-known tuners! Imagine that! At best the idea is laughable.

1.3 Naked Rhythm and a Short Imaginative History on the Pan and it Frequency Range as I see it!

My Definition: **Naked Rhythm** is that powerful driving force of *'fully exposed musical expressions'* that empowers people of any culture to invent and produce for themselves instruments of music that fully expresses their feelings, desires and struggles.

The steelpan is a perfect example of a product of Naked Rhythm.

The highest note on the 'High D Tenor' steelpan the $F^{\#}_6$ corresponds to the highest notes normally played on the Clarinet, the Oboe and the Mandolin. The lowest note on the 'Nine Bass' pan, the A_1, sits above the lowest notes on the Bass Tuba and the Bass Viol. The overlap of the musical range found on the pan instruments is similar to that found among wind instruments and string instruments.

Color combinations is what it is all about on this instrument that evolved from a desire by the people on the Caribbean Island of Trinidad in their desire to generate '***Naked Rhythm***' on the town streets and in the backyards of their homes. Even in its precursor, the '***Tamboo Bamboo***' and the *concept changing* '***Biscuit Tin,***' this Naked Rhythm of *'fully exposed musical expressions'* had become a significant driving force. The spontaneity of the Tamboo Bamboo and its players jostling on the roadway for a good spot to 'tap' their bamboo and this lone character standing there while the others moved on just to enjoy that more pleasing sound from that 'good spot.' 'I shall return to it!' he shouts then moves on! Then who was it that picked up that empty bin when his bamboo ruptured? He beat that bin with whatever next came to hand. Beating it into shape and tone, not knowing that he had taken the first steps on a long journey that continues to this day. The road to Pan — that which was once a steel drum now beaten and transformed into a pan — had begun and as pan lives, there can be no sweeter tones that those that can be expressed on this instrument when played to expose and reveal their nakedness in true calypso rhythm, classical music, church music and panorama vibes. In Pan Ramajay this musical nakedness is the issue, addressed by the tenors, argued to the fullest by the guitars and to every question posed, the cello and bass provide an answer. Play on! Play on! Says the biscuit tin beater!

1.4 Finding the Answers

These are the questions: 'What is the Pan?' How does it work? Exactly what is it? I found the answers not by asking any pan maker, tuner or panist but by posing these questions to the Pan itself! Exactly what are you? How do you work? I know this seems like a strange thing to be doing but if you immerse yourself deeply into anything, that thing soon acquires a personality of its own. But these questions, personal in nature, were not asked in words but in 'deeds.' My questions were all prefaced with 'Show me how!' I let the pan itself show me how it worked, what it is and even how it must have come about! The Pan sitting in a corner is dumb! You can't get an answer that way. You must play the notes, play its skirt, change its surroundings (ambient temperature and the like), excite it like nobody had done before, force or 'squeeze' the answers out of it. I learnt to be patient. Many times the answers were buried in a lot of noise. When for example I visited a pan yard (almost always incognito) I had to ignore the sound of the music (and that is very hard) in order to catch that particular sound or set of tones that carried the information I was seeking. Many times also, not even I knew what I was seeking; then something happened, something new, something strange or something that I knew was missing from previous sounds that I heard. My readers should not ask me to define clearly for them what these sounds were. They were often very subtle and always difficult to put into words. The pan does not speak in words so how could I! Did I say 'speak' yes I did for we shall soon learn that the Pan has a *voice* in fact many voices! The Pan also comes in different '*accents*!'

While the Pan 'told' me about itself, the two pan makers, Bertie and Randolph, with whom I held private discussions, told me some of what they did to the pan. They were the modern 'biscuit tin' beaters. I met Bertie very late in life after I had completed the bulk of my work but I met Randolph earlier. I begin the next Section with Randolph.

1.5 Persons who Share a Deep Dedication to Pan

I enjoyed the collaboration with former pan maker, tuner, arranger and band leader Randolph Leroy Thomas, Inventor of the *Grooveless Pan*. He was a good friend and a dedicated family man with an unmatched community spirit. His steelband '*Moods*' was a band that I could walk through freely during practice sessions while listening for those '*hard to describe things*', beside the music, that allowed me to write so much about these Pan instruments. With other bands I stood unnoticed on the outskirts but with an equally attentive ear — I listened, but very rarely was it the music I was seeking! If you want to learn all aspects of the pan you must attend the practice sessions. Listening only to the well-rehearsed pieces at the final performance is not enough. Players in the bands I visited may not recall seeing me in their pan yard because it was my policy to know the instruments not the players. I felt welcome at The Steel Orchestra, Courts Sound Specialists of Laventille, a steelband managed by Pan Trinbago's Secretary Richard Forteau and led by his son, Rudo Forteau. It was through Richard Forteau that I gained entry and walked the hallowed halls of Pan Trinbago. By invitation therefore, I fell into the company of real friends of the steelpan — Former President Arnim Smith, Former President Patrick Arnold, Keith Diaz, Melville Bryan, Fitzroy Henry, Allan Augustus, Trevor Reid, Diane DeCuruew-Ridley, Cecilia Zena Moore, Helen Scanterbury-James, Beverly Ramsey-Moore ....

I thank Mrs. Maureen Manchouck and her staff at NIHERST especially Kala Sookhram and Althea Maund; of Pan Trinbago, Patrick Arnold, Richard Forteau, Melville Bryan and Fitzroy Henry for the opportunities they afforded me to present my work to Pan Makers and Tuners by way of Seminars and Conferences. I appreciate the contacts, some brief, others lengthy, that I made with Tuners — the entire company of men and women who attended the 1999 2-Day Steelpan Seminars at the Holiday Inn (now Capital Plaza), Port of Spain and in Tobago, among them, the gifted adjudicator and educator, Merle Albino-de Coteau, Members of the Steelpan Tuner's Guild of TT, Bertrand Kellman, Tony Slater, Phillip Morris, Jimmy Phillips, Denzil Fernandez, Michael 'Scobie' Joseph ....

On Bertie Marshall, I have not said enough in my paper dedicated to him (Achong 2000d) for I understand only too well his tough stance on pan preparation. We have never disagreed on anything related to the Steelpan! Together, we share a mutual interest in the Steelpan. The 'Great Man', one of the 'Giants', is a source of wisdom and the holder of a superb pair of ears for pan tones and its music. He made a great impression on me and still does. Readers will read more about Bertie in this book. (Please note that some of the references to Bertie made in this book were written before his passing in 2012. I prefer to leave them in their original form.)

1.6 Naming the Instruments by Type and a Glimpse at its Beginning

In the Pan family there are many members differing by names chosen to define musical range and purpose. While the range of the tenor pan corresponds better with the human soprano voice than the human tenor voice and there is a recent attempt to rename the tenor pan the '*soprano pan*' (and many have already done so thus adding to the *non-standardization problem*) the present author feels no urging to follow this move. This simple attempt at name changing does not even attempt to rename the 'tenor bass' (the only oxymoron found among pans) as the '*baritone pan*,' which should follow from the same reasoning. The *guitar pan,* formerly the *cuatro pan,* received it name because of its early use principally for strumming. Lacking any formal standardization procedure, I have chosen to use throughout this work, the *de facto* (traditional) standard names such as the '*tenor pan*' and '*tenor bass*'. Each musical instrument has its own history of development whether we know it fully or not.

If there is to be standardization, then the names to be adopted should be the original native names (not used in this work) such as '*Ping Pong*' for example, that make no mention of other instruments or the human voice. Pan has evolved over the years with improvements in tonality, musical range and utility. This could be a genuine reason for renaming the instruments but at the same time, Pan should not be encumbered by unnecessary baggage. The unpublished works of pan historian and friend, the late Oscar 'Bogart' Pile (1922-2008), should be collated and published. His work and others from the early pan pioneers will shed much light on this matter.

It was from Oscar Pile that I learnt about Tanty Willie (see Achong 2000d) and the old lorry chassis in her backyard. It was on Tanty Willie's old lorry chassis that the young Oscar and his musically minded friends met and by choosing their preferred section of the chassis, beat out 'sounds of steel' thereby creating perhaps the first '*improvised*' Steel Orchestra — I call it the 'Willie Band'! There is so much to be said about '*improvisation*' in pan music. This is only a 'hint' of what the broader picture of 'Pan Beginnings' really looked like. Don't despise the early beginning of the Steelpan because I see today young men and women, on television, beating out music on garbage cans as did the early pan pioneers of the 1930s. Oscar Pile was the only historian from whom I learnt 'first hand' anything clear and understandable about the history of Pan — too many versions of the 'beginning' only brought confusion, to my mind anyway.

I cannot cover the history of the Steelpan in a book such as this but I include just enough of its history to place this work in its proper perspective and to credit those who worked in developing the instrument on which this book focuses. I was born in the town of San Fernando, Trinidad, but except for the steelbands located in my home town (now a City), I lack sufficient information on the development of the steelpan in the Southern areas of the Island of Trinidad to allow me to write a commentary worthy of the efforts in the South. I regret this unfortunate omission. As a youth I often visited the yard of the close-to-home *Free French Steelband* and recall some other well known South bands such as *Bataan* the 'base' for 'pan man' Horace 'Nickady' Nicholas, *Hatters* which together with *Broadway Syncopators* were the 'base' for George 'Bigger' Braithwaite, *Cavaliers* and *Southern Marines*. My only active participation in steelpan music did however, take place in my community band, when as a boy, (without my parent's knowledge or consent) I played the *'iron'* in the *Melody Makers Steel Orchestra*, formerly located at the corner of Marryat Street and Coffee Street, San Fernando. As I recall, the then 'captain' of the band was an excellent bass player, tuner and pan maker. I recall also on one Carnival Day as the band, Melody Makers with me on one of the irons which I personally painted in the band colors two days earlier, was about to enter Skinners Park, a man entered the band, took away my iron, leaving me virtually 'locked out' because in those day you could not go on stage unless you were a player. So I lost my only chance of gaining the credit of appearing 'on stage' with a Steel Orchestra! Since then I have always been part of the audience.

There are two elderly gentlemen of the North, 'well known' in the early days of the steelpan development and whom I have chosen to represent the early *'pan men'* — Kirton 'Eddie Boom' Moore of *The Renegades Steel Orchestra* and Hugh 'Dasheen' Hackett of *The Invaders Steel Orchestra*. 'Eddie Boom' was a bass player in his band while 'Dasheen' was a *Doo Doop* (2- or 3-note pan) player. I wish to add, especially for the older readers who may have witnessed the early days of the steelpan development, the following bits of information gleaned from Moore and Hackett; it was from the grounds of the *Boyack and McKenzie Company*, in the area of *Tugs and Lighters* in the town of Cocorite located on the North Western Coasts of Trinidad that many of the early pan makers located in and around the Capital City of Port of Spain obtained their steel drums. In my 1999 Steelpan Seminar delivered in Port of Spain to pan makers and tuners, I used this aspect of the history of Pan as a preface to my lectures! These 'drum collectors' counted it a joy to lift the drums, full or empty, over fences and for long distances, such was their love and commitment to the instrument. The statute of limitation on these activities has long expired so it is safe to disclose these 'Pan secrets' and I can reassure 'Dasheen' that Magistrate Chin is no longer on the Bench!

1.7 On the Shoulders of Giants — those who saw 'Gems in Steel'

Little did 'Eddie Boom' and 'Dasheen' know that their shoulders which bore these steel drums and the shoulders of all the men such as George 'Bigger' Braithwaite whose broad shoulders took his instrument along High Street, Coffee Street, unto Royal Road and back, carried the mighty weight of a national treasure, a future National Instrument — an instrument destined to give joy and pride to an emerging nation of musically minded people — in Trinidad we say *'it's music in we blood*!'

The development and form of the musical instrument described in this book rests on the shoulders of many dedicated men who saw *'gems in steel.'* They all stand tall but some are *'Giants*!' In this company of 'Giants' one finds, in no special order: Victor 'Totee' Wilson, Carlton 'Zigilly' Barrow, Sonny Roach, George 'Bigger' Braithwaite, Neville Jules, Anthony 'Tony' Williams, Bertrand 'Bertie' Marshall, Belgrave Bonaparte, Elliot 'Ellie' Mannette, Lincoln Noel, Rudolph 'Hammer' Charles, Bertrand 'Birch' Kellman, Herman Guppy, Lloyd Gay, …. Wilson's 1939 four-note *'Ping Pong'* (the name he gave to the instrument) can be considered the *'Model-T'* of Pan; not because of any claim to being the first but for what followed — as the Ford Model-T applied a stamp to a transportation concept, all the early Tenor Pans were called by the name 'Ping Pong.'

There is another class of Giants without which the Steelpan would not have become the popular musical instrument that it is today. I refer to the *Giants among Panists*. Portions of this book rest on the shoulders of these Giants because, with pairs of sticks, they have explored, at the deepest level, the musical capabilities of the Steelpan. I have derived much inspiration from the musical works and achievements of these great men. In this Class of Giants one finds: Sonny Roach, Belgrave Bonaparte, Emmanuel 'Cobo Jack' Riley, Len 'Boogsie' Sharpe, Ken 'Professor' Philmore, Robert 'Robbie' Greenidge, Ray Holman, Bertrand 'Birch' Kellman, Darren Sheppard, Liam Teague, Clyde 'Lightning' George, 'Eddie Boom' (the bassist), …. Sonny Roach, the winner of the 1946

Island-wide (Trinidad) Ping Pong competition (beating the indefatigable Ellie Mannette into second place), was tuner and panist — a brilliant fellow!

There are the 'Giants' among Band Leaders or Captains — Oscar 'The Peace Maker' Pile (*Casablanca*), Belgrave Bonaparte (*Southern Symphony*, where *Chords* first entered Pan Music on a sound, professional basis), Bertie Marshall (*Highlanders,* a band significant for its *many innovations*), Rudolph Charles (*Desperadoes*) ....

There are the 'Giants' among Arrangers — Clive Bradley (*Desperadoes*), Jit Samaroo (*Renegades*)**,** Dr. Pat Bishop (*Exodus, Desperadoes*), Pelham Goddard (*Invaders, Exodus*), Neville Jules (*Trinidad All Stars*), Leon 'Smooth' Edwards (*Trinidad All Stars*) ....

The description of Oscar Pile as 'The Peace Maker' is my personal assessment of this 'Giant' based on my discussions with him, and his description of his involvement in the events that took place in the early days of Pan. Oscar Pile was a personal friend, my senior.

CHAPTER 2

The Rawform — Preparation and Treatment

2.1 The Rawform

Two basic styles of drums are used in the classical steelpan making process:

(i) those with non-removable head (*tight head*), with permanently attached top and bottom covers and
(ii) the removable head (*open head*), in which the top head or cover is secured by means of a separate closing ring with either a bolted or lever-locking closure.

These drums are factory made with expanded rolling hoops in the drum body that stiffen the cylinder and provide a low friction surface for rolling filled containers. Steel drums manufactured specifically for steelpan construction follow the basic designs for drums built for industrial use. Details are given in Figure 2.1. Steel thickness and metal quality do not form part of the current standard.

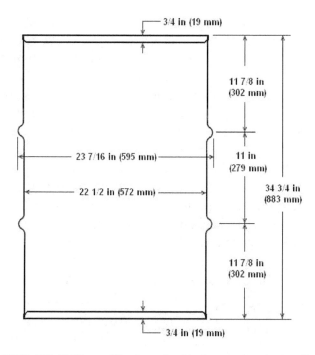

Fig. 2.1. ANSI MH2 1997 specifications for the Conventional 55-gallon drum.

2.2 The Seams or Chimes

The seam or chime that form the rim of the pan needs to be looked at in some detail because it is important in maintaining static and dynamic stability to the instrument and is often a source of problems in the pan-making process.

The drum seaming operation requires the cylindrical skirt, a top head blank, a bottom head blank and a series of forming stations for preparing and finishing the seams. Some details are given in Figure 2.2. The seaming apparatus includes a seaming chuck that receives the blank top or bottom head and the end of the cylindrical skirt. The chuck includes an anvil portion and a peripheral lower anvil wall. The seaming apparatus also includes a seaming roll having a seaming surface for engaging the peripheral curl of the skirt end in a seaming operation to compress the peripheral curl against the peripheral flange of the top or bottom head against the lower anvil wall of the seaming chuck.

During forming the bottom chime is sealed with a non-hardening seaming compound, and applied in conformance to standard manufacturing quality procedures, to ensure no leakage. Seaming compound is omitted for double seam/welded bottom chimes. It is the bottom head that is used in pan making so that when the indented pan is annealed (*burned*) the sealing compound is destroyed by oxidation increasing the possibility of a loose seam. This is a well-known problem that arises from the intensity of the hammer-peening process of *sinking*. The triple-seamed chime is advantageous in this respect as it reduces the possibility of seam-loosening. Whenever this problem arises the final tuning of some outer pan notes may be impossible. The solution is for the pan maker to weld the seam preferably before sinking or to rework the chime after burning. The latter solution requires a forming station with matching chuck and roll.

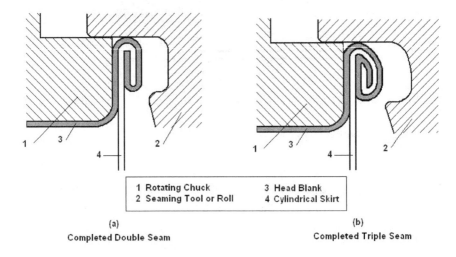

Fig. 2.2. Cross-section of the finishing chuck and roll on (a) Double-seamed chime and (b) Triple-seamed chime. The Seaming Tool is shown as it is being withdrawn from the finished chime.

UN specifications require the bottom chime be triple seamed, *or* either double-seamed or double-seamed *and* welded, if the double seam drum meets UN test criteria. These test criteria involve a drop test of the water-filled drum from a height of 1.8 m (for 55 Gal drums) unto a hard surface with impact point on the chime that is more likely to fail.

2.3 Steel Gauges

Table 2.1. Gauge No. and Sheet Steel Thicknesses

Gauge no.	Minimum Thickness	
	in.	mm.
12	0.0946	2.40
16	0.0533	1.35
18	0.0428	1.09
19	0.0378	0.960
20	0.0324	0.823
22	0.0269	0.683
24	0.0209	0.531
26	0.0159	0.404
28	0.0129	0.328
29	0.0115	0.292

Most drums used for pan making are made of commercial-grade cold-rolled, low-carbon, sheet steel. Over the years, the cost and weight of steel drums have been reduced owing to technological advances, such as the introduction of the triple-seam chime in the early 1980s. Improvements in cold-rolled steel chemistry, surface quality, and gauge control have also contributed to a reduction in cost and weight. Until the early 1960s, most tight-head drums were made of steel 0.0428 in. (1.1 mm) thick (formerly 18-gauge). These were particularly good times for the local steelpan makers of Trinidad for better instruments are produced from the lower gauge steel. There has since been a shift to a lighter-gauge drum with a steel thickness of 0.043 inch (1.1 mm) in the top and bottom heads and 0.030 in. (0.8 mm) in the body (formerly known as the 20/18 drum, now marked as 1.1/.8/1.1). Currently, 55-gal (208 L) drums of 0.0378-in. (1.0-mm) steel thickness are being manufactured to transport hazardous materials, and 55-gal drums of 0.030-in. (0.8-mm) thickness or thinner are used for non-hazardous materials. Both types have been used in the steelpan making industry in Trinidad and Tobago and other Caribbean islands. The drums designed to carry hazardous materials are preferred for their greater thicknesses despite the dangers posed by recycled drums of this type. At the time of writing, there is a move to curtail the use of drums used for carrying hazardous materials.

Low-carbon steels by definition contain less carbon than other steels (tool steel for example) and are inherently easier to cold-form due to their soft and ductile nature.

2.4 General Properties of low-carbon steel and stainless steel

2.4.1 Low-carbon steel and stainless steel

Table 2.2. General Properties of Low-Carbon and Stainless Steels

Properties	Carbon Steels	Stainless Steels
Density (1000 kg/m^3)	7.7	7.75-8.1
Elastic Modulus (GPa)	190-210	190-210
Poisson's Ratio	0.27-0.3	0.27-0.3
Thermal Expansion (10^{-6}/K)	11-16.6	9.0-20.7
Thermal Conductivity (W/m-K)	24.3-65.2	11.2-36.7
Specific Heat (J/kg-K)	450-2081	420-500
Tensile Strength (MPa)	276-1882	515-827
Yield Strength (MPa)	186-758	207-552
Percent Elongation (%)	10-32	12-40
Hardness (Brinell 3000kg)	86-388	137-595
Carbon Content (wt% C)	0.05 – 0.3	—

For good cold-forming properties, the low-carbon steel used in steelpan making should have carbon content around 0.12 wt% C and not outside the range (0.1 to 0.15) wt% C. *The instrument's performance is more tolerant of a higher carbon content (within the range) than a lower one, particularly if it falls below the range; in which case tuning the inner notes on the tenor will be very difficult.*

Table 2.2 lists the typical properties of two varieties of steels at room temperature (25°C). Although low-carbon steel is the most widely used material in pan making, stainless steel is included in the table for purpose of comparison. The wide ranges of ultimate tensile strength, yield strength, and hardness are largely due to different heat treatment conditions. The surface hardness can be improved by a process called carburizing, which involves heating the alloys in a carbon-rich atmosphere.

2.4.2 Table of Constants

Table 2.3 Table of Constants

Material	Density kg·m^{-3} ρ	Young's Modulus Gpa $\equiv 10^9$ N·m^{-2} Y	Poisson's Ratio ν	Velocity of sound in the material m·s^{-1} c	Characteristic Impedance x10^6 rayls ρc	Thermal Coefficient of Linear Expansion x 10^{-6} °C^{-1} α_T
Steel	7700	207	0.29	6100	47	11 - 13
Nickel	8800	210	0.31	5850	51.5	13
Brass	8500	104	0.37	4700	40	18.7
Aluminum	2700	68.3	0.34	6300	17	20 –25
Rubber (soft)	920	(8 – 50) x10^{-4}	0.4 – 0.5	570 – 1440	0.53 – 1.32	–
Air (20°C)	1.21	–	–	343	0.000415	–

While low-carbon steel is the common metal used in steelpan production, other metals such as brass and aluminum have been tried. In addition nickel is used in the nickel plating and chroming of the instruments. The material constants for these metals, rubber (for stick making) and air (which is the medium into which the sounds of the instrument are propagated) are shown in Table 2.3. These constants will be used in the development of various stages of the work in this book. The definitions of these constants will be given as required in the text.

2.5 Sinking: Indenting the Pan Face by Hammer Peening

The classical process of steelpan production begins with the indentation of the top face of a '55-gallon' steel drum by hammer peening. The process involves the use of a heavy ball-peen hammer used to subject the drumhead to repeated impacts. The hammer velocity is such that each impact produces plastic deformation of the surface, thereby inducing a compressive stress. The surface to be indented is traversed at a rate and in such a manner as to give the required coverage and form to the final pan face. The process is usually applied manually and is therefore subject to limitations of control. Mechanized impactors employing an air pressure gun allows for more repeatable impact characteristics.

The ball-peen or engineer's hammer is a type of peening hammer used in metalworking and is distinguished from 'point-peen', 'claw', and 'chisel-peen' hammers by having a hemispherical head. The original function of this hammer was to 'peen' riveted or welded material so that it will exhibit the same *elastic* behavior as the surrounding material. Specifically, striking the metal imparts a compressive stress at the point of impact, which results in strain hardening of that area. Strain hardening raises the elastic limit of a material into the plastic range without affecting its ultimate strength. A strain-hardened material will not deform under the same low stresses as a non-hardened material. Most metals can be 'worked' by such methods until they lose all of their ductile characteristics and become strong but brittle. During sinking the pan maker is careful to avoid overworking the pan face into this brittle state. For this reason, greater care must be exercised with mechanized hammers.

Each hammer blow that strikes the drumhead surface imparts to the surface a noticeable indentation. These indentations create residual compressive stresses at and slightly beneath the surface, which enable the pan face to better resist any fatigue or stress corrosion that it might be exposed to once in service. This pre-stressing is an added bonus in the sinking process because it is known that cracks will not initiate or propagate in a compressively stressed zone. This increases the life of the final pan. The specific properties of the residual compressive stress layer are dependent on the specific hammer peening parameters and the tensile strength of the steel being peened. In fact, as will be shown in later chapters, residual stresses are important in the dynamical behavior and stability of this musical instrument. Despite the great importance of the peening process in pan making, the techniques of residual stress management is still largely an art.

2.6 Obliquity

In order to achieve the desired form and depth of indentation during sinking, and to avoid the occurrence of *flapping* (or *buckling*) which is possible on thin 'over-worked' material under conditions of high compressive stress, hammer peening (see Figure2.3) is executed with much '*obliquity*' ('*stretching*' or '*scratching*' action). In addition to the stretching across the impacted face under plastic deformation, there is a redistribution of in-plane stresses. Proper *stress-relief annealing* reduces this problem.

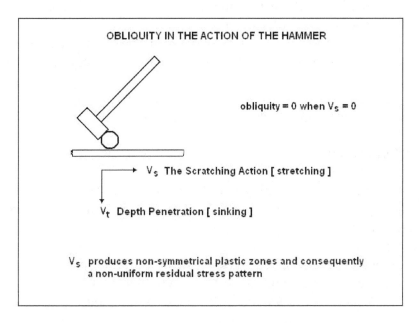

Fig. 2.3. Obliquity in hammer peening action, showing the two components of hammer velocity.

While it is possible, as the history of the pan certainly shows, to produce high quality pan instruments without detailed metallurgical information on the rawform material, it will not be cost-effective to try this on a commercial basis. The final state of the prepared instrument and its dynamical behavior when played depends on the stress and heat treatment history of the material. For these reasons, the *Pan Making Process Control Schedule* should include the following details:

2.7 Pan Making Process Control Schedule

1. Knowledge of the carbon content and metallurgical condition of the rawform material.
2. Any pre-treatment, stress relief, heat treatments or surface finishing performed on the item.
3. The sketch showing preferred (could be standard) note layout.
4. Note templates with preferred shapes and sizes.
5. The hammer material, weight, metallurgical condition (hardness), diameter and profile.
6. Pan face thickness profile.
7. Coverage. Nearly 100% of the pan face should be hammer peened thereby ensuring that the residual stress distribution becomes more uniform.
8. Details of any post-sinking treatment, e.g. annealing and surface finishing such as chroming.

2.8 Saturation

The initial rough forming with the heavy hammer is followed by a more precise, controlled peening with a lighter hammer. The goal here is to obtain a smooth concave surface and to bring the material to *saturation*. Saturation is a technical term and corresponds to the state where for any given intensity of peening, the pan face has a uniform distribution and consistent magnitude of the *compressive residual stresses*. Saturation corresponds to coverage that is very close to 100%. The pan maker uses two cues to determine this state, one visual and the other audible. The visual cue is the smoothness and uniform '*gray color*' of the pan face after peening. The audible cue is perhaps the most dependable one for this musical instrument. As the pan face is indented the tone generated by the impacts gradually changes. When saturation is reached, the pan face will generate when struck lightly at almost any point, a consistent mellow *bell-like tone*. Continued peening brings little changes to this tone although these additional impacts will ensure that those areas that were not properly impacted receive the required treatment.

When saturation condition is reached, higher impact energies will result in deeper penetration. Care must be exercised at this point because non-uniformity, impurities or the presence of deep indentations from stamping by the drum manufacturer may cause the now thin pan face to develop cracks.

2.9 Residual Stress

Residual stresses are caused by plastification of a material on a micro-level and are present in a metallic object that is free of external loads. They are generated by virtually all manufacturing processes. They add to applied loads and are particularly insidious because they satisfy force equilibrium and, therefore, offer no external evidence of their existence. Early pan makers were placed in a quandary because of these hidden stresses. The instabilities that were produced by these stresses led to the belief that the pan had a life of its own. One early solution to this dilemma was the burial of the pan for a few weeks and on its 'exhumation', the pan was found to be miraculously stable. The fact of the matter was that the pans in burial were given sufficient time for stress relaxation in the steel to run its course.

If residual stresses were not important in pan dynamics we would not be considering it at all. All manually or machine engineered steelpans are stressed to some extent, as a result of their manufacture and to a much lesser extent in-service. For the casual pan maker it is not necessary to know in detail, or even at all, the precise level of that stressing because it is always well within the ultimate capabilities of the finished steelpan, so that mechanical failure is rare. Failure can result however if mechanical changes such as reducing skirt length is made to the tuned instrument.

Fig. 2.4. Stress concentration at the indent.

Residual stresses on the steelpan are largely introduced during the peen forming and tuning processes. These stresses produced during the hammer impacts with the pan face are caused by plastification of the material on a micro-level, which results in the distortion of the pan face. As illustrated in Figure 2.4, the impacted material in the immediate region of contact is subjected to stresses beyond the yield point of the steel resulting in plastic deformation. The surrounding region meanwhile is only deformed elastically. To maintain the cohesion between these two regions the stretched layers are set to compressive stresses. These compressions are compensated by tensile stresses in the elastically strained region. When the peening load is removed the pan face recovers elastically but does not return to its original position or shape since part of the cross-section has yielded — the pan face remains permanently deformed. The corresponding residual stresses are negative at the top surface — negative in the sense of the stress induced by the applied load.

In order to form the panface, the face is either indented by hammer peening (traditional way) or by press forming. In both cases the material is stretched. If the material was simply stretched elastically, it will be under tension and return to its original flat shape after stretching. However, the material is stretched beyond its yield point which means that the material undergoes plastic flow. This puts the material that has yielded under compression. The yielded material does not return to its original shape. Therefore to form the pan face and notes, which are permanent shapes, the material must yield and be placed under compression.

On the fully indented pan with all notes formed and tuned (also by hammer peening) the pan face, seam and skirt exists in static force equilibrium. The rim and skirt exists in a state of hoop stress that occurs when the rim and skirt undergo expansion and contraction during the sinking process. Temporarily clamping the rim during sinking will not change the appearance of the hoop stresses because on removal of the clamps the rim and skirt will be required to supply the equilibrating forces. The skirt and rim can also suffer noticeable distortion when the clamps are removed.

2.10 Load Analysis of the Chime

2.10.1 Load Analysis of the Chime before Sinking

During the sinking of the pan face the resultant forces of the hammer impacts are transmitted to the skirt through the chime. One of the effects of these forces is to open the chime.

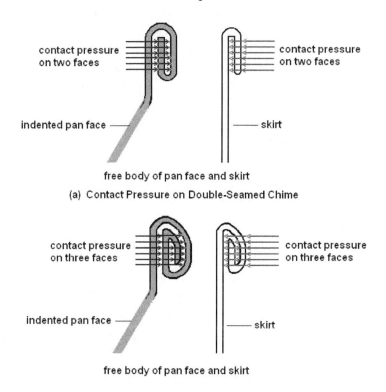

Fig. 2.5. Free-body cross-sectional view of the indented pan face and the skirt in the area of the chime or rim.

The detailed stress variation within the chime is extremely complicated; as a result, we shall use some simplifying assumptions which are usually made in routine analysis and design of connected structures. The sketch in Figure 2.5 shows the cross section of a double-seamed chime assembly comprising the pan face and skirt that fasten these two components together. The free body view of the pan face and skirt demonstrates the loading due to contact forces and the restoring forces due to the spring-like action of the curved elements (labeled A, B and C in Figure 2.6). In reality because of its compactness and highly curved geometry, there are complex stress patterns and force distributions within the chime. There will be high local stresses around the elements A, B and C but we simplify the illustration and analysis by considering these elements as acting as equivalent 'C-springs' or 'C-clamps'. Taken around the circumference of the skirt, each element of length δL of the chime can be treated in this manner. In addition a flow analogy is used to visualize how stress is transmitted through the loaded components. In the illustration and analysis, the restoring forces P_A, P_B and P_C effectively replace the elements A, B and C respectively. We need only to consider these restoring forces and the contact forces F_a ... F_d between the elements labeled #1 to #5.

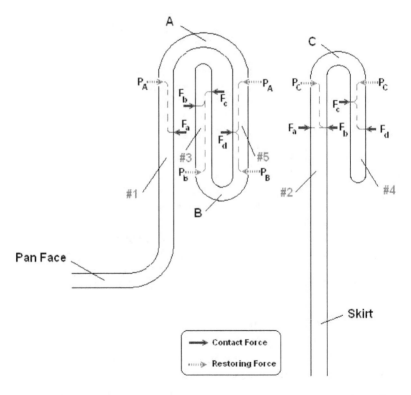

Fig. 2.6. Free body view of the chime before sinking. All forces are for unit length along the run of the chime.

In the seam-forming process, the chime is pre-stressed (*tightened*) between the anvil of the rotating chuck and the seaming tool. This pre-stress is sufficient to ensure a good seal for the purposes for which the drum was designed. In the process the elements #1 - #5, A, B and C are deformed and on release from the chuck a state of deformation is retained. This state before sinking is illustrated in Figure 2.6 with all the constraints for the initial deformations necessary to preserve the geometric integrity of the assemblage. In this way *compatibility* is assured. In addition, Figure 2.6 shows all forces necessary to guarantee *equilibrium* of each free body member. The load on each component is a function of the initial tightening and the external load applied during and after sinking of the pan face. The component loads cannot be found immediately because the assembly is statically indeterminate. Resolution requires consideration of *compatibility*, *equilibrium* and the *constitutive* laws of all deformable components, whose behavior here is assumed to be elastic and isothermal. The isothermal property can be assured because in this metal-to-metal structure all components are good thermal conductors in close physical contact.

2.10.2 Compatibility

After tightening the compressions of elements #2, #3 and #4 are δ_2, δ_3 and δ_4 respectively, while the combined compression of the three elements is δ. If there is no seam separation, compatibility requires

$$\delta = \delta_2 + \delta_3 + \delta_4. \tag{2.1}$$

The compression of elements #1 and #5 (with free or exposed surfaces) are relevant during seam tightening when the entire chime is compressed. When the chime is released from the seaming tool the outer faces of the chime are free as in Figure 2.6 so that these two elements no longer remain in compression. For this reason they are not counted in equation (2.1).

2.10.3 Equilibrium

The static force equilibrium will now be considered for each numbered element. All forces F_a, F_b, F_c, F_d, P_A, P_B and P_c may vary (in magnitude) along the run of the chime. They can be expressed in the form $\mathbf{F}_j = \mathbf{f}_j\, \delta L$ and $\mathbf{P}_j = \mathbf{p}_j\, \delta L$ respectively, where $\mathbf{f}_j$, and $\mathbf{p}_j$, are the force intensities (or force per unit length) and δL is an increment of length along the run of the chime. The force intensities are like stresses (force per unit area). In static analysis of the assembly, it must be kept in mind that in each element (component) the forces are balanced. To assist this exercise the reader can follow the *force paths* or *flow* within each element drawn as dotted lines in Figure 2.6. The flow analogy is useful when visualizing how stress is transmitted through a loaded component. In this analogy, force paths in the component are likened to streamlines in a fluid channel whose shape is similar to that of the component — fluid enters and leaves the channel at locations which correspond to the areas where the external forces are applied to the component. Readers who are familiar with control theory will see the connection to '*Through Variables.*'

Force equilibrium requires the following expressions for the respective elements:

#1. $\qquad\qquad\qquad \mathbf{F}_a = \mathbf{P}_A.$ \hfill (2.2)

#2. $\qquad\qquad\qquad \mathbf{F}_b = \mathbf{P}_C + \mathbf{F}_a.$ \hfill (2.3)

#3. $\qquad\qquad\qquad \mathbf{F}_c = \mathbf{P}_B + \mathbf{F}_b.$ \hfill (2.4)

#4. $\qquad\qquad\qquad \mathbf{F}_c = \mathbf{P}_C + \mathbf{F}_d.$ \hfill (2.5)

#5. $\qquad\qquad\qquad \mathbf{F}_d = \mathbf{P}_B + \mathbf{P}_A.$ \hfill (2.6)

2.10.4 Constitutive Laws

Since the elements #2, #3 and #4 are loaded by compressive forces they all undergo compressive deformation δ_i as discussed earlier. If k_i is the stiffness of the ith element then one can write the constitutive equations

$$\mathbf{F}_a = k_2\, \delta_2, \qquad \mathbf{F}_b = k_3\, \delta_3, \qquad \mathbf{F}_d = k_4\, \delta_4. \qquad (2.7a, b, c)$$

The elements #2 and #4 are formed from the top of the skirt and should have identical stiffnesses making $k_2 = k_4$. Element #3 is formed from the edge flange of the pan face. If the pan face and skirt are made from identical material of equal gauge then one may assume equal stiffness throughout the structure, $k_2 = k_3 = k_4 = k$. If k_e is the equivalent stiffness of the three elements in physical contact and in series then one also has

$$\frac{1}{k_e} = \frac{1}{k_2} + \frac{1}{k_3} + \frac{1}{k_4}, \tag{2.8a}$$

or equivalently

$$C_e = C_2 + C_3 + C_4 = \Sigma C_i, \tag{2.8b}$$

where each element has *compliance* (reciprocal stiffness) C_i and where C_e is the effective compliance.

In the case where the elements are of equal stiffness one may write $k_e = k/3$. Since there are free faces on elements #1 and #5 these two elements cannot be included in this stiffness expression. The equivalent stiffness of the chime assembly is therefore determined by the three elements #2, #3 and #4.

These equations can now be solved to remove the indeterminacy giving the component loads:

$$\mathbf{P}_A = k_2\,\delta_2, \tag{2.9}$$

$$\mathbf{P}_A + \mathbf{P}_C = k_3\,\delta_3, \tag{2.10}$$

$$\mathbf{P}_A + \mathbf{P}_B = k_4\,\delta_4. \tag{2.11}$$

These equations lead to

$$\mathbf{P}_B = k_4\,\delta_4 - k_2\,\delta_2, \tag{2.12}$$

$$\mathbf{P}_C = k_3\,\delta_3 - k_2\,\delta_2. \tag{2.13}$$

$\mathbf{P}_A$, $\mathbf{P}_B$ and $\mathbf{P}_C$ together form a distributed initial load or *preload* that is set as the chime is tightened during the seam forming process.

The degree of preloading for a given steel material is determined by the compressions δ_2, δ_3 and δ_4.

Comparing equations (2.9), (2.10) and (2.11), one observes that the least tightly loaded element is #2, which corresponds to the top of the skirt entering the seam. This is also the joint most subject to loosening during sinking. The inner elements #3 and #4 are more tightly bound as seen from equations (2.10) and (2.11). We can go a step further in verifying this conclusion. Since the chime is an assembly held together by compression, $\mathbf{P}_B$ and $\mathbf{P}_C$ cannot be negative. Therefore from equations (2.12) and (2.13) respectively, if one assumes equal stiffness of the elements, one finds the necessary conditions $\delta_4 > \delta_2$ and $\delta_3 > \delta_2$. This shows that the inner elements #3 and #4 are more tightly bound within the chime.

2.10.5 Load Analysis of the Chime after Sinking

The sinking (indenting) of the pan face by hammer peening is essentially a destructive process since it is generally applied to drums that were not manufactured or tested for that purpose. When the rawform (drum) is manufactured specially for pan making, the sinking process must still be regarded as a destructive process because of the high stresses applied to the material. The seam arrangement in Figure 2.6 is required to sustain heavy loads during sinking without undergoing seam separation. This requirement can only be met if the externally applied load does not exceed the preload. We will assume that during sinking the seam has not separated but that the process has left the pan face in a state of residual compressive stress that tends to curl the pan face inwards (to make it more concave) and that the seamed top section of the skirt has also been displaced radially inwards towards the center of the pan face. This inward distortion of the top of

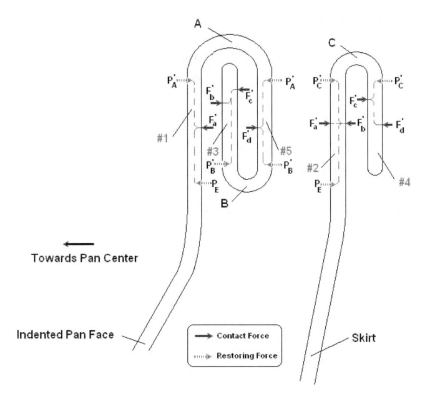

Fig. 2.7. Chime after sinking. In this perspective representation, the seam elements which on the real pan will be bent inward towards the pan center are displayed vertically for ease in viewing the forces.

the skirt is elastic in nature and provides the restoring force that prevents the pan face from further inward curling. The final sate after sinking is shown in Figure 2.7 with the distortions at the top of the skirt much exaggerated for clarity. Included in this figure is the external loading $\vec{P}_E$ provided by the indented pan face and an equal but opposite $\vec{P}_E$ produced by the distorted skirt. These forces are *external* only with respect to the chime but they are internal to the full pan assembly. Sinking is expected to loosen the chime and alter its geometry somewhat so in Figure 2.7 the new forces are identified by a prime (').

2.10.6 Compatibility

After sinking, the compressions for elements #2, #3 and #4 are δ'_2, δ'_3 and δ'_4 respectively while the combined compression of the three elements is δ'. Compatibility requires

$$\delta' = \delta'_2 + \delta'_3 + \delta'_4. \tag{2.14}$$

2.10.7 Equilibrium

The static force equilibrium after sinking, with the introduction of the external loading $\mathbf{P_E}$ gives:

$$\mathbf{F'_a} = \mathbf{P'_A} - \mathbf{P_E}. \tag{2.15}$$

$$\mathbf{F'_b} = \mathbf{P'_C} + \mathbf{F'_a} + \mathbf{P_E}. \tag{2.16}$$

$$\mathbf{F'_c} = \mathbf{P'_B} + \mathbf{F'_b}. \tag{2.17}$$

$$\mathbf{F'_c} = \mathbf{P'_C} + \mathbf{F'_d}. \tag{2.18}$$

$$\mathbf{F'_d} = \mathbf{P'_B} + \mathbf{P'_A}. \tag{2.19}$$

2.10.8 Constitutive Laws

The stiffness constants k_i are unlikely to change significantly during sinking but may change during the annealing that follows. One can readily write the constitutive equations

$$\mathbf{F'_a} = k_2 \delta'_2, \quad \mathbf{F'_b} = k_3 \delta'_3, \quad \mathbf{F'_d} = k_4 \delta'_4, \tag{2.20a, b, c}$$

which describes the loading on each element.

These equations can now be solved to remove the indeterminacy giving the component loads:

$$\mathbf{P'_A} - \mathbf{P_E} = k_2 \delta'_2, \tag{2.21}$$

$$\mathbf{P'_A} + \mathbf{P'_C} = k_3 \delta'_3, \tag{2.22}$$

$$\mathbf{P'}_A + \mathbf{P'}_B = k_4 \, \delta'_4. \quad (2.23)$$

Using equations (2.21), (2.22) and (2.23), one can also write

$$\mathbf{P'}_C + \mathbf{P}_E = k_3 \, \delta'_3 - k_2 \, \delta'_2, \quad (2.24)$$

$$\mathbf{P'}_B + \mathbf{P}_E = k_4 \, \delta'_4 - k_2 \, \delta'_2. \quad (2.25)$$

Referring to equation (2.21) we see that once again element #2 has the lowest resultant loading. Now it is even possible for the compression of #2 to drop to zero ($\delta'_2 = 0$) and for the interfaces to separate as will be the case if $\mathbf{P}_E = \mathbf{P'}_A$ (refer to equations (2.15) and (2.20a)). The possibility of this occurring can be reduced by making the preload $\mathbf{P}_A$ sufficiently large so that its reduction during sinking (and annealing) to the new value $\mathbf{P'}_A$ leaves it still large enough to guarantee $\mathbf{P'}_A > \mathbf{P}_E$. This condition can be met by proper choice of pan face material (thickness and elastic properties) and good seam-forming practice. The critical value of the external loading $\mathbf{P}_E^*$ is therefore the preload $\mathbf{P'}_A$.

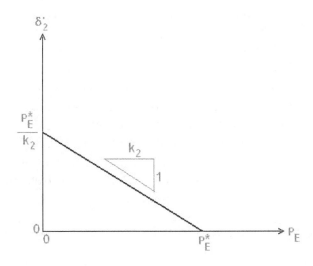

Fig. 2.8. Compression δ'_2 is plotted versus $\mathbf{P}_E$.

The compression δ'_2 is plotted versus $\mathbf{P}_E$ in Figure 2.8. The graph indicates that compression becomes zero ($\delta'_2 = 0$) when the external load reaches the critical value $\mathbf{P}_E^*$. Since δ'_2 cannot be negative it follows that element #1 must lose contact with element #2. Thus seam separation occurs and the remaining seam takes the entire external load as can be inferred from equations (2.24) and (2.25). If δ'_2 goes to zero then from equations (2.24) and (2.25) one observes that elements #3 and #4 will then be loaded by the resultant forces $\mathbf{P}'_C + \mathbf{P}_E$ and $\mathbf{P}'_B + \mathbf{P}_E$ respectively. Because of the external loading $\mathbf{P}_E$, these two elements could be subjected to greater compression after sinking than before sinking.

One observes that as the outer (leftmost) seam separates, the load is shifted towards the inner seam. The triple-seamed chime is therefore more reliable in this respect because should seam separation occur there will then be two remaining seams to take the load.

2.10.9 Extension of the Equations to the Triple-Seamed Chime

Extension of the analysis to the case of the triple-seamed chime is straightforward and can be done by simple inspection of the equations for the double-seamed chime. This is left as an exercise for the reader. The main advantage of the triple-seamed chime has been stated earlier — it provides an additional seam for taking up the external load in the event of failure at one of the interfaces. In Figure 2.5, observe the differences in the geometry of these two types of chimes. The triple-seamed chime, in addition to its 7-layer structure compared with the 5-layer design for the double seam chime, has a more curved and rolled-up shape. Together, these two features give the triple seam chime greater reliability. Obviously, for the foregoing reasons it is better to select or construct drums with triple-seamed chimes for pan manufacture.

2.11 Chime Rotation and Welded Chimes

Chime Rotation is a term introduced here that refers to the chime being rotated under loading generated during hammer peening impacts and can be significant when the pan face is indented to the depths required for the high-end pans. The cause of this rotation may be appreciated from the sketches in Figure 2.9 (a) which show the rotation grossly exaggerated with the impact force F_i equilibrated by the force F_s from the skirt resting on the ground or other support. Because these two forces are directed along different lines of action there exists a resultant bending moment M_i the direction of which is such as to unfold the chime (by rotation in an anti-clockwise direction in Figure 2.9 (a)). There is therefore a tendency for the outer joint between elements #2 and #3 to separate as the chime partially unfolds. To prevent this happening, the chime can be strengthened before sinking by running a fillet weld (see Figure 2.9 (b)) along the outer joint and skirt. Using triple-seamed chimes with their additional layering, improved geometry and tighter seam reduces this problem significantly even without welding.

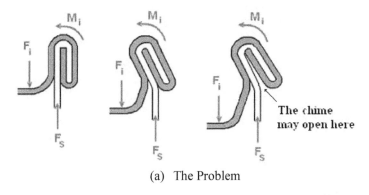

(a) The Problem

Fig. 2.9 (a). As shown from left to right, indenting to greater depths the pan face may lead to opening of the chime.

As an improvement technique, after welding, the skirt should be lightly hammer peened (refer to Figure 2.9 (b)), preferably with a small pneumatic hammer, in the area confined to just below the *weld toe* and around the *weld run* to supply beneficial compressive stresses just under the skirt outer surface. Peening confers a favorable residual stress distribution that increases the allowable loads in the region of the chime during indentation of the pan face. As all pan makers certainly know, the steelpan is a unique instrument held together under very high internal stresses. Anyone who has witnessed the rather 'brutal' process of sinking will certainly be reminded of this. Peening may restore the welded area of the welded elements back up to or above their original fatigue strengths (see Figure 2.10).

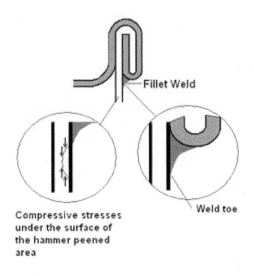

(b) The Solution

Fig. 2.9 (b). Placing a fillet weld circumferentially around the chime can solve this problem.

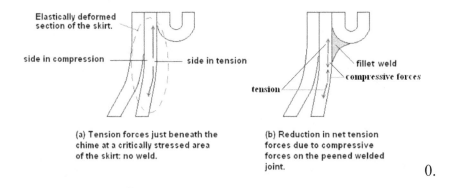

(a) Tension forces just beneath the chime at a critically stressed area of the skirt: no weld.

(b) Reduction in net tension forces due to compressive forces on the peened welded joint.

Fig. 2.10. Enlarged section of the pan face and skirt in the area around the chime showing the tensile forces and compressive forces for chimes with (a) no weld and (b) welded seam after peening.

2.12 Role of the Skirt in Maintaining Static and Dimensional Stability

One of the questions frequently asked in steelpan manufacture concerns the optimum length of the skirt especially on the high-end (tenor) pans. The tenor pan has been manufactured with skirt lengths from approximately 30 cm down to as low as 10 cm. While there are dynamical problems to be addressed in answering this question we shall address only the static stability in this Chapter. All pans made from drums cut to under one-third (⅓) the drum length i.e. 30 cm or less, will be referred to here *as short-skirted pans*.

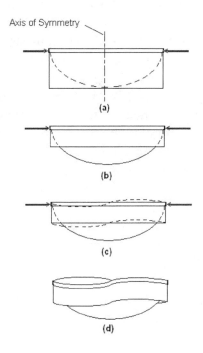

Fig. 2.11. Progression towards *flexural-torsional buckling on the steelpan structure*.

The hidden residual stresses have profound effects on the dimensional stability of the pan. If the free end of the finished short-skirted pan were to be cut off so as to significantly shorten its length or to place an edge design (such as scallops) the *roundness* of the skirt and chime could be significantly altered as the assembly buckles. This problem is illustrated in Figure 2.11 beginning with a fully indented and formed pan in (a) and the progression to the buckled state in (d) when the skirt length is reduced by cutting and removal of a significant section of the skirt. The resulting changes in note frequencies will be addressed in a later chapter but here we are concerned only with the pan distortion and changes to the hidden stresses.

When the skirt is cut or altered some of the stressed material is removed. This results in strain changes due to the stress redistribution in the remaining material. Since no material was removed from the highly stressed indented pan face the remaining material on the skirt and the chime will be required to provide the constraint required to maintain static equilibrium. From energy considerations the assembly undergoes a transition from a stable state to an unstable state (a *limit state*) consistent with energy lost (potential energy loss) in the cut-off and energy used in the redistribution of stresses and changes in geometry. The final state is therefore not necessarily consistent with that required for a tuned state of the pan or for the shape of the skirt to remain cylindrical and the rim (chime) as a circle set in a plane. If the skirt length is significantly reduced the result is an out-of-plane rotation of the chime together with a twisting of the entire assembly. The assembly suffers what is referred to as a *flexural-torsional buckle* shown in Figure 2.11 panel (d). This type of failure occurs suddenly in an assembly such as the pan with non-symmetrical cross-section, one axis of symmetry and constructed of members with a much greater in-plane bending stiffness than torsional or lateral bending stiffness.

2.13 Simple Experiments using Homemade Mini-Pans — Tin-Can experiments on a shoestring budget

The reader can verify a number of buckling results by performing some simple experiments. These experiments I call my 'Tin-Can experiments on a shoestring budget!' In engineering this is called 'Modeling.' The author, with his technical background, finds the modeling of the mini-pans using tin-cans or soda cans relatively simple but the reader who attempts them will, in short order, be something of a 'tin-smith' himself.

Take two cans the size of tin-cans (soda cans) made of steel or aluminum and cut them to form miniature versions of the pans shown in Figure 2.11 panels (a) and (b). Make sure than the skirts are cut to different lengths at least in the ratio 3:1. The indented shape of the face is not necessary for this experiment but if you desire this detail on your model for more realism you can use the bottom ends of empty aerosol cans; however you may find that greater manually applied forces are required to conduct the experiment. Make sure that the aerosol can is completely empty before attempting to cut it and exercise due caution.

Taking each miniature pan in turn, grasp the closed end around the chime between the thumb and first finger of both hands, curling them around the model. Now in order to check the in-plane stiffness, try to distort (crush) the 'pan face' by pressing inwards to simulate the inward compressive forces shown in Figure 2.11. Be careful that you **do not** compress the open end of the pan because that will be similar to using your real full-size tenor pan as a chair by sitting on the upright open end, a sure way to destroy a good pan. Some may find crushing the miniature pans difficult others may not. If you succeeded and one of the model pans crumbled, you have witnessed a classic case of flexural-torsional buckling.

Which pan was easier to buckle? You should find that it was the pan with the shorter skirt.

If you did not succeed don't feel disappointed because you can now demonstrate an important property of the short-skirted pan. Grasp one of the model pans between thumb and first fingers with each hand on diametrically opposite sides of the model then try to twist the pan face and skirt in the manner depicted in Figure 2.11 (c) (use a piece of cloth to avoid cutting your hands on the sharp edges of the model). This one proves to be much easier and demonstrates that the pan assembly has a greater in-plane bending stiffness than torsional or lateral bending stiffness. This property together with the application of compressive stress is the basic requirement for flexural-torsional buckling to occur. Once again you should find that the pan with the shorter skirt was easier to twist showing that by shortening the skirt torsional stiffness is reduced. This is the key to understanding the structural instability that limits the design and construction of the steelpan.

If you tried this experiment using cans with flat end covers and repeated with cans having indented end covers (pressurized cans) you should have observed that the miniature pans with indented faces required greater force to twist and to buckle. But you must not conclude that stability against buckling on the real pans can always be increased by increasing the *depth of indentation* because the compressive forces exerted by the indented pan face also increases. *In fact, tenor pans indented to greater depths are generally more prone to buckling. For this reason, for each depth of indentation on a given pan there will be a lower limit to the skirt length that ensures stability.* Imperfections (loose regions along the chime) and non-uniformities (crookedness and variations in elastic properties) within the assembly will affect the stability so that it is not possible to obtain any simple solution to this problem that will yield a value for this minimum skirt length. *However there is a minimum skirt length for each individual pan.* Guidelines can however be set based on the physics of the problem as discussed here and from empirical data on real pans. Obtaining reliable empirical data on steelpans is either prohibitively costly or invasive and destructive. The latter voids the sample instrument for use as a musical instrument or use in any subsequent buckling tests.

Flexural-torsional buckling by compressive loads may be predicted using energy methods in which the energy equation is formulated by summing the strain energy and the potential energy of the loads. Setting the second variation of the total potential energy equation equal to zero provides the equilibrium position where the assembly transitions from a stable state to an unstable state. To accurately predict the buckling response of the thin shell pan structure the methodology must incorporate either the measured imperfections in the structure and loading, or accurate statistical approximations to the imperfections. The *linearized form* of these equations leads to an eigenvalue problem in which the pan transitions from a stable eigenstate to an unstable one. The geometrical form of the buckled pan shown in Figure 2.11 panel (d) represents the *lowest buckling eigenstate*. More complex geometrical forms representing higher eigenstates are also possible but with diminished probability.

2.14 Pan face with Cutout

If the central area of the pan face that normally contains the inner notes on a tenor pan is removed, then the structure becomes more unstable against flexural-torsional buckling. This can be easily verified on your tin-can models. Using one of your depressurized cans with indented bottom, drill a starting hole in the bottom at the radial position where, to scale, the model tenor will contain the inner notes. Half way out from the center will do. Now by using a nibbling tool, a jigsaw with a fine-toothed metal cutting blade, or rotary tool, cut out a neat circular hole. *Save the cutout*. Now mark out in proportion, the length of the skirt that will form a miniature tenor and cut the side of the can circumferentially along your mark. You now have a mini-tenor with a circular cutout. Now make another mini-tenor just like the first but without the cutout. See Figure 2.12 for details.

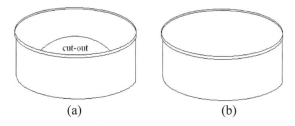

Fig. 2.12. The indented mini-pans; (a) with a central cutout (a hole in the middle), (b) with complete pan face.

Test 1:

Now take the cutout which you saved and try to mate it with the hole on the pan face. The starting hole for cutting will serve as a reference point. You will surely find that it does not match right around with the edges even if you make allowances for the metal cuttings lost by using the cutting tool. If you have an old full-sized pan which in its day was properly tuned and you can afford to experiment with it, then take your rotary tool (nibbler or jigsaw) and neatly cut out a note *along the true note boundary* or along the groove. Now try to mate them up again. *They don't match!* Try other notes to make your experiment convincing. If you have the skill you can map out (in 3-D) the shape of the note before and after cutting. In all cases and to varying degrees, the notes, like the mini-pan cutout, will change shape once the in-plane stresses along the cut-line are removed by cutting. If you were able to map out the note shape before and after cutting, you will be able to decide for yourself that the note was under compression on the pan face. Without the mapping you will have to depend on the edges alone to make your assessment. The bottoms of commercially made tin-cans are indented before being fastened by the seam so that the internal stresses are not too strong. Enjoy yourself!

Test 2:
Repeat the compression and twisting tests on both mini-tenors. You should find that the tenor with the cutout is much easier to buckle into the shape shown in Figure 2.13.

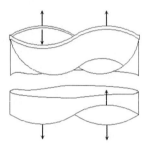

Fig. 2.13. An exploded cutaway view of the pan with cutout under torsion and after buckling. Arrows indicate directions of displacement.

This establishes two facts:

(1) *Buckling Criticality depends on structural details.*
(2) *The central part of the pan face* (the section that was cut off) *is very necessary in maintaining torsional rigidity to the pan structure and its ability to resist buckling.*

The reason why I asked for you to cut out the hole in the middle before cutting the 'skirt' is because if you reverse the order the mini-pan may buckle prematurely; it gets very 'fragile' without the middle section. For the same reason *do not* use a pair of shears in these experiments.

2.15 Additional Degrees of Freedom: New modes with Cutout

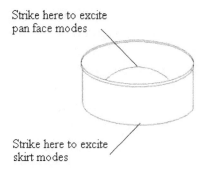

Fig. 2.14. Exciting vibrational modes on the skirt and on the pan face with cutout.

The real pan face with similar cutout, if used to form notes, will be very prone to the excitation of an entirely new set of vibrational modes where the free inner edge executes relatively large displacements. As illustrated in Figure 2.14 these modes can be excited by tapping the inner edge with a stick in the same manner that the skirt modes can be excited by tapping the edge of the skirt. ***If these two edges are struck sufficiently hard with <u>glancing blows</u>, torsional modes can be excited.*** These are similar to the modes set up on a wine glass when the rim is stroked with the finger. All these new modes, resulting from the cutout, add additional degrees of freedom to the pan thereby further complicating its normal-mode frequency spectrum.

You can check on the existence of these modes on your mini-pan with cutout by tapping on the points indicated on Figure 2.14 using a small mini-stick (without the rubber tip) or a pencil (not the eraser end). On your mini-pan these (untuned) modes will be at high frequencies; this is the reason for not using rubber on the contact end of your stick or pencil.

2.16 Stress Loading on the Pan Assembly

Let us now look closer at the stress loading on the pan assembly. For simplicity we shall assume that the pan face in its compressive state of stress exerts a uniformly distributed force intensity p_e around the rim of the skirt, as shown in Figure 2.15. While in practice the stress distribution is unique to each pan, the somewhat symmetrical array of notes and the uniform coverage of the peening across the pan face make this assumption one that is close to reality. The compressive action of the pan face which pulls the upper rim of the skirt inwards is equilibrated by the *hoop stress* — a purely elastic restoring force distribution produced by the inwardly bent chime and top rim of the skirt. The *hoop stress* or *tangential stress* is distributed non-uniformly down the length of the skirt as shown in Figure 2.15, panel (a), with a stress concentration in the area around the chime and falling to zero at the bottom free end (lower rim) of the skirt.

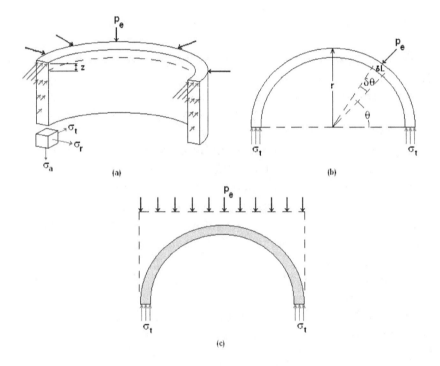

Fig. 2.15. Hoop stress (σ) and compressive force intensity (p_e) distributions on the pan skirt. The skirt thickness is exaggerated for clarity.

This fall-off to zero of the hoop stress from top to bottom allows for a further simplification in which the tangential stress σ_t in the skirt is considered to be uniform and confined mainly around a narrow strip of width z around the top of the skirt (refer to Figure 2.15, panel (a)). The variable z plays the role of *effective skirt length*.

Note: The effective skirt length is a mathematical construct; if you cut the skirt of a working pan to this length the skirt material that remains may not be able to supply the required hoop stress without buckling.

Since the assembly is in static equilibrium then with the uniformity assumption we can consider a section such as in (b) of Figure 2.15 for analysis. Since the skirt measurements satisfy the condition $D/t > 25$ where D is either the inner diameter D_i or outer diameter D_o and t $(= D_o - D_i)$ is the thickness, the analysis is carried out assuming the *thin-cylinder approximation* in which the radial stress is zero, $\sigma_r = 0$. Since the lower end (the bottom) of the skirt is free, the axial stress is also zero, $\sigma_a = 0$. At an angle θ as shown in the illustration, the component of force $p_e \delta L$ in the direction of the stress σ_t is $p_e sin(\theta) \delta L$. Integrating around the semi-circular section of radius r, with $\delta L = r\, \delta\theta$, one gets,

$$\text{Total force} = p_e r \int_0^\pi \sin(\theta)\,d\theta$$

$$= 2\, p_e\, r$$
$$= p_e D, \qquad (2.26)$$

where D $(= 2r)$ is the diameter of the skirt. For this thin-walled skirt, it really does not matter here if the inner diameter D_i or outer diameter D_o is used for D. In the free-body analysis with the total force given by $p_e\, D$, the illustration depicted in (c) of Figure 2.15 is therefore useful because p_e can then be considered to be effectively distributed uniformly along the diameter of the skirt. With the system in equilibrium one has

$$p_e\, D = \sigma_t\, (2tz), \qquad (2.27)$$

and finally,

$$\sigma_t = \frac{p_e D}{2 t z}. \qquad (2.28)$$

We can obtain useful information from equation (2.28), restricted of course by the assumptions made in its derivation. It is clear from this equation that the hoop stress σ_t is more likely to approach critically high values for thin-walled skirts (having small values or t) or more generally for those having large D/t ratios. The possibility for static and geometrical instability is therefore increased with the use of large diameter drums manufactured with thinner gauge steel (gauge # > 20).

While the present simple model will not provide us with an independent expression for the effective skirt length z, its value is expected to decrease as the actual skirt length is reduced. Equation (2.28) shows that reducing z increases the hoop stress, thereby providing us with the qualitative result that the assembly will approach *buckling criticality* as the skirt length is shortened. The condition for failure however, is not given by equation (2.28). Observe that equation (2.28) does not contain any elastic or material constants for the skirt. This is a result of using the thin cylinder approximation, which is obeyed by both the modeled miniature pans and the real steelpans. The reader can verify these observations using the model pan experiment discussed earlier by choosing cans with thinner or thicker walls, by varying the length and by using aluminum and steel cans.

2.17 Guidelines for Buckling Avoidance

To determine the onset of buckling or the critical loading $\mathbf{p}_{crt}$ we cannot simply replace σ_t by the critical stress σ_{crt} for the material. *Buckling failure is a structural problem.* The deflection shape of the structure adjusts itself to one that minimizes the total energy of the assembly depending on the geometry and loading. For this shell structure (pan face + skirt) the character of the buckling and load levels that lead to instability are governed by the imperfections in either the structural parts or loading introduced during seaming, sinking and shaping. In the following discussions some guidelines are suggested and should be followed.

1. *The pan maker should be concerned with details.* Proper sizing of the members to resist buckling is easily compromised if seaming details are inadequately designed.

Pan makers often leave this decision up to the drum makers who in fact do not design their drums with the steelpan in mind. For example, *if the chime is required to be moment-resistant so as to resist chime rotation, then it should be of the triple-seamed design or double-seamed with adequate pre-stress, fillet welded and peened.*

2. The steelpan is susceptible to buckling because of its construction as an assemblage of a thin-walled cylindrical shell (skirt) and an indented shell (pan face) which subjects the structure to high residual stresses. If the pan maker wants to shorten the skirt there is very little that can be done to alter this basic design because of the distinct roles played by each of the two substructures in the vibrational dynamics of the instrument. Some pan makers in attempting to use very short skirt lengths on the tenor pan have resorted to the use of stiffeners (*stringers*) welded to the chime and top end of the skirt. Because of variations in localized stress concentrations in these complex, short-skirted, welded assembly the fabrication and tuning processes cannot be repeated with sufficiently tight tolerances for high quality instruments to be produced on a consistent basis. In addition there are acoustical problems associated with the use of these very short skirt lengths. Using thickness values from Table 2.1 in equation (2.28) one finds that the use of #18 gauge steel in place of #20 gauge for the skirt, with all other quantities remaining unchanged, reduces the hoop stress by 24.5%. This is a significant decrease, which contributes towards increasing the safety margin against buckling. The recommendation is for the use of thicker and longer skirts on the high end pans for increased stability against buckling.

3. As the span (diameter) of an element become larger, there is a greater tendency for instability to occur. The author had the rare opportunity of witnessing master pan tuner Bertie Marshall of Trinidad tune an over-sized tenor pan scaled up approximately x2 in all dimensions except for shell thickness. The pan maker who earlier worked on the instrument through its sinking, forming and burning stages could not sink the central area of the pan face to the depths required for proper tuning of the inner notes. Despite this limitation, Marshall

was able to tune the outer notes to produce very loud well modulated tones. The difficulty experienced with this large tenor was the tendency to buckle during sinking. This problem became even more severe during the hammer-peening tuning operation. Local stability for the inner notes was lacking and global stability of the instrument was marginal. Equation (2.28) shows that the skirt hoop stress is proportional to the ratio D/t. In order to keep the hoop stress within safe limits, doubling the diameter requires a corresponding increase in thickness. The skirt on the pan presented to Marshall for tuning should have been made with gauge #12 steel (and the pan face to #18 or #16) to allow the proper depth of indentation to be safely achieved.

4. Because the cold-formed steel members — pan face and skirt — are designed with large diameter-to-thickness ratios, it is not uncommon in the manufacture for the critical buckling stresses to be much lower than the material yield stress. Therefore, buckling will, very likely, dominate the behavior of any pan designed with larger pan faces to hold significantly more notes than the present maximum around thirty. With the common drum-indenting process the use of materials with higher yield stress than the commonly used low-carbon steel will not entirely remove this problem. Recall that the buckling problem is structural. As an example the Pang range of pans made by Felix Rohner with their larger-than-normal pan face, uses nitrided steel pan faces and stainless steel skirts. But in his fabrication process the pan face is deep-drawn from a flat sheet of low-carbon steel by hydroforming, gas-nitrided, then fitted to the skirt with a welded chime. This represents a combination of good fabrication processes that guard against buckling and provides a good base structure on which to form stable notes. The use of fillet welds with after-weld peening would have further improved the product (see Section 2.11).

2.18 Stress Corrosion Cracking (SCC)

It will be instructive at this point to discuss an additional problem, that of fracture that usually occur along the top of the chime and in the stamped areas on the pan face. This problem occurs particularly when poor quality material is over worked. The problem can originate from a combination of a number of sources (i) corrosion (ii) abrasion (iii) over-tightening of the chime during manufacture (iv) residual stresses on the pan face before and after indenting. The effects of residual stresses and corrosive environment are closely interrelated. **To be an effective agent for corrosion, the stress must be tensile as opposed to compressive**. The more highly stressed regions of the pan will become *anodic* (relative to nearby, low-stressed sections) and *corrosive cells* (an electrolytic process) will be set up due to differences in local stress levels. Since the entire pan face is cold worked, the more highly curved and strongly stressed areas such as *welds, grooves, bore edges* and *chime*, will be corroded in preference to uniform sections. The grooves are concave on the top side of the pan face so that cracking will begin (if it does) on the tensile underside of the grooves. Similarly, cracking may be seen on the tensile outer face of the chime.

SCC is the failure of a structure subjected to the combined actions of stress and a corrosive environment. In the case of brass, the residual stresses in the cold-worked material combine with traces of ammonia in the environment to cause the failure. The problem has been observed in many different alloys and environments, e.g. Al-Cu, Al-Zn-Mg, stainless steels, magnesium alloys in the presence of chloride ions, mild steels with hydroxyl ions (caustic solutions). Regardless of whether the pan rawform is recycled steel drums or straight from the factory material, the prior exposure of the drums to toxic chemicals, chemical treatment for hardening, and continued exposure to harmful environment sets up the possibility for this type of problem. The build-up of corrosion products in confined spaces on the pan face and chimes can generate significant stresses that should not be overlooked.

2.19 Some Sections of the Pan Subjected to High Localized Stresses

Examples of areas on the pan subjected to high localized compressive and tensile stresses are (a) the outer layer of the chime (b) the grooves and (c) the bore holes on the bore pan. These areas are identified in Figure 2.16.

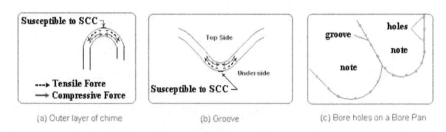

(a) Outer layer of chime   (b) Groove   (c) Bore holes on a Bore Pan

Fig. 2.16. Some sections subjected to high stresses. (a) The outer layer of the chime, (b) the grooves between notes and (c) areas around the holes on the bore pan.

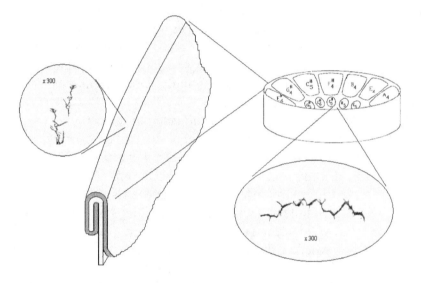

Fig. 2.17. Typical patterns of Stress Corrosion cracking on the chime and pan face of the steelpan. Left unattended these microcracks can grow to visibly large cracks under the right conditions.

High tensile stresses arise on the outer regions of the exposed layer of the chime. This region is prone to SCC activity as illustrated in Figure 2.17. For the grooves, SCC activity begins on the underside of the groove where the stress is tensile, then progresses through the material to the top side. The crack may propagate along the groove and be visible from both sides (see Figure 2.17). On the bore pan, some pan makers groove the pan in addition to drilling the bore holes. *This compounds the problem* for the following reason. When a plate of metal (or a shell) containing a hole (see Figure 2.18), a notch or a crack, is subjected to tensile or compressive stresses, the stress surrounding the 'flaw' is amplified. The amplification is dependent on the orientation and geometry of the flaw. The flaw may be wholly within the material or be visible at its surface.

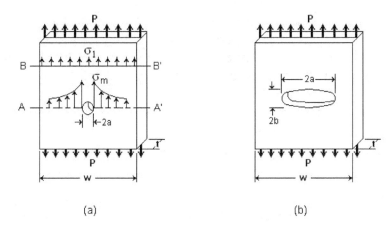

Fig. 2.18. (a) Stress concentration around a circular hole and (b) configuration for an elliptical hole in a stressed plate. Drawn for Tensile Stress. Reverse the direction of the 'arrows' for compression.

Figure 2.18 (a) shows the case for a circular hole in a metal plate (the same applies for non-metallic solids). In this example, the plate is subjected to a uniform tensile force P, which produces a nominal stress $\sigma_1 = P/(tw)$ away from the hole (such as along the plane BB'). The stress along the plane AA' rises sharply around the hole and maximizes to

$$\sigma_m = K_t \sigma_1$$

at the hole surface and decreases to the nominal applied stress (if $a \ll w$) with increasing distance from the hole. The constant K_t is the *stress concentration factor*, where $K_t = 3$ in the case of a circular hole and is independent of the properties of the material. The same treatment applies for Compressive Stress.

The region immediately surrounding bore holes on the bore pan will therefore be subjected to high levels of stress. When for example the bore pan is constructed by first forming the grooves (which itself induces high localized stresses) and then a hole is introduced, the possibility for failure is increased. If this instrument is subjected to repeated re-tuning fatigue failure is more likely in areas along the groove. In forming and tuning bore notes, it is possible and safer, to avoid grooving by relying entirely on blocking by hammer peening — *the grooveless bore pan.*

When the 'flaw' is a crack, approximated by a slender elliptical cutout in the plate, (see Figure 2.18 (b)) with semi-major axis = a and semi-minor axis = b, oriented with the major axis perpendicular to the applied stress, the maximum stress located at the *crack tip* is given by

$$\sigma_m = K_t \sigma_1,$$
$$K_t = \left(1 + 2\frac{a}{b}\right).$$

When $a = b$, the hole is circular. A crack is represented by the condition $b \ll a$ so that $\sigma_m \gg \sigma_1$. Therefore very high levels of stress appear at the crack tips.

It should also be noted that stress concentration also occurs at sharp corners or wherever there are abrupt changes in geometry. *For this reason, the author recommends the use of fillet welds (rounded (concave) welds) at the chime-skirt boundary in order to reduce stress concentrations in the weldment (see Section 2.11).*

2.20 Mechanical Failure

Stress corrosion cracks propagate over a range of velocities depending on the combination of material type, residual stress and chemical environment. The transition from a relatively slow crack growth rate associated with stress corrosion to the fast crack propagation rates associated with purely mechanical failure occurs when

$$\sigma \left(C + L_p\right)^{\frac{1}{2}} = K_c, \qquad (2.29)$$

where K_c = fracture toughness, σ = stress, C = crack length and L_p = length of the plastic zone associated with the crack. Typical values for K_c (MPa-m$^{1/2}$): Aluminum alloy (7075) = 24, Steel alloy (4340) = 50. (see Tada et al. 2000)

Griffith (1962) and Barenblatt (1962) have shown that for a crack modeled as a narrow elliptical cutout of length C in a plate of thickness t, the reduction in stress energy V due to a remote load or residual tensile stress σ is given by

$$V = \frac{\pi C^2 \sigma^2 t}{4E} \qquad (2.30)$$

where E is the Young's modulus of the plate. The surface energy of the plate is always positive because the atoms of the metal are less bound on the surface. Therefore, any increase in the length of the crack is accompanied by an increase in the surface energy of the plate. If the length of the crack increases by δC, the surface area A increases by 2δA = 2tδC because two new surfaces are opened up (one δA on each side) at the tip of the crack. The surface energy increases by 2SδA where S is the surface energy per unit area (for mild steel S ≈ 2.2 Jm^{-2}). If the decrease in tensile stress energy equals (in magnitude) the increase in surface energy then the crack can propagate without any net change in energy. In this case the crack can grow spontaneously. When δV = 2SδA one gets from equation (2.30) the critical stress for spontaneous crack propagation

$$\sigma_{crit} = \left(\frac{4ES}{\pi C}\right). \qquad (2.31)$$

Pan makers and players have observed these spontaneous, often puzzling appearances of cracks on their instruments during preparation or at arbitrary times while in service. *The presence of tensile stresses on the pan face (in particular) is bad; for this reason, the compressive stresses set up by hammer peening works to the pan maker's advantage in reducing cracking.*

Prior to sinking, if SCC was initiated by environmental conditions and residual stress, crack growth may result in localized stress relief and the crack may cease to propagate as the crack tip stress intensity falls below K_{scc} before K_c is reached. During the indenting (sinking) process the rapid buildup of stress on the chime and the pan face may allow the stress corrosion cracks to reach the critical size for fast mechanical fracture. This is an annoying problem for pan makers who rely on used drums for pan production. It usually results in wasted material or recourse to welding of the cracked area. While many pan makers now rely on specially fabricated drums for pan production, precautions against SCC must still be observed.

2.21 Control of SCC

The control of SCC begins at the fabrication stage. The often used method of water quenching after stress-relief-anneal (burning) subjects the pan surfaces to the aggressive action of high temperature steam. Even the application of layers of nickel and chromium (chroming) by electroplating, which can provide long term protection is susceptible to problems if not carefully performed. *Hydrogen embrittlement* may occur during the initial stages of the electroplating process when hydrogen is released. Hydrogen tends to be attracted to regions of *high triaxial tensile stress* (stress directed along three directions) where the metal structure is dilated (opened). It is therefore drawn to the regions ahead of cracks or notches that are under stress. The dissolved hydrogen then assists in the fracture of the metal, possibly by assisting in the development of local plastic deformation.

> *Caution for makers of chrome bore pans: Due to stress concentrations (3 x nominal stress) around the small holes drilled in the preparation of bore pans, makers are cautioned to delay drilling these holes until the instruments have been pre-tuned and chromed. This will reduce the hydrogen embrittlement problem noted above. In addition the pan maker must ensure that all cracks are properly repaired before the pan enters any of the chemical cleaning processes prior to chroming.*

Hammer peening introduces surface compressive stresses that are beneficial for the control of SCC. Therefore, **the traditional indenting process is itself, a method of controlling SCC.** In fact, properly peened pan faces are observed to show very few incidences of SCC. The uniformity with which the hammer-peening process is applied is important if it is to be effective. When combined with proper stress-relief annealing, adequate protection can be provided without any additional procedure to the production process. Care must then be exercised in the chroming process to follow if this option is taken.

Chemical corrosion inhibitors may be effective at controlling SCC but may prove to be unattractive on a musical instrument mainly because of their toxicity and possible health hazard. *In addition, on the carbon steel used for pan production, inhibitors that contain nitrates, hydroxides or carbonates may create the necessary conditions for stress corrosion cracking.*

The interested reader should consult specialized publications on corrosion and cracks for example: Callister (1994), Hertzberg (1996), Newman and Procter (1990), Newman (1995), National Physical Laboratory (2000) and Parkins (2000).

2.22 A Brief Descriptive Introduction to Crystalline Structure and some Rudiments of Metallurgy

2.22.1. Crystal Structure

We now take a short introduction to Crystalline Structure of the material used in pan manufacture and the rudiments of metallurgy that would be useful to the pan maker. Not often does one find the pan maker who excels in the knowledge of the material (usually low-carbon steel) which he uses in the manufacture of steelpans. The pan maker usually takes for granted that steel drums, the most common rawform, would perform satisfactorily and that the end product would be acceptable. However, I know firsthand that in the country of Trinidad and Tobago, the pan makers 'know their steel' and as soon as the process of sinking (indenting) begins they can tell whether or not the metal being worked on is suitable. Their art has been superbly developed! This situation is similar to what one finds in the woodworking industry. Wood is a product derived from trees which are objects found in botany yet woodworkers and carpenters know the physical properties of spruce, pine, mahoe (blue mahoe), cedar, apamat (pink poui) etc that apply to their craft. I also know these wood types firsthand from my woodworking experience.

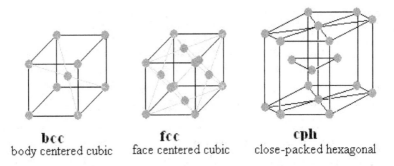

bcc
body centered cubic

fcc
face centered cubic

cph
close-packed hexagonal

Fig. 2.19. The building blocks or Unit Cells for some materials and metals. Examples of these materials are : BCC, soft ductile metals like copper, gold and silver; FCC less ductile but strong such as iron; and for CPH, zinc which is brittle.

Most common metals have either a *face-centered cubic* (fcc) and *body-centered cubic* (bcc) or a *close-packed hexagonal* (cph) crystalline structure formed by the arrangement of the atoms. The major differences between these structures is in the building blocks or *Unit Cells* as shown in Figure 2.19. The *simple cubic* system (sc) consists of one lattice point on each corner of the cube. Each atom at a lattice point is then shared equally between eight adjacent cubes, and the unit cell therefore contains in total one atom ($1/8 \times 8 = 1$). This simple structure is not found in natural materials however. The *body-centered cubic* system (bcc) has one lattice point in the center of the unit cell in addition to the eight corner points. It has a net total of 2 lattice points per unit cell ($1/8 \times 8 + 1 = 2$). The *face-centered cubic* system (fcc) has lattice points on the faces of the cube, that each gives exactly one half contribution, in addition to the corner lattice points, giving a total of 4 lattice points per unit cell ($1/8 \times 8 = 1$ from the corners plus $1/2 \times 6 = 3$ from the faces). The close-packed hexagonal (cph) is related to the fcc. These differences in the number of atoms per unit cell lead to differences in the physical properties of the bulk material. For example bcc metals are soft and ductile; fcc metals (such as iron) are less ductile and hard while cph metals are brittle. Many other features depend upon the crystal structure of metals, such as density, deformation processes, alloying behavior, vibration damping and much more. The mass density of the metal is determined by the atomic mass of the atoms forming the unit cell and the volume of the cell.

Except in a few instances, metals are crystalline in nature and, except for single crystals they contain internal boundaries known as *grain boundaries*. When a grain is *nucleated* during processing (as in solidification of the molten metal or *annealing* after *cold working*), the atoms within each growing grain are lined up in a specific pattern that depends upon the crystal structure of the metal. With growth, each grain will eventually impinge on others and form an *interface* or *boundary* where the atomic orientations are different. This results in grain formation with random orientations everywhere within the solid metal. With iron or steel, individual grains will be magnetized but the randomness in their orientations ensures that the bulk magnetization is zero. These grains can be observed by polishing the surfaces of specimens of the metal. Grain size is normally quantified by a numbering system which runs from *coarse* $N = 1\text{-}5$ to *fine* $N = 5\text{-}8$. The size number N is derived from the formula $N=2n-1$ where n is the number of grains per square inch at a magnification of 100. Pan makers may not possess the microscope and polishing equipment needed to make measurements of grain sizes but during sinking (indenting) the hammer impacts 'polish' the surface which allows the 'sinker' to obtain good visual information by observing the light reflected from the pan face. Un-worked areas of the pan face reflect ordinary sunlight differently compared with 'work hardened' areas. I shall refine this description in the next paragraph.

2.22.2. The Importance of Dislocations to Pan Making and Note Dynamics

Metals are often stronger when they have defects. The defects encountered in the low carbon steel used in pan manufacture (and other metals) are: (i) *point defects*: resulting from vacancies (absence of an iron atom) and interstitials impurities (such as the addition of carbon atoms) (ii) *linear defects: dislocations* (edge, screw, mixed types), (iii) *grain boundaries* and (iv) *extended defects*: pores, cracks (see Sections 2.18 – 2.20). Grain size has an important effect on physical properties and as first shown by Hall and Petch the strength of a material can be increased by reducing the grain size. Small grain sizes give better strength and toughness while larger grain sizes give better workability. Hall-Petch strengthening is based on the observation that grain boundaries impede *dislocation* movement and that the number of dislocations within a grain have an effect on how easily dislocations can traverse grain boundaries and travel from grain to grain. So, by changing grain size one can influence dislocation movement and yield strength. For example, heat treatment after *plastic deformation* and changing the *rate of solidification* (*water quenching* for smaller grain sizes or *air cooling* for larger grain sizes) are ways to alter grain size. These observations are important for the sinking (indenting) and annealing (burning) processes carried out on the pan. As the pan face is work hardened, the grain size decreases. What the pan maker or sinker observes is the changing quality of grayness of the surface of the pan face. He can hammer peen to obtain uniformity in the grayness. This 'quality of grayness' is somewhat subjective, being dependent on the visual acuity of the individual pan maker and the color and intensity of the light incident upon the pan face but we are not interested in quantifying this property of the of the surface so each pan maker/sinker must acquire and develop his own visual acuteness to these changing properties of the pan face. The sound of the hammer impacts is also a function of the hardness of the area of pan face that is struck. By combining the aural and visual inputs the pan maker learns to 'sink' by ear and sight! For a description of this, see 'Saturation' in Section 2.8.

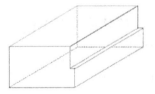

Fig. 2.20. Edge dislocation

An edge dislocation as depicted in Figure 2.20 is a defect where an extra half-plane of atoms is introduced mid way through the crystal, distorting nearby planes of atoms. To get another picture for this, imagine inserting a half-sheet of paper into a stack of paper. The half-sheet fits alright until you get to the edge of the half-sheet where the edge is clearly visible. When enough force or shear stress is applied from one side of the crystal structure, this extra plane passes through planes of atoms breaking and joining bonds, one or a few atoms at a time, until it reaches the grain boundary. The energy required to break a single atomic bond is far less than that required to break all the bonds on an entire plane of atoms at once. This simple model of the mechanism involved in moving a dislocation shows that *plasticity* is possible at much lower stresses than that required to fracture an entire perfect crystal. In ductile materials, the movement of dislocations as described is the mechanism for plastic deformation and gives rise to the characteristic malleability of metals.

When these metals are subjected to *'cold working'* ('cold' here refers to relatively low temperatures compared to the material's melting temperature) *the dislocation density increases* due to the formation of new dislocations. The consequent increasing overlap between the strain fields of adjacent dislocations gradually increases the resistance to further dislocation motion. This causes a hardening of the metal as deformation progresses. This effect is known as *strain hardening* or *work hardening*. In addition, adding pinning points that inhibit the motion of dislocations, such as alloying elements, or the addition of carbon to iron, can introduce stress fields that ultimately strengthen the material by requiring a higher applied stress to overcome the pinning stress in order to continue dislocation motion.

The importance of dislocation density and pinning sites to Magnetomechanical Damping (the damping mechanism in note vibration dynamics) is dealt with in Section 9.7.

The effects of strain hardening can be removed or reduced by appropriate heat treatment (*annealing or 'burning' in pan makers' jargon*) which promotes the recovery and recrystallisation of the material. Next we examine these processes with particular application to the Steelpan.

2.23 Low Temperature Stress Relief Anneal — Burning

2.23.1 Eutectoid Reaction in Carbon Steel

Pure iron (Fe) melts around 1500 °C and around 1100 °C it changes to the body-centred-cubic (bcc) δ-phase. At lower temperatures it changes from the α-phase which has a body-centered-cubic (bcc) lattice to the face-centered-cubic (fcc) γ-phase just below 912 °C. The situation is quite different with a little bit of added carbon (*carburizing*) —somewhat more than 0.1 weight % that forms a Fe-C (Iron-Carbon) system. The *eutectoid reaction* describes the phase transformation of one solid into two different solids. In the Fe-C system, there is a *eutectoid point* at approximately 0.8 wt % C, 723°C (see Figure 2.21). The phase in the middle portion of Figure 2.21 just above the *eutectoid temperature* T_e for plain carbon steel is known as *Austenite* (γ).

Now consider what happens as the austenite phase is cooled through the eutectoid temperature $T_e = 723°C$. Austenite containing 0.8 wt % C changes into *Ferrite* (α) (iron containing almost no carbon) and *Cementite* (Fe_3C, containing 25% carbon, i.e. one in every four atoms in Fe_3C is a carbon atom). Hence carbon atoms must diffuse together to form Fe_3C, leaving ferrite. This mixture of ferrite and cementite is called *Pearlite* (because of its pearly appearance) which grows in a lamellar or plate-like form (alternate layers of 88% ferrite and 12% cementite) consuming the austenite as it goes. Ferrite is soft iron.

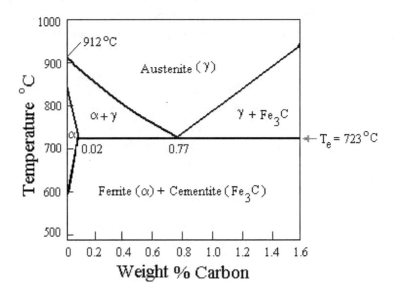

Fig. 2.21. Phase diagram below 1000 °C for steel up to 1.6 wt% C.

The rate of cooling dictates the structure and properties of the steel. If the steel cools too slowly, the cementite will precipitate in the middle of large areas of soft ferrite. Slow cooling produces a more workable or ductile steel. If the steel in quenched and made to pass through the triangle ($\alpha + \gamma$) on the left of Figure 2.21 as fast as possible, the ferrite and cementite are formed together at the same time uniformly. The cementite is dispersed finely and evenly throughout the ferrite producing *Martensite Steel,* which is hard, brittle and denser than austenite.

The microstructures of steel vary considerably with carbon content, with increasing amounts of the hard, brittle, cementite being present in steels of higher carbon content. These variations in microstructure lead to significant changes in physical properties. The steel required for drum and steelpan production must display adequate ductility for shaping. This requires a low carbon content, typically up to around 0.1 - 0.2 wt % carbon with adequately slow cooling in the austenite (γ) $\rightarrow$ ferrite (α) + cementite (Fe_3C) transition.

2.23.2 Annealing

Annealing is a heat treatment process in which the material is exposed to elevated temperature for an extended period and then slowly cooled. It is used to relieve stresses, increase softness, ductility and toughness, or to produce specific microstructure.

Full Anneal — a transformation to austenite, then furnace cooled to coarse pearlite to produce a relatively soft and ductile material (refer to Figure 2.22 for the range of temperatures used, typically 800-920°C, Red-Orange on the color chart).

Process Anneal — used to revert effects of work hardening by *recovery* and *recrystallization* and to increase ductility. Heating is usually limited to avoid excessive grain growth and oxidation. Process anneal is used to treat low-carbon steels (< 0.25 wt% Carbon). Refer to Figure 2.22 where one sees that in process anneal the work piece takes on a dull red color.

Stress-Relief-Anneal — used to eliminate or minimize stresses arising from plastic deformations, non-uniform cooling and phase transformations between phases with different densities. Annealing temperatures are relatively low so that useful effects of cold working are not eliminated.

2.23.3 Low-Temperature Stress-Relief-Anneal for the Steelpan

In the manufacture of the steelpan by hammer peening large non-uniform stresses can develop over the pan face. Stress-relief-anneal serves to redistribute and minimize these stresses to present an improved, stable material for tuning. However, by restricting the annealing temperature T_a to values

$$T_a < T_e - 170 \; °C, \qquad (2.32)$$

(which is *below the nominal temperatures for Process Anneal*, see Figure 2.22), the beneficial properties acquired by the pan face under hammer peening are not eliminated. The condition in (2.32) was first given in the author's Pan Maker's Handbook, 1999a. Let us now see how I arrived at this condition. The recrystallization temperature of low-carbon steel is around 1000°F ≡ 538°C. In the low-temperature stress-relief anneal to be applied to the material in pan preparation in order to retain the beneficial effects of work hardening (see for example Section 2.21 on SCC) it is important to avoid the recrystallization that occurs in Process Anneal. Taking the recrystallization temperature as the *ceiling temperature* (upper limit) for stress relief anneal and the eutectoid temperature T_e = 710 °C (the value used in the 1999 Handbook), this gives a difference of 710 − 538 = 172 °C. Rounding this value to 170 °C, one gets the stated condition $T_a < T_e - 170 \; °C$. The small difference between T_e = 710 °C used in the Handbook and the value 723 °C in Figure 2.22 is not critical. We now get $T_a < 540$ °C.

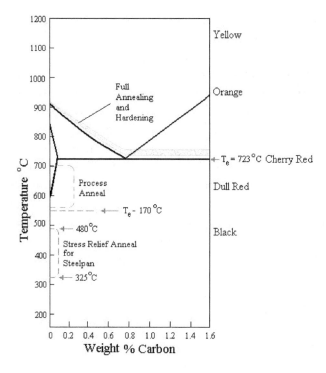

Fig. 2.22. Phase-transitions in the vicinity of the eutectoid indicating heat treatment temperatures for a variety of annealing processes. The upper temperature limit $T_e - 170$ °C and recommended range for annealing the pan is indicated. The indicated colors show that the steel glows cherry red at the eutectoid temperature. In Stress Relief Anneal the pan must remain 'black' in color — DO NOT ALLOW ANY AREAS ON THE PAN TO GLOW RED!

- *This author recommends stress-relief annealing temperatures within the range 325 – 480 °C with a maximum holding time of 20 minutes, followed by cooling in still air to ambient temperature.*

If temperature is determined visually, the pan maker must ensure that no part of the pan under heat treatment glows in daylight (with a red or dull red color). For speed and to reduce cost, some pan makers use hand-controlled gas-fired torches and look for the 'blue steel' appearance on the pan face. This method is risky as it can raise the temperatures on areas of the pan face to excessively high values in addition to producing non-uniform treatment over the area of the pan face.

Figure 2.23 shows the temperature distribution over a Double Second pan under construction during the stress-relief-anneal process fired by wood burning. Similar temperature distributions are obtained on larger pan instruments. The relatively lower temperature at the central region of the pan face in Figure 2.23 is desirable because of the reduced material thickness and the need for lower damping capacity in this area (see Chapter 9). Improperly controlled gas-fired annealing furnaces or torches can produce significantly higher temperatures over areas of the pan face that render the finished material too soft for proper tuning. Because of the thinness of the pan face (especially near the center), great care must be exercised in controlling the furnace temperatures and annealing time. Annealing time on a controlled wood-fired furnace is around 20 minutes, followed by air cooling to ambient temperature.

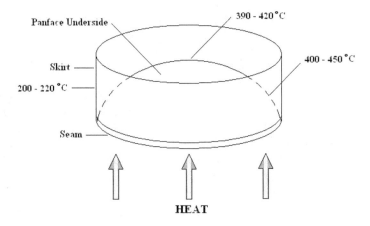

Fig. 2.23. Temperature distribution over one member of a Double Second pan during the heating phase of Low-temperature Stress-Relief-Anneal.

Note on Factory Products: Commercial factory produced steelpans do not normally carry any information on the production procedure that might be helpful to the experienced professional player or researcher. Tonal qualities, dynamic and static stability, as well as longevity of the finished instrument are strongly dependent on the production methods. In Trinidad and Tobago, the instrument purchaser can freely consult with the small-scale pan maker even visit his workshop to observe the production procedure. In dealing with the small-scale pan maker, experienced players can also make recommendations on preferred gauge of steel, skirt length, notes layout, chroming (optional) and even annealing procedure. Commercial scale pan makers should at least provide details on the rawform material and annealing procedures to the buyer. The author's personal instrument (of choice) is a heavy gauge, un-chromed, loud sounding *grooveless tenor* — the product of the late master pan maker Randolph Leroy Thomas.

2.24 Chroming

It has become common practice today, after *first-tuning*, to chrome the higher frequency pans (tenors and seconds) and to retune afterwards (*second-tuning*). Chroming is essentially the electrolytic deposition of nickel onto the steelpan surface followed by a flash of chromium to produce a highly reflective finish. The deposited metal layer therefore consists mainly of nickel. Chroming is done mainly for aesthetics and to reduce rusting without much consideration for the effect on dynamics and on tonal quality.

2.24.1 Effects of Coating on the Material Properties of Notes

To consider the effect of coating elasticity on the note resonant frequency, the effective Young's modulus E_{eff} and density ρ_{eff} of a uniformly coated note are expressed as

$$E_{eff} = \alpha E_c + \beta E_s$$

$$\rho_{eff} = \alpha \rho_c + \beta \rho_s$$

where E_c and E_s are the Young's modulus of the coating and the steel, respectively, ρ_c and ρ_n are the density of the coating and steel, respectively, and α and β are the fractional thicknesses of the coating and the steel portion of the note, respectively ($\alpha + \beta = 1$). Since the coating consists mainly of nickel with a final flash of chrome, the bulk properties of the coating can be taken as that of nickel. $E_{nickel} = 210$ *GPa*, $\rho_{nickel} = 8800$ *Kg/m³* while for the steel the corresponding values are lower, $E_s = 207$ *GPa*, $\rho_s = 7700$ *Kg/m³*. The chroming process therefore leaves the Young's modulus essentially unchanged but the effective density of the note is increased.

2.24.2 Negative Effect of Chroming on Tonality

The chroming process used on the steelpan is well known by the better pan makers to reduce the musical brightness of steelpan tones. Compared to steel, nickel possesses greater magnetostrictive properties and the purity of the metal greatly reduces the occurrence of defects. These factors increase the damping capacity of nickel compared to that of low-carbon steel (see Section 9.7). The layers of nickel deposited (topside and bottom side) on the surfaces of the notes *increases* the damping losses at all modal frequencies resulting in diminished tonality and reduced acoustical output for a given level of stick impact.

2.25 Powder Coating and some Negative Effect on Tonality

Powder Coating is a process recently introduced to pan finishing. The powder used for the process is a mixture of finely ground particles of pigment and polymeric resin electrostatically charged (positively with respect to ground) and sprayed onto electrically grounded pans. Prior to final tuning, the pan is cleaned and pretreated in a similar manner to chromed pans. The coated pans are then placed in a convection and/or infrared oven for curing at a temperature between 140 and 220 °C. Convection curing using hot air is the simpler method for most pan manufacturers. The result is a high quality coating over the entire surface of the pan (pan face and skirt, inside and outside) with an attractive finish, excellent durability and resistant to chipping and abrasion.

Environmental advantage: Compared to chroming, the coating process generates negligible environmentally unfriendly substances; there is no venting to the atmosphere and over-spray powder is collected and re-used.

Dynamical disadvantage: There are two dynamical disadvantages associated with powder coating of the notes. The first is dealt with in Chapter 11 on the receptance method as applied to flexible coatings. That analysis shows that powder coating or any type of paint coating results in a decrease in the frequency of a note by mass-loading. This has to be compensated for by an increase in the rise of the note and shaping. The second disadvantage cannot be removed by any process other than coating removal. *The coating is responsible for an additional component of mechanical resistance which is primarily associated with energy losses taking place through the mechanical flexing of the coating material. The higher modes (partials) are more severely affected because of their shorter generalized wavelengths (see Sections 13.30 – 13.32).* The energy loss in the vibrating coating shows up as a decrease in the loudness of the tone for a given impact and a decrease in the duration of the tone — *the tone is slightly muted.* The severity of both effects increases as the coating thickness increases. See Chapter 12 for effects on acoustical output.

2.26 Nitriding

Case hardening of carbon steel can be carried out using carbon by first heating the material to the desired temperature followed by immersion into powdered carbon (or heavy oil — a hydrocarbon) for a time period determined by the depth of case required.

- *The author gained much practical experience in these processes through blacksmithing while working as a trade apprentice (see 'Becoming a Good Tuner' in Section 14.33). In the making of 'cold chisels' I would douse the tip of the hot work piece into the powdered coal in the cooler corners of the forge (furnace) or into a bucket of heavy oil (a readily available commodity on the Texaco Refinery). I thank my four supervisors at that 'Trade School' led by Mr. Williams.*

Nitriding is a case hardening process that involves the diffusion of nitrogen into the surface layers of low-carbon steel. Gas nitriding is carried out in an ammonia atmosphere at 490-550°C. Components to be nitrided are sealed in a gas-tight container and heated for periods of between 6 and 120 hours, depending on the case depth required. Nitriding may also be carried out in a bath of molten salts, the glow discharge of plasma and by ion implantation. In gas nitriding, ammonia (NH_3) splits into hydrogen and nitrogen and the nitrogen reacts with the steel penetrating the surface to form nitrides. At about 6 wt% N, a compound Fe_4N, gamma prime (γ') is formed. At nitrogen contents greater than 8 wt%, the equilibrium reaction product is Fe_3N, epsilon (ε).

Nitrided cases are stratified (see Figure 2.24). The outermost layer (the *compound zone*) can be all γ' and if this is the case, it is referred to as the *white layer*. Such a surface layer is undesirable: it is very hard and is so brittle that it may spall (fracture) in use. Special nitriding processes are used to reduce this layer or make it less brittle. The ε layer (*diffusion zone*) of the case is hardened by the formation of the Fe_3N compound, and below this layer (the *transition zone*) there is some solid solution strengthening from the nitrogen in solid solution.

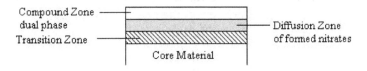

Fig. 2.24. Nitrided case showing the stratification. Not drawn to scale.

Nitriding takes place in the ferritic (α) state rather than the austenitic state used for carburizing. This is possible since ferrite has a much higher solubility for nitrogen than it does for carbon. The advantage of nitriding in the ferritic state is that any previous heat treatment of the component is not disrupted and there is little distortion of the final component shape. All shaping, stress relieving, hardening and tempering are therefore carried out before nitriding. In addition nitrided components are extremely resistant to abrasion, have high fatigue strengths and good anticorrosion properties. These are important properties in steelpan production where nitriding can be used as a *prefinishing process* that imparts longevity to the tuned state of the notes. While the nitrided product is hardened steel, final shaping and tuning can still be carried out and chroming is not required.

A newly developed low-temperature (below 400°C) gas-nitriding process at the universities of Utrecht and Groningen may prove to be even better as a prefinishing process for steelpans. This method offers finer control on stratification thicknesses, smaller average crystallite sizes for greater ductility and pore-free top surface layer for better corrosion protection. Because of the layered structure of the nitrided surface, the thinness of the pan face, and the fact that both sides of the pan face are nitrided, the use of lower temperatures is an advantage.

To date, the only commercial application of nitriding in steelpan production has been done by Schärer and Rohner (2000). In their procedure, a flat sheet of low-carbon steel is first deepdrawn by hydroforming into a spherical form. The work piece is then heated in an ammonia filled furnace to a temperature of 580 °C and nitrided for 7 to 12 hours then slowly cooled down to ambient temperature. The work piece is than welded to a stainless steel skirt (see Schärer et al. 2000).

CHAPTER 3

Non-Linear Dynamical and Statical Analysis of Elastic Shell Structures on the Steelpan

3.1 Introduction

In this Chapter a non-linear analysis of the thin, shallow, domed-shaped notes on the steelpan is given. The main findings of this work were first reported in Achong (1999b). The non-linear behavior of these structures has been previously reported by Achong (1996b and 1998) and Achong and Sinanansingh (1997). What is in fact interesting, indeed remarkable, is that this musical instrument makes effective use of the quadratic and cubic non-linearities of shells (see Yu 1963, Evensen 1963 and Grossman et al. 1969) even though the pan makers have been unaware of this behavior. Pan makers have often used expressions such as 'the pan has a life of its own' when confronted with the curious behavior of the instrument during manufacture. The author will shortly comment on these 'curious behavior.'

In the work by Achong, the vibrations of notes on the steelpan were reduced to the solution of a system of ordinary differential equations containing quadratic non-linear terms. While single notes were studied in Achong (1996b), in Achong and Sinanansingh (1997), non-linearly coupled sub-structures were analyzed. These coupled sub-structures included *sympathetic pairs* and *note-skirt* systems. The dynamics of both these systems were found to be consistent with quadratic type non-linearity and in the case of the former there was strong evidence for internal resonances. The inverse problem of parameter estimation can be found in Achong (1998). The non-linear behavior of the steelpan notes were investigated further by showing that chaotic motion is possible (see Achong 1999c) under intense harmonic excitation (see Chapter 18).

Rossing et al. (1996) have given a brief history of these instruments while describing some aspects of the spectral structure of their tones. Using holographic interferograms, Rossing et al. (1995) have also illustrated the complex motions that can be set up on the pan face and skirt. Hansen (1995) has used computer animations to illustrate the normal modes and the linear coupling between note sections.

In this Chapter, the non-linear statical and dynamical equations will be developed for these notes. To avoid any misunderstanding, it is made clear that except in the case of the fundamental mode (the *key-note*) the non-linear formulations in this Chapter do not provide the pan maker with simple formulas into which numerical substitutions can be made for the calculation of the octave or higher note frequencies or the relative magnitudes of the partials. There are good reasons for avoiding the presentation of frequency formulas for the upper partials and they are all related to the tuning method that has to be applied to these modes on the steelpan (details would be given later). The relative magnitudes can be found but would involve computations beyond the reach of the average pan maker. This should not discourage the pan maker because this entire book is written with him in mind. The approach will be to begin with an elastically supported spherical cap under compressive and thermal stresses, impose shape deformations on the cap to simulate the note-shaping process, and then solve the resulting non-linear dynamical equations to yield expressions for the modal frequencies and coupling coefficients. It will be shown that this approach provides explanations for a very broad range of effects observable on the pan during and after tuning.

To facilitate the analysis in this Chapter and throughout this work, certain terms must be defined as follows:

Definitions:
Mechanical Stress: (Symbol σ) Stress is defined as 'force per unit area'. Stress normal to the plane containing the area is usually denoted '*normal stress*' and can be expressed as

$$\sigma = F_n / A$$

where

σ = *normal stress* (units: (Pascal, Pa), N/m^2, (pounds per square inch, psi))
F_n = *normal component of force (units:* (Newton, N), (pound force, lb$_f$))
A = *area (units:* (square meter, m^2), (square inch, in^2))

Referring to the sketches below, the body can be placed under *tensile* stress '*under tension*' or *compressive* stress '*in compression*'. The area A lies along the line aa. Stress parallel to the plane is denoted '*shear stress*'.

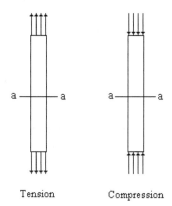

Tension   Compression

Mechanical Strain: (Symbol ε) Strain is defined as '*deformation of a solid due to stress*' and can be expressed as

$$\varepsilon = \delta l / l_0$$

where

ε = *strain* (units: dimensionless)
δl = *change in length* (units: m, in)
l_0 = *initial length* (units: m, in)

Elastic deformation: A deformation of a body in which the applied stress is small enough so that the object retains its original dimensions once the stress is released.

Plastic deformation: A deformation of a body caused by an applied stress which remains after the stress is removed.

Hooke's Law: Linear relations between components of stress and components of strain are known as Hooke's law.

Young's modulus: (Symbol E) Imagine an elemental cube with sides parallel to a set of rectangular coordinates (x,y,z) and subjected to the action of normal stress σ_z uniformly distributed over opposite sides in the xy-plane.

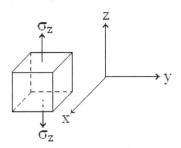

The unit of *elongation* in *tension* (or *contraction* if in *compression*) is given according to Hooke's law by

$$\varepsilon_z = \sigma_z / E,$$

where E is the *modulus of elasticity* or *Young's modulus* (units: (Pa) N/m^2, (pounds per square inch) psi).

Poisson's ratio: (Symbol ν) When the elemental cube is stretched along the z-axis, the elongation is accompanied by lateral strain components (compressions) perpendicular to the z-axis. The ratio of lateral compression ($-\varepsilon_x$, $-\varepsilon_y$) to the longitudinal elongation (ε_z) is *Poisson's ratio*,

$$v = -\frac{\varepsilon_x}{\varepsilon_z}, \quad v = -\frac{\varepsilon_y}{\varepsilon_z}.$$

Young's modulus and Poisson's ratio in *tension* are the same as in *compression*.

3.2.1 Note Preparation and Dynamic Behavior

In order to develop a consistent and applicable theoretical model for the steelpan notes it is necessary to consider the preparation of these shell-like steel structures. Each note forms but a sub-structure of a complex array of similarly prepared shallow shells over the indented face of a steel drum (Achong 1996b). The structure of these notes, depicted in Figure 3.1, differ only in the details that give each note its particular frequency and position on the musical scale. The family of steelpans includes the high-range *tenor*, the mid-range *cello* and the low-range *bass*. Pans such as the *double second*, the *guitar* and others, fill in to cover (with overlap) the musical range from G_1 (48.999 Hz) to G_6 (1567.98 Hz).

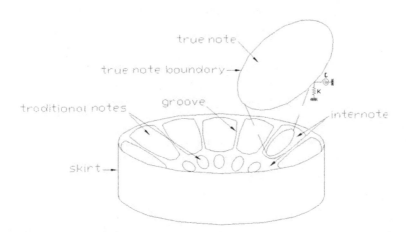

Fig. 3.1. Typical arrangement of notes on the face of a tenor steelpan. The elliptical area of mode localization is shown enlarged and elastically supported.

After marking the boundaries of the *traditional notes*, pan makers add the grooves (if required) then peen along the marks from the top of the pan face so as to further indent those areas. During this process as the marked areas are indented, the notes are seen to rise out of the pan face — the notes are *erected*. This is the correct method both practically and theoretically because this allows the *internote* areas to be further work hardened while the note areas remain relatively more ductile and of lower stiffness. *Since hammer-peening work hardens the material, the note areas are surrounded (bounded) by the stiffer internote.* **This is good structural engineering put into practice by the pan makers.**

3.2.2 Boundary Conditions, Internal Stresses and Advanced Tuning

The hammer peening to indent the pan face and to form or tune the notes, like shot-peening (see for example Niku-Lari 1981) or ball forming (see for example Johnson 1982), induce residual compressive stresses in the material which are partially reduced and redistributed by tempering. The evidence for the existence of these residual compressive stresses on the steelpan comes directly from the observation of two effects (Achong 1997).

The first is the (infrequent) occurrence of *localized buckling* (termed '*flapping*' by pan makers for the 'paper-like' behavior displayed by the affected area) in small areas of the note (usually around 2 cm across) during the tuning process. This is the first of the 'curious behavior' observed by the pan maker. Localized buckling is produced by the excessive compressive stresses in the region of interest and the resulting reduction (to zero) of the effective dynamic stiffness.

The second effect is the small upward shift in the frequency of the notes after the newly completed pans are made (the second 'curious behavior'). This tendency to '*run sharp*' is observable (to the trained ear) just one day after manufacture and the frequency shift may slowly increase during the first week. The author has interpreted this shift as a direct result of the reduction in residual compressive stresses through stress relaxation. The decrease in dynamic stiffness by residual compressive forces produces a note of frequency lower than it would have been otherwise. Stress relaxation can therefore produce this increase in note frequency. A simple destructive test for the existence of the compressive stresses comes by cutting the skirt on the tuned pan. If the material removed from the skirt is excessive, the whole rim and pan face may be distorted but the general tendency is for the frequencies of the notes to increase and the pan must then undergo extensive retuning.

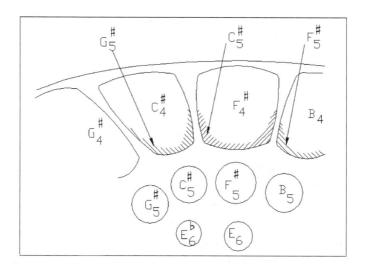

Fig. 3.2. Details of note arrangement showing musical tones that may be excited on the pan face with Advanced Tuning.

Each note, by its connection to the rest of the pan face, will be characterized by a set of hidden boundary conditions describing the note edges, and by unknown residual (compressive) stresses. The usual procedure of separating the edge supports into independent translational and rotational springs (see Figure 3.1) as suggested by Achong (1996b) for the areas of localization, although possible in principle, may not be easily achievable in practice, where, as expected, it will not be possible to independently vary or control each of these two elastic parameters. In practice also, it is found that it is not required that the support be constant along the boundary of the *traditional note* (defined by the grooves). In fact, pan makers, on purpose, create variations in edge supports when for example, sections (or separate *domains*) of the same traditional note are tuned to different frequencies. This is illustrated in Figure 3.2. In cases where the notes are tuned in the manner indicated in Figure 3.2, *domain interaction* is deliberately incorporated into the note dynamics (see Achong 1999b). This *advanced form of tuning — Advanced Tuning —* was used by the late Randolph Thomas on the outer notes of his tenor and second pans. It goes beyond *Complex Tuning* which requires the keynote, octave and twelfth to be set up on the note.

As an all-metal instrument, thermal stresses will also play an important role in the system dynamics. This is in fact strongly supported by the following 'layman' observation (Achong 1997). Steel orchestras, when performing outdoors have been using canopies to protect the steelpans (mainly the bass) from direct sunlight. The frequencies of the notes are lowered as the temperature is increased with the bass pans being more greatly affected (by showing a greater percentage frequency shift). Temperature changes can also affect the tonal structure by modifying the relative amplitudes of the partials as well as the amplitude and frequency modulations.

From the preceding discussion, one sees that each note produced by the combined processes of sinking, shaping, tempering and tuning will be unique (Achong 1996a). This uniqueness has to do with the elastic parameters of the peened material, the form (geometrical shape) of the note, note dimensions (size), edge supports and internal stresses. In this respect, *no two steelpans, or two notes, are identical*. This uniqueness poses special problems for the analysis, which, as a result, must handle shells of diverse shapes, unknown internal stresses and non-uniform edge supports.

3.3 Observations

Achong (1996b) reported the *confinement* (*mode localization*) of the vibratory motion of the steelpan note to an elliptical region defined within the area — the *traditional note* — bordered by the groove (see Figure 3.1). This elliptical area defines the *True Note* (Achong 2000a) while the entire area bounded by the groove*s* is the *Traditional Note* (see Figure 3.1). The grooves are not essential (Achong 1996b) although they assist in blocking the note to reduce inter-note coupling: (the special role played by grooves will be dealt with later). Investigation by the author of many types of steelpans (tenors, seconds, cellos etc, the bass excluded for reasons to be given later in Chapter 14) gives a mean aspect ratio of $a/b = 1.27 \pm 0.08$ for the elliptical planform defining the area of localization. The peening action applied during tuning is carefully applied to the boundary that defines the true note (see Figure 3.1).

Achong (1996b) has given unmistakable evidence for the non-linear nature of the vibratory modes excited within these areas of localization, by showing the occurrence of the *Jump Phenomenon* and *Hopf Bifurcation* on a properly tuned note of a tenor pan. This type of behavior can be observed on notes that show strong coupling between the first two modes and have also been shown by Achong [loc. cit.] to be a direct consequence of quadratic non-linearity on these shell-like structures. It has been found that the second mode can only be of significant intensity when the corresponding linear frequency is approximately twice the linear frequency of the first mode. The oscillatory systems therefore possess *internal resonances* (i.e. they are systems with commensurate linearized natural frequencies). When the second mode to first mode frequency ratio is (typically) within 2 ± 0.006, quadratic couplings are strong, resulting in deep amplitude and frequency modulations and accounts for the distinctive tonal structure of the instrument.

Notes that display a relatively weak second mode tend to display more rapid, low level, amplitude (and frequency) modulations. They also show a somewhat larger departure from harmonicity (second mode typically at the end of the range 2 ± 0.02). In this case, the modulations on the first mode are still linked directly to the second mode in a manner that is consistent with quadratic non-linear coupling. Notes produced with these weak mode-coupling characteristics however, lack the musical luster and color of notes with strong couplings.

For variations on a pan, good pan makers create a mixture of notes with varying degrees of mode coupling (although they lack the understanding of this non-linear process). *I must insert a rider to the latter comment because since my Seminars to Pan Makers and Tuners of Trinidad and Tobago in1999, many pan makers/tuners have begun to identify tonal characteristics of the pan with these non-linear processes even making use of such terms as 'parametric excitations!'*

When a note is played with the stick, the tonal structure depends on the intensity of the impact. A simple description of the tonal changes brought about by varying the impact is not possible because both amplitude and frequency modulations are involved. When the note is played softly however, the amplitude-time history shows a simpler structure. The changes occur at a fundamental level because an upward scaling (amplification) of the amplitude profiles for the note played softly will not reproduce the profiles for the same note played loudly. These features are all consistent with non-linear mode coupling. In addition, pitch glides (upward and downward) over the duration of the tone, consistent with non-linear interaction has been reported (see earlier publications by the author).

The present author has consistently observed that during the initial *attack phase* of the tone, the first mode begins below the set frequency then rapidly rises towards the correct value. The interpretation is that the large amplitude excursions occurring during this brief initial period produces *soft spring* behavior of the material which lowers the vibrational frequency. The stick remains in contact with the note for an appreciable fraction of the duration of this effect which last no more than one to two periods of note surface oscillation (this must not be confused with *pitch glide* for which the duration is much longer). This observation is consistent with non-linear interactions (quadratic to be exact) on the steelpan notes.

3.4 Non-Linear Analysis

3.4.1 The Basic Shell Structure

In the analysis that follows, the non-linear dynamics are developed for the shell-like region where the motion is localized, as shown in Figure 3.1. This region is assumed as having a basic spherical form (see Figure 3.3), which can then be distorted during the tuning process into the desired shape. While this procedure of starting with a spherical form is not necessary, the strategy leads to some convenience in the analytical development, especially as it is desirable to incorporate the tuning process in which the notes are changed from one shape to another (for a continuation of this discussion see 'Comment' in Section 14.25.5). In addition to this, the *'rise'* (defined as H_0 in Figure 3.3) is a readily noticeable feature of the dome-shaped notes. It will therefore be beneficial to regard the rise as a *distinguished parameter* and to keep it separated from other parameters defining the shape (or form) of the shell. By not concealing the rise within some general shape-function, some aspects of the role played by this physically meaningful parameter may be determined even without completely solving the final equations.

One may ask the question: How complex must be the mechanical model and hence the mathematical model to properly describe the dynamical behavior of these notes? If notes having regions of localization that are circular in planform show similar behavior to those with elliptical planforms (and they do), then the model geometry can be considerably simplified. In the present case, a completely satisfactory description of the problem can be obtained by restricting the analysis to regions displaying axisymmetric properties on a circular planform (recall that the mean aspect ratio is 1.27, not too far from unity). While this restriction has the effect of removing the aspect ratio (the ratio a/b of the major to minor semi-axes) as a tuning parameter, it still allows the note dynamics to be fully studied. Pan makers have however, experienced greater difficulty in tuning the circular notes for two reasons; (i) the degeneracy it introduces and (ii) the restriction $a = b$ denies them the opportunity of varying the ratio a/b and thereby gaining an extra tuning parameter. The use of the $5/4^{ths}$ –Law or the $9/8^{ths}$-Rule avoids this problem (see Chapter 14).

Consider the note on the pan face as a domain $N = N(R, \theta, \phi)$ with boundary ∂N. The shell geometry is depicted in Figure 3.3. R is the mid-surface radius (with $R = R_0$ = constant, when the form is perfectly spherical), a is the planform radius, H_0 is the rise, and h is the thickness. It will be convenient to define the ratio H_0/h as the 'rise factor.' W, u_ϕ and u_θ are respectively, the transverse, azimuthal and radial displacements, and are functions of the space coordinates and time. Since only axisymmetric deformations are considered, all displacements and stresses are independent of the variable ϕ, and $u_\phi = 0$. A position coordinate r is defined as $r = R \sin\theta$. As shown in Achong (1996a), the relative dimensions of these structures satisfy the criteria for treatment as shallow shells:

$$a/h \geq 20, \quad R/h \geq 20, \quad \text{and} \quad a/H_0 \geq 5.$$

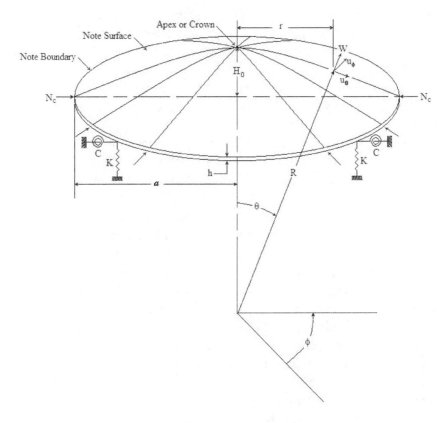

Fig. 3.3. The shell geometry and boundary conditions of the notes on a steelpan.

3.4.2 **Non-linear Shallow Shell Theory**

Instead of analyzing the shell-note system beginning with the basic stress-strain equations as I did in my initial (unpublished but successful) work on the problem, I prefer to use the procedure I adopted in my 1999b paper. This procedure which allowed me to quickly get to the equations relevant to the steelpan, used previously published work in the area, a procedure suited to the requirements for journal publication but when used here, will require that the reader gain access to these (two) publications and read the contents. However, these two papers do require some mathematical and engineering sophistication (*no more, no less I suppose, than is required here*). The analysis begins with the basic shell equations given by Connor (1962) and by Grossman et al. (1969) for the axisymmetric motion of a thin homogeneous spherical shell (in dimensionless form)

$$\frac{1}{12}\nabla^4 W + 2(1+\nu)\left(\frac{a}{2R_0}\right)\left(\frac{a}{h}\right)^2\left[\left(\frac{\partial}{\partial x}+\frac{1}{x}\right)u + 4\left(\frac{a}{2R_0}\right)W\right]$$

$$+ (1+\nu)\left(\frac{a}{h}\right)\left(\frac{a}{2R_0}\right)\left(\frac{\partial W}{\partial x}\right)^2 - \left(\frac{a}{h}\right)\left(\frac{\partial}{\partial x}+\frac{1}{x}\right)\left[\frac{\partial W}{\partial x}\left(\frac{\partial}{\partial x}+\frac{\nu}{x}\right)u\right]$$

$$+ 2(1+\nu)\left(\frac{a}{2R_0}\right)W\frac{\partial W}{\partial x} + \left(\frac{h}{2a}\right)\left(\frac{\partial W}{\partial x}\right)^3\right] + \frac{\partial^2 W}{\partial \tau^2} = 0,$$

(3.1a)

$$\frac{\partial}{\partial x}\left(\frac{\partial}{\partial x}+\frac{1}{x}\right)u + 2(1+\nu)\left(\frac{a}{2R_0}\right)\frac{\partial W}{\partial x} + \left(\frac{h}{2a}\right)\left(\frac{\partial}{\partial x}+\frac{1-\nu}{x}\right)\left(\frac{\partial W}{\partial x}\right)^2 = 0.$$

(3.1b)

where $u(x,\tau)$ and $W(x,\tau)$, in units of shell thickness h, are the radial and transverse displacements respectively, $x = r/a$, $\tau = \gamma t$,
$\gamma^2 = \dfrac{Eh^2}{\rho a^4 (1-\nu^2)}$, $\nabla^4 = \left(\dfrac{\partial^2}{\partial x^2}+\dfrac{1}{x}\dfrac{\partial}{\partial x}\right)^2$, with E being Young's modulus, ρ the shell density and ν denotes Poisson's ratio. Equation (3.1a) represents the dynamical equilibrium condition for the forces acting on an infinitesimal element of shell while (3.1b) is the compatibility condition for the displacement fields $u(x,\tau)$ and $W(x,\tau)$.

Equations (3.1) include the first order effects of bending and stretching, but contains no rotational (torsional) or longitudinal inertia terms. Torsional oscillations on a steelpan note is absent during normal stick excitation because there is no 'twist' or 'pre-twist' involved. To purposely excite torsional modes, considerable torque will be required to twist the note. Stick-note impacts possess neither the forces nor the energies necessary in order to make torsional modes relevant to the dynamics of a sounding steelpan note supported by the pan face. These impacts will not excite torsional modes in the attached skirt either (the skirt being much more massive).

If the edge or boundary ∂N of the shell is fixed in the longitudinal direction and elastically supported by translational and rotational springs having, respectively, *distributed stiffness K* (N/m^2) and *C* (Nm/m) as in Figure 3.1, the necessary boundary conditions are

$$[u]_{x=1} = 0, \quad C\left[\frac{\partial W}{\partial x}\right]_{x=1} = -\frac{D}{a}\left[\frac{\partial^2 W}{\partial x^2} + \frac{v}{x}\frac{\partial W}{\partial x}\right]_{x=1},$$

$$K[W]_{x=1} = \frac{D}{a^3}\left[\frac{\partial}{\partial x}\left(\frac{\partial^2 W}{\partial x^2} + \frac{1}{x}\frac{\partial W}{\partial x}\right)\right]_{x=1},$$

(3.2a - c)

where D is the *flexural rigidity* defined as $D = Eh^3/12(1-v^2)$. In general, K and C may not be constant along the edges but to retain the axisymmetric nature of the analysis, their constancy is required. For the clamped edge, $C = \infty$, $K = \infty$, making $[\partial W/\partial x]_{x=1} = 0$, $[W]_{x=1} = 0$.

By symmetry, the following conditions hold at the pole

$$[u]_{x=0} = 0,$$

$$[\partial W/\partial x]_{x=0} = 0. \qquad (3.3a,b)$$

3.5 Forced Oscillations and Stick Impacts

In order to introduce the reader to the theory of stick-note interactions, a simplified discussion of stick impacts is presented here. This serves to introduce some of the basic principles and serves as a precursor to the full discussion presented in Chapter 13.

Forced oscillations (for steady state or bifurcation studies) are considered by including a harmonically applied surface load that is symmetrical about the *pole* (the *apex* or *dome* of the note as in Figure 3.3) and normal to the surface. Stick impacts may also be considered by including a short duration surface load applied normal to the surface over an area (the *contact-area*) $A_c = \pi\varphi_c^2/4$ where φ_c is the *stick-width*. To maintain the symmetry of the motion being considered here, the mid-impact point must be at the pole (in the terminology of the panist, this point on the note is referred to as the '*sweetspot*'). Since stick impacts made in the normal playing action of the panist are relatively weak (i.e. they produce no permanent deformation of the note surface), the requirement that the exciting force be applied at the sweetspot only, can be dropped. This will be done in Chapter 13 on Stick-Note interactions.

Since both impact and continuous harmonic loading will not be applied together, the general form of the load can be written as $z(x) p(\tau)$, where $z(x)$ is a *distribution function* describing the distribution of the applied load over the surface and $p(\tau)$ is a sinusoidal function for harmonic loading or a pulse for stick impacts. The forcing term to be added to the right hand side of (3.1a) can therefore be expressed as $\tilde{z}(x) p(\tau)$, where

$$\tilde{z}(x) = \frac{(1-v^2)}{E}\left(\frac{a}{h}\right)^4 z(x).$$

For harmonic loading

$$p(\tau) = \sin(\Omega \tau), \qquad (3.4)$$

where $\Omega = \omega/\gamma$ with ω as the external driving frequency. On the steelpan, sinusoidal excitation may be applied acoustically or by attaching an electromagnetic vibrator at some point remote from the note being excited.

For stick impacts, the force-time history $p(\tau)$ can be modeled by a half-sine function

$$p(\tau) = \sin(2\pi\tau/3\gamma\tau_c), \quad 0 \leq \tau \leq 3\gamma\tau_c/2$$
$$= 0, \qquad \text{otherwise.} \qquad (3.5)$$

where τ_c is the *contact-time*. Contact time is dependent on the impact velocity, stick tip radius and the material used on the stick tip. The effects of the hand during delivery complicate the general problem. Further details on the impact problem are given in Chapter 13.

For stick impacts, if the applied force is assumed to be uniform over a *contact area* $A_c = \frac{1}{4}(\pi \varphi_c^2)$, where φ_c is the *contact width*, then one has

$$z(x) = 1 \quad |x| \leq \frac{\varphi_c}{2a}$$

$$= 0 \quad |x| > \frac{\varphi_c}{2a}.$$

(3.6)

3.6 Internal Damping

Since the dynamical equations will prove to be non-linear, implying the possibility of *internal resonances*, the shell material may be subjected to several vibrational frequencies at the same time. In the analysis by Achong (1998), the damping coefficient μ was assumed to be independent of frequency and therefore the same for each excited (non-linear) mode. Not only was this assumption confirmed experimentally [*loc. cit.*], it also proved to be effective in allowing the integration of the non-linear equations to proceed (see Section 5.7 for more details). The inclusion of internal damping adds to the left-hand side of (3.1a) the term $+ \breve{\mu} \dfrac{\partial W}{\partial \tau}$, where $\breve{\mu} = \mu \gamma (1 - v^2) a^4 / (E h^3)$ with μ as the damping coefficient. It should be noted that the damping coefficient is a temperature dependent parameter.

3.7 Compressive and Thermal Stresses

3.7.1 Compressive in-plane Loading

To allow for residual compressive stresses that develop during the manufacture and tuning of the instrument, the next modification is the inclusion of a uniform compression $-N_c$ ($N \cdot m^{-1}$) applied radially along the shell boundary. This adds a constant in-plane stress σ_c (=

$-N_c/h$) to the stress components $\sigma_{\theta\theta}$ and $\sigma_{\phi\phi}$, which in turn introduces to the left hand side of (3.1a), the extra terms

$$+ \breve{N}_c \nabla^2 W - 2\breve{N}_c a^2 /(hR_0),$$

where

$$\breve{N}_c = N_c a^2 (1-v^2)/Eh^3$$

3.7.2 Uniform Temperature Change

The steelpan in use, especially outdoors, may rarely experience uniform temperature even over the pan face alone. However, because the entire instrument is made of steel, one can make the reasonable assumption of uniform temperature (and uniform temperature change) over the area of a single note. Because of the small thickness of the material (around 0.3 mm) one can also assume that the temperature does not vary through the shell thickness. The thermal stress analysis is thereby simplified by not having the shear forces that would otherwise have appeared had there been a significant temperature gradient across the shell thickness.

For a uniform temperature rise δT the affected shell stress-strain relations (including the effects of compression) are

$$\sigma_{\theta\theta} = \frac{E}{(1-v^2)} [\varepsilon_{\theta\theta} + v\varepsilon_{\phi\phi} - (1+v)\alpha_T \delta T] + \sigma_c,$$

$$\sigma_{\phi\phi} = \frac{E}{(1-v^2)} [\varepsilon_{\phi\phi} + v\varepsilon_{\theta\theta} - (1+v)\alpha_T \delta T] + \sigma_c, \quad (3.7a,b)$$

where α_T is the thermal expansion coefficient. These stress-strain relations lead to simple expressions for the thermally induced in-plane stress resultants

$$N_{\theta\theta} = N_{\phi\phi} = \frac{hE\alpha_t \delta T}{(1-v)}.$$

As in the case of in-plane compressive loading, thermal loading will produce two additional terms on the left-hand side of (3.1a). These terms are

$$+ \check{N}_T \nabla^2 W - 2\check{N}_T a^2 /(hR_0),$$

where

$$\check{N}_T = \alpha_T \delta T (1+v)\left(\frac{a}{h}\right)^2.$$

Combining the effects of in-plane loading and uniform temperature rise, the modification to equation (3.1a) is the addition of the terms

$$+ (\check{N}_c + \check{N}_T)\nabla^2 W - 2(\check{N}_c + \check{N}_T)a^2 /(hR_0).$$

One immediately observes from this result that temperature changes will produce effects identical to those observed for changes in the compressive forces.

3.8 The Shape Function

In the shaping or forming of each shell or note during tuning, the tuner finds a shape that imparts the desired tonal character to the note. Consider now the shell to be deformed symmetrically about the pole such that $R = R_0 + q(x) \cdot H_0$, where $q(x)$ is the *shaping function* representing a small (dimensionless) distortion of the shell mid-surface and $H_0 = a^2/2R_0$. Along the boundary of the shell, $q(1) = 0$. The *Gaussian curvature* K_G and the *radius of curvature* R_c of the mid-surface of this deformed shell will vary with the angle θ as

$$K_G = \frac{1}{R_c} = \frac{R^2 + 2(dR/d\theta)^2 - R(d^2R/d\theta^2)}{[R^2 + (dR/d\theta)^2]^{\frac{3}{2}}}. \qquad (3.8)$$

Since $q(x) \cdot H_0 \ll R_0$, by substituting $R = R_0 + q(x) \cdot H_0$ and dropping in (3.8), all terms higher than first order in $q(x) \cdot H_0/R_0$, the quotient

$Q(x) \doteq R_0/R_c$, defined here as the **shape function**, can be expressed as

$$Q(x) = 1 - 2\left(\frac{H_0}{a}\right)^2 q(x) - \frac{1}{2}\frac{d^2 q(x)}{dx^2}, \qquad (3.9)$$

Note: wherever the symbol $\doteq$ appears it reads 'defined as.'

The shaping is assumed to take place on an initially spherical cap for which the shape function is equal to unity ($Q(x) = 1$) everywhere on the spherical surface. Of course there are an infinite number of routes to the desired note shape, starting from an initially spherical cap is just one of these. Analytically speaking, this is a very convenient route. An equally unique but different route is also followed by the boundary conditions leading to the final state. All other routes are acceptable. *This gives each steelpan note its own history — a unique history, followed exactly by no other note anywhere or at any time* (see Section 3.14).

On the notes of the steelpan, the ratio H_0/a (or more precisely, *the rise-to-planform radius ratio*) takes values typically around 1/40, so that the second term in $Q(x)$ may be relatively small. For the deformed shell, the variable curvature $Q(x)/R_0$ replaces $1/R_0$ in the development of the new equations to replace the perfectly spherical shell equations (3.1 a, b).

3.9 Modified Dynamical Equations

By including forcing, damping, in-plane loading, temperature change and shell deformation into the system of non-linear dynamic equations, the new set of equations are:

$$\frac{1}{12}\Delta^4 W + 2(1+v)\left(\frac{a}{2R_0}\right)\left(\frac{a}{h}\right)^2 \left[Q(x)\left(\frac{\partial}{\partial x} + \frac{1}{x}\right)u + 4\left(\frac{a}{2R_0}\right)Q(x)^2 W\right]$$
$$+ (1+v)\left(\frac{a}{h}\right)\left(\frac{a}{2R_0}\right)\left(\frac{\partial W}{\partial x}\right)^2 Q(x) - \left(\frac{a}{h}\right)\left(\frac{\partial}{\partial x} + \frac{1}{x}\right)\left[\frac{\partial W}{\partial x}\left(\frac{\partial}{\partial x} + \frac{v}{x}\right)u\right]$$

$$+ 2(1+v)\left(\frac{a}{2R_0}\right)Q(x)W\frac{\partial W}{\partial x} + \left(\frac{h}{2a}\right)\left(\frac{\partial W}{\partial x}\right)^3 \Bigg] + (\check{N}_c + \check{N}_T)\Delta^2 W$$

$$- 2(\overline{N}_c + \overline{N}_T)\left(\frac{a^2}{hR_0}\right)Q(x) + \frac{\partial^2 W}{\partial \tau^2} + \check{\mu}\frac{\partial W}{\partial \tau} = \check{z}(x)\rho(\tau),$$

(3.10a)

$$\frac{\partial}{\partial x}\left(\frac{\partial}{\partial x} + \frac{1}{x}\right)u + 2(1+v)\left(\frac{a}{2R_0}\right)Q(x)\frac{\partial W}{\partial x} + \left(\frac{h}{2a}\right)\left(\frac{\partial}{\partial x} + \frac{1-v}{x}\right)\left(\frac{\partial W}{\partial x}\right)^2 = 0$$

(3.10b)

3.10 Statical and Dynamical States

3.10.1 MDOF Solution of the Non-Linear Equations

On inspecting equations (3.10) one clearly sees the appearance of linear, quadratic and cubic terms in the displacement $W(x, \tau)$. This means that in addition to the natural modes at frequencies ω_n ($n = 1, 2, 3, ...$), *parametric mode* components at *harmonic* frequencies $m\omega_n$ ($m = 2, 3$) and at *combination frequencies* $\omega_{n1} \pm \omega_{n2}$ (where n_1 and n_2 are small integers) will be present. However, the pan maker can tune the notes to ensure the close harmonicity of the natural modes $\omega_n \approx n\omega_1$ to achieve a reduction in the number of spectral components and in so doing, set the conditions necessary for the generation of internal resonances. While it is possible to obtain a solution involving all the spectral components, for the purposes of the present work, the lead taken by the pan maker will be followed by applying the condition $\omega_n \approx n\omega_1$ ($n = 2, 3, 4, ...$). The use of the 'approximately equal' sign '$\approx$' rather than the 'equal' sign '=' will be fully explained in Chapter 14 where tuning scenarios are discussed.

Experimental results in Achong (1996b) show that when a steelpan note is played with a stick, only the first three (and occasionally four) frequency components are of sufficient amplitudes to be of musical interest. This holds true over the entire family of steelpans. Therefore, in order to solve equation (3.10) for the deflection, it will be assumed that the variable $W(x, \tau)$ may be expressed in separable form as the sum of a space-dependent function $\psi_0(x)$ representing the *static state* and three space- and time-dependent functions $\psi_i(x)$ and $w_i(\tau)$ respectively representing the *dynamical state* of the system. Thus, for this multi-mode (MDOF) system, one can write the following truncated series expansion

$$W(x,\tau) = \psi_0(x) + \sum_{i=1}^{N} \psi_i(x) w_i(\tau), \qquad (3.11)$$

where the modal coordinates (mode shapes) ψ_i ($i = 1, 2, 3$ for $N = 3$) and static state $\psi_0(x)$ must satisfy both the boundary conditions in (3.2a,b) and the conditions (3.3a,b) at the pole, the modal coordinates $w_i(\tau)$, are unspecified functions of time to be determined. Higher modes ($i > 3$), *by assumption*, do not contribute significantly to the system response. However, the extension to four modes ($N = 4$) is straightforward but to keep the expressions as compact as possible this will only be done at the final stages of the *multi-time analysis*.

3.10.2 General Solution Procedure

When $W(x, \tau)$ is substituted from (3.11) into (3.10b), (3.10b) is solved for $u(x,t)$ by successive (double) integration and by employing the conditions of (3.3a,b). Using this solution for $u(x,t)$ in (3.10a), performing the conventional Galerkin averaging (pre-multiplying (3.10a) by the nth modal function and integrating over the interval [0, 1]) and consolidating terms, yield the equations for the dynamic state. In deriving the coupling parameters in the dynamic equations, close (not necessarily exact) harmonicity $\omega_n \approx n\,\omega_1$ is assumed. This procedure will be given the necessary elaboration in Chapter 8 for the SDOF case where the formulation takes on a simpler form.

3.10.3 Definition of Functionals

Arising in the general solution of the MDOF differential equations (3.10a, b) is a set of functionals L, M, P, S, V, X, Y and Z in the form $G(variable_1, variable_2, ...)$. Some of these functionals contain double integrals as a result of solving for u in (3.10b). The functionals are

$$L(A) = \nabla^4 A, \quad M(A) = A, \quad (3.12, 13)$$

$$P(A,B) = \left[\left(\frac{d}{dx} + \frac{1}{x} \right) \left(\frac{1}{x} \int_0^x \left(\int_0^x A\, dx \right) x\, dx - x \left[\int_0^x \left(\int_0^x A\, dx \right) x\, dx \right]_{x=1} \right) \right] B, \quad (3.14)$$

$$S(A,B) = \left[\left(\frac{d}{dx} + \frac{1}{x} \right) \left(\frac{1}{x} \int_0^x \left(\int_0^x \left(\frac{d}{dx} + \frac{1-v}{x} \right) A\, dx \right) x\, dx - x \left[\int_0^x \left(\int_0^x \left(\frac{d}{dx} + \frac{1-v}{x} \right) A\, dx \right) x\, dx \right]_{x=1} \right) \right] B, \quad (3.15)$$

$$V(A) = \left[\left(\frac{d}{dx} + \frac{1}{x} \right) A \right], \quad X(A) = -\nabla^2 A, \quad (3.16, 17)$$

$$Y(A,B) = \left(\frac{d}{dx} + \frac{1}{x} \right) \left(A \left(\frac{d}{dx} + \frac{v}{dx} \right) \left(\frac{1}{x} \int_0^x \left(\int_0^x B\, dx \right) x\, dx - x \left[\int_0^x \left(\int_0^x B\, dx \right) x\, dx \right]_{x=1} \right) \right), \quad (3.18)$$

$$Z(A,B) = \left(\frac{d}{dx} + \frac{1}{x} \right) \left(A \left(\frac{d}{dx} + \frac{v}{x} \right) \left(\frac{1}{x} \int_0^x \left(\int_0^x \left(\frac{d}{dx} + \frac{1-v}{x} \right) B\, dx \right) x\, dx \right.\right.$$
$$\left.\left. - x \left[\int_0^x \left(\int_0^x \left(\frac{d}{dx} + \frac{1-v}{x} \right) B\, dx \right) x\, dx \right]_{x=1} \right) \right). \quad (3.19)$$

The Galerkin averaging performed over the nth mode yields a set of averaged functionals identified by the over-bar ($\overline{}$) as illustrated for the generic functional G:

$$\overline{G}_n(var_1,...) = \int_0^1 G(var_1....) \psi_n\, x\, dx \Big/ \int_0^1 \psi_n^2\, x\, dx, \quad (3.20)$$

It should be noted that the Galerkin averaging procedure involves surface integrals over the area of the note surface. In the example given, this appears as

$\int_0^{2\pi}\int_0^1 G(\text{var}_1\ldots)\psi(x,\theta)x\,dx\,d\phi \Big/ \int_0^{2\pi}\int_0^1 \psi_n^2\,x\,dx\,d\phi$ but as a result of the assumed axisymmetric properties of the motion and the planform, each integration with respect to ϕ will lead to the factor 2π which cancels to yield the result in (3.20).

3.10.4 The Static State

The statical equation in differential form is obtained by using $W(x,\tau) = \psi_0(x)$ in equations (3.10 a, b) with the stress terms in general form. The result is the force equilibrium equation given by

$$\frac{1}{12}\nabla^4\psi_0 + 8(1+\nu)\left(\frac{H_0}{h}\right)^2\left\{Q^2\psi_0 - \frac{1}{2}(1+\nu)P(Q\psi_0',Q)\right\} - (\check{N}_c+\check{N}_T)\nabla^2\psi_0$$

$$+ (1+\nu)\left(\frac{H_0}{h}\right)\left\{S(\psi_0'^2,Q) + Q\psi_0'^2 + 2Y(\psi_0',Q\psi_0') - 2V(Q\psi_0\psi_0')\right\}$$

$$+ \frac{1}{2}Z(\psi_0',\psi_0'^2) + \frac{1}{2}V(\psi_0'^3) = 4(\check{N}_c+\check{N}_T)\left(\frac{H_0}{h}\right)Q,$$

(3.21)

where $(\bullet)' = d(\bullet)/dx$. The special case of $(\check{N}_c+\check{N}_T)(H_0/h)=0$, arising when the compressive and thermal stresses are zero or the note surface is flat ($H_0 = 0$), has the trivial solution $\psi_0(x) = 0$ (*everywhere zero* over the note surface). Equation (3.21) describes the surface displacement due to changes in internal stresses at the note boundary and due to changes in temperature of the note material.

For a steelpan just sitting there un-played, equation (3.21) describes the response of the note surface to changes in ambient temperature and changes in the internal stresses arising, for example, through the effects of aging. Equation (3.21) therefore defines the '*quiescent state*' of a note.

3.10.5 Static Force Distribution

Associated with the static displacement at each point on the note surface is a *Static Force* (see Section 8.18 for further discussions), directed *upward* and *normal* to the note surface at that point. This force distribution over the note surface, in dimensionless form, is given by the term $4(\breve{N}_c + \breve{N}_T)\left(\dfrac{H_0}{h}\right)Q(x)$. One can therefore write the dimensionless Static Force at a point on the note surface as

$$f_0(x) = 4(\breve{N}_c + \breve{N}_T)\left(\dfrac{H_0}{h}\right)Q(x). \qquad (3.22)$$

This equation has an amazing simplicity in form yet it carries very important information. For the note in its initial spherical form with $Q(x) = 1$, signifying constant curvature, the force at any point on the note surface is equal to $4(\breve{N}_c + \breve{N}_T)\left(\dfrac{H_0}{h}\right)$, which is constant over the surface. When the note is tuned and shaped into its final form a static force distribution is set up over the note surface proportional to the function $Q(x)H_0/h$. This is an important result because it reveals to us that the shape function $Q(x)$ not only describes the departure of the note shape from the perfect spherical form but it also describes the force distribution that shapes the note surface in the static equilibrium (note at rest) or in its quiescent state.

3.10.6 The Shape Function, Q(x)

The surface displacements described by (3.21) depend on the geometrical shape (3-Dimensional form) of the note surface through the shape function $Q(x)$. An interesting question therefore naturally arises: *Are there any shapes other than the flat plate ($H_0 = 0$) for which the displacement produced by changes in temperature and residual stress is everywhere zero?* The answer is simple and in the negative because the only other condition apart from $H_0 = 0$ that satisfies the question is for the shape function $Q(x)$ itself to be zero. Recall that for a perfectly spherical cap, $Q(x) = 1$. To satisfy the conditions of the question, on writing $z(x) = \{q(x) + h\psi_0(x)/H_0\}$, one must have

$$Q(x) = 1 - 2\left(\frac{H_0}{a}\right)^2 z(x) - \frac{1}{2}\frac{d^2 z(x)}{dx^2} = 0, \tag{3.23}$$

for which the solution is

$$z(x) = \frac{1}{2}\left(\frac{a}{H_0}\right)^2\left(1 - \cosh\left(i 2\left(\frac{H_0}{a}\right)x\right)\right). \tag{3.24}$$

The presence of the hyperbolic cosine with *imaginary* argument shows that for *real* notes such a surface is impossible.

This should not be looked upon as just a curious mathematical exercise because it is important to find ways of increasing the stability of the note against changes in temperature and residual stresses. The general problem can therefore be stated in terms of the minimization of $\psi_0(x)$ while retaining all the other geometrical requirements such as the need to have $H_0 \neq 0$. This is clearly an optimization problem that requires the planform be at least elliptical in form for there must be at least one other variable to adjust in order to perform the optimization. The ratio of the semi-axes on an elliptical planform — the *aspect ratio* — provides the additional variable but a word of caution is appropriate here. There is a stronger requirement in the tuning of the notes for the aspect ratio to be close to the value 5/4 or 9/8 (see Sections 14.25 and 14.26). The lesson here is that *it is impossible to optimize the pan in each and every way.*

3.11 The Pan Jumbie

In order to preserve and record some aspects of the traditional attempts of the pan makers in coming to grips with the mechanical behavior of the steelpan, I shall give a description of the underlying forces and stresses controlling the notes on the instrument using, where I deem appropriate, the idiom of these excellent craftsmen. In the vernacular, the term '*Pan Jumbie*' an expression used in pan making circles in Trinidad and Tobago, is very descriptive and has its equivalent meaning in the terminologies of physics and engineering. The meaning given below applies to the statical behavior of the notes but in Chapter 17, a more general meaning is given which embraces the entire instrument as a system under internal stresses.

Returning to equation (3.21), the shape of the stressed note in its final form, *tuned or untuned*, is described by the radius

$$R = \underbrace{R_0 + H_0 q(x)}_{\text{set by the pan maker}} + \underbrace{h\psi_0(x)}_{\text{set by the internal stress fields}} \qquad (3.25)$$

Equation (3.25) shows that the equilibrium shape of the note is dependent on both the form imposed by the pan maker in shaping the note (the $R_0 + H_0 q(x)$ terms) and that induced by the stresses (the $h\psi_0(x)$ term). In practice, it will not be possible to separate these two contributions by direct measurement. However, in the case of the thermally induced stress field one can alter the temperature of the instrument to measure its contribution to the second term in (3.25). It is clear however, that *note shapes are determined not only by the pan maker but also by the underlying mechanism* that controls the statical equilibria of these shell structures.

It is the existence of the states described by (3.21) and the presence of the second term in (3.25) that led the early pan makers to the belief that '*the pan has a life of its own*'. In the vernacular, (3.21) *describes that 'life'*. In another colloquial expression (also native to Trinidad and Tobago) the instrument is said to *possess* a '*Pan Jumbie.*' It is a historical fact that some early pan makers buried the pan in the ground, when unearthed days later the pan could be tuned quickly and easily. The scientific explanation is that the pan burial rather than '*exorcising*' the Jumbie, gave the pan the time required for *stress relaxation* to take place (see Section 2.9).

In fact the 'Pan Jumbie' is nothing more than the hidden stress fields and associated static force distributions, which can change with time and are affected by ambient temperature (see Section 17.20). These fields and forces, particularly just after *First Tuning*, affect note shape, note frequencies as well as the tonality of the sounding note. Once more, in the vernacular, equation (3.21) is the '*manifestation*' of the 'Pan Jumbie' on the individual notes.

Distortion may occur if the internal stresses are not reduced and properly distributed over the pan face. This is the bane of pan makers and tuners for it brings annoying and unpredictable changes to the tonal frequencies. Stress-relief annealing will reduce these stresses when the pan is heated to the recommended temperature, held there long enough, and slowly cooled to room temperature (see Chapter 2). Finally, to the early pan makers, *fire* it seemed, could tame the Jumbie. In scientific jargon tempering relaxes the residual stresses.

On the pan, it is physically impossible to reduce the residual stress fields and the thermally induced stresses to zero. In the vernacular, it is impossible to remove or 'exorcise' the Pan Jumbie! *The Pan Jumbie is ubiquitous*!

3.11.1 Discussion on the Static State

The solutions I gave in Achong (1999b) (see, for example, equations (23) and (24) of that paper) were obtained using the full expression for $W(x, \tau)$ given by (3.11). In that formulation the static displacement amplitude A_0 of the function $\psi_0(x)$ cannot be independently determined because $\psi_0(x)$ is left as an undetermined function to be found by solving the highly non-linear equation in (3.21). The following discussion seeks a resolution for this problem, which arises from the non-linear nature of the system. *In full mathematical rigor this problem cannot be avoided.*

3.11.2 Case 1: Zero Compressive and Thermal Stresses

In the case of zero compressive and thermal stresses, the static displacement function is identically zero, $\psi_0(x) = 0$. The note surface takes on the shape defined by the function g(x) where

$$g(x) = H_0\{(1-x^2) + q(x)\}, \qquad (3.26)$$

and

$$Q(x) = 1 - 2\left(\frac{H_0}{a}\right)^2 q(x) - \frac{1}{2}\frac{d^2q(x)}{dx^2}. \qquad (3.27)$$

The first term in (3.26) describes the initial spherical form while the second term describes the shaping function imparted to the note surface by the pan maker/tuner.

3.11.3 Case 2: Non-Zero Compressive and Thermal Stresses

When the compressive and thermal stresses are non-zero, the note surface is displaced by an amount given by the static displacement function which is now non-zero, $\psi_0(x) \neq 0$. The dynamical equations must then be obtained for the new note shape defined by

$$g(x) = H_0\{(1-x^2) + q(x) + h\psi_0(x)/H_0\}, \quad (3.28)$$

which consists of two parts

$$g(x) = \underbrace{H_0\{(1-x^2)+q(x)\}}_{\text{Set by the Tuner}} + \underbrace{h\psi_0(x)}_{\text{Set by compressive/thermal stresses}}$$

and the new shape function

$$Q(x) = 1 - 2\left(\frac{H_0}{a}\right)^2 \{q(x)+h\psi_0(x)/H_0\} - \frac{1}{2}\frac{d^2}{dx^2}\{q(x)+h\psi_0(x)/H_0\}. \quad 3.29)$$

In order to solve the equations (which will yield $\psi(x)$ and $\psi_0(x)$), both the magnitude A_0 of the static displacement function $\psi_0(x)$ at the vertex ($x = 0$) of the note and the form of the function $\psi_0(x)$ must be known. But $\psi_0(x)$ cannot be determined before the statical equations are solved! *This is an inherent feature of this non-linear instrument, which operates under stress. This is not unlike the 'which came first, chicken or the egg?' paradox!*

How can this problem be resolved?

Since there is no exact (closed-form) solution to the general non-linear problem set by (3.10), a good approximation must be sought. To resolve the problem therefore, one can use the following procedure:

(i) Begin with *Case1* (zero stress, $A_0 = 0$) and solve the differential equations (3.10a, b) to yield all the quadratic and cubic parameters. This solution takes

$W(x,\tau) = \sum_{i=1}^{N} \psi_i(x) w_i(\tau)$. The static term $\psi_0(x)$ does not appear (does not exist) because *the static displacement amplitude A_0 is zero.*

(ii) Define the compressive/thermal stresses (or stress fields).

(iii) Substitute the parameters obtained in (i) in the dynamical equation with time-dependent terms set to zero to obtain the closed-form static displacement amplitude equation with the stresses present. Solve this static equation to yield the amplitude A_0 of the static displacement. This step will not determine the form of $\psi_0(x)$ only its amplitude A_0.

(iv) Assume an *admissible function* for $\psi_0(x)$ that satisfies the boundary conditions. This admissible form for $\psi_0(x)$ together with A_0 is now used in g(x) to determine the *new note shape*.

(v) To obtain the new set of quadratic and cubic parameters, solve the dynamical equations for the note under stress *with its new shape* defined by (3.28). This solution also takes $W(x,\tau) = \sum_{i=1}^{N} \psi_i(x) w_i(\tau)$; the static term $\psi_0(x)$ does not appear because *the static displacement (with $A_0 \neq 0$) is now included* in the new note shape.

(vi) The quadratic and cubic parameters obtained in this way will not contain $\psi_0(x)$ explicitly as they do in Achong (1999b).

(vii) Notice that in step (iii) the parameters used to determine A_0 are those corresponding to the initial note shape. This is the correct procedure because it is the *initial* shape that is distorted by the applied stresses.

When we deal with engineering designs in Chapter 8 this procedure will be adopted and given further clarification.

3.12 The Dynamical State in MDOF Representation

3.12.1 The General Dynamical Equations

It is important that the analysis of the vibrational motion of an excited steelpan note be carried out by considering all the degrees of freedom that are important in the use of these shells as musical instruments. Each mode (corresponding to key-note, octave or twelfth) contributes one degree of freedom. Normally three or four modes of vibration are important so the analysis takes the route followed by a Multi-Degree of Freedom (MDOF) system. If the external force $p(\tau)$ (applied continuously or by impact) is resolved into its temporal *Fourier components* $F_n(p(\tau))$, the modal equations derived from (3.10a,b) and (3.11) are a set of dimensionless second-order Ordinary Differential Equations, ODEs, given by

$$\frac{d^2 w_n}{d\tau^2} + \mu_n \frac{dw_n}{d\tau} + \omega_n^2 w_n + \sum_{i,j=1}^{3} \alpha_{ij,n} w_i w_j + \sum_{i,j,k=1}^{3} \beta_{ijk,n} w_i w_j w_k = f_0 + p_n, \quad (n = 1, 2, 3)$$

(3.30)

where $\frac{d^2 w_n}{d\tau^2}$ is the inertial (acceleration) term, $\mu_n \frac{dw_n}{d\tau}$ represents viscous damping with $\mu_n \doteq \breve{\mu}$, $\omega_n^2 w_n$ is the usual structural stiffness term (which includes the effects of thermal and compressive stresses), $\sum_{i,j=1}^{3} \alpha_{jk,n} w_j w_k$ represent quadratic stiffness, $\sum_{i,j,k=1}^{3} \beta_{ijk,n} w_i w_j w_k$ represents the cubic stiffness, and p_n are the normalized modal external forces, with

$$p_n = F_n(p(\tau)) \int_0^1 \breve{z}(x) \psi_n x \, dx \bigg/ \int_0^1 \psi_n^2 x \, dx.$$

(3.31)

Equation (3.30) represents a set of three non-linear coupled equations (or four non-linear coupled equations if there are four tuned modes on the note). The modal equations are coupled by the non-linear terms with coefficients $\alpha_{ij,n}$ and $\beta_{ij,n}$.

When an external force p_n is applied (by stick impacts for example), if struck from the underside it adds to or if struck on the top in the normal way, subtracts from the static force f_0 to produce the required modal excitation. Because of the non-linear operation of the pan, the maximum intensity to which a particular note can be played before tonality deteriorates depends on the value of f_0. It is well known especially on the lower pans that striking a note too vigorously result in poor tonality. This topic will be discussed in more detail in Chapter 8.

The method of *Multiple Scales* (see Nayfeh 1973 and Kevorkian 1987) may be used to construct a uniformly valid, asymptotic expansion of the modal equations as done by Achong (1996b, 1997, and 1998) where only the quadratic (even-order) couplings are retained. This procedure is employed and discussed in Chapter 4.

The modal driving force function will be fully discussed in Chapter 13 which deals with stick-note interaction. The procedure for obtaining numerical solutions of ψ_0, ψ_n and the corresponding eigenfrequencies ω_n will involve lengthy iterations and extensive use of differential equation solvers. Although these solutions do not form part of the work covered in the present book, one may add that in solving for the eigenfrequencies corresponding to trial values for the spring constants K and C, it is necessary to define *detuning parameters* σ_n (where $\omega_n = n\,\omega_1 \pm \sigma_n$). As explained in Chapter 14, the detuning parameters determine the tonal structure of a sounded note. In practice the tuner sets the spring constants K and C by hammer peening. Readers interested in seeing how this is done are referred to the paper Achong (1995) where solutions are given for flat elliptical plates. For the pan, these elliptical plates are replaced by ellipsoids on elliptical planforms supported by elastic supports K and C.

3.12.2 Quadratic Coupling Coefficients

In order to consolidate coefficients formed by the permutation of the subscripts on $\alpha_{jk,n}$ and $\beta_{ijk,n}$ (not including the mode designator, n) an asterisk will be used; for example, $\alpha^*_{jk,n} = \alpha_{jk,n} + \alpha_{kj,n}$.

3.12.2.1 Square-Term Coefficients

The coefficient for the only term of the form $\alpha_{jj,n} w_j^2$ (the quadratic interaction of mode j with itself), is found in mode2 for $j = 1$, and is given by

$$\alpha_{11,2} = 2(1+v)\left(\frac{H_0}{h}\right)\left\{\overline{Y}_2(\psi'_1, Q\psi'_1) + \frac{1}{2}\overline{M}_2(Q\psi'^2_1) - \frac{1}{2}\overline{S}_2(\psi'^2_1, Q) - \overline{V}_2(Q\psi_1\psi'_1)\right\}.$$

$$(3.32)$$

It will be shown in Chapters 4, 5 and 6 that this coupling coefficient plays a key role in determining the amplitude of the second mode as it controls the energy transferred from mode1 to mode2 *via internal resonance*. In the limit $H_0 \to 0$, as the shell tends towards the flat plate, the terms with H_0/h as a prefactor will be reduced to zero. On these dome-shaped notes, the rise-factor H_0/h will therefore be the main parameter controlling the $\alpha_{11,2}$ coefficient for the second mode. This parameter is modified during the tuning process to set the relative strength of the second mode (the octave). Increasing $\alpha_{11,2}$, increases the strength of the octave. The energy transfer of this parametric excitation is illustrated by the *Product Rule*

$$\boxed{\text{Mode1}} \quad \times \quad \boxed{\text{Mode1}} \quad \to \quad \boxed{\text{Mode2}} .$$

3.12.2.2 Cross-Term Coefficients

The coefficients $\alpha^*_{12,1}$ (mode1), $\alpha^*_{23,1}$ (mode1), $\alpha^*_{13,2}$ (mode2), and $\alpha^*_{12,3}$ (mode3), for cross terms of the form $\alpha^*_{jk,n} w_j w_k$ are given by

$$\alpha^*_{jk,n} = (1+v)\left(\frac{H_0}{h}\right)\{\overline{Y}_n(\psi'_j, Q\psi'_k) + \overline{Y}_n(\psi'_k, Q\psi'_j) + \overline{M}_n(Q\psi'_j, \psi'_k)$$
$$- \overline{S}_n(\psi'_j \psi'_k, Q) - \overline{V}_n(Q\psi_j, \psi'_k) - \overline{V}_n(Q\psi_k, \psi'_j)\},$$
$$(j \neq k). \qquad (3.33)$$

The energy transfers for these parametric excitations are illustrated by the Product Rule

$$\boxed{\text{Mode } j} \quad \times \quad \boxed{\text{Mode } k} \quad \to \quad \boxed{\text{Mode } n} .$$

These coupling coefficients determine the energy transfers; from mode2 back to mode1 ($\alpha^*_{12,1}$), from modes 2 and 3 to mode1 ($\alpha^*_{23,1}$), from modes 1 and 3 to mode2 ($\alpha^*_{13,2}$) and finally, from modes 1 and 2 to mode3 ($\alpha^*_{2,13}$). In the absence of strong cubic non-linearity, the term $\alpha^*_{12,3}\ w_1\ w_2$, will generate, and transfer energy to mode3 through a combination resonance. This is the mechanism suggested by the present author in 1996 for third mode excitation on the steelpan notes when only quadratic non-linearity is assumed. In fact numerical modeling suggests that on all steelpan notes this is the main mechanism, exceeding any transfers through the cubic coupling. This is to be expected because the cubic forces arise from in-plane stretching which couples weakly to the transverse motion of the vibrating note surface. The cross-terms in (3.33) will all vanish as $H_0 \rightarrow 0$.

For those readers with more mathematical taste, rather than the *quadratic form* in w, we could equally have used the *symmetric bilinear form* (in w_1 and w_2). This will bear out the fact that $\alpha_{12,3}\ w_1\ w_2$ is equal to $\alpha_{21,3}\ w_2\ w_1$ *(observe the symmetry in the subscripts)*.

A general observation on all coefficients $\alpha_{ij,n}$ is their dependence on the static state ψ_0 (through the shape function $Q(x)$). These coefficients are therefore dependent on the compressive and thermal stresses. *This is important because not only is the frequency altered by changes to any of these stresses but so are the couplings that are second order in the modal coordinates. It should also be noted that this dependence on ψ_0 means that the partials are dependent on the Quiescent State of the note.* I shall have more to say on this later.

3.12.3 Cubic Coupling Coefficients

Of all the cubic coefficients, $\beta_{111,3}$ is singled out for special mention because this one determines the generation of an internal resonance at ω_3. This coefficient is expressed as

$$\beta_{111,3} = \frac{1}{2}\overline{Z}_3\left(\psi'_1, \psi'^2_1\right) - \frac{1}{2}\overline{V}_3\left(\psi'^3_1\right). \qquad (3.34)$$

In this expression, the effect of the rise-factor is not immediately obvious (dependence comes only through the effect of the rise factor on the modal coordinates ψ_n). In fact, the terms involving the cubic coefficients persist even at the flat plate limit. Compared to the quadratic coefficients, the cubic coefficients (on the pan) are consistently lower in magnitude and this explains why pan makers have always experienced great difficulty in obtaining strong third modes on the instrument.

In model the coefficients for the terms $\beta^*_{113,1} w_1^2 w_3$ and $\beta^*_{223,1} w_2^2 w_3$ are given by

$$\beta^*_{jj3,1} = \overline{Z}_1(\psi'_j, \psi'_j \psi'_3) + \frac{1}{2}\overline{Z}_1(\psi'_3, \psi'^2_j) - \frac{3}{2}\overline{V}_1(\psi'^2_j \psi'_3) \quad (j = 1, 2). \tag{3.35}$$

The coefficient $\beta^*_{123,2}$, for the cubic term $\beta^*_{123,2} w_1 w_2 w_3$ in mode2 is given by

$$\beta^*_{123,2} = \overline{Z}_2(\psi'_1, \psi'_2 \psi'_3) + \overline{Z}_2(\psi'_2, \psi'_1 \psi'_3) + \overline{Z}_2(\psi'_3, \psi'_1 \psi'_2) - 3\overline{V}_2(\psi'_1 \psi'_2 \psi'_3) \tag{3.36}$$

Finally, in mode3, corresponding to the term $\beta^*_{122,3} w_1 w_2^2$, is the coefficient

$$\beta^*_{122,3} = \overline{Z}_3(\psi'_2, \psi'_1 \psi'_2) + \frac{1}{2}\overline{Z}_3(\psi'_1, \psi'^2_2) - \frac{3}{2}\overline{V}_3(\psi'_1 \psi'^2_2). \tag{3.37}$$

3.12 4 Small-displacement Modal Frequencies

For small displacements (amplitudes), the modal frequencies ω_n for axisymmetric modes are given by the equation

$$\omega_n^2 = \frac{1}{12}\overline{L}_n(\psi_n) + 8(1+v)\left(\frac{H_0}{h}\right)^2 \left\{ \overline{M}_n(Q(x)^2 \psi_n) - \frac{1}{2}(1+v)\overline{P}_n(Q(x)\psi'_n, Q(x)) \right\}$$
$$- (\breve{N}_c + \breve{N}_T)\overline{X}_n(\psi_n). \tag{3.38}$$

The modal frequencies are seen to depend on the compressive and thermal stresses through the term with $(\breve{N}_c + \breve{N}_T)$ as a prefactor. The modal frequencies are also seen to depend on the rise-factor (H_0/h) and on the form of the note surface through the shape function $Q(x)$, both of which are varied during tuning as the note is shaped by hammer peening. $Q(x)$ is also a function of the stresses.

Generally, the frequencies will increase with the rise-factor. If $Q(x)$ tends to increase the overall curvature of the note, the frequencies may increase. Equation (3.38) is sufficiently detailed for extensive use on the subtleties of pan dynamics. For example, the human ear can easily detect changes in note frequency brought about by small temperature changes; these frequency changes are accounted for in (3.38).

The small-amplitude fundamental frequency f_1 in Hertz, can be found from

$$f_1 = \frac{\omega_1 h}{2\pi a^2} \sqrt{\frac{E}{\rho(1-v^2)}}. \qquad (3.39)$$

This is a *'first-approximation'* formula which will be improved upon in later Sections of this book. Unlike the small-amplitude frequency defined above, the non-linear (large amplitude) frequencies are functions of time (being dependent on the modal interactions) and must be determined dynamically from the time derivative of the phases. In general the non-linear sounding frequency will not be equal to f_1 because of the *pitch glides* and *frequency modulations* (see Achong 1996b) that characterize the tones of the steelpan.

3.13 Tuning the Pan with a Blowtorch

Using (3.38), one can explain the operation of the unorthodox 'blowtorch' method used by some pan makers to fine-tune the instrument. Equation (3.38) readily shows that $\delta\omega_n \propto -\delta\tilde{N}_c$, that is, if the compressive stress in increased ($\delta\tilde{N}_c$ positive) then the modal frequency is reduced ($\delta\omega_n$ negative) and vice versa. Since the effect of reducing the compressive stress $\tilde{N}_c$ in (3.38) is an increase in frequency, fine tuning of the instrument can be done by heating individual notes with a blowtorch then allowing the notes to cool naturally to ambient temperature. Localized heating will produce a redistribution and reduction of the residual compressive stresses (*stress relieving*). After cooling, when the treated note is sounded, because the modal frequencies will increase, there will be a 'sharpening' of the tone. *This method can only be used to raise the frequency of the note.*

However, if the temperature of the note is raised high enough (see Section 2.24 for the limits), the material tends to soften. This is a reversal of the work hardening achieved through peening. *The result, in this case is a reduction in frequency and a degrading of the note material.*

The blowtorch method cannot be highly recommended as a tuning technique for the following reasons

(i) accidental overheating of the note may cause irreversible changes to the material microstructure,
(ii) all modes on the treated note are affected in the process but not necessarily in the manner that may lead to good tonality,
(iii) nearby notes are affected by the process.

Some of these points will become clearer in later Sections of this book.

3.14 The History of a Note

When the blowtorch procedure is taken together with the initial peening, shaping and tempering of the pan, one sees that the final tuned state (characterized by frequency) of an individual note, can be arrived at through infinitely many different ways. It can be said therefore, that *the tuned state has a history*. The conclusion is that the modal frequencies are not uniquely determined by the note geometry and the spring constants (K and C) defining the boundary. The same conclusion was arrived at in Achong (1996a). It clearly shows that *boundary conditioning* (setting K and C) alone is insufficient for setting the modal frequencies of the notes on the steelpan.

3.15 Buckling

If the small-amplitude frequency for the first mode under the condition of zero compressive and thermal stresses is defined as ω_{10}, a *buckling parameter s*, can be defined as

$$s = (\breve{N}_c + \breve{N}_T)\frac{\overline{X}_1(\psi_1)}{\omega_{10}^2}. \tag{3.40}$$

Using (3.38), the small amplitude frequency ω_l for model on the stressed note can then be written as

$$\omega_1 = \omega_{10}(1-s)^{\frac{1}{2}}, \qquad (3.41)$$

where

$$\omega_{10}^2 = \frac{1}{12}\overline{L_1}(\psi_1) + 8(1+v)\left(\frac{H_0}{h}\right)^2\left\{\overline{M_1}(Q(x)^2\psi_1) - \frac{1}{2}(1+v)\overline{P_1}(Q(x)\psi_1',Q(x))\right\}$$

(3.42)

Buckling then occurs for $s = 1$, in which case the lowest mode frequency is reduced to zero as the global thermal expansion and/or compressive stress cancels out the structural stiffness for model. Since the structural stiffness goes to zero, the linear restoring force vanishes. Such cancellation can be observed in small regions on the note area. But this is not allowed to occur over the entire note. The pan maker can correct this compressive stress-induced buckling ('flapping') on the pan by peening with much obliquity ('stretching') the regions slightly away from the affected area. Proper stress-relief annealing during manufacturer can reduce the tendency to buckle.

3.16 Ellipsoidal Notes and the Pan Maker's Formula

While the note dynamics can be understood from the present analysis with the restriction to symmetrical motion on a circular planform, greater flexibility in tuning is allowed on notes with elliptical areas of confinement. On an elliptical planform, the second and third natural modes can be more readily tuned to the required relationship with the first mode, by employing two modes one having the minor axis and the other having the major axis as nodal diameters respectively. For more discussions on this aspect of the note dynamics see Sections 14.25 to 14.28.

To deal fully with ellipsoidal shapes, the coordinate space must be increased. This will yield equations that are much more complicated than that presented here but is worth doing especially for the practical application of the results. However, this refinement will leave the non-linear form of equation (3.14) unchanged. In such an exercise, carried out for an ellipsoidal shell on an elliptical planform having semi-major axis a and semi-minor axis b, it will be found useful to produce a 'semi-general' solution containing the *aspect ratio* $\frac{a}{b}$ of the planform as an adjustable parameter in the same manner that the *rise-factor* $\frac{H_0}{h}$ appears in the present equations. It will then be possible to avoid performing the numerical solutions on the non-linear equations in order to see how the aspect ratio affects the musical interval between partials. A neat solution to this problem is given by the $5/4^{ths}$ –Law and the $9/8^{ths}$-Rule (see Sections 14.25 – 14.28).

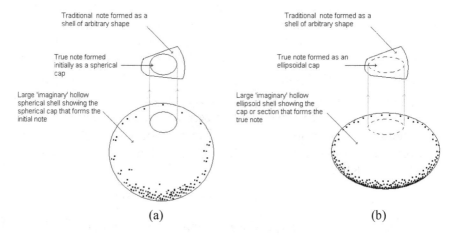

Fig. 3.4. (a) Initial spherical note formed as a cap taken from a large imaginary hollow spherical shell. (b) The spherical shell is squashed or stretched into an ellipsoid from which the ellipsoidal cap is taken to form the ellipsoidal note. For size, these imaginary spherical and ellipsoidal shells can be as large as 5 m (15 feet) across.

In the theoretical development of the note system discussed here, it is assumed that one begins with a spherical shell (or cap) which is then deformed (shaped) into an ellipsoidal shell which forms the basic shape of the true note (refer to Figure 3.4). The final shape of the true note is then determined dynamically as the tuned modes on the vibrating note determine the shape of the true note boundary. For a picture of this shaping process we refer to Figure 3.4(a) where the initial spherical cap contained within the traditional note (bordered by grooves) can be imagined as a small cap with a circular base (planform) cut out of a large 'imaginary' spherical shell and fastened to the traditional note. In reality of course this large spherical shell does not exist and one does not actually cut out and fasten anything. What I really want you to have in mind is the shape of that initial spherical cap forming the note. It is a cap having a large radius of curvature equal to that of the large imaginary spherical shell. I suggest you read this paragraph over if you haven't yet got the picture!

Now to shape the initial spherical cap, we go to Figure 3.4(b) where our large imaginary spherical shell has been squashed or stretched into a large imaginary ellipsoidal shell. The ellipsoidal shell forming the note (within the traditional note) is taken as a small cap having an elliptical base (planform) cut from the large imaginary ellipsoidal shell (remember that in reality we do no cutting and fastening). The ellipsoidal shell forming the basic shape of the true note now rests on an elliptical planform within the traditional note. The note dynamics then determine the final shape of the true note boundary (which will be elliptical).

For elliptical planforms, closed-form solutions similar to equation (3.39) are not generally possible. However, because the aspect ratio of the planforms used on the steelpan notes is close to unity ($a/b = 5/4$ see Section 14.25) or $a/b = 9/8$ if the option of the *third* is used on the bass, see Section 14.27), approximations are possible that can explain the qualitative aspects of note dynamics and provide accurate quantitative results. Consider the spherical shell on a circular planform of radius r_c. This shell is now distorted (perturbed) into one having an elliptical planform with semi-major axis a and semi-minor axis b. The equation of this ellipse can be written in polar form as

$$r = a(1 + k^2 sin^2 \phi)^{-\frac{1}{2}}, \qquad (3.43)$$

where $k^2 = (a/b)^2 - 1$, the origin is at the centre of the ellipse and the angle ϕ is measured counter-clockwise from the positive major axis. To determine the radius r_c of the initial circular planform for these very shallow shells, we can adopt the approach of Lord Rayleigh (1945) who pointed out that for irregularly shaped plates the fundamental frequency is best approximated by the fundamental frequency of a circular plate having a radius equal to the average radius of the irregular plate. The average radius of the elliptical planform is given by

$$r_c = \frac{a}{2\pi}\int_0^{2\pi}(1 + k^2 \sin^2 \phi)^{-\frac{1}{2}}d\phi. \tag{3.44}$$

As a numerical example for $a/b = 1.25$ and $a = 1$ *(unit of length)*, $b = 0.8$, the radius of the circular planform that we have perturbed is equal to $r_c = 0.892$.

The first modification we can apply to equation (3.39) is to replace a with the radius r_c. That is the easy part, now comes the hard part. If it were possible to obtain an exact closed-form solution, all this division of the solution into parts will not be necessary. The perturbation of the spherical cap into an ellipsoidal cap changes not only the shape of the planform but also the stiffness of the shell; essentially changing ω_1^2. In order to see what goes on here we take as an example the analysis of the clamped elliptical plate in the paper Achong 1995. In that paper the *"modified support technique"* (equation (21b) in that paper) gives the fundamental mode frequency of the elliptical plate as

$$f = f_c[A_1 + k^4 A_4/\gamma_2]^{\frac{1}{2}}, \tag{3.45}$$

where f_c is the corresponding circular plate frequency and

$$A_1 + \frac{k^4 A_4}{\gamma_2} = \frac{a}{2b}\left(1 + \left(\frac{a}{b}\right)^2\right) + \frac{a}{2\pi b \gamma_2}\left(\left(\frac{a}{b}\right)^2 - 1\right)^2 \int_0^{2\pi} \frac{\sin^2 2\phi}{1 + \left(\left(\frac{a}{b}\right)^2 - 1\right)\sin^2 \phi} d\phi, \tag{3.46}$$

which I have written out fully in terms of the *aspect ratio* a/b of the elliptical planform. The value of γ_2 depends on the aspect ratio but its value $\gamma_2 = 2.82$ obtained numerically by a minimization procedure in the paper of 1995 gives a good approximation for a range of aspect ratios not far from unity as are in fact found on the pan. The second term in equation (3.46) contains an *elliptic integral* and the value of this term is small in comparison with the first term and it can be regarded as a 'correction term.'

The striking aspect of equations (3.45) and (3.46) is that the fundamental frequency of the elliptical plate can be expressed in terms of the corresponding circular plate frequency and the aspect ratio a/b of the planform. This is fine for the flat plate but when the spherical shell is perturbed into an ellipsoidal shell as obtained in the tuning process of the pan notes, life is not so easy. This is where the hard part comes in. We can't go into all the details here but readers can see that already with the flat plate in some instances such as with γ_2, the aspect ratio gets *lost* in some numerical computation. Even the elliptic integral in equation (3.46) which, when evaluated for each value of the aspect ratio a/b, produces just a numerical value (just a number), and should be seen as another instance where the aspect ratio gets 'lost.' This is an indication (not a proof) that an exact closed-form solution is not possible. But we can still move ahead. Let us first simplify equation (3.46) by retaining only the first term; that is we keep A_1 and drop the rest. Now if we define the *ellipticity* ε of the elliptical planform as $\varepsilon = (a/b) - 1$, we can express A_1 as a series in ε up to second order by

$$A_1 = \frac{a}{2b}\left(1 + \left(\frac{a}{b}\right)^2\right) = (1 + 2\varepsilon + (3/2)\varepsilon^2). \qquad (3.47)$$

We can then write the approximate fundamental frequency of the elliptical plate as

$$f = f_c(1 + 2\varepsilon + (3/2)\varepsilon^2)^{\frac{1}{2}}. \qquad (3.48)$$

If we try to improve this expansion formula in ε by including the second term in equation (3.46) (the *correction term*), the elliptic integral and γ_2 will halt our progress. This happens on a grander scale when we try to find a second-order expansion formula for the frequency of the perturbed spherical shell or the perturbation of one ellipsoidal shell to another ellipsoidal shell! In other words, we cannot use analytical methods to follow *completely and exactly* the note shaping procedure carried out by the pan maker. This is not a failure of the analytical methods but represents instead the complexity of the process which will in reality involve many more variables than are used here — such as the exact shape of the note surface that changes with each application of the hammer, the unknown internal stress distributions and the evolving boundary conditions.

All is not lost but we must be prepared to sacrifice some accuracy. In obtaining the solution for the spherical shell deformed by the Shape Function $Q(x)$ in Section 3.8, we altered the single radius of curvature R. But now, for the perturbed shell, on elliptical planform, there are two principal radii of curvature R_x and R_y. Since numerical solutions provide the only way through the resulting 'mess' there will be no way to assist the pan maker with a formula that will be useful in tuning the notes unless some precision is sacrificed. It was at this point that I decided to settle for the 'best' result while maintaining those aspects of the spherical shell solutions that can be easily understood geometrically. With this understanding, the resulting second-order fundamental frequency equation for the shallow shell ellipsoid can be expressed as

$$f = f_c(1 + 2\varepsilon + 4\varepsilon^2)^{\frac{1}{2}}. \qquad (3.49)$$

The coefficient of the quadratic term in this expansion (the 4) is found to depend explicitly on the corresponding root of the frequency equation for the spherical shell (for an example of this type of equation see equation (3.42)). This coefficient is therefore a very complex function of the aspect ratio of the note, with the value 4 being a good approximation. The factor 2 in the linear term with ε is however quite robust. Combining the easy part where the replacement $a \mapsto r_c$ is made in equation (3.39) with the hard part as expressed by equation (3.49) and using $\varepsilon = (a/b) - 1$, the resulting frequency equation for the fundamental frequency of the pan note on elliptical planform (the true note) is given by

$$f_1 = \frac{\omega_1}{2\pi}\left(\frac{E}{\rho(1-v^2)}\right)^{\frac{1}{2}} \frac{h}{r_c^2}\left(3 - 6\frac{a}{b} + 4\left(\frac{a}{b}\right)^2\right)^{\frac{1}{2}}. \qquad (3.50)$$

The value for ω_1 is derived from equations (340), (3.41) and (3.42) which are shallow shell equations. In this approximation it is assumed that the rise-factor H_0/h remains constant in the perturbation.

In the example given earlier, where $a = 1$, $b = 0.8$ and $r_c = 0.892$, squaring gives $r_c^2 = 0.796$ from which one finds that $r_c^2 \cong ab$; the equality holds when $a = b$ but the approximation is quite good for all elliptical planforms of low ellipticity as obtained on the pan notes. We can now replace r_c^2 with the product ab in equation (3.50) to give the Pan Maker's Formula:

The *Pan Maker's Formula*:

$$f_1 = \frac{\omega_1}{2\pi}\left(\frac{E}{\rho(1-v^2)}\right)^{\frac{1}{2}} \frac{h}{ab}\left(3 - 6\frac{a}{b} + 4\left(\frac{a}{b}\right)^2\right)^{\frac{1}{2}}. \qquad (3.51)$$

Equation (3.51) represents the best available approximate closed-form solution for the key-note frequency of a pan note. A version of this formula first appeared in the author's work, *The Pan Makers' Handbook* 1999.

Finding a more precise solution will amount to the *effective absorption* of the factor $\left(3 - 6\frac{a}{b} + 4\left(\frac{a}{b}\right)^2\right)^{\frac{1}{2}}$ into the expression for ω_1 which, by equation (3.42) means its absorption along with H_0/h into the functions $\bar{M}_1$ and $\bar{P}_1$. These two functions then take on more general forms for integration over the three dimensional domain $N = (R, \theta, \phi)$. With this generalization we lose track of the easily identified geometrical variables a, b, H_0 and h. As a result, we lose our ability to follow the effect that each of these variables has on the note frequency during the tuning process (except by using lengthy numerical methods). In my opinion it is far better to sacrifice some precision and generality by using the procedures adopted here, where one begins with a shallow shell of spherical form then deform the shell into an ellipsoid. This method not only predicts accurately the qualitative behavior of the note, but also yields good quantitative accuracy bearing in mind that the solution assumes that the pan maker has achieved perfect blocking of the note. Perfect blocking will ensure that the note boundary ∂N remains fixed (suffers no displacement or rotation). While the pan maker hammer peens the boundary in order to block (tighten) the note, the result is never perfect. This means that the boundary of an excited note will execute small vibrations *which makes it possible for note-note interactions to take place (such as on the Marshall Pairs)*.

Imperfect blocking results in energy losses as the note boundary is set into small vibrations. In this case, the spring constants K and C must both be finite, resulting in a lowering of the note frequency compared to what obtains with a fixed (or clamped) boundary. In later Sections of this book, the energy losses through the boundary, the material losses within the note domain, and the acoustic radiation (itself a loss to the air medium) are all taken into account to determine their effects on note frequency.

Comment: *Exactly what do I mean by 'it is far better to sacrifice some precision?' We are in fact speaking about precision to within less than one percent and at worse (for ellipticity larger than those found on a typical steelpan note) just a few percent of the exact frequency of the note. We have therefore sacrificed very little by way of precision when using equation (3.51). Typical aspect ratios on the pan notes will therefore give us good precision when using the Pan Maker's Formula. The formula does however, presuppose good pan making practices and excellent blocking.*

CHAPTER 4

The Steelpan as a System of Non-Linear Mode-Localized Oscillators: Theory, Simulations and Experiments

4.1 Mode Localization

In studying the vibrational motion of the notes on the pan it was discovered and reported in Achong (1996b) for the first time that the pan operates as a system of non-linear mode-localized vibrators. In response to an external transient impulse (stick impact), the motion remains confined mostly to the true note around the point of application of the disturbance. Mention of the system as a set of localized vibrators was made in Achong (1996a) but there, the system was modeled linearly for the purpose of determining fundamental mode shapes. As shown in Achong (1996a), the motion is confined on the note to an area bounded by an elliptical nodal line. For all notes, these boundaries are located within the area defined by the grooves, with the grooves lying *outside* the boundary of the true note..

In studies of linear mode localization it was shown (Hodges 1982, Pierre and Dowell 1987 and Wei and Pierre 1988a & b) that weak structural irregularities might lead to confinement of free and forced vibrations. In these studies, the localized vibrations and wave confinement resulted from some mistuning of the sub-assemblies. For non-linear mode confinement (Vakakis and Cetinkaya 1993,

Vakakis et al. 1993 and King and Vakakis 1995) in contrast to the linear case, mode confinement occurs in weakly coupled structures even in the absence of structural disorder. The main mechanism is the non-linear relation between amplitude and frequency that occurs during non-linear free oscillation. Each vibrating note (substructure) on the pan is an ideal system for displaying non-linear phenomena because of the shell curvature (producing quadratic non-linearities) and stretching of the midsurface (cubic non-linearities). In addition, the notes are coupled through areas of the pan face (the *internote*) that differ only in curvature, thickness and the stiffness.

For a theoretical statement that gives convincing proof of mode localization on the steelpan, see Section 6.2.1. The supporting experimental evidence is also given in Chapter 6.

4.2 Non-Linearities in other Musical Instruments

Non-linearities are also to be found in woodwinds, brass and bowed string instruments (McIntyre et al. 1983). The 'pitch-flattening' effect of bowed-string instruments (McIntyre and Woodhouse 1979), originates in the non-linear characteristics of the frictional force ('slip and stick') exerted by the bow on the string. The large amplitude behavior of the clarinet is also non-linear. The rounding or squaring of the periodic pressure waveform of the clarinet is due to the time-smearing effect of reflection from the bell back to the reed and the steepening effect of rapid puffs of air past the reed (McIntyre et al. 1983). Non-linear effects such as the higher type Raman waves found on the bowed string are known to be musically important as they lend color to the sound (Lawergren 1980).

4.3 Scope of the Chapter

This Chapter is concerned with the temporal aspects of the note vibrations on the steelpan and does not address the spatial problem of mode shapes except in a limited way in order to justify the use of the present method of analysis. The method is based on the non-linear analysis of Chapter 3. By considering the region on the note to which the motion is confined, vibrational analysis may be performed on this shell-like structure (see Figure 3.3) with the surrounding areas of the note and pan face replaced by equivalent springs to set the boundary conditions. A linear analysis of this type has been done for flat elliptical plates by Achong (1995). There are difficulties in extending the technique covered in that paper from the flat elliptical plate to the notes on the steelpan. The two main difficulties that one encounters in the extended analysis are (i) the determination of the exact surface geometry of the note and (ii) the determination of the appropriate boundary conditions. It has been shown by Achong (1996a) that there is no unique note geometry or unique set of boundary conditions that determines the fundamental frequency of a note on the steelpan. This Chapter therefore temporarily sets aside these difficulties to address the equally important aspects of time-histories and spectra of the vibrations on the steelpan.

4.4 Time-Domain Analysis

The time-history of a steelpan tone may be divided into two phases (i) the *impact phase*, and (ii) the *free oscillation phase*. The impact phase is of short duration, lasting less than the period of a typical fundamental mode vibration, and describes the time when the stick remains in contact with the note. The free oscillation phase on the other hand, describes the vibrational phase from the moment the stick leaves the pan to the end of the tone. The free oscillation phase shows a fast initial rise in amplitude of the vibration followed by slow amplitude modulations and decay.

4.4.1 Impact Phase

For the full theory of the impact phase, refer to Chapter 13. For the analysis in this Chapter, some essential points of the Impact Theory given in Chapter 13 are brought forward and stated here.

On the steelpan, note excitation by stick impact represents a case of *impulsive loading* where the force is applied over a time interval shorter than the period that characterizes the motion of the note surface. The initial movement of the note depends on the velocity of the stick and interaction between the stick and the note. The impact problem is complicated by the effects of the hand action, the position of the impact point on the note, the contact area between stick and note, the nature of the materials in contact and the duration of the impact. The simple theory of impulsive excitation shows that *contact-area frequency band limiting* arises when the width of the contact area (*stick-width*) is greater than the generalized half-wavelength of the mode in question. This effect is put to use when choosing the stick size appropriate for each pan type (larger stick widths are required for the lower pans). *Contact time* produces a band limitation for frequencies higher than that for which one-half cycle has the same duration as the impact. Both types of frequency limitation can be controlled by the panist during the delivery of the impact to produce a brighter or a more rounded tone.

Excitation due to impact often yields a half-sine shaped force and it is possible to mathematically model the stick impacts on the steelpan using this approximation. In any case, because of physical limitations on stick-width and contact-time, the driving-force Fourier series will be convergent and sharply band-limited (see Chapter 13 for full details).

4.4.2 Free Vibration Phase

In the present Chapter, the approach chosen to analyze the free vibration phase of steelpan notes is that suited to *multi degree-of-freedom (MDOF) non-linear systems* displaying amplitude changes on time scales that are long compared to the periods of the modes of vibration. It is important to grasp this notion of time scales early and to clearly understand that in the dynamics of note vibrations there are aspects that can be described on short time-scales while there are other aspects that occur on longer time-scales. This analysis covers the temporal aspects of the motion and since there are several free parameters involved, there is a wealth of possible cases that can be modeled.

For consistency with the experimental methods described in this Chapter where the vibration detection system is responsive only to the transverse motion of the notes and because the main component of motion is transverse, a model representing only the transverse displacement of the note surface is adopted. This means that longitudinal displacements in the plane of the note surface are not considered. The weaker cubic non-linearites are related to these in-plane displacements. The vibrations take place in the neighborhood of a static-equilibrium configuration represented by the shell-like note at rest. Because of the curvature and the stretching of the midsurface of the note, the first non-linear terms of the Taylor expansions of the differential equations of motion results in a non-linear system of equations.

The transverse displacement of a note in the neighborhood of a static-equilibrium (see Section 3.10) can be expressed in separable form as

$$w(r,t) = \sum_{n=1}^{\infty} \psi_n(r) u_n(t) \qquad (4.1)$$

where $\psi_n(r)$ are appropriate spatial functions (mode shapes) satisfying the boundary conditions of the note, n is the mode number, and $u_n(t)$ are unknown functions of time only.

4.4.3 The 3-DOF Note —Key-note, Octave and Twelfth

In order not to overburden this analysis only the quadratic terms due to curvature of the note surface will be retained in the non-linear part of u_n while the smaller cubic terms due to stretching of the midsurface will be neglected. This is a reasonable approximation on these shallow shell structures which, when played in the usual manner with the stick, will experience only small transverse displacements and small midsurface stretching. We also consider the note after impact to be a free non-linear oscillator subject to an initial displacement. In later analyses, the cubic non-linearities will be introduced.

We have made the explicit assumption that the motion of the note surface is in some small neighborhood of static equilibrium (the *Quiescent Point*) and to do this, we shall introduce a small gauge parameter ε, $0 < \varepsilon < 1$. It is also assumed that the damping term is of the same order in ε as the quadratic term. For a note with its first mode (the fundamental) tuned as the key-note (ω_1), the second mode to the octave ($\omega_2 \approx 2\omega_1$) and the third mode to the musical twelfth ($\omega_3 \approx 3\omega_1$), the governing equations, taken from equation (3.30) in Chapter 3 are

$$\frac{d^2 u_n}{dt^2} + \omega_n^2 u_n + \varepsilon \left[2\mu_n \dot{u}_n - \sum_{j=1}^{3} \sum_{k=1}^{3} \alpha_{j,k,n} u_j u_k - f(t) \right] = 0. \quad (4.2)$$

Here u_n are the displacements; the dots refer to differentiation with respect to time t; ω_n are the natural frequencies of the linearized system with $\omega_1 < \omega_2 < \omega_3$; μ_n are the damping coefficients; α_{jkn} are the quadratic parameters with $\alpha_{jkn} = \alpha_{kjn}$; $f(t)$ is a short duration external impulse (approximately half-sine shaped) which is set to zero after impact for the free system. The factor 2 appearing in the decay term is inserted for algebraic simplicity later in the analysis. The higher untuned modes ($n > 3$) of the note do not interact significantly with the system under study provided that their natural frequencies are not close to an integer multiple of the fundamental mode frequency. Since we are considering small oscillations about the Quiescent State, the static force f_0 does not enter equation (4.2). This statement will later be refined to include the *Tuning Temperature*.

4.5 Parametric Excitations and Internal Resonances

Equation (4.2) as a force equation describes the inertial forces per unit mass $\ddot{u}_n$, the linear restoring forces $\omega_n^2 u_n$, the stick impact force $f(t)$ and a number of internal *parametric forces* given by $\alpha_{jkn} u_j u_k$. Since only quadratic non-linearity is operative in this analysis, these parametric forces are all quadratic in form. The strongest of these parametric forces is *the interaction of the first mode with itself*, described by $\alpha_{112} u_1^2$. If the first mode vibrations are described approximately by a cosine function $u_1 \sim cos\,(\omega_1 t)$ then $u_1^2 \sim cos^2(\omega_1 t) = \frac{1}{2}[1 + \cos(2\omega_1 t)]$, which shows that the term $\alpha_{112} u_1^2$ describes a *parametric excitation* at twice the frequency ($2\omega_1$) of the first mode in addition to a constant (DC) term (see Chapter 7 for more details). Similarly the term $\alpha_{121} u_1 u_2$ describes a parametric excitation at frequency ($\omega_2 - \omega_1$) while the term $\alpha_{123} u_1 u_2$ describes a parametric excitation at frequency ($\omega_1 + \omega_2$). These can be verified from simple trigonometry where the product of two cosines cos(A)cos(B) can be expressed as the sum of terms in cos(A-B) and cos (A+B).

If the second natural mode (mode2) on a note is tuned so that $\omega_2 \approx 2\omega_1$ (the octave), the frequency of the parametric excitation $\alpha_{112}u_1^2$ will be close to the second mode through the frequency-doubling interaction of mode1 *with itself*. This means that parametric excitation $\alpha_{112}u_1^2$ can resonate with mode2 and in the process, transfer energy from the first mode (mode1) to the second mode (mode2). This interaction is described as an *internal resonance*. The second mode therefore resonates parametrically with the first mode through the coupling described by the parameter α_{112}. The parametric excitation $\alpha_{121}u_1u_2$ at frequency $(\omega_2 - \omega_1) \approx \omega_1$, will resonate with the first mode in another internal resonance. Mode1 and mode2 therefore interact quadratically to transfer energy back to mode1.

If the third natural mode (mode3) on the note is tuned so that $\omega_3 \approx 3\omega_1$ (the twelfth), the parametric excitation $\alpha_{123}u_1u_2$ at frequency $(\omega_2 + \omega_1) \approx 3\omega_1$ will resonate with mode3. Mode1 and mode2 therefore interact quadratically to transfer energy to mode3. There is another parametric excitation $\alpha_{231}u_2u_3$, at frequency $(\omega_3 - \omega_2) \approx \omega_1$, which transfers energy from mode2 and mode3 back to mode1. Finally, the parametric excitation $\alpha_{132}u_1u_3$ transfers energy from mode1 and mode3 to mode2. There are higher parametric excitations such as $\alpha_{224}u_2^2$ and $\alpha_{235}u_2u_3$ that will interact with the 4th and 5th modes *if and only if* they were tuned to the respective frequencies $\omega_4 \approx 2\omega_2$ and $\omega_5 \approx \omega_2 + \omega_3$. However, since by assumption, only the first three modes (partials) are correctly tuned these last two interactions will not take place. However, these two parametric excitations will still exist and be detectable at very low levels on the note but they will not interact with any of the normal modes.

4.6 Multi Time-scale Analysis Applied to the Free Phase

In the multi time-scale procedure developed by Nayfeh and Mook (1979), one defines $t_0 = t$, $t_1 = \varepsilon t$, where the main oscillatory behavior at frequencies ω_n are associated with the fast time scale t_0, while amplitude and phase modulations due to damping and non-linearities take place on the slow time scale t_1. In addition, the time derivative is $d/dt = D_0 + \varepsilon D_1$ where $D_n = \partial/\partial t_n$.

The procedure allows the independent variable u_n to be expanded in the form (*ansatz*)

$$u_n = u_{n0}(t_0,t_1) + \varepsilon u_{n1}(t_0,t_1) + O(\varepsilon^2) \qquad (4.3)$$

By substituting (4.3) into (4.2), transforming time derivatives and equating coefficients in like powers of ε, one obtains the following set of equations

order ε^0,

$$D_0^2 u_{n0} + \omega_n^2 u_{n0} = 0 \qquad (4.4)$$

order ε^1,

$$D_0^2 u_{n1} + \omega_n^2 u_{n1} = -2D_0(D_1 + \mu_n)u_{n0} - \sum_{j=1}^{\infty}\sum_{k=1}^{\infty} \alpha_{jkn} u_{j0} u_{k0} \qquad (4.5)$$

The general solution of (4.4) takes the form

$$u_{n0} = A_n(t_1) e^{i\omega_n t_0} + cc \qquad (4.6)$$

where cc is the complex conjugate of the preceding terms. A_n can be expressed as

$$A_n = \tfrac{1}{2} a_n e^{i\phi_n} \qquad (4.7)$$

where a_n and ϕ_n are functions of the slow time t_1 and represent the amplitude and phase of the nth Fourier component of the displacement respectively.

To study the internal resonances the second and third non-linear modes are described by the *detuning parameters* σ_1 and σ_2 where

$$\omega_2 = 2\omega_1 + \varepsilon\sigma_1, \quad \omega_3 = \omega_2 + \omega_1 + \varepsilon\sigma_2. \tag{4.8}$$

These detuning parameters for the higher partials (above the key-note) on the steelpan were introduced for the first time in my 1996 paper (Achong 1996b). The detuning parameters describe how close the second and third modes are to a harmonic relation with the first mode. If $\sigma_1 = 0$ and $\sigma_2 = 0$, $\omega_2 = 2\omega_1$ and $\omega_3 = 3\omega_1$, in which case the modes are in a perfect harmonic relation. **Steelpans with notes of good tonality are never tuned to perfect harmonicity — the detuning parameters must never be set to zero** (see Chapters 10 and 14). This requirement follows directly from the non-linear mode of operation of the steelpan as first reported in 1996 (*loc. cit.*).

Clarification: *It is important at this point to make a clear distinction between the term 'detuning' used here and the term 'mistuning.' Readers are very familiar with the term 'mistuning' which refers to a 'frequency shift', 'an error in frequency' or an 'offset in frequency' occurring on a note when compared with the correct frequency or frequencies on the musical scale. The 'mistuning' of a note may be the result of a number of reasons — carelessness on the part of the tuner, mishandling of the instrument, changes in ambient temperature etc. Mistuning can apply to any one or all of the partials on a note. Mistuning always degrades the quality of a note and that of the instrument. Mistuning is never deliberate (well at least not among the tuners that I know)!*

On the other hand, 'detuning' is deliberate. Detuning applies only to the higher partials (the octave and the twelfth) but never to the key-note. If the key-note is 'off' then it is mistuned. Detuning does not apply to the 'third' (above the octave) if that musical note is used as a higher partial on the bass. If the 'third' is 'off' then it is mistuned.

Detuning is applied to the octave and twelfth to ensure that these partials are NOT tuned to the second and third harmonics of the key-note respectively. Tuning to the harmonic produces the 'Pung' tone (see Section 14.24). Detuning these two partials is also done in order to set the tonality of the note as we shall see in later Sections.

The solvability conditions are now obtained by substituting (4.6) into (4.5) and eliminating the resultant *secular terms*. In general, secular terms are of the type t^n for systems whose integrable parts are non-linear, but here, they are of the *t-linear* ($n = 1$) secular type. Secular terms grow without limit and lead to instabilities. They must be removed by a *renormalization* procedure. This procedure in our case, equates the secular terms to zero. The substitution of (4.7) and (4.8) and the separation of real and imaginary parts, convert these solvability equations to

$$a_1' = -\mu_1 a_1 + \frac{\alpha_{121}^*}{4\omega_1} a_1 a_2 \sin\gamma_1 + \frac{\alpha_{231}^*}{4\omega_1} a_2 a_3 \sin\gamma_2$$

$$a_2' = -\mu_2 a_2 + \frac{\alpha_{112}}{4\omega_2} a_1^2 \sin\gamma_1 + \frac{\alpha_{132}^*}{4\omega_2} a_1 a_3 \sin\gamma_2$$

$$a_3' = -\mu_3 a_3 - \frac{\alpha_{123}^*}{4\omega_3} a_1 a_2 \sin\gamma_2$$

$$\phi_1' = -\frac{\alpha_{121}^*}{4\omega_1} a_2 \cos\gamma_1 - \frac{\alpha_{231}^*}{4\omega_1} \frac{a_2 a_3}{a_1} \cos\gamma_2$$

$$\phi_2' = -\frac{\alpha_{112}}{4\omega_2} \frac{a_1^2}{a_2} \cos\gamma_1 - \frac{\alpha_{132}^*}{4\omega_2} \frac{a_1 a_3}{a_2} \cos\gamma_2$$

$$\phi_3' = -\frac{\alpha_{123}^*}{4\omega_3} \frac{a_1 a_2}{a_3} \cos\gamma_2 . \tag{4.9a-f}$$

where $\alpha_{jkn}^* = \alpha_{jkn} + \alpha_{kjn}$, $(*)' = \frac{d}{dt_1}(*)$, and

$$\gamma_1 = \phi_2 - 2\phi_1 + \sigma_1 t_1, \quad \gamma_2 = \phi_3 - \phi_2 - \phi_1 + \sigma_2 t_1. \tag{4.10}$$

The following key can be used to identify the quadratic coupling parameters:

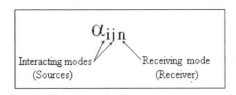

Equations (4.9a-c) describe the rate of growth and decay or the *amplitude modulation* of the modal amplitudes a_1, a_2 and a_3. Equations (4.9d-f) describe the variation in phase or the *frequency modulations* of the respective modes. The parameters ω_n, μ_n, σ_1, σ_2 and α_{jkn} allow the full range of modulation features observed on a steelpan to be modeled mathematically. The adjustment of parameters is the computational equivalent of the art and practice of tuning the pan as done by the pan maker. Parameter adjustment (from the author's perspective) is however, much easier to master.

4.7 Solution for 4-DOF Notes — Key-note, Octave, Twelfth and Second octave

4.7.1 Single Note with Quadratic and Cubic Non-linearities: Free Vibration

The case corresponding to a note for which the first four partials (fundamental or key-note (ω_1), octave (ω_2), twelfth (ω_3), second octave (ω_4)) are tuned and where both quadratic and cubic non-linearities are considered is described by the following set of equations:

$$\frac{d^2 u_n}{dt^2} + \omega_n^2 u_n + \varepsilon \left(2\mu_n u - \sum_j^4 \sum_k^4 \alpha_{ijn} u_i u_k - \sum_i^4 \sum_j^4 \sum_k^4 \beta_{ijkn} u_i u_j u_k \right) = 0, \quad (4.11)$$

where β_{ijkn} are the cubic coupling parameters.

$$\omega_2 = 2\omega_1 + \varepsilon\sigma_1, \ \omega_3 = 3\omega_1 + \varepsilon(\sigma_1 + \sigma_2), \ \omega_4 = 4\omega_1 + \varepsilon\sigma_3. \quad (4.12\text{a-c})$$

The following key can be used to identify the coupling coefficients:

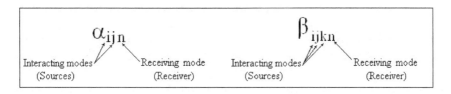

$$a'_1 = -\mu_1 a_1 + \frac{\alpha^*_{121}}{4\omega_1} a_1 a_2 \sin\gamma_1 + \frac{\alpha^*_{231}}{4\omega_1} a_2 a_3 \sin\gamma_2 + \frac{\alpha^*_{341}}{4\omega_1} a_3 a_4 \sin\gamma_6 + \frac{\beta^*_{2231}}{8\omega_1} a_2^2 a_3 \sin\gamma_4 - \frac{\beta^*_{1241}}{8\omega_1} a_1 a_2 a_4 \sin\gamma_8$$

$$a'_2 = -\mu_2 a_2 + \frac{\alpha^*_{132}}{4\omega_2} a_1 a_3 \sin\gamma_2 - \frac{\alpha^*_{112}}{4\omega_2} a_1^2 \sin\gamma_1 - \frac{\alpha^*_{242}}{4\omega_2} a_2 a_4 \sin\gamma_5 + \frac{\beta^*_{1232}}{8\omega_1} a_1 a_2 a_3 \sin\gamma_4 - \frac{\beta^*_{1142}}{8\omega_1} a_1^2 a_4 \sin\gamma_8$$

$$a'_3 = -\mu_3 a_3 - \frac{\alpha^*_{123}}{4\omega_3} a_1 a_2 \sin\gamma_2 + \frac{\alpha^*_{143}}{4\omega_3} a_1 a_4 \sin\gamma_6 + \frac{\beta^*_{1113}}{8\omega_3} a_1^3 \sin\gamma_3 + \frac{\beta^*_{2213}}{8\omega_3} a_1 a_2^2 \sin\gamma_4$$

$$a'_4 = -\mu_4 a_4 + \frac{\alpha^*_{224}}{4\omega_4} a_2^2 \sin\gamma_5 - \frac{\alpha^*_{134}}{4\omega_4} a_1 a_3 \sin\gamma_6 + \frac{\beta^*_{1124}}{8\omega_4} a_1^2 a_2 \sin\gamma_8 + \frac{\beta^*_{3324}}{8\omega_4} a_3^2 a_2 \sin\gamma_7$$

$$\phi'_1 = -\frac{\alpha^*_{121}}{4\omega_1} a_2 \cos\gamma_1 - \frac{\alpha^*_{231}}{4\omega_1} \frac{a_2 a_3}{a_1} \cos\gamma_2 - \frac{\alpha^*_{341}}{4\omega_1} \frac{a_3 a_4}{a_1} \cos\gamma_6 - \frac{\beta^*_{2231}}{8\omega_1} \frac{a_2^2 a_3}{a_1} \cos\gamma_4 - \frac{\beta^*_{1241}}{8\omega_1} a_2 a_4 \sin\gamma_8$$

$$\phi'_2 = -\frac{\alpha^*_{132}}{4\omega_2} \frac{a_1 a_3}{a_2} \cos\gamma_2 - \frac{\alpha^*_{112}}{4\omega_2} \frac{a_1^2}{a_2} \cos\gamma_1 - \frac{\alpha^*_{242}}{4\omega_2} a_4 \cos\gamma_5 - \frac{\beta^*_{1232}}{8\omega_1} a_1 a_3 \cos\gamma_4 - \frac{\beta^*_{1142}}{8\omega_1} \frac{a_1^2 a_4}{a_2} \cos\gamma_8$$

$$\phi'_3 = -\frac{\alpha^*_{123}}{4\omega_3} \frac{a_1 a_2}{a_3} \cos\gamma_2 - \frac{\alpha^*_{143}}{4\omega_3} \frac{a_1 a_4}{a_3} \cos\gamma_6 - \frac{\beta^*_{1113}}{8\omega_3} \frac{a_1^3}{a_3} \cos\gamma_3 - \frac{\beta^*_{2213}}{8\omega_3} \frac{a_1 a_2^2}{a_3} \cos\gamma_4$$

$$\phi'_4 = -\frac{\alpha^*_{224}}{4\omega_4} \frac{a_2^2}{a_4} \cos\gamma_5 - \frac{\alpha^*_{134}}{4\omega_4} \frac{a_1 a_3}{a_4} \cos\gamma_6 - \frac{\beta^*_{1124}}{8\omega_4} \frac{a_1^2 a_2}{a_4} \cos\gamma_8 - \frac{\beta^*_{3324}}{8\omega_4} \frac{a_3^2 a_2}{a_4} \cos\gamma_7.$$

(4.13a-h)

$$\gamma_1 = \phi_2 - 2\phi_1 + \sigma_1 t_1, \qquad \gamma_2 = \phi_3 - \phi_2 - \phi_1 + \sigma_2 t_1,$$

$$\gamma_3 = 3\phi_1 - \phi_3 - (\sigma_1 + \sigma_2)t_1, \qquad \gamma_4 = 2\phi_2 - \phi_3 - \phi_1 + (\sigma_1 - \sigma_2)t_1,$$

$$\gamma_5 = 2\phi_2 - \phi_4 + (2\sigma_1 - \sigma_3)t_1, \qquad \gamma_6 = \phi_4 - \phi_1 - \phi_3 - (\sigma_1 + \sigma_2 - \sigma_3)t_1,$$

$$\gamma_7 = 2\phi_3 - \phi_2 - \phi_4 + (\sigma_1 + 2\sigma_2 - \sigma_3)t_1, \quad \gamma_8 = 2\phi_1 + \phi_2 - \phi_4 + (\sigma_1 - \sigma_3)t_1.$$

(4.14a-h)

If the detuning parameter σ_2 is redefined according to $\omega_3 = 3\omega_1 + \varepsilon\sigma_2$, then

$$\gamma_1 = \phi_2 - 2\phi_1 + \sigma_1 t_1, \qquad \gamma_2 = \phi_3 - \phi_2 - \phi_1 + (\sigma_2 - \sigma_1)t_1,$$

$$\gamma_3 = 3\phi_1 - \phi_3 - \sigma_2 t_1, \qquad \gamma_4 = 2\phi_2 - \phi_3 - \phi_1 + (2\sigma_1 - \sigma_2)t_1,$$

$$\gamma_5 = 2\phi_2 - \phi_4 + (2\sigma_1 - \sigma_3)t_1, \qquad \gamma_6 = \phi_4 - \phi_1 - \phi_3 + (\sigma_3 - \sigma_2)t_1,$$

$$\gamma_7 = 2\phi_3 - \phi_2 - \phi_4 + (2\sigma_2 - \sigma_1 - \sigma_3)t_1, \quad \gamma_8 = 2\phi_1 + \phi_2 - \phi_4 + (\sigma_1 - \sigma_3)t_1.$$

(4.15a-h)

Only the rare, high-end, quality pan from a gifted tuner will require the set of equations (4.13), (4.14) and (4.15) for a description of its note dynamics.

4.8 Signal Processing

4.8.1 Short Time Fourier Transform

Because it is the objective of the work in this Chapter to determine and analyze the sound production mechanisms of the steelpan, it is necessary to choose a signal processing technique that presents a valid representation of the time-varying signals and its basic components. The Short Time Fourier Transform (STFT) (see Allen and Rabiner 1977, Schafer and Rabiner 1973 & 1978) finds application in the evaluation of slowly time-varying components of quasi-periodic signals, such as those occurring in speech processing, vibration analysis, and musical tone analysis. The STFT of a signal u(t) is defined as

$$S(t,\omega) = \int_{-\infty}^{+\infty} [u(t')\overline{g}(t'-t)]e^{-j\omega t'} dt', \qquad (4.16)$$

where ω is the *analyzing frequency*. The STFT is thus the Fourier Transform (FT) of the product of the signal u(t') and a shifted 'analysis window' $\overline{g}(t'-t)$ (the overbar denotes complex conjugation). This pre-windowing suppresses all signals outside a small interval around the analysis time *t* and the STFT tells us how strongly a neighborhood around the time-frequency point (t,ω) contributes to the signal. The signal is assumed stationary when seen through this window. Figure 4.1 illustrates the pre-windowing operation. The STFT then is a measure of how close in the frequency domain is the frequency this sampled signal to the analyzing frequency ω.

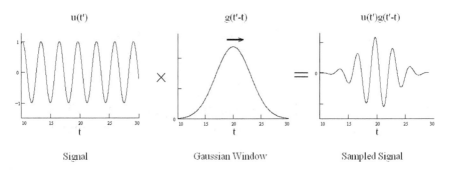

Fig. 4.1. Pre-windowing the signal around the analysis time t.

This transform is linear by definition and, in addition preserves frequency shifts and time shifts up to a phase factor (Hlawatsch and Boudreaux-Bartels 1992). These linear properties allow for the decomposition of the pan signal into a sum of elementary STFT contributions.

The decomposition depends on the choice of analysis window. A short window offers good time resolution, while good frequency resolution requires a long window. The uncertainty principle (Gabor 1946 and Papoulis 1974) prohibits windows with arbitrarily short duration and arbitrarily narrow bandwidths. Maximized concentration in time-frequency is obtained with the use of a Gaussian window function (Helstrom 1966 and Bastiaans 1980) which can be taken as

$$g(t) = (\pi \gamma_g^2)^{\frac{1}{4}} \exp(-t^2/2\gamma_g^2), \quad (4.17)$$

where the variance γ_g^2 has to be chosen with care in order to obtain the desired frequency-time resolution.

If the signal components appear at frequencies ω_n (n = 1, 2, 3,...), the STFT (expressed as $S_u^{\{n\}}$) is maximized and phase shift is minimized when $\omega \approx \omega_n$. An important point worth mentioning here is that when computing the phase sequence $\phi_n(t) = arg(S_u^{\{n\}})$ for each component, use is made of the inverse tangent which (on your computer) is a many-to-one transformation restricting the phase to the interval $[-\pi/2, \pi/2]$. In general all the inverse functions of sine, cosine, and tangent are multi-valued functions. This can produce a phase ambiguity which has to be resolved using a suitable unwrapping procedure. In practice, when $S_u^{\{n\}}(t,\omega)$ is maximized, with $(\omega_n - \omega)t$ not near $-\pi/2$ or $\pi/2$, the unwrapping process is relatively simple.

In simple practical terms, the phase ambiguity problem appears in this way. As the computation of the STFT of a recorded (or live) sample progresses, a discrete sequence of phase values is computed. On inspecting this sequence one may find that at some point in the sequence, the angle increases towards the value $\pi/2$ say, then on the next entry on the sequence, the phase switches to $-\pi/2$ (or very close) — the phase has wrapped around by 180 degrees or π. A computer routine can be added to the STFT program to catch and unwrap these phase switches.

For a discretized signal with sampling period Δt, the STFT at time $t = m\Delta t$ is defined as

$$S(m,\omega) = \sum_{m'=-\infty}^{+\infty} [u(m') \overline{g}(m'-m)] e^{-j\omega m'}. \quad (4.18)$$

The convention of normalizing Δt to unity is used here. This is the form suitable for the analysis of the sampled data obtained in the present work.

4.8.2 STFT of Velocity and Displacement

The STFT of the displacement u and its time derivative $\dot{u}$ (velocity), are related linearly by

$$S_{\dot{u}}^{\{n\}} = -j\omega_n S_u^{\{n\}}, \qquad (4.19)$$

where the factor -j (= $\sqrt{(-1)}$) indicates a -90° phase shift. Equation (4.19) shows that velocity data will show a high-frequency emphasis (proportional to ω_n). For (4.19) to be applicable in the present analysis, both the amplitude and frequency ω_n must vary slowly on the timescale t_1, and they must be at least quasi-stationary in the analysis window. If these conditions are satisfied then with the help of (4.19), velocity STFT may be used to compute the displacement STFT. The high-frequency emphasis inherent in the velocity data makes it advantageous to record the velocity of the vibrating note and make use of this emphasis to help in resolving the weaker higher modes.

The compatibility of the STFT and the multi time-scale analysis is now very clear, for the experimental data can be compared with the multi time-scale analysis through the 'equivalence' $A_n \equiv S_u^{\{n\}}$ or $a_n \equiv |S_u^{\{n\}}|$ and $\phi_n \equiv arg\left(S_u^{\{n\}}\right)$.

4.9 Experimental and Computational Methods

The selection of steelpans for analysis was done somewhat by random from among a number of similar, musically excellent instruments in the possession of a pan maker. From among the hundreds of notes examined, covering a range of pan types, those chosen for presentation in this analysis, show the rich variety of time variations produced by the steelpan notes. All pan tones were stored in digitized form on computer hard discs. The vibrational modes were excited by impact using standard pan sticks. A small rubber tipped stick is used on the higher pans while for the lower pans a larger and softer tip is used. The softer the tip the more the impact energy is concentrated in the lower frequencies. By using a thin strip of foil on the tip of the stick together with the metallic pan face, a simple 'switching circuit' contact-time (make-to-break) measuring apparatus was employed.

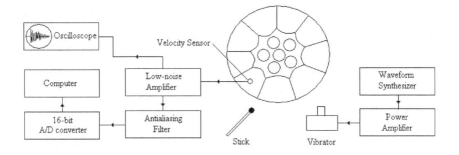

Fig. 4.2. The experimental setup for the determination of steelpan responses.

Velocity rather than displacement measurements were made because of the simplicity of the experimental set-up required and there was the added benefit of the frequency emphasis offered to the higher frequency modes which improved the signal-to-noise-ratio for these weaker signal components.

The velocity transducer was of the electromagnetic type, the output voltage of which is directly proportional to the transverse velocity of the vibrating note. By using the note itself as the active element, the transducer was self-tuned. The essential features of the set-up shown in Figure 4.2, consisted of a small electromagnetic transducer, low-noise differential input preamplifier, anti-aliasing filters, 16-bit A/D converter, computer and data storage devices. The software/hardware combination allowed a choice of sampling rates in the range 11 to 44 KHz. In most cases, the lower rate was found to be sufficiently fast.

To determine the frequency-response curves for the system under periodic excitation, the steelpans were excited by an electrodynamic vibrator attached to either the center of the pan face or to the skirt, and driven by a power amplifier. Acoustic excitation has also been used for the bass pans. The power amplifier was driven by a sinusoidal waveform produced by a stable multifunction waveform synthesizer with 0.001 Hz resolution. To determine the steady-state amplitudes, the responses were analyzed in 16 Kbyte bins at 0.1 Hz steps (0.02 Hz steps near unstable regions, see Chapter 18 on Exotic Responses).

For maximum accuracy all computer software representing the data analyses, were checked using independent electronically generated synthesized waveforms having known time and frequency structures. The variance in the STFT computations was set with $\gamma_g = T_1$ where T_1 equals one waveform period of the analyzing frequency used for the first mode component, and the Gaussian window was truncated to a width of $8T_1$. The same window was used for all modes on a note, giving the same resolution at all locations in the time-frequency plane.

The discrete displacement values u_j were obtained from the sampled velocities $\dot{u}_j$ using a multi-step, 4th order Adams-Moulton Predictor-Corrector integration method with mop-up, taken from the author's home-brew assortment of numerical solvers. Readers interested in developing their own software routines can seek the help of the following references: Abramowitz and Stegun (1972), Jeffreys and Jeffreys (1988), Press et al. (1992), Shampine (1994) and Shampine and Gordon (1975).

A straightforward 4th order Adams-Bashforth or Adams-Moulton method can also be used. For readers following this procedure, a cautionary note should be added here on integrating the velocity data to obtain the note displacements. As it is with all multistep numerical integration methods, errors in earlier steps can feed into later calculations with unfavorable consequences. With discretized values of the velocity, the initial velocity which should correctly be zero but with the use of electronic digitizing circuitry (analog to digital A/D converters) to record the data, this zero may appear digitally as ± 1 bit or greater. In fact the entire data may be shifted up or down by one bit or even more. In 8-bit sampling for example, this amounts to a fractional error of $±1/256 = ±0.00390$ (and much smaller for 12-bit and 16-bit sampling). By itself, this is quite a small error, which can be ignored in presenting the velocity data. But when the data is integrated, this 'zero error' accumulates with each step to produce a linear component (proportional to time t) in the computed displacement data. This artifact can easily be spotted because at the end of the sampled tone, the note displacement should return to zero. If at the end of the tone, a large displacement is observed in the computation, one can easily remove the artifact with a mop-up procedure which subtracts from the displacement data a linear function with the opposite slope.

To model the notes, equations (4.9a-f) were integrated numerically using a *fixed-step* 4th order *Runge-Kutta routine* (see for example Arfken 1985) to produce discretized values for a_n and φ_n at time steps of 0.1. *Variable step* methods such as the Runge-Kutta-Gill method are not recommended here because of the need to preserve phase data and to re-construct the modal components in both amplitude and phase. (*Note: the variable step method is still useable but one must record the step sizes along with the computed output in order to reconstruct the required time-series. This method adds a bit more complication to the process.*) A 4th order method with the recommended time step (0.1) is sufficiently accurate and stable for working with the non-linear note dynamics under normal stick excitation but it fails under strong continuous sinusoidal excitation (for an example of this type of problem, see Cartwright and Piro 1992) as required to observe the exotic features of the note dynamics. In the latter case, an 8th order Runge-Kutta or an 8th order *Finite Difference Method* (preferably both, as a check) should be employed with care.

4.10 Results and Discussion

4.10.1 Numerical and Experimental Results

Note: Readers should pay attention to the detailed structure of the tones generated by the note vibrations and to the explanations given for even the most subtle features of the tones. These subtle features enrich the sound of this instrument.

Measurement of the contact time using the *electrical-contact method* gives the total time duration (from make-to-break) that the stick remains in contact with the note. In Chapter 13 it is shown that the total time in contact with the note $T/2$ is equal to $3\tau_c/2$ where τ_c is the *contact-time* and T is the period of the equivalent half-sine pulse. Experimental data showed that T/2 is shorter than a typical period of oscillation on the tenor pan $0.3\,ms \leq T/2 \leq 0.6\,ms$ and of the order of a period on the bass $4\,ms \leq T/2 \leq 8\,ms$. These results show that the contact-times fall within the range: Tenor, $0.2\,ms \leq \tau_c \leq 0.4\,ms$; Bass, $2.67\,ms \leq \tau_c \leq 5.3\,ms$.

In producing the steelpan tones by the normal way of stick impacts, no attempt was made to quantify the impacts except in the musical manner from 'very soft' (*pianissimo*) to 'loud' (*forte*) as judged from the acoustical output.

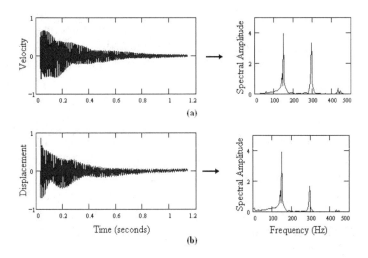

Fig. 4.3. Time histories and frequency spectra for the **D$_3$** (146.83 Hz) note played 'forte': (a) surface velocity and (b) surface displacement.

Computations done on the experimental velocity data and the derived displacement data agree with equation (4.15) in both magnitude and phase (including the -90°shift). Significant savings in computational costs can therefore be realized by using (4.15) to compute the displacement STFT once the velocity STFT is maximized and the phase unwrapped. Typical velocity and displacement data together with the corresponding spectra are shown in Figure 4.3 for a note excited by stick impact to the sweetspot (see Chapter 13). The narrowness of the spectral peaks is an important feature and the high frequency emphasis in the velocity data is evident from the spectral amplitudes. The peak for the second mode at 293.66 Hz is for the displacement spectra is ½ the height of the corresponding peak for the velocity spectra. A weak third mode around 440 Hz just rises above the baseline in the displacement spectra. This is in agreement with equation (4.15), which gives the ratio $\left| S_{\ddot{u}}^{\{n\}} / S_{\dot{u}}^{\{n\}} \right| = \omega_n$. In normalized units (rounded to the nearest integer) $\omega_1 = 1$, $\omega_2 = 2$, $\omega_3 = 3$, so that the height of the displacement peaks will fall off by the factor 1, ½, ⅓ when compared to the corresponding peaks on the velocity spectra.

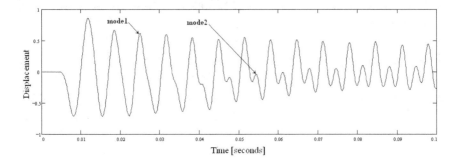

Fig. 4.4. The first 0.1s of the **D₃** note surface displacement showing the rapid development of the first mode and the slower growth of the second mode. The second mode becomes visible after five cycles of the first mode.

This is a well-modulated tone with a strong second mode (mode2) obtained from the **D₃** note on a tenor bass. Observe the amplitude modulations on both the velocity and the displacement time histories of the note vibration. Figure 4.4 shows the first 0.1 second of this tone at higher time resolution. The weak third mode cannot be resolved on the plots in the time domain but can just be resolved in the frequency domain on the spectral plots (Fourier Transform). Observe the fast rise of mode1 and the slower growth of mode2, which becomes visible after five cycles of mode1. This slower growth of the second mode is typical of the notes on the steelpan and will be fully explained using the theory developed here.

Observe if you could, the longer period of the first cycle of vibration. This is a general feature on this non-linear system and can be better observed on tones with slower rise-times (those that take a few initial cycles to maximize). This initial lengthening of the period produces an initial reduction in the tonal frequency. This effect is explained in Chapters 7 and 13, where it is shown that because of the quadratic restoring forces (which are generally stronger than the cubic forces), the notes vibrate like *softening springs.* This means that as the displacement increases, the frequency of oscillation is reduced. Initially, the impacted note will vibrate with large amplitude which subsequently decays. The note therefore commences vibration with a lowered frequency.

All numerical computations on the system equations (9a-f) were done with parameter values chosen to closely (but not necessarily exactly) model the tones produced on the pan. In the numerical modeling, the amplitude-time and frequency-time structures were found to be very sensitive to the detuning parameters — as the detuning parameter is reduced the modulation period increased. The practical interpretation is that the higher modes are not tuned in exact harmonic sequence by the pan maker if the 'natural' modulation features, so characteristic of the steelpan sound, are to be obtained.

4.10.2 B_4 Note

Figure 4.5(a) presents an example of one of the 'simplest' tone structure observed on the pan and seen here on the B_4 (493.9 Hz) note of a tenor played at a *forte* level. This simple structure as seen here on a bore pan can be seen more readily on the 'normal' pans. However, this simple structure is not typical of good, well-modulated B_4 notes. Observe in Figure 4.5 (a), the small modulations on the displacement envelope produced by *mode1 × mode2* interaction. Under higher time resolution Figure 4.5 (b) shows an almost sinusoidal type of motion because the second mode is relatively weak. Pan maker Bertie Marshall refers to this as an example of 'Simple Tuning'.

The STFT analysis of the tone is shown in Figure 4.6 (a, c, e, f). The velocity STFT's were maximized at f_1 = 493.68 Hz (mode1) and f_2 = 976.9 Hz (mode2). In Figure 4.6 (a), mode1 shows a rapid attack followed by an almost smooth exponential decay, a low level quasi-periodic (*amplitude modulated*) mode2 and the absence of a third mode component. Figures 4.6 (c, e, f) show the phase and frequency modulations. Only very small modulations (down to noise level) are observed in the mode1 phase ϕ_1, while relatively strong phase modulation is seen on ϕ_2 for mode2. Therefore, the mode1 frequency f_1 remains essentially constant throughout the tone (Figure 4.6 (e)) while the second mode frequency f_2 is strongly modulated (*frequency modulated*) as seen in Figure 4.6(f). Observe in panels (e) and (f) the modal frequencies begin lower than the nominal values of 493.68 Hz and 976.9 Hz respectively, then rapidly rises to the values set by the tuner.

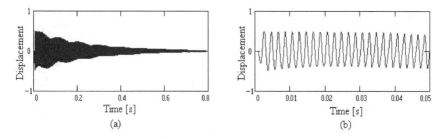

Fig. 4.5. Displacement time history of the displacement on a simply tuned B_4 note played forte. Low resolution showing the modulated envelope. (b) High time resolution showing essentially mode1 displacements. Mode2 is not resolved.

This non-linear system was modeled numerically and the results shown along with the phase diagrams in Figures 4.6 (b) and 4.6 (d). Modeling parameters: $\alpha_{211} = \alpha_{121} = 0.0025$, $\alpha_{112} = 0.007$, $\alpha_{123} = \alpha_{213} = 0$, $\alpha_{132} = \alpha_{312} = 0$, $\alpha_{231} = \alpha_{321} = 0$, $\mu_1 = \mu_2 = 0.0006$, $\mu_3 = 0$, $\sigma_1 = -0.008$, $\sigma_2 = 0$; initial amplitudes: $a_1 = 1$, $a_2 = a_3 = 0$. In order to reduce the complexity of the numerical modeling, computation begins the instant the first mode maximizes thus avoiding the more complex impact phase. Special numerical computations will be carried out in Section 13 to deal with the impact phase.

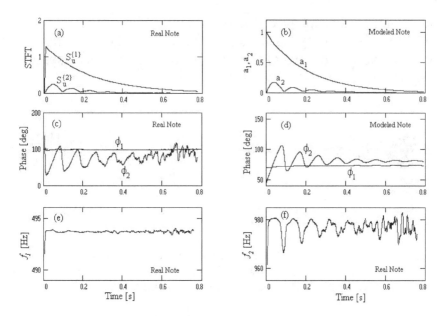

Fig. 4.6. STFT of the **B**$_4$ data in panels (a), (c), (e) and (f) showing amplitude, phase and frequency as functions of time. Amplitude and phase for numerically modeled note in panels (b) and (d).

Observe the strong similarities in the details of the phase diagrams obtained from non-linear theory and from experiment (compare panels (c) and (d)), with the experimental phase data for mode2 becoming noisy only as the signal dropped to an 'inaudible' level. The design parameters for the modeled note were chosen to provide good match between $S_u^{\{1\}}$ and a_1 and between $S_u^{\{2\}}$ and a_2 (compare panels (a) and (b)).

4.10.3 $F_4^\#$ Note

The tone structure in Figure 4.7 (a) for this $\mathbf{F}_4^\#$ (369.99 Hz) note played *forte*, shows a modulated decaying amplitude for mode1 and a weak modulated mode2 component. STFT's were maximized at f_1= 367.3 Hz (= $\mathbf{F}_4^\#$-13 cents) and f_2= 743.2 Hz (= $\mathbf{F}_5^\#$+7 cents). There was a small mis-tuning (by -13 cents) of the key-note at the time of the experiment.

Although somewhat similar to the Figure 4.6 (a) structure, the added modulation features produced an audibly discernible frequency modulation and a slow upward frequency glide on mode1 (Figure 4.7 (e)). A downward glide plus frequency modulation is seen on mode2 (Figure 4.7 (g)). The numerically modeled system represented in Figure 4.7 (b, d. f, h) reproduces these modulations and glides as can be seen from the changing phase slopes in Figure 4.7 (d) (compared with Figure 4.7 (c)). With its low-level amplitude modulations but strong frequency modulations (FM) this note when sounded generates a good example of a FM-dominated tone.

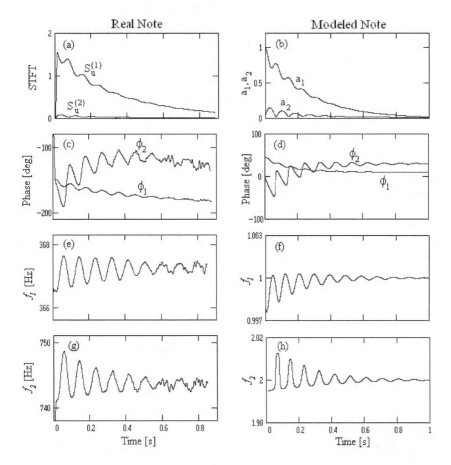

Fig. 4.7. The tone structure for a $\mathbf{F}_4^{\#}$ note played *forte*. Left panels for the real note and right panels for the numerical model with normalized modal frequencies.

The amplitude modulations clearly show the continuous exchange of energy between the two modes. The modal frequencies of the modeled note have 'small amplitude' values of $\omega_1 = 1$ and $\omega_1 = 2$

(plus the detuning). Modeling parameters: $\alpha_{211} = \alpha_{121} = 0.035$, $\alpha_{112} = 0.01$, $\alpha_{123} = \alpha_{213} = 0$, $\alpha_{132} = \alpha_{312} = 0$, $\alpha_{231} = \alpha_{321} = 0$, $\mu_1 = \mu_2 = 0.0006$, $\mu_3 = 0$, $\sigma_1 = 0.01$, $\sigma_2 = 0$; Initial amplitudes: $a_1 = 1$, $a_2 = a_3 = 0$.

4.10.4 E_4^b Note

A properly tuned, strongly modulated and more complex tone structure for an E_4^b (311.1 Hz) note played *forte* shown in Figure 4.8. Figures 4.9 (left panels), show the amplitude and phase histories of the sounded note while the simulated results are shown in Figures 4.9-right panels. All three experimental modes have been closely modeled, with a more exact matching on mode1 still possible by a slight increase in α_{211} and α_{121}. In fact, by tweaking the parameters during the computations while maintaining the same patience and care as exercised by the good tuner it is possible to obtain near perfect matching to the real note characteristics. It is only by the absence of the initial attack that the mathematical simulation can be easily distinguished from the steelpan data in these figures. STFT maximized with $f_1 = 311.1$ Hz, $f_2 = 624.0$ Hz, $f_3 = 930.6$ Hz. Modeling parameters: $\alpha_{211} = \alpha_{121} = 0.01$, $\alpha_{112} = 0.014$, $\alpha_{123} = \alpha_{213} = 0.01$, $\alpha_{132} = \alpha_{312} = 0.005$, $\alpha_{231} = \alpha_{321} = 0.005$, $\mu_1 = \mu_2 = 0.0006$, $\mu_3 = 0.0008$, $\sigma_1 = 0.002$, $\sigma_2 = 0.004$; Initial amplitudes: $a_1 = 1$, $a_2 = a_3 = 0$.

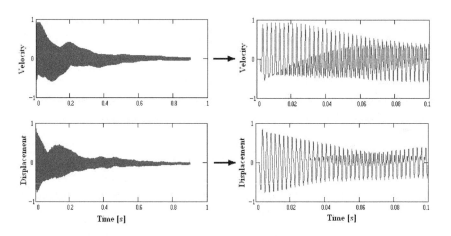

Fig. 4.8. Velocity and displacement of an excited E^b_4 note played forte. On the high time-resolution plots observe the presence of a stronger mode2 component on the velocity data.

Observe in Figure 4.9 top left panel (almost the same as the top right panel), that as mode1 initially rises in magnitude and begins its first descent that energy is transferred to mode2 (a process controlled by coupling parameter α_{112}) which slowly grows in magnitude. Mode2 reaches maximum amplitude before mode1 reaches its first minimum. Mode1 then begins its second ascent while mode2 descends as energy is transferred back to mode1 (a process controlled by α_{121}). These energy transfers continue throughout the lifetime of the tone as the system looses energy through damping and acoustical radiation. Stronger coupling (larger α_{112} and α_{121}) increases the energy transfers and the depth of modulation. In the mean time, mode3 receives energy from the coupling of mode1 and mode2 as determined by the parameter α_{123}. Mode3 loses energy back to mode1 (determined by α_{231}) and to mode2 (determined by α_{132}).

The rate of the amplitude modulations seen on mode1 and mode2 are determined by the detuning parameter σ_1. The rate being slower as σ_1 is reduced or equivalently, the closer ω_2 is to $2\omega_1$. Similarly, the modulation rate of mode3 is determined by the value of detuning parameter σ_2.

The real and modeled phase data are in good agreement. Notice that the large swing on ϕ_2 that occurs around t = 0.2 s, coincides with the rapid change in the magnitude of mode2 which also occurs around t = 0.2 s. This feature is well reproduced in the modeled note. The corresponding frequency changes on mode2 are seen also at this time (around 0.2 s) as a fast frequency excursion upward then downward. Mode1 shows only small frequency modulations that correspond to the times of minimum amplitude of mode1.

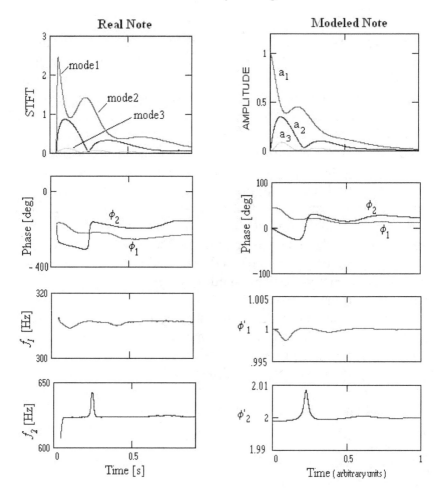

Fig. 4.9. Comparison of experimental data and numerical modeling for the E^b_4 note. The left panels, show the displacement STFT, phase and frequency histories of the real note. The right panels show the corresponding results for the numerical model.

This E_4^b note gives a good example of an AM-dominated (Amplitude Modulation-dominated) tone. It is a general feature of the tones on the steelpan that tones can be categorized as being FM-dominated (Frequency Modulation-dominated) or AM-dominated on either ends of the modulation 'spectrum'. The tones categorized as being 'best' on any steelpan are always AM-dominated. But 'best' is subjective so that it is not uncommon to find players with a preference for FM-dominated tones.

4.11 Effects of Stick Impact on Tonal Structure

The tone structures are shown for a **D$_3$** (146.8 Hz) note on the bass played *forte* (Figure 4.10 (a)) and *piano* (Figure 4.10 (c)). Many of the notes on the various types of pans, when played *forte* or *fortissimo* ('very loud') produced tones with time-structures between those of Figure 4.10 (c) and those of Figure 4.10 (a). The numerically modeled non-linear modes are shown in Figures 4.10 (b) and 4.10 (d). The *piano* level was modeled with an initial a$_1$ = 0.5, while the equivalent *forte* level had an initial a_1 = 1.0. The similarities between the real pan tone structure and the mathematical tone structure are remarkable. For emphasis, the parameters were chosen to produce a simulated mode3 component at an amplitude level higher than that obtained on the original tone. STFT maximized at f_1= 146.9 Hz, f_2= 293.0 Hz, f_3= 438.0 Hz. Modeling parameters: $\alpha_{211}=\alpha_{121}$= 0.0125, α_{112}= 0.025, $\alpha_{123}=\alpha_{213}$= 0.015, $\alpha_{132}=\alpha_{312}$= 0.005, $\alpha_{231}=\alpha_{321}$= 0.01, $\mu_1=\mu_2=\mu_3$ = 0.0006, σ_1= -.002, σ_2= -.01

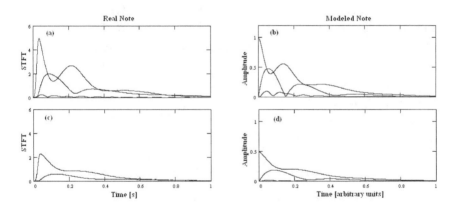

Fig. 4.10. Variation of amplitude with time for two different impact forces on the **D$_3$** note: (a) experimental and (b) numerical, for an impact corresponding to the pan played *forte*: (c) experimental and (d) numerical for the pan played *piano*.

The significant increase in the level of the second mode component when the more strongly non-linear notes are played with more vigor (compare Fig. 4.10 (a) and Fig. 4.10 (c), severely limits, especially on the bass, the levels at which the notes can be played by the panist. A dominant second mode on the bass is musically, undesirable. The non-linear theory shows that *as the initial amplitude of mode1 is increased (by playing louder), significantly more energy is spilled over into the second mode*. *In a linear system this will not occur*. This explains the difficulty that pan makers have struggled with in the development of the steelpan as they tried to make a 'louder' bass pan (the physically largest of the pans). (*See Chapter 14 for a useful remedy for this problem*). The increase in the relative amplitude of the higher modes as the instrument is played louder is of a fundamental nature on this strictly non-linear instrument and applies to all types of steelpans.

An estimate of the energy ratio can be made by integrating $|S_u^{\{n\}}(t,\omega)|^2$ over the duration of the note. From the *piano* to the *forte* level, the percentage of total energy in mode2 of this D_3 note rose from 11.3% to 21.7% respectively. Similar results were obtained for other notes tested in this manner.

The observation here is that the tonal quality is dependent on the manner in which the impact is delivered. This effect is applied by the panist with great effectiveness to the 'roll' which consists of a succession of single strikes of equal power. On the pan, the 'diminuendo roll' produces a gradual rounding of the tone as the intensity of the impact is reduced while the 'crescendo roll' produces a steadily brightening, lively sound as the impact intensity is gradually increased. On a properly tuned note, a more rounded tone with reduced amplitude modulation is produced at the piano level while a strongly amplitude modulated brighter tone is produced at the forte level.

4.12 Area of Confinement — the True Note

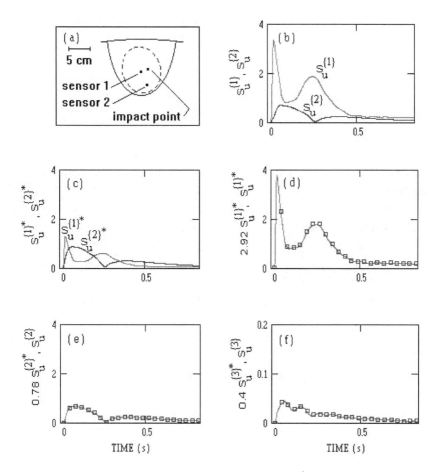

Fig. 4.11. Two-point modal measurement on an E_4^b tenor note: (a) sketch illustrating the placements of sensor 1 and sensor 2 (data identified by an asterisk *), the impact point and the boundary of confinement (ellipse); (b) sensor 1 data; (c) sensor 2 data; (d), (e) and (f) show sensor 2 data (—) normalized by least squares factors to match sensor 1 data (□).

A limited report is presented here for the confinement of vibration and for the mode shapes. Figure 4.11 (a) shows a sketch of the E_4^b note with one sensor (#1) located at the apex (crown) of the note and the other (#2) at approximately two thirds the distance from apex to the nodal line. The elliptical nodal line shown as the dotted ellipse in Figure 4.11 (a), determined by a Chladni method, represents the boundary of the localized vibrations — defined as the

True Note (see Section 3.3). Generally, the orientation, size and shape of these boundaries, within the regions marked by the grooves, depend on the preparation, the shaping and the tuning of the note. The grooves, while serving the purpose of reducing the interaction between neighboring notes, are only partially responsible for the confinement, as pans with similar vibrational properties have been constructed without grooves (see Section 14.35). The pan face undergoes curvature changes, inelastic strain and damage through the action of hammering.

Figures 4.11 (b) and 4.11 (c) show the Fourier components at the two sensor locations. Though at first sight the two diagrams appear dissimilar, the amplitudes can be scaled as in Figures 4.11 (d-f), and made to appear at equal levels. The exact match throughout the entire time-history in Figures 4.11 (d-f), shows that the mode shape (the set of scaling factors) for each spectral component (mode) can be obtained by mapping the surface with the sensor even though the modes are non-linear. In addition, the matching shows that the parameters (α_{jkn}, μ_n, and σ_n) can be obtained from the data acquired at a single location on the note and then combined with the mode shapes to produce the entire temporal/spatial character of the vibrations (i.e. to determine fully, the solution to equation (4.1)). The single-point parameter determination used in this work is therefore justified.

CHAPTER 5

The Steelpan as a System of Non-Linear Mode-Localized Oscillators: Coupled Sub-Systems, Simulations and Experiments

5.1 Introduction

This Chapter is a sequel to Chapter 4 where the dynamics of the steelpan notes were developed as systems of non-linear mode-localized oscillators. This Chapter examines the coupled note-note and note-skirt systems on the steelpan modeled as a plexus of non-linear oscillators interconnected by linear mechanical filters. The tonal qualities of a note depend on the degree of coupling and the closeness in frequency of the excited modes on the interacting subsystems. Modes above the fundamental (the partials) are produced by internal resonances and combination resonances.

Chapter 4 described the physical structure of the steelpan and examined the response of the notes to impacts produced by striking the notes with the stick. In that Chapter, each note was seen to function as a non-linear system for which the governing equations for note vibrations contained only linear and quadratic terms. These vibrations are confined to an elliptically shaped *true note* area. The exchange of energy between resonances on a note produces amplitude as well as frequency modulations.

Situations always arise on the steelpan where the mechanical coupling between subsystems (notes and skirt) is important. When the pan is being tuned for example, some notes may, by chance, have almost the same fundamental frequency as the desired frequency of the note to be tuned. The coupling of these notes makes it extremely difficult for the pan maker to tune the note. Coupling between note and skirt produces a similar difficulty. In the latter case, the coupling remains after tuning is completed and this degrades the tonal quality.

5.2 Theoretical Development

5.2.1 The Combinatorics and Fundamental Properties of the System

The following categorization of the musical instrument defined as the Pan, is independent of the material (metal) from which it is constructed — steel, brass, aluminum or any other metal. Many versions of this instrument have appeared in the past and there exists at present many new versions and others may be added to that list in the future. The term *Pan* therefore refers singly and collectively, to those instruments obeying the dynamical equations and satisfying the physical description contained in this work.

Consider the system of N-connected domains Ω_1, Ω_2, ... Ω_N on the pan (see Figure 5.1) . All of these domains, except one (the cylindrical skirt), are of similar geometry (describing the shallow shell or cap-like notes) but they differ in geometrical details (size, rise etc.) and in elastic properties. The domains are connected by means of elastic elements, defined here and in earlier publications by the author (see Achong and Sinanansingh 1997) as the *internotes* (and collectively as the *internote),* represented by the pan face exclusive of the notes (*true notes*) (see Section 3.3). The connection of *internotes* forms the domain Ω_0. All notes are considered non-linear systems while the physically largest element, the skirt, is modeled linearly.

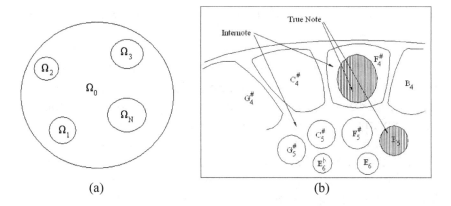

Fig. 5.1. (a) The N+1 domains of the system, (b) a section of a typical tenor steelpan.

To each domain is assigned (by the *tempering, forming* and *tuning processes*) a **set** of *unique parameters* satisfying the following conditions:

1. On a given pan, no two sets of parameters are equal.
2. For its use as a percussion musical instrument, on a given domain the set contains the parameters that define the frequencies of the vibrational modes corresponding to that domain. The set also contain parameters that define the internal quadratic and cubic modal couplings, damping, acoustic radiation etc.
3. Despite the fact that the number of elements in a set is quite large, a **reduced set** can always be found that is suitable for musical purposes. The reduced set suffices because on the domains representing the notes, only the keynote (unison), the octave and possibly the twelfth but rarely the second octave are directly tunable.
4. Practical limitations will always be sufficient to ensure that no two or more pans have exactly the same set of parameters. Within musically acceptable limits however, two or more pans of the same **type** may be considered **equivalent**. These musically acceptable limits are determined by the subjective nature of our sense of hearing.
5. The musical equivalence in (4) applies to the reduced set and defines, in the restricted sense of applying to one pan

type, what is usually referred to as a pair (or set) of **blended** *pans.*

Since blocking is never perfect, some small vibrations are always found along the domain boundaries. This results in transmission losses and results in some measure of coupling between domains. The transmission conditions, which describe processes in Ω_0 (the internote), as influenced by the N domains, are assumed to produce linear paths connecting the N domains. On the steelpan, this condition of linearity is made possible by the process of hammering the *internotes* to produce a stiffened indented pan face with local resonant frequencies higher than note frequencies. In more precise terms the immediate internote area enclosing a note is mechanically stiffer than the enclosed note. In this way, the *internotes* are made to function as linear mechanical filters at the note frequencies (see Section 14.11 for details). This observation requires some further discussion. To achieve this in a simple descriptive way, we proceed as follows:

5.2.2 The Internote as a network of Linear Mechanical Filters

It is necessary that the internote, consisting of all areas of the pan face exclusive of the true notes, contain no regions possessing local modes of vibration in resonance or in 'near resonance' with any of the keynotes or higher partials corresponding to the tuned notes. For this reason the indenting (sinking) process is designed to ensure a smooth, evenly peened and very stiff pan face. Failure to achieve this, particularly in the inner regions of the pan face will present the tuner with immense problems during the tuning of these areas. This problem on the middle region of the pan has been observed on experimental designs with two notable cases being recorded one by the author (see Bertie Marshall's attempt to tune a 'very large pan' in Achong 2000b) and on the aluminum pan by Murr et al. (2006). The grooving process helps to achieve the desired conditions in the critical areas immediately outside the true notes but the same can be achieved by hammer peening without the aid of a punch. Greater peening skill is required to prepare and tune a grooveless pan however. With the pan face properly prepared, the transmission process across the pan face in response to striking a note can be understood with the use of an equivalent lumped-parameter system representing the elements along a signal path from the sounding note to a remote point on the pan face. The pan face then appears as a network of *linear mechanical filters*. For further discussions see Chapter 14, observe the special case for *Advanced Tuning* in Section 14.42.1.

5.2.3 The Dynamics of the System

In considering the vibrations of the sub-systems of the steelpan, the work of Chapter 4 is extended to include the two most frequently encountered cases of domain interaction on the properly constructed pan: (i) two-domain Note-Note interaction and (ii) two-domain Note-Skirt interaction. At any time, in any one of these interactions, one domain may be regarded as the *source* and the other as the *receiver*. The roles of source and receiver are interchangeable but generally, the principle of reciprocity does not apply to the transmission process.

On the high-end pans one also finds the *triple* (or *whole note*), for example $\{G_4, G_5, G_6\}$ which opens the possibility for three-domain interaction. While these interactions can be established experimentally by externally driving the outer note (G_4) sufficiently strong at its fundamental frequency, with stick excitation (of the G_4) at the normal level of excitation, the second octave (G_6) is too weakly excited to be of musical importance. If a pan is prepared and tuned with strong coupling of the triple notes, mode confinement will suffer to the extent that tone duration will be drastically shortened. *This is not a recommended practice. Nothing new, exciting or of musical importance comes from it so it is not considered here.*

As in Chapter 4, only quadratic non-linearities are considered and they appear, in the system of equations, to the first order in the gauge parameter ε. There are two sets of quadratic terms to consider. The first of these contain products describing interactions between components of the same domain (the α-terms) and those describing the non-linear interaction between the source and receiver domains (the *β-terms*). There will also be terms describing linear interactions between the two domains (the *Γ-terms*). The spatial separation of the two domains requires the introduction of complex coupling coefficients $\boldsymbol{\beta} = \beta\, e^{i\beta}$ and $\boldsymbol{\Gamma} = \Gamma\, e^{i\delta}$ to account for the phase shifts produced by time delays on transmission across the connecting domain Ω_0.

On a 3-D system such as the steelpan, there is in general, the possibility of multiple paths between source and receiver, with each path producing its own amplitude- and phase-modified signal at the receiving domain. These multiple paths will be of particular importance during and immediately following the initial transients produced by the stick impact. Since however, the typical dimension (L) of any substructure (domain) on the pan satisfies the condition $L \ll c/f$ (where c is the sound velocity in steel and f is the signal frequency), while the note is sounding, a single pair of phase and amplitude values may be used to describe the resultant signal for each frequency component arriving at the receiver domain.

The notes on a steelpan are excited by stick impact, which produces a short duration *Impact Phase* followed by a longer duration *Free Vibration Phase*. As in equation (4.1) of Chapter 4, the transverse vibration displacement fields on domain d can be expressed in a form separable in space and time as

$$w_d(\mathrm{r},t) = \sum_{n=1}^{\infty} u_{nd}(t)\, \psi_{nd}(\mathrm{r}), \qquad (5.1)$$

where $\psi_{nd}(r)$ are appropriate spatial functions (mode shapes) satisfying the boundary conditions of the domain, n is the mode number, and $u_{nd}(t)$ are unknown functions of time only. Solutions are sought for the component $u_{nd}(t)$ on the coupled system using a version of equation (4.2) modified to include domain-domain coupling. The governing equations are

$$\ddot{u}_{nd} + \omega_{nd}^2 u_{nd} + \varepsilon\left[2\mu_{nd}\dot{u}_{nd} - \sum_{j=1}^{\infty}\sum_{k=1}^{\infty} \alpha_{jkn}^{\{d\}} u_{jd} u_{kd} - \sum_{j=1}^{\infty}\sum_{k=1}^{\infty}\sum_{p=1}^{2} \beta_{jp,kp}^{\{nd\}} u_{jp} u_{kp} - \sum_{j=1}^{\infty} \Gamma_{jd}^{\{nd\}} u_{j\bar{d}} - f_d(t) \right] = 0.$$

(5.2)

where d defines the source domain and $\bar{d}$ the receiver domain ($\bar{d} = 1(2)$ when d = 2(1)); $\bar{p} = 1(2)$ when $p = 2(1)$; u_{nd} are the displacements; the dots refer to differentiation with respect to time t; ω_{nd} are the natural frequencies of the linearized subsystems with

$\omega_{1d} < \omega_{2d} \ldots < \omega_{\infty d}$; μ_{nd} are the damping coefficients; $\alpha_{jkn}^{\{d\}}$ are the quadratic coupling constants of the domain d with $\alpha_{jkn}^{\{d\}} = \alpha_{kjn}^{\{d\}}$; $\beta_{jp,k\bar{p}}^{\{nd\}}$ are the quadratic coupling constants linking domain d and domain $\bar{d}$, $\Gamma_{jd}^{\{nd\}}$ are the linear coupling constants linking domain d and domain $\bar{d}$, $f_d(t)$ is a short duration external impulse which is set to zero after impact for the free system.

5.3 The Multi Time-scale Procedure

5.3.1 Theory

In the multi time-scale procedure (see Chapter 4), one defines $t_o = t$, $t_1 = \varepsilon t$, where the main oscillatory behavior occurring at frequencies ω_n are associated with the fast time-scale t_0, while amplitude and phase modulations due to damping and non-linearities take place on the slow time-scale t_1. Also, the time derivative is $d/dt = D_0 + \varepsilon D_1$ where $D_n = \partial/\partial t_n$. The procedure allows the independent variable u_n to be expanded in the form

$$u_{nd} = u_{n0d}(t_0, t_1) + \varepsilon u_{n1d}(t_0, t_1) + O(\varepsilon^2).$$

By substituting this equation into equation (5.1), transforming time derivatives and equating coefficients of like powers of ε, one obtains the following set of equations for the coupled note-note or note-skirt system during the free vibration phase

order ε^0,

$$D_0^2 u_{n0d} + \omega_{nd}^2 u_{n0d} = 0 \tag{5.3}$$

order ε^1,

$$D_0^2 u_{n1d} + \omega_n^2 u_{n1d} = -2D_0(D_1 + \mu_{nd})u_{n0d} + \sum_{j=1}^{\infty}\sum_{k=1}^{\infty} \alpha_{jkn}^{\{d\}} u_{j0d} u_{k0d}$$

$$+ \sum_{j=1}^{\infty}\sum_{k=1}^{\infty}\sum_{p=1}^{2} B_{jp,k\bar{p}}^{\{nd\}} u_{j0p} u_{k0\bar{p}} + \sum_{j=1}^{\infty} \Gamma_{j\bar{d}}^{\{nd\}} u_{j0\bar{d}}. \quad (5.4)$$

The general solution of (5.3) takes the form

$$u_{n0d} = A_{nd}(t_1) e^{i\omega_{nd} t_0},$$

where

$$A_{nd} = \tfrac{1}{2} a_{nd} e^{i\phi_{nd}},$$

with a_{nd} and ϕ_{nd} being functions on the slow time-scale t_1 and representing the amplitude and phase of the nth Fourier component of the displacement respectively.

5.3.2 Case 1: Note-Note Interaction

5.3.2.1 Marshall Pairs

The interacting pair of notes of importance on the steelpan is the combination of an outer note and an inner note tuned to the octave (refer to Figure 5.1b where the pairs {B_4; B_5} and {$F_4^\#$; $F_5^\#$} for example, can be identified). These neighboring notes are usually tuned to operate in *sympathetic vibration*, with the octave being excited when the lower frequency keynote is played. On some steelpans, sympathetic-pairs of this type can be found that are almost entirely dependent on note-note coupling for tonal quality and structure. In recognition of Pan maker Bertram 'Bertie' Marshall, who introduced these sympathetic-pairs for 'reinforcements' as he originally described the tuning method, the present author will hereafter, refer to these as 'Marshall-Pairs' (see Achong 2000c). In the system of equations governing the coupled pair of notes, the note of lower frequency (domain 1) is described as a 3-DOF system, and the higher note (domain 2) as a 2-DOF system. This is a sufficient description, as the third mode on the higher note and the fourth mode on the lower note have been observed on most steelpans to be very low in amplitude and will therefore produce relatively weak interaction products in combination resonances.

5.3.2.2 Solvability Equations

The resonances studied here, correspond in domain 1 to an *internal resonance* with $\omega_{21} \approx 2\omega_{11}$, a *combination resonance* with $\omega_{31} \approx \omega_{11} + \omega_{21}$, and in domain 2, to *internal resonances* with $\omega_{12} \approx 2\omega_{11}$ and $\omega_{22} \approx 2\omega_{12}$. The closeness of these resonances are described by the *detuning parameters* $\sigma_1, \sigma_2, \sigma_3$ and σ_4, where

$$\omega_{21} = 2\omega_{11} + \varepsilon\sigma_1 \quad , \quad \omega_{31} = \omega_{11} + \omega_{21} + \varepsilon\sigma_2$$

$$\omega_{12} = 2\omega_{11} + \varepsilon\sigma_3 \quad , \quad \omega_{22} = 2\omega_{12} + \varepsilon\sigma_4. \qquad (5.5\text{a-d})$$

Readers may use the key below to identify the coupling parameters.

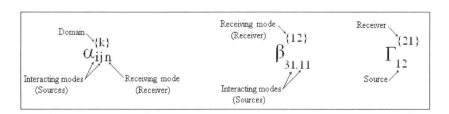

The solvability conditions are obtained from equations (5.2) to (5.4) by the procedure outlined in Chapter 4. The separation of real and imaginary parts, converts these solvability equations to

$$a'_{11} = -\mu_{11}a_{11} + \frac{\alpha_{121}^{\{1\}*}}{4\omega_{11}} a_{11} a_{21} \sin\gamma_1 + \frac{\alpha_{231}^{\{1\}*}}{4\omega_{11}} a_{21} a_{31} \sin\gamma_2 + \frac{\beta_{12,11}^{\{11\}}}{4\omega_{11}} a_{12} a_{11} \sin(\gamma_1 + \gamma_3 + \theta_\beta)$$

$$+ \frac{\beta_{12,31}^{\{11\}}}{4\omega_{11}} a_{12} a_{31} \sin(\gamma_2 - \gamma_3 + \theta_\beta) + \frac{\beta_{22,31}^{\{11\}}}{4\omega_{11}} a_{22} a_{31} \sin(\gamma_5 + \theta_\beta)$$

$$a'_{21} = -\mu_{21}a_{21} - \frac{\alpha^{\{1\}}_{112}}{4\omega_{21}}a^2_{11}\sin\gamma_1 + \frac{\alpha^{\{1\}*}_{132}}{4\omega_{21}}a_{11}a_{31}\sin\gamma_2 + \frac{\beta^{\{21\}}_{21,22}}{4\omega_{21}}a_{21}a_{22}\sin(2\gamma_3+\gamma_4+\theta_\beta)$$

$$+ \frac{\beta^{\{21\}}_{22,12}}{4\omega_{21}}a_{22}a_{12}\sin(\gamma_3+\gamma_4+\theta_\beta) + \frac{\Gamma^{\{21\}}_{12}}{2\omega_{21}}a_{12}\sin(\gamma_3+\delta_\Gamma)$$

$$a'_{31} = -\mu_{31}a_{31} - \frac{\alpha^{\{1\}*}_{123}}{4\omega_{31}}a_{11}a_{21}\sin\gamma_2 + \frac{\beta^{\{31\}}_{12,11}}{4\omega_{31}}a_{12}a_{11}\sin(\gamma_3-\gamma_2+\theta_\beta) + \frac{\beta^{\{31\}}_{22,11}}{4\omega_{31}}a_{22}a_{11}\sin(\gamma_5+\theta_\beta)$$

$$\phi'_{11} = -\frac{\alpha^{\{1\}*}_{121}}{4\omega_{11}}a_{21}\cos\gamma_1 - \frac{\alpha^{\{1\}*}_{231}}{4\omega_{11}}\frac{a_{21}a_{31}}{a_{11}}\cos\gamma_2 - \frac{\beta^{\{11\}}_{12,11}}{4\omega_{11}}a_{12}\cos(\gamma_1+\gamma_3+\theta_\beta)$$

$$- \frac{\beta^{\{11\}}_{12,31}}{4\omega_{11}}\frac{a_{12}a_{31}}{a_{11}}\cos(\gamma_2-\gamma_3+\theta_\beta) - \frac{\beta^{\{11\}}_{22,31}}{4\omega_{11}}\frac{a_{22}a_{31}}{a_{11}}\cos(\gamma_5+\theta_\beta)$$

$$\phi'_{21} = -\frac{\alpha^{\{1\}}_{112}}{4\omega_{21}}\frac{a^2_{11}}{a_{21}}\cos\gamma_1 - \frac{\alpha^{\{1\}*}_{132}}{4\omega_{21}}\frac{a_{11}a_{31}}{a_{21}}\cos\gamma_2 - \frac{\beta^{\{21\}}_{21,22}}{4\omega_{21}}a_{22}\cos(2\gamma_3+\gamma_4+\theta_\beta)$$

$$- \frac{\beta^{\{21\}}_{22,12}}{4\omega_{21}}\frac{a_{22}a_{12}}{a_{21}}\cos(\gamma_3+\gamma_4+\theta_\beta) - \frac{\Gamma^{\{21\}}_{12}}{2\omega_{21}}\frac{a_{12}}{a_{21}}\cos(\gamma_3+\delta_\Gamma),$$

$$\phi'_{31} = -\frac{\alpha^{\{1\}*}_{123}}{4\omega_{31}}\frac{a_{11}a_{21}}{a_{31}}\cos\gamma_2 - \frac{\beta^{\{31\}}_{12,11}}{4\omega_{31}}\frac{a_{12}a_{11}}{a_{31}}\cos(\gamma_3-\gamma_2+\theta_\beta) - \frac{\beta^{\{31\}}_{22,11}}{4\omega_{31}}\frac{a_{22}a_{11}}{a_{31}}\cos(\gamma_5+\theta_\beta),$$

$$a'_{12} = -\mu_{12}a_{12} + \frac{\alpha^{\{2\}*}_{121}}{4\omega_{12}}a_{12}a_{22}\sin\gamma_4 + \frac{\beta^{\{12\}}_{31,11}}{4\omega_{12}}a_{31}a_{11}\sin(\gamma_2-\gamma_3+\theta_\beta)$$

$$+ \frac{\beta^{\{12\}}_{22,21}}{4\omega_{12}}a_{22}a_{21}\sin(\gamma_3+\gamma_4+\theta_\beta) - \frac{\beta^{\{12\}}_{11,11}}{4\omega_{12}}a^2_{11}\sin(\gamma_1+\gamma_3+\theta_\beta)$$

$$- \frac{\Gamma^{\{12\}}_{21}}{2\omega_{12}}a_{21}\sin(\gamma_3+\theta_\beta),$$

$$a'_{22} = -\mu_{22}a_{22} - \frac{\alpha^{\{2\}}_{112}}{4\omega_{22}}a^2_{12}\sin\gamma_4 - \frac{\beta^{\{22\}}_{31,11}}{4\omega_{22}}a_{31}a_{11}\sin(\gamma_5+\theta_\beta)$$

$$- \frac{\beta^{\{22\}}_{21,21}}{4\omega_{22}}a^2_{21}\sin(2\gamma_3+\gamma_4+\theta_\beta) - \frac{\beta^{\{22\}}_{21,12}}{4\omega_{22}}a_{21}a_{12}\sin(\gamma_3+\gamma_4+\theta_\beta),$$

$$\phi'_{12} = -\frac{\alpha_{121}^{\{2\}*}}{4\omega_{12}}a_{22}\cos\gamma_4 - \frac{\beta_{31,11}^{\{12\}}}{4\omega_{12}}\frac{a_{31}a_{11}}{a_{12}}\cos(\gamma_5+\theta_\beta) - \frac{\beta_{11,11}^{\{12\}}}{4\omega_{12}}\frac{a_{11}^2}{a_{12}}\cos(\gamma_1+\gamma_3+\theta_\beta)$$

$$-\frac{\beta_{22,21}^{\{12\}}}{4\omega_{12}}\frac{a_{22}a_{21}}{a_{12}}\cos(\gamma_3+\gamma_4+\theta_\beta) - \frac{\Gamma_{21}^{\{12\}}}{2\omega_{12}}\frac{a_{21}}{a_{12}}\cos(\gamma_3+\delta_\Gamma),$$

$$\phi'_{22} = -\frac{\alpha_{112}^{\{2\}}}{4\omega_{22}}\frac{a_{12}^2}{a_{22}}\cos\gamma_4 - \frac{\beta_{31,11}^{\{22\}}}{4\omega_{22}}\frac{a_{31}a_{11}}{a_{22}}\cos(\gamma_5+\theta_\beta) - \frac{\beta_{21,21}^{\{22\}}}{4\omega_{22}}\frac{a_{21}^2}{a_{22}}\cos(2\gamma_3+\gamma_4+\theta_\beta)$$

$$-\frac{\beta_{21,12}^{\{22\}}}{4\omega_{22}}\frac{a_{21}a_{12}}{a_{22}}\cos(\gamma_3+\gamma_4+\theta_\beta).$$

(5.6a-j)

where the prime denotes d/dt_1; θ_β and δ_Γ represent the phase angles corresponding to the β and Γ coefficients in each term; $\alpha_{jkn}^{\{d\}*} = \alpha_{jkn}^{\{d\}} + \alpha_{kjn}^{\{d\}}$; and

$$\gamma_1 = \phi_{21} - 2\phi_{11} + \sigma_1 t_1, \qquad \gamma_2 = \phi_{31} - \phi_{21} - \phi_{11} + \sigma_2 t_1$$

$$\gamma_3 = \phi_{12} - \phi_{21} + (\sigma_3-\sigma_1)t_1, \qquad \gamma_4 = \phi_{22} - 2\phi_{12} + \sigma_4 t_1$$

$$\gamma_5 = \gamma_1 - \gamma_2 + 2\gamma_3 + \gamma_4. \qquad (5.7\text{a-e})$$

Varying the values in the parameter set (ω, μ, σ, α, β, Γ) allow the full range of modulation features observed on the coupled note-note system to be modeled mathematically.

5.3.3 Case 2: Note-Skirt Interactions

A case often encountered on the pan is the interaction between the skirt and the note being played. When this occurs, it is usually the case that a single excited mode on the skirt will interact with the note. Overcoupling however, can have undesirable effects, as the tonal quality of the note is lost.

The skirt when left at its full un-cut length for the lower frequency pans (the bass instruments) is a cylindrical shell with two circumferential ridges (the rolling hoops) (see Figure 5.2). These ridges serve as stiffeners on the original steel drum. As if by design, these stiffened cylindrical shells were 'made to order' for this instrument. Because of the stiffeners, high frequencies will excite 'local' modes in which vibration occurs predominantly in a small section (between stiffeners) of the stiffened cylinder. This tends to reduce note-skirt coupling in many cases.

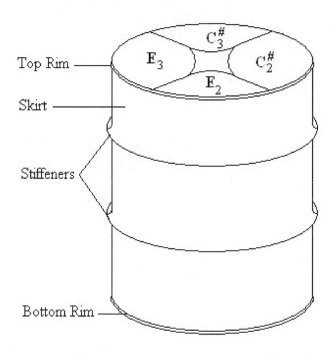

Fig. 5.2. Sketch of a typical bass pan. Skirt length = 88 cm, diameter = 57 cm.

Two resonances, corresponding to the second and third non-linear modes, are considered for the note (domain 1, modeled as a 3-DOF system). At the levels of excitation attained on the pan while being played, no non-linear effects have been detected experimentally on the skirt. A single, linear mode is therefore considered for the skirt (domain 2, modeled as a 1-DOF system). To express quantitatively the nearness of these resonances one defines the detuning parameters σ_1, σ_2 and σ_3 according to

$$\omega_{21} = 2\omega_{11} + \varepsilon\sigma_1 \; , \quad \omega_{31} = \omega_{11} + \omega_{21} + \varepsilon\sigma_2 \; , \quad \omega_{12} = \omega_{11} + \varepsilon\sigma_3 \, .$$

(5.8a-c)

Applying these conditions to the system equations yields the following solvability equations

$$a'_{11} = -\mu_{11}a_{11} + \frac{\alpha_{121}^{\{1\}*}}{4\omega_{11}} a_{11}a_{21}\sin\gamma_1 + \frac{\alpha_{231}^{\{1\}*}}{4\omega_{11}} a_{21}a_{31}\sin\gamma_2 + \frac{\beta_{12,21}^{\{11\}}}{4\omega_{11}} a_{12}a_{21}\sin(\gamma_1 - \gamma_3 + \theta_\beta)$$
$$+ \frac{\Gamma_{12}^{\{11\}}}{2\omega_{11}} a_{12}\sin(\gamma_3 + \delta_\Gamma),$$

$$a'_{21} = -\mu_{21}a_{21} - \frac{\alpha_{112}^{\{1\}}}{4\omega_{21}} a_{11}^2\sin\gamma_1 + \frac{\alpha_{132}^{\{1\}*}}{4\omega_{21}} a_{11}a_{31}\sin\gamma_2 - \frac{\beta_{12,11}^{\{21\}}}{4\omega_{21}} a_{12}a_{11}\sin(\gamma_1 - \gamma_3 + \theta_\beta),$$

$$a'_{31} = -\mu_{31}a_{31} - \frac{\alpha_{123}^{\{1\}*}}{4\omega_{31}} a_{11}a_{21}\sin\gamma_2 + \frac{\beta_{12,21}^{\{31\}}}{4\omega_{31}} a_{12}a_{21}\sin(\gamma_3 - \gamma_2 + \theta_\beta),$$

$$\phi'_{11} = -\frac{\alpha_{121}^{\{1\}*}}{4\omega_{11}} a_{21}\cos\gamma_1 - \frac{\alpha_{231}^{\{1\}*}}{4\omega_{11}} \frac{a_{21}a_{31}}{a_{11}}\cos\gamma_2 - \frac{\beta_{12,21}^{\{11\}}}{4\omega_{11}} \frac{a_{12}a_{21}}{a_{11}}\cos(\gamma_1 - \gamma_3 + \theta_\beta)$$
$$- \frac{\Gamma_{12}^{\{11\}}}{2\omega_{11}} \frac{a_{12}}{a_{11}}\cos(\gamma_3 + \delta_\Gamma),$$

$$\phi'_{21} = -\frac{\alpha_{112}^{\{1\}}}{4\omega_{21}} \frac{a_{11}^2}{a_{21}}\cos\gamma_1 - \frac{\alpha_{132}^{\{1\}*}}{4\omega_{21}} \frac{a_{11}a_{31}}{a_{21}}\cos\gamma_2 - \frac{\beta_{12,12}^{\{21\}}}{4\omega_{21}} \frac{a_{12}^2}{a_{21}}\cos(2\gamma_3 - \gamma_1 + \theta_\beta)$$
$$- \frac{\beta_{12,11}^{\{21\}}}{4\omega_{21}} \frac{a_{12}a_{11}}{a_{21}}\cos(\gamma_1 - \gamma_3 + \theta_\beta),$$

$$\phi'_{31} = -\frac{\alpha_{123}^{\{1\}*}}{4\omega_{31}} \frac{a_{11}a_{21}}{a_{31}}\cos\gamma_2 - \frac{\beta_{12,21}^{\{31\}}}{4\omega_{31}} \frac{a_{12}a_{21}}{a_{31}}\cos(\gamma_3 - \gamma_2 + \theta_\beta),$$

$$a'_{12} = -\mu_{12}a_{12} - \frac{\Gamma_{11}^{\{12\}}}{2\omega_{12}} a_{11}\sin(\gamma_3 + \delta_\Gamma), \quad \phi'_{12} = -\frac{\Gamma_{11}^{\{12\}}}{2\omega_{12}} \frac{a_{11}}{a_{12}}\cos(\gamma_3 + \delta_\Gamma),$$

$$(5.9\text{a-h})$$

where

$$\gamma_1 = \phi_{21} - 2\phi_{11} + \sigma_1 t_1, \quad \gamma_2 = \phi_{31} - \phi_{21} - \phi_{11} + \sigma_2 t_1, \quad (5.10\text{a-c})$$

5.4 Energy Exchanges between Domains

5.4.1 Note-Note Exchanges between Marshall Pairs

When the outer note (d = 1) is played at the *sweetspot*, the first mode (nd = 11 pronounced 'one-one' not 'eleven') is excited while the second mode (nd = 21 pronounced 'two-one not 'twenty one') is initially excited at a very low level. Energy is transferred from mode (nd = 11) to mode (nd = 21) and to mode (nd = 12) on the inner note. The quadratic response of the inner note allows the disturbance received from mode (nd = 11) to interact with mode (nd = 12). This transfer of energy allows the inner note to begin vibrating at its first natural frequency ω_{12}. This is non-linear coupling involving the terms in equation 1 with coefficient β. Meanwhile mode (nd = 21) on the outer note transfers energy to mode (nd = 12) which is the first mode on the inner note. This is linear coupling involving the terms in equation 1 with the coefficient Γ. Then mode (nd = 12) interacts non-linearly with mode (nd = 11) to return energy to mode (nd = 11) on the outer note. Mode (nd = 12) also couples energy linearly back to mode (nd = 21) on the outer note. These exchanges continue as the tone loses energy through material damping in the steel, transmission losses and through radiation of acoustical energy. The radiated sound which one hears is actually a loss effect although it constitutes the main purpose for the system operating as a musical instrument. Acoustical radiation contributes only a small fraction of the total losses and is not included in equation (5.1)! The reader may find this surprising but it will be dealt with later.

The major energy exchange processes including those involving the second mode on the inner note, mode (nd = 22), are shown in Figure 5.3. In addition to these excitations, the third mode on the outer note (nd = 13) receives energy from the quadratic interaction of mode (nd = 11) and mode (nd = 12). This third mode corresponds to the musical twelfth but in sympathetic pairs this mode is usually weak. When the notes are tuned to emphasize sympathetic vibrations, the second mode or octave (nd = 21) on the outer note is sacrificed because it is adjusted to transfer energy to the inner note unison (nd = 12). In this way when the outer note is played one hears the inner note as the octave.

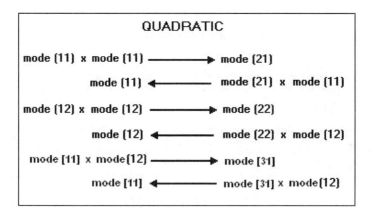

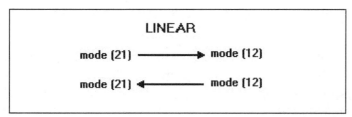

Fig. 5.3. Major energy exchange processes on a sympathetic pair of notes.

Note: mode 12 is pronounced 'mode one-two', mode 31 is pronounced 'mode three-one' etc.

Dynamically, the energy transfers by quadratic interactions take place through the generation of parametric vibrations (oscillations) as follows; when mode 11 interacts quadratically with itself as *mode 11 × mode 11*, a parametric vibration is excited at frequency equal to $2\omega_{11}$. Since the frequency of this parametric excitation is close to the frequency of mode 21, an *internal resonance* is produced between the parametric excitation and mode 21. This effectively transfers energy from mode 11 to mode 21. As a second example; when mode 11 interacts quadratically with mode 12 a parametric excitation is produced at frequency $\omega_{11} + \omega_{12}$ which is close to ω_{31}. This produces a *combination resonance* (mode 11 combines with mode 21) to form a resonance with mode 31). All the other quadratic interactions in Figure 2 operate in a fashion similar to one or the other of these two examples. The linear exchanges are straightforward.

5.4.2 Note-Skirt Exchanges

The note-skirt interactions are all linear. While the notes on the pan face are tuned to the musical scale the modes on the skirt are untuned. Through *coincidence*, a skirt mode may lie close in frequency to a tuned mode on a note. The closeness of these two frequencies and the degree of linear coupling then determine the dynamics of the affected note.

5.5 Experimental and Computational Methods

5.5.1 General Procedure

The methods for data acquisition and note excitation were the same as those described in Chapter 4. Two velocity transducers were used however to simultaneously monitor each of the two interacting regions. Two sets of data were acquired for each note-note pair by exciting each note, in turn, by stick impacts. For the note-skirt interaction, impacts were applied only to the note. The velocity data were analyzed using the Short-Time Fourier Transform (STFT) with the Gaussian window set as in Chapter 4 and the corresponding displacement amplitudes and phases deduced from the transformed velocity data. The nth Fourier component in domain d is represented by S_{nd}. As shown in Chapter 4, the multi-time analysis can be compared with the experimental data through the 'equivalence' $a_{nd} \equiv |S_{nd}|$ and $\phi_{nd} \equiv arg(S_{nd})$.

Equations (5.6a-j) and (5.9a-h) were integrated numerically using a fourth order Runge-Kutta routine to produce discretized values for a_{nd} and ϕ_{nd} at time steps of 0.1. (In some numerical analyses, time steps of 0.05 and 0.025 were used.). All numerical computations on the equation system (5.6a-j) and (5.9a-h) were done with parameter values chosen to closely (but not necessarily exactly) model the tones produced on the pan. Following the procedure in Chapter 4, the stick impacts were tabulated in the musical manner from 'very soft' (*pianissimo*) to 'loud' (*forte*) as judged from the acoustical level of the tone.

5.5.2 Experimentally and Theoretically generated Tonal Structures

5.5.2.1 Note-Note coupling of a $\{E_4 ; E_5\}$ Pair: Playing the E_4 Note

The first example tones shown in the velocity-time profiles of Figure 5.4, were taken on the $\{E_4;E_5\}$ Marshall Pair found on a tenor. Kinetic energy and hence the square of the velocity, is directly related to the acoustical radiation of the notes. When the E_4 note is struck (Figure 5.4a) the inner E_5 note responds in sympathy (Figure 5.4b) at a level that maybe classified musically as soft. But the most noticeable feature in Figure 5.4(a) and Figure 5.4(b) is that *the velocity responses are symmetrical about the zero level*. This means that the vibrations are taking place in an essentially *symmetrical potential well* (see Chapter 8) which implies that the natural second mode (octave) on this E_4 is weak. This is the reason why the tuner has chosen to pair these E_4 and E_5 notes in order to strengthen (reinforce) the octave in the tone. One observes in both Figures 5.4a & 5.4b, that the modal velocities undergo slow periodic modulations as energy is exchanged between the notes. One should observe here that for a unit area of note surface, to produce a given velocity or amplitude of vibration, more energy is required on the higher frequency note. This means that for a given degree of coupling and energy transfer larger velocity and amplitude modulations are expected on the lower frequency note (E_4 in this case).

Note: Readers should not take it to mean that all Marshall Pairs or $\{E_4;E_5\}$ pairs in particular will show this symmetry. This is a special case selected from among many and used here for the purpose of showing what tonal features are possible on the pan. It represents a good example for teaching purposes. In fact, all the pan tone examples shown in this book were selected for just this purpose.

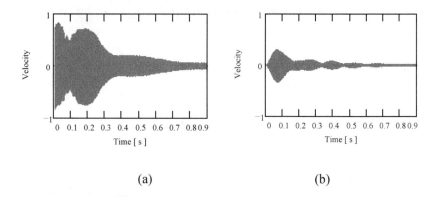

Fig. 5.4. The {E_4;E_5} sympathetic pair on a tenor. (a) Velocity-time history for the played E_4 note as the source and (b) the corresponding response from the E_5 note as receiver.

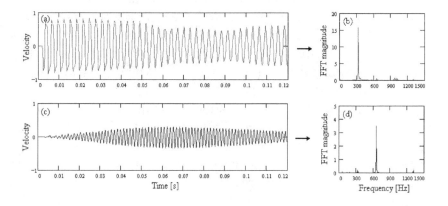

Fig. 5.5. The {E_4;E_5} pair in higher time resolution and the corresponding frequency spectra. (a) and (b) show the dominance of the keynote on the E_4 member; (c) and (d) show the velocity and spectrum respectively, for the E_5 member responding in sympathy with the E_4.

The higher time resolution display in Figure 5.5 shows very 'clean' vibrations on the played E_4 member and an equally clean response from the E_5 member. What these higher resolution plots and the spectra clearly show is that for this particular {E_4;E_5} Marshall-Pair when the E_4 note is played the first partial (the keynote) is produced by the E_4 note while the second partial (the octave) is produced exclusively by the E_5 note. This is a classic example of a properly tuned Marshall Pair. It demonstrates unambiguously, the following aspects of the steelpan theory set out in this book:

1) On almost all musical instruments, sympathetic responses are of the linear type requiring both the source and the receiving (responding) members to be tuned to the same (or almost the same) frequency. The steelpan however produces both linear and non-linear types of sympathetic responses. In fact, on a given pan, the non-linear or quadratic type of response is the one mostly observed.
2) When a note is excited by stick impact or driven by an external source (even by another note excited on the same pan), the note will respond linearly and non-linearly (quadratically).
3) The stick excited note (E_4) produces a strong excitation of its first natural mode (the key-note at the musical E_4 = 329.63 Hz) and a parametric excitation at twice this frequency (659.26 Hz). Both these components of excitation are transmitted across the internote to the E_5 note.
4) The parametric excitation on the E_4 note does not induce any appreciable resonance from the second mode on the E_4 note because the coupling $\alpha_{112}^{\{1\}}$ is weak. As a result, the E_4 note generates no audible *resident octave* (see Section 13.2).
5) The component at 329.63 Hz that reaches the E_5 note from the E_4 note drives the E_5 note to produce a non-linear (quadratic) response from E_5 at 659.26 Hz (dependent on the coupling $\beta_{11,11}^{\{12\}}$) which excites the first mode or the key-note on the E_5 note. The weaker parametric component at 659.26 Hz arriving at the E_5 note from the E_4 note and dependent on the coupling $\Gamma_{21}^{\{12\}}$ also excites the E_5 key-note. Since the resident octave on the E_4 note is very weak, the contribution from the latter is negligible.
6) The resident octave on the E_5 note is absent because the coupling determined by $\alpha_{112}^{\{2\}}$ is weak. The absence of resident octaves on both notes is achieved by using large detuning on these modes. This explains what the tuner accomplishes by hammer peening as he sets the pair into a

state of reliance on the higher member of the Marshall Pair for the production of the octave or second partial (in this case the E_5 note).

7) The manner in which the E_5 note is excited by the E_4 note is best described as an *excitation by a sub-harmonic* (a totally non-linear effect). To the extent that detuning can be considered small, the E_4 can be regarded as the sub-harmonic of the E_5. See Chapter 14 where the tuning restrictions require the *stretching* or *compressing* of the octave (on a well tuned pan, strict harmonicity is not allowed since the modes interact).

8) The result, consistent with the theory, is the generation of a clean, well modulated key-note on the E_4 note without a resident octave, and a clean octave provided by the E_5 note, also without a resident octave which would otherwise have provided a second octave component.

9) In the above explanations the small detuning on all the modes (parametric and normal) are ignored in order to keep the discussion simple. They are however important in determining the levels and rates of modulations on the generated tones.

5.5.2.2 Note-Note coupling of a $\{E_4 ; E_5\}$ Pair: Playing the E_5 Note

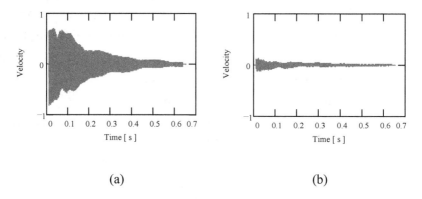

(a) (b)

Fig.5.6. (a) Velocity-time history for the played E_5 note as the source and (b) the corresponding response from the E_4 note as receiver.

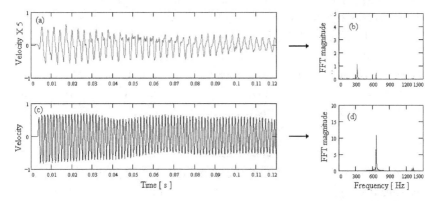

Fig. 5.7. The $\{E_4;E_5\}$ pair in higher time resolution and the corresponding frequency spectra. (a) and (b) show the E_4 member; (c) and (d) show the velocity and spectrum respectively, for the E_5 member responding in sympathy with the E_4. For clarity, the velocity scale in (a) is expanded X5.

When the E_5 note is struck, acting as the source (Figure 5.6(a)), and the E_4 note acts as the receiver (Figure 5.6(b)), the E_4 note shows very low but audible levels of excitation. For an understanding of the exchange processed in this case one has to look at the higher time resolution plots in Figure 5.7 where for clarity, the velocity scale for the E_4 plot is expanded X5. Compare the slow rise of the octave E_5 in Figure 5.5c as it receives energy through quadratic coupling with the key-note on E_4 with the rapid rise of the key-note E_4 in Figure 5.7a when the E_5 note is played. This rapid rise in E_4 shows that excitation of E_4 is through direct transfer of energy from the impact point on E_5 through the action of a Fourier component (see Chapter13 for details) of the contact force delivered by the stick to the E_5 note and transmitted through the internote to the E_4 note in a time of approximately 25 microseconds. Players who listen attentively can hear this low-level excitation of an outer note when an inner note is played. This is not a true note-note interaction and being of very low intensity the sound produced in this manner is of no musical concern. However, as in the present example the interaction of this low-level excitation on E_4 with the higher member E_5 of the Marshall Pair produces modulations on the E_5 key note (as seen in Figure 5.6a that are desirable for the generation of musically pleasing tones.

To interpret the amplitude modulations seen in Figure 5.6 take a close look at the level of the FFT magnitude for second octave on the E_5 note at around 1318.5 Hz in Figure 5.7(d). This mode is barely discernible which means that it couples weakly with the E_5 key-note (at around 659.26 Hz. However, the E_5 key-note couples linearly with the octave mode (around 659.26 Hz) on the E_4 note which it first excites. In addition the weakly excited key-note on E_4 (around 329.63 Hz) interacts quadratically with its octave on the E_4 note. There is a weaker coupling (set by $\beta_{12,11}^{\{11\}}$) between the key-note on E_4 (mode 11) with the key-note on E_5 (mode 12) made possible through a *combination resonance* between these two modes which produces a *parametric excitation* at frequency close to that of the E_4 key-note (mode 11). This parametric excitation transfers energy from the E_5 keynote (mode 12) to the E_4 keynote (mode 11) despite the wide difference in their frequencies. In addition, since the E_4 note is already excited, there is energy transferred by quadratic coupling ($\beta_{11,11}^{\{12\}}$) from the E_4 key-note to the E_5 key-note. The net results of all these interactions are the modulations shown in Figure 5.6 and Figure 5.7. (*Readers may wish to read this a second time because there is so much happening simultaneously every time a note is played.*)

Were these interactions absent, the tonal qualities of these two notes would be uninteresting. Because the time duration of each note when played and acting as the main source is not unduly affected by note-note coupling, the author classifies this note pair in the 'good' category.

When the tonal structures for these two members of this Marshall Pair are compared, one sees that for this combination of notes, reciprocity clearly does not apply — although these two notes are coupled dynamically, playing one member is quite different from playing the other.

Note: *Readers who have covered potential wells in Chapter 8 can use the results in Figure 5.5 as a good example of vibration within a symmetrical potential well. The results clearly show that when the quadratic and cubic coupling are weak then the potential well is the result of a single force, the linear restoring force that generates the fundamental mode. Excitations within this well will display* *symmetry (about the axis through zero velocity) in velocity and in displacement (about the axis through zero displacement).*

5.5.3 Note-Note Coupling on a Pair of A_4 and A_5 Tenor Notes

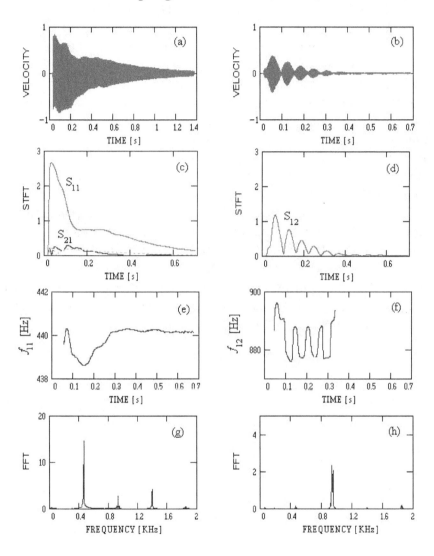

Fig. 5.8. Comparison of experimental results for the coupled A_4 and A_5 notes on a tenor pan when A_4 is played *forte*: (a) A_4 velocity time-history, (b) A_5 velocity time-history, (c) STFT of A_4 component, (······, S_{31}), (d) STFT of A_5 component, (e) modulation of f_{11} (= 440.0 + $\psi'_{11}/2\pi$ Hz), (f) modulation on f_{12} (= 881.0 + $\phi'_{12}/2\pi$ Hz).

On the tenor steelpan tested, the A_4 (440.0 Hz), note which is an outer note, was tuned, by the pan maker, to couple strongly to the A_5 (880.0 Hz) inner note. The inner note was actually tuned higher than 880 Hz by +1.97 cents or 881 Hz. This small detuning on the inner A_5 note is necessary because when played as the A_5 keynote, this note must sound in-tune. The two notes act as a Marshall Pair. The tone structures for the A_4 note played *mezzo forte* (moderately loud) are shown in Figure 5.8(a) (the velocity time-history) and in Figure 5.8(c) (the STFT amplitude profile). Figure 5.8(c) shows an initially rapidly decaying amplitude profile followed by a period of almost constant amplitude then by a period of slow decay. The frequency modulation accompanying these amplitude changes is shown in Figure 5.8(e). Notice the initial fall and rise in frequency immediately after impact.

The corresponding structures for the A_5 note as it responds to the impact on the A_4 note (Figures 5.8(b), 5.8(d) and 5.8(f)), show a strongly modulated 881 Hz component. These strong and rapid modulations are often observed for sympathetic pairs. The rapid modulation is a result of the small detuning of the inner note at just +1.97 cents. Larger detuning will result in a slower modulation rate. STFT's were maximized at f_{11}= 440 Hz and f_{12}= 881 Hz.

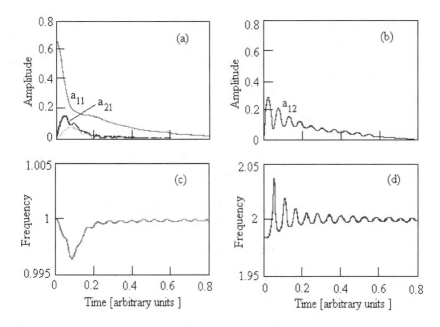

Fig. 5.9. Comparison of analytical results for the coupled A_4 and A_5 notes on the simulated tenor pan when the A_4 note is played *forte*: (a) amplitudes of A_4 components (a_{11}, a_{21}, a_{31}), (d) amplitude of A_5 component, (e) modulation on ω_{11} ($= 1 + \phi'_{11}$), (f) modulation on ω_{12} ($= 2 + \phi'_{12}$).

The interaction process can be understood from the numerically modeled system, the results for which are shown in Figure 5.9. The numerical model reproduces the main amplitude and frequency modulations observed on the real system (compare Figures 5.8 and 5.9). The amplitude modulations clearly show the continuous exchange of energy between the two notes. The main channel for energy transfer from A_4 to A_5 is through the term $-(\beta^{\{12\}}_{11,11} a^2_{11} / 4\omega_{12}) \sin(\gamma_1 + \gamma_3 + \theta_\beta)$ in equation (5.6(g)). This represents a non-linear (quadratic) coupling of the fundamental on the A_4 note to the fundamental on the A_5 note. The reverse coupling of these two modes is through the term $+ (\beta^{\{11\}}_{12,11} a_{12} a_{11} / 4\omega_{11}) \sin(\gamma_1 + \gamma_3 + \theta_\beta)$. The periodicity of these two non-linear terms depend on the detuning parameter σ_3 (refer to equations (5.7a-c)). The frequency modulations on these two modes are similarly accounted for by the terms containing the coupling constants $\beta^{\{11\}}_{12,11}$ and $\beta^{\{12\}}_{11,11}$ in equations (5.6d) and (5.6i) respectively. The frequency modulations are more pronounced on the model (Figures 5.9(c) and 5.9(d)) than they are on the real note (Figures 5.8(e) and 5.8(f)).

Modeling parameters:
A_4 note (domain 1): $\alpha_{211} = \alpha_{121} = 0.065$, $\alpha_{112} = 0.03$, $\alpha_{123} = \alpha_{213} = 0.06$, $\alpha_{132} = \alpha_{312} = 0.001$, $\alpha_{231} = \alpha_{321} = 0.03$, $\mu_{11} = 0.0008$, $\mu_{21} = 0.005$, $\mu_{31} = 0.002$, $\sigma_1 = \sigma_2 = 0.003$, $\beta^{\{11\}}_{12,11}1 = 0.02$, all other ß=0.001, $\Gamma^{\{21\}}_{12} = 0.012$: Initial amplitudes: $a_{11} = 0.65$, $a_{21} = a_{31} = 0$.
A_5 note (domain 2): $\alpha_{211} = \alpha_{121} = 0.001$, $\alpha_{112} = 0.001$, $\mu_{12} = 0.0008$, $\mu_{22} = 0.0008$, $\sigma_3 = 0.03$, $\sigma_4 = 0.001$, $\beta^{\{12\}}_{11,11}2 = 0.12$, all other $\beta = 0.001$, $\Gamma^{\{12\}}_{21} = 0.06$: Initial amplitudes: $a_{12} = 0.02$, $a_{22} = 0$.

5.5.4 Note-Skirt Interaction on the Bass D_3

Tone structures are shown for the D_3 (146.8 Hz) note on a bass pan played at the *forte* level in Figure 5.10 and at the *piano* level in Figure 5.12. In both cases there are note-skirt interactions between the fundamental mode on the note and a mode of frequency 179 Hz which was found to be confined mainly to the lower third portion of the skirt between the lower stiffener and the bottom rim. To excite this mode on the skirt by striking the note on the pan face, there had to be sufficiently strong coupling of the note to this subsection of the skirt.

5.5.4.1 Forte Level

On a normal level of amplitude resolution (Figure 5.10(a)) there appears nothing unusual about the tone structure of this note. The non-linear interaction between the fundamental resonance corresponding to {nd} = {11} and the internal resonance {nd} = {21}, show up as slow but pronounced modulations of the amplitudes S_{11} and S_{21} as the two modes constantly exchange energy. On the frequency plot (Figure 5.10(c)) one observes the corresponding low frequency amplitude modulations discussed in Chapter 4.

Under higher resolution (Figure 5.10(b)), a faster low-level modulation is observed on the amplitude profile S_{11}. On the frequency plot Figure 5.10(c), the corresponding frequency modulation is quite significant. The depth of frequency modulation on the fundamental mode is

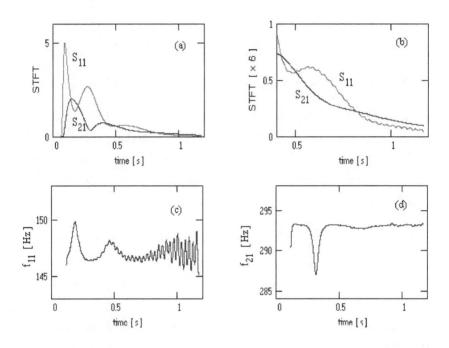

Fig. 5.10. Experimental results for the bass D_3 note played *forte* with skirt coupling: (a) displacement STFT, (b) STFT at higher resolution, (c) frequency modulation on f_{11} (= 146.9 + $\phi'_{11}/2\pi$ Hz), (d) frequency modulation of f_{21} (= 294.0 + $\phi'_{21}/2\pi$ Hz).

seen to grow steadily as the tone decays. The depth of frequency modulation increases to as much as 2.5 Hz, representing a 1.7% change in frequency of the tone. While this surely represents significant changes in intonation, it occurs when the intensity of the tone has fallen to low levels. Nevertheless, this modulation was clearly audible as a warble, whenever the note was played. This warble could be stopped by clamping the lower rim of the skirt, clearly indicating that the effect was due to note-skirt coupling.

There are no corresponding modulations of any significance on the higher modes.

The velocity STFT's were maximized at $f_{11} = 146.9$ Hz (mode1) and $f_{21} = 294$ Hz (mode2). This note-skirt system was modeled numerically and the results shown along with the frequency diagram in Figures 5.11(a-d). Modeling parameters were:
$\alpha_{211} = \alpha_{121} = 0.0125$, $\alpha_{112} = 0.025$, $\alpha_{123} = \alpha_{213} = 0.015$, $\alpha_{132} = \alpha_{312} = 0.005$, $\alpha_{231} = \alpha_{321} = 0.01$, all ß $= 0.001$, $\Gamma_{12}^{\{11\}} = 0.003$, $\Gamma_{11}^{\{12\}} = 0.004$, $\mu_{11} = \mu_{21} = \mu_{31} = 0.0006$, $\mu_{12} = 0.0004$, $\sigma_1 = -0.002$, $\sigma_2 = -0.01$, $\sigma_3 = -0.045$. Initial amplitudes: *forte* level; $a_{11} = 1$, $a_{21} = a_{31} = 0$, $a_{12} = 0.08$

Observe the strong similarities in the details of the frequency diagrams obtained theoretically (Figure 5.11(a, c, d)) and experimentally (Figure 5.10(a, b, c)). The frequency modulation characteristics are properly reproduced in the mathematical synthesis. The non-linear domain-to-domain coupling constants $\beta_{jp,kp}^{\{nd\}}$ are quite small (ß $= 0.001$) resulting in an essentially linear note-skirt interaction.

The modulation, which appears on the amplitude profile a_{11} (the theoretical equivalent to S_{11}) is described by the term $\left(\Gamma_{12}^{\{11\}}/2\omega_{11}\right)a_{12}\sin(\gamma_3 + \delta_\Gamma)$, which appears in the expression for a'_{11} (equation (5.9a)). The angle γ_3 contains a term $(\omega_{12} - \omega_{11})t_1/\varepsilon$ (see equations (5.8c) and (5.10c)) which shows that the modulation is the result of a 'beat' effect between the modes $\{nd\} = \{11\}$ and $\{nd\} = \{12\}$ on a time-scale t_1 with angular frequency $|(\omega_{12} - \omega_{11})/\varepsilon|$.

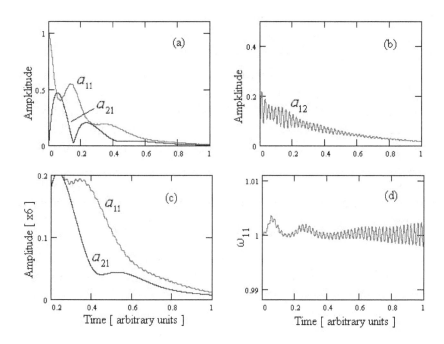

Fig. 5.11. Analytical results of the simulated **D**$_3$ note played *forte* with skirt coupling: (a) amplitudes of note components, (b) amplitude of skirt component, (c) note components under higher resolution, (d) frequency modulation on ω_{11} (= $1 + \phi'_{11}$).

The steady growth in the level of frequency modulation seen in Figure 5.11(d) as the tone decays can be explained with the term $-\left(\Gamma_{12}^{\{11\}} a_{12} / 2\omega_{11} a_{11}\right)\cos(\gamma_3 + \delta_\Gamma)$, which appears in the expression for the frequency ϕ'_{11} (equation 5.9(d)). Because of the long persistence of the skirt vibrations and the faster decay of the note vibrations (as an example, see Figure 5.14(a,c)), the amplitude ratio a_{12}/a_{11} actually increases as the tone decays, so increasing the level of the frequency modulation. The cosine factor accounts for the periodicity.

5.5.4.2 Piano Level

The experimental results for the **D**$_3$ note excited at the *piano* level is shown in Figure 5.12, while in Figure 5.13 the numerically modeled note is shown for the same modeling parameters used at the *forte* level but with initial amplitudes; $a_{11} = 0.5$, $a_{21} = 0$, $a_{31} = 0$, $a_{12} = 0.04$. Comparing Figures 5.12(a, b & c) with Figures 5.13(a, c

& d), one finds that all the amplitude modulation and frequency modulation features for this note played at the piano level can be accounted for in the theory. One also observes that towards the end of the tone, the depth of frequency modulation on the fundamental mode ({nd}={11}), produced by the note-skirt coupling, is greater when the note is played at the *piano* level than when it is played at the *forte* level. This is a direct result of the greater amplitude ratio a_{12}/a_{11} (or its equivalent S_{12}/S_{11}) expected in the dying stages of the tone in the former case.

In Chapter 4 it was shown that the tonal structure of the steelpan note is very dependent on the intensity of the impact, with a greater percentage of the energy going into the higher modes (the higher partials) when the note is played louder. With linear coupling between note and skirt it is now observed that the frequency modulation features produced by this coupling becomes more significant as the note is played softer.

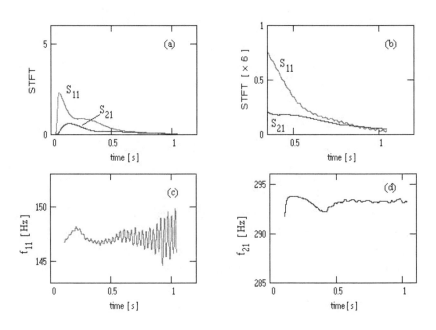

Fig. 5.12. Experimental results for the bass D_3 note played *piano* with skirt coupling: (a) displacement STFT, (b) STFT at higher resolution, (c) frequency modulation on f_{11} (= 146.9 + $\phi'_{11}/2\pi$ Hz), (d) frequency modulation of f_{21} (= 294.0 + $\phi'_{21}/2\pi$ Hz).

Note: Since this type of note-skirt interaction occurs naturally on the instrument, it is perfectly acceptable to allow these interactions when they occur since they are low-level effects. To some, these modulations may add 'naturalness' to the instrument. Of course one has to be close to the instrument in order to hear it whenever it occurs. As described in the Pan Maker's Handbook, one can always apply some mass-loading to the skirt to remove this effect if so desired.

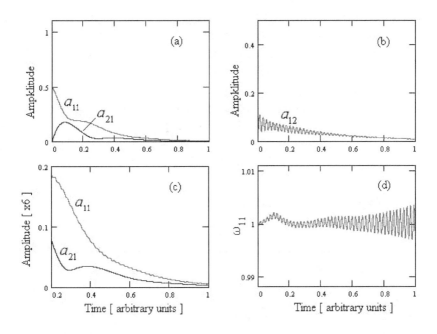

Fig. 5.13. Analytical results of the simulated D_3 note played *piano* with skirt coupling: (a) amplitudes of note components, (b) amplitude of skirt component, (c) note components under higher resolution, (d) frequency modulation on ω_{11} (= $1 + \phi'_{11}$).

5.5.5 Note-Skirt Coupling on the $F_3^{\#}$ Note of a Double-Second Steelpan

The 'double-second' instrument consists of a pair of steelpans with notes of frequencies in the musical range $F_3^{\#}$ (185.0 Hz) to A_5 (880.0 Hz). The double-second tested, carried a skirt of length 25 cm, diameter 57 cm and sheet thickness 0.085 cm. During the tuning of this note, the tuner experienced great difficulty as the frequency approached the required $\mathbf{F}_3^{\#}$ at 185.0 Hz.

Figure 5.14 shows the time-histories and frequency spectra for the $\mathbf{F}_3^{\#}$ note and for the skirt on this instrument. Excitation was done using the stick and by striking in turn, the note and then the skirt. Figures 5.14b and 5.14d represent spectra for the velocity data so they show a high frequency emphasis (proportional to frequency) over the corresponding spectra for the displacements. The relative amplitudes of the components on the skirt spectra depend on time as well as the location of the transducer monitoring the motions of the skirt. Of immediate importance here is the much longer duration of the skirt excitation over that of the note and the near coincidence of the 186.0 Hz (fundamental) f_{11} component on the note and the 183.0 Hz (dominant) f_{12} component on the skirt. The closeness in frequency of these two components is indicated by the two vertical arrows in in Figure 5.14(d).

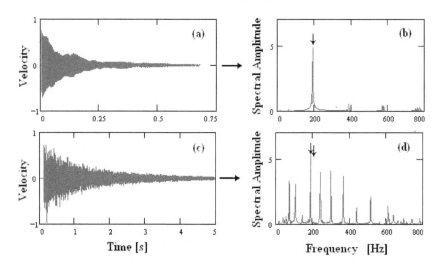

Fig. 5.14. Experimental time histories and spectra for the $\mathbf{F}_3^{\#}$ note and the skirt on the double-second pan: note time-history, (b) note spectrum; (c) skirt time-history, (d) skirt spectrum. The spectral lines of the interacting modes are identified by vertical arrows and the frequency spacing indicated by the double arrows in (d).

For the note played *forte*, Figure 5.15 shows the displacement amplitudes for three note components (S_{11}, S_{21}, and S_{31}) and for the 183 Hz component (S_{12}) of the skirt. The velocity data from which these results were computed, were obtained by monitoring the note and the skirt simultaneously. There are some important features in these results for this case of strong note-skirt coupling.

In Figure 5.15(b), the skirt first responds to the impulse imparted directly to the note by the stick, with an initial rapid rise in displacement amplitude. This is followed at first by a short duration decay, then the motion is fed by the energy transferred from the note to the skirt. This transfer is accompanied by a rapid decay of the motion on the note (see Figure 5.15(a) where S_{11} decays rapidly). The decay on the note is halted somewhat as energy is transferred from the skirt back to the note, but decay continues until the amplitude of the first mode drops to almost zero after 0.6 s. Thereafter the motion of the note is controlled by energy transfers from the skirt.

Accompanying these amplitude modulation features are the changes in the frequency f_{11} of the fundamental mode on the note. Figure 5.15(d) shows the frequency (obtained from the time derivative of the phase ϕ_{11}) as it changes from a value varying around 186 Hz for the first 0.6 s to a value varying around 183 Hz (the value for the skirt component) for the remainder of the tone duration. This shows that the *pumping action* of the skirt on the note dominates the note dynamics after 0.6 s.

Of direct importance are the very low levels observed for both the internal resonance ($\omega_{21} \approx 2\omega_{11}$) and the combination resonance ($\omega_{31} \approx \omega_{11} + \omega_{21}$). Since these are the resonances that produce the partials on the steelpan, this note produces a rather dull tone. The fact that these resonances are at such low levels signify the absence of strong mode confinement on this $F_3^\#$ note — a direct result of the strong note-skirt coupling. Mode confinement, necessary on the steelpan for the tonal quality of the instrument, can therefore be destroyed when it is possible to simultaneously excite dominant modes of nearly similar frequencies on the skirt that couple strongly to modes on the note.

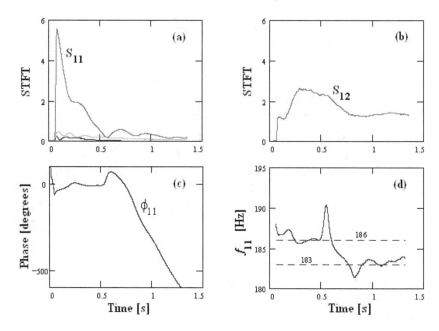

Fig. 5.15. Experimental results for the double-second $F_3^{\#}$ note played forte with skirt coupling. (a) note displacement STFT, (S_{21}, S_{31}). (b) STFT of the skirt component. (c) phase-time response of the first mode on the note. (d) frequency modulation on f_{11} (= 186.0 + $\phi'_{11}/2\pi$ Hz)

The velocity STFT's were maximized at f_{11} = 186 Hz (mode1) and f_{21} = 374 Hz (mode2). This note-skirt system was modeled numerically and the results shown along with the frequency diagram in Figures 5.16a-d. *Modeling parameters*: $\alpha_{211} = \alpha_{121} = 0.001$, $\alpha_{112} = 0.005$, $\alpha_{123} = \alpha_{213} = 0.001$, $\alpha_{132} = \alpha_{312} = 0.001$, $\alpha_{231} = \alpha_{321} = 0.001$, all $\beta = 0.0$, $\Gamma_{12}^{\{11\}}=0.0016$, $\Gamma_{11}^{\{12\}}=0.0033$, $\mu_{11}= \mu_{21} = \mu_{31} = .001$, $\mu_{12} = 0.0003$, $\sigma_1= -0.01$, $\sigma_2 = -0.003$, $\sigma_3 = -0.01$: *Initial amplitudes*: *forte* level; $a_{11} = 1$, $a_{21} = a_{31} = 0$, $a_{12}=0.0$.

The good agreement between Figure 5.15 and Figure 5.16 confirms the applicability of the present theory to the coupled note-skirt system on the steelpan. The strength of the note-skirt coupling is determined by the values for $\Gamma_{jd}^{\{nd\}}$. While the values used here for these coupling coefficients (0.0016 and 0.0033) are somewhat smaller than those for the D_3 note-skirt coupling on the bass (0.003 and 0.004 respectively) it should be noted that the coupled modes in the present example are closer in frequency (186 Hz and 183 Hz) than the coupled modes are on the bass (147 Hz and 179 Hz). The higher partials remained strong on the **D**$_3$ bass note while the higher partials were almost insignificant on the **F**$_3^{\#}$ double-second note in addition to the shortened duration of the **F**$_3^{\#}$ keynote.

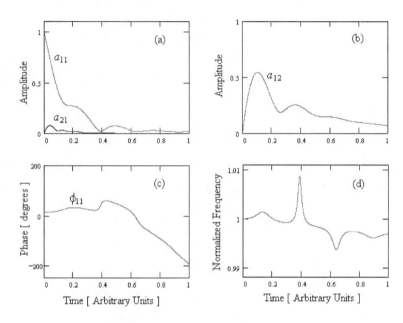

Fig. 5.16. Analytical results of the simulated **F**$_3^{\#}$ note played *forte* with skirt coupling: (a) amplitudes of note components, (b) amplitude of skirt component, (c) time-history of phase ϕ_{11}, (d) frequency modulation on ω_{11} (= $1 + \phi'_{11}$).

5.6 Modal Frequencies on a Clamped-Free Cylindrical Skirt

The strategy adopted here, in investigating the note-skirt resonances, is to calculate the modal frequencies on the skirt treated as a clamped-free circular cylinder and to search for coincidences on the musical scale of frequencies (those to which the pan is tuned). The structure of the steelpan consists of a cylinder (the skirt) closed at one end by an indented circular plate (the pan face) and with the other end fully or partially opened. Partially opening one end is a practice followed by some makers in constructing the bass. One realizes that since the indented pan face is generally stiffer than the skirt and because of the crimped rim (chime), the pan face-skirt boundary, to a first approximation, could be treated as fixed (clamped). The open end of the skirt is essentially free. In a more accurate development of the theory, the skirt-pan face structure should be considered as a two-component system (or three-component if one end is partially opened) coupled by a set of rotational and translational springs. Bearing in mind that in practice the excitation levels on the instrument are relatively small and that pan makers generally use secure rims on their instruments, the clamped-free approximation allows for a reasonably accurate assessment of the note-skirt resonance problem.

A further approximation is to ignore the presence of stiffeners on the skirt. Stiffeners will generally shift the modal frequencies upwards and introduce new higher modes. The presence of stiffeners only affects the results for the lower pans that employ at least two stiffeners on the skirt in most cases.

Because of the introductory nature of the present analysis, a new theoretical formulation specially tailored for the vibrations of the steelpan skirt (with non-ideal pan face-skirt supports) will not be presented here. Instead, a fairly accurate closed-form solution for the frequencies of a clamped-free cylinder developed by Soedel (1980) will be used. When applied to the steelpan skirt, this closed-form approximation has been found by the author to be in excellent agreement with the more exact cubic and sextic frequency equations developed by Sharma (1974) for the fixed-free cylinder. The Soedel formulation is much easier to use as it involves less computational effort. The linear version of the Sharma equation (loc cit) which assumes zero hoop and shear strains, is too inaccurate for use on the present system.

For a cylindrical skirt of length L, radius R, thickness h, steel density ρ, Young's modulus of elasticity E and Poisson's ratio ν, the Soedel formulation (valid for transverse dominated deflections) is given in equation (5.11). The parameters η_m are the roots of the analogous clamped-free beam problem with m (1, 2, 3, ..) representing the axial mode numbers. The index n (0, 1, 2, 3, ...) are the circumferential wave numbers identifying the *swaying* ($n = 1$), *ovalling* ($n = 2$) and *breathing* ($n > 2$) modes.

$$f_{mn} = \frac{1}{2\pi}\left(\frac{Y}{\rho}\right)^{\frac{1}{2}}\left[\frac{\eta_m^4}{R^2 L^4 \left(\frac{n^2}{R^2}+\frac{\eta_m^2}{L^2}\right)^2} + \frac{h^2}{12(1-\nu^2)}\left(\frac{n^2}{R^2}+\frac{\eta_m^2}{L^2}\right)^2\right]^{\frac{1}{2}}. \quad (5.11)$$

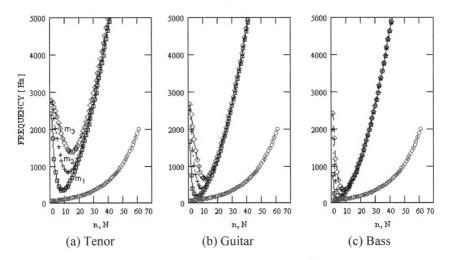

Fig. 5.17. Natural frequencies for the skirts on the tenor, guitar, and bass instruments as functions of axial and circumferential mode numbers m and n respectively. The lower slowly rising red curve on each panel represents a plot of the frequencies of notes on the musical tempered scale versus a pseudo index N.

In Figure 5.17, skirt natural frequencies are plotted for three classes of steelpans: tenor (L = 210 mm, R = 290 mm, h = 1 mm), guitar (L = 450 mm, R = 290 mm, h = 1 mm) and bass (L = 880 mm, R = 290 mm, h = 1 mm), with *Young's modulus* 207 GPa, *Poisson's ratio* 0.3 and *density* 7700 kg/m^3.

To gain some physical insight into the results shown in Figure 5.17, one can use the strain energy approach. The strain energy of the vibrating skirt consists of bending strain energy and stretching strain energy. Sketches of these energies are shown in Figure 5.18. As the axial wave number m increases, the flexibility decreases (becoming more inflexible) so increasing the frequency. This is seen more clearly in Figure 5.17(a) for the tenor skirt as m increases. At low circumferential mode numbers n, the stretching strain energy dominates. As n increases, stretching strain energy rapidly decreases while bending strain energy increases. The frequency of vibration is approximately proportional to the square root of the total strain energy as shown by the similarity in behavior of the total strain energy curve in Figure 5.18 and the frequency curve in Figure 5.17. The minimum total strain energy corresponds to the lowest vibrational frequency.

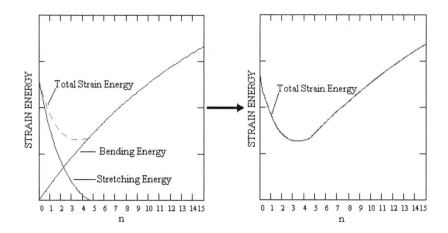

Fig. 5.18. Variation of strain energy components and total strain energy with circumferential mode number n.

Comparing Figures 5.17 and 5.18 shows that the shorter skirts (tenor range) are more strongly dominated by stretching strain energies at low values of n. As the axial mode number is increased, the shorter skirt shows a greater increase in stretching and bending energies. Since the swaying ($n = 1$) and the ovalling ($n = 2$) modes are very dependent on the stretching strains the constraint provided by the fixed end is crucial in determining these frequencies. This means that the fixity of the rim on the high (tenor range) pans is more important for these modes dominated by stretching strains than it is for the lower (bass range) pans. It is unlikely however that in the normal playing of these instruments especially the upper range, short-skirt pans, that the swaying or ovalling modes will be excited to any significant level.

Some theoretical modal shapes for the skirt vibrational modes are shown in Figure 5.19. For emphasis and better visibility, the modal amplitudes in Figure 14 have been greatly exaggerated. The *ovalling mode* ($m =1$, $n = 2$) is shown in Figure 5.19a while three *breathing modes* with $n = 5$ are shown in Figures 5.19(b, c & d). These are some of the low order modes. Higher modes show more complex structures. The reader should note that Figure 5.19 presents 'snapshot pictures' of the vibrations at an instant in time. The real dynamic picture will contain the motion showing outward and inward movements of the skirt as it vibrates. .

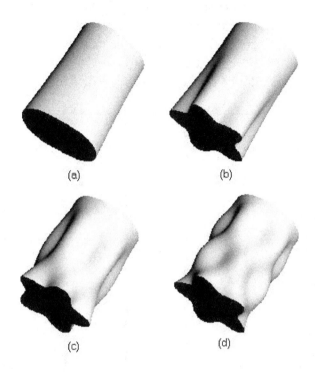

Fig. 5.19. Modal shapes for vibrational modes on the skirt. The rim is at the top while the free end is at the bottom. (a) Ovalling, $(m, n) = (1, 2)$; (b) $(m, n) = (1, 5)$; (c) $(m, n) = (2, 5)$ (d) $(m, n) = (3, 5)$. All amplitudes exaggerated for emphasis.

5.7 Statistical Study of Coincidences

Without reference to the degree of coupling between the played notes on the pan face and the natural modes on the skirt, one can look for coincidences and near-coincidences on these two sets of frequencies. One can search within defined frequency bandwidths Δf_j for coincidences that exist between the skirt modes and the note frequencies on the pan. This will allow one to confirm analytically, and to provide some explanation for, the observation by pan makers that these annoying coincidences turn up 'more often' on the midrange pans. The reader must note that coincidences are generally rare.

Figure 5.20 shows the mode frequencies for the three selected skirts ($h = 1$ mm) along with the frequencies of the notes on the musical scale. For each skirt, counts are made for the number of coincidences with the musical scale within bandwidths of $\Delta f_j = 2, 4, 8, 12, 16$ Hz. Upper and lower frequency limits were set for each instrument: Tenor ($C_4 = 261.63$ Hz to $G_6 = 1568$ Hz), Guitar ($D_3 = 145.83$ Hz to $B_4 = 493.88$ Hz) and Bass ($C_2 = 65.4$ Hz to $A_3 = 220$ Hz).

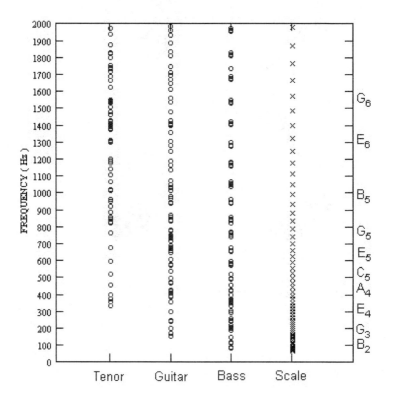

Fig. 5.20. Overlay of mode frequencies for three selected skirts and the frequencies of the notes on the musical scale.

Table 5.1 shows the number of coincidences for the three ranges of instruments including an additional set of results for a tenor skirt of length 15 cm (6 inches). Tenor skirt lengths usually fall within the range 15 – 21 cm. In these sets of results, coincidences were sought between skirt frequencies and all note frequencies on the instruments (for inner and outer notes). There is a small excess of coincidences on the mid-range guitar, a result which agrees with the pan makers' observation. However, because the note-skirt resonance effect is controlled by the degree of note-skirt coupling, where stronger coupling is expected between the outer notes and the skirt, it will be useful to repeat the search without the inner notes. This was done for the tenor and guitar and the result appears in Table 5.2. On the bass there are only a few inner notes employed so their exclusion does not affect the results in any significant way.

In Table 5.2, one sees a marked decrease in coincidences when the outer notes alone are counted (the more likely notes to exhibit strong note-skirt coupling in practice), especially on the tenor. This explains the almost complete absence in practice, of bothersome note-skirt resonances on the high range steelpans.

In the results of Tables 5.1 & 5.2, one clearly sees a relatively high number of coincidences on the bass. When a pan maker uses the fashionable 'straight skirt' (without stiffeners as analyzed here) the skirt resonances are known to appear. This is the reason why the straight skirt has not 'caught on' among pan makers who prefer instead, the traditional stiffened skirt. Having two stiffeners reduces the effective length, and for the higher axial modes effectively divides the skirt into three short sections. This has the effect of raising the modal frequencies of the skirt and brings the distribution of the higher modes closer to that of the shorter pans. This reduces the number of coincides significantly (as obtained in practice).

Bandwidth Hz	Number of Coincidences					
	Tenor L=21cm, (15cm)		Guitar L = 45 cm		Bass L = 88 cm	
2	2 (1)	1* (3)*	3	2*	3	1*
4	3 (3)	1* (3)*	4	3*	6	2*
8	3 (4)	4* (5)*	10	7*	9	3*
12	10 (6)	6* (6)*	11	8*	9	5*
16	11 (10)	9* (6)*	14	8*	9	5*

Table 5.1. Number of frequency coincidences obtained at different bandwidths. Inner and outer notes included. Bracketed values in the tenor column are for a skirt of length 15 cm. Values with an asterisk (*) are for skirt thickness h = 1.5 mm; all other results are for h = 1 mm.

Bandwidth Hz	Number of Coincidences				
	Tenor L=21cm, (15cm)		Guitar L = 45 cm		Bass L = 88 cm
2	2 (0)	1* (0)*	0	2*	3	1*
4	2 (0)	1* (0)*	1	2*	6	2*
8	3 (0)	2* (0)*	7	4*	9	3*
12	4 (0)	3* (0)*	7	5*	9	5*
16	4 (1)	4* (0)*	7	5*	9	5*

Table 5.2. Number of frequency coincidences obtained at different bandwidths. Inner notes excluded. Bracketed values in the tenor column are for a skirt of length 15 cm. Values with an asterisk (*) are for skirt thickness h = 1.5 mm all other results are for h = 1 mm.

Increasing the thickness h, from 1 mm to 1.5 mm, reduces the number of coincidences on all instruments as can be seen in Tables 5.1 & 5.2 (results identified by an asterisk (*)). However, segmenting the skirt with stiffeners (stringers or rolling hoops) is the more effective way of avoiding note-skirt resonances as it results in much larger upward shift in the resonant frequencies.

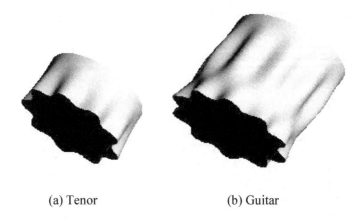

(a) Tenor   (b) Guitar

Fig. 5.21. Resonant modes on two pan skirts. (a) Mode (1, 9) on a tenor skirt (L = 21 cm, h = 1mm) at 293.11 Hz in resonance with the $\mathbf{D}_4$ (293.66 Hz) note. (b) Mode (2, 10) on a guitar (L = 45 cm, h = 1 mm) at 348.65 Hz in resonance with the $\mathbf{F}_4$ (349.23 Hz) note.

Two examples of resonant modes on the skirts of the model tenor ($L = 21$ cm, $h = 1$ mm) and the model guitar ($L = 45$ cm, $h = 1$mm) are shown in Figure 5.21. One observes that the free end (the bottom) of the skirt will always be an anti-nodal line. This makes the free end an ideal location for mass-loading as a means of tuning-out these resonances when they do arise. Careful choice of mass (always the minimum required) attached to the free end will shift these resonances sufficiently away from the note frequency being affected. The reader is reminded that the amplitudes of the modal displacements in Figure 5.21 are greatly exaggerated for visibility. On a real pan these vibrations are imperceptible to the eye but can be sensed by touch. Also, on real tenor and guitar pans these two modes D_4 and F_4 may not be ones in resonance on the skirts because of differences in skirt length, thickness, density and elastic constants that characterize the particular instruments.

5.8 Partially Opened Skirts

Some makers partially open the lower end of the skirt on their basses by cutting a central hole (circular or square) in the end plate. This provides an additional constraint on what is normally the free end, which will raise the natural frequencies of the skirt. On the bass, this means reducing the possibility of coincidences with the low frequency bass notes. Partially opening the lower end also increases the overall rigidity of the structure (instrument). There are therefore some advantages to be gained by partially opening the lower end of the skirt.

5.9 Chapter Summary

The motion of the coupled note-note or note-skirt system retains some of the characteristics of the single note dynamical system, as expected, when the coupling coefficients are small or when the mode frequencies are not closely related harmonically. The modulation characteristics of the moderately or strongly coupled systems are quite different to those of the uncoupled system. Unique tonal qualities are obtained on note pairs in sympathetic vibration with the second octave often showing deep amplitude and frequency modulations.

It is an interesting fact in the history and development of the steelpan that the steel drums used as the rawform for most steelpans have provided many desirable characteristics for the successful development of the instrument. As the present author has said in many seminars on the instrument, 'the steel drum was made to order for the steelpan.' The presence of the stiffeners on commercial drums has served to reduce the effective lengths of the skirt and to dynamically partition the skirt at the higher frequencies. This has allowed for the proper construction of the bass as it reduces the possibility for note-skirt resonances. The additional constraint provided by the partially opened end on some basses further reduces this possibility. In *The Pan Makers' Handbook* the author has suggested simple mass-loading procedures for eliminating the occasional note-skirt resonances that may threaten to make an otherwise good pan useless.

CHAPTER 6

The Steelpan as a System of Non-linear Mode-Localized Oscillators: the Inverse Problem — Parameter Estimation

6.1 Introduction

In Chapters 4 and 5 the physical structure of the steelpan was described and an examination made of the responses of the notes and other sub-sections to impacts produced by striking the notes with the stick. Each note functions as a non-linear system for which the governing equations for note vibrations contain linear and quadratic terms. Quadratic non-linearities arise from the curvature of the notes, which are formed as shallow shell-like domes on the indented face of a steel drum. The exchange of energy between resonances on a note produces amplitude as well as frequency modulations.

This Chapter is concerned with the specific *inverse problem* of estimating the parameters for the analytical model developed for the steelpan in Chapters 3, 4 and 5. The techniques developed in this Chapter add to the body of knowledge on inverse problems of vibrating systems (see for example Lancaster and Maroulas 1987, Starek and Inman 1992, 1995 and the review papers by Gladwell 1986, 1996) and to the area of *model updating* (see the survey by Mottershead and Friswell 1993).

6.2. Theoretical Development

The non-linear theory for the notes on the steelpan developed in previous Chapters is employed here in the inverse problem of parameter estimation. A practically feasible procedure is now developed that yields the note parameters from the time-history data of individual notes.

6.2.1. Phase Flow

After some algebraic manipulations of equations (4.9a-c) in Chapter 4 to eliminate the sines, one arrives at the equation

$$\frac{1}{2}\frac{d}{dt_1}\left[a_1^2 + v_2 a_2^2 + v_3 a_3^2\right] = -\left[\mu_1 a_1^2 + \mu_2 v_2 a_2^2 + \mu_3 v_3 a_3^2\right]. \quad (6.1)$$

where

$$v_2 = \frac{\omega_2}{\omega_1}\frac{\alpha^*_{121}}{\alpha_{112}}, \quad v_3 = \frac{\omega_3}{\omega_1}\left(\frac{\alpha^*_{132}\alpha^*_{121}}{\alpha^*_{123}\alpha_{112}} + \frac{\alpha^*_{231}}{\alpha^*_{123}}\right). \quad (6.2)$$

It is not possible to get a complete, closed-form solution to equation (6.1) for the case $\mu_1 \neq \mu_2 \neq \mu_3$. However, a reasonable simplification is to assume equal damping for the three modes $\mu_1 = \mu_2 = \mu_3 \doteq \mu$. This assumption is justified by the following consideration. Damping in metals at low stress levels is due primarily to magnetoelastic hysteresis, which in the present frequency range of interest, is independent of frequency (see Harris (1987) and Chapter 9). The steel used in the manufacture of steelpans exhibit little internal damping because of the low stress levels involved during a vibration cycle. The first modes for the notes on the steelpans are all located in the frequency range 69.3 Hz ($C_2^\#$) on the low end, to 1396.9 Hz (F_6) on the high end. For the most part, it is only the first three modes of vibration on each note that are of sufficient amplitude to be of significant musical interest. On any particular note therefore, the frequency range over which the damping is required, is somewhat limited. Observation of many steelpan tones shows that the duration of these tones are all of the order of one second. While this latter observation, taken alone, cannot accurately define the damping coefficients for this non-linear instrument, it does imply that the degree of damping is not expected to be highly variable over the frequency range of the instrument.

With the equal damping assumption, (6.1) can be integrated to give

$$E(\tau) = E(0)\, e^{-2\mu\tau}, \qquad (6.3)$$

where

$$E(\tau) = a_1^2 + v_2 a_2^2 + v_3 a_3^2, \qquad (6.4)$$

and τ (in units of the time scale t_1) is the time measured from the instant that E maximizes. The latter occurs some time after the stick has lost contact with the note.

Were the damping coefficients of the second and third modes to be written as $\mu_2 = \mu_1 + \delta\mu_2$, $\mu_3 = \mu_1 + \delta\mu_3$, to account for differences in damping coefficients, then (6.3) must be replaced by

$$E(\tau) = E(0)\, e^{-2[\mu_1 \tau + g(\tau)]},$$

with

$$g(\tau) = \int_0^\tau \frac{\delta\mu_2 v_2 a_2^2 + \delta\mu_3 v_3 a_3^2}{a_1^2 + v_2 a_2^2 + v_3 a_3^2}\, d\tau', \qquad (6.5a,b)$$

where τ' is a dummy variable over the interval $[0, \tau]$. If $\delta\mu_2$ and $\delta\mu_3$ are significantly different from zero, then $E(\tau)$ will not follow an exponential law. It ought to be possible to test, empirically, the applicability of these equations to the steelpan notes.

From equations (6.3) and (6.4) one gets,

$$\frac{a_1^2}{B_1} + \frac{a_2^2}{B_2} + \frac{a_3^2}{B_3} = e^{-2\mu\tau}, \qquad (6.6)$$

where

$$B_1 = E(0), \quad B_2 = \frac{E(0)}{v_2}, \quad B_3 = \frac{E(0)}{v_3}. \qquad (6.7a,b,c)$$

Equation (6.6) shows that under equal damping, the modal amplitudes $a_n(\tau)$ are not independent of each other but that *a weighted sum of the squares of the modal amplitudes should follow an exponential decay law*. The weights in the summation are the coefficients $1/B_i$, $i = 1, 2, 3$. For a conservative system ($\mu = 0$), the solutions lie on an ellipsoid in the six-dimensional phase space $(a_1, a_2, a_3, \phi_1, \phi_2, \phi_3)$. For a dissipative system however, such as the notes on the steelpan, this ellipsoid slowly collapses as the tone decays.

From an energy standpoint, equation (6.6) describes the partition of energy amongst the three modes and shows that the total vibrational energy, *expressed by the sum of squares of the modal amplitudes*, decays exponentially with time.

- *Equation (6.6) is a clear statement of the phenomenon of non-linear mode localization as it expresses the fact that the vibrational motions of the tuned modes of a sounding note are mutually coupled thereby confining the energy to a well defined domain called the true note.*

Energy is slowly lost (on a time scale of a second) from the domain by acoustical radiation and transmission across the note boundary. Energy is dissipated within the domain by magnetomechanical damping and appears as heat.

- *It is this confinement of vibrational energy to well defined domains that makes possible, the operation of the steelpan as a plexus of tuned shells on a larger indented shell (the pan face).*

6.2.2. Frequency-Amplitude Relation

Equations (4.9d-f) in Chapter 4 can be reduced to

$$\phi_1' a_1^2(\tau) - \frac{\omega_2}{\omega_1} \frac{\overset{*}{\alpha}_{121}}{\alpha_{112}} \phi_2' a_2^2(\tau) - \frac{\omega_3}{\omega_1} \left\{ \frac{\overset{*}{\alpha}_{231}}{\overset{*}{\alpha}_{123}} - \frac{\overset{*}{\alpha}_{132} \overset{*}{\alpha}_{121}}{\overset{*}{\alpha}_{123} \alpha_{112}} \right\} \phi_3' a_3^2(\tau) = 0 .$$

(6.8)

Equation (6.8), shows the relationship of the frequency modulations ϕ_n' to the amplitudes $a_n(\tau)$. Examples of this frequency-amplitude dependence as found on the steelpan were given in the experimental and numerical data of Chapters 4 and 5.

6.3. Solution to the Inverse Problem

Before proceeding with the inverse problem, the observation data are defined.

6.3.1. Observation Data.

The data provided by observation of the steelpan are in the form of displacement (or velocity) time-histories of the vibrating notes. The notes are set into vibration by impact using a standard rubber-tipped stick. Velocity measurements can be made using a set-up consisting of a small electrodynamic velocity transducer, low-noise amplifier, antialiasing filter, A/D converter and a desktop computer. This raw data can be analyzed using the Short-Time-Fourier-Transform (STFT) (discussed fully in Chapter 4) to produce complex spectral components $S_{\dot{u}}^{\{n\}}$ for the velocity $\dot{u}$. These velocity STFT components are linearly related to the STFT $S_u^{\{n\}}$ for displacement u by, $S_{\dot{u}}^{\{n\}} = -j\omega_n S_u^{\{n\}}$. In the present analysis, there exists the correspondence $a_n \equiv |S_u^{\{n\}}|, \varphi_n \equiv \arg(S_u^{\{n\}})$. The inverse problem based on this correspondence is given below.

6.3.2. Inverse Parameter Value Problem.

Given the observation data in the above form, determine the values of $(\omega_n, \mu_n, \sigma_1, \sigma_2, \alpha_{jkn})$;

Remark. An obvious question that arises is that of the uniqueness of $(\omega_n, \mu_n, \sigma_1, \sigma_2, \alpha_{jkn})$ recovered from the observation data.

To see more clearly what parameters can be determined, equation (6.5) must be written in the more explicit form

$$a_1^2(\tau) - a_1^2(0)e^{-2[\mu_1\tau + g(\tau)]} + \frac{\omega_2}{\omega_1}\frac{\alpha_{121}^*}{\alpha_{112}}[a_2^2(\tau) - a_2^2(0)e^{-2[\mu_1\tau + g(\tau)]}] +$$

$$\frac{\omega_3}{\omega_1}\left(\frac{\alpha_{231}^*}{\alpha_{123}^*} + \frac{\alpha_{132}^*\alpha_{121}^*}{\alpha_{123}^*\alpha_{112}}\right)[a_3^2(\tau) - a_3^2(0)e^{-2[\mu_1\tau + g(\tau)]}] = 0.$$

(6.9)

From equations (6.8) and (6.9), one sees that from the experimental data, the α parameters cannot be determined individually but only in the combined form of ratios $\alpha_{121}^*/\alpha_{112}$, $\alpha_{132}^*/\alpha_{123}^*$ and $\alpha_{231}^*/\alpha_{123}^*$. This, at least partially, answers the question on the uniqueness of the α parameters.

The use of the slow time τ ($= \varepsilon t$) in equation (6.9) means that in practice, where it is the real time (or fast time) t that is measurable, only the products $\varepsilon\mu_n$ can be determined from the experimental data. Similarly, for the detuning parameters, only the products $\varepsilon\sigma_n$ can be determined.

The frequencies ω_n (and frequency modulations) are easily recovered by maximizing the STFT's as described fully in Chapters 4 and 5. These frequency values will be unique for each note.

6.3.3. The Mirror Functions and a New Signal Processing Technique

Normally the STFT is maximized by choosing the analyzing frequency that gives the maximum $|S_u^{\{n\}}|$. But when there is moderate or strong amplitude modulation on the signal, this method becomes insensitive to small changes in the analyzing frequency. A much more accurate signal processing method is developed here which incorporates the system equations with the STFT process. The result is a very precise phase-sensitive technique with special application to the modulated steelpan tones.

From equation (6.8) one can define two functions, *Mirror Functions*, M_1 and M_2

$$M_1(t) = \phi_1' a_1^2(t), \qquad (6.10)$$

and

$$M_2(t) = -A\,\phi_2' a_2^2(t) - B\,\phi_3' a_3^2(t), \qquad (6.11)$$

Observe that $M_1(t)$ is dependent *only* on the phase and amplitude of mode1 while $M_2(t)$ is dependent *only* on the phase and amplitude of mode2 and mode3. On a suitable time plot these functions should appear as 'mirror images' of each other once the correct values for A and B are obtained. As will be seen in the examples to follow, the matching of the mirror functions $M_1(t)$ and $M_2(t)$ provides a very sensitive check on the correctness of the analyzing frequencies ω_n used in the STFT analysis. The analytical power of this method lies in the strong phase dependence of these mirror functions — observe that the functions depend on the time rate of change of phase ϕ_n'; that is on the frequency modulation of the modes.

6.3.4. Minimization and Discretization

Values for $\varepsilon\mu_n$, $(\omega_2 \alpha_{112} / \omega_1 \alpha_{121}^*)$ and $(\omega_3/\omega_1)(\alpha_{132}^* \alpha_{121}^* / \alpha_{123}^* \alpha_{112} + \alpha_{231}^* / \alpha_{123}^*)$ are determined by minimizing $[E(t) - E(0)e^{-2[\varepsilon\mu_1 t + g(\varepsilon t)]}]^2$. The values of A and B are determined by minimizing $[M_1(t) + M_2(t)]^2$. A second value for $(\omega_2 \alpha_{112} / \omega_1 \alpha_{121}^*)$ is found from A, while a value for $(\omega_3/\omega_1)(\alpha_{231}^*/\alpha_{123}^* - \alpha_{132}^* \alpha_{121}^* / \alpha_{123}^* \alpha_{112})$ can be obtained from B.

Experimental data will normally be obtained or stored in discretized form because of sampling. The real functions $E(t)$ and $M_m(t)$ ($m = 1, 2$) will be represented by the sequences

$$E_j, M_{m,j}, \quad j = 0, \ldots, N-1$$

where N represents the number of data points in the whole sample. The procedure for solving the inverse problem of parameter estimation therefore requires the minimization of the residuals

$$K_E = \frac{1}{N} \sum_{j=0}^{N-1} [E_j - E_0 e^{-2(j\varepsilon\mu_1\delta t + g_j)}]^2 \quad K_M = \frac{1}{N} \sum_{j=0}^{N-1} [M_{1,j} + M_{2,j}]^2$$

(6.12a,b)

where δt is the sampling interval. Time derivatives of the phase are estimated using the phase change over successive discrete time samples.

6.4. Simulation

On completing the minimization procedure, the parameters and parameter ratios can be used to simulate the steelpan response during the period of free vibrations (more precisely, from the instant that E maximizes to the end of the tone).

It was shown in Chapter 4 that tonal structure (frequency and amplitude) depends on the manner in which the stick impact is delivered. The level of the second mode increases significantly in comparison with the first mode when the note is played with more vigor. The note simulation must therefore consider this. Following the procedure adopted in Chapters 4 and 5, a note judged to have been played at the *forte* level (loud) can be simulated in the numerical experiments by assuming an initial amplitude for the first mode as $a_1(0) = 1$. Similarly, a note at the *piano* level (soft) will have $a_1(0) = 0.5$.

The non-uniqueness of the α-parameters allows a wide range of values that may be acceptable in the simulation. However, the α-ratio values determined in the minimization procedure must be satisfied. In addition, the time scale in the simulation is arbitrary, but in this case, it is necessary to keep the ratio of the detuning parameters consistent with the results obtained in the minimization procedure.

6.5 Example Applications

6.5.1 General Remarks

The algebraic simplicity of the results in the previous section allows for the straightforward application of the inverse procedure to the vibrations of the steelpan notes. Two examples are taken from the example set of Chapter 4. The first example corresponds to a note for which there is a weak second mode and negligible higher modes, while in the second example there is a strong second mode and a comparatively weaker third mode. These examples are typical of those found on this instrument. Note excitation was done in the normal way for this instrument, by striking the note with the stick and velocity recordings made in the manner described earlier for *observation data*.

Derivatives with respect to real time t replace derivatives with respect to τ since the factor ε cancels out across equation (6.8). The sampling rate for the data was 11 KHz. Sampling faster produced no additional information. The procedures for setting the parameters for the Gaussian window and the variance in the STFT computations were the same as those used in Chapter 4. For the simulation of steelpan responses, Equations (4.9a-f) were integrated numerically using a fourth order Runge-Kutta routine which produced the discretized values for a_n and ϕ_n at time steps of 0.1.

Minimization of equation (6.12a) was first done assuming different decay coefficients and then by assuming equal decay coefficients with g_j set to zero. It was necessary to perform separate minimization for each case because of the non-linear nature of the problem. The results presented here were first reported by the author in Achong (1998). The only changes made in the present analysis were (i) the higher tolerance set in the minimization procedure and (ii) a small offset DC voltage correction to the sampled data on the $F_4^{\#}$ note. This did not significantly change the results; however, improvements were obtained in the deviations between *E(t)* defined by equation (6.3) and *E(t)* defined by equation (6.5).

The two tones used as examples were chosen because of their large modulations which will put the theory to the most stringent test. The tone of the sampled $F_4^{\#}$ note is a good example of frequency modulation at its best while the tone of the sampled E_4^{b} note is an excellent example of amplitude modulation.

6.5.2. The $F_4^\#$ Note on a Tenor Pan

The tone structure (modal components) for the $F_4^\#$ (369.99 Hz) note played *forte*, is shown in Figure 6.1. This particular note shows a modulated first mode component and a weak, modulated, second mode. Higher modes were not present. Because of a small mistuning of this note at the time of the experiment, STFT's were maximized at f_1=367.3 Hz and f_2= 743.2 Hz for a frequency ratio $f_2/f_1 (=\omega_2/\omega_1) = 2.0234$. The product $\varepsilon\sigma_1$= 54.0 rad/s ≡ 8.6 Hz.

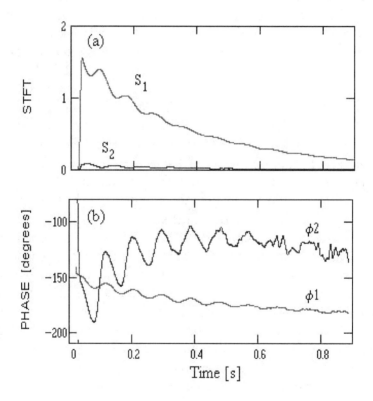

Fig. 6.1. Observation data for the $F_4^\#$ note in the form of Fourier components: (a) the amplitudes $|S_n|$; (b) the phase angles $\arg|S_n|$.

$E(t)$ reached a maximum some 13.8 ms after the stick made contact with this note. This time interval is approximately five times the period of the first mode. The minimization of the residual K_E yielded the values $\varepsilon\mu_1 = \varepsilon\mu_2 = 3.18$ s^{-1}, $\alpha^*_{121}/\alpha_{112} = 56.0$ under the equal damping assumption and $\varepsilon\mu_1 = 3.16$ s^{-1}, $\varepsilon\mu_2 = 3.28$ s^{-1}, $\alpha^*_{121}/\alpha_{112} = 56.0$ otherwise. A previous analysis (Achong 1998) of this data overlooked a rather small zero offset error (two digitizing steps) on the digitized data leading to slightly smaller coefficients (for example; $\varepsilon\mu_1 = \varepsilon\mu_2 = 3.17$ s^{-1}, $\alpha^*_{121}/\alpha_{112} = 53.4$). The corrected data are used in the present analysis.

In Figure (6.2) the function $E(t)$ from equation (6.3) is seen to follow the exponential decay function $E(0)e^{-2\varepsilon\mu t}$ very closely. Figure (6.3) shows the percentage deviation between $E(t)$ defined in equation (6.3) and $E(t)$ according to equation (6.5). This deviation was computed to higher tolerances than what I used in Achong (1998) thus yielding a deviation that is less than 0.1% throughout the duration of the tone. It is therefore reasonable to conclude that *there is no significant difference between the damping coefficients for the two modes on this note.*

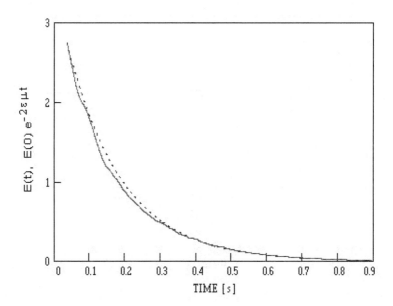

Fig. 6.2. The functions $E(t)$ (solid curve) and $E(0)e^{-2\varepsilon\mu t}$ (dotted curve) for the $F^\#_4$ note. The theory requires these two functions to be equal.

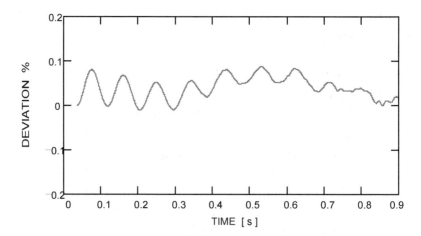

Fig. 6.3. The percentage deviation between $E(t)$ defined by equation (6.3) and $E(t)$ defined by equation (6.5a) for the $\mathbf{F}^{\#}_4$ note. Equal damping on the three modes requires the deviation to be zero.

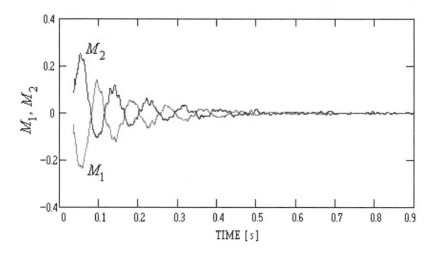

Fig. 6.4. The mirror functions $M_1(t)$ and $M_2(t)$ for the $\mathbf{F}^{\#}_4$ note. Notice the mirror functions are images of each other about the 'horizontal' time axis drawn through $M_1(t) = M_2(t) = 0$.

Minimization of the residual K_M yielded the value $\alpha^*_{121}/\alpha_{112} = 48.0$. This value is some 16.7% lower than that obtained by minimizing K_E. The mirror functions $M_1(t)$ and $M_2(t)$ are plotted in Figure 6.4. While adjustments to the value of A ($= \omega_2 \alpha_{112}/\omega_1 \alpha^*_{121}$) in the minimization process will produce changes to the magnitude of the function $M_2(t)$, it will not alter the *form* of $M_2(t)$. There is a fair degree of detailed matching in the form of the functions $M_1(t)$ and $M_2(t)$ seen in Figure 6.4. This strongly suggests that the analytical model can be applied with confidence to this musical instrument.

6.5.3 $F_4^{\#}$ Simulation

The non-linear response of the $\mathbf{F}_4^{\#}$ note was modeled numerically by integrating equations (4.9a,b,d,e) with the parameters; $\alpha_{121}^{*} = 0.16$, $\alpha_{112} = 0.0033$, $\varepsilon\sigma_1 = 0.01$, $\mu_1 = 0.0006$, $\mu_2 = 0.00062$.

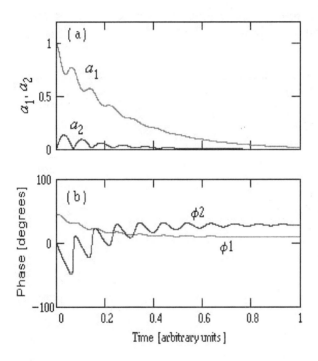

Fig. 6.5. Numerical simulation of the $\mathbf{F}_4^{\#}$ note: (a) amplitudes, (b) phase angles.

The mean parameter ratio for $\alpha_{121}^{*}/\alpha_{112}$, obtained by minimization of the residuals, is satisfied by these α-parameters. To simulate the note played *forte*, the initial (dimensionless) displacement on the first mode was set at unity. The simulated amplitudes a_1, and a_2 are shown in Figure 6.5(a) while the corresponding phases ϕ_1 and ϕ_2 are shown in Figure 6.5(b). There is marked similarity between the real note data of Figure 6.1 and the simulated results in Figure 6.5.

6.5.4 The E_4^b Note

A more complex tone structure is shown in Figure 6.6 for the E_4^b (311.1 Hz) note played *forte*. To determine these components the STFT's were maximized with $f_1 = 311.1$ Hz, $f_2 = 624.0$ Hz, $f_3 = 930.6$ Hz. The corresponding frequency ratios are $f_2/f_1 = 2.006$ and $f_3/f_1 = 2.991$ with $\varepsilon\sigma_1 \equiv 1.8$ Hz and $\varepsilon\sigma_2 \equiv -4.5$ Hz.

On this note, E(t) reached a maximum 16.5 ms after the note was struck (approximately five times the period of the first mode). The minimization of the residual K_E yielded the values $\varepsilon\mu_n = 3.53$ s^{-1}, (n = 1, 2, 3), $\alpha^*_{121}/\alpha_{112} = 2.89$ and $(\alpha^*_{231}/\alpha^*_{123} + \alpha^*_{132}\alpha^*_{121}/\alpha^*_{123}\alpha_{112}) = 1.24$ under the equal damping assumption, and $\varepsilon\mu_1 = 3.52$ s^{-1}, $\varepsilon\mu_2 = 3.72$ s^{-1}, $\varepsilon\mu_3 = 3.52$ s^{-1}, $\alpha^*_{121}/\alpha_{112} = 2.89$ and $(\alpha^*_{231}/\alpha^*_{123} + \alpha^*_{132}\alpha^*_{121}/\alpha^*_{123}\alpha_{112}) = 1.24$ otherwise (notice that both analyses yield the same α-ratios). In Figure 6.7 the function $E(t)$ from equation (6.3) is seen for this note also, to closely follow the exponential function $E(0)e^{-2\varepsilon\mu t}$.

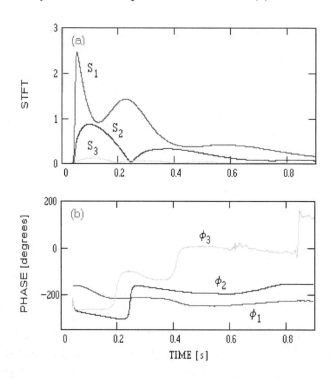

Fig. 6.6. Observation data for the E_4^b note in the form of Fourier components: (a) amplitudes $|S_n|$, (b) the phase angles arg(S_n).

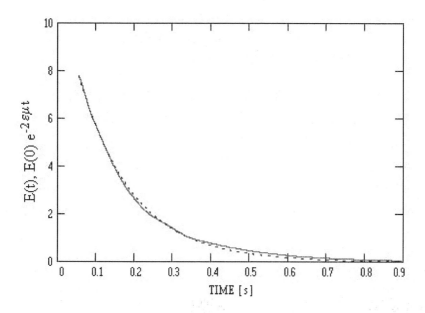

Fig. 6.7. The functions $E(t)$ (——) and $E(0)e^{-2\varepsilon\mu t}$ (- - -) for the E_4^b note. Theory requires agreement between these two curves.

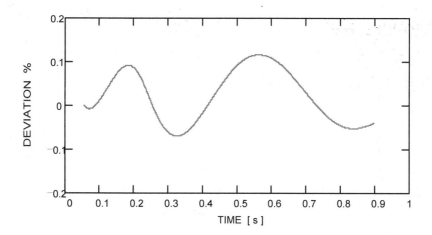

Fig. 6.8. The percentage deviation between E(t) defined by equation (6.3) and $E(t)$ defined by equation (6.5) for the E_4^b note. Equal damping on the three modes requires the deviation to be zero.

The deviation between $E(t)$ defined by equation (6.3) for equal damping and $E(t)$ according to equation (6.5), is plotted in Figure 6.8. The absolute magnitude of this deviation remains less than 0.12 % for the duration of the tone. Here also, it is clearly demonstrated that the equal damping assumption which leads to the exponential decay of $E(t)$ is applicable to the steelpan notes.

Minimizing the residual K_M yielded the values $\alpha^*_{121}/\alpha_{112} = 2.49$ and $(\alpha^*_{231}/\alpha^*_{123} - \alpha^*_{132}\alpha^*_{121}/\alpha^*_{123}\alpha_{112}) = 0.54$. As with the $\mathbf{F}_4^\#$ note, the value for $\alpha^*_{121}/\alpha_{112}$ obtained by minimizing K_F is less than the value obtained by minimizing K_E by 16%. Combining the two sets of results for the parameters one also gets the values $\alpha^*_{231}/\alpha^*_{123} = 0.89$ and $\alpha^*_{132}/\alpha^*_{123} = 0.14 \text{ or } 0.12$ (the latter values corresponding to $\alpha^*_{121}/\alpha_{112} = 2.49 \text{ or } 2.89$).

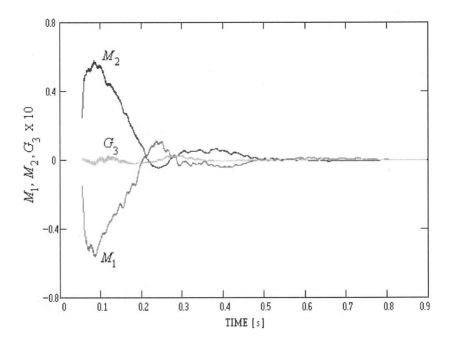

Fig. 6.9. The mirror functions $M_1(t)$, $M_2(t)$ and function $G_3(t)$ for the $\mathbf{E}_4^b$ note with mode2 maximized at $f_2 = 624.0$ Hz.. Notice the mirror functions are images of each other about the 'horizontal' time axis drawn through $M_1(t) = M_2(t) = 0$.

In Figure 6.9 the mirror functions $M_1(t)$ and $M_2(t)$ are plotted along with the contribution $G_3(t) = -B\phi_{3'}a_3^2(t)$ (scaled up x10) by the third mode to $M_2(t)$. From Figure 6.9 it is clear that in this example, it is the second mode that largely determines the form of the function $M_2(t)$.

6.5.5. E_4^b Simulation

The non-linear response of the E_4^b note was modeled numerically by integrating equations (4.9a-f) with the parameters; $\alpha_{121}^* = 0.047, \alpha_{112} = 0.019, \alpha_{123}^* = 0.014, \alpha_{231}^* = 0.012, \alpha_{132}^* = 0.0009, \mu_1 = 0.00067, \mu_2 = 0.00067, \mu_3 = 0.00067, \varepsilon\sigma_1 = 0.0028, \varepsilon\sigma_2 = -0.0048$. The parameter ratios obtained by minimization of the residuals are satisfied by these parameters. To simulate the note played *forte*, the initial (dimensionless) displacement on the first mode was set at unity.

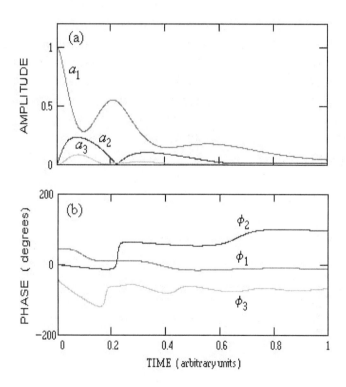

Fig. 6.10. Numerical simulation for the E_4^b note: (a) amplitudes a_n, (b) the phase angles ϕ_n.

The simulated amplitudes a_1, and a_2 are shown in Figure 6.10(a) (compare with Figure 6.6(a)) while the corresponding phases for ϕ_1 and

ϕ_2 are shown in Figure 6.10(b) (compare with Figure 6.6(b)). There are strong similarities between the real and simulated amplitude and phase structures for the first two modes that dominated the dynamics of this note. The third mode is simulated reasonably well in amplitude but the phase shows expected variations from the observation data as the vibration decays, mainly because of the weakness of this mode.

6.5.6 Optimizing the STFT

To demonstrate the sensitivity of the present method to changes in the analyzing frequency used in the STFT, the analyzing frequency for the second mode was reduced from the optimized value of $f_2 = 624.0$ Hz to a new value of 623.4 Hz — a frequency reduction of just under 0.1 % — and the Fourier component for the second mode recalculated. With this being the only change to the analysis, the new results are shown in Figure (6.11). There is now no matching of the mirror functions $M_1(t)$ and $M_2(t)$. The form of $M_2(t)$ has changed completely. This change was brought about mainly by the phase component $\phi_2(t)$ as there were only very small changes to the amplitude $a_2(t)$. In addition to maximizing the STFT and minimizing the phase in the usual way, the matching of these two mirror functions serves as a sensitive check on the accuracy of the mode frequencies.

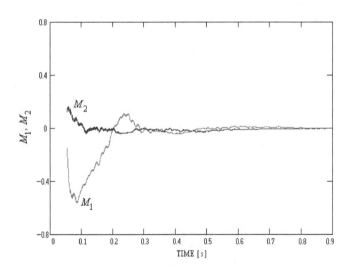

Fig. 6.11. The functions $M_1(t)$ and $M_2(t)$ for the $\mathbf{E}_4^b$ note with mode2 maximized at $f_2 = 623.4$ Hz

6.5.7 The Damping Coefficients

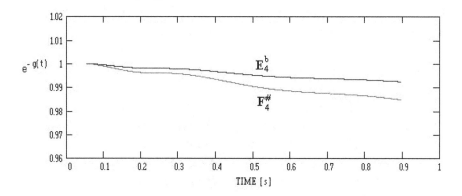

Fig. 6.12. The function $e^{-g(t)}$ for the E_4^b and $F_4^\#$ notes. The damping coefficients are all equal when $e^{-g(t)} = 1$.

The damping mechanism discussed in Chapter 9 is consistent with the observation that the damping coefficient is the same for all the audible modes on a given note — *confirmed in Figure 6.3 and Figure 6.8 to one part in a thousand (1 in 1000).* The differences in damping coefficients are measured by the function $g(\tau)$ in equation (6.5a). The damping coefficients are exactly equal when $g(\tau) = 0$ or equivalently, $e^{-g(\tau)} = 1$. Plots of the function $e^{-g(t)}$ for the E_4^b and $F_4^\#$ notes are shown in Figure (6.12). For the E_4^b note, $e^{-g(t)}$ remains in the interval [0.993, 1] while on the $F_4^\#$ note the interval is [0.985, 1].

6.6 Comparison of Note Dynamics

In comparing these two notes, one ought to look at the ratio $\alpha_{112}/\alpha_{121}^*$ for which the average value on the $F_4^\#$ note is 0.02 while on the E_4^b note it is 0.37. This shows that in both cases the coupling constant α_{112} which is a measure of the coupling of mode1 energy into mode2 is less than α^*_{121} which is a measure for the reverse coupling of energy from mode2 back to mode1. The process for energy exchange is however much more effective on the E_4^b note; this accounts for the more complex structure obtained on this E_4^b note and explains its much greater brilliance (musically).

6.7 Equal Damping and Summary of Analytical Technique

The model parameters for the non-linear vibrations of the notes on the steelpan as developed in the analyses of Chapters 4 and 5 can be computed by the inverse process developed here.

- *It has been verified that approximately equal damping exists for all the tuned modes on a note.*
- *Equal damping leads to the result that a weighted sum of the squares of the modal amplitude follows an exponential decay law. This decay law was closely obeyed on the two notes chosen as examples. The same results were obtained on numerous other notes studied by the author.*

Minimization procedures gave estimates for the decay coefficients and the weights from which the α-parameter ratios were computed. The simulated tonal structures using model parameters consistent with the analysis closely matched the real data.

In essence the computations are relatively simple. After computing the STFT for the tone signal (velocity or displacement time-history) the amplitude and phase data are used in the expressions for the residuals K_E and K_M which are then minimized. The minimization leads to estimation of the α-parameter ratios and decay constants. The matching of the two mirror functions plays the additional role as a very sensitive check on the accuracy of the analyzing frequencies used in the STFT computation.

6.8 Confirmation of the Mode-Localization or Mode Confinement Phenomenon

The experimental demonstration of the mirror functions introduced here is valid confirmation of confinement on the sounding notes of the steelpan. These results show that each normal mode on a tuned note is localized within some region or domain on the pan face referred to as the *true note*. This is in marked contrast to the vibrations that occur on an untuned pan before final preparation. Mode-localization or confinement requires that the vibrational modes of a tuned vibrating note be so closely related that the continuous exchange of motional energy between them ensures that the energy, except what is lost by transmission and acoustical radiation, remains within the defined region. The total vibrational energy decays exponentially with time. The energy lost through internal magnetomechanical damping is dissipated as heat in the material forming the note. Without mode confinement, the steelpan as a tuned musical instrument would not have been possible.

It is important for the experimentalist to bear in mind when measuring residual stress distributions on the pan faces of untuned pans, especially in the early stages of preparation, that there are no well-defined domains on the pan face of these unfinished pans with the full properties of a note. On a fully prepared, tuned pan, these domains are properly defined statically and dynamically but only approximately defined visually except when a Chladni pattern is employed. One should not use unfinished pans to assign properties to the finished product.

CHAPTER 7

Parametric Excitations

7.1 Theoretical Basis

In Chapter 3 it was shown that non-linearities are a natural aspect of the dynamics of the steelpan. These non-linearities are also responsible for much of the uniqueness in its sound. When a note on the pan is partially tuned so that the modal frequencies are not close to harmonicity, ω_n is not close to $n\omega_1$, it is possible to describe the dynamics of the system by a set of independent equations, one equation for each mode. Since there exists no mutual coupling between the modes in this case, the quadratic cross-terms and the mixed cubic terms are all zero. If w_n are the generalized coordinates (displacements) of the set of n $(1, 2, 3, ...)$ independent normal modes, the non-linear modal equations are of the form

$$\ddot{w}_n + \mu_n \dot{w}_n + \alpha_{1n} w_n + \alpha_{2n} w_n^2 + \alpha_{3n} w_n^3 = f_0 + f_n(\tau), \qquad (7.1)$$

where the over-dot represents differentiation with respect to τ, $\ddot{w}_n$ is the inertia term, $\mu_n \dot{w}_n$ represents damping, $\alpha_{1n} w_n$ is the linear stiffness, $\alpha_{2n} w_n^2$ and $\alpha_{3n} w_n^3$ are the quadratic and cubic stiffness respectively, f_0 is a static force produced by internal stresses while $f_n(\tau)$ is the external excitation. The α–parameters are dependent on the geometry of the shell, the elastic properties of the shell, the boundary conditions, internal compressive stresses and temperature. The quadratic terms arise from the shell curvature while the cubic terms arise from the stretching of the shell mid-surface. Because of this non-linear structure of the steelpan dynamics, it is now shown that this dynamics involve *mechanical parametric oscillators.*

7.2 SDOF Solutions

For the purpose of the present work, equation (7.1) can be reduced to a Single-Degree-of- Freedom (SDOF) equation representing a note tuned to the required fundamental (primary frequency = ω) but with all higher modes ($n = 2, 3, 4, ...$) 'untuned' and well away in frequency from $n\omega$. This second requirement removes the possibility of internal resonances (Chapter 3) and corresponds to the experimental situation where the higher modes are sufficiently separated in frequency from the parametric excitations to allow the latter to be spectrally resolved. When driven sinusoidally at a forcing frequency Ω close to the primary frequency, the effects of the higher, untuned modes can be neglected. When compressive stress and thermal effects are neglected, and by dropping all subscripts except on the α parameters, the reduced equation has the form

$$\ddot{w} + \mu \dot{w} + \alpha_1 w + \alpha_2 w^2 + \alpha_3 w^3 = F \cos\Omega\tau, \qquad (7.2)$$

where F now represents the magnitude of the sinusoidal driving force. With reference to the formulation in Chapter 3, in the notation used here, $\omega_0 = \sqrt{\alpha_1}$, $\alpha_2 = \alpha_{11,2}$, $\alpha_3 = \beta_{111,3}$. For an appropriate choice of parameters $\mu, \alpha_1, \alpha_2, \alpha_3, \Omega$ and F equation (2) can be integrated numerically and the spectral components extracted. However, we seek an analytical solution in order to identify the parametric modes of vibration of the type that equation (7.2) describes.

In any study on the musical aspects of the steelpan, periodic solutions of the system dynamics play a fundamental role. Because the system under consideration undergoes *forced* vibrations, at best, the solutions should include a *driven* mode $w \sim \cos(n\omega\tau)$ and a *companion* mode $w \sim \sin(n\omega\tau)$. To reduce the appearance of complexity in the derived equations, and without loss of generality, the companion modes will be suppressed in the following procedure.

The Harmonic Balance Method (HBM) (for example, see Mickens 1981) is used in the solution of equation (7.2). HBM is based on the assumption that for a given sinusoidal excitation there exists a steady-state solution that can be approximated to satisfactory accuracy by means of a finite Fourier series. Consequently, the displacements take on a set of amplitudes and phases for all frequency components. Enough harmonics must be used so that the Fourier series constructed from these harmonic amplitudes and phases can reproduce a reasonable replica of the time domain solution. If the system equation such as equation (7.2) is not available but instead there exists data in the form of a time series for the displacements obtained experimentally then the HBM has to be implemented numerically in an iterative process.

Since the HBM assumes a periodic solution of equation (7.2) to exist, $w(t)$ can be expanded as a superposition of harmonics (a Fourier series):

$$w(\tau) = \sum_{n=0}^{\infty} a_n (e^{in(\omega\tau+\phi)} + e^{-in(\omega\tau+\phi)}), \qquad (7.3)$$

where the fundamental component ω is the playing frequency (the key-note) of the sounding note. For computational purposes, the Fourier series has to be truncated to a suitable degree N high enough to represent accurately the solution $w(t)$. In the present study it is sufficient to continue the summation in equation (7.3) up to the fifth harmonic. In the methodology of HBM, assuming that the system is driven at the primary mode frequency, $\Omega = \omega$, equation (7.3) is substituted into equation (7.2).

On performing all the differential and algebraic operations described in equation (7.2), constant terms and terms of like frequencies or 'harmonics' (ω, 2ω, 3ω...) including the forcing terms are consolidated and equated to zero. This is the 'balancing' procedure where the sum of the terms associated with each frequency component (including zero frequency for the constants) must vanish independently. One can also extract from the computation, the non-linear frequency of the vibrating system (see Sections 7.3 and 8.11.6). After some algebra, there ensue the following expressions:

$$a_0 = -\frac{\alpha_2}{2\alpha_1}a_1^2 + O(a_1^4), \tag{7.4}$$

$$a_1 = \frac{F}{\mu\omega}, \tag{7.5}$$

$$w(\tau) = a_0 + a_1\cos(\omega\tau + \phi) + \frac{\alpha_2}{6\alpha_1}a_1^2\cos 2(\omega\tau + \phi) + \frac{\alpha_3}{32\alpha_1}a_1^3\cos 3(\omega\tau + \phi)$$
$$+ \frac{\alpha_2\alpha_3}{480\alpha_1^2}a_1^4\cos 4(\omega\tau + \phi) + \frac{\alpha_3^2}{1024\alpha_1^2}a_1^5\cos 5(\omega\tau + \phi) + \ldots\ldots \tag{7.6}$$

where a_1 is the amplitude of the primary resonance. In these equations,

$$\omega = \omega_0(1 - \mu^2/2\omega_0^2)^{1/2} \tag{7.7}$$

is the *damped* linear frequency while $\omega_0 = \alpha_1^{1/2}$ is the *undamped* linear frequency. Equation (7.5) gives an expression for the amplitude a_1 of the driven mode that is consistent with simple principles of physics. The amplitude a_1 is proportional to the applied impulse per oscillation F/ω (the greater the driving impulse, the larger the amplitude), and inversely proportional to the damping coefficient μ (the greater the damping, the smaller the amplitude).

7.3 Restoring Forces

The analysis also yields the expression for the *primary mode restoring force*. This is retrieved from the algebraic expressions by recognizing that for a strictly linear system, the restoring force is equal to the negative of the product of the stiffness and the displacement, -$\omega^2 w$. As an equation of forces, equation (7.2) in its expanded form is well suited for this procedure. The real component of w in its linear form is equal to $a_1\cos(\omega\tau + \phi)$ and ω^2 is recognized as the *linear stiffness*. Observe that damping changes the linear stiffness from ω_0^2 to ω^2. The presence of quadratic and cubic non-linearites will also cause a change in the stiffness of the primary mode and thereby introduce a shift in the system's natural frequency. In the HBM expansion of the system equation, all terms related to the primary stiffness are consolidated to yield the restoring force up to $O(a_1^4)$

$$F_{primary} = -\left(\omega_0^2 - \frac{\mu^2}{2} + \left(\frac{3\alpha_3}{4} - \frac{5\alpha_2^2}{6\alpha_1}\right)a_1^2\right)a_1 \cos(\omega\tau+\phi). \quad (7.8)$$

This expression for the primary restoring force yields the *non-linear frequency ω^* with damping* for the primary mode as

$$\omega^* = \omega_0\left[1 - \frac{\mu^2}{2\alpha_1} + \left(\frac{3}{4}\frac{\alpha_3}{\alpha_1} - \frac{5}{6}\left(\frac{\alpha_2}{\alpha_1}\right)^2\right)a_1^2\right]^{1/2}. \quad (7.9)$$

Compare equation (7.9) with equation (7.7) which gives the *linear frequency with damping*.

7.4 Frequency-Amplitude Dependence

Equation (7.9) shows that in addition to the frequency shift produced by the $-\mu^2/2\alpha_1$ term, which also occurs in the linear case with damping, the last two amplitude-dependent terms produce a shift which is the combined effect of the cubic and quadratic non-linearities. This equation will be used in Chapter 8 where a deeper analysis is possible. For the moment it is sufficient to note that as a result of the frequency-amplitude dependence, **initially, *as the note is played, the tone begins slightly flat, quickly rising in frequency (over the first few (one to two) cycles) with frequency modulations imposed as the tone develops and decays.*** These modulations take us beyond equation (7.9).

7.5 Drift

The coefficient a_0 given by equation (7.4) represents a 'drift' in the response; this is a direct effect of the quadratic (even-order) non-linearity. Under constant-amplitude harmonic loading (F = constant), the drift appears as a constant component of the deflection of the note surface. Under the impulse loading that occurs during the normal playing of the notes (which, in its fullness, requires the solution of equation (7.1)), there is a time-dependent drift. For a 3-Degree-of-Freedom (3-DOF) system, with second and third normal modes tuned close to the corresponding harmonic of the first mode, the solution of equation (7.1) shows the dominant drift term to be (ignoring smaller higher order terms)

$$drift \approx -\frac{1}{2}\left(\frac{\alpha_{21}}{\alpha_{11}}a_1^2 + \frac{\alpha_{22}}{\alpha_{12}}a_2^2 + \frac{\alpha_{23}}{\alpha_{13}}a_3^2\right) \qquad (7.10)$$

where, in α_{mn}, m is the non-linear coefficient index while n is the mode number, and the time-dependent modal amplitudes a_n are modulated as energy is exchanged among the modes.

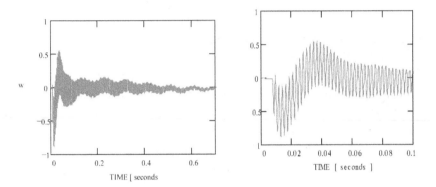

Fig. 7.1. Body motion on the A_4 note on a bore tenor pan played fortissimo. Wobble frequency approximately 11.5 Hz. Displacements in units of note thickness h.

After stick impact, the note surface will execute a slow 'wobbling' drift with a frequency under 20 Hz. This effect is better described as *body motion*. An example of this motion with significant displacement is shown in Figure 7.1. Most notes show milder body motion than that seen in the Figure 7.1 example.

7.6 Parametric Excitations with a^n and $a_m a_n$ Amplitude Dependencies. Heterodyning

7.6.1 Parametric Excitations

Equation (7.6) shows that $w(\tau)$ consists of a number of vibration components which appear at harmonics of the primary frequency; $n\omega$ (n

= 2, 3, 4, 5 ...). These components, with sharply decreasing amplitude are the *parametric excitations* (see Chapter 4) of the note surface:

Parametric excitation at frequency 2ω: $\quad \dfrac{\alpha_2}{6\alpha_1} a_1^2 \cos 2(\omega\tau + \phi)$,

Parametric excitation at frequency 3ω: $\quad \dfrac{\alpha_3}{32\alpha_1} a_1^3 \cos 3(\omega\tau + \phi)$,

Parametric excitation at frequency 4ω: $\quad \dfrac{\alpha_2 \alpha_3}{480\alpha_1^2} a_1^4 \cos 4(\omega\tau + \phi)$,

Parametric excitation at frequency 5ω: $\quad \dfrac{\alpha_3^2}{1024\alpha_1^2} a_1^5 \cos 5(\omega\tau + \phi)$.

No special or 'extra' fine-tuning is required to produce these parametric excitations as they appear directly from the non-linearities of the instrument. However, to properly observe them in the presence of the higher tuned partials, their spectral peaks must be adequately resolved, so some detuning is necessary (see below). *A word of caution is necessary here; these weak parametric excitations must not be confused with the normal modes or partials. They are however the means by which energy can be transferred from the fundamental mode to the higher modes by the process of internal resonance,*

Parametric modes may have been observed on the steelpan by researchers in the field and some have been mistaken for weak normal modes or reported as split modes. They have also been reported by pan producers with the claim that the notes on their steelpans have been tuned to as high as the 9th partial. Many of these reports are erroneous because: (a) the amplitude of these excitations decrease rapidly with increasing harmonic number, and (b) similar effects are observed when spectral analysis is carried out on tones that have been *over-amplified* (and distorted) electronically, subjecting the analysis to the non-linearities of the analyzer itself. Effect (b) is the most likely culprit in these reported cases. Simply put, they are artifacts of the spectral analysis.

7.6.2 Double Peaks in Pan Spectra

To best observe these parametric excitations, the second and third normal modes must be tuned well away from integer multiples of the primary resonance. They are therefore difficult to observe on a properly tuned pan (with near harmonic tuning), or may give additional peaks or structure to the spectral components. An example on a real pan is shown in Figure 7.2. The double peak on the spectrum that appears in the range 180 to 192 Hz is created by a parametric excitation at 184.60 Hz (peak c, slightly detuned from 2 x 92.40 = 184.80 Hz.) and by the second normal mode (n = 2) at 191.19 Hz (peak d). The second mode is very much detuned (see Chapter 4) producing a poor tone from this $F^{\#}_2$ note. However, the author did this intentionally by detuning this note prior to taking the measurements, in order to increase the separation between the parametric excitations and the normal modes. When these double-peaks appear around the second (third) mode frequency, it is a clear indication that the detuning is large resulting in a poor sounding note with weak second (third) partial.

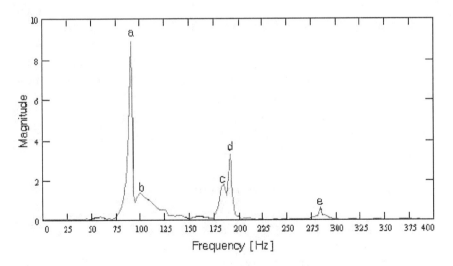

Fig. 7.2. Spectrum for $F^{\#}_2$ note on a bass. The first mode (a) is at 92.40 Hz. The lower component (c) of the double peak (roughly at the middle of the figure) corresponds to the parametrically excited vibration at 184.60 Hz (slightly detuned from 2 x 92.40 = 184.80 Hz). The higher frequency component (d) is the second mode at 191.19 Hz. A low-level third mode (e) sits at 284.67 Hz.

7.6.3 Combination Frequencies: Heterodyning

If the reader should look carefully at the base of the fist mode peak in Figure 7.2, there would be seen a weak broadened peak at 99 Hz (peak b). This is formed by the non-linear interaction of the first mode at 92.40 Hz (peak a) and the second mode at 191.19 Hz which produces a parametric excitation at $f_2 - f_1$ =191.19 – 92.40 = 98.79 Hz (plus a small detuning). This peak at 99 Hz was verified as real and not an artifact arising from noise for example, as its position was tracked when the temperature of the pan was progressively increased from 27.5°C to 56°C (see Figure 5 in Achong 1999b). It appeared consistently at the difference frequency $f_2 - f_1$ (subject to a small detuning). This is an example of parametrically induced combination frequencies $f_m \pm f_n$ with an $a_m a_n$ amplitude-dependence law. This means that the amplitude of the 99 Hz excitation in Figure 7.2 is proportional to a_1^3, which accounts for its small amplitude. The coupling coefficient corresponding to the $f_1 + f_2$ excitation is too low for this combination mode to show any discernible structure around the third mode peak in Figure 7.2. For another example on the E_4^b tenor note see Figure 8 of Achong (1999b).

These combination frequencies are the result of the *heterodyne* aspect of steelpan non-linear operation involving the (vector) products $w_m w_n$. The present SDOF treatment does not allow complete treatment of these combination resonances, but the 2-DOF and 3-DOF treatments clearly show the appearance of the combination components along with the usual harmonic terms appearing in equation (7.6).

7.6.4 Further Checks and Confirmation

As a further check on these low-level excitations, the linearity of the signal detecting and processing equipment was verified using simultaneous two-frequency excitation on a linear vibrating system. The a_1^n dependence of the amplitude on mode number n, given by equation (7.6), has also been readily verified on numerical simulations.

7.6.5 No Evidence for Frequency Splitting

The reader is reminded that the double-peaks (for example the peaks 'c' and 'd' in Figure 7.2) ought not to be called 'split modes' or be seen as examples of 'frequency splitting' because each peak has a separate and distinctly different origin. The same applies to the combination resonances. Claims to discovery of new spectral types in pan sounds must always be fully substantiated by proper modal identification. The El Paso groups, Murr et al. (1999) and Ferreyra et al. (1999) have made claims to frequency splitting on the steelpan notes without proper modal identification being reported. This makes their conclusions questionable. 'Splitting' implies that a single mode or component is altered to show up in two or more distinct states having different energies and frequencies. These new components must therefore correspond to unique sets of modal numbers: for example mode2 splits into mode2a and mode2b (each with its unique set of modal numbers). If this effect were to exist on the steelpan, it would very likely have rendered the instrument useless for musical purposes. Pan makers would be kept busy trying to remove the splitting. Frequency splitting has never been observed on the thousands of pans tested or listened to by the present author and is at variance with accepted shell theory for these metal note structures. The present author sees the claims by the El Paso groups as a misidentification of normal modes and parametric excitations.

7.7 Chapter Summary

When a steelpan note is played, in addition to the normal modes, a number of low-level parametric modes are excited at harmonically related frequencies (plus some small detuning) and in combinations $f_m \pm f_n$ (plus some small detuning). When the note is driven at the first mode frequency, the amplitudes of the harmonically related parametric excitations at frequency nf_1 follow an a_1^n power law. The amplitude of the combination components at frequencies $f_m \pm f_n$ follow an $a_m a_n$ law. Parametric excitations can lead to internal resonances and energy transfers between modes allowing for complex tonal structures.

CHAPTER 8

The SDOF Model of steelpan notes: Quality Factor, Hardening and Softening effects, Potential Wells and Frequency Shifts

8.1 Introduction

It has been shown in Chapters 4 and 5 that the tonal structures of the steelpan notes are the result of non-linear vibrations of shallow shells on the pan face of the instrument. For example, all the first and second mode amplitude- and frequency-modulation features observed on the real notes can be synthesized in the non-linear model involving internal resonances. Perhaps the most convincing demonstration of the effect of internal resonances on this instrument comes during the tuning process itself. The moment that the tuner has correctly shaped the notes and set the right boundary conditions and in-plane stresses, the note begins to 'sing' loudly with a beautiful resonance. This is the moment when the modes are tuned to a nearly perfect *key-note-octave-twelfth* relationship.

The global view provided by the set of note equations, allows both the main musical features as well as important subtleties to be understood. They therefore provide physicists, engineers and capable pan makers, with an efficient basis for describing those aspects of the steelpan that are of interest to present concerns on the note dynamics.

The heuristic procedure that has typified pan making, namely 'hit and miss' and 'trial and error' should now become a thing of the past. The equations set out by the author can explain what has been seen and predicts what are yet to be seen on the steelpan.

8.2 The Static State of the Note as a SDOF System

The static state of the SDOF system is described by the same equation given for the MDOF system in Chapter 3, namely

$$\frac{1}{12}\nabla^4\psi_0 + 8(1+v)\left(\frac{H_0}{h}\right)^2\left\{Q^2\psi_0 - \frac{1}{2}(1+v)P(Q\psi_0',Q)\right\} - (\check{N}_c + \check{N}_T)\nabla^2\psi_0$$

$$+ (1+v)\left(\frac{H_0}{h}\right)\left\{S(\psi_0'^2,Q) + Q\psi_0'^2 + 2Y(\psi_0',Q\psi_0') - 2V(Q\psi_0\psi_0')\right\}$$

$$+ \frac{1}{2}Z(\psi_0',\psi_0'^2) + \frac{1}{2}V(\psi_0'^3) - 4(\check{N}_c + \check{N}_T)\left(\frac{H_0}{h}\right)Q = 0,$$

(8.1)

where $Q = Q(x)$ is the *shape function* (not to be confused with the Quality Factor).

The dimensionless surface displacement function $\psi_0(x)$ must satisfy the same pole and boundary conditions imposed on the modal coordinate $\psi(x)$ describing the mode shape of the fundamental mode. In fact the static equation (8.1) is a special case of the dynamical equation (3.10a) with the time dependent terms set to zero and with $\psi_0(x)$ replacing $\psi(x)$. It is therefore admissible to write

$$\psi_0(x) = A_0\psi(x), \qquad (8.2)$$

where A_0 is the amplitude (in units of note thickness h) of the dimensionless static displacement of the note at the apex arising from the application of thermal and/or compressive stresses to the system.

The pole and boundary conditions are also satisfied by the function

$$g(x) = \{(1-x^2) + q(x)\},$$

which describes the normalized shape (in units of the rise H_0) of the note under zero stress. If the note is subjected to compressive and thermal stresses, one can expect the displaced surface to be described by the new function $(H_0 + hA_0)g(x)$. Therefore another admissible function is

$$\psi_0(x) = A_0 g(x). \tag{8.3}$$

In practice, the shape of each steelpan note and its boundary and pole conditions are unique. It is therefore impossible to write down a general modal function $\psi(x)$ that applies exactly to notes of all shapes. The best one can do is to find functions whose parameters can be adjusted to match the boundary conditions and provide a good fit to the dynamical and statical equations. Therefore, of the two suggested functions for $\psi_0(x)$, equation (8.3), which tracks the note shape during the tuning process is expected to provide a better description of the note surface distorted under stress. If the note is under compressive/thermal stress and the stress changes, the displacement amplitude will undergo a change δA_0.

8.3 Dynamical Equations

In the general multi-mode problem, numerical solution can be sought by the standard method of choosing an appropriate set of orthogonal trial functions satisfying equations (3.10a, b) and the boundary and pole conditions. In the present analysis, a simpler approach is used which assumes that the pan maker/tuner can achieve perfect *blocking* of the note (equivalent to infinite spring constants along the note boundary). Therefore, while the notes on the pan face are constrained in a manner somewhere between *freely simply supported* and *clamped*, the assumption is that the ideal state of perfect blocking or clamped constraint is achieved. One observes here that because the ideal is never fully achieved in practice, coupling to other parts of the pan face and skirt *always* occur to some degree.

It will be assumed here that $\psi(x)$ takes the form of the fundamental mode solution for the small amplitude, free (unforced), axisymmetric vibration of the clamped spherical shell with a modified *geometric parameter*. An immediate consequence of the axisymmetric assumption is that the effects of aspect ratio (for ellipsoidal notes) are suppressed. The modal function (mode shape) is given by

$$\psi(x) = N_0 \left\{ J_0(K\,x) + \frac{J_1(K)}{I_1(K)} I_0(K\,x) - \left[J_1(K) \frac{I_0(K)}{I_1(K)} + J_0(K) \right] \right\}, \tag{8.4}$$

where the normalizing factor N_0 is chosen for the convenience of having

$$\int_0^1 \psi^2 x\, dx = 1, \tag{8.5}$$

and K is the first root of

$$[J_0(K) I_1(K) + I_0(K) J_1(K)] K \left[\frac{\lambda^4 + K^4 (1-v)}{\lambda^4} \cdot \frac{1}{2} - 1 \right] + 2 J_1(K) I_1(K)(1+v) = 0. \tag{8.6}$$

Notes: (i) *Do not confuse this K with the spring constant along the note boundary.*

(iii) *A function of a variable x is usually expressed as f(x). The root of a function f(x) is that value of x that makes the function take on the value zero i.e. f(x)= 0. The root of a function is also referred to as a 'zero' of that function (since it makes the function zero). Some functions may have only one root, others may have many roots. The roots of a function can be real, imaginary or complex.*

J_0 and J_1 are Bessel functions of the first kind while I_0 and I_1 are modified Bessel functions of the first kind, with $\lambda^2 = [12(1-v^2)]^{\frac{1}{2}} [2H_0/h]$ as the geometric parameter.

8.3.1 Case I: Zero Compressive/Thermal Stress

In order to make the modal function in equation (8.4) (which is exact for perfectly spherical shells) applicable to the case of shaped shells forming the pan notes, the geometric parameter λ is redefined by replacing R_0 with an equivalent radius R_{eq} which equals the radius of that perfect spherical shell (on the same planform) having the same mid-surface area as that of the shaped shell. For the case of zero compressive/thermal stress, one can readily show that

$$R_{eq} = R_0 \left[\int_0^1 \left(\frac{dq}{dx} - 2x \right)^2 x \, dx \right]^{-\frac{1}{2}}. \tag{8.7}$$

The proof is as follows. Consider the general note shape in the Figure 8.1. A circular band of note surface of width ds and radius r forms an element of surface area $dA = 2\pi r ds$. The width ds is given by $ds = [dg^2 + dr^2]^{1/2}$ where g $(= H_0 g(x))$ for the note under zero compressive/thermal stress is given by the expression $g = H_0[q(x) + (1-x^2)]$ and where the radial distance $r = xa$. Using the approximation $2R_0 H_0 = a^2$ to eliminate H_0, and integrating dA over the note surface gives for the area of the note mid-surface

$$A = 2\pi \int r \, ds$$

$$A = 2\pi a^2 \int_0^1 \left[1 + \frac{a^2}{4R_0^2} \left(\frac{dq}{dx} - 2x \right)^2 \right]^{\frac{1}{2}} x \, dx.$$

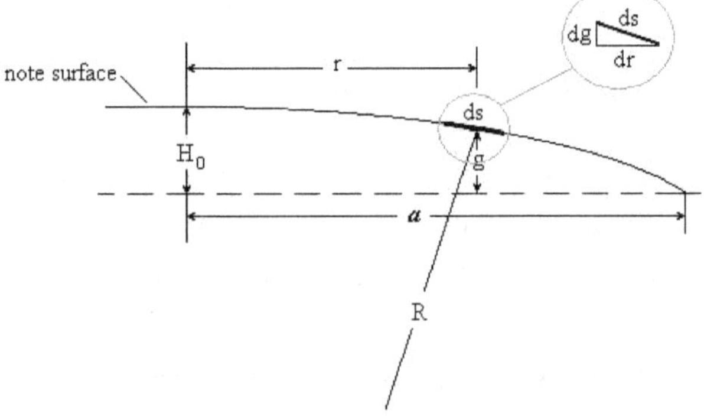

Fig. 8.1. Section of a general note shape showing an element of mid-surface area. The radius of curvature R varies with r for an arbitrarily shaped note but is constant with $R = R_0$ for a spherical cap.

For spherical caps, $q(x) = 0$ and $dq/dx = 0$ for x over the interval $[0, 1]$. In general, for these shallow shells, one finds that $\frac{a^2}{4R_0^2}\left(\frac{dq}{dx} - 2x\right)^2 \ll 1$ at all points on the surface. Using this in the well known approximation $(1+\delta)^{\frac{1}{2}} \approx 1 + \frac{1}{2}\delta$ for $\delta \ll 1$, allows A to be written as

$$A = 2\pi a^2 \int_0^1 \left[1 + \frac{a^2}{8R_0^2}\left(\frac{dq}{dx} - 2x\right)^2\right] x\, dx.$$

$$= \pi a^2 \left[1 + \frac{a^2}{4R_0^2} \int_0^1 \left(\frac{dq}{dx} - 2x\right)^2 x\, dx\right] \quad (8.8)$$

For a spherical cap of radius R_{eq}, equation (8.8) is easily integrated to give the mid-surface area

$$A_{sphr\,cap} = \pi a^2 \left[1 + \frac{a^2}{4R_{eq}^2}\right]. \quad (8.9)$$

If the mid-surface area A of the shaped note equals the mid-surface area $A_{sphr\,cap}$ of the equivalent spherical cap then by comparing (8.8) and (8.9) one gets

$$\frac{1}{R_{eq}^2} = \frac{1}{R_0^2} \int_0^1 \left(\frac{dq}{dx} - 2x\right)^2 x\, dx,$$

from which equation (8.7) follows directly.

The geometric parameter can now be redefined as

Zero Stress: $\lambda^2 = [12(1-v^2)]^{\frac{1}{2}} \left[\int_0^1 \left(\frac{dq}{dx} - 2x\right)^2 x\, dx\right]^{\frac{1}{2}} \left[\frac{2H_0}{h}\right].$ (8.10)

This geometric parameter now depends on the *form (geometry)* of the shell mid-surface through the *shaping function q(x)* (which describes the departure of the note geometry from the spherical cap). It should be clear that this definition will always result in the exact value of λ and the precise mode shape $\psi(x)$ whenever the shaping function takes the form $q(x) = b(1 - x^2)$ since this represents a change from one spherical form to another. For other shaping functions describing the note geometry, close approximations for the mode shape should be obtained. *Essentially, shaping the note during tuning is now equivalent to varying q(x).*

8.3.2 Case II: Non-zero Compressive/Thermal Stress

In the case of the note under compressive/thermal stress g(x) is replaced by $(H_0 + hA_0)g(x)$ which is the same as $H_0[q(x) + (1-x^2)] + h\psi_0(x)$ therefore $q(x)$ must be replaced by the new shaping function $\{q(x) + h\psi_0(x)/H_0\}$ in equation (8.10) and in the expression for $Q(x)$. The geometric parameter in this case is given by

Non-Zero Stress:

$$\lambda^2 = [12(1-v^2)]^{\frac{1}{2}} \left[\int_0^1 \left(\frac{d}{dx}(q(x) + h\psi_0(x)/H_0) - 2x \right)^2 x\, dx \right]^{\frac{1}{2}} \left[\frac{2H_0}{h} \right].$$

(8.11)

Since all tuned pan notes will be under stress at all times, (8.11) always apply. It should be clear from this expression for the geometric parameter that if the temperature of the pan changes or the compressive stresses are altered by aging or by the application of external forces from such sources as clamps or other attachments for example, the mode shape will be altered. This in turn implies that there will be a change in the note frequency.

8.4 Solving the SDOF Equation for the Coupling Parameters

When $W(x, \tau)$ is substituted from equation (3.11) (for $N = 1$, single mode), equation (3.10b) is solved for the shaped shell by integrating twice and employing the boundary and pole conditions (equations (3.2a-c)). This operation yields

$$u(x,\tau) = -2(1+v)\left(\frac{H_0}{a}\right)w(\tau)E(x) - \left(\frac{h}{2a}\right)[w(\tau)]^2 G(x),$$

where

$$E(x) = \frac{1}{x}\int_0^x e(x)\,x\,dx - x\left\{\int_0^x e(x)\,x\,dx\right\}_{x=1}, \quad \text{with } e(x) = \int_0^x Q\left(\frac{d\psi}{dx}\right)dx,$$

$$G(x) = \frac{1}{x}\int_0^x g(x)\,x\,dx - x\left\{\int_0^x g(x)\,x\,dx\right\}_{x=1}, \quad \text{with } g(x) = \int_0^x \left(\frac{d}{dx} + \frac{1-v}{x}\right)\left(\frac{d\psi}{dx}\right)^2 dx.$$

(8.12a, b, c)

Note: As is often the case with a long intricate analysis, one may 'run out' of suitable symbols to express new functions. Such is the case in equation (8.12c) where a new function g(x) is defined. This is a 'local function' used only within equation (8.12c). Do not confuse this function with g(x) used elsewhere to define the note shape.

On carrying out the conventional Galerkin averaging on equation (3.10a) (that is, multiplying by $\psi\,x$ and integrating with respect to x over the interval $[0,1]$) and using the normalizing condition in equation (8.5), the following SDOF non-linear prototype o.d.e (ordinary differential equation) is obtained

$$\frac{d^2 w}{d\tau^2} + \bar{\mu}\frac{dw}{d\tau} + \alpha_1 w + \alpha_2 w^2 + \alpha_3 w^3 = f_0 + \overline{f}_s(\tau), \qquad (8.13)$$

where

$$\alpha_1 = \frac{1}{12}M_1 + 8(1+v)\left(\frac{H_0}{h}\right)^2\left(M_2 - \frac{1}{2}(1+v)M_3\right) - (\check{N}_0 + \check{N}_T)M_4 \quad (8.14)$$

$$M_1 = \int_0^1 (\Delta^4 \psi) \psi \, x \, dx, \qquad M_2 = \int_0^1 Q^2 \psi^2 \, x \, dx,$$

$$M_3 = \int_0^1 \left[\left(\frac{d}{dx} + \frac{1}{x} \right) E \right] Q \psi \, x \, dx, \quad M_4 = -\int_0^1 (\Delta^2 \psi) \psi \, x \, dx,$$

$$\alpha_2 = (1+v) \left(\frac{H_0}{h} \right) (M_5 - 2 M_6), \qquad (8.15)$$

$$M_5 = \int_0^1 \left[\left(\frac{d\psi}{dx} \right)^2 \cdot \left(\frac{d}{dx} + \frac{1}{x} \right) G \right] Q \psi \, x \, dx$$

$$M_6 = \int_0^1 \left(\frac{d}{dx} + \frac{1}{x} \right) \left[Q \psi \frac{d\psi}{dx} - \frac{d\psi}{dx} \left(\frac{d}{dx} + \frac{v}{x} \right) E \right] \psi \, x \, dx$$

$$\alpha_3 = \frac{1}{2} M_7, \qquad (8.16)$$

$$M_7 = -\int_0^1 \left(\frac{d}{dx} + \frac{1}{x} \right) \left[\left(\frac{d\psi}{dx} \right)^3 - \frac{d\psi}{dx} \left(\frac{d}{dx} + \frac{v}{x} \right) G \right] \psi \, x \, dx$$

$$f_0 = 4 (\breve{N}_0 + \breve{N}_T) \left(\frac{H_0}{h} \right) M_8,$$
(8.17)
$$M_8 = \int_0^1 Q \psi \, x \, dx$$

$$\bar{f}_s(\tau) = f_s(\tau) M_9, \qquad (8.18)$$
$$M_9 = \int_0^1 z(x) \psi \, x \, dx$$

For any reasonably practical note that the pan maker can produce, the normalized damping coefficient $\breve{\mu} = \mu\gamma(1-\upsilon^2)a^4/(Eh^3)$ is constant over the surface of the note. The $M_1 \ldots M_9$ functionals are the SDOF versions of the functionals $\overline{G}_n(\text{var}_1 \cdots)$ found in the MDOF analysis given in Section 3.10.3.

8.5 Buckling (Flapping) Analysis and the Static State of the Note

8.5.1 Flapping Analysis

The Buckling problem was treated in the MDOF analysis but an analysis in the SDOF case is done here in order to look at this important problem using a simpler set of equations. In the case of large compressive in-plane loading or at a high enough temperature, the expression for α_1 (the stiffness parameter), equation (8.14), shows that *negative* stiffness is possible if the following inequality is satisfied

$$(\breve{N}_c + \breve{N}_T) M_4 > \frac{1}{12} M_1 + 8(1+v)\left(\frac{H_0}{h}\right)^2 \left(M_2 - \frac{1}{2}(1+v) M_3\right). \quad (8.19)$$

This phenomenon can be observed on the steelpan during the tuning process and reveals itself as an area (smaller than the size of a typical note) of localized buckling (called *flapping* because of the paper-like behavior of the affected area).

- Flapping, in this case, is due to the compressive loads induced by hammer-peening and shaping of the note.
- *Flapping will not occur under tensional loading.*

Buckling under thermal loading is an unlikely situation on the steelpan but is still an open possibility. For the buckled state of the system under consideration, values for the critical temperature and critical compressive load can be obtained by setting $\alpha_1 = 0$. These values will be dependent on the shell geometry. Steelpan notes normally operate in the *pre-buckling* state where the induced stresses set conditions for the dynamic state when the note is sounding.

Notice from the left-hand-side of equation (8.19) that increasing the temperature of the tuned note has the same effect as increasing compressive loading. This fact is important for the pan maker/tuner as it implies that the same modifications in the spectrum (timbre) of a note normally achieved by peening can also accompany changes in temperature of the finished pan.

- *Temperature changes can temporarily modify the tonality of a note in the same manner as peening achieves in a more permanent way. Because of this, a finely tuned pan is best played under the same temperature conditions as it was tuned. Since temperature is such an important parameter for the steelpan, commercial producers (at least) should indicate the temperature at which tuning was done and a range of temperatures over which the instrument is expected to perform at its best.*

To consider the problem further, the *buckling* or *flapping parameter* s is defined in the SDOF notation as

$$s = (\breve{N}_c + \breve{N}_T)\frac{M_4}{\alpha_0}, \qquad (8.20a)$$

where

$$\alpha_0 = \frac{1}{12}M_1 + 8(1+v)\left(\frac{H_0}{h}\right)^2\left(M_2 - \frac{1}{2}(1+v)M_3\right). \qquad (8.20b)$$

For the system under zero compressive and thermal stress ($s = 0$) the angular frequency of vibration is equal to $\sqrt{\alpha_0}$. From equations (8.17) and (8.20a), the force f_0 can be expressed as

$$f_0 = s\beta, \qquad (8.21)$$

with

$$\beta = 4\alpha_0 \left[\frac{H_0}{h}\right]\frac{M_8}{M_4},\qquad(8.22)$$

and the dynamical equation (8.13) can be written as

$$\frac{d^2w}{d\tau^2} + \breve{\mu}\frac{dw}{d\tau} + \alpha_0(1-s)w + \alpha_2 w^2 + \alpha_3 w^3 - s\beta = f(\tau).\quad(8.23)$$

From equation (8.23) one gets for the normalized frequency of the note

$$\text{frequency} = (\alpha_0(1-s))^{\frac{1}{2}}$$

which goes to *zero* when $s = 1$. In the note dynamics, the note stiffness is proportional to the square of the frequency; thus one can write

$$\text{stiffness} \sim \alpha_0(1-s)$$

which goes to *zero* when $s = 1$. If the note stiffness is zero, then it can be displaced by the 'slightest touch!' This is the '*Flapping Phenomenon.*' In technical language this is called '*Buckling.*' Although it is not desired on any pan note, it is very interesting to observe the response of the section of note material that 'flaps!' It behaves like a piece of tissue paper but you have to remember that it is made of steel. When you see it for the first time you are sure to play with it for a while.

When the buckling parameter is made equal to one, $(s = 1)$ one gets from equation (8.20a) the critical stress condition for flapping as

$$(\breve{N}_c + \breve{N}_T)_{crit} = \frac{\alpha_0}{M_4}.$$

Notice that both the residual compressive stress $\breve{N}_c$ and the thermal stress $\breve{N}_T$ contribute to this effect so that increasing the ambient temperature increases the possibility for flapping. This happens when $\breve{N}_c + \breve{N}_T$ reaches the critical value equal to α_0/M_4. We also see that since the critical stress is directly proportional to α_0/M_4 that by equation (8.20b) and the definitions of M_1, M_2, M_3 and M_4, the critical stress depends on the curvature of the note surface *as it vibrates* in the lowest mode, through $\Delta^4\psi$ and $\Delta^2\psi$ *(where ψ is the fundamental mode shape)*, and on the note surface shape through Q. Generally, the tuner will find it more unlikely for buckling to occur in areas on the inner notes (unless the inner areas of the pan face have been 'thinned out' too severely by 'over sinking') because these notes are dynamically stiffer, the note surfaces are assigned greater curvature, and subjected to lower compressive stresses. In practice, only a small section of the note surface will buckle (flap) because the tuner cannot easily set up sufficiently strong compressive stresses along the entire note boundary but he can achieve this over a small 'patch' on the note. It is therefore possible to correct the state of the section of note surface that has buckled by peening the areas around that small section to reduce the internal compressive stresses sufficiently to restore stiffness to the affected area. In fact this is exactly what the tuner does.

Flapping usually occurs on thin 'over-worked' material and is more likely on notes under conditions of high compressive stresses. The problem, when it occurs, is easily corrected by hammer peening with much *'obliquity'* (*'stretching'* or *'scratching'* action) somewhat away from the affected area on the note to redistribute the in-plane stresses. Proper *stress-relief annealing* reduces this problem. The apprentice tuner should not panic when this problem occurs and should not rush to reshape the entire note.

The effects of the buckling parameter on the behavior of the notes are summarized in Table (8.1).

TABLE 8.1

Buckling Parameter S	State	Behavior
s < 1	Pre-Buckling Linear restoring force is negative, opposing displacement.	Typical behavior under normal ambient temperature and residual stresses.
s = 1	Buckling (*Flapping*) Linear stiffness vanishes $\alpha_0(1-s) = 0$. Only the weaker, non-linear Forces remain.	This state usually confined to a small area of the note during the tuning process. Produced by excessive compressive stresses at the boundary of the affected area. Affected area loses its dynamic stiffness and displays a "paper-like" response to small external forces. The area "flaps" like a sheet of paper. Removed by hammer peening (*stretching*) the note surface in an area away from the affected region.
s > 1	Post-Buckling Linear restoring force changes sign, assisting displacement.	May follow buckling but requires excessive ambient temperatures and/or extreme levels of residual compressive stresses. Unlikely occurrence on the pan.

8.5.2 Static State of the Note

It should be pointed out that the product sβ represents an *out-of-plane* (orthogonal) force which distorts the note surface upward i.e. it raises the *apex* of the note. The static problem (*note at rest*) can be addressed by setting the time derivatives in equation (8.23) to zero. For the *static case*, which represents a *local equilibrium state*, the displacement amplitude is therefore governed by

$$\alpha_0(1-s)w_0 + \alpha_2 w_0^2 + \alpha_3 w_0^3 - s\beta = 0 , \quad (8.24)$$

where w_0 is the displacement measured at the apex (recall here that these displacements are in units of note thickness h). Therefore one has the equality $A_0 = w_0$ for the amplitude of the static displacement function $\psi_0(x)$. This allows us to write

$$\alpha_0(1-s)A_0 + \alpha_2 A_0^2 + \alpha_3 A_0^3 - s\beta = 0 , \quad (8.25)$$

It is clear from equation (8.25) that the force f_0 (= $s\beta$) is responsible for the displacement because when $f_0 = 0$, $A_0 = 0$.

In the perturbation scheme, for a given s value, once the parameters α_j ($j = 1, 2, 3$) and β are determined from equations (8.14), (8.15), (8.16) and (8.22), the cubic equation (8.25) can be solved algebraically, yielding A_0 as the real root. A_0 is then updated by setting $A_{0i} = A_0$. When the parameter s is altered to $s + \delta s$ by a change in temperature for example, using the new β and α_j parameters obtained for the updated shaping function, equation (8.25) is again solved to determine A_{0f}. The required change in the displacement amplitude is then obtained as $\delta A_0 = A_{0f} - A_{0i}$.

The force f_0 varies during the tuning process and influences the final note shape. The path taken by f_0 can be found by calculating f_0 at each step of the perturbation process described above. *This force is always present on a note and is partly responsible for the observation by early pan makers that 'the pan seems to have a life of its own'* (see Achong 1999b). This behavior (see Section 2.9) is one of the steelpan subtleties known mainly to the pan makers. There is a well documented story (Achong 2000d) described to me by Bertie Marshall in a 2000 interview when I also met the Master Tuner for the first time. Bertie described an experiment in which he attached a system of springs and weights to the notes of a pan in an attempt to influence the frequencies of the partials on the notes. In fact what Bertie was really attempting to do, was to influence this *'peculiar behavior'* of the notes. Among pan makers, Marshall came the closest to discovering the static force f_0. Observe from equations (8.21) and (8.22) that this force vanishes as $H_0 \rightarrow 0$ (the geometrically flat note surface).

8.6. Note Deformation under Thermal/Compressive Stresses

If δs is the change in buckling parameter arising from a temperature increase and/or an increase in the in-plane compression, and δA_0 is the note displacement (measured at the apex) produced as a result, then using equation (8.25) one can write

$$\delta A_0 = \frac{\delta s\,(\beta + \alpha_0 A_0)}{\alpha_0(1-s) + 2\alpha_2 A_0 + 3\alpha_3 A_0^2}. \qquad (8.26)$$

The corresponding change in the static force is

$$\delta f_0 = \beta \delta s.$$

Equation (8.26) can be expressed as the sum of two terms,

$$\delta A_0 = 4\delta s\,\frac{H_0 M_8}{h M_4}\left(\frac{\alpha_0}{\omega'^2}\right) \;+\; \delta s\,A_0\left(\frac{\alpha_0}{\omega'^2}\right), \qquad (8.27)$$

$$\underbrace{\phantom{4\delta s\,\frac{H_0 M_8}{h M_4}\left(\frac{\alpha_0}{\omega'^2}\right)}}_{\text{due to Bending}} \qquad \underbrace{\phantom{\delta s\,A_0\left(\frac{\alpha_0}{\omega'^2}\right)}}_{\text{due to Reduction in Stiffness}}$$

where $\omega'^2 = \alpha_0(1-s) + 2\alpha_2 A_0 + 3\alpha_3 A_0^2$.

(i) In equation (8.27), the first term on the right-hand-side (normally the larger of the two terms) is the component of surface displacement due to *bending* of the mid-surface of the note.

(ii) The second term is the displacement due to the *reduction in stiffness* of the note structure. This can be deduced from equation (8.25) where $\alpha_0(1-s)$ is the linear stiffness. When the note is subjected to an increase in temperature or compressive stress the buckling parameter changes by δs and the stiffness changes by $-\alpha_0 \delta s$. The negative sign indicates a reduction in note stiffness.

Due to bending and reduced stiffness, the note becomes more convex upwards (see Figure 8.2) as the temperature or compressive stress is increased. This surface displacement results in a change in the note geometry and is a contributing factor to the resulting change in note frequency that accompanies temperature or stress changes. Because all steelpan notes possess a dome shape, represented by the non-zero value of the rise-to-thickness ratio H_0/h in the first term, all pan notes are subject to this effect.

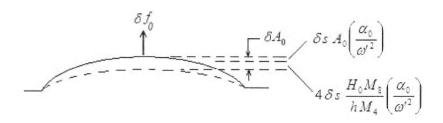

Fig. 8.2. Note displacement (exaggerated for clarity) produced by a change in temperature and/or change in in-plane stress.

8.7 Frequency Shifts: Why is the bass pan more greatly affected by temperature and residual stress?

Since there is a reduction in dynamic stiffness as the temperature or residual stress increases, the note frequency will be correspondingly reduced. However, this reduction in frequency is partially offset by an increase in frequency due to the increase in the rise of the note under stress. This increase offsets some of the reduction that comes from the reduced stiffness. To determine the SDOF version of equation (3.38), begin with equation (8.14). For the note tuned by the pan maker at ambient temperature T_0 (which now becomes the *Tuning Temperature* T_t) that makes a transition between two nearby stress states, one has

$$\omega_i^2 = \alpha_0 - (\check{N}_c + \check{N}_T)_i M_{i4},$$

$$\omega_f^2 = \alpha_0 - (\check{N}_c + \check{N}_T)_f M_{f4}, \qquad (8.28a, b)$$

where the subscripts i and f refer to the 'initial' and 'final' states respectively. For small changes in thermal loading $\check{N}_T$ and small changes in residual compressive loading $\check{N}_c$, made independently, and on substituting $\omega_f^2 - \omega_i^2 = 2\omega_i \delta\omega$ (considered as the difference between two squares) into equation (8.28), the respective frequency changes are given by

Thermal Stress: $$\delta\omega = -\frac{\alpha_T(1+v)}{2\omega_i}\left(\frac{a}{h}\right)^2(\Delta T_f M_{4f} - \Delta T_i M_{4i}),$$

Compressive Stress: $$\delta\omega = \frac{(1+v^2)}{2\omega_i E}\left(\frac{a}{h}\right)^2(\sigma_{cf} M_{4f} - \sigma_{ci} M_{4i}),$$

(8.29 a, b)

where $\sigma_c = -N_o/h$ is the compressive stress along the note boundary, $\Delta T_i = T_i - T_0$, $\Delta T_f = T_f - T_0$ with T_i and T_f as the initial and final temperatures respectively. In general, M_4 decreases as the stress or buckling parameter increases. The changes to M_4 represent the change brought about by the change in geometry of the note under compressive and thermal stresses. If this change is omitted in equations (8.28a, b) by making $M_{4i} = M_{4f}$ then the calculated values for frequency shifts associated with temperature and stress changes will be overestimated.

Notice that the frequency shift is directly proportional to the ratio $(a/h)^2$ for temperature changes and for residual stress changes. This means that notes of larger area or of thinner material will be found to exhibit greater frequency-temperature and frequency-stress dependence. This explains why the bass pans, with their large notes (greater "a" values), suffer the greatest reduction in note frequency when played in direct sunlight. It was for this reason that canopies were introduced. The use of heavy gauge steel (giving greater "h" values in the tuned state) on the bass significantly reduces this problem. *The use of heavy gauge steel on all pans, provide greater stability against changes in frequency.*

8.8 Applying the Method to Small and Large Stress Changes

8.8.1 Small Changes in Temperature and Compressive Stress

For small changes in temperature or compressive stress a simpler approach is to work with the buckling parameter then make use of the fractional frequency shift expression

$$\frac{\delta\omega}{\omega} = -\frac{\delta s}{2(1-s)}, \qquad (8.30)$$

obtained from expression $\omega^2 = \alpha_0(1-s)$. Using equation (8.20a)

$$\delta s = \alpha_T \, \delta T \, (1+v)\left(\frac{a}{h}\right)^2 \frac{M_4}{\alpha_0}, \qquad \text{Thermal Stress}$$

$$= -\frac{\delta\sigma_c}{E}(1+v^2)\left(\frac{a}{h}\right)^2 \frac{M_4}{\alpha_0}, \qquad \text{Compressive Stress.}$$

(8.31)

Equations (8.30) and (8.31) with $\alpha_1 = \alpha_0 (1-s)$ give the final result for the fractional change in frequency

$$\frac{\delta\omega}{\omega} = -\frac{\alpha_T \delta T(1+v)}{2}\left(\frac{a}{h}\right)^2 \frac{M_4}{\alpha_1}, \qquad \text{Thermal Stress}$$

$$= \frac{\delta\sigma_c(1+v^2)}{2E}\left(\frac{a}{h}\right)^2 \frac{M_4}{\alpha_1}, \qquad \text{Compressive Stress.}$$

(8.32)

Since $\omega^2 = \alpha_1$, equations (8.29) and (8.32) are identical when the change in M_4 is sufficiently small. In equation (8.32), an increase in compressive stress means that $\delta\sigma_c$ is negative so that an increase in temperature or compressive stress brings about a decrease in frequency.

8.8.2 The Method for Large Stress Changes

The preceding results can be applied to small stress changes such as may result from a few degrees change in temperature or to the change in compressive stress that comes about between first and second tuning. If the temperature changes are of the order of tens of degrees then the computation must proceed in a stepwise fashion, updating all parameters that depend on A_0 after each step, and updating A_0 and $\psi(x)$ as well throughout the computation. It is unlikely that this process will be required for large changes in compressive stress because, in practice, this can only be achieved by hammer peening which produces note shape changes that require the recalculation of all parameters for the new shape. This recalculation then yields the new frequency directly.

When the computations are carried out in a stepwise fashion for a note that experiences a large temperature change, the parameters dependent on A_0 or equivalently, ψ_0, will gradually change throughout the process. Although the linearity $\delta\omega \propto \delta T$ will be preserved at each step, when the entire range of temperature change is covered, the changes brought about by the note deformation will produce a non-linear frequency-shift-temperature relation. Of course, this non-linear relationship will go unnoticed if the frequencies were determined directly for the initial shape then again for the final shape (if the final shape is known).

As an additional result of the stepwise computation, the note shape at each step can be found by adding the function $\delta A_0 \psi(x)$ to the previous note shape. It should now be quite clear that the computation allows the entire path of the note to be followed from the initial state to the final state.

Note: A much more detailed analysis of the frequency dependence on temperature is given in Chapter 9 where the effects of changes in elastic moduli are taken into account. The results of that analysis are fully consistent with experimental data.

8.9 Use of other Materials — Brass and Aluminum

Various researchers have experimented with alternative materials for the manufacture of pans; brass (Murr et al. 2004), aluminum (Murr et al. 2006), stainless steel (Murr et al. 2008). This is an exciting area of research where the theory of operation of this percussion instrument should serve as a guide towards the use of alternative rawform metal. Brass has been an alternative metal of choice. One observes however that brass has a Young's modulus (104 Gpa) approximately half that of steel (207 Gpa). Equation 8.32 shows that for notes of similar geometry, size and thickness, undergoing similar changes in residual stress, the brass note will suffer a 100% greater change in frequency shift compared to the steel note. The temperature coefficient of expansion (α) for brass is 19 x 10^{-6} /°C; compared with the value for low carbon steel of 12 x 10^{-6} /°C. For all other parameters equal, the brass note will suffer a 58% *greater* frequency shift as the temperature of the note changes. Brass is therefore seen to be much *less stable* than steel against changes in ambient temperature and residual stress. Since brass is softer than steel, when used as the rawform for pans, a percussion instrument, the notes will have a much *shorter lifetime* in the tuned state. When aluminum is used in the construction of pans, frequency shifts around 92% greater (compared to the shifts expected for steelpans) can be expected.

For a given set of parameters, geometry, dimensions, residual stress and temperature, the fundamental frequency of a note is approximately proportional to $(E/\rho(1-v^2))^{1/2}$. With a density of 8500 Kg/m^3 for brass and 7700 Kg/m^3 for steel together with the elastic constants given in Table 2.3, the brass note will be approximately 30% lower in frequency. Additional lowering of the frequency of the brass note relative to steel comes about through the dependence of the *frequency constant* α_1, (see equation (8.14)) on the *mode shape* (ψ) which in turn depends on the *geometrical factor* (λ) and Poisson's ratio (v). For a given planform size (note size), the brass note must be hammer peened with a greater rise to thickness ratio H_0/h in order to be tuned to the same frequency as the steel note. Brass notes therefore call for a different shape compared to the steel notes of similar frequency. Note shape affects most of the dynamical parameters so that a pan maker must readjust to the brass material. That will not be difficult for a skilled tuner or pan maker. *The theory developed here is applicable to all rawform materials.*

In the case of Aluminum, while the value of $(E/\rho(1-v^2))^{1/2}$ is just over 1 % lower than that for steel (use the physical constants in Table 2.3 to verify this) a further lowering comes from the value for the *frequency constant* α_1. But the real problem with aluminum (and its alloys) comes from three different quarters. The first is related to the low melting point of aluminum (660 °C) and the absence of any clearly visible signs that indicates when a sample of the metal is about to melt. Unlike steel which changes color when heated, aluminum remains unchanged in color. This poses a problem for the aluminum pan maker and can almost rule out the successful application, on a production basis, of stress relaxation (tempering) in controlling the stress fields on the aluminum pan face. Controlled stress relief can be done during manufacturing by heat-treating the parts in an oven, followed by gradual cooling.

The second problem, one that rears itself on the brass pan as well, is the difficulty in setting up the conditions for 'Blocking' (see Chapter 14) particularly on the inner notes of the instrument. The internote on a steelpan requires extensive peening in order to ensure good Blocking (Tightening). On soft metals like brass and aluminum, without the benefits of work hardening, this poses serious problems for the tuner. Material failure can occur at a faster rate than on the normal low-carbon steel. .

The third problem, perhaps the most important one, a *structural limitation* which arises with all aluminum alloys, is their fatigue strength. Unlike steel, aluminum alloys have no well-defined fatigue limit. This means that fatigue failure eventually occurs, under even the very small cyclic loadings that occur during normal use as an aluminum pan. It certainly is the cause of the failure mentioned at the end of the last paragraph. *Aluminum pan makers must therefore design and sell their instruments for a fixed life that is relatively shorter than the life of a standard steelpan.*

The combined effects of oven-controlled stress relief during manufacture and the short life may not auger well for economical production and cost effectiveness when compared with the production methods for the steel instrument. But I am not too worried about these economic matters. After all, my steelpan research and costs incurred in preparing this book were all met 'out-of-pocket' with a rather shallow pocket 'to boot!' so I may not be the best judge on these money matters.

The 'beauty' of using low-carbon steel is derived from the work hardening properties that it presents to the pan maker and its long life under cyclic loading. These properties are fully exploited in the tuning (and repeated re-tuning) of the steel versions of the instrument.

8.11 Potential Energy, Internal Forces, Note Geometries, Potential Wells

8.10.1 Potential Energy

Eliminating damping and forcing gives the Hamiltonian H = K + U for equation (8.23) as $H = \frac{1}{2}\dot{w}^2 + \frac{1}{2}\alpha_0(1-s)w^2 + \frac{1}{3}\alpha_2 w^3 + \frac{1}{4}w^4 - s\beta w$ with the kinetic energy $K = \frac{1}{2}\dot{w}^2$ and potential energy

$$U = \frac{1}{2}\alpha_0(1-s)w^2 + \frac{1}{3}\alpha_2 w^3 + \frac{1}{4}w^4 - s\beta w \qquad (8.33)$$

One sees that because of the terms involving β and α_2 the potential energy function satisfies the condition $U(w) \neq U(-w)$. This means that **the energy variations for upward note displacements are not the same as for downward displacements.** *It is in fact easier to displace the note surface downwards than it is to displace the surface upwards.* In the limit, as $H_0 \to 0$ (flat plate), one finds that $\alpha_2 \to 0$, $\beta \to 0$, so the asymmetry of U is removed in the flat plate case.

An example of the motion in the asymmetrical potential well of the steelpan notes is seen in Figure 8.3a,b, which shows the displacement w (in units of note thickness h) for the D_4 note on a cello. The note was excited *fortissimo* (very loud) in order to achieve sufficient travel into the higher regions of the well. Larger displacements are clearly seen as the note surface moves downward (corresponding to negative *w* values).

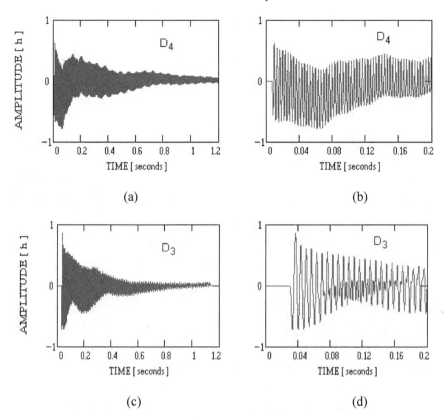

Fig. 8.3. Motion in asymmetrical potential wells. (a) Displacements on the D_4 note of a cello pan played fortissimo. (b) The initial displacements on the D_4 note under higher time resolution. (c) Displacements for the D_3 note on a bass played fortissimo. (d) The initial displacements on the D_3 note under higher time resolution. All displacements are in units of note thickness h.

Figures 8.3c,d show displacements for a D_3 bass note played fortissimo. When excited to the fortissimo level, these two notes produce tones characterized by strong amplitude modulations. This indicates strong levels of mode coupling, resulting from relatively large α_2 and α_3. This is precisely the condition required for strongly asymmetrical potential wells and asymmetry in the displacements (as clearly shown in Figure 8.3). Striking the notes from the underside of the pan gave similar results as in Figure 8.3 showing that the asymmetry is not the result of the direction of the initial force vector describing the stick impact.

8.10.2 Linear and Non-linear Internal Forces

Differentiating the energy expression in equation (8.33) with respect to the system's degree of freedom gives the internal forces $f_{int} = -\partial U/\partial w$

$$f_{int} = -\alpha_0 (1-s) w - \alpha_2 w^2 - \alpha_3 w^3 + s\beta. \tag{8.34}$$

The first term represents the linear restoring force responsible for the first mode resonance (the *tonic*) at frequency $\omega = \sqrt{\alpha_0(1-s)}$. The linear force is associated with the *bending* of the mid-surface of the note. It is clear from this expression, that for $s = 1$ (*the flapping condition*), the first mode restoring force $f_1 = -\alpha_0(1-s)w$ is *identically zero* hence the *paper-like* behavior of the flapping region. The terms $-\alpha_2 w^2$ and $-\alpha_3 w^3$ represent the internal quadratic and cubic forces (per unit mass) with *driving frequencies* at $\omega_2 \approx 2\omega$ and $\omega_3 \approx 3\omega$ respectively. These are the forces responsible for the parametric excitations discussed in Chapter 4 and Chapter 7. These forces can generate internal resonances at frequencies 2ω and respectively provided that the second and third normal modes are close to these frequencies. It is clear from the factor (H_0/h) in the expression for α_2 (see equation (8.15)) that the parametric excitation at $\approx 2\omega$ arises because of the curvature of the shell and is therefore dependent on the form (geometry) of the shell.

These internal forces are very important because they determine all that is interesting and unique on the steelpan. They turn up in every area of the note dynamics. Figure 8.4 shows plots of the linear force, quadratic force, cubic force and the sum of all three forces for a model note with its convex face upwards. In these plots, for emphasis and clarity, the quadratic and cubic forces are illustrated with relative magnitudes greater than what is obtained in practice. The linear and cubic forces are odd functions of the note surface displacement because they both change sign as the movement switches from upwards (positive) to downwards (negative). The quadratic force is an even function of the note surface displacement. The resulting equation represented by the sum of these three forces is asymmetrical about the rest position ($w = 0$). The linear and cubic forces always act in such a direction as to restore the surface to its rest position. On the other hand the quadratic force is always directed downwards, acting to restore the surface to the rest position when the displacement is upwards but acting so as to increase any downward displacement. For a given magnitude of resultant force, this asymmetry results in greater downward displacement compared with the upward displacement (see panel (d) in Figure 8.4). The static force $s\beta$ is always directed upwards (in the direction from planform to apex) producing a stress dependent displacement. It is easier to distort these notes downward.

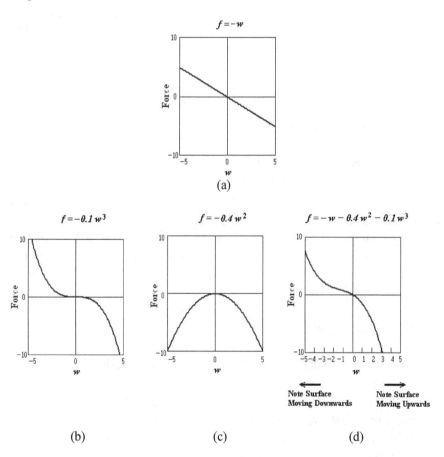

Fig. 8.4. Normalized internal forces on the vibrating note (a) linear restoring force (b) cubic force (c) quadratic force and (d) sum of all three forces. Note shape is convex upwards.

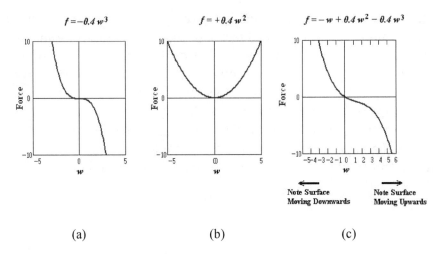

Fig. 8.5. Normalized internal forces on the vibrating note (a) cubic force (c) quadratic force and (d) sum of all forces including the linear force. The quadratic parameter is negative ($\alpha_2 < 0$) in this case.

In the system described in Figure 8.4 the coupling parameters α_1, α_2 and α_3 are all positive. However, it is possible on notes with surfaces having both positive and negative curvature for α_2 to take on negative values, even zero. Figure 8.5 shows the case for $\alpha_2 < 0$. For a given magnitude of resultant force, the asymmetry results in greater upward displacement compared with the downward displacement (see panel (c) in Figure 8.5). It is easier to distort these notes upward.

8.11 Response of the Note to External Excitation

Experimental work on the steelpan usually includes excitation of the notes by means of an acoustic exciter or by an electromechanical device. When the objective is the measurement of modal frequencies, care must be taken to excite the notes to sufficiently small oscillations for the note dynamics to be regarded as linear. Large amplitude excitations on a properly tuned note will always allow the note to respond in a manner consistent with its non-linear dynamics. It is therefore necessary to analyze the response of the notes to excitations in the two regimes (i) the linear regime and (ii) the non-linear regime.

8.11.1 Linear Frequency Response

Consider the case where the quadratic and cubic forces are so small in comparison with the linear force that their effects on the note dynamics can be neglected. This state is approached for sufficiently small displacements of the note surface i.e. by playing the note very softly. Additionally, since the driving forces are all weak in these cases, by considering these small vibrations about the statically displaced state (the rest or quiescent state) the dependence on the static force f_0 can be removed. For a sinusoidal driving force $\bar{f}_s = F\cos(\omega\tau)$, equation (8.13) is therefore reduced to that of a simple damped oscillator

$$\frac{d^2w}{d\tau^2} + R_m \frac{dw}{d\tau} + \omega_0^2 w = F\cos(\omega\tau), \qquad (8.35)$$

where the substitutions $\omega_0 = \sqrt{\alpha_1}$ (with the zero subscript is used here to identify the frequency of the undamped oscillator) and $R_m = \bar{\mu}$ have been made (the reason for the latter substitution will soon become clear). The solution to this equation consists of two parts, a *transient* term and a *steady-state* term. The duration of the transient term is set by the decay coefficient while the steady state term essentially describes the long-term state of the system.

8.11.2 The Transient Term

The transient term is expressed as

$$w = e^{-\alpha\tau}(A_1 e^{-i\omega_d\tau} + A_2 e^{i\omega_d\tau}), \qquad (8.36)$$

where the amplitudes A_1 and A_2 are in general complex and the frequency of damped oscillation ω_d is defined by $\omega_d = \sqrt{\omega_0^2 - 2\alpha^2}$ with $\alpha = R_m/2$. After sufficient time has elapsed, $\alpha\tau \gg 1$, the damping term $e^{-\alpha\tau}$ makes the transient term negligibly small leaving only the steady-state *term whose frequency equals that of the driving force*. The linear frequency with damping can be written as

$$\omega_d = \omega_0 (1 - R_m^2 / 2\omega_0^2)^{\frac{1}{2}}. \tag{8.37}$$

Whenever a note on the pan is played by stick excitation the note vibrates in the *transient mode*. As a result, the intensity of the tone will show a fast initial rise then gradually decay. However, because the note dynamics is always non-linear, the transient mode is more complicated than the expression given here for the transient term. If a note is played very softly the displacements are small and the frequency of the sounding note corresponds to the damped frequency ω_d. *The small displacement undamped frequency ω_0 is never heard when a note is played.*

8.11.3 The Steady State Term

The steady-state solution is easily obtained by replacing the sinusoidal driving force by its complex form $F = Fe^{i\omega\tau}$, taking the complex solution in the form $w = Ae^{i\omega\tau}$ and making use of the differential operator $\frac{d}{d\tau}(\bullet) = i\omega(\bullet)$. Equation (8.35) then becomes

$$(-A\omega^2 + iA\omega R_m + A\omega_0^2)e^{i\omega\tau} = Fe^{i\omega\tau}. \tag{8.38}$$

Since this equation is true for all times, A must satisfy

$$A = \frac{F}{i\omega R_m + (\omega_0^2 - \omega^2)}, \tag{8.39}$$

giving the complex displacement w as

$$w = \frac{-iFe^{i\omega\tau}}{\omega[R_m + i(\omega - \omega_0^2/\omega)]}. \tag{8.40}$$

The denominator in (8.40) contains a factor which defines the *complex mechanical impedance* Z_m of the reduced system

$$\mathbf{Z}_m = R_m + i(\omega - \omega_0^2/\omega) = R_m + iX_m = Z_m e^{i\phi}, \qquad (8.41)$$

where the *mechanical reactance* X_m is defined as $X_m = (\omega - \omega_0^2/\omega)$. It is now possible to explain the substitution $R_m = \bar{\mu}$ but first, the following observation. From equation (8.41), $\mathbf{Z}_m$ is analogous to the electrical complex impedance, ω_0^2 is analogous to the reciprocal of the electrical capacitance while X_m is analogous to the series combination of the capacitance with a unit of electrical inductance (because the equations are written in terms of unit mass). The *mechanical resistance* is therefore defined by R_m and just as in an electrical oscillatory circuit where the electrical resistance damps the oscillations, so too in the present system it is R_m or equivalently $\bar{\mu}$ (as the *damping coefficient*) that damps the vibration of the note. The magnitude of the mechanical impedance is

$$Z_m = (R_m^2 + X_m^2)^{\frac{1}{2}}, \qquad (8.42)$$

and the phase angle ϕ is

$$\phi = \tan^{-1}\frac{X_m}{R_m} = \tan^{-1}[(\omega^2 - \omega_0^2)/(\omega R_m)]. \qquad (8.43)$$

Using the mechanical impedance, the complex displacement takes on the form

$$w = \frac{-iFe^{i(\omega\tau-\phi)}}{\omega Z_m}. \qquad (8.44)$$

Using the identity $e^{-i\frac{\pi}{2}} = -i$ in equation (8.44) gives

$$w = \frac{Fe^{i(\omega\tau-\phi-\frac{\pi}{2})}}{\omega Z_m}. \qquad (8.45)$$

The actual (measurable) displacement w is equal to the real part of equation (8.45) expressed as

$$w = \frac{F}{\omega Z_m}\cos(\omega\tau-\phi-\pi/2), \qquad (8.46)$$

where $F/\omega Z_m$ is the maximum displacement or *displacement amplitude*). The phase angle between the displacement and the driving force is $(\phi+\pi/2)$.

The complex velocity $v = dw/d\tau = i\omega w$ is found from equation (8.44) as

$$v = \frac{Fe^{i(\omega\tau-\phi)}}{Z_m}, \qquad (8.47)$$

with real part

$$v = \frac{F}{Z_m}\cos(\omega\tau-\phi), \qquad (8.48)$$

where F/Z_m is the maximum velocity referred to as the *velocity amplitude*. This equation shows that the angle between the velocity and the driving force is ϕ. A comparison between equation (8.46) and equation (8.48) shows that the displacement *lags* behind the velocity by $\pi/2$ or 90°.

Equation (8.43) shows that for low frequencies ($\omega < \omega_0$) the phase angle ϕ is positive so that the velocity lags behind the driving force. At high frequencies ($\omega > \omega_0$) the phase angle is negative with the velocity leading the driving force. When $\omega = \omega_0$ the phase angle is zero and the velocity and driving force are in phase with each other. At this frequency the mechanical reactance X_m vanishes and the mechanical impedance Z_m has its minimum value $Z_m|_{min} = R_m$.

At this frequency — the *velocity resonance frequency*— the velocity amplitude takes on its maximum value F/R_m.

While the velocity amplitude will reach its maximum for a driving frequency ω_0 the displacement amplitude maximizes at a slightly different frequency. This *displacement resonance frequency* is obtained by differentiating equation (8.46) with respect to ω and equating the differential to zero. The result is

$$[2\omega^2 + R_m^2 - 2\omega_0^2]\omega = 0. \qquad (8.49)$$

This equation has two roots

(i) the simple root $\omega = 0$, which corresponds to a constant static force F applied to the system which acts as a linear spring to produce a displacement equal to F/ω_0^2 and

(ii) ω equal to the frequency of *damped oscillation* $\omega_d = \sqrt{\omega_0^2 - R_m^2/2}$ which is the frequency corresponding to *displacement resonance*.

It is important to distinguish between *velocity resonance* and *displacement resonance* because all real systems (defined by $R_m \neq 0$) are damped. If the resonance frequency of a pan note is to be measured then the experimental method determines whether the measured value gives ω_0 (by the *velocity method*) or ω_d (by the *displacement method*). By carefully using both methods, the mechanical resistance of the note can be measured using

$$R_m = \sqrt{2(\omega_0^2 - \omega_d^2)}.$$

8.11.4 Power Relations and the Resonance Curve

The external system (or agency) that drives the oscillating system supplies power to the driven system. In steady state, when the input power is averaged over time (at least over one whole cycle of oscillation) the power supplied is equal to the power dissipated by the internal resistance of the driven system. The driven system (the note) must adjust both the amplitude and the phase of the oscillation to achieve this balance.

The instantaneous power supplied to the system is equal to the product of the instantaneous driving force and the velocity. If P_i is the instantaneous power then using the real parts of the complex expressions for force and velocity gives

$$P_i = \frac{F^2}{Z_m}\cos(\omega\tau)\cos(\omega\tau - \phi). \qquad (8.50)$$

The average power P over one period $T = 2\pi/\omega$ of the driving force is given by

$$P = \frac{\int_0^T P_i d\tau}{T}$$
$$= \frac{F^2}{2Z_m}\cos(\phi) \qquad (8.51)$$

The expression $\cos(\phi)$ is called the *mechanical power factor* and since $\cos(\phi) = R_m/Z_m$, the average power can be expressed as

$$P = \frac{F^2 R_m}{2Z_m^2}$$
$$= \frac{F^2 R_m}{2[R_m^2 + (\omega - \omega_0^2/\omega)^2]}. \qquad (8.52)$$

The average power maximizes when the denominator in equation (8.52) is a minimum and this occurs for $\omega = \omega_0$ which is the same condition that maximizes the velocity. At this frequency, $Z_m = R_s$, $X_m = 0$, $\cos(\phi) = 1$ and $P_{\max} = F^2/2R_m$.

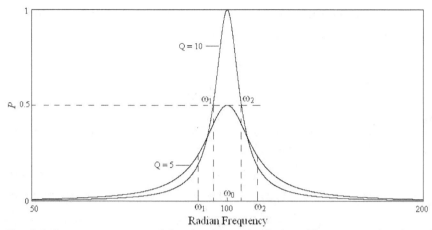

Fig. 8.6. Resonance curves of the simple mechanical oscillator approximation of the note system plotted with low Q values which broadens the peaks for greater clarity and emphasis.

A normalized plot of P versus frequency is shown in Figure (8.6) for two systems having the same resonance frequency but different mechanical resistance and driven with the same driving force amplitude F. The curve of larger maximum amplitude was plotted for $P_{max} = F^2/2R_m = 1$ while the second curve was plotted with the mechanical resistance increased by a factor of two. Observe that the peak on the lower curve is reduced to 0.5 as a result of doubling the mechanical resistance. The curve for the system with greater damping is broader along the frequency axis because the sharpness of the resonance curve is primarily dependent on R_m.

8.11.5 The Quality Factor, Q and Frequency Bandwidth, B

A precise definition of the *width* or *sharpness* of the resonance curve is given in terms of the *Quality Factor Q or Q-factor*, defined as the ratio of the resonance frequency ω_0 to the width of the resonance curve at half-maximum power $\omega_2 - \omega_1$. By definition

$$Q = \frac{\omega_0}{\omega_2 - \omega_1}. \qquad (8.53a)$$

The width of the resonance curve at half-maximum power expressed as $B = (\omega_2 - \omega_1)/2\pi$, or equivalently as

$$B = \frac{\omega_0}{2\pi Q}. \qquad (8.53b)$$

is defined as the *frequency bandwidth* (in Hertz) where $\omega_0/2\pi$ is the resonant frequency in Hertz..

Since $P_{max} = F^2/2R_m$ and $P = F^2 R_m / 2Z_m^2$, the power is at half-maximum when $Z_m^2 = 2R_m^2$. The condition $Z_m^2 = 2R_m^2$ can be written in the form $\omega^2 - \omega_0^2 = \pm \omega R_m$. Solving for the two values of ω satisfying this condition gives $\omega_2 - \omega_1 = R_m$ and hence

$$Q = \frac{\omega_0}{R_m}. \qquad (8.54)$$

Another very instructive derivation is possible; it is based on the definition of the quality factor as

$$Q = \omega \frac{\langle E \rangle}{\langle P \rangle}, \qquad (8.55)$$

where $\langle E \rangle$ is the average energy stored per cycle, $\langle P \rangle$ is the average power dissipated per cycle, and ω is the radian oscillation frequency. The average power dissipated per cycle is the same as the power supplied per cycle to maintain oscillation. This definition of Q applies at all frequencies so that at the resonance frequency ω_0 one has

$$\langle E \rangle = \frac{1}{2}\omega_0^2 |A|^2 = \frac{F^2}{2R_m^2},$$

$$\langle P \rangle = \frac{F^2}{2R_m}. \qquad (8.56a,b)$$

The quality factor is therefore given by

$$Q = \omega_0 \frac{F^2/2R_m^2}{F^2/2R_m} = \frac{\omega_0}{R_m}. \qquad (8.57)$$

From this inverse relationship between Q and R_m, it should now be clear that high Q is synonymous with low losses and vice versa.

On the steelpan the Q values are relatively high but display much variability depending on

(i) the musical range of the instrument,
(ii) on the choice of material,
(iii) the hammer peening and stress relief processes and
(iv) the operating temperature of the finished instrument.

In general the Q is lowest on the low-end instruments and highest on the high-end instruments with values falling within the range $20 \leq Q \leq 110$. The quality factor decreases with increasing operating temperature. These aspects are discussed in Chapter 9.

8.11.6 Non-Linear Frequency, Hardening and Softening Springs

In the linear dynamics, by solving the linear equation (8.35), the linear frequency with damping was determined to be

$$\text{Linear: } \omega_d = \omega_0 \left(1 - \frac{R_m^2}{2\omega_0^2}\right)^{\frac{1}{2}}.$$

In order to examine the case for the non-linear system the expression for the *non-linear frequency* with damping must be culled from the HBM analysis employed in Chapter 7. On solving the corresponding non-linear dynamical equations by the Harmonic Balance Method, the non-linear frequency with damping $\omega*$ is found to be

Non-Linear: $$\omega^* = \omega_0 \left[1 - \frac{R_m^2}{2\omega_0^2} + \left(\frac{3}{4}\frac{\alpha_3}{\alpha_1} - \frac{5}{6}\left(\frac{\alpha_2}{\alpha_1}\right)^2 \right) a_1^2 \right]^{1/2},$$

(8.58)

where a_1 is the displacement amplitude of the first mode (tonic). *Some words of clarification*: Although equation (8.58) was obtained in the HBM analysis of a SDOF system it can just as well be obtained from the analysis of a MDOF system using the method of *Multiple-Time Scales* employed in Chapter 4. For sufficiently low levels of excitation $a_1 \to 0$, the non-linear frequency with damping is equal to the linear frequency with damping

$$\omega^* \to \omega_d = \omega_0 (1 - R_m^2 / 2\omega_0^2)^{\frac{1}{2}}.$$

Just as the linear stiffness is given by ω_d^2, the non-linear stiffness is given by ω^{*2}. The frequency equation shows that, depending on the values of the α-parameters, the system stiffness may display a *hardening effect* (increase in non-linear frequency with amplitude) or a *softening effect* (a decrease in non-linear frequency with amplitude). The conditions for these two opposing effects are

$$\frac{3}{4}\frac{\alpha_3}{\alpha_1} - \frac{5}{6}\left(\frac{\alpha_2}{\alpha_1}\right)^2 > 0 \quad \text{Hardening},$$

$$\frac{3}{4}\frac{\alpha_3}{\alpha_1} - \frac{5}{6}\left(\frac{\alpha_2}{\alpha_1}\right)^2 < 0 \quad \text{Softening}. \quad (8.59\text{a, b, c})$$

$$\frac{3}{4}\frac{\alpha_3}{\alpha_1} - \frac{5}{6}\left(\frac{\alpha_2}{\alpha_1}\right)^2 = 0 \quad \text{Linear}.$$

These effects can be understood from the directions of the quadratic force and the cubic force relative to the direction of the dominant linear force.

Figure (8.4) shows that the cubic force acts in the same direction as the linear restoring force effectively increasing the restoring force and by implication, increasing the dynamic stiffness of the fundamental mode of the note. It is clear from the term $3\alpha_3/4\alpha_1$ in the frequency equation (8.58) that the cubic non-linearity is responsible for the hardening effect of the note.

On the other hand, for *positive* quadratic coupling α_1, the quadratic forces always act in the same direction, *opposing* the linear restoring force when the deflection is downward but *assisting* when the note surface displacement is upward. If the linear and quadratic forces alone were acting then the note will be softer (reduced stiffness) when pushed downwards but harder (stiffer) when pulled upwards. Over one whole cycle of vibration the note will show a softer behavior. To see this, look at the cases where there exist only cubic and linear forces. Whether they act singly or together, in one complete cycle the note surface is displaced equally above and below the rest position (except for the slight reduction due to damping as the motion progresses). In the cases where the quadratic force acts alone or together with the linear force, in one complete cycle the downward displacement always exceeds the upward displacement. For negative quadratic coupling α_1, the same effect is present but one must switch around upward with downward; in one complete cycle the *upward* displacement always exceeds the *downward* displacement.

As a result of the linear and non-linear forces there are three types of resonance responses to harmonic forcing: the note behaves as

(i) a softening spring,
(ii) a linear spring or
(iii) a hardening spring.

These responses are shown in Figure 8.7. The peak of the resonance curve for the softening nonlinearity bends to the left, since the natural frequency of the system decreases with increasing amplitude, while for hardening nonlinearity the curve bends to the right.

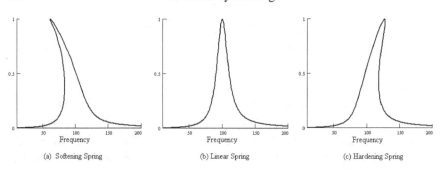

Fig. 8.7. Frequency response plots for a non-linear spring showing hardening and softening effects.

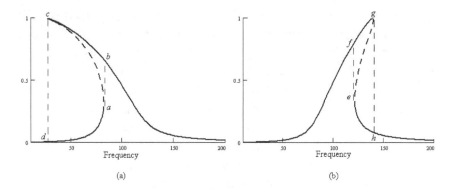

Fig. 8.8. Bifurcation and Jump Phenomenon on the normalized response of (a) the softening system and (b) the hardening system. Notice that these curves are not tilted symmetrically about the linear resonance curve.

The linear response curve is *single-valued*. This means that for all values of the driving force amplitude, there is a well-defined single value for the response function for each value of the driving frequency. For the non-linear system, the dependence of the response on the non-linearity increases with the driving force amplitude. For low levels of the driving force, the response curve shows a small degree of tilt and the response remains single valued. As the driving force increases the tilt increases until a critical driving force is reached when at the point "*a*" on the response curve in Figure 8.8a, the tangent (slope) becomes infinite. This critical point can be reached by varying some parameter(s) in the non-linear term of the response function or by varying the driving force. Once the point of *infinite tangency* is reached the system *bifurcates* as it moves from a *single-valued state* to a *multi-valued state*, from a *stable domain* to an *unstable domain*. The full lines on the response curve correspond to stable solutions of the response function. The dotted line describes an unstable region that *cannot be accessed* by the system. The unstable region is bounded by points of infinite tangency "*a*" and "**c**". Experimentally it is impossible to find the system in a state along the region of the dotted line.

If the system in Figure 8.8a is excited with sufficient driving force to guarantee bifurcation and the driving frequency beginning at zero is slowly increased the system follows a path along the curve from "*o*" up to the point "*a*". If the driving frequency and amplitude are held constant the response can suddenly jump from "*a*" to "*b*". This is called the *Jump Phenomenon* and is accompanied by a sudden change in the amplitude of oscillation. With the system at "*b*", if the frequency (not the amplitude) of the driving force is now slowly reduced, the system follows the path along the response curve from "*b*" to "*c*". But "*c*" is also a point of infinite tangency (an *unstable point*) so the system can jump from "*c*" to end on the stable point "*d*". The system displays *hysteresis* since the path depends on the history, a result that follows from the multi-valued property of the system.

A similar interpretation holds for the hardening system in Figure 8.8b where bifurcation and jumps also exist. The notes on the steelpan possess these natural properties that can allow them to display a variety of interesting dynamics. *It is remarkable that these exotic behavior are found on the steelpan known mostly for its use as a musical instrument.* These matters are fully discussed in Chapter 18.

8.12 Note Geometries, Potential Wells and Critical Points

To best examine the steelpan note system dynamics in the neighborhood of a *local equilibrium point* (w_0), the motion can be viewed in the system's potential well. This allows a 'visual' picture of the note surface movements to be presented. In this representation the *critical points* of the note dynamics can be discussed.

8.12.1 Critical Points and their Properties

A differentiable function $f = f(x)$ has *fixed points* (also called *stationary points* or *turning points*) at all points x_0 that satisfy $f'(x_0) =$

0 where $(\bullet)' = d(\bullet)/dx$. A fixed point is a point that does not change upon application of a normalization (*scaling*) operation, a set of differential operations etc, it is an *invariant*. The function can be dependent on a number of parameters each one of which may be considered to be the dependent variable x. For example on the steelpan note, the buckling parameter may be considered as the dependent variable if the temperature or residual stress is altered. If a variable is slightly displaced from a fixed point, the system may

(i) return to the fixed point ('*asymptotically stable*' or '*superstable*'),
(ii) move away ('*unstable*'), or
(iii) move in a neighborhood of the fixed point but not approach it ('*stable*' but not '*asymptotically stable*').

Fixed points are also called *critical points* or *equilibrium points*. The path of the system in the space (*phase space*) describing the state of the system is referred to as the *trajectory*. A trajectory passing through at least one point that is not a critical point cannot cross itself unless it is a *closed curve*, in which case it corresponds to *a periodic solution* or a *periodic orbit*. When a pan note is played, the state of the vibrating surface is a series of periodic orbits. When the pan is exposed to changing ambient temperature the surface undergoes changes in state that could be described as *open* and the trajectory is *an open curve*.

A stationary point can be an *extremum* (a *minimum* or a *maximum*) of the function f. An extremum can be *local* (applying over a given region) or *global* (applying over the entire domain of the function). If f is twice differentiable ($f''(x)$ exists) the test for maximum or minimum can be stated:

(i) $f'(x_0) = 0$, $f''(x_0) > 0$, the point x_0 is a minimum.
(ii) $f'(x_0) = 0$, $f''(x_0) < 0$, the point x_0 is a maximum.

In addition if

(iii) $f'(x_0) = 0$, $f''(x_0) = 0$ and $f'''(x_0) \neq 0$, then x_0 is a *saddle point*.

8.12.2 Potential Energy Function and Potential Wells

Potential wells are very common in nature. Whenever you walk downhill in a valley, reach the bottom and ascend on the other side you have walked through a gravitational potential well. When a simple oscillator such as a pendulum swings it moves from its highest point of greatest potential energy, descends to its lowest position (lowest potential energy) and ascends up to another point of maximum potential energy. The bob of the pendulum executes this motion *in a potential well*. A child on a swing executes motion in a potential well.

A simple undamped oscillator can be modeled as a mass m attached to a spring of *spring constant k*, it obeys the equation $m\ddot{w} + kw = 0$, where w is the deflection of the spring, $\ddot{w}$ is the acceleration of the mass and $-kw$ the restoring force exerted on the attached mass. The ratio k/m is equal to the square of the radian frequency of oscillation, $\omega^2 = k/m$. The potential energy stored in the spring is given by $U = kw^2/2$ which is a parabolic function. A plot of the potential energy U versus the displacement w is shown in Figure 8.9a.

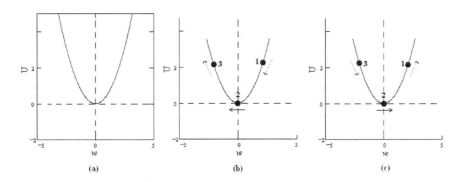

Fig. 8.9. Potential well of a simple oscillator. A small mass is pictured as moving within this well.

The potential energy U is symmetrical about the axis through $w = 0$ and there is one turning point located at ($U = 0, w = 0$). This turning point is at the bottom of the *potential well* and represents a *local minimum* or *equilibrium point*. In Figure 8.9b, if the motion of the mass m in the well begins at 1, it naturally proceeds towards the point of minimum potential energy at 2 then rises to position 3 where it momentarily stops, then (as in Figure 8.9c) it retraces its *trajectory* passing through 2 back to 1 to complete one cycle of oscillation. Since the system is undamped this path is retraced indefinitely. The trajectory described in this well is *stable* because the mass *always returns to the local equilibrium point*. If the motion were damped, the potential well will still be parabolic with a single local equilibrium point at $w = 0$ but the displacements will gradually decrease until the mass finally comes to rest at the bottom of the well. So that *a linear system with damping is stable, in fact it is asymptotically stable* because $w \to 0$ (the equilibrium point) as $t \to \infty$. The local minimum in this system is also a *global minimum* because there is no other for all w.

To study the non-linear oscillatory note systems that are found on the steelpan we shall use the potential energy function given in equation (8.33). Since it is required here that the case of zero stress ($s = 0$) be considered it is convenient to define $\alpha_{10} \doteq \omega_0^2$ as the symbol for the α_1 parameter when $s = 0$. By normalizing equation (8.33) with respect to ω_0^2, the potential energy can be written in the convenient form

$$U = \frac{(1-s)w^2}{2} + \frac{aw^3}{3} + \frac{bw^4}{4} - sBw, \qquad (8.60)$$

where
  s is the buckling parameter,
  $a = \alpha_2/\alpha_{10}$,
  $b = \alpha_3/\alpha_{10}$ and
  $B = \beta/\alpha_{10}$.
Potential wells are plotted in Figure 8.10 for different sets of parameters (a, b, c, s, B).

In Figure 8.10a the parameters define a linear system such as the simple oscillator under zero residual stress and zero thermal stress. (b) represents a combination of linear and cubic forces in the system under zero stress loading. This represents a flat unstressed plate. The systems in (a) and (b) are characterized by symmetrical wells with a single critical point at ($U = 0, w = 0$). The systems in (a) and (b) are both stable because trajectories (or *orbits*) will always return to the local minimum.

The system in (c) has a combination of linear and quadratic forces under zero stress loading. The local equilibrium point remains at ($U = 0$, $w = 0$) but there now exists a second critical point. This second critical point is a *local maximum* located at $w = -2$. In this system, trajectories restricted to $w > -2$ all follow parabolic paths and are stable but those for $w < -2$ follow *hyperbolic paths*. Any system entering a hyperbolic trajectory will never return to the local minimum and are regarded as *unstable*.

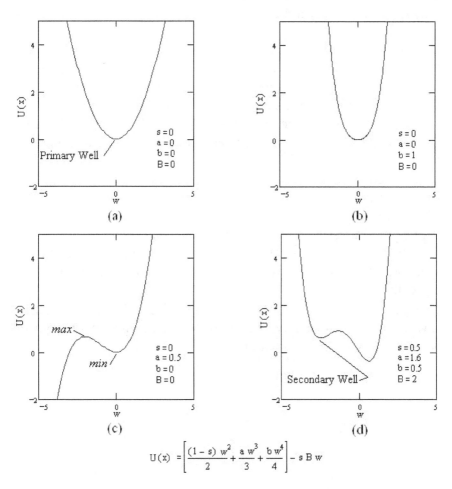

$$U(x) = \left[\frac{(1-s)\,w^2}{2} + \frac{a\,w^3}{3} + \frac{b\,w^4}{4} \right] - s\,B\,w$$

Fig. 8.10. Potential wells for the non-linear oscillatory note systems on the pan.

Whereas in the cases 8.10a and 8.10b where there were for each non-zero U value, two w values of equal magnitude, there now exists in 8.10c as many as three *different* values of w having the same U value. The system has *bifurcated*.

Figure 8.10d shows a more realistic note system having linear, quadratic and cubic forces acting simultaneously while the system is placed under both compressive stress and thermal stress. All notes on the pan experience these forces and stress loading while being played or excited in any way. The orthogonal static force $f_0 = s\beta$ associated with the potential energy component $-s\beta w$ produces a displacement of the local minimum in the *primary well* placing it at the position ($U = -0.377, w = 0.64$). Observe two things

(i) the local minimum in the primary well is now negative and its position displaced upwards relative to the local minima in the other three cases (see Figure (8.10d) and
(ii) there now appears a *secondary well* with a critical point or local minimum at ($U = 0.90, w = -1.3$). Another bifurcation has occurred with the generation of the second local minimum.

Since the primary well contains the lowest potential energy, the most stable state of the system is at the bottom of the primary well. Therefore all notes will have their surfaces displaced upwards by virtue of the stress loading and their *equilibrium state* (*quiescent state, rest state, or ground state*) will be located at the bottom of the primary well. When a note is played, vibrations will occur with displacements about this equilibrium state.

Figure 8.11a shows a stable trajectory executed over the path bb′ and an unstable trajectory beginning at a, passing through both the local minimum and the maximum and

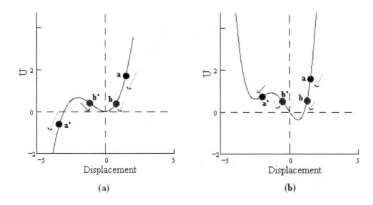

Fig. 8.11. Other examples of potential wells possible on non-linear systems.

continuing on to a'. There is nothing to stop the trajectory continuing on to -∞. A real system cannot physically do this especially for the pan system; however, what it means is that the downward displacement can be excessively large. *This system does not exist on the pan.*

If the trajectories are restricted to the primary well such as shown by bb' in Figure 8.11b, the system will remain stable. *However if the note is played too vigorously and excitation follows the path aa' then the system enters the secondary well.* The system may remain in the secondary well for some time while executing oscillations there at a frequency *different* to that for oscillations in the primary well. Or the note may execute oscillations spanning both wells with a complicated motion having frequency components unrelated to the frequency obtained in the primary well. *This is the reason for the annoying 'Boiing' sound on poor quality bass notes played excessively loud.*

8.12.3 Conditions for the existence of a Secondary Well and the Stability of Steelpan Notes

The static state of the note is crucially important in determining the response of the note to an external force. The conditions for the generation of strong upper partials (octave and twelfth) may also lead to the creation of a secondary well, in which case, playing the note loudly could result in off-tune annoying tones. Such a situation could exist even on the tenor, particularly on the bore tenor especially when too many holes are drilled along the grooves.

In studying the stability conditions for the static state it will be convenient to replace the note displacement variable w with w_0 in the equation for the potential energy. On differentiating the potential energy function given in equation (8.60) with respect to w_0, one gets for $U' = 0$

$$(1-s)w_0 + aw_0^2 + bw_0^3 - sB = 0. \tag{8.61}$$

The three *turning points* (critical points) can be obtained as the real roots of equation (8.61).

Case I: Zero Stress, $s = 0$

Consider first the case for $s = 0$, we seek the roots of

$$w_0 + aw_0^2 + bw_0^3 = 0. \tag{8.62}$$

The three real roots are

$$w_0 = 0, \qquad \text{Minimum of the Primary Well}$$

$$w_0 = \frac{-a + \sqrt{a^2 - 4b}}{2b}, \qquad \text{Local Maximum}$$

$$w_0 = \frac{-a - \sqrt{a^2 - 4b}}{2b}, \qquad \text{Minimum of the Secondary Well}$$

with $a^2 > 4b$, $b \neq 0$ and $s = 0$.

$$\tag{8.63a,b,c}$$

Of special concern here is the *discriminant* of the polynomial (8.62). *A discriminant is a quantity, usually invariant under certain classes of transformations, which characterizes certain properties of the roots of an equation.* A polynomial discriminant is the product of the squares of the differences of the polynomial roots. Defining the discriminant of a polynomial of degree n as D_n, the discriminant of (8.62) is $D_2 = a^2 - 4b$. Two real roots emerge when $D_2 > 0$ is satisfied. The necessary condition for the existence in real space of the local maximum and the secondary well is $a^2 > 4b$ (with $b \neq 0$). By requiring $U'' > 0$ (*the condition for the turning point to be a minimum*) shows that $a^2 > 4b$ is a *necessary and sufficient condition* for the formation of the secondary well when s = 0.

If $b = 0$ and $s = 0$, as in Figure 8.10c, then the bottom of the primary well is at $w_0 = 0$, the local maximum is at $w_0 = -1/a = -2$ and there is no secondary well.

No matter what the shape or boundary conditions of the note may be, the parameter b (or α_3/α_{10} to be precise) is *never equal to zero*. Because of this, the situations in Figure 8.10c and Figure 8.11a never arise on the pan. Neither does the case of the simple oscillator in Figure 8.10a because of damping and non-linearities.

Case II: Non-zero Stress, $s \neq 0$

For the general case, including stress loading $s > 0$, the *necessary condition* for the existence of the secondary well, determined from equation (8.61) through the requirement on its discriminant, is

$$D_3 > 0,$$

where, in explicit algebraic form

$$D_3 = 4bs^3 - (27B^2b^2 + 12b - 18abB - a^2)s^2 + (12b - 18abB - 2a^2 + 4Ba^3)s + a^2 - 4b.$$

(8.64a,b)

In this case the *sufficient condition* ($U' = 0$, $U'' > 0$), in explicit algebraic form, is too complicated a set of expressions to serve as a useful object in the present discussion. As we shall see, the *linearized form* of (8.64) is very useful and can serve to illustrate a procedure often used in stability analysis of systems in the neighborhood of a critical point. The condition (8.64) reduces to $a^2 > 4b$ for $s = 0$.

$$U = \left[\frac{(1-s)w_0^2}{2} + \frac{aw_0^3}{3} + \frac{bw_0^4}{4} \right] - sBw_0$$

$$a = 0.895315, \quad b = \frac{a^2}{4}, \quad B = 1.52236$$

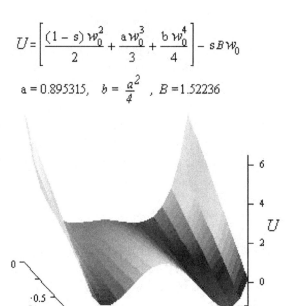

Fig. 8.12. Potential well of a note system satisfying $a^2 = 4b$ at $s = 0$, progressing towards the buckling state as s increases from zero to unity.

To assist in the further analysis, a 3-D plot of the potential well for a modeled note is shown in Figure 8.12. The details of the modeling procedure are left for Section 8.15. The note was modeled so that the condition $a^2 = 4b$ is just satisfied. For $s = 0$, *this system is at the critical point for the formation of a secondary well.* As s increases a secondary well develops and the depths of both the primary and the secondary wells increase as s increases up to the buckling point $s = 1$. *When the system buckles ('flaps' in steelpan parlance) it can easily move from one well to the other with the application of near zero external force because the linear force (normally the largest of all the forces) vanishes.*

For $s = 1$, the condition for the existence of a secondary well obtained from condition (8.64) reduces to *$27Bb^2 < 4a^3$*. A simple check shows this necessary condition is satisfied by the parameters in Figure 8.12.

If s were to increase from s = 0 by a small amount $\delta s \ll 1$, then the linearized form of condition (8.64)

$$(12b - 18abB - 2a^2 + 4Ba^3)\delta s + a^2 - 4b > 0, \qquad (8.65)$$

can be used to determine whether the secondary well can develop. The use of linearized forms near critical points is an established procedure in system stability tests. For $\delta s \neq 0$, the inequality $a^2 > 4b$ even if it is satisfied, no longer serves as a condition for the formation of the secondary well. Condition (8.65) must be used instead.

Applying the equality $a^2 = 4b$ to condition (8.65) reduces (8.65) to the simple form

$$aB < 2, \text{ or equivalently, } 2\alpha_{10}^2 > \alpha_2 \beta. \qquad (8.66)$$

Note: *This 'simple looking' condition is very important on the pan as we shall see presently.*

A simple check shows that condition (8.66) is satisfied by the parameters in Figure 8.12. In all cases of numerical modeling of notes by the author, when $a^2 = 4b$, the inequality $aB < 2$ was consistently obeyed. In addition, because the linear force almost always exceeds the quadratic force on the notes of the pan, $\alpha_{10} > \alpha_2$ is almost always satisfied for note shapes commonly found on the pan. *There are exceptions however where for a broad range of note shapes, α_2 can exceed α_{10} and even take on negative values as well (see Sections 8.21 – 8.23).* Because of the wide range of possible note shapes, it cannot be generally shown that condition (8.66) is always satisfied. What we have just verified however, is that in the *neighborhood* of the critical point for s = 0, defined by $a^2 = 4b$, a small increase in the buckling parameter (through an increase in the compressive stress or temperature) makes possible the formation of a secondary well provided the condition (8.66) is satisfied.

Bass players have observed that when the pans are exposed to direct sunlight for long periods (as occur on Carnival days) the notes on the bass not only decrease in pitch but they often produce the 'boiing' sound when played vigorously. When the hot notes are struck hard with the stick, the surface is driven down towards the position of the secondary well. The vibration of these notes is a good example of the double-well oscillations described here.

8.13 Conditions on the Forces related to the Key-note (Tonic) and the Octave

Condition (8.66) is written in a form that allows one to see that it represents a product (or ratio) of forces, where β determines the magnitude of the static force $f_0 \doteq s\beta$ (which is adjusted while tuning to set the *quiescent state*), α_{10} determines the linear restoring force (which is adjusted in tuning the frequency of the tonic) while α_2 determines the quadratic force (that couples the tonic to the octave). There are therefore very powerful methods available for determining the stability of a note under the constraint of these various forces. *It is therefore important for the reader to keep in mind that despite the somewhat complicated appearance of some of the equations or conditions set out here, the underlying motive is to seek relationships (simple ones wherever possible) among the internal forces on the notes.* **The relationships sought are those that can guarantee the stability of the array of tuned notes on the pan face.**

Caution: On the real pan, the tuner, while tuning, has no way of knowing the α-parameters, nevertheless, a note should not be tuned with parameters satisfying $\alpha_2^2 \geq 4\alpha_{10}\alpha_3$ if the risk of instabilities associated with the system entering the buckling mode is to be avoided. Because s is never zero in practice, it will be difficult for any pan maker to bring a note to the condition $\alpha_2^2 \geq 4\alpha_{10}\alpha_3$ without the note buckling. The condition usually satisfied on the steelpan notes in the tuned state is $\alpha_2^2 < 4\alpha_{10}\alpha_3$ but with $s > 0$, many notes also satisfy condition (8.64) giving them a secondary well. When the potential well displays a very symmetrical form, the sounded note is dull and almost monotone. It will be shown later that *large α_2 values are required for strong second partials* (the octaves) and this leads to asymmetrical wells even the generation of a secondary

Secrets of the Steelpan

well. It will further be shown that *a properly tuned note is very prone to instabilities of the kind described by the jump phenomenon and other more subtle forms of bifurcations.*

8.14 Numerical Computations

The corresponding potential wells can be constructed using equation (8.60) after solving for the system parameters α_n ($n = 1, 2, 3$) and β. Numerical solvers on a computer are required and in addition, the reader should possess some analytical and computational skills. The routines are somewhat tedious (but unavoidably so) especially the double integrals defining $E(x)$ and $G(x)$ in equation (8.12b, c). The entire routine can be executed in Mathcad©. Mathcad© may prove to be uneconomical in some cases where the general purpose resident integration routines are used. Other more economical quadrature procedures can be written in the Mathcad© program to speed up the computation.

The solution procedure runs as follows: *(All readers are advised to read these instructions whether or not they intend to do the computations themselves as the instructions contain vital information on the tuning process.)*

(i) These calculations should begin with $s = 0$, for which $A_0 = 0$, then repeated by incrementing s by a small step each time until the desired maximum s value is reached. On each step the shape of the note must be corrected using the function $A_0 \psi_0$.

(ii) Take $v = 0.3$ for steel. If you wish to experiment with another material such as brass for example ($v = 0.37$), merely changing v here will not fully achieve this. The corresponding material constants (Young's modulus, Poisson's ratio and density) for that new material must also be used wherever they appear in the other formulas.

(iii) Assuming $H_0/h = 3$ (or any other suitable value) choose the shape you wish to give the note by defining $q(x)$.

(iv) The function $q(x)$ sets the shape of the note. *This replicates the note shaping process of tuning.* Numerical experiments can therefore be carried out to determine the effects of note shape (form) on the dynamics and tonality of the note. (Tonality is used here in a restricted sense because only one frequency component, the key-note, is involved.)

(v) Substitute $q(x)$ into equation (8.10) to yield λ *if $s = 0$ (or into equation (8.11) if $s > 0$)*.

(vi) Substitute λ into equation (8.6). Obtain the root K through a suitable iterative procedure. *It is very important to ensure correct convergence in your routine here otherwise the K value will be useless*. Substitute K into equation (8.4) to define the mode shape $\psi(x)$.

If you choose to work in Mathcad © the following WHILE loop may be used to obtain K: here, *estk* is the *estimate for K*. Be careful of the starting value for *estk* (in this sample routine I am using the starting value for *estk* as 5). Define the function DEL(*estk*) equal to the left side of equation (8.6) with K replaced by *estk*. The loop ends with the required K value as k. The values shown at the end of the routine are typical and are inserted here only for illustration purposes.

$$k := \begin{vmatrix} estk \leftarrow 5 \\ \text{while } |DEL(estk)| \geq 0.0000001 \\ \qquad estk \leftarrow estk - \dfrac{DEL(estk)}{\dfrac{d}{destk}DEL(estk)} \end{vmatrix}$$

$$DEL(k) = 7.105 \cdot 10^{-15}$$
$$k = 4.296$$
$$K := k$$

Note: The variable k is used here as a local variable in the Mathcad© routine for computing K. Do not confuse with k used in the function $q(x)$.

(vii) Use equation (8.5) to normalize the mode shape function and thereby determine N_0 defined in equation (8.4).
(viii) Obtain the values for the functionals $M_1 \ldots M_9$.
(ix) Determine ω_0 using the appropriate M_i values and calculate β.

(x) Determine the values for α_1, α_2 and α_3.
(xi) Set a value for s or equivalently $(\breve{N}_C + \breve{N}_T)$. *This action replicates another aspect of the tuning process.* Hammer peening not only shapes the note, it modifies the stress distribution over the note area and along its boundaries i.e. it sets the $\breve{N}_c$ value. Changing the s value can also simulate the effects of changes in temperature because it changes the $\breve{N}_T$ value. *To re-emphasize a point already made, changes due to $\breve{N}_c$ cannot be distinguished from changes due to $\breve{N}_T$.*
(xii) Solve equation (8.25) for A_0, depending on the value of s.
(xiii) Update the note shape with the new $A_0\psi_0$. Repeat the process for the new s value.

You will observe from the above procedure that having chosen a basic note shape and note parameters, the computations will provide you with α_1, α_2 and α_3 and f_0. α_1 determines the frequency of the note. Also you observe that as s increases the note shape changes with $A_0\psi_0$. You can experiment by changing the shaping function $q(x)$ or any parameter that suits your interest.

The reader may be surprised to learn that the procedures (i) to (xiii) all have their counterpart in the real process of tuning as carried out by the tuner. It takes some time for anyone to become sufficiently familiar with the mathematical procedures of the simulation and the physical processes involved in tuning the pan to see these relationships at a glance. However do not be discouraged, just plod on. It takes a while, sometimes years before a tuner really gets 'the hang' of pan tuning anyway! For those who are really interested in all this, they could take some comfort in knowing that the updating of the note shape by means of $A_0\psi_0$ (see (i) and (xiii)) each time the stress (defined by s) is changed is a result of (the 'work' of) the *ubiquitous Pan Jumbie*! For more on this see Section 17.20.

8.15 Modeling Real Notes

8.15.1 Shaping Functions and Note Shapes

Real notes are modeled in the SDOF representation, beginning with an initially spherical cap with rise factor H_0/h typical of notes found on the instrument. This shape is then modified to *simulate tuning* by using one of three shaping functions

$$q(x) = k\,(1 - \cos(\pi(x-1))), \tag{8.67a}$$

$$q(x) = k\,(1 - 2.4x^2 + 1.4x^3), \tag{8.67b}$$

$$q(x) = k\,(x - 2.4x^2 + 1.4x^3). \tag{8.67c}$$

In designing the note shapes in this study, the note surface is formed as the *surface of revolution* produced by these functions. Since the notes are assumed to be perfectly blocked, at the note boundary (x = 1), a necessary condition for q(x) is that q(1) = 0. The functions chosen for q(x) are completely arbitrary and reflect the fact that a wide range of note shapes is possible (a fact known to the master pan maker). The static and dynamic responses of notes having shapes determined by these design functions will be studied in various sections of this book. The note shape, *with height expressed in units of note thickness*, is given by

$$g(x) = \frac{H_0}{h}\left\{(1-x^2) + q(x)\right\}.$$

Examples of these note shapes are plotted in Figure 8.13 (not drawn to scale) for three values of k in the two of the three shaping functions. Positive values of the *shaping parameter k*, increases the rise of the dome and the steepness of the note profile. Negative k values produce a flattening of the dome eventually forming an indentation at the pole. Almost every steelpan built today employ note surfaces having positive curvature. The notes on the early steelpans were indented so that the final note shape possessed negative curvature. It is possible to form and tune the notes with surfaces having both positive and negative curvature. Some are plotted here for the purposes of studying the potential wells but they will be further examined later for their tonal properties.

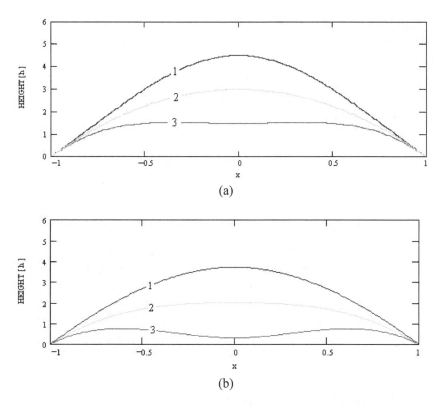

Figure 8.13. Height scale expanded for visual clarity.
(a) Function (8.67a): k = 0.5 (curve 1), k = 0 (curve 2, spherical), k = -0.5 (curve 3).
(b) Function (8.67b): k = 0.2 (curve 1), k = -0.35 (curve 2), k = -0.9 (curve 3).

With the application of the shaping function, which simulates the shaping process, the final rise factor is equal to $(H/h) = (H_0/h)(1 + k)$ in the case of equations (8.67a & b), where H_0/h is the rise factor of the initial spherical cap. The analytical equations takes care of this change as seen from the original differential equations where the rise factor always appear as the product $(H_0/h)Q(x)$. Therefore, in seeking any relationship between note frequency and rise factor, the final value of the rise factor after shaping, H/h, must be used. Although this may seem to be just a linear scaling adjustment, not only is it correct, this quantity is of more practical value because in practice H/h is the measured quantity.

8.15.2 Parameters for the Modeled Potential Wells

Bifurcation and potential well studies are now carried out for notes shaped by the function (8.67b). Some of the general features found here can also be seen on notes shaped by the other functions. From equation (8.61), the critical points are determined as roots of the equation U′ = 0. In order to distinguish these special values of w_0, they will be defined by the new variable Z_i where the subscript i = 1 will define *the bottom of the primary well*, i = 2 defines *the local maximum* and i = 3 the *bottom of the secondary well*. The equation then takes the form

$$(1-s)Z + aZ^2 + bZ^3 - sB = 0, \qquad (8.68)$$

where s now becomes the variable parameter. The onset of bifurcation is signaled by the appearance of three real roots for equation (8.68). The *critical value s** of the buckling parameter that defines the onset of bifurcation, $D_3 = 0$, is equal to the real root of the equation

$$4bs^3 - (27B^2b^2 + 12b - 18abB - a^2)s^2 + (12b - 18abB - 2a^2 + 4Ba^3)s + a^2 - 4b = 0. \qquad (8.69)$$

After deciding on the *shaping function q(x)*, for each value of the *shaping parameter k*, the *rise-to-radius ratio* and *height-ratio H_0/h*, the note parameters (a_1, a_2, a_3, β) are computed numerically. From each of these parameter sets the values of a, b and B are determined. *If the process of pan making was easy it would have been reflected here but it isn't. The whole art of pan making is centered right here, in the determination of the parameter set (a_1, a_2, a_3, β) which defines the various forces found on the note.* But this applies only to a monotone note for there are other modes (partials) to tune and many more parameters to set. This is left to the MDOF analysis.

8.15.3 The Quiescent State

When the buckling parameter is varied, the bottom of the primary well, traced out by Z_1, moves outwards (upwards on the pan face). This displacement must be included in any expression for the note shape because, while the displacement can be varied, it cannot be eliminated as long as $s > 0$. In the SDOF treatment, the expression for the rise H of the note at the apex measured from the plane through the note boundary (the *planform*) is therefore given by

$$H = H_0 + H_0 \, q(0) + h \, Z_1. \tag{8.70}$$

This equilibrium position represents the *quiescent point* about which the note will execute its vibrational motion after being impacted by the stick. *The real root of equation (8.68) therefore has a very direct physical meaning in terms of what one observes visually as the dome shape of a note.* The Quiescent State for a note of given geometrical form in phase space is described by H from equation (8.70), the buckling parameter s and the static force f_0.

It should also be noted that $A_0 = Z_1$. In the models that follow, the reader should pay attention to the paths taken by Z_1 since they show the outward movement of the apex of the note (the *sweetspot*) as the buckling parameter (due to a combination of compressive and thermal stresses) is varied. During tuning or aging, as the stresses vary along the note boundary, the note surface moves upward or downward in response. Remember that Z_1 (or A_0) is expressed in units of note thickness h so you can get the actual movement by multiplying Z_1 by h in millimeters. As you view the plots, you can assume $h = 0.3$ mm to get a feel for the actual displacement of the apex of the note as it is tuned. Of course you must add to this any changes in shape resulting from the shaping function which in practice is done with the hammer.

8.15.4 Some Remarks on the Compressive Stresses

For dynamical as well as statical reasons, it is important to fully understand the requirement of uniformity of the compressive stress around the note boundary. As can be seen in Chapter 14 on the tuning process, the tuner carefully hammer peens the note boundary in the *shaping-tuning* process. Although this may not be obvious to someone casually observing the actions of the trained tuner, in addition to note shaping, the tuner carefully sets the boundary conditions of the note with as close as possible uniformity in stress distribution in order to achieve near perfect blocking. *Stresses that are random in distribution, direction and magnitude will define neither a boundary nor a note.* Once near perfect blocking is achieved (for perfect blocking is not possible because of internal losses), the note rings out with a loud tone when played with the stick. The greater the degree of blocking the louder is the tone. Good quality instruments satisfy these conditions.

During the initial stages of pan making when the areas bordered by the grooves are formed prior to burning, the stress distribution over the pan face display a high degree of randomness in the distribution of internal stresses (compressive and tensional). The magnitudes of these residual stresses will generally be reduced during burning (stress relief anneal). This randomness will preclude the existence of specific areas of well defined frequencies or the existence of localized motion when these areas are struck. These observations on the initial randomness are consistent with Peekna and Rossing (2000) where the residual stresses were measured for an untuned tenor pan in the early stages of processing before and just after annealing. However, the situation is completely different on a properly tuned pan characterized by notes of well-defined tonal frequencies that originate from localized areas of the pan face. Such clearly defined characteristics can only be associated with equally clearly defined parameters and conditions.

When for example the note boundary is determined by the Chladni method or by Holographic Interferometry, the nodal lines so obtained are contours of equal dynamic stiffness. These contours can be distorted by changes in note shape, thickness or internal stress. *It has been shown in this book that dynamic stiffness is a function of the stress applied internally along the note boundary.* The well-defined boundary nodal lines are indicative of the uniformity of the boundary stresses.

8.16 Modeled Notes

Figures 8.14 to 8.17 show the bifurcation diagrams and potential wells (in 3-D representation) for notes shaped as in Figure 8.13 for $H_0/h = 3.2$ and rise-to-radius ratio of 1:31. The temperature dependence of the note static and dynamic behavior for normal changes of ambient temperatures is more important to the frequency of vibration than to the bifurcation and buckling problem. It will therefore be assumed that the notes are kept at the temperature at which they were tuned so making $N_T = 0$. The effects of temperature on frequency will be considered separately.

Case 1

Figure 8.14 shows the result for the note initially shaped as a shallow spherical cap as in Figure 8.13a using steel as the pan face material. For this note, $a^2 - 4b = -0.102$ which means that the critical value of the buckling parameter $s*$ is greater than zero, in fact $s* = 0.416288$ here. From the definition of the buckling parameter and the normalized compressive force per unit length along the boundary, N_c, and using $\sigma_c = -N_c/h$ one can write

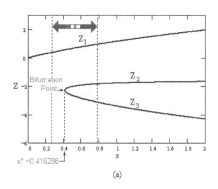
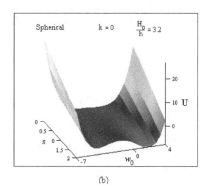

Fig. 8.14. (a) Bifurcation plot (b) Potential well.

$$s = -\frac{\sigma_c(1-v^2)}{E}\left(\frac{a}{h}\right)^2 \frac{M_4}{\omega_0^2}. \tag{8.71}$$

Recall that the parameter "a" that appears in equation (8.71) is the radius of the note. If the material is steel, $E = 207$ GPa, $v = 0.3$, for brass, $E = 104$ GPa, $v = 0.37$. With $a = 3$ cm, $h = 0.3$ mm and $H_0/h = 3.2$, for the note modeled as a spherical cap, one gets

Steel: $\quad s = -0.0053\sigma_c,$ \hfill (8.72)

Brass: $\quad s = -0.01\sigma_c,$

with σ_c in units of MPa (1MegaPascal = 10^6 N·m^{-2}). For a steelpan in thermal equilibrium at the temperature at which it was initially tuned the modeled note will buckle, $s = 1$, for a critical compressive stress

$$\sigma_{crit} = -189 \text{ MPa} \quad (Steel)$$
$$= -100 \text{ MPa} \quad (Brass).$$

Because of the lower critical stress for brass, *greater care must be exercised when forming the brass pan face where low temperature annealing must be carried out even during the sinking process.* If the numerical value of σ_c exceeds these critical values the note enters the post-buckling phase. For typical notes of steel on the pan the compressive stresses along the note boundary fall within the range (*observe the use of the absolute value $|\sigma_c|$ here*)

$$50 \text{ MPa} \leq |\sigma_c| \leq 150 \text{ MPa}.$$

With $\sigma_{crit} = -189$ MPa, this gives for the modeled steel note, $0.26 \leq s \leq 0.79$. To give meaning to these quantities the range of s values for this note design is shown on the bifurcation plot Figure 8.14a..

Case II

The results for a note shaped by the function $q(x) = 0.2(1 - 2.4 x^2 + 1.4 x^3)$ starting from the initial spherical cap with $H_0/h = 3.2$ ending with $H/h = 3.84$ are shown Figure 8.15. This note shape represents a form having greater positive curvature than the spherical cap as shown in Figure 8.13b. With $a = 3$ cm, $h = 0.3$ mm and $H_0/h = 3.2$, one gets

$$\text{Steel:} \quad s = -0.00348 \, \sigma_c, \quad (8.73)$$
$$\text{Brass:} \quad s = -0.0068 \, \sigma_c,$$

$$\sigma_{crit} = -288 \text{ MPa} \quad (Steel)$$
$$= -147 \text{ MPa} \quad (Brass).$$

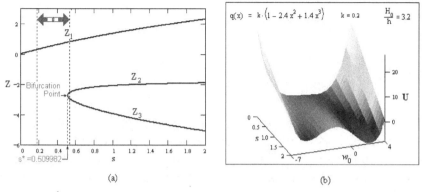

Fig. 8.15. (a) Bifurcation plot (b) Potential well.

Observe that the higher curvature, which imparts greater flexural stiffness to the notes, produces an increase in the value of the critical stress as well as an increase in note frequency. The bifurcation point is now located at $s^* = 0.50992$ which requires a compressive stress of -147 MPa in order to develop a secondary well. This value is on the upper end of the range of stresses imparted to the boundaries of typical notes in the tuned state. Figure 8.15b, shows details of the well as s increases from zero to $s = 0.52$, the maximum allowed at the top of the stress range $\sigma_c = -150$ MPa. Although this is a usable design form, the tuner will experience some difficulty increasing the compressive stresses by peening along the boundary to make this a pleasant sounding note characterized by strong modulations associated with strong partials. Increasing the magnitude of σ_c will be required in order to achieve a reduction in note frequency.

Case III

Figure 8.16 shows the results for a shaping function $q(x) = -0.9(1 - 2.4\ x^2 + 1.4\ x^3)$ starting from the initial spherical cap with $H_0/h = 3.2$ ending with $H/h = 0.32$. This represents a form having both positive and negative curvature as seen in Figure 8.13b. It is unusual for a pan note but is a useful exercise here. With $a = 3$ cm, $h = 0.3$ mm and $H_0/h = 3.2$, one gets

Steel: $\quad s = -0.0104\,\sigma_c,$ (8.74)
Brass: $\quad s = -0.0186\,\sigma_c,$

$$\sigma_{crit} = -97 \text{ MPa} \quad (\textit{Steel})$$
$$= -54 \text{ MPa} \quad (\textit{Brass}).$$

By shaping the note into a form having both positive and negative curvature, the effective flexural stiffness is reduced (see Section 8.20 for the frequencies associated with this design). Of the three designs, this note is more easily buckled although the critical buckling parameter for the formation of the secondary well is now close to the value 2 ($s^* = 1.969611$).

This example demonstrates the fact that buckling is possible without the formation of a secondary well. In the pre-buckling phase $s < 1$, *where all pan notes operate*, the potential well of the present design, has a very symmetrical form (see Figure 8.16b), similar to that of a flat plate. This similarity is due to the presence of regions of positive and negative curvature, which acting together reduces the overall flexural stiffness. If a note is shaped into this form the primary well will take on too close a symmetrical profile to allow for the generation of strong higher partials. Although the presence of compressive stresses along the boundary *can assist in shaping the well thereby increasing the strengths of the higher partials,* the tuner will not be able to peen the boundary of this note to the degree required before the onset of buckling.

Notes possessing this and similar shapes having both positive and negative curvature are not employed on the steelpan for precisely these reasons — a fact unknown to the pan makers who stick only to shapes of positive curvature. These reasons obtained from the static behavior of the pan would not have been known to pan makers but they nevertheless, by their training and experience in the art, have avoided these shapes because pan tuning is all about approaching the conditions for *good tonality*, not the opposite. Anyone trying to use these shapes would soon give up!

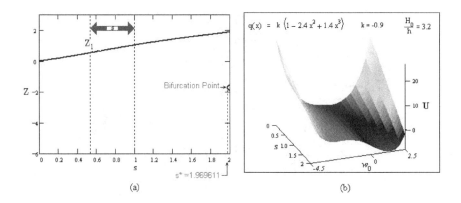

Fig. 8.16. (a) Bifurcation plot (b) Potential well.

Special Case IV

Figure 8.17 shows the results for the shaping function $q(x) = -0.35(1 - 2.4 x^2 + 1.4 x^3)$ starting from the initial spherical cap with $H_0/h = 3.2$ ending with $H/h = 2.08$. This note was specially modeled to an *optimized* shape for steel that maximizes the amplitudes of the octave and the twelfth and is fully discussed in Section 8.21. The optimization will not be quite as perfect for brass. (***This is an important point which the reader ought not to miss. A tuner who has grown accustomed to tuning pans of steel must spend some time 're-training' on brass before he becomes proficient on brass pans.***) The optimized form possesses a somewhat flattened mid-area with positive curvature on the outer regions (see Figure 8.13b). With $a = 3$ cm, $h = 0.3$ mm and $H_0/h = 3.2$, one gets

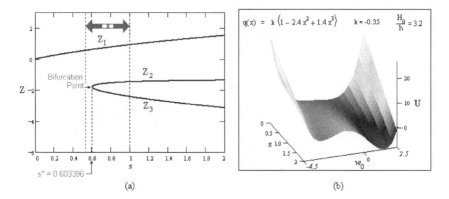

Fig. 8.17. (a) Bifurcation plot (b) Potential well.

$$\text{Steel:} \quad s = -0.0106\,\sigma_c, \quad (8.75)$$
$$\text{Brass:} \quad s = -0.0199\,\sigma_c,$$

$$\sigma_{\text{crit}} = -95 \text{ MPa} \quad (Steel)$$
$$= -50 \text{ MPa} \quad (Brass).$$

The bifurcation point is located at $s^* = 0.603396$, which corresponds to a compressive stress of -57 MPa for steel and approximately -30 MPa for brass. With such low stress limits for bifurcation, the potential energy plots for real notes of this design will almost certainly possess a secondary well and display relatively strong non-linearites. The design criterion was the maximization of the second and third partials by geometric optimization. As explained earlier a note tuned to do precisely this may also be characterized by a double well potential. However it will be very difficult for any pan maker (manual or robotic) to tune a note to the precision possible in this numerical computation. ***Tuning cannot be achieved by simply stamping the metal into shape.***

Remark: *There is something quite subtle and important in the above paragraph that I hope has caught the attention of the reader. For those who did and those who did not notice, I revealed in that paragraph the fact that the relative strengths of the partials —key-note, octave and twelfth— are determined by the geometry or form of the note surface. To demonstrate this as it occurs in practice I will choose one of the leading tuners in Trinidad, at the time of writing and use one of his pans for the* *demonstration. I choose Master Tuner Herman Guppy. The pan, or pans, two of them, a Double Second (see Figure 1.3) and a Four Cello; the band, Tropical Angel Harps. Resident tuner for this band, Phillip Morris, himself an accomplished tuner, brought these pans to my attention. There are notes on these pans whose tones are truly the sound of 'Angel harps' simply marvelous. I have stared at these notes and marveled at their form, too subtle to describe. It's not the smoothness of the surfaces or the rise of the notes. To fully appreciate them you must get in close, tap them with your thumb, listen, and watch them vibrate. Beautiful! Great craftsmanship!*

Not satisfied? Want some more of these fine notes/ See Figure 1.2 on the Four Cello by Master Tuner Bertram Kellman. Sorry but you must hear this one yourself!

8.17 Comparison with the Euler Load on a Strip of Note Material

It is good for the reader to get a 'feel' for the strength of the compressive stresses to which the note material is subjected when in use on the finished pan. To this end we now switch our attention briefly to the critical loading (the *Euler Load*) of a flat strip of material as it buckles under compression. Consider a flat strip of steel plate of length L having the same thickness h as the pan face being held under compressive load σ between both ends. Refer to Figure 8.18 for details. No change is visible when the compressive load first increases from zero — the strip is stable, there is no buckling, and no out-of-plane displacement. The load-displacement equilibrium path is thus characterized by a vertical segment on the load-displacement plot this is the *primary path*, which lasts until the increasing load reaches the critical *Euler load*

$$\sigma_{crit} = \pi^2 \, Eh^2/(12L^2), \qquad (8.76)$$

which is a constant, characteristic of the particular strip.

When the load reaches the Euler load, buckling suddenly takes place without any further load increase, and lateral deflections grow instantaneously in either equally probable direction as illustrated in Figure 8.18c. On buckling therefore, the equilibrium path bifurcates into two symmetric secondary paths as the load increases beyond the critical point.

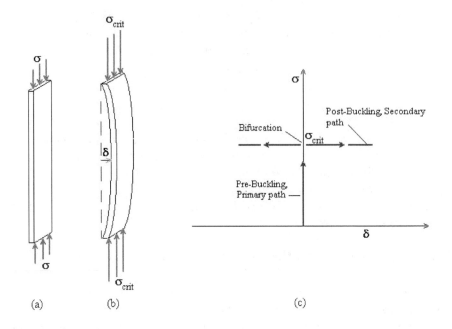

Fig. 8.18. (a) and (b) Buckling of a metal strip under compressive loading. (c) Load-displacement path from the pre-buckling state on to the post-buckling state.

If a strip is taken from a similar piece of material as the notes modeled in the previous examples, $h = 0.3$ mm and on using $L = 2a = 6$ cm (where a is the note planform radius), one gets $\sigma_{crit} = 4.3$ MPa (steel), 2.1 MPa (brass). What we see is that the steelpan notes will buckle under compressive loads some 20 to 70 times larger than the buckling loads of a flat strip made of the same note material. It is the dome-shaped structure of the notes that gives them this increased load bearing property. This increased stiffness is also associated with the audio frequencies generated by these notes on excitation.

8.18 The Pre-stressed State, Mechanical Bias and De-localization

8.18.1 The Pre-stressed State

In practice as well as in the modeling procedure, the compressive stress at the note boundary is a *free parameter*. In fact as further discussed in Chapter 14, the pan maker or tuner uses this free parameter to tune the notes of the pan. Each note on a pan must be independently tuned so that the *quiescent point* of operation is stable and well positioned in state space (the space where the quiescent point, thermal and compressive stresses are the coordinates). We now proceed to explore this state space and to define a new term — *Mechanical Bias*.

During the tuning process, compressive in-plane stresses produced by hammer peening, especially to the internote area of the pan face, together with thermally induced stresses, sets the note into a *pre-stressed state*. Because thermal stresses change under variation in ambient temperature the stressed state is not fixed. *The pre-stressed state determines the stress range in which the note will operate.*

Since the bottom of the primary well corresponds to the static state of the note surface (note at rest), the note surface moves outwards as the boundary compressive stress is increased or when the temperature of the pan is increased. This static displacement given by Z_1 is produced by the static force $f_0 = s\beta$ acting orthogonal to the surface at the apex. For $\delta T = 0$, that is when there is no change in the thermal stress, the static force is due entirely to the compressive stress σ_c and is given by

$$f_0 = -\frac{4\sigma_c(1-v^2)}{E}\frac{a^2 H_0 M_8}{h^3}. \tag{8.77}$$

This is f_0 in its dimensionless form. Recall that f_0 defined in equation (8.21) represents in normalized (dimensionless) units a force per unit mass. On taking the mass of the note to be $m_n = \pi a^2 h \rho$ where ρ is the density of the note material, and employing the normalization parameter $\gamma^2 = Eh^2/[\rho a^4(1-v^2)]$ gives for this force in dimensional form

$$F_0 = -4\pi \sigma_c H_0 h M_8. \tag{8.77}$$

For the notes designed in the previous sections, one gets

Steel: $F_0 = -3.62\,\sigma_c M_8$ Newtons,
Brass: $F_0 = -3.62\sigma_c M_8$ Newtons, (8.78a, b)

with σ_c in units of MPa. M_8 depends on the note shape, rise-factor and Poisson's ratio of the material. For these design shapes, taking a compressive *pre-stress* design $\sigma_c = -80$ MPa (steel), $\sigma_c = -40$ MPa (brass), one has

Case I	Steel:	$F_0 = 329$,	Newtons
	Brass:	$F_0 = 164.8$,	
Case II	Steel:	$F_0 = 388.6$,	
	Brass:	$F_0 = 195.8$,	
Case III	Steel:	$F_0 = 179.8$,	
	Brass:	$F_0 = 87.9$,	
Special Case IV	Steel:	$F_0 = 256.6$,	
	Brass:	$F_0 = 126.2$,	

Notice how much F_0 depends on the note shape and type of material.

While f_0 represents the (Galerkin) average static orthogonal force over the surface of the note, considered to act normal to the note surface at the apex, the static force distribution (see Chapter 3) over the surface is described by

$$f(x) = 4(\check{N}_c + \check{N}_T)\left(\frac{H_0}{h}\right)Q(x), \qquad (8.79)$$

where

$$Q(x) = 1 - 2\left(\frac{H_0}{a}\right)^2 \{q(x) + h\psi_0(x)/H_0\} - \frac{1}{2}\frac{d^2}{dx^2}(q(x) + h\psi_0(x)/H_0),$$

with

$$\psi_0 = A_0 g(x).$$

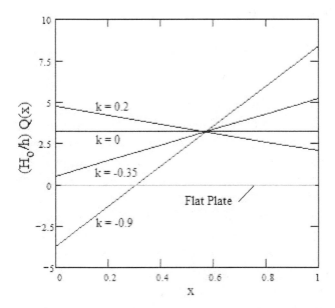

Fig. 8.18. Normalized form of the static force distribution over the surfaces of the modeled notes. Observe the constant value for the flat plate $(H_0/h)Q(x) = 0$, and for the spherical cap $(k = 0)$, $(H_0/h)Q(x) = 3.2$.

From (8.79), it is clear that the quantity $(H_0/h)Q(x)$ describes the form of the static force distribution over the surface of the note. The shaping function therefore determines the force distribution over the surface. The form of the force distributions for the four modeled notes are shown in Figure 8.18 by plotting $(H_0/h)Q(x)$ as a function of x using the ratio $H_0/a = 1/31$ (a typical value on the pan). For the flat plate used here as a reference, the force is zero everywhere on the surface because $H_0 = 0$. The distributions all appear as linear functions of x because (i) the small H_0/a ratio when squared makes the second term in $Q(x)$ negligibly small (ii) $q(x)$ (hence $g(x)$ and ψ_0) is a cubic which yields a linear function for the second derivative in the second term. The linearity obtained here for force distribution on these perfectly smooth note surfaces is not expected in practice where hammer marks are often seen randomly covering the note surfaces. The region on the plot for $k = -0.9$ where the force takes on negative values corresponds to the region on the note surface where the curvature is negative. Observe that for $k = 0$, the perfectly spherical surface, the force distribution is constant over the surface as expected.

8.18.2 Mechanical Bias and De-localization

Compressive in-plane stresses produced by hammer peening (especially to the internote area of the pan face), together with (ambient) temperature-induced stresses, sets the note into a *pre-stressed state*. The pre-stressed state determines the stress range in which the note will operate. It should also be observed that as the loading is increased, the bottom of the primary well moves outwards (upwards on the pan face). Since the bottom of the well corresponds to the static state of the note surface (note at rest), this means that the note surface moves outwards as compressive stress in increased or when the temperature of the pan is increased. This static displacement is given by w_0 and is produced by the static force $s\beta$ (orthogonal to the surface). This force acts as a *mechanical bias* set by the *pre-stressed state* of the note.

When the note is played, the applied stick impulses add or subtract from the mechanical bias, causing vibrations of the note surface. When the pan face is driven at the appropriate frequency by an attached electromechanical vibrator or driven acoustically, there will be essentially no mechanical motion except for the imperceptible vibration of the *true note* area.

In practice, because of imperfect blocking, $s\beta$ and the static position of the note surface w_0, depend on the changes occurring over the entire instrument. In other words, <u>**in practice the mechanical bias is not fully determined locally, there is some de-localization**</u>. When for example in the process of tuning, a couple notes have already been tuned, it is normal to see the tuner return to correct a note that has drifted off because of changes to its mechanical bias. *This continues throughout the entire tuning process until all mechanical biases have been set, the notes are properly blocked and all the notes are correctly tuned.*

- *De-localization of the static force distribution or equivalently the mechanical bias on the note surface is responsible for the changes in frequency on a remote note as the pan is tuned. When a note is being tuned, the mechanical bias on a remote note may be altered. This affects the vibrational characteristics of the remote note. This effect is a readily observed on the pan during the tuning process.*

- *It is imperative that the mechanical bias of the pre-stressed state be kept stable or the note dynamics will be altered. The high variability of the mechanical biasing on the pre-burn pan is the main reason for stress relief annealing (burning).*
- *The mechanical biasing concept introduced here is very useful because on a tuned pan, each note is assigned a particular bias consistent with its other parameters that determine the character and frequency of the tone it generates.*
- *These biases can be changed globally by temperature changes, by cutting the skirt, clamping the skirt, and <u>by adding or removing attachments from the pan</u>.*
- *Because of the de-localization of the static force distribution,* **as a rule, the steelpan as a tuned instrument cannot be dismantled into fractional parts — pan face, skirt and chime.**

The compressive pre-stressed state is critical especially on the low-end pans. For basses constructed with thin material, compressive pre-stress has to be kept low to avoid buckling. When the notes on such a bass is struck intensely the 'boiing' sound is likely to be heard. Good basses are those made with heavier gauge steel thereby allowing the notes to be operated at higher compressive stress ranges consistent with the intense forcing that are needed for truly booming bass sounds. **This is the key to good steelpan bass construction**.

Since $\beta \to 0$ for the flat plate, mechanical biasing exists by virtue of the curvature of the note characterized by the rise factor (H_0/h) and the existence of the compressive forces $\breve{N}_c$ and $\breve{N}_T$.

- *The pan face of the steelpan can therefore be considered as a sub-section consisting of an array of well-defined domains (the notes) set to different levels of mechanical biasing (pre-stressed states) compared to those levels found on the stiffer internote domain.*
- *In the mechanical-biasing interpretation, it is interesting that pan makers have found this clever method by which they establish areas on the pan face that are set to respond to*

impacts in different stress ranges, display high degrees of localization and oscillate at distinct frequencies.

Definition: *The Mechanical Bias of a steelpan note is the resultant static force sβ acting orthogonally to the note surface, produced by the thermal stresses and the residual compressive stresses.* In addition to the effect of stresses, this static force depends on the geometry, size and thickness, material density and elastic properties of the note.

Statical Importance: The rest state of a steelpan is a static equilibrium of many forces distributed over all the domains of the instrument. The mechanical coupling of these domains (notes, internotes, chime and skirt) guarantees the stability of the system. If the chime opens and fails, some or all notes are placed out-of-tune. The same happens if the skirt on a previously tuned instrument is cut or if attachments are mounted on the skirt. These failures or alterations produce a redistribution of the internal forces including the mechanical bias on the notes.

Dynamical Importance — Upper Limit on the Stick-Note Contact Force: The Mechanical Bias sets the stress range of operation of a note. For the dynamics of a note to remain within the bounds associated with the production of audio tones that are characterized as 'musical' and 'normal' for the instrument, the force applied by stick impact must generate stresses that fall well within the defined stress range. For proper execution of the note dynamics, the panist must ensure that stick-note impacts satisfy the condition,

$$F_c \ll |4\pi \sigma_c H_0 h M_8|$$

where F_c is the *contact force* applied by stick impact. This condition, as stated, applies at the Tuning Temperature. *This condition imposes an upper limit on the force with which the player should impact the note with the stick.* For each note this force upper limit exists. At the system level, when the note is played, the applied force F_c appears as a short duration transient change in the static force, to which the system responds and is set into vibration. When the energy introduced into the system by the impact is dissipated by internal damping and acoustic radiation, the static force returns to its original value at the end of the tone.

With high levels of excitation, the motion of the note surface takes the note into the regions of the potential well (even into the secondary well if it exists) where the non-linearities are more manifest. The audio sound then becomes distorted and more complex. This happens long before the maximum force limit $|4\pi\sigma_c H_0 h M_8|$ is reached.

- As a general rule, the condition $F_c \ll |4\pi\sigma_c H_0 h M_8|$ tells us that notes with greater rise H_0 and greater thickness h can be played harder since this allows for greater stick-note contact forces.

Caution: *For some notes especially those on the higher pans, the upper limit for the contact force can be quite high (see examples below). If as an experimenter you wish to use the onset of distortion such as the 'boiing' sound to measure this force the method may prove to be destructive. The application of large contact forces can off-tune a note since it acts like a hammer blow! Only on a poorly performing bass with thin pan face material can this method work. In this case, the force upper limit is quite low and the use of excessive forces will, at worse, result in the loss of an already poorly performing instrument anyway.*

An example of the mechanical bias on a model pan using the previous four note designs in steel is shown in Figure 8.19.

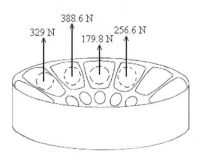

Fig. 8.19 Mechanical Bias on the modeled notes of a steel tenor pan. (N ≡ Newtons)

A typical stick impact on a mid-range note played *forte* produces a peak impact force of around 40 N and an average force of 20 N (see Chapter 13). This impact when applied to the top face of the note will act in a direction to oppose the mechanical bias and cause a downward displacement of the note surface. As a result of the impact, the note executes damped vibrational motion *about the quiescent* point (represented by the rest position of the note surface). The greater the level of mechanical bias, the higher the stress range of operation and the greater the stick impact that the note can withstand without executing motion into the secondary well (if it exists) or creating undesirable tonal frequencies. Large amplitude vibration under high levels of forcing will be discussed in Chapter 18 on *Exotic Effects*.

8.19 Effects of Hammer Marks and Small Indentations or Humps

Hammer marks are the small humps and indentations made on the note surface and pan face during the sinking, shaping and tuning processes. These hammer marks are distributed randomly over the note surface and are of arbitrary shapes and sizes. Hammer marks, by their sharp bends and curves are characterized by their high local stiffnesses. As a result, they increase the overall stiffness of the note. This is the reason corrugated steel sheets are resistant to bending along a line perpendicular to the run of the corrugation. The pan maker unwittingly compensates for this increased stiffness during the shaping process of tuning. If you attempt to flatten or 'smooth out' these hammer marks, the note frequency will be altered. Small hammer marks, although they may not be visually pleasing, do not alter the overall performance of the sounding note. When done in excess however, they do present problems to the tuner especially in tuning the octave and twelfth. Problems arise when the size of the indentations approach the *generalized wavelength* (see Chapter 13) of a tuned mode. Such large indentations alter the shape and location of the nodal lines. The effect of hammer marks on stick impact is discussed in Section 13.14.4.

8.20 The Frequency Characteristics of Modeled Notes

The solution procedure for the α-parameters involves successive numerical solutions of the equations for each modification of the design form g(x) and since the state of stress on the note is set by the buckling parameter, for each change in value of the buckling parameter s. The Young's modulus and Poisson's ratio are chosen as E = 207 GPa, ν = 0.3 (typical for steel), or E = 104 GPa, ν = 0.37 (typical for brass). Clamped note boundaries are assumed. The *clamped* (or *fixed*) boundary is an ideal condition requiring perfect *blocking* of the note. Tuners and pan makers try to approach this condition as best they could unless note-note coupling is desired for sympathetic pairing. Pan makers refer to this process as *blocking* or *tightening*. In practice, the boundaries of pan notes lie somewhere between what engineers refer to as *simple supports* and *clamped supports*.

8.20.1 Small Amplitude Frequencies of Steel and Brass Notes: Curvature Effects

To illustrate the potential of the present steelpan dynamical theory, several notes having clamped boundaries (perfectly blocked) are analyzed for a range of note shapes in brass and in steel. Frequencies are obtained under zero compressive/thermal stress from equation (8.14) through the normalized frequency relation $\omega^2 = \alpha_1$ by the numerical procedure outlined in Section 8.14. The reduced forms of equation (8.14) are given in equations (8.80) and (8.81)

Dome Shaped Notes

$$\omega = \left[\frac{1}{12}M_1 + 8(1+\nu)\left(\frac{H_0}{h}\right)^2\left(M_2 - \frac{1}{2}(1+\nu)M_3\right)\right]^{\frac{1}{2}}, \quad (8.80)$$

Flat Plate:

$$\omega_0 = \left[\frac{1}{12}M_1\right]^{\frac{1}{2}}. \quad (8.81)$$

From equation (8.80) we see that if the note is designed with $M_2 = (1+v)M_3/2$ then the note frequency will be the same as that of the flat plate given by (8.81). Since this condition can be satisfied for different note shapes it shows that notes of different shapes can be designed to have the same frequency. The only elastic constant involved here is Poisson's ratio v.

8.20.2 Spherical form

The dependence of the fundamental frequency on note shape and rise factor, H/h, for a spherical form ($q(x) = 0$) is shown in Figure 8.20(a) while the note shape is illustrated in Figure 8.20(b) (see Figure 8.13(b), curve #2). The spherical form serves as the reference shape in this analysis. The ordinates of Figure 8.20(a) are the ratios of the (renormalized) radian frequencies ω, of the notes to that of a flat plate ω_0, having the same planform as the note. The curves for both brass and steel are almost parabolic with brass having significantly lower frequency at any given value of H/h. For a given value of H/h, the curvature of any one of these spherical notes is constant and positive over the whole surface.

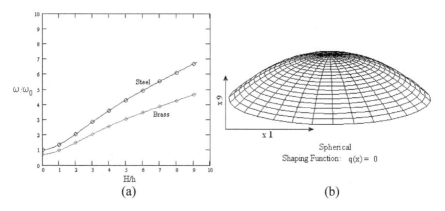

Fig. 8.20. Notes in the shape of shallow spherical shells, $q(x) = 0$. (a) Ratio of the note frequency to that of the flat plate on the same planform, (b) Note shape with the height on a x 9 scale for clarity.

8.20.3 Shaping Function q(x) = 0.5 k(1 + cos(π (x-1)))

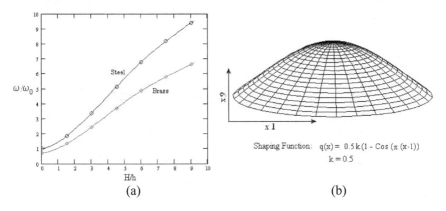

Fig. 8.21. Notes in the shape modified by the shaping function q(x). (a) Ratio of the note frequency to that of the flat plate on the same planform, (b) Note shape with the height on a x 9 scale for clarity.

For the family of notes having the shape determined by the shaping function q(x) = k(1 + cos(π (x-1))), with *k = 0.5*, the results are shown in Figure 8.21 (see Figure 8.13(a), curve #1). The surfaces of these notes possess greater positive curvature when compared with the spherical notes. The curvature changes over the surface being greatest at the apex of the note. *This increase in curvature results in an increase in frequency for any given ratio H/h when compared to the corresponding note having a spherical form.* This dependence of frequency on note shape is consistent with the tuning/shaping practices of the tuner.

The results in Figure 8.22 are obtained for an unusual shape having an inner region of negative curvature and an outer region of positive curvature (see Figure 8.13(a), curve #3). This is achieved by setting *k = -0.5* in the shaping function q(x) = .k(1 + cos(π (x-1)). Pan makers, normally, do not use this combination of curvatures. The common practice is to shape the notes convex upwards with positive but variable curvature over the surface. The curves now show the frequency first increasing for low vales of H/h, reaching a local frequency maximum for *H/h = 2.35*, on to a local minimum at *H/h = 2.9*, then increasing for lager values of *H/h*. This behavior is the result of the opposing effects that positive and negative curvature have on the frequency of the note. If the central region of these notes were indented much further by setting k < -0.5, the frequency over a range of *H/h* values can be made equal to or less than the frequency of the flat plate ($\omega \leq \omega_0$).

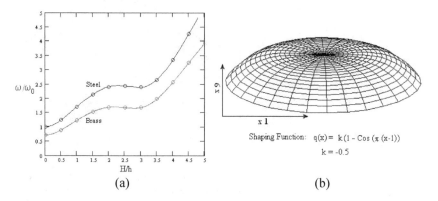

Fig. 8.22. Notes in the shape set by the shaping function q(x) to produce positive and negative curvature. (a) Ratio of the note frequency to that of the flat plate on the same planform, (b) Note shape with the height on a x 9 scale for clarity. The central region of the note surface is indented.

8.20.3.1 Observations: Quiescent State and System Stability

All notes can be formed as convex upward or convex downward (concave) with equal results. For this reason a Pan can be played by striking the top-side or under-side of the notes. Notes are normally shaped convex upwards with positive but varying curvature over the surface but notes can also be shaped with a combination of positive and negative curvature. The combination of curvatures can reduce the dependence of the note frequency on the *rise factor H/h* which we shall define as $y \doteq H/h$ for our purposes here. In fact at the *turning points* (*max* and *min*) of the $\omega(y)/\omega_0$ function (see the curves in Figure 8.23(a)) the variation of frequency with rise factor vanishes. Slopes $\frac{d}{dy}(\frac{\omega}{\omega_0})$ of the frequency ratio versus H/h curves in Figure 8.22(a) are plotted in Figure 8.23(b) for steel and brass. *At the points where the slope is zero, the note possesses low dependence on the rise factor H/h. This occurs at H/h = 0 (the flat plate), and at the points H/h = 2.35 (2.17) and H/h = 2.9 (2.80) on our dome shaped notes. The bracketed values are for brass.*

In the design represented in Figure 8.22 the note will display this type of stability fairly well over the range $2.3 \leq H/h \leq 2.9$ (steel). However, arbitrary use of positive and negative curvature combinations will not always guarantee this property. At a point of inflection $\left(\frac{d^2}{dy^2}\left(\frac{\omega}{\omega_0}\right) = 0\right)$ on the frequency curves Figure 8.22(a), the slope function $\frac{d}{dy}\left(\frac{\omega}{\omega_0}\right)$ of Figure 8.23(b) is at a minimum or maximum. For maximum stability of this type, the quiescent point of operation must be at or in the neighborhood of the point where the slope in Figure 8.23b is at a max or min. Approximately midway ($H/h = 2.64$ for steel) between the max and min points on the curves in Figure 8.22(a) is a point of inflection. The point $H/h = 2.64$ (2.55) is a global minimum for the slope function plotted in Figure 8.23b for steel (brass). There is another inflection point at $H/h = 0.9$ (0.86) where the slope is at a local maximum. However in the neighborhood of this second inflection point the frequency of the note is not stable against variation in the rise factor.

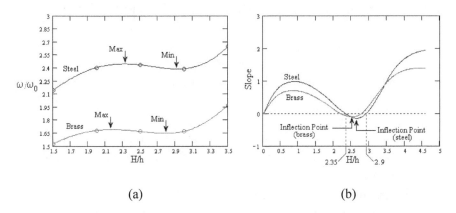

Fig. 8.23. (a) Enlarged section of Figure 8.22(a) around the min/max area. (b) Slopes of the frequency ratio versus H/h curves in Figure 8.22(a). The shift in position of the stationary points (max, min and inflection) from steel to brass is due to the difference in Poisson's ratio for the two materials.

This note as a shallow shell structure having both positive and negative curvature on the surface, displays some properties of the flat plate at the points $H/h = 2.35$ (2.17) and $H/h = 2.9$ (2.80). However, the differences lie in the values of the quadratic parameter α_2, which is zero for the flat plate but non-zero and relatively large in the neighborhood of these stationary points. This means that the vibrating note with these *H/h* values will induce relatively strong parametric excitations and second mode (octave, if tuned properly) unlike the flat plate.

While it will not be really practical to tune notes to specific shapes as we can do in our modeling, what we gain from this is the knowledge that the behavior of the note to retain a tuned frequency depends on the geometrical shape or form given to the tuned note. While these considerations are seen to depend on the single elastic parameter ν, the other material and elastic parameters (density and Young's modulus) are needed in order to set the frequency. We shall have more to say on the ν-dependence shortly.

8.20.3.2 Effects due to Thermal/Compressive Stresses

Consider the steel note, with similar arguments for the brass note. With the presence of thermal/compressive in-plane stresses, while the frequencies will be altered throughout the entire range of *H/h* values, numerical simulations show that in the range *2.3 ≤ H/h ≤ 2.9* (*the precise location of this range depends on the thermal/compressive stresses*), the notes suffer greater changes in frequency produced by stress variations than notes with rise factors just outside this range. This is due to the following dynamical effects:

(i) When the thermal/compressive stress is increased, the note is forced outward by the static force f_0, thus increasing the rise factor.

(ii) An increase in the rise factor in this range *2.3 ≤ H/h ≤ 2.9* produces a small *decrease* in the note frequency, *unlike what happens outside this range* (see Figure 8.23(a)).

(iii) Accompanying any increase in the thermal/compressive stress is a *reduction in the stiffness* of the note, which brings about a *reduction* in the note frequency.

(iv) It follows that within the range *2.3 ≤ H/h ≤ 2.9* the note frequency suffers a frequency reduction due to change in geometry and a frequency reduction due to decrease in dynamical stiffness. On the pan notes, the frequency change due to stress-induced stiffness variation *always exceeds* the

accompanying frequency change due to stress-induced geometrical variation.
(v) Outside the range $2.3 \leq H/h \leq 2.9$ the *reduction* in frequency due to a *decrease in stiffness* is partially compensated for by an *increase* in frequency due to *changes in geometry*.
(vi) Similar arguments hold for a decrease in thermal/compressive stresses.

It turns out that the region $2.3 \leq H/h \leq 2.9$ (or similar regions on other designs using positive and negative curvature) which first appears to be an ideal location for the quiescent point of the note (*because of the low sensitivity to changes in H/h*) is in fact *not globally optimal*.

- **Note**: *The reader should note here that a problem has arisen in trying to find globally optimized designs on the steelpan. Similar problems arise in other areas of operation of the steelpan when optimization is sought. One has to be very cautious in making claims to optimization on the pan.*

8.20.4 Shaping Function $q(x) = k(1 - 2.4x^2 + 1.4x^3)$

The shaping function $q(x) = k(1 - 2.4x^2 + 1.4x^3)$ with $k = -0.5$ produces a note shape with positive curvature on the outer region and negative curvature on the inner region of the note surface. While the function $q(x)$ used here is mathematically different from the cosine function used in the previous design they produce similar note shapes (compare Figure 8.22(b) and Figure 8.24(b)). The frequency curves in Figure 8.24(a) are also similar to those in Figure 8.22(a).

The stationary points on the frequency curves in Figure 8.24(a) are inflection points. Using a reasonably thorough numerical search of the frequency function in the neighborhood of $k = -0.5$ showed that this shaping function produces no max-min points, only an inflection point on each curve. Over the range $2.6 \leq H/h \leq 3.4$, the frequency variation is very small for both materials. The inflection point is located at $H/h = 2.94$ for brass and at $H/h = 3.09$ for steel. Each inflection point on Figure 8.25(b) is located at slope = 0.

The difference in position of the inflection point is the result of the difference in Poisson's ratio for brass $\nu = 0.37$ and steel $\nu = 0.3$. Young's modulus is not involved. The reason why Poisson's ratio is involved and not Young's modulus is that *the position of the inflection point depends only on the geometry (shape or form) of the note surface not on the size (scale) of the note*. The inflection point is a *scale invariant* property. Since the Poisson's ratio is the ratio of orthogonal changes in lengths of the note material under stress, it describes changes in note *shape*. Since the Young's modulus which relates stress to strain for these homogeneous and isotropic materials, steel and brass, it describes changes in size (*scale*) of the stressed notes. ***The reader must see these comments not only as mathematical details but also as technical points since they involve physical properties of the note material — the elastic constants of the note material and their roles.***

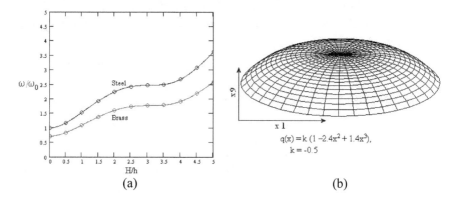

Fig. 8.24. Notes in the shape set by the shaping function q(x) to produce positive and negative curvature. (a) Ratio of the note frequency to that of the flat plate on the same planform, (b) Note shape with the height on a x 9 scale for clarity. The central region of the note is indented.

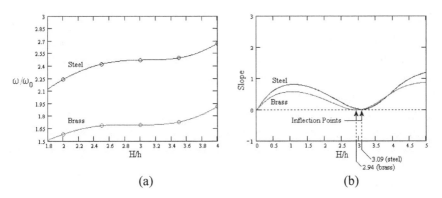

Fig. 8.25. (a) Enlarged section of Figure 8.24(a) around the min/max area. (b) Slopes of the frequency ratio versus H/h curves in Figure 8.24(a). The shift in position of the inflection points from steel to brass is due to the difference in Poisson's ratio for the two materials.

8.20.4.1 Temperature Effects

Tuning a note (brass or steel) with this shaping function and placing the quiescent point at the inflection point produces a note with better temperature stability than the previous example involving the cosine function. The reason is that the frequency changes due to stress-induced changes in rise factor are minimal around the inflection point in Figure 8.25b. The frequency change is now due almost entirely to changes in note stiffness induced by the stress. However, *the inflection point obtained here is not globally optimal.* There are points more stable against temperature changes located in regions where the frequency increases with H/h, because this increase partially offsets the reduction in frequency associated with the decrease in stiffness.

8.20.4.2 Observation

Despite the stronger dependence on temperature of notes shaped and tuned around the stationary points these notes can be useful in the following way. If it could be guaranteed that in use, the tuned note (or instrument as a whole) will be subjected only to small variations in temperature around the *Tuning Temperature T_t*, then these notes by their low dependence on rise factor should remain in the tuned state longer than usual. One route of the note from the tuned to the untuned state is by slow gradual reshaping by stick impacts made most often in the neighborhood of the apex (sweetspot). With the instrument operating around T_t, the note must first work its way out of the neighborhood of the stationary point before significant detuning can take place.

Although this analysis focused only on the neighborhood of stationary points this is appropriate because these are the only distinguishing geometrical characteristics for the note shapes. The results and note characteristics obtained here are independent of the size of the note. They are all scale invariant (independent) properties. They therefore apply to Pans of all types.

These observations are important in Pan making because the pan maker must be informed of the existence or non-existence of optimized note shapes. Optimization must be carefully defined because there is no globally optimized state of a note. Some requirements for one type of optimization may conflict with the requirements for another type.

8.21. More Shapes and more Results

Additional numerical results are presented in Figures 8.26–8.31. The design forms are plotted in Figures 8.26(a, b) for a range of values for the parameter k. Figures 8.27(a, b) show two unusual geometries for Pan notes. Figure 8.27(b) is similar in form to the Pang notes used by Rohner and Schärer (2000), and it is for this reason that this shape is included in the analysis. Design frequencies are shown in Figures 8.28(a, b). Observe that frequency is not uniquely determined by note geometry. For a given in-plane stress, the desired frequency can be obtained (for example) from two designs for each of the two trial functions. For example Figure 8.28(b) shows that for $s = 0$, a note having the geometry involving trial function (8.67c) with $k = -1.139$, has the same frequency as the spherical cap ($k = 0$). As expected, the design frequency decreases as the buckling parameter s (or compressive stress) increases.

Secrets of the Steelpan 343

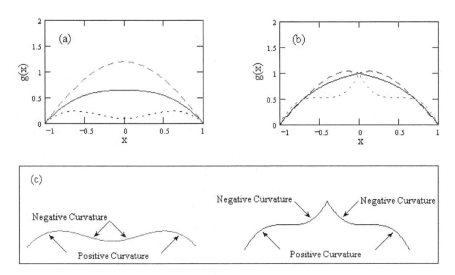

Fig. 8.26. (a) g(x) using eqn.(8.67b), for k = 0.2 (– – –); k = -0.35 (———); k = -0.9 (- - - -): (b) g(x) using eqn.(8.67c), for k = 0.6 (– – –); k = -0.35 (———); k = -2.0 (- - - -). (c) Regions of positive and negative curvature on the note surface

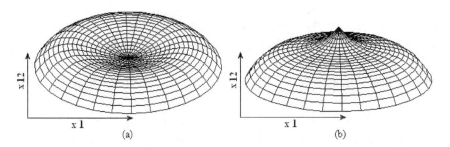

Fig. 8.27. (a) Dimple geometry for function (8.67b), k = -0.9, (b) Nipple geometry for function (8.67c), k = -2.0.

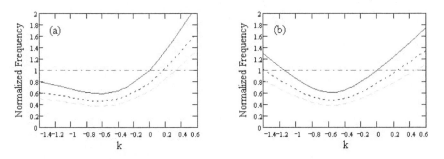

Fig. 8.28. Normalized frequency: s = 0, (———); s = 0.4, (- - -); s = 0.6, (– – –). Using function (8.67b): (b) Using function (8.67c).

With the application of the shaping function, which simulates the shaping process, in the case of shaping functions (8.67a) and (8.67b), the final rise factor is equal to $(H/h) = (H_0/h)(1 + k)$, where H_0/h is the rise factor of the initial spherical cap. When shaping function (8.67c) is used, $H = H_0$. The analytical equations takes care of the change in rise as seen from the original differential equations where the rise factor always appear as the product $(H_0/h)Q(x)$. Therefore, in seeking any relationship between note frequency and rise factor, the final value of the rise factor after shaping, H/h, must be used. Although this may seem to be just a linear scaling adjustment, not only is it correct, this quantity is of more practical importance because in practice, H/h is the measurable quantity. The initial H_0/h could be lost through shaping.

Figure 8.29 shows the frequencies for the design function $q(x) = k(1 - 2.4x^2 + 1.4x^3)$ with k taking on a range of values $-2 \leq k \leq 0.4$ while the rise factor cover the range $0 \leq H/h \leq 10$. The case $k = 0$ applies to the spherical cap. The curves illustrate the way in which frequency can vary with note shape. First refer to Figure 8.28(b), one sees that the frequency as a function of k for $H/h = 3.2$ there is a minimum at approximately k = -0.55. Second, on Figure 8.29 begin on the curve for $k = 0.4$ and work your way to each curve successively as k goes through the values 0.4, 0.2, 0, -0.1, and finally to -0.35. Notice that the frequency curves progressively moves downward and the frequency decreases for any given value of H/h. But for $k = -0.6$, the curve returns to cross the $k = -0.35$ curve and that the frequencies are increasing faster for $H/h > 6.6$. If k were to continue to decrease below –0.6 the frequency curves progressively move upwards and finally to the position shown for k = -2 (for clarity, the intermediate curves for $-0.6 > k > -2$ are not shown in Figure 8.29).

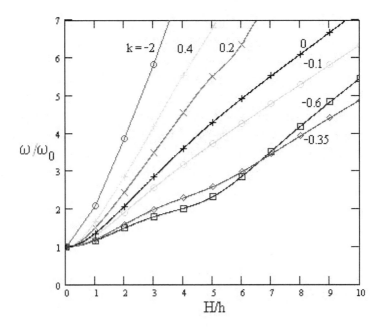

Fig. 8.29. Frequency plots of notes shaped with the shaping function $q(x) = k(x - 2.4x^2 + 1.4x^3)$. For large negative k values these notes possess a central nipple of high local stiffness.

The reduction in frequency as *k* moves from 0.4 down to –0.35 is the result of the canceling effects of positive and negative curvature. Therefore, the curves first move downward. When the central region of negative curvature dominates the note dynamics, the curves move upward. This is the reason why the curve for *k = -2* lies so high on Figure 8.29.

These changes in the frequency curves should be correlated with the changes in note shape as *k* goes from positive to negative values. Figure 8.26(b) shows what happens. The note begins to develop a central *nipple* and at *k = -2*, this nipple is well developed. The Pang instruments employ this nipple shape (often called a 'dome,' a feature seen on 'gongs' and other musical instruments found in the Gamelan orchestra of oriental origin). The nipple is a region of high negative curvature. This high curvature imparts high stiffness to the central region, making the note as a whole a dynamical area of high overall stiffness. Since the square of the frequency is directly related to the stiffness, the frequency is high for these shapes. Therefore, to use these notes on the steelpan the area of the note (true note) must be made larger than on other designs. In addition, larger compressive stresses are required along the note boundary. This could prove to be a problem on the lower frequency notes on the Standard Pan. This explains why notes of a given frequency on the Pang are larger than those found on the Standard Pan that employ positive curvature throughout without the nipple. *The need for higher compressive stresses is not a problem on the thicker nitrided steel material used on the pang. The advantage of using these nipple shapes with their stiffer central region is that they can better withstand repeated stick impacts and remain tuned for a longer time.*

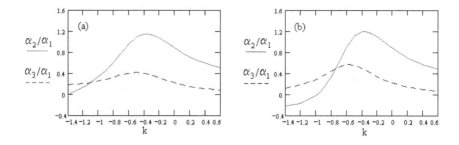

Fig. 8.30. Alpha parameter ratios: α_2/α_1, (———); α_3/α_1, (- - - -). (a) Using function (8.67b), (b) Using function (8.67c).

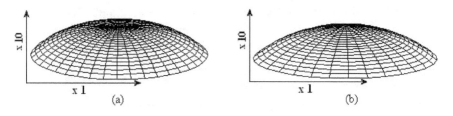

Fig. 8.31. (a) Geometry of optimal note using (8.67b), k = -0.35. (b) Geometry of optimal note using equation (8.67c), k = -0.35.

Computed values for normalized parameters α_2/α_1 and α_3/α_1 are shown in Figure 8.30. The parameter ratio α_2/α_1 peaks at approximately the same k value of -0.35 (geometries shown in Figure 8.31) while the parameter ratio α_3/α_1 peak at k values of -0.494 and -0.610 for function (8.67b) and function (8.67c) respectively. *It is clear from these results that it is not always* *possible to maximize the quadratic (α_2) and the cubic (α_3) interaction parameters simultaneously.*

8.22 Can the Note Frequency be made Amplitude Independent?

All the notes on the steelpan investigated by the present author, with the exception of notes producing the 'pung tone' (see Chapter 14), have been found to show amplitude-frequency dependence. At first the amplitude-independent condition given in equation (8.59c) may seem to be a desirable design criterion for the steelpan notes but it may be difficult to achieve on a regular and permanent basis because of the influence of the unknown in-plane loads and environmental temperature variation. By numerical computations for the case of the clamped perfect spherical shell under zero in-plane loading and zero temperature change this amplitude-independent condition has been found to be satisfied at the critical rise factor $(H_0/h)_{crit} = 0.5587$. This represents a shell that is much shallower than those found on pans ($H_0/h \approx 3$ is a typical rise factor on a Tenor pan).

For perfect shells under compressive loading and/or subject to an increase in temperature, α_1 decreases, thereby causing a *decrease* in the critical rise factor. The shell must therefore be even shallower in practice for the amplitude-independent condition to be satisfied. For rise factors in the range 2 to 4, and a wide range of shell shapes, the present author has found that it is possible to satisfy equation (8.59c). In practice, satisfying equation (8.59c) will be a tall order indeed for the Pan tuner. However, the more important aspects of frequency correctness and obtaining a sufficiently strong second mode easily take preference over any desire for amplitude-independence of the frequency. In fact, frequency-amplitude dependence is responsible for the natural sound of the instrument.

Figure 8.32 shows plots of the coefficient difference *D(k)* (refer to equation (8.58) defined by

$$D(k) = \frac{3}{4}\frac{\alpha_3}{\alpha_1} - \frac{5}{6}\left(\frac{\alpha_2}{\alpha_1}\right)^2. \tag{8.82}$$

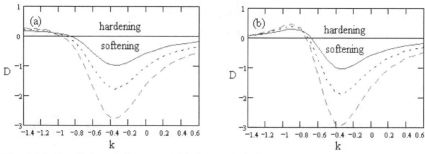

Fig. 8.32. Coefficient difference D(k) for s = 0, (—); s = 0.4, (- - - -); s = 0.6, (– – –).
(a) Using function (8.67b), (b) Using function (8.67c).

According to the conditions given in equation (8.59), when $D(k) > 0$ (the *hardening condition*), the dynamical *stiffness* of the note *increases* with displacement amplitude whereas when $D(k) < 0$ (the *softening condition*), the dynamical *stiffness decreases* with displacement amplitude. For the two design notes in Figure 18.32, in the more useful range of the design parameter, $k > 0.6$, the behavior is that of a softening spring. Frequency-amplitude dependence disappears for $k = -0.9$ for shaping function (8.67b) and $k = -0.7$ for shaping function (8.67c). The exact value of k at which this happens depends on the thermal/compressive stresses through the parameter s.

With both design functions, the use of large negative k value, as seen in Figure 8.32, produce in addition to the low values for the coupling parameters, a weak dependence of $D(k)$ on the buckling parameter s. This means that in this case, there is a weak $D(k)$-temperature dependence. For $k \approx -1.05$ in function (8.67b) and $k \approx -0.8$ and $k \approx -1.4$ in function (8.67c), $D(k)$-temperature dependence almost vanishes. There is also a sharp reduction in $D(k)$-temperature dependence as k increases positively producing very convex (upwards) shapes. *It is therefore possible to design notes with small temperature dependence. However, this condition is satisfied at parameter values that result in poor tonal quality. One must point out that this behavior is all a result of geometry and not material properties of the note. It applies to notes of all materials (metals).*

8.23 Special comments on Nipple Shaped Notes: The Pang

The Pang family of instruments is manufactured with gas-nitrided steel and characterized by the 'dome' or 'nipple' at the center of the notes. This distinguishing feature can be seen on the instruments given in Rohner and Schärer (2000), These instruments, except for the Hang, are played with rubber tipped sticks having an additional layer of felt covering for extra softness. For the Ping version (equivalent to the Tenor) the tip radius is larger than the Tenor stick being closer in size to the sticks used on the midrange Guitar pans. From equation (13.63), one sees that the increased radius (R_s) and reduced elastic modulus (E_s) the contact-time τ_c on the Ping is generally longer than the contact-time for impacts on the Tenor. The contact-width is also greater for these sticks. Longer contact-time and greater contact-width result in increased attenuation of the higher partials (see Chapter 13). Notice again on Figure 8.30b that as the k is reduced and the nipple develops that the cubic and quadratic (normalized) parameters α_2/α_1 and α_3/α_1 are reduced. A low value for the quadratic coupling parameter means low energy transfer from the fundamental (mode1) to the octave (mode2) and the twelfth (mode3). When these two effects are combined, they give to the Ping and other Pang members a mellow tone with weaker higher partials than the Tenor and other comparable pans. This is certainly, the sound of the Pang tones heard in practice.

Figure 8.32b shows that these notes are of the hardening type. In addition for $k = -2$ the quadratic parameter α_2 takes on negative values compared to the positive values for $k >-0.844$ for $H/h = 4$ (the value of k for which α_2 changes sign increases with H/h). So that for $H/h = 4$ and $k = -0.844$ the quadratic coupling parameter α_2 ($\equiv \alpha_{112}$) vanishes and so does the energy transfer from mode1 (the key note) to mode2 (the octave). The locus of points satisfying $\alpha_2 = 0$ is shown in Figure 8.33. If the quiescent state of operation of a note lies along this locus, there will be no direct energy transfer from the fundamental (key note) to the octave. The main mechanism for the octave excitation, the parametric excitation set by α_2 and internal resonance, mode1 → mode2, will be inoperative.

This design provides the tuner with a wide range of tuning possibilities on the intensities of the higher partials. The quiescent point can be set close to or away from the $\alpha_2 = 0$ curve to give the desired level of mode1 ↔ mode2 coupling. For example on Figure 8.33, if during tuning the quiescent point moves through the positions q_1 (k = -0.3), q_2 ($k = -0.9$), q_3 (k = -1.1), q_4 ($k = -1.8$), with

$H/h = 3.2$ in all cases, then, from Figure 8.30(b), the ratio α_2/α_1 takes on the values, 1.18, 0.185, -0.063, -0.207 respectively. If the note is tuned on the musical scale and the detuning parameter properly set at each location, the tone will move from strong octave (q_1), weak octave (q_2), almost inaudible octave (q_3) and finally to weak octave (q_4).

In Figure 8.33, the point at $H/h = 0$ on the curve ($\alpha_2 = 0$) does not describe a flat plate instead it describes an initially flat plate ($H_0 = 0$) reshaped by the function (8.67c) with $k = -1.8$. The shaping function (8.67c) does not alter the rise at the apex. This note, depicted in Figure 8.34, has the same α-parameter values as the flat plate, $\alpha_1 = 8.696958$, $\alpha_2 = 0$ and $\alpha_3 = 4.85168$. This note, of unusual shape, will not be found on the steelpan because of the absence of quadratic coupling as required for a strong octave and reasonably strong twelfth.

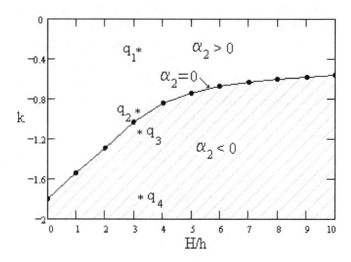

Fig. 8.33. Parameter Space showing regions of positive and negative (shaded region) coupling constant α_2 separated by the locus of points along which $\alpha_2 = 0$, for the shaping function (8.67c). Trial quiescent points are denoted by q_n for $H/h = 3.2$.

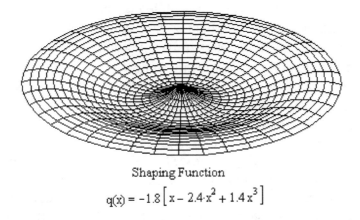

Shaping Function

$q(x) = -1.8 \left[x - 2.4 \cdot x^2 + 1.4 x^3 \right]$

Fig. 8.34. Modeled note (clamped along the boundary), shaped by the function $q(x)$ from an initially flat plate. This note, with $k = -1.8$, has the same α_1, α_2 and α_3 values as the flat plate. This note also has the same fundamental frequency (keynote) as the flat circular plate (clamped at the boundary).

In Section 8.4 the quadratic coupling parameter is defined as

$$\alpha_2 = (1+v)\left(\frac{H_0}{h}\right)(M_5 - 2M_6),$$

with

$$M_5 = \int_0^1 \left[\left(\frac{d\psi}{dx}\right)^2 - \left(\frac{d}{dx} + \frac{1}{x}\right) G \right] Q\psi \, x \, dx,$$

$$M_6 = \int_0^1 \left(\frac{d}{dx} + \frac{1}{x}\right) \left[Q\psi \frac{d\psi}{dx} - \frac{d\psi}{dx}\left(\frac{d}{dx} + \frac{v}{x}\right) E \right] \psi \, x \, dx,$$

where E, G and Q are all functions determined by the geometrical form of the note surface. Observe that the integrals M_5 and M_6 are determined only by the form of the note surface and the mode shape ψ for mode1. The quadratic parameter vanishes, $\alpha_2 = 0$, when $H_0 = 0$ (the flat plate) or for the dome shaped notes when $M_5 = 2 M_6$. The region of Figure 8.33 where $\alpha_2 > 0$, satisfies $M_5 > 2 M_6$, the region where $\alpha_2 < 0$ satisfies $M_5 < 2 M_6$ while the boundary between these two regions, the line along which $\alpha_2 = 0$, satisfies $M_5 = 2 M_6$.

It is shown in Section 8.10 that for notes with $\alpha_2 > 0$ it is easier to distort the note surface downward while for $\alpha_2 < 0$ it is easier to distort the note surface upward. For $\alpha_2 = 0$, the distortions (vibrations) are symmetrical about the quiescent (rest) point (similar to the flat-plate vibrations).

In addition if the impact point is at the apex of the note then since nodal lines for mode2 and mode3 run through this point these modes are not excited (except as discussed in Chapter 13, at very low levels because of the effect of losses on the nodal lines and asymmetry in the contact force over the contact-area). However because $\alpha_3 \neq 0$, mode3 (if properly tuned) can be weakly excited by mode1 through cubic interaction. Note that $\alpha_3 \equiv \beta_{111,3}$ in the MDOF analysis. Weak coupling between mode1 and mode2 then becomes possible by the quadratic interaction between mode1 and mode3 (through the parameter α_{132} computed in the MDOF analysis not in the SDOF analysis used here). To initially excite the octave or twelfth to any significant degree with this design will require the impact point to be *off the apex*. However, the parametric resonance, mode1 x mode1→ mode2, will still be inoperable.

The Pang tones are not unlike the tones produced by early steelpans of the 1950's with their 'simple tuning' which did not rely on strong octaves and higher partials. These Early Pans, like the Pang, were also played with sticks having larger tips than present day Tenor sticks and were also covered in felt or entirely wrapped in cotton cloth.

CHAPTER 9

Thermal and Compressive Stresses: Damping: Microstructural Control and Engineering Designs

9.1 Introduction

In this Chapter the effects of Thermal and Compressive stresses and temperature itself on note dynamics are analyzed. This all-metal instrument is subject to frequency and other tonal variations as ambient temperature varies and as the internal stresses relax due to aging. The latter effect is mainly noticeable immediately after tuning since the effect decreases with time. We also examine the mechanisms of damping and its dependence on the microstructure of the steel material used in pan production. The Chapter closes with some engineering note designs.

9.1.1 The Tuning Temperature

At this point it will be appropriate to formally define the *Tuning Temperature* T_t, although this terminology was already used in Chapter 8. Because of its importance, a formal definition is given:

- The **Tuning Temperature** T_t, is that temperature at which a steelpan was last tuned.

Since note frequencies and modal couplings are functions of temperature the author recommends that the Tuning Temperature should be made available to the owner or player of the instrument.

9.2 Dependence of Frequency on In-plane Stress

When a note makes a transition, $\Sigma_i \to \Sigma_f$, between two states of stress Σ_i and Σ_f produced thermally and/or by changes to the internal residual stresses of the system, the fractional frequency shift is determined as follows: If the initial and final states of the note are characterized by normalized compressive and thermal forces per unit length $(\check{N}_c + \check{N}_T)_i$ and $(\check{N}_c + \check{N}_T)_f$ along the note boundary, the following relations exist for the radian frequencies

$$\omega_i^2 = \alpha_{0i}(1-s_i), \qquad \omega_f^2 = \alpha_{0f}(1-s_f)$$

$$s_i = (\check{N}_c + \check{N}_T)_i \frac{M_{4i}}{\alpha_{0i}}, \quad s_f = (\check{N}_c + \check{N}_T)_f \frac{M_{4f}}{\alpha_{0f}}.$$

(9.1a-d)

If the change in temperature and/or the compressive stress is sufficiently small, one can write

$$\omega_f^2 - \omega_i^2 = (\omega_f + \omega_i)(\omega_f - \omega_i) \approx 2\omega_i \delta\omega,$$
$$(\check{N}_c + \check{N}_T)_f - (\check{N}_c + \check{N}_T)_i = \delta\check{N}.$$

(9.2a, b)

Using the expressions in equations (9.1) and (9.2) one gets for $s \neq 1$ the fractional change in frequency

$$\frac{\delta\omega}{\omega_i} = \underbrace{-\frac{\delta\check{N} M_{4f}}{2(1-s_i)\alpha_{0i}}}_{\text{due to change in note stiffness}} + \underbrace{\frac{1}{2(1-s_i)}\left\{\left(\frac{\alpha_{0f}}{\alpha_{0i}}-1\right) + s_i\left(1-\frac{M_{4f}}{M_{4i}}\right)\right\}}_{\text{due to change in note shape}}.$$

(9.3)

In response to changes to the in-plane stress, the first term on the right side of equation (9.3) represents the component of fractional frequency shift due to the change in *note stiff*ness, while the second term is that due to the change in *note shape*. Recall that the first mode stiffness goes to zero for $s = 1$ this means that as s approaches unity the change in frequency becomes very large. In any event equation (9.3) is not applicable for $s = 1$. The first term is numerically larger than the second term but they are both of the same order of magnitude. If the second term is omitted, the frequency shift will be overestimated by up to x10 (one order of magnitude) depending on the initial note geometry and how far apart the initial and final states are in phase space.

Although equation (9.3) was derived for the single mode system, it is written in *parameterized form* so it will apply to other modes on the note. This parameterized form will hold generally and exactly if there is no coupling between the modes. However, since the steelpan is usually tuned to obtain good modulation (detuning parameters $|\sigma_1|, |\sigma_2| > 0$), the mode-mode coupling is sufficiently weakened to allow application of equation (9.3) to all the tuned modes on the pan. The mode shapes for the higher modes are asymmetrical however so this will call for modifications to the expressions used for calculating the parameters in equation (9.3).

Changes in temperature are equivalent to changes in the compressive force. However, if the exact cause for the change of state is known then one can write the fractional frequency shift for $s \neq 1$ as

Thermal:

$$\frac{\delta\omega}{\omega_i} = -\frac{\alpha_T \, \delta T (1+\upsilon)}{2(1-s_i)} \left(\frac{a}{h}\right)^2 \frac{M_{4f}}{\alpha_{0i}} + \frac{1}{2(1-s_i)}\left\{\left(\frac{\alpha_{0f}}{\alpha_{0i}}-1\right) + s_i\left(1-\frac{M_{4f}}{M_{4i}}\right)\right\},$$

Compressive:

$$\frac{\delta\omega}{\omega_i} = \frac{\delta\sigma_c(1-\upsilon^2)}{2(1-s_i)E}\left(\frac{a}{h}\right)^2 \frac{M_{4f}}{\alpha_{0i}} + \frac{1}{2(1-s_i)}\left\{\left(\frac{\alpha_{0f}}{\alpha_{0i}}-1\right) + s_i\left(1-\frac{M_{4f}}{M_{4i}}\right)\right\},$$

(9.4a,b)

where δT and $\delta\sigma_c$ are the changes in temperature and compressive stress, respectively. For an increase in temperature δT is positive while an increase in compressive stress makes $\delta\sigma$ negative. I should point out that since σ_c is negative an increase in compressive stress actually refers to the modulus of $\delta\sigma_c$. Equations (9.4a, b) are the SDOF versions of equations (23) and (24) respectively in Achong (1999b) in a form that allows for easier computation.

For changes in temperature from T_i to T_f, one has the exact relation

$$\omega_f^2 = \omega_i^2 + \left\{(\alpha_{0f} - \alpha_{0i}) + s_i\alpha_{0i}\left(1 - \frac{M_{4f}}{M_{4i}}\right)\right\} - \alpha_T(T_f - T_i)(1+\upsilon)\left(\frac{a}{h}\right)^2 M_{4f}. \quad (9.5)$$

Since the approximate expression for frequency in Hertz is given by

$$f = \frac{\omega}{2\pi}\left(\frac{Eh^2}{\rho a^4(1-\upsilon^2)}\right)^{\frac{1}{2}}, \quad (9.6)$$

multiplying both sides of equation (9.5) by $Eh^2/\{4\pi^2\rho a^4(1-v^2)\}$ gives the relation between the initial and final frequencies f_i and f_f as

$$f_f^2 = f_i^2 + \left[\left\{(\alpha_{0f} - \alpha_{0i}) + s_i\alpha_{0i}\left(1 - \frac{M_{4f}}{M_{4i}}\right)\right\} - \alpha_T(T_f - T_i)(1+\upsilon)\left(\frac{a}{h}\right)^2 M_{4f}\right]\frac{Eh^2}{4\pi^2\rho a^4(1-\upsilon^2)}, \quad (9.7)$$

Corrections to equation (9.6) for ellipsoidal notes on elliptical planforms are given in the *Pan Maker's Formula*, equation (3.51), but all this is not necessary here. However for those who would like to see the complete version of equation (9.7) based on the Panmaker's Formula, here it is

$$f_f^2 = f_i^2 + \left[\left\{(\alpha_{0f} - \alpha_{0i}) + s_i\alpha_{0i}\left(1 - \frac{M_{4f}}{M_{4i}}\right)\right\} - \alpha_T(T_f - T_i)(1+\upsilon)\left(\frac{a}{h}\right)^2 M_{4f}\right]$$

$$\times \frac{Eh^2\left[3 - 6\frac{a}{b} + 4\left(\frac{a}{b}\right)^2\right]}{4\pi^2(ab)^2\rho(1-\upsilon^2)}.$$

We continue our discussion using the simpler form given in equation (9.7). Equation (9.7) describes the frequency change for a tuned (or untuned) note as a function of operating temperature. Generally, *a well-tuned steelpan will perform optimally at the Tuning Temperature T_t.*

Equation (9.7) has the parabolic form $y^2 = a_0 - a_1 x$, which is plotted in Figure 9.1 for arbitrary values of a_0 and a_1. Expressions for a_0 and a_1 can be obtained from equation (9.7). Since the note frequencies take on only positive values and the temperature covers a limited range, the solutions for the note frequencies are found only in the portion of the curve indicated by the solid line in Figure 9.1a. When equation (9.7) is plotted on a graph of f_f versus T_f, the graph displays the form sketched in Figure 9.7b for an arbitrary set of parameters. Equation (9.7) predicts a *decrease in frequency with increasing temperature as well as an increase in slope of the curve with temperature*; since the slope is a negative quantity, this means that the modulus of the slope increases.

Remark: *The term a_0 is a complicated function which varies slowly with temperature (due mainly to changes in note surface shape) and, in practice, is not strictly constant in the plot of f_f versus T_f.*

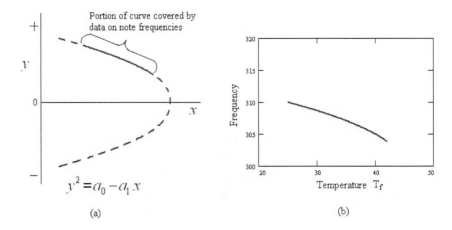

Fig. 9.1. Graphs showing the variation of note frequency with temperature. (a) General shape of the frequency-temperature response curve. (b) A typical response.

9.3 Dependence of Young's Modulus and Poisson's Ratio on Temperature

The frequency of a vibrating note is dependent on the elastic constants of the note material. So far, it has been implicitly assumed that the elastic moduli and Poisson's ratio for the steel material are independent of temperature. There is not a wealth of information in the literature on the variation of the elastic moduli of carbon steel with temperature. Data is available in a number of handbooks, but often only over a limited temperature range. Koster and Metallk (1948) produced reliable data for a number of metals over a wide temperature range. Their results show that the elastic modulus for steel in the temperature range 0°C to 200°C decreases at the rate of approximately -0.05 GPa per degree. For $E = 207$ GPa at 20°C this gives a temperature coefficient of $\delta E = -2.42 \times 10^{-4}$ °C^{-1}. On using equation (9.6), since frequency is proportional to $E^{\frac{1}{2}}$, the fractional change in frequency resulting from the temperature dependence of E is

$$\frac{\delta f}{f} = \frac{\delta E}{2E}$$
$$= -\frac{2.42 \times 10^{-4} \, \delta T}{2} \qquad (9.8)$$
$$= -1.21 \times 10^{-4} \, \delta T.$$

Obtaining sufficiently precise measurements of Poisson's ratio that allows for temperature dependence is particularly difficult. Poisson's ratio, defined as $v = E/2G - 1$, a simple function of the *elastic modulus* (E) to *shear modulus* (G) ratio E/G, reflects the type of interatomic-bonding in the material better than any elastic constant. The Poisson's ratio can be found by combining direct measurements of E and G as functions of temperature for the same sample piece. This method is however inherently less accurate than the method which involves striking a disc test-piece and measuring the vibration frequencies of the axisymmetric 'diaphragm' mode and the lower principal mode. The ratio of these frequencies, coupled with the disc thickness to diameter ratio, gives the Poisson's ratio.

One of the best methods of measuring the dependence of elastic constants on temperature is the *ultrasonic pulse sing-around method* (Fukuhara and Sanpel 1993). By ultrasonic pulse excitation, longitudinal (compressive) and transverse (shear) waves are generated in a rod-shaped metal specimen heated in an inert atmosphere of Argon. In order to prevent spurious signals by *mode conversion* (which tends to occur at the ends or edges of vibrating bodies), the far end of the rod is terminated with an impedance matching ultrasonic waveguide. Measured mode velocities, compressive v_p and shear v_s, are then used to calculate the elastic moduli and Poisson's ratio using the following relations

$$\rho v_s^2 = G, \quad \rho v_p^2 = \left(\frac{4G - E}{3G - E}\right) G, \quad v = \frac{1}{2} \frac{\left(\frac{v_p}{v_s}\right)^2 - 2}{\left(\frac{v_p}{v_s}\right)^2 - 1}$$

where ρ is the density, G is the shear modulus, E is Young's modulus and ν is Poisson's ratio.

Table 9.1

Material	Chemical composition (mass %)							Hardness (HB)
	C	Si	Mn	P	S	Cr	Ni	
AISI SAE 1010	0.11	0.24	0.65	0.017	0.01	0.12	-	83

C — Carbon, Mn — Manganese, Si — Silicon, P — Phosphorus, S — Sulphur, Cr — Chromium, Ni — Nickel.

The carbon steel used by Fukuhara and Sanpel is specified in Table 9.1. The composition shown here is close to the compositions found on the low-carbon steel used in pan construction. The reported results give:

Young's modulus 206.6 GPa at 20 °C, 158.7 GPa at 600 °C; Shear modulus 80.9 GPa at 20°C, 60.7 GPa at 600°C.

If linearity is assumed over the temperature range, the temperature coefficients for Young's modulus and shear modulus are given by the respective values,

$$\delta_E = \Delta E /(E \Delta T) = -3.993 \times 10^{-4} \,°C^{-1},$$
$$\delta_G = \Delta G /(G \Delta T) = -4.262 \times 10^{-4} \,°C^{-1}.$$

If the temperature coefficient of Poisson's ratio is defined as $\delta_\nu = \delta\nu/\nu_i$ one obtains for a temperature change $\Delta T = T_f - T_i$ in degree Celsius

$$v_i = \frac{E}{2G} - 1,$$

$$v_f = \frac{E(1+\delta_E \Delta T)}{2G(1+\delta_G \Delta T)} - 1,$$

$$\delta v = v_f - v_i = \frac{E}{2G}(\delta_E - \delta_G)\Delta T,$$

$$\frac{\delta v}{v_i} = \left(1 + \frac{1}{v_i}\right)(\delta_E - \delta_G)\Delta T,$$

finally
$$\delta_v = \left(1 + \frac{1}{v_i}\right)(\delta_E - \delta_G) \, °C^{-1}. \qquad (9.9)$$

If Young's modulus and the shear modulus track each other closely so that $\delta_E = \delta_G$, then, from equation (9.9), the Poisson's ratio temperature coefficient δ_v is zero. However, this is not the case for low-carbon steel, where these two elastic moduli decrease and Poisson's ratio increases with increasing temperature. To see this, we need to be a bit more technical (for just a moment). The fact is the Poisson's ratio of low-carbon steel is linked to its covalent bonding. The observation of a comparatively large *positive* temperature coefficient for Poisson's ratio would therefore suggest the activation of a shear mode in deformation at high temperatures. Both δ_E and δ_G are *negative*, so look again at equation (9.9), in order for δ_v to be positive, one must have $|\delta_G| > |\delta_E|$. This condition is satisfied in the data for the AISI SAE 1010 steel. The results are therefore in accordance with the activation of a shear mode at high temperatures and a positive Poisson's ratio coefficient (but these technical details need not concern us any further). We can now apply the results directly to the low-carbon steel used on the pan.

By using equation (9.6) and $\omega_i^2 = \alpha_{0i}(1-s_i)$ together with $\alpha_0 = \frac{1}{12}M_1 + 8(1+v)\left(\frac{H_0}{h}\right)^2\left(M_2 - \frac{1}{2}(1+v)M_3\right)$ one can easily show that a change in v brings about a fractional frequency change given by

$$\frac{\delta f}{f_i} = \frac{v_i \, \delta v}{(1-v_i^2)} + \frac{4\delta v}{\alpha_{0i}}\left(\frac{H_0}{h}\right)^2 \{M_2 - (1+v_i)M_3\}, \qquad (9.10)$$

where the second term arises from the dependence of α_0 on v. Combining equations (9.8), (9.9) and (9.10) gives the expressions for the fractional frequency shift resulting from changes to Young's modulus and Poisson's ratio for the low-carbon steel (and other metals that are useable for pan construction) notes on the steelpan as

$$\frac{\delta f}{f_i} = \left[\frac{v_i^2}{(1-v_i^2)} + \frac{4v_i}{\alpha_{0i}}\left(\frac{H_0}{h}\right)^2 \{M_2 - (1+v_i)M_3\}\right]\left(1+\frac{1}{v_i}\right)(\delta_E - \delta_G)\Delta T + \frac{\delta_E \Delta T}{2}, \qquad (9.11)$$

for a temperature change of ΔT °C. If the nominal value of v_i for steel is taken as 0.29, using the temperature coefficients for SAE 1010 low-carbon steel one can write

$$\frac{\delta f}{f_i} = 1.2 \times 10^{-4} \left[0.0918 + \frac{1.16}{\alpha_{0i}}\left(\frac{H_0}{h}\right)^2 (M_2 - 1.29 M_3)\right]\Delta T - 1.997 \times 10^{-4} \Delta T \qquad (9.12)$$

For an increase in temperature, the first term on the right side of equation (9.12) resulting from the change in Poisson's ratio, *increases* the frequency while the second term resulting from the change in Young's modulus *decreases* the frequency. It is therefore necessary to take the analysis a step further to see which way the temperature dependence of the elastic parameters affects the note frequency.

For the notes modeled in Sections 9.11.2 and 9.11.4, it will be shown that in the first term on the right side of equation (9.12), the factor in square brackets is always much less than unity; typically in the interval 0.10 to 0.13. According to the mechanisms considered so far, the effect of temperature on the note frequency through the temperature dependence of the elastic constants, is therefore largely due to the changes in Young's modulus (the second term on the right side of equation (9.12)). Frequency changes due to the temperature dependence of Poisson's ratio, is an order of magnitude smaller.

The linear shift expressed by equation (9.12) due to the temperature dependence of Poisson's ratio and Young's modulus can be incorporated into equation (9.7) with the result

$$f_f^2 = f_i^2 + \left[\left\{(\alpha_{0f} - \alpha_{0i}) + s_i \alpha_{0i}\left(1 - \frac{M_{4f}}{M_{4i}}\right)\right\} - \alpha_T \Delta T(1+\upsilon_i)\left(\frac{a}{h}\right)^2 M_{4f}\right] \frac{E_i h^2 [1+(2\varphi\delta_\nu + \delta_E)\Delta T]}{4\pi^2 \rho a^4 (1-\upsilon_i^2)}$$

,
(9.13)

with

$$\Delta T = T_f - T_i, \quad \varphi = 0.0918 + \frac{1.16}{\alpha_{0i}}\left(\frac{H_0}{h}\right)^2 (M_2 - 1.29 M_3),$$

where, on typical notes, $0.10 \leq \varphi \leq 0.13$ depending on note shape and boundary conditions.

9.4 Including the Effects due to Direct Linear Expansion/Contraction (Scaling) of the Note

There is a major advantage of using the dimensionless procedure; only when it is necessary to return to real time in seconds or lengths in meters is it necessary to re-normalize so that standard units can be used. Because of the use of dimensionless terms and expressions throughout the analysis carried out up to this point, we have avoided the scaling problems that arise when working with different dimensions from note to note (pan to pan) and to dimensional changes due to thermal expansion or contraction. For the isotropic materials used in pan making, length ratios are invariant under temperature changes. The only quantities in the frequency equation that are subject to scaling due to temperature changes are the note thickness h, the note size a, and the density ρ where they appear in equation (9.13) as the factor $h^2/\rho a^4$. Because density varies as (length)$^{-3}$, the factor $h^2/\rho a^4$ scales *linearly* with length. The factor $h^2/\rho a^4$ must therefore be replaced by $h^2(1+\alpha_T \Delta T)/\rho a^4$. This refinement puts the frequency equation in the form

$$f_f^2 = f_i^2 + \left[\left\{(\alpha_{0f} - \alpha_{0i}) + s_i\alpha_{0i}\left(1 - \frac{M_{4f}}{M_{4i}}\right)\right\} - \alpha_T \Delta T(1 + v_i)\left(\frac{a}{h}\right)^2 M_{4f}\right] \frac{E_i h^2[1 + (2\varphi \delta_v + \delta_E + \alpha_T)\Delta T]}{4\pi^2 \rho a^4 (1 - v_i^2)}$$

(9.14)

where very small terms appearing as products of temperature coefficients δ_v, δ_E and α_T are neglected. Observe that if one uses the modified form of the equation, corrected according to the *Pan Maker's Formula*, $h^2(3 - \frac{6a}{b} + 4\left(\frac{a}{b}\right)^2)^{\frac{1}{2}}/\rho(ab)^2$ scales the same way with temperature as $h^2/\rho a^4$ where *the aspect ratio a/b (a dimensipnless quantity) is temperature invariant,*.

In equation (9.14), for the sum of coefficients $(2\varphi \delta_v + \delta_E + \alpha_T)$, one has

(i) the coefficient of linear expansion for steel $\alpha_T = +1.2 \times 10^{-5}$ °C^{-1},
(ii) the temperature coefficient of Young's modulus $\delta_E = -3.993 \times 10^{-4}$ °C^{-1}
(iii) the effective coefficient due to temperature dependence of Poisson's ratio $2\varphi\delta_v \approx +(2.4 \text{ to } 3.12) \times 10^{-5}$ °C^{-1}.

This gives for the coefficient sum,

$$(2\varphi\delta_v + \delta_E + \alpha_T) = (-3.56 \text{ to } -3.63) \times 10^{-4} \text{ °C}^{-1},$$

which is not significantly different from the temperature coefficient for the Young's modulus. One therefore finds that dimensional scaling (expansion or contraction) due to temperature changes does not have a significant effect on the note frequency when compared to other larger effects. Even the change brought about by the temperature dependence of Poisson's ratio is more significant. The layman's statement that "the note frequencies fall as the steelpan is heated because the notes expand and grow larger" has some elements of truth but it overlooks the more significant thermal mechanisms.

In Chapter 12 which deals with acoustic radiation it is shown that the free-air medium produces a loading on both sides of the vibrating note. Due to changes in air density with temperature, this introduces an additional frequency shift which brings a modification to equation (9.14) giving it its final form

$$f_f^2 = f_i^2 - 4.572 \cdot 10^{-7} f_i^2 \frac{a}{h} \Delta T$$
$$+ \left[\left\{ (\alpha_{0f} - \alpha_{0i}) + s_i \alpha_{0i} \left(1 - \frac{M_{4f}}{M_{4i}} \right) \right\} - \alpha_T \Delta T (1 + \upsilon_i) \left(\frac{a}{h} \right)^2 M_{4f} \right] \frac{E_i h^2 [1 + (2\varphi \delta_v + \delta_E + \alpha_T) \Delta T]}{4\pi^2 \rho a^4 (1 - \upsilon_i^2)}$$

(9.15)

The modification introduced by acoustic radiation is given by the second term on the right side of (9.15) where one sees that notes with larger a/h ratios (as found on the bass) are more greatly affected. While the factor $(-4.572 \cdot 10^{-7})$ makes this term a small correction to the frequency shift, the presence of this term in equation (9.15) is important since on the pan, as a musical instrument, we are mainly interested in the acoustical radiation. Once again we see that the acoustical radiation into 'free air' plays a minor role in the note dynamics! However, if conditions are set up to affect the 'free air' nature of the air medium such as the incorporation horns (or partial horns when some surrounding or nearby structure is incorporated) or acoustic resonators (pipes for example), the coupling between the note and the 'restricted medium' will be greater (see Section 12.22).

Some Important Observations: In Section 14.25 it is shown that for the notes on the high-end pans tuned in the standard fashion Keynote-Octave-Twelfth, the musical interval between the Twelfth (Fifth above the octave) and the Octave is approximately equal to $(a/b)^2$ where a/b is the aspect ratio of the note. Similarly, in Section 14.26 it is shown that for the bass tuned in the fashion Keynote-Octave-Third, the interval between the Third and the Octave is also approximately equal to $(a/b)^2$. These two results are described as the $5/4^{ths}$-*Law* and the $9/8^{ths}$-*Rule* respectively. For our present purposes, we make the observation that since the aspect ratio a/b is dimensionless (being the ratio of two lengths defining the elliptical planform of the true note), to the extent that the $5/4^{ths}$-Law and the $9/8^{ths}$-Rule are obeyed, **changes in temperature will not affect the musical interval between the Twelfth and the Octave on the high-end pans and the interval between the Third and the Octave on the**

low-end pans. This constancy of the musical interval occurs despite changes to the frequencies of all the partials on the temperature affected note. In addition, the *Steelpan Law of Ratios* (see Section 14.25) will be unaffected by changes in temperature. The relative amplitudes of the partials will however be affected by temperature because the non-linear coefficients that define the mutual coupling of the partials are all subject to change under temperature variations. ***The timbre of a pan note is therefore a function of temperature.*** [However, I must qualify my statements with the technical refinement that the pan as a whole is subject to changes in environmental temperature and as a result, the *Stress Fields* over the pan face and *Hoop Stress* on the chime and skirt will all be affected. This can produce stress changes on each note and result in additional frequency shifts — an effect associated with the *ubiquitous Pan Jumbie* (see Section 17.20). The temperature dependence of the partials is therefore very complex so that the *Steelpan Law of Ratios*, the $5/4^{ths}$-*Law* and the $9/8^{ths}$-*Rule* are all subject to some dependence on temperature but the effect is expected to be quite small for reasonable changes in temperature to which the instruments are expected to be subjected in normal use.]

9.5. Experimental Observations

Foreword: *In the discussions that follow, the terms 'close harmonicity' and 'harmonicity' will be used in describing the ratios of higher modes to the fundamental. However, the use of these terms <u>does not</u> imply that the higher modes are harmonics of the fundamental mode. The normal modes on the steelpan, tuned or untuned, are not natural harmonics of the fundamental mode.*

The experiments described here were all performed on notes selected on the basis that they showed larger than normal detuning on the octave. The purpose for this was to reveal the presence of parametric modes if they appeared and to track their movements in the frequency domain as the temperature is varied. It is very difficult to resolve the much weaker parametric modes from the normal modes on notes with small, even normal detuning because of the merging of the spectral peaks.

9.5.1 Thermal Effects on Frequency Spectra

To confirm the theoretical results obtained in the previous Sections, steelpans were subjected to temperature changes in the range 23.5 °C to 57 °C, and at each *thermal state*, the surface velocity data generated by stick impact were recorded. The experimental method for data collection and handling can be found in Chapter 4. Displacement data were computed by integration while the spectral data were generated by taking the Fourier transform. The frequency modulations associated with the non-linear modal interactions are expected to be much smaller than the thermally/compressively induced shifts in frequency. This makes it possible to obtain the frequency shifts from the Fourier Transform averaged over the entire tone duration.

9.5.1.1 The Tenor

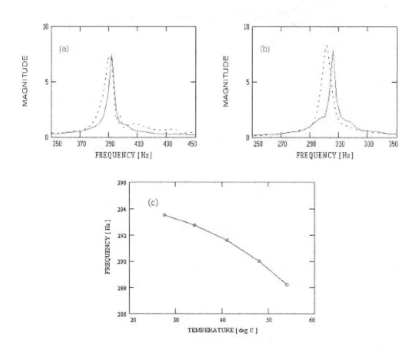

Fig. 9.2. First mode peaks on the tenor for (a) the **G**$_4$ note at 27.5° C (—) and at 54° C (- - -), (b) the **D**$_4$ note at 27.5° C (—) and at 54° C (- - -); (c) frequency of the **D**$_4$ note as a function of temperature.

Figures (9.2a, b) show the shifts in first-mode peaks for a G_4 note (elliptical planform minor axis x major axis ≈ 10 cm x 13 cm) and the D_4 note (planform: 10.5 cm x 13 cm) on the tenor. The G_4 note (393.2 Hz at 27.5 °C) shifted downward in frequency at a rate of -0.014 Hz/deg to present a -0.1 % change in frequency at the final temperature of 54 °C. The D_4 note dropped from 293.5 Hz at 27.5 °C to 288.2 at 54 °C, representing an average rate of -0.2 Hz/deg and an overall frequency change of -1.8 %.

The frequency of the D_4 note on the same tenor, as a function of temperarure is shown in Fgure 9.2(c). The experimental results in Figure 9.2(c) confirm the theoretical predictions of Section 9.2. These rates of frequency decrease with increasing temperature are typical of the values for notes on other tenor pans.

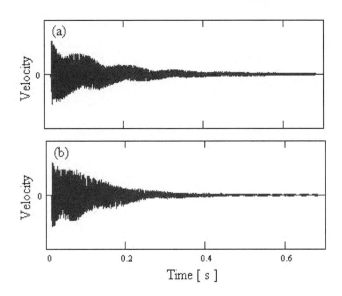

Fig. 9.3. Velocity-time graphs for the G_4 tenor note at (a) 27.5° C and (b) 54° C. Observe the changes in the amplitude profile — effects that produce changes in timbre. Compared with (a), the tone in (b) has been degraded by the increase in temperature of the pan.

A secondary result, observable on the spectral data, is the broadening of the spectral peaks as the temperature is increased. Corresponding to this increase in frequency bandwidth, there was a reduction in the duration of the sounded tone for both these notes.

This is of importance because it implies an increase in damping as the temperature increases.

The note surface velocity-time histories for the G_4 note are shown in Figure 9.3. The data obtained at 27.5°C represents the expected profiles for a well-modulated note (see details in Chapters 4 - 6) under normal (tropical) temperatures. At 54°C, the modulations are clearly different, indicating, from the shape of the profile, that tonality (measured by the depth of modulation) has deteriorated. The frequencies of the first mode and second mode shifted from their initial values at 27.5°C of f_1 = 393.2 Hz, f_2 = 792.3 Hz to final values at 54°C of f_1 = 392.8 Hz, f_2 = 790.0 Hz. The frequency ratio f_2/f_1, shifted from 2.015 to 2.011, representing a change in the *detuning parameter*. The detuning parameter together with the *coupling parameters* (see details and other dependencies in Chapters 4 – 6) determines the structure of the tone. The change in modal damping is barely discernible here from the tone duration but can be seen in the frequency bandwidth analysis.

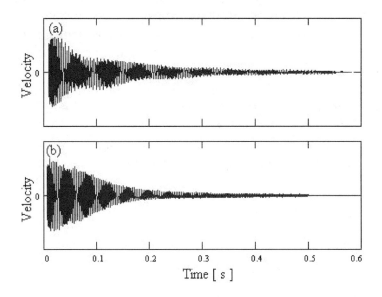

Fig. 9.4. Velocity-time graphs for the D_4 tenor note at (a) 27.5° and (b) 54° C. Observe the reduction in tone duration and changes in the shape of the amplitude profile as the temperature is increased.

In Figure 9.4 the note surface velocity-time histories for the D_4 note show similar changes in the tonal characteristics with temperature. On this note the frequency ratio f_2/f_1, shifted from 2.018 to 2.039 representing a greater change in the detuning parameter. ***The tonal structure progressively deteriorates as the temperature is increased above the Tuning Temperatute.***

The parametric modes were not resolved on either of these two tenor notes.

9.5.1.2 The Bass

Figure 9.5 shows the complete spectra (below 400 Hz) at 27.5 °C (full line) and at 56 °C (dotted line) for the $\mathbf{F}_2^{\#}$ note (planform minor x major axes = 18 cm x 27 cm) on a bass pan. The *aspect ratio* for this note is equal to $\frac{27}{18} = 1.5$, a value that does not comply with the $9/8^{ths}$-Rule for the bass or even the $5/4^{ths}$-Law for the high-end pans (see Sections 14.25 and 14.26). This means that one can expect large detuning on the higher partials. This is exactly what I needed here in order to properly resolve any parametric excitations from the normal modes. This note was chosen specially for this reason.

On the scale of Figure 9.5, peak broadening is unobservable but by plotting the velocity data as in Figure 9.6, one can observe the decrease in duration when compared with the longer persistence of the vibrations at the lower temperature. Also by comparing the two plots in Figure 9.6, notice the changes to the modulated velocity envelopes. These changes result from the thermally produced modifications to the modal coupling and, more importantly, the increase in vibration damping with temperature.

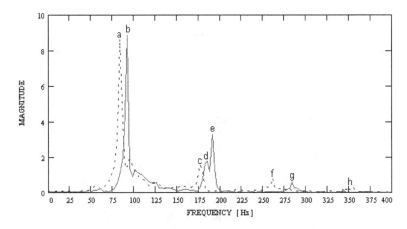

Fig. 9.5. Spectra of the $F_2^{\#}$ bass note at 27.5° C (—) and at 56° C (- - -).

In Figure 9.5, the first mode (key-note) peak labeled b, at 92.40 Hz is shifted downward (peak a) to 84.34 Hz. This represents a rate of -0.28 Hz/deg or a frequency change of -8.7 %. The second mode (octave) peak e (191.19 Hz), is shifted down to c (177.57 Hz) for a change of -7.1 %. The third mode g (284.67 Hz) is shifted down to f (261.35 Hz) for a change of -8.2 %.

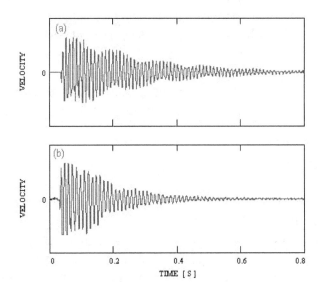

Fig. 9.6. Velocity time graphs for the $F_2^{\#}$ bass note at (a) 27.5° C and (b) 56° C. Amplitude modulations (related to the timbre) and tone durations are clearly modified by temperature as seen on this note.

In Figure 9.5, the peak labeled d (184.60 Hz) on the 27.5 °C data corresponds to the *parametrically generated* vibration controlled by the quadratic coupling coefficient $\alpha_{11,2}$. This non-linear mode will be observed with small detuning close to $2\omega_1$ ($\equiv 2 \times 92.40 = 184.80$ Hz). At 56 °C, the corresponding parametric mode is not observable and the octave is much weaker both of these observations indicate a reduction in $\alpha_{11,2}$. The cubic parametric modes are unobservable at both temperatures. Notice however the appearance at 56 °C, of a fourth mode h, at 354.14 Hz, very likely a normal mode as the frequency is not close to multiples of the first mode frequency or any linear combination of lower frequencies.

The frequency ratio f_2/f_1 on the $F_2^\#$ note increases from 2.069 at 27.5 °C to 2.105 at 56 °C. Closer harmonicity (smaller detuning) will be required were this a note on a higher frequency pan, such as the tenor or on a better tuned bass. The present note displays relatively weak second mode as a result of this lack of close harmonicity and results in a reduction in energy transferred between first and second modes. In any event, dominating second modes are not required on the bass. This particular $F_2^\#$ note was chosen for display here because it clearly shows the *parametric mode* (labeled d). If the detuning on the second mode was made smaller then the profile for d would have merged with the profile for the second mode, e, making it impossible to resolve the parametric mode.

As predicted by equation (9.4), the percentage frequency shifts on the bass (with larger *a/h* ratios) are consistently higher than those on the tenor.

9.5.1.3 The Cello

Similar observations were made on a steelpan cello at temperatures of 23.5 °C, 34.5 °C, 44 °C, 50 °C and 57 °C. This particular pan was selected not on the basis of tonal qualities but rather to clearly show the appearance of parametric excitations. On a well-tuned cello with good tonal qualities, because of the small degree of detuning (close harmonicity), the spectral peaks for these excitations would have have been located too close to the normal modes peaks to allow proper resolution of the individual peaks. The results are shown in Figures 9.7a - f for the E_3^b note, where, for clarity, only the data at 23.5 °C, 44 °C and 57 °C are shown on the spectral plots.

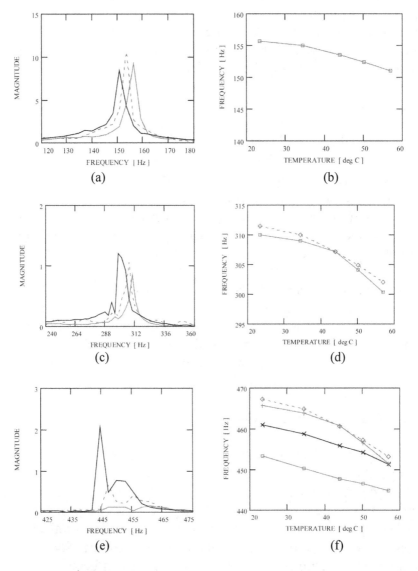

Fig. 9.7. The E_3^b note on the cello: (a), (c) and (e) first second and third normal mode peaks, respectively at 23.5, 34, 44, 50 and 57 °C. (b), (d) and (f) show the complete frequency-temperature plots. Dotted lines in (d) and (f) are the plots of $2f_1$ and $3f_1$ respectively. Points marked by x in (f) are the parametric excitations represented by the higher frequency components of the double peaks in (e). The solid line in (f) with points marked by +s is a plot of $f_1 + f_2$.

In Figure 9.7(e), double peaks appear for the third mode. The lower frequency peak on each plot represents the normal mode while the higher frequency peak represents the parametric excitation produced by either (i) cubic non-linearity at $3f_1$ or (ii) a quadratic interaction between the key-note and octave at $f_1 + f_2$. Notice in Figure 9.7(f) how closely the plot of $3f_1$ runs in relation to the plot of $f_1 + f_2$. This could make it difficult by frequency considerations alone to decide between the two mechanisms. However, cubic excitations are always very weak and difficult to detect so the parametic interaction appearing in Figure 9.7e more likely represents the normally stronger quadratic interaction of key-note and octave. The fact that this low intensity spectral peak can be tracked on the spectra as the temperature changes is proof of its reality. The lack of coincidence of this excitation (marked by 'x' in Figure 9.7(f)) and the plot of $f_1 + f_2$ (marked by '+'), except at the high temperature end-point, is due to the natural detuning that occurs on the system.

Parametric excitations due to quadratic non-linearities are not observable on the spectral data for the octave in Figure 9.7(c), most likely due to merging and not to low levels of excitation because the octave is quite strong showing strong interaction between key-note and octave. This is consistent with the observed closeness of the curve for the octave frequency and the plot of $2f_1$ in Figure 9.7(d). Of course exact harmonicity is to be avoided!

9.5.1.4 General Observations

Equation (9.7) predicts the decrease in frequency with increasing temperature as well as the increase in the absolute value of the slope of the curve with temperature as clearly shown in the experimental curves (compare Figure 9.1 with the right panels of Figure 9.7).

The close similarity between the form of the theoretical curve (Figure 9.1) and the experimental curves (Figure 9.7) relating frequency and temperature verifies two physical effects:

(i) Increasing the temperature of the note material introduces thermal stresses that result in *a reduction in dynamic stiffness*. Associated with this reduction in dynamic stiffness is a decrease in modal frequency.

(ii) Thermal stresses produce *a distortion in the shape of the note mid-surface* with resulting changes in modal frequencies.

Similar effects are expected for changes in compressive stress.

9.6 Dependence of Q-Factor, Mechanical Resistance and Damping Capacity on Temperature

9.6.1 Experimental Results

On the velocity-time histories of the excited notes studied here there is evidence of increased internal losses of the note material as the temperature is increased. To quantify these changes, the quality factor of the notes were determined and shown in Table 9.2. Recall that the quality factor Q of an oscillator is a measure of the stored energy per cycle to the power dissipated per cycle of oscillation (see Section 8.11.5). The larger the Q, the smaller the losses, the lower the damping and the longer the duration of the tone. As the temperature increases the Q decreases while mechanical resistance R_m increases for all the notes.

Table 9.2

Steelpan	Note	Temperature °C	Frequency f Hz	Bandwidth* B Hz	Quality Factor Q = f/B	Mechanical Resistance $R_m = 2\pi B$ s^{-1}
Tenor	G_4	27.5	393.2	3.8	102.7	24.1
		54.0	392.8	4.9	80.8	30.6
	D_4	27.5	293.5	3.9	76.2	24.2
		54.0	288.2	5.8	50.0	36.2
Cello	E^b_3	23.5	152.4	3.1	49.6	19.3
		44.0	150.6	3.5	43.2	21.9
		57.0	148.0	3.9	37.8	24.6
Bass	$F^\#_2$	27.5	92.4	3.6	25.8	22.5
		56.0	84.3	3.9	21.6	24.5

* Bandwidths were measured at the $1/\sqrt{2}$ points by interpolation on the spectral peaks.

Table 9.3

Steelpan	Note	Temperature °C	Damping Capacity Q^{-1}	Average Damping Capacity by Instrument Type Q^{-1}	Average Damping Capacity Coefficient $\delta Q^{-1}/\delta T$ °C^{-1}
Tenor	G_4	27.5	$\times 10^{-3}$ 9.8	$\times 10^{-3}$ (13.8 ± 3.8)	(2.1 ± 0.6) × 10^{-4}
		54.0	12.4		
	D_4	27.5	13.1		
		54.0	20.0		
Cello	E^b_3	27.5	20.2	(23.3 ± 3)	
		44.0	23.2		
		57.0	26.5		
Bass	$F^{\#}_2$	27.5	38.8	(42 ± 4)	
		56.0	46.0		

Notice in Table 9.2 that the Q is highest on the tenor (around 100) and lowest on the bass (around 20). The mechanical resistance R_m however, is fairly constant with an average value around 25 ± 2 s^{-1}. The mechanical resistance is dependent on the material and the treatment it receives which will not differ wildly among the notes used in our experiment. (*Note: The value 25 ± 2 s^{-1} measures the combined losses from mechanical damping, acoustic radiation and transmission losses across the note boundary. On a well prepared note, mechanical damping contributes, by far, the largest fraction of the total losses.*)

A useful parameter to consider is the *total loss capacity* or *damping capacity* Q^{-1}. Although this is the reciprocal of the quality factor and carries the same information, it is a term widely used in the study of material damping for comparing losses under different loading conditions (thermal, magnetic or stress). Table 9.3 shows the total damping capacity for the sampled notes on three instrument types. Observe that the damping capacity increases as one move from tenor to cello, on to the bass. This is expected because the Q decreases as one moves from tenor to bass. One can also define an average rate of increase of damping capacity with temperature. This *Damping Capacity Coefficient* has the positive value given by

Damping Capacity Coefficient of a Steelpan Note:
$$\delta Q^{-1}/\delta T = (2.1 \pm 0.6) \times 10^{-4} \text{ °C}^{-1}.$$

For an explanation of the positivity of the damping capacity coefficient when only the magnetomechanical damping (MMD) is considered see Section 9.9. The total loss includes acoustical radiation, magnetomechanical, and transmission losses. From the dependence of radiation resistance on temperature given in Chapter 12, acoustical radiation losses will *decrease* with temperature but this represents a much smaller change than the *increase* due to MMD. Transmission losses across note boundaries will be temperature dependent if *blocking* loses effectiveness with temperature. We now examine this possibility.

The nodal line which defines the boundary of the true note is *a locus of equal dynamic stiffness*. In setting the static parameters for this nodal line, the pan maker/tuner hammer peens and blocks the note with particular attention given to the approximate boundary of the true note (not to be confused with the grooves). It is not necessary to completely peen along the entire boundary because the true note is established dynamically within the bounds set by the static conditions (note thickness, elastic constants, compressive stresses, homogeneity of the note material, and note surface shape). Experience shows that this is true in practice. It is also true to say that the dynamics which involves mode coupling 'helps' the tuner in defining the true note. Blocking, by hammer peening, sets the compressive stresses along the boundary and in turn, the note modal frequencies. Thermal stress will therefore affect the modal frequencies of the note and the non-linear coupling between the modes. The data in Figure 9.7 reveals this by the changes in the amplitude of the higher modes relative to the first mode as the temperature is increased. The amplitude of the higher modes is determined mainly by quadratic coupling with the first mode (the key note or tonic). As a result of the changes in coupling, mode localization (see Sections 4.1 and 6.8) will be affected making the vibrational energy less confined to the true note area at the elevated temperature. To understand this more clearly, one must take note of the fact that the mode-mode couplings on a note depends on the detuning which changes with temperature. If the detuning brings the modes too close to harmonicity the amplitudes of higher modes (partials) will decrease (as they do in the case of the pung tone; see Section 14.24). One must note the fact that blocking is not only set by peening along the boundary but is also set dynamically by mode confinement. Since temperature is seen to affect the latter then it is possible for blocking to be degraded by an increase in temperature and to bring about an increase in damping capacity.

As a subtle point, it should be noted that at times, one can find a particular note that sounds 'better' when played at a temperature different from the Tuning Temperature. This can happen because the tuner cannot always set each note perfectly when working at a particular temperature but overall, the notes on a pan should sound their 'best' at the Tuning Temperature. Musical qualities like 'better' or 'best' even 'perfect' are all subjective so this has to be decided upon by the tuner or panist. It is hard to please everyone on all the notes. The tuner can always re-tune any note that requires some fine adjustment.

9.7 Damping Mechanisms

9.7.1 General Methods of Energy Dissipation

Damping is the energy dissipation property of a material under cyclic stress induced by vibration. Vibration damping is usually divided into five different damping mechanisms. They include

- (i) internal material damping,
- (ii) interface damping (rubbing or friction damping),
- (iii) radiation damping,
- (iv) energy losses occurring as a result of transmission across boundaries of structures, and
- (v) viscous damping caused by viscoelastic material or by surrounding fluid (air).

Internal discontinuities can also produce reflections that convert transverse vibrations into longitudinal vibrations resulting in mode conversion that robs the primary (transverse) mode of energy. *This is precisely the role played by the grooves (which lie outside the boundary of the true note) in restricting energy transfer out of the true note area. The bore holes on the bore pan play a similar role.* Internal friction of metals is due to the internal mismatch in the material microstructure. Two or more of the above listed mechanisms may be operating simultaneously in a vibrating system.

Consequently, the effects of the various energy loss mechanisms are usually lumped together and represented by some convenient damping mechanism. The most commonly used mechanism for representing energy dissipation is to assume the existence of dissipative forces that are a function of velocity. This is done in rheological modeling involving dashpots (see Chapter 13). For most systems however, energy is dissipated hysteretically by yielding or plastic straining of the material. The stick rubber tip for example displays this hysteretic behavior (see Chapter 13).

- *One should emphasize here that as a musical instrument, the main output of the pan is its acoustical radiation but, as an energy-loss mechanism, in this Section we treat this aspect (acoustical radiation) simply as a damping mechanism. It is therefore important to reduce the effects of other damping mechanisms in order to raise the relative level of acoustical radiation to maximize the acoustical output from the pan.*

9.7.2 Magnetomechanical Damping (MMD)

Magnetic domains are regions inside a material such as steel that are magnetized in different direction so that the net magnetization is nearly zero. The domains are separated by *domain walls*.

For the steel notes of the steelpan, internal damping of the vibrating notes is mainly attributed to the vibration-induced movement of *magnetic domain walls*, through the irregular energy distribution generated by their interaction with *structural defects*. When domain wall rotation is irreversible, a fraction of the energy is dissipated as an internal friction and appears eventually as heat (Cochardt, 1953). This, together with *acoustical radiation damping* and losses across the note boundary (*transmission losses*) are responsible for the damping of an excited note. It has been shown (see Section 6.5.7) that the total damping is insensitive to the frequency of oscillation on a given note.

MMD in steel is known to increase *linearly* with strain amplitude, ε, thus the damping losses increases more rapidly than stored energy per cycle of vibration which increases as the square of the amplitude ($\sim \varepsilon^2$). To see this, consider the linear dependence of MMD on strain amplitude (~ε) as the *coupling strength*. Then the damping losses increases as

$$\text{MMD Losses} \sim (\text{coupling strength})(\varepsilon^2) \sim \varepsilon^3.$$

MMD damping losses therefore increases as the third power of the strain while stored energy increases as the second power of the strain. This *cubic dependence on strain amplitude* does not introduce non-linearities in the frequency response with the production of third harmonics because the magnetic domain walls move in such a way as to ensure that the stress-strain (σ-ε) loops at each ε are *similar* (see sketch in Figure 9.8). ***This self-similarity is important as it guarantees the spectral purity of the sounding note on the pan.*** Were it not for this *self-similarity* of the (σ-ε) loops, the audio tones on all the notes on all the pans (tenor to bass) would be 'ringing out' with high pitched oscillations due to the preponderance of third harmonic components.

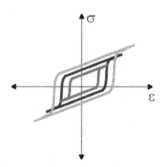

Fig. 9.8. Self-similarity of stress-strain loops. Each loop is just a larger or smaller version of its neighbor.

- ***Through this subtle effect of self-similarity, the steelpan has been 'rescued' from an excess of metallic sounds that would have rendered it unsuitable as a tuned, melodic instrument.***

In general, the amplitude of the (σ-ε) loop varies as ε^n and the area enclosed by the loop is a measure of the energy dissipation. At low stress levels, the magnetomechanical energy dissipation is proportional to σ^n, where $n \geq 3$. At high stress, n decreases. The stress at which this decrease commences being higher the greater the hardness of the material. For the low-carbon steel on the pan under normal playing conditions, $n = 3$ applies.

MMD depends on: (i) the magnetomechanical coupling factor describing the efficiency of converting elastic to magnetic energy, (ii) the magnetic anisotropy describing the difficulty of magnetic moment rotation, (iii) the Young's modulus, (iv) the magnetization, (v) the magnetostriction and (vi) the crystallographic texture of the material. For more information on these mechanisms, readers should consult some additional literature such as Frank et al. (1969) and Coronel and Beshers (1988). How domain walls move depends on the presence of *inclusions* or *pinning sites*, such as crystal imperfections, stress concentrations*, voids and cracks. MMD is therefore affected by the dislocation structure of cold-work during sinking. Pinning sites act as anchors to the walls since the magnetostatic energy decreases when domain walls attach to the pinning sites. This drop in energy indicates a bond or an attachment. By restricting the motion of the domain walls, damping is reduced. Reduction in damping is required here because the pan maker wants to produce instruments having high acoustic output. These properties and hence the damping characteristics of the material can be optimized through *microstructural control*. **This is an important aspect of steelpan construction.**

* The stress concentration around bore holes on the bore pan does not reduce the damping capacity of the outer notes because these holes are normally located outside the boundary of the true note. In addition note vibration is minimized at the true note boundary. However, the inner notes on a bore tenor may have bores along the true note boundary. The stress concentrations around these notes can restrict domain wall movement thereby reducing damping. The result is an increase in the relative loudness of the inner notes on the bore pan. The outer notes receive their benefits (increased loudness) from the bore holes when the stress concentrations (or holes) act as scattering sites for waves transmitted away from the notes and through the internote (see Sections 14.12.3 and 14.12.4).

9.8 Microstructural Control

The traditional hammer peening process of pan making is in fact a form of microstructural control. Work hardening is one of the beneficial aspects of hammer peening which should be retained by careful application of the heat treatment (stress relief anneal, see Section 2.23) that follows sinking and forming. The advantage of Traditional Sinking (hammer peening) over Press Forming (hydroforming, spin forming etc.) of the pan face is the controlled application of work hardening whereby greater work hardening can be (and is) applied to the inner areas of the pan face where the higher notes are located. By this method, where dislocations are introduced by cold-working, the damping capacity of the inner notes can be reduced with positive results on the acoustic output. Refer to Section 14.12.5 for a continuation of this discussion on this important aspect of '*pan face preparation*' as it relates to tuning the pan and isolating the notes.

Heat treatment always increases the damping capacity of materials. During heat treatment the number of defects, such as dislocations, decreases and, thus, the internal stresses in the material decreases. As a consequence of the internal stress relief, the damping capacity increases (Smith and Birchak, 1968, 1969). It is well known to the better pan makers that excessive burning (application of excessively high temperatures or prolong heating) severely degrades the tonal qualities of the tuned notes. In fact these notes display high damping that can readily be inferred from the shortened duration and the resulting lower average intensity of the tones. All these factors were considered in establishing the temperature range for 'Burning' (annealing) given in Section 2.23.

9.9 The Vibrating Note at Elevated Temperatures

When the temperature of the pan is increased by tens of degrees above normal room temperature (in more precise terms, above the *Tuning Temperature*) the damping increases. This condition is only temporary because the damping returns to its original level as the pan is cooled back to room temperature. MMD at room temperature and just above is a process that is affected by thermal activation; where the barriers (defects, dislocations from cold-work etc) lose their effectiveness in restraining the domain walls as the temperature is increased. *The increase in thermal energy at elevated temperatures weakens the attachment of domain walls to the pinning sites. The damping capacity of the note material therefore increases with temperature.* This explains the positive damping capacity coefficient $\delta Q^{-1}/\delta T = (2.1 \pm 0.6) \times 10^{-4}$ °C^{-1} obtained in Table 9.3 for pan notes (*cf.* Achong 1999b). *Of direct importance to the sounding tones, the tone duration and the Q of the note are both reduced.* These effects are more noticeable on the low-end pans as the previous examples clearly show (see Figures 9.3 and 9.4 for the tenor and Figure 9.6 for the bass).

9.10 The Transition Period between First and Second Tuning

Immediately after *First Tuning*, the instrument goes through a rather complex metallurgic process as the stresses are relieved and redistributed resulting in changes to the *modal frequencies*, the *coupling coefficients* and the *surface shape*. The most easily detected change is that the notes of a recently tuned pan will *run sharp* overnight. For changes in compressive stress from σ_{ci} to σ_{cf}, one has the exact relation

$$\omega_f^2 = \omega_i^2 + \left\{ (\alpha_{0f} - \alpha_{0i}) + s_i \alpha_{0i} \left(1 - \frac{M_{4f}}{M_{4i}} \right) \right\} + \frac{(\sigma_{cf} - \sigma_{ci})(1 - v^2)}{E} \left(\frac{a}{h} \right)^2 M_{4f}.$$

(9.16)

Multiplying both sides of equation (9.16) by $Eh^2/\{4\pi^2 \rho a^4 (1-v^2)\}$ converts to frequency in Hertz giving the relation between the initial and final frequencies f_i and f_f as

$$f_f^2 = f_i^2 + \left[\left\{ (\alpha_{0f} - \alpha_{0i}) + s_i \alpha_{0i} \left(1 - \frac{M_{4f}}{M_{4i}} \right) \right\} + \frac{(\sigma_{cf} - \sigma_{ci})(1 - v^2)}{E} \left(\frac{a}{h} \right)^2 M_{4f} \right] \frac{Eh^2}{4\pi^2 \rho a^4 (1 - v^2)}$$

(9.17)

If one is interested only in the fractional change in frequency for small changes in compressive stress, one makes use of equation (9.4b) as reproduced below.

$$\frac{\delta f}{f_i} = \underbrace{\frac{\delta \sigma_c (1-v^2)}{2(1-s_i)E} \left(\frac{a}{h}\right)^2 \frac{M_{4f}}{\alpha_{0i}}}_{\text{due to change in note stiffness}} + \underbrace{\frac{1}{2(1-s_i)} \left\{ \left(\frac{\alpha_{0f}}{\alpha_{0i}} - 1\right) + s_i \left(1 - \frac{M_{4f}}{M_{4i}}\right) \right\}}_{\text{due to change in note shape}},$$

Observe here that stress relaxation modifies (increases) the dynamical stiffness of the note and alters the geometrical form (shape) of the note.

Owing to stress relaxation which commences immediately after tuning, the compressive stress distributed along the boundary and stresses throughout the note will decrease (overnight). Since compressive stress is *negative* this makes $\sigma_{ci} < \sigma_{cf}$, which makes $f_f > f_i$, — the note runs sharp *after* stress relaxation.

One readily derives from equation (9.4b) that larger notes or notes of thinner material undergo a larger fractional change in frequency for a given change in compressive stress. These notes will therefore be more susceptible to the effects of stress relaxation during the transition period that follows first tuning in particular and after tuning in general. In designing a steelpan that is less susceptible to changes in internal stresses, the important parameter to consider is the ratio of note size to note thickness a/h. Decreasing this ratio reduces the frequency dependence on stress relaxation.

The formal similarity between equation (9.7) for the frequency dependence on temperature changes and equation (9.17) for the frequency dependence on changes in compressive stress indicates that if one could alter and measure σ_c as a control variable, plots similar to those found for f vs. T could be obtained for f vs. σ_c. The same conclusion can be reached by comparing equation (9.4a) and equation (9.4b) for the frequency shifts.

Since the sequence of changes during stress relaxation is unique to each note on a pan (as determined by the particular values taken up by the s, σ and M parameters), it will be instructive to display the results for a note, which after *First Tuning* showed many changes in the frequency spectra. The sample note chosen for display here is one that showed changes to the first three normal modes as well as the parametric modes. It will however be typical of most notes. Observations were made on a newly constructed tenor pan immediately after First Tuning and then later, after being kept at an approximately constant temperature of 23°C for 24 hours. The shifts in the spectral peaks corresponding to first, second and third modes for the E_4^b note are shown in Figure (9.9a-c) respectively.

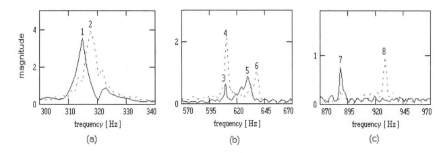

Fig. 9.9. The effects of stress relaxation on the frequency components of an E_4^b tenor note: —, before relaxation; - - -, after relaxation. (a) First mode showing an upward shift after relaxation; (b) changes to the second normal modes (peaks 3 and 4) and the parametric excitations (peaks 5 and 6); (c) shift in frequency of the third normal mode.

- In Figure 9.9a, the first mode shows a shift upwards from its initial frequency of $f_1 = 314.84$ Hz (peak 1) to $f_1^* = 317.68$ Hz (peak 2), a shift of +2.84 Hz.
- In Figure 9.9b the second mode natural frequency (peaks 3 and 4 respectively) shows a shift from $f_2 = 609.59$ Hz to $f_2^* = 610.55$ Hz (a shift of +0.96 Hz).
- The peak labeled 5, at 629.94 Hz, corresponds to the slightly detuned parametrically excited mode expected at $2f_1$ (= 629.68 Hz). Twenty-four hours later, this parametric mode is observed as peak 6 at 637.94 Hz, now more detuned from the value of $2f_1^*$ (= 635.36 Hz). The sign (direction) of these frequency shifts indicate a *reduction* in compressive stress $\delta\sigma_c > 0$ (recall that σ_c is negative), *consistent with compressive stress relaxation*. The parametric excitations at peaks 5 and 6 are clear demonstrations of the quadratic non-linearity that governs the dynamics of steelpan notes.
- In Figure 9.9c, the frequency for the third natural mode moved from $f_3 = 888.62$ Hz (peak 7) to $f_3^* = 928.58$ Hz (peak 8). This large shift may be related to sensitive dependence of this particular note to changes in surface shape (through the connection of ψ_0 to the compressive

stress). No parametric excitation resulting from cubic non-linearities was large enough to be observable.

I should point out that parametric excitations and the corresponding peaks in the frequency spectrum are more easily observed during the early stages of tuning. When tuning has progressed to the final stages, the spectral peaks of the parametric excitations merge with the corresponding peaks of the normal modes and are either totally or partially hidden.

9.11 Engineering Designs

9.11.1 General design considerations

Four notes will be modeled in this Section, the $C^{\#}_6$, D_4, B_4 and the $F^{\#}_2$ Bass note. These notes will be analyzed to determine their frequency dependence on temperature and changes in compressive stress. For low carbon steel, $\alpha_T = 12 \times 10^{-6}$ °C^{-1}, E = 207 GPa, ρ = 7750 Kg·m^{-3}, ν = 0.3, Yield strength typically in the region of 200 MPa and Ultimate tensile strength 380 MPa. The design parameters and note characteristics are tabulated in the Tables 9.3 and 9.4. In these designs, the design stress σ_c is determined by the note shape and buckling parameter, using

$$\sigma_c = -\frac{s\,E}{(1-\upsilon^2)}\left(\frac{h}{a}\right)^2 \frac{\alpha_0}{M_4}. \qquad (9.18)$$

In addition, the mechanical bias F_0 describing the quiescent point of operation of the sounding note is obtained from

$$F_0 = -4\pi\sigma_c H_0 h\, M_8 = \frac{4\pi\,s\,E\,H_0 h^3 M_8}{(1-\upsilon^2)\,a^2}\left(\frac{\alpha_0}{M_4}\right). \qquad (9.19)$$

Observe the strong dependence of F_0 on the note thickness h (to the third power) when expressed as a function of the buckling parameter s. F_0 is also seen to depend directly on the rise H_0. Although the frequency of these shallow shell notes on the pan increases with the rise, quite a large rise is used on the bass together with strong compressive stresses to lower the frequency. If you look at the first expression $F_0 = -4\pi\sigma_c H_0 h M_8$ you can see why **increasing $|\sigma_c|$ (which implies making σ_c more negative), H_0 and h will always increase the mechanical bias. Increasing the mechanical bias allows the note to operate with stronger stick impacts without audio distortion.** Recall that when the note is struck by the stick the impact force subtracts (adds if played from the underside) from the mechanical bias over a period equal to the make-to-break contact time.

The component of fractional frequency shift κ due to change in note shape is given by

$$\kappa = \frac{1}{2(1-s_i)}\left\{\left(\frac{\alpha_{0f}}{\alpha_{0i}}-1\right) + s_i\left(1-\frac{M_{4f}}{M_{4i}}\right)\right\}, \qquad (9.20)$$

where κ must be calculated from the parameters describing the initial and final states of each note. Computing the value of κ is fully tractable but it is somewhat laborious. These are the steps; (i) Initially set $s = 0$. Choose a shaping function $q(x)$ and solve equation (8.10) for λ. (ii) Use this λ to solve equation (8.6) for K. (iii) Use K to define $\psi(x)$ in equation (8.4). (iv) Normalize using equation (8.5). Use ψ to determine M_j with ($j = 1, 2 ...8$) by numerical integration (this involves equations (8.12a, b, c)). (v) Use M_j, in equations (8.14), (8.15) and (8.16) to determine α_1, α_2 and α_3 (since $s = 0$, $\alpha_0 = \alpha_1$). (vi) Use equation (8.22) to determine β. (vi) Define an initial state of temperature or internal stress using s_i. (vii) Use equation (8.25) to determine A_0. (viii) Using A_0, define $\psi_0(x)$ in equation (8.11) and determine a new value for λ. (ix) Return to step (ii) and repeat the steps leading to the new set M_j. (x) Using equation (8.20b) with the new M_j set (which includes M_{4i}) determine α_{0i}. (xi) Define the final state s_f. (xii) Repeat steps (vii) to (x) with s_f replacing s_i; determine M_{4f} and α_{0f}. Now calculate κ using equation (9.20). I use this algorithm in my program package to calculate frequency changes produced by note shaping.

For symmetrical modes on circular planform the fundamental frequency of the note is obtained using

$$f = \frac{1}{2\pi}\left(\frac{\alpha_0(1-s)E}{\rho(1-\upsilon^2)}\right)^{\frac{1}{2}}\frac{h}{a^2}. \qquad (9.21a)$$

For elliptical planforms the key-note frequency can be written as

$$f = \frac{1}{2\pi}\left(\frac{\alpha_0(1-s)E}{\rho(1-\upsilon^2)}\right)^{\frac{1}{2}}\frac{h}{ab}\left(3 - 6\frac{a}{b} + 4\left(\frac{a}{b}\right)^2\right)^{\frac{1}{2}}. \qquad (9.21b)$$

Equations (9.21b) and (3.51) are equivalent.

9.11.2 Notes Designed with Low Mechanical Bias

Negative k values in the shaping function $q(x) = k(1 - 2.4x^2 + 1.4x^3)$ were use to give the finished note shapes less curvature in the middle portion of the surface compared to the initial spherical cap The note designs are shown in Table 9.3. Reducing the curvature reduces the frequency. The notes in Table 9.3 were designed with low compressive stresses and low mechanical bias F_0. Since typical stick impacts for the mid-range pans produce maximum forces around 40N, of the five designs, only the tenor notes $C^\#_6$ and D_4 (with h = 0.4mm) can be played loudly without distortion. All other notes in Table 9.3, *particularly the bass note*, must be played softly.

Observe the variations in temperature-dependent fractional frequency shift among the designs, in particular pay attention to the x10 greater shift on the $F^\#_2$ bass note when compared to the $C^\#_6$ tenor note. Since the shifts given by κ depend on the initial and final states (unspecified in the designs) they are not computed in the tables.

TABLE 9.3

Notes designed with the shaping function $q(x) = k(1 - 2.4x^2 + 1.4x^3)$. T = 23°C

Note	Frequency Hz	Dimensions	Parameters † (initial values)	Fractional Frequency Shift $\Delta\omega/\omega$	Initial Stress σ_c MPa	Mechanical Bias F_0 Newtons
$C^\#_6$	1108.73	$a = b = 3.728$cm $h = 0.3$mm, $H_o/h = 3.2$, $k = -0.35$ $A_0 = 0.47322$	$s = 0.325028$ $\alpha_0 = 52.591$ $\alpha_2 = 47.849$ $\alpha_3 = 12.516$ $\beta = 88.7297$ $M_4 = 7.719$ $M_8 = 0.88635$ $\varphi = 0.1192$	$-0.0031\ M_{4f}\ \delta T$ $+ \kappa$	-32.62	104.7
B_4	493.88	$a = b = 5.586$cm $h = 0.3$mm, $H_o/h = 3.2$, $k = -0.35$ $A_0 = 0.47322$	$s = 0.325028$ $\alpha_0 = 52.591$ $\alpha_2 = 47.849$ $\alpha_3 = 12.516$ $\beta = 88.7297$ $M_4 = 7.719$ $M_8 = 0.88635$ $\varphi = 0.1192$	$-0.0074\ M_{4f}\delta T$ $+ \kappa$	-14.54	46.5
D_4	293.66	$a = b = 8.168$cm $h = 0.4$mm, $H_o/h = 3.2$, $k = -0.35$ $A_0 = 0.66455$	$s = 0.44595$ $\alpha_0 = 58.225$ $\alpha_2 = 49.620$ $\alpha_3 = 12.368$ $\beta = 105.383$ $M_4 = 7.570$ $M_8 = 0.88635$ $\varphi = 0.11919$	$-0.0098\ M_{4f}\delta T$ $+ \kappa$	-18.7	106.8
		$a = b = 7.244$cm $h = 0.3$mm, $H_o/h = 3.2$, $k = -0.35$ $A_0 = 0.47322$	$s = 0.325028$ $\alpha_0 = 52.591$ $\alpha_2 = 47.849$ $\alpha_3 = 12.516$ $\beta = 88.7297$ $M_4 = 7.719$ $M_8 = 0.88635$ $\varphi = 0.1192$	$-0.0083\ M_{4f}\delta T$ $+ \kappa$	-8.64	27.7
$F^\#_2$	92.50	$a = b = 14.225$cm $h = 0.4$mm, $H_o/h = 2.5$, $k = -0.30$ $A_0 = 0.44235$	$s = 0.32019$ $\alpha_0 = 43.340$ $\alpha_2 = 39.303$ $\alpha_3 = 10.539$ $\beta = 67.571$. $M_4 = 7.337$ $M_8 = 0.97199$ $\varphi = 0.12345$	$-0.0326\ M_{4f}\delta T$ $+ \kappa$	-3.4	21.3

† These parameters are weakly dependent on the rise to radius ratio H_0/a.

9.11.3 Intensity (Loudness) Problems with the Bass Notes and the 'Wobbly Effect'

What has just been observed here with respect to the limitations on the stick impacts on the bass note for the designs using low mechanical bias is an example of a general problem encountered on the bass steelpans. Owing to the acoustical requirement that these notes be of large area (πab) in order to increase the acoustic output and the dynamical requirements that the area be large but the thickness (h) not be excessively large in order to obtain the desired low frequencies, the compressive stress σ_c along the boundary and the mechanical bias on the note surface are restricted to relatively low values (when compared to the notes on the high-end pans). There are physical upper and lower limits to the thickness h that can be used to produce these instruments. But large h values are required to increase the mechanical bias and allow for strong stick impacts and loud bass tones. Increasing the operating temperature increases the mechanical bias but its negative effects on tonality (as seen in the experimental data) remove this procedure as a viable option. The best that can be done in this situation of competing requirements, is to increase the thickness as much as possible by using a lower gauge steel for the pan face (#16 perhaps) as the initial rawform and to apply as much compressive stress as possible along the boundary by hammer peening while staying away from the buckling limit. Observe that the mechanical bias is directly proportional to the buckling parameter s.

This problem is related to what I define as the '*Wobbly Effect*' which is more often observed on the higher pitched pans. For example, the C_4 note, the lowest on the tenor, and depending on template sizing, can sometimes be allocated too small an area on the panface. In order to tune such a note to C_4 on the musical scale, the tuner applies concentrated peening along the note boundary which raises the level of compressive stress. Increasing the compressive stress compensates for the reduced area and lowers the note frequency to the desired value. Sometimes, the compressive stress, being high, reduces the stiffness of the note and the supporting internote to the point where the note, when played, becomes 'wobbly.' The observant tuner (or panist) may have noticed this effect on some of the pans brought for tuning. I myself have seen this on quite good, professionally finished pans. However, while this is not a critical problem, on the standard pan, with its diameter typically around 22 inches, this problem can be removed by increasing the pan diameter by an extra 2 inches. If this is done, the pan maker must not be tempted to add extra notes for then, other problems may arise.

9.11.4 Notes Designed with High Mechanical Bias

Before discussing these designs I should point out that pan makers may not be able to achieve these very high compressive stresses and mechanical biases unless good material is used along with good pan preparation and proper hammer peening.

For variety, the designs in Tables 9.4 and 9.5 make use of a variation of the first shaping function expressed as $q(x) = k(x - 2.4x^2 + 1.4x^3)$ and in addition, greater compressive stress is applied along the note boundary. Although this new shaping function appears different from the first one used in Table 9.3, the two functions have identical curvature (defined by the second derivative) which define the bending moments in the shell-shaped notes.

In the second design, the tenor note $C^{\#}_6$ can sustain even stronger impacts compared with the note in the first design. One of the E_3 designs uses an ellipsoidal note on an elliptical planform tuned in the ***Key-note-Octave-Twelfth*** format (see Section 14.25) with $a/b = 5/4$. In this design the compressive stress and mechanical bias are calculated using $\sqrt{ab}$ in place of a in equation (9.18) as is appropriate for ellipsoidal notes (see Section 3.16). The quiescent point for the bass note $F^{\#}_2$ has been improved but due to space limitations on the pan face, to provide sufficiently high mechanical bias, elliptical planforms must be used. We see this in the following way: When using an ellipsoid, the frequency will increase unless the compressive stress is also increased. With the ellipsoid, we can therefore increase the compressive stress by peening thereby setting up the required high mechanical bias.

TABLE 9.4

Notes designed with the shaping function
$$q(x) = k(x - 2.4x^2 + 1.4x^3). \ T = 23°C$$

Note	Frequency Hz	Dimensions	Parameters †	Fractional Frequency Shift $\Delta\omega/\omega$	Initial Stress σ_c MPa	Mechanical Bias F_0 Newtons
$C^\#_6$	1108.73	$a = b = 3.83$cm $h = 0.4$mm, $H_o/h = 3.2$, $k = -0.3$ $A_0 = 0.47322$	$s = 0.563574$, $\alpha_0 = 55.7011$ $\alpha_2 = 49.5984$ $\alpha_3 = 15.496$ $\beta = 85.073$ $M_4 = 8.5034$ $M_8 = 0.83016$ $\varphi = 0.1025$	$-0.0029\ M_{4f}$ $\delta T + \kappa$	-91.82	489.0
		$a = b = 3.64$cm $h = 0.37$mm $H_o/h = 3.2$, $k = -0.3$ $A_0 = 0.47322$		$0.0029\ M_{4f}$ $\delta T + \kappa$	-84.5	386.2
E_3	164.81	$a = b = 10.08$cm $h = 0.4$mm, $H_o/h = 2.5$, $k = -0.2$ $A_0 = 1.100$	$s = 0.681791$ $\alpha_0 = 74.18819$ $\alpha_2 = 51.1348$ $\alpha 3 = 12.0868$ $\beta = 152.8709$ $M_4 = .95764$ $M_8 = 0.99515$ $\varphi = 0.12067$	-0.0204 $M_{4f}\delta T + \kappa$	-26.0	125.1
		$a = 11.451$cm $b = 10.179$cm $h = 0.4$mm, $H_o/h = 2.5$, $k = -0.2$ $A_0 = 1.100$			-22.68	109.1
		$a = b = 9.867$cm $h = 0.4$mm, $H_o/h = 2.5$, $k = -0.3$ $A_0 = 0.81897$	$s = 0.596933$ $\alpha_0 = 53.71865$ $\alpha_2 = 43.7990$ $\alpha_3 = 12.2598$ $\beta = 90.200$ $M_4 = 7.27632$ $M_8 = 0.92030$ $\varphi = 0.11588$	-0.0427 $M_{4f}\delta T + \kappa$	-16.46	76.1

† These parameters are weakly dependent on the rise to radius ratio H_0/a.

TABLE 9.5

Notes designed with the shaping function
$q(x) = k(x - 2.4 x^2 + 1.4 x^3)$. T = 23°C.

Note	Frequency Hz	Dimensions	Parameters †	Fractional Frequency Shift $\Delta\omega/\omega$	Initial Stress σ_c MPa	Mechanical Bias F_0 Newtons
$F^{\#}_2$	92.50	$a = b$ =13.171cm h = 0.4mm, H_o/h = 2.5, k = -0.3 A_0 = 0.81897	s = 0.596933 α_0=53.71865 α_2 = 43.7990 α_3 = 12.2598 β = 90.200 M_4 = 7.27632 M_8 = 0.92030 φ = 0.11588	-0.0760 $M_{4f}\delta T + \kappa$	-8.54	50.6
		$a = b$ =13.458cm h = 0.4mm, H_o/h = 2.5, k = -0.2 A_0= 1.100	s = 0.681791 α_0=74.18819 α_2 = 51.1348 α_3 = 12.0868 β = 152.8709 M_4 = 6.95764 M_8 = 0.99515 φ = 0.12067	-0.0364 $M_{4f}\delta T + \kappa$	-14.60	73.0
		a = 19.00cm b = 16.891cm h = 0.566mm H_o/h = 2.5, k = -0.2 A_0= 1.100	s = 0.681791 α_0=74.18819 α_2 = 51.1348 α_3 = 12.0868 β =152.8709 M_4 = 6.95764 M_8 =0.99515 φ = 0.12067	-0.0257 $M_{4f}\delta T + \kappa$	-45.47	455.2

† These parameters are weakly dependent on the rise to radius ratio H_0/a.

Since the design parameters calculated for the circular planform can be used for elliptical planforms having low aspect ratios (close to unity) the final design in Tables 9.5 uses an elliptical planform with aspect ratio a/b = 9/8 to allow for tuning in the **Key-note-Octave-Third** format (see Sections 14.25 and 14.26). A thickness h = 0.566 mm (thicker than normal) is used to achieve a mechanical bias of 455.2 N with reduced fractional frequency shift for this $F^{\#}_2$ bass note. Notice the relatively large thickness that is required to bring the bass note up to the biasing level of the tenor. This is expected because of the much larger surface area of the bass note. This note is designed to be played very intensely without distortion.

In practice, good bass construction calls for a heavy gauge rawform, adequate indentation to raise the level of residual compressive stresses across the pan face and properly applied peening along the note boundary. This well designed note also displays lower temperature-frequency dependence.

From Tables 9.3, 9.4 and 9.5, the function φ, which appears in the frequency equation (9.15), is seen to take on values within the interval [0.10, 0.13]. In practice, for any reasonable note shape and boundary conditions, one can safely assume a value for φ within this small range.

CHAPTER 10

Mode Locking on the Non-Linear Notes of the Steelpan

10.1 Introduction

The steelpan as a musical instrument of the percussion family, with rigid vibrators, has been shown to operate as a system of non-linear mode-localized oscillators. Each note consists of a shallow dome-shaped shell formed on the indented face of the steelpan . The first mode of each note is tuned according to the musical scale with the second mode as an upper octave (the *resident octave*) and the third mode as a musical twelfth (the *resident twelfth*). The unique tonality obtained on this instrument is supplied by the amplitude and frequency modulations produced by the non-linear quadratic and cubic interactions between the tuned modes on a note (or between two sympathetic notes). To obtain acceptable tonality however, the second and third modes must never be tuned as exact harmonics of the first mode.

In the non-musical (exotic) applications, under continuous sinusoidal excitation the instrument has been shown to display Hopf bifurcation and the jump phenomenon (see Chapter 18 and Achong 1996b). Using electronic synthesis, the instrument has also shown interesting chaotic behavior (see Chapter 18).

The purpose of this analysis is to show that the vibrational state of a steelpan note, when played by striking with the stick, remains essentially in the *acquisition mode* (in the terminology of Control Theory) but under the right conditions, may correspond to the oscillations of *locked modes* (Achong 2003). The treatment considers interaction of the first two (tuned) modes and is limited to quadratic non-linearities only.

10.2. Modal Equations

Following the analysis of Chapter 4, the governing equations for these rigid vibrators with u_n as the modal displacements are described by equation (4.2). For the purposes of this analysis, it is sufficient to consider only the free oscillation phase for the following reasons: Generally for normal playing action on this percussion musical instrument, the duration of the initial *impact phase* is less than one period of oscillation of the fundamental (first) mode. In addition, the first mode takes a few periods of oscillation to rise to maximum amplitude while the second mode, as it receives energy from the first mode through quadratic coupling, reaches its maximum somewhat later.

For *phase locking* to occur the natural frequencies ω_1 and ω_2 of the first and second modes respectively, must be nearly harmonically related as described by the detuning parameter σ where $\omega_2 = 2\omega_1 + \varepsilon\sigma$. In the present context, $\Omega \doteq \varepsilon\sigma$ is the *initial frequency detuning* and ε is a gauge or order parameter. To solve the set of equations in (4.2), the multi-time method (see Chapter 4) is used. Assuming a set of solutions (for zeroth order in ε) of the form

$$u_{n0} = \tfrac{1}{2} a_n(t_1) e^{i(\omega_n t_0 + \phi_n(t_1))} + cc,$$

where a_n and ϕ_n are functions of the slow time t_1 (= εt). The (free) system equations are a reduced set of equations (4.9) and (4.10) of Chapter 4 describing two coupled modes

$$a_1' = -\mu_1 a_1 + \frac{\alpha_{121}^*}{4\omega_1} a_1 a_2 \sin\gamma_1, \quad a_2' = -\mu_2 a_2 - \frac{\alpha_{112}}{4\omega_2} a_1^2 \sin\gamma_1$$

$$a_1\phi_1' = -\frac{\alpha_{121}^*}{4\omega_1} a_1 a_2 \cos\gamma_1, \quad a_2\phi_2' = -\frac{\alpha_{112}}{4\omega_2} a_1^2 \cos\gamma_1. \quad (10.1\text{a-d})$$

where $\alpha_{jkn}^* = \alpha_{jkn} + \alpha_{kjn}$, the prime denotes $\frac{d}{dt_1}$, and

$$\gamma_1 = \phi_2 - 2\phi_1 + \sigma t_1. \quad (10.2)$$

10.3 Growth and Decay of Modal Amplitudes

From equations (10.1a,b) the following conditions are obtained:

(a) Mode1: The amplitude a_1 grows when $(\alpha_{121}^*/4\omega_1)a_2 \sin\gamma_1 > \mu_1$; which requires that $\sin\gamma_1 > 0$.

(b) Mode2: The amplitude a_2 grows when $-(\alpha_{112} a_1^2/4\omega_2 a_2) \sin\gamma_1 > \mu_2$; which requires that $\sin\gamma_1 < 0$

(c) The complements of (a) and (b) are the conditions for decay.

Mode coupling is clearly evident in these conditions. As $\sin\gamma_1$ alternates between +1 and -1, energy is exchanged between the two modes and the modal amplitudes and frequencies are modulated. The modulation rates are described by the slowly varying phase angle γ_1.

10.4 Mode Locking

From equations (10.1c,d) if one defines

$$e_{f1} \doteq -(\alpha_{121}^* a_2/4\omega_1)\cos\gamma_1,$$

and

$$e_{f2} \doteq (\alpha_{112} a_1^2/4\omega_2 a_2)\cos\gamma_1,$$

one can write

$$\phi_1(t_1) = -\frac{\alpha^*_{121}}{4\omega_1} \int a_2 \cos\gamma_1 \, dt_1 = \int e_{f1} \, dt_1,$$

$$\phi_2(t_1) = -\frac{\alpha_{112}}{4\omega_2} \int \frac{a_1^2}{a_2} \cos\gamma_1 \, dt_1 = \int e_{f2} \, dt_1. \quad (10.3a, b)$$

Equations (10.3a, b) show that the action of the non-linear shell oscillators is that of an integrator generating the phase angles ϕ_n of the oscillator signals $\tfrac{1}{2}a_n(t_1)e^{i(\omega_{n t0} + \phi_n(t_1))}$. This is precisely the role played by the *voltage-controlled oscillator* (VCO) in an electronic phase-locked loop (see for example Gardner 1979). In the case of the steelpan however, because of the non-linear dynamics, the notes are *displacement-controlled oscillators* (DCO's). In the sense of servo theory, e_{f1} and e_{f2} are *error displacements* with γ_1 as the *phase error*.

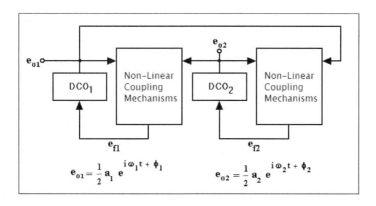

Fig. 10.1. Model of the coupled non-linear modes on a steelpan note. Mode 1 on the left and mode 2 on the right.

The equivalent loop model is shown in Figure 10.1. Here, the error signals correspond to the observed amplitude modulations. An essential difference between the operation of the present system and that of an electronic phase-locked loop is that in the latter, only phase information (and not energy) is transferred to the VCO after comparison is made between the VCO frequency and the reference frequency. On a steelpan note however, both phase information and energy are transferred among the various tuned vibrating modes.

10.5 The Lock or Synchronous Mode

By the definition of 'lock', the system is *locked* or in the *synchronous mode*, if

$$\phi'_n = 0.$$

From the cosine in the integrand of equations (10.3a, b), this requires that ϕ_n arrive at one of the stable nulls $\gamma_1 = \pi(4m \pm 1)/2$. In practice, the conditions for steady state are less precise and may be more realistically defined by the conditions $|\phi'_n| \le \delta_\omega$ and $|\phi_n - 2m\pi| \le \delta_\phi$. But this is a *steady state* condition that cannot be maintained over the duration of the tone driven initially by an impact. The system will therefore constantly be in the *acquisition mode*, with smooth passages through the synchronous mode if the conditions are right. This behavior produces frequency modulations that exceed the frequency limit δ_ω.

If the present system is required to lock 'harmonically', with $\omega_2 \approx 2\omega_1$, a clearer understanding of the operation of this system can be obtained by considering that initially, the system is not in lock but that the frequency relation is closely harmonic. The quadratic non-linearity, described by the coupling parameter α_{112}, will generate from model (with displacement u_1), a constant term and a second harmonic term:

$$u_1^2 \approx (\cos \omega_1 t)^2 = \frac{1}{2}(1 + \cos 2\omega_1 t). \tag{10.4}$$

Identify in equation (10.4) the constant term of magnitude ½ and the second harmonic term ½$\cos(2\omega_1 t)$. On using the full expression for u_1 this constant term will be replaced by a slowly varying component, the *drift term* (see Chapter 7). The second harmonic component at $2\omega_1$ will beat against the second mode at ω_2. Another component (the *combination* component) at frequency $\omega_2 - \omega_1$ generated through the quadratic coupling defined by the parameter $\alpha_{121} (\equiv \alpha_{211})$ will beat against the first mode at ω_1. Under these conditions the error displacements will consist of two beat components of low frequency $\cong |\omega_2 - 2\omega_1|$. These error displacements, by generating the phase changes in equations (10.1a,b), will produce changes in the instantaneous frequencies $\omega_1 + \phi_1'$, $\omega_2 + \phi_2'$ of mode1 and mode2 respectively, and at some point these frequencies will be harmonically related and lock may result. While the error displacements may assume levels sufficient to attain lock, the system will be losing energy through internal damping, transmission losses and acoustic radiation. Therefore the locked state can only be *transitional*. These changes show up as the amplitude and frequency modulations of the decaying musical tones of the instrument.

Mode locking with a 1:2 frequency ratio occurs when

$$\omega_2 + \phi_2' = 2(\omega_1 + \phi_1') \qquad (10.5)$$

which may be written

$$\omega_2 - 2\omega_1 = 2\phi_1' - \phi_2' \qquad (10.6)$$

and finally as

$$\Omega = \left(\frac{\alpha_{112} \, a_1^2}{4 \, \omega_2 \, a_2} - \frac{\alpha_{121}^*}{2 \, \omega_1} a_2 \right) \cos \gamma_1 \; . \qquad (10.7)$$

Since $-1 \leq \cos \gamma_1 \leq +1$, this locking condition is equivalent to

$$|\Omega| \leq \left| \frac{\alpha_{112} \, a_1^2}{4 \, \omega_2 \, a_2} - \frac{\alpha_{121}^*}{2 \, \omega_1} a_2 \right| \; . \qquad 10.8)$$

The condition given by equation (10.8) provides less detail than equation (10.7) on the synchronous operation but it is a useful condition not requiring the phase data. The expression on the right-hand side of equation (10.8) gives the greatest frequency separation between the second mode signal at ω_2 and the frequency-doubled signal at $2\omega_1$ in order to attain lock. This expression is therefore the *pull-in range*, which, for the present system, is dependent on the modal amplitudes (an interesting non-linear behavior).

$$\text{Pull-in Range} = \left| \frac{\alpha_{112}\, a_1^2}{4\, \omega_2\, a_2} - \frac{\alpha_{121}^*}{2\, \omega_1} a_2 \right|. \tag{10.9}$$

Mode locking therefore requires large values of the coupling parameter α_{112} or the modal amplitude a_1 and small values of α_{121}^* and a_2. In typical phase–locked loops, the reference oscillator is of stable and fixed frequency. In the present system the first mode acts as the reference but its frequency is modulated by $\phi_1' [= -(\alpha_{121}^* a_2 / 4\omega_1) \cos \gamma_1]$ which effectively reduces the pull-in range as the second term in equation (10.9) shows.

10.6 Analysis of Real and Simulated $F^\#_4$ and $E^\flat_4$ Notes

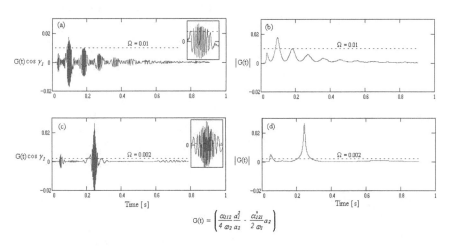

Fig. 10.2. Locking condition determined for a real $F^\#_4$ note (a) and (b) and a real $E^\flat_4$ note (c) and (d). Observe the rare occasions (emphasized in the insets) when $|G(t)|$ exceed the detuning parameter Ω (in normalized units) allowing the possibility of attaining the lock state.

The locking conditions in the form of equation (10.7) and the equivalent form equation (10.8) are shown in Figure (10.2) for two sampled notes $\mathbf{F}^{\#}_4$ and $\mathbf{E}^{\flat}_4$. In Figure 10.2(a) the condition of equation (10.7) expressed as $\Omega = G(t) \cos(\gamma_1)$ is satisfied during the time period 0.09 to 0.1 s as the $\mathbf{F}^{\#}_4$ system makes smooth passages through the synchronous mode (see details in inset on Figure 10.2(a)). Figure 10.2(b) shows that synchronous operation is possible over this time interval but describes the passages in less detail. In Figure 10.2c the condition of equation (10.7) expressed as $\Omega = G(t) \cos(\gamma_1)$ is satisfied during the time period 0.2 to 0.23 s as the $\mathbf{E}^{\flat}_4$ system makes smooth passages through the synchronous mode (see details in inset on Figure 10.2(c)). Figure 10.2(d) describes these synchronous passages in less detail.

The locking conditions on the simulated $\mathbf{F}^{\#}_4$ and $\mathbf{E}^{\flat}_4$ notes are shown in Figure 10.3(a-d). The simulations are in complete agreement with the real system. The experimental data of the real and simulated notes verify the theoretical conclusion that on steelpan notes, the system makes only smooth passages through the synchronous (locked) mode and remains essentially in the acquisition mode. The acquisition mode is accompanied by frequency and amplitude modulations that characterize the tones of the sounding notes.

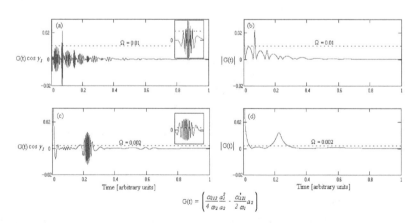

Fig. 10.3. Locking condition determined for the simulated $\mathbf{F}^{\#}_4$ note (a) and (b) and the simulated $\mathbf{E}^{\flat}_4$ note (c) and (d). Observe the rare occasions (emphasized in the insets) when $|G(t)|$ exceed the detuning parameter Ω allowing the possibility of attaining the lock state.

10.7 Mode Locking on the Pung To*ne*

It is clear that on this musical instrument, where significant amplitude and frequency modulations are necessary for good tonality, the sounding note will remain in the acquisition mode. However, during the tuning of the instrument, a note can be placed in the state where the frequency of mode2 is exactly equal to the second harmonic of mode1 ($\omega_2 = 2\omega_1$, equivalent to making $\Omega = 0$). This produces a musically unpleasant tone, the 'pung tone' in which the fundamental (mode1) after the initial rapid attack, decays rapidly in intensity, with mode2 in the meanwhile rising more slowly then finally decaying to zero. To be precise, this is the *2-mode Pung Tone* (see Section 14.24). There are no additional amplitude modulations and the frequencies remain stable throughout the duration of the tone. Figure 10.4 shows a simulation of this tone where these properties are clearly seen. In Figure 10.4(b), $|G(t)| \geq \Omega$ (= 0) is satisfied, confirming that the pung tone is a classic example of mode locking.

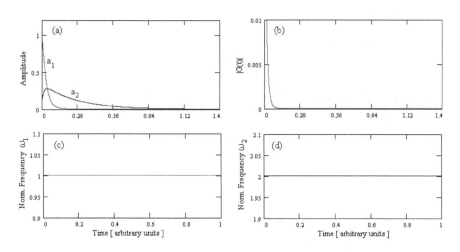

Fig. 10.4. The free phase of a simulated pung tone: (a) amplitude time-history, (b) locking condition showing $|G(t)| \geq \Omega$ (= 0), (c) mode1 normalized frequency and (d) mode2 normalized frequency.

The case of the *3-mode Pung Tone* (see Section 14.24) is somewhat different. In this case the combination resonance formed by the non-linear interaction of mode2 and mode3 with mode1 (determined by the parameter α_{231}) results in the transfer of phase information on this resonance to mode1, that alters the frequency of mode1 for a short duration (see Chapter 14, Figure 14.28). There is no change in the frequency of mode2 during that short period however.

This analysis adds further clarification to the *often-confusing* reference to 'harmonics' or '*tuning the harmonics*' by pan makers. **On a properly tuned steelpan instrument, the higher modes are never tuned as harmonics of the fundamental.** While the first two higher modes above the fundamental are tuned as the upper octave and the twelfth, they **must not** be tuned with the precision $\omega_2 = 2\omega_1$, $\omega_3 = 3\omega_1$. On this non-linear instrument where the tuned modes are coupled by internal resonances there must be some detuning of the partials — the octave and twelfth must be *stretched* or *compressed* (see Chapter 14). Tuning modes to the exact harmonic results in mode locking which generates the poorly sounding pung tones.

On the Pan, *as a rule*, all partials above the key-note must be stretched or compressed. This means that only the key-notes on a tuned pan follow the adopted 12-TET musical scale exactly. There is no way to get around this by having all the partials tuned exactly on the musical scale without producing a 'dud.'

CHAPTER 11

Vibrational Analyses of Mass Loaded Plates and Shallow Shells by the Receptance Method with Application to the Steelpan

11.1 Introduction

The effects of mass-loading on the fundamental frequency of circular and elliptical plates have been studied by a number of workers: Goel (1975) presented exact solutions, in terms of Bessel functions, for the natural frequencies of the circular plate on elastic supports with a central mass. Grossi et al. (1986) and Sonemblum et al. (1989) applied optimized Rayleigh-Ritz procedures to clamped and simply supported plates carrying concentrated central masses. Liew (1992) has analyzed the vibration of circular plates on line and ring supports carrying concentrated masses using the pb-2 Rayleigh-Ritz method. In Achong (1994), an optimized Rayleigh-Ritz method was applied to mass-loaded circular and elliptical plates on elastic supports. Although all these papers deal with plates they are relevant to the shallow shells found on the pan as a limiting case when the rise of the shell tends to zero.

The present analysis seeks approximate solutions for the fundamental frequencies of vibrating mass-loaded plates and shallow shells using the receptance method (Bishop and Johnson 1960). As seen in the open literature, this method has been applied to the vibration of a variety of mechanical systems; Wilken and

Soedel (1976a, b), Azimi et al. (1984), and Azimi (1988a, b). Azimi, in [1988a], used the method to study the symmetrical vibrational modes of circular plates for a wide range of edge support conditions, and in (1988b), to determine the frequency equation with mass loading at the center. In my own work on this problem, Achong (1996a), I applied the receptance method to circular and elliptical plates as well as the shallow shells found on the steelpan. This work is included in this Chapter.

Also included in the present analysis, is a method to determine the normalized transverse displacements (mode shapes) of vibrating plates and shallow dome-shaped shells *by frequency measurements only*. This method of using *frequency-only measurements* to determine mode shapes is a new and interesting procedure developed here specifically for the steelpan but can be applied to other musical instruments with vibrating surfaces.

11.2. Receptance Method Applied to the Mass-Loading Problem

11.2.1 The Mass-Loaded Plate

The following treatment of the mass-loaded plate is given only as an introduction to the analysis. Mass loaded plates or rather 'free' mass loaded plates are not found on the steelpan. However, their dynamical behavior closely approximates the dynamics of the shallow shells that form the notes on the steelpan. Consider now, as shown in Figure 11.1, a total of N concentrated masses attached to a plate at arbitrary positions, producing a total of (N+1) sub-systems. X_P and X_M are displacement vectors while F_P and F_M are force vectors for plate and concentrated mass respectively.

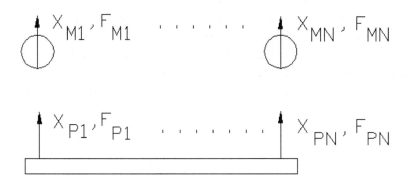

Fig. 11.1. The plate and concentrated masses joined at N co-ordinates.

In the absence of any externally applied force, and so long as the masses remain coupled to the plate, the system satisfies the following compatibility and equilibrium conditions

$$X_P - X_M = 0, \quad F_P + F_M = 0. \tag{11.1}$$

When the forces vary sinusoidally with frequency ω,

$$X_M = [\alpha] F_M, \quad X_P = [\beta] F_P, \tag{11.2}$$

where $[\alpha]$ and $[\beta]$ are the receptance matrices of the masses and plate respectively. Equations (11.1) and (11.2) give the frequency equation of the mass-loaded plate as

$$Det([\alpha] + [\beta]) = 0, \tag{11.3}$$

here Det is the determinant of matrices.

11.3.1 The Elliptical Plate

In anticipation of the receptance analysis for the shallow ellipsoidal shells that form the notes (true notes) on the steelpan, and in order to guide the thoughts of the reader on the present treatment of elliptical plates, I point out that because of the relatively small rise found on these notes, the elliptical plate forms a good approximation to the ellipsoidal shells for the receptance analysis. For this reason we consider the elliptical plate at this point. It will however, be incorrect to use the elliptical plate to fully determine the frequencies of the vibrational modes of the ellipsoidal shell. Despite this, there are some aspects of the shell vibration that can be dealt with to good approximation by using the simpler geometry of the elliptical plate.

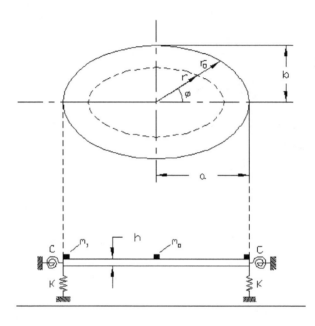

Fig. 11.2. Elliptical plate carrying point-mass m_0 at the centre and ring-mass m_1 along the edge attached to spring supports C and K.

The analysis for the elliptical plate (see Figure 11.2) gives an approximation to the shallow ellipsoidal shells on elliptical planforms representing the true notes on the pan. For the elliptical plate initially at rest, and undamped, the harmonic response at the point (r_i, ϕ_i), to a force $F(r_j, \phi_j; t) = F_j \sin \omega t$ applied at (r_j, ϕ_j) is given by

$$w(r_i, \phi_i; t) = \frac{F_j}{\rho h} \sum_{n=0}^{\infty} \sum_{m=0}^{\infty} \frac{W_{nm}(r_i, \phi_i) W_{nm}(r_j, \phi_j)}{Q_{nm} \omega_{nm}} \int_0^t \sin(\omega \tau) \sin[\omega_{nm}(t - \tau)] d\tau,$$

(11.4)

where

$$Q_{nm} = \int_0^{2\pi} \int_0^{r_0} W_{nm}^2(r,\phi) r \, dr \, d\phi, \qquad (11.5)$$

ω_{nm} are the natural frequencies of the plate, ρ is the density, h is the thickness, r_0 is the plate boundary, and $W_{nm}(r,\phi) = W_m(r)\cos n(\phi - \phi_{nm})$ are the normal mode shapes of the plate. Using (11.4), the plate receptances in modal series form can be written directly;

$$\beta_{ij} = \frac{w(r_i,\phi_i;t)}{F(r_j,\phi_j;t)} = \frac{1}{\rho h} \sum_{n=0}^{\infty} \sum_{m=0}^{\infty} \frac{W_{nm}(r_i,\phi_i) W_{nm}(r_j,\phi_j)}{Q_{nm}(\omega_{nm}^2 - \omega^2)}, \qquad (11.6)$$

with the reciprocity condition $\beta_{ij} = \beta_{ji}$ satisfied. The receptance of a concentrated mass M_j attached to the plate at (r_j, φ_j), is given by

$$\alpha_{jj} = \frac{w(r_j,\phi_j;t)}{F(r_j,\phi_j;t)} = -\frac{1}{M_j \omega^2}. \qquad (11.7)$$

The frequency equation (11.3) of the mass-loaded plate can be written as

$$\text{Det} \begin{bmatrix} \beta_{11}+\alpha_{11} & \beta_{12} & \beta_{13} & \cdots & \cdots \\ & \beta_{22}+\alpha_{22} & \beta_{23} & \cdots & \cdots \\ & & \beta_{33}+\alpha_{33} & \cdots & \cdots \\ & \cdot & \cdot & \cdot & \cdots \\ \text{(Symmetric)} & \cdot & & \cdot & \beta_{NN}+\alpha_{NN} \end{bmatrix} = 0.$$

(11.8)

Equations (11.6), (11.7) and (11.8) combine to give the eigenfrequencies of the mass-loaded elliptical plate. These eigenvalues can only be found numerically and require the mode shape for each term counted in the series. The problem is simplified however, for the case where the fundamental mode ($m = n = 0$) dominates the series in (11.6). This is possible if the attached masses produce only small changes in the natural frequencies of the plate. For this special case, (11.8) reduces to the simple form

$$1 + \sum_{j=1}^{N} \frac{\beta_{jj}}{\alpha_{jj}} = 0. \qquad (11.9)$$

If the boundary of the elliptical plate is defined as $r_0 = a(1 + k^2 \sin^2 \phi)^{-\frac{1}{2}}$ where $k^2 = (a/b)^2 - 1$ with semi-axes a and b, it may be assumed as in Achong (1995), that the *iso-deflection contour lines* (contours or lines of equal displacement) correspond to the family of concentric ellipses $r = a \xi (1 + k^2 \sin^2 \phi)^{-\frac{1}{2}}$, with the variable ξ ($= r/r_0$) having the value 0 at the plate center and 1 at the boundary. For the case where (11.9) applies, writing the fundamental frequency and mode shape of the unloaded plate as ω_0 and W_0 respectively, we first obtain from (11.5) the expression

$$Q_0 = 2\pi ab \int_0^1 W_0^2(\xi) \xi \, d\xi,$$

and from (11.6), (11.7) and (11.9), we get the frequency equation

$$\left(\frac{\omega_0}{\omega}\right)^2 = 1 + \frac{\sum_{j=1}^{N} \mu_j W_0^2(\xi_j)}{2 \int_0^1 W_0^2(\xi) \xi \, d\xi}, \qquad (11.10)$$

where $\mu_j = \dfrac{M_j}{M_p}$ is a normalized *loading ratio*, with $M_p = \rho \pi abh$ being the mass of the plate.

If ω_j is the frequency for the plate when loaded with a single mass M_j, it follows from (11.10) that the frequency ω of the plate with all N masses attached is given by

$$\frac{1}{\omega^2} = \sum_{j=1}^{N}\left(\frac{1}{\omega_j^2}\right) - (N-1)\frac{1}{\omega_0^2}. \qquad (11.11)$$

For the plate with a single mass M attached at the center, (11.10) gives

$$\left(\frac{f_0}{f}\right)^2 - 1 = \frac{M\,W_0^2(0)}{2\,M_p\int_0^1 W_0^2(\xi)\xi d\xi}, \qquad (11.12)$$

where $\omega\,(rad/s) = 2\pi f\,(Hz)$. We emphasize here that this result applies to cases with small mass-ratios μ, which is the condition laid down for (11.9).

We note that (11.10) may be written in the general form

$$\left(\frac{\omega_0}{\omega}\right)^2 = 1 + \frac{1}{M_0}\sum_{j=1}^{N} M_j\,(W_0^2)_j, \qquad (11.13)$$

where $M_0 = M_p <W_0^2>$ is the first-mode equivalent mass, and $<W_0^2> = \frac{1}{A}\int_A W_0^2 dA$ is the spatial average with the domain A as the area of the plate. Equation (11.13) allows solutions to the problem for plates of arbitrary shapes.

11.3.2 Thin, Shallow Shells

We now develop an approximate analysis applicable to thin shallow shells having spherical or ellipsoidal shapes similar to those obtained on the steelpan notes. The section of a note on a tenor steelpan (for example), bounded by the azimuthal nodal line for the first mode, has an elliptical planform, and may be typically represented by the following parameter ratios: aspect ratio $(a/b)_{max} \approx 1.25$, thickness ratio $(b/h) \approx 10^2$, $(R/h) \approx 1900$, and $(b/H_0) \approx 40$, where R is the smallest radius of curvature and H_0 is the central elevation or rise of the mid-surface of the shell above the projected base plane (the planform). In addition, following Rekach (1978), and Lim and Liew (1994), the thin shallow shell parameters, in our notation, should satisfy the conditions

$$b/h \geq 20, \quad R/h \geq 20, \quad \text{and} \quad b/H_0 \geq 5.$$

All these limits are satisfied on the steelpan notes. The following simplifications can therefore be made in our analysis:

(i) The shallowness of the shells allows the use of a system of coordinates generated by the projection of the mid-surface of the shell unto the base plane (planform). In this simplification, the equation of contour lines for the shallow ellipsoidal shell is the same as that for the corresponding flat elliptical plate under similar boundary conditions (see Bucco and Mazumdar 1983).

(ii) In addition to the radial force and radial (transverse) deflection on the vibrating shell, there are the in-plane forces and deflections. One expects the radial force to dominate the shell-mass interaction when the mass-loaded shell is vibrating in the fundamental mode. The receptances of the shell and the concentrated mass may therefore be determined by the radial interaction force only. Both the radial and in-plane forces are necessary however, for the determination of the natural frequencies and mode shapes of the unloaded shell. Wilken and Soedel (1976a) have used a similar simplification for the case of ring-stiffened cylindrical shells.

Under these assumptions, with spatial averaging carried out over the projected area, the frequency equation for the shell is found to be identical to (11.10) where M_p is the mass of a flat plate equal in area to the projected area of the shell on the base plane.

As a check on the validity of this result, we make use of the general expression for the first natural frequency of a linear elastic system

$$\omega_0 = 1/\sqrt{M_0 C_0}, \qquad (11.14)$$

where M_0 and C_0 are the first-mode equivalent mass and compliance respectively. Equation (11.14) is applicable to all systems, irrespective of structure, as it follows from the general physical properties of all linear elastic systems. We make use an asterisk to distinguish quantities for the shell from the corresponding quantities for the plate. For the unloaded uniform shell,

$$M_0^* = \frac{M_s}{S} \int_S W_0^{*2} \, dS = M_s <W_0^{*2}>,$$

where M_s is the shell mass, S is the shell mid-surface area, and

$$W_0^{*2} = V_0^2 + U_0^2 + W_0^2,$$

with V_0 and U_0 as the in-plane deflections. The structural configuration of the mass-loaded shell represents a combination of a continuous system — the shell — and a set of discrete point masses, with an equivalent mass given by

$$M_{0L}^* = \underbrace{\frac{M_s}{S} \int_S W_0^{*2} \, dS}_{\text{continuous}} + \underbrace{\sum_{j=1}^{N} M_j (W_0^{*2})_j}_{\text{discrete}}. \qquad (11.15)$$

Since the natural frequency of the loaded shell is $\omega = 1/\sqrt{M_{0L}^* C_0}$, we obtain from (11.14) and (11.15)

$$\left(\frac{\omega_0}{\omega}\right)^2 = 1 + \frac{1}{M_0^*} \sum_{j=1}^{N} M_j (W_0^{*2})_j. \qquad (11.16)$$

For very shallow shells, the first mode is bending-dominated and primarily associated with transverse motion. In this case, if we can neglect the contributions of in-plane deflections to the change in frequency of the shell produced by the loading, and if $M_s \approx M_p$ (as satisfied by the steelpan notes considered here), then (11.16) will reduce to (11.13). Equation (11.16) does not require these assumptions however.

11.3.3 The Powder-Coated Note

Some steelpan notes are painted or powder-coated (see Section 2.25 for a discussion on powder coating). This coating may not add any degree of stiffness to the note but can introduce only mass loading to the note surface. In this case the coated note represents a combination of a of a continuous paint coating and another continuous system — the note material (steel) —, with an equivalent mass given by

$$M^*_{0L} = \frac{M_s}{S} \int_S W_0^{*2} \, dS + \int_S \rho_c t_c W_0^{*2} \, dS, \qquad (11.17)$$

where ρ_c and t_c are the density and thickness of the coating respectively. Both of these quantities may change with position on the note surface. One gets from this, the frequency equation for the coated note

$$\left(\frac{\omega_0}{\omega}\right)^2 = 1 + \frac{1}{M_0^*} \int_S \rho_c t_c W_0^{*2} \, dS. \qquad (11.18)$$

For a uniform coating of mass M_c, the frequency equation reduces to

$$\left(\frac{\omega_0}{\omega}\right)^2 = 1 + \frac{M_c}{M_0^*} \langle W_0^{*2} \rangle$$

$$= 1 + \frac{M_c}{M_s}. \qquad (11.19)$$

Expressed in Hertz, the frequency f_c of the uniformly coated note is given in terms of the frequency without coating f_0 by

$$f_c = \frac{f_0}{\sqrt{1+\dfrac{M_c}{M_s}}}. \tag{11.20}$$

If the coating is made excessively thick and/or stiff, then the mode shape and the compliance will both be affected. For (11.20) to be applicable the mass of the deposited coating must be kept small in relation to the mass of the note and powder coating material of low stiffness must be used. What is more important however is for the coating to exert negligible effect on the note dynamics. Having said all his, one must realize that the frequency shift of (11.20) may not be observed directly because the tuning process will automatically compensate for the effects on modal frequencies produced by the coating. However, slow drifts in frequency may occur if the curing process for the coating is not properly carried out (see Section 2.25) and the mechanical properties of the coating undergo large changes as it ages.

From these observations it is clear that we must consider the effects of using coatings with appreciable stiffness. Equation (11.18) can be used to cover the case where the coating is non-uniform so we need only consider the case where the coating is uniform but of appreciable stiffness. In this case the stiffness of the coated note will be greater than the uncoated note or equivalently, the compliance of the coated note C_c will be less than the compliance of the uncoated note $C_c < C_0$. Repeating the analysis gives the frequency equation for the case of stiff coating as

$$f_c = \frac{f_0}{\sqrt{\dfrac{C_c}{C_0}\left(1+\dfrac{M_c}{M_s}\right)}}. \tag{11.21}$$

Observe from equation (11.21) that the reduction in compliance when the coating is applied will partially compensate for the frequency reduction effect of the mass loading. However, as the coating ages under normal environmental conditions the compliance of the coating may undergo irreversible changes (most likely becoming more compliant, effectively increasing C_c) which will call for re-tuning of the instrument. Coating materials that show signs of *chalking* (see Section 12.21) with age are more susceptible to this problem. These changes may occur even while the instrument is kept in storage.

11.4 Approximate Mode Shape Determination

11.4.1 Fundamental Mode

If the shell or elliptical plate is driven by an external vibrator, with a test mass placed first at the center $\xi = 0$ then at an arbitrary point ξ, one obtains from (11.10) for the plate, or from (11.16) for the shell,

$$w(\xi) = \frac{W_0(\xi)}{W_0(0)} = \left[\left\{\left(\frac{f_0}{f}\right)^2 - 1\right\}_\xi\right]^{\frac{1}{2}}, \qquad (11.22)$$

where $w(\xi)$ is the normalized mode amplitude at position ξ. Equation (11.22) allows approximate mode shapes to be found by attaching a small test mass at selected positions on the structure and measuring the modal frequencies.

11.4.2 Generalizing to Higher Modes

Under normal excitation of steelpan notes by stick impact, the fundamental mode usually dominates. However, when driven by an external vibrator, higher modes can be made to dominate by driving the system at the desired resonant frequency. One can therefore choose a mode above the fundamental to dominate the series in (11.6) which will give the general forms for (11.21) and (11.22) for the (driven) n^{th} mode of frequency f_n as

$$f_{n,c} = \frac{f_n}{\sqrt{\frac{C_{cn}}{C_n}\left(1 + \frac{M_c}{M_s}\right)}}, \qquad (11.23)$$

$$w_n(\xi) = \left[\left\{\left(\frac{f_n}{f}\right)^2_\xi - 1\right\}\right]^{\frac{1}{2}}. \qquad (11.24)$$

From (11.23) one should note that the effects of aging discussed in Section 11.3.3, depends on the vibrational mode. The changes in frequency as the coating ages will therefore vary from one partial to another. Since aging will bring about structural changes in the coating material, the effects will be more noticeable on the higher partials.

On the Pan, where internal resonances are likely to excite a number of normal modes, for (11.23) and (11.24) to be usable one must ensure that the levels of excitation from the external source are not excessive. If a number of modes are simultaneously excited then the reduced frequency formula given by (11.9) does not apply since a number of terms are present in the series in (11.6). In this case, simple solutions are not possible since the mode shapes of all excited modes must then be known. While (11.23) can be used to determine the shift in frequencies of the key-note, octave and twelfth when they are individually excited by an external sinusoidal source, it gives only an approximation to these frequency shifts when these three modes are all excited by stick impacts. In the same way, equation (11.24) gives the mode shape when each mode is excited singly and not the shape of the note surface when all three modes are excited simultaneously.

11.5 Experimental Data on the Steelpan

The effects of attached concentrated masses on the fundamental frequencies of the steelpan have been investigated experimentally by the author in Achong (1996a) and Achong et al. (1993). The experimental arrangement consisted of a tenor pan suspended horizontally by means of cords fastened to the rim, and excited by an oscillator-driven electromagnetic vibrator attached to the center of the pan face.

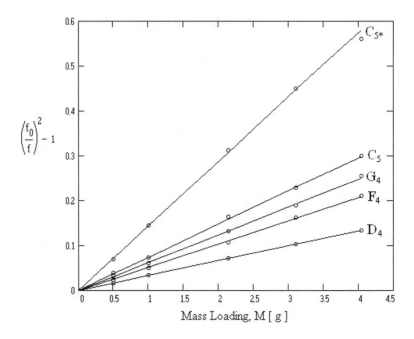

Fig. 11.3. Experimental values of $(f_0/f)^2 - 1$ for notes on the steelpan when loaded with central masses M having small contact areas. The straight lines are least squares fit to the data points.

The microphone for a sound level meter was placed 1 m above the pan face and resonance determined by observing, on an oscilloscope, the maximum response of the microphone to the sound generated by the note in resonance. The resonances were well pronounced and audibly loud (75 - 80 dB). With the notes having a quality factor Q, typically around 100, resonances were determined to within ±0.1 Hz using a well referenced digital frequency counter. Test masses, in the form of small ceramic magnets, were attached to the desired positions on the note surface.

Figure 11.3 shows the experimental data for mass-loading at the anti-nodal point (co-ordinate center) for the following 'outer' notes on a tenor steelpan: C_5 ($f_0 = 523.0$ Hz), G_4 ($f_0=392.0$ Hz), F_4 ($f_0=349.2$ Hz) and D_4 ($f_0=293.6$ Hz). The data labeled C_5* were obtained for the D_5 ($f_0 = 587.3$ Hz) 'inner' note, re-tuned by the author to C_5. The linearity displayed in Figure 11.3 is consistent with (11.19) and this suggests that the present theory is applicable to the domed shaped notes on the steelpan.

In the following data for the C_5 and C_{5*} notes, the shell is defined as that sub-section enclosed by the azimuthal nodal line (elliptical or circular in shape), determined by a Chladni method: C_5; $a = 5.5$cm, $b = 4.75$cm, $h = 0.046$cm, $H = 0.13$cm, $M_p = 29.7$ g: C_{5*}; $a = b = 4.75$cm, $h = 0.032$cm, $H = 0.09$cm, $M_p = 17.5$ g, where H is the rise of the domed shell above the plane containing the nodal line, and M_p is the mass of a flat plate bounded by the nodal line. The geometries of these two notes of equal frequencies are clearly different and observe in particular, that the pan face is thinner in the central region. From the slopes of the best-fit lines in Figure 11.3, with the maximum displacement normalized to unity, $W_0^*(0) = 1$, and taking $M_s \approx M_p$, we obtain the following estimates for the spatial average $<W_0^{*2}>$,

$$<W_0^{*2}> = 0.45 \pm 0.01 \quad \text{for } C_5$$
$$= 0.40 \pm 0.01 \quad \text{for } C_{5*},$$

which, within the margin of error, show the mode shapes to be different for the two notes.

The results demonstrate that there is no unique geometry or unique set of boundary conditions that determines the fundamental frequency of a note on the steelpan.

Note: The boundary of the inner D_5 note re-tuned by the author to C_5 was re-shaped from its original elliptical form into a circular form. This was done not only to ensure that the fundamental mode shape is different from that on the outer C_5 note but also to ensure that the second and third modes do not lie close to the harmonics of the fundamental. See Sections 14.25 – 14.26 where the $5/4^{ths}$-Law and the $9/8^{ths}$-Rule are discussed. This guarantees that the fundamental mode will dominate the series in equation (11.6).

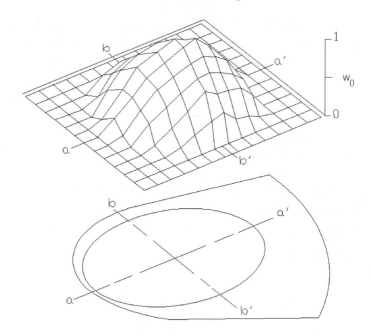

Fig. 11.4. Composite diagram of the $F_4^\#$ note showing azimuthal nodal line (ellipse) and the 3-D plot of normalized mode amplitudes (the vertical scale for W_0 is exaggerated for clarity).

The normalized mode amplitudes computed from (11.22) for the $\mathbf{F}_4^\#$ note (f_0 = 370.0 Hz), are shown as a 3-D plot in Figure 11.4. In obtaining this data, the use of a small ceramic magnet (mass = 2 g) as the test mass, allowed the load to be quickly and easily repositioned. The slight asymmetry about the two axes on the 3-D plot is due to local variations in mechanical and geometrical properties produced by hammering the notes. In other tests, such variations were observed to produce distortions in the radial nodal lines of the higher vibrational modes.

The ellipse drawn on the surface of the note in Figure 11.4 represents the azimuthal nodal line determined by a Chladni method. The physical data on this note are: H = 0.10 cm, h = 0.05 cm, a = 5.6 cm, b = 5.1 cm, and M_p = 34.5 g. The slanted orientation of the axes on the note surface is typical of many of the notes on a steelpan and represents the result of the 'tuning by shaping' process used by the pan maker to obtain the desired tonal properties of each note. This particular $\mathbf{F}_4^\#$ note with its low rise-factor H/h = 2 and low aspect ratio a/b = *1.098*, produces weak higher partials (see Chapter 14). This note was tuned this way by the author in order to emphasize the fundamental mode (key-note) only.

11.6 Chapter Summary

Useful applications of the receptance method have been presented for thin shallow shells and the analytical approximations are seen to be applicable to the notes on the steelpan. Once the mode shape for the unloaded system is known, the present method allows the fundamental frequencies for the mass-loaded system to be determined using very simple equations. Estimates for the parameter $<W_0^2>$ can be obtained from measured modal data (frequency domain) based on the response of the vibrating system to mass loading. The vibration mode amplitudes may also be computed from frequency measurements on the loaded system. The method can be applied to other geometries and boundary conditions to study local vibrations in fairly complicated structures.

CHAPTER 12

Acoustics of the Steelpan

12.1 The Air Column semi-enclosed by the Skirt and Pan Face

We now examine the possibility for the air column partly enclosed by the skirt to execute cavity vibration at frequencies that are harmonically related to an excited note. The walls formed by the pan face and skirt are not rigid as is usually the case for classical air columns but this effect produces little change in the present consideration. In addition, resonance phenomena only occur if *standing waves* can be set up effectively in the air column. The standing waves must draw their energy from the note placed at the top of the air column. This situation is very unlikely on the high-end pans where the skirt length is shorter than the radius of the skirt and the pan face extends most of the way into the column.

Column resonances are more likely on the low-end bass instruments with their much longer skirts. Treating the bass pan as a tube with one open end, radius r and length L (end-corrected to $L + 0.6r$), the resonant frequencies at an ambient temperature of $23°$ C are given by

$$f_n = n \frac{86}{L + 0.6r} \quad n = 1, 3, 5, 7, \ldots \text{ (odd)},$$

with dimensions in meters. Resonances between note and air column are only possible if the column frequency falls within the frequency bandwidth of the note vibration which is around 4 Hz (see Table 9.2). For a bass having $L = 0.88$ m, $r = 0.29$ m, the first three resonances occur at 81.6 Hz, 244.8 Hz, 407.97 Hz. Only the lowest resonance is close to the bass notes $\mathbf{D}^{\#}_2$ (77.78 Hz) and $\mathbf{E}_2$ (82.4 Hz). However, the second resonance at 244.8 Hz is close enough to $\mathbf{B}_3$ (246.94 Hz) which is the octave of the $\mathbf{B}_2$ (123.47 Hz) note on the bass. In addition, most bass pans are played with their open ends just a few centimeters above the floor level. The column then approaches a tube closed at both ends with a shift of the lower resonances towards higher frequencies but with little radiation from the open end.

General Remarks: In practice, because of the relatively large opening at the base of these pan skirts, column resonances have not contributed any noticeable increase in acoustical response on these instruments. This is good, because these resonances would have resulted in an unpleasant 'booming' sound quality when particular notes are played. The air column will contribute mainly *mass loading* to the vibrating note and a small (mostly imperceptible) addition to the stiffness especially on bass pans with partially opened bottom ends..

12.2 Acoustic Terms and Standards of Reference

We now present the terms and standards of reference appropriate for our discussion on the acoustic radiation of our musical instrument. Occasional references may be made to the International Organization for Standardization (ISO), the International Electrotechnical Commission (IEC) and the American National Standards Institute (ANSI). We begin by looking at the basic response of the human ear to sound pressure, some psychoacoustic effects, then follow this up with a discussion of the quantities used to measure the sound output of the steelpan.

Sound is by (i) *technical definition*, the oscillation in pressure, stress, particle displacement, particle velocity, etc. in a medium, or the superposition of such propagated oscillations, and by (ii) *common definition*, the auditory sensation evoked by the oscillation described in (i) (refer to ANSI S1.1-1994).

The human ear is a marvelous device, possessing very high sensitivity over a relatively broad range of frequencies — the audio range of frequencies — which extend from tens of Hertz up to approximately 20 kHz depending on the individual listener. Generally the upper frequency limit decreases with age. For a variety of reasons, a person may also suffer permanent increase in the threshold of audibility — Permanent Threshold Shift or Permanent Hearing Loss (refer to ANSI S3.20-1995). The latter is commonly referred to as 'hard-of-hearing.' For example, the present author can hardly detect the alarm on his digital watch but his grandson detects it in the adjoining room — a fact of life. Such impairment may also come as a result of excessive exposure to high levels of noise — an occupational hazard.

12.3 Sound Pressure and Sound Pressure Level (SPL)

Sound Pressure is the minute fluctuations in atmospheric pressure that accompany the passage of a sound wave; from the feeble buzz of a mosquito to the roar of a jet engine. These pressure fluctuations drive the tympanic membrane of the ear into vibrations which are then transmitted to the inner ear to produce, in the brain, the sensation of audible sound. For a steady sound, the sound pressure is that value averaged over a period of time or for one of varying pressure, as the root-mean-square (rms) sound pressure at a point during a given time interval. The unit of measure is the Pascal (Pa), where $1 \text{ Pa} \equiv 1 \text{ N·m}^{-2}$ (refer to ANSI S1.1-1994). The weakest sound that can be heard by a person with good hearing in a very quiet environment is expressed as a sound pressure of 20 micropascals (20 µPa) — approximately equal to the pressure disturbance at the ear created by a mosquito at a distance of 2 meters.

Because of the very wide range of pressures encountered in everyday life, a compressed or *logarithmic* scale is adopted. In the logarithmic scale to base 10, the time-averaged-square of the pressure with reference to the square of the lowest level of audibility p_{ref} = 20 µPa, is expressed in units of decibels (dB). By this, one gets for sound pressure p, the *Sound Pressure Level* (symbol: L_p)

$$L_p = 10 \log \left(\frac{p^2}{p_{ref}^2}\right) dB$$

where it is understood that the log function is to base 10.

12.4 Sound Intensity and Sound Intensity Level

Sound Intensity, I, and Sound Pressure at a point in air as the medium are related by the expression:

$$I = \frac{p^2}{2\rho_0 c}$$

where

I = Sound Intensity (units: $Watt \cdot m^{-2}$)
p = sound pressure (Pa)
ρ_0 = density of air ($kg \cdot m^{-3}$)
c = speed of sound in air ($m \cdot s^{-1}$).

The standard threshold of hearing can therefore be stated in terms of pressure and the sound intensity in decibels can be expressed in terms of the sound pressure: *Sound Intensity Levels* are defined with respect to the lowest audible level of intensity $I_{ref} = 10^{-12}$ watt·m^{-2} and expressed in units of decibels (refer to ANSI S.1-1994):

$$L_i = 10 \log \left(\frac{I}{I_{ref}}\right) = 10 \log \left(\frac{p^2}{p_{ref}^2}\right) = 20 \log \left(\frac{p}{p_{ref}}\right) \; dB$$

where

L_I = sound intensity level (dB)
I = sound intensity ($W \cdot m^{-2}$)
$I_{ref} = 10^{-12}$ - reference sound intensity ($W \cdot m^{-2}$)

With this logarithmic scale, doubling the intensity increases the sound level by 3 dB ($\equiv 10 \log(2) = 10 \cdot (0.301) = 3$ dB). The range of sound intensities that the human ear is capable of hearing spans the interval 10^{-12} $W \cdot m^{-2}$ to 100 $W \cdot m^{-2}$. On the logarithmic scale this interval equals 0 dB to 140 dB (observe the compression in the numbers used to express the range of values). To accommodate such a great span in intensities, the ear operates according to a logarithmic law by which it effectively compresses the sound intensity levels. The logarithmic sound intensity level scale adopted in the definition therefore matches the human sense of hearing.

Note*: The use of base 10 is chosen for convenience in the definition and its choice does not imply that the compression mechanism used by the ear also follows the base 10 logarithms. The simple conversion factor $\log_B A$, converts logarithms to base A into logarithms to base B.*

12.5 Loudness

Loudness is the judgment of sound intensity by the human senses as such it is a subjective measure. In terms of the sound intensity level one perceives 0 to 20 dB sound as *very faint*, 70 to 80 dB as *loud* and 140 dB as *deafening* or *ear shattering*. But one might say that it is possible for a subject to judge whether or not two sounds of different pitch are equally loud. But pitch also is subjective so any procedure based on 'pitch' will be unreliable. In order to quantify loudness in a repeatable way, frequency must replace pitch i.e. a well defined sound of fixed frequency (1 kHz is standard) must be chosen as the reference. Because the human ear operates in pairs and the sense of hearing also displays directional properties, the mode of presentation of the test sound must be clearly defined. For these and other reasons, some unexplained, the early 1933 Fletcher-Munson Curves of equal-loudness levels (*isophones*) (Fletcher and Munson 1933) determined by pure tones delivered by headphones is not equivalent to the later 1956 Robinson-Dodson Curves determined by frontal incidence of pure tones delivered by loud speaker in an anechoic (free-field) chamber (Robinson and Dodson 1956). The revised ISO 226:2003 standard *Equal-Loudness Contours* (see Figure 12.1) also differs from both the 1933 and 1956 curves but remains the most reliable results to follow. Of concern here is that the reader be made aware of the existence of these two earlier equal-loudness curves in order to avoid possible confusion.

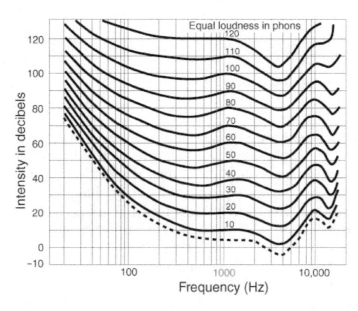

Fig. 12.1. ISO 226:2003 equal-loudness contours.

An *equal-loudness contour* is a measure of sound pressure level (SPL) in dB, over the audible frequency spectrum, for which a listener perceives a constant loudness. The unit of measurement for loudness levels is the *phon*, and by definition two pure tones that have equal phons are equally loud. Also by definition, *the loudness level in phons is numerically equal to the SPL in decibels at 1kHz.* As seen in Figure 12.1, the human ear is most sensitive around 3 kHz to 4 kHz which means that in judging the bass and tenor pans for equal loudness, greater SPL will be required from the bass notes.

12.6 Bass Loss Problem

Observe on the family of equal-loudness curves that the ear is less sensitive at low frequencies and that this *discrimination against the lows* becomes steeper for softer sounds. When this is combined with the *inverse square law* (see Section 12.11.2), *the sound further from the source is not only perceived as less loud but also as being deficient in the bass frequencies.*

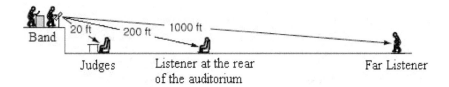

Consider the typical setting for a panorama pan competition in a large, 200 ft long open-air auditorium as sketched above, where the judges are seated at the front a distance of 20 ft from the band. Listeners are located throughout the auditorium except for a far listener located 1000 ft away from the band. Assume that the judges hear both the low C_2 (65.406 Hz) on the Bass and the high G_6 (1568.0 Hz) on the Tenor, at the same loudness of 80 phons. Because the human ear discriminates against the low frequencies, the dB levels required at the location of the judges are: 90 dB at 65.406 Hz and 78 dB at 1568.0 Hz. Using the inverse square law, relative to the position of the judges, the sound intensity at all frequencies will fall by 20 dB at the rear of the open-air auditorium and by 34 dB at the position of the far listener. The intensities and loudness (in phons) at the three locations are tabulated as follows:

	20 ft	200 ft	1000 ft
C_2 (65.406 Hz), 90 dB, 80 phons		70 dB, 55 phons	56 db, 34 phons
G_6 (1568 Hz), 78 dB, 80 phons		58 dB, 60 phons	44 db, 44 phons
Difference = 0 phons		Difference = 5 phons	Difference = 10 phons

While the judges perceive the C_2 and G_6 tones with equal loudness (difference = 0 phons), the listener at the rear perceives the G_6 tone to be the louder by 5 phons while the far listener perceives the G_6 to be the louder by 10 phons. By using the rule of thumb that the power must be increased by approximately a factor of 10 to sound twice as loud, the far listener will perceive the G_6 to be *twice as loud* as the C_2 tone.

It can be seen from this example that location is important as it affects one's perception of the bands' performance. One will almost always find the far listener to be in disagreement with the judges on the performances of the bands. If extra loud basses are used to please the listener at the rear of the auditorium, the band is sure to lose points with the judges who will surely find the band to be unbalanced with the basses dominating.

It will not be out-of-place to comment here on a practice at the Trinidad and Tobago Panorama Competitions to amplify the bands and in doing so, to pass the signals through selective filters with bass and treble boosts in the name of bringing the music to all listeners at the performance. These sound systems, with microphones placed willy-nilly around the stage do more harm than good to the sound. Worst of all they completely destroy the *Chorus Effect* (see Chapter 15).

12.7 Total SPL for a number of Incoherent Sources

Note: Since we are discussing a musical instrument it is important here to distinguish between the following:

(a) the common usage of the word *coherent*, synonymous with *lucid, logical* and *consistent* and
(b) as used in this work, the scientific meaning of the word *coherent* — *two sources of acoustic radiation are said to be coherent if the waves emitted from them have the same frequency and mutually they show zero or constant phase difference.*

Incoherent sources do not satisfy one or both of these two requirements on frequency and phase. Independent sources of sound are mutually incoherent.The very nature of the pan notes as shallow domes supported elastically by the pan face which in turn is supported elastically (almost rigidly by the chime) to the skirt, all of which are immersed in a fluid medium (air) that they may radiate acoustically, makes for an intrinsically incoherent system of audio sources (notes). The notes simply cannot maintain a high degree of coherence over the duration of a sounding tone (~ 1 second). Two wavetrains generated by successive stick-note impacts will be mutually incoherent. The note as an acoustic source radiates waves that are modulated both in amplitude and frequency by mechanisms that are coupled non-linearly. Furthermore the waves consist of a number of partials where the phase relation between any pair of partials is subject to continuous variation over the duration of the tone generated by stick impact. The only tone that is almost free of these modulation effects—the *Pung Tone* — is not employed on the steelpan because of its short duration and the unpleasantness of its sound. Even this special tone is incoherent.

When sound produced by a number of independent sources, arrive at a point in the medium of propagation, the combined effect results from the addition of acoustic energy at the point. Since the sources are independent and therefore incoherent, the sound waves arrive at the point, with random phases. The resultant intensity — energy per unit area per unit time — is therefore the sum of the individual intensities. Since intensity is proportional to the square of the pressure one can also use the sum $\sum p_i^2$. The equation for the resultant sound pressure level of *n* incoherent radiating sources is

$$L_p = 10 \log \left(\frac{\sum_1^n p_i^2}{p_{ref}^2} \right) \text{ dB}.$$

In terms of the *sound pressure levels* produced at a point in the medium by each source acting individually, since $\frac{p_i^2}{p_{ref}^2} = 10^{\frac{L_i}{10}}$ one can also write for the resultant *sound pressure level, SPL*

$$L_p = 10 \log \left(\sum_{i=1}^n 10^{\frac{L_i}{10}} \right) dB.$$

The steelpans forming a steel orchestra and the notes on each pan are independent, incoherent sources of sound — each note works independently. This independence is not the result of there being different players, but because the notes themselves are inherently incoherent. This applies even on the Marshall Pairs for while the two notes forming a pair are mechanically coupled, when a member (usually the lower member) is played, the frequencies of the partials on both notes change continually during the duration of the tone — they are not coupled to the extent required for coherence. The resultant sound pressure level at a point in the medium can therefore be obtained from a summation of terms involving the SPL produced by each source as we have just shown.

12.8 Measurement of Sound Level

It is often required to make sound level measurements using a *Sound Level Meter*. Because the human ear discriminates against low frequencies (see Figure 12.1), any measurement of the subjective response to sound pressure must be adjusted to match the sensing characteristics of the ear. This weighted measurement of sound pressure is called *sound level*, as compared to *sound pressure level*, which is an unweighted, objective measurement of sound pressure. Sound level is measured with a sound level meter.

Changes in sound pressure $\Delta p = p_2 - p_1$, can be expressed as changes in sound intensity level:

$$\Delta L_i (dB) = 20 \left[log\left(\frac{p_2}{p_{ref}}\right) - log\left(\frac{p_1}{p_{ref}}\right) \right] = 20 log\left(\frac{p_2}{p_1}\right)$$

Common microphones such as the dynamic microphone produce an output voltage which is proportional to the sound pressure. By this proportionality, when used in a sound level meter, changes in sound intensity incident on the microphone can be calculated from

$$\Delta L_i = 20 log\left(\frac{V_2}{V_1}\right) dB.$$

where V_1 and V_2 are the voltages produced by the microphone in response to pressures p_1 and p_2, respectively. For a number, n, of independent sources one has

$$\begin{aligned} L_i(dB) &= 10 log\left(\frac{\sum_1^n V_i^2}{V_{ref}^2}\right) \\ &= 10\left[log(\textstyle\sum_1^n V_i^2) - log(V_{ref}^2)\right] \\ &= 10 log(\textstyle\sum_1^n V_i^2) - constant, \end{aligned}$$

where the value of V_{ref} (or the *constant*) is determined by calibration.

Consider now the audio range of frequencies divided into a number (N) of narrow frequency bands. Following what we have already said, the sources in each band, and the sources from band to band, are independent and as a result, the generated pressure disturbances are uncorrelated (incoherent). To each band is assigned a *weight*, the magnitude of which depends on the response of the ear. For each band, the average voltage produced over the band in response to the pressure is then scaled (weighted) according to the assigned weights w_i. An analogue or digital sound meter displays 10 times the logarithm of the sum of weighted squares $\sum_1^N (w_i V_i)^2$ while the term involving V_{ref}^2 appears as a constant offset voltage which is taken up in the calibration of the display scale. For the *weighted response* one has

$$sound\ level = 10 log \sum_{i=1}^{N} (w_i V_i)^2 - constant.$$

The weighting is carried out by an electronic *weighting network*. When a flat response network is used (all $w_i = 1$), the sound level meter measures the SPL. There are three (sometimes four) networks, A, B and C corresponding to the inverse of the 40, 70 and 100 dB equal loudness contours, respectively (see Figure 12.1). These networks allow the sound meter to largely ignore lower frequency sounds in a manner similar to the way our ears work.

The standard sound meter also incorporates *time-weighting*. In this case the frequency weighted AC signal from the network is converted to DC by a root-mean-square (rms) circuit incorporating an integrator. The integrating time determines the time-weighting: Slow, S, (1 second) and Fast, F, (125 ms). Refer to the International Electrotechnical Commission, Paper IEC 61672:2003 for more information on the Standards adopted there.

12.9 Acoustical Radiation from the Steelpan

Each steelpan has a unique acoustical radiation pattern because each pan is crafted differently thereby creating surfaces varying in geometry, elastic properties and dynamical stiffness. When a note is struck, energy is coupled mechanically to the internote, to other notes and to the skirt. The sounding pan is therefore a very complex three dimensional vibrating object. The vibration of this complex shell structure produces acoustical radiation in the surrounding medium from which the structure, in turn, experiences both reactive loading and damping. Radiation from the front or outward faces of the structure will be in anti-phase with radiation from the corresponding back face.

In matrix formulation, the equation governing this coupled structural-acoustic system can be written compactly as

$$(S - \omega^2 M)u - Ap = f, \qquad (12.1)$$

where S is a stiffness matrix, M is a mass matrix, u is a displacement vector for points (*nodes*) on the pan ω is the radian frequency of the radiation, A is a structural-acoustic coupling matrix, p is a nodal sound pressure at a point in the medium, and f is an external force vector driving the system. Despite the simple appearance of this equation, the component parts, matrices S, M and A are all very complicated. This usually makes direct solutions in closed-form difficult or impossible so that solutions are mainly sought by numerical analysis such as Finite Element Method (FEM), and Boundary Element Method (BEM).

The force vector f is usually imparted by stick impact, which generates a number of vibrational motions of frequencies, magnitudes and phases varying both in time and with position on the pan surfaces. For normal excitation with the stick, equation (12.1) must therefore be solved simultaneously for a range of frequencies over the time duration of the excitation. The radiation pattern from the sounding pan, played with the stick, is therefore a complex frequency dependent structure changing in both space and time as the tone develops and decays.

In practice, it will not be physically meaningful to use instantaneous sound level measurements to determine the radiation pattern of the pan. This is because (i) one cannot be sure which is the most meaningful time to make the measurement (ii) travel times to the nodal point varies for different sections of the system and (iii) acoustical measurements are only meaningful when taken over a number of cycles of the particular vibration. Where there exists time-dependence of amplitude and/or frequency, as is the case for the pan notes, the averaging time must be even longer. This problem is made worse if the walls of the room enclosure are not totally sound absorbing (anechoic). However, if f represents a forcing at constant amplitude and frequency, the results obtained from sound level measurements will be meaningful once the initial transients have settled, and equation (12.1) could be more easily applied.

The skirt section offers two important contributions to the radiation field; (i) by its length it offers a time delay in the transmission through the air medium for the relative travel times from the front and back faces to an external point in the air medium (allowing for the possibility of reinforcement from these two out-of-phase sources), (ii) it increases the size of the radiating surface by acting as a soundboard. As a soundboard, the skirt must act passively at the sounding frequencies, without strong resonances, which will otherwise seriously affect the tonal characteristics and the radiation pattern.

The complex nature of the acoustical sources on the pan and the non-linear nature of the vibration process, produce acoustical radiation patterns that change throughout the duration of the sounding tone. As vibrational energy is exchanged among non-linear modes on the sounding note, it is possible during short periods within the tone duration for the octave to be the more dominant mode of vibration. The radiated acoustic field varies accordingly. Asymmetrical patterns are also to be expected because of asymmetries in the pan geometry and vibrational properties.

Copeland et al. (2001) have reported on their measurements of acoustic radiation produced by individually excited pan notes. Their results, presented in 'false color' plots, are in qualitative agreement with listeners' assessment that the pan sounds somewhat louder when listened to directly above or below the sounding note. However, the results do not support those reported by Muddeen and Copeland (2000) in which the acoustic radiation field showed strong dependence on 'elevation angle' measured above and below the plane of the instrument and unexpected strong minor lobes with deep minima, sometimes dropping down to zero (perfect *nulls*)! If one places his/her ear in the direction of one of these zeros (nulls), no sound would be heard! This type of spatial complexity in the sound radiation pattern of pans (with perfect nulls) has never been observed by the present author, nor have these radiation patterns been observed aurally by pan makers or even by the casual listener. However, these radiation patterns are commonly found for real and computer simulated radio frequency antennas. I should also point out that in practice, transmission losses from the sounding note that spreads across the pan face material, will (as losses are known to do especially in complex radiating sources) cause the minima (nulls) in the radiation pattern to be *filled* in. I would have thrown blame for these 'oddities' on the *Cepstrum* technique (see Muddeen and Copeland, 2000) used in acquiring and processing the data but the perfect 'left-right' symmetry displayed in all the reported polar plots, an effect which the Cepstrum software could not have created as an artifact, causes me to place the blame elsewhere and to label it of unknown origin! Despite the claim in their 2000 paper, that the *"rotational resolution of the experiment was 30° (of arc), which precluded the detection of small variations in the radiation pattern"* most of the plots showed features that require angular resolutions very much smaller than 30° (just a few degrees of arc in most cases and as little as around *1°* for the fine details in the minor lobes). The only reliable and useable result that emerges from these experiments is from the 2001 paper which as already stated is in agreement with listener's perception of enhanced loudness of the sounding note above and below the pan face.

12.10 Acoustical Radiation from a Single Note

The problem of acoustic radiation from a vibrating note observed at large distances is now addressed. Because the steelpan is a coupled system involving the *notes, internote* and *skir*t, each with its own dynamic and radiative characteristics, it is not possible to obtain exact mathematical expressions for the acoustic radiation pattern for the instrument as a whole. This is especially true for the pan face, which exhibits varying stiffness across its surface. Some simplification is necessary. As seen in Chapter 5, when the note-skirt coupling is strong, note dynamics is controlled by the skirt and the affected note cannot be properly tuned. *A good note (musically) is always one with weak note-skirt coupling.* While the note functions as the *active radiator*, the skirt acts only as a *passive radiator*, providing added color to the timbre. If the skirt contribution to the acoustical output were to be entirely removed (subtracted), this will alter the timbre of the sounding note and modify the radiation pattern in a manner that depends on the particular note played.

The dynamically stiff internote areas are poor radiators at the fundamental frequencies of the notes while possessing very complex spatial responses to these frequencies. To excite the internote areas normally requires larger driving forces compared to those normally applied to the notes during stick impact. This is easily demonstrated by playing the internote with the stick. Since the notes on the pan face are tuned to different frequencies with frequency spacing that greatly exceeds the bandwidth of each note, expressed as $|f_n - f_m| \gg B$ (see Section 8.11.5), if sympathetic vibration is absent on both the pan face and the skirt (see Chapter 5), and if normal levels of note excitation are considered, the steelpan can be taken as a single source radiator. In this approximation, the acoustic radiation from the skirt is ignored and the pan face is treated as a stiffened surface acting as a baffle. If acoustical radiation into the top half-space alone is considered (see Figure 12.2) then the vibrating note is treated essentially as a baffled loudspeaker.

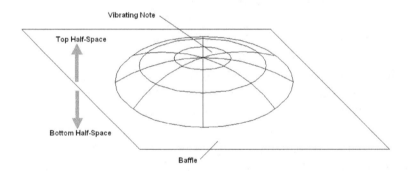

Fig. 12.2. The reduced form of the steelpan as a source of acoustical radiation.

In the case of the excitation of a single mode of finite bandwidth, the properties that will be described are the *acoustical pressure*, the *radiation directivity, mass loading, acoustical radiation power, acoustic efficiency, acoustical reaction force* and *acoustic impedance*. Because the rise H_0 of a typical note is just a few millimeters and the rise-to-radius ratio $H_0/a \approx 1/30$, is small, it is acceptable to consider a plane (flat) vibrating note limited by a closed boundary on which the amplitude of vibration vanishes. This boundary condition, where $w_n = 0$ along the boundary of the *true note*, corresponds to the baffled condition. We assume that the note is in contact with air, a light fluid, such that the total power radiated by the note is sufficiently weak. By this is meant that the modes of the note are weakly perturbed by the loss through acoustical radiation. The domain of validity of this "light fluid" regime is such that the loss due to acoustical radiation can be neglected in the vibrational dynamics of the note. However, we wish to retain these losses in the analysis that follows.

Quantitatively, any appreciable loss of the note vibrational energy due to radiation must occur on a time scale much larger than the inverse of the *local modal density*. If internal material losses and other losses affecting the frequency bandwidth are included, this statement is equivalent to

$$|f_{n+1} - f_n| \gg B,$$

where $f_{n+1} - f_n$ is the difference between two consecutive eigenfrequencies of the note (such as the key-note and octave) and B is the frequency bandwidth of the note. Since the steelpan notes are tuned with modal frequencies close to harmonicity, one has

$$|f_{n+1} - f_n| \approx f_1,$$

where f_1 is the fundamental frequency. Hence, the condition to be satisfied is

$$f_1 \gg B,$$

which is equivalent to the requirement that the Quality Factor (Q) of the note be much greater than unity

$$\frac{f_1}{B} = Q \gg 1.$$

As shown in Section 9.6, Q-values typically fall within the range 20 to 100, which meets the requirement for the present analysis.

In the weak note-to-air coupling regime studied here, each mode radiates essentially independent of each other. This occurs despite the coupling that exists between modes on the note itself. We therefore address the radiation by a single mode (*eigenmode*). A further simplification is required because each mode of the sounding tone exhibits both amplitude and frequency modulations. While the amplitude modulations can readily be dealt with, the frequency modulations must be sufficiently small to allow the *spatial coherence* *effects across the note surface to be easily handled. This is especially true for higher frequency modes where the spatial structure of the vibrating surface (mode shape) can be quite complex.

* *While we consider the sounding note excited by stick impact as radiating on a whole as an incoherent source, under constant single frequency external forcing of constant magnitude, one needs to consider the mutual coherence of sections of the note surface as it vibrates.*

Because of all these complications, the basis of the decomposition will be:

(i) The eigenmodes of vibration of the note are essentially the same as that for the fluid (air) replaced by a vacuum.
(ii) For a given eigenmode at frequency ω, the amplitude of vibration $w(x,y)$ and velocity $v(x,y)$ of the note are given by the dynamical equations and the temporal dependence $e^{-j\omega t}$ is implicit in these equations.
(iii) Along the note boundary the transverse displacement and velocity both vanish: $w(x,y)|_{boundary} = 0$, $v(x,y)\,)|_{boundary} = 0$ (*perfect blocking*).
(iv) Frequency modulation is suppressed by assuming well-defined (fixed) modal frequencies (*eigenfrequencies*). The justification for this assumption is as follows: The greatest spatial separation between two points on the note is *2a*. Therefore the greatest time separation for acoustic radiation (two signals) arriving at a point P in the air medium from any pair of points on the note surface is *2a/c*. If one takes a typical value for notes on the pan as $2a \approx 0.1$ m then, with the speed of sound in air c = 340 $m \cdot s^{-1}$ one gets the maximum difference in arrival times as $\Delta t = 2a/c \approx 3 \times 10^{-4}$ s. Because of the frequency modulation and the difference in arrival times, signals arriving at P from the two points will

differ slightly in frequency. In order to constructively add to the pressure field at the point P, *the two signals must overlap in the frequency domain*. Therefore, since each signal has a frequency bandwidth B, *coherence problems arise* when the rate of frequency modulation $|\delta f/\delta t|$ satisfies

$$|\delta f/\delta t| \geq B/\Delta t.$$

Taking a typical frequency bandwidth B of around 3Hz (see Table 9.2), this requires

$$|\delta f/\delta t| \geq B/\Delta t = 10 \; kHz \cdot s^{-1}.$$

Since such fast frequency modulation rates (10 $kHz \cdot s^{-1}$) do not occur on the pan (the maximum FM rate $|\delta f/\delta t|_{max}$ being around 100 $Hz \cdot s^{-1}$), coherence problems *do not* arise and one is justified in suppressing frequency modulations in determining the acoustic pressure field (despite the existence of FM in steelpan tones).

Note: The result obtained in (iv) above is important as it demonstrates that the frequency modulations generated on a well tuned pan can be *faithfully recorded* and heard by a listener located at points remote from the pan location. In addition, frequency modulation then becomes an important contributory factor in the *Chorus Effect* in Steel Orchestras and Ensembles (see Chapter 15).

(v) In the following analysis the Rayleigh integral method (Rayleigh 1896) is adopted. The Rayleigh integral is an approximate radiation integral in which it is assumed that the radiating surface is flat and lies in an infinite, flat, rigid baffle. This method for calculating the sound pressure field gives very accurate results when compared to the more accurate but more computationally intensive Boundary Element Method (see for example Wu and Seybert 2000).

As a reminder to the reader, the term 'note' means the 'true note' and not the whole area contained within the borders of the grooves — which is the 'traditional note.' Generally, areas of

the internote are also contained within the borders of the grooves.

12.11 Acoustical Pressure at a remote point in the air medium—the Far Field

12.11.1 The Flat Radiator Embedded in a Rigid Surface (the Infinite Baffle)

The geometrical arrangement of source (pan note) and receiver (observer or listener) is shown in Figure 12.3. The surface containing the source lies in the X-Y plane ($z = 0$ plane) while observations are made in the X_0-Y_0 plane. For the baffled vibrating source, each infinitesimal element of area $dA = dxdy$ at position coordinates (x, y) (in the source plane) contributes to the acoustical pressure (the *pressure phasor*) **p** at the point $P(x_0, y_0)$ (in the observing plane). Acoustical radiation is considered only in the semi-infinite space of positive z (the top half-space above the note). At large distances from the source, the complex acoustic pressure in the sound field radiated by a source of angular frequency ω is given by the Rayleigh integral

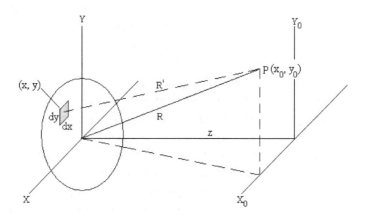

Fig. 12.3 1. Coordinate system for acoustical radiation from a steelpan note lying in the X-Y plane. The z-axis is normal to the note surface at the apex and points outwards from the front or top face of the note. The *Source Plane* contains X and Y while the *Observing Plane* contains X_0 and Y_0.

$$p = \frac{jz_0 \, k e^{j\omega t}}{2\pi} \iint v_n(x,y) \frac{e^{-jkR'}}{R'} dx \, dy \qquad (12.2)$$

where $z_0 = \rho_0 c$ is the *characteristic impedance* of the air medium, ρ_0 is the air density, c is the speed of sound in air, k $(= \omega/c = 2\pi/\lambda)$ is the *wave number* with λ as the wavelength of the sound in air, and ω is the angular frequency of vibration of the note. The integral is dependent on the relative amplitudes and phases of the normal velocity $v_n(x,y)$ at points (x,y) on the surface of the source. In equation (12.2) one can define a function

$$\Phi_n = \frac{e^{j\omega t}}{2\pi} \iint v_n(x,y) \frac{e^{-jkR'}}{R'} dx \, dy \qquad (12.3)$$

which is called the *velocity potential*, with

$$p = j\omega \rho_0 \Phi_n,$$

while $(e^{-jkR'}/R')$ is a *Green's function* (you don't have to know why it is called by that name in order to continue with the analysis, just think of it as one of those 'naming of notions' that mathematicians like to use in order to give credit to each other; this one, like others in the genre is credited, rightfully so, to British selt-taught mathematician George Green circa 1830). Green's functions and the mathematical operations associated with them are very powerful analytical tools.)

Using the system of coordinates in Figure 12.3, the distance R' can be written as

$$R' = z \left[1 + \frac{(x_0-x)^2}{z^2} + \frac{(y_0-y)^2}{z^2} \right]^{\frac{1}{2}}. \qquad (12.4)$$

On expanding this expression one gets

$$R' = z + \frac{x_0^2 + y_0^2}{2z} - \frac{x_0 x + y_0 y}{z} + \frac{x^2 + y^2}{2z} + \cdots.$$

From the *characteristic far-field condition* $z \gg \frac{\pi(x^2+y^2)_{max}}{\lambda}$ where, in the case of a circular radiator of radius a, $\pi(x^2+y^2)_{max}$ corresponds to the area, πa^2 of the source, the term $\frac{(x^2+y^2)}{2z}$ can be neglected. This result, together with $R = [z^2 + x_0^2 + y_0^2]^{\frac{1}{2}} \approx z + \frac{x_0^2+y_0^2}{2z}$ gives

$$R' \approx R - \frac{x_0 x + y_0 y}{z}. \tag{12.5}$$

Equation (12.3) can therefore be written as

$$\Phi_n = \frac{e^{j(\omega t - kR)}}{2\pi R} \iint v_n(x,y) e^{jk\left(\frac{x_0 x + y_0 y}{z}\right)} dx\, dy.$$

By defining the *spatial frequencies* or *wave numbers* $k_x = -kx_0/z$ and $k_y = -ky_0/z$, the velocity potential can be written in the form

$$\Phi_n = \frac{e^{j(\omega t - kR)}}{2\pi R} \iint v_n(x,y) e^{-j(k_x x + k_y y)} dx\, dy. \tag{12.6}$$

The reason we want the information in the *spatial frequency* or *wave number* domain is because it is directly correlated to the angle the signal is coming from relative to the observing plane. These angles with respect to the observing plane are defined by $-x_0/z$ and $-y_0/z$. The double integral in (12.6) represents the 2-D *Spatial Fourier Transform* $\mathfrak{F}[v_n(x,y)]$ of the normal velocity evaluated at spatial frequencies k_x and k_y. Thus

$$\mathfrak{F}[v_n(x,y)] = \iint v_n(x,y) e^{-j(k_x x + k_y y)} dx\, dy, \tag{12.7}$$

which allows the velocity potential to be expressed as

$$\Phi_n = \frac{e^{j(\omega t - kR)}}{2\pi R} \mathfrak{F}[v_n(x,y)] \tag{12.8}$$

and the *pressure phasor* as

$$p = \frac{j z_0\, k e^{j(\omega t - kR)}}{2\pi R} \mathfrak{F}[v_n(x,y)]. \tag{12.9}$$

Equation (12.9) shows that the radiation acoustic pressure is directly related to the spatial Fourier transform of the velocity normal to the source surface. Physically, this means that spatial coherence (effects) between different points on the note play a major role. In practice, the numerical determination of the Fourier transform for sources with boundaries of arbitrary shapes is a difficult problem, precisely due to the presence of these spatial coherence effects, especially for the higher modes for which the spatial structure of eigenmodes (mode shapes) and the velocity distribution over the source surface are particularly complex (complicated).

The formulation given in equation (12.9) applies to a flat radiator in free air so it is necessary to consider the shallow shell shaped notes in this fashion. This treatment of the vibrating note will be developed next.

12.11.2 The Model Note Embedded in a Rigid Surface Radiating in Free Air

Note: We have adopted the Rayleigh Integral method and its underlying assumptions especially the infinite rigid surface requirement, therefore, since the pan face and skirt do not meet this ideal perfectly, one should expect, in practice, some deviations in the measured field from those predicted in the following analysis. The smaller the note area in relation to the pan face, the better will be the agreement.

Because of anti-phase motion of each half of the note surface in the case of the octave and the twelfth, if the characteristic size or radius of the note a, satisfies $a < \lambda$, observed from afar at a distance $R >> \lambda$, the net volume displacement of the medium (air) for these modes approaches zero (cancels out). As a result the far-field acoustic intensity for these and higher (*anti-phase*) modes, vanishes. This is shown in Figure 12.4 for waves arriving at the point P. For the octave, points such as O on one half of the note can be matched with another point O' on the other half which moves in anti-phase with the first. Summing the contributions of all these pairs on the note, results in total cancellation of the acoustic field at P. This holds for all points in the far field. The same situation arises for the twelfth mode which also displays this anti-phase motion. These two modes, defined in Section 14.2 as the *resident octave* and *resident twelfth, are therefore inefficient acoustical radiators.* Since the entire surface of the octave note in a Marshall Pair (for example the C_5 in a [C_4, C_5] pair) vibrates in phase, it provides an *acoustical advantage* over the acoustically inefficient resident octave. (*Please take special note of this fact.*)

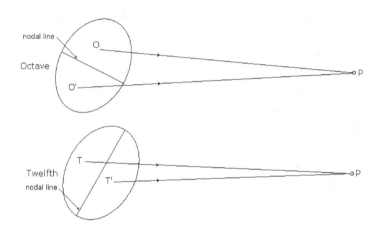

Fig. 12.4. Cancellation of the far field acoustical radiation at a point P by out-of-phase waves arriving from points O and O' for the octave (top) and points T and T' (bottom) for the twelfth.

Note: *On the bass pans one may find that the Third is used in place of the Twelfth. On the Third, the note surface vibrates in the same manner as the Twelfth (which is now absent) so, for the same reason, the Third is also acoustically inefficient.*

For the fundamental mode (the key-note) all points on the note surface move together in phase. This allows us to write the surface velocity v_n in terms of the fundamental frequency ω and the displacement normal to the note surface w_n as $v_n = j\omega\, w_n$. For the octave and twelfth, half the area of the note surface moves in-phase while all the points on the other half move out-of-phase with respect to the first half. The complexity of this phase pattern increases with mode number and becomes difficult to predict when other components of the pan (the pan face, other notes and the skirt) may interact with these modes. The perfect blocking assumption will remove the effect of the latter. Progress towards a resolution of these problems can be made if one includes the fact that;

- *The characteristics of the sound wave produced by a vibrator depend on the volume of air displacement and not on the shape details of the vibrator.*

When the note vibrates in the fundamental mode, with a mode shape having maximum displacement at the apex (center), dropping to zero at the boundaries (*perfect blocking*), one can replace the system with an equivalent vibrating piston (a *simple piston*) that produces the same *volume displacement amplitude* as the true source (see Figure 12.5).

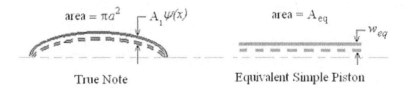

Fig. 12.5. Source as the vibrating true note and the equivalent simple piston.

In Section 8.3 the mode shape for the fundamental mode in the SDOF approximation for a note on circular planform is given by

$$\psi(x) = J_0(K x) + \frac{J_1(K)}{I_1(K)} I_0(K x) - \left[J_1(K) \frac{I_0(K)}{I_1(K)} + J_0(K) \right], \quad (12.10)$$

where $x = r/a$. The product of A_1 and the mode shape $\psi(x)$ describes the displacement amplitude of the note as it vibrates, in terms of the distance x measured from the 'center' or apex of the note. It is important to note that *the function $\psi(x)$ is a maximum at the apex ($x = 0$) and falls to zero at the boundary of the note ($x = 1$)*. Consider now a note of planform radius a vibrating with angular frequency ω and displacement $w_{max} = A_1\psi(0)$ at the apex. The mode shape average is given by

$$\overline{\psi} = \frac{\int_0^a \psi(r) 2\pi r \, dr}{\pi a^2} = 2 \int_0^1 \psi(x) x \, dx, \tag{12.11}$$

while the average displacement of the surface is $A_1 \overline{\psi}$. If the equivalent simple piston is of surface area A_{eq} and its displacement amplitude is w_{eq} then, the volume displacement amplitude of the piston is equal to that of the real note when

$$w_{eq} A_{eq} = A_1 \overline{\psi} \, \pi a^2, \tag{12.12}$$

where πa^2 is the *planform area,* used as an approximation to the surface area of the note. If the note planform is elliptical with a' and b' being the semi-major and semi-minor axes then one can replace πa^2 with the area $\pi a' b'$ or what amounts to the same thing, making $a^2 = a'b'$. Since the aspect ratio a'/b' ($= 1.27 \pm 0.08$) is not far from unity, we can replace the elliptical planform with a circular planform of equal area, consistent with the 'equal volume of air displacement' principle above.

Note: For those interested in the vibration of elliptical and circular plates, refer to my work in Achong (1995) where it is shown how an elliptical plate of low ellipticity can be transformed into an equivalent circular plate having the same vibrational frequency.

It is convenient to make $A_{eq} = \pi a^2$ which makes $w_{eq} = A_1 \overline{\psi}$. With this equivalent piston embedded in the rigid baffle but free to move as a driven vibrator, the flat source requirement for the Rayleigh integral is met. As the piston vibrates, all points on the piston execute the same displacement, with w_{eq} replacing w_n and v_n replaced by $v_{eq} = j\omega \, w_{eq}$. The radiation will therefore be symmetrical about the z-axis so it is sufficient to specify the point P by two coordinates as P(R, ϕ) and the surface area element as $dA = r \, dr \, d\phi$ as shown in Figure 12.3.

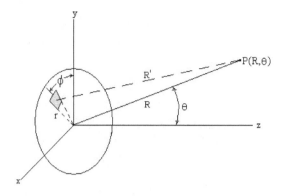

Fig. 12.6. Coordinate system for acoustical radiation from an equivalent simple piston.

From the geometry of Figure 12.6, the distance R' is equal to

$$R' = \left(R^2 + r^2 - 2Rr\sin\theta\cos\phi\right)^{\frac{1}{2}}. \qquad (12.13)$$

At large distances from the baffled note ($R \gg r$), an approximate expression for R' can be obtained by expanding the right side of equation (12.13) in a power series. On retaining only the first two terms in this series, one gets

$$R' = R - r\sin\theta\cos\phi. \qquad (12.14)$$

Equation (12.14) is a special case (due to the symmetry) of equation (12.5). Observe that for P sufficiently distant from the source, the difference in distance $R' - R = -r\sin\theta\cos\phi$ is independent of R. The same holds true for any pair of points on the note surface. This means that the relative phase of the pressures at P produced by any pair of points on the note surface is independent of R.

The advantage of using the simple piston representation of the true note is that the complication of using the mode shape function (12.10) directly into equation (12.9) is avoided. However, the mode shape function is required in order to determine w_{eq} and v_{eq}. With v_{eq} replacing $v_n(x,y)$ in (12.9) and taking $R' \approx R$ for $R \gg r$, equation (12.9) is cast into the more convenient form

$$p = \frac{j\rho_0 c\, k e^{j(\omega t - kR)}}{2\pi R} v_{eq} \iint e^{jkr \sin\theta \cos\phi} r\, dr\, d\phi. \qquad (12.15)$$

If the radius of the equivalent piston is taken as a, (12.15) can be written as

$$p = \frac{j\rho_0 c\, k e^{j(\omega t - kR)}}{2\pi R} v_{eq} \int_0^a r\, dr \int_0^{2\pi} e^{jkr \sin\theta \cos\phi}\, d\phi. \qquad (12.16)$$

To solve the second integral in (12.16), use is made of the standard integral relation

$$J_m(x) = \frac{(-j)^m}{2\pi} \int_0^{2\pi} e^{jx\cos\phi} \cos(m\phi)\, d\phi, \qquad (12.17)$$

where J_m is the mth order Bessel function. Using (12.17) in (12.16) for $m = 0$ (the lowest order), one gets

$$p = \frac{j\rho_0 c\, k e^{j(\omega t - kR)}}{2\pi R} v_{eq} \int_0^a r\, [2\pi J_0(kr \sin\theta)]\, dr. \qquad (12.18)$$

To solve the integral in (12.18) use is made of another integral relation between the *zeroth order* Bessel function J_0 and the *first order* Bessel function J_1

$$\int x J_0(x)\, dx = x J_1(x),$$

which gives for the pressure phasor

$$p = \frac{j\rho_0 c\, k a^2 e^{j(\omega t - kR)}}{2R} v_{eq} \left[\frac{2J_1(ka \sin\theta)}{ka \sin\theta} \right]. \qquad (12.19)$$

From (12.19), the result for the pressure amplitude is

$$p = \frac{\rho_0 c\, k a^2}{2R} v_{eq} \left[\frac{2 J_1(ka \sin\theta)}{ka \sin\theta} \right]. \qquad (12.20)$$

Observe that the sound pressure falls inversely proportional to the distance from the sound source, $p \propto 1/R$.

The time-averaged acoustical intensity I (power per unit area) defined as

$$I = \frac{p^2}{2 \rho_0 c},$$

can now be expressed as

$$I = \frac{\rho_0 c\, k^2 (\pi a^2)^2}{8 \pi^2 R^2} v_{eq}^2 \left[\frac{2 J_1(ka \sin\theta)}{ka \sin\theta} \right]^2. \qquad (12.21)$$

Using $k = \frac{\omega}{c}$ one gets

$$I = \frac{\rho_0 \omega^2 (\pi a^2)^2}{8 \pi^2 c R^2} v_{eq}^2 \left[\frac{2 J_1(ka \sin\theta)}{ka \sin\theta} \right]^2. \qquad (12.22)$$

Equation (12.22) describes the *far-field* acoustical radiation.

Equation (12.22) shows the following:

(i) The intensity is directly proportional to the density of the air medium.
(ii) The *intensity decreases as the inverse square of the distance* to the note.
   This is the **Inverse Square Law** of acoustical radiation.
(iii) The intensity is directly proportional to the *square* of the frequency of the sounding note (inversely as the square of the wavelength).
(iv) The intensity is directly proportional to the *square* of the note surface velocity.

(v) It must be carefully noted that the intensity is proportional to the *square of the area* of the radiator and not linearly as the area. For this reason, notes of larger true note area (for a given frequency) can generate more intense sounds. Increasing the area by a factor of two (x 2) increases the intensity by a factor of four (x 4) or +6db. Compare this with the use of two similar pans played simultaneously, here the intensity is doubled or increased by only +3db. So that the sound intensity produced by two pans can also be achieved by increasing the (true note) area of the notes on a single pan by a factor √2 or an increase of 41%. Economically, this may seem a good way of reducing the size of a steel orchestra while maintaining a high sound level as is often suggested by some advocates of this idea but it is well known that the full tonal characteristics of an orchestra comes from the combination of many of the same instrument in sections. *High sound level is not the reason for creating a large orchestra. The reason for having a large orchestra is the 'Chorus or Ensemble Effect' (see Chapter 15).*

12.11.3 The Transition from Near Field to Far Field

The far field region approximation given by equation (12.14) can be improved to include the position where the transition from *Near Field* to *Far Field* occurs by retaining the second order term in the series expansion. For $\phi = 0$, the improved equation is

$$R' = R - r\sin\theta + \frac{r^2 \cos^2\theta}{2R}. \quad (12.23)$$

The transition between far field and near field is normally taken as the point in the medium (air) where the *phase error* introduced by neglecting the third term in (12.23) corresponds to a path length of $\lambda/16$, where λ is the wavelength of the sound in air. Thus we get for the transition point between far field and near field, the relation

$$\frac{r^2 \cos^2\theta}{2R} = \frac{\lambda}{16}.$$

For $\theta = 0$, we get the minimum distance R_{ff} (where the subscript *ff* stands for *far field*) that may be considered as far-field (or the maximum for near-field) as

$$R_{ff} = \frac{8r^2}{\lambda} = \frac{2D^2}{\lambda}.$$

or in terms of the frequency f and sound velocity c,

$$R_{ff} = \frac{2D^2 f}{c}, \tag{12.24}$$

where $D = 2r$ is the diameter of the source. Using $D = 2\sqrt{(ab)}$ where a and b are the semi-axes of a true note on the pan, from tenor to bass, with $c = 340$ ms^{-1}, gives a range of values for R_{ff} satisfying

$$1.4\text{cm} \leq R_{ff} \leq 3\text{cm},$$

with an average value $R_{ff} \approx 2$cm (a more accurate estimate is not necessary here). This result will be of concern to us when we consider *blocking* and the interaction between notes in Section 14.15.

12.11.4 Radiation Patterns for the Vibrating Note

Using equation (12.21) and $A_{eq} = \pi a^2$, the intensity along the z-axis ($\theta = 0$) is expressed as

$$I_0 = \frac{\rho_0 c k^2}{8\pi^2 R^2} v_{eq}^2 A_{eq}^2. \tag{12.25}$$

allowing the intensity in the direction θ to be given by

$$I = I_0 \left[\frac{2J_1(ka\sin\theta)}{ka\sin\theta} \right]^2. \tag{12.26}$$

The *Directional gain* D in decibels can also be defined

$$D = 10 \log_{10} \frac{I}{I_0} = 20 \log_{10} \left[\frac{2J_1(ka \sin \theta)}{ka \sin \theta} \right] \text{ db.} \qquad (12.27)$$

The term *Directivity function* $D(\theta)$ is used to describe the quotient

$$\frac{2J_1(ka \sin \theta)}{ka \sin \theta}.$$

Polar radiation patterns are shown in Figure 12.7 for a number of values of ka $(= 2\pi a/\lambda)$.

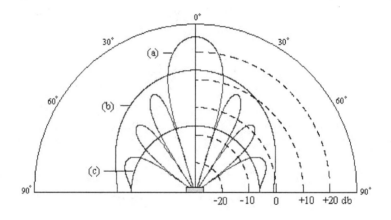

Fig.12.7. Polar far-field radiation patterns, D plotted against θ, at different frequencies for an equivalent simple piston modeling the note vibration. (a) $\lambda = 0.5a$, (b) $\lambda = 2a$, (c) $\lambda = 20a$.

At long wavelengths (low frequencies) for example $\lambda = 20a$, the radiation pattern is almost spherically symmetrical (pattern (c) in Figure 12.7). As the frequency is increased the radiation is more directed along the principal axis (z-axis, $\theta = 0$), as in pattern (b), $\lambda = 2a$ in Figure 12.7.

At even higher frequencies (pattern (a), $\lambda = 0.5a$) side lobes (or *minor lobes*) develop and the radiated power is mostly confined to the central lobe. In example (a), the maximum of the first secondary lobe is approximately 17db below the maximum on the main lobe.

In the author's experience while walking around a range of pans — tenors, quitars, basses — excited externally to produce constant displacement of the vibrating note, I have never detected these side lobes. If they existed then there would have been directions in which the sound of the vibrating note would have disappeared entirely or be reduced to the lower level of acoustic radiation produced by the skirt. To check this possibility one simply mount the exciter close to the sounding note and reduce the level of excitation to ensure that the sound heard is essentially produced by the note alone. In order to be sure, the pan should preferably be a well tuned, loud sounding tenor similar to what I have used in my own tests. Acoustic directivity with side lobes similar to (a) have never been detected on the many steepans that I have listened to in the 'panyards.'

On a tenor pan, a typical outer note $F_4 = 349.23$ Hz, the true note equivalent radius is approximately $a \approx 4$cm. Using a sound velocity in air of 340 m/s at 20 °C give the ratio $\lambda/a = 24.3$. For the D_6 note ($f = 1174.66$ Hz, $a \approx 2.5$cm), $\lambda/a = 11.6$. On the cello pan the F_3 note ($f = 164.8$ Hz, $a \approx 10$cm), $\lambda/a = 20.6$. On the $F^{\#}_2$ bass note ($f = 92.5$ Hz, $a \approx 13$cm), $\lambda/a = 25.3$. Within the limits of applicability of the present analysis, the radiation pattern for the notes on the steelpan should therefore be represented by (c) in Figure 12.7 and in Figure 12.8.

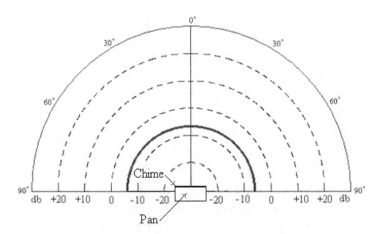

Fig. 12.8. Polar far-field radiation pattern applicable to notes on the steelpan, D plotted against θ, for $\lambda = 20a$. The horizontal line at 90° lies in the plane containing the chime.

The pan note satisfying $\lambda = 20a$ therefore *radiates almost isotropically* into the surrounding air medium. An isotropic radiation pattern is expected for all sources satisfying $\lambda \gg a$ *i.e. where the size of the source is much smaller than the wavelength.* With a typical pan it will take very careful listening and a keen ear to detect any small changes in the sound intensity with direction produced in the top half-space of a played note that may arise from the finite size of the pan face and as a result of the pan face and skirt acting as passive radiators. This suggests a radiation pattern similar to Figure 12.8 for the far field. The reader can readily verify this observation. However, if the ear is placed close to the note, the radiation corresponds to the *near field* and equation (12.21) is not applicable. In any case since the near field in within approximately 3 cm of the note surface, placing your ear this close to the note will cause your head to modify the near field.

Note: *Since we have to employ the product 2ka later on, we use the above examples to establish that for the notes found on the steelpan the condition $2ka \lesssim 1$ is satisfied. The approximate equality applies to the very high frequency notes on the tenor pan.*

12.11.5 Effects of Mode Shape on the Radiation Pattern — Shaded Source and the Absence of Minor Lobes

The mode shape for the fundamental mode sketched in Figure 12.5 maximizes at the apex and drops to zero at the boundary. This means that on a sounding note the outer regions of the note surface are deiven with lesser amplitude. An acoustic source with this property is said to be '*shaded*' and will produce a beam pattern having lower minor lobes than one which is driven uniformly over its radiating surface (as in the case of the equivalent flat piston). *The beam pattern will therefore show weaker minor lobes than the idealized pattern of Figure 12.7 for $\lambda = 0.5a$. In cases where $\lambda \sim 20a$ where there are no side lobes, 'shading' will simply reduce the intensity levels at the 'sides' as θ approaches 90°. This will result in increased directivity in the forward and backward directions.* **Since the conditions for the pan notes satisfy $\lambda \sim 20a$ we can readily understand why minor lobes are not detectable in the radiation patterns for pan notes with the pattern being more closely like that** *shown in Figures 12.8 and 12.9 (*Figure 12.9 does however include an additional effect that we shall deal with next*).* Already we see that steelpan radiation patterns with strong minor lobes as reported by Muddeen and Copeland (2000) are *not* to be expected.

12.12 Effects of Finite Pan Face and Bottom Radiation; the Hass Effect or Precedence Effect

An important role played by the skirt and pan face is to prevent the anti-phase sound waves emanating from the back (bottom) face of a note from interfering destructively with those from the front (top) face; these typically cause cancellations and significantly alter the level and quality of sound at low frequencies. At any point in the air medium situated some distance from the pan there is a delay in the arrival of the sound from the top (*top radiation*) and bottom (*bottom radiation*) of the note. The phase shift that this produces in the two arriving signals depends on the frequency of the sound, the phase shift being less at the lower frequencies. If the phase shift produced by differences in travel distance equals 180° the two signals will then be in-phase and will add constructively. But this will not occur everywhere. With an infinitely large skirt, this interference would be entirely prevented. A sufficiently long skirt sealed at the bottom can approach this behavior. However, pan skirts are all of finite length and are opened at the bottom. Closing the bottom severly loads the notes especially the bass.

With a finite pan face and skirt, the bottom radiation from the sounding note produces partial cancellation in the forward direction. The net result is a reduction in the transmitted intensity particularly at large angles of θ around 90° — this corresponds to the plane containing the chime (top rim) and extended all around the pan (see Figure 12.8). As a result of this direction dependent reduction in intensity, the radiation is not perfectly isotropic but appears to be more confined to the forward (and backward) direction — somewhat closer to that shown in Figure 12.7 pattern (b). The changes in the Directivity function depends on the individual pan and on the particular note played and may not be apparent to the average listener in a typical room. Figure 12.9 shows what one can expect for a typical test. Observe the scale in decibels is chosen to cover around ±3 db in order to emphasize the effect.

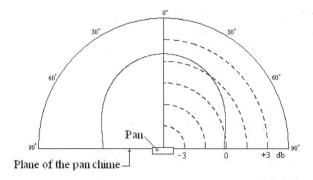

Fig. 12.9. Approximate polar far-field radiation pattern for shaded notes on the steelpan with bottom radiation. Observe the greater forward directivity and absence of side lobes.

With a finite pan face, the location of the sounding note will have the affect of making the polar radiation pattern asymmetrical. This effect is greater for the outer notes lying close to the edge of the pan or the chime. Some lop-sidedness is therefore to be expected in practice. This effect is not very critical either in solo performances or when the instruments are used in a band.

One question the reader may ask is, 'is there any role played by the *Precedence Effect* or the *Hass Effect* in all this (Hass 1951, 1972; Wallach et.al. 1949)?' The Precedence Effect is a *psychoacoustic effect* in which after one hears an initial signal the brain *suppresses* any later arrival of the *same* signal for a time period of 30 to 40 milliseconds. By masking the second signal, the brain can process a signal mixed with echoes in order to determine the direction of the source of the initial signal. Normally we are not aware that this goes on *in our brain* but if the second sound arrives after 40 milliseconds we perceive it as a distinct echo. What we are conscious of is our ability to determine, even in noisy conditions, the direction of a source and on which we can focus our hearing and attention. When we listen to a set of pans especially close up, the Precedence Effect will operate to allow us to focus our attention on an *individual pan* being played. The music arranger, of a steelband, during practice, uses this to determine the location in the band of an off-tuned pan or note. It really does not matter if the second sound came from beneath the pan or as an echo. What this teaches us is that when it comes to the sense of hearing, we cannot only consider the nicely drawn up and accurate physics of the system; we must also include the psychoacoustics, that's where *'we'* become involved. We did this in Section 12.6 when we considered the relative loudness of the bass and the tenor at the location of the Judges, the listener at the rear of the auditorium and at the position of the far listener. We will be wrong to ignore the behavior of our sense of hearing.

With reference to Chapter 15 which deals with the *Chorus Effect*, the Precedence Effect will *not* destroy the Chorus Effect for the first 40 milliseconds because the Chorus Effect is produced by the superposition of a number of *independently* produced voices. In the case of our steel orchestra, each of these voices possesses a distinct tonal structure. Our brain treats these distinct sounds *not* in the manner of the Precedence Effect (*which applies to the same sound repeated*) but in a manner that results in the Chorus Effect.

12.13 Mechanical Impedance of the Radiating Mass Loaded Note

A pan note free of paint or powder coating, vibrating freely in a vacuum will experience no loading except for magnetomechanical damping. Mass loading appears naturally when the note vibrates in air with the generation of acoustical radiation. Paint coatings applied to the note surfaces (top and bottom) will also be responsible for mass loading as described in Section 11.3.3. These effects can be studied in steady state motion by driving the note sinusoidally by means of an external electromechanical vibrator attached to a remote point on the steelpan. The driving frequency can be made to correspond to the fundamental (key-note) of the note under investigation.

Once again to avoid the complications of the mode shape and the velocity distribution over the note surface, the analysis is carried out in the equivalent simple piston formulation. In order to retain the 'note perspective' however, reference will be made to the note surface not to the piston surface. Consider a coated note, represented now by a simple coated piston, excited by the application of a sinusoidal driving force $\mathbf{f} = fe^{j\omega t}$ of frequency ω and of constant magnitude f. The vibrating note will radiate acoustical energy into the air medium around it. The note therefore exerts a force $\mathbf{f}_r = Z_r v_{eq} e^{j\omega t}$ on the medium and the medium in turn exerts an equal and opposite reaction force on the note. Here $Z_r = R_r + jX_r$, is the acoustical impedance loading of the air medium, with resistive component R_r and reactive component X_r. Both R_r and X_r are in units of $kg \cdot s^{-1}$. Since we are carrying out a strictly SDOF analysis, the differential equation for the note (equivalent piston) vibrating in air can be written

$$(m_n + m_c)\frac{d^2w}{dt^2} + (R_m + R_c)\frac{dw}{dt} + S_{eff}w = (f - Z_r v_{eq})e^{j\omega t}, \quad (12.28)$$

where m_n and m_c are the *equivalent mass* of the note and coating respectively, defined for the generic note of mass m by

$$m_{eqv} = 2m \int_0^1 \psi^2 x\, dx$$

$$= m\langle \psi^2 \rangle, \quad (12.29)$$

This formulation applies to both the note material (the steel component) and coating because the coating is assumed to evenly cover the note surface, is rigidly attached to the note and vibrates at each point, in unison with the note surface. Equation (12.29) can be generalized for uneven coatings as shown in Section 11.3.3. R_m is the mechanical resistance of the note, R_c is the mechanical resistance of the coating and S_{eff} is the effective stiffness of the coated note. It should be noted here that $S_{eff} = \frac{1}{C_{eff}}$ where C_{eff} is the effective compliance of the mass loaded note. The solution of equation (12.28) for the complex, *steady-state* velocity of the note surface is given by

$$u_{eq} = \frac{f}{R_m + R_c + R_r + j\left[\omega(m_n + m_c) + X_r - \frac{S_{eff}}{\omega}\right]}. \quad (12.30)$$

The mechanical impedance of the vibrating (coated) note radiating into the air is given by the denominator on the right side of (12.30). By writing $X_r = m_r \omega$ the concept of an *equivalent radiation mass* m_r can be introduced, consistent with the mass-loading produced by the air medium in contact with the note. It is also clear from (12.30) that this form for X_r is dimensionally correct. One can now write for the mechanical impedance

$$Z_m = R_m + R_c + R_r + j\left[\omega(m_n + m_c + m_r) - \frac{S_{eff}}{\omega}\right], \quad (12.31)$$

and

$$v_{eq} = \frac{f}{Z_m}. \quad (12.32)$$

12.14 Acoustic Power Output and Acoustic Efficiency

Under steady-state motion the external agency which drives the note sinusoidally, supplies energy to the note at a rate equal to the rate of loss of energy through internal losses in the note material (determined by R_m), internal losses in the coating (determined by R_c) and acoustical energy losses (determined by R_r). If v_{rms} is the root-mean-square velocity of the note surface, the *acoustic power* P_r is given by

$$P_r = R_r v_{rms}^2,$$

where, from equation (12.32)

$$v_{rms} = \frac{f}{\sqrt{2 Z_m Z_m^*}}.$$

Finally one has

$$P_r = \frac{R_r f^2}{2\left[(R_m+R_c+R_r)^2 + \left(\omega(m_n+m_c+m_r) - \frac{S_{eff}}{\omega}\right)^2\right]}. \quad (12.33)$$

Since power is lost in proportion to the resistive components of the impedance, with radiation losses being the desired output from the sounding note, one has for the *acoustic efficiency*, η

$$\eta = \frac{R_r}{R_m+R_c+R_r}. \quad (12.34)$$

With R_c in the denominator of the expression for η, *the* acoustic efficiency of a pan note *decreases* when the note is coated with a layer of paint*. The acoustic efficiency also decreases when the magnetomechanical resistance R_n is increased. In order to increase the acoustic efficiency, R_r must be increased while all other resistive losses must be reduced. Acoustical radiation is desired although in principle it is an energy loss for the vibrating note. It is necessary therefore to obtain an expression for the acoustic impedance. This can be obtained from the equation for the acoustical reaction force.

* *It is important to note that while the coating (powder coating for example) used on a pan note is permanently attached, the placing of any object on the surface such as the 'mat' described in Section 13.15.10, will result in additional losses. If the note is covered with a sheet of removable felt for example, then portions of this covering may participate in the motion of the note surface albeit in a random fashion. This motion will add to the losses and reduce the acoustic efficiency.*

12.15 Acoustical Reaction Force and Acoustic Impedance in Free Air

With reference to Figure 12.10, consider a pair of area elements $dA = rdrd\theta$ and $dA' = sdsd\phi$ on the vibrating note surface. The element dA acting as the *source* produces an incremental pressure dp_r in the medium immediately above dA' acting as the *receiver*. The total pressure at dA' produced by the rest of the note surface is

$$\boldsymbol{p}_r = \frac{j\rho_0 ck}{2\pi} v_{eq} e^{j\omega t} \iint \frac{e^{-jkr}}{r} dA. \qquad (12.35)$$

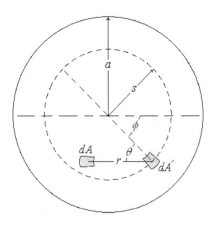

Fig. 12.10. Coordinate system for a pair of surface elements on the note surface.

Associated with this acoustic pressure is a reaction force on the element dA' of $-p_r dA'$ and a total reaction force over the entire note surface of

$$\mathbf{f}_r = -\iint p_r dA'. \qquad (12.36)$$

Combining (12.35) and (12.36) gives

$$\mathbf{f}_r = -\frac{j\rho_0 c k}{2\pi} v_{eq} e^{j\omega t} \iint dA' \iint \frac{e^{-jkr}}{r} dA. \qquad (12.37)$$

The solution of equation (12.37) can be simplified by observing that the surface elements dA (= $rd\theta dr$) and dA' (= $sd\phi ds$) play interchangeable roles as *source* and *receiver* and that the same holds for all such pairs over the entire note surface. Because of this symmetry it is sufficient to restrict the integration range for dA so that $r \leq s$ and subsequently to multiply the result by the factor 2. The region contained within the radius s comprises points where $-\pi/2 \leq \theta \leq \pi/2$ and $0 \leq r \leq 2s\cos\theta$. The integration with respect to dA' is completed over the entire surface with $0 \leq \phi \leq 2\pi$, $0 \leq s \leq a$. With this procedure, one obtains

$$\mathbf{f}_r = -\frac{j\rho_0 c k}{\pi} v_{eq} e^{j\omega t} \int_0^{2\pi} d\phi \int_0^a s ds \int_{-\frac{\pi}{2}}^{\frac{\pi}{2}} d\theta \int_0^{2s\cos\theta} e^{-jkr} dr. \qquad (12.38)$$

The integral with respect to ϕ is independent of the other integrals, is straightforward, and yields the factor 2π. The other integrals are solved in the order *right-to-left*. The first integral yields

$$\int_0^{2s\cos\theta} e^{-jkr} dr = \frac{j}{k}(e^{-j2ks\cos\theta} - 1).$$

In the second integral one part yields, $-\frac{j}{k}\int_{-\frac{\pi}{2}}^{\frac{\pi}{2}} d\theta = -\frac{j\pi}{k}$ and the other part $\frac{j}{k}\int_{-\frac{\pi}{2}}^{\frac{\pi}{2}} e^{-j2ks\cos\theta} d\theta$ can be integrated as a power series in $\cos\theta$ by expanding the exponential using

$$e^{-x} = 1 - x + \frac{x^2}{2!} - \frac{x^3}{3!} + \cdots = \sum_{n=0}^{\infty} \frac{(-x)^n}{n!}.$$

On integrating term-by-term with respect to θ the result is a complex (real and imaginary) power series, $f(s)$, in s. The third and final integral, $\int_0^a sf(s)ds$, consists of a series of simple integrals which can be integrated term-by-term. The final expression for the force contains a complex power series in $2ka$ consisting of a resistance function $\mathcal{R}(2ka)$ (the real component) and a reactance function $j\mathcal{X}(2ka)$ (the imaginary component) as

$$\mathbf{f}_r = -\rho_0 c\, \pi a^2 v_{eq} e^{j\omega t}[\mathcal{R}(2ka) + j\mathcal{X}(2ka)], \quad (12.39)$$

where

$$\mathcal{R}(2ka) = \frac{1}{2}\left[\frac{(2ka)^2}{4} - \frac{(2ka)^4}{4^2 \cdot 6} + \frac{(2ka)^6}{4^2 \cdot 6^2 \cdot 8} - \cdots\right],$$

$$\mathcal{X}(2ka) = \frac{4}{\pi}\left[\frac{2ka}{3} - \frac{(2ka)^3}{3^2 \cdot 5} + \frac{(2ka)^5}{3^2 \cdot 5^2 \cdot 7} - \cdots\right]. \quad (12.40a, b)$$

Using

$$\mathbf{f}_r = -v_{eq} e^{j\omega t} Z_r. \quad (12.41)$$

one gets for the acoustic radiation resistance R_r and acoustic radiation reactance X_r

$$R_r = \rho_0 c \pi a^2 \mathcal{R}(2ka),$$
$$X_r = \rho_0 c \pi a^2 \mathcal{X}(2ka),$$

with the *acoustic impedance* expressed as

$$Z_r = R_r + jX_r,$$

It has already been established that for the notes found on the steelpan $2ka \leq 1$ (see Section 12.11.4). One can therefore retain only the lowest terms in equations (12.40a, b) to write the note acoustic resistance and reactance as

$$R_r = \tfrac{1}{2}\rho_0 c \pi k^2 a^4,$$
$$X_r = \tfrac{8}{3}\rho_0 c k a^3. \quad (12.42a, b)$$

The acoustic resistance and reactance are in units of $kg \cdot s^{-1}$ as expected.

Using equations (12.42a,b) and $kc = \omega$ we arrive at expressions for the *acoustic radiation efficiency* of the coated note:

$$\text{Acoustic Radiation Efficiency} \quad \eta = \frac{\frac{1}{2c}\rho_0 \pi \omega^2 a^4}{R_m + R_c + \frac{1}{2c}\rho_0 \pi \omega^2 a^4}, \quad (12.43)$$

and the *equivalent radiation mass*

$$\text{Equivalent Radiation Mass} \quad m_r = \frac{8}{3}\rho_0 a^3. \quad (12.44)$$

Observe here that the equivalent radiation mass is dependent only on the density of the medium (air) and the size of the note: it is independent of frequency. This result is not surprising because it is the acoustic reactance ($X_r = m_r \omega$) that depends on the frequency. As a result of the air density dependence, the acoustic mass loading will decrease as the ambient temperature rises. This means that there will be, albeit small, increase in the note frequency resulting from the decrease in air density as the temperature rises. For completeness, we shall return to this effect (see Section 12.19).

12.16 Note Response to Continuous External Excitation`

Using $kc = \omega$, $v_{eq} = j\omega w_{eq}$ and $w_{eq} = A_1 \bar{\psi}$ equation (12.25) can be written as

$$I_0 = \frac{\rho_0 \omega^4}{8\pi^2 cR^2} A_1^2 \bar{\psi}^2 (\pi a^2)^2.$$

If the note in steady state motion is kept vibrating with displacement amplitude $A_1 \bar{\psi}$ by a constant amplitude externally applied driving force $\mathbf{f_e} = f_e e^{j\omega t}$ (defined at the note location), then one has

$$A_1 \bar{\psi} e^{j\omega t} = \frac{f_e e^{j\omega t}}{\omega Z_m},$$

which allows the expression

$$I_0 = \frac{\rho_0 \omega^2}{8\pi^2 cR^2} \left(\frac{f_e^2}{(R_m + R_c + R_r)^2 + \left(\omega(m_n + m_c + m_r) - \frac{S_{eff}}{\omega}\right)^2} \right) (\pi a^2)^2. \tag{12.45}$$

When for example the notes on the pan are excited by an electromagnetic vibrator attached to the pan, and the far field is monitored with a sound level meter for purposes of measuring resonance frequencies, one normally varies the driving force to the note under test in order to set an appropriate sound intensity level. This is clearly demonstrated in equation (12.45) where $I_0 \propto f_e^2$. Under constant forcing, the note will vibrate with constant displacement magnitude and at a distance R from the note, produce a fixed intensity level I_0 set by the resistive losses and mass loading on the note as seen from the corresponding terms in equation (12.45).

Depending on the relative magnitudes of the frequency dependent terms $\omega(m_n + m_c + m_r)$ and $\frac{S_{eff}}{\omega}$ the note behaves either *mass-like* or *spring-like*. To illustrate this distinction, consider how *a small child, low in mass, can bounce around joyfully on a sponge pillow but an adult, high in mass, finds no bouncing pleasure, no 'springiness' in such a pillow.* In this simple representation of the note one has resonance when the mass and stiffness terms are equal — the reactance is identically zero— thus giving the frequency of resonance as

$$\omega_0 = \sqrt{\frac{S_{eff}}{m_n + m_c + m_r}}$$

$$= \frac{1}{\sqrt{(m_n + m_c + m_r)C_{eff}}}.$$

At resonance the vibrating note behaves resistively while the intensity I_0 maximizes to

$$I_{0,max} = \frac{\rho_0 \omega_0^2}{8\pi^2 cR^2} \left(\frac{f_e^2}{(R_m + R_c + R_r)^2} \right) (\pi a^2)^2. \tag{12.46}$$

At resonance

$$A_1 \overline{\psi} = \frac{f_e}{(R_m + R_c + R_r)\omega_0},$$
(12.47)

which is the expression for the average displacement of the note surface under the action of force of amplitude f_c. From (12.46) and (12.47) the maximum acoustic intensity is given by

$$I_{0,max} = \frac{\rho_0 \omega_0^4}{8\pi^2 cR^2} A_1^2 \overline{\psi}^2 (\pi a^2)^2.$$
(12.48)

12.17 Transmission Losses across Note Boundaries

It is very clear from these equations that the acoustic intensity of the note vibrating in the fundamental (resonant) mode is increased when the resistive losses or dissipation losses are minimized. R_m is the parameter that describes only the magnetomechanical losses in the note material so we can at this point include the *transmission losses* across the note boundary (both losses occurring simultaneously) by replacing R_m with the sum $R_m + R_t$ (see equations (12.46) and (12.47)). The former, R_m, is set by the choice of low-carbon steel, work hardening and annealing (burning) while the latter, R_t — the *transmission loss parameter* — is set by blocking. Equations (12.43), (12.46) and (12.47) must now be modified to read

$$\eta = \frac{\frac{1}{2c}\rho_0 \pi \omega^2 a^4}{R_m + R_t + R_c + \frac{1}{2c}\rho_0 \pi \omega^2 a^4},$$
(12.49)

$$I_{0,max} = \frac{\rho_0 \omega_0^2}{8\pi^2 cR^2}\left(\frac{f_e^2}{(R_m + R_t + R_c + R_r)^2}\right)(\pi a^2)^2.$$
(12.50)

$$A_1 \overline{\psi} = \frac{f_e}{(R_m + R_t + R_c + R_r)\omega_0},$$
(12.51)

It was convenient to work without making reference to the transmission losses because the Rayleigh integral method requires that the note move within an infinite rigid plane. To satisfy this requirement, of a vibrating surface within a rigid plane, the transverse displacement and velocity of the note must be zero along the boundary. This condition implies that there is no energy transferred from the note to the supporting pan face which amounts to the same thing as zero transmission losses. Equations (12.49), (12.50) and (12.51) are therefore applicable in the low transmission loss regime, precisely where a properly prepared tuned pan should operate.

12.18 Equivalent Electrical Circuit

It is possible to represent the externally driven, coated, single-mode note with all its losses and mass loading as an equivalent electrical circuit as shown in Figure 12.11. The sinusoidal forcing is expressed as the real part of f_e, expressed as $\text{Re}(f_e e^{j\omega t}) = f_e \cos(\omega t)$ and set up as an AC voltage source of amplitude f_e (in Volts) and angular frequency ω. The dissipative components are the resistive elements R_m, R_c, R_t and R_r (in Ohms) connected in series. The reciprocal of the effective stiffness is represented as a *compliance* in the form of a *capacitance* $1/S_{eff}$ (in Farads) while the mass loading is the series connection of *inductances* (in Henrys) lumped together as the sum of equivalent masses $m_n + m_c + m_r$. The velocity v_{eq} corresponds to the *loop current* (in Amperes) in the circuit.

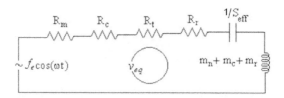

Fig. 12.11. Equivalent series electrical circuit for a linear single-mode note under constant non-resonant sinusoidal forcing.

The circuit of Figure 12.11 is the *hardware* implementation of the equation

$$v_{eq} = \frac{f_e \cos(\omega t)}{R_m + R_c + R_t + R_r + j\left(\omega(m_n + m_c + m_r) - \frac{S_{eff}}{\omega}\right)}.$$

At resonance, $\omega = \omega_0$, the inductive reactance (*mass term*) cancels the capacitive reactance (*stiffness term*) resulting in the *purely resistive* circuit shown in Figure 12.12.

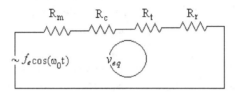

Fig. 12.12. Equivalent electrical series circuit for the single-mode note at resonance.

At resonance

$$v_{eq} = \frac{f_e \cos(\omega_0 t)}{R_m + R_c + R_t + R_r}.$$

Once again, by reducing the values of the dissipative elements R_m, R_c, R_t and R_r, the note surface velocity v_{eq} is increased. However, by reducing R_r, acoustic radiation is suppressed. One should therefore *increase* R_r ($= \frac{1}{2}\rho_0 c \pi k^2 a^4$) in order to increase the intensity of the radiated sound. The variable most appropriate for this purpose is the radius a, which means that one should increase the physical size of the note.

There is another reason for representing the linear single-mode note as an equivalent electrical circuit — a subtle one. Observe in Figure 12.12 how simple the system becomes at resonance as the complications of the reactive stiffness and mass loading are removed: their effects now only contained in ω_0. This is precisely what happens in the mechanical system of the steel notes (in the linear approximation). The stiffness of the steel note depends on the elastic constants, the residual compressive stress constraint, the density of the steel and on the geometry of the note surface. But, *the details on how these elements are formed do not matter at resonance* since the terms representing them vanish at resonance.

- This explains why some pans may show a large number of hammer marks on the notes and pan face leading one to believe that the notes will sound awful when played but to one's surprise they play beautifully. The eye having been deceived leads one to believe that all those indentations (those details) will result in a harsh mixture of tones. *The lesson here is to judge a pan with your ear not with your eye.*

From these remarks it must not be construed that 'anything goes'. Just the opposite is the case. For the hammer marks are simply a record of the pan maker's determined effort to bring the instrument to a state of perfection. The ear and not the eye tells us that he did just that.

- *It should now be equally clear that the quality of manufacturing by the pan maker and the quality of peening by the tuner determine the intensity and loudness of a note.*
- It is also clear that losses introduced by painting or powder-coating the note (through R_c) will reduce the intensity and loudness of the note. While one can operate the note without a coating (equivalent to setting $R_c = 0$) it is not possible for $R_m + R_t$ to be reduced to zero (because in that case, if the note is operated in a vacuum it then becomes a perpetual motion machine which nature forbids). Since the acoustic radiation resistance R_r cannot be eliminated (unless the note is operating in a vacuum), there is a finite upper limit to the intensity of a note vibrating in a medium (air). In the vacuum the intensity is zero.
- Although we are using the steady state results, if these measures are taken to maximize the steady state intensity then when the note is excited by stick impact, the acoustic output will also be maximized.

12.19 Some Numerical Examples on Model Notes

Prefatory Remark: The notes on the steelpan radiate acoustically from both the top and bottom surfaces of the note equally in opposite direction and opposite phase. This means that as the note vibrates it suffers acoustic mass loading on both surfaces (top and bottom). This should be kept in mind.

In Section 9.6 typical values for mechanical resistance of pan notes are tabulated. These values are listed in units of s^{-1} so they must be converted to values having units of $kg \cdot s^{-1}$ using the equivalent mass of the notes. Using equation (12.10) and the associated expressions found in Section 8.3 one can calculate the mechanical resistance in the required units for a note of equivalent mass m_n using

$$R_m \text{ (in } kg \cdot s^{-1} \text{ units)} = m_n R_m \text{ (in } s^{-1} \text{ units)}. \qquad (12.52)$$

In solving the integrals in equation (12.11) for $\bar{\psi}$ and in equation (12.29) for $\langle \psi^2 \rangle$ the value of K used in equation (12.10) is found as the first root of

$$[J_0(K) I_1(K) + I_0(K) J_1(K)] K \left[\frac{\lambda^4 + K^4 (1-v)}{\lambda^4} \frac{}{2} - 1 \right] + 2 J_1(K) I_1(K)(1+v) = 0$$

and the geometric parameter λ (in the case of zero compressive stress along the note boundary) determined from

$$\lambda^2 = [12(1-v^2)]^{\frac{1}{2}} \left[\int_0^1 \left(\frac{dq}{dx} - 2x \right)^2 x \, dx \right]^{\frac{1}{2}} \left[\frac{2H_0}{h} \right].$$

(T*he geometric parameter and the wavelength are represented by the same symbol* λ *so do not confuse them.*) The effect of compressive stress on the note shape is neglected here in order to keep the present analysis simple (see Section 8.6). For our examples we choose notes having a rise-factor of $H_0/h = 3.2$ tuned with shaping functions

Note 1: $q(x) = b(1 - 2.4x^2 + 1.4x^3)$, $b = -0.35$
Note 2: $q(x) = b(x - 2.4x^2 + 1.4x^3)$, $b = -2.0$
Spherical cap: $q(x) = 0$.

The form (shape) of the note surface is described by the function $y(x) = (H_0/h)[1 - x^2 + q(x)]$. The initial form as a spherical cap and the final form of the tuned notes are shown in Figure (note form). These note shapes are also discussed in Section 8.15.

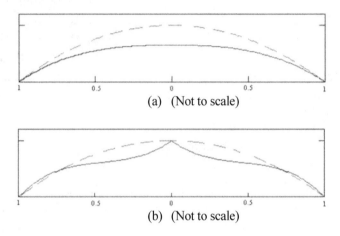

Fig. 12.13. (a) The initial note shaped as a spherical cap (- - -); the finished shape for Note 1 (—), (b) The initial note shaped as a spherical cap (- - -); the finished shape for Note 2 (—).

These geometries were chosen for this analysis in order to show as well, that the visual appearance of a note does not give a reliable indication of its performance as an acoustic radiator. It is clear that the finished shapes of Note 1 and Note 2 are very different in appearance. But we ought to be careful in our interpretations here because the present analysis treats the note in the formulation of the simple piston which removes precisely those features that make the notes visibly different. Also, by using equation (12.10), we take with it the assumptions made in its development. If we refer to that development we see that there too, an equivalent representation, specifically the representation as an equivalent spherical cap, is adopted (all for the sake of simplicity). What we find therefore is that our present results should tell us if by choosing different note shapes, these shapes can be represented by *different* spherical caps. It is this difference, if it exists, that we seek.

Table 12.1

Parameter	Spherical Cap	Tuned Note 1	Tuned Note 2
$\bar{\psi}$	0.3454	0.3980	0.3500
$\langle \psi^2 \rangle$	0.3037	0.3464	0.3082
m_n (kg)	3.2500×10^{-3}	3.7060×10^{-3}	3.2947×10^{-3}
m_r (kg)	0.183×10^{-3}	0.183×10^{-3}	0.183×10^{-3}
R_m (kg·s^{-1})	0.0780	0.0889	0.0791
R_r (kg·s^{-1}) at 246.94 Hz (**B$_3$**)	0.029	0.029	0.029
K	4.5988	4.2962	4.6521
λ	4.7080	4.0027	4.5169
b	0	-0.35	-2

For our note material we assume a note thickness $h = 0.3$ mm, $H_0 = 3.2 \times h$, so for a steepness of 1/40, one gets $a = 3.84$ cm. Using $\rho_n = 7750$ kg·m^{-3}, gives $m_n = 10.7 \langle \psi^2 \rangle$ gm. For the air medium at 20°C, the air density takes the value $\rho_0 = 1.204$ kg·m^{-3}. Since the tuning process will involve taking the same piece of material and shaping it into the forms illustrated in Figure 12.13, the same mass, 10.7 gm, must be used for each note. From the tabulated values for R_m in Table 9.2 we use the value R_m (in s^{-1} units) ≈ 24 s^{-1} as typical for room temperature notes. The latter assumes similar anneal processing of these notes. Other parameters: *steepness* = H_0/a = 1/40, *Poisson's ratio* = 0.29. For these parameters and designs, one gets Table 12.1.

1. Equation (12.48) shows that by increasing the mode shape average $\bar{\psi}$ the acoustic radiation intensity can be increased, which is desirable. For the two notes having the shapes described in the above example, <u>a given displacement amplitude A_1</u> (measured at the apex) and given frequency, from the results in Table 12.1, Note 1 will be 29.3% (1.1 db) more intense than Note 2. This difference arises because $\bar{\psi}$ is different for these two notes. *To this extent therefore, these two notes perform differently as equivalent simple piston acoustic radiators.*

Comment: *In Section 8.21 the shaping function used on Note 1 was designed to optimize the relative intensities of the second and third partials. All round, this is a good note shape design. The note shape used on Note 2 is similar to the form found on the Pang variety of steelpan instruments. While these two examples are mere demonstrations, the proof is in the equation for the acoustic intensity (equation (12.48)) that the tuning/shaping process can be used to optimize the acoustic intensity of the instrument. The pan maker/tuner can achieve this indirectly through shaping which in turn influences the dynamics that establishes the final mode shape and its average value $\bar{\psi}$. However, the optimization is not unique, for many note shapes and mode shapes can produce the same $\bar{\psi}$. The general tuner invariably gets close to an optimized shape for the set of note parameters characterizing particular notes. The experienced tuner will always demand proper note preparation so that an optimized shape can be arrived at quickly.*

Note: *It is important for me to put some emphasis on what has just been demonstrated here. One of the attributes of a Master Tuner is his ability to tune notes that not only sound better than those tuned by the general tuner but they sound louder as well. What are the secrets? Since I promised to unlock (and expose) all the secrets of the pan, this one is no exception. They are simple really, once you find out what they are! First of all, as stated above, the master will always demand proper note preparation.* **This is where the traditional art of sinking by hammer peening is far superior to the press forming process** *(a view I have long held, and expressed to pan makers/tuners of Trinidad and Tobago over the years). Once satisfied with the preparation, he then blocks (tightens), shapes and tunes the key-note and partials, all in a series of hammer peening actions. The example given immediately above shows that proper note shape can give an extra decibel (or more) in tone intensity. This increase is audibly noticeable. But the bulk of the acoustic power contribution comes from* **proper blocking**. *Traditional hammer peening (by hand) allows the maker/tuner to apply his own skills to this process. Consider the hand peened car bodies produced by the makers of Rolls Royce and*

Bently of yesteryear —far superior to today's mass produced, easy on the die, quick for marketing, soft-bodied cars. Some may say 'but they look good!' Such remarks might be appropriate for cars but no one goes around testing cars with a pan stick! I hope that my readers judge a pan by its musical performance.

2. For the notes tuned to B_3 (246.94 Hz), vibrating with <u>*a displacement amplitude $A_1 \bar{\psi}$*</u> equal to two thirds the note thickness, $A_1 \bar{\psi} = 0.2$ *mm*, at a temperature of 20 °C, using equation (12.48) gives the maximum acoustic power at a distance of 2 meters from any one of the model notes as

$$I_{0,max} = 77.4 \text{ db}.$$

Note: *Observe the difference between this case where $A_1 \bar{\psi}$ is used as against the case in (1) above where A_1 is used (the words above are underlined so that this difference will not be missed).*

Equation (12.47) shows that to maintain Note 1 in steady state vibration with an amplitude of 0.2 mm requires a driving force of amplitude $f_e = 0.0372$ *N* and slightly smaller values for the other notes because of their lower R_m. This driving force at a frequency of 246.94 Hz must not be confused with either the contact force on impact or its Fourier component at 246.94 Hz. This driving force f_e is that required to *maintain* oscillation at a constant displacement amplitude. Just that (small) driving force required to compensate for the losses.

3. The equivalent acoustic radiation mass is $m_r = 0.183$ gm. From Section 11.3.2 we see that the frequency of the vibrating note is reduced under mass loading. Since acoustic radiation is the only loading on an unpainted note ($m_c = 0$), and the note is loaded equally on both the top and bottom surfaces, the frequency ω^* of the radiation loaded note is given by

$$\omega^* = \frac{\omega}{\sqrt{1+\frac{2m_r}{m_n}}}, \quad f^* = \frac{f}{\sqrt{1+\frac{2m_r}{m_n}}} \qquad (12.53a,b)$$

where f is the frequency in Hz ($\omega = 2\pi f$) of the free (unloaded) note and the factor 2 in the term under the square root sign enters because the note is mass loaded on both the upper and lower radiating surfaces. From equation (12.53) we get for our design notes $f^*/f = 0.9833$, for a fractional frequency change equal to -1.67%. If our design notes were tuned in a vacuum (neglect for the moment, the complications involved in doing this) to the B_3 (246.94 Hz) note on the cello, the frequency of these notes will be lowered by 4.12 Hz on exposure to air at 20 °C. But this effect goes unnoticed in practice simply because the tuner will in fact tune the note to 246.94 Hz in air. But if the pan, tuned accurately in air at 20 °C, were placed in a vacuum, the B_3 note will then vibrate at a frequency of 251.13 Hz although it probably will not be heard.

Using equation (12.44) and equation (12.53b) it is easily shown that if the ambient temperature changes, the frequency shift δf resulting from air density change $\delta \rho_0$ is

$$\frac{\delta f}{f} = -\frac{4a^3}{3m_n}\delta\rho_0,$$

which on taking the temperature coefficient of air density as δ_0 reduces to

$$\frac{\delta f}{f} = -\frac{4a}{3\pi\rho_n h}\delta_0 \Delta T, \qquad (12.54)$$

where ΔT is the change in temperature. Further if one takes for the air medium $\rho_0 = 1.164$ kg·m^{-3} at 30°C and $\rho_0 = 1.247$ kg·m^{-3} at 10°C one gets the approximate temperature coefficient for air density ,

$$\delta_0 = -0.00415 \; kg \cdot m^{-3} \cdot °C^{-1}.$$

Finally

$$\frac{\delta f}{f} = 2.286 \cdot 10^{-7}\frac{a}{h}\delta T. \qquad (12.55)$$

We see in equation (12.55) that the fractional change in frequency varies directly as the ratio a/h which means that large notes of thin material are more greatly affected by changes in air density. But one needs to find out the extent of these changes. Using the values in our design, $a/h = 38.4/0.3$, gives

$$\frac{\delta f}{f} = 2.93 \cdot 10^{-5} \delta T.$$

For a temperature increase of 10°C, typical for outdoors, this equation gives

$$\frac{\delta f}{f} = 0.0293\ \%.$$

For our model notes tuned to B_3 this corresponds to a rise in frequency of 0.073 Hz due to *changes in acoustic radiation damping alone*. There are, however larger effects (see Chapter 9) that will mask this frequency shift.

The effect of acoustic mass loading given by equation (12.54) can be included in the frequency equation (9.15) obtained in Section 9.4 to yield the improved equation

$$f_f^2 = f_i^2 + \left[\left\{(\alpha_{0f} - \alpha_{0i}) + s_i \alpha_{0i}\left(1 - \frac{M_{4f}}{M_{4i}}\right)\right\} - \alpha_T \Delta T (1 + v_i) \left(\frac{a}{h}\right)^2 M_{4f}\right] \frac{E_i h^2 [1 + (2\varphi \delta_v + \delta_E + \alpha_T)\Delta T]}{4\pi^2 \rho a^4 (1 - v_i^2)}$$
$$- \frac{8 f_i^2}{3\pi \rho}\left(\frac{a}{h}\right)\delta_0 \Delta T\ ,$$

(12.56)

where it is understood that ρ is the density of the note material (steel). This equation can be obtained through the reverse of the following operation: In equation (12.56) consider only the air density change. This gives $f_f^2 = f_i^2 - \frac{8 f_i^2 a}{3\pi \rho\, h}\delta_0 \Delta T$ which on using the difference between two squares is equivalent to $2 f \delta f = -\frac{8 f^2 a}{3\pi \rho\, h}\delta_0 \Delta T$, same as equation (12.54). Now begin with (12.54) reverse the procedure then include the other effects given in (9.15).

12.20 Acoustic Radiation Efficiency

12.20.1 Uncoated Notes

The mechanical resistance $R_m = 24\ s^{-1}$ determined experimentally, in fact gives the sum $R_m + R_t + R_r$ for an uncoated, un-chromed note (see Section 9.6.1). Since we will be using this value as the typical value for all pans at normal room temperature, and since it is impossible to divide this value into the three components R_m, R_t and R_r we take it as representing an equivalent sum of mechanical resistance due to internal material losses and transmission losses (this representation is already used in the example notes in Section 12.19 and in Table 12.1. Thus we write for the acoustic radiation efficiency of the uncoated note

$$\eta = \frac{\frac{1}{2c}\rho_0 \pi \omega^2 a^4}{R_m m_n + \frac{1}{2c}\rho_0 \pi \omega^2 a^4}$$

$$= \frac{\frac{1}{2c}\rho_0 \pi \omega^2 a^4}{R_m (\pi \rho_n a^2 h)\langle \psi^2 \rangle + \frac{1}{2c}\rho_0 \pi \omega^2 a^4}$$

$$\eta = \frac{\rho_0 \omega^2 a^2}{2 R_m c \rho_n h \langle \psi^2 \rangle + \rho_0 \omega^2 a^2}. \tag{12.57}$$

12.20.2 Paint-Coated (Powder-Coated) Notes

For a paint-coated note with coating density ρ_c, mechanical resistance R_c and coating thickness h_c, we get

$$\eta = \frac{\rho_0 \omega^2 a^2}{2c(R_m \rho_n h_n + R_c \rho_c h_c)\langle \psi^2 \rangle + \rho_0 \omega^2 a^2}, \tag{12.58}$$

where the note thickness h_n does not include the coating. In addition, due to the stiffness of the coating, S_{eff} shows a small increase. One sees right away that because of the additional losses due to the coating, the acoustic efficiency is reduced. The efficiency also decreases as the coating thickness and coating density are increased. Choosing, low-loss and light-weight coating is preferable but may cause some conflicts with the required wear resistant properties that are also desired. *Conflicting requirements such as these are bound to show up when choosing coating materials from among commercial products that are not specifically designed for steelpan notes.*

12.20.3 Chrome-Plated or Nickel-Plated Notes

An equation similar to (12.58) exists for chrome-plated notes. Since these steel notes are essentially nickel plated with a flash of chromium, one can write

$$\eta = \frac{\rho_0 \omega^2 a^2}{2c(R_{m,st}\rho_{st}h_{st} + R_{m,ni}\rho_{ni}h_{ni})\langle \psi^2 \rangle + \rho_0 \omega^2 a^2}, \quad (12.59)$$

where the subscripts $st \equiv steel$ and $ni \equiv nickel$ distinguish the two metals. The Young's modulus for nickel (E_{ni} = 210 GPa) is only slightly higher than that for low-carbon steel. Elastically, when the chromed note vibrates transversely, to a first approximation it behaves as a slightly thicker steel material. *But the nickel provides greater magnetomechanical damping (MMD) than an equivalent thickness of the steel forming the note i.e. $R_{m,ni} > R_{m,st}$.* The acoustic efficiency, as equation (12.59) shows, will always be reduced when the notes are chromed or nickel plated. The efficiency also decreases as the coating thickness is increased.

12.20.4 Acoustic Efficiency of Notes

We now arrive at the following results for the acoustic radiation efficiency:

(i) For our model notes tuned to **B**$_3$ (246.94 Hz) on the cello, at 20 °C, with c = 343 $m \cdot s^{-1}$, ρ_0 =1.204 $kg \cdot m^{-3}$, R_m = 24 s^{-1}, using equation (12.57) the acoustical efficiencies are:

Note 1   η = 0.245 ≡ 24.5 %
Note 2   η = 0.267 ≡ 26.7 %
Sph. Cap η = 0.27 ≡ 27.0 %

So that 24.5% of the total energy loss on our model note1 is lost through acoustical radiation. The efficiencies of Note 1 and Note 2 differ by only 0.022. Since, as a musical instrument, the acoustical output must be maximized, it is clear that all effort should be made to increase η by ensuring that R_m is reduced as much as possible. Well applied *work hardening* and *indenting* (sinking) followed by good *stress relief anneal* (burning) practices will accomplish this. Overheating or prolong heating, even at the recommended temperatures, will increase R_m. Chroming or powder-coating will improve the visual appearance of our note but they will degrade the acoustical efficiency. Of course one must weigh these two conflicting attributes carefully — *what satisfies the eye may not always be pleasant to the ear!*

(ii) When the acoustical resistance is relatively small,

$$\rho_0 \omega^2 a^2 \ll 2c(R_{m,st}\rho_{st}h_{st} + R_{m,ni}\rho_{ni}h_{ni})\langle\psi^2\rangle$$

the acoustic efficiency η increases in proportion to $(\omega a)^2$. Stated thus

$$\eta \propto (\omega\, a)^2.$$

This relation is written as the square of a product because it can be generally stated that high frequency notes are usually small in area while low frequency notes are generally large. Therefore, **one should not use the direct relationship between η and a^2 to make the misleading statement that larger notes are more efficient.** For a given frequency however, in comparing *similarly prepared* notes, one can with high degree of certainty on the outcome make the statement that the larger of two such notes will be found to be more efficient.

- *Notice how carefully I have worded these statements on the acoustic efficiency. You should take the same care in using the notion of acoustic efficiency.*

(iii) The acoustic efficiency can be increased by reducing the thickness h but this must be done with care because problems such as buckling may arise. Because of these problems larger notes should be made of thicker material (steel).

(iv) At low efficiency levels ($\eta < 0.5$) the acoustical efficiency is directly dependent on the air density ρ_0 and inversely dependent on the sound velocity c. Air density decreases with temperature while the velocity of sound increases with temperature therefore efficiency decreases as the temperature rises. For the conditions obtained on all steelpans these relationships hold true; in fact over the normal range of temperatures that the instrument is subjected, the efficiency-temperature relation is fairly linear as demonstrated for our model notes in Figure 12.14.

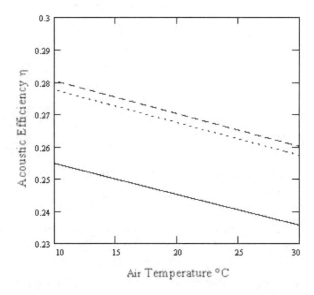

Fig. 12.14. Acoustic efficiency as a function of air temperature for (a) model note1 (—), (b) model note 2 (····), (c) spherical cap (- - -).

In these plots air density in units of $kg \cdot m^{-3}$ is corrected for temperature changes in the range 10 to 30 °C using

$$\rho_0(T) = 1.247 - 0.00415(T - 10),$$

while the velocity of sound in units of $m \cdot s^{-1}$ is corrected using

$$c(T) = 337.3 + 0.585(T - 10),$$

with temperature T in °C.

Pans are more acoustically efficient when played in cold dry air (indoors or outdoors). But one ought to remember that the acoustic mass loading and the frequencies of the notes are temperature dependent as well. For this reason, the acoustical advantage gained by playing the pan in cold air may be offset by the resulting shift (upward) in the note frequencies. *It is always best to play the pan at the temperature at which it was tuned.* If necessary, a skilled tuner can adapt his/her tuning methods to take account of these effects.

At a given temperature, the moisture present in the atmosphere decreases the air density because the molecular weight of water is smaller than the average molecular weight of dry air. This results in a small decrease in the acoustic efficiency with relative humidity. However, we will not belabor this point since the reader can obtain the data on air density and relative humidity elsewhere to satisfy his/her curiosity.

12.21 A Few Hints on Selecting Coating Formulation and Note Material

(i) Coating a note by liquid painting or powder coating reduces the acoustical efficiency. As a guide, if coating is necessary, ensure that the mechanical resistance R_c of the coating falls well below the value 24 s^{-1}. Since R_c is essentially resistance to bending, the coating must be sufficiently flexible. Since one of the aims in the powder coating industry is to make the coating resistant to abrasion, the curing process is designed to *harden* the coating. This reduces flexibility and may increase R_c. Powder coating formulations should therefore be chosen to maximize flexibility and reduce bending losses. The latter is however, not one of the typical parameters specified for commercial raw materials used in powder coating. In addition the powders should be of the *thermosetting type* with low molecular weight to reduce mass loading. Avoid *acrylics* because of their high hardness and poor flexibility. *Epoxies* are subject to embrittlement — a defect that could adversely affect the vibration of the notes — and may discolor (*chalk* or *whiten*) in prolong or repeated exposure to sunlight. The material degradation associated with chalking will manifest itself as changes in note tonality as the pan ages.

(ii) The use of higher density note material will increase ρ_n and reduce the acoustic efficiency unless the loss in the new material is lower than that of low carbon steel. Brass for example, when compared to steel, through its higher density alone will reduce the efficiency by the factor 0.906. This must be interpreted properly: If the efficiency of a steel note is η_{steel} and only the density is changed in the efficiency formula then the efficiency of the brass note will be $\eta_{brass}= \eta_{steel}(0.906)$.

For chrome-plated notes, the drop in acoustic output that the author and some pan makers have observed when comparing pans before and after chroming is the result of two changes made to the note:

1. Chroming is nickel plating followed by a flash of chromium. Nickel shows greater magnetomechanical energy dissipation than low-carbon steel; as a result the MMD it introduces is greater than that for an equivalent thickness of low-carbon steel. The resistance term $R_{m,ni}$ which appears in the denominator on the right side of equation (12.59) reduces the acoustic efficiency.
2. The density of nickel (8800 $kg \cdot m^{-3}$) is greater than that of steel (7750 $kg \cdot m^{-3}$). Therefore, the layers of nickel added to both sides of the steel note increases the mass term

appearing in the denominator on the right side of equation (12.59) which again reduces the acoustic efficiency.

The energy loss of a pan note varies in proportion to:

Bare-metal note: $R_m \rho_n h_n \langle \psi^2 \rangle \pi a^2 + \frac{\pi \rho_0 \omega^2 a^4}{2c}$.

Powder Coated (painted) note:
$(R_m \rho_n h_n + R_c \rho_c h_c) \langle \psi^2 \rangle \pi a^2 + \frac{\pi \rho_0 \omega^2 a^4}{2c}$.

Chromed or Nickel Plated Note:
$(R_{m,st} \rho_{st} h_{st} + R_{m,ni} \rho_{ni} h_{ni}) \langle \psi^2 \rangle \pi a^2 + \frac{\pi \rho_0 \omega^2 a^4}{2c}$.

Energy loss is seen here to increase when the notes are coated.

12.22 Using Horns or other Attachments to modify the Radiation Characteristics

It is possible (but not recommended by the author) to attach horns or make use of partial horns formed by surrounding structure in order to modify the acoustic radiation characteristics of the pan. Any horn attachment must, of necessity, be large (around 12 feet or 4 m) in order to effectively modify the free air radiation characteristics of the pan. Attachments of these types using standing waves to enhance the radiation from pan notes have been tried (for example the Rocket pan by Rudolph Charles) and suggested in at least one patent (see the G-Pan in Chapter 17). Enhanced radiation, even in specific directions, means that there is less energy imparted to the standing waves which interact directly with the vibrating note making the standing wave less stable and the frequency of the note less defined. This happens because any increase in energy outputted from the instrument must come from somewhere; in this case it comes from the standing waves. Altogether this makes the instrument more difficult to maintain; certainly it will be difficult to master. See Section 17.23 for more details.

CHAPTER 13

Stick-Note Impact — Impact Phase

13.1 Introduction

This Chapter on Stick-Note impact is the longest in this book. I devoted much time and effort in developing the material covered here because I believe that the small fraction of a second taken by a panist to play a note, call this 'panist's time' is equivalent to the one hour of 'tuner's time' spent in preparing the note. This certainly makes good sense when, for example, you listen to a Bertrand 'Birch' Kellman tenor played by Len 'Boogsie' Sharpe. *You ought to be as appreciative of the tuner as you are of the panist*! I believe that the same in-depth treatment given to the pan should be given to the stick despite the apparently simpler construction of the stick. Readers are in for a surprise when they read through this Chapter and discover the many secrets that lay hidden in a pair of pan sticks! My role is to unlock and reveal these secrets.

There are a number of essential factors to consider in the analysis of the stick and the stick-note impact. In order to make a complete study, the procedure to be followed in this Chapter begins with a thorough treatment of the stick and tip under *static* conditions followed by the *dynamic* analysis of the stick-note impact with the note in its simplified form as a SDOF (Single Degree of Freedom) system. Initially, the impact is treated as a free collision (no *Hand Action*) of stick tip and note, a situation found mainly in the playing action of the low-end pans. A more general treatment then follows with Hand Action included in the form of a generalized force F_H which remains fully under the control of the player. While this latter treatment applies to all pan notes it accounts for the hand action used mainly on the high-end pans. Finally the work sees further generalization when the note is presented fully as a MDOF (Multiple Degree of Freedom) system. All the obvious and subtle aspects of playing the pan are therefore covered.

At first it seems unlikely that the real or apparent complexity of playing the pan could ever be captured by mathematical equations. But to understand that it is possible, one must set aside the activities of the mind of the player or the multitude of decisions that he can make. One only needs to consider the action *taken* and *played out*. The action 'played out' is a physical sequence of activities consisting of a hand-stick action which accelerates the stick towards the note, makes an impact, and executes controlled *stick retrieval*. This action or force F_H, called here the *Hand Action*, a physical force, although under full control of the player and therefore arbitrary, can always be represented by some well chosen mathematical function.

Such a treatment as briefly outlined above when placed within the bounds and rules of *Music* and the *Musical Scale*, is capable of defining the strengths and limitations of the steelpan (and its sticks) as a musical instrument.

The musical scale does not dictate the dynamics of the notes of the pan. This latter statement is hard to comprehend by someone who is conditioned to think only in relation to an accepted musical scale. The present author has allowed himself greater freedom. As we shall see, and as experience surely teaches, the proper use of the Hand Action allows the player to fulfill the requirements for 'good music' from the *dynamics of* the pan. Of course, the ability of the player to accomplish this successfully depends on the physical properties of the selected pair of sticks and the tuned state of the instrument.

To assist the reader, simple versions of the system are treated first, followed by a gradual increase in the system complexity until the system is fully developed. Example solutions are given as the treatment develops. One will find for example, an increase in the complexity of the expressions for the *contact-time* as the analysis progresses. The author has made great efforts to find closed-form solutions throughout the analysis. In the most general of cases however, only numerical solutions are possible. Numerical solutions can offer a very high degree of precision.

To introduce the analysis, we begin with the basics, so we first look at the rubber that forms the tip of the stick.

13.2 Rubber Compositions, Stick Aging and Tip Material Properties

Natural rubber or *caoutchouc* — meaning 'weeping wood' after the manner in which the latex is collected — is latex produced in trees (mainly *Hevea Brasiliensis* a tree native to South America). The structure of natural rubber consists of *cis*-1,4-polyisoprene (carbon and hydrogen composition) about 94% and non-rubber components such as proteins and lipids. *Cis* is Latin for 'on this side' so that cis-1,4 means that the atoms are bonded on the same side of the carbon-carbon double bond (C=C) (see Figure 13.1) and the monomer is linked in the chain through carbon atoms numbered 1 and 4.

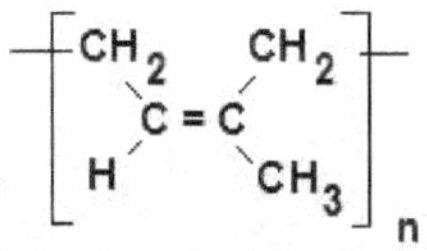

single repeat unit

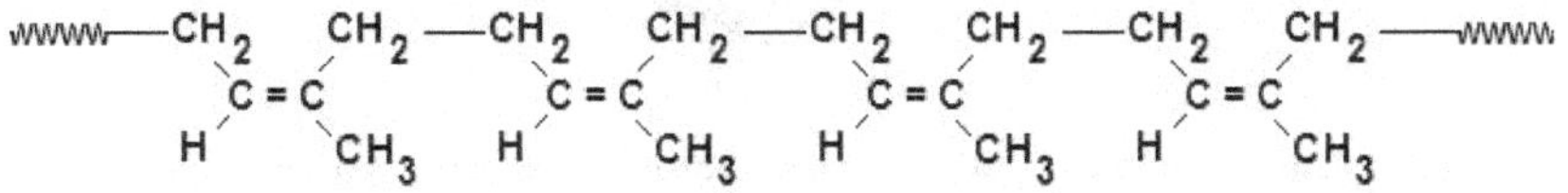

polymer chain of connected repeat units

Fig. 13.1. The cis-1,4-polyisoprene repeat unit of natural rubber. The number of these repeat units is the number n which can be in the thousands forming a long polymer chain.

Rubber is natural rubber latex that has been *vulcanized* with sulfur. This chemical process, in its simplest form is brought about by heating the natural rubber with sulfur to convert the rubber into a more durable material with higher tensile strength and greater resistance to abrasion. Synthetic rubber also has the *cis*-1,4-polyisoprene composition (with other elements e.g. chlorine, fluorine, nitrogen or silicon) but without the protein and lipids. These rubber compounds consist of one kind of molecule (an *isoprene*) joined together in a long chain to form a larger, longer, flexible molecule (a *polymer*). Vulcanization provides covalent crosslinks, chemically bonding the polymer chains together into one molecule.

Due to the unsaturation of carbon–carbon (C=C) double bonds of its structure, rubber deteriorates when exposed to sunlight, ozone (O_3) and oxygen (O_2). Pan players generally attribute the gradual loss in the strength of the stick tips to be the result of '*fatigue*' when in reality this 'fatigue' is nothing more than a slow *oxidation* (meaning 'to combine with oxygen') taking place at the available double bonds of the rubber molecules. Aging of rubber is essentially an oxidative process, which weakens the links along the chain. *Hydrogenation* (a *Reduction* process — the opposite of Oxidation) has been used to reduce the saturation of *diene* (a molecule containing two carbon-carbon double bonds) polymers in order to enhance the thermal and oxidative resistance of the polymer.

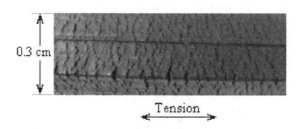

Fig. 13.2. This is a close-up view of a section of used auto battery rubber 'tie-down' clamp. Observe the cracks that developed perpendicular to the direction of the applied tension. Elevated temperatures in the engine compartment increased the rate of this oxidation related process. (Note the scale of the cracks.)

Examples of silicone rubber tips are shown in Figure 13.3.

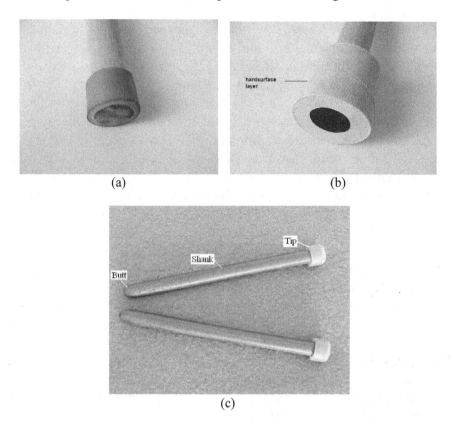

Fig. 13.3. (a) Tenor stick with silicone rubber tip. (b) Guitar stick with artificial rubber tip. (c) A pair of small tenor sticks with ebony wood (African black wood) shank and silicone rubber tip. Shank length: 15 cm (6 inches).

Ozone plays a much more important role in the degradation of polymers containing C=C double bonds of the kind found in conventional rubber. In saturated polymers, it initiates oxidation. Cracking along the rubber surface (see Figure 13.2), aligned perpendicular to the direction of the applied stress, develops more rapidly with ozone than with oxygen and exposes increased surface area to oxidation. Elevated temperatures enhance this process. Silicone polymer molecules generally do not contain any C=C double bonds and thus cannot be attacked by ozone. Given natural aging processes, silicone rubber is virtually totally resistant to oxygen and ozone. This type of rubber is fast becoming the rubber of choice over the conventional rubber in the manufacture of pan sticks.

Rubber (an *elastomer*) can 'bounce' because it can be stretched to many times its original size and return to its original shape without permanent deformation. It is the *'spaghetti-like'* or *'hairball'* arrangement of the long chain molecules that accounts for this property (see Figure 13.4 (a)). This random or disordered arrangement of the chains corresponds to a state of low energy and high *entropy* (a measure of disorder). [The universe and everything in it, in time, tends towards states of greater entropy. For this reason, entropy is even used as a means of describing the arrow of time.] When rubber is stretched, the chains tend to align themselves in the direction of the applied stress (see Figure 12.4 (b)) and the process increases the potential or stored energy of the system. This is a state of lower entropy. When the applied stress is removed the rubber naturally returns to the disordered spaghetti arrangement increasing its entropy as it returns to its original shape. Rubber has a *'memory'* of the original shape but not a perfect or immediate one so that the return to the original shape (the *'effect'*) lags well behind the removal of the stress (the *'cause'*). The rubber *'creeps'* slowly back to its original shape. The final 'hairball' arrangement will not be the same in the minute details as the original but any hairball (from a given person's head) is as good as any other from the same head (!); same with rubber. Owing to this memory, rubber displays the property of *hysteresis*.

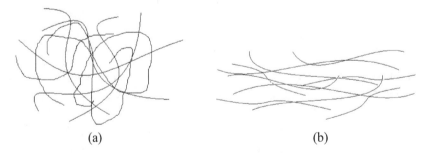

(a) (b)

Fig. 13.4. (a) Normal state, disordered arrangement of chains. (b) Stretched state, chains tend to align in the direction of the applied stress.

If the rubber is stretched far enough the chains will line up in a sufficiently ordered state for the rubber to *crystallize* — becomes *glassy*. *Amorphous* (disordered) polymers when held above their *glass transition temperature* T_g are soft and pliable but below T_g they are hard and glassy (they can be easily shattered by impact). At room temperature natural and synthetic rubber are above their glass transition temperature. Stick tips will therefore harden as the temperature is reduced well below normal room temperature.

As a stick tip ages, the *p-index* (a measure related to the hysteresis, to be fully defined in Section13.6.2) of the tip material tends to increase and the hysteretic property becomes more noticeable. In addition, as the tip rubber deteriorates with age (mainly through oxidation), the elastic constant E decreases. This in turn reduces the tip stiffness and the *contact force* of the stick tip. To compensate for the reduction in contact force with older sticks, the player must strike the notes harder (i.e. with greater impact velocity).

- **Caution: To avoid rapid deterioration, pan sticks should not be exposed to direct sunlight for long periods or stored close to active ultra violet (UV) lamps, running electric motors or other ozone generators.**

Readers requiring more information on the structure and chemistry of rubber can consult the following publications; Wade (2006), Moss and Smith (1995), Barrows and Eberlein (2005), Saunders (1964) and Zweifel and Nantz (2007).

13.3 Protective Chemicals

Certain chemical additives confer resistance to heat, sunlight, oxygen, and ozone. Added to rubber compounds in small amounts (1–2 percent), the amines *paraphenylene diamines*, act as powerful antioxidants. Diamines such as *alkyl-aryl paraphenylene diamines* prevent cracking. A few percent of microcrystalline paraffin wax in the mix formulation does the same job because it blooms to the surface and forms a protective skin providing good protection from oxygen and ozone. This waxy coating can be observed on new rubber components for example, auto CV joint boots, isolator bushings and seals (the author is an auto mechanic among other things so these items come readily to mind). Some of the sheet rubber used on wrapped sticks can also be seen to possess this waxy coating with its white translucent appearance.

- **Caution: Since natural rubber is a hydrocarbon product, stick tips made with this material must not be exposed to petroleum vapors or stored close to petroleum-based products such as gasoline, kerosene, greases and oils.**

13.4 Impact Abrasion

Abrasion is the loss of structure by mechanical forces from foreign elements. Stick tips suffer abrasion because of the stick-note impacts when the instrument is played. Some stick tips are manufactured from rubber tubing and sponge balls that carry a hard outer layer. *Hardsurfacing* is designed to provide impact and abrasion resistance to the tubing and ball (see Figure 13.2b and Figure 13.5a, b). If the abrazed area penetrates through the *hardsurface* layer, then progression of tip loss can be rapid since this layer is very thin. Once pass the hardsurface, abrasion quickly destroys the softer underlying structure of the tip. Abrasion of the rubber surface, like cracking (especially on wrapped sticks, where the tip rubber is held in a permanently stretched state), exposes new surfaces for oxidation. The wear resistance qualities of the stick tip are some of the major factors that determine the life expectancy of a stick. The tenor bass tip in Figure 13.5b and the bass tip in Figure 13.5c were constructed using similar rubber balls. On the tenor bass tip in Figure 13.5b the differences in structure of the inner section and the outer hardsurface layer are clearly revealed.

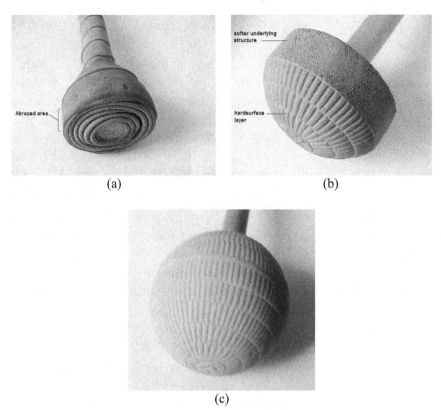

Fig. 13.5. (a) Cello stick with wrapped tip. (b) Tenor Bass stick with tip cut from ball of artificial rubber. (c) Bass tip made from a ball of the same artificial rubber material as in (b).

13.5 Basic Stick-Note Interaction

13.5.1 General Remarks

Remark: In the following analyses the term 'stick' is often used interchangeably with the term 'stick tip.'

The sound of a steelpan depends on the dynamics of the excited note and the type of impact that initiates the note vibrations. It also depends on the note-note and note-skirt interactions but since the stick loses contact with the note after a brief interval, it is possible to separate these problems.

On impact, the note excitation is initiated by a force $F(t)$ exerted by the stick for a time interval $0 < t < \tau_c$ over an area $A_c = \pi c^2$. Here, τ_c is the *contact-time* and A_c is the *contact-area*, with c representing the one-half the *stick contact-width*. Here it is assumed that the contact area is circular. If the contact area is not circular, as often is the case, then A_c represents the *equivalent* circular contact area. It is known that contact-time depends on the type of pan being played. Measurements made by the author (Achong 1996b) have shown that contact-times are shorter than a typical period of note oscillation on the tenor pan ($0.2 \; ms \leq \tau_c \leq 0.4 \; ms$) and of the order of a period on the bass ($2.7 \; ms \leq \tau_c \leq 5.3 \; ms$). Contact-time and contact-area are dependent on the impact force and the material used on the stick tip. The effects of the hand during delivery complicate the general problem. The empirical values for the duration of contact measured from '*make*' to '*break*' using the *electrical contact method* (see Achong 1996b) actually measures $3\tau_c/2$ not τ_c as defined here.

13.5.2 **Time-History of a Sounding Tone — the Two Phases**

The time-history of a steelpan tone may be divided into two phases (i) the *impact phase* or *driven phase*, and (ii) the *post-impact* or *free oscillation phase*. The impact phase is of short duration, lasting less than the period of a typical fundamental mode of vibration, and describes the time when the stick remains in contact with the note. The free oscillation phase on the other hand, describes the vibrational phase from the moment the stick leaves the pan to the end of the tone. The time-history of a sounding tone shows a fast initial rise in amplitude of the vibration followed by slow amplitude modulations and decay.

On the steelpan, note excitation by stick impact represents a case of *impulsive loading* where the force is applied on a small area of the note surface over a time interval shorter than the period that characterizes the motion of the note. The initial movement of the note depends on the velocity of the stick and interaction between the stick and the note. The impact problem is complicated by

(a) the position of the impact point on the note,
(b) the contact area between stick and note,
(c) the effects of the hand action,
(d) the nature of the materials in contact, and
(e) the duration of the impact.

As reported by Achong (1996b), the simple theory of impulsive excitation shows that *contact-area frequency band limiting* arises when the *contact-width* φ_c is greater than one ½ the *generalized wavelength* λ_g of the mode in question (see Section 13.30 for an in-depth study);

$$\varphi_c > \lambda_g /2. \tag{13.1}$$

This effect is put to use when choosing the stick size appropriate for each pan type (larger contact widths are required for the lower pans in order to attenuate annoying high frequency modes). This accounts for the player's choice of larger sticks for the bass where high frequency components must be limited and smaller sticks for the tenor where the necessary high partials must not be unduly affected.

In Achong 1996b, one also finds that *Contact-time frequency band limiting* occurs at frequencies f, higher than that for which one-½ cycle of note vibration has the same duration as the impact. The relation is

$$f > 1/(2\tau_c). \tag{13.2}$$

Equation (13.2) is the *temporal* complement to the *spatial* expression given in (13.1). During the delivery of the impact, to produce a brighter or a more rounded tone, the player can control these two types of frequency limitations.

Excitations due to impact often yield an approximate ½-sine shaped force function and it is possible to mathematically model the stick impacts on the steelpan using this approximation. In any case, because of physical limitations on contact-width and contact-time, the driving-force Fourier series will be convergent and sharply band-limited. We shall return to these band-limiting effects later and develop them fully.

13.6 Static Analysis of the Stick

13.6.1 Stick Non-Linearity

As in the case of piano hammers, measurements show that the compliance of steelpan sticks do not follow Hooke's Law which calls for a linear relation between the applied force and the tip displacement. In addition, in deformation cycles, as the sticks are loaded and unloaded, the sticks show varying degrees of hysteresis. Because of this type of non-linearity, the *stick compliance C* (defined in terms of the *compression X* and *force F*, as $C = X / F$), will depend on the strength of the impact.

13.6.2 Hysteresis

Definition: Hysteresis is the lagging of an effect behind its cause.

A typical loading-unloading cycle for the pan stick with hysteresis is shown in Figure 13.6.

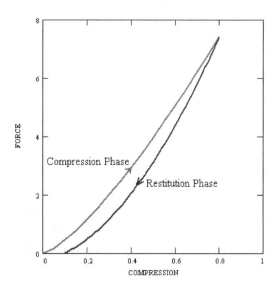

Fig. 13.6. Loading-unloading cycle of a typical pan stick. Compression phase and Restitution phase.

It is known that hysteresis is encountered in many phenomena like phase transitions, ferromagnetism, plasticity, superconductivity, in the absorption and desorption of moisture by wood, as well as in various biological systems. The term hysteresis was introduced into the scientific vocabulary about 115 years ago by, Alfred Ewing (1895) with the following definition: 'When there are two quantities M and N, such that cyclic variations of N cause cyclic variation of M, then if the changes of M lag behind those of N, we may say that there is hysteresis in the relation of M and N.' For the pan stick there is hysteresis in the relation between the contact force applied to the rubber tip and the tip deformation.

The loading-unloading curves of Figure 13.6 can be fitted to a *power law* of the form

$$F = k_1 X^p, \qquad (13.3)$$

with the *index* p > 1 and where k_1 is the *loading curvature* of the loading-unloading curves. Because of hysteresis, the retention of part of the distortion from a previous compression phase makes the pan sticks appear softer during the restitution phase. The *p-index* for the restitution phase is therefore larger than that for the compression phase.

The natural and artificial gum material used either in the form of tubing or flat sheets for stick production, show intrinsically non-linear compliance. Some sticks are made by wrapping (stacking) layers of rubber material unto a wooden, bamboo or aluminum shank. These layers are always in a stretched state, which results in inter-layer pressure and stack compression. This fact, together with the 'slipping' between layers as the tip is deformed on impact, greatly complicates any analysis of the wrapped sticks. Because of these factors, the wrapped sticks do not deform elastically, being dependent on the loading path and the accompanying energy dissipation. The dependence on the loading path (hysteresis) implies that the stick tip possesses a *memory*. Mathematically this means that the compression and restitution phases of a compression-restitution cycle must be described with different values of the p-index. After the removal of the load, the stick tips will eventually return to their original shape but in tests carried out by the author some tips took as long as twenty (20) minutes to do this.

13.6.3 Measurement Methods

The author and his assistant (Achong 2000e and Achong and Rosemin 2000) carried out a series of experiments on pan sticks to determine their hysteresis properties. Sticks were selected from among private and industrial pan makers and the samples contained both used and new sticks. The rubber tips were either of the wrapped variety, made from rubber tubing or fashioned from sponge balls. This method of selection allowed for a fair spread of stick parameters.

The compression/restitution cycles under load were carried out using a simple jig (see Figure 13.7) for applying weights unto the rubber tip and measuring the displacements with a travelling microscope. At the end of the cycle, the final displacement was measured before the rubber returned to its initial shape. The loading surfaces were flat and of sufficient area to avoid dimpling of the rubber.

The mechanical characteristics of the rubber were obtained by measuring the compression produced by a known force applied by mass loading. The stick compliance $C = X/F$ can be measured at any point in the loading. However, for a variable force such as obtained during impact, as the rubber is compressed, the force on the note increases to a maximum when the compression is greatest. It is at this point that the energy transfer from stick to note is also at its peak. The effective compliance C_{eff} corresponding to the maximum force F_{max} and maximum compression X_{max} can be found from the expression,

$$C_{eff} = X_{max}/F_{max}.$$

STATIC MEASUREMENTS

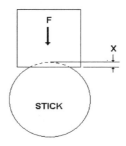

Fig. 13.7. Static measurements involving the applied force F and compression X.

13.6.4 The P-index in Static Deformation

The compression/restitution cycles of the rubber tips are expected to display hysteresis properties. Examples are shown in Figure 13.8 for a bass stick, which employed a sponge ball as the tip and in Figure 13.9 for a 'mini pan' stick using commercial rubber tubing. As seen in these figures, the rubber, during restitution as the load is gradually removed, does not retrace the path taken during the compression phase. There is also a residual compression after the load was completely removed. These are the expected features of hysteresis (a lagging effect).

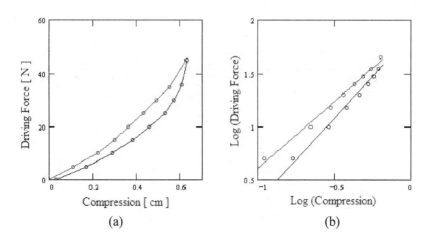

Fig. 13.8. Loading-Unloading curves for the pan stick, compression (red) and restitution (blue) for a new bass stick (54 mm diameter tip). (a) Plots on linear scales. (b) Plots on Log-Log scales

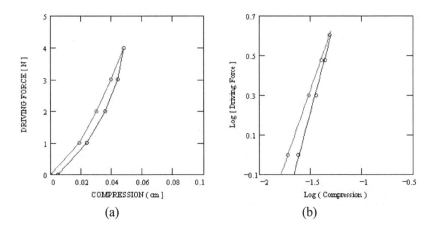

Fig. 13.9. Loading-Unloading curves, compression and restitution for a new mini stick. (a) Plots on linear scales. (b) Plots on Log-Log scales

Table 13.1

p-index		Stick Description
Compression	Restitution	
1.48	1.62	Cello (new) white rubber tubing
1.49	1.94	Mid (new) rubber tubing
1.48	1.74	Meditation (new) rubber tubing
1.26	1.58	Tenor Bass (new) ½ rubber ball
1.66	2.28	Mini (used) rubber tubing
1.46	1.83	Tenor (used) 7 layers of yellow glove
1.09	2.26	Bass (used) 54 mm diameter ball
1.05	1.46	Cello (used) 11 layers, football inner tube
1.20	1.64	Cello (used) 11 layers, unknown rubber
1.49	1.56	Tenor (used) 5 layers, football inner tube
1.09	1.45	D-Second (used) 7 layers football inner tube
1.23	1.86	Tenor (used) 12 layers, glove rubber
1.35	1.68	Bass (new) 54 mm diameter ball
Mean 1.33 ± 0.05	Mean 1.76 ± 0.07	
Mean P-index over compression and restitution 1.55 ± 0.06		

On taking the logarithm of both sides of equation (13.3)

$$log(F) = p\,log(X) + log(k_1), \qquad (13.4)$$

which on a graph of *log(F)* versus *log(X)* produces a straight line. The straight lines of Figures 13.8b & 13.9b are in agreement with equation (13.4) and verify the power-law relation. Values for the p-indices can be determined from the log-log slopes of Figures 13.8b and 13.9b. For the bass stick of Figure 13.8, the p-indices are: compression, *p = 1.26*; restitution, *p = 1.58*. For the mini stick of Figure 13.9, the *p-indices* are compression, *p = 1.49*; restitution, *p = 1.94*. Table 13.1 gives a list of p-indices for random selection of thirteen new and used sticks.

With reference to Table 13.1, the p-indices on restitution and on compression are statistically different while the overall average p-index of *1.55 ± 0.06* is consistent with the 3/2 index of Hertzian contact theory (Hertz 1882)

13.7 Statical Analysis of the Stick-Note System

13.7.1 Model Stick

The stick is modeled as an impactor in the form of an equivalent spherical ball. The surfaces of the note and impactor are given analytically in the coordinate system of the principal axis which passes through the initial point of contact O and runs normal to the tangent plane at O (see Figure 13.10). This coordinate system is fixed in space at the point of first contact. Since the impactor is assumed to be initially spherical, the principal axis runs along a diameter to the sphere.

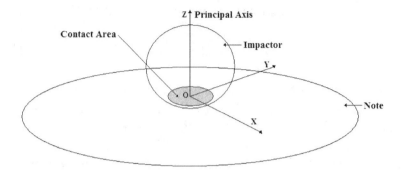

Figure 13.10. 1 Coordinate system for the stick tip (impactor) and the note surface during impact.

Since the note surface is generally ellipsoidal with principal radii R_x and R_y, the contact area will be elliptical over the note surface and centered at the impact point. The distance z of the impactor from the x-y plane at $z = 0$ at the moment of contact may be expressed in the form

$$z = Ax^2 + By^2. \tag{13.5}$$

For all typical note-stick combinations on the steelpan $(R_x, R_y) \gg R_s$, where R_s is the radius of the impacting sphere. It is therefore reasonable to assume that the spherical impactor contacts a flat note surface. On this basis, one can assume axisymmetry of the contact surface. This reduces the contact area to a circular form with $r^2 = x^2 + y^2$ and equation (10.5) reduces to

$$z = Ar^2. \tag{13.6}$$

If the two bodies, note (ellipsoidal) and stick, are pressed together by a normal force F_z an elliptical contact area is generated. The normal pressure $P_z(x, y)$ on the contact surface is in general a semi-ellipsoid (Hertz 1882).

$$P_z(x) = \begin{cases} \sigma_{z0}\sqrt{1-\left(\dfrac{x^2}{a^2}+\dfrac{y^2}{b^2}\right)}, & \text{for } \left(\dfrac{x^2}{a^2}+\dfrac{y^2}{b^2}\right)^{\frac{1}{2}} < 1 \\ 0, & \text{for } \left(\dfrac{x^2}{a^2}+\dfrac{y^2}{b^2}\right)^{\frac{1}{2}} \geq 1 \end{cases}$$

(13.7)

where a and b are the semi-axes. Shown in Figure 13.11 are the stick tip modeled as a rubber sphere and the note in cross-sectional view, with greatly exaggerated displacement and note thickness.

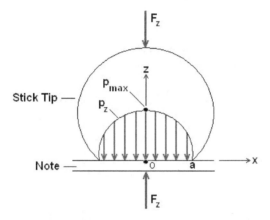

Fig. 13.11. Cross-sectional view of the stick tip modeled as a rubber sphere in contact with the note.

The Cartesian coordinate system is defined with the y-axis normal to the sketch plane. Both components deform but with the note of steel, the indentation into the steel is some five orders of magnitude (a hundred thousand times) smaller than that of the rubber sphere. The contact area extends a distance **a** from the z-axis of symmetry. The contact pressure and loading severity are maxima on this axis. The contact pressure drops to zero along the boundary of the contact zone. In the axisymmetric case with $a = b = c$, the contact area is circular while equation (13.7) reduces to a semi-spheroid pressure distribution:

$$P_z(x) = \begin{cases} \sigma_{z0}\sqrt{1-\dfrac{x^2}{c^2}}, & \text{for } x < c \\ 0, & \text{for } x \geq c \end{cases} \qquad (13.8)$$

where c is the radius of the circular contact area on the x-y plane at O and σ_{z0} is the surface stress acting on unit contact area at $z = 0$. Since the surface integral of $P_z(x)$ over the contact area $A_c = \pi c^2$, must equal the force F_z, the stress σ_{z0} can be readily determined from equation (13.8) as follows:

$$\begin{aligned} F_z &= \int_{A_c} P_z \, ds \\ &= \int_0^c P_x(x)(2\pi x) dx \\ &= 2\pi \int_0^c \sigma_{z0} (1-\frac{x^2}{c^2})^{\frac{1}{2}} x \, dx \\ &= 2\pi \sigma_{z0} \frac{c^2}{3}, \end{aligned}$$

$$(13.9)$$

where *ds* is the element of surface area and finally

$$\sigma_{z0} = \frac{3 F_z}{2\pi c^2}. \qquad (13.10)$$

When the integration is carried out for the elliptical contact area having semi-axes *a* and *b*, by using equation (13.7) the result is

$$\sigma_{z0} = \frac{3 F_z}{2\pi ab}, \qquad (13.11)$$

with $A_c = \pi ab$. It should be noted here that for both cases the surface stress σ_{z0} is equal to F_z divided by $\frac{2}{3} A_c$.

Using equations (13.8) and (13.10), the pressure distribution can now be written in the form

$$P_z(x) = \begin{cases} \dfrac{3F_z}{2\pi c^2}\sqrt{1-\dfrac{x^2}{c^2}}, & \text{for } x < c \\ 0, & \text{for } x \geq c \end{cases} \quad (13.12)$$

Kalker (1990) gave a solution of this problem of relating σ_{z0} and F_z to the displacements of the impacting bodies in terms of three dimensionless parameters α, β and γ. For the stick-note impact problem there is considerable simplification of Kalker's equations because of the vast differences in the elastic moduli of the rubber stick and the steel notes. With reference to Table 2.3 of Constants, Young's modulus for the steel notes has the value $E_n = 207$ GPa, while the corresponding value for the rubber tips of the sticks is $E_s = (8 \text{ to } 50) \times 10^{-4}$ GPa. Regardless of chemical composition or temper treatment, steel has a Poisson ratio of approximately 0.3. Rubber compositions have Poisson ratios typically between 0.4 and 0.5. If ξ_s and ξ_n are the respective indentations into the stick tip and note material, one can readily write

$$\frac{\xi_n}{\xi_s} = \frac{E_s(1-v_n^2)}{E_n(1-v_s^2)}. \quad (13.13)$$

Since E_s is some five orders of magnitude smaller than E_n (i.e., $E_s/E_n \approx 10^{-5}$), in typical stick-note impacts $\xi_n \approx 10^{-5}\,\xi_s$. With very good accuracy one can therefore use the condition $\xi_n \ll \xi_s$ to simplify the Kalker equations. Using the coefficients A and B from equation (13.5), the simplified expressions for Kalker's coefficients α, β and γ are

$$\alpha = \frac{a^2(A+B)E_s}{F_z(1-v^2)}, \quad \beta = \frac{a^2(A+B)}{\xi_s}, \quad \gamma = \frac{A}{A+B}.$$

(13.14a, b, c)

Using the semi-axes a and b in equation (13.7) the other expressions for these coefficients are

$$\alpha = \frac{3}{2\pi}(1-k^2)^{\frac{1}{2}} G(k), \quad \beta = \frac{G(k)}{H(k)}, \quad \gamma = \frac{H(k)-K(k)}{G(k)},$$

where $k = \left(1 - \frac{b^2}{a^2}\right)^{\frac{1}{2}}$, for $b \leq a$,

(13.15a, b, c)

and where $G(k)$ and $H(k)$ are complete elliptical integrals of the first and second kind respectively and $K(k)$ a combination of these given by

$$\left.\begin{array}{l} G(k) = \displaystyle\int_0^{\pi/2} (1-k^2 \sin^2 \phi)^{\frac{1}{2}} d\phi, \\[2mm] H(k) = \displaystyle\int_0^{\pi/2} \frac{d\phi}{(1-k^2 \sin^2 \phi)^{\frac{1}{2}}}, \\[2mm] K(k) = \dfrac{H(k) - G(k)}{k^2}. \end{array}\right\}$$ (13.16a, b, c)

On solving for F_z from (13.14), (13.15) and (13.16) one finds

$$F_z = \frac{2\pi E_s}{3(1-v_s^2)} \left(\frac{1}{A}\right)^{\frac{1}{2}} \xi_s^{\frac{3}{2}} S(k),$$ (13.17)

where

$$S(k) = \frac{1}{(1-k^2) H(k)} \left(1 - \frac{K(k)}{H(k)}\right)^{\frac{1}{2}}.$$

Equation (13.17) is consistent with the Hertz [1882] solution showing the three-halves (3/2) power law relationship between the applied force and the displacement. The function $S(k)$ shows that the force-displacement relationship is dependent on the ratio of the semi-axes of the elliptical contact surface. This is an indication that the force-displacement relation depends on the shape of the contact area.

For circular contact areas ($a = b$, $k = 0$, $A = B$), $G(0) = \pi/2$, $H(0) = \pi/2$, $K(0) = \pi/4$, and $S(0) = 2^{1/2}/\pi$. For the case of circular contact areas, Equation (13.17) simplifies to

$$F_z = \frac{4 E_s}{3(1 - v_s^2)} \left(\frac{1}{2A} \right)^{\frac{1}{2}} \xi_s^{\frac{3}{2}}, \qquad (13.18)$$

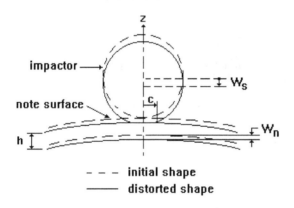

Fig. 13.12. Stick tip compression W_0 and note displacement W_n on a note of thickness h. Not drawn to scale.

We now show that in the deformation of stick tips that can be modeled as spherical rubber impactors, the deformation obeys equation (13.6). As illustrated in Figure 13.12, the impactor distorts the initial shapes of impactor and note producing a displacement W_s of the impactor (stick tip) and W_n on the note. In Figure 13.13, consider the circular impactor section of radius R_s. At the moment of impact the impactor makes contact with the note at the point O. During the impact, either as a consequence of the impact or as a result of the impact and the ongoing vibratory motion, the note surface travels a distance W_n. Meanwhile, as the impact point moves from O to O' the impactor is deformed with a displacement W_s along the principal axis. The radius of the contact area is $r = c$

and the displacements W_s and W_n are measured along the principal axis (at $r = 0$). From simple geometrical properties of the circle and with reference to Figure 13.13, one finds

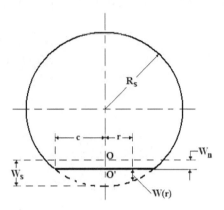

Fig. 13.13. Geometry of the deformed stick tip.

$$c^2 = (2R_s - (W_s - W_n))(W_s - W_n). \tag{13.19}$$

For small deformations, $R_s \gg (W_s - W_n)$, Equation (15) reduces to

$$c^2 = 2R_s(W_s - W_n) \tag{13.20}$$

and finally,

$$W_s - W_n = \frac{1}{2R_s} c^2 \tag{13.21}$$

Equation (13.6) and equation (13.21) are identical in form, with the coefficient A given by

$$A = \frac{1}{2R_s}. \tag{13.22}$$

The surface shown as the dotted curved line in Figure 13.13, is described by the equation

$$W(r) = (W_s - W_n) - Ar^2. \tag{13.23}$$

This equation is of the form

$$z(r) = \xi - Ar^2. \tag{13.24}$$

Since equation (13.24) has the same form as equation (13.6), the previous analysis leading to equation (13.18) is applicable to the stick-note impacts.

There are some informative articles and survey papers on these impact problems that can be found in Okrouhlik (1994). Among these is the work by Steuermann (1939) and it is instructive to look at his formulation of this problem. For axisymmetric polynomial surfaces of the more general form

$$z(r) = \xi - A_n r^{2n}, \quad n = 1, 2, \cdots \tag{13.25}$$

produced by the action of a normal force F_z, Steuermann obtained the force displacement law

$$F_z = \frac{4En}{(1-\nu^2)(2n+1)} \left(\frac{1 \cdot 3 \cdots (2n-1)}{2 \cdot 4 \cdots 2n \cdot A_n} \right)^{\frac{1}{2n}} \xi^{\frac{2n+1}{2n}}. \tag{13.26}$$

Comparing equation (13.24) and equation (13.25), one observes that the case $n = 1$ applies to the stick-note system considered here and equation (13.26) reduces to

$$F_z = \frac{4E_s}{3(1-\nu_s^2)} \left(\frac{1}{2A_1} \right)^{\frac{1}{2}} \xi_s^{\frac{3}{2}}. \tag{13.27}$$

With $A_1 = A$, equation (13.18) and equation (13.27) are identical. It is now possible to confidently apply equation (13.14) (or equation (13.27)) to the stick-note problem with $\zeta_s = (W_s - W_n)$. By making use of equation (13.22) one can now write

$$F_z = \frac{4E_s}{3(1-v_s^2)} R_s^{\frac{1}{2}} (W_s - W_n)^{\frac{3}{2}}. \qquad (13.28)$$

We now proceed to give a discussion of equation (13.28).

When the rubber impactor strikes the note and is compressed along the principal axis (see Figure 13.14), this compression is accompanied by a lateral bulging perpendicular to this axis. This bulging increases the stiffness of the impactor and is taken into account by the factor $(1 - v_s^2)$ in the denominator of the force equation. For a given impact force F_z, the effective distortion $(W_s - W_n)$, is greater for softer impactors (having lower E_s values). For a given applied force, stick tips of larger radius R_s experience smaller effective distortion.

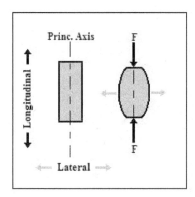

Fig. 13.14. Lateral bulging of a sample compressed longitudinally.

The force F_z results from the impact of note and stick and as a result F_z is time dependent and not a constant. Since one is dealing with a percussion musical instrument, the object of applying a force F_z normal to the note surface is to produce an initial displacement W_n of the note at the point of application thereby exciting note vibrations and the production of the audible tone. The note displacement W_n must not be confused with the elastic indentation into the steel material ξ_n suffered by the note material on impact. By reference to equation (13.13) ξ_n is some five orders of magnitude smaller than the indentation into the rubber tip of the stick.

13.7.2 The p-index in Compression and Restitution

A comparison of equation (13.28) and equation (13.3) ($F = k_1 X^p$) shows that for the rubber sticks used on this instrument, the 3/2-index in equation (13.28) must be replaced with the index p. It is now possible to incorporate the hysteretic behavior of the stick tips into our force-displacement equations but in order to do this we must first write the diusplacements W_s and W_n in dimensionless form by writing $W_s = w_s R_s$, $W_n = w_n h$. In this way the stick distortion w_s is measured as some fraction of its radius R_s while the note displacement w_n is measured in units of the note thickness h. Use of the dimensionless form for the distortion is necessary because p is not necessarily rational and its use as an index can produce dimensional problems. With this formulation one gets

$$F_z = \frac{4 E_s}{3(1-v_s^2)} R_s^2 \left(w_s - \frac{h}{R_s} w_n \right)^p. \tag{13.29}$$

The value of the *p-index* used in equation (13.29) will depend on whether the tip is in compression or in restitution.

13.8 Dynamical Analysis of the Stick-Note System

13.8.1 Analysis of the Linearized Form

Recalling the normalized (dimensionless) SDOF dynamical equation (8.13)

$$w_{,\tau\tau} + \overline{\mu} w_{,\tau} + \alpha_1 w + \alpha_2 w^2 + \alpha_3 w^3 = f_0 + \overline{f}_s(\tau), \tag{13.30}$$

the stiffness terms are linear, quadratic and cubic in decreasing order of magnitude. In (13.30) I have used the shortened notation $w_{,\tau\tau} = \frac{d^2 w}{d\tau^2}$, $w_{,\tau} = \frac{dw}{d\tau}$. The *static state* can be considered by setting the time derivatives in equation (13.30) to zero. The problem of finding the note displacement on application of a fixed external force is greatly simplified by retaining only the linear stiffness term $\alpha_1 w$. In order to allow the reader to grasp all the important details, this analysis will begin with a linearized treatment followed by the full non-linear analysis. A useful approach to analyzing a non-linear equation is to study its *linearized equation*, which is obtained by replacing the non-linear terms by linear approximations.

If an external force F is applied normal to the note surface at the sweetspot then in dimensionless form the linearized static equation obtained by replacing the non-linear form by a linear approximation is

$$\alpha_1 w = f_0 + f, \qquad (13.31)$$

where, from equations (8.14) and (8.17)

$$\alpha_1 = \frac{1}{12} M_1 + 8(1+v) \left(\frac{H_0}{h}\right)^2 \left(M_2 - \frac{1}{2}(1+v) M_3\right) - (\check{N}_c + \check{N}_T) M_4,$$

$$f_0 = 4(\check{N}_c + \check{N}_T) \left(\frac{H_0}{h}\right) M_8. \qquad (13.32a, b)$$

In equation (13.31) f and f_0 are the normalized expressions for external force F and the internal force F_0 respectively, the note is of unit mass and the displacement w is in units of note thickness h. On re-normalization of equation (13.31) the resulting note displacement W_n, is expressed as

$$W_n = \frac{a^2 (1-v_n^2)}{\alpha_1 \pi h^3 E_n} F_0 + \frac{a^2 (1-v_n^2)}{\alpha_1 \pi h^3 E_n} F, \qquad (13.33)$$

the re-normalized stiffness is $\alpha_1 \dfrac{E_n h^2}{\rho_n a^4 (1-v_n^2)}$ and the note is treated as having circular planform radius a and mass $m_n = \pi a^2 h \rho_n$.

Observe from equation (13.33) that in the linearized case, W_{n0} is equal to the sum of the upward directed displacement due to the static force F_0 produced by residual stress or temperature change and the displacement produced by the applied force F. From equation (13.32b) the displacement produced by F_0 is proportional to the rise factor (H_0/h) and the static stress $(\check{N}_c + \check{N}_T)$. As seen from the factor a^2

on the right hand side of equation (13.33), for a given applied force, notes of larger area undergo greater displacement. Generally, and as a result of this area dependence, the surfaces of the larger bass notes are more easily displaced than the surfaces of the smaller tenor notes. By the $1/h^3$ factor also on the right hand side of equation (13.33), thicker notes suffer smaller displacement and must generally be played with greater vigor. With the typical forces involved in normal stick excitation, note displacements are generally small because of the large value for the Young's modulus of steel E_n that appears in the denominator of the right hand side of equation (13.33).

With reference to equation (13.32a), the presence of the linear stiffness α_1 in equation (13.33) shows that the note displacement produced by the external force is reduced if the rise factor H_0/h is increased. This is because increasing the *rise factor* (raising the dome) increases the stiffness of the note. *This is the explanation for the observation well known to pan players that highly raised notes feel stiffer on impact and require greater force to play.*

On the other hand if the temperature of the pan increases then the term in α_1 involving $\check{N}_T$ will increase, producing a reduction in the note stiffness and resulting in a greater deflection of the note. This is an easily observed effect on the larger notes of the bass pan when the instrument is played outdoors and exposed to direct sunlight for a long period. Through the term in α_1 involving $\check{N}_c$, an increase in the compressive forces along the note boundary will reduce the note stiffness and result in greater note displacement. Identical adverse effects on note dynamics occur when the temperature of the instrument is too high or the residual compressive stresses are too high.

13.8.2 Analysis of the Non-linear Form

As seen in equation (13.33), in the linear approximation the note displacement is directly proportional to the applied force. If the non-linear quadratic and cubic stiffness terms are included, then the solution for the displacement will involve terms in F^2 and F^3 and the magnitude of W_n will then depend on the *direction* of the applied force. As a result of the non-linearity *it is easier to displace the note surface downwards than to displace it upwards*. We proceed now to verify these statements (see also Section 8.10.2).

On including the quadratic and cubic terms in the expression for the stiffness and retaining the static force f_0, equation (13.31) is modified to read

$$\alpha_1 w + \alpha_2 w^2 + \alpha_3 w^3 = f_0 + f, \qquad (13.34)$$

where, from equation (8.15)

$$\alpha_2 = (1+v)\left(\frac{H_0}{h}\right)(M_5 - 2M_6),$$

and from equation (8.16)

$$\alpha_3 = \frac{1}{2} M_7.$$

If the coefficients α_1, α_2 and α_3 satisfy the conditions $\alpha_1 > \alpha_2$, $\alpha_1 > \alpha_3$ (a condition that applies on the steelpan), then for small displacements, equation (13.34) can be solved using the *Frobenius Method* (George Frobenius (1848-1917) developed this method in 1873) by assuming a series solution of the form

$$w = \sum_{n=0}^{\infty} s_n f^n \qquad (13.35)$$

On substituting (13.35) into (13.34) and retaining terms up to third order in f, the coefficients s_i are found to be

$$s_0 = \frac{1}{\alpha_1} f_0 - \frac{\alpha_2}{\alpha_1^3} f_0^2 - \frac{\alpha_3}{\alpha_1^4} f_0^3,$$

$$s_1 = \frac{1}{\alpha_1 + 2 s_0 \alpha_2 + 3 s_0^2 \alpha_3},$$

$$s_2 = -\frac{\alpha_2 + 3\alpha_3 s_0}{\left(\alpha_1 + 2s_0 \alpha_2 + 3s_0^2 \alpha_3\right)^3},$$

$$s_3 = -\left(2 s_2 \alpha_2 + 6\alpha_3 s_0 s_2 + \alpha_3 s_1^2\right) s_1^2. \qquad (13.36\text{a-d})$$

From equation (13.36a) the static displacement S_n in re-normalized form due to the force F_0 is given by

$$S_n = \frac{a^2(1-v_n^2)}{\alpha_1 \pi h^3 E_n} F_0 - \frac{\alpha_2}{\alpha_1^3}\left(\frac{a^2(1-v_n^2)}{\pi h^3 E_n}\right)^2 \frac{F_0^2}{h} - \frac{\alpha_3}{\alpha_1^4}\left(\frac{a^2(1-v_n^2)}{\pi h^3 E_n}\right)^3 \frac{F_0^3}{h^2}. \qquad (13.37)$$

Observe in equation (13.37) that because of the quadratic and cubic terms the static displacement is smaller than that obtained in equation (13.33) for the linear case.

Applying the condition $\alpha_1 > \alpha_2$, $\alpha_1 > \alpha_3$ to equations (13.36a-d) followed by a substitution into equation (13.35) then re-normalizing one gets an improved expression (compare with equation (13.33)) that reads

$$W_n = S_n + \frac{a^2(1-v_n^2)}{\alpha_1 \pi h^3 E_n} F - \frac{\alpha_2}{\alpha_1^3}\left(\frac{a^2(1-v_n^2)}{\pi h^3 E_n}\right)^2 \frac{F^2}{h} - \frac{\alpha_3}{\alpha_1^4}\left(\frac{a^2(1-v_n^2)}{\pi h^3 E_n}\right)^3 \frac{F^3}{h^2}. \qquad (13.38)$$

Since the displacement S_n is produced by residual stresses or temperature changes, once the note is already tuned and the temperature held constant, the reference note surface is one that is already displaced by S_n, therefore the measurable displacement $\widehat{W}_n$ on application of an external force F_z is given by

$$\widehat{W}_n = \frac{a^2(1-v_n^2)}{\alpha_1 \pi h^3 E_n} F_z - \frac{\alpha_2}{\alpha_1^3}\left(\frac{a^2(1-v_n^2)}{\pi h^3 E_n}\right)^2 \frac{F_z^2}{h} - \frac{\alpha_3}{\alpha_1^4}\left(\frac{a^2(1-v_n^2)}{\pi h^3 E_n}\right)^3 \frac{F_z^3}{h^2}, \qquad (13.39)$$

where $\widehat{W}_n = W_n - S_n$. The expression for $\widehat{W}_n$ given by equation (13.39) is the required note displacement to be used for W_n in equation (13.29 24). Making this substitution in equation (13.29 24) gives

$$F_z = \frac{4E_s}{3(1-v_s^2)} R_s^{\frac{1}{2}} \left[W_s - \frac{a^2(1-v_n^2)}{\alpha_1 \pi h^3 E_n} F_z + \frac{\alpha_2}{\alpha_1^3}\left(\frac{a^2(1-v_n^2)}{\pi h^3 E_n}\right)^2 \frac{F_z^2}{h} + \frac{\alpha_3}{\alpha_1^4}\left(\frac{a^2(1-v_n^2)}{\pi h^3 E_n}\right)^3 \frac{F_z^3}{h^2} \right]^{\frac{3}{2}}$$

(13.40a)

$$W_s = \left(\frac{3(1-v_s^2)}{4E_s R_s^{\frac{1}{2}}}\right)^{\frac{2}{3}} F_z^{\frac{2}{3}} + \frac{a^2(1-v_n^2)}{\alpha_1 \pi h^3 E_n} F_z - \frac{\alpha_2}{\alpha_1^3}\left(\frac{a^2(1-v_n^2)}{\pi h^3 E_n}\right)^2 \frac{F_z^2}{h} - \frac{\alpha_3}{\alpha_1^4}\left(\frac{a^2(1-v_n^2)}{\pi h^3 E_n}\right)^3 \frac{F_z^3}{h^2}.$$

(13.40b)

If the tip of a pan stick is placed on the sweetspot of a note and a force F_z (which includes the component of the stick weight along the z-axis) is applied to the stick, then the resulting stick compression is given by W_s in equation (13.40b). The complexity of the force-displacement relations in equation (13.39) and equation (13.40b) is the result of combining a non-linear musical instrument (steelpan note) with a non-linear stick. The first term (obeying a 2/3-power law) in equation (13.40b) is the displacement due to the elastic response of the stick tip while the remaining terms arise from the note displacement in response to the applied force.

Since the note moves on its support the reader will no doubt be asking how are the support conditions along the note boundary (the boundary conditions) introduced into the expression for the note displacement W_n. The dependency on support conditions enters through the stiffness parameters α_1, α_2 and α_3. The functions M_i (i = 1··· 8) that enter the expressions for the stiffness parameters depend on the boundary conditions. As well, one should recall that α_2 depends not only on the note boundary conditions but also on the note shape and that α_2 goes to zero as the note loses its dome geometry and becomes a flat plate. The coefficient α_3 never goes to zero even as the dome shape tends to the flat plate because the note material *always stretches* as it vibrates or is deformed by application of an external force.

If (i) the compressive forces along the note boundary and/or (ii) the note temperature is sufficiently high, α_1 can go to zero with the result that the note loses dynamic stiffness and is very easily displaced (for any finite force F, $\widehat{W}_{n0} \to \infty$, as $\alpha_1 \to 0$). The limit $\widehat{W}_{n0} \to \infty$, that appears under the condition $\alpha_1 \to 0$, in the practical situation should be taken to mean that the displacement becomes large. This is the phenomenon of 'flapping' discussed earlier and is more likely to be observed over a small patch of the note. It is hardly likely that a pan maker will hammer peen an entire note until the whole note 'flaps' for that is not in the process of pan making.

It is easily verified, by reversing the direction of the applied force in equation (13.39) that *the force applied on the top face of the note produces a greater displacement than a force of equal magnitude applied from under the pan face* (see Section 8.10). This asymmetry in the displacement amplitude is preserved during the free vibration of the note surface. When the note is played, this asymmetry is easily detectable but as the vibration decays, towards the end of the tone the note dynamics become closer to that of a simple oscillator where the displacements about the static (rest) state are symmetrical. For sufficiently small amplitude of vibration, the non-linear terms in the note dynamical equations are negligible in comparison to the linear terms reducing the system to a simple oscillator. This brings us to the dynamics of the note and stick under impact.

13.9 Stick-Note Impact Dynamics

13.9.1 Origin of the Contact Force

The basis of the impact theory is the generation of transient stress pulses introduced in the note material, tip material and the shank when a mechanical impact is applied over a small patch of the note surface. The stress pulses propagate into both the impactor (stick tip) and the note with spherical wavefronts as compression (P) and shear (S) waves. In addition, surface waves, or Rayleigh waves with cylindrical wavefronts, travels along the note and tip surfaces away from the impact point. The P and S waves are partially reflected by interfaces with differing acoustic impedances, such as internal discontinuities (the rubber-shank interface for example) or external boundaries. The transmitted and reflected waves are, in turn, reflected at the free surfaces and propagate back into the objects to be partially reflected again by internal defects or boundaries. Therefore, a transient resonant condition develops by the multiple reflections of the waves.

The speeds of the P and S waves in a material are given in terms of the Compressional modulus M, Shear modulus G, Young's modulus E, Poisson ratio v, and density ρ by

$$\text{S-wave speed,} \quad V_s = \sqrt{\frac{G}{\rho}}$$

$$= \sqrt{\frac{E}{2\rho(1+v)}}$$

$$\text{P-wave speed,} \quad V_p = \sqrt{\frac{M}{\rho}}$$

$$= \sqrt{\frac{E(1-v)}{\rho(1+v)(1-2v)}} \quad (13.41\text{a, b})$$

with the condition $V_p > V_s$ satisfied (see Table 13.2), allowing the compressive wavefront to travel ahead of the shear wavefront. From the factor $(1 - 2v)$ in the denominator of equation (13.41b), it follows that the upper limit on the value of Poisson's ratio is 0.5. Rubber has a value for v between 0.4 and 0.5.

TABLE 13.2

$E = 8 \times 10^5$ Nm^{-2}, $\rho = 920$ kg m^{-3}		
Poisson's Ratio v	V_p (ms^{-1})	V_s (ms^{-1})
0.4	43.16	17.62
0.45	57.43	17.32

As v approaches 0.5 the material becomes incompressible in the sense that under compression there is no change in volume. A good (but approximate) demonstration of this is a *water baby* (a balloon filled with water). When compressed between the hands, the water baby bulges at the sides keeping the volume essentially constant. For this reason it is very difficult to fit a rubber bung into an undersized hole. Anyone who has tried to insert a rubber grommet into a properly sized hole knows of this problem. Cork on the other hand has a Poisson ratio $v \approx 0$ making it useful for sealing wine bottles.

The contact pressure distribution described by equation (13.8) and illustrated in Figure 13.11 describes a static compression state or one in which the compression is carried out at a sufficiently slow rate for the stress fields to develop fully. In the analysis to follow it will be assumed, and later verified, that the stress fields are well developed during the stick-note contact.

13.9.2 The Stick-Note Model in the SDOF Representation

In this section, a model is developed for the stick-note system during impact. The purpose of this model is to guide our thinking and the reader should not run out shouting 'eureka! we have found the mechanical model on which sticks and notes can be built without steel drum or rubber.' At best, the model is a good approximation to the real system but it lacks certain features that are not easily sketched or included in a diagram.

When the pan is played manually with the stick there are two forces, both of which, for normal contact, are directed along the principal axis. The first of these is the force F_z generated by elastic deformation of the stick impactor and the note. The second is the force F_H imparted by the hand of the player. It is assumed that these two forces are directed along the principal axis and it is further assumed that there are no tangential forces. As a result there are no tangential stresses and no slipping or partial slipping (no part of the contact area slides across the note surface). The normal playing action of the pan player ensures that the latter assumption applies in practice (the player does not drag the stick across the note surface). To appreciate the importance of these two forces, consider a note being played with light control from the hand so that the stick simply falls unto the note and freely rebounds. Compare this with the case where there is deliberate hand control so that the tip of the stick in addition to its rapid motion towards the note is either forced unto the note after impact or is rapidly withdrawn by the player. These are two extreme cases of the playing action.

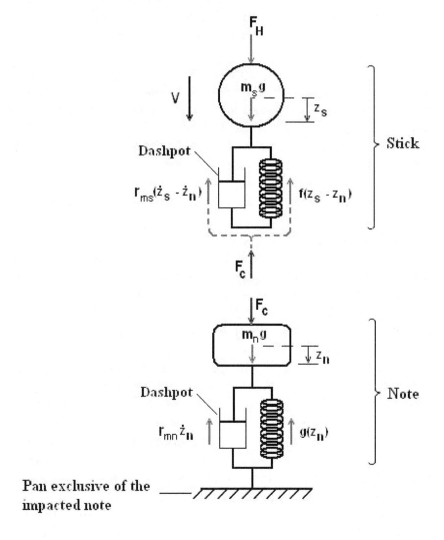

Fig. 13.15. Model stick-note system.

To assist in the analysis of the system in the impact phase a model is set up as shown in Figure 13.15 with all the details and major attributes of the real system. In later sections dealing with the more general MDOF system more subtle but important details will be added to the system. The note is modeled as a mass m_n attached to a *dashpot* which implements the damping mechanism within the note and in parallel with the dashpot is a massless non-linear spring representing the system stiffness for which the restoring force is given by the function $g(z_n)$. The elementary impedance element in mechanics is the dashpot, which may be approximated mechanically by a plunger in a cylinder of gas or liquid. The spring-dashpot combination in the modeled representation of the stick-note system is similar in principle to the *spring-over-shock* damping system employed on automobiles. At any time the spring and dashpot (shock absorber) in parallel combination are subject to the same displacement. This will not be the case for the series connection of these two elements.

Constant mechanical impedance means that the velocity produced is always linearly proportional to the force applied to the dashpot element. From this elemental relation, the damping force $r_{mn}\dot{z}_n$ is proportional to the velocity $\dot{z}_n$ of the note, where r_{mn} is the *mechanical resistance* of the note describing the dissipative properties of the vibrating note. Note dissipation arises mainly from the magnetomechanical losses associated with the vibration of the material, transmission losses across the note boundary and to a lesser extent losses through acoustical radiation of sound waves. The over-dot (˙) represents differentiation with respect to ordinary time t. The variable z_n represents the displacement of the center of mass of the modeled note (located approximately at the apex) from its position at the instant of impact. For completeness, the weight of the note $m_n g$ is included where g is the acceleration due to gravity and the z-axis is assumed to be vertical. The weight of the note plays a minor role in the note dynamics because its contribution is not significant and could be neglected in most cases. The mass-spring-dashpot system is rigidly supported by the pan, which serves as the frame of reference for all displacements. We could be more precise by supporting the note on springs having spring constants K and C as done in Section

3, Figure (3.2) but for the present purposes we set these constants to large values so that we can ignore the small displacements and bending along the note boundary. The mass of a typical pan is sufficiently large for us to regard it as fixed during the impact although a player might choose to move the pan in a rhythmic motion for attention by the audience.

Consider the stick tip as consisting of an equivalent spherical impactor of mass m_s attached to (i) a dashpot to implement the internal losses produced during distortion of the tip and (ii) a non-linear spring that implements the departure from Hooke's law and the hysteresis effects. For the stick dashpot, the damping force $r_{ms}(\dot{z}_s - \dot{z}_n)$ is proportional to the relative velocity of the mass m_s with respect to the note surface. Where r_{ms} is the *mechanical resistance* which describes the dissipative properties of the tip. The spring provides a restoring force given by the function $f(z_s - z_n)$ where z_s is the displacement of the center of mass of the impactor measured from its position at the instant of contact. The function $f(z_n - z_s)$ models the force-displacement behavior of the stick tip including its hysteresis properties. Through the swinging action of the hand, the stick impacts the note with a velocity V_0 and during the impact a force F_H is applied with the hand. By means of the applied force F_H the player controls the impact as required by the musical demands, vary the contact time and even break stick contact with the note. The player can interrupt the impact dynamics at will. *In fact it is only through F_H and V_0 that the player enters into the dynamics of the steelpan.* The weight of the stick impactor $m_s g$ is included because of its significance to the player in controlling the playing action.

All displacements are functions of time, $z = z(t)$. For compatibility in relating the model to the real system we must have $z_s \equiv W_s$ and $z_n \equiv W_n$. A free body representation of the stick-note system is employed in Figure 13.15 in order to identify the contact force F_c between stick and note during impact. F_c replaces the force F_z used in the static analysis.

Using the free body representation with g as the earth's gravitational acceleration, one gets the set of equations:

Contact force: $\quad F_c = f(z_s - z_n) + r_{ms}(\dot{z}_s - \dot{z}_n)$. $\hspace{2em}$ (13.42)

Stick: $\quad m_s \ddot{z}_s + r_{ms}(\dot{z}_s - \dot{z}_n) + f(z_s - z_n) = F_H + m_s g$. $\hspace{1em}$ (13.43)

Note: $\quad m_n \ddot{z}_n + r_{mn}\dot{z}_n + g(z_n) = F_0 + F_c + m_n g$. $\hspace{2em}$ (13.44)

On using equation (13.42), equation (13.44) can also be written as

$$m_n \ddot{z}_n + r_{mn}\dot{z}_n + g(z_n) = F_0 + f(z_s - z_n) + r_{ms}(\dot{z}_s - \dot{z}_n) + m_n g.$$
$\hspace{25em}$ (13.45)

Where r_{mn} is the *mechanical resistance* describing the dissipative properties of the note.

Comment on symbols used for Mechanical Resistance: In this Section, the symbol r_m is used to denote the Mechanical Resistance. Here, r_m is expressed in units of mass per unit time (kg·s^{-1}). In Section 8.11.3 and elsewhere the symbol R_m is used for the Mechanical Resistance per Unit Mass. R_m is expressed in units of reciprocal time (s^{-1}). The terms are related but the use of these two symbols is just a matter of mathematical convenience.

The expression for $g(z_n)$ can be found from equation (13.34) after re-normalization. F_0 is the re-normalized form of the static force f_0 arising from residual and thermal stresses. The initial displacement and subsequent vibration of the note following the impact takes place relative to the static state. Therefore for the dynamic state (SDOF) one gets

$$g(z_n) = \frac{\pi h E_n}{a^2 (1-v_n^2)} \left(\alpha_1 h^2 z_n + \alpha_2 h z_n^2 + \alpha_3 z_n^3 \right). \hspace{2em} (13.46)$$

If the effects of changing temperature and residual stresses are to be included then f_0 (or F_0) must be re-inserted in equation (13.46). Of course, changes in temperature and residual stresses will modify the parameters α_j ($j = 1, 2, 3$). The reason for all this is that the original static state is no longer available since the state of the note is dependent on temperature and residual stresses. We will deal with these matters in later Sections.

Similarly the expression for $f(z_s - z_n)$ is found from equation (13.28), giving

$$f(z_s - z_n) = \frac{4 E_s}{3(1-v_s^2)} R_s^{\frac{1}{2}} (z_s - z_n)^{\frac{3}{2}}. \qquad (13.47)$$

Finally, using the equivalence $z_s \equiv W_s$ and $z_n \equiv W_n$, and the equations (13.43) to (13.47), the following equations can be written describing the *impact phase* of the stick-note system in the SDOF representation:

13.9.3 Impact Phase: SDOF (Single-mode)

13.9.3.1 Without Stick Memory Non-Linearity — No Hysteresis

$$m_s \ddot{W}_s + r_{ms}(\dot{W}_s - \dot{W}_n) = F_H + m_s g - \frac{4 E_s}{3(1-v_s^2)} R_s^{\frac{1}{2}} (W_s - W_n)^{\frac{3}{2}}, \qquad (13.48a)$$

$$m_n \ddot{W}_n + r_{mn}\dot{W}_n + \frac{\pi h E_n}{a^2(1-v_n^2)}\left(\alpha_1 h^2 W_n + \alpha_2 h W_n^2 + \alpha_3 W_n^3\right) = \frac{4 E_s}{3(1-v_s^2)} R_s^{\frac{1}{2}} (W_s - W_n)^{\frac{3}{2}} +$$
$$+ r_{ms}(\dot{W}_s - \dot{W}_n) + F_0 + m_n g \qquad (13.48b)$$

$$F_c = \frac{4 E_s}{3(1-v_s^2)} R_s^{\frac{1}{2}} (W_s - W_n)^{\frac{3}{2}} + r_{ms}(\dot{W}_s - \dot{W}_n). \qquad (13.48c)$$

13.9.3.2 With Stick Memory Non-linearity — Hysteresis

The use of a $\frac{3}{2}$-power law to describe stick compression and restitution, removes the memory or hysteretic aspect of the stick behavior. To remove this shortcoming, the hysteresis properties of the stick will now be included as explained in the derivation of equation (13.29). This will involve changing the $\frac{3}{2}$ index to p, which then takes up different values for restitution ($p = p_r$) and for compression ($p =$

p_c). With this improvement, problems relating to hysteresis through the use of soft and hard rubber, wrapped sticks and the aging of sticks, can then be addressed. Using the dimensionless displacements $w_s \equiv W_s/R_s$ and $w_n \equiv W_n/h$, the results are

$$m_s \ddot{w}_s + r_{ms}(\dot{w}_s - \frac{h}{R_s}\dot{w}_n) = \frac{F_H}{R_s} + \frac{m_s g}{R_s} - \frac{4E_s}{3(1-v_s^2)} R_s \left(w_s - \frac{h}{R_s} w_n\right)^p,$$
(13.49a)

$$m_n \ddot{w}_n + r_{mn}\dot{w}_n + \frac{\pi h^3 E_n}{a^2(1-v_n^2)}\left(\alpha_1 w_n + \alpha_2 w_n^2 + \alpha_3 w_n^3\right) = \frac{4E_s}{3(1-v_s^2)} \frac{R_s^2}{h}\left(w_s - \frac{h}{R_s} w_n\right)^p +$$
$$+ \frac{r_{ms} R_s}{h}(\dot{w}_s - \frac{h}{R_s}\dot{w}_n) + \frac{F_0}{h} + \frac{m_n g}{h}.$$

(13.49b)

These two *dependent* differential equations can only be solved numerically and will require in addition to the values for the elastic constants, mass and geometric parameters, an independent expression for F_H as well as the initial velocity V_0 of the stick on impact. The latter two requirements are under the full control of the player. If the note was in a state of vibration from a previous impact then the note velocity and displacement at the instant of impact are required to complete the integration.

13.9.4 Free Vibration Phase: SDOF (Single-Mode)

When the player applies an *upwardly directed* force F_H of sufficient magnitude the stick moves away from the note surface. When the stick falls freely unto the note surface without hand control it will rebound on its own volition. After stick-note separation, equations (13.49a) and (13.49b) are no longer dependent, the contact force drops to zero, and equation (13.49b) with the contact force components on the right hand side equal to zero describes the *free vibration phase* of the note. On neglecting the small contribution due to the weight of the note, this free phase is described by the equation

$$m_n \ddot{w}_n + r_{mn}\dot{w}_n + \frac{\pi h^3 E_n}{a^2(1-v_n^2)}\left(\alpha_1 w_n + \alpha_2 w_n^2 + \alpha_3 w_n^3\right) = \frac{F_0}{h}. \quad (13.50)$$

To reproduce the dynamics for a struck note, equations (13.49a, b) must first be solved for the contact phase then all parameters, including the value of w_n at the instant of stick-note separation, are passed to equation (13.50) which is then solved for a smooth continuation of the note vibration. This is exactly what takes place on the real system. In fact if you were to play a note on the real pan then rest the stick gently unto the note surface to damp its motion you can reproduce this as well by returning to equations (13.49a, b), passing the parameters and applying the appropriate force function F_H.

Dividing through by m_n ($= \pi a^2 h \rho_n$) in equation (13.50), replacing the time variable t in the derivatives with the dimensionless variable $\tau = \gamma t$, and by making the substitution $\mu = r_{mn}/(\gamma\, m_n)$ where $\gamma^2 = E_n h^2 / \left[\rho_n a^4(1-v_n^2)\right]$, returns the equation (13.30) (with $\overline{f}_s(\tau)$ set to zero for the free phase).

Equation (13.50) describes the single-mode (SDOF) free vibration of a steelpan note for which the natural modes of higher frequencies are far removed from any harmonic relationship with the fundamental. Untuned or partially tuned notes fall into this category. Since the impact phase lasts for only a fraction of the period of the fundamental mode of vibration, equation (13.50) describes almost the entire vibrational state of the sounding note.

Each time the note is played equations (13.49a, b) and equation (13.50) must be solved. The roll is therefore a series of repeated solutions of these equations, carried out with a time interval between impacts that is shorter than the duration of the tone. Although these equations have brought us a long way towards understanding the dynamics of stick-note interaction there are some subtleties of the roll that can only be addressed with the full MDOF multi-mode solution. These will be addressed in Section 13.24.

It is important to re-emphasize here that this general analysis of the steelpan notes applies to all states of the notes whether or not the natural frequencies of the modes of vibration agree with the musical scale. *The musical scale does not dictate the dynamics.*

13.9.5 Modeling the Hand Action in solving the Stick-Note Dynamic Equations

The hand action of the bass player is close to that of accelerating a rubber ball towards the note then releasing the ball to fall freely unto the note. The ball then rebounds and moves away from the note. One could therefore simplify the solution of the coupled equations (13.48a, b) by setting F_H to zero. The hand actions of the tenor player are more deliberate and controlled with the possibility for contact to be broken earlier than in the case of a free rebound. The force F_H must therefore be retained in any solution of the equations that replicate the tenor playing action. In general however, one should retain F_H for all pans because the player is free to modify the impacts even on the bass.

13.9.6 Soft-Stick Hard-Note Approximation

As a further simplification we can also solve equations (13.48a, b) using the soft-stick hard-note approximation to obtain typical values for the impact time and impact width. In this approximation we use the physical fact that the stiffness of the notes on a pan is much greater than the stiffness of the rubber tips on the stick and apply the condition $z_s \gg z_n$. On taking the time derivative of $z_s \gg z_n$ one obtains the other condition $\dot{z}_s \gg \dot{z}_n$. The first inequality is obvious while the second requires a little thought. During impact with *stick-note contact maintained*, z_s and z_n are stick and note displacements respectively. They also take place over *the same time interval*. If the first inequality ($z_s \gg z_n$) is valid then the second ($\dot{z}_s \gg \dot{z}_n$) must also be valid. Applying these conditions, equation (13.49a) then reads

$$m_s \ddot{w}_s + r_{ms} \dot{w}_s = \frac{F_H}{R_s} + \frac{m_s g}{R_s} - \frac{4E_s}{3(1-v_s^2)} R_s w_s^p, \quad (13.51a)$$

while the contact force is given by

$$F_c(t) = \frac{4E_s}{3(1-v_s^2)} R_s^2 w_s^p(t) + r_{ms} R_s \dot{w}_s(t). \quad (13.51b)$$

Using numerical methods, equation (13.51a) can be solved independently of equation (13.49b). On solving equation (13.51a) numerically for $w_s(t)$ and $\dot{w}_s(t)$, the *contact force history* can be obtained from equation (13.51b). In this way the dependence of contact force on the hand action F_H can be obtained.

13.10 Examples of Modeled Stick-Note Impacts

Note: *Before we proceed with the discussions on the time-histories shown in Figure 13.16 we take note of the following detail applied in the numerical computations. The indices p_c and p_r take on different values during the compression phase and restitution phase respectively. However, it is physically impossible for this index to change instantaneously at the turning point between the two phases. What really happens in practice, in the neighborhood of this transition, is that the index smoothly changes from p_c to p_r. This transition is a physically complex process involving the microstructure of the rubber and the details of the tip construction (layering for example). The cells in the foamy rubber for example after having air squeezed out of them in compression must now be refilled during restitution. Because of the large number of these cells, on average, this is a smooth process during the turn-around. We avoid these complications by simply allowing the index to change smoothly from p_c to p_r in the transition region during simulation. To implement this procedure properly, the numerical calculations are first allowed to run completely through the compression phase to determine the time it takes for the stick tip to stop momentarily (t_{max}). The calculations are then repeated with a suitable smooth 'transition function' introduced in the neighborhood of t_{max}, and centered on t_{max} that allows the index to change smoothly from p_c to p_r. All the graphically displayed time-histories for stick-note impacts in this work apply this process numerically in the neighborhood of the 'peaks' except of course when hysteresis is absent ($p_c = p_r$).*

The following examples are obtained by numerically solving equation (13.51a) and equation (13.51b). The two examples use typical parameter values for soft sticks tips used on the mid- to low-range pans; $E_s = 8 \times 10^5 \, \text{Nm}^{-2}$, $v_s = 0.4$, $m_s = 0.032$ kg, $R_s = 0.02$ m, initial impact velocity $V_0 = 0.7$ m·s^{-1}. The tips are assumed to be dissipation free with mechanical resistance $r_m = 0$. The weight of the tips, $m_s g$ (= 0.32 N), is also neglected. The modeled impacts assume $F_H = 0$, that is the tip is allowed to strike the note and rebound freely. Figure 13.16 shows the contact force history in the soft-stick hard-note approximation for two cases, a typical tip with $p_c = 1.33$, $p_r = 1.76$ and the case $p_c = p_r = 1$.

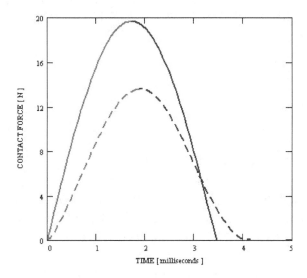

Fig. 13.16. Force profiles for (a) $p_c = 1.33$, $p_r = 1.76$ (dashed curve) and (b) $p_c = p_r = 1$ (solid curve). In the compression phase, the contact force rises towards the maximum while in the restitution phase the contact force decays to zero from the maxcimum. In both plots $F_H = 0$, no losses, stick weight neglected.

For $p_c = p_r = 1$ the force profile is symmetrical, attaining a maximum force $F_{max} = 19.7$ N some 1.73 ms after initial contact. At ½-maximum ($F_{max}/2$) the width of the force-time curve is 2.29 ms. For $p_c = 1.33$, $p_r = 1.76$ the profile is asymmetrical with the compression phase lasting 1.95 ms, restitution phase lasting 2.16 ms with $F_{max} = 13.6$ N, The width at ½-maximum is 2.21 ms. Observe that the duration of the force profile measured from the instant contact is made (the '*make*') to the instant when contact is broken (the '*break*'), increases as the p-index increases. Observe the '*decay tail*' in Figure 13.16 on the profile for $p_r = 1.76$. This tail which prolongs the restitution phase for $p_r = 1.76$ is absent on the profile for $p_r = 1$.

13.11 Notes Impacted with Negligible Hand Action ($F_H = 0$)

13.11.1 The Reduced Equation

In this case we will first examine the solutions for a non-dissipative stick, $r_{ms} = 0$, operated with little hand action, $F_H = 0$ and treat the stick weight contribution as negligible. Equation (13.51a) then reduces to

$$\ddot{w}_s = - \frac{4E_s}{3(1-v_s^2)m_s} R_s w_s^p \ . \qquad (13.52a)$$

To properly handle the effects of hysteresis the p value must be changed during the impact as the rubber goes from compression to restitution. The solution must therefore be carried out numerically in two parts (a *piece-wise* solution). However, a reliable closed-form solution is sought so a further simplification will be made that allows the use of equation (13.52a) to derive simple, but remarkably accurate and useful, expressions for the impact-time and the impact-width.

13.11.2 Contact Force in the Linearized Model

In order to simplify the analysis a linearized form of equation (13.52a) will be employed. This linearization removes the memory aspects of the stick but its advantage is that it allows for simple (but quite accurate) closed-form solutions. On rewriting equation (13.52a) with p =1 one gets the linearized form

$$\ddot{w}_s = - \frac{4E_s}{3(1-v_s^2)m_s} R_s w_s , \qquad (13.52b)$$

which is of the general form

$$\ddot{w}_s = - \omega^2 w_s , \qquad (13.53a)$$

or equivalently in dimensional length units

$$\ddot{W}_s = -\omega^2 W_s, \qquad (13.53b)$$

with

$$\omega^2 = \frac{4E_s R_s}{3(1-v_s^2)m_s}, \qquad (13.54)$$

which describes the *stiffness* of the stick tip. Equation (13.53b) describes simple sinusoidal motion of angular frequency ω and for which the solution is a sinusoidal of the form

$$W_s = A\sin(\omega t), \qquad (13.55)$$

where A (= V_0/ω) is the maximum displacement of the non-dissipative stick tip surface during the impact. If the weight $m_s g$ were included in equations (13.52a, b) it produces an additional displacement $m_s g/\omega^2$ which equals the compression of the stick impactor resting on the note surface.

The simple sinusoidal approximation applies so long as the deformations during impact are kept sufficiently small. We are however only concerned with the first '½ wavelength' of this sinusoidal solution which describes the initial compression followed by restitution of the rubber tip as illustrated in the sketch in Figure 13.17 panel (a). In Figure 13.17, the period $T = 2\pi/\omega$. The stick makes contact with the note at $t = 0$ and breaks contact at $t = T/2$. Equation (13.56) describes, in a reduced form, the contact force F_c during impact. A

$$F_c(t) = \frac{4E_s}{3(1-v_s^2)} R_s^2 \, w_s^p(t) \qquad (13.56)$$

linear version of this equation shows the force (for $p = 1$) proportional to the stick displacement w_s. Therefore since the displacement obeys a ½-sine law so does the force as

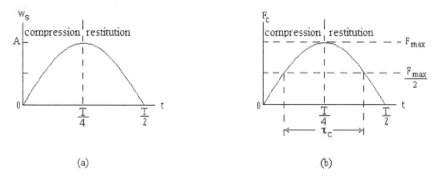

Fig. 13.17. (a) Compression-Restitution time history for a stick tip displaying linear stiffness characteristics. (b) The Force-Time history for the stick in (a).

shown in Figure 13.17 panel (b). In order to relate in a simple way the contact-time to the other stick parameters for the real stick, one can therefore assume that the force-time history of the stick impact follows an approximate ½-sine law

$$F_c = F_{max} \sin(\omega t), \quad 0 \le t \le T/2, \quad (13.57)$$

where

$$F_{max} = \frac{4 E_s R_s}{3(1-v_s^2)} A = m_s \omega V_0 . \quad (13.58)$$

Equation (13.58) reveals the expected dependence of the maximum contact force on the stick mass and impact velocity.

Another useful form for the maximum contact force for $p = 1$ can be obtained from equation (13.58) and equation (13.54) and it reads

$$F_{max} = \frac{4}{3} R_s^2 V_0 \left(\frac{\pi \rho_s E_s}{(1-v_s^2)} \right)^{\frac{1}{2}} . \quad (13.59)$$

The maximum contact force is determined by the choice of stick through the parameters: stick tip radius R_s, stick rubber density ρ_s, Elastic Modulus of the rubber E_s, and Poisson's ratio of the rubber

v_s. The panist decides on the magnitude of the maximum contact force by the impact velocity V_0 through hand action.

13.11.3 Non-linear Form for F_{max} with No Losses

Returning to the non-linear form, equation (13.52a) can be solved for the velocity which can then be used to obtain the maximum displacement $w_{s(max)}$ and finally an expression for F_{max}. Temporarily dropping the 's' subscript for convenience, acceleration d^2w/dt^2 can be written as $v\,dv/dw$ where the velocity $v = dw/dt$. The solution is as follows:

$$\frac{d^2w}{dt^2} = v\frac{dv}{dw} = -\omega^2 w^p$$

$$\int_{v_0}^{v} v\,dv = -\omega^2 \int_0^w w^p\,dw$$

$$v^2 - v_0^2 = -\frac{2\omega^2}{p+1} w^{p+1},$$

where v_0 is the dimensionless form of V_0 given by $v_0 = V_0/R_s$ and the p-index corresponds to the compression phase of the stick impact. One can therefore write

$$V^2 - V_0^2 = -\frac{2(\omega R_s)^2}{p+1} w^{p+1}. \qquad (13.60)$$

When the stick displacement is at its maximum (i.e. maximum compression), the velocity is zero ($V = 0$) so one obtains from equation (13.60) (reinserting the s subscript)

$$w_{s(max)} = \left(\frac{p+1}{2}\right)^{\frac{1}{p+1}} \left(\frac{V_0}{\omega R_s}\right)^{\frac{2}{p+1}} \quad \text{for all } p, \qquad (13.61)$$

$$w_{s(max)} = \frac{V_0}{\omega R_s} \quad \text{for } p=1.$$

Therefore the physical meaning of the dimensionless ratio $V_0/\omega R_s$ is that when $p = 1$ it measures the ratio of maximum compression of a non-dissipative tip to the tip radius.

When the stick displacement is at its maximum, equation (13.52a) shows that the acceleration is also at a maximum. Therefore multiplying both sides of equation (13.52a) by m_s gives the maximum contact force

$$F_{max} = m_s \omega^2 R_s w^p_{s(max)}, \qquad (13.62a)$$

from which one gets

$$F_{max} = m_s \omega^2 R_s \left(\frac{p+1}{2}\right)^{\frac{p}{p+1}} \left(\frac{V_0}{\omega R_s}\right)^{\frac{2p}{p+1}},$$

and finally

$$F_{max} = \frac{4}{3} R_s^2 V_0^{\frac{2p}{p+1}} \left(\frac{E_s}{1-v_s^2}\right)^{\frac{1}{p+1}} \left(\frac{\pi \rho_s (p+1)}{2}\right)^{\frac{p}{p+1}}, \qquad (13.62b)$$

Observe from equations (13.62 a ,b) that in general:

- the maximum contact force F_{max} scales as the square of the stick tip radius R_s,
- the maximum contact force is proportional to $V_0^{\frac{2p}{p+1}}$,
- the maximum contact force is proportional to $w^p_{s(max)}$.

Caution: Concerning the first point above, there is still a lot more to come in later Sections so please <u>do not</u> make the hasty conclusion that in order to make the pan sound louder you simply increase the radius of the tip.

Numerical methods must still be used to obtain the force-time history in the non-linear case with hysteresis. By looking at the increased complexity (though mild) of equation (13.62b) (cf. equation (13.59)) the reader should see good reason for proceeding with the linear approximation. But simplicity is not the compelling reason for using the linear form. The fact is that the linear form gives a very good description of the impact process. It ignores the hysteretic behavior of the stick tip but where that aspect may modify the stick parameters (contact-time for instance) it could be dealt with in a special analysis. Notice that the linear approximation equation (13.59) is recovered by setting $p = 1$ in equation (13.62b).

For values of p on the interval [1, 2], it can readily be shown from equation (13.62b) that for the dimensionless ratio $V_0/\omega R_s < 0.3$, F_{max} decreases monotonically with p while for $V_0/\omega R_s > 0.6066$, F_{max} increases monotonically. The former condition is obtained for all stick impacts made in the normal stick excitation of the steelpan while the latter condition requires unrealistically large values for the manually applied stick impact velocity V_0. For the impact solution shown in Figure 13.16, $V_0/\omega R_s = 0.038$.

As an example, using the typical values, $E_s = 8 \times 10^5$ N·m^{-2} (soft rubber), $v_s = (0.4, 0.45)$, $\rho_s = 920$ kg·m^{-3}, $R_s = 0.015$ m, $V_0 = (1.0$ m·s^{-1}, 1.5 m·s^{-1}), in Equation (59+d), Figure 13.18 gives the F_{max} values for $V_0/\omega R_s = (0.125, 0.122)$. Observe the larger F_{max} values for the stiffer stick tip material ($v_s = 0.45$). Observe from Figure F_{max} that for $V_0 = 1.5$ m·s^{-1}, $p = 1$, $v_s = 0.4$, $F_{max} = 23.6$ N while for $p = 1.33$ (typical for the compression phase of the stick tip), $F_{max} = 18.1$ N. The assumption $p = 1$ therefore overestimates the maximum impact force by some 23 % in this example.

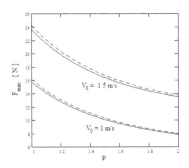

Fig. 13.18. F_{max} as a function of the compression p-index and Poison's ratio ; (—) $v_s = 0.4$, (- - -) $v_s = 0.45$.

13.11.4 Aging and Impact Force

The results shown graphically in Figure 13.18 explains the well known effect that as the stick ages it gradually acquires a 'dead feel' in the hands of the player. As a stick ages the p-indices of the rubber tip increases. A given stick, as it ages, will therefore progressively move towards the right on the curves of Figure 13.18. So that *for a given impact velocity one will generally find that older sticks will impart lower impact forces to the pan notes.*

13.11.5 Contact Times

Continuing with the linear form, by using the *boxcar function* $B_c(a,b)$, sketched in Figure 13.19(a), the ½-sine contact force expression in equation (13.57) can be written more elegantly as

$$F_c = F_{max} \sin(2\pi t/T) \, B_1(0, T/2). \qquad (13.63)$$

The boxcar function $B_1(0,T/2)$ limits the sine function which is continuous on the interval $(-\infty, +\infty)$ to the finite interval $(0, T/2)$ as shown in Figure 13.19 (b).

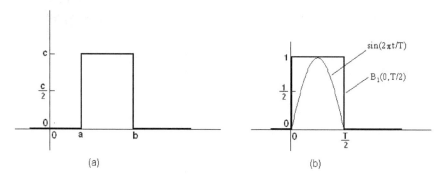

Fig. 13.19. (a) The boxcar function. (b) The product of the sine function and the boxcar function produces the ½-sine function.

The contact force reaches a maximum when $\sin(\omega t) = 1$ which corresponds to the time

$$t_{max} = \frac{\pi}{2\omega}.$$

This ½-sine law leads directly to two simple relationships:

1. The first is that for the sine function of angular frequency ω, the *contact-time*, measured at ½-maximum ($F_{max}/2$) occurs at points $2\pi/3$ radians apart giving

$$\tau_c = \frac{2\pi}{3\omega}. \quad (13.64)$$

   (*When used for tips with $p > 1$, this relation underestimates the contact-time.*)

2. The second is that for this linear approximation, the angular frequency is related to the *effective mass* and effective compliance by

$$\omega^2 = \frac{1}{M_{eff} C_{eff}}, \quad (13.65)$$

where $M_{eff} = m_s$.
Equation (13.64) and equation (13.65) combine to give

$$\tau_c = \frac{2\pi}{3} (M_{eff} C_{eff})^{1/2} \quad (13.66)$$

from which an estimate of the contact-time can be made. The compliance C_{eff} can be obtained using the experimental procedure developed in Section 13.6.3.

Using the relation $\omega^2 = \dfrac{4 E_s R_s}{3(1-v_s^2) m_s}$, equation (13.66) and taking the effective mass of the stick as that of a rubber sphere of density ρ_s and radius R_s, the *purely theoretical formula* for the contact-time (for $p = 1$) reads

$$\text{contact-time} \quad \tau_c = \frac{2\pi^{\frac{3}{2}}}{3}\left(\frac{(1-v_s^2)\rho_s}{E_s}\right)^{\frac{1}{2}} R_s. \qquad (13.67)$$

This equation predicts that for a given rubber material the contact time increases linearly with the radius of the stick tip R_s. If a rubber material having higher elastic constant E_s is used (density remaining constant) then the contact time decreases. Players can readily verify these observations qualitatively. In terms of the tip stiffness equation (13.67) can also be written as

$$\tau_c = \frac{2\pi}{3}\left(\frac{m_s}{stiffness}\right)^{\frac{1}{2}}. \qquad (13.67b)$$

In which case the player sees that the contact time increases with the mass of the stick but decreases as the stiffness of the stick tip increases. In addition, if it is required, the effective compliance (*reciprocal stiffness*) is given by

$$C_{eff} = \frac{1}{m_s \omega^2} = \frac{3(1-v_s^2)}{4E_s R_s}.$$

13.11.6 Effects associated with Stick Dissipation

For completeness, the effects of internal dissipation in the stick tip rubber material must be considered. In the following analysis, where appropriate, quantities affected by stick tip dissipation will be distinguished from their non-dissipative values by the use of the prime (′) symbol.

In the linear model, when the mechanical resistance r_{ms} in retained, equation (13.53b) reads

$$\ddot{W}_s + \frac{r_{ms}}{m_s}\dot{W} = -\omega^2 W_s. \qquad (13.68)$$

By writing $\alpha = r_{ms}/(2m_s)$, the solution of this equation is given by

$$W_s = Ae^{-\alpha t} \sin(\omega_d t). \quad (13.69)$$

Observe that the introduction of stick tip losses produces an exponential (decay) factor $e^{-\alpha t}$; this feature is retained in the more refined analyses that comes later. Equation (13.48c) in the hard-note soft-stick approximation with $p = 1$ reduces to

$$F'_c = \frac{4E_s}{3(1-v_s^2)} R_s W_s + r_{ms} \dot{W}_s. \quad (13.70)$$

The expression for the contact force with tip dissipation is made more complicated by the velocity dependent second term in equation (13.70). Substituting equation (13.69) in equation (13.70) yields

$$F'_c = \frac{4E_s R_s}{3(1-v^2)} Ae^{-\alpha t}\sin(\omega_d t) + r_{ms} A\omega_d e^{-\alpha t}\cos(\omega_d t) - r_{ms}\alpha Ae^{-\alpha t}\sin(\omega_d t)$$

,
$$(13.71)$$

where $\omega_d = \sqrt{(\omega^2 - \alpha^2)}$ is the radian frequency with dissipation, $A\omega_d = V_0$ and $\frac{4E_s R_s}{3(1-v^2)} A$ is the expression for the maximum contact force F_{max} *without* dissipation. With $r_{ms} = 2m_s\alpha$ the last term in equation (13.71) is seen to be a small force component in α^2.

Since we are dealing with a real physical system (i.e. ω_d is positive real), the condition $\alpha < \omega$ must be satisfied. In addition experience informs us that the stick tip is more *spring-like* than *damper-like* and, as will be demonstrated for the pan sticks, the stronger condition $\alpha \ll \omega$ is also satisfied. By using the condition $\frac{dF'_c}{dt} = 0$ on equation (13.71), it can be shown that for sufficiently small damping, the contact force *with* dissipation maximizes after initial contact at a time t'_{max} given by

$$t'_{max} = \frac{\pi}{2\omega} - \frac{\alpha}{\omega^2}, \qquad (13.72)$$

compared to the time $t_{max} = \pi/2\omega$ *without* dissipation (small terms in $(\alpha/\omega)^2$ are neglected).

The maximum contact force with dissipation is given by

$$F'_{max} = F_{max}(1 - 2\alpha^2/\omega^2)e^{-\alpha\pi/2\omega_d}, \qquad (13.73)$$

which is less than F_{max}. The contact-time τ'_c with dissipation measured at points where the *contact force* drops to half maximum is given to a good approximation by

$$\tau'_c = \tau_c (1 - \sqrt{3}\alpha/2\omega), \qquad (13.74)$$

where τ_c is the contact-time *without* dissipation. This can be compared with the slightly longer 'contact time' $\tau'_c = \tau_c(1 - \alpha/2\omega)$ measured at points where the *displacement* drops to half maximum. For a tip with dissipation amounting to $\alpha/\omega = 0.1$, the difference between these two estimates is just 3.6 %. It is important for us to observe these small differences here because in later analyses where p > 1, we shall find it much simpler (mathematically) to estimate contact times using the displacement response even though contact-time is defined as the duration between points where the contact-force drops to half maximum. To do this properly we use the relationship between force and displacement in order to make the appropriate corrections but more on that later.

In partial summary, some effects of stick dissipation for *p = 1* are:

1. The maximum contact force is reduced, $F'_{max} < F_{max}$.
2. Force maximum occurs at an earlier time during impact, $t'_{max} < t_{max}$.
3. The contact-time is decreased, $\tau'_c < \tau_c$.
4. While the tip displacement returns to zero at a time $t_{d,0} = \pi/\omega_d$ after the initial contact is made, the contact force

returns to zero at a slightly earlier time given by $t_{f,0} = \frac{\pi}{\omega_d} - \frac{2\alpha}{\omega_d^2}$. This happens because the cosine term in (13.71) goes negative after the contact force passes its maximum and begins its descent to zero. The cosine term then drops the force to zero a little earlier. For those interested in what takes place during the short time interval $\frac{2\alpha}{\omega_d^2}$; first of all at $t = t_{f,0}$ the stick tip begins its ascent from the note surface with a small residual compression and with its bottom suface still in contact with (just touches) the note. This continues for a time $\frac{2\alpha}{\omega_d^2}$ during which the contact force remains zero because the center of mass of the tip rises at the same rate (the rebound velocity V_r) as the tiny compressed portion of the tip expands to its undeformed shape. The rebound velocity to good approximation (neglecting terms in $(\alpha/\omega)^2$) is given by $V_r = V_0\sqrt{1 - 2\pi\alpha/\omega}$ so the small residual compression can be expressed as $\delta W_s = 2V_r\alpha/\omega_d^2$. This residual compression is quite small for all stick-note impacts (< 1% of the tip radius). *This effect, which results from the slowing down of the tip response by the damping force, must not be confused with the residual compression produced by hysteresis. There is no hysteresis for the case p = 1 considered here.* The Coefficient of Restitution (see Section 13.13) for this tip is given by $\varepsilon_r = \sqrt{1 - 2\pi\alpha/\omega}$ where $2\pi\alpha/\omega$ is the fractional energy dissipated during impact.

Let us obtain estimates for the relative changes produced by dissipation. For example using the value *α/ω = 0.1* for a lossy tip, one finds that *(2πα/ω)100%* = 63% of the energy is lost during impact. The coefficient of restitution is ε_r = *0.61*. The radian frequency ω_d is just *0.5 %* smaller than ω without dissipation, contact-time decreases by *8.6 %* while the maximum force is reduced by *16 %.* This *16%* reduction in contact force is significant. Observe that dissipation in the rubber tip of the stick has a greater effect on the contact force than on the contact-time. The decrease in contact-time by *8.6 %* will hardly produce any noticeable effect on a sounding note because the dynamical response of the note is very dependent on the applied force; the *16 %* reduction in the contact force will have a far greater effect on tonality. *Players certainly would have noticed that lossy sticks greatly reduce the sound intensity of the played note while still allowing control on the contact time — i.e. lossy sticks (not the really 'dead' ones) still allow the player the ability to play the notes.*

13.11.7 Initial Contact Force

When the stick dissipation is sufficiently small so that second and third order terms in α/ω can be neglected, and the boxcar function introduced to define the impact pulse, equation (13.71) can be written as

$$F'_c = \frac{4E_s R_s V_0}{3(1-v^2)\omega_d} e^{-\alpha t} \sin(\omega_d t) B(0, 3\tau_c/2) + r_{ms} V_0 e^{-\alpha t} \cos(\omega_d t) B(0, 3\tau_c/2), \quad (13.75)$$

The resistive component of this contact force is given by

$$F_i(t) = r_{ms} V_0 e^{-\alpha t} \cos(\omega_d t) B(0, 3\tau_c/2). \quad (13.76)$$

At the instant of stick-note contact (the '*make*'), t = 0, equation (13.76) shows that there is an *initial contact force*

$$F_i = r_m V_0. \quad (13.77)$$

This is the familiar opposing force experienced by anyone who has tried to expand or compress an auto shock absorber or a bicycle tire pump by applying a rapid initial motion.

Observe from equation (13.76) that unlike the maximum contact force F_{max}, *the resistive contact force $F_i(t)$ is independent of the radius of the stick tip*. The initial force F_i depends only on the mechanical resistance r_m and on the initial velocity of impact V_0. (*Note: The MDOF analysis is required to fully understand this force.*)

Figure 13.20 shows the contact force history obtained from a numerical solution of equations (13.51a) and (13.51b) for stick with tip parameters; $\tau_c = 2.4$ ms, $\omega = 868$ rad·s^{-1}, $r_m = 1$ kg·s^{-1}, $m_s = 0.031$ kg, $p = 1$. With an initial impact velocity $V_0 = 1.48$ m·s^{-1}, the impact without losses ($r_m = 0$, solid curve) one gets $F_{max} = 39.8$ N, $F_i = 0$. With losses (dashed curve) F_{max} is reduced by 2.9% (in agreement with the result one obtains from equation (13.73)), while the initial contact force is $F_i = 1.48$ N (in agreement with equation (13.77)). Note that in this example $\alpha/\omega = 0.019$ which is about 5 times smaller that in the example given in Section 13.11.6.

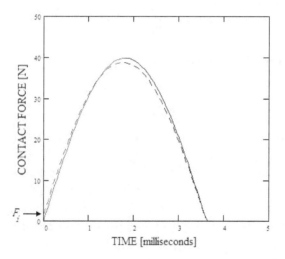

Fig. 13.20. Contact-force histories: (——) $r_m = 0$; (- - -) $r_m = 1.0$ kg·s^{-1} where F_{max} is reduced by 2.9%.

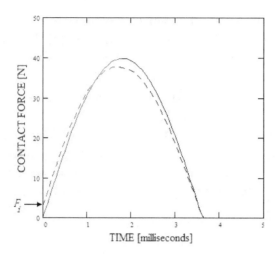

Fig. 13.21. Contact-force histories: (—) $r_m = 0$; (- - -) $r_m = 2.0$ kg·s^{-1}.

Figure (13.21) shows the force history for a tip with $r_m = 2$ kg s^{-1}, obtained from a numerical solution of equations (13.51a) and (13.51b), giving $F_i = 2.96$ N (in agreement with equation (13.77)). Observe in both Figure 13.20 and Figure 13.21 that the contact force maximizes earlier and the break also occurs earlier (barely discernible on the time-scale on Figure 13.21) with tip dissipation. These contact force time histories can also be obtained directly using the following equation obtained by combining equations (13.76) and (13.62b)

$$F_c(t) = \frac{4}{3} R_s^2 V_0^{\frac{2p}{p+1}} \left(\frac{E_s}{1-v_s^2}\right)^{\frac{1}{p+1}} \left(\frac{\pi \rho_s (p+1)}{2}\right)^{\frac{p}{p+1}} e^{-\frac{r_{ms}}{2m_s}t} \sin(2\pi t / 3\tau_c) B(0, 3\tau_c / 2)$$
$$+ r_{ms} V_0 e^{-\frac{r_{ms}}{2m_s}t} \cos(2\pi t / 3\tau_c) B(0, 3\tau_c / 2),$$

(13.78)

where the first term gives the main component of the contact force while the second term gives the contribution from the resistive forces.

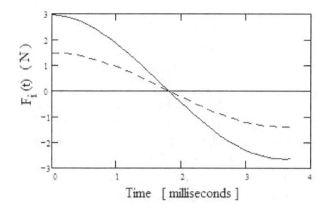

Fig. 13.22. Resistive forces for the two cases with $V_0 = 1.48$ m·s^{-1}: solid curve (—) $r_m = 2.0$ kg·s^{-1}; dashed curve (- - -) $r_m = 1.0$ kg·s^{-1}.

Observe from Figure 13.22 that the cosine profile defines a force that is positive for ½ of the make-to-break duration and negative for the other ½ duration. This, as we shall see in more detail later, means that the resistive force is very ineffective in exciting vibrations at low frequencies.

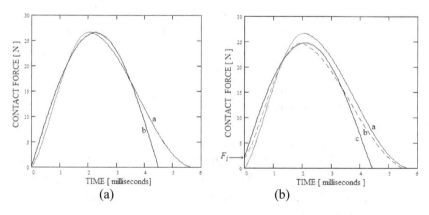

Fig. 13.23. (a), (b). Left Panel: Contact-force histories for $p_c = 1.33$, $p_r = 1.76$, $V_0 = 1$ m·s^{-1}, $E_s = 1.5 \times 10^6$ N·m^{-2}, $R_s = 0.02$ m, $\rho = 920$ kg·m^{-3}: (a) numerical solution or (—) $r_m = 0$; (b) ½-Sine formula, $r_{ms} = 0$. Right Panel: Contact-force histories for $p_c = 1.33$, $p_r = 1.76$, $V_0 = 1$ m·s^{-1}, $E_s = 1.5 \times 10^6$ N·m^{-2}, $R_s = 0.02$ m, $\rho = 920$ kg·m^{-3}: (a) Numerical Simulation (—) $r_m = 0$; (b) Numerical Simulation (- - -) $r_m = 2.0$ kg·s^{-1}, (c) ½-Sine formula, $r_{ms} = 2.0$ kg·s^{-1}.

Figure 13.23(a) shows the contact force histories, obtained from a numerical solution of equations (13.52a) and (13.52b), for stick with tip parameters $m_s = 0.031$ kg, $\omega = 1243$ rad·s^{-1}, $r_m = 0$, $p_c = 1.33$, $p_r = 1.76$. With an initial impact velocity $V_0 = 1$ m·s^{-1}, impact curve (a) one gets $F_{max} = 26.52$ N maximizing at 2.05 ms after 'make', $\tau_c = 2.996$ ms. Using the ½-Sine formula equation 13.78 with $p = 1.33$, $\tau_c = 3.0$ ms gives $F_{max} = 26.52$ N at 2.15 ms.

Figure 13.23(b) shows the contact force histories, obtained from a numerical solution of equations (13.52a) and (13.52b), for stick with tip parameters $m_s = 0.031$ kg, $\omega = 1243$ rad.s^{-1}, $r_m = 2$ kg·s^{-1}, $\alpha/\omega = 0.026$ where $\alpha = r_m/(2m_s)$, $p_c = 1.33$, $p_r = 1.76$. With an initial impact velocity $V_0 = 1$ ms^{-1}, the impact without losses, $r_m = 0$, curve (a) one gets $F_{max} = 26.52$ N maximizing at 2.05 ms after 'make', $\tau_c = 2.996$ ms, $F_i = 0$. With losses, curve (b) F_{max} is reduced to 24.64 N at 1.95 ms, $\tau_c = 3.02$ ms, while the initial contact force is $F_i = 2$ N (in agreement with equation (13.77). Using the ½-Sine formula equation (13.77) with $p = 1.33$, $\tau_c = 3.02$ ms gives $F_{max} = 24.76$ N at 2.11 ms, $F_i = 2$ N.

The curves in Figure 13.23(a) and Figure 13.23(b) show that the ½-Sine formula gives a good time-history of the impact except for the decay tail of the profile in the restitution phase. In later studies we shall find that with hand action, the retrieval force applied to the stick has the effect of removing this tail. The retrieval force causes the force profile to decay more rapidly to zero giving the profile a more symmetrical appearance about the peak.

Another feature produced by the hysteretic behavior seen on the decay tail in Numerical Solution and not captured in the ½-Sine solution is the increased duration to the 'break'. Look closely at the tail on Figure 13.23(b) and there the solid curve (——— (a)) is seen to persist slightly longer than the dashed curve (- - - (c)). This feature which is observed at low levels of the contact force profile (towards the end) is not important in the excitation of modal vibrations on the note and will be ignored in the analyses to follow.

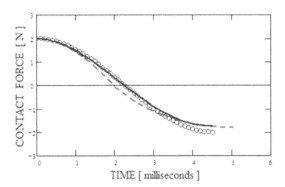

Fig. 13.24. Resistive force profiles for $r_{ms} = 2$ kg·s^{-1}, $V_0 = 1$ m·s^{-1}: dashed curve (- - -) obtained by numerical solution; solid curve (———) the exponential decay ½-cosine approximation with $\tau_c = 3.02$ ms; and the curve marked by circles (oooo) for the undamped ½-cosine approximation with $\tau_c = 3.02$ ms.

The resistive force component obtained for the numerical solution displayed in Figure 13.23(b) is shown in Figure 13.24 along with the ½-cosine approximations. The dashed curve (- - -) is obtained for the numerical solution with $r_{ms} = 2$ kg·s^{-1}, the solid curve (—) is the exponential decay ½-cosine approximation with $\tau_c = 3.02$ ms and the curve marked by circles (oooo) is the undamped ½-cosine approximation with $\tau_c = 3.02$ ms (without the exponential decay factor). In the numerical solution the velocity at 'make' is $V_0 = 1$ m·s^{-1} while the velocity at the 'break' is $V_r = -0.870$ m·s^{-1}. In the ½-cosine approximation with the exponential decay factor included, the velocity of the tip at 'make' is $V_0 = 1$ ms^{-1} while the velocity at the 'break' is in good agreement at $V_r = -0.864$ ms^{-1}. The undamped ½-cosine approximation overestimates the resistive force on the tail of the impact profile to a greater extent than the (damped) exponential decay ½-cosine approximation.

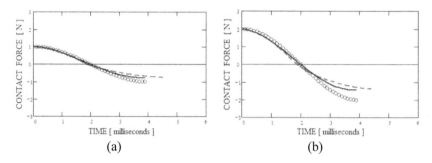

Fig. 13.25. Resistive force obtained by for (a) $r_{ms} = 1$ kg·s^{-1}, $V_0 = 1$ m·s^{-1}, (b) $r_{ms} = 2$ kg·s^{-1}, $V_0 = 1$ m·s^{-1}, pre-stress = 4.35 psi, $F_H = 2$ N (see text for details). Numerical solution, dashed curve (- - -); solid curve (———) the damped exponential ½-cosine with $\tau_c = 2.65$ ms; and the curve marked by circles (oooo) for the undamped ½-cosine also with $\tau_c = 2.65$ ms.

The final model stick investigated here is one for which the full analysis is discussed later in this chapter. The results are presented at this point because this stick is closer to the real sticks obtained in practice having pre-stress and controlled by hand action. The pre-stress in this case is 4.35 psi (pounds per square inch) and the hand action provides a retrieval force of 2 N directed upward away from the note. The retrieval force begins at the 'make' and continues throughout the duration of the impact. The results are presented in Figure 13.25 for two values of the mechanical resistance. The damped ½-cosine approximation, the solid curve (———) and the curve marked by circles (oooo) for the undamped ½-cosine approximation closely follow the numerical solutions shown as the dashed curves (- - -) through the compression phase and approximately half-way along the restitution phase, deviating along the impact tail. The solid curve was obtained using the *effective coefficient of restitution (eCOR)* (see Section 13.15.9) to determine the rebound velocity and to set the decay constant in the exponential decay factor. In particular, for case (b) (refer to the caption for Figure 13.25), with hand action and pre-stress, the 'damping coefficient' α in the exponential decay factor increased from $\alpha = r_{ms}/2m_s = 32.258$ s^{-1} to $\alpha = -2\ln(eCOR)/3\tau_c = 83.448$ s^{-1}. The damped ½-cosine approximation is very good in this case. In both the eCOR method and the numerical solution one finds $V_r = -0.717$ m·s^{-1} (the –ve sign indicates that it is opposite in direction to V_0).

Loosely wrapped sticks are expected to display greater dissipation than a homogeneous ball of the same material. Losses within the wrapped stick arise from the energy dissipation associated with inter-layer slippage and changes in stack compression. The conclusion is that lossy sticks produce a non-zero initial contact force and a reduction in the maximum contact-force. Other effects are discussed in Section 13.14.

13.11.8 Contact-width

Case 1: $p = 1$, $r_m = 0$, $F_H = 0$.

Let us now look at the *contact-width* φ_c. In Section 13.7.1, equation (13.20) it was shown that the radius c of the contact area varies with the stick and note deformation as

$$c = [2R_s (W_s - W_n)]^{\frac{1}{2}}. \tag{13.79}$$

It is important to emphasize at this point that during the impact the deformations W_s and W_n vary with time making r_c time dependent, $r_c = r_c(t)$. Therefore contact-width $\varphi_c(t) = 2 c(t)$ is also a function of time. For the case $W_s \gg W_n$ one gets

$$\varphi_c(t) = [8 R_s W_s]^{\frac{1}{2}}. \tag{13.80}$$

If the deformation W_s in equation (13.55) is differentiated with respect to time one gets the stick tip velocity

$$\dot{W}_s = \omega A \cos(\omega t), \tag{13.81}$$

where ωA is the maximum velocity which occurs on this cosine function first at $t = 0$. If the stick tip impacts the note with an initial velocity V_0 (normal to the pan face at the point of contact at time $t = 0$) then V_0 corresponds to this maximum velocity, $V_0 = \omega A$. Therefore the maximum distortion A is equal to V_0/ω. Combining this with equations (13.55) and (13.81) one gets for the time development of the contact width,

$$\varphi_c(t) = \left(\frac{8R_sV_0}{\omega}\right)^{\frac{1}{2}} (\sin(\omega t))^{\frac{1}{2}}, \qquad (13.82)$$

which is shown in Figure 13.26.

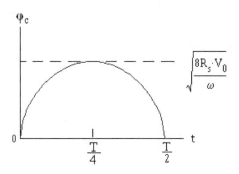

Fig. 13.26. Contact width as a function of time.

Since $\varphi_c(t)$ changes during the impact it is appropriate to define the contact-width as the value of $\varphi_c(t)$ when the contact force $F(t)$ maximizes. This corresponds to the maximum value of $\varphi_c(t)$ which occurs at the time $t = T/4$ after contact is made between stick and note (refer to Figure 13.26. Therefore one can write

$$contact-width \; \varphi_c = \left(\frac{8R_sV_0}{\omega}\right)^{\frac{1}{2}}. \qquad (13.83)$$

If stick dissipation is included then ω_d replaces ω in equation (13.83). If the same example $\alpha = \omega/10$ is used here then dissipation will increase the contact-width by only 0.25%. Knowing the initial impact velocity and the value of ω from empirical results, then with the help of Equation 13.64(61) the contact-width can be calculated. Alternately, using equation (13.83) and following the procedure adopted in formulating equation (13.66) one gets the fully theoretical results

Contact-width: $\varphi_c = (8V_0)^{\frac{1}{2}} \left(\dfrac{\pi(1-v_s^2)\rho_s}{E_s} \right)^{\frac{1}{4}} R_s,$ (13.84)

Contact Area: $A_c(t) = (\pi \varphi_c^2 / 4) \sin(\omega t).$ (13.85)

Hereafter, by definition, φ_c written without the time variable refers to the contact-width. Observe that in the linear approximation without hand control the impact-time is dependent only on the size of the stick tip and its material properties. However the contact-width is dependent on these same properties of the stick but in addition is also dependent on the impact velocity. *In the linear approximation ($p = 1$), the impact velocity determines the extent to which the stick tip material is spread across the note surface during impact but does not affect the time it takes to do it!*

Another useful form for the contact-width makes use of the compliance C_{eff}, one gets

$$\varphi_c = [8V_0 R_s]^{\frac{1}{2}} [m_s C_{eff}]^{\frac{1}{4}},$$

which, together with equation (13.85) shows that

1. the contact area increases with stick radius
2. the contact area increases with stick tip mass
3. the contact area increases with stick tmpact velocity and
4. by making the tip more compliant (softer) the contact area is increased.

This form is more useful to the player or stick maker.

Case 2: $p \geq 1$, $r_m = 0$, $F_H = 0$

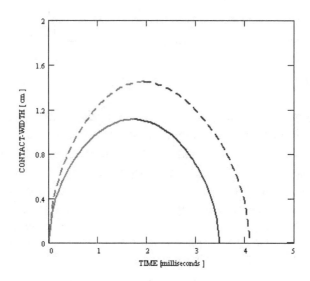

Fig. 13.27. Numerical solution for stick contact width (a) $p_c = 1.33$, $p_r = 1.76$ (dashed curve), (b) $p_c = p_r = 1$ (solid curve). Tip radius $R_s = 2$ cm, initial impact velocity $V_0 = 0.7$ m·s^{-1}, $E_s = 8 \times 10^5$ N·m^{-2}.

The contact-width and contact-area are measured when the tip distortion is a maximum:

$$\varphi_c = \left(8 R_s W_{s(max)}\right)^{\frac{1}{2}}.$$

Using equation (13.61) with $W_{s(max)} = R_s w_{s(max)}$, one gets

$$\varphi_c = \sqrt{8}\, R_s \left(\frac{p+1}{2}\right)^{\frac{1}{2(p+1)}} \left(\frac{V_0}{\omega R_s}\right)^{\frac{1}{p+1}}, \quad (13.86)$$

and

$$A_c = 2\pi R_s^2 \left(\frac{p+1}{2}\right)^{\frac{1}{(p+1)}} \left(\frac{V_0}{\omega R_s}\right)^{\frac{2}{p+1}}. \quad (13.87)$$

For the numerical solution illustrated in Figure 13.16, the contact-width history is shown in Figure 13.27 The values, contact-width =

1.11 cm for $p_c = p_r = 1$ and contact-width = 1.44 cm for $p_c = 1.33$, $p_r = 1.76$ are in agreement with equation (13.86) where $p = p_c$.

Writing $p_c = p$, we examine the following cases:

Case 3: $p \geq 1$, $r_m \geq 0$, $F_H = 0$

Since $F_{max} \propto W^p_{max}$ on using equation (13.73), $F'_{max} = F_{max}(1 - 2\alpha^2/\omega^2)e^{-\alpha\pi/2\omega_d}$, which applies for $p > 1$ to a good approximation, one gets

$$W_{s(max)} = \left(\frac{p+1}{2}\right)^{\frac{1}{p+1}} \left(\frac{V_0}{\omega R_s}\right)^{\frac{2}{p+1}} e^{-\frac{\alpha\pi}{2p\omega}} \left(1 - 2\frac{\alpha^2}{\omega^2}\right)^{\frac{1}{p}}, \qquad (13.88)$$

where ω replaces ω_d in the exponential. This leads to

$$\varphi_c = \sqrt{8} \; R_s \left(\frac{p+1}{2}\right)^{\frac{1}{2(p+1)}} \left(\frac{V_0}{\omega R_s}\right)^{\frac{1}{p+1}} e^{-\frac{\alpha\pi}{4p\omega}} \left(1 - \frac{\alpha^2}{p\omega^2}\right),$$

and

$$A_c = 2\pi R_s^2 \left(\frac{p+1}{2}\right)^{\frac{1}{(p+1)}} \left(\frac{V_0}{\omega R_s}\right)^{\frac{2}{p+1}} e^{-\frac{\alpha\pi}{2p\omega}} \left(1 - \frac{2\alpha^2}{p\omega^2}\right), \qquad (13.89\text{a, b})$$

or in their final form

$$\varphi_c = 8^{\frac{1}{2}} R_s V_0^{\frac{1}{p+1}} \left(\frac{p+1}{2}\right)^{\frac{1}{2(p+1)}} \left(\frac{\pi\rho_s(1-v_s^2)}{E_s}\right)^{\frac{1}{2(p+1)}} e^{-\frac{\alpha\pi}{4p\omega}} \left(1 - \frac{\alpha^2}{p\omega^2}\right),$$

$$A_c = 2\pi R_s^2 V_0^{\frac{2}{p+1}} \left(\frac{p+1}{2}\right)^{\frac{1}{(p+1)}} \left(\frac{\pi\rho_s(1-v_s^2)}{E_s}\right)^{\frac{1}{p+1}} e^{-\frac{\alpha\pi}{2p\omega}} \left(1 - \frac{2\alpha^2}{p\omega^2}\right).$$

$$(13.90\text{a, b})$$

These are the most general closed-form expressions for the contact-width and contact area in all cases where $F_H = 0$. Observe that in general the contact-area is proportional to $V_0^{\frac{2}{p+1}}$. Equations (13.90a, b) can also be used when $F_H > 0$ *provided that* F_H is applied *after* the contact force maximizes. If F_H is applied earlier then both the contact force and the contact-area are affected by the hand action and they can be determined by solving equation (13.51a) numerically. There are no closed-form solutions for a general force function F_H but closed-form solutions are possible for special cases.

13.11.9 Limits on the Linear Approximation

For equation (13.84) to be consistent with empirical values for the contact-width an upper limit must be established for the initial velocity V_0. This will ensure that the contact force is kept within the bounds consistent with the linear approximation. Contact force increases as the impact velocity is increased and for a given contact force, the linear relation predicts larger compressions than the non-linear relation ($p > 1$). The disagreement increases with the magnitude of the force. Using the linear approximations for all impact velocities may produce unphysical results where the contact-width may even exceed the diameter of the tip. To establish this limit the following elastic constants and density for the soft rubber used on pan sticks will be used in equation (13.66) and equation (13.84): $E_s = 1.5 \times 10^6$ N·m^{-2}, $v_s = 0.45$, $\rho_s = 920$ kg·m^{-3}. The following simple relations are obtained.

Contact-time $\tau_c = 0.82\, R_s$ milliseconds, (R_s in centimeters).
(13.91)

Contact-width $\varphi_c = 0.56\, R_s\, (V_0)^{\frac{1}{2}}$ centimeters, (V_0 in meters/second).
(13.92)

Let us first establish that equation (13.91) gives reasonably accurate values for the contact times. Table 13.3 compares the theoretical results with the empirical values for the contact-time for a range of sticks and playing action for each stick category.

TABLE 13.3

Stick Type	R_s (cm)	Contact-time τ_c (ms)			Empirical value	
		$E=8\times10^5$ N·m^{-2} (softer rubber)	$E=2\times10^6$ N·m^{-2} (harder rubber)	Equation (13.91)	T/2 [ms]	$\tau_c = T/3$ [ms]
Bass	3	3.36	2.51	2.46	4 to 8	2.7 to 5.3
Cello	2	2.24	1.42	1.84	1.8 to 3	1.2 to 2.0
Tenor	0.8	0.90	0.57	0.74	0.3 to 0.6	0.2 to 0.4

The empirical values for the duration of contact using the electrical contact method (as used in Achong 1996b) actually measures T/2 not τ_c as defined here but the contact-time can be obtained from $\tau_c = T/3$. The agreement in Table 13.3 is quite good for the bass and reasonably good for cello pans but equation (13.91) gives an overestimate for the tenor pans. This overestimate for the tenor appears because the empirical values for the contact-time are affected by the rapid stick withdrawal used in the playing action on high-end pans. This action produces a deliberate reduction in the contact–time. In addition the present analysis made the assumption $F_H = 0$ which applies more closely to the playing action on the mid-range and low-end pans.

Empirical results using the author's *stick print* technique (made with lightly coated stick tips similar to taking a fingerprint) employed by the author on a range of sticks (with spherical or almost spherical tips) show that the contact-width for normal tone intensities is approximately one-quarter the diameter D_s of the stick tip, $\varphi_c \approx D_s/4$. We will adopt this formula only as a 'rule-of-thumb' relation that we can use in the following way to set an upper limit to the impact velocity. Using our rule-of-thumb, let us set as a reasonable margin of applicability, the condition $\varphi_c < D_s/2$. Substituting into equation (13.92) gives

$$0.56\ R_s\ (V_0)^{1/2} < 0.5\ D_s, \qquad (13.93)$$

and finally

$$V_0 < 3.2 \text{ m·s}^{-1}. \qquad (13.94)$$

In practice, for any manually applied stick impact under normal playing action, this stick velocity upper limit is satisfied, implying that the linear approximation holds well in practice.

13.11.10 Non-linear Treatment of Contact Time

13.11.10.1 General Solution of the Tip Displacement-Time Problem

The linear analysis carried out with $p = 1$, afforded limited understanding of the stick-note impact especially with respect to the dependence on impact velocity. The non-linear treatment while not particularly difficult is somewhat lengthy. Nevertheless, for its importance in subsequent work it must be dealt with here.

In the following analysis, without any risk of confusion of the symbols, the notation is simplified by writing the dimensionless tip compression w_s as w. In order to proceed with the integration involved, it is also necessary to treat only the case $r_{ms} = 0$ (r_{ms} will be re-introduced later). Equation (13.60) shows that for all values of the p index,

$$V^2 - V_0^2 = -\frac{2(\omega R_s)^2}{p+1} w^{p+1}, \qquad (13.95a)$$

from which the following velocity expression is derived:

$$\frac{dw}{dt} = \frac{V_0}{R_s}\left(1 - \frac{2}{p+1}\left(\frac{\omega R_s}{V_0}\right)^2 w^{p+1}\right)^{\frac{1}{2}}. \qquad (13.95b)$$

Equation (13.95b) can be integrated to yield the time for the tip to be compressed an amount w,

$$t = \frac{R_s}{V_0}\int_0^w \left(1 - \frac{2}{p+1}\left(\frac{\omega R_s}{V_0}\right)^2 w^{p+1}\right)^{-\frac{1}{2}} dw. \qquad (13.96)$$

Making use of equation (13.61) in equation (13.96) to eliminate $\omega R_s/V_0$ we have

$$t = \frac{R_s}{V_0} \int_0^w \left(1 - \left(\frac{w}{w_{max}}\right)^{p+1}\right)^{-\frac{1}{2}} dw. \qquad (13.97)$$

Equation (13.97) can be solved by first expressing the integrand as a binomial series. Using the binomial expansion

$$(1-x)^{-r} = \sum_{k=0}^{\infty} \frac{(r)_k}{k!} x^k$$
$$= 1 + rx + \tfrac{1}{2} r(r+1)x^2 + \tfrac{1}{6} r(r+1)(r+2)x^3 + \ldots$$

the case for $r = \tfrac{1}{2}$ gives

$$(1-x)^{-\tfrac{1}{2}} = 1 + \tfrac{1}{2}x + \tfrac{3}{8}x^2 + \tfrac{5}{16}x^3 + \tfrac{35}{128}x^4 + \tfrac{63}{256}x^5 + \tfrac{231}{1024}x^6 + \ldots$$

In the expanded form, equation (13.97) can now be written as

$$t = \frac{R_s}{V_0} \int_0^w \left(1 + \tfrac{1}{2}\left(\frac{w}{w_{max}}\right)^{p+1} + \tfrac{3}{8}\left(\frac{w}{w_{max}}\right)^{2(p+1)} + \tfrac{5}{16}\left(\frac{w}{w_{max}}\right)^{3(p+1)} + \ldots\right) dw.$$

Proceeding with the integration, term by term, gives

$$t = \frac{R_s}{V_0}\left(w + \frac{1}{2(p+2)} w_{max}^{-(p+1)} w^{p+2} + \frac{3}{8(2p+3)} w_{max}^{-2(p+1)} w^{2p+3} + \frac{5}{16(3p+4)} w_{max}^{-3(p+1)} w^{3p+4} + \ldots\right). \qquad (13.98)$$

For $w = x w_{max}$ where $0 \le x \le 1$, one gets

$$t = \frac{R_s w}{V_0}\left(1 + \frac{1}{2(p+2)} x^{p+1} + \frac{3}{8(2p+3)} x^{2(p+1)} + \frac{5}{16(3p+4)} x^{3(p+1)} + \ldots\right). \qquad (13.99)$$

For computational purposes, equation (13.99) can be written using a recurrence relation. Thus

$$t = \frac{R_s w}{V_0} \sum_{n=0}^{\infty} \frac{y_n x^{n(p+1)}}{n(p+1)+1}, \qquad (13.100)$$

where

$$y_0 = 1 \ and \ for \ n \geq 1, \ y_n = \frac{(2n-1)}{2n} y_{n-1}.$$

Equation (13.100) can be written in the equivalent form

$$t = \frac{R_s w_{max}}{V_0} \sum_{n=0}^{\infty} \frac{y_n x^{n(p+1)+1}}{n(p+1)+1}. \qquad (13.101)$$

Equation (13.101) is the solution for the time, measured from the instant of stick-note contact ('make'), for the tip to compress an amount w expressed as a fraction x of the maximum compression w_{max}.

Equation (13.101) can be used to solve the problem of tip displacement as a function of time, $w = w(t)$. While the procedure is lengthy as it involves solving equation (13.101) for the time t for each value of w expressed as a fraction $x = w/w_{max}$, it will be simpler for the general reader than solving equation (13.51a) numerically. However, while the solution of equation (13.51a) requires a numerical ODE solver, it has the advantage of including losses due to the mechanical resistance and the effects of hand action by the player. The following Mathcad© routine can be used to complete the summation in equation (13.101).

SUMMATION IMPLEMENTED in MATHCAD©

The summation in equation (13.101) is determined for N terms as follows:

DEFINE p
p := 1.33   {or any other value}

DEFINE x and y_0
x:= 0.6   {or any other fraction}
The y_n variable is represented by y, beginning with y = 1

$$\text{sum}(N) := \begin{vmatrix} s \leftarrow x \\ y \leftarrow 1 \\ \text{for } n \in 1..N \\ \quad \begin{vmatrix} y \leftarrow y \cdot \dfrac{2 \cdot n - 1}{2 \cdot n} \\ s \leftarrow s + y \cdot \left[\dfrac{x^{n \cdot (p+1)+1}}{n \cdot (p+1)+1} \right] \end{vmatrix} \end{vmatrix}$$

N := 1000
sum(N) = 0.6319148879

The lines of this routine can be modified to find the values of the other summations found in this Chapter.

We now look at some special cases.

13.11.10.2 Case 1: Displacement Profile

The displacement-time profile for the compression phase can be obtained using equation (13.101). If there is no hysteresis then the profile is symmetrical so equation (13.101) also determines the profile for the restitution phase. The situation is different for a hysteretic tip.

At the end of the compression phase parameterized by the index $p = p_c$, the tip enters the restitution phase parameterized by the index $p = p_r$. Since the maximum displacement w_{max} is the same for both phases, the restitution phase will follow the correct path from maximum displacement to the point where the displacement reaches w when the velocity V_r replaces V_0 in the restitution phase: using (13.95a) this procedure gives

$$V_r = \left(\frac{p_c+1}{2}\right)^{\frac{p_r+1}{2(p_c+1)}} \left(\frac{2}{p_r+1}\right)^{\frac{1}{2}} \left(\frac{V_0}{\omega R_s}\right)^{\frac{p_r+1}{p_c+1}} \omega R_s. \qquad (13.102)$$

Equation (13.102) simply answers the question 'with what velocity must the tip impact the note to attain the same compression w_{max} if its compression p-index is replaced by p_r?' V_r is the rebound velocity at the end of the restitution phase. Using this trick I have saved myself a lot of algebra.

Beginning at the 'make', the time taken for the tip to reach a displacement $w = x\, w_{max}$ (where $0 \leq x \leq 1$) in the restitution phase is

$$t = \frac{R_s w_{max}}{V_0} \sum_{n=0}^{\infty} \frac{y_n}{n(p_c+1)+1} + \frac{R_s w_{max}}{V_r} \sum_{n=0}^{\infty} \frac{y_n\left(1-x^{n(p_r+1)+1}\right)}{n(p_r+1)+1}. \qquad (13.103)$$

The first term gives the time to reach maximum compression while the second term gives the time taken from maximum compression to reach the displacement w in restitution.

13.11.10.3 Case 2: Contact Time from 'make' to 'break', without Hysteresis

In this case, without hysteresis, the p-indices for compression p_c and for restitution p_r are equal, $p_c = p_r$. The displacement profiles for the compression and restitution phases are symmetrical about a line drawn through the point of maximum displacement and parallel to the displacement axis. The 'make–to–break' contact time $\tau_{m\text{-}t\text{-}b}$ is therefore twice the time taken from the 'make' to maximum compression $w = w_{max}$, $x = 1$. Accordingly

$$\tau_{m-t-b} = \frac{2R_s w_{max}}{V_0} \sum_{n=0}^{\infty} \frac{y_n}{n(p_c+1)+1}. \qquad (13.104)$$

Substituting the expression for w_{max} in equation (13.104) gives

$$\tau_{m-t-b} = \left(\left(\frac{p_c+1}{2}\right) \frac{\pi \rho_s (1-v_s^2)}{E_s}\right)^{\frac{1}{p_c+1}} \frac{R_s}{V_0^{\frac{p_c-1}{p_c+1}}} S_{1,p_c}, \qquad (13.105)$$

where

$$S_{1,p_c} = 2 \sum_{n=0}^{\infty} \frac{y_n}{n(p_c+1)+1}.$$

Observation: *Equation (13.105) shows that the contact time from make to break without hysteresis, varies with the impact velocity as $V_0^{\frac{1-p_c}{p_c+1}}$. For $p_c = 1$, there is no velocity dependence in agreement with the analysis for τ_c given in earlier Sections. For $p_c > 1$, the make-to-break contact time decreases as the velocity increases.*

Computer evaluation of the summation in equation (13.105) reveals that the sum $S_{1,p}$ converges very slowly for all values of the p-index. To obtain values compatible with the exact solution for $p_c = 1$, where $\tau_{m-t-b} = \pi/\omega$ the summation must be continued up to n = 1.5 x 10^7 (fifteen million) in Double Precision Arithmetic. Table 13.4 shows the results for a range of p-indices. In Table 13.4 a comparison of the results for $p_c = 1$ is made with the exact solution.

TABLE 13.4

p-index p_c	S_{1,p_c}
1	3.1406 (for 10^6 terms) * 3.14130 (for 1.5×10^7 terms) Exact value = π = 3.1415926...
1.1	3.09431
1.2	3.05182
1.3	3.01256
1.33 (average for stick tips in compression)	3.00136
1.4	2.97618
1.5 (Hertz index)	2.94237
1.6	2.91085
1.7	2.88141
1.76 (average for stick tips in restitution)	2.86465
1.8	2.85383

* For $p_c = 1$ the integral in equation (13.98) can be written as $\int_0^1 (1-x^2)^{-\frac{1}{2}} dx$, which gives

$$S_{1,1} = 2\int_0^1 (1-x^2)^{-\frac{1}{2}} dx.$$ Substituting $x = \sin\theta$ gives $S_{1,1} = 2\int_0^{\pi/2} d\theta = \pi$.

The case for Hertzian impact where $p_c = p_r = 3/2$ (the Hertz index) was evaluated by Timoshenko and Goodier (1970) with the result

$$\tau_{m-t-b} = 2.94 \left(\frac{1.25\sqrt{2}\,\pi\rho_s(1-v_s^2)}{E_s} \right)^{\frac{2}{5}} \frac{R_s}{(2V_{in})^{\frac{1}{5}}}$$

where the 'incoming velocity' V_{in} (in the terminiogy of Timoshenko and Goodier) is equal to V_0 in our notation. This result is in agreement with Table 13.4 for $p_c = 3/2$ and with equation (13.105).

13.11.10.4 Case 3: Contact Time at ½-Maximum Points, without Hysteresis

The contact-time τ_c used throughout this work is defined as the time duration separating points on the contact force profile where the force is at ½-maximum $F_{max}/2$. Since in general, the force-displacement relation gives $F_{max} \propto w_{max}^p$ (see equation 13.62a), points on the profile corresponding to $F_{max}/2$ occur for displacements equal to $w_{max}/2^{1/p}$. Therefore, in equation (13.99), $x = 2^{-\frac{1}{p_c}}$. Substituting this expression into equation (13.99) gives the time $t_{\frac{1}{2}}$ from 'make' to the first point on the (compression) profile where the force equals $F_{max}/2$. Thus

$$t_{\frac{1}{2}} = \frac{R_s w_{max}}{V_0} \sum_{n=0}^{\infty} \frac{y_n 2^{-\left(n+\frac{n+1}{p_c}\right)}}{(n(p_c+1)+1)}. \qquad (13.106)$$

By symmetry of the compression and restitution phases ($p_c = p_r = p$ in the present case), the contact-time at ½-maximum is therefore given by

$$\tau_c = \tau_{m-t-b} - 2 t_{\frac{1}{2}}. \qquad (13.107)$$

Using equations (13.105), (13.106) and (13.107) one can write

$$\tau_c = \left(\left(\frac{p_c+1}{2}\right)\frac{\pi \rho_s (1-v_s^2)}{E_s}\right)^{\frac{1}{p+1}} \frac{R_s}{V_0^{\frac{p_c-1}{p_c+1}}} S_{2,p_c}, \qquad (13.108)$$

where

$$S_{2,p_c} = 2\sum_{n=0}^{\infty} \frac{y_n}{n(p_c+1)+1}\left(1 - \frac{1}{2^{n+\frac{n+1}{p_c}}}\right).$$

Observation: Equation (13.108) shows that the contact-time at ½-maximum also varies with the impact velocity as $V_0^{\frac{1-p_c}{p_c+1}}$. For $p_c = 1$, there is also no velocity dependence in agreement with the analysis in earlier sections. For $p_c > 1$, the contact-time decreases with increasing velocity.

TABLE 13.5

p-index p_c	S_{2,p_c}
1	2.094104 (for 1.5x10^7 terms) Exact value = $2\pi/3$ = 2.094395…
	$S_{2,p}/S_{1,p}$ = 0.666636 Exact value = 2/3 = 0.666666…
1.1	1.97776
1.2	1.87344
1.3	1.77938
1.33 (p_c average for stick tips)	1.75295
1.4	1.69419
1.5	1.61671
1.6	1.54594
1.7	1.48107
1.76 (p_r average for stick tips)	1.44469
1.8	1.42140

For $p_c = 1$, the results tabulated in Table 13.5 are in good agreement with the exact values. *For large values of n, the expression* $2^{-(n+\frac{n+1}{p_c})}$ *in the summation in equation (13.108) may produce overflows on a desktop computer.* In practice however, it is not necessary to calculate the sum to the precision in Table 13.5 so this problem is not of any real concern.

13.11.10.5 Case 4: Contact Time from 'make' to 'break', with Hysteresis

In the case with hysteresis, the p-index for the compression phase p_c is not equal to the index for the restitution phase p_r. This produces displacement profiles for the compression and restitution phases that are asymmetrical about a line drawn through the point of maximum displacement. The 'make–to-break' contact time $\tau_{m\text{-}t\text{-}b}$ is therefore the sum of the times taken for these different phases.

Using V_r in equation (13.98) for the restitution phase and V_0 for the compression phase gives

$$\tau_{m\text{-}t\text{-}b} = \frac{R_s w_{\max}}{V_0} \sum_{n=0}^{\infty} \frac{y_n}{n(p_c+1)+1} + \frac{R_s w_{\max}}{V_r} \sum_{n=0}^{\infty} \frac{y_n}{n(p_r+1)+1}, \tag{13.109}$$

and finally

$$\tau_{m\text{-}t\text{-}b} = \left(\left(\frac{p_c+1}{2}\right)\frac{\pi\rho_s(1-v_s^2)}{E_s}\right)^{\frac{1}{p_c+1}} \frac{R_s}{V_0^{\frac{p_c-1}{p_c+1}}} \frac{S_{1,p_c}}{2}$$

$$+ \left(\frac{p_r+1}{p_c+1}\right)^{\frac{1}{2}} \left(\left(\frac{p_c+1}{2}\right)\frac{\pi\rho_s(1-v_s^2)}{E_s}\right)^{\frac{2+p_c-p_r}{2(p_c+1)}} \frac{R_s}{V_0^{\frac{p_r-1}{p_c+1}}} \frac{S_{1,p_r}}{2}.$$

$$\tag{13.110}$$

The first term in equation (13.110) gives the time from 'make' to the maximum compression while the second term gives the time from the maximum to the 'break'. Equation (13.110) reduces to equation (13.105) when $p_r = p_c$ (no hysteresis). Table 13.4 can be used to obtain the values for the summations in equation (13.110) for a range of (p_c, p_r) combinations.

Observation: *Equation (13.110) shows that with hysteresis, the time duration from 'make' to maximum displacement (and maximum force) varies with the impact velocity as $V_0^{\frac{1-p_c}{p_c+1}}$ while the remaining period to the 'break' varies as $V_0^{\frac{1-p_r}{p_c+1}}$. For $p_r = p_c = 1$, there is no velocity dependence in agreement with the analysis in earlier sections. For $(p_c, p_r) > 1$, the contact time decreases with increasing velocity.*

13.11.10.6 Case 5: Contact Time at ½-Maximum Points, with Hysteresis

The results obtained for preceding cases are now used to solve this problem. The ½-maximum points are located at the points where $x = 2^{-\frac{1}{p_c}}$. The time taken from 'make' to the first ½-maximum point is obtained from equation (13.106) as

$$t_{\frac{1}{2}}^{\{comp\}} = \frac{R_s w_{max}}{V_0} \sum_{n=0}^{\infty} \frac{y_n}{(n(p_c+1)+1)2^{n+\frac{n+1}{p_c}}} . \qquad (13.111)$$

Similarly, the time from the second ½-maximum point located on the restitution phase to the 'break' is given by

$$t_{\frac{1}{2}}^{\{rest\}} = \frac{R_s w_{max}}{V_r} \sum_{n=0}^{\infty} \frac{y_n}{(n(p_r+1)+1)2^{\frac{np_r+n+1}{p_c}}} . \qquad (13.112)$$

One can write

$$\tau_c = \tau_{m-t-b} - \left(t_{\frac{1}{2}}^{\{comp\}} + t_{\frac{1}{2}}^{\{rest\}} \right). \qquad (13.113)$$

From equations (13.109), (13.111), (13.112) and (12.113) one gets

$$\tau_c = \frac{R_s w_{max}}{V_0} \left\{ \sum_{n=0}^{\infty} \frac{y_n}{n(p_c+1)+1} - \sum_{n=0}^{\infty} \frac{y_n}{(n(p_c+1)+1)2^{n+\frac{n+1}{p_c}}} \right\} +$$

$$\frac{R_s w_{max}}{V_r} \left\{ \sum_{n=0}^{\infty} \frac{y_n}{n(p_r+1)+1} - \sum_{n=0}^{\infty} \frac{y_n}{(n(p_r+1)+1)2^{\frac{np_r+n+1}{p_c}}} \right\}$$

Finally, after some simplification

$$\tau_c = \left(\left(\frac{p_c+1}{2}\right)\frac{\pi\rho_s(1-v_s^2)}{E_s}\right)^{\frac{1}{p_c+1}} \frac{R_s}{V_0^{\frac{p_c-1}{p_c+1}}} \frac{S_{2,p_c}}{2} +$$

$$\left(\frac{p_r+1}{p_c+1}\right)^{\frac{1}{2}}\left(\left(\frac{p_c+1}{2}\right)\frac{\pi\rho_s(1-v_s^2)}{E_s}\right)^{\frac{2+p_c-p_r}{2(p_c+1)}} \frac{R_s}{V_0^{\frac{p_r-1}{p_c+1}}} \frac{S_{2,p_r}}{2}$$

(13.114)

where

$$S_{2,p_r} = 2\sum_{n=0}^{\infty} \frac{y_n}{n(p_r+1)+1}\left(1 - 2^{-\left(\frac{np_r+n+1}{p_c}\right)}\right).$$

Equation (13.114) reduces to equation (13.108) when $p_r = p_c$ (no hysteresis). Table 13.5 can be used to obtain the values for the summations in equation (13.114) for a range of (p_c, p_r) combinations.

Observation: Equation (13.114) shows that with hysteresis, the portion of the ½-maximum contact-time in the compression phase varies with the impact velocity as $V_0^{\frac{1-p_c}{p_c+1}}$ while in the restitution phase the variation goes as $V_0^{\frac{1-p_r}{p_c+1}}$. For $p_r = p_c = 1$, there is no velocity dependence while for $(p_c, p_r) > 1$, the contact time decreases with increasing velocity.

General Observation: In all cases, the contact time is directly proportional to the tip radius R_s.

13.12 Scattering of Stress Waves in the Stick Tip and Shank

At this point, in order to move forward, we must look at other physical activities taking place within the tip. We must investigate the propagation and scattering of the stress waves that produce the pressure fields within the tip.

13.12.1 A Simplified Model

In this Section we are primarily interested in the reduction of impact energy transmitted from the tip to the shaft and towards the player's hand. This energy lost from the impact area cannot be recovered and is eventually dissipated as heat mainly within the shaft. We are therefore not too concerned with the absorption mechanisms within the shaft material itself. We are however, concerned with reducing the energy that *leaves* the tip during impact by transmission down the shaft. This enables us to focus mainly on the rubber tip and the piece of shaft material within the tip. Once we have optimized the tip by reducing stress waves transmission into the shaft then the bulk of the shaft extending into the player's hand plays a lesser role. However, there will always be sufficient stick-note contact information transferred from the shank to the hand to provide the *tactile feedback* necessary for good stick control (see Section 13.22). To see how the tip optimization could be effected we must look at the propagation and scattering of stress waves within the tip.

Technically, the scattering of stress waves by interfaces in a layered elastic solid such as the wrapped pan stick, can be properly investigated by using a *finite element discretization analysis* (FEA) applied to the near field (stress field). The transient response is then obtained by applying Fourier methods from which the reflected, refracted and direct stress waves can be studied. Because of the small size of the stick tip there is no far field to consider except that associated with high acoustic frequency components that travel down the shank. These disturbances that propagate along the shank allow the player's hands to feel the contact sensation. To get at the information we desire, the FEA procedure will be bypassed for a simpler, heuristic, approach. The approach suffers one drawback it considers the effects of plane waves on flat boundaries whereas within the stick tip one finds almost spherical waves impinging on curved interfaces. In addition, stick impacts are transient events so that the generation of regions of zero stress wave amplitude or *nodes* is just a transitory event on timescales of a very small fraction of a second at most. Despite the resulting loss of precision, the results are satisfactory and they agree with observations made by panists over the years that the pan has been around as a musical instrument.

When the tip makes contact with the note, two major responses occur in the tip material. First, the tip surface at the point of impact begins to move inward, compressing the rubber. This motion begins with the initial velocity $v = V_0$ and decreases to $v = 0$ when the point of maximum compression $w = w_{max}$ is reached. The second event is the rapid propagation of *stress waves* into the tip medium with velocity $v_p = \sqrt{M/\rho}$ where M is the compressional modulus and ρ is the density of the medium. In all stick-note impacts $V_0 \ll v_p$ so that the inward moving tip surface trails behind the rapidly advancing compressive stress waves.

For waves of wavelength λ to be reflected by an object its width must satisfy the relation *width* $> \lambda$. For a shank of diameter $d = 1$ cm, $v_p = 50$ ms^{-1} for the rubber, this condition is satisfied for waves of frequency $f > v_p / d = 5$ kHz. *The following discussion is therefore restricted to the high frequency wave components of the impact stress.*

Caution: *Readers must not associate or confuse these high frequency stress waves with the note frequencies. These stress waves are related to the impact (transient) dynamics within the stick tip.*

On impact quasi-spherical wavefronts will emanate from the small impact region and spread (*diverge*) into the rubber and shank material. Due to anisotropy (if it exists) in the rubber and/or shank material where the waves propagate with different velocities in mutually perpendicular directions, *refraction* (change in the direction of wave propagation) will occur. As the incident wave (I) travels through the medium, it impinges on its first interface A→B (see Figure 13.28) between the first and second layers of the wrapped stick or at the rubber-shank boundary. Because of *acoustic impedance* mismatch, a reflected wave (R) is generated in the first medium (A) and a transmitted wave (T) is propagated into the second medium (B). Repeated transmissions/reflections — *scattering* — occur within the tip during the transient lifetime of the wave pulse.

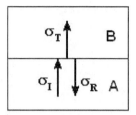

Fig. 13. 28. Scattering (transmission/reflection) at an interface.

The ratios of the respective magnitudes of these waves depend on the *characteristic impedances*, $z = \rho v_p$, of the two media and on the *angle of incidence* of the incident wave. The geometry of the tip rubber is either spherical (or almost so) or cylindrical while that of the shank is cylindrical (solid or hollow). Therefore, in general, the incident waves will impinge on curved interfaces with a wide range of incident angles. For incidence other than *normal* (perpendicular to the interface), the transmitted wave is refracted.

Further complications may arise with differences in the porosity and elastic structure of the materials used in stick construction. For example, anisotropic materials such as wood and bamboo (major constituents: cellulose fibre imbedded in a lignin matrix) with their grain structure, or rubber sponge balls with their internal honeycomb structure, give rise to situations where waves propagated parallel to the surface travel with a different velocity to waves propagated in a perpendicular direction. The movement of fluid (air) between the voids in these materials gives rise to both *resistive* and *reactive* components to the characteristic impedance, both of which generally depend on frequency.

Consider again the Figure 13.28, if σ represents the stress amplitude then the ratio of transmitted to incident stress amplitude is given by

$$\alpha_T \doteq \frac{\sigma_T}{\sigma_I} = \frac{2\rho_B v_{pB}}{\rho_A v_{pA} + \rho_B v_{pB}}, \quad (13.115)$$

while the ratio of reflected to incident stress amplitude is

$$\alpha_R \doteq \frac{\sigma_R}{\sigma_I} = \frac{\rho_B v_{pB} - \rho_A v_{pA}}{\rho_A v_{pA} + \rho_B v_{pB}}. \quad (13.116)$$

For *continuity* at the interface

$$\sigma_I + \sigma_R = \sigma_T, \quad 1 + \alpha_R = \alpha_T. \quad (13.117)$$

Consider the following special cases:

Case (i): If $\rho_B v_{pB} = \rho_A v_{pA}$ then

$$\sigma_R = 0, \quad \sigma_T = \sigma_I.$$

There is no reflection at the interface of two media having the same characteristic impedance as the wave is completely transmitted across the interface: for example, a *rubber → rubber* interface (same rubber of course on a wrapped stick for example).

Case (ii): If $\rho_B v_{pB} \ll \rho_A v_{pA}$, for example a *rubber → air* interface or a *wood → air* interface, there is almost total reflection with almost no transmission. Approximately zero transmission of the stress waves into the air medium is expected because the rarefied air cannot support the stress incident upon it. In this case, one has

$$\sigma_R \approx -\sigma_I, \quad \sigma_T \approx 0.$$

In this case, the reflected wave amplitude is almost equal to that of the incident wave and 180° out of phase with the incident wave (the negative sign denotes this out-of-phase condition). The result, the reflected and incident waves cancel at the interface producing a node.

Case (iii): If $\rho_B v_{pB} \gg \rho_A v_{pA}$, for example an *air* $\rightarrow$ *rubber* interface or an *air* $\rightarrow$ *wood* interface, then

$$\sigma_R \approx \sigma_I, \quad \sigma_T \approx 2\sigma_I.$$

The result is an *antinode* at the interface.

Table 13.6 shows the properties of air (at normal temperature and pressure) and a number of materials used for stick construction.

TABLE 13.6

Material	Young's Modulus N·m^{-2}	Density Kg/m^3 ρ	Velocity m·s^{-1} v_p	Characteristic Impedance kg·m^{-2}·s or *rayls* ρv_p
Air T = 20°C. P_0 = 1.013 x 10^5 N·m^{-2}	-	1.21	$v_p = \sqrt{\frac{\gamma P_0}{\rho}} = 343$ $\gamma = 1.402$	415
Soft Rubber	(0.8 – 5) x 10^6	920	(0.57 – 1.44) x 10^3	(0.53 –1.32) x 10^6
Pine Wood	0.85 x 10^{10}	450	3.5 x 10^3	1.58 x 10^6
Oak Wood	1.1 X 10^{10} (along grain)	720	4 x 10^3	2.88 x 10^6
Bamboo (depends on species and age)	(1–1.3) x 10^{10} (parallel to long axis)	660-720	4.3 x 10^3	2.95 x 10^6
	(0.35-0.55) x 10^{10} (perpendicular to long axis)		2.6 x 10^3	1.8 x 10^6
Carbon Fibre Composite (CFC)	13 x 10^{10} (Standard Grade)	1600 (typical)	9.5 x 10^3	15 x 10^6 (typical)
Aluminum	7.1 x 10^{10}	2700	6.3 x 10^3	17 x 10^6

Using the data in Table 13.6 the transmission ratios for the interfaces found on typical stick tips are shown in Table 13.7.

TABLE 13.7

	Transmission Ratio σ_T/σ_I						
	Air	Rubber	Pine	Oak	Bamboo	CFC	Aluminum
Air →	1	1.9991	1.9995	1.9997	1.9997 (1.9995)	1.9999	1.9999
Rubbe →	0.00087	1	1.2490	1.5039	1.5128 (1.3067)	1.8809	1.8942
Pine →	0.00052	0.751					
Oak →	0.00029	0.4961					
Bamboo →	0.00028 (0.00046)	0.4872 (0.6933)					
CFC →	0.00006	0.1191					
Aluminum →	0.00005	0.1058					

Bracketed ( ) quantities are for stress waves travelling perpendicular to the longitudinal axis of bamboo.

The reflection ratios for these interfaces are shown in Table 13.8.

TABLE 13.8

	Reflection Ratio σ_R/σ_I						
	Air	Rubber	Pine	Oak	Bamboo	CFC	Aluminum
Air →	0	0.9991	0.9995	0.9997	0.9997 (0.9995)	0.9999	0.9999
Rubber →	-0.9991	0	0.2490	0.5039	0.5128 (0.3067)	0.8809	0.8942
Pine →	-0.9995	-0.2490					
Oak →	-0.9997	-0.5039					
Bamboo →	-0.9997 (-0.9995)	-0.5128 (-0.3067)					
CFC →	-0.9999	-0.8809					
Aluminum →	-0.9999	-0.8942					

Bracketed ( ) quantities are for stress waves travelling perpendicular to the longitudinal axis of bamboo.

We shall make use of these tabulated data later in our discuissions.

13.12.2. Refraction and Reflection

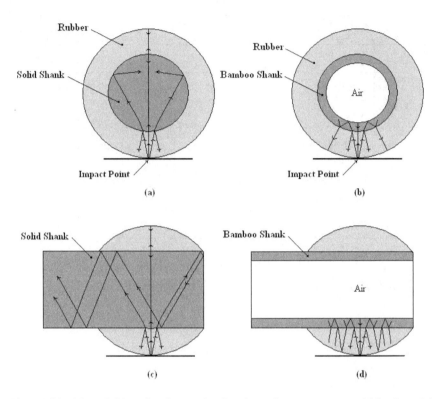

Fig. 13.29. (a) and (c) reflection and refraction of stress waves within the stick with solid shank. (b) and (d) reflection and refraction of stress waves within the stick with hollow shank.

Refraction is the change in direction of propagation of a wave due to a change in its velocity. Refraction is essentially a surface phenomenon commonly observed when a wave travels from one medium to another. For the stress waves generated in the tip during stick-note impact, refraction occur at the *rubber→ air, rubber→ wood* and *wood→* air interfaces. For normal (perpendicular) incident angle there is no refraction. Figure 13.29 shows how these waves (depicted as rays) on leaving the point of impact are refracted and reflected at the interfaces within the tip. The directions of travel (propagation) in Figure 13.29 are based on Snell's law of refraction $(sin\theta_A)/(sin\theta_B) = v_A/v_B$ relating the incident angle θ_A and the refracted angle θ_B to the ratio of velocities v_A/v_B for waves moving from medium A into medium B. For all reflected waves, the angle of reflection equals the angle of incidence. Observe in Figure 13.29, that there are no waves propagated into the air medium.

Note: The rays drawn in Figure 13.29 strictly apply to high frequency stress waves in homogeneous shanks and rubber tips (unwrapped). With bamboo, the longitudinal and radial velocities are different and with solid wood, the grain structure (of fibres) and porosity complicates the propagation of stress waves. In both cases the stress waves are dispersed within the shank so one must take Figure 13.29 as a simplified representation of a rather complex phenomenon involving dissipative and dispersive effects. In addition, the waves that leave the impact area and travel down the shank constitute a major part of the energy lost because these waves do not return to the impact area to contribute to the stress field (or pressure field, see Figure 13.11) in the contact region. It is this pressure field that produces the contact force. From this it is clear that shank losses reduce the contact force.

Solid Shank: For the solid shank in Figure 13.29(a), the refraction (bending of the rays at the interfaces) and reflections at the *rubber→ wood* and *wood→ rubber* interfaces result in considerably more stress energy being transferred to the shank. The waves within the shank are propagated down the shank (see Figure 19.29(c)), towards the hand, by repeated reflections at the *wood → air* interface (formed at the surface of the shank). Considerable energy can therefore be lost in this way to the solid shank. Although almost no energy is transferred from the surface of the shank to the surrounding air medium, along the portion of the shank where the player holds the stick, stress waves will be refracted into the fleshy material of the hand in contact with the shaft. By this, the player can make tactile judgments on the stick-note contact and adjust his hand action.

Hollow Shank: In the case of the hollow shank however, (Figures 13.29 (b) and (d)), the waves suffer multiple reflections within the thin annular cross-section of the shank with a large fraction of the stress energy being transmitted back to the rubber (Figure 13.29(d)). The hollow shank therefore allows the stress waves to be concentrated within the rubber tip in a region close to the impact point. This is the desired result because the stresses around the impact point are responsible for the *Contact Force* which excites the note.

Although a smaller fraction of the impact energy is transmitted into the hollow shank material compared to energy transmitted into the solid shank, the annular construction of the hollow shank allows the stress waves to be concentrated closer to the shank outer surface. This gives the player's hand a better 'feel' for the impact. In addition the stress energy propagated towards the butt end of the solid shank is quickly absorbed by the shank material. Tactile feedback is therefore much better with the hollow shank. Many players of the high-end pans (with their smaller sticks) have expressed their experiences to me concerning this effect. Of course sensations such as these will vary from player to player and the effect will not be very noticeable on the lower pan instruments where the tips are larger and the hand action is different (see Section 13.17).

13.12.3 Effective Tip Size Reduction

Observe in Figure 13.29 (d) the stress concentration that develops around the contact point especially when a hollow shank is used. This stress concentration is related to the *'proximity effect'* (see Section 13.21.4) and is enhanced on *thin-layered tips* mounted on hollow shanks. When playing the pan notes with thin-layered tips (such as *single wrapped tips* formed by stretch fitting a short length of rubber tubing unto the end of the shank, see Figure 13.3) the stress concentrations during impact around the point of contact can be quite high especially when hollow shanks are used. Contact width and contact times are reduced since the more intense pressure field (see Sections 13.7.1 and 13.15.3) extends over a smaller area around the contact point. *The <u>total contact force</u> (the product of pressure and contact area) measured over the contact area is unaffected.* By employing a measuring technique based on the 'stick print' method (see Section 13.11.9 and Figure 13.39) the *effective contact areas* are found to be reduced by factors of ½ and better over the solid ball of rubber (the exact value depends on rubber stiffness, number of layers and tip geometry). *The stick behaves essentially as one having a reduced radius (smaller effective radius)* *but having the same mass.* The corresponding *effective radius reduction factor* is approximately $1/\sqrt{2} \approx 0.7$ or better (here, smaller is better). By employing these effects, tenor stick construction can be optimized and combined with fast hand action to achieve the desired short contact times required when playing the *Marginal Notes* on the tenor (see Section 13.27.8). Since *contact-time* is directly proportional to the tip radius R_s (see equations (13.67) and (13.114)), *contact time is reduced in proportion to the tip radius reduction factor*. However, the actual radius R_s, not the reduced radius, is used to calculate the contact force which is the product of the *enhanced* contact pressure and the *reduced* contact area. These two effects essentially cancel themselves out in the product.

13.12.4 Optimum Design Criterion

Note excitation is maximized when the stress pulse produced in the impacted rubber develops the force field distribution shown in Figure 13.11 with minimum loss to the shank. *Shank Loss* is minimized when the resultant stress magnitude at the *rubber → shank* interface is minimized. It is not physically possible to produce a perfect node at this interface but by proper design, the optimum condition can be closely realized. The *optimum design criterion* therefore calls for the *minimization* of the stress magnitude at the *rubber → shank* interface.

13.12.5 Design Examples

We are now in a position to examine the propagation of the stress pulse generated in the tip on impact. Consider the three designs in Figure 13.30: (a) a loosely wrapped tip on a solid wooden shank with air trapped between layers, (b) a tightly wrapped rubber tip on a solid wooden shank and (c) a tightly wrapped tip on a hollow shank.

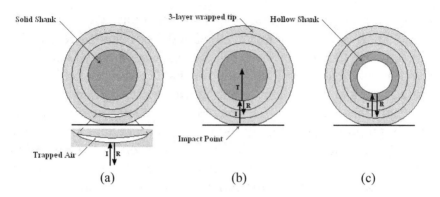

Fig. 13.30. Reflection and transmission at interfaces on the stick tip examples,

Example (a): When impact is made, stress waves travel into the outermost rubber layer towards the air inclusion. At the *rubber→ air* interface $\sigma_T = 0.00087\ \sigma_I$, $\sigma_R = -0.9991\sigma_I$ giving $\sigma_{resultant} = \sigma_I - 0.9991\sigma_I = 0.0009\ \sigma_I$, which represents a node. While there are other paths for the waves emanating from the contact region, strong impedance mismatch will always exist at the *rubber→ air* interface for all these waves. The condition in *case (ii)* is therefore satisfied with the formation of a node at the interface. The formation of a node at this interface is to be expected because the rarefied air cannot support the stress incident upon it. There is no stress pulse transmission beyond the trapped air into the underlying rubber layers. This confinement of the impact-induced stress drives the outermost layer into vibration in the manner of a stretched rubber membrane. These vibrations are readily felt by the player and *the note is poorly excited.* **It is therefore important that the layers of the wrapped stick be wrapped tightly to exclude trapped air between layers.**

As the wrapped stick ages and is used repeatedly for playing the instrument, the wrapping becomes loose and air enters the spaces between layers. The compressive stress during stick-note impact will then be confined mainly to the outer layers, reducing the effectiveness of the stick.

Example (b): In this case, due to good mechanical contact between the rubber layers and with $\rho_B v_{pB} = \rho_A v_{pA}$ for the *rubber→ rubber* interfaces, the waves propagate towards the shank without reflection

($\sigma_R = 0$). At the *rubber* → *wood* interface, $\sigma_R/\sigma_I = 0.2490$ (Pine), $\sigma_T/\sigma_I = 1.2490$ (Pine), the amplitude of the stress wave passing at normal incidence into the wooden shank is increased by a factor 1.2490. At the opposite side of the shank, the *wood* → *rubber* interface produces a reflected wave of magnitude $\sigma_R = -0.2490 \times 1.2490\ \sigma_I = -0.311\ \sigma_I$. This reflected wave returns to the opposite *wood* → *rubber* interface and is transmitted into the rubber with amplitude $\sigma_T = 0.751 \times (-0.311)\ \sigma_I = -0.2336\ \sigma_I$. If one ignores the small time delay between the original incident wave at the *rubber* → *wood* interface and the returning wave, the resultant amplitude at the interface for this single path is

$$\sigma_{resultant} = \sigma_I + 0.2490\ \sigma_I - 0.2336\ \sigma_I = 1.015\ \sigma_I,$$

down from $1.2490\ \sigma_I$.

Similarly for a solid aluminum shank one gets

$$\sigma_{resultant} = 1.715\ \sigma_I,$$

down from $1.8942\ \sigma_I$.

While the magnitude of the resultant wave at the *rubber* → *shank* interface is reduced, the design is not optimized. There are many other paths taken by the stress waves within the tip. These multiple paths are complicated by the angles of incidence, reflection and refraction but still do not lead to an optimized design.

Example (c): In this design, the shank is hollow. For wood, bamboo, carbon-fibre composite and aluminum shanks, the wave transmitted into the shank material is almost totally reflected at the *shank* → *air* interface (see Figure 13.30(c)). In this design the resultant wave at the *rubber* → *shank* interface and the resultant wave transmitted into the air in the hollow must be determined after multiple transmission/reflection at the interfaces.

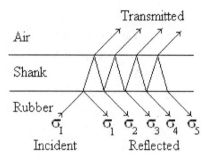

Fig. 13.31. Multiple transmission/reflection at the rubber-shank-air interfaces. Angles exaggerated for clarity.

Figure 13.31 shows a stress wave of amplitude σ_I incident at the *rubber→ shank* interface of a hollow shank. A cascade of reflections and transmissions follow at the *rubber→ shank, shank → rubber* and *shank→ air* interfaces. The shank thickness is sufficiently small for time delays to be ignored. In addition, since the amplitude of the waves transmitted across the *shank→ air* interface is very small we can ignore the contribution from these waves when they are reflected from the *air → shank* interface on the opposite side of the hollow. Assuming normal incidence, and using the symbols α_{Txy}, α_{Rxy} to denote transmission and reflection ratios at the interface $x \to y$ respectively, one obtains

$$\sigma_1 = \sigma_I \, \alpha_{Rrs}$$
$$\sigma_2 = \sigma_I \, (\alpha_{Trs} \, \alpha_{Rsa} \, \alpha_{Tsr})$$
$$\sigma_3 = \sigma_2 \, (\alpha_{Rsr} \, \alpha_{Rsa})$$
$$\sigma_4 = \sigma_2 \, (\alpha_{Rsr} \, \alpha_{Rsa})^2$$
$$\sigma_5 = \sigma_2 \, (\alpha_{Rsr} \, \alpha_{Rsa})^3$$
$$\ldots\ldots\ldots$$
$$\sigma_m = \sigma_2 \, (\alpha_{Rsr} \, \alpha_{Rsa})^{m-2}$$

(s ≡ shank, r ≡ rubber, a ≡ air)

Summing these reflected components gives

$$\sigma_{reflected} = \sigma_I \alpha_{Rrs} + \sigma_I (\alpha_{Trs} \alpha_{Rsa} \alpha_{Tsr}) \sum_{n=0}^{\infty} (\alpha_{Rsr} \alpha_{Rsa})^n.$$

Since $0 < (\alpha_{Rsr} \alpha_{Rsa}) < 1$, the summation converges to give

$$\begin{aligned}\sigma_{resultant} &= \sigma_I + \sigma_{reflected} \\ &= \sigma_I + \sigma_I \alpha_{Rrs} + \frac{\sigma_I (\alpha_{Trs} \alpha_{Rsa} \alpha_{Tsr})}{1 - \alpha_{Rsr} \alpha_{Rsa}},\end{aligned} \qquad 13.118$$

where $\sigma_{resultant}$ is the resultant wave amplitude at the *rubber→shank* interface.

Similarly, the resultant amplitude of the wave transmitted into the air in the hollow of the shank is given by

$$\sigma_{transmitted} = \sigma_I \alpha_{Trs} \alpha_{Tsa} + \frac{\sigma_I (\alpha_{Trs} \alpha_{Rsa} \alpha_{Rsr} \alpha_{Tsa})}{1 - \alpha_{Rsr} \alpha_{Rsa}} \qquad 3.119$$

Using the data in Tables 13.7 and 13.8, equations (13.118) and (13.119), a list of resultant and transmitted stress amplitudes is presented below. The object is to minimize both $\sigma_{resultant}$ and $\sigma_{transmitted}$.

Pine:
$$\sigma_{resultant} = 8.314 \times 10^{-4} \sigma_I.$$
$$\sigma_{transmitted} = 8.647 \times 10^{-4} \sigma_I.$$

Oak:
$$\sigma_{resultant} = 9.092 \times 10^{-4} \sigma_I.$$
$$\sigma_{transmitted} = 8.636 \times 10^{-4} \sigma_I.$$

Bamboo: *Radial direction*
$$\sigma_{resultant} = 9.421 \times 10^{-4} \sigma_I.$$
$$\sigma_{transmitted} = 8.668 \times 10^{-4} \sigma_I.$$

CFC: $\sigma_{resultant} = 1.578 \times 10^{-3} \sigma_I$.

$\sigma_{transmitted} = 1.051 \times 10^{-3} \sigma_I$.

Aluminum: $\sigma_{resultant} = 1.789 \times 10^{-3} \sigma_I$.

$\sigma_{transmitted} = 8.944 \times 10^{-4} \sigma_I$.

From these results, shanks made of hollow pine, hollow oak or bamboo should give superior performance over CFC and Aluminum. Statistically, there is essentially no difference in the performance of hollow pine, hollow oak and bamboo. There is a simple explanation for this: If the acoustic characteristic impedance of the shank material is equal (or nearly equal) to that of soft rubber, then the stress waves will propagate without reflection to the *shank→ air* interface where they will be almost totally reflected. Consequently, a node will develop at the *shank→ air* interface. This satisfies the optimum design criterion. A check of Table 13.6 shows that unlike the values for aluminum and CFC the acoustical impedances of pine, oak and bamboo are all close to that of soft rubber.

Some panists are known to favor bamboo and other hollow sticks (hollow aluminum for example) for the higher pans because they are superior to the solid ones when playing these instruments. Hollow sticks are generally of the bamboo variety. Hollow pine (or other wood) sticks are not used because they are unavailable but they can be made at home by drilling a hole down the longitudinal axis of the shank to a depth just beyond the tip (see Figure 13.32 (a)). Adding small perforations to the hollow section of this shaft to provide contact with air on the inner surface of the rubber is not a good way to increase internal stress wave reflection. This procedure will only weaken the structure. When making a hollow pine stick (for example) one has to be careful to avoid later splitting or warping of the shank. An 'end plug' or 'end ring' can be inserted on the tip end of the bore. An end plug made of lead or other metal can be used to 'stiffen' the tip and to restore 'weight' balance to the stick. A metal ring inserted firmly (or glued) into the bore opening will serve to stiffen the tip end. Bamboo, when properly cured by drying to low moisture content does not exhibit warping and splitting problems because of its natural anatomical structure and the presence of 'bamboo nodes' along the longitudinal axis of the Culm. When using bamboo however, to avoid later splitting caused by repeated or heavy use, one should cut the shank so that a 'bamboo node' exists at the tip end of the shank (see Figure 13.32 (b)).

Fig. 13.32. Partial cut-away views of two sticks. (a) Author designed hollow wooden stick. (b) Bamboo stick.

In the case of hollow CFC or aluminum shank, there exists large impedance mismatch at the interface with rubber and the interface with air. This means that the pulse component entering the shank suffers repeated reflections within the shank material which, for other than normal angles of incidence and reflection, produces waves travelling up and down along the length of the shank in the manner of an *'acoustic pipe'*. This produces the familiar ringing tones associated with hollow aluminum shanks. The player's hand and the rubber tip on the other end act as dampers for these vibrations.

13.12.6 Recommendations

If one can find or design a rigid material with characteristic impedance equal to or close to that of soft rubber then, because of impedance matching, a hollow shank made of this material will offer superior performance in stick-note impacts. Perfect impedance matching is not essential.

13.13 The Coefficient of Restitution (COR) of Stick Tips

13.13.1 What is the COR?

In most everyday impacts between two objects, some kinetic energy remains after the collision. The Coefficient of Restitution (COR) is a quantity used to define the fraction of the initial kinetic energy that remains after the collision. The COR is close to 1.00 if very little kinetic energy is lost. If the collision is perfectly elastic, COR = 1.00 and there is no energy lost. On the other extreme, for example when a piece of soft putty falls to the floor, practically all the initial kinetic energy is lost, COR $\cong$ 0, and the putty does not rebound. In most common examples such as a rubber ball dropped unto a hard flat surface, the ball rebounds. Some energy is lost so that the rebound velocity is less than the velocity with which it impacted the surface. In this case the COR is less than 1.00. For a few common objects: a properly inflated basketball has COR = 0.6, a baseball COR = 0.55, a golf ball impacting a driving club COR = 0.83, and a regulation tennis ball COR = 0.728. These balls are designed to provide good rebound required by the specific sport. The COR for pan sticks is a very useful quantity to consider here because it plays an important role in the tactile feedback to the player and in addition it can easily be measured.

We now perform the analysis to obtain the coefficient of restitution of the stick tip in collision with the steel note. Here as in the soft-stick hard note assumption the note displacement and by implication, the rebound velocity of the note will be set to zero. Application of the laws of mechanics tells us that the average force $\vec{F}_{avg}$ during impact is equal to the rate of change of linear momentum $\dfrac{\Delta \vec{P}}{\Delta t}$,

$$\vec{F}_{avg} = \frac{\Delta \vec{P}}{\Delta t}, \qquad (13.120)$$

where $\Delta \vec{P}$ is the change in linear momentum during the time interval Δt. The time interval Δt for the impact measured from first contact ('make') to end of contact ('break') when the stick rebounds is equal to $\tau_{m\text{-}t\text{-}b}$. In addition, $\Delta \vec{P} = m_s \Delta \vec{V}$ where $\Delta \vec{V}$ is the change in velocity of the stick due to the impact. Putting these relations into equation (13.120) gives

$$\vec{F}_{avg} = \frac{m_s \Delta \vec{V}}{\tau_{m-t-b}}. \tag{13.121}$$

If the tip rebounds with a velocity $\vec{V}_r$ *directed upward* away from the note surface, then since the initial velocity $\vec{V}_0$ is *directed downward* towards the note, one gets for the change in velocity

$$\Delta \vec{V} = \vec{V}_r - \vec{V}_0 \quad \text{(vector equation)}$$
$$\Delta V = V_0 + V_r, \quad \text{(scalar equation)} \tag{13.122}$$

where V_0 and V_r are the initial and final 'scalar velocities' or speeds respectively. Substituting (13.122) in (13.121) gives, in scalar form

$$V_r = \frac{F_{avg} \tau_{m-t-b}}{m_s} - V_0. \tag{13.123}$$

The Coefficient of Restitution (COR) ε_r of the stick tip is defined as: *the ratio of the speed of separation after impact to the speed of approach before impact*:

$$\varepsilon_r = -\frac{\vec{V}_r}{\vec{V}_0}$$
$$= \frac{V_r}{V_0}. \tag{13.124}$$

Since kinetic energy is proportional to the velocity squared (KE = $mv^2/2$), it follows from Equation (13.124) that the percentage kinetic energy loss during impact is given by

$$\text{Percentage of KE Lost} = (1 - \varepsilon_r^2)100\%. \tag{13.125}$$

The Newton coefficient of restitution expressed by equation (13.124) assumes that ε_r is dependent only on the *ratio* of the velocity between contact points at the end of the impact to the velocity at incidence. The Newton coefficient of restitution is assumed to be independent of the *magnitudes* of these velocities but depends on the shape and physical properties of the two impacting objects. In practice the coefficient of restitution is dependent on the magnitude of the incident velocity. Since the physical properties of the rubber material used in stick tip manufacture are temperature dependent, the COR will vary with temperature. For an elastic impact $\varepsilon_r = 1$ (closely but not exactly approximated by two impacting pieces of diamond) while for a totally inelastic collision such as when using soft putty, $\varepsilon_r = 0$. When soft putty impacts a surface there is no rebound, all the kinetic energy is lost as indicated by equation (13.125) for $\varepsilon_r = 0$. In an elastic collision, both momentum and kinetic energy are conserved while in an inelastic collision momentum is conserved but kinetic energy is not. Stick-note impacts are inelastic so kinetic energy is lost in all stick impacts on the pan placing them somewhere between these two extremes.

Equations (13.123) and (13.124) yield

$$\varepsilon_r = \frac{F_{avg}\, \tau_{m-t-b}}{m_s V_0} - 1. \tag{13.126}$$

Equation (13.126) can be inverted to yield

$$F_{avg} = \frac{m_s V_0}{\tau_{m-t-b}}(1+\varepsilon_r), \tag{13.127}$$

so once the COR for the tip and the contact time (make-to-break) are known the average impact force can be found.

13.13.2 The COR Equation by Energy Balance

13.13.2.1 General Nature of the approach

We first consider the general case that occurs in practice where the tip is not simply a ball of rubber but a combination of tip and shank. The shank, particularly the portion that extends into the tip must be included for a full treatment of the energy balance problem.

During impact, the initial kinetic energy $\frac{1}{2}m_s V_0^2$ is converted into other forms of energy in the compression phase and in the restitution phase until, at the 'break' the tip rebounds with kinetic energy $\frac{1}{2}m_s V_r^2$. In the compression phase, potential energy is stored in the compressed tip, while mechanical work is done against the internal frictional forces. In the restitution phase, a part of the stored potential energy is converted into kinetic energy while work is again done against the internal frictional forces. The work done over the two phases cannot be recovered so this results in energy loss. During the course of the impact stress energy is transferred to the shank material at the core of the tip. This energy is dissipated in the shank and results in additional energy loss.

13.13.2.2 Hysteretic Losses

To determine the energy lost due to hysteresis, consider the hysteresis cycle in Figure 13.33. The energy E_H lost during the hysteresis cycle is equal to the area enclosed by the hysteresis loop in Figure 13.33. Thus

$$E_H = \oint F dW = m_s (\omega R_s)^2 \oint w^p dw. \qquad (13.128)$$

Integration around the loop consists of the path through the *compression phase* to maximum compression W_{max}, followed by the return path through the *restitution phase*. Observe on Figure 13.33 the small *residual compression* $R_s \delta_w$ at the end of the restitution phase. The tip rebounds with this small compression which decreases to zero as the tip slowly returns to its original shape.

Typically: $\delta_w \approx 0.004$ *for Small Mini Sticks.*
≈ 0.01 *for Bass Sticks*

Solving the loop integral in equation (13.128) gives

$$E_H = m_s(\omega R_s)^2 \left\{ \frac{w_{max}^{(p_c+1)}}{p_c+1} - \left(\frac{w_{max}^{(p_r+1)}}{p_r+1} - \frac{\delta_w^{p_r+1}}{p_r+1} \right) \right\}, \qquad (13.129)$$

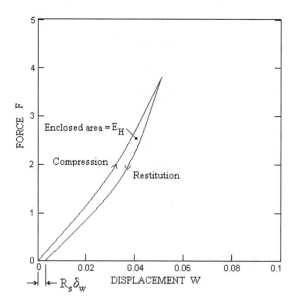

Fig. 13.33. Hysteresis cycle.

The last term on the RHS of (13.129) can be obtained by following the tip as it rebounds with a residual compression δ_w and completes the restitution phase in its 'upward' path away from the impacted note surface.

The dimensionless residual compression δ_w, which vanishes ($\delta_w = 0$) in the absence of hysteresis ($p_c = p_r$), is an unknown function of the p-indices and other material quantities and depends on the internal structure of the rubber material. The 'spaghetti-like' structure of the long chain molecules forming the rubber, when stretched or compressed requires some time to return to its original configuration. This is one of the underlying causes of hysteresis on the stick tip. *In the case of wrapped sticks, the residual compression is partly due to inter-layer slippage. The layers require more time than the duration of the restitution phase to return to the original state before slippage. Even so, slip is not fully reversible. The rubber balls used on the low-end pans generally possess a sponge-like, partially air-filled, structure, which tends to display larger δ_w. This is partly due to the slow refilling of the air expelled from the internal spaces during compression.*

The stored residual potential energy that the stick tip takes with it on the rebound, as a fraction of the initial kinetic energy is obtained from equation (13.129) as

$$\delta E_{residual} = 2\left(\frac{\omega R_s}{V_0}\right)^2 \frac{\delta_w^{p_r+1}}{p_r+1} = \frac{E_s \delta_w^{p_r+1}}{V_0^2 \pi \rho_s (1-v_s^2)}\left(\frac{2}{p_r+1}\right). \quad (13.130)$$

After the 'break', as the tip leaves the note surface, the stored residual energy is converted into internal mechanical work and eventually to heat. This energy cannot be recovered and is lost.

When the small residual compression is ignored, equation (13.129) reduces to

$$E_H = m_s(\omega R_s)^2 \left\{\frac{w_{max}^{(p_c+1)}}{p_c+1} - \frac{w_{max}^{(p_r+1)}}{p_r+1}\right\}, \quad (13.131)$$

When $p_c = p_r$, there is no hysteresis so that during restitution the tip retraces the path taken during compression, the enclosed area is zero, making $E_H = 0$ in this case.

13.13.2.3 Mechanical Work

During impact the work done *against* the forces associated with the mechanical resistance of the tip material is given by

$$Work = r_{ms}R_s\left\{\left[\int_0^{w_{max}} V dw\right]_{comp} + \left[\int_{w_{max}}^{\delta_w} V dw\right]_{rest}\right\}. \quad (13.132)$$

The subscripts '*comp*' and '*rest*' refer to the compressive phase and the restitutive phase, respectively. This mechanical work appears as heat in the rubber material. It is therefore irrecoverable in the stick-note impact process.

13.13.2.4 Shank Absorption

The process of shank absorption is too complicated for a full treatment to be done here; however, it is dealt with adequately for our purposes in Section 13.12. Complications arise because of the localized stresses around the portion of shank inserted into the rubber ball or tubing. Regions of localized stress concentrations act as *scattering centers*. Stress waves generated in the rubber tip during impact, travel to the shank at the core of the tip. These waves are partially transmitted through the shank, partially reflected (*scattered*) at the shank-rubber boundary and partially absorbed by the shank material. In the case of wrapped sticks, stress waves are scattered at the rubber-to-rubber and the rubber-to-shank interlayer boundaries. The vibrations transmitted along the shank from the tip to the butt end of the shank held by the hand can be felt by the player. *Shank absorption is generally reduced by the use of hollow shanks. This is mainly due to the removal of otherwise absorbent shank material by hollowing.*

Shank absorption is a transient process, confined mainly to the early part of the compression phase. We use the symbol E_{SA} to denote this unknown energy loss due to shank absorption.

13.13.2. Energy-Balance Equation

The energy-balance (conservation of energy) equation takes the form

$$\tfrac{1}{2}m_s V_0^2 - \tfrac{1}{2}m_s V_r^2 = m_s(\omega R_s)^2 \left\{ \frac{w_{max}^{(p_c+1)}}{p_c+1} - \left(\frac{w_{max}^{(p_r+1)}}{p_r+1} - \frac{\delta_w^{p_r+1}}{p_r+1} \right) \right\} + E_{SA}$$

$$+ r_{ms} R_s \left\{ \left[\int_0^{w_{max}} V dw \right]_{comp} + \left[\int_{w_{max}}^{\delta_w} V dw \right]_{rest} \right\}$$

(13.133)

Using $\varepsilon_r = V_r/V_0$ in equation 13.133 gives

$$\varepsilon_r^2 = 1 - 2\left(\frac{\omega R_s}{V_0}\right)^2 \left\{ \frac{w_{max}^{(p_c+1)}}{p_c+1} - \left(\frac{w_{max}^{(p_r+1)}}{p_r+1} - \frac{\delta_w^{p_r+1}}{p_r+1}\right) \right\} - \frac{2E_{SA}}{m_s V_0^2}$$

$$- \frac{2r_{ms} R_s}{m_s V_0^2} \left\{ \left[\int_0^{w_{max}} V dw\right]_{comp} + \left[\int_{w_{max}}^{\delta_w} V dw\right]_{rest} \right\}.$$

(13.134)

We now consider some special cases.

Case 1: COR of Tip with no Resistive Losses, no Shank Absorption and no Hysteresis

Method 1: Energy-Balance Method

In this case the p-index for compression equals the p-index for restitution, $p_c = p_r = p$, $E_{SA} = 0$, $\delta_w = 0$ and $r_{ms} = 0$. From equation 13.134

$$\varepsilon_r = 1.$$

Method 2: Velocity Method

Equation (13.60) shows that in this case, the velocity of the center of mass of the tip during impact is given by

$$V^2 - V_0^2 = -\frac{2(\omega R_s)^2}{p+1} w^{p+1}.$$

(13.135)

At the 'make' and at the 'break' when the tip surface displacement is zero, $w = 0$, equation (13.135) gives the tip velocities as

$$V = \pm V_0.$$

(3.136)

This means that in vector quantities, the tip rebounds with a velocity $\vec{V} = \vec{V_r} = +\vec{V_0}$ *directed upward*, away from the note surface, while the initial velocity $\vec{V} = -\vec{V_0}$ is *directed downward* towards the note surface. This means that the impact velocity is numerically equal to the rebound velocity giving

$$\varepsilon_r = \frac{V_r}{V_0} = \frac{V_0}{V_0} = 1. \qquad (13.137)$$

For all non-hysteretic, loss-free tips the COR is equal to unity, $\varepsilon_r = 1$. This situation never arises in practice.

Case 2: COR of Tip with Hysteresis no Shank Absorption and no Resistive or Residual Losses

In this case, the p-index for compression and the p-index for restitution are different, $p_c \neq p_r$. The COR can be found using three methods. The first makes use of equation (13.126) and requires solving for F_{avg} using the force equation, the second uses the energy-balance method equation (13.134), while the third method (which is much simpler) solve for the rebound velocity V_r directly.

Method 1: Average-Force Method

Equation (13.51b) gives the contact force for the loss free tip as

$$F_c(t) = \frac{4E_s}{3(1-v_s^2)} R_s^2 w_s^p(t).$$

With $\omega R_s = \sqrt{E_s/(\pi \rho_s (1-v_s^2))}$ and $m_s = 4\pi \rho_s R_s^3/3$, equation (13.51b) can be written as

$$F_c(t) = m_s \omega^2 R_s^2 w_s^p(t). \qquad (13.138)$$

The average force during impact can now be obtained by integrating the contact force with respect to time over the compression and restitution phases of the impact and dividing by the make-to-break contact time $\tau_{m\text{-}t\text{-}b}$. Thus

$$F_{avg} = \frac{\left[\int_0^{t_{max}} F_c \, dt\right]_{comp} + \left[\int_{t_{max}}^{\tau_{m\text{-}t\text{-}b}} F_c \, dt\right]_{rest}}{\tau_{m\text{-}t\text{-}b}}, \quad (13.139)$$

where the integration over the compression phase sets $p = p_c$ while the integration over the restitution phase sets $p = p_r$, with t_{max} as the time taken to reach maximum compression.

Using equation (13.95b), the integral for the compression phase in equation (13.139) can be expressed as

$$\left[\int_0^{t_{max}} F_c \, dt\right]_{comp} = \int_0^{t_{max}} m_s \omega^2 R_s w^{p_c} \, dt$$

$$= \frac{m_s \omega^2 R_s^2}{V_0} \int_0^{w_{max}} w^{p_c} \left(1 - \left(\frac{w}{w_{max}}\right)^{(p_c+1)}\right)^{-\frac{1}{2}} dw. \quad (13.140)$$

Expanding the integrand in equation (13.140) as a binomial series then integrating gives

$$\left[\int_0^{t_{max}} F_c \, dt\right]_{comp} = \frac{m_s \omega^2 R_s^2 w_{max}^{(p_c+1)}}{(p_c+1)V_0} \sum_{n=0}^{\infty} z_n$$

where $\quad (13.141)$

$$z_n = \frac{z_{n-1}(2n-1)}{2n+2}, \quad z_{-1} = -2.$$

Similarly, for the restitution phase with $\delta_w = 0$

$$\left[\int_{t_{max}}^{\tau_{m\text{-}t\text{-}b}} F_c \, dt\right]_{rest} = \frac{m_s \omega^2 R_s^2 w_{max}^{(p_r+1)}}{(p_r+1)V_r} \sum_{n=0}^{\infty} z_n, \quad (13.142)$$

where V_r is given by equation (13.102).
Using these results in equation (13.139) gives

$$F_{avg}\,\tau_{m-t-b} = m_s\,\omega^2 R_s^2 \left(\frac{w_{max}^{(p_c+1)}}{V_0(P_c+1)} + \frac{w_{max}^{(p_r+1)}}{V_r(P_r+1)}\right) \sum_{n=0}^{\infty} z_n. \quad (13.143)$$

Substituting equation (13.143) into equation (13.126) and using the expressions for w_{max} and V_r we get after some simplification

$$\varepsilon_r = \left(\frac{1}{2}\sum_{0}^{\infty} z_n - 1\right) + \frac{1}{2}\left(\sum_{n=0}^{\infty} z_n\right)\left(\frac{p_c+1}{2}\right)^{\frac{p_r+1}{2(p_c+1)}}\left(\frac{2}{p_r+1}\right)^{\frac{1}{2}}\left(\frac{V_0}{\omega R_s}\right)^{\frac{P_r-p_c}{p_c+1}}. \quad (13.144)$$

It can be shown that the infinite series
$\sum_{n=0}^{\infty} z_n = 1 + \frac{1}{4} + \frac{1}{8} + \frac{5}{64} + \frac{7}{128} + \frac{21}{512} + \frac{33}{1024} + \dots$ converges to the value 2
(see below), which reduces equation (13.144) to

$$\varepsilon_r = \left(\frac{p_c+1}{2}\right)^{\frac{p_r+1}{2(p_c+1)}}\left(\frac{2}{p_r+1}\right)^{\frac{1}{2}}\left(\frac{V_0}{\omega R_s}\right)^{\frac{P_r-p_c}{p_c+1}}. \quad (13.145)$$

When $p_r = p_c$, one gets $\varepsilon_r = 1$ as in Case 1

- **Physicist's Proof**: Consider the stick-note system where there is no energy loss during impact. From the physics of the system, this impact is perfectly elastic so $\varepsilon_r = 1$. Now consider equation (13.144) which applies to the system where the only losses possible are hysteretic losses. For the case $p_c = p_r$ there are no hysteretic losses and equation (13.144) reduces to $\varepsilon_r = \sum_0^{\infty} z_n - 1$. Since $\varepsilon_r = 1$ it follows that $\sum_0^{\infty} z_n = 2$ is true.

  Mathematician's Proof: Using a 1–1 correspondence, one can show that the infinite series $\sum_0^{\infty} z_n$ is equal to $2s$ where s is the geometric series $\frac{1}{2} + \frac{1}{4} + \frac{1}{8} + \frac{1}{16} + \dots \frac{1}{2^n} + \dots$. Multiply this series by 2 to give $2s = 1 + \frac{1}{2} + \frac{1}{4} + \frac{1}{8} + \frac{1}{16} + \dots \frac{1}{2^n} + \dots$, then, by inspection, $2s = 1 + s$ which leads to $s = 1$ and $\sum_0^{\infty} z_n = 2$ which was to be proved.

Method 2: Energy-Balance Method

With $E_{SA} = 0$, $\delta_w = 0$ and $r_{ms} = 0$, equation (13.134) gives

$$\varepsilon_r^2 = 1 - 2\left(\frac{\omega R_s}{V_0}\right)^2 \left\{ \frac{w_{max}^{(p_c+1)}}{p_c+1} - \frac{w_{max}^{(p_r+1)}}{p_r+1} \right\}.$$

On substituting for w_{max} from equation (13.61), one gets after some simple algebra

$$\varepsilon_r = \left(\frac{p_c+1}{2}\right)^{\frac{p_r+1}{2(p_c+1)}} \left(\frac{2}{p_r+1}\right)^{\frac{1}{2}} \left(\frac{V_0}{\omega R_s}\right)^{\frac{p_r-p_c}{p_c+1}}. \quad (13.146)$$

Equation (13.145) and equation (13.146) are identical.

Method 3: Velocity Method

This method is straightforward as it makes direct use of the expression for V_r given in equation (13.102):

$$\varepsilon_r = \frac{V_r}{V_0} = \left(\frac{p_c+1}{2}\right)^{\frac{p_r+1}{2(p_c+1)}} \left(\frac{2}{p_r+1}\right)^{\frac{1}{2}} \left(\frac{V_0}{\omega R_s}\right)^{\frac{p_r-p_c}{p_c+1}}, \quad (13.147)$$

identical to the result in Equation (13.145). This simpler Method serves to verify the procedures of Methods 1 and 2. However, Method 2 will be found more convenient for cases where pre-stress and losses are included.

Finally

$$\varepsilon_r = \left(\frac{p_c+1}{2}\right)^{\frac{p_r+1}{2(p_c+1)}} \left(\frac{2}{p_r+1}\right)^{\frac{1}{2}} \left(\frac{V_0^2 \, \pi \rho_s (1-v_s^2)}{E_s}\right)^{\frac{p_r-p_c}{2(p_c+1)}}. \quad (13.148)$$

Observations: Equation (13.148) shows that with hysteresis ($p_c < p_r$) the COR increases with the impact velocity as $V_0^{\frac{p_r - p_c}{p_c + 1}}$. The COR increases with tip material density and decreases with tip elastic constant. For $p_c = p_r$ these dependencies all vanish so they are purely hysteretic effects.

TABLE 13.9

p_c	p_r	ε_r		
		$V_0 = 0.7$ m·s^{-1}	$V_0 = 1.0$ m·s^{-1}	$V_0 = 1.5$ m·s^{-1}
1	1	1	1	1
1.2	1.2	1	1	1
1.2	1.6	0.435	0.464	0.499
1.3	1.6	0.551	0.577	0.608
1.3	1.7	0.452	0.481	0.516
1.33	1.76	0.432	0.461	0.497
1.4	1.8	0.469	0.498	0.533

Some examples are shown in Table 13.9 for $E_s = 5 \times 10^6$ N·m^{-2}, $\rho_s = 920$ kg·m^{-3}. The COR analysis of the tip requires further improvement but this requires the inclusion of pre-stress applied during the manufacture of the tip. Additional refinements to the stick dynamics, including Hand Action are also required before entering the general COR analysis. *(When Hand Action is included one should speak of the 'Effective COR' instead of the COR).* We shall find that the COR values in Table 13.9) are generally lower than the values obtained for real pan sticks. The reason as we will also see is the omission in the analysis of pre-stress found on all pan sticks. The analysis of the wrapped stick will deal with this problem for all sticks.

13.14 Wrapped Sticks

13.14.1 Basic Ideas on the Wrapped Stick

The case for wrapped sticks is complicated analytically by slippage between layers, inter-layer forces and variation in applied tension to the rubber during wrapping. Because of these complications the elastic properties are subject to much variation. In particular, the slippage between layers that occurs during impact increases the hysteretic effects. The tension applied to the stretched banding rubber during wrapping subjects the tip to compressional stresses. A close analogy here is the soccer ball, which is pumped up to increase the internal pressure. The greater the pressure, the stiffer the ball and the greater is its COR. To gain some insight into the effects of these stresses consider the superball[©].

The superball is an extremely elastic bouncy ball invented by N. Stingley. First manufactured in 1965, it soon became a very popular toy. It is made of the synthetic rubber polymer polybutadiene, vulcanized with sulfur at a temperature of 165 °C and at a pressure of 1,200 psi (pounds per square inch). This manufacturing process which sets a very high compressive pre-stress, gives the superball a very high COR. Dropped from shoulder height, a superball will bounce nearly all the way back; thrown down on a hard surface, it can rebound to over 30 meters. It is dangerous to cut this ball open with a knife because it can rapidly burst open causing serious eye injury. The same holds true for the compressed intermediate layers of a 3- or 4-piece wound golf ball (I learned this from my wife who tried it as a child!). To observe this effect safely on the pan stick, wearing safety glasses, take a tightly wrapped stick tip and by using a sharp knife or razor, quickly, but carefully, cut the top two or three layers right through in a direction parallel to the shank. The rubber will rapidly unwind as the compressive stresses are removed. If you are too timid (I hope you are) take the TV advice — *'don't try this, we are professionals.'*

The more tightly the banding rubber is wrapped unto the shank, the greater is the COR and stiffness of the tip. This allows the stick maker or player to vary the tip properties and resulting contact times.

In all stick construction, the tip is attached to the end of the shank by compression forces between the rubber and the shank. Therefore, all stick tips are in a state of pre-stress. The manufacturers of the rubber or 'sponge' balls commonly used as stick tips normally set the balls in a state of internal pre-stress to increase their capacity for bouncing.

13.14.2 Single Layer Stretch-Fitted or Force-Fitted Tip

The simplest version of the wrapped stick is one in which a single piece of rubber tubing is *stretch-fitted* unto the end of the shank (see Figure 13.3(a)). The rubber tubing is simply stretched radially, fitted over the shank and released. For the thicker section of tubing, the shank is forced into the diametrically smaller hole of the tubing. They are held together by friction generated by the compressive forces between rubber and shank. The principle of operation on impact is the same as for the multi-layered tip which follows.

13.14.3 The Basic Multi-layer Wrap

Figure 13.34 (a) shows the banding rubber as it is wrapped unto the end of the shank. In the *Basic Wrap*, the layers are placed directly above each other. This produces a cylindrically shaped tip. In a more *complex wrap*, the band is moved back and forth along the shank to produce a rounded tip. The free end of the band is pulled to stretch the rubber and to apply a tension T_0 while wrapping. To keep the other end of the band in place on the shank the stick maker using his thumb, presses down on the rubber with a force of magnitude F_t and relies on the frictional forces $\mu_{rs}F_t$ and $\mu_{tr}F_t$ between the rubber-shank and thumb-rubber interfaces to produce the required restraint (μ_{rs} and μ_{tr} are respectively the rubber-shank and thumb-rubber coefficients of static friction). Since the rubber is flexible (and it is assumed to be *perfectly* flexible), all tensional forces are directed tangentially as shown in Figure 13.34(b). To be '*perfectly flexible*' means that the force required to '*bend*' the banding rubber is zero.

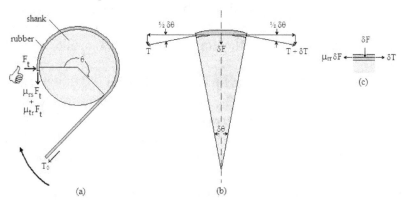

Fig. 13.34. (a) Banding rubber wrapped unto the end of the shank. (b) A small piece of banding rubber (enlarged) at position specified by the angles θ and $\theta + \delta\theta$. (c) Frictional force at rubber-rubber interface. For clarity the shank, rubber thickness and illustrated hand are not drawn to scale.

If the tensional forces at the ends of a section of banding rubber are T and $T + \delta T$ as in Figure 13.34(b), then the radial component of force directed normal to the small section at its center is

$$\delta F = (T + \delta T) \sin\tfrac{1}{2}\delta\theta + T \sin\tfrac{1}{2}\delta\theta. \qquad (13.149)$$

For $\delta\theta \to 0$ and $\delta T \to 0$, Equation (wrap 1) reduces to

$$\delta F = T\delta\theta. \qquad (13.150)$$

For a static radial force δF exerted normal to the shank surface by the stretched rubber, the frictional force (refer to Figure 13.34(c) for the rubber-rubber interface) is of magnitude

$$\mu_{rs}\delta F = \delta T, \qquad (13.151)$$

where μ_{rs} is the coefficient of *static* friction (or *sliding* friction if slipping occurs while wrapping) between rubber and shank surfaces. Normally, the banding rubber is not allowed to slide along the shank surface or over the previous layer of rubber. The stick maker's action is to set down layer upon layer while maintaining an essentially constant tension — *wrapping tension* — T_0 on the stretched band. The constancy of T_0 is however, not necessary.

On completion of the first layer, the second layer is laid down as the stick maker removes the thumb and allows the frictional forces to keep the layers in place. For the second and subsequent layers, the rubber-rubber coefficient of static friction μ_{rr} replaces μ_{rs} as in Figure 13.34(c). On completion of the wrap, the end of the band is tucked under the topmost layer or under a separate layer on the shank where it is held in place by friction. When a new layer is laid down, the radius of the existing tip is slightly reduced and the tangential stress is also slightly modified. Since sticks are normally wrapped with few layers, these small displacements and tangential stress increments are ignored. The small number of layers and step-wise increase in tip radius (in units of band thickness) also means that the present problem cannot be effectively modeled by a set of differential equations. In addition, the compressive Young's modulus of the shank is sufficiently high for the shank radius to remain essentially unchanged during the wrapping process.

We are interested in the normal forces δF and the compressional stresses they generate in the completely wrapped tip. If the width and the thickness of the stretched banding rubber are b and t respectively (see Figure 13.35(a)), then the *wrapping stress* over the cross-sectional area of the stretched band is

$$\sigma_t = \frac{T_0}{bt}. \tag{13.152}$$

When the wrapping process is completed, because of the assumed *perfect flexibility* of the rubber layers, the resultant normal compressive force on each small section of a layer is the sum of the δF forces produced by the layers wrapped *directly above* it. These forces are depicted in Figure 13.35(b). The outer, free surface of the tip experiences none of these forces while the shank surface experiences the greatest compressive force.

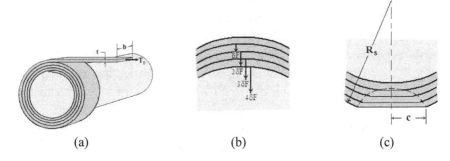

Fig. 13.35. (a) Wrapping tension and band dimensions. (b) Normal forces exerted by the rubber layers. (c) Layers deformed during impact.

Before impact, the interfaces between layers follow a smooth spiral curve where each interface can be assigned an approximate radius R_m, with m as the interface number ($m = 0, 1, 2 \ldots$ where $m = 0$ corresponds to the rubber-shank interface). For an N-layered tip with R_N as the radius of the free outer surface, one has $R_N = R_s$ where R_s is the stick tip radius. During impact with a flat surface, the layers are flattened in the region around the point of contact as shown in Figure 13.35(c). This region is enclosed by the dotted curve in Figure 13.35(c). In the region where the layers are flattened, the radius of curvature is very large and this results in a reduction in the normal compressive forces. This effect is confined to the region defined by the contact-area.

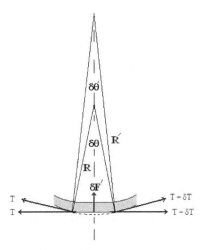

Fig. 13.36. Diagram showing the forces on a deformed layer during impact.

When the radius of curvature is changed on impact from R to R' as shown in Figure 13.36, the angle subtended by a small section of the banding rubber changes from $\delta\theta$ to $\delta\theta'$, with $\delta\theta > \delta\theta'$. The radial compressive force is reduced from δF to $\delta F'$ where

$$\delta F' = \delta F \frac{\delta\theta'}{\delta\theta}$$

$$= \delta F \frac{R}{R'}$$

$$= T_0 \delta\theta \left(\frac{R}{R'}\right). \qquad (13.153)$$

The distortion of the smooth spiral structure produces restoration forces that act to restore the distorted region to its original geometrical form. These forces which arise from the distortion of the layered structure under tension must not be confused with the forces arising from the elastic compression of the rubber that follow the w^p-law as previously discussed. The *radial restoration force* δF_r

produced by the small section of banding rubber shown in Figure 13.36 is equal in magnitude to the difference $\delta F - \delta F'$. Thus

$$\delta F_r = \delta F - \delta F$$
$$\delta F_r = T_0 \delta\theta \left(1 - \frac{R}{R'}\right). \tag{13.154}$$

This restoration force acts in the direction opposite to the radial compressive force δF and is directed towards the impacted surface (the note). $\delta F_r = 0$ when $R' = R$ (no distortion) and increases to $\delta F_r = T_0\, \delta\theta$ when the distorted section is perfectly flat ($R' = \infty$).

13.14.4 Hitting a Local Hump or Depression on the Note

Since the restoring force δF_r arises from the distortion of the rubber layers, it is necessary to consider the effect on δF_r of the localized distortions on the note surface itself. Localized *humps* and *pits* (or *dimples*) are normal features of the hammer peening process. If the tip strikes a localized hump on the note surface it is possible for the distorted outer layer(s) to acquire *negative curvature* (see Figure 13.37(a)). In this case

$$\delta F_r = T_0 \delta\theta \left(1 + \frac{R}{|R'|}\right). \tag{13.155}$$

Striking areas such as these on the note surface produces a greater restoring force and increases the local contact pressure. Similarly, when a depression (or hammer mark) as in Figure 13.37(b) on the note surface coincides with the impact point, the distorted radius R' while remaining positive, is reduced and so too is the restoring force and local contact pressure. By these changes in impact force, the player can actually 'feel' these uneven areas as the stick makes contact with the note. When playing the dome shaped notes on the pan, particularly the relatively smaller inner notes on the high-end pans, the impact is of the type shown in Figure 13.37(a).

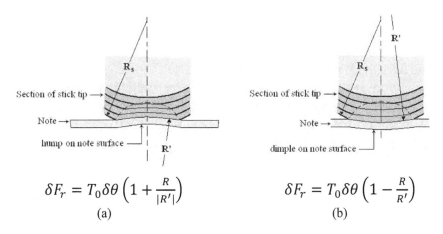

Fig. 13.37. Hump Distortion of layers on striking a hump (a) or a depression (b) on the note surface.

Since the restoring force at a given interface is additive by virtue of the layers directly above it, by assuming *perfect flattening* one gets for the maximum restoration force at the center of the contact area

$$\delta F_{r(\max)} = nT_0\delta\theta, \qquad (13.156)$$

where n is the number of flattened layers with $n < N$. The small integer n depends on the impact velocity but in numerical calculations it can be set at a suitable value less than N. The maximum pressure $\sigma_{r(max)}$ exerted on the impacted surface (note) by this small section of banding rubber of area $bR_s\delta\theta$ is given by

$$\sigma_{r(max)} = \frac{\delta F_{r(max)}}{bR_s\delta\theta}$$

$$= \frac{n}{bR_s\delta\theta}T_0\delta\theta$$

$$= \frac{n}{bR_s}T_0,$$

and finally

$$\sigma_{r(max)} = \frac{nt}{R_s}\sigma_t. \qquad (13.157)$$

The maximum pressure on the impacted surface is therefore equal to a fraction (nt/R_s) of the wrapping stress applied to the banding rubber during wrapping. This remarkable behavior results from the assumption that the banding rubber is perfectly flexible. This assumption is very closely approached in practice. For the shrink-fit tip, $n=1$

$$\sigma_{r(max)} = \frac{t}{R_s}\sigma_t. \qquad (13.158)$$

> As an example, static loading of the 7-layer wrapped cello stick illustrated in Figure 13.5(a) showed flattening of the outer four layers (n = 4) when a load of 45N (approximately 10 lb weight) was applied. A maximum force of 45N is possible for a strong stick-note impact with this stick. For this tip R_s = 2 cm and for the banding rubber, $t \approx 1$ mm, $b \approx 1.3$ cm. For a typical wrapping tension of 1 pound-force (approximately 4.5 N) this gives $\sigma_{r(max)}$ = 4(4.5)/(0.013x0.02) = 6.9 x 10^4 N·m^{-2} = 10 psi (pounds per square inch). To this pressure must be added the pressure due to elastic compression of the rubber.
> **Note:** 1 psi = 6.9 x 10^3 N·m^{-2}

If perfect flattening is not assumed then one has

$$\sigma_{r(max)} = \frac{t\sigma_t}{R_s}\sum_{m=1}^{N}\left(1 - \frac{R_m}{R'_m}\right), \qquad (13.159)$$

where N is the number of layers

$$N = \frac{R_s - R_{shank}}{t}, \text{ (rounded to the nearest integer)}$$

and in which one observes that the undistorted inner layers with $R'_m = R_m$ do not contribute to the restoring force or contact pressure attributed to pre-stress.

If the wrapping tension varies from layer to layer, one can write in final form

$$\sigma_{r(max)} = \frac{1}{bR_s} \sum_{m=1}^{N} T_m \left(1 - \frac{R_m}{R'_m}\right), \qquad (13.160)$$

where T_m is the tension in the mth layer. Inter-layer friction allows for variations in the wrapping tension. This general formula also applies to the impacts on humps and dimples in Figure 13.37.

13.14.5 The Crisscross Wrap

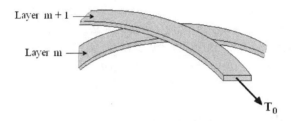

Sticks are often wrapped with the layers forming a crisscross pattern that results in a rubber ball at the end of the shank. The wraps are not perfect but by using a thin banding rubber and many turns, the ball can be perfected. If the wrapping tension remains constant for each layer, with the overlapping crisscross pattern, on impact the restoring forces (which are always normal to the applied wrapping tension) will still act radially outward and be additive as obtained with the basic wrap. For a perfectly wrapped ball, equation (13.160) applies and is valid in practice for tips wrapped in this manner. This means that the small local deformations due to crisscrossing are not taken into account. It is impractical to do otherwise because not only will the corrections turn out to be comparatively small, if they could be calculated, but they will vary with each crisscross whether hand or machine wrapped.

Comments: Equation (13.160) reveals that the contact pressure arising from the distortion of the layers of the wrapped stick on impact varies

   (i) *directly with the wrapping tension,*
   (ii) *inversely with the width b of the banding rubber,*
   (iii) *inversely with the tip radius R_s.*
   (iv) *Although the band thickness t does not appear explicitly in the equation, by using thinner bands the number of layers N required for a given tip radius R_s is increased. In fact, since $N = (R_s - R_{shank})/t$, using thinner banding rubbers for wrapping can increase the contact pressure.*

Observations (i) to (iv) explain the following: (a) Why the effective compression stiffness of the tip increases when the tip is wound with greater wrapping tension. (b) The effective stiffness of the finished tip is also greater when a narrower banding rubber is used. (c) The resulting increase in contact pressure as the number of wraps is increased is better observed for the tenor sticks where the tip radius R_s is smaller.

13.14.6. Feel and Responsiveness

By wrapping the inner layers with greater tension than that for the outer layers, the stick maker can create a tip with a hard 'core' and a soft 'mantle' as shown in Figure 13.38. Also by selecting different rubber materials for core and mantle, the responsiveness and 'feel' of the stick-note impact can be varied. A harder mantle can improve the responsiveness of the note on impact while a softer mantle can reduce it.

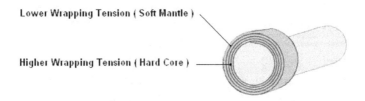

Fig. 13.38. Varying the wrapping tension to produce a hard core and soft mantle. Positions of 'hard' and soft' can be reversed for the opposite effect.

13.14.7 Wrapped Stick with a Felt or other Lossy Overlay

In the early days of pan making players dealt with the high untuned modes on the notes by wrapping their sticks with soft cloth or felt material. The Pang line of pans by Felix Rohner also used felt tipped sticks in order to reduce the levels of the high partials. This was done as a matter of choice because (as explained to me by Felix himself) the ears of the Swiss players were often affected by the loudness of the pans and the high pitched components of sound that the instruments produced. The felt or cloth materials were fibrous and low in density. A layer or two of this material will contribute only a small fraction of the total mass of the tip. Therefore it contributes only a small fraction of the total kinetic energy of the impact. On the other hand, the compression of these fibrous materials during impact will result in the absorption of a significant fraction of the total impact energy. This absorbed energy amounts to a loss and appears as heat within the felt (or cloth) layers. Such layers are best treated as *lossy layers* or *lossy overlays*. Their overall effect is to add a new component of resistance to the mechanical resistance r_{ms} of the stick tip. These lossy overlays do not provide any significant restoring forces because of their resistive (lossy) behavior. *In principle the stick tip with a lossy overlay is approximately equivalent to the stick without the overlay but with the lossy material (a mat) placed over the note surface or restricted to the area of contact.* See Figure 13.39.

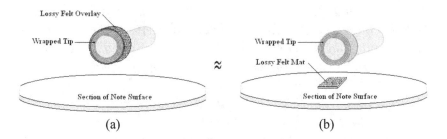

Fig. 13.39. (a) Wrapped rubber tip finished with an overlay of felt. (b) An approximate equivalent where the felt is in the form of a small mat on the note surface.

Provided that the density of the overlay is sufficiently small, during impact, the only change to the dynamical equations in cases (a) and (b) is the increase in r_{sm}. After impact, the mat may participate in some motion along with the note surface depending on the mass of the mat or more precisely that fraction of the mass that moves along with the note. If this mass is appreciable (which is not the case in the assumptions made here), then the note frequency will be reduced due to mass loading (see Chapter 11).

I am not inclined to recommend either case (a) or (b) because the overlay (or mat) material must be lossy to be effective. For example, the hammer on the piano is used during and after impact with the string(s) but no part of the hammer is carried along with the string. During impact the hammer losses set the contact-times, after impact the hammers provide the damping that helps to stop the strings. On the other hand the pan sticks are only active during impact. While damping may be useful on the sticks for the lower pans, stick losses should be minimized on the high-end pans. The lighter sticks used on the tenor already reduces the impact energy, tip losses only worsens the situation. If the mat is used to provide longer contact-times on some notes while the bare rubber tip is used on the uncovered notes, the transition between these covered and uncovered notes may pose a problem with the *tactile feedback* to the player. *In addition the hand action of the player will be restricted since the matted notes will always be subjected to longer contact times without the possibility of fast excitations when necessary or as the music demands.*

Note: *On the use of mats, with my objections already given above, I must come clean. I have often used these mats (usually a piece of the non-skid material used in cupboard drawers) to increase contact times during my research. But being aware of its effect on the driving force during impact, I have been able to perform my contact-time work without problems. But these were specific laboratory-type applications with corrections made for the other effects of the mat. This is certainly not possible when notes with mats are used in actual musical performances. It is in these live musical applications where I have serious reservations on their use. We will see later in this Chapter with the MDOF analysis why we need to be concerned.*

13.15 Contact Force Analysis of the Wrapped Stick

13.15.1 Introduction

The main purpose of this analysis on wrapped sticks is to develop the techniques for calculating the contact pressure and to indicate the formal methods of attack on the problem. The following treatment of the wrapped stick sets aside the complications of slippage caused by variation in wrapping tension and inter-layer forces by treating the wrapped tip as a pre-stressed spherical ball. Therefore, in this treatment the static state of pre-stress applied to the tip by the wrapping process is not modified by slippage during the impact. This state will however change gradually with time as the tip rubber ages (oxidizes), as the stick is used and as slippage redistributes the internal stresses (all part of aging).

13.15.2 The Contact Area

The shape of the contact area between tip and note depends on the tip design as illustrated in Figure 13.39. The wrapped stick with cylindrical tip produces a contact area resembling a distorted ½ ellipse as shown in Figure 13.39(a). The contact area for this design is usually small. For the single wrap tips, the stick maker usually sands the edge of the tip giving it a rounded shape. This increases the contact area by giving it a more elliptical shape as shown in Figure 13.39(b). Tips with a ball-like shape as in Figure 13.39(c) produce circular shaped contact areas.

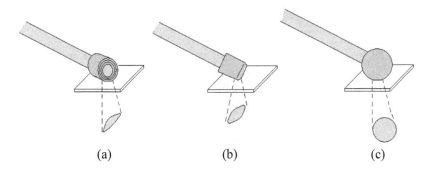

Fig. 13.39. Contact areas for various tip designs produced by the author's stick print method.

Elliptical and other non-circular shapes can be represented by an equivalent circular contact area which produces the same contact-force. In all cases, the pressure distribution arising from the distortion of the layers on impact maximizes at the center and falls to zero along the boundary of the contact area. Smaller contact areas can be realized in the designs of Figure 13.39 (a) and (b) as discussed in Section 13.12.3.

13.15.3 Pressure Distribution

It is assumed that (i) the contact area is circular and (ii) during impact the pressure distribution due to pre-stress within the distorted region bounded by the contact area is similar in form to that arising directly from compression and restitution as illustrated in Figure 13.40 (compare with Figure 13.11) where z and x are position coordinates. In support of (ii), there is no compelling physical reason for the two pressure distributions appearing in the same volume of rubber to be sensibly different. Physically, the two pressure distributions (fields) must be additive.

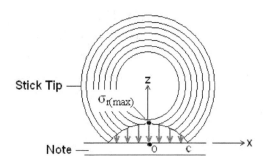

Fig. 13.40. Pressure distribution within a wrapped tip distorted on impact.

As a result, the equation for the combined pressure distribution is a modification of equation (13.12) given by

$$P_z(x) = \begin{cases} (\sigma_{z0} + \sigma_{pre})\sqrt{1 - \dfrac{x^2}{c^2}}, & \text{for } x < c \\ 0, & \text{for } x \geq c. \end{cases} \quad (13.161)$$

where

$$\sigma_{pre} \doteq \sigma_{r(max)}$$

is *the pre-stress for the wrapped stick fully compressed during impact* and σ_{z0} is the normal stress (defined by equation (13.10)) in the absence of pre-stress (and where the symbol '$\doteq$' means 'defined as'). This definition assumes implicitly that the elastic modulus E_s is unaffected by the pre-stress which in turn requires $\sigma_{pre} \ll E_s$. This latter requirement is met for the pre-stress levels obtained on the wrapped sticks.

Repeating the analysis for the contact force with the tip mechanical resistance included gives

$$F_c = m_s\omega^2 R_s w^p + \frac{4\pi}{3}\sigma_{pre} R_s^2 w + r_{ms} R_s v, \quad (13.162)$$

and

$$F_{max} = \underbrace{m_s\omega^2 R_s w_{max}^P}_{\text{impulsive term}} + \underbrace{\frac{4\pi}{3}\sigma_{pre} R_s^2 w_{max}}_{\text{pre-stress term}} \quad (13.163)$$

At maximum compression, the tip velocity is zero ($v = 0$).

13.15.4 General Impact Dynamics with Pre-Stress and Hand Action Included

In the sketch below the initial stick velocity on impact V_0 is directed vertically downwards and the retrieval force F_H acts vertically upward. In all configurations F_H and V_0 lie along the normal to the note surface at the point of impact. If by virtue of the pan face being inclined to the horizontal, the normal makes an angle of ϕ to the vertical, the weight $m_s g$ entering the equations must be replaced by $m_s g \cos\phi$. For the nine-bass where some pans are arranged with their skirt axis horizontal ($\phi = 90°$), there will be no stick weight contribution to the impact force.

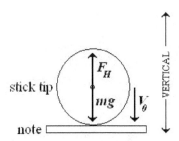

In any complete treatment of the stick-note problem the hand action must be included for it is only in this way that one can include the freedom of the player to control and execute the desired impact. Technically, this means that F_H is an arbitrary force function. Musically on the other hand, F_H must be well defined in its magnitude, duration and timing. This is another subtle aspect of the stick-note interaction.

Equation (13.51a) must be modified accordingly, beginning with

$$\frac{d^2 w}{dt^2} = -\omega^2 w^p - \frac{4\pi\sigma_{pre} R_s}{3 m_s} w - \frac{r_{ms}}{m_s}\frac{dw}{dt} + \frac{g\cos\phi}{R_s} - \frac{F_H}{m_s R_s}, \qquad (13.164)$$

$$\frac{d^2 w}{dt^2} = v\frac{dv}{dw},$$

$$v\frac{dv}{dw} = -\omega^2 w^p - \frac{4\pi\sigma_{pre} R_s}{3 m_s} w - \frac{r_{ms}}{m_s}\frac{dw}{dt} + \frac{g\cos\phi}{R_s} - \frac{F_H}{m_s R_s}, \qquad (13.165)$$

where F_H is positive for a 'lifting' upward force or negative for a 'pressing' downward force. The freedom of the player in striking the note in any manner that seems fit is expressed here by the arbitrary nature of the force function F_H. *In choosing a suitable function however, one should be guided by normal hand actions of the good player and the type of pan being played.* From equation (13.165) one gets

in compression

$$\int_{v_0}^{0} v\,dv = -\omega^2 \int_{0}^{w_{max}} w^{p_c}\,dw - \frac{4\pi\sigma_{pre}R_s}{3m_s}\int_{0}^{w_{ma}} w\,dw - \frac{r_{ms}}{m_s}\int_{0}^{w_{max}}vdw\bigg|_{comp} + \frac{g\cos\phi}{R_s}\int_{0}^{w_{max}} dw - \frac{1}{m_s R_s}\int_{0}^{w_{max}} F_H\,dw$$

$$v_0^2 = \frac{2\omega^2}{p_c+1} w_{max}^{p_c+1} + \frac{4\pi\sigma_{pre}R_s}{3m_s} w_{max}^2 + \frac{2r_{ms}}{m_s}\int_{0}^{w_{max}}vdw\bigg|_{comp} - \frac{2g\cos\phi}{R_s} w_{max} + \frac{2}{m_s R_s}\int_{0}^{w_{max}} F_H\,dw,$$

(13.166a)

in restitution

$$\int_{0}^{v_r} v\,dv = -\omega^2 \int_{w_{max}}^{\delta_w} w^{p_r}\,dw - \frac{4\pi\sigma_{pre}R_s}{3m_s}\int_{w_{max}}^{\delta_w} w\,dw - \frac{r_{ms}}{m_s}\int_{w_{max}}^{\delta_w}vdw\bigg|_{rest} + \frac{g\cos\phi}{R_s}\int_{w_{max}}^{\delta_w} dw - \frac{1}{m_s R_s}\int_{w_{max}}^{\delta_w} F_H\,dw$$

$$v_r^2 = \frac{2\omega^2}{p_r+1}(w_{max}^{p_r+1} - \delta_w^{p_r+1}) + \frac{4\pi\sigma_{pre}R_s}{3m_s}(w_{max}^2 - \delta_m^2) + \frac{2r_{ms}}{m_s}\int_{\delta_w}^{w_{max}}vdw\bigg|_{rest}$$

$$-\frac{2g\cos\phi}{R_s}(w_{max} - \delta_w) + \frac{2}{m_s R_s}\int_{\delta_w}^{w_{max}} F_H\,dw,$$

(13.166b)

where v_0 and v_r are the dimensionless forms of the impact velocity V_0 and the rebound velocity V_r given by $v_0 = V_0/R_s$, $v_r = V_r/R_s$, respectively. To complete the integral $\int vdw$ we use the following approximation, with good results.

Solutions for the Integral $\int vdw$

The special case $p_c = p_r = 1$, gives a ½-sine solution for the tip displacement-time history. This solution also gives good results in other applications so it is useful and instructive to obtain a solution of the integral $\int vdw$ for this case. If we assume

$$w = w_{max}\sin(\omega t),$$

then we can write for the velocity

in Compression: $\quad v = v_0 \cos(\omega t),\ 0 \leq \omega t \leq \pi/2$,

in Restitution: $\quad v = v_r \cos(\omega t),\ \pi/2 \leq \omega t \leq \pi - \delta_w / w_{max}$.

The range limit $\pi - \delta_w / w_{max}$ at the end of the restitution phase is found in the following way. Without hysteresis, the restitution phase is completed when the tip is fully restored to its original shape. This occurs when

$$\omega t_{break} = \pi,$$

where t_{break} is the time to break contact *without* hysteresis. However, with hysteresis, restitution ends (contact is broken) with the tip retaining a residual compression δ_w given by

$$\delta_w = w_{max} \sin(\pi - \omega t'_{break}), \qquad (13.167)$$

where t'_{break} is the time to break contact when hysteresis is present. Since $\delta_w / w_{max} \ll 1$, equation (13.167) is satisfied for

$$\omega t'_{break} = \pi - \delta_w / w_{max}.$$

It can be shown from the series expansion for $\sin(\omega t'_{break})$ that this result is accurate to order $\left(\frac{\delta_w}{w_{max}}\right)^3$ which can be compactly written as $O\left(\frac{\delta_w}{w_{max}}\right)^3$. The result ($\omega t'_{break} < \pi$) shows that with hysteresis, contact is broken just short of complete restoration of the tip to its original shape.

These equations give

$$\int v\, dw = v_0 w_{max} \omega \int \cos^2(\omega t)\, dt$$

On making the substitution $\theta = \omega t$ and writing $\cos^2 \theta = \frac{1}{2}(1 + \cos(2\theta))$ one gets for the integral in the compression phase

$$\left| \int_0^{w_{max}} v dw \right|_{comp} = \frac{v_0 w_{max}}{2} \int_0^{\pi/2} (1+\cos(2\theta)) d\theta$$

$$= \frac{\pi v_0 w_{max}}{4}.$$

Finally,

$$\frac{1}{v_0 w_{max}} \left| \int_0^{w_{max}} v dw \right|_{comp} = \frac{\pi}{4}. \qquad (13.168)$$

Similarly, for the integral in the restitution phase, one gets

$$\left| \int_{\delta_w}^{w_{max}} v dw \right|_{rest} = \frac{v_r w_{max}}{2} \int_{\pi - \frac{\delta_w}{w_{max}}}^{\pi/2} (1+\cos(2\theta)) d\theta$$

$$= -\frac{\pi v_r w_{max}}{4} + v_r \delta_w.$$

Finally,

$$\frac{1}{v_r w_{max}} \left| \int_{\delta_w}^{w_{max}} v dw \right|_{rest} = -\frac{\pi}{4} + \frac{\delta_w}{w_{max}}. \qquad (13.169)$$

Since the compression-restitution time history for $(p_c, p_r) > 1$ is not exactly a ½-sine function, the exact solution in the general case will yield a factor slightly different from $\pi/4$ which appears in both equations (13.168) and (13.169). However, the small term, δ_w/w_{max}, in the restitution phase will remain essentially unchanged. We verify this by noting that for low levels of losses, using equation (13.95b) the integrals can be expressed as:

In Compression $p_c \geq 1$;

$$\frac{1}{v_0 w_{max}} \left| \int_0^{w_{max}} v dw \right|_{comp} = \int_0^1 (1 - x^{p_c+1})^{\frac{1}{2}} dx$$

which can be integrated numerically to yield

$$\frac{1}{v_0 w_{max}} \left| \int_0^{w_{max}} v\,dw \right|_{comp} = \begin{cases} \frac{\pi}{4}, & p_c = 1 \\ \frac{\pi}{4} + 0.02282, & p_c = 1.33 \end{cases}.$$

In Restitution $p_r \geq 1$;

$$\frac{1}{v_r w_{max}} \left| \int_{\delta_w}^{w_{max}} v\,dw \right|_{rest} = -\int_0^1 (1 - x^{p_r+1})^{\frac{1}{2}} dx + \int_0^{\frac{\delta_w}{w_{max}}} (1 - x^{p_r+1})^{\frac{1}{2}} dx.$$

Solving the first integral on the right side numerically and expanding the integrand in the second integral as a series before integrating then retaining only the dominant term (since $\delta w/w_{max} \ll 1$) gives

$$\frac{1}{v_r w_{max}} \left| \int_{\delta_w}^{w_{max}} v\,dw \right|_{rest} = -\begin{cases} \frac{\pi}{4}, & p_r = 1 \\ \frac{\pi}{4} + 0.04470, & p_r = 1.76 \\ \frac{\pi}{4} + 0.06842, & p_r = 2.3 \end{cases} + \frac{\delta_w}{w_{max}} - O\left(\frac{\delta_w}{w_{max}}\right)^{p_r+2}.$$

By comparing these results with equation (13.168) and equation (13.169), it is clear that the ½-sine approximation gives the required values for the integrals to acceptable levels of accuracy (within approx 8% error) for all the p-indices found on the stick tips.

13.15.5 Details of the Hand Action and Stick Retrieval — Advanced and Delayed Stick Retrieval

The force F_H entering these equations must be applied *during* the impact. Forces applied to the stick before contact only serve to modify the stick trajectory prior to impact and to vary V_0. In the normal playing action on the instrument, when it is necessary to produce a soft, muted tone, F_H is used to 'press down' (lightly enough) the stick unto the note. When used in this fashion the direction of the force must be reversed to retrieve the stick. F_H is used most often as a 'retrieving' force. As a retrieving force it is applied only after contact is made (after the 'make') and maintained for (at least) the remaining duration of the impact (up to the 'break'). The player decides the moment of application of F_H and the magnitude of F_H. As noted earlier, in the strictest technical sense, F_H is entirely arbitrary, being left to the discretion and purpose of the player. There is no general solution for the integral containing F_H in the integrand but reasonable, practical assumptions can be made on possible forms of the function F_H based on the following:

(i) When F_H is zero during impact, the stick simply falls towards the note, striking it with some initial velocity V_0. Any non-zero F_H applied to the stick before impact serves only to change this initial impact velocity. When however, F_H is non-zero during impact the situation is different.

(ii) The hand action force F_H is used by the player to modify the timbre of the note by making subtle changes to the relative strengths of the partials. To achieve this, the contact-time τ_c is varied. The longest contact time is obtained when $F_H = 0$ or when F_H is directed towards the note to further prolong the impact. Increasing contact times decreases the relative strengths of the higher partials (and high untuned modes). All retrieving actions shorten the contact times and increase the relative strengths of the higher partials (and high untuned modes).

(iii) When F_H is applied, the magnitude of the maximum contact force is modified depending on the time of application during impact. The trained player is consciously aware of this effect. By the auditory and tactile feedback available to him, he makes the necessary adjustments to F_H during play to produce the desired impact force.

(iv) Contact times are very short, lasting only a fraction of a millisecond to a few milliseconds at most. *This short time does not allow the playing action for each generated tone to be complicated.* For the experienced player the playing action is, for the most part, *pre-determined* for each required style of play and for each musical composition or parts thereof. *Modifications are subtle. To put it simple, the trained panist knows how to select and use a pair of sticks.*

(v) It is truly marvelous that while hand action during contact for each sounding note is simple, the combination of a series of impacts used to generate a musical *sentence* or *phrase* can be quite complex. It is this complexity that fascinates both player and listener. *This complexity belongs to the music.*

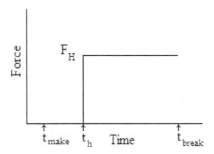

Fig. 13.41. Hand Action applied as a step function at time t_h between make and break.

(vi) Ours is the simple task. A simple and effective form for the hand action is the application of a constant retrieval force after the 'make' but before the tip reaches maximum compression. F_H therefore takes on the form of a *step* or *Heaviside function* as shown in Figure 13.41. For a given impact velocity this has the effect of reducing both the maximum contact force and the contact-time. If the retrieval force is applied after maximum compression then the maximum contact force is unaffected but the contact-time is reduced. The latter is a case of '*Delayed stick retrieval*,' while the former can be called '*Advanced stick retrieval.*'

(vii) These two retrieval options should be given formal definitions:

Advanced stick retrieval occurs when the retrieval force is applied *before* the contact force maximizes. The retrieval therefore commences in the stick compression phase and may also be called '*early stick retrieval*'.

Delayed stick retrieval occurs *after* the contact force has maximized. This retrieval commences in the restitution phase and may be called '*late stick retrieval.*'

Neglecting the body antics and stick waving that usually accompany the playing of the instrument, neither of which contributes to the stick-note impact although it has an 'impact' on the audience, normal hand action consists mainly of a rapid acceleration of the stick towards the note followed by a quick retrieval of the stick. On the low-end pans, the hand action usually allows the stick to complete its free compression and restitution from 'make' to 'break' (see the sketches in Figure 13.41) before the stick is retrieved. However, on all pans especially on the top-end pans the panist may choose to quickly retrieve the stick before the stick breaks contact with the note on its own volition. This action reduces the contact-time τ_c of the impact, which by equation (13.66b) means that the tip stiffness is effectively increased. By this deliberate action the panist makes the stick tip perform as a stiffer tip which extends the frequency response of the stick-note system by increasing the cut-off-frequency $f_c = 1/2\tau_c$, allowing for the generation of stronger higher partials.

It is indeed interesting that the hand action of the panist can modify in a dynamic way the effective properties of the stick. The slow response that may otherwise arise in the restitution phase of the tip due to hysteresis can be removed by rapidly withdrawing the stick after impact is made. When the panist reverses the direction of the hand action F_H in order to lift the stick away from the note, from the moment that the stick breaks contact with the note the motion of the stick is arbitrary — the panist can wave the stick around before the next impact. *The equations derived here in no way remove the freedom of the panist in choosing the style, manner or intensity of play.*

The sketches of Figure 13.42(a) show, in the ½-Sine approximation, how the application of a retrieving force (essentially directed upwards away from the note) at times t_{h1}, t_{h2} or t_{h3} causes an early break with the impacted note. Instead of the free path (solid line in Figure 13.42(a)) between 'make' and 'break' the force history is made to follow a quicker route towards the break (characterized by $F_c = 0$) as show by the dotted lines in Figure 13.42(a).

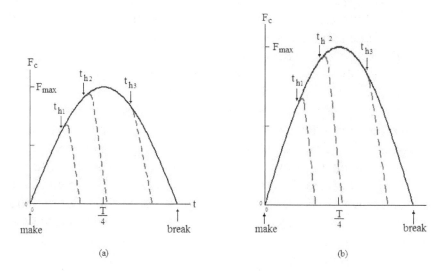

Fig. 13.42. Contact force time histories. (a) Low impact velocity. (b) For larger impact velocity.

There is a short delay after t_h for F_c to begin its descent to zero (refer to Figure 13.42(a) for details). This delay (in the response) occurs because the point of application of the hand action force F_H is at the center of mass of the stick tip while the contact force F_c appears at the moving stick-note interface. This delay is longer for softer, less responsive sticks. When the time of application of the retrieval force t_h satisfies $t_h < T/4$ the maximum force is reduced resulting in reduced intensity of the generated sound. For short retrieval times ($t_h < T/4$), the panist can compensate for the expected reduction in maximum contact force by increasing the impact velocity V_0 to restore the force as shown in Figure 13.42(b). *This becomes a 'natural' action of the trained panist.* When $t_h \geq T/4$ the maximum force is unchanged.

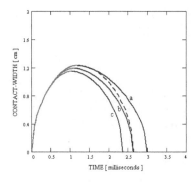 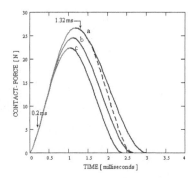

Fig. 13.43. Time histories of Contact-width and Contact-force for four cases of guitar or cello pan stick impacts.

Figure 13.43 shows a set of model impacts on the guitar or cello pan obtained by numerically solving equation (13.164) with $E_s = 2 \times 10^6$ N·m^{-2}, $\sigma_{pre} = 0$, $R_s = 0.015$ m, $p_c = .33$, $p_r = 1.76$, $V_0 = 1.48$ m·s^{-1}, $r_{ms} = 0$, $Cos\phi = 0$. Hand action forces F_H in cases (b) and (c) are applied 0.2 ms after 'make' and maintained until 'break'.

For cases (a), (b), and (c) in Figure 13.42 the results are:

(a) $F_H = 0$ (*stick rebounds on its own volition*), make-to-break duration $\tau_{m-t-b} = 2.99$ ms, $\tau_c = 1.58$ ms and $F_{max} = 26.56$ N. Cut-off frequency $f_c = 316.46$ Hz, just above $\mathbf{E}^b{}_4$ at 311.13 Hz.

For the case plotted as a dashed curve (- - -), parameters are the same as in case (a) except that the force $F_H = 4.77$ N is applied 1.32 ms after the 'make'. Since the force maximizes 1.04 ms after the 'make', this means that the retrieval force is applied 0.28 ms into the restitution phase. In this case, only the time duration in the restitution phase is affected. Here, $\tau_{m-t-b} = 2.64$ ms, $\tau_c = 1.49$ ms and $F_{max} = 26.56$ N (same as for case (a)).

(b) $F_H = 2.17$ N, $\tau_{m-t-b} = 2.62$ ms, $\tau_c = 1.40$ ms and $F_{max} = 24.53$ N. Cut-off frequency $f_c = 357.14$ Hz, just above $\mathbf{F}_4$ at 349.26 Hz.

(c) $F_H = 4.77$ N, $\tau_{m-t-b} = 2.38$ ms, $\tau_c = 1.29$ ms and $F_{max} = 22.37$ N. Cut-off frequency $f_c = 387.60$ Hz, just below $\mathbf{G}_4$ at 392.00 Hz.

These impacts with $\sigma_{pre} = 0$, were designed to determine, specifically, the effects of hand action on this stick. We make some further observations:

(i) A *delayed retrieval* of the stick shortens the contact-time but leaves the maximum force unaffected. *The experienced panist will acquire knowledge of this fact through experience and use it to achieve the desired tonality changes.*
(ii) Greater contact forces and lower contact times are possible by introducing some pre-stress (say by *re-wrapping the wrapped stick with greater wrapping tension and/or change of banding rubber*).
(iii) Observe that the make-to-break duration changes more rapidly with F_H than the 'rise time' from 'make' to F_{max}. This is consistent with the observed increase in the degree of symmetry of the profiles as F_H increases.

The above examples partly demonstrate the range of impact control available to the panist. *The panist can therefore vary the two main aspects of stick-note impact (i) the impact force and (ii) the frequency band-limiting applied to the higher modes.*

13.15.6 Solutions of the Integral $\int f_H dw$; Advanced Retrieval and Delayed Retrieval

If the step-function form of the hand action introduced in the example above is used here, one has to decide at what point after the 'make' to apply F_H. If one decides to commence retrieval in the compression phase (*Advanced stick retrieval*) when the compression reaches a fraction f of the maximum one gets

$$\text{for compression} \qquad \int_{fw_{max}}^{w_{max}} F_H \, dw = F_H (1 - f) w_{max},$$

for restitution $\quad \int_{\delta_w}^{w_{\max}} F_H dw = F_H(w_{\max} - \delta_w).$

Note that it is the fraction f being defined here not w_{max} which is yet to be determined.

If the retrieval begins in the restitution phase (*Delayed stick retrieval*) one gets

for compression $\quad \int F_H dw = 0,$

for restitution $\quad \int_{\delta_w}^{fw_{\max}} F_H dw = F_H(fw_{\max} - \delta_w).$

This procedure appears at first to be somewhat artificial. So what is the procedure followed by the player? During practice, the player strikes a sequence of notes in the execution of a new phrase and repeats the phrase a few times, each time refining the impact for each note. The player, using his musical experience, then settles for the best impact for each note. To use this procedure here, one must perform a series of numerical integrations on equation (13.164) (and the full equations for the excited note vibrations for completeness) with each solution corresponding to a different choice of function F_H. Copying the player, by the tone generated, one then chooses the hand action best suited to the musical needs. But this also, only comes by experience. With some computational experience one can also decide on the optimum fraction f and force *function* F_H. *Variations* are introduced by switching among several force functions thereby changing on each execution ever so small changes in timbre. Our procedure is therefore not artificial; instead it matches the real action of the player. Other techniques related to the impact point on the note surface will be discussed in later Sections.

13.15.7 The Compression and Restitution Formulas

By including the shank absorption losses $E_{SA}^{\{comp\}}$ and $E_{SA}^{\{rest\}}$ that occur during compression and restitution respectfully, from equation (13.166a) and equation (13.166b) one obtains

Compression Phase:

$$V_0^2 = \left(\frac{2}{p_c+1}\right)(\omega R_s)^2 w_{max}^{p_c+1} + \frac{4\pi\sigma_{pre} R_s^3}{3m_s} w_{max}^2 + \left(\frac{\pi r_{ms} R_s V_0}{2m_s} - 2R_s g\cos\phi\right) w_{max}$$

$$+ \frac{2R_s}{m_s}\int_0^{w_{max}} F_H\, dw + \frac{2E_{SA}^{\{comp\}}}{m_s}.$$

(13.170)

Restitution Phase:

$$V_r^2 = \left(\frac{2}{p_r+1}\right)(\omega R_s)^2 (w_{max}^{p_r+1} - \delta_w^{p_r+1}) + \frac{4\pi\sigma_{pre} R_s^3}{3m_s}(w_{max}^2 - \delta_w^2) - \left(\frac{\pi r_{ms} R_s V_r}{2m_s} + 2gR_s\right) w_{max}$$

$$+ \left(\frac{2r_{ms} R_s V_r}{m_s} + 2R_s g\cos\phi\right)\delta_w + \frac{2R_s}{m_s}\int_{\delta_w}^{w_{max}} F_H\, dw - \frac{2E_{SA}^{\{rest\}}}{m_s}.$$

(13.171)

By adopting the step-function form for the hand action there are two cases to consider; (1) retrieval begins during compression, (2) retrieval begins during restitution. Since the end of compression is the beginning of restitution, the third case where retrieval begins at the instant of maximum compression ($f = 1$) is covered by case (1) and case (2).

To best cover these cases, the variable fraction f is replaced by two new variables f_{cm} and f_r for compression (cm) and restitution (r) respectively, where:

Case 1; Retrieval begins during the Compression Phase ($f_r=1$, $0 \leq f_{cm} \leq 1$)

Case 2; Retrieval begins during the Restitution Phase ($f_{cm}=1$, $0 \leq f_r \leq 1$)

Case 3; Retrieval begins at the end of the Compression Phase $f_{cm} = f_r = 1$

Compression Phase:

$$V_0^2 = \left(\frac{2}{p_c+1}\right)(\omega R_s)^2 w_{max}^{p_c+1} + \frac{4\pi\sigma_{pre}R_s^3}{3m_s} w_{max}^2 + \frac{2E_{SA}^{\{comp\}}}{m_s}$$

$$+ \left(\frac{\pi r_{ms} R_s V_0}{2m_s} - 2R_s g \cos\phi + \frac{2R_s}{m_s} F_H(1-f_{cm})\right) w_{max}.$$

(13.172)

Restitution Phase:

$$V_r^2 = \left(\frac{2}{p_r+1}\right)(\omega R_s)^2 (w_{max}^{p_r+1} - \delta_w^{p_r+1}) + \frac{4\pi\sigma_{pre}R_s^3}{3m_s}(w_{max}^2 - \delta_w^2) - \frac{2E_{SA}^{\{rest\}}}{m_s}$$

$$- \left(\frac{\pi r_{ms} R_s V_r}{2m_s} + 2R_s g \cos\phi - \frac{2R_s f_r}{m_s} F_H\right) w_{max} + \left(\frac{2r_{ms} R_s V_r}{m_s} + 2R_s g \cos\phi - \frac{2R_s}{m_s} F_H\right)\delta_w.$$

(13.173)

Case (1) is typical of the playing action on the high-end pans while case (2) applies mainly to the low-end pans.

Note: Equations (13.172) and (13.173) can be used to show that for $p_r = p_c = 1$ *(no hysteresis), zero pre-stress, no tip weight contribution, but with damping included, the rebound velocity is given by* $V_r \cong V_0\sqrt{1 - 2\pi\alpha/\omega}$, *same as in Section 13.11.6. This means that for the tip with $p = 1$ and with damping, the COR is given by* $\varepsilon_r \cong \sqrt{1 - 2\pi\alpha/\omega}$.

13.15.8 The Stick Compression Formula

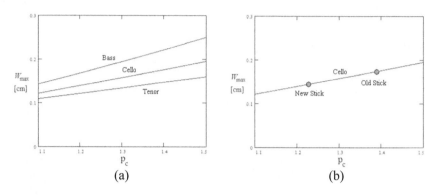

Fig. 13.44. (a) Typical plot of tip compression W_{max} (in centimeters) versus p_c for sticks on the bass, cello and tenor with $\sigma_{pre} = 0$ and $r_m = 0$. (b) Progression to the right as a typical Cello stick in use, ages.

It is interesting and informative to look first of all, at how the compression w_{max} depends on the compressive p-index p_c. As a stick ages, the rubber material acquires larger values for the compressive and restitutive p-indices. As a result the tip will appear softer on impact and the compression will increase for a given impact velocity. Figure 13.44 shows a plot of equation (13.174) for typical bass, cello and tenor sticks with an impact velocity of $V_0 = 1.5$ ms^{-1}. The plots appear approximately linear over the small range of the p_c index. The increase in compression with p_c and hence with age, is clearly shown. *Generally, as a stick is used and ages, its position on the plot will gradually move towards the right. One finds that it becomes easier to compress a stick tip as the stick ages — the tip becomes softer.*

When $\sigma_{pre} = 0$ and $r_m = 0$, equation (13.170) gives

$$w_{max} = \left(\frac{p_c+1}{2}\right)^{\frac{1}{p_c+1}} \left(\frac{V_0}{\omega R_s}\right)^{\frac{2}{p_c+1}}. \qquad (13.174)$$

This solution is denoted by w_0

$$w_0 = \left(\frac{p_c+1}{2}\right)^{\frac{1}{p_c+1}} \left(\frac{V_0}{\omega R_s}\right)^{\frac{2}{p_c+1}}. \tag{13.175}$$

Therefore, in this case

$$\frac{w_{max}}{w_0} = 1.$$

Returning to the general case with pre-stress and internal losses, with $m_s = \frac{4}{3}\pi \rho_s R_s^3$ we define the new parameters

$$a = \frac{\sigma_{pre} w_0^2}{\rho_s V_0^2}, \quad b = \frac{1}{p_c+1}, \quad c = \frac{3 r_{ms} w_0}{8 \rho_s R_s^2 V_0} - \frac{2 R_s w_0 g \cos\phi}{V_0^2} + \frac{3 F_H (1 - f_{cm}) w_0}{2\pi \rho_s R_s^2 V_0^2}, \quad g_c = \frac{3 E_{SA}^{\{comp\}}}{2\pi \rho_s R_s^3 V_0^2},$$

where a is a measure of the pre-stress for a given tip material and impact velocity; b is a simple function of the compressive p-index; c is a measure of the mechanical resistance of the tip, tip weight contribution and hand action; g_c is the fraction of impact energy absorbed by the shank during compression. These parameters allow Equation (13.172) to be written in the form

$$\left(\frac{w_{max}}{w_0}\right)^{\frac{1}{b}} + a\left(\frac{w_{max}}{w_0}\right)^2 + c\frac{w_{max}}{w_0} + g_c = 1. \tag{13.176}$$

With $x \doteq w_{max}/w_0$, equation (13.176) can be written as

$$a x^2 + x^{\frac{1}{b}} + c x + g_c - 1 = 0. \tag{13.177}$$

Note: As the alert reader would have noticed, I have defined the variable x in different ways in the analyses found in this book. I have chosen to do this rather than use a new symbol (possibly Greek) each time. One can easily run out of new symbols in work such as this. I believe the reader can easily keep track of the meaning attached to x in each case. I also believe most readers would prefer to see an algebraic equation written in the familiar variable (or 'unknown') x.

Equation (13.177) is the *Stick Compression Formula*. The original second order differential equation (13.162) describing the stick tip compression during impact has now been reduced to the algebraic expression (13.177). Increasing the pre-stress σ_{pre}, increases the coefficient a, which in turn, *reduces* the compression x — the tip appears harder to compress.

The general equations for the contact width and contact area in terms of x are

$$\varphi_c = R_s\sqrt{8w_0 x}, \quad A_c = 2\pi R_s^2 w_0 x. \quad (13.178a, b)$$

13.15.9 The Stick Restitution Formula

The *Stick Restitution Formula* will contain the unknown rebound velocity V_r. Defining the new parameters $b_r = \frac{1}{p_r+1}$, $g_r = \frac{2E_{SA}^{\{rest\}}}{m_s V_0^2}$ (for the fraction of impact energy absorbed by the shank during restitution),

$$c_1 = \frac{3 r_{ms} w_0}{8\rho_s R_s^2 V_0}, \quad c_2 = \left(\frac{2R_s w_0 g \cos\phi}{V_0^2} - \frac{3 f_r F_H w_0}{2\pi \rho_s R_s^2 V_0^2}\right), \quad c_3 = \left(\frac{2R_s w_0 g \cos\phi}{V_0^2} - \frac{3 F_H w_0}{2\pi \rho_s R_s^2 V_0^2}\right),$$

and new variable $y \doteq \frac{\delta_w}{w_0}$, with $\varepsilon_r^* = V_r/V_0$ one gets from equation (13.171) the *Stick Restitution Formula*

$$a(x^2 - y^2) + \left(x^{\frac{1}{br}} - y^{\frac{1}{br}}\right) - (c_1 \varepsilon_r^* + c_2)x + \left(\tfrac{4}{\pi} c_1 \varepsilon_r^* + c_3\right)y - g_r - \varepsilon_r^{*2} = 0.$$

(13.179)

Typically: $y = \delta_w/w_0 \approx 0.03$ *Small Mini Sticks*,
≈ 0.12 *Bass Sticks*.

The shank absorption parameters g_c and g_r are small fractions that are not easily measured but can be reduced as discussed in Section

13.12. The variable y takes on a constant value for a given impact and is determined by a measured or assumed value for the residual compression δ_w. Once y is known and x is obtained as a root of equation (13.177), the value for ε_r^* is obtained by solving equation (13.179) as a quadratic in ε_r^*.

In fact, the Stick Restitution Formula is essentially a formula for the COR ε_r. But there is a caveat. The COR for an object impacting a given surface is normally defined without the object being acted upon by an external agency during impact. In our case, during impact, the stick is acted upon by the player and by some component of the earth's gravitational attraction (the weight). For this reason, the symbol for the COR in equation (13.179) is 'starred' with an asterisk. The value ε_r^* is really the '*effective COR*' (eCOR) which is dependent on the player's hand action. To recover the value for the COR ε_r, one must set $F_H = 0$ and $\phi = 90°$, which results in $c = c_1$, $c_2 = 0$, $c_3 = 0$. This gives

$$a\left(x^2 - y^2\right) + \left(x^{\frac{1}{b_r}} - y^{\frac{1}{b_r}}\right) - c\varepsilon_r\left(x - \frac{4y}{\pi}\right) - g_r - \varepsilon_r^2 = 0. \tag{13.180}$$

The value of x obtained as a root of equation (13.177) must be substituted in equation (13.180) (a quadratic in ε_r) to solve for the COR ε_r. The COR is the real positive root of equation (13.180). Readers should observe that we have transformed the original second order differential equations (shown in integral form in equations (13.166a, b)) into a pair of algebraic equations in equation (13.177) and equation (13.179) or in reduced form, equation (13.180).

13.15.10 Inclusion of Absorption Mats for Experimental purposes

Stick (tip) resistive losses and Shank Absorption losses occur naturally. Although they have been seen to act negatively on the impact, they do have real use in bringing the transient motion of the rubber tip to a quick end. As natural effects they are useful in this respect. But it is somewhat difficult to vary these losses for experimental purposes. This is the reason for using the absorption mats in Section 13.20 when it is necessary to investigate the effects of damping on stick behavior. While it is not a recommended procedure for the instrument, the effect of the absorption mat (or lossy overlay) can very easily be included in the Compression and Restitution equations in the following way: If the mat absorption losses that occur during compression and restitution are represented by $E_{MA}^{\{comp\}}$ and $E_{MA}^{\{rest\}}$ respectfully, then the terms g_c and g_r can be rewritten as

$$g_c = \frac{2\left(E_{SA}^{\{comp\}} + E_{MA}^{\{comp\}}\right)}{m_s V_0^2}, \quad g_r = \frac{2\left(E_{SA}^{\{rest\}} + E_{MA}^{\{rest\}}\right)}{m_s V_0^2}.$$

In addition to their application to the mats, these modifications can be used to investigate the sticks with felt overlay.

13.16 Solutions for the Stick Compression Formula

The non-mathematical reader may defer the reading of the following Section on the Solution Methods. Anyone interested in designing sticks will however find the analysis very useful.

13.16.1 Solution Methods

The required root of equation (13.177) can be found by a number of ways (i) by *Iteration*, (ii) by transforming (13.177) into an *Infinitely Nested Radical* and (iii) by writing (13.177) as a *Recurrence Formula*.

Method (i): Iteration

One sets up the iteration function

$$f(x) = ax^2 + x^{\frac{1}{b}} + cx + g_c - 1,$$

where $0 < x < 1$ for pan sticks. Let the root $x = x_0$ of $f(x) = 0$ exist in the vicinity of $x = x_1$ (an initial *trial value* or an '*approximate zero*' of $f(x)$). A safe starting value is $x_1 = 0.5$. Then in a sequence of steps (n = 1, 2, ...) update the trial value using the Newton-Raphson method

$$x_{n+1} = x_n - \frac{f(x_n)}{f'(x_n)}, \text{ where } f'(x_n) = 2ax_n + \frac{1}{b}x_n^{\frac{1}{b}-1} + c,$$

until the value x_n converges to the desired root. The process can be terminated when $|f(x_n)| \leq \kappa$, where κ is a small number representing the tolerance of the iteration. For greater accuracy set a tighter tolerance (smaller values of κ, say 10^{-4}, 10^{-5}, 10^{-6}). At each step (each value of n), the approximation to the root must improve.

NEWTON–RAPHSON ROUTINE implemented in MATHCAD® MathSoft, Inc.

The Stick Compression Formula is solved for a range of values of pre-stress expressed as fractions of the elastic modulus: $\sigma_{pre} = sE$. The dimensionless displacement w_0 is written as w, g_c as gc, while V_0 is written as V, The rubber density is ρ, Young's modulus, E.

DEFINE ALL PARAMETERS
c, b, gc, w etc.
DEFINE RANGE
s := 0.0, 0.01 .. 0.1
DEFINE FUNCTIONS

$$a(s) := \frac{s \cdot E \cdot w^2}{\rho \cdot V^2}$$

$$f(x) := a(s) \cdot x^2 + x^{\frac{1}{b}} + c \cdot x + gc - 1$$

WORK OUT x values in a WHILE loop. Be CAREFUL IN CHOOSING THE STARTING VALUE (estx). Choose estx < 1. Set tolerance: κ = 0.0000001 or any suitably small value.

$$x(s) := \begin{vmatrix} estx \leftarrow 0.5 \\ \text{while } |f(estx)| \geq 0.0000001 \\ \quad estx \leftarrow estx - \frac{f(estx)}{\frac{d}{destx} f(estx)} \end{vmatrix}$$

Calculate maximum displacements: wmax(s) := w·x(s)

The Newton-Raphson method is known to converge to the wrong value unless necessary precautions are taken. To this end, the following conditions are included: Since in our case $f(x)$ is a monotonic function increasing in the interval [0, 1] one finds that

(i) $f'(x)$ does not change sign (where f' denotes first derivative of f with respect to x),

(ii) there is no point of inflection in this interval (this means
$f''(x_n) = 2a + \frac{1}{b}(\frac{1}{b}-1)x_n^{\frac{1}{b}-2}$ does not change sign) and

(iii) $f(x_n)f''(x_n) > 0$, (where f'' denotes second derivative)

therefore the sequence converges to the desired root x_0.

Method (ii): Nested Radical

In the following analysis where *Nesting* is involved, the symbol d will be used to denote the '*depth*' of nesting. To simplify the algebra and to make the development easier to follow, we temporarily set $c = 0$ and $g_c = 0$.

Depth 0 (d = 0): From (13.177), when $\sigma_{pre} = 0$, $c = 0$ and $g_c = 0$, $x = 1$, thus $w_{max} = w_0$.

Higher Depths — Nesting

Solutions of the stick compression equation (13.177) are sought for the pre-stress parameter a in the range $0 \leq a \leq 1$. In the range $0 \leq a \leq 1$, the higher depth equations take a very interesting form. To find these equations, write equation (13.177) in two equivalent forms

$$x^2 = [1-ax^2]^{2b}, \qquad x = [1-ax^2]^b.$$

Substitute the expression for x given by the second equation into the right side of the first equation then continue this process repeatedly. After an infinite number of substitutions one gets

$$x^2 = \left[1 - a\left[1 - a\left[1 - a\left[\ldots\ldots x^2 \ldots\ldots\right]^{2b}\right]^{2b}\right]^{2b}\right]^{2b}. \quad (13.181)$$

The expression on the right side of equation (13.181) is an *Infinitely Nested Radical* ($d = \infty$) with a *seed* x^2 at the heart of the nest. (It is tempting to call 'x^2' the 'egg' in the nest instead of the 'seed' but this would introduce an extraneous and false notion.)

The nested radical extends to infinite *depth* but good results are possible for a *finite depth* (*Finitely Nested Radical*). The seed can be obtained from a solution of lower nesting depth. The zeroth-depth ($d = 0$) solution gives, seed = $x^2 = 1$. This gives good results for the pan stick problem with $0 \leq a \leq 1$. Using the $d = 0$ solution as the seed in the *Depth 6* nest, we find

$$x^2 = \left[1 - a\left[1 - a\left[1 - a\left[1 - a\left[1 - a\left[1 - a\right]^{2b}\right]^{2b}\right]^{2b}\right]^{2b}\right]^{2b}\right]^{2b}. \quad (13.182)$$

This elegant equation is the 'classic form' of a nested radical. In general, the estimate at depth d will be denoted by the *convergent* $x^{\{d\}}$ (do not read this as 'x to the power $\{d\}$'; in this notation, $\{d\}$ is just a superscripted label employed to keep track of the depth) and the corresponding estimate for w_{max} is given by $w_{max}^{\{d\}} = w_0 x^{\{d\}}$. Figure 13.45 shows an example of the convergence of the Nested Radical.

Side Note: *It would have been just as easy for me to have defined the variable b as $p_c + 1$ instead of $\frac{1}{p_c + 1}$. In the early development of the present analysis I had done this but I chose to invert b for the sake of equation (13.182). To me, this equation 'looks better' the way it appears in (13.182).*

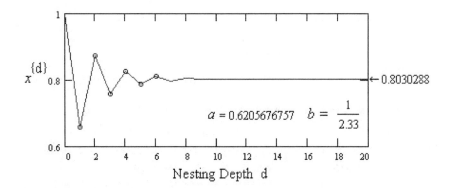

Fig. 13.45. Convergence of $x_{max}^{\{d\}}$ with increasing depth. The first few convergents are identified by the 'o' symbol.

Comment: *In Figure 13.45 and in all such graphical representations of the convergents $x^{\{d\}}$ versus the depth, the solutions are the discrete values located at the abscissas d = 0, 1, 2, 3, …. The lines joining these values on the graph are inserted for convenience to allow the reader to visually follow the trend of the convergents as d increases.*

We now derive an expression by which the exact value may be found. The exact value is that obtained as the depth grows to infinity, $x^{\{d\}} \to x_{exact}$ as $d \to \infty$. One property of the finite depth solution is that as the depth increases the values of the convergents $x^{\{d\}}$ oscillate about the exact value (see Figure 13.45), with $x^{\{d\}} > x_{exact}$ for *even* depth and $x^{\{d\}} < x_{exact}$ for *odd* depth. Hence, x_{exact} lies between $x^{\{d\}}$ and $x^{\{d-1\}}$. For any two consecutive convergents $x = x^{\{d-1\}}$ and $x = x^{\{d\}}$ at least one satisfies

$$|x_{exact} - x| \leq \tfrac{1}{2}|x^{\{d\}} - x^{\{d-1\}}|.$$

One also finds that the convergents to x_{exact} for all $d = 0, 1, 2, 3, …$ satisfy

$$\tfrac{1}{2}(x^{\{2d+1\}} + x^{\{2d\}}) > x_{exact} > \tfrac{1}{2}(x^{\{2d+2\}} + x^{\{2d+1\}}),$$

where $\tfrac{1}{2}(x^{\{d-1\}} + x^{\{d\}})$ is the *Running Mean* or *Moving Average (MA)*.

From these results one can write with rapidly increasing accuracy as *d* increases

$$x_{exact} = \tfrac{1}{2}(x^{\{d-1\}} + x^{\{d\}}), \qquad (13.183)$$

or if one wants to do a little better

$$x_{exact} = \tfrac{1}{4}(x^{\{d-1\}} + 2x^{\{d\}} + x^{\{d+1\}}). \qquad (13.184)$$

However, I should caution the reader against extending these interpolation formulas for low *d* values.

For low d values, the estimate is good to the 4th decimal place: for the example in Figure 13.45, at d = 9, equation (13.183) gives x_{exact} = 0.8030859, while for d = 20, equation (13.183) gives x_{exact} = 0.8030287 (compare with x_{exact} = 0.8030288 obtained by iteration in Method (i)).

The '*oscillation*' about a fixed point — '*bracketing a fixed point*' — with diminishing magnitude of the difference $\left|x^{\{d\}} - x_{exact}\right|$ — an '*attractive fixed point*' — as seen in Figure 13.45, is an indication of convergence of the nested radical. A necessary and sufficient condition for convergence is that $a^{(2b)^d}$ be bounded (the proof is simple but we will not overindulge ourselves with it; however, if you have a mathematically incisive mind, a quick look at equation 13.182 should convince you that this condition is true). For further reading on these matters, see the related works by Herschfeld (1935) and by Jones (1995). In the present problem, one has $0 \le a \le 1$, $0 < b < 1$, which ensures that $a^{(2b)^d}$ is bounded. Numerical analyses show that as *a* approaches unity from *below*, the rate of convergence slows down dramatically, so for finite *d*, the depth must be increased to attain a high level of accuracy. When $a > 1$, the nest '*blows-up*' (becomes *unstable*) at some high depth $d = d_u$ where d_u decreases as *a* increases above unity. However, the nested radical method of solving the present problem, is *stable,* when the stated conditions on *a* and *b* are satisfied.

Note: *Some of the mathematical notions employed here will be used in Chapter 18, where the exotic aspects of steelpan dynamics are discussed.*

Method (iii): Recurrence Relation

The method by which the nested radical was set up from equation (13.177) suggests a more flexible approach, a recursive one, more suitable for computer programming. The Nested Radical for compression can be written as a Recurrence Relation in the depth d

$$x^{\{d\}} = \left[1 - a(x^{\{d-1\}})^2 - c x^{\{d-1\}} - g_c\right]^b, \quad d \geq 1. \quad (13.185)$$

$$w_{max} = w_0 x^{\{d\}} \text{ as } d \to \infty.$$

The form in equation (13.185) can be embedded in a *'for'*, *'while'*, or *'until'* loop of a computer program. The loop can be terminated when $|x^{\{d\}} - x^{\{d-1\}}| \leq \kappa$ where κ is suitably small or, the loop can simply be terminated at a sufficiently large depth. In all physically realizable conditions on the stick tips, one finds that $0 < c < 1$, which ensures that $c^{(2b)^d}$ is bounded. The previous statements on convergence and stability apply to the recurrence formula.

Since the zeroth depth solution is $x^{\{0\}} = 1$, and $x^{\{1\}}$ must be real, equation (13.185) requires the condition $(a + c + g_c) < 1$. But since this result is based on the lowest order of approximation and therefore the least accurate, it does not achieve anything of significance. In fact it can be entirely avoided, allowing the method to be used even if this condition is violated by assuming a smaller zeroth solution (starting value). An efficient computational routine can therefore be written with the starting value $x^{\{0\}}$ satisfying $x^{\{0\}} < \frac{1}{2a}\left[\sqrt{c^2 + 4a(1 - g_c)} - c\right]$. Two sample computations are shown in Figure 13.46. Observe the rapid convergence to the exact value in addition to the decrease in the displacement as the mechanical resistance increases.

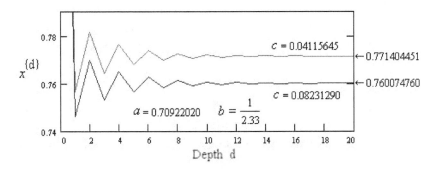

Fig. 13.46. Convergence of the recurrence relation for $g_c = 0$, $r_{ms} = 1$ kg·s^{-1} (top plot) and for $r_{ms} = 2$ kg·s^{-1} (bottom plot). The exact values of $x^{\{d\}}$ shown on the right side were obtained by Method (i).

RECURRENCE METHOD in MATHCAD®

DEFINE a, b, c and g_c
DEFINE starting value x_0. Ensure that
$x_0 < \frac{1}{2a}\left[\sqrt{c^2 + 4a(1 - g_c)} - c\right]$
DEFINE maximum depth. In this example, maxd = 50
DEFINE range variable d
The following example appears in Figure 13.46.
$a := 0.70922020 \quad b := \frac{1}{2.33} \quad c := 0.04115645 \quad g_c := 0$

$\frac{1}{2a}\left[\sqrt{c^2 + 4a(1 - g_c)} - c\right] = 1.159$

$x_0 := 1$
maxd := 50
d := 1..maxd

$x_d := [1 - a \cdot (x_{d-1})^2 - c \cdot x_{d-1} - g_c]^b$

$x_{exact} := \frac{x_{maxd} + x_{maxd-1}}{2}$
$x_{exact} = 0.7714044508$

The Preferred Method

Solution methods (ii) and (iii) are both subject to the conditions $0 \leq a \leq 1$ and $0 \leq c \leq 1$. Since a varies as $V_0^{\frac{2(1-p_c)}{p_c+1}}$ while c varies as $V_0^{\frac{1-p_c}{p_c+1}}$, with $p_c > 1$, these conditions are easily breached for low impact velocities: *there is no remedy*. Iteration Method (i) is therefore the preferred solution method because it is not subject to any condition on the values of a and c other than practical ones.

13.16.2 Impact Force

In obtaining the form for F_{max} when using equation (13.163), small quadratic terms in σ_{pre}/E_s are neglected to yield

$$F_{max} = \frac{4}{3}R_s^2 V_0^{\frac{2p}{p+1}} \left(\frac{E_s}{1-v_s^2}\right)^{\frac{1}{p+1}} \left(\frac{\pi \rho_s (p+1)}{2}\right)^{\frac{p}{p+1}} + \frac{4}{3}\pi \sigma_{pre} R_s^2 V_0^{\frac{2}{p+1}} \left(\frac{\pi \rho_s (p+1)(1-v_s^2)}{2E_s}\right)^{\frac{1}{p+1}}.$$

(13.186)

Equation (13.186) shows that pre-stress produces an *increase* in the maximum contact force (compare equation (13.186) with equation (13.62b)). The player or stick maker, as is the common practice, adjusts the wrapping tension (which sets the pre-stress) to achieve the desired range of contact forces. *In doing this, he adjusts the second term in equation (13.186)* **(isn't that nice!)**.

Maybe I should say a little more about (13.186) and the player. *In making a wrapped stick, the player chooses the stick tip radius R_s appropriate for the pan type; he chooses the wrapping (banding) rubber which determines E_s, ρ_s, v_s and p; he determines the width and thickness of the banding rubber along with the applied wrapping tension to set the range for σ_{pre}; then finally, when he plays he applies a contact velocity V_0 to produce the sound intensity of the tone appropriate for the music.*

In the case of a bass stick made from a commercial rubber (sponge) ball, the same choices are made but now the pre-stress σ_{pre} is determined by the ball manufacturer. Some players may choose to carefully remove the hard surface outer layer of the ball (see Section 13.4). This process reduces the pre-stress and makes the ball softer.

13.16.3 Effective and Dynamic Tip Stiffness

Observe from equation (13.177) that pre-stress produces a *reduction* in the compression, which is expected because of the *increase* in effective or dynamic tip stiffness. For example in the case of $p_c = 1$, when pre-stress is applied through wrapping, by comparing equation (13.62b) and equation (13.186), the effective stiffness of the tip is increased from $m_s \omega^2$ to

$$\text{effective stiffness} = m_s \omega^2 \left(1 + \frac{\pi \sigma_{pre}(1-\upsilon_s^2)}{E_s} \right).$$

$\omega^2 = \dfrac{E_s}{(\pi \rho_s (1-\upsilon_s^2)) R_s^2}$ is the *stiffness parameter*. This *effective stiffness*, is what one senses when the stick tip is squeezed between the fingers. The increase in stiffness by the application of pre-stress to a wrapped tip is an effect that is readily observed and is used to the stick makers' advantage in setting the 'softness' or 'hardness' of the wrapped stick. *Wrapping the tip tighter increases its stiffness. The increase in stiffness due to pre-stress is more noticeable for softer rubber (lower elastic modulus E_s).*

In the general case, the *dynamic stiffness* of the stick tip depends on the impact velocity and is given by

$$\text{dynamic stiffness} = m_s \omega^2 \left(1 + \pi \sigma_{pre} \left(\frac{(1-\upsilon_s^2)}{E_s} \right)^{\frac{2}{p_c+1}} \left(\frac{\pi \rho_s (p_c+1)}{2} \right)^{\frac{1-p_c}{p_c+1}} V_0^{\frac{2(1-p_c)}{p_c+1}} \right).$$

This expression for the dynamic stiffness applies to cases where the second term in the brackets is much smaller than unity and $V_0 \neq 0$. Observe here that in practice ($p_c > 1$) the dynamic stiffness of the wrapped stick, for a given value of pre-stress σ_{pre}, *decreases* (the tip *softens*) as the impact velocity V_0 increases. This velocity dependence means that players can vary the tip stiffness dynamically by varying the impact velocity. However, the velocity dependence is not a strong one, with the fractional stiffness variation going only as $V_0^{\frac{2(1-p_c)}{p_c+1}} \approx V_0^{-0.28}$.

13.16.4 A Softening Effect Discovered on the Wrapped Sticks

In my work on the steelpan I have often observed that nature has set things up in favor of the panist. For example, as the equation for dynamical stiffness of wrapped sticks shows, when the impact velocity increases, the tip becomes dynamically softer — a subtle '*softening effec*t' and one in the player's favor. The only limitation is now set by the swiftness of the hands of the player. One may argue that it would have been better for nature to have set things the other way by making the tip dynamically stiffer (harder) when it is played swiftly. But then the player will be fighting (and you will then literally see him/her struggling) to control the unwanted untuned high modes of the note that this 'hardening' effect would have introduced. Nature did it right by inserting its own measures — the *Softening Effect* — to control this, leaving the panist free to exploit the richness of the high tones on the tenor. We saw that this softening depends on the velocity as $V_0^{\frac{2(1-p_c)}{p_c+1}} \approx V_0^{-0.28}$, if the velocity dependence was much stronger than this (with a number much larger than 0.28) then we will run into problems when we play fast. It turns out just right. But the story isn't over yet, nature didn't make the wrapped sticks, we did! Now we know why wrapped sticks are so good! They are the best pan sticks in my opinion. I marvel at these things whenever I discover them and it is a pleasure to share them with you, the readers.

13.16.5 Contact Time for Normal and Wrapped Tips no Hysteresis with $r_{ms} = 0$ and $E_{SA} = 0$

Using equation (13.166a), the expression for the contact time from 'make' to 'break' on a pre-stressed tip is given by

$$\tau_{m-t-b} = \frac{2R_s}{V_0} \int_0^{w_{max}} \left[1 - \frac{2}{p_c+1}\left(\frac{\omega R_s}{V_0}\right)^2 w^{p_c+1} - \frac{4\pi\sigma_{pre} R_s^3}{3 m_s V_0^2} w^2 \right]^{-\frac{1}{2}} dw.$$

(13.187)

In order to make the integration in equation (13.187) tractable, in the binomial expansion of the integrand some small terms are discarded and the expression for w_{max} without pre-stress is used. The approximate result is

$$\tau_{m-t-b} \approx \left(\left(\frac{p_c+1}{2}\right)\frac{\pi\rho_s(1-v_s^2)}{E_s}\right)^{\frac{1}{p_c+1}} \frac{R_s}{V_0^{\frac{p_c-1}{p_c+1}}} S_{1,p_c}$$

$$- \frac{\sigma_{pre}}{2\rho_s}\left(\left(\frac{p_c+1}{2}\right)\frac{\pi\rho_s(1-v_s^2)}{E_s}\right)^{\frac{3}{p_c+1}} \frac{R_s}{V_0^{\frac{3(p_c-1)}{p_c+1}}} S_{3,p_c}$$

(13.188)

where

$$S_{1,p_c} = 2\sum_{n=0}^{\infty} \frac{y_n}{n(p_c+1)+1}.$$

Despite the approximations made in deriving this formula for the 'make-to-break' contact time the results are very accurate because the approximation procedure was carefully chosen. It does require a fair amount of mathematical experience and physical knowledge in order to make the proper choices in doing this type of analytical work. Examples of this physical knowledge can be taken from the work in this Chapter that precedes the present Section. The reader should attempt a derivation of equation (13.188) using the steps outlined above.

13.16.6 Contact Time for Normal and Wrapped Tips with Hysteresis, for $r_{ms} = 0$ and $E_{SA} = 0$

Employing the methods used in deriving equation (13.110) and equation (13.188), the contact time (m-t-b) for the wrapped tip with hysteresis is given by the approximation

$$\tau_{m-t-b} \cong \left(\left(\frac{p_c+1}{2} \right) \frac{\pi \rho_s (1-v_s^2)}{E_s} \right)^{\frac{1}{p_c+1}} \frac{R_s}{V_0^{\frac{p_c-1}{p_c+1}}} \frac{S_{1,p_c}}{2}$$

$$+ \left(\frac{p_r+1}{p_c+1} \right)^{\frac{1}{2}} \left(\left(\frac{p_c+1}{2} \right) \frac{\pi \rho_s (1-v_s^2)}{E_s} \right)^{\frac{2+p_c-p_r}{2(p_c+1)}} \frac{R_s}{V_0^{\frac{p_r-1}{p_c+1}}} \frac{S_{1,p_r}}{2}$$

$$- \frac{\sigma_{pre}}{4\rho_s} \left(\left(\frac{p_c+1}{2} \right) \frac{\pi \rho_s (1-v_s^2)}{E_s} \right)^{\frac{3}{p_c+1}} \frac{R_s}{V_0^{\frac{3(p_c-1)}{p_c+1}}} S_{3,p_c}$$

$$- \frac{\sigma_{pre}}{4\rho_s} \left(\frac{p_c+1}{2} \right)^{\frac{5-p_r}{2(p_c+1)}} \left(\frac{p_r+1}{2} \right)^{\frac{1}{2}} \left(\frac{\pi \rho_s (1-v_s^2)}{E_s} \right)^{\frac{6+p_c-p_r}{2(p_c+1)}} \frac{R_s}{V_0^{\frac{2p_c+p_r-3}{p_c+1}}} S_{3,p_r}.$$

(13.189)

The contact-time τ_c cannot be expressed exactly in simple closed form in this case, but employing the method used in deriving equation (13.114) and dropping some small non-linear terms one gets to good approximation

$$\tau_c = \left(\left(\frac{p_c+1}{2}\right)\frac{\pi\rho_s(1-v_s^2)}{E_s}\right)^{\frac{1}{p_c+1}}\frac{R_s}{V_0^{\frac{p_c-1}{p_c+1}}}\frac{S_{2,p_c}}{2}$$

$$+\left(\frac{p_r+1}{p_c+1}\right)^{\frac{1}{2}}\left(\left(\frac{p_c+1}{2}\right)\frac{\pi\rho_s(1-v_s^2)}{E_s}\right)^{\frac{2+p_c-p_r}{2(p_c+1)}}\frac{R_s}{V_0^{\frac{p_r-1}{p_c+1}}}\frac{S_{2,p_r}}{2}$$

$$-\frac{\sigma_{pre}}{4\rho_s}\left(\left(\frac{p_c+1}{2}\right)\frac{\pi\rho_s(1-v_s^2)}{E_s}\right)^{\frac{3}{p_c+1}}\frac{R_s}{V_0^{\frac{3(p_c-1)}{p_c+1}}}S_{4,p_c}$$

$$-\frac{\sigma_{pre}}{4\rho_s}\left(\frac{p_c+1}{2}\right)^{\frac{5-p_r}{2(p_c+1)}}\left(\frac{p_r+1}{2}\right)^{\frac{1}{2}}\left(\frac{\pi\rho_s(1-v_s^2)}{E_s}\right)^{\frac{6+p_c-p_r}{2(p_c+1)}}\frac{R_s}{V_0^{\frac{2p_c+p_r-3}{p_c+1}}}S_{4,p_r},$$

$$(13.190)$$

where

$$S_{4,p_c} = 2\sum_{n=0}^{\infty}\frac{y_n}{n(p_c+1)+3}\left(1-2^{-\left(n+\frac{n+1}{p_c}\right)}\right), \quad S_{4,p_r} = 2\sum_{n=0}^{\infty}\frac{y_n}{n(p_r+1)+3}\left(1-2^{-\left(\frac{np_r+n+1}{p_c}\right)}\right),$$

$$y_0 = 1 \text{ and for } n \geq 1, \ y_n = \frac{(2n-1)}{2n}y_{n-1}.$$

Based on this formulation, a linear dependence of contact-time on pre-stress is expected. Observe in equation (13.188), equation (13.189) and equation (13.190) that the contact time *decreases* as the pre-stress *increases*. This explains the player's observation that the *'responsiveness'* of the wrapped stick is improved by re-wrapping the tip with greater tension on the banding rubber.

13.17 Numerical Modeling of Stick-Note Impacts

13.17.1 Numerical Solutions Using Closed-form Equations

For a range of tip and impact parameters, equation (13.190) is used to model a selection of bass, cello and tenor sticks. In the case of the cello, one stick (Case (b)) is modeled by numerically integrating equation (13.164). This serves the purpose of demonstrating the reliability of equation (13.190) in calculating the contact-time and to show that the linear relationship with pre-stress holds good.

Bass

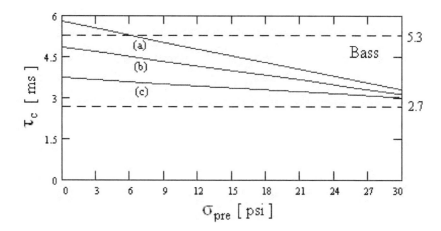

Fig. 13.47. Contact-time versus pre-stress for bass sticks $R_s = 3$ cm, $\rho_s = 920$ kg·m^{-3}, $p_c = 1.33$, $p_r = 1.76$, $v_s = 0.4$; (a), $V_0 = 1$ m·s^{-1}, $E_s = 1 \times 10^6$ N·m^{-2}, (b) $V_0 = 2$ m·s^{-1}, $E_s = 1 \times 10^6$ N·m^{-2}, (c) $V_0 = 2$ m·s^{-1}, $E_s = 2 \times 10^6$ N·m^{-2}. Dashed lines define the practical range.

On the bass, where softer tips (with lower E_s values) can be found, modeling can involve lower impact velocities and lower elastic constants. The slower actions on the bass are modeled in Figure 13.47 with an impact velocity of 1 m·s^{-1}. The bass sticks are usually not of the wrapped variety so that lower pre-stress is expected. Lower pre-stress means longer contact times. The graphs in Figure 13.47 display these properties. One should be careful to note the good confirmation of the known details and the hand action (F_H close to zero as in free fall and rebound) usually associated with the bass (and cello) sticks.

Cello

For the cello sticks in Figure 13.48 the contact times without hand action fall within the experimental range or just above. This is expected because the lower-end pans are played with almost a free-fall action of the stick unto the notes. Hand action, which is always necessary, when applied with a quickened retrieval allows the sounding tones to be adjusted for control of the partials.

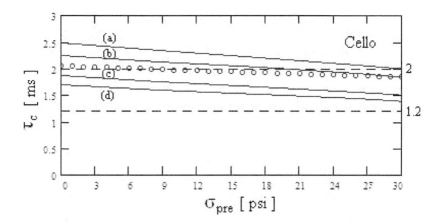

Fig. 13.48. Contact-time versus pre-stress for cello sticks; $R = 2$ cm, $E_s = 2 \times 10^6$ N·m^{-2}, $\rho_s = 920$ kg·m^{-3}, $p_c = 1.33$, $p_r = 1.76$, $v_s = 0.4$; (a) $V_0 = 2$ m·s^{-1}, (b) $V_0 = 3$ m·s^{-1} (c) $R_s = 1.5$ cm, $V_0 = 2$ m·s^{-1}, (d) $R_s = 1.5$ cm, $V_0 = 3$ m·s^{-1}. Solution by Numerical Integration for case (b) shown as (o o o). Dashed lines define the practical range.

Numerical integration of equation (13.164) for case (b) with $F_H = 0$, $\cos\theta = 0$ and $r_{ms} = 0$ is shown in Figure 13.48. Even here, in this more precise solution, the linear dependence on pre-stress is observed. There is only a slight over estimate of the contact-time using equation (13.190) at low values of pre-stress.

Tenor

The dependence of contact-time on pre-stress, impact velocity and p-indices described by equation (13.190) is shown in Figure 13.49 for four tenor sticks. As expected, in all cases represented here, contact-time is seen to decrease linearly with pre-stress. With reference to the caption, (cases (a) & (b)) when the impact velocity is increased the contact-time decreased. In the cases (c), $p_c = p_r = 1.5$ and (d) $p_c = p_r = 1$, both of which produce symmetrical displacement-time profile and with $V_0 = 3$ ms^{-1} come closest to the upper limit of the experimental contact-times.

- The contact-times calculated for these model sticks, with σ_{pre} taking values even above the maximum value for these sticks ($\sigma_{pre,max} \approx 20$ psi), *are **between two to three times** the experimental values*. Recall that equation (13.190) is only valid for impacts with $F_H = 0$.
- **This demonstrates the necessity for hand action (retrieval force) in playing the tenor.**
- *Hand action can reduce the contact times to the experimental values <u>only if</u> stick retrieval begins in the compression phase and maintained for the remainder of the impact.* **This action is in fact used by the trained tenor player.**

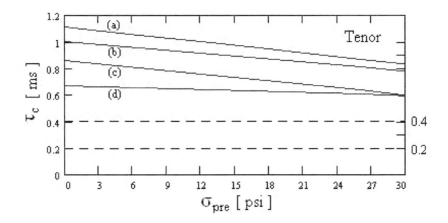

Fig. 13.49. Contact-time versus pre-stress for tenor sticks; $R = 0.8$ cm, $E_s = 1.5 \times 10^6$ N·m^{-2}, $\rho_s = 920$ kg·m^{-3}, $v_s = 0.4$: (a) $p_c = 1.33$, $p_r = 1.76$, $V_0 = 2$ m·s^{-1}, (b)) $p_c = 1.33$, $p_r = 1.76$, $V_0 = 3$ m·s^{-1} (c)) $p_c = 1.5$, $p_r = 1.5$, $V_0 = 3$ m·s^{-1}, (d) $p_c = p_r = 1$, $V_0 = 3$ m·s^{-1}. Dash lines define the practical range.

For the 'brightest' possible tone on the tenor, the notes must be played very quickly (***presto***). This action increases the impact velocity, so that with the quick retrieval that follows, the note can still be played with the required force.

Remarks: *I think it necessary for me to repeat with some emphasis the results just obtained.*

- Stick action <u>without</u> retrieval force produces contact times consistent with contact times found for the low-end pans such as the cello and bass.
- However, this action, which amounts to a free fall that allows the stick to rebound on its own volition, produces contact times that are <u>too long</u> for playing the high-end pans such as the tenor.
- **This makes it quite clear from theoretical considerations alone, that the hand action to be used on the tenor <u>must be different</u> from the hand action used in playing the bass.**
- Retrieval forces are necessary in the hand action used in playing the high-end pans.
- It must also be pointed out that the correct hand action to be applied in playing a particular pan depends on the properties of the stick tip (radius of the tip being a major one of these).

13.17.2 Numerical Solutions Using the General ODE

In the following numerical analyses, solutions are obtained for the general ODE given by equation (13.164). These solutions incorporate all parameters of the stick tip and the hand action of the player.

13.17.2.1 Hand Action on the Tenor

The previous analyses using the closed-form solutions demonstrated that the tenor pan (representing the range of high-end pans) must be played with **swift** and **effective** hand-action. This style of play is very different from the style used by players on the low-end pans. *The short duration contact times that the notes of the tenor demand cannot be obtained using the style of play used on the lower pans.* These facts are well known through experience to the trained player, tuner and pan maker but it is obtained here purely on principles of physics/mathematics. In this treatise, it is absolutely necessary to demonstrate this because *all musical aspects of the instrument depend on these rudiments of stick-note interaction.*

- It is sometimes suggested by pan innovators that the range of notes contained on the pans forming the 'voices' of pan orchestras can be freely extended. If this were practical, then fewer players may be required in an ensemble! *If one were to extend the range of the middle range pans for example, one will surely find that a single pair of sticks will not work effectively.* The reader should try playing a tenor pan with a cello stick! The present analysis on Contact-times clearly demonstrates the impracticability of this suggestion. In a later Section on Contact-width Wavelength Band-limiting (Section 13.30) these stick-note problems are further clarified. Switching sticks during play is hardly an option.

13.17.2.2 Numerical Modeling of Stick-Note impacts on the Tenor

Numerical solutions of equation (13.164) yield contact width and contact force histories for tenor stick impacts as shown in Figure 13.50. Solutions of equation (13.164) yield tip displacements w which on substituting into equation (13.80) as $W_s = R_s w$, give the contact width as a function of time. Substituting the solutions for displacements into equation (13.162) give the contact force as a function of time.

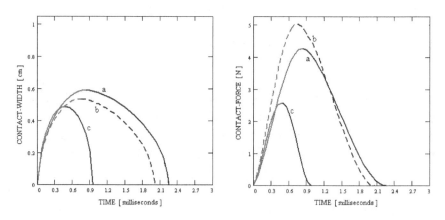

Fig. 13.50. Time histories of Contact-width and Contact-force for three cases of tenor stick impacts. In (a) $\sigma_{pre} = 0$, $F_H = 0$, and (b), $\sigma_{pre} = 8.7$ psi, $F_H = 0$ and in (c) $\sigma_{pre} = 0$, $F_H = 2N$ (directed upward).

In these model stick impacts, $E_s = 1.5 \times 10^6$ N·m^{-2}, $R_s = 0.008$ m, $p_c = 1.33$, $p_r = 1.76$. For cases (a), (b) and (c) in Figure 13.50 the results are:

(a) $F_H = 0$, $\sigma_{pre} = 0$, $V_0 = 1$ m·s^{-1}, producing a make-to-break duration = 2.24 ms, $\tau_c = 1.156$ ms and $F_{max} = 4.27$ N.

(b) $\sigma_{pre} = 0.04\, E_s = 8.70$ psi, $F_H = 0$, $V_0 = 1$ m·s^{-1}, producing a make-to-break duration = 2.0 ms, $\tau_c = 1.08$ ms and $F_{max} = 5.04$ N. Observe the differences between cases (a) and (b): when pre-stress is applied the contact-time and the contact-width are both reduced. This is expected since pre-stress increases the dynamical stiffness of the tip with a resulting increase in contact-force. This is consistent with player's experience where wrapping the tips with increased tension—wrapping tighter—increases the contact-force. The stick (b) is also more responsive by reason of its greater stiffness.

(c) $F_H > 0$, the differences are appreciable. Here, $\sigma_{pre} = 0$, $F_H = 2$ N (directed away from the note, applied 0.06 ms after 'make' and maintained throughout the remainder of the impact), $V_0 = 1$ m·s^{-1}, make-to-break duration = 0.95 ms, $\tau_c = 0.54$ ms and $F_{max} = 2.56$ N. With hand action, the contact-time is greatly reduced at the expense of a reduction in contact force. This can be compensated for by increasing the impact velocity.

Although we shall have occasion to look fully at the excitation of the partials in Sections 13.24 - 13.27 dealing with the MDOF analysis, it can be mentioned here that the contact-time $\tau_c = 0.54$ ms, corresponds to a *Cut-off Frequency* of $f_c = 1/2\tau_c = 926$ Hz. This means that all partials (including fundamental or key-note) above **B**$^\flat_5$ (= 932.33 Hz) will not be significantly excited directly by this impact. In order to properly excite the inner notes on the tenor above **B**$^\flat_5$, faster stick retrieval is necessary.

Observe in these examples the effectiveness of hand action (F_H) in reducing both the contact-time and the contact-width. Increasing F_H is also seen to make the force and contact width profiles more symmetrical (*because the restitution phases are shortened by stick retrieval*). This tendency for the profiles to become mores symmetrical as the contact-time enters the normal time domain created for it by the tenor players (0.2 ms ≤ τ_c ≤ 0.4 ms with good sticks) indicates that the ½-sine approximation (not used in these numerical computations), which is a perfectly symmetrical function, when used for the force profile is truly a good choice.

13.17.2.3 Excitation of the Marginal Notes: Effective Tip Radius Reduction

The *Marginal Notes* (see Section 13.27 for a definition and full treatment) on the tenor, $\mathbf{E}^{\flat}_6$ and higher, require contact-times shorter than 0.4 milliseconds. The panists play these notes by rapid alternation of impacts using the two sticks. In a single application the hand action is one of high impact velocity followed by a very rapid lifting of the stick. It turns out that in order to enter the domain of contact times $\tau_c < 0.4$ milliseconds, stick retrieval must begin *before* the tip attains maximum compression. When the 'hardness' of the tip is increased, this allows the tip to reach maximum compression earlier but then these hardened tips cannot be used on the lower notes of the tenor! It is clearly the panist who solves this problem by his hand action.

Without Effective Tip Radius Reduction

We now model this action for a single impact. In order to properly excite the *Marginal Notes* on the tenor very fast stick retrieval is necessary, *with $\tau_c = 0.2$ milliseconds considered as best achievable in practice*. Figure 13.51 shows a model impact on the tenor with a stick tip having $R_s = 0.008$ m, $p_c = 1.33$, $p_r = 1.76$, $E_s = 2 \times 10^6$ N·m^{-2}, $\sigma_{\text{pre}} = 0.1\ E_s$. Impact velocity $V_0 = 0.8$ m·s^{-1}. In this model, stick retrieval commenced 0.053 milliseconds after initial contact is made with the note. This means that the force profile will follow the free compression dynamics for the first 0.053 milliseconds and thereafter deviate from it as the tip comes under the influence of the hand applied retrieval force.

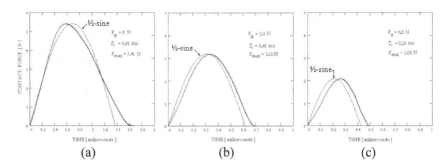

Fig. 13.51. Contact-Force time histories for three cases of a tenor stick impact showing dependence on hand retrieval force F_H. Half-Sine models of the Contact-Force profiles are also shown.

For cases (a), (b) and (c) in Figure 13.51 the results are:

(a) $F_H = 0$, $F_{max} = 5.41$ N, $\tau_c = 0.91$ milliseconds. Cut-off frequency $f_c = 549.45$ Hz, just below $\mathbf{C}^{\#}_5$ at 554.37 Hz.
(b) $F_H = 3.0$ N, $F_{max} = 3.18$ N, $\tau_c = 0.41$ milliseconds. Cut-off frequency $f_c = 1219.51$ Hz, just below $\mathbf{E}^{\flat}_6$ at 1244.51 Hz.
(c) $F_H = 6.0$ N, $F_{max} = 2.08$ N, $\tau_c = 0.28$ milliseconds. Cut-off frequency $f_c = 1785.71$ Hz, just above $\mathbf{A}_6$ at 1760 Hz.

The first observation one can make from these results is the wide range in contact-time (0.91 – 0.28 ms in our examples) that the player can make simply by varying the retrieval force. In the modeling of Figure 13.51 a retrieval force of $F_H = 6.0$ N (directed upward) is required to achieve the contact-time of 0.28 milliseconds, suitable for exciting the Marginal Notes. Because the stick is being retrieved by the hand, the tip compression is reduced; this reduction, combined with the retrieving force results in a lowering of the contact-force. If the retrieval force is too large, the tip barely touches the note. This model impact gives a 'make-to-break' duration of 0.48 milliseconds. Observe the almost symmetrical profiles for contact width and contact time when hand retrieval is included. Also shown in Figure 13.51 are the ½-Sine force profiles with the same contact-time τ_c. Observe that the ½-Sine force profile in example (a) maximizes later while in (c) it maximizes earlier than the more exact model profile. These time shifts (approximately 50 microseconds in these two examples) are negligible when the ½-Sine function is used in stick-note contact modeling.

If one wonders how it is possible for the tenor player to apply this much force (6 N), you are reminded that this force is applied for the very short period of (0.48 - 0.05) milliseconds (or approximately 430 microseconds if that sounds more convincing). In other words since each contact lasts 480 microseconds, a tenor player playing mainly in the Marginal Zone must play these notes 2083 times in order to remain in contact with these notes for an accumulated time of 1 second! In fact if you add up the actual time that the stick remains in contact with the notes on any pan in a typical 10 minute playing session, you will be amazed at the result! It is very short indeed but I leave this as an exercise for the reader. You may be led to the conclusion that a player 'hardly touches' the notes while playing! Astonishing!

With Effective Tip Radius Reduction

In Section 13.12.3 we saw that tenor sticks having single layer tips or tips wrapped with just a few layers of rubber, especially when mounted on hollow shafts, can produce, dynamically, *an effective reduction in tip radius*. Taking a typical *tip radius reduction factor* of 0.7, the design values are now given by:

(a) $F_H = 0$, $F_{max} = 5.41$ N, $\tau_c = 0.64$ milliseconds. Cut-off frequency $f_c = 781$ Hz, just below $\mathbf{G_5}$ at 783.99 Hz.

(b) $F_H = 3.0$ N, $F_{max} = 3.18$ N, $\tau_c = 0.29$ milliseconds. Cut-off frequency $f_c = 1724$ Hz, just below $\mathbf{A_6}$ at 1760 Hz.

(c) $F_H = 6.0$ N, $F_{max} = 2.08$ N, $\tau_c = 0.2$ milliseconds. Cut-off frequency $f_c = 2500$ Hz, below $\mathbf{E_7}$ at 2637 Hz.

Without hand action ($F_H = 0$), case (a) above gives a contact time of 0.64 ms which is too long for the excitation of the Marginal Notes on the tenor. In order to play the Marginal Notes on the tenor, the panist must be able to achieve on a consistent basis a contact time of 0.3 ms.

Secrets of the Steelpan

- *We find therefore that with proper hand action (cases (b) and (c) above) the **single-layer tips** (see Figure 13.3) favored by the tenor panists are well suited for producing the short contact times needed on the Marginal notes.*

Remark: *I wish to emphasize the last result for its importance in the selection and production of tenor sticks. It is not because of the unavailibity of very good commercially made sticks that the finest tenor players have been driven to the use of small single layer tips such as those shown in Figure 13.3 but it is because these sticks are close to ideal and well suited for the required purpose. These players have discovered experimentally, what is expressed in the numerical results of this Section.*

- **The effective reduction of contact area offered by single layer tips**, *combined with their **small size** (as the results in (a), (b) and (c) above have shown) serve to provide the short contact times required for playing the inner notes of the tenor pan.*
- *Just as the theoretical results of this Section teaches us that it becomes increasingly difficult to approach contact time below 0.3 milliseconds **it also teaches us that there must exist a practical upper limit to the frequency of playable notes that can be placed on the high-end pans** (tenors). This problem will be tackled later in this Chapter.*

13.17.2.4 Numerical Modeling of Stick-Note impacts on the Guitar and Cello Pans

In Section 17.17.1, solutions were obtained for the stick-note impacts using a stick tip of radius 1.5 cm, suitable for the guitar or cello pan. For some longer duration impacts more suitable for the lower guitar and cello notes (especially the latter), a larger diameter tip is now tried. Figure 13.52 shows a set of model impacts on the guitar/cello pan with $R_s = 2$ cm, $E_s = 1.5 \times 10^6$ N·m^{-2}, $p_c = 1.33$, $p_r = 1.76$, $V_0 = 1.48$ m·s^{-1}. In all cases, hand action forces F_H are applied 0.05 ms after 'make' and maintained until 'break'.

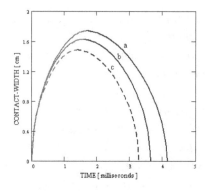 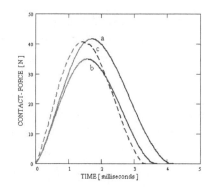

Fig. 13.52. Time histories of Contact-width and Contact-force for three cases of guitar /cello stick impacts The dashed curves (c) demonstrate clearly how the application of pre-stress by wrapping the tip more tightly can reduce contact times and increase the contact force.

For cases (a), (b), and (c) in Figure (13.52) the results are:

(a) $F_H = 0$ N, $\sigma_{pre} = 0$, make-to-break duration = 4.14 ms, τ_c = 2.19 ms and $F_{max} = 41.7$ N. Cut-off frequency $f_c = 228.31$ Hz, just above $\mathbf{B}^\flat_3$ at 223.08 Hz.

(b) $F_H = 6.9$ N, $\sigma_{pre} = 0$, make-to-break duration = 3.63 ms, τ_c = 1.99 ms and $F_{max} = 34.92$ N. Cut-off frequency $f_c = 251.26$ Hz, just below $\mathbf{C}_4$ at 261.63 Hz.

(c) $F_H = 8.4$ N, $\sigma_{pre} = 0.04$ E_s, make-to-break duration = 3.28 ms, $\tau_c = 1.87$ ms and $F_{max} = 40.55$ N. Cut-off frequency $f_c = 267.38$ Hz, just above $\mathbf{C}_4$ at 261.63 Hz.

In case (c) some pre-stress is added to reduce the contact-time and increase the contact-force. On the wrapped sticks this corresponds to the procedure of re-wrapping the tip with greater tension applied to the banding rubber. Pre-stress can also be found in molded rubber balls of the type used in making sticks for the low-end pans. The reduction in contact-width is a good feature on this stick especially on the higher notes of the cello pan.

13.17.2.5 Numerical Modeling of Stick-Note impacts on the Bass Pan

Figure 13.53 shows a set of examples for the bass pan with p_c = 1.33, p_r = 1.76, σ_{pre} = 0.02 E_s = 4.35 psi, E_s = 1.5 x 10^6 N·m^{-2}. Since tips on the bass are mainly of the molded rubber ball type some pre-stress is added in the modeling. In all cases studied here for the bass, hand action forces F_H are applied 0.05 ms after 'make' and maintained until 'break'. Readers may wonder if it is at all possible for the player to commence application of the retrieval force 0.05 ms after 'make', but all that is needed is for the player to anticipate the 'make'. Sometimes this may result in the retrieval commencing before contact is made, in which case the impact velocity is reduced while F_H is applied throughout the impact. There is therefore nothing special about the 0.05 ms after contact is made and it is perfectly possible. It should be noted however, that it takes some time after the retrieval force is applied for the stick to actually break contact with the note.

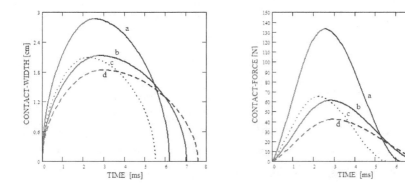

Fig. 13.53. Time histories of Contact-width and Contact-force for four cases of bass stick impacts.

For cases (a), (b), (c) and (d) in Figure 13.53 the results are:

(a) R_s = 0.03 m, F_H = 3 N, V_0 = 2 m·s^{-1}, make-to-break duration = 6.2 ms, τ_c = 3.4 ms and F_{max} = 133.3 N. This is an example of a very strong impact that may not be sustainable by all bass notes without producing distortions in the sound. *To handle such a strong impact without distortion of the sound,* the quiescent point of the bass note must be set with mechanical bias appreciably greater than 133.3 N.(see Section 8.15.3 dealing with the quiescent state). This example is used here to show what is possible on the bass and the need for the pan maker to ensure good production practices on the bass. A *heavy-handed* player can easily exceed the allowable stick impact force using typical bass sticks.

(b) $R_s = 0.03$ m, $V_0 = 1$ m·s^{-1}, $F_H = 1$ N, make-to-break duration = 7.05 ms, $\tau_c = 3.90$ ms and $F_{max} = 61.33$ N. Cut-off frequency $f_c = 128.20$ Hz, just below $\mathbf{C}_3$ at 130.81 Hz.

(c) For comparison, a tenor bass stick is given here with $R_s = 0.025$ m, $V_0 = 1.5$ m·s^{-1}, $F_H = 3$ N, make-to-break duration = 5.55 ms, $\tau_c = 3.05$ ms and $F_{max} = 65.05$ N. Cut-off frequency $f_c = 163.93$ Hz, just below $\mathbf{E}_3$ at 164.81 Hz.

(d) Finally, the case is shown with $R_s = 0.03$ m, $V_0 = 0.7$ m·s^{-1}, $F_H = 0$, make-to-break duration = 7.6 ms, $\tau_c = 4.2$ ms and $F_{max} = 41.83$ N. This is a case without hand assisted retrieval which typically produces longer contact times. This characterizes a slow hand action where the stick is dropped unto the note and allowed to rebound freely. Cut-off frequency $f_c = 119.05$ Hz, just below $\mathbf{B}_2$ at 123.47 Hz.

It is clear from the cut-off frequencies for mode excitation obtained in these examples that the bass pan operates in the frequency band-limited region of the contact-force spectrum. This is what bass notes are all about—no 'ringing' tones. This is also what bass sticks are all about — why their large size and relatively soft feel!

13.18 General COR Formula for all Sticks

13.18.1 Energy Balance Method and Velocity Method

Using the preceding analyses a complete treatment of the COR is now possible. It is important to treat this matter thoroughly because as we shall see, the COR is closely tied to the players' ability to participate in the stick-note impact process. In addition it allows the player to adjust his/her hand action for the best note excitation in each case. This is what playing music on the pan is all about! Well, there is more to the music I must admit.

Method I: Energy Balance Method

For the wrapped stick and all other sticks, the general formula for the COR obtained from the energy-balance equation is given by

$$\varepsilon_r^2 = 1 - 2\left(\frac{\omega R_s}{V_0}\right)^2 \left\{ \frac{w_{max}^{p_c+1}}{p_c+1} - \left(\frac{w_{max}^{p_r+1}}{p_r+1} - \frac{\delta_w^{p_r+1}}{p_r+1}\right) \right\} - \frac{4\pi\sigma_{pre}R_s^3}{3m_s V_0^2}\delta_w^2$$

$$- \frac{2E_{SA}}{m_s V_0^2} - \frac{\pi r_{ms} R_s w_{max}}{2m_s V_0} - \varepsilon_r \left(\frac{\pi r_{ms} R_s w_{max}}{2m_s V_0} - \frac{2 r_{ms} R_s \delta_m}{m_s V_0} \right)$$

(13.191)

Here, the total energy lost through shank absorption is the sum $E_{SA} = E_{SA}^{\{comp\}} + E_{SA}^{\{rest\}}$.

Equation (13.191) can be written in the form

$$\varepsilon_r^2 = 1 - \delta_H - \delta_{SA} - \delta_{MR},$$ (13.192)

where δ_H is the fractional energy lost by hysteresis, δ_{SA} is the fractional energy lost by shank absorption while δ_{MR} is the fractional energy lost by virtue of the mechanical resistance of the tip material. The term on the right side of equation (13.191) with ε_r as a prefactor, forms part of δ_{MR} and represents that fraction of work done in the restitution phase. The terms containing δ_w represent the residual internal energy of the partly restituted tip on rebound as a fraction of the initial impact energy.

Note: *As a prelude to the discussion on stick design later in this work, it should be noted here that in order to increase the COR, these energy losses must be reduced.*

Using $\omega R_s = \sqrt{E_s/(\pi \rho_s (1-v_s^2)}$ and $m_s = \frac{4}{3}\pi\rho_s R_s^3$ with some rearrangement, equation (13.191) can be written as

$$\varepsilon_r^2 + \varepsilon_r \left(\frac{3r_{ms} w_{max}}{8\rho_s V_0 R_s^2} - \frac{3r_{ms}\delta_m}{2\pi\rho_s V_0 R_s^2} \right) = 1 - \frac{2E_s}{V_0^2 \pi \rho_s (1-v_s^2)} \left\{ \frac{w_{max}^{p_c+1}}{p_c+1} - \left(\frac{w_{max}^{p_r+1}}{p_r+1} - \frac{\delta_w^{p_r+1}}{p_r+1} \right) \right\}$$
$$- \frac{\sigma_{pre}\delta_w^2}{\rho_s V_0^2} - \frac{3E_{SA}}{2\pi\rho_s R_s^3 V_0^2} - \frac{3r_{ms} w_{max}}{8\rho_s V_0 R_s^2}.$$
(13.193)

The COR is the positive real root of the quadratic equation (13.193). It should be observed that in equation (13.193) no correction is made to the tip mass for that portion of the shank located within the rubber tip.

Method 2: Velocity Method

The velocity method gives a result equivalent to the Stick Restitution Formula (with $F_H = 0$, $\phi = 90°$) in the form

$$\varepsilon_r^2 + \varepsilon_r \left(\frac{3r_{ms} w_{max}}{8\rho_s V_0 R_s^2} - \frac{3r_{ms}\delta_m}{2\pi\rho_s V_0 R_s^2} \right) = \frac{E_s}{\rho_s V_0^2} \left(\left(\frac{2}{p_r+1} \right) \frac{(w_{max}^{p_r+1} - \delta_w^{p_r+1})}{\pi(1-v_s^2)} + \frac{\sigma_{pre}}{E_s}(w_{max}^2 - \delta_w^2) \right)$$
$$- \frac{3E_{SA}^{\{rest\}}}{2\pi\rho_s R_s^3 V_0^2}.$$
(13.194)

The COR is the positive real root of the quadratic equation (13.194).

13.18.2 Comparison of Methods

For $E_{SA} = 0$, Figure 13.54 compares the two methods with the exact solution. The exact solutions can be obtained by two methods (a) Iterating the Stick Compression Formula to yield w_{max} ($= xw_0$) and (b) by numerically integrating the differential equations. The latter method proceeds as follows: For the compression phase

$$\frac{d^2 w}{dt^2} = -\omega^2 w^{p_c} - \frac{4\pi\sigma_{pre} R}{3m_s} w - \frac{r_{ms}}{m_s}\frac{dw}{dt},$$

which on integrating yields w_{max} as a function of σ_{pre}. The corresponding values for the rebound velocity V_r, are found from the numerical integration of the differential equation for the restitution phase. This second integration proceeds downwards from w_{max} until w reaches zero (the 'break'). If there is measurable residual compression then integration ceases when $w = \delta_w/R_s$. The rebound velocity V_r is found from the numerically determined value of dw/dt at the break. The COR is then given by V_r/V_0.

Further analysis of equation (13.193) and equation (13.194) reveals that whenever w_{max} is underestimated this leads to an overestimate of the COR by the energy-balance method and an underestimate by the velocity method (see Figure 13.54). The converse also holds.

Very precise estimates of the COR are obtained by increasing the depth d. Figure 13.55 shows the results for $d = 6$ and $d = 20$.

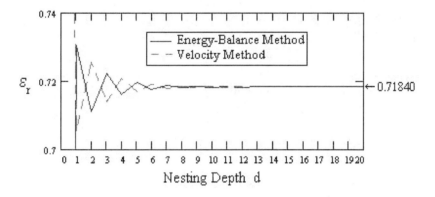

Fig. 13.54. Fluctuations in the COR versus the depth for for tip material with $E_s = 5 \times 10^6$ N·m^{-2}, $\rho_s = 920$ kg·m^{-3}, $v_s = 0.4$, impact velocity $V_0 = 1$ m·s^{-1}. $\sigma_{pre}/E_s = 0.07$, $r_{ms} = 0$.

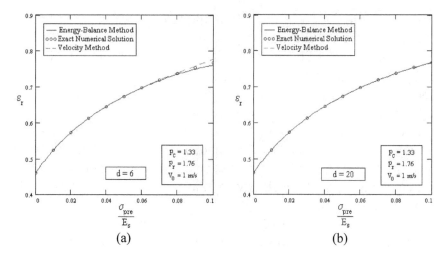

Fig. 13.55. COR as a function of pre-stress for tip material with $E_s = 5 \times 10^6$ N·m^{-2} (hard rubber), $\rho_s = 920$ kg·m^{-3}, $v_s = 0.4$, impact velocity $V_0 = 1$ m·s^{-1}. $r_{ms} = 0$, (a), Depth 6; (b) Depth 20.

Having demonstrated that the solution methods for the COR are consistent and accurate, one can rely on the Energy Balance Method or the Velocity Method for all such calculations.

13.18.3 Equivalence of the Two COR Equations

If one treats w_{max} and ε_r as the two unknowns then there are three equations, (13.177), (13.193) and (13.194) defining these two unknowns. These quantities appear over-defined. The resolution of this mathematical problem is simple and demonstrates the consistency of the two methods of obtaining the COR.

The computations displayed earlier show that equations (13.193) and (13.194) give equal values for ε_r once the correct value for w_{max} is substituted. The question naturally arises, are they *independent*? They are not, as the following analysis shows: construct a difference equation

[right side of equation (13.194)] − [right side of equation (13.193)] = *residual*,

it being understood that the left sides of (13.193) and (13.194) are equal. If the two equations are equivalent, *residual* must be identically zero. Thus

$$\left[\frac{E_s}{\rho_s V_0^2}\left(\left(\frac{2}{p_r+1}\right)\frac{w_{max}^{p_r+1}}{\pi(1-v_s^2)}+\frac{\sigma_{pre}}{E_s}w_{max}^2\right)-\frac{3E_{SA}^{\{rest\}}}{2\pi\rho_s R_s^3 V_0^2}\right]$$

$$-\left[1-\frac{2E_s}{V_0^2\pi\rho_s(1-v_s^2)}\left\{\frac{w_{max}^{p_c+1}}{p_c+1}-\frac{w_{max}^{p_r+1}}{p_r+1}\right\}-\frac{2r_{ms}}{8\rho_s V_0 R_s^2}w_{max}-\frac{3E_{SA}}{2\pi\rho_s R_s^3 V_0^2}\right]=residual$$

which reduces to

$$\frac{E_s}{V_0^2\pi\rho_s(1-v_s^2)}\left\{\frac{2}{p_c+1}\right\}w_{max}^{p_c+1}+\frac{\sigma_{pre}}{\rho_s V_0^2}w_{max}^2+\frac{2r_{ms}}{8\rho_s V_0 R_s^2}w_{max}+\frac{3E_{SA}^{\{comp\}}}{2\pi\rho_s R_s^3 V_0^2}-1=residual \quad (13.195)$$

Using the expressions for w_0 and the parameters a, b, c and y_c, equation (13.195) further reduces to

$$ax^2+x^{\frac{1}{b}}+cx+y_c-1=residual. \qquad (13.196)$$

The expression on the left side of equation (13.196) is found in the Stick Compression Formula equation (13.177), and it is equal to zero. Therefore, $residual = 0$. Equation (13.193) (by the Energy Balance Method) and equation (13.194) (by the Velocity Method) are found to be equivalent. It is therefore sufficient to take equation (13.193) and the Stick Compression Formula equation (13.177) as the pair of independent equations. Equation (13.177) can then be solved iteratively and the result used in equation (13.193) (with $w_{max} = xw_0$) to determine the COR of the stick. This procedure is adopted in the following illustrations of the dependence of the COR on pre-stress, velocity and losses.

Comment: *I hope that readers, through this exercise, have learnt one of the techniques I employ to verify the correctness and consistency of my equations. The consistency shown in the above example between two sets of equations involving many terms and derived by different methods, would not have been possible if important physical effects were neglected in the derivations. Rigor always pays off in the end!*

13.19 Dependence of COR on Elastic Modulus, Pre-stress and Impact Velocity — Effect on the 'Nuances of Touch'.

Figure 13.56 shows that for $\delta_w = 0$, $r_{ms} = 0$ and $E_{SA} = 0$ and a given value of pre-stress the COR decreases with increasing Young's modulus (E_s) of the tip rubber. The rubber found on typical pan sticks fall in the soft rubber range E_s around 1.5×10^6 N·m^{-2} with pre-stress under 20 psi (wrapped and normal tips). By increasing the wrapping tension on the wrapped sticks, the player generates more 'bounce' from the stick. This is confirmed in Figure 13.56 where the COR is seen to increase with pre-stress.

The dependence of the COR on pre-stress and impact velocity is illustrated in Figure 13.57. The COR shows greatest velocity dependence when $\sigma_{pre} = 0$. This dependence decreases as σ_{pre} increases with a small dependence for $\sigma_{pre} \geq 20$ psi (with the set of parameters seen in the caption of Figure 13.57). This latter observation is also consistent with the behavior of the Superball$^{©}$ which, with its very high pre-stress, shows a consistently high COR at all manually produced velocities.

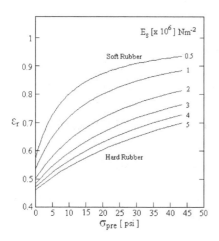
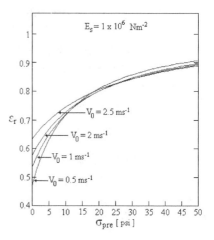

Fig. 13.56. COR as a function of pre-stress and Young's modulus with $p_c = 1.33$, $p_r = 1.76$, $\rho_s = 920$ kg·m^{-3}, $V_0 = 1$ m·s^{-1}, $\delta_w = 0$, $r_{ms} = 0$ and $E_{SA} = 0$.

Fig. 13.57. COR as a function of pre-stress and impact velocity with $p_c = 1.33$, $p_r = 1.76$, $\rho_s = 920$ kg·m^{-3}, $r_{ms} = 0$ and $E_{SA} = 0$.

The Nuances of Touch

A good panist can make a good stick play better but a bad stick only makes a good panist 'sound bad!'

I expect the alert reader to be now saying 'you can't discuss nuances of touch here because that is a matter for the panist and his music!' If you said as much then you are almost right. The music is on the sheets, perhaps stored in the panist's head, but so long as it remains there, no one can talk about nuances! To put the music into the air so that the panist and the audience can hear and appreciate the 'player's touch' you must use a pair of sticks on the pan. Just as one can tune 'pung notes' on a pan which cannot be altered in tonality no matter who plays such notes, there are 'dud sticks' that no panist can make good even by using them on a competition grade pan. A good panist can easily find his hand actions severely restricted, and even lose his touch when caught in the unfortunate situation of playing with the wrong sticks, mis-matched sticks or badly prepared sticks.

So while we cannot address too strongly here the relationship between the nuances and the music — a topic better handled by the panist himself — we are perfectly well positioned to describe the role of the stick as the panist executes his hand action as influenced by the music.

The good panist usually prepares his sticks himself particularly when wrapped sticks are used. There is quite an 'art' to *Wrapping Sticks*, but the science is very certain and the performance quite predictable. When a stick for use on the mid to high pans is carefully prepared, the *pre-stress is normally around 10 psi*. From Figure 13.57 one sees that with a pre-stress of 10 psi, the panist, by varying the impact velocity, can make changes to the COR by roughly ± 5%. This may appear as a small variation but in the hands of a trained panist it offers that fine control which contributes greatly to the '*nuances of touch.*' Observe that by using stick tips with lower pre-stress (softer tips), greater *fine control on the COR is possible — up to ± 15%*. What does this mean in practical terms? Using Figure 13.57, one gets for the stick operating nominally with a COR of 0.7, pre-stress = 10 psi, the COR can be *increased* by 10% simply by increasing the impact velocity from 0.5 m·s^{-1} to 2.5 m·s^{-1}.

This translates into a *reduction* in impact energy loss of 20%. The figures for a softer stick operating nominally with a COR of 0.6, pre-stress = 5 psi, gives an *increase* in COR of 30% and a *reduction* in energy loss of 34% when the panist increases the impact velocity from 0.5 m·s^{-1} to 2.5 m·s^{-1}. This 'energy loss' must be properly interpreted because the total energy applied in the stick-note system is 25 times greater at 2.5 m·s^{-1} than at 0.5 m·s^{-1} (energy increasing as the square of the velocity) so far greater actual energy is available, and lost, at the higher velocity. The panist can 'work up quite a sweat' in a 10-minute performance.

See how much wider control on the COR is availale on the softer stick. When the COR is too high (greater than 0.75) the panist gives up control of the impact to the stick. It might be easier for the reader to think of the *'responsiveness'* and *'bounce'* of the stick in response to the hand actions of the panist. The softer tip (wrapped with lower tension for example) is more responsive to the changes in hand action. With the stiffer tip (greater pre-stress) there is more 'bounce,' all impacts are alike with the production of a consistently 'bright' sound on each impact. See Table 13.9 for a pre-view of the summary of this Section.

We see from this analysis that stick tip preparation is very important; if the tip is made too 'stiff' by applying too much pre-stress the panist loses dynamical control of the COR. This explains why tips with high pre-stress (and their hard 'feel') tend to generate a consistent 'ping' tone no matter how hard or soft the impact; the panist has great difficulty varying the tonality to suit the mood of the music. The stick must be *voiced* to suit the pan, the player, and the music; see Section 14.44.2.

13.20 The Inclusion of Mechanical Resistance, Residual Compression, Shank Absorption and Lossy Overlay

The dependence of the COR on tip mechanical resistance r_{ms} is illustrated in Figure 13.58. The values of the COR show the expected decrease as r_{ms} increases. Soft rubber materials with low mechanical resistances are desirable in the design of efficient sticks for all pans but particularly the high end pans.

The losses due to shank absorption are difficult to calculate and to measure experimentally. The residual compression can be measured for individual sticks by taking each stick through a hysteresis cycle. It is however useful to lump the three losses, residual compression, shank absorption and mechanical resistance together to determine their effect on the COR. It may also be desirable to introduce the absorption mat or lossy overlay here since this is a replaceable item whose properties can be easily varied. If one takes

$$\delta = \delta_H + \delta_{SA} + \delta_{MR} + \delta_{MA}$$

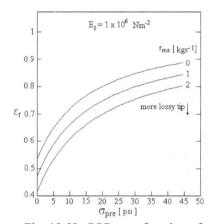 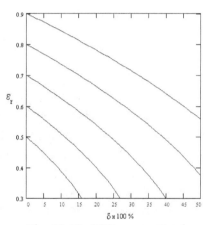

Fig. 13.58. COR as a function of pre-stress and mechanical resistance with $p_c = 1.33$, $p_r = 1.76$, $\rho_s = 920$ kg·m^{-3} and $E_{SA} = 0$.

Fig. 13.59. COR versus Total Losses (see Text).

as the total fractional energy lost through these four agencies, where δ_{MA} represent the fraction for the overlay or mat, one gets for the COR

$$\varepsilon_r = \sqrt{\varepsilon_{rh}^2 - \delta},$$
$$\varepsilon_r = \varepsilon_{rh} \text{ when } \delta = 0,$$

and where ε_{rh} is the COR when only hysteretic losses with zero residual compression are considered. The effects on COR values are shown in Figure 13.59. Since the absorption mat is replaceable, one can test the stick with and without the mat to determine the fractional energy lost by mat absorption. By using samples of tip wrapping rubber as the absorption mat, the absorption losses of the samples can be found by repeating the tests, with and without the rubber mat. I found this to work effectively but since my results are specific only to those rubber samples in my possession these results are not reproduced here. In these tests the 'Swinging Stick Method' (see Section 13.21) was used with the mat or rubber sample affixed to the impact plate.

If ε_{r1} is the COR without the mat and ε_{r2} is the COR with the mat then, provided that the initial impact velocity is the same in both cases, one gets

$$\delta_{MA} = \varepsilon_{r1}^2 - \varepsilon_{r2}^2.$$

Remember that a single layer of matting or sheet of wrapping rubber works like the single-wrap stick so that the 'proximity effect' of the comparatively harder impact plate will affect your measurement as it does for the single layer stick tip. The mat or wrapping rubber affixed to the impact plate appears harder than actual just as when you squeeze a single-wrap stick tip it feels soft at first but as you squeeze it down towards the shank it feels harder. This is more readily observed when the single layer of rubber is thin and very soft.

Example: To use Figure 13.59 for a rough estimate on a typical wrapped stick with E around 0.5×10^6 N·m^{-2}, first use the $E = .0.5 \times 10^6$ N·m^{-2} curve in Figure 13.56 for $\sigma_{pre} = 10$ psi (for a strong impact or lower for a soft impact). This gives $\varepsilon_{rh} = 0.8$ for $\delta = 0$. Locate the curve in Figure 13.59 with the value $\varepsilon_{rh} = 0.8$ on the ordinate for $\delta = 0$ (along the vertical COR axis). This is the curve you will use in your estimate. Decide, from the condition of the tip, on a reasonable value for the fractional loss δ. If one takes $\delta = 0.1$ ($\equiv 10\%$), the selected curve in Figure 13.59 gives $\varepsilon_r \approx 0.74$, or 0.735 using $\varepsilon_r = \sqrt{\varepsilon_{rh}^2 - \delta}$. This agrees with the value $\varepsilon_r = 0.73$ found experimentally for the wrapped stick illustrated in Figure 13.5(a) (see Section 13.21.4).

Partial Summary:

- Wrapped sticks allows the COR to be adjusted by varying the wrapping tension which sets the value of σ_{pre} (i.e. wrapping the tip tighter increases the COR).
- Contact force on the wrapped stick can be adjusted by varying the wrapping tension.
- Some amount of pre-stress is always required in the manufacture of pan sticks if COR values around 0.7 are to be obtained.

13.21 Experimental Determination of COR

13.21.1 My 'Swinging Stick Method' and the Swinging Stick COR Formula

In this method, the stick is used as a pendulum by suspending it from a fulcrum attached to the end of the shank. For wooden shanks, the fulcrum can be made by driving two small steel pins into the end of the shank at diametrically opposite points. The stick is then hung tip downward with each pin resting in a V-notch formed from two small pieces of a discarded band saw blade (or something similar). The teeth on the band saw blade are made of hardened steel therefore they can serve as excellent bearing surfaces. Two V-notches cut into two small graphite blocks can also be used to make excellent fulcrums. The accuracy of your measurements will depend on the quality of the fulcrum and how freely the suspended stick oscillates. Quality here means workmanship. The stick when set to oscillate about the fulcrum must move in a single plane. First, operate the pendulum without a strike plate or impact plate so that the pendulum swings 'freely'. If the pins and/or notches are not diametrically opposite and their axes not truly in-line, the stick will try to execute a figure-8 motion or in a really bad construction the pins will hop about within the notches or hop out of the notches. The reader should feel free to use any improved design such as one using micro (or mini) bearings with a stick attachment that accommodates different shank sizes. Make it sturdy, lightweight and frictionless as possible.

Theory

The theory is very simple. The experimental procedure requires the measurement of only two angles, one fixed while the other depends on the COR of the stick under test. Consider the stick with its axis inclined at an angle ϕ_i to the vertical as shown in Figure 13.60. The stick is then released from this initial rest position allowing it to rotate about the axis of rotation at the fulcrum. Allow the stick to fall freely. Do not push or impede the stick in any way. The tip makes contact with the fixed impact plate with an initial contact velocity V_i. The stick then rebounds with a velocity V_f as contact is broken with the plate then swings through a maximum angle ϕ_f (see Figure 13.60 for more details). In the Center-of-Mass (CM) coordinates, the corresponding velocities are $V_{i,cm}$ and $V_{f,cm}$ respectively. Measured from the axis of rotation, the distance to the point of impact is given by R while the distance to the center-of-mass is R_{cm}. The following equations readily follow:

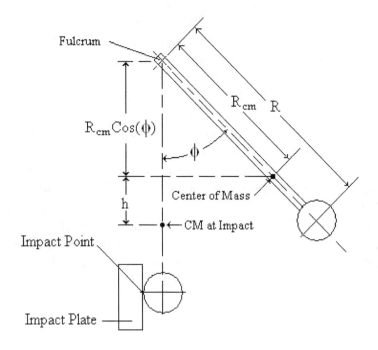

Fig. 13.60. Experimental setup to determine the COR of a fully assembled stick.

$$V_{i,cm} = V_i \frac{R_{cm}}{R}, \qquad V_{f,cm} = V_f \frac{R_{cm}}{R},$$

giving the COR as

$$\varepsilon_r = \frac{V_f}{V_i} = \frac{V_{f,cm}}{V_{i,cm}}.$$

If the center-of-mass falls through a vertical distance h_i on the downswing and rises a vertical distance h_f on the upswing then the principle of energy conservation requires

$$\text{Downswing:} \qquad Mgh_i - \delta E_i = \tfrac{1}{2} MV_{i,cm}^2,$$
$$\text{Upswing:} \qquad \tfrac{1}{2} MV_{f,cm}^2 - \delta E_f = Mgh_f,$$

where M is the total mass of the stick. Energy losses due to air resistance and support friction at the fulcrum are represented by δE_i and δE_f on the downswing and upswing respectively. These equations yield

$$\varepsilon_r = \frac{V_{f,cm}}{V_{i,cm}} = \left(\frac{h_f}{h_i}\right)^{\frac{1}{2}} \left(\frac{1 + \dfrac{\delta E_f}{Mgh_f}}{1 - \dfrac{\delta E_i}{Mgh_i}}\right)^{\frac{1}{2}}. \qquad (13.198)$$

Using Figure 13.60 which shows the center-of-mass dropping a vertical distance h as it swings through an angle ϕ, one gets $h = R_{cm}[1-\cos\phi]$. From this result, using equation 13.198 one gets

$$\varepsilon_r = \left(\frac{1-\cos\phi_f}{1-\cos\phi_i}\right)^{\frac{1}{2}} \left(\frac{1 + \dfrac{\delta E_f}{Mgh_f}}{1 - \dfrac{\delta E_i}{Mgh_i}}\right)^{\frac{1}{2}}.$$

If the suspended stick is treated as a damped simple oscillator performing only a fractional cycle in each swing, then the results of Section 8.11 allow us to take $Mgh = <E>$ where $<E>$ is the average energy *stored* per cycle and δE as the energy *lost* per fractional cycle. In terms of the average power dissipated per cycle $<P>$, one can write $\delta E = <P>\delta t$ where δt is the time taken for the fractional cycle swing. Since $<P> = R_m<E>$ where R_m is the mechanical resistance (to swinging motion) of the system, one can write

$$\varepsilon_r = \left(\frac{1-\cos\phi_f}{1-\cos\phi_i}\right)^{\frac{1}{2}} \left(\frac{1+R_m\delta t_f}{1-R_m\delta t_i}\right)^{\frac{1}{2}}. \qquad (13.199)$$

In practice and in the exact ('large angle') theory, the time for each swing δt depends on the angle of swing, making δt_i slightly larger than δt_f. In the damped simple oscillator ('small angle') approximation $\delta t_f = \delta t_i$, which, in the low loss approximation $R_m \delta t \ll 1$, allows the energy loss factor to be written as

$$\left(\frac{1+R_m\delta t_f}{1-R_m\delta t_i}\right)^{\frac{1}{2}} \approx (1+2R_m\delta t_i)^{\frac{1}{2}} \approx 1+R_m\delta t_i. \qquad (13.200)$$

Equation (13.200) demonstrates the fact that the effect of energy losses cannot be completely removed and that it accumulates with successive swings. It is important therefore that while air friction cannot be eliminated (unless one takes the trouble of enclosing the apparatus in a vacuum chamber which is not recommended), the fulcrum must be made as frictionless as possible.

Assuming negligible losses one can take

$$\varepsilon_r = \left(\frac{1-\cos\phi_f}{1-\cos\phi_i}\right)^{\frac{1}{2}},$$

which, by simple trigonometry, reduces to

$$\varepsilon_r = \frac{\sin\tfrac{1}{2}\phi_f}{\sin\tfrac{1}{2}\phi_i} \quad . \tag{13.201}$$

I call this the '*Swinging Stick COR Formula.*'
The impact velocity is given by

$$V_0 = \sqrt{2gR(1 - \cos\phi_i)},$$

same as $\quad\quad V_0 = 2\sin\left(\tfrac{1}{2}\phi_i\right)\sqrt{gR}, \tag{13.202}$

Because of the exclusion of losses, estimates of COR based on equation (13.201) are subject to a systematic error of $(-100R_m\delta t_i)$ % (the estimates are *lower* than the true value). For the purposes of steelpan sticks, equation (13.201) can safely be used if particular attention is paid to the fulcrum to reduce R_m as much as possible. *If graphite blocks are not used in the construction, a small quantity of dry graphite lubricant such as the quick-drying type used for lubricating auto door locks can be applied to reduce the rubbing friction at the fulcrum.* The only measurements required is the initial angle ϕ_i and the maximum angle of rebound ϕ_f. When comparing sticks it is advisable to use the same initial angle ϕ_i (say 45°).

Note: *Where required, the acceleration due to gravity can be taken as* $g = 10 \; m \cdot s^{-2}$.

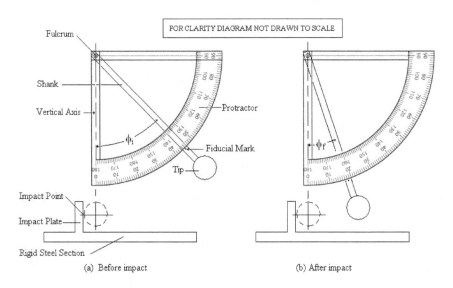

Fig. 13.61. Practical arrangement using a plastic protractor and impact plate.

Details of the apparatus are shown in Figure 13.61. The rigid steel section in Fgure 13.61 can be made of heavy (or dense) wood to which a metal impact plate is fitted. A fiducial mark is placed on the surface of the stick shank along a line parallel to the axis of the shank. This fiducial mark serves as a reference point for the measurement of the angle of swing. Align the axis of the shank so that in the vertical position the fiducial mark coincides with 0° on the protractor while the tip just touches the impact plate. The plane of the protractor must be perpendicular to the axis of rotation at the fulcrum. The plane of the impact plate must be vertical and perpendicular to the plane of the protractor.

13.21.2 Approximate Formula and Simple Stick Tip COR Meter

Remark*: At the First International Conference on the Science and Technology of the Steelpan (ICSTS 2000) held in Trinidad, the attending Secondary School students asked me to write a book on the Science of the Steelpan especially for schools. I have not yet done this but some Sections of the present book have been written with these students in mind. This sub-Section, on a Simple COR Formula and COR Meter is one that I have written especially for* *these young students to allow them to study some physical properties of pan sticks in the classroom or at home.*

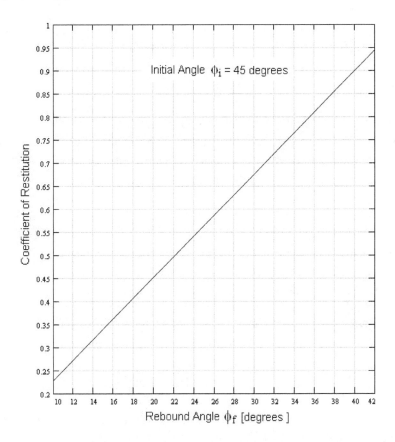

Fig. 13.62. Plot of COR versus Rebound Angle for pan tips suspended on the jig shown in Figure 13.61

For those requiring a quick and easy formula for calculating the COR without the use of an electronic calculator or trigonometric tables, a good approximation (based on small angle approximation) is given by the linear expression

$$\varepsilon_r \cong \frac{\phi_f}{\phi_i}$$

accurate to within 2 percent (quite good!). Since COR is dimensionless (just a number), this formula should be read, 'the

COR is equal to the *ratio* of the rebound angle to the initial angle.' Therefore it will be wrong to say that ε_r is a function of ϕ_f, but it would be correct to say that it is a function of (in fact equal to) the ratio ϕ_f/ϕ_i. If you like using an initial angle ϕ_i of 45° as suggested, then simply use the equivalent approximation

$$\varepsilon_r \cong 0.022\phi_f$$

where the final angle ϕ_f is in degrees (of arc).

This linear form plotted in Figure 13.62 makes the measurement exercise very easy, so now everyone can compare pairs of sticks within minutes using this formula and the jig shown in Figure 13.61. If you want you can calibrate your 'protractor' to read the COR directly when using an initial angle of 45°. You would then have a neat '*COR Meter*' for your sticks, courtesy '*yours truly.*' This COR Meter will be ideal for voicing and balancing your sticks (see Section 14.45).

The tips of bass sticks made from whole sponge balls can be suspended using a length of thread or lght string and swung as a simple pendulum as another form for your COR Meter. Easy does it!

13.21.3 COR Values for an Assortment of Tips

Some commercial sticks are made by stretching a piece of rubber tubing over one end of the shank (see Figure 13.3). Depending on the ratio (*tt/sr*) of the tubing thickness (*tt*) to shank radius (*sr*), these sticks may be classified as (i) *thin-layered* (*tt/sr* < *1*) (for example Figure 13.3(a) or (ii) *thick-layered* (*tt/sr* ≥ *1*) (for example Figure 13.3(b)). This construction is equivalent to a single-layer wrapped stick. The result is a somewhat harder tip not only because of the pre-stress (applied by forcing the shank into the tubing for a tight fit) but also due to the close proximity of the relatively hard shank to the tip surface — there is no accumulated compression over a number of layers. This *proximity effect* is more severe for thin-layered tips.

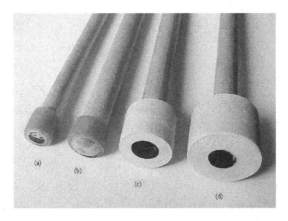

Fig. 13.63. Samples (a) and (b) are thin-layered (silicone rubber) while (c) and (d) are thick-layered (silicone hard-surfaced rubber).

Despite the increase in tip stiffness, a noticeable result of the proximity effect and the reduction in the relative thickness of the tubing (see Figure 13.63) is the decrease in the COR values for the thin-layered tips. This is a direct result of the absorption of a significant fraction of the impact energy by the (wooden) shank. This absorbed energy is dissipated mainly as heat in the shank This is energy that would otherwise have been stored as potential energy in the compressed rubber. When impact energy is stored in the rubber during the compression phase it is made available in the restitution phase as kinetic energy. Equation (13.201) still applies for these sticks because the losses due to energy absorption by the shank is an *internal* process that affects the system only by lowering the kinetic energy and the rebound velocity V_f. Once V_f is reduced the COR value drops accordingly.

The thin-layered sticks are not energy efficient and the player must adjust his/her playing style when using these sticks since there is a reduction in the energy delivered to the note and in particular to the desired modal components or partials.

For the new sticks shown in Figure 13.63 the experimental error of ±4% for the COR does not include the small but unknown uncertainty due to air viscosity and fulcrum losses. Experimental COR values determined to an accuracy of ± 4%: Tip (a) $\varepsilon_r = 0.50$; Tip (b) $\varepsilon_r = 0.53$; Tip (c) $\varepsilon_r = 0.59$; Tip (d) $\varepsilon_r = 0.67$.

Sample (a) treated as a tightly-fitted thin-layered stick will produce a pre-stress of approximately 5 psi on a hard impact. Using

$E_s = 1 \times 10^6$ N·m^{-2} in Figure 13.56 for $\sigma_{pre} = 5$ psi gives $\varepsilon_{rh} \approx 0.65$. By interpolating on Figure 13.59 for a rough estimate or using $\varepsilon_r = \sqrt{\varepsilon_{rh}^2 - \delta}$ with $\varepsilon_r = 0.50$ gives the value $\delta = 0.173 \equiv 17.3\%$ for the fractional energy loss. This loss, most of which should be due to shank absorption, will no doubt increase as this stick deteriorates in use. The COR for the selection of stick tips shown Figure 13.64 are: (a) Wrapped Cello, $\varepsilon_r = 0.73$; (b) Tenor Bass, $\varepsilon_r = 0.69$; (d) Bass, $\varepsilon_r = 0.70$.

The experimental values for the impact velocities attained by the sticks under test ranged from 0.9 m·s^{-1} for the small mini sticks with $R = 14$ cm, to 1.28 m·s^{-1} for the cello and bass sticks with $R = 28$ cm. In all tests, the initial angle ϕ_i was set to 45°.

(a) $\varepsilon_r = 0.73$ (b) $\varepsilon_r = 0.69$ (c) $\varepsilon_r = 0.70$

Fig. 13.64. (a) Seven-layer wrapped tip for cello. (b) Cut ball tip for Tenor Bass. (c) Hard surfaced rubber sponge ball tip for Bass.

The COR values for well wrapped multi-layer sticks were always found to be in the high range around 0.7 and slightly better but dependent on the quality of the banding rubber used to make the tip. Re-wrapping tips with used (old) rubber is not always a good idea because the old banding rubber may show varying elastic properties along its length and across its width. The wrapping tension has to be varied somewhat randomly during re-wrapping when using used rubber. For best results always use new rubber.

13.22 Tactile Feedback and Impact Force

13.22.1 Feedback — Tactile, Auditory and Visual

When a steel orchestra or a pan ensemble performs, the players rely on *auditory* and *visual feedback* in order to play in *synchrony*.

As is well known to the bandleader or conductor, starting simultaneously does not necessarily dictate synchrony. This is a frequent problem during practice sessions. A conductor, when used, can provide an additional communication link to ensure proper timing. Even the rhythmic swaying of the players to the musical sound provides timing information needed for synchronization. The individual player must at all times be able to hear his/her own instrument. When the overall sound intensity of the many instruments is high (for example at a Panorama Performance) one can find players bending closer to their instruments to increase local auditory feedback. Generally, the players in pan ensembles and full orchestras have trained themselves to keep the tempo by adjusting to the delays in auditory feedback that naturally occur for sound transmission across the distances separating the players.

Synchrony is not all; *tonality* is of great importance in any performance — solo or orchestral. Players generate tonality on the individual instrument and by the combined sound of all the instruments. To the player striking the notes, tonality requires a combination of *tactile* and auditory feedback. Tactile feedback must be achieved in the millisecond duration of stick contact while auditory feedback lasts a thousand times longer as it spans the entire second of the sounding tone.

The overriding mechanism responsible for the tonality of a sounding note is non-linear modal interaction. This means that the tuner, who sets the parameters for this mechanism, is chiefly responsible for the tonal qualities of a note. However, the tone generated by this mechanism depends on how the note is impacted by the stick. This is the reason for the great length of this Chapter; *stick-note impact is crucial*. The player when seen leaning towards the instrument is not only sharpening his/her auditory acuity but also his/her *mechanoreceptors* for feedback in fine motor control and the activation of related hand muscles. The feel of the impact is dependent on the magnitude of the contact force relative to the weight of the stick and the pressure sensations transmitted through the shank to the hand. *Lightweight hollow shanks (for example those made of bamboo) are superior to solid shanks in this regard (see Section 13.12).*

13.22.2 Impact Force and Hand Control

The impact force maximizes when the rebound velocity equals the incident velocity (in magnitude), $V_r = V_0$ or equivalently $\varepsilon_r = 1$. If the duration of the impact is assumed constant, then the ratio of the contact force F_ε when the COR equals ε to the contact force F_1 when the COR equals 1, is given by the approximation (refer to equation (13.127)

$$\frac{F_\varepsilon}{F_1} \approx \frac{1+\varepsilon}{2}. \qquad (13.203)$$

This simple approximation in (13.203) is useful for comparing pan sticks on the basis of the COR as shown in Table 13.9.

It is important to point out that in stick-note impacts on the low-end pans, where the hand action is less impulsive the effective COR (the eCOR) is somewhat lower than the value measured using a fixed impact plate. This is the result of the movement of the note surface on impact and the resulting energy transfer to the note to set it into vibration. The sensation for the player, especially on these low-end pans, is a softer impact. In contrast, on the high-end pans with the more deliberate hand action, the retrieving force applied by hand action increases the rebound velocity while decreasing the contact-time. This increases the effective COR and gives the sensation to the hand and effect on the note, of a stiffer tip.

TABLE 13.9

COR ε_r	Contact Force Ratio $100(1+\varepsilon_r)/2$ %	Tactile Feedback	**Result**
0	50 %	Dead. Like playing the notes with soft putty.	Tip 'sticks' to the note restricting vibration.
$0.2 < \varepsilon_r < 0.35$	60 to 67.5%	Like playing with very soft felt-tipped sticks. Mushy feel,	Muted, under-modulated tone.
$0.35 < \varepsilon_r < 0.5$	67.8 to 75%	Soft touch, becoming livelier towards the top of this COR range.	Moderately strong partials, increasing in intensity at the top of this COR range.
$0.5 \leq \varepsilon_r \leq 0.75$	75 to 88%	Gives the player best control of the tone.	**Strong partials* well modulated. I recommend this COR range.**
> 0.75	> 88%	Excessive bounce. Tone always very bright. Less impact control available to the player.	Very metallic tones as ε_r approaches 0.8. Tip properties determine tonality.

* Assumes a properly tuned note.

13.22.3 Simple Formula Combining Rebound Angle and Contact Force Ratio

A simple formula relating the contact force ratio in Section 13.22.2 with the rebound angle can be obtained by combining equation (13.203) with the expression $\varepsilon_r \cong \frac{\phi_f}{\phi_i}$. By taking an initial angle ϕ_i of 45° and rebound angle ϕ_f in degrees, one gets for the contact force ratio defined in Section 13.22.2, expressed as a percentage,

$$\left(\frac{f_\varepsilon}{f_1}\right) 100\% = 50 + \frac{10}{9}\phi_f \%.$$

Using this simple formula and the jig in Figure 13.61 the contact force ratio can be easily estimated and Table 13.9 used as a 'look-up' table to categorize the stick under test. The composite plot in Figure 13.65 does all this for you. Make sure each pair of sticks fall close together in the region $0.5 \leq COR \leq 0.75$.

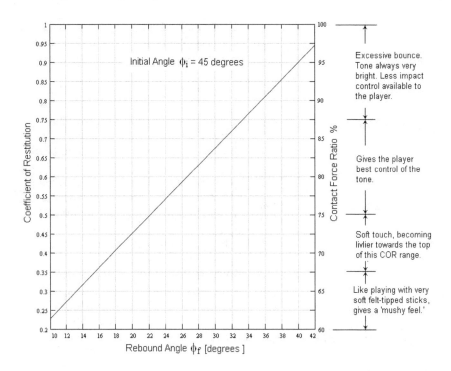

Fig. 13.65. Composite plot showing the COR and Contact Force Ratio versus the Rebound Angle for an initial angle of 45 degrees. Note that contact force ratio and COR fundamentally (and to a good approximation) depend only on the *ratio* of ϕ_f to ϕ_i.

13.23 Contact Pressure Distribution in Impact Dynamics

13.23.1 Condition for use of the Statical Contact Pressure Distribution Formula

During impact, the stress field in the compressed region of the tip defined by a circular area of diameter φ_c develops in a time τ_s given by

$$\tau_s = \varphi_c / V_p,$$

where V_p is the velocity of the compression waves within the stick tip. After this time has elapsed, the displacement of the tip in compression will reach its statical value and all the tip material in the region defined by the contact area will be *causally connected* for the remainder of the impact. This causal connection is the physical requirement that allows the stress field to produce a clearly defined contact force at the stick-note interface. The *static pressure distribution* formula can therefore be applied to the impact *dynamical problem* provided that the contact-time satisfies the condition $\tau_c \gg \tau_s$ which gives

$$\tau_c \gg \varphi_c / V_p.$$

Using equation (13.66) and equation (13.84), this condition can be written as

$$V_0 \ll V_p \left(\frac{\pi^{\frac{5}{2}} (1-v_s)}{18(1-2v_s)^{\frac{1}{2}}} \right),$$

This condition is independent of the radius of the stick tip so it applies to all sticks used on the steelpan. For typical values of the Poisson's ratio one gets

$$V_0 \ll \begin{cases} 1.3 \, V_p & \text{for } v_s = 0.4 \\ 1.69 \, V_p & \text{for } v_s = 0.45 \end{cases},$$

or simply,

$$V_0 \ll V_p . \tag{13.204}$$

We have already shown that for all manually applied stick impacts under normal playing action, $V_0 < 3.2$ m·s^{-1}, so that with $V_p = 43$ m·s^{-1} (see Table 13.2) condition (13.204) holds well in practice. The *statical* pressure distribution formula can therefore be used in the stick-note impact *dynamical* problem as long as the initial impact velocity V_0 is small compared to the velocity of the compressional waves V_p.

13.23.2 Time-dependent Contact Pressure Distribution

For the statical contact problem with an applied force F_z the pressure distribution over the contact area of radius c was found in Section 13.7 to be

$$\text{Static Case: } P_z(x) = \frac{3F_z}{2\pi c^2}\left(1 - \frac{x^2}{c^2}\right)^{\frac{1}{2}} \tag{13.205}$$

This describes a distribution which maximizes to $P_z(0) = 3F_z/(2\pi c^2)$ at the center ($x = 0$) of the contact area and drops to zero along the boundary ($x = c$) of the contact area.

When the pressure distribution given by equation (13.205) is applicable ($V_0 \ll V_p$), the static force F_z can be replaced with the time-dependent force $F_c'(t)$, giving the pressure distribution

$$\text{Dynamic Case: } P_c(x,t) = \frac{3F_c'(t)}{2\pi c^2}\left(1 - \frac{x^2}{c^2}\right)^{\frac{1}{2}}, \tag{13.206}$$

where $\pi c^2 = A_c$, $c^2 = 2R_s^2 w_{s,max}$ and

$$F_c'(t) = \left[\frac{4}{3}R_s^2 V_0^{\frac{2p}{p+1}}\left(\frac{E_s}{1-v_s^2}\right)^{\frac{1}{p+1}}\left(\frac{\pi\rho_s(p+1)}{2}\right)^{\frac{p}{p+1}} + \right.$$

$$\left.\frac{4}{3}\pi\sigma_{pre}R_s^2 V_0^{\frac{2}{p+1}}\left(\frac{\pi\rho_s(p+1)(1-v_s^2)}{2E_s}\right)^{\frac{2}{p+1}}\right] e^{-\frac{r_{ms}}{2m_s}t} \sin(2\pi t/3\tau_c) B(0,3\tau_c/2)$$

$$+ r_{ms} V_0 e^{-\frac{r_{ms}}{2m_s}t} \cos(2\pi t/3\tau_c) B(0,3\tau_c/2),$$

(13.207)

In order to keep the following development simple, we temporarily withhold the use of the general expression for F_c' by suppressing the pre-stress and dissipation terms. Later, these terms will be inserted to give the full expression.

Since the contact force maximizes with $w_s = w_{s,max}$, $\dot{w}_s = 0$, using equation (13.51b), one gets

$$F_{max} = \frac{4E_s}{3(1-v_s^2)} R_s^2 w_{s,max}^p.$$

Finally one gets for the pressure distribution

$$P_c(x,t) = \frac{E_s w_{s,max}^{p-1}}{\pi(1-v_s^2)} z(x) \sin(2\pi t/3\tau_c) B_1(0,T/2),$$

where

$$z(x) = \left(1 - x^2/c^2\right)^{\frac{1}{2}}$$

and

$$P_c(x) = \frac{E_s w_{s,max}^{p-1}}{\pi(1-v_s^2)} z(x). \qquad (13.208)$$

The spatial average of the contact pressure over the contact area, is given by

$$\overline{P}_c = \frac{\int_{A_C} P_c(x)ds}{\int_{A_C} ds}$$

$$= \frac{E_s w_{s,max}^{p-1}}{\pi(1-v_s^2)} \left[\frac{\int_{A_C} z(x)ds}{\int_{A_C} ds} \right]$$

$$= \frac{E_s w_{s,max}^{p-1}}{\pi(1-v_s^2)} \left[\frac{\int_c \left(1-\frac{x^2}{c^2}\right)^{\frac{1}{2}} 2\pi x dx}{\int_c 2\pi x dx} \right]$$

$$= \frac{E_s w_{s,max}^{p-1}}{\pi(1-v_s^2)} \left[\frac{2}{3}\right].$$

(13.209)

Comment: *This method of finding the average contact pressure of the stick-note impact in the SDOF analysis will be referred to and improved upon in the MDOF analysis. In equation (13.209) observe the factor [⅔] in square brackets for future reference.*

Therefore, the spatial average of the contact pressure — the pressure amplitude — is given by

$$\overline{P}_c = \frac{2E_s}{3\pi(1-v_s^2)} w_{s,max}^{p-1}.$$ (13.210)

$$\left\{ \text{For dissipative pre-stressed tips}: \overline{P}_c = \frac{2E_s}{3\pi(1-v_s^2)} w_{s,max}^{p-1} + \frac{2\sigma_{pre}}{3} + \frac{r_{ms}V_0}{A_c} \right\}$$

In particular, for p = 1

$$\overline{P}_c = \frac{2E_s}{3\pi(1-v_s^2)} \qquad (13.211)$$

Therefore:

- In the SDOF model, parameterized by p = 1, with $F_H = 0$, the pressure amplitude of the stick-note impact is constant and determined only by the tip parameters E_s and v_s.

Since force = (pressure x area) the contact force at time t during the impact is obtained from the integral $\int_{A_c} P_c(x,t)\,ds$ where ds is an element of area on the note surface. This contact force for $r_{ms} = 0$, is equal to

$$(2E_s/3\pi(1-v_s^2))\, w_{s,max}^{p-1}\, A_c \sin(\omega t)\, B_1(0,T/2).$$

- In the SDOF model, for p = 1 with $F_H = 0$, stick-note impacts can be described as a constant pressure amplitude $2E_s/3\pi(1-v_s^2)$ applied over a small patch on the note surface which quickly grows in area from zero to a maximum A_c and just as quickly the area reduces to zero. The form of the area function is the ½-sine function $A_c\sin(\omega t)\, B_1(0,T/2)$.
- Equation (13.210) and equation (13.211) show that $\overline{P}_c = \overline{P}\,|_{p=1}\, w_{s,max}^{p-1}$. Since $w_{s,max} < 1$ this result implies that the average contact pressure maximizes as p approaches unity (consistent with the results shown in Figure 13.18).

Partial Summary: The set of ideas and concepts developed so far underlies the SDOF description of the Impact Phase. Stick-note impacts generally follow a power law parameterized by the p-index with different p values for the compression phase and the restitution phase. The impact is locally well modeled by the linearized form (setting p = 1) of the equations. This feature allows for simplification of the impact process and provides closed-form solutions that can be easily used by stick makers. The analysis of impacts on the more general MDOF multi-mode note system can now be done with the help of this clear interpretation of the impact in the SDOF case.

13.24 MDOF Analysis of the Stick-Note Contact Phase

13.24.1 Generalization of the Pressure Distribution Function

The formulations for the average force F_{avg} and F_{max} developed in the discussions on the coefficient of restitution are inadequate for use in the present work on multi-mode modal interactions. The COR is a useful quantity in simple impact problems such as obtained in the SDOF stick-note system and it serves as the appropriate parameter for determining the level of tactile feedback that the player may experience. However, these models, despite their somewhat complicated mathematical appearance, are still *too simplified* for many practical situations that arise in the complex multi-mode system of the steelpan. *The contact or impact phase of the multi-mode stick-note system is not a simple impact problem.* However, the treatment in the previous Sections remains valid within its limits of applicability.

In this Section attention is paid to the fact that when struck by the stick, a note executes a number of modal vibrations (multi-mode vibrations). It is the transfer of energy from the impacting stick that sets the note surface into vibration. Each mode vibrates at a particular frequency and must be excited by vibrational energy at a frequency corresponding to that of the excited mode.

Because the note is being driven into vibration in the stick-note interaction, the modal response of the impacted note must be considered in formulations involving the pressure distribution function. So far, the analysis has been restricted to the SDOF system having just one excited mode with the additional restriction that impacts be made to the single sweetspot located at the apex of the note. To deal with impacts at any arbitrary point on the note surface the *mode shape* ψ_m must be included and this will change the way in which the surface integral of the pressure distribution is to be carried out.

In solving the integral $\int_0^{A_c} P_c ds$ in Section 13.23.2 it was assumed (implicitly) that the note presents a constant modal response over the area of the impact. This assumption is approximately true for the fundamental mode in the SDOF case for sufficiently small contact areas centered at the apex. However, the assumption cannot be generally true because when the note vibrates, the displacement maximizes at the antinodes and decreases to zero (*or near zero when losses on the note are considered*) at the note boundary or along nodal lines.

Using the system of coordinates described in Section 3.4.1, the stick impact point on the note surface can be specified by the coordinate set (r_i, ϕ_i). At this location the contact pressure is distributed within a circular region of radius $c(t)$ as shown in Figure 13.66. The perspective for the diagram in Figure 13.66 is the projection unto the plane passing through the note boundary and normal to the z-axis.

A new variable χ, with $\chi^2 = r_i^2 + r^2 - 2r_i r \cos(\phi_i - \phi)$, replaces x in equation (13.208). The contact pressure distribution can now be written as

$$P_c(r,\phi) = \frac{E_s \, w_{s,\max}^{p-1}}{\pi(1-v_s^2)} z(r,\phi), \qquad (13.212)$$

$$\left\{ \text{For dissipative pre-stressed tips}: P_c(r,\phi) = \left(\frac{E_s}{\pi(1-v_s^2)} w_{s,\max}^{p-1} + \sigma_{pre} + \frac{3r_{ms}V_0}{2A_c} \right) z(r,\phi) \right\}$$

where $z(r,\phi) = \left[1 - 4\chi^2 / \varphi_c^2 \right]^{\frac{1}{2}}$

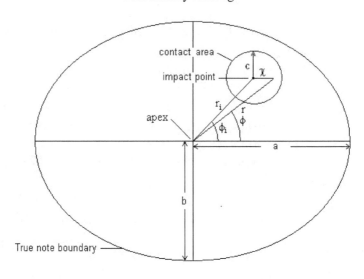

Fig. 13.66. Circular contact area with impact point at coordinates (r_i, ϕ_i).

13.24.2 A Quick Comparison between SDOF and MDOF

The advantage of the SDOF (Single Degree Of Freedom) analysis of the stick-note contact phase is the simplicity it offers in some of the equations thereby making closed-form solutions possible. All the results obtained in the SDOF analysis can be obtained from the MDOF (Many Degrees Of Freedom) treatment. The MDOF analyses are mathematically more difficult, may not always yield closed-form solutions, but they allow all the interacting modes of vibration to be included. Their main advantage, when applied to the impact phase, is that they allow for the treatment and explanation of the subtleties of pan playing in which, for example, the player can emphasize certain modes. In the SDOF analysis, the impact point was limited to the sweetspot, now in the higher dimensional MDOF analysis *the impact can be anywhere on the note surface*. Now that we can choose the impact point anywhere on the note, with the help of equation (13.212), *we can unlock the secrets of the professional player but we may not all be able to apply them in practice with the same level of perfection.*

To proceed further with the MDOF analysis it is necessary that the mode shapes of all excited vibrations be considered because *stick-note impacts are impulsive interactions between the stick and the normal modes of vibration of the no*te. The impact provides the forces that excite these normal vibrational modes. *It does this in a manner that depends on both the spatial and the temporal aspects of each vibrational mode.* Since the stick contact force is pulse-like its Fourier components imparts the initial energy to each mode during the impact. However, since there is a partitioning of the impact energy, *the modes are not equally excited.*

Now the note is excited by two agencies, namely the driving forces generated by the ½-sine function and the forces generated by the ½-cosine function associated with tip losses. In the SDOF analysis, these two agencies were seen to be fundamentally different. However, there were no compelling reasons to treat these two sets of forces separately by *decoupling* them. In anticipation of the results to be obtained in the MDOF analysis, these two forces must be treated separately even though they both arise from stick-note impacts because they produce two distinctly different audio sounds from the sounding note — *one musical, the other noisy.*

As a general remark, all pans and sticks are not created equal. However, all pans and all sticks operate under the same set of principles. The following impact analysis applies to all sticks and to all pans whether tuned or untuned. In a general sense all pans are tuned but the title 'tuned pan' will be reserved for pans for which there is that special relationship among the note frequencies that correspond to the musical scale.

13.24.3 Modal Equivalent Mass

The *Modal Equivalent Mass* is an important quantity in the dynamics of the vibrating steelpan note because a note (the true note) when it is excited to produce the key-note and higher partials, sets up on its surface a complex mixture of time-dependent shapes. To each partial (key-note, octave and twelfth) there is a corresponding mode of vibration and mode shape ψ_m on the surface of the note. Since the amplitude of vibration for each of these modes varies across the surface of the note, if one considers the note surface to be made up of small sections, these sections do not contribute equally to the kinetic energy of the vibrating note nor do they contribute equally to the acoustical radiation of the note.

The driving forces $p_m(\tau)$ — or the *load participation factors* — that selectively excite each mode on impact, are normalized forces per unit mass obtained from the contact pressure distribution given in equation (13.212). To obtain the force per unit mass requires the use of the *modal equivalent mass* of the note *for each mode* because displacement on the vibrating note varies over the note surface and in particular nodal lines (in the ideal limit) do not vibrate at all. The note mass (in physical units of kg) is given by

Note mass:

$$\begin{aligned} m_n &= \int_A \rho_n h \, ds \\ &= \rho_n h \int_A ds \\ &= \rho_n h A, \end{aligned} \qquad (13.213)$$

with h is the note thickness (assumed constant over the surface of the note), ρ_n is the note material density and A is the surface area of the note. On the other hand, the *modal equivalent mass* of the note vibrating in the mth mode, defined as

Modal equivalent mass: $\quad m_{eqv}^{\{m\}} = \int_A \rho_n h \psi_m^2(r,\phi) \, ds,\quad$ (12.214)

represents that mass which, when vibrating with displacement equal to the amplitude of the mth mode has the same dynamical effect (same kinetic energy) as the vibrating note. In general, for any kind of dynamic loading, a larger $m_{eqv}^{\{m\}}$ leads to lower modal (and hence physical) responses and vice versa. In equation (13.214) the symbol $\{m\}$ on the modal equivalent mass $m_{eqv}^{\{m\}}$ is used as a *label* to identify the mth mode. In this definition, ψ_m is the mth (arbitrarily scaled) mode shape having no units. When the density and thickness are constant over the note surface, using equation (13.213) and equation (13.213), the *modal equivalent mass* can also be written as

$$m_{eqv}^{\{m\}} = m_n \frac{\int_A \psi_m^2(r,\phi)\,ds}{\int_A ds} \quad (13.215)$$

$$= m_n \langle \psi_m^2 \rangle,$$

where the bracket function $\langle X \rangle$ represents the *mean value* of the function X over the defined area (in this case A).

Equation (13.215) shows that the equivalent mass is equal to the product of the mass of the note and the average value of the square of the mode shape function over the note surface. If the modal response is constant over the note surface ($\psi_m = 1$ everywhere over the note) then the equivalent mass equals the mass of the note (as obtained for the SDOF case).

13.24.4 The Impact Equations in the MDOF Representation

In order to present the terms in the MDOF non-linear dynamical equations in a compact form, the analysis replaces the ordinary time variable t with a normalized time variable $\tau = \gamma t$, where $\gamma^2 = E_n h^2 / [\rho_n a^4 (1 - v_n^2)]$. The reader should not experience any difficulty switching between these two time variables because the use of normalized time always involves the simple substitution of τ/γ for the variable t.

If the external force $p(\tau)$ is applied continuously or by impact, the modal equations for note vibrations derived from equation (3.30) are a set of second-order ODEs (one ODE for each value of the modal number m) given in dimensionless form by

$$\frac{d^2 w_m}{d\tau^2} + \mu_m \frac{dw_m}{d\tau} + \omega_m^2 w_m + \sum_{i,j=1}^{N} \alpha_{ij,m} w_i w_j + \sum_{i,j,k=1}^{N} \beta_{ijk,m} w_i w_j w_k = f_0 + p_m(\tau),$$

$$(m = 1, 2, 3, \ldots N) \quad (13.216)$$

where m is the mode designator or mode number (in the musical context, m refers to the set of partials, first, second, third etc, associated with the note: *not all partials may be present on a given note*), w_m is the displacement of the note surface in the mth mode,

$\dfrac{d^2 w_m}{d\tau^2}$ is the inertial term (acceleration), $\mu_m \dfrac{d w_m}{d\tau}$ represents damping, $\mu_m = \dfrac{r_m}{m_{eqv}^{\{m\}} \gamma}$ with r_m as the mechanical resistance of the note, $\omega_m^2 w_m$ is the usual structural stiffness term (which includes the effects of thermal and compressive stresses), f_0 is the normalized static force due to thermal and compressive stresses which sets the quiescent point of the note system, $\sum_{i,j=1}^{3} \alpha_{jk,n} w_j w_k$ represent quadratic stiffness, $\sum_{i,j,k=1}^{3} \beta_{ijk,n} w_i w_j w_k$ represents the cubic stiffness. If f_m is the modal frequency of the mth mode then $\omega_m = \dfrac{2\pi_m f_m}{\gamma}$.

Driving Forces

To obtain the normalized driving forces per unit mass, the following operations are performed on the RHS of equation (13.212):

(i) divide by $\gamma^2 h$ (to be consistent with the dimensionless inertial term in equation (13.216)),
(ii) perform the replacement $t \mapsto \tau/\gamma$
(iii) perform a Galerkin average (see Section 8.4) of the pressure distribution function $z(r, \phi)$ over the note surface area A,
(iv) divide by the note equivalent mass $m_{eqv}^{\{m\}}$ for the corresponding mode,
(v) multiply by the ½-sine function, which describes the temporal aspect of the impact.

These operations transform $P_c(r, \phi)$ into $p_m(\tau)$. For zero pre-stress the result is

$$p_m(\tau) = \frac{E_s(1-\upsilon_n^2)}{\pi E_n(1-\upsilon_s^2)} \left(\frac{a}{h}\right)^4 w_{s,max}^{p-1} \frac{\int_{A_c} z(r,\phi)\psi_m(r,\phi)ds}{\int_A \psi_m^2(r,\phi)ds} \sin\left(\frac{2\pi\tau}{3\gamma\tau_c}\right) B_1(0,3\gamma\tau_c/2),$$

(13.217)

and with pre-stress

$$p_m(\tau) = \left(\frac{E_s}{\pi(1-\upsilon_s^2)} w_{s,max}^{p-1} + \sigma_{pre}\right) \frac{(1-\upsilon_n^2)}{E_n}\left(\frac{a}{h}\right)^4 \frac{\int_{A_c} z(r,\phi)\psi_m(r,\phi)ds}{\int_A \psi_m^2(r,\phi)ds} \times$$

$$\sin\left(\frac{2\pi\tau}{3\gamma\tau_c}\right) B_1(0,3\gamma\tau_c/2),$$

(13.218)

where $ds = r\,dr\,d\phi$, $A_c = 2\pi R_s^2 w_{s,max}$ is the contact-area of the stick-note impact, $A = \pi ab$ is the area of the note, a and b are respectively the major and minor semi-axes of the note, $z(r, \phi)$ is the contact pressure spatial distribution function, $\psi_m(r,\phi)$ is the mode shape of the mth mode. Since the pressure distribution function is zero everywhere outside the contact-area A_c centered at the impact point, the integral $\int_{A_c} z(r,\phi)\psi_m(r,\phi)ds$ is confined only to the area of contact as indicated.

The factor $sin(2\pi\tau/3\gamma\tau_c)B_1(0,3\gamma\tau_c/2)$ describes the temporal aspect of the impact, while the integral quotient $\int_{A_c} z(r,\phi)\psi_m(r,\phi)ds / \int_A \psi_m^2(r,\phi)ds$ describes the spatial aspect. Observe that only the spatial aspect of the impact is expressed in integral form. Integration of the temporal aspect over time is done in the solution of equation (13.216), an ODE in which all the derivatives are with respect to normalized time.

Returning to the SDOF analysis in Section 13.23.2, one can readily see that the integral quotient $\int_{A_c} z(r,\phi)\psi_m(r,\phi)ds / \int_A \psi_m^2(r,\phi)ds$ used here in the MDOF case, is a generalization of the SDOF expression $\int_{A_c} z(x)\,ds / \int_{A_c} ds = 2/3$ (see equation (13.209) and the comment made there concerning the bracketed two thirds), where the note presents a constant (unity) modal response $\psi_m(r,\phi)=1$ over the impact area. This integral quotient plays an important role in the stick-note interaction so it deserves the special treatment that follows.

13.24.5 The Stick-Note Impact Function describing the 'Player's Action'

The steelpan is a percussive musical instrument where the player *selects* the impact point on the note surface in order to generate a desired tonal effect. *In 'playing the Instrument' it is not sufficient to merely 'strike the notes.'* A special function is now defined which describes this selection of impact point; it will be called the *Stick-Note Impact Function S(m,r,ϕ)*. The function $z(r,\phi)$ defines both the contact pressure spatial distribution and the impact point on the note, while the *value* of the integral quotient $\int_{A_c} z(r,\phi)\psi_m(r,\phi)ds / \int_A \psi_m^2(r,\phi)ds$ determines its contribution to the magnitude of the modal forces $p_m(\tau)$. *The operation or 'Player's Action' of applying contact pressure with the stick over an area A_c centered at a specific point (r,ϕ) on the surface of a <u>tuned</u> note of area A is expressed in symbolic notation by*

$$S(m,r,\phi) = \frac{\int_{A_c} z(r,\phi)\psi_m(r,\phi)ds}{\int_A \psi_m^2(r,\phi)ds}. \qquad (13.219)$$

This action by the player, *assigns a value* to the function $S(m,r,\phi)$. In the SDOF system the value assigned to the Stick-Note Impact Function is simply 2/3 (see Section 13.23.2 and equation 13.209).

The integral $\int_A \psi_m^2(r,\phi)ds$ is a normalization factor and it is customary (as in the SDOF analysis) to normalize the mode shape functions so that $\int_A \psi_m^2(r,\phi)ds = 1$, which allows one to conveniently write

$$S(m,r,\phi) = \int_{A_c} z(r,\phi)\psi_m(r,\phi)ds.$$

However, if this is done here for each mode then the relative magnitudes (*mode-to-mode*) of $S(m,r,\phi)$ will be lost. In order to preserve the relative levels of modal excitation on impact, we will **not** perform this normalization in the MDOF analysis.

$S(m,r,\phi)$ and hence, the magnitude of the driving force for a given mode (the mth mode) maximizes when the impact point coincides with a sweetspot (where $|\psi_m(r,\phi)|$ is a maximum) and minimizes when the impact point falls on or in the neighborhood of a nodal line (where $|\psi_m(r,\phi)|$ is a minimum). Since (i) the contact area is of finite size (contact not confined only at a single point), (ii) the mode shape $\psi_m(r,\phi)$ changes sign across a nodal line and (iii) $|\psi_m(r,\phi)|$ is not necessarily symmetrical about the nodal line, the impact point need not fall exactly on a nodal line for $S(m,r,\phi)$ to be at a minimum. It is sufficient for the impact point to be in the neighborhood of the nodal line for this minimization to occur.

'True Note' defined by the Stick-Note Impact Function

The boundary of the *true note* (which always lie within the *traditional note*) is a nodal line, generally elliptical, along which $S(m,r,\phi)$ is a minimum. Using the Stick-Note Impact Function one can clearly define the boundary of the true note as the *locus of all points for which $S(m,r,\phi)$ is a minimum for all tuned modes on the note. In addition, the area enclosed by this locus is a minimum (this last condition excludes points remote from the note).* What all this demonstrates is the fact that by using a sufficiently small stick tip one can determine the true note boundary by 'sounding' the note in the general location of the boundary.

13.24.6 Mode Emphasis and De-emphasis by Control of the Impact Point — The Panist making use of the Stick-Note Impact Function

The player decides which note to strike and the point on the note surface at which to make the impact. For a proper understanding of this aspect of the impact, the note surface must not be viewed simply as a dome-shaped metal shell. Instead it must be viewed as a surface on which various mode shapes develop once the note has been struck and excited. The first three normal modes are shown in Figure 13.67 along with sketches of their approximate mode shapes. For each mode there is at least one sweetspot corresponding to the anti-nodal point or the point of maximum displacement. *For maximum initial excitation of a particular mode, the impact must be made at the sweetspot corresponding to that particular mode.* The expert player with knowledge gained through experience with a particular pan, can emphasize individual modes by striking at the corresponding sweetspot. This is needed in the proper execution of a roll on the tenor. Here, as the roll progresses, the player can gradually shift the impact point around the note surface to a point close to or on the corresponding sweetspot to emphasize the chosen mode while de-emphasizing others. *This is one of the tricks in the art of pan playing.*

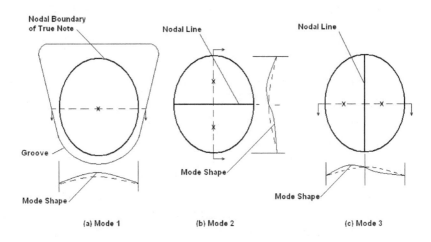

Fig. 13.67. Location of the true note within the grooved area and the nodal lines associated with mode 2 and mode 3. The true note nodal boundary is the same for all modes. Sweetspots are marked by an X. The dashed curves show the note surface at rest. Modal displacements change direction every half cycle.

For its importance we now give further details on $S(m,r,\phi)$. These details are fully incorporated into and covered by the integral $\int_{A_C} z(r,\phi)\psi_m(r,\phi)ds$ where the function $z(r,\phi)$ describes the location of the impact point and 'center' of the normalized pressure distribution over the contact area. The use of the function $\psi_m(r,\phi)$

for a particular mode identified by mode number m, ensures that the integral provides the impact force that initially excites that particular mode. The *product* of $z(r,\phi)$ and the mode shape function $\psi_m(r,\phi)$ is an *overlap function* which maximizes when the impact point corresponds to the sweetspot for the mth mode and minimizes when the impact point falls on a nodal line corresponding to the mth mode or on the true note boundary. The overlap integral taken over the contact area A_c is always zero when the contact area lies entirely outside the true note boundary because $\psi_m(r,\phi)$ is zero everywhere outside the true note for the lossless system or one that is perfectly blocked at the boundaries. This explains why a note cannot always be excited by merely striking at any arbitrary point within the area bounded by the groove (the *traditional note*). *The impact point must fall within the true note area.* Taking the integral of the overlap function over the contact area A_c (of width φ_c) sums the contribution from all points of contact between stick and note for each mode separately. In practice, blocking is not perfect thus making $\psi_m(r,\phi)$ take on small values immediately outside the note boundary.

Emphasis and de-emphasis can only be effective if the panist is allowed full freedom to exercise his/her repertoire of stick actions. If restrictions are introduced, say by poor choice of sticks, the subtle tonal enrichment that normally flows from the hands of the panist will surely be lost.

13.24.7 Assigning values to the Impact Function $S(m,r,\phi)$

Case 1: $p=1$, $r_m=0$, $\sigma_{pre}=0$, $F_H=0$

Using

$$\varphi_c^2 = 8R^2 V_0 \left(\frac{\pi(1-v_s^2)\rho_s}{E_s}\right)^{\frac{1}{2}}, \quad A_c = \pi\varphi_c^2/4 \text{ and } V_p = \sqrt{\frac{E_s(1-v_s)}{\rho_s(1+v_s)(1-2v_s)}},$$

gives

$$\varphi_c = R_s \left[\frac{V_0}{V_p}\right]^{\frac{1}{2}} \left[\frac{8\pi^{\frac{1}{2}}(1-v_s)}{(1-2v_s)^{\frac{1}{2}}}\right]^{\frac{1}{2}}, \quad A_c = \frac{\pi R_s^2 V_0}{V_p}\left[\frac{2\pi^{\frac{1}{2}}(1-v_s)}{(1-2v_s)^{\frac{1}{2}}}\right].$$

Using this expression for A_c and with $A = \pi ab$, it readily follows from *dimensional analysis* performed on equation (13.217) that

$$\frac{\int_{A_c} z(r,\phi)\psi_m(r,\phi)ds}{\int_A \psi_m^2(r,\phi)ds} \propto \frac{A_c}{A} \propto \frac{R_s^2 V_0}{ab V_p}. \quad (13.220)$$

This is an important result: it tells us that the Stick-Note Impact function depends directly on the ratio of the cross-sectional area of the stick tip to the area of the true note (R_s^2/ab) — *in practical terms, larger notes require larger sticks*. Because of its importance to the impact force the result in equation (13.220) will be obtained in the form of an equality using a more rigorous method.

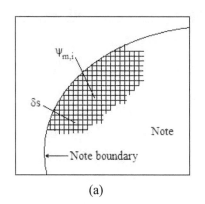 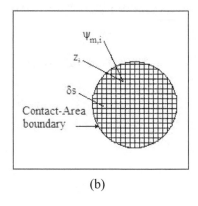

(a)   (b)

Fig. 13.68. True note (a) and contact-area (b) divided into small area elements.

Using simple quadrature, the integrals in equation (13.220) can be evaluated numerically as follows: Divide the contact-area A_c into a large number N_I of small elements each of area δs, giving $A_c = N_I \delta s$ as in Figure 13.68. Similarly divide the note surface area A into

N_2 elements each or area δs to give $A = N_2 \, \delta s$. Both $N1$ and $N2$ must be sufficiently large (δs sufficiently small) to ensure that the areas are well covered. Label the elements (1, 2 ...i...N) and for the ith element the corresponding values z_i and ψ_i as shown in Figure 13.68. Along nodal lines the values of ψ_i are all zero and ψ_i changes sign on either side of the nodal line except in the case of the note boundary. For the note boundary it is assumed that the note is perfectly blocked so that ψ_i is zero everywhere outside the note. This means that the net contribution of products $z_i \psi_i$ in the neighborhood of nodal lines will be small even vanishingly small.

In the limit as $(N_1, N_2) \to \infty$, $\delta s \to 0$, integrals can be transformed into summations as follows:

$$S(m,r,\phi) = \frac{\int_{A_c} z(r,\phi) \psi_m(r,\phi) ds}{\int_A \psi_m^2(r,\phi) ds} \equiv \frac{\lim \left\{ \sum_1^{N_1} z_i \psi_{m,i} \, \delta s \right\}}{\lim \left\{ \sum_1^{N_2} \psi_{m,i}^2 \, \delta s \right\}} = \frac{\lim \left\{ \dfrac{\sum_1^{N_1} z_i \psi_{m,i}}{N_1} A_c \right\}}{\lim \left\{ \dfrac{\sum_1^{N_2} \psi_{m,i}^2}{N_2} A \right\}}$$

$$= \frac{\langle z \psi_m \rangle}{\langle \psi_m^2 \rangle} \left(\frac{A_c}{A} \right)$$

$$= \frac{\langle z \psi_m \rangle}{\langle \psi_m^2 \rangle} \left(\frac{R^2 V_0}{abV_p} \right) \left(\frac{2\pi^{\frac{1}{2}}(1-v_s)}{(1-2v_s)^{\frac{1}{2}}} \right).$$

(13.221)

Case 2: $p \geq 1$, $r_m \geq 0$, $\sigma_{pre} = 0$, $F_H = 0$

Using equations (13.90) and (13.221) gives

$$\frac{\int_{A_c} z(r,\phi) \psi_m(r,\phi) ds}{\int_A \psi_m^2(r,\phi) ds} = \frac{\langle z \psi_m \rangle}{\langle \psi_m^2 \rangle} \left(\frac{A_c}{A} \right)$$

$$= 2 \frac{\langle z \psi_m \rangle}{\langle \psi_m^2 \rangle} \left(\frac{R_s^2}{ab} \right) \left(\frac{V_0}{V_p} \right)^{\frac{2}{p+1}} \left(\frac{\pi(p+1)(1-v_s)^2}{2(1-2v_s)} \right)^{\frac{1}{p+1}} e^{\frac{\alpha\pi}{2p\omega}},$$

(13.222)

where the factor $(1- 2\alpha^2/p\omega^2)$ is neglected but it can be reinserted for completeness. The exponential factor

$$e^{-\frac{\alpha\pi}{2p\omega}} \approx 1 - \frac{3r_{ms}}{16pR_s^2}\left(\frac{\pi(1-v_s^2)}{E_s\rho_s}\right)^{\frac{1}{2}}$$

gives an additional dependence on the tip properties.

Equations (13.221) and (13.222) show that:

- During stick-note impact there are well defined forces (modal forces) driving each tuned mode found on the note.
- The amplitudes of the modal driving forces per unit mass for the mth mode is proportional to the mean value $<z\psi_m>$ of the product $z\psi_m$ of the pressure distribution function and the mode shape divided by the mean value of the square of the mode shape function $<\psi_m^2>$.
- While the distribution function z is always positive, ψ_m changes sign across nodal lines. The mean $<z\psi_m>$ can therefore be zero if the impact point is in the neighborhood of a nodal line of that particular mode. Selected modes can therefore be *de-emphasi*zed by stick impacts made along the corresponding nodal lines. Striking away from the nodal lines preferably at the antinodes (sweetspots) can *emphasize* these modes. It should be noted that the apex of the note, which corresponds to the sweetspot for the fundamental (*key-note*) coincides with the intersection of the nodal lines for the *octave* and the *twelfth*. This means that striking the key-note sweetspot de-emphasizes the initial excitation of the octave and twelfth. However since the dominant modality for mode excitation is through quadratic excitation generated by the key-note, the apex is still the best impact point for maximum excitation of *all* the partials.

Case 3: $p \geq 1$, $r_m \geq 0$, $\sigma_{pre} \geq 0$, $F_H = 0$

In this slightly more general case

$$S(m,r,\phi) = \frac{\int_{A_c} z(r,\phi)\psi_m(r,\phi)ds}{\int_A \psi_m^2(r,\phi)ds}$$

$$= \frac{\langle z\psi_m \rangle}{\langle \psi_m^2 \rangle}\left(\frac{A_c}{A}\right) \quad (13.223)$$

$$S(m,r,\phi) = \frac{\langle z\psi_m \rangle}{\langle \psi_m^2 \rangle}\left(\frac{2R_s^2 w_0 x}{ab}\right),$$

where x is obtained from the stick compression formula. Using equation (13.223) in (13.218) and with $w_{s(max)} = w_0 x$ gives

$$p_m(\tau) = \left(\frac{E_s}{\pi(1-\upsilon_s^2)}w_{s(max)}^p + \sigma_{pre}w_{s(max)}\right)\frac{(1-\upsilon_n^2)}{E_n}\left(\frac{a}{h}\right)^4\frac{\langle z\psi_m \rangle}{\langle \psi_m^2 \rangle}\left(\frac{2R_s^2}{ab}\right)e^{-\frac{\alpha\tau}{\gamma}} \times$$

$$\sin\left(\frac{2\pi\tau}{3\gamma\tau_c}\right)B_1(0, 3\gamma\tau_c/2)$$

$$+$$

$$\left(\frac{3r_{ms}V_0}{4\pi R_s^2}\right)\frac{(1-\upsilon_n^2)}{E_n}\left(\frac{a}{h}\right)^4\frac{\langle z\psi_m \rangle}{\langle \psi_m^2 \rangle}\left(\frac{2R_s^2}{ab}\right)e^{-\frac{\alpha\tau}{\gamma}}\cos\left(\frac{2\pi\tau}{3\gamma\tau_c}\right)B_1(0, 3\gamma\tau_c/2).$$

$$(13.224)$$

Notice in equation (13.224) that $p_m(\tau)$ is expressed as the sum of the ½-sine function and the ½-cosine function. This separation into two forces was also done in the SDOF analysis in equation (13.78). The reasons for doing this will soon become clear. If the Shank Losses are neglected and the expression in equation (13.88) is used, one can write equation (13.224) more explicitly and to a good approximation as

$$P_m(\tau) = 2V_0^{\frac{2p}{p+1}} \frac{\langle z\psi_m \rangle}{\langle \psi_m^2 \rangle} \left(\frac{a}{h}\right)^4 \left(\frac{R_s^2}{ab}\right) \left(\frac{(1-\upsilon_n^2)}{E_n}\right) \left(\frac{E_s}{\pi(1-\upsilon_s^2)}\right)^{\frac{1}{p+1}} \left(\frac{\rho_s(p+1)}{2}\right)^{\frac{p}{p+1}} \times$$

$$\left(1 + \sigma_{pre} V_0^{\frac{2(1-p)}{p+1}} \left(\frac{\rho_s(p+1)}{2}\right)^{\frac{1-p}{p+1}} \left(\frac{\pi(1-\upsilon_s^2)}{E_s}\right)^{\frac{2}{p+1}} e^{-\alpha\left(\frac{\tau}{\gamma} + \frac{\pi}{2\omega}\right)}\right) \times$$

$$\sin\left(\frac{2\pi\tau}{3\gamma\tau_c}\right) B_1(0,3\gamma\tau_c/2)$$

$$+$$

$$\frac{3r_{ms}V_0}{2\pi ab} \left(\frac{(1-\upsilon_n^2)}{E_n}\right) \left(\frac{a}{h}\right)^4 \frac{\langle z\psi_m \rangle}{\langle \psi_m^2 \rangle} e^{-\frac{\alpha\tau}{\gamma}} \cos\left(\frac{2\pi\tau}{3\gamma\tau_c}\right) B_1(0,3\gamma\tau_c/2)).$$

(13.225)

This form for the driving forces is very useful as it allows both qualitative and quantitative determination of the effects on the initial excitation of the partials of almost all the stick and note impact parameters. The exact form in equation (13.224) will give more precise estimates in numerical solutions.

Observe the following with reference to equation (13.225):

The ½-sine modal driving forces

- The normalized modal driving forces per unit mass are proportional to $V_0^{\frac{2p}{p+1}}$ and $E_s^{\frac{1}{p+1}}$. The player can vary V_0 for each impact, and decide its contribution by the choice of stick, which determines the p-index (compression). The $E_s^{\frac{1}{p+1}}$ dependence means that these forces *increase* with the elastic modulus of the tip rubber and by implication, these forces increase with the tip stiffness.
- The normalized modal forces are proportional to R_s^2/ab. This shows that the larger the ratio of the stick cross-sectional area to the area of the note surface, the stronger is the mode excitation. However, this result must be taken with some caution because *wavelength band limiting* (which will

be treated in the Section 13.30) places restrictions on the size of the stick tip.

The ½-cosine driving forces due to tip mechanical resistance

- The normalized driving forces per unit mass due to tip mechanical resistance are proportional to V_0 and r_m. When the mechanical resistance of the tip is increased the magnitudes of these forces also increase. As a stick age and its mechanical losses increase, these forces will increase.
- These driving forces are independent of tip radius, density and elastic modulus.

The fact that these two types of forces display so diverse dependencies on stick and impact parameters suggests that they are fundamentally different. To more fully understand the differences Fourier analyses of these forces must first be carried out.

Case 4: $p \geq 1$, $r_m \geq 0$, $F_H > 0$

In this general case equation (13.222) and the ½-sine, ½-cosine functions, which describe the temporal development of the contact area, can still be used provided certain conditions related to the timing of the hand action F_H are met. This case involves issues that affect the magnitudes of the contact forces and the spectral components of the forces. For these reasons the following sections on Fourier analyses of the Impact Phase must be studied before application of the present results to the real cases obtained in practice involving hand action F_H.

13.25 Spectral Distribution of the Contact Force — the Primary Forces generated by Impact

13.25.1 General Aspects of the Problem

The analysis and numerical computations in this Section will be carried out with a high degree of rigor in order not to miss the subtle aspects of stick-note excitations. Our goal here is to find out what is possible with the combination of note, stick and player. It is here that the actions of the finest panists can be put to the test.

In this section where repeated reference to modal frequency in Hertz (Hz) must be made, we temporarily set aside the use of normalized time τ and make use of ordinary time t once again.

Whereas in the SDOF analysis where, for example in equation (13.78) the contact force was expressed as the sum of two components — the 'normal' impact force containing the ½-sine function and the resistive force component containing the ½-cosine function — in the following MDOF analysis these two components will be treated separately. The reason for this is that the sound generated by stick-note impact consists of the desired musical component and a noise component.

Upon impact with the surface of the note, stress waves of different frequencies, phases and amplitudes are generated and propagating wavefronts are created in both the stick tip and the note material. The ½-sine force–time function is therefore equivalent to the summation of a number of these continuous sinusoidal force-time functions with different frequencies, amplitudes and phases. The frequency content of the impact is therefore a function of the duration and magnitude of the impact.

A *Fourier Expansion* is usually defined for a periodic function $f(t)$ in terms of an infinite sum of sines and cosines. The sine and cosine components of the force-time function are the Fourier components of the function. Although the ½-sine function is non-periodic and, in practice, only a finite number of sine and cosine components are generated on impact, the terminology still applies. What happens is that the sines and cosines with their individual amplitude and phase, on summation, cancel themselves out for $t < 0$, $t > 3\tau_c/2$ while generating the ½-sine function on the interval $[0, 3\tau_c/2]$.

Although the modal sub-systems described in equation (13.216) respond selectively to the frequency components of the impact forces, it will not be complete to select a single force component before the integration and place it on the right-hand side of (13.216) in order to simplify the analysis. This is not the mathematically correct or the physically proper way of treating this damped non-linear system driven by impact. The reasons are:

(i) each mode, while characterized by a modal frequency f_m and Quality Factor Q, is responsive to a range of frequencies centered at f_m corresponding to the intrinsic frequency bandwidth (f_m/Q) of the mode,
(ii) the impact force frequency spectrum is not uniform and in addition contain zeros at well defined frequencies and
(iii) the system is non-linear because the vibrating modes, when properly tuned, interact with each other.

If for example the chosen frequency corresponds to a zero on the spectrum, because of the system bandwidth and asymmetries (in phase as well as amplitude) about the zero, the system can still give some small response to forces on either side of the zero. The damping term in equation (13.216) will ensure that the sub-system ('sub' here referring to the fact that a note on a pan is just one of many that comprise the whole system) responds to all impact force frequency components over the mode bandwidth. Inserting a single frequency component on the right-hand side of equation (13.216) will defeat the proper function of the damping term and the full response of the sub-system over the specified range of frequencies.

13.25.2 The Fourier Transform

To help the general reader on the mathematical concepts and procedures used in this section, the following texts are recommended: Bracewell (1999), Press et al. (1992), Morse and Feshbach (1953), Abramowitz and Stegun (1972), and Acton (1990).

Definition of the Fourier Transform

The *Fourier Transform* is a generalization of the complex Fourier Expansion. For a function $f(t)$, the Fourier *transform* $F(k)$ is defined as

$$F(k) = \int_{-\infty}^{\infty} f(t) e^{-2\pi i k t} dt, \quad \text{(in the frequency domain)}, \quad (13.226)$$

and its *inverse*

$$f(t) = \int_{-\infty}^{\infty} F(k)e^{2\pi i k t} dk, \quad \text{(in the time domain)}. \qquad (13.227)$$

It is usual to include a scaling factor of $(2\pi)^{-\frac{1}{2}}$ to restore symmetry of the transform and its inverse when the frequency is used in place of k. Because of the existence of the transform and its inverse, the information content of the transform $F(k)$ is the same as that of the function $f(t)$. When the analysis is carried out in the t-domain (time domain) the function $f(t)$ is used while for analysis in the k-domain (frequency domain) the function $F(k)$ is used. On obtaining the Fourier transform of the impact function we will be working in the frequency domain to obtain information on the frequency content of the impact forces bearing in mind that the system dynamical equations can be solved in the time domain.

13.25.3 Application to the Impact Problem

For the purposes of this analysis on the spectral content of the driving forces generated by the impact, we begin by using the contact force expression given in equation (13.75) written in the form

$$F_c' = \frac{4E_s R_s V_0}{3(1-v^2)\omega_d} \left[sin(\omega_d t) + \frac{2\alpha}{\omega}\left(1-\left(\frac{\alpha}{\omega}\right)^2\right)^{\frac{1}{2}} cos(\omega_d t) \right] e^{-\alpha t} B(0, 3\tau_c/2),$$

(13.228)

where once again, $\alpha = r_{ms}/2m_s$. For good sticks having tips made of low-loss rubber, we only need to consider the cases $(\alpha/\omega) < 1/10$. In this case the exponential factor $e^{-\alpha t}$ can be neglected for the time being. The exclusion of the exponential factor will not significantly alter the Fourier transform when the losses are sufficiently low. For old used sticks or what we define as 'Dead Sticks' the exponential factor must be retained. We must take care of all possibilities seeing that pan sticks come in all varieties having a wide range of properties. In the case of low-loss sticks, one can also neglect terms that are second order in (α/ω) which further simplifies equation (13.228) to

$$F'_c = \frac{4E_s R_s V_0}{3(1-v^2)\omega} \left[sin(\omega t) + \frac{2\alpha}{\omega} cos(\omega t) \right] B(0, 3\tau_c/2)$$

(13.229)

Through the application of the Fourier Transform on the force-time function shown in Figure (13.17), the frequency content of the impact can be determined. To obtain the Fourier transform of the ½-sine force function $sin(2\pi t/3\tau_c) B_1(0, 3\tau_c/2)$ given in equation (13.59), the function will be converted to the product of a cosine function and the *rectangle* or *gate* function Π(x) which is shown in Figure 13.69.

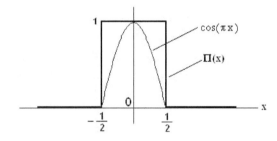

Fig. 13.69. Product of the 'origin-shifted' ½-sine function and the gate function Π(x).

This conversion to the 'origin-shifted' form is required in order to make use of a result from the *modulation theorem* on Fourier Transform that greatly simplifies the transform analysis of the ½-sine function. To achieve the sine-cosine conversion the pulse in Figure 13.17(b) is *shifted* to the left along the time axis by $3\tau_c/4$ and for mathematical convenience, a new variable x is introduced; *please note that this variable x is used locally in Section 13.25 (and all its sub-sections) and is not related to variables by the same 'name' used in other Sections of this book.* Except for the change of variable, the new ½-cosine form is functionally and practically equivalent to the ½-sine function describing the force-time history of the impact. Simply think of the impact as occurring $3\tau_c/4$ earlier.

The new form for the force history is $cos(2\pi k_0 x)\Pi(x)$, with $k_0 = ½$. The modulation theorem allows the Fourier transform of the function $[cos(2\pi k_0 x) f(x)]$ to be expressed as

$$\Im_x[cos(2\pi k_0 x) f(x)](k) = \tfrac{1}{2}[F(k-k_0)+F(k+k_0)], \quad (13.230)$$

where the symbol $\Im$ is used to denote the Fourier transform (or more explicitly, *the operation of taking the Fourier transform*), $F(k)$ is the Fourier transform of $f(x)$ and $k = 3f\tau_c/2$ with f being the frequency of the spectral component. With $f(x) = \Pi(x)$, the standard form for the Fourier transform of the gate function can be employed to obtain the right side of equation (13.230). This transform is given by

$$\Im_x[\Pi(x)](k) = sinc(\pi k),$$

where the unnormalized *sinc* function is known under different names depending on the context as the *sine cardinal (sinus cardinalis), impulsive sine, instrumental function* or *sampling function* with

$$sinc(\pi k) = \frac{sin(\pi k)}{\pi k}.$$

Impulsive sine is most appropriate in the present context. It should be noted that the impulsive sine is equivalent to j_0 — the zeroth order spherical Bessel function of the first kind. Using these results and definitions, one gets

$$\Im_x[cos(2\pi k_0 x)\Pi(x)](k) = \frac{1}{2}\left[\frac{sin(\pi(k-k_0))}{\pi(k-k_0)} + \frac{sin(\pi(k+k_0))}{\pi(k+k_0)}\right].$$

(13.231)

On using $k_0 = ½$ the Fourier transform $G(k)$ for the ½-sine contact force is now given by

$$G(k) = \frac{1}{2}\left[\frac{\sin(\pi(k-\tfrac{1}{2}))}{\pi(k-\tfrac{1}{2})} + \frac{\sin(\pi(k+\tfrac{1}{2}))}{\pi(k+\tfrac{1}{2})}\right], \quad (13.232)$$

or equivalently

$$G(k) = \frac{1}{2}[sin\,c(\pi(k-\tfrac{1}{2})) + sin\,c(\pi(k+\tfrac{1}{2}))]. \quad (13.233)$$

The absolute value of the function $G(k)$ is plotted in Figure 13.70. In Figure 13.70 if $\tau_c = 0.2$ ms (the contact time for a tenor impact), $k = 5$ corresponds to 16.7 kHz.

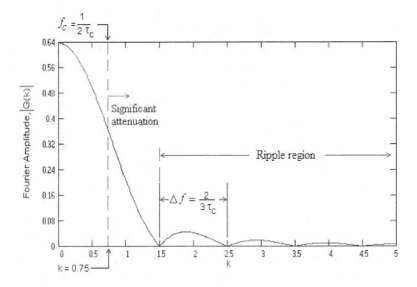

Fig. 13.70. Fourier transform of the ½-sine function. Observe the steep roll-off in amplitude as the response enters the ripple region.

Interpretation of the G(k) Spectral Plot — the Primary Forces

The amplitudes on the spectral plot of the function $G(k)$ are proportional to the sinusoidal driving forces — the *Primary Forces* — generated by the ½-sine impact force spanning continuously from zero through the entire range of audio frequencies (0 — 20 kHz). The impacted note responds to these sinusoidal forces by vibrating mainly at frequencies corresponding to its tuned resonant modes. The note will also show transient non-resonant responses to all other driving forces within the spectrum. The note will also respond by exciting the natural untuned modes (untuned by the tuner or pan maker) at lower amplitude levels.

In Figure 13.70, notice the *roll-off* in amplitude function $|G(k)|$ as the frequency increases, with a magnitude of 0.360 at $k = 0.75$, which corresponds to $f = 1/2\tau_c$ (refer to equation (13.2)). The frequency above which, significant attenuation occurs is defined as the *Cut-off-Frequency* $f_c = 1/2\tau_c$. Observe the 'ripples' which (see Figure 13.70) appear in the region $k > 1.5$. Also observe that the zeros of G(k) occur at $k = (2n+1)/2$, $(n = 1,2,3 \ldots)$ or at frequencies $f_n = (2n+1)/3\tau_c$ at frequency intervals of width $\Delta f = 2/3\tau_c$. These zeros indicate that in the limit $f_n/Q \rightarrow 0$ (where Q is the Quality factor of the note), impact energy *will not* be imparted to modes on the note that are tuned to frequencies $f_n = (2n+1)/3\tau_c$.

We have therefore made two important observations:

1. There is a *Cut-off Frequency* above which the driving force for mode excitation falls off rapidly; *Cut-off-Frequency* $f_c = 1/2\tau_c$. (Observe here that the *contact-time* τ_c used here and elsewhere in this book is defined dynamically at the *half-maximum* points of the *contact-force* F_{max}. If one were to use the layman's definition of contact time, which simply measures the time of physical contact between note and stick, which is the *make-to-break* time $\tau_{m\text{-}t\text{-}b}$, then one would get an incorrect value for f_c.)
2. There are zeros in the driving force spectrum which means that not all modes can be excited by an impact of a given duration; the modes that cannot be excited are of frequencies $f_n = (2n+1)/3\tau_c$, $(n = 1,2,3 \ldots)$.

Before these results are applied to the tuned notes of the steelpan, there is one more important aspect of the function $G(k)$ to be noted. The case of $k = 0$ on the spectrum corresponds to zero frequency or the DC signal in an electronic system. The value $G(0) = 2/\pi = 0.63662...$ should therefore be equal to the mean (DC) value of the ½-sine function $sin\,(\pi x)$ over the interval [0,1]. This is in fact the case, as $\int_0^1 \sin(\pi x)\,dx = 2/\pi$ which can be readily verified from elementary integrals. In Figure 13.71 this mean value is plotted in relation to the ½-sine function. This exercise also explains the amplitude scale used for the $G(k)$ plot in Figure 13.70.

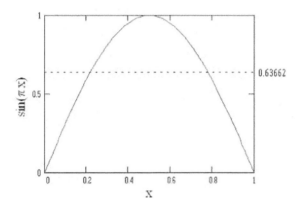

Fig. 13.71. Plot of the ½-sine function. The average magnitude of the function is shown by the dotted line.

Compare the value 0.63662 to the average value of the exponential decay ½-sine approximation using the model stick in the previous example;

$$\frac{\int_0^{3\frac{\tau_c}{2}} e^{-\alpha t} \sin \frac{2\pi t}{3\tau_c}\,dt}{\frac{3\tau_c}{2}} = 0.62897.$$

The closeness of these two values may be taken as reasonable justification for the use of the simplified ½-sine formulation without the exponential decay. But this is only good for low-loss tips. These considerations are important because on impact the $G(0)$ force opposes the mechanical bias and moves the note away from its quiescent state. In simple, less technical language, $G(0)$ displaces the note surface during stick-note impact.

13.25.4 Improved Formulation and Dead Sticks

When the exponential decay factor $e^{-\alpha t}$ is inserted, one gets in the *time domain* a multiplication of an exponential function with a ½-sine function. This can be readily dealt with because *a multiplication in the time domain corresponds to a convolution in the frequency domain and vice versa.* The Fourier transform of the exponential decay ½-sine function is therefore given by

$$\mathfrak{J}_x[e^{-2\pi k_c |x|} \cos(2\pi k_0 x)\Pi(x)](k) = \left[\mathfrak{J}_x[e^{-2\pi k_c|x|}](k) * \mathfrak{J}_x[\cos(2\pi k_0 x)\Pi(x)]\right]$$
$$= \left[\frac{1}{\pi}\left(\frac{k_c}{k^2+k_c^2}\right) * \frac{1}{2}[\operatorname{sinc}(\pi(k-\tfrac{1}{2})) + \operatorname{sinc}(\pi(k+\tfrac{1}{2}))]\right]$$

(13.234)

where $k_c = \dfrac{3\tau_c\, r_{ms}}{8\pi m_s}$ and the symbol $f * g$ denotes the *convolution* of the functions f and g defined by

$$f * g = \int_{-\infty}^{\infty} f(k')g(k-k')dk',$$

where

$$f(k) = \frac{1}{\pi}\left(\frac{k_c}{k^2 + k_c^2}\right),$$
$$g(k) = G(k).$$

Observe the integral limits [-∞, +∞]. For readers interested in solving the integral, when evaluated numerically, ensure that the limits of the integration cover a suitably large range in (- and +) k (for example [-5, 5]). Since $f(k)$ is a symmetrical, sharply peaked *Lorentzian* function with half-width (i.e. the magnitude falls to half the peak value) at $k = \pm k_c$, in numerical solutions the step-size δk must be made suitably small (for example $\delta k \leq 0.001$). The convolution will be *incorrect* if it is restricted to positive (or negative) k only such as [0, 5] (or [-5, 0]). The functions defined here, f, g and $f * g$ are even functions, $f(k) = f(-k)$, $g(k) = g(-k)$, however, we will plot them only in the positive half-space because k represents the (normalized) frequencies of the *physical forces* generated by the stick-note impact.

Good Sticks versus Dead Sticks

At this point I must insert some comments on the players' choice of sticks or more precisely what influences this choice. A pan stick can be accepted or rejected by a player based on any of the following; (1) appearance (2) weight (3) length of shank (4) type of shank (wood, metal, solid, hollow) (5) size or radius of tip (6) condition of wrapping rubber (tight or loose, worn or new) (7) type of rubber (natural or artificial) (8) softness of tip (9) ability to play to the player's liking (10) inability to play at all (dead stick). We have already taken most of these characteristics into the analysis of sticks, save for the first and the last; so what makes a stick a *dead stick*? These characteristics except for the first, 'appearance,' can be quantified or have their properties defined (natural versus artificial (silicone) rubber for example). Appearance is in the eye of the player but it is not entirely subjective for as the player would say 'there is something about that stick that I like (or don't like).' I grew up among musicians and I know that they can be very particular about certain things especially with their music which comes first. On the pan, our musicians would always avoid the dead stick so we need to know why!

For the values of mechanical resistance found on *good low-loss tips* ($r_{ms} < 1$ kg·s^{-1}), the modifications to the force spectrum that the improved formulation produces, as Figure 13.72(a) shows, are too small to be of practical importance and may be ignored. This means that players and stick makers can choose from among a range or variety of low-loss tip material to obtain acceptable characteristics for their sticks.

However, the situation changes when *lossy* or *dead sticks* are considered as in Figure 13.72(b). For dead sticks, the driving forces for mode excitation, located in the region of importance ($k < 0.75$), are significantly reduced. ***This is the main reason why dead sticks***

are rejected by players. The reduction in amplitude continues in the ripple region with some shifting of the zeros and peaks.

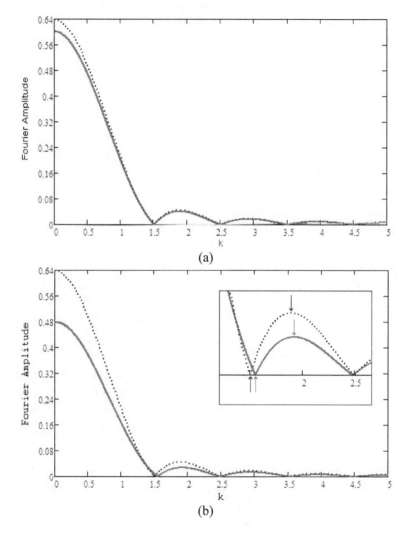

Fig. 13.72. Plot of the function $|G(k)|$ dotted line (......) and the function $|f * g|$ for the exponential decay ½–sine function solid line (——) with (a) $r_{ms} = 1$ kg·s^{-1} and (b) $r_{ms} = 5$ kg·s^{-1}. Observe the small frequency hift in the ripple region of the spectrum in (b) highlighted in the insert.

ROUTINE FOR NUMERICALLY COMPUTING $f * g$

The convolution integral defined here, converges very rapidly and is well suited for numerical computation. For the accuracy required in this work, it is sufficient to use brute force simple quadrature and a large number of points. However, for the reader's sake, a standard integration procedure, *Durand's Rule*, of the *Newton-Cotes* variety will be used in the sample procedure given here. Other quadrature rules such as the more familiar *Simpson's 3/8 Rule* can be used. The Durand's Rule is straightforward, quite accurate and is easily implemented.

Using the functions $f(k)$ and $G(k)$ defined in the text, we obtain $[f * g]_n$ by Durand's rule for $n := 0, 1, \ldots N$ as

$$[f * g]_n = \delta k \frac{e^{-2\pi k c}}{2\pi} \left(\tfrac{2}{5}(fg_{n,0}+fg_{n,N}) + \tfrac{11}{10}(fg_{n,1}+fg_{n,N-1}) + \sum_{j=2}^{N-2} fg_{n,j} \right)$$

where

$$fg_{n,j} = \left(\frac{k_c}{(j\delta k)^2 + k_c^2} \right) \left[\operatorname{sinc}\left(\pi\left((n-j)\delta k + \tfrac{1}{2}\right)\right) + \operatorname{sinc}\left(\pi\left((n-j)\delta k - \tfrac{1}{2}\right)\right) + \operatorname{sinc}\left(\pi\left((n+j)\delta k + \tfrac{1}{2}\right)\right) + \operatorname{sinc}\left(\pi\left((n+j)\delta k - \tfrac{1}{2}\right)\right) \right].$$

One can take, for example, $\delta k = 0.001$, $N = 5000$ or $\delta k = 0.0005$, $N = 14000$, depending on the accuracy required. The values of $[f * g]_n$ can be plotted as a function of k $(= n\delta k)$. Evaluation can easily be done in Mathcad®.

13.25.5 Forces due to Mechanical Resistance

The Fourier transform $M(k)$ of the function $[\sin(\omega t) + (2\alpha/\omega)\cos(\omega t)]B(0, \pi/\omega)$ takes on the complex form

$$M(k) = G(k) + i\frac{2\alpha}{\omega}H(k), \qquad (13.235)$$

where

$$H(k) = \frac{1}{2}\left[\operatorname{sinc}\left(\pi\left(k - \frac{1}{2}\right)\right) - \operatorname{sinc}\left(\pi\left(k + \frac{1}{2}\right)\right)\right].$$

The factor i ($=\sqrt{-1}$, *imaginary unity*) in equation (13.235) indicates that the spectral components in $i\frac{2\alpha}{\omega}H(k)$ are phase shifted by 90° or $\pi/2$ with respect to the real components of $G(k)$. This is expected from the orthogonality of the sine and cosine functions. A plot of the absolute value of the function $H(k)$ is shown in Figure 13.73.

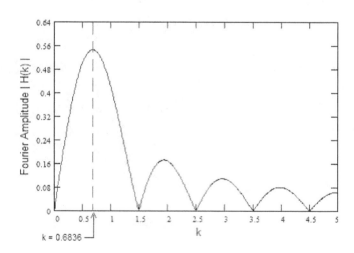

Fig. 13.73. Plot of $|H(k)|$ as a function of k.

Interpretation of the H(k) Spectral Plot

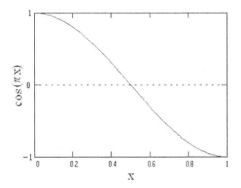

Fig. 13.74. Plot of the ½-cosine function. The average magnitude of the function is shown by the dotted line.

Referring to Figure 13.74 the average for the cosine function over the interval [0,1] is zero, $\int_0^1 \cos(\pi x)\,dx = 0$, so that the component of driving force supplied by the cosine term for $k = 0$ (corresponding to zero frequency) must also be zero. Compare this result (the zero value) with the average for the exponential decay ½-cosine using the model stick in the previous example

$$\frac{\frac{\alpha}{\omega}\int_0^{3\frac{\tau}{2}} e^{-\alpha t} \cos\frac{2\pi t}{3\tau}\,dt}{\frac{3\tau}{2}} = 3.73 \cdot 10^{-5},$$

which is 'practically' zero.

The spectral plot of the absolute value of the function H(k) shows the relative amplitude of the sinusoidal driving force components generated by the ½-cosine impact force. Here also if $\tau_c = 0.2$ ms (the contact time for a tenor impact), $k = 5$ corresponds to 16.7 kHz so that the spectral frequencies of these driving forces span continuously through the audio range of frequencies. Notice that for the ½-cosine force-time function the driving force amplitude is zero at zero frequency as expected. The mechanical resistance produces high frequency driving force components of greater magnitude than the ½-sine force-time function in the ripple region ($k > 1.5$) of the spectrum. However, this is not useful in enhancing the levels of normal mode excitation because the tuned modes are located mainly in the region $k < 0.75$. From the peak on H(k) at $k = 0.68362181...$, which corresponds to the frequency $f_p = 2(0.6836)/3\tau_c$, down to the first zero at $k = 1.5$ the roll-off is faster than that obtained for $G(k)$ giving greater attenuation of the driving forces over the same spectral range

When the exponential decay factor is included, $H(k)$ is replaced by

$$h(k) = \left[\frac{1}{\pi}\left(\frac{k_c}{k^2 + k_c^2}\right) * H(k)\right], \qquad (13.236)$$

but here too, as shown in Figure 13.75, the changes to the force spectrum *for good stick tips* are too small to be of practical importance. **The situation changes however when lossy, dead sticks are considered.**

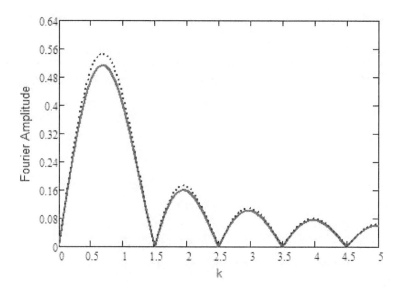

Fig. 13.75. Plot of the function $|H(k)|$ dotted line (......) and the function $|h(k)|$ for $r_{ms} = 1$ kg·s^{-1} solid line (———).

Whereas $G(0)$ is non-zero and produces a net displacement of the note surface from its quiescent state during impact, $H(0)$ is identically zero. The resistive forces therefore do not contribute to the net displacement of the note surface during impact. One can easily understand this from Figure 13.74 which shows that the average value of the ½-cosine function is zero.

Remark: From the spectral properties of the resistive forces it can be concluded that the mechanical resistance of stick tips *cannot* be used to enhance the modal driving forces during impact. This raises an important question; *can the force-time history of a stick tip be customized to produce enhanced modal response from the pan notes?* This question will be answered in the following Sections.

13.26 Effect of Hand Action F_H on the Contact Force Spectrum

The truncation of the free compression-restitution force history of the stick-note impact by the manual application of a retrieving force modifies the high frequency force components. This means that in the 'ripple' region of the force spectrum the peaks are shifted. If the contact-time is too short these high frequency waves may excite untuned very high frequency, but audible, vibrational modes on the note. The panist may take advantage of these high frequency modes to add 'metallic' ringing tones to the sound. *A sharp, crispy style of playing can therefore give the sounding tones on the pan a 'rich metallic' sound.*

> *I once observed a pair of young tenor panists use the butt end of their sticks to add metallic harshness to a 'roll' with exciting and useful effect (these panists can be seen in Figure 1.4 front, right). They executed this roll with much showmanship by crouching low with eyes to the level of their respective pan while I smiled broadly and nodded my head in appreciation! I clearly noticed that they played "off center" or away from the sweetspot of the note; this action emphasized the higher modes as required. Well done!*

The reduced contact-time shifts the cut-off-frequency upward allowing higher frequency key-notes to be excited. *This is the reason why the panist plays the higher tenor notes with shorter contact times.* To incorporate these impacts (with F_H) into the linear model an equivalent ½-sine force-time curve can be fitted to the truncated curve while ensuring that both curves have the same contact-time. By still adopting the ½-height points as a measure of contact-time this construction is illustrated in Figure 13.75 for the case where $t_h > T/4$. When the stick retrieval force (hand action) is applied at time t_h after stick-note contact is made, the contact force profile takes the path along the dotted curve in Figure 13.76(a). Similar constructions can be done for other cases but the ½-sine curve should maximize at the same the maximum force as the truncated curve. This is done in Figure 13.76(b). A more refined procedure is not necessary because that will mainly affect the ripple region, which is not usable for the excitation of tuned modes of usable acoustic strength.

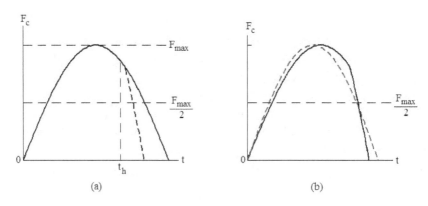

Fig. 13.76. (a) (—) Contact force history for $F_H = 0$; (- - -) contact force history, $F_H > 0$ for $t \geq t_h$.
(b) (—) Contact force history, $F_H > 0$ for $t \geq t_h$; (- - -) fitted ½-sine force profile.

The constructed (or *fitted*) ½-sine curve will produce the required contact-force and cut-off-frequency but the peaks in the ripple region will be slightly displaced from those produced by the truncated curve. As explained previously this is not a problem because the high frequency metallic sounds can still be excited. However, the latter is a minor aspect of the musical tone anyway (well, to some but not all panist or listeners). Technically there will always be a small shift (in time) of the peak on the fitted F_c curve when the symmetrical ½-sine function is substituted for the asymmetrical hand-modified impact curve (refer to Figure 13.76(b)) but in these cases since the shift is a very small fraction of the period of the excited note, the effect is musically insignificant.

The only 'exact' solution is a numerical one but then the hand action must be precisely known. In any case the exact form of F_H is arbitrary and entirely 'in the hands of the panist'. If the panist decides to 'double strike' or act awkwardly in striking the note and that is the intended style fitted to the musical score then one is free to do so. However, these can be dealt with anyway by the proper choice of F_H.

Conclusion: *For hand actions that are intended mainly for reducing the duration of the stick-note impacts the ½-sine force history can be applied.*

13.27 Contact Force Produced by the ½-Sine Force Function

13.27.1 General Application to the Impacts on all Pans

In the following sections, answers will be found to the question 'Why do we find some sticks more suitable than others for playing particular pans?' The analysis of the previous section shows that except in the case of a very lossy 'dead' stick (where stick dissipation cannot be neglected), the frequency content of the impact can be adequately described by the Fourier transform of the ½-sine pulse. Using this result, the effects of contact-time on the *initial* excitation of notes on the pan are now fully examined.

In terms of spectral frequency $f = 2k/3\tau_c$ with f in Hertz and τ_c in seconds, one can write

$$G(f) = \frac{1}{2}\left[\operatorname{sinc}\left(\pi\left(\frac{3f\tau_c}{2} - \frac{1}{2}\right)\right) + \operatorname{sinc}\left(\pi\left(\frac{3f\tau_c}{2} + \frac{1}{2}\right)\right)\right].$$

In plotting graphs of attenuation or system response over a wide frequency range it is customary to plot the normalized response versus frequency on log-log or linear-log axes. In adopting the latter procedure here, the function *G(f)* is normalized with respect to *G(0)* in obtaining the ordinates [*G(f)/G(0)*]. Since frequency $f = 2k/3\tau_c$, the abscissas are given explicitly by *log[2k/3τ_c]* of *log(f)*. Figure 13.77 shows the general form of the impact-force spectrum along with some of the terms used to identify parts of the spectrum. The curve shows the relative amplitude of the driving forces as a function of frequency. Observe that the driving force is large and constant at low frequencies. As the curve enters the *knee* region, the force begins a rapid reduction to zero then it enters the *ripple region*. By definition, the *Cut-off-Frequency* on the spectrum is located at $f_c = 1/2\tau_c$ below the *knee* on the down-slope of the spectrum. The high-frequency *roll-off* beyond the knee is a highly desirable feature used effectively on the steelpan as a percussive musical instrument. This feature shows that the rubber tips perform effectively as natural low-pass filters for the driving forces generated on impact.

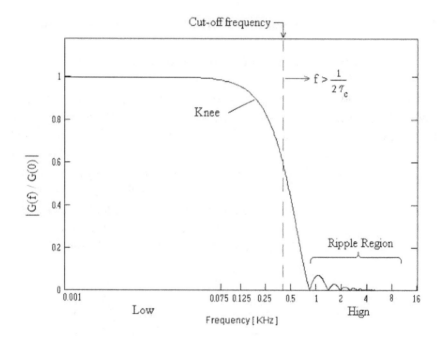

Fig. 13.77. Plot of $[G(f)/G(0)]$ as a function of frequency. The curve shows the relative amplitude of the driving forces as a function of frequency.

All modal driving force magnitudes quoted in this section are with respect to the zero frequency driving force component normalized to unity. At the cut-off frequency the magnitude of the force falls to 0.566 while the size of the ripples in the ripple region is lower than 0.07.

13.27.2 The Tenor

When the analysis is done for stick impacts on the tenor, curves similar to that shown in Figure 13.77 are obtained. The plots in Figure 13.78 and Figure 13.79 were done for $\tau_c = 0.2$ and 0.4 millisecond respectively. These τ_c values are at the lower and upper ends of the range of contact-times obtained for the tenor pans.

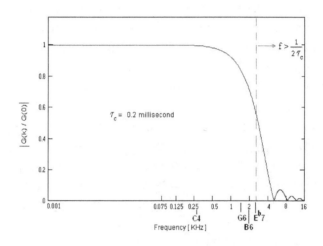

Fig. 13.78. Plot of $[G(f)/G(0)]$ as a function of frequency for Tenor pan with $\tau_c = 0.2$ millisecond.

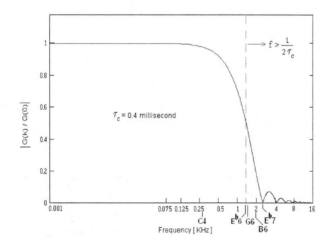

Fig. 13.79. Plot of $[G(f)/G(0)]$ as a function of frequency for Tenor pan with $\tau_c = 0.4$ millisecond.

- For $\tau_c = 0.2$ millisecond, the driving force for the G_6 note at 1567.98, is down to 0.809, the B_6 at 1975.5 Hz is down to 0.7 while the $E^\flat_7$ mode (the upper octave of the $E^\flat_6$ note) at 2489.02 Hz falls just inside the cut-off limit at $f_c = 2500$ Hz with a force magnitude of 0.566.
- For $\tau_c = 0.4$ millisecond the $E^\flat_6$ note at 1244.51 Hz falls just inside the cut-off limit at 1250 Hz with a driving force magnitude of 0.569 while the G_6 falls just beyond the cut-off limit. The $E^\flat_7$ is now smack on the 'zero' response of the curve. If this note was present on the tenor and played with this tenor stick and with this contact-time you will get no response!
- This means that *the $E^\flat_7$ note is at the physical upper limit for excitation by manually applied stick-note impacts on the steelpan. It is the highest note that can be placed on a tenor pan, but it is subject to severe limitations.* The player can only excite this note using a very good stick with a quick (*veloce*) playing action with rapid withdrawal of the stick. Even playing with the shortest contact-time manually possible, the excitation force will be diminished by 3 decibels (the acoustic attenuation to be dealt with later is even worse than this). This is not a practical option for consistency in excitation.
- This Upper Frequency Limit $E^\flat_7 \equiv 2489.02$ Hz for the stick-pan combination that defines the instrument shall be called the **Steelpan Cut-Off Frequency.**
- The driving force for the lowest tenor note, the C_4 at 261.63 Hz is at 0.996 (for $\tau_c = 0.2$ ms) and 0.977 (for $\tau_c = 0.4$ ms) and is therefore more than adequately excited.

Observations*: The picture that emerges from these purely theoretical considerations of the stick-note impact problem is consistent with the player's choice of sticks and playing action. The player must deliberately reduce the contact-time when playing the inner notes of the tenor in order to achieve adequate modal* *response and a sufficiently loud tone. It also identifies a fundamental limitation of the tenor pans.*

- Using the *ideal* tenor sticks it will *not* be physically possible to manually play notes tuned to frequencies higher than the $E^\flat_7$, certainly not with the repeatability required for music. Some mechanical assistance will be required, similar to the piano action, in order to go even as high as $E^\flat_7$ on the musical scale. This observation can easily be checked and confirmed by the reader on a good quality tenor pan by playing notes around G_6.
- All practical sticks are subject to internal losses making them less than ideal or optimum. In practice therefore it becomes harder to achieve good response from the hi-end notes with real sticks.
- Since the tenor pan contains the highest frequency notes found on this musical instrument, the $E^\flat_7$ note represents an upper bound for the steelpan. Making a physically larger or smaller instrument or larger/smaller set of notes will not remove or affect this limit.
- The existence of this upper bound is independent of the characteristics of the notes such as (a) the metal used or the properties of the metal, (b) the shape or form of the note, (c) the support conditions (boundary conditions) of the note or any other parameter as defined in the note analyses of the present work.
- There are some zeros in the spectrum that may prevent the initial excitation of higher octaves of the tones. In fact the G_7 musical note (upper octave of the G_6) cannot be directly excited (to any useful level) by hand action employing the typical tenor sticks. How these high octaves are excited is dealt with in the section on Mode Interactions.

13.27.3 Dead Stick versus Good Stick on the Tenor

Figure 13.80 shows the force spectrum for a dead stick having r_{ms} = 5 kg·s^{-1}, τ_c = 0.4 ms and a cut-off frequency of f_c = 1250 Hz which is just above $E^\flat_6$ at 1245 Hz. This means that this dead stick will not be usable on notes above $E^\flat_6$ and in addition all notes including $E^\flat_6$ and lower will also suffer serious reduction in excitation levels.

Observe that the **E**$^b_7$ at 2490 Hz is smack on the 'zero' on the dead stick response curve at 2500 Hz (just a little shy).

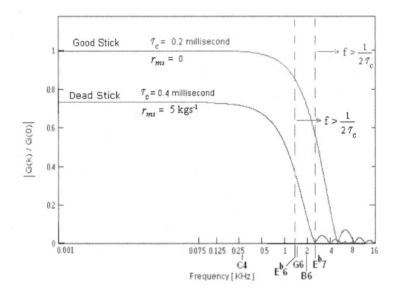

Fig. 13.80. Plot of $|G(f)/G(0)|$ for a good stick with $r_{ms} = 0$, $\tau_c = 0.2$ ms, $f_c = 2500$ Hz, and a $|f*g|/|G(0)|$ for a dead stick with $r_{ms} = 5$ kg·s^{-1}, $\tau_c = 0.4$ ms, $f_c = 1250$ Hz.

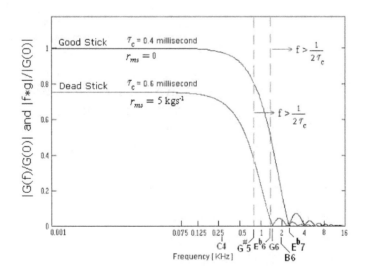

Fig. 13.81. Plot of $|G(f)/G(0)|$ for a good stick with $r_{ms} = 0$, $\tau_c = 0.4$ ms, $f_c = 1250$ Hz, and a $|f*g|/|G(0)|$ for a dead stick with $r_{ms} = 5$ kg·s^{-1}, $\tau_c = 0.6$ ms, $f_c = 833.3$ Hz.

Figure 13.81 shows the force spectrum for a dead stick having r_{ms} = 5 kg·s^{-1}, τ_c = 0.6 ms and a cut-off frequency of f_c = 833.3 Hz which is just above $\mathbf{G^\#_5}$ at 830.61 Hz. This means that this dead stick will not be usable on notes above $\mathbf{G^\#_5}$ and in addition all notes including $\mathbf{G^\#_5}$ and lower will also suffer serious reduction in excitation levels. Observe that the $\mathbf{G_6}$ note is about smack on the 'zero' on the dead stick response curve (just a little shy under actually). **You will not hear a thing on the $\mathbf{G_6}$ with this dead stick!** *I need to correct my last statement; you will only hear noise (to be explained shortly).* The notes $\mathbf{E_6}^\flat$ and higher are performing just as badly, all in the ripple region. A player would a lot sooner replace his sticks before they degrade to this extent. This example demonstrates and quantifies the trend that an aging stick undergoes or the performance of a stick that has been very poorly constructed.

13.27.4 Marginal Notes and the Marginal Zone

All sticks are subject to internal losses. Because of this, if we take the example of the tenor sticks which play the highest notes on the pan, then in normal use, the real stick lies somewhere between the Dead Stick and the Good Stick (r_{ms} = 0). For computational purposes I have defined the 'Good Stick' as possessing the idealized property of zero losses, r_{ms} = 0. This ideal stick, my 'Good Stick', will therefore not be found naturally; all real sticks as used by players will therefore have responses somewhere between those plotted for Good and Dead sticks in Figure 13.80 and Figure 13.81. Because of this the band-limiting restrictions on the upper frequency of playable notes must be taken as a fundamental property of the Stick-Note combination that constitutes the steelpan as a musical instrument.

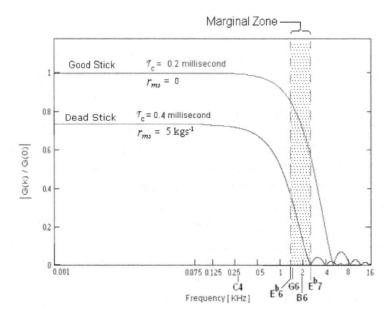

Fig. 13.82. Plot showing the location of the region defining the Marginal Zone on the Tenor.

For these theoretical and technical reasons, it is necessary to classify all notes on the tenor pan (as our first example) whose defining frequency (key-note) falls within the musical range $E^b{}_6$ to $E^b{}_7$ as *Marginal Notes*. This can be understood more clearly by studying the plots in Figure 13.80 where the contact-time $\tau_c = 0.2$ millisecond (best possible) and contact-time $\tau_c = 0.4$ millisecond (worse case on the tenor) clearly shows this band of frequencies (or notes) $E^b{}_6$ to $E^b{}_7$ as falling into the heavily attenuated range. What it means in practice is that these *Marginal Notes* are only weakly excited directly by stick impact. It is for these reasons that the E_6 is the highest note on the Low 'C' Tenor, while it is the $F^{\#}{}_6$ on the High 'D' Tenor.

On all pan-types, tenor to bass, the Marginal Notes are to be found within the frequency band defined by the top and bottom notes,

$$\text{\textit{Top Marginal note} frequency} = \frac{1}{\tau_c},$$

$$\textit{Bottom Marginal Note frequency} = \frac{1}{2\tau_c}.$$

where τ_c is the contact-time for the pan-stick combination. The Marginal Notes are found in the frequency band defined as the *Marginal Zone* (see Figure 13.82. The Marginal Zone spans one octave. The top of the Marginal Zone corresponds to the first zero on the force spectrum, were the frequencies of these zeros are given by $f_{0,n} = \frac{2n+1}{3\tau_c}, n = 1, 2, 3 \ldots$ These zeros are all located in the ripple region.

While the concept of Marginal Notes and Marginal Zone apply to all pans, the concept is most useful at the top-end of the musical scale for the tenor instrument because one can always use a tenor stick and tenor hand action to excite the Marginal Notes found on all the lower instruments. The Marginal Zone on the tenor therefore defines the absolute limit of the pan-stick instrument.

Driving Force Attenuation in the Marginal Zone:

Observe in the linear-log plot of Figure 13.82 that the section of the force spectrum curve between the cut-off frequency $f_c = \frac{1}{2\tau_c}$ to the first zero at $f_{0,1} = \frac{1}{\tau_c}$ is *approximately linear* (a straight line of negative slope). This allows for a simple formula relating the attenuation of the force components in the Marginal Zone. Also observe that the interval between f_c and $f_{0,1}$ is exactly one octave. Expressed first as a fraction of the force at zero frequency, then in units of decibels, the attenuation of the contact force amplitude delivered to the note at a frequency f, satisfying $\tfrac{1}{2} \leq f\tau_c < 1$ (that is f falls within the Marginal Zone), by a stick-note impact of contact-time τ_c, is given by

$$\textit{Driving Force Attenuation} = 10 \log \left[\frac{\log\left(\frac{1}{f\tau_c}\right)}{\log(4)} \right] db, \quad (13.237)$$

where the logarithms are to base 10. A more precise formula but also a more complicated one is possible from the equation describing the force spectrum. This precision is not necessary, especially as it will involve the computation of convolution integrals that will not introduce any new information on the quantity we are concerned with — a ratio of amplitudes expressed in decibels.

For contact-time values covering the range possible with tenor sticks (Good (low-loss) and Dead (lossy)) in the hands of a good tenor panist, the attenuations in the Marginal Zone are shown in Table 13.10:

Table 13.10 gives a very accurate representation of what takes place among the Marginal Notes on a tenor pan during stick impact. It highlights the physical limitations of this percussion instrument and for design purposes, can be used to set the upper limit for the tuned key-note frequency. In Table 13.10 the driving force attenuation is divided into three shaded regions in order to highlight the levels of excitation expected:

Table 13.10 Driving force attenuation for 'Good' and 'Dead' sticks.
NP — Not Playable because they lie in the ripple region.
Everything in the darkly shaded region is in Dead Stick Territory.

Note	Frequency f (Hz)	Type of Stick Tip			
		Good $\tau_c = 0.2$ ms Attenuation (db)	Good $\tau_c = 0.3$ ms Attenuation (db)	Good $\tau_c = 0.4$ ms Attenuation (db)	Dead $\tau_c = 0.6$ ms Attenuation (db)
E^b_6	1244.51	—	-1.47	-2.98	-6.76
E_6	1318.51	-0.17	-1.75	-3.36	-7.72
F_6	1396.91	-0.36	-2.03	-3.77	-8.950
$F^\#_6$	1479.98	-0.56	-2.33	-4.22	-10.67
G_6	1567.98	-0.78	-2.64	-4.73	-13.56
$G^\#_6$	1661.22	-1.00	-2.99	-5.30	NP
A_6	1760.00	-1.23	-3.37	-5.97	NP
B^b_6	1864.65	-1.48	-3.78	-6.75	NP
B_6	1975.53	-1.74	-4.23	-7.70	NP
C_7	2093.53	-2.02	-4.74	-8.93	NP
$C^\#_7$	2217.46	-2.32	-5.32	-10.63	NP
D_7	2349.32	-2.64	-5.98	-13.48	NP
E^b_7	2489.02	-2.98	-6.76	-24.98	NP
E_7	2637.02	-3.36	-7.72	NP	NP

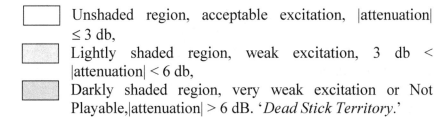

☐ Unshaded region, acceptable excitation, |attenuation| ≤ 3 db,

▨ Lightly shaded region, weak excitation, 3 db < |attenuation| < 6 db,

▧ Darkly shaded region, very weak excitation or Not Playable, |attenuation| > 6 dB. '*Dead Stick Territory.*'

Note: *The modulus or absolute value of the attenuation denoted by the modulus bars | | is used here in order to reduce the confusion that may arise (for some readers) with the negative values and the 'less than' 'greater than' conditions.*

Important notes:

(a) $F^\#_6$ highest note found on the Tenor with acceptable excitation at the mid-range contact time (0.3 ms).
(b) $G^\#_6$ highest note frequency for which an acceptable level of excitation (with less than 3db (absolute value) attenuation) can be expected at the mid-range contact time (0.3 ms) for a low-loss tenor stick played across the tenor range by a good panist.

While the 'Dead Stick' is totally useless, its inclusion here serves as a reference for what can be considered a good or useable stick. Since in practice the contact-time obtained by a panist on the tenor falls in the range 0.2 ms ≤ τ_c < 0.4 ms, as the Table shows, unless these Marginal Notes are played consistently with contact times at the bottom of the range (0.2 ms), the excitation levels can suffer serious attenuation. It is perhaps best to use the mid-value τ_c = 0.3 ms as a reasonable guide to what can be expected in the stick-note generation of tones by the tenor panist. Table 13.10 shows that notes below $G^\#_6$ are well handled while notes above $G^\#_6$ can be expected to show undesirably low levels of excitation. In stick-note impact simulations (of the kind discussed in Section 13.17), it becomes increasingly difficult to attain values for τ_c approaching 0.2 ms. For reasonable levels of contact-force, as 0.2 ms is approached, stick retrieval requires increasingly greater hand action F_H. Tenor players can easily relate their experience with this conclusion. Because of this difficulty, strong or acceptable excitation in the Marginal Zone cannot always be expected from the player or pan.

Based on these observations, especially since the losses on real sticks will further increase the attenuation, I recommend that for reliability and evenness in sound levels (within acceptable bounds) across the whole range of tenor notes, the upper limit — or the (tentative) *practical cut-off* — on the tenor be set at $G^{\#}_6$. Acoustical considerations may further reduce this upper limit as we shall soon look into.

To properly interpret the entries in Table 13.10, when a force amplitude is attenuated by -3db, its value has been *halved* and at -6db, it has been reduced to a *quarter* of its value. When the Good stick is played with $\tau_c = 0.2$ milliseconds (*best possible*), a -3 db attenuation is reached at around $E^{\flat}_7$. When the attenuation values are more negative than -3 db, there is reason for concern because the notes will not be adequately excited. For example, with this same stick when played with a slower hand action $\tau_c = 0.4$ milliseconds, the attenuation is at -24.98 db so the value of the contact force component is reduced by a factor 0.003175. The note will not be heard. It is precisely for this reason that the $E^{\flat}_7$ note must be considered to be the *Absolute Cut-Off* for notes on the steelpan. Real sticks lie somewhere between the Good (Lively) Stick and the Dead Stick. Observe in Table 13.10 that for the Dead Stick, notes above $G^{\#}_6$ are not playable. In fact the driving force for all the notes above $G^{\#}_6$ will be highly attenuated.

It is clear from these results that the notes in the Marginal Zone must be played with the shortest contact times. Since the worse case contact-time on the tenor with good sticks is normally around 0.4 milliseconds, using a *tolerable attenuation* of around -3 db one can readily understand (especially the tenor players) why the Low 'C' Pan has a top note at E_6 (attenuation of -3.36 db for $\tau_c = 0.4$ ms) and why the High 'D' Tenor top note is the $F^{\#}_6$ (attenuation of -4.73 db for $\tau_c = 0.4$ ms). On the patented design for the G-Pan Soprano (see Chapter 17) one finds a top note of B_6 (attenuation of -7.70 db or a force reduction by a factor of 1/6 for $\tau_c = 0.4$ ms) which is quite severe attenuation (**you must apply a stick contact force <u>six times</u> normal to obtain an acceptable acoustic output(!)**). Two problems arise here (i) the player in attempting to strike the note this hard may find his hand action unduly affected if this B_6 note is one of a series of notes to be played according to the requirements of the music, (ii) the level of *Stick Noise* (see Section 13.28.2) will be very high and disturbingly audible. One may try to make use of the *acoustical advantage* that the larger notes on the patented G-Pan provide to compensate for this loss; while this will help this note one must remember that the low frequency notes on the same pan can also make use of this acoustical advantage, so *relative to them*, the driving force for the B_6 note is still -7.70 db down (Dead Stick territory). If these high notes are not physically larger then there is no acoustical advantage to be gained so the B_6 faces severe problems!

Acoustial Attenuation in the Marginal Zone:

Players and tuners would also be interested in the acoustical radiation output of the notes in the Marginal Zone. We have already seen how severe the attenuation can be for the driving force but, sadly, as it turns out the acoustic attenuation is even more severe. With reference to equation (12.46), the maximum acoustic output intensity I_0 of a note of given surface area is proportional to the square of the *product* of the note frequency ω (or f in Hertz) and the external driving force f_e. It is this *squared relationship* that makes the acoustic attenuation more severe. Using the proportionality $I_0 \propto (f \, f_e)^2$ and Table 13.10 we can readily obtain the attenuation in acoustic radiation output. This relationship shows that the *acoustic output increases* with frequency f but as Table 13.10 shows, the driving *force f_e decreases* with frequency in the Marginal Zone. When the true note surface area A is included one gets $I_0 \propto (f A f_e)^2$.

Combining equation (13.237) with $I_0 \propto (f A f_e)^2$ one gets for the acoustic intensity ratio between a note of area A_2 and frequency f_2 and another note, *also in the Marginal Zone*, of area A_1 and frequency f_1

$$Acoustic\ Intensity\ Ratio = 20\ log \left[\frac{f_2 A_2 \log(f_2 \tau_c)}{f_1 A_1 \log(f_1 \tau_c)}\right]\ db, \quad (13.238)$$

Table 13.11 Acoustic attenuation for notes of equal area over a range of contact times relative to the $E^{\flat}_6$ note played with $\tau_c = 0.2$ ms. Entries in the un-shaded region are acceptable levels of acoustic output. INA: Inaudible (attenuation < -20 db). NP: Not Playable.

Note	Frequency f (Hz)	Type of Stick Tip			
		Good	Good	Good	Dead
		$\tau_c = 0.2$ ms	$\tau_c = 0.3$ ms	$\tau_c = 0.4$ ms	$\tau_c = 0.6$ ms
		Attenuation (db)	Attenuation (db)	Attenuation (db)	Attenuation (db)
$E^{\flat}_6$	1244.51	Ref	-2.9	-5.9	-13.5
E_6	1318.51	0.2	-3.3	-9.1	-16.4
F_6	1396.91	0.3	-3.7	-13.3	-19.3
$F^{\#}_6$	1479.98	0.4	-4.1	-15.5	INA
G_6	1567.98	0.5	-4.5	-18.6	INA
$G^{\#}_6$	1661.22	0.5	-4.8	INA	NP
A_6	1760.00	0.6	-5.2	INA	NP
$B^{\flat}_6$	1864.65	0.6	-5.6	INA	NP
B_6	1975.53	0.5	-6.0	INA	NP
C_7	2093.53	0.5	-6.3	INA	NP
$C^{\#}_7$	2217.46	0.4	-6.7	INA	NP
D_7	2349.32	0.2	-7.1	INA	NP
$E^{\flat}_7$	2489.02	0.1	-7.5	INA	NP
E_7	2637.02	-0.2	-7.8	NP	NP

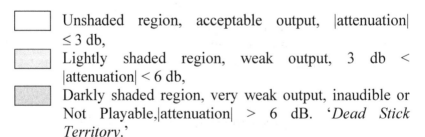

Unshaded region, acceptable output, |attenuation| ≤ 3 db,

Lightly shaded region, weak output, 3 db < |attenuation| < 6 db,

Darkly shaded region, very weak output, inaudible or Not Playable, |attenuation| > 6 dB. '*Dead Stick Territory.*'

where we shall be taking f_2 as the higher note frequency. Due care must be exercised in the use of this equation since it applies only to those notes that lie along the linear roll-off on the *(driving force) vs (log-frequency)* plot. It does not apply to the notes in the *ripple region* for they are not playable. It is also assumed that all stick impact parameters including the impact velocity are the same when applied to each note.

The acoustical output of a note depends on the surface area of the true note and the contact-time of the stick impact so in order to compare notes of different frequencies in the Marginal Zone, the acoustic output of the $E\flat_6$ note played with a contact-time equal to 0.2 ms is taken as the reference. This reference '*tone*' is located in the upper left corner of Table 13.11. All notes in the Zone are then assigned the *same surface area* allowing only the frequency to change from note to note. In practice the higher notes are made smaller in area with a resulting decrease in acoustic output as the frequency increases. With the many choices available in note sizes, let us first use $E\flat_6$ as the reference note and consider notes of equal surface area. In addition, the human ear shows a natural variation in sensitivity at the higher prequencies (see Section 12.5) but we leave this effect out of our present calculations.

Table 13.11 shows the relative attenuation of the acoustic intensity of the notes using equation (13.238) for the same set of contact times as in Table 13.10. The decrease in driving force is greater than the increase in frequency as one moves upward in the marginal zone for the longer contact times (0.3 ms and 0.4 ms) but for $\tau_c = 0.2$ *ms* these changes effectively *cancel themselves out* resulting in essentially no change ($\lesssim 0.5$ *db*) in acoustic output across the Marginal Zone. Observe on the first row of Table 13.11 that on the refereence note $E\flat_6$, the acoustic output decreases significantly as the contact-time is increased. For the 'dead stick', all the notes are in the 'dead' zone. For the good stick with $\tau_c = 0.4$ ms all notes except the $E\flat_6$ note are in the 'dead' zone. This means that when the panist plays with little hand action resulting in long contact times ($\tau_c = 0.4$ ms or greater) only the notes located on the outer and middle areas of the tenor pan face can be adequately excited; the inner or central notes cannot be excited. The Marginal Notes require $\tau_c = 0.3$ ms or shorter. Observe the severity of the attenuation at $\tau_c = 0.4$ ms where the acoustic intensity drops in excess of -20 db on the $G^{\#}_6$ note making this note inaudible.. All higher notes are either inaudible (INA) or not playable (NP). Because of this problem, tenor players must perfect their stick action to produce consistently short contact times. I know that they work hard to achieve this. As it turns out, the much recommended contact-time of $\tau_c = 0.2$ ms given in earlier Sections of this work turns out to be optimum for maximizing the acoustic output of the Marginal Notes.

Although the entries in Table 13.11 are correct for notes of equal area, the first column appears *glaringly unnatural* for this instrument for it implies that all the notes in the Marginal Zone sound almost equally loud when the contact-time is very short! This situation is caused by the assumption of *equal area* for the notes in the marginal zone. To present a more realistic picture *it is now assumed that the areas of the notes decrease linearly as the frequency increases, dropping to half the surface area over one octave*. The results are shown in Table 13.12. These results are closer to what is observed for real tenor pans.

The large 'dead' areas in Tables 13.11 and 13.12 explain why the high notes on the tenor are so hard to play. Recall the difficulty experienced by players in playing the high-end notes of the tenor with adequately short contact times. Because the mathematical equations developed in this Chapter for stick-note impacts describe *very closely* the actions of the player and the designs of the stick, this same difficulty was seen in the numerical simulations in Section 13.17. No player can consistently produce contact times of *0.2 ms* with sticks that must also be used on the lower tenor notes which require longer contact times. However *0.3 ms* is easier to achieve. The B_6 note on the patented G-Pan is seen to fall way down (in fact 9db down) in the 'dead' zone for the normal *0.3 ms* contact-time. Pan makers must therefore build their instruments and sticks to operate in accordance with these purely physical limitations.

Using Table 13.12, we see why pan makers have stopped at $F^{\#}_6$ as the highest note on the tenor. Using the normal playing action of the good tenor panist who can consistently achieve a contact-time of 0.3 ms, the $F^{\#}_6$ note is already 5.2 db down from the $E^{\flat}_6$ reference note. The G_6 note and all higher notes are in the dead zone, which means that for practical purposes they cannot be played! This is consistent with the pan makers' observation.

Table 13.12 Acoustic attenuation for notes of decreasing area. The note area is assumed to decrease linearly with increasing frequency dropping to half the surface area over one octave. Entries in unshaded areas are acceptable levels of acoustic output. INA: Inaudible (attenuation < -20 db). NP: Not Playable.

Note	Frequency $f\ (Hz)$	Type of Stick Tip			
		Good	Good	Good	Dead
		$\tau_c = 0.2$ ms	$\tau_c = 0.3$ ms	$\tau_c = 0.4$ ms	$\tau_c = 0.6$ ms
		Attenuation (db)	Attenuation (db)	Attenuation (db)	Attenuation (db)
E^b_6	1244.51	Ref	-2.9	-5.9	-13.5
E_6	1318.51	-0.2	-3.7	-9.5	-16.8
F_6	1396.91	-0.5	-4.5	-13.0	INA
$F^\#_6$	1479.98	-0.8	-5.2	-16.6	INA
G_6	1567.98	-1.1	-6.1	INA	INA
$G^\#_6$	1661.22	-1.5	-6.8	INA	NP
A_6	1760.00	-1.9	-7.7	INA	NP
B^b_6	1864.65	-2.4	-8.6	INA	NP
B_6	1975.53	-3.0	-9.0	INA	NP
C_7	2093.53	-3.6	-9.8	INA	NP
$C^\#_7$	2217.46	4.3	-10.8	INA	NP
D_7	2349.32	-5.1	-11.8	INA	NP
E^b_7	2489.02	-6.0	-12.8	INA	NP
E_7	2637.02	-7.0	-13.8	NP	NP

☐ Unshaded region, acceptable output, |attenuation| ≤ 3 db,

▒ Lightly shaded region, weak output, 3 db < |attenuation| < 6 db,

▓ Darkly shaded region, very weak output, inaudible or Not Playable,|attenuation| > 6 dB. '*Dead Stick Territory.*'

The analytical procedures for estimating contact-time as discussed earlier, show that the contact-time on the Low and Mid range pans can be accurately determined theoretically from the tip and impact parameters (in good agreement with experimental values) while the contact-time on the high-end pans is largely under the control of the panist. With some knowledge of the retrieving force applied by the panist and time of application of the retrieval, the contact-time can be computed in all cases. Technically, what this means is that so long as the stick consists of a shank and a soft tip (to satisfy tonality requirements), apart from using low-loss material on the tip, reducing tip size etc, the final value of contact-time remains a function of the stick action of the player.

- *In answer to the question of 'custom designing the contact–force profile' (see Section 13.25.5) it can clearly be seen that after the proper choice of tip material, shank and manner of construction (wrapping) it is the hand action of the panist that ultimately determines the contact-force profile and tonal responsiveness. Contact-force profiling is therefore a matter for the panist! I have described how he exercises this control and provided the analytical description for the playing action and the response of the note to his actions but exactly how the panist does it in each stroke of the stick is entirely 'in his hands.' He is even free to exercise any measure of awkwardness if that is his style or if clumsiness is called for in the music!*

The playing of Marginal Notes on the tenor is therefore a special technique to be acquired by the panist with swift hands. This conclusion can easily be verified by observing the special *veloce* action of the professional tenor panist. On the Low-end pans the stick action allows for a contact based more on 'free fall' of the stick so that contact-time is more a function of tip parameters and impact velocity. This also is noticeable in the action of the professional bassists.

The Marginal Notes on the low-end pans include those high notes such as the C_4 (a tenor note by definition) on the bass which are not effectively excited by the sticks. These will be dealt with in the Sections that follow.

13.27.5 The Cello

For the mid-range cello pans, the impact-force spectrum for $\tau_c = 1.2\ ms$ and $\tau_c = 2.0\ ms$ are shown in Figures 13.83(a) and 13.83(b).

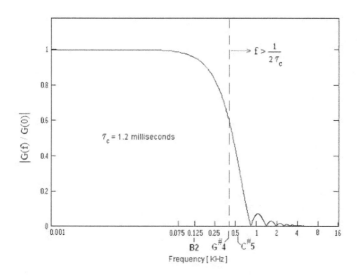

Fig. 13.83(a). Plot of $[G(f)/G(0)]$ as a function of frequency for the Cello pan with $\tau_c = 1.2$ milliseconds.

- For $\tau_c = 1.2\ ms$, $f_c = 416.67\ Hz$. This means that all notes between $G^\#_4$ (415.30 Hz) and $C^\#_5$ (554.37 Hz, the highest note on the cello) inclusive, are *frequency band-limited*.
- At $\tau_c = 2\ ms$, $f_c = 250\ Hz$, frequency band-limiting begins just above the B_3 (246.94 Hz) note. The observation here is that the notes on the cello pan are located just around the knee of the contact-force spectrum. The higher notes on the cello as well as their higher partials will therefore be frequency band-limited on initial excitation with the stick. The $C^\#_5$ now falls just beyond the first zero (at 500 Hz) in the ripple region which means that this note cannot be excited with this longer (2 ms) contact-time.
- Almost all notes on the cello have their higher partials frequency band-limited. This observation can also be stated by saying, 'all notes on the cello are played on the knee of

the impact-force spectral response'. This is one of the two effects that are responsible for the mellow tone of the cello (see the section on *wavelength band-limiting* for the other effect).

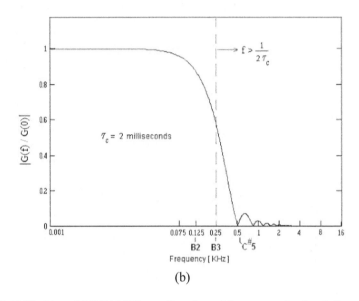

Fig. 13.83(b). Plot of $[G(f)/G(0)]$ as a function of frequency for the Cello pan with $\tau_c = 2$ milliseconds.

Observations: As the effects of frequency band-limiting are examined for pans of decreasing note frequency it is observed that the instruments operate closer to the knee of the impact-force spectrum. This is a clear indication that the steelpan is a band-limited instrument. This is essential for this all-metal percussion instrument to produce pleasant well-rounded tones. After all, striking a piece of metal usually produce annoying high frequency sound, many components of which are not tuned to the musical scale. In fact on a steelpan note, only the first few, usually no more than three, modes are tuned to the musical scale. The other normal modes are left untuned and must be removed from the sounding tone by band-limiting the excitation mechanisms. *Steelpans must therefore, of necessity, operate close to the knee of the impact-force spectrum.* It shall be seen that on the bass, where band-limiting is more critical in order to produce low booming tones, that this is certainly the case.

For comparison, in Figure 13.84 the impact-force spectrum for a dead cello stick with $r_{ms} = 5$ kg·s^{-1} is plotted together with the impact-force spectrum for a good cello stick. It is assumed that the contact-time of 2 milliseconds is the same for both sticks. In practice it is difficult to obtain small contact times with the use of dead sticks. Because of the low level of sound output, there is a tendency for the panist to lift the stick late, resulting in somewhat longer contact times. Observe the large drop in the magnitude of the driving forces produced by the dead stick over the frequency range of the cello pan. Similar results are obtained for dead sticks used on the other pans.

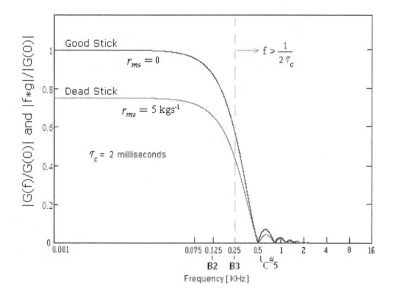

Fig. 13.84. Normalized spectra shown for a good Cello stick tip and a dead Cello stick. The contact-time is taken to be equal in both cases.

13.27.6 Marginal Notes; the Cello and its Accent

Based on the definition of Marginal Notes given earlier, using the contact-time values one will simply get C_4 to $G^{\#}_4$ but the cello is designed with higher notes, all working in the band-limited region. The range of the Marginal Zone must therefore be extended to $C^\#_5$. On the Cello, all notes from C_4 to $C^\#_5$ (a total of 14 notes) are therefore Frequency Band Limited. On the Four Cello (G_2 to $C^\#_5$, 31 notes) this represents almost half the total number or notes on the Cello. Such a large number of band-limited notes satisfies the requirement for a mellow instrument but relies on hand-action to retrieve the stick quickly in order to excite these notes to usable levels. Cello players know that the stick action for these pans falls somewhere between the tenor and the bass and does require practice especially where varying moods must be accommodated. The Cellos are very *'moody'* instruments, controlling (along with the Guitar and Quadraphonic) the middle register in the orchestra as a whole, so with their higher notes properly band-limited they are prevented from sounding like the low end of the tenors—*they have a distinctive accent*. They can *'grumble'* in the background, if that is the mood of the musical piece or form the *bridge* to the tenors in the lead up to a state of joyous excitement! Exhilarating when you hear it!

To comment further on the moody aspects of the cellos I include the following as a 'touch up' piece I felt compelled to do during my review of this section which was done two days after the 2012 Trinidad Panorama Final. Listen to the steel orchestra *Trinidad All Stars* performing *Destra's 'Play Yourself Crazy.'* Listen carefully to the *'answers'* given by the cellos and basses to the *'demanding questions'* rich in melody and meaning posed by the tenors!! For each note played by the frontline tenors the cellos gave a ready answer in *'toe-to-toe'* fashion at the back! As the nursery rhyme goes 'I can do it too, fancy little sailor' where I have altered the words to suit this band which is well known for its depiction of fancy sailors at Carnivals. Just beautiful! No wonder All Stars retained their crown as the champion steelband.

13.27.7 **The Bass**

For the Bass, as shown in Figure 13.85(a) & (b), the notes cover a relatively narrow range of frequencies from 49 Hz to 261.63 Hz.

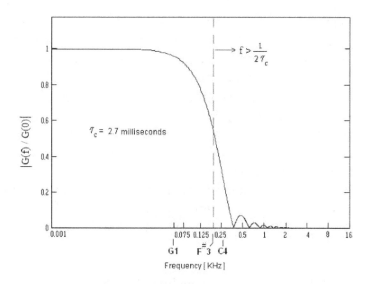

Fig. 13.85 (a). Plot of $[G(f)/G(0)]$ as a function of frequency for the Bass pan with $\tau_c = 2.7$ millisecond.

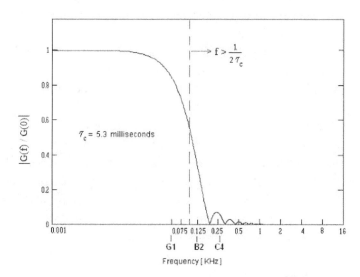

Fig. 13.85(b). Plot of $[G(f)/G(0)]$ as a function of frequency for the Bass pan with $\tau_c = 5.3$ milliseconds.

- Using the shortest contact-time for the bass $\tau_c = 2.7$ ms (Figure 13.85(a)), the cut-off frequency is at 185.19 Hz almost coinciding with the $F^{\#}_3$ note at 185.00 Hz. Frequency band-limiting essentially begins at the $F^{\#}_3$ note and extends to the C_4 note affecting seven (7) of the thirty (30) notes. All notes starting at $F^\#_3$ and extending up to C_4 will have all their upper partials frequency band-limited. The driving force for the C_4 note in particular is down to 0.282.

- For τ_c = 5.3 ms (Figure 13.85(b)), f_c = 94.34 Hz, with frequency band-limiting starting just above the $F^\#_2$ (92.50 Hz) and affecting the fundamental modes on a total of eighteen (18) notes. Notes on which the fundamental mode is band-limited are described here as being *fully band-limited*. All the upper partials on the notes of the bass are now frequency band-limited. All notes from $F^\#_3$ to C_4 fall within the ripple region and are severely frequency band-limited.

Observations: The strong reduction in modal driving force for notes on the bass instrument at frequencies above $F^\#_3$ (185.00 Hz) seems to suggest that these notes should either be played with a cello stick or be removed from the six-bass and nine-bass instruments. When these higher notes on the bass are played the tones are so weak that they usually cannot clearly be heard across the span of a typical-size steel orchestra. *They are kept because they are used as the octaves in sympathetic pairs.* The slightly smaller stick tips used on the tenor-bass may allow their use on this instrument. Many of the notes on the bass are not adequately driven by manual stick impacts. This is one of the reasons for the low level of acoustical output from this rather large musical instrument. *This is a fundamental problem related to the principle of operation of this impact driven bass percussion instrument. This problem can only be handled by proper choice of sticks. If the size of the notes is increased, stick size must also be increased.*

13.27.8 Marginal Notes — Bass

Based on the definition of Marginal Notes given earlier, using the contact-time values one simply gets G_2 to $F^\#_3$ but the Bass is designed with higher notes, all working in the band-limited region. The range of the Marginal Zone must therefore be extended to C_4 or $C^\#_4$ (to include all Basses). On the Standard Bass, all notes from G_2 to C_4 (a total of 18 notes) are therefore Frequency Band Limited.

This band-limiting action applies also to the higher frequency modes corresponding to the higher partials as we shall soon discuss.

13.27.9 Playing the Tenor with a Bass Stick

It is interesting to look at the result of playing the tenor with a bass stick. The result is well known in practice for the excitation is extremely poor. This is seen in Figure 13.86 where the tenor range is superimposed on the force spectrum produced by a bass stick impact. The tenor frequencies lie entirely within the ripple region of the spectrum where mode excitation is very low. All mode excitations will be fully band-limited. *Contact noise* (see the Sections to follow) will dominate the sound generated.

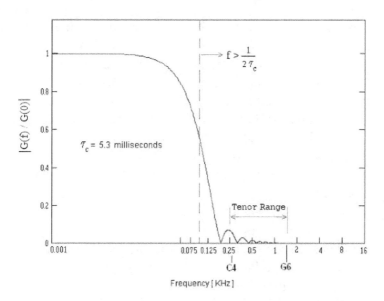

Fig. 13.86. When excited with a bass stick the tenor pan frequencies fall within the ripple region of the driving force spectrum.

There is a region on the contact-force spectrum below the lowest bass note which is always present in the stick-note impact. These low frequency components go into the very weak excitation of the low modes of the skirt. However, the modal density of the skirt is very low at these frequencies — which expressed in simple terms means that there are very few vibrational modes on the skirt at these low frequencies. The energy transfer that result from these low frequency contact forces propagated from the impact point to the skirt do not represent note-skirt interaction. Note-skirt interaction (see Chapter 5) represents energy transfer *between* the vibrating note and the skirt. It is also incorrect and misleading to describe all responses by the skirt as sympathetic vibration.

13.27.10 The Unused Region of the Contact Force Spectrum below the Bass Note Frequencies

When the note is struck, broadband energy is transferred to all areas of the pan; their spectrum being given by the force spectra some of which we have plotted. Because the spectrum is continuous below the lowest bass frequency extending down to 0 Hz, a variety of modes can be excited. But since they are below the lowest bass frequency, they are well outside the frequency bandwidths of the notes. As a result, their effect is small. Because the point impacts made by the stick are applied asymmetrically with respect to the pan face-chime-skirt system, these low modes can be of the swaying type (see Section 5.6). For the researcher or pan maker interested in investigating these modes, one should be careful to not confuse these modes with the low frequency motion that may arise when the entire pan oscillates (rocks side-to-side) on its supports when being played or subjected to a single impact. *This rocking motion is not a property of the pan*! This problem of 'false' modal identification may occur on the bass resting on rubber supports — the usual 'feet' of the bass pan. These vibratory motions are sub-sonic and therefore inaudible in the range below 20 Hz. On the guitar and tenor these motions are clearly visible under most playing conditions (sometimes induced by the player in a rhythmic fashion to attract attention). These 'body motions' do not affect the characteristics of the played note.

13.27.11 Summary of Frequency Band-limiting on all Pans

The effect of frequency band-limiting on steelpans is summarized in Table 13.13. Observe that for each pan type that the number of partials (modes) excited on impact is reduced as the contact–time is increased. Even the fundamental on some notes can be band-limited as seen on the cello and bass where the contact-times are longer. Most of the notes on the bass are played in this *fully band-limited* fashion but then this is exactly what is required on these low-end pans. While all notes on the tenor are played without band-limiting of the fundamental mode, the table shows that the tenor player, by controlling the contact-time can increase or decrease the number of impact-excited modes on almost all the notes.

Table 13.13

Pan	τ_c $f_c = \frac{1}{2}\tau_c$	Frequency Band-limited Fundamental Modes and the Number of Partials N that can be Excited on Impact				
		Fully Band-limited	N = 1	N = 2	N = 3	N = 4
Tenor	0.2 ms 2500 Hz	-	E_6-G_6 (4)	A_5-E^b_6 (7)	E^b_5-$G^\#_5$ (6)	D_4-D_5 (13)
	0.4 ms 1250 Hz	-	E_5-G_6 (16)	A_4-E^b_5 (7)	E_4-$G^\#_4$ (5)	D_4-E^b_4 (2)
Cello	1.2 ms 416.37 Hz	A_4-$C^\#_5$ (5)	A_3-$G^\#_4$ (12)	$C^\#_3$-$G^\#_3$ (8)	B^b_2-C_3 (3)	-
	2 ms 250 Hz	C_4-$C^\#_5$ (14)	C_3-B_3 (12)	B^b_2-B_2 (2)	None	-
Bass	2.7 ms 185.19 Hz	$F^\#_3$-C_4 (7)	$F^\#_2$-F_3 (12)	B_1-F_2 (7)	G_1-B^b_1 (4)	-
	5.3 ms 94.34 Hz	G_2-C_4 (18)	G_1-$F^\#_2$ (12)	-	-	-

Any partial of frequency f satisfying $f = (2n+1)/3\tau_c$ (n = 1, 2, 3, ...) *cannot* be excited by stick impact. These are the zeros of the impact force spectrum. A bracketed number ( ) is the number of notes in the indicated musical range.

13.27.12 Extending the Musical Range of Steelpans

The natural limits set by frequency band limiting of the notes on the top end of the tenor pan shows that notes above G_6 cannot be adequately excited by direct hand controlled stick impacts. The use of smaller tenor sticks allows for some extension upward in the musical scale but at reduced intensity. Since a larger rise on the note can always be used to compensate for an increase in note planform size, the use of a larger diameter pan face allows larger inner notes to be constructed. Some of these inner notes can be made to sound almost as loud as traditional outer notes. The Pang range of pans (which appeared in the 1990's) is one of the first to successfully use these larger notes and pan diameters. An even earlier, very loud pan, measuring 29 inches (72 cm) in diameter is shown being demonstrated by one of its makers, Fitzroy Henry, in Figure 13.87. For a given musical note (on the musical scale) the larger notes are however, still subject to the same frequency band limiting as the smaller notes. *Band limiting cannot be avoided.* In fact, it is necessary since it is used to limit the excitation levels of unwanted tones.

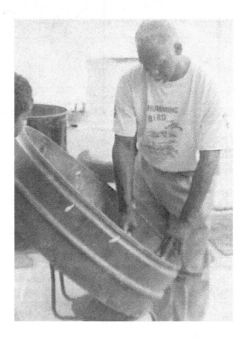

Fig. 13.87. A large 29-inch (72 cm) diameter pan demonstrated by one of its makers, Fitzroy Henry.

It is always possible to extend the range downward on the musical scale as seen from the plots of modal driving force versus frequency. However as the pan notes are made to operate further to the left of the knee of the response curve it is more likely that higher untuned natural modes will be excited. The problem is similar to that experienced when a guitar or cello pan is played with a tenor stick. Although the tuner can vary the frequencies of these higher modes these natural modes cannot be completely removed from the note dynamics. For this reason the steelpan, as a musical instrument, is operated close to the knee as a system of band-limited vibrators. Excessive excitation of these untuned modes can produce noise (a psychoacoustic effect) in the ear of the listener (see Chapter 16). Therefore if the tenor range is extended downward the characteristics of the sticks must be adjusted. This may in turn affect the fidelity of the higher notes when played with the same sticks.

By comparison, the wide range of the piano is made possible by the use of individual hammers, one for each note. Each hammer is individually crafted to optimize its band-limiting characteristics and impact force suited for each string (or set of strings). This is not possible on the normal manual two-stick manner of playing the pan and the suggestion that the player can switch sticks during play is not a practical option.

13.28 Stick Contact Noise and Tip Mechanical Resistance

13.28.1 Origin of the Stick Contact Noise

Tip losses determined by the mechanical resistance r_{ms} has been shown in the SDOF analysis to produce an initial contact force $F_i = r_{ms}V_0$, (for p = 1). In the MDOF analysis the contact force produced by the tip losses consists of a spectrum of forces described by the Fourier transform of the loss component of the contact force.

The Fourier transform that corresponds to the loss term in equation (13.235) can be expressed as

$$H^*(k) = i\frac{2\alpha}{\omega}H(k)$$

$$= i\frac{\alpha}{\omega}\left[\operatorname{sinc}\left(\pi\left(k-\frac{1}{2}\right)\right) - \operatorname{sinc}\left(\pi\left(k+\frac{1}{2}\right)\right)\right].$$

In terms of spectral frequency $f = 2k/3\tau_c$ with f in Hertz, τ_c in seconds and substituting the expressions for α and ω, one can write

$$H^*(f) = i\frac{3r_{ms}}{8R_s^2}\left(\frac{1-v_s^2}{\pi\rho_s E_s}\right)^{\frac{1}{2}}\left[\operatorname{sinc}\left(\pi\left(\frac{3f\tau_c}{2}-\frac{1}{2}\right)\right) - \operatorname{sinc}\left(\pi\left(\frac{3f\tau_c}{2}+\frac{1}{2}\right)\right)\right].$$
(13.239)

The best way to view and compare these spectral forces graphically is to plot the ratio $|H^*(f)/G(0)|$ for a variety of tips. This plot will give the ratios of the resistive forces generated by the ½-cosine term to the maximum contact force generated by the ½-sine term and are shown in Figure 13.87. These relative magnitudes depend on r_{ms}, R_s, E_s, ρ_s and v_s. However, it must be emphasized that the force amplitudes shown here are measured *relative* to the maximum modal driving force component and are not absolute values. The latter depend only on the product $r_{ms}V_0$. Relative values are used here because one is really interested in the acoustical output of the sounding note which consists of the key-note (and higher partials) excited by the ½-sine function and would like to have the noise component (excited by the ½-cosine function) reduced.

Figure 13.88 shows the relative force spectra generated by the function $|H^*(f)|$ for stick tips used on

(a) the tenor pan with $r_m = 1$ kg·s^{-1}, $R_s = 0.8$ cm, $\alpha/\omega = 0.112$, $\tau_c = 0.2$ ms, peak at $f_p = 2.28$ kHz,
(b) the mid-range cello pan with $r_m = 1$ kg·s^{-1}, $R_s = 2$ cm, $\alpha/\omega = 0.018$, $\tau_c = 2.2$ ms, peak at $f_p = 207$ Hz and
(c) the bass pan with $r_m = 1$ kg·s^{-1}, $R_s = 3$ cm, $\alpha/\omega = 0.008$, $\tau_c = 3.4$ ms, peak at $f_p = 134$ Hz.

The main peak on the force spectrum is located at the frequency f_p given by

$$f_p = 0.4557479/\tau_c.$$

The constant 0.4557479 is obtained by analysis of the function $|H^*(f)|$. Observe that for all three stick tips, the force spectrum amplitude begins on zero at zero frequency, rises to a maximum (134 Hz for the bass stick, 207 Hz for the cello stick, 2.28 kHz for the tenor stick) then falls rapidly into the ripple region at high frequencies. Because of their spectral characteristics, these forces are not effective in driving the normal modes on the pan. However, they can drive low-level high frequency transient vibrations of the stick and note material at the stick-note interface, which in turn produce a *sharp percussive noise* which can best be described as a *clap*.

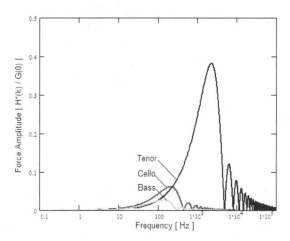

Fig. 13.88. Spectral component $|H^*(f)|$ normalized with respect to $|G(0)|$. Bass stick, $R_s = 3$ cm, $\tau_c = 3.4$ ms, peak at 134 Hz; Cello stick, $R_s = 2$ cm, $\tau_c = 2.2$ ms, peak at 207 Hz; Tenor stick, $R_s = 0.8$ cm, $\tau_c = 0.2$ ms, peak at 2.28 kHz.

13.28.2 Stick Contact Noise (SCN) or Stick-Note Clap (SNC)

Whenever the steelpan is played with a stick one can hear a short duration 'clap' noise as the stick makes contact with the note. The sound of stick-note clap is similar to that generated by striking the palm of your hand with one or two fingers (DO NOT clap with your palms, this rapidly releases the air trapped between both palms creating a loud noisy outburst). The flesh on the fingers and palms is lossy, low-stiffness material, fitting exactly the requirements for generating this type of sound. In fact some of the characteristics observed on stick-note clap can be demonstrated using your finger and the palm of your hand. Equation (13.239) describes the spectral components of the forces generating this noise. The intensity of the clap depends on the stick tip construction and the material used. The factor α/ω essentially measures the ratio [mechanical resistance/(stiffness)$^{1/2}$] so that equation (13.239) predicts that stick tips having high loss and low stiffness will generate greater stick noise relative to the sounding key-note. Old, used sticks with their high losses and low stiffness are well known to generate this noise making them useless for playing the inner notes of the tenor pan. This noise is heard together with the sounding key-note particularly on impact with the small inner notes of the high-end pans. The same sound is generated if the stick impacts the internote areas of the pan.

Observe in Figures 13.88 and 13.89 that the contact noise peak at frequencies above the knee for each type of tip. These examples used the same tip material for the tenor, cello and bass stick tips. While the material properties used here will produce acceptable contact noise on the bass and cello pan, it will prove to be very noisy on contact with the inner notes of the tenor pan. Heavily used sticks can rapidly become lossy with an accompanying increase in contact noise. In order to avoid this problem the panist finds that as the tips age s/he must change the tenor stick tips earlier than the bass stick tips. Loosely wrapped sticks (tenor versions in particular) with their intrinsically higher losses must be re-wrapped to reduce this noise. This noise is compounded on the wrapped stick if the outer layer becomes loose allowing the layer to vibrate as a membrane during impact (see Section 13.12).

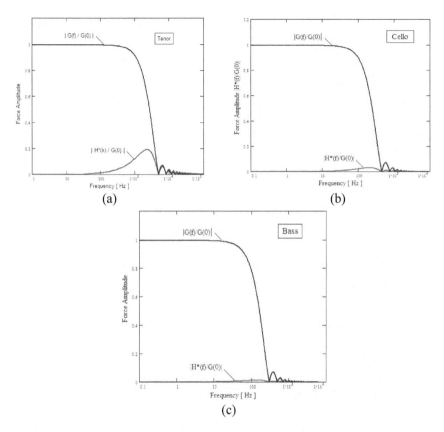

Fig. 13.89. Normalized contact noise driving force spectrum $|H(f)/G(0)|$ compared with normalized modal driving force spectrum $|G(f)/G(0)|$ using the same tip material (a) tenor, (b) cello, (c) bass.

13.28.3 Some Physical Considerations — the Tenor Stick Example

The SDOF analysis has shown that the resistive force $F_i(t)$ begins (at $t = 0$) on an amplitude maximum. Certainly, no force can develop instantaneously. How can this be reconciled with the limits placed on the time development of the contact forces by the finite velocity of the compressional stress waves V_p within the tip? To get some idea of the time for stress wave development, consider a tenor stick with $\varphi_c \approx 0.25$ cm. For a typical p-wave velocity $V_p = 50$ ms^{-1}, one gets the time for stress wave development as $\tau_s = \varphi_c / V_p = 50$ microseconds (50 μs). This is the earliest time after the 'make' that the stick contact force spectrum is open to physical interpretation. This applies to the normal contact force, which obeys the ½-sine law and the resistive force, which obeys a ½-cosine law. Translated into frequency this time period of 50 μs corresponds to 20 kHz in the frequency domain. This means that in the driving force spectrum the first components to develop are the high frequency components starting around 20 kHz followed by the lower frequency components. What appears as an instantaneous force F_i at $t = 0$ in the SDOF analysis is in reality a rapid rise measured in tens to hundreds of microseconds of a number of spectral components described by the function $H^*(f)$ beginning first with the high frequency components and progressing towards lower frequency components. Because there will be insufficient time during the impact for low frequency force components to fully develop, there is a low-frequency −3db cut-off for stick noise given by

$$f_{min} = 0.198767/\tau_c.$$

The constant 0.198767 is obtained by numerical analysis of the function $|H^*(f)|$. For practical purposes one can take $f_{min} \approx 0.2/\tau_c$ (or 1 kHz for $\tau_c = 0.2$ ms, just below the D_6 (1174.66 Hz) note).

This scenario is consistent with the force spectrum shown in Figure 13.88 where the spectral amplitude falls off rapidly with frequency below the peak at f_p ($= 0.4557479/\tau_c$) (or 2.28 kHz in our example). These transient forces drive low-level non-resonant vibrations of the note and tip material in the immediate neighborhood of the impact point. These short duration vibrations and the short acoustic wavetrain (*wavelets*) they generate in the surrounding air medium consist of a band of frequencies (essentially covering the range $f_{min} \approx 0.2/\tau_c$ to $f_{max} \approx 1/\tau_c$ or 1 kHz to 5 kHz in our example) with peak amplitude at f_p ($= 2.28$ kHz). The upper frequency f_{max} corresponds to the first zero in the ripple region of the $H^*(f)$ function. These vibrations are of short duration for two main reasons:

1. Firstly, the cosine profile defines a force that is positive for ½ the make-to-break duration and negative for the other ½ duration (see Figure 13.74). Therefore the cosine function produces no net displacement of the note.

2. Secondly, the excitation frequencies are higher than many of the note frequencies on the pan (on the tenor G_6 is at 1.56798 kHz) thus giving a non-resonant (low response) condition on the note.

The human ear does not distinguish the individual frequencies within the noise band; instead one hears a short duration 'clap' produced by the superposition of these wavelets at the eardrum. Since one is dealing with a non-resonant process, striking any part of the pan face produces the clap. *Put this to the test by using one finger of your right (left) hand to strike different parts of the palm or fingers on the left (right) hand while listening to the sound of the clap. Sounds the same way each time!* This explains the brief 'clap' sound of the stick noise.

13.28.4 Solution to the Stick-Note Clap Problem

When a pan note is improperly blocked much of the impact energy is lost across the note boundary resulting in a low intensity heavily damped tone. This may result in relatively louder contact noise levels. While Figure 13.89 shows that the relative magnitude of the modal driving forces delivered to the tuned modes of the note are larger than those driving the contact noise components, which is good for the generation of strong relatively noise-free key-notes and partials, this advantage can easily be lost by improper note preparation and poor blocking. Whereas the intensity and tonal characteristics of the tuned key-note and partials depend on the location of the impact point, note preparation and blocking, *contact noise do not*. This can easily be verified by striking the inner notes and internote areas with a lossy tenor stick. Almost the same level of noise is generated by these impacts. To reduce the effects of contact noise on the inner notes of the high-end pans and to increase the intensity of the sounding key-note the tuner must ensure that the notes are properly blocked (*tightened*). Difficulty in achieving proper blocking will always occur when the inner section of the pan is not indented to the required depth and/or the pan face is not properly annealed. *Good preparation is essential*!

The use of low-loss tip material especially on the stick tips for the tenor and high-end pans helps in reducing stick-note clap. Re-wrapping with increased tension or changing to new rubber and increasing the tension works on wrapped tips.

At all times, avoid the use of lossy overlays on the stick tip. As the author has earlier recommended do not use absorption mats which not only has the propensity for increasing stick noise but also damps the vibration of the notes — a muting effect. The latter is unpredictable and since a tone already sounded cannot be recalled, this could prove embarrassing for the panist!

13.29 Dynamical Equations for the Two Types of Vibrations Produced by Stick-Note Contact

As the typical listener can readily verify, whenever pan notes are played there are two distinctly different types of percussive sounds generated by stick-note impacts:

13.29.1 The Major Sound — Engineering Formulas

The *major sound*, lasting around one second, and representing the desired tones, are *the musical key-note and accompanying higher partials* that characterize the sounding note. The vibrations generating these sounds are driven by the spectral forces arising from the ½-sine pulse imparted to the note on impact. Low-level resonant vibrations are also excited and may be heard when these spectral forces propagate to other areas of the pan face and skirt (skirt excitations are discussed in Chapter 5). The note vibrations generating the desired tones are described by the following set of coupled dimensionless non-linear equations:

$$\frac{d^2 w_m}{d\tau^2} + \mu_m \frac{dw_m}{d\tau} + \omega_m^2 w_m + \sum_{i,j=1}^{N} \alpha_{ij,m} w_i w_j + \sum_{i,j,k=1}^{N} \beta_{ijk,m} w_i w_j w_k = f_0 +$$

$$2 V_0^{\frac{2p_c}{p_c+1}} \frac{\langle z \psi_m \rangle}{\langle \psi_m^2 \rangle} \left(\frac{a}{h}\right)^4 \left(\frac{R_s^2}{ab}\right) \left(\frac{(1-\upsilon_n^2)}{E_n}\right) \left(\frac{E_s}{\pi(1-v_s^2)}\right)^{\frac{1}{p_c+1}} \left(\frac{\rho_s(p_c+1)}{2}\right)^{\frac{p_c}{p_c+1}} \times$$

$$\left(1 + \sigma_{pre} V_0^{\frac{2(1-p_c)}{p_c+1}} \left(\frac{\rho_s(p_c+1)}{2}\right)^{\frac{1-p_c}{p_c+1}} \left(\frac{\pi(1-\upsilon_s^2)}{E_s}\right)^{\frac{2}{p_c+1}} e^{-\alpha\left(\frac{\tau}{\gamma}+\frac{\pi}{2\omega}\right)} \sin\left(\frac{2\pi\tau}{3\gamma\tau_c}\right) B_1(0,3\gamma\tau_c/2) \right.$$

$$(m = 1, 2, 3, \ldots). \qquad (13.240)$$

Impact Phase and Free Phase

Because of the presence of the Box Function B_1 (which defines the range of the *Impact phase*), on the right side of equation (13.240), the *Free Phase* given by

$$\frac{d^2 w_m}{d\tau^2} + \mu_m \frac{dw_m}{d\tau} + \omega_m^2 w_m + \sum_{i,j=1}^{N} \alpha_{ij,m} w_i w_j + \sum_{i,j,k=1}^{N} \beta_{ijk,m} w_i w_j w_k = 0,$$

(13.241)

follows after the end of the *Impact Phase*.

The static force f_0 and the coefficients ω_m, $\alpha_{ij,m}$ and $\beta_{ijk,m}$ appearing in these equations depend on note geometry, boundary conditions, temperature and residual stresses. Since the zero-frequency component of the ½-sine driving force is non-zero, this force produces a temporary displacement of the note from its quiescent point that is dependent on f_0. The Mechanical Bias f_0 determines the maximum impact force that the note can withstand without generating unpleasant (distorted) sounds.

Observe clearly the roles played by the stick parameters (R_s, E_s, ρ_s, v_s, and p) and the impact velocity of the stick V_0. The note size and geometry enter explicitly through a, b and h and implicitly through ω_m, $\alpha_{ij,m}$ and $\beta_{ijk,m}$. The contact time τ_c is determined by the stick parameters, the impact velocity and hand action of the player and to a lesser extent, by stick losses.

These equations completely describe the stick-note interaction and modal vibrations that generate all the tonal features for single notes on the steelpan for all manner and style of playing. *(The equations for note-note (sympathetic) and note-skirt interactions are given in Sections 5.3.2 and 5.3.3.)* The modes excited here are 'global' in the sense that they involve significant vibration of the whole note.

Numerical Solution

The procedures followed in the numerical methods used to solve equations (13.240) and (13.241) provide excellent explanations for the excitation and vibrational processes that take place on an impacted note. Numerical integration proceeds from the initial state of the system $w_m(0)$ at $\tau = 0$ and in a step-wise fashion provides updated values $w_m(n\delta t)$ at times $\tau = \delta\tau, 2\delta\tau, 3\delta\tau...N\delta\tau$ at very short intervals $\delta\tau$ over the required duration $N\delta\tau$. It is equivalent to a series of high-speed snapshots of the real stick-note system from the instant of impact until the completion of the sounding tone. During the impact on the real note, the modal sub-systems (modes) with their individual frequencies and intrinsic bandwidths respond selectively to the frequency components of the impact force. Similarly, in the numerical solution of the equation, as the numerical integration progresses, the chosen modal sub-system described by the left-hand side of equations (13.240) and (13.241) and identified by the subscript m, will respond selectively to the frequency components of the temporal function on the right-hand side. By virtue of the damping term on the left side of equations (13.240) and (13.241) the numerical system will display vibrations over a range of frequencies consistent with the bandwidths of the vibrational modes of the system.

All aspects of the development obtained on the real note including frequency and amplitude modulations, generation and interactions of the partials and decay of the note vibrations are produced in the solution.

Engineering Formulas for Excited Partials in Standard (MKS or SI) Units

Instructions for use of the Equations:

(i) *If the temperature and boundary stresses differ from those obtained at the time of tuning then all affected parameters including the modal frequencies and note shape must be corrected before solving the equations. Refer to the relevant sections of this book dealing with these topics.*

(ii) *The modal displacements W_m are measured from the note surface in the Quiescent State therefore the Mechanical Bias F_0 does not appear explicitly in the equations (this assumes that all necessary corrections in (i) have been carried out). If corrections have not been made for changes in operating conditions (including the temperature of the note) then F_0*

appears explicitly and all dynamical parameters correspond to the prevailing conditions.

With modal masses $m_{eqv}^{\{m\}}$ in kilogram (kg), time t in seconds (s), modal displacements W_m in meters (m), impact velocity V_0 in m·s^{-1}, note mechanical resistance $r_{mn}\left(=\mu_m \gamma\, m_{eqv}^{\{m\}} \equiv R_{mn} m_{eqv}^{\{m\}}\right)$ in kg·s^{-1}, stick radius R_s in meters, elastic modulus of the stick tip E_s in N·m^{-2}, tip pre-stress σ_{pre} in N·m^{-2}, the tip density ρ_s in kg·m^{-3}, linear spring constants $k_m^{\{1\}}\left(=\omega_m^2 \gamma^2 m_{eqv}^{\{m\}}\right)$ in N·m^{-1}, quadratic spring constants

$$k_{ij,m}^{\{2\}} = \left(\frac{\alpha_{ij,m}\gamma^2 m_{eqv}^{\{m\}}}{h}\right) \text{ in } \text{N·m}^{-2}, \text{ cubic spring constants}$$

$$k_{ijk,m}^{\{3\}} = \left(\frac{\beta_{ijk,m}\gamma^2 m_{eqv}^{\{m\}}}{h^2}\right) \text{ in N·m}^{-3}, \text{ tip mass } m_s \text{ in kg, tip mechanical}$$

resistance r_{ms} in kg·s^{-1}, the tip stiffness parameter ω^2 in s^{-2}, contact time τ_c in seconds, the set of coupled dynamical equations for the tuned modes $m = 1, 2, 3\ldots N$ are given by

Impact Phase and Free Phase:

$$m_{eqv}^{\{m\}}\frac{d^2 W_m}{dt^2} + r_{mn}\frac{dW_m}{dt} + k_m^{\{1\}}W_m + \sum_{i,j=1}^{N} k_{ij,m}^{\{2\}}W_i W_j + \sum_{i,j,k=1}^{N} k_{ijk,m}^{\{3\}}W_i W_j W_k =$$

$$2\pi \frac{\langle z\psi_m \rangle}{\langle \psi_m^2 \rangle} V_0^{\frac{2p_c}{p_c+1}} R_s^2 \left(\frac{E_s}{\pi(1-v_s^2)}\right)^{\frac{1}{p_c+1}} \left(\frac{\rho_s(p_c+1)}{2}\right)^{\frac{p_c}{p_c+1}} \times$$

$$\left(1+\sigma_{pre}V_0^{\frac{2(1-p_c)}{p_c+1}}\left(\frac{\rho_s(p_c+1)}{2}\right)^{\frac{1-p_c}{p_c+1}}\left(\frac{\pi(1-v_s^2)}{E_s}\right)^{\frac{2}{p_c+1}}\right) e^{-\frac{r_{ms}}{2m_s}\left(t+\frac{\pi}{2\omega}\right)}\sin\left(\frac{2\pi t}{3\tau_c}\right) B_1(0, 3\tau_c/2).$$

The frequency of the key-note, in units of Hertz, is given by

$$f_1 = \frac{1}{2\pi}\sqrt{\frac{k_1^{\{1\}}}{m_{eqv}^{\{1\}}}}.$$

A term-by-term description of the driving forces on the right side of the Engineering Formula now follows for completeness (*you will find that all aspects of the stick and impact conditions have been included)*:

- $2\pi \dfrac{\langle z\psi_m \rangle}{\langle \psi_m^2 \rangle} V_0^{\frac{2p_c}{p_c+1}} R_s^2 \left(\dfrac{E_s}{\pi(1-v_s^2)} \right)^{\frac{1}{p_c+1}} \left(\dfrac{\rho_s(p_c+1)}{2} \right)^{\frac{p_c}{p_c+1}}$

- $\dfrac{\langle z\psi_m \rangle}{\langle \psi_m^2 \rangle}$; The function z handles the details of the stick impact point on the note surface and the force distribution over the contact area. The mode-shape function ψ_m identifies the excited vibrational mode. $\langle z\psi_m \rangle$ is an average taken over the contact-area A_c while $\langle \psi_m^2 \rangle$ is an average taken over the entire note surface.

- $V_0^{\frac{2p_c}{p_c+1}}$; This is the velocity factor that incorporates the compressive p-index and impact velocity V_0.

- $R_s^2 \left(\dfrac{E_s}{\pi(1-v_s^2)} \right)^{\frac{1}{p_c+1}} \left(\dfrac{\rho_s(p_c+1)}{2} \right)^{\frac{p_c}{p_c+1}}$: This factor shows the dependence on stick tip radius R_s, tip rubber density ρ_s, compression p-index p_c and elastic constants E_s and v_s.

- $\left(1 + \sigma_{pre} V_0^{\frac{2(1-p_c)}{p_c+1}} \left(\dfrac{\rho_s(p_c+1)}{2} \right)^{\frac{1-p_c}{p_c+1}} \left(\dfrac{\pi(1-v_s^2)}{E_s} \right)^{\frac{2}{p_c+1}} \right)$: This is the pre-stress factor, which incorporates the stick tip parameters, impact velocity and the pre-stress σ_{pre}. For wrapped sticks the pre-stress is determined by the wrapping tension, the width and thickness of the banding rubber (see Section 13.14).

- $e^{-\frac{r_{ms}}{2m_s}\left(t+\frac{\pi}{2\omega}\right)} \sin\left(\dfrac{2\pi t}{3\tau_c} \right) B_1(0, 3\tau_c/2)$

- $e^{-\frac{r_{ms}}{2m_s}\left(t+\frac{\pi}{2\omega}\right)}$ is the exponential decay factor associated with the mechanical resistance r_{ms} of the tip material and is active during the impact phase. This term is important in describing the impact produced by all sticks used on the pan particularly sticks with lossy tips. This factor determines whether a stick is 'good' or 'dead'.

- $\sin\left(\dfrac{2\pi t}{3\tau_c}\right) B_1(0, 3\tau_c/2)$ is the ½-sine factor that describes the impulsive (pulse-like) nature of the stick-note impact. The Boxcar function $B_1(0,3\tau_c/2)$ limits the duration of the impact, from *make* to *break*, to $3\tau_c/2$. The contact-time τ_c is determined by the stick tip parameters, impact velocity and especially on the high-end pans, the hand action of the player.

13.29.2 The Minor Sound — Stick-Note Clap

The *minor sound*, of lower intensity, is the *clap (*contact noise) of very short duration, tens of milliseconds at most. There are no internal resonances associated with the excitations generating the clap. As a result the non-linear stiffness related to the coupling coefficients $\alpha_{ij,m}$ and $\beta_{ijk,m}$ will be zero in the ODEs describing these excitations. Since the amplitude of the zero frequency component of the ½-cosine driving force is zero, there is no displacement from the quiescent point so the static force f_0 does not appear in the ODEs. Since the ½-cosine driving force produces no net displacement of the note surface from the quiescent point it does not contribute to the excitation of the tuned modes of vibration. In addition the mode designator 'm' must be replaced by 'N' to indicate that the equations describe the transient noise vibrations at radian frequencies ω_N.

Since the clap equations do not describe the tuned modes, what meaning must be given to $\langle z\psi_N \rangle$ and $\langle \psi_N^2 \rangle$? First, consider the following two readily verifiable aural observations (i) and (ii) and their interpretation (iii):

(i) The clap produced by stick-note contact is generated by and radiated from a small area around the point of contact (the impact point) — *the noise source is highly localized.*

(ii) The short duration sound of the clap is of a *'non-musical'* nature, unrelated to the tuned modes of the note.

(iii) The related vibrations are spatially restricted and the radiated sound decays rapidly with time, indicative of relatively strong damping. This rapid damping causes the vibrational motion to rapidly decay spatially (on the note and tip surfaces) and hence creates a tendency for the vibration to be localized near the impact point. Therefore, the modes of vibration generating the clap are 'not global' they are 'local' in the sense that they do not involve significant vibration of the entire note. In addition the tip material is also set into a transient state of vibration that is partly responsible for the sound of the clap. Here also the effect is heavily damped and spatially localized. This explains (i) and (ii) above.

Since the mode shapes for the noise vibrations are undetermined and the frequencies span a continuous band (with zeros), a reasonable assumption is to use for all clap driving forces the SDOF result $\langle z\psi_N \rangle / \langle \psi_N^2 \rangle = 2/3$. The implicit assumption made here is that the averaging is carried out over the contact area. This is strictly true for $\langle z\psi_N \rangle$ but extended to include $\langle \psi_N^2 \rangle$ because of the spatial localization of these transient vibrations in the immediate neighborhood of the contact point. One thus obtains for the transient response that generates the clap off the tip and note surface or pan face:

$$\frac{d^2 w_N}{d\tau^2} + \mu_N \frac{dw_N}{d\tau} + \omega_N^2 w_N = \frac{r_{ms} V_0 a^4 \rho_n (1-v_n^2)}{m_{eqv} E_n h^2 R_s} e^{-\alpha\frac{\tau}{\gamma}} \cos\left(\frac{2\pi\tau}{3\gamma\tau_c}\right) B_1(0, 3\gamma\tau_c/2),$$

(13.242)

where m_{eff} is the mass of the region (of area $\approx A_c$) on the pan face or tip executing the transient motion that generates the clap. Observe in

(13.242) that the right side of the equation describes the contact force which is the same for the tip excitation and the note suface excitation. The frequencies ω_N that appear in the clap equation (13.242) are contained in the spectrum described by the function $H^*(f)$.

Observe once again that the forces that excite and drive these vibrations are proportional to the stick tip mechanical resistance r_{ms} and the initial velocity V_0. Because all tip materials are lossy, the forces in (13.242) and the clap they generate are always present during impact. *All sticks generate some level of contact noise. Dead sticks are the worse offenders!*

Engineering Formulas for Stick-Note Clap in Standard (MKS or SI) Units

The ½-cosine forces excite areas in the neighborhood of the contact area to a shallow depth (because of strong damping) in the rubber tip and a small area on the note surface. The effective mass will be equal to the mass of the excited region. This is consistent with the SDOF approximations made earlier for the clap modes. With the equivalent mass m_{eqv} in kilogram (kg), time t in seconds (s), displacement W_N in meters (m), mechanical resistance of the excited material $r_m (= \mu_N m_{eqv} \gamma)$ kg·s^{-1}, impact velocity V_0 in m·s^{-1}, radian frequency of stick noise ω_N in s^{-1}, tip mechanical resistance r_{ms} in kg·s^{-1}, linear spring constant of the vibrating material $k_N^{\{1\}} (= \omega_N^2 m_{eqv} \gamma^2)$ N·m^{-1}, contact time τ_c in seconds, the set of independent dynamical equations for the clap excitations are given by

Impact Phase and Free Phase

$$m_{eqv}\frac{d^2 W_N}{dt^2} + r_m \frac{dW_N}{dt} + k_N^{\{1\}} W_N = r_{ms} V_0 e^{-\frac{r_{ms}t}{2m_s}} \cos\left(\frac{2\pi t}{3\tau_c}\right) B_1(0, 3\tau_c/2).$$

13.29.3 Effect of note material losses

The nodal lines that form dynamically on the vibrating note surface can be understood as the spatial counterpart to the zeros on the Fourier transform of the impact force-time function. A mode cannot be excited by point (zero width) impacts along its nodal lines on the surface of the note. Similarly an ideal mode (zero frequency bandwidth) receives no energy from an impact if its frequency falls on one of the zeros of the impact force spectrum.

In practice a real note experiences losses of energy as it vibrates, in the following ways;
  (i) Internal mechanical losses (which increases with the use of powder coating, chrome plating or nickel coating) increase in proportion to A (the surface area of the note).
  (ii) Acoustical Radiation losses (which increases approximately as the product f^2A^2, where f is the frequency of the note).
  (iii) Transmission losses across imperfect note boundaries.

In practice, because of these losses within the note material, there will be some *small levels* of vibration along nodal lines and along the true note boundary. This means that the same losses that give a note a finite value for the Q-factor is also responsible for the small vibrations along nodal lines. With losses, the mode shape $\psi_m(r,\phi)$ extends beyond the ideal boundary. This has two consequences:

  (i) The first is that energy of the excited note is lost across the true note boundary, which implies that *a note can never be fully blocked in practice despite the skill and experience of the pan maker or tuner. This observation is important in pan making and makes possible the interactions between separated domains of the pan.*
  (ii) The second effect is that when combined with the finite area of stick-note contact, it is possible to impart a small level of excitation to a mode by impact along a nodal line as well as along the true note boundary even when the contact point lies outside the boundary. However, the level of excitation rapidly diminishes as the impact point moves outward away from the boundary. This low-level mode of excitation is useful for experimental purposes whereby excitation of a note can be carried out using an electromechanical vibrator connected to a remote spot on the pan.

13.30 Contact-Width Wavelength Band-Limiting

13.30.1 The Basic Nature of Wavelength Band-Limiting

The mode shapes generated on the note surface can be quite complex when taken singly or all together. If the contact-width spans a number of points corresponding to maximum displacements (antinodes) of a given mode, the excitation level is diminished. In general, the spacing of antinodes for a given mode decreases with increasing modal frequency. Higher frequency modes are therefore more likely to experience greater constraints coming from the width of the stick contact on the note surface. It will therefore be important for us to look at this problem. The constraints put on the excitation of high frequency modes are certainly incorporated into the design of the sticks used for playing the pan. It contributes to the decision to use large tips on the bass and small tips on the tenor. Just as contact-time leads to frequency band-limiting, so does contact-width lead to *wavelength band-limiting*. The first is a temporal limiting mechanism while the latter is a spatial limiting mechanism.

13.30.2 The Generalized Wavelength of a Spatially Periodic Function

For a spatially periodic function such as a simple sinusoidal $y(x) = A \sin(2\pi x/\lambda)$, the wavelength λ is clearly defined and remains constant for all x. The wavelength is also independent of the amplitude A of the sine function. The wavelength can easily be measured from crest to crest or from the separation between alternate zeros of $y(x)$.

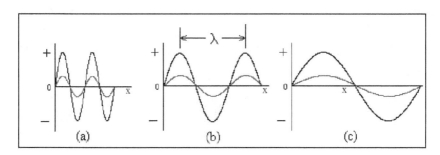

Fig. 13.89. The sine function at three different wavelengths and amplitudes.

This sine function is plotted in Figure 13.90 for three different wavelength values. By comparing the two waveforms seen in each of the panels in Figure 13.90 observe that as the amplitude is reduced the wavelength remains constant but the curvature is reduced. By comparing the panels (a), (b) and (c) in order, observe that as the wavelength λ increases the curvature decreases. It should be possible to use these relationships between wavelength and curvature to define the wavelength for an arbitrary periodic function.

For more general spatially periodic functions such as the mode shape functions on the notes, we are faced with a problem in defining the wavelength because the distance from crest to crest may change with position on the note surface. To find a way to do this, return to the sine function and consider the curvature defined as the second derivative of y with respect to x;

$$\text{Curvature} \quad \frac{d^2 y}{dx^2} = -\frac{(2\pi)^2}{\lambda^2} A \sin(2\pi x / \lambda).$$

The curvature of the function increases with the amplitude, A, of the sine function as observed previously. By dividing both sides of the equation by $y(t)$, this dependence is removed. This allows for a definition of wavelength λ as

$$\frac{1}{\lambda^2} = -\frac{1}{(2\pi)^2} \frac{1}{y} \frac{d^2 y}{dx^2}. \tag{13.243}$$

Having found a relationship that is independent of the amplitude, equation (13.243) can be raised to the level of a general formula by introducing the subscript g to denote the *generalized wavelength* λ_g at a point x

$$\frac{1}{\lambda_g^2} = -\frac{1}{(2\pi)^2} \frac{1}{y} \frac{d^2 y}{dx^2}. \tag{13.244}$$

For spatially periodic functions, $-(1/y)d^2y/dx^2$ is always positive so that the generalized wavelength is *always real*.

If equation (13.244) is a reliable definition for the wavelength of general functions then we can put it to a simple test. Consider the Bessel function $j_0(x)$ which appears in the Fourier transform of the ½-sine force function and also appears in the solution for the mode shape function $\psi(x)$ in Section 8.3. This function is plotted in Figure 13.91. The function is oscillatory and the period slowly shortens as x increases. The period will eventually become the constant 2π as $x \to \infty$ (large values of x).

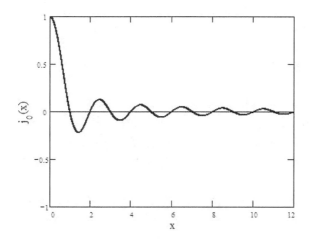

Fig. 13.91. Plot of the Bessel function $j_0(x)$.

With $y(x) = j_0(x)$, applying equation (13.244) gives

$$\frac{1}{\lambda_g^2} = \frac{1}{(2\pi)^2}\left[1 - \frac{1}{x}\frac{j_1(x)}{j_0(x)}\right],$$

$$\lambda_g = 2\pi\sqrt{2}, \qquad x \to 0$$
$$= 2\pi, \qquad x \to \infty$$

where $j_1(x)$ is the first order Bessel function of the first kind. Equation (13.244) yields for the generalized wavelength the values

$\lambda_g = 2.83\pi$ for $x \to 0$ and $\lambda_g = 2\pi$ for large values of x. These values can be compared with the values obtained from the zeros of $j_0(x)$ which occur at 2.405, 5.520, 8.654, 11.792, ... $(n-¼)\pi$ as $n \to \infty$. The generalized wavelength for low values of x is given approximately by $\lambda_g = 8.654 - 2.405 = 6.249$ or $\lambda_g = 11.792 - 5.520 = 6.249$, both of which are close to $2\pi = 6.284$. For large values of x, $\lambda_g = (n-¼ +2)\pi - (n-¼)\pi = 2\pi$ in exact agreement with equation (13.244). Equation (13.244) works well for the function $y(x) = j_0(x)$ in determining the generalized wavelength at a point x. Maybe the reader can find other periodic or quasi-periodic functions to try out equation (13.244).

13.30.3 Generalized Wavelength on the Note Surface

(i) A Simple Straightforward Approach

Unlike the one-dimensional functions $y(x) = A \sin(2\pi x/\lambda)$ and $y(x) = j_0(x)$, the mode shape ψ_m for transverse vibrations of a note is a three-dimensional surface formed dynamically on the ellipsoidal surface of the vibrating note. Because the dome shaped note is a shallow shell, points on the note surface can be mapped, by projection, unto points (r, ϕ) on the plane passing through the note boundary as illustrated in Figure 13.92. This projection reduces the dimension by one giving a two-dimensional representation $\psi_m(r, \phi)$ for the mode shape function for which there should be two generalized wavelengths. To define the generalized wavelengths using equation (13.244) the mode shapes are expressed as $\psi_m(\zeta, \xi)$ using two orthogonal coordinates ξ and ζ (equivalent to the familiar (x, y) ordered pair in Cartesian coordinate systems) where $\xi = r \sin\phi$ and $\zeta = r \cos\phi$ (see Figure 13.92). This allows the generalized wavelength in each of these coordinates to be written as

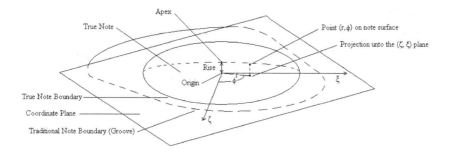

Fig.13.92. Note geometry with the Rise exaggerated for clarity.

$$\frac{1}{\lambda_{g,\xi}^2} = -\frac{1}{4\pi^2}\frac{1}{\psi_m}\frac{\partial^2 \psi_m}{\partial \xi^2},$$

$$\frac{1}{\lambda_{g,\zeta}^2} = -\frac{1}{4\pi^2}\frac{1}{\psi_m}\frac{\partial^2 \psi_m}{\partial \zeta^2}. \quad (13.245a, b)$$

For modes symmetrical with respect to the apex of the note (which corresponds on projection, to the origin of the ζ, ξ coordinates), one finds that $\lambda_{g,\zeta} = \lambda_{g,\xi}$. With reference to the mode shapes in Figure 13.67 the generalized wavelength of a particular mode is defined as twice the distance between adjacent anti-nodes (sweetspots) or twice the distance between consecutive nodal lines.

The reader must not confuse the generalized wavelength of a vibrational mode with the wavelength (in air) of the acoustical vibrations that propagate away from the note. The scale of the generalized wavelength on the note surface is in millimeters or centimeters while the scale of the acoustical waves heard by the listener is in meters.

(ii) **A More Formal Approach**

There is the well know operation that can be used on a time periodic function y(t) where the taking of the derivative of the function with respect to time $\frac{dy}{dt}$ is replaced by the operation $j\omega y$ where $\omega = 2\pi/T$ is the frequency and T is the period. For spatially periodic functions there is an equivalent operation. If ψ(x) is a spatially periodic function with spatial 'period' or wavelength λ where the wave number is $k = 2\pi/\lambda$, then the derivative $\frac{d\psi}{dx}$ can be replaced by the operation $jk\psi$. If this operation is performed twice (that is to take the second derivative) one gets

$$\frac{d^2\psi}{dx^2} = -k^2\psi,$$

which gives

$$\frac{1}{\lambda^2} = -\frac{1}{4\pi^2\psi}\frac{d^2\psi}{dx^2},$$

same as in equation (13.245).

(iii) Generalized Wavelength by Spatial Fourier Transform

Since the mode shape $\psi(\zeta, \xi)$ describes the spatial structure of the displacements over the note surface, one can determine the wavelengths of this structure using the spatial Fourier transform. We have

$$\Psi(\mathbf{k}) = \mathfrak{J}_x[\psi(\mathbf{x})](\mathbf{k})$$

where $\mathbf{x}$ is a generalized coordinate standing for the pair (ζ, ξ) and $\mathbf{k}$ is the wave number (Fourier transform variable). Since the structure is projected unto the plane (ζ, ξ) there are in general two wavelengths corresponding to $\lambda_{g,\zeta} = 2\pi/k_\zeta$ and $\lambda_{g,\xi} = 2\pi/k_\xi$ as before. However, we cannot reduce this expression for the spatial Fourier transform into an equation like (13.245) unless a function is specified for ψ. The power of this method lies in its ability to handle more complex spatial functions such as those that occur for the higher untuned modes on the note surface.

13.31 The Condition for Suppressing Unwanted High Frequency Modes

Contact-width wavelength band-limiting is the spatial complement to the temporal aspect of *contact-time frequency band-*

limiting. While frequency band-limiting applies to modal vibrational frequencies satisfying the condition $f \geq 1/2\tau_c$, contact-width wavelength band-limiting takes place when the generalized wavelength of a mode satisfies the condition

$$\varphi_c \geq \frac{\lambda_g}{2}, \qquad (13.246)$$

see the work in Achong (1996b) and Achong (2000a). To see this, it must be recalled that over one generalized wavelength, the mode shape function is *positive* over one ½-wavelength and *negative* over the other. It is therefore clear that if the contact-width φ_c spans an entire generalized wavelength for the mth mode, the integral $\int_{A_c} z(r,\phi)\psi_m(r,\phi)ds$ over the contact-area will then be minimized, possibly to zero. Since the Stick-Note Impact Function $S(m,r,\phi)$ given by equation (13.219) is proportional to this integral, the modal driving force for the mode in question, will be similarly minimized. This mode and all higher modes having generalized wavelengths shorter than φ_c will therefore be strongly attenuated and at normal levels of intensity their contributions to the tone of the sounding note will be reduced possibly to inaudible levels.

Since the most general expression for the contact width is given by

$$\varphi_c = R_s\sqrt{8w_0 x},$$

where x is obtained as the root of the Stick Compression Formula, one has

$$R_s\sqrt{8w_0 x} \geq \frac{\lambda_g}{2}, \qquad (13.247)$$

as the condition that allows wavelength band-limiting to be effective. **All modes satisfying equation (13.247) will be wavelength band-limited.** Using the expression for the generalized wavelength, one can write this in the equivalent form

$$\frac{R_s}{\pi}\sqrt{8w_0 x} \geq \left(-\frac{1}{\psi_m}\frac{\partial^2 \psi_m}{\partial \xi^2}\right)^{-\frac{1}{2}} \qquad (13.248)$$

Using equation (13.90a), equation (13.247) can be written to good approximation when $\sigma_{pre} = 0$ as

$$\lambda_g \leq 4(2^{\frac{1}{2}})R_s V_0^{\frac{1}{p_c+1}} \left(\frac{p_c+1}{2}\right)^{\frac{1}{2(p_c+1)}} \left(\frac{\pi \rho_s (1-v_s^2)}{E_s}\right)^{\frac{1}{2(p_c+1)}} e^{-\frac{\alpha \pi}{4 p_c \omega d}} \left(1 - \frac{\alpha^2}{p_c \omega^2}\right),$$

or for $r_{ms} = 0$, p = 1,

$$\lambda_g \leq 4(2^{\frac{1}{2}})R_s V_0^{\frac{1}{2}} \left(\frac{\pi \rho_s (1-v_s^2)}{E_s}\right)^{\frac{1}{4}}, \qquad (13.249a, b)$$

with λ_g and R_s in meters and V_0 in meters/second.

If $\lambda_{g,\xi}$ is the longer of the two generalized wavelengths given by equation (13.245) then this condition can be stated in terms of the mode shape function as

$$\left(-\frac{1}{\psi_m}\frac{\partial^2 \psi_m}{\partial \xi^2}\right)^{-\frac{1}{2}} \leq \frac{8^{\frac{1}{2}}}{\pi} R_s V_0^{\frac{1}{p_c+1}} \left(\frac{p_c+1}{2}\right)^{\frac{1}{2(p_c+1)}} \left(\frac{\pi \rho_s (1-v_s^2)}{E_s}\right)^{\frac{1}{2(p_c+1)}} e^{-\frac{\alpha \pi}{4 p_c \omega d}} \left(1 - \frac{\alpha^2}{p_c \omega^2}\right)$$

or for $r_{ms} = 0$, $p_c = 1$,

$$\left(-\frac{1}{\psi_m}\frac{\partial^2 \psi_m}{\partial \xi^2}\right)^{-\frac{1}{2}} \leq \frac{8^{\frac{1}{2}}}{\pi} R_s V_0^{\frac{1}{2}} \left(\frac{\pi \rho_s (1-v_s^2)}{E_s}\right)^{\frac{1}{4}}, \qquad (13.250a, b)$$

with position coordinates ζ and ξ in meters.

Some important observations must be made here:

- When a stick of tip radius R_s impacts the note with velocity V_0, all modes of vibration satisfying equation (13.250a) fall within the cut-off region and cannot be excited to levels suitable for musical purposes by stick-note impact. Using a stick tip of even larger radius extends the cut-off to longer generalized wavelengths and lower modes. Lower modes produce acoustical vibrations of lower frequency therefore

the attenuation may affect all modes above the first two or three modes giving the tone a more mellow sound.
- *For this reason the low-end pans are played with sticks having tips of large diameter in order to de-emphasize the higher modes and produce a low pitch sonorous tone. The player imparts a greater impact velocity V_0 in order to increase the intensity of the tone <u>but doing so also extends the cut-off downwards to lower modes.</u>*
- If the size of a note is increased for a given frequency, then the generalized wavelengths will also increase. Equation (13.250) shows that in order to limit the higher (untuned) modes in a manner similar to that achieved on the smaller note then (i) the stick size must be increased proportionately or (ii) a softer rubber (lower E_s) be used or (iii) a denser rubber (greater ρ_s) be used. Using a larger diameter stick is the best option.
- One can verify that changing these parameters in the manner indicated above also increases the contact-time which will provide increased frequency band-limiting. *There is therefore no conflict between these two band-limiting mechanisms—contact-time frequency band-limiting and contact-area wavelength band-limiting. However, as we shall see below, when losses are included there can arise some conflict when lossy tips or mats are used in an attempt to 'optimize' performance.*

13.32 The Spatial and Temporal Conditions for Initial Mode Excitation and Choice of Sticks

13.32.1 The Guiding Principles

The stick serves two purposes (1) to excite the required vibrational modes and (2) to suppress unwanted modes. The latter was dealt with in the previous section, now we seek the guiding principles by which the *desired* tones are *generated (as opposed to being suppressed)*.

Spatial Condition

The complement to equation (13.247) is **the condition for initially exciting the mth mode by stick impact**, it reads

$$\left(-\frac{1}{\psi_m}\frac{\partial^2 \psi_m}{\partial \zeta^2}\right)^{-\frac{1}{2}} > \frac{R_s}{\pi}\sqrt{8w_0 x}. \qquad (13.251)$$

Notice that in writing this condition *the shorter of the two generalized wavelengths is used*. In order to easily compare sticks used on different sized notes, we normalize the coordinates by defining $y = \zeta/\breve{a}$ which allows equation (13.251) to be written in the form

$$\left(-\frac{1}{\psi_m}\frac{\partial^2 \psi_m}{\partial y^2}\right)^{-\frac{1}{2}} > \frac{R_s}{\pi\,\breve{a}}\sqrt{8w_0 x}, \qquad (13.252)$$

where $\breve{a}$ is equal to the semi-major axis of the true note. This notation is used only in equation (13.252) in order to avoid confusion with the parameter 'a' which appears in the Stick Compression Formula below. The Stick Compression Formula and the expressions on which equation (13.252) rely are reproduced here for easy reference:

$$a x^2 + x^{\frac{1}{b}} + c x + g_c - 1 = 0,$$

$$a = \frac{\sigma_{pre} w_0^2}{\rho_s V_0^2}, \quad b = \frac{1}{p_c + 1}, \quad c = \frac{3 r_{ms} w_0}{8\rho_s R_s^2 V_0} - \frac{2 R_s w_0 g \cos\phi}{V_0^2} + \frac{3 F_H (1 - f_{cm}) w_0}{2\pi\,\rho_s R_s^2 V_0^2}, \quad g_c = \frac{3 E_{SA}^{\{comp\}}}{2\pi\,\rho_s R_s^3 V_0^2},$$

$$w_0 = \left(\frac{p_c + 1}{2}\right)^{\frac{1}{p_c+1}} \left(\frac{V_0}{\omega R_s}\right)^{\frac{2}{p_c+1}}, \quad \omega^2 = \frac{4 E_s R_s}{3(1 - v_s^2) m_s}.$$

One should pause for a moment to make a close inspection of equation (13.252). The condition to be satisfied for mode excitation given by (13.252), as simple as it appears, contains a large amount of important information.

- *Equation (13.252) states, in the most general way, the spatial condition that must be satisfied for the excitation, by stick-note impact, of the mth vibrational mode on a steelpan note.*
- *This condition takes into account all the note parameters through the modal function ψ_m, all the stick (rubber) parameters including tip radius R_s and pre-stress, and all the impact parameters such as the weight of the stick tip, shank absorption, impact velocity and hand action F_H.*
- ***This is the condition that governs the choice of sticks for all the different types of pans.***

To a good approximation, in the absence of hand action and pre-stress, one can also write

$$\left(-\frac{1}{\psi_m}\frac{\partial^2 \psi_m}{\partial y^2}\right)^{-\frac{1}{2}} > \frac{8^{\frac{1}{2}}}{\pi}\frac{R_s}{\tilde{a}}V_0^{\frac{1}{p_c+1}}\left(\frac{p_c+1}{2}\right)^{\frac{1}{2(p_c+1)}}\left(\frac{\pi \rho_s(1-v_s^2)}{E_s}\right)^{\frac{1}{2(p_c+1)}}e^{-\left(\frac{\alpha\pi}{4p_c\omega}\right)}\left(1-\frac{\alpha^2}{p_c\omega^2}\right)$$

(13.253)

Equation (13.253) without the hand action F_H, describes more closely the stick impacts found on the lower pans but also gives some reasonable qualitative results for the higher pans.

Equation (13.252) and Equation (13.253) state two of the most useful and informative results obtained here for the stick-note interaction and the influence of the player on the tonal quality of the sounding note. They explain, for example, why the notes of a tenor cannot be played with a bass stick. The following results follow directly from the condition (13.253):

- The left side of this inequality relates purely to the note dynamics while the right side relates to the choice of stick size, stick material properties and to the action of the player in imparting an impact velocity to the stick. This condition is therefore only partially set by the choice of stick because the panist can make variations to V_0 during play. The player can therefore vary the *timbre* of a note by varying the hand action to suppress or excite higher partials as desired.

- Because the generalized wavelengths for notes on the tenor are shorter than those found on the lower pans, stick tips with smaller radii are required on the high-end pans.
- Since the loss parameter α is proportional to the tip resistance r_{ms}, the last two factors on the far right of equation (13.253), $e^{-\left(\frac{\alpha\pi}{4 p_c \omega}\right)} \left(1 - \alpha^2 / p_c \omega^2\right)$ show that by increasing the tip loss, the contact-width is reduced. *This makes it easier to satisfy the condition given by equation (13.253) which is the spatial condition for mode excitation. This allows <u>higher</u> modes to be excited*! The underlying reason for this is that during impact, part of the impact energy is lost as heat due to the mechanical resistance; this loss represents energy that would have otherwise been used to further compress the tip. However, as we saw earlier, tip loss increases the contact-time because it slows down the impact; this longer contact-time *suppresses* the higher modes.

- **These two conflicting effects that accompany stick losses tell us that stick losses <u>cannot</u> be used to optimize stick performance. This lesson should be applied to the use of lossy material such as lossy overlays or 'covers' (as suggested for the G-Pan, see Chapter 17).**

From equation (13.252) one finds:

- Most importantly, through hand action, the player can reduce the right side of the inequality by applying a greater retrieving force F_H which increases the coefficient c; doing this will allow modes of shorter wavelengths (higher frequencies) to be *initially* excited. When it is necessary to suppress the higher modes, F_H is reduced allowing for a greater contact area. **This is precisely the action taken by the player.**
- The conditions are not fixed by note and stick parameters there are subtle controls left to the panist such as the magnitude of the force F_H, the impact velocity V_0 and the

time of commencement of stick retrieval during the impact (determined by the fraction f_{cm}).
- Higher modes can be initially excited by increasing the pre-stress (which increases the coefficient a) by wrapping the tip with greater tension.
- Observe that the tip weight term $-2R_s w_0 g \cos\phi / V_0^2$ in the parameter c has the effect of increasing x and thereby reducing the modal frequencies that can be initially excited. On the high-end pans the player normally compensates for the weight by applying a slightly greater F_H. However, the effect of the stick weight is desirable on the low-end pans where the almost 'free fall' stick action applied by the panist allows the weight of the stick to reduce the level of the high frequencies. A close study of the action of the bass panist shows that the stick weight is in fact incorporated in the player's stick action.
- Losses introduced through r_{ms} and g_c generally reduce the contact width but because of the accompanying decrease in contact force, tip losses should be reduced as much as practicably possible.

The experienced player executes note impacts according to a set of rules, to wit, those practical rules consistent with equation (13.252).

Temporal Condition

The frequency condition to be satisfied for initial excitation is $f < 1/2\tau_c$. In terms of the period of vibration $T_m = 1/f_m$, the temporal complement to equation (13.252) giving the condition for initial excitation of the mth mode can be expressed as

(a) *General case:* $T_m > 2\tau_c$

$$f_m < 1/2\tau_c, \text{ or as } f_m < f_c. \tag{13.254}$$

In the general case with hand action, the contact-time and hence the upper limit on f_m must be determined by numerical solution of equation (13.164).

(b) Special case $F_H = 0$: Applicable on the low-end pans.

Using equation (13.190) for a tip in which the shank and mechanical resistance losses are negligible, gives

$$f_m < \frac{1}{2} \left\{ \left[\left(\frac{p_c+1}{2} \right) \frac{\pi \rho_s (1-v_s^2)}{E_s} \right]^{\frac{1}{p_c+1}} \frac{R_s S_{2,p_c}}{2V_0^{\frac{p_c-1}{p_c+1}}} + \left(\frac{p_r+1}{p_c+1} \right)^{\frac{1}{2}} \left[\left(\frac{p_c+1}{2} \right) \frac{\pi \rho_s (1-v_s^2)}{E_s} \right]^{\frac{2+p_c-p_r}{2(p_c+1)}} \frac{R_s S_{2,p_r}}{2V_0^{\frac{p_r-1}{p_c+1}}} \right.$$

$$- \frac{\sigma_{pre}}{4\rho_s} \left[\left(\frac{p_c+1}{2} \right) \frac{\pi \rho_s (1-v_s^2)}{E_s} \right]^{\frac{3}{p_c+1}} \frac{R_s S_{4,p_c}}{V_0^{\frac{3(p_c-1)}{p_c+1}}}$$

$$\left. - \frac{\sigma_{pre}}{4\rho_s} \left(\frac{p_c+1}{2} \right)^{\frac{5-p_r}{2(p_c+1)}} \left(\frac{p_r+1}{2} \right)^{\frac{1}{2}} \left(\frac{\pi \rho_s (1-v_s^2)}{E_s} \right)^{\frac{6+p_c-p_r}{2(p_c+1)}} \frac{R_s S_{4,p_r}}{V_0^{\frac{2p_c+p_r-3}{p_c+1}}} \right\}^{-1}$$

(13.255)

By considering only those impacts without the application of a retrieval force ($F_H = 0$), the upper limit on f_m given by (13.255) are lower than the values obtained in practice, particularly on the high-end pans. As the analyses with hand action have shown, contact times are reduced with the application of hand action retrieval force. This, in turn, *increases* the upper limit on f_m. We have already demonstrated by numerical examples in Section 13.14.2 how the player can increase the upper limit on f_m thereby allowing higher frequency modes to be better excited. By doing this the tone takes on greater *brilliance*.

(c) Special case, $p_c = p_r = 1$, $F_H = 0$

$$f_m < \frac{3}{4\pi^{\frac{3}{2}} R_s} \left(\frac{E_s}{(1-v_s^2)\rho_s} \right)^{\frac{1}{2}}.$$

As obtained for the spatial condition, the left side of these inequalities relates purely to the note dynamics. In principle it is possible to express f_m or T_m in terms of the mode shape function ψ_m but this can only be done in closed-form for special cases. On a tuned pan, f_m are the frequencies on the musical scale so we know their values. What we may not know are the frequencies of the untuned modes so it is very important for the tuner to reduce the intensities of these modes. Observe that the RHS of the condition in (13.255) depends on the tip radius, the pre-stress and on the material and elastic properties of the stick tip. For $F_H = 0$, once a stick is chosen the temporal condition is set. However, this only arises because the panist has chosen that style of play which allows the stick to impact the note and rebound without hand control. The panist regains control by deliberate application of hand action and impact velocity to vary the contact-time. This is the *General case* (a), the style of play associated with good pan playing.

Most of the effects of soft and hard sticks, large and small sticks are well known to the pan maker and panist: the conditions obtained here for initial mode excitation confirm all these effects but in addition give the physical explanation for them. These spatial and temporal conditions for initial mode excitation tell us that:

(i) The softer the stick tip (lower E_s and σ_{pre}) the less likely it is for a higher mode (higher partial) to be initially excited. Therefore tones produced with soft sticks are generally weaker in the higher partials and in untuned higher modes.

(ii) Increasing the wrapping tension T_0 (which increases the pre-stress), increases f_c allowing higher partials to be initially excited as well as the unwanted higher untuned modes.

- Small diameter sticks (small R_s) increases f_c allowing these sticks to produce tones richer in higher partials.
- Large diameter (large R_s) sticks produce tones weaker in the higher partials. This effect is very noticeable because both spatial and temporal band limiting depends linearly on the radius R_s.

- Sticks with lower density rubber (lower ρ_s) with their larger f_c, are seen from these two conditions to allow for the generation of higher frequency modes. However, this choice lowers the mass of the stick, which may not allow the panist to impart sufficient energy into the stick impact so lowering the overall sound intensity. One can easily demonstrate this by using a low-density foam ball as the stick tip.
- Striking the note harder by increasing the impact velocity V_0 is not always an effective way of increasing the intensity of the higher partials. The spatial condition in this case becomes more restrictive. However, the plus side to this velocity dependence is that it gives the panist the means of adjusting the impact to get some control on the partials. *It is in fact here that the good panist can excel. The author thinks this is what is known in pan circles as a 'good touch'. It is more than simply having a good pair of sticks.*

The reader must use the spatial and temporal conditions cautiously. They apply only to the *initial excitation* of the modes. As discussed in Chapters 3 – 6, energy exchanges through parametric resonances driven mainly by the initial excitation of the fundamental mode (the key-note) is the principal modality for the excitation of higher modes (partials) on the steelpan. This means that the pan maker/tuner is chiefly responsible for the tonal qualities of the note. *For each second of tone generated by the panist with a stick impact lasting a fraction of a millisecond, the pan maker/tuner must spend one hour in making hammer impacts.*

The formulas for mode excitation by stick impacts are obtained as conditional statements (inequalities). Because of this, there is much leeway in the choice of sticks in order to achieve a particular tonal response. For while two notes are never identical but with some effort can be made to produce almost similar tones, much less effort is required in producing two sticks that will allow almost identical excitation. Simply put, the inequalities in equation (13.252) and equation (13.254), make stick making a much simpler exercise than pan making. *It also means that the bounds on the choice of sticks are less restrictive than the bounds on the choice of pans for the production of good musical tones. This explains why the subtleties of stick choice especially between good sticks are largely a matter of personal taste.*

The spatial and temporal conditions act simultaneously in restricting the initial excitation of a mode during impact. *Both conditions must be satisfied for a mode to be initially excited to levels adequate for musical purposes.* If one or both are not satisfied the result is significant attenuation in the initial excitation of the particular mode. When the notes are played with the normal rubber tipped sticks the untuned high frequency vibrations that accompany the tones generated when the notes are struck by a sharp hard object are almost entirely eliminated by the mechanisms of contact-time frequency band-limiting and contact-width wavelength band-limiting.

When equations (13.252) and (13.254) are combined with the results for the COR of the tip (cf. Table 13.9), one has the statements of the guiding principles for the selection and construction of sticks suitable for use on the steelpan.

13.32.2 Use of Other Objects for Note Impacts

For a typical tenor pan with $\tau_c = 0.2$ ms, frequency band-limiting begins at 2.5 kHz. To raise this to 20 kHz (the audible upper limit) requires a contact-time of 0.2 (2.5/20) ms = 0.025 ms which is one-eight (1/8) times smaller. Such small contact-times can only be achieved with a hard impactor. This can be achieved by using a tip material such as hard rubber with a Young's modulus sixty-four (64) times larger than the average E_s value for pan sticks. Equation (13.252) also applies for other hard objects such as the bare shank of the stick. For example, if the shank is made of aluminum for which $E = 7.1 \times 10^{10}$ N·m^{-2} then by striking the note with the shank instead of the rubber tip, the RHS of equation (13.252) is decreased by the factor 1/300. This guarantees the excitation of all the high frequency audible modes of vibration on a note played with the shank or an equivalent hardwood or metallic impactor. The tones generated with hard objects having small size or radius will therefore be characterized by their high frequency content and the metallic ringing sounds they generate. *One must be especially careful when using sticks that generate these high metallic tones. In solo performance the problem does not arise but in orchestral use, these* high untuned modes generate noise that are particularly annoying (see Chapter 16).

13.32.3 The Very Lossy, Dead Stick

Very lossy sticks generally show a larger change in p-index from compression to restitution. As the rubber ages or deteriorates, old, used sticks tend towards this state and become softer in the process. Contact-times and contact-widths may increase well beyond the values typical for normal sticks in the particular pan category and, the maximum contact force is reduced. This results in greater attenuation of the higher partials by frequency and wavelength band-limiting and the presentation of a low intensity (soft) almost monotone sound (fundamental only).

13.33 Why is Band-Limiting Essential on the Steelpan?

The steelpan as fine a musical instrument as it is at the time of writing still must undergo improvements and modifications to ensure that it delivers the tones required for the changing musical tastes of players and listeners. The performance of these impact-driven (percussion) instruments is straightforwardly affected by the presence of undesirable vibrations in their transient responses, due to the inherent excitation of several normal and parametric modes. Even on a fully and properly tuned steelpan, the majority of the normal modes are left untuned. In practice, these instruments are assembled into steel orchestras, which as a direct result, influence even more the generation of undesired tones in a rather complex and unpredictable manner (see Chapter 16).

The traditional approaches to minimizing the effects of undesired modal vibrations focus on either the positioning of the notes of the system, in order to obtain acceptable dynamic characteristics, or using soft padded sticks. For example the Pang made by Felix Röhner of Switzerland is played with padded felt-tipped sticks similar to those used on the pans found in Trinidad and Tobago around the 1950's. Each one of the methods for controlling the levels of undesired vibrations is subjected to a number of disadvantages and drawbacks. Positioning notes on the pan face or over two or more pan faces on multiple-pan instruments is limited.

Notes are not considered closely related to each other if they are near each other in the chromatic scale. This is the basis of the *Circle of Fifths*. The arrangement of notes on the tenor for example follows the Circle of Fifths (in reverse order) in order to reduce the coupling between neighboring notes. However, it drops the need for decoupling the notes by placing the octaves adjacently on the inner notes in order to provide some degree of sympathetic vibration. Therefore, the solution to the problem of unwanted vibration is not a simple one.

13.34 Playing the Roll — The Tremolando

Keywords: Impact velocity: determines impact force and loudness as the roll progresses.
Rapidity: rate of impacts, gives accents and pulse to the roll.

An important and useful playing action on this percussion instrument is the *roll* or *tremolando* ($\tilde{\sharp}$), where the player using two sticks, one in each hand, alternates impact between two areas on *the same note* in a rapid action. Similar to the roll played in this way is the rapid alternation of the impacts *between two notes* ($\sqcap$). By varying the impact points, the fundamental, the upper octave or the twelfth on a note can be emphasized. So that during the roll, the accomplished player can move the impact points around the note surface to obtain very subtle variations in tonality or timbre. In addition the impact velocity can be gradually increased in a crescendo or reduced in a diminuendo. The impact velocity can be controlled independently of the rapidity.

To account for the two impact points and any changes made to their positions, coordinates for two such impact points labeled i and j are shown in Figure 13.93. It is also possible for the contact areas to be different as a result of dissimilarity in stick tip geometry, material properties, the subtle effects of using different hands (left and right) or changes in impact velocities as indicated by the radii c_i and c_j.

Because of the changes made by the panist to each impact during the roll, a strictly analytical solution of equation (13.240) is clearly not possible in the case of the roll. However, the roll, with all its variations, can easily be handled in a numerical solution since the impacts can be introduced at any time $n\delta\tau$, at any location specified by the impact coordinates, along with the appropriate changes to the impact parameters made on the RHS of equation (13.240). All roll actions can be followed and computed in the numerical solution. Equation (13.240) therefore completely describes the roll which is perhaps the most complex playing action on the steelpan.

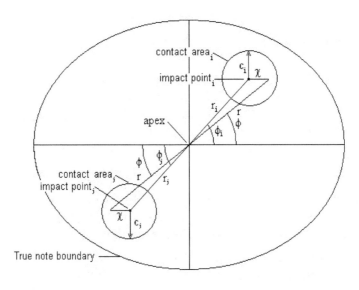

Fig. 13.93. Two impact points on the tenor note that may be used in executing the roll.

Assuming the availability on computer of a numerical solver for ordinary differential equations, the solution procedure for the roll runs as follows:

(i) Choose a pair of sticks through the parameter set (E_s, v_s, R_s, ρ_s, r_s, p_r, p_c). These parameters determine the elastic and material properties of the tip and its size. For wrapped stick tips select a value for the pre-stress σ_{pre} to simulate the setting of the wrapping tension. Follow the lead of the professional player with a choice of identical sticks — 'voiced sticks.'

(ii) Choose the pan by the values in the parameter set (E_n, v_n, ρ_n, h). If the thickness h varies from note to note then the choice of h can be done in (iii).

(iii) Specify the note or notes to play by the values in the set (a, b, h) and for each mode (usually two or three) on each note, select the values in the set (ω_m, μ_m, $\alpha_{ij,m}$, $\beta_{ijk,m}$). Setting the modal frequencies ω_m automatically sets the detuning parameters

(iv) Insert at the required times and locations on the note the series of impacts with the desired contact-times and the impact velocities V_0 to achieve the desired intensity variations (crescendo, diminuendo or whatever).

(v) Choose a small time-step $\delta\tau$ for the numerical integration. Begin the solution of the *Impact Phase* equations (one for each mode) with the first impact. Since the modal equations on a given note are dependent, they must be solved simultaneously. After a number of time-steps $3\gamma\tau_c/2\delta\tau$ has elapsed in the computation, the impact phase is complete. Pass all parameters and w_m (amplitudes and phases) over to the *Free Phase* equations (13.241) and continue the solutions until the arrival of the next impact. On the next impact, return to the *Impact Phase* equations passing once more the updated w_m (amplitudes and phases)* while specifying all the required impact parameters. Continue alternating between the *Impact Phase* equations and the *Free Phase* equations until the roll is complete. The roll *must* end on the *Free Phase equations* (13.240).

(vi) The solutions corresponding to the modal displacements of the vibrating note surface are the set of discrete time series consisting of the amplitudes and phases for $w_m(n)$, $n = 0$, 1, 2, ...N.

(vii) Since the computations are all done in normalized time τ, conversion to real time t is accomplished with the transformation $\delta\tau = \gamma\delta t$.

(viii) In these computations the static force (mechanical bias) f_0 is only needed if the pan operates at a temperature different to the temperature at which it was tuned. In which case the modal frequencies ω_n must be adjusted for the expected frequency shifts and the coupling parameters ($\alpha_{ij,m}$, $\beta_{ijk,m}$) adjusted for changes in the note shape. This may seem complicated but the pan does all this for itself when the temperature changes away from the Tuning Temperature T_t.

* While these computations yield only the displacement amplitudes and not the phases directly, it is important to maintain the order in the amplitude sequence generated for each mode as the computations alternate between the Impact Phase and Free Phase otherwise the relative phases of the of the vibrating modes will be affected.

13.35 Strumming

Strumming is the action of repeatedly playing the same notes or chord in a rhythmic (*ritmico*) manner as done on the string guitar or similar instrument. It is from this mode of play that the guitar pan acquired its name. The solution procedure on a numerical solver is similar to that for the roll except for the use of one or possibly two notes and the differences in the application of the impacts. When two notes are strummed, the numerical solutions must be carried out simultaneously for each note but the two sets of equations must run independently.

13.36 Playing Notes with Sympathetic Interaction

The sympathetic pairs $\{\mathbf{B}_4;\mathbf{B}_5\}$, $\{\mathbf{F}_4^{\#}, \mathbf{F}_5^{\#}\}$, $\{\mathbf{G}_4^{\#};\mathbf{G}_5^{\#}\}$ and other similar pairs found on the tenor, double second and in fewer numbers on lower pans are very interesting dynamically and musically. In this book, Chapter 5 is dedicated to this aspect of note-note interaction while Chapter 14 deals with the tuning aspects. It is worth noting here that there is no special method to be used for impacts on sympathetic pairs. We choose the $\{\mathbf{B}_4;\mathbf{B}_5\}$ pair for our discussion but the same holds for the other pairs. We consider two cases:

Case (i) *Weak or non-existent Resident Octave on the B_4 Note.*

Generally, to be useful, such pairs are tuned with *strong internote coupling*. There is no reciprocity in sympathetic vibrations here because the interactions among the modes are non-linear. This means that striking the B_4 note causes the sympathetic excitation of the coupled B_5 note even though the resident octave on the B_4 note is absent (or weak because of detuning). Striking the B_5 note does not sympathetically excite the B_4 note — this is what the absence of reciprocity means. Some players may claim that it does, to a small extent. But what they are hearing is not sympathetic vibration. Instead it is a direct result of linear, non-sympathetic, transfer of energy from the impact point on the B_5 note to the B_4 note via the coupling path made open by the tuner to allow coupling of the two notes. In fact the sympathetic excitation of the B_5 when the B_4 is played, results in a tonal frequency slightly different from the frequency of the B_5 note when it is excited by direct impact. In numerical simulation, the equations for these two coupled notes together with all their associated partials must be solved simultaneously.

Case (ii) *Strong or Moderately Strong Resident Octave on the B_4 Note.*

Generally, such pairs are *not* tuned with strong internote coupling. The individual notes are properly blocked. In this case striking the B_4 note excites the resident octave and weakly excites the nearby B_5 note non-linearly. The nearby B_5 is excited sympathetically. Striking the B_5 note will sympathetically and linearly excite the resident octave on the B_4 note. The B_4 key-note is not excited. If internote coupling is strong (an inadvisable suggestion) then strong interactions, linear and non-linear will exist between the two notes forming the pair. Strong coupling of two modes of equal frequency on closely spaced notes is unwise because of the energy it robs from the lower key-note (B_4 in our example) whenever that lower key-note is the desired tone. It is also difficult to re-tune (or reproduce) such pairs consistently. In numerical solutions, the equations for the coupled pair and their partials must be solved simultaneously. By varying the coupling, between members of the pair the effect of blocking on tonality can be investigated.

13.37 A Standard Measure for Tip Compression (TC)

13.37.1 The Classification of Sticks

At the time of writing, stick manufacturers have failed to come up with a system that will give us some real information about their sticks, or the means for comparing sticks produced by different manufacturers. The division of sticks into the general classes; Bass Sticks, Cello Sticks and Tenor Sticks are well known but there is no subdivision within the classes by a well defined methodology. This section brings some remedy to this situation in an easily understood manner for both manufacturers and users. The method is directly related to the mechanism by which steelpan tones are generated by stick-note impacts making it highly reliable and well interpreted.

13.37.2 Matching a Pair of Sticks

Also lacking, is a clearly defined system for pairing sticks within a class. Color and other cosmetic qualities are also used in pairing but these are not really effective. Of course the reason for this is the absence of proper classification. Stick makers try to match their sticks into equal pairs by weight, length, shank material, tip material, wrapped or unwrapped, and tip size. The method for stick classification introduced here, adds to this list by including an aspect related to stick-note impact dynamics. In selecting a pair of sticks one must ensure that the members of the pair not only look alike but also play alike. In my early investigation of pan sticks I felt the need for assigning a number to these sticks that gave some measure of the softness of the tips. I soon came up with the procedure that follows.

13.37.3 The Measure

Throughout these analyses of stick impact the compression is seen to play a principal role in determining the contact-area, contact-time and contact force. For this reason, it is appropriate here to introduce a standard measure for the compression. This must be done in a manner that is applicable to all sticks. To allow the measure to apply to the small tenor sticks and to be applicable to the much larger bass sticks a reference load of 1 kg is chosen. While larger loads will allow easier measurements of the loaded tip, the shank of the tenor sticks will impede compression (the proximity effect).

Definition: *The Tip Compression (TC) is defined as the fractional deformation of the stick tip under a static load of 1kg, multiplied by 1000. The deformation is the total displacement along a vertical diameter (the principal axis) produced by a 1 kg load applied to the top surface of the tip resting on a smooth hard surface (see Figure 13.93 for details). The fractional deformation is the ratio of the deformation of the loaded tip to the diameter of the free tip measured along the principal axis. Accordingly, for a fractional deformation of 0.08 under a load of 1kg, the Tip Compression value is TC = 80. Since tip properties vary with temperature, a reference temperature of 23 °C is recommended.*

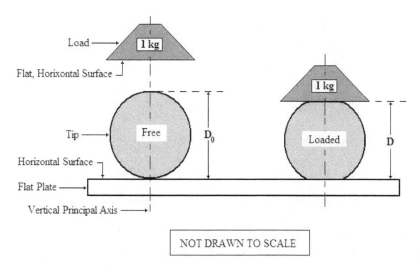

Fig. 13.94. Measurement Setup for TC.

In the test setup (see Figure 13.94), the tip must be placed between two horizontal flat surfaces of sufficient area to allow for unobstructed compression and the formation of the top and bottom contact areas. If D_0 is the diameter of the free tip and D is the diameter under a load of 1 kg, the TC value can be evaluated using the following expression

$$deformation = D_0 - D$$

$$TC = \frac{deformation}{D_0} \, 1000$$

$$TC = \left(1 - \frac{D}{D_0}\right) 1000.$$

Homemade sticks show large variability in compression values while commercial stick manufacturers offer no reliable scientific data on the properties of their sticks. The following typical values were obtained for an assortment of homemade and commercial sticks:

TC = 81 (soft bass stick, illustrated in Figure 13.5(c)),
TC = 47 (hard bass stick),
TC = 45 (cello),
TC = 48 (double second),
TC = 40 (tenor, single layer),
TC = 80 (soft tenor stick, multi layer).

Softer tips show larger TC values.

13.37.4 Application of TC Values

In orchestral applications it may be necessary to standardize the sticks for each section or voice. In the string section of an orchestra, the individual violinist can adjust the bow tension and rosin. Wrapped pan sticks can be similarly adjusted by re-wrapping and adjusting the wrapping tension. TC values can therefore be used to standardize the sticks used in sections of the steel orchestra.

CHAPTER 14

INSIDE PAN TUNING — FREQUENCY RANGE, METHODS OF TUNING, PRINCIPLES OF STEELPAN OPERATION, Tuning Scenarios and the Tonal Structure of Steelpan Notes

14.1 Introduction

Inside Pan Tuning takes a look at the tuning processes of the steelpan from 'inside' the instrument. Readers who have acquired a good understanding of the pan by reading the previous Chapters should all be capable of seeing the instrument from this perspective — it gives the best view possible of the tuning process. As you read this Chapter if there are areas of the pan dynamics and operation that you don't feel too comfortable with I recommend that you review those Sections dealing with those topics. Make good use of the Index and Contents and the Cross References contained in the Chapters. It would help greatly to your understanding if you were to have your personal steelpan close to you as you read. In this way you can go to the instrument and with the aid of the 'outside view' that it provides, get a complementary picture of the instrument as it goes through the processes described from the 'inside,' in this Chapter. The 'Inside View' requires the definitions and proofs of a number of Laws and Rules that apply specifically to the instrument. All these Laws and Rules are established in this Chapter but they all rest on the theory and dynamics discussed in the previous Chapters.

The principles and methods of tuning the steelpan are presented here with the following prefatory remarks;

(1) The principles and methods apply *specifically* to the steelpan.
(2) They *do not* provide a general coverage applicable to *all musical instruments* nor do they contain a 'blow by blow' commentary of the hammer peening process involved in tuning the pan. For the latter, which is an acquired skill, readers should consult the pan makers and tuners who with their knowledgeable peening actions are best suited to the task. In any case, with what force and where to strike the note surface varies with each note and with each round of tuning — there is no set pattern that fits all notes at all times. Exactly where to strike or peen a note on its surface cannot be generalized because of the complex nature of the tuning process brought about by the many tuning parameters. It is for similar reasons that this work does not contain a guide to the playing of the pan, a musical talent, for which the many skilled panists are much better suited.
(3) **Unison Tuning** is the method of choice for tuning the steelpan rather than the *discrimination of beats* which is the *classical method.* The *Unison Method* is dependent upon **pitch-matching** of the key-notes to the musical scale and **tonal judgments** made aurally by the tuner on the *total sound* of the partials. The classical method will be found unreliable on the steelpan because of the natural modulations (both AM and FM) present in pan tones.

The reader will therefore find that the tuning methods given here differ from those used in the tuning of other musical instruments. These differences arise because of the peculiar properties of the steelpan and the principles of its operation. Therefore, in order to maintain that perspective in an otherwise very wide field we must first define the Pan. This will be followed by the definitions of three standard systems of tuning. After all this we go fully 'inside the Pan.'

14.2 Definitions I

1) **The Steelpan or Pan**

    The **Steelpan** or **Pan** is a plexus of tuned shells called by the traditional name '*notes*' formed on the surface of a larger indented steel shell called the ***pan face***. This definition was used in the paper, Achong 2000b, but in this Chapter the use of the word 'plexus' will be fully clarified. A plexus is, by definition, 'a *structure in the form of a network*.' Generally, the instrument is not seen in this way and players of this musical instrument, for the most part are only aware of the '*traditional notes*.' What is hidden from direct view is the *interconnection* of these notes (to be more precise, the t*rue notes*) through the *internote*. By the phenomenon of ***non-linear mode localization*** (see Chapters 4, 5 and 6) the tuned modes of a sounding note are mutually coupled thereby confining the total vibrational energy to a well defined *spatial domain* called the ***true note*** *(see my introductory remarks in the Preface to this book)*. In my writings, the *true note* is referred to as the *note* while the larger area usually bordered by grooves, carry the designation, ***traditional note***. The domain referred to as the ***internote*** consists of all areas on the pan face exclusive of the true notes. ***Energy confinement*** within the true notes — the underlying principle of operation of the steelpan — makes it possible for a number of tuned notes to be placed on the same pan face. The 'network' or 'plexus' picture is seen when one considers the fact that perfect '*blocking*' of these true notes is not practically possible. This results in vibrational energy transfers within the network of notes via the internote. Owing to the great effort of the tuner and pan maker to minimize these energy transfers, except for the much needed Marshall Pairs, players only hear the sound of the notes.

2) **Categorization:**

   (a) Under the general category of **Pitched Percussion Instruments**, the **Steelpan** or **Pan** finds a position under the sub-category of **Idiophones**, and as a sub-class, **Vibration of Shells**.

   (b) The musical instrument called a **Pan** is dynamically different from a Drum which is an *Unpitched Percussion Instrument* falling under the sub-category of *Membranophones.*. The Pan operates mainly on the principle of excitation of a number of non-linearly coupled modes of vibration of thin shallow shells formed on a metal surface. This definition applies to the traditional multi-note instruments as well as the single-note versions, sometimes referred to as **Dew Drops**, formed on individually tuned single-note pans built from tin cans. So its name is not a matter of convenience or random choice but is based on well defined operational principles. Although these aspects were not known by the early innovators who gave Pan its name they were correct in choosing a name that shows its novelty and uniqueness.

   It is a pity that so many people around the world are misled by the incorrect name — the *Steel Drum* — into the belief that the instrument is a drum, which would place it in the wrong sub-category of Membranophone. This term 'steel drum', used mainly in the United States, applies only to the source of the material used in the construction of the instrument in the same manner as 'trees' or 'wood' is the material source for the Violin. The Violin is not a 'tree' and the Steelpan is not a 'steel drum.' The author states categorically, **the steelpan is not a drum**. It is true that in the 'Rum and Coca-Cola' days of the late 1940s, 50s and early 60s, American tourists to Trinidad and Tobago saw what did appear to be steel drums being played by the Islanders. But lack of understanding or appearance is not a good reason or basis for naming a thing. This 'other name' is not used in Trinidad and Tobago, the instrument's country of origin where there is no confusion on the identity of the steelpan (see however, Chapter 17 where there is an attempt to lead us backward with the more confusing, oxymoronic name, the 'steelpan drum!').

Despite all this, there are patents and websites in particular, where, based on supposed visual similarities to the drum, one finds arguments on whether the pan is something of a unique hybrid of membranophone and idiophone — *quite a contradiction of terms.* The drum membranophone consists of a 2-D membrane (*linear* in operation) stretched under tension while the pan idiophone consists of 3-D shallow metal shells (*non-linear* in operation) under compression.

3) **Steelpan Types**

The musical instruments called *Steelpans* are members or *species* of a family of instruments of the same *genus* that differ mainly in their musical ranges. The *types* or *species* of the *genus* Pan are:

- **Tenor**: *High Tenor, Low Tenor, Double Tenor*
- **Double Second.**
- **Quadraphonic.**
- **Guitar**: *Double Guitar, Triple Guitar*
- **Cello**: *Four Cello, Triple Cello*
- **Bass**: *Tenor (High) Bass, Six Bass, Nine Bass, 12-Bass (rare).*

There are other less popular types and other names given to the early versions of the instrument as for example: the ***Ping Pong,*** a forerunner of today's Tenor and the ***Doo Doop****,* a bass pan with two or three notes, played with a single stick to augment the rhythm section of a steelband. One also finds the '***Dew Drops***' a generic name for a collection of single-note pans tuned in the 'tenor' range, originally made from 1-quart motor oil tins or similar steel containers. All these instruments fall under the genus, Pan.

4) **Uniqueness in Operation and Structure**
   The pan is unique among melodic musical instruments. The pan, essentially a system of shallow shells, all arranged on a larger shell or pan face, derives this uniqueness from the following properties which also defines the instrument:

   (a) The **notes** (*the true notes, not the traditional notes*) form a system of non-linear *mode-localized oscillators*. This non-linear mode of operation is dynamic in nature, results from the shell structure, and is responsible for all the musical and exotic properties of the instrument.
   (b) The tuned vibrational modes on the note are *mutually coupled*. This non-linear coupling is responsible for mode-localization and the *confinement* of vibrational energy within the area defined as the **true note**.
   (c) The *true note* is contained within an area called the '*traditional note*' usually bordered by grooves.
   (d) All areas of the pan face *exclusive* of the *true notes*, under normal levels of excitation, consist of a linear system of connected domains defined as the **internote**.
   (e) The notes can be arranged by *tuning* and *blocking* to operate independently of each other or as **sympathetic (Marshall) pairs**.

5) *By function and definition,* **the steelpan is a single, fully assembled unit**. *Because of the de-localization of the stress distribution over the instrument (see Section 8.18),* **as a rule, the steelpan, as a tuned instrument, cannot be dismantled — detachable parts are not allowed (not by authoritative decree or fiat but by virtue of the instrument's mode of operation).** The idea of using removable parts may seem attractive but it is fraught with dangers. See Section 8.18.2 for this important property.

   Because of its importance I include the following *caution* to the readers and pan makers:

   - Stress de-localization on the instrument occurs because it is practically impossible to completely block the notes on the pan so that stress changes produced at source points anywhere on the pan can potentially alter the stress distribution on the notes. ***When it comes to improving the stability of the steelpan and preserving the tuned state of a 'Competition Grade' steelpan, the only good detachable part is an eliminated one!*** An example of an 'eliminated part' is the lower portion of the skirt which is cut off from the original drum (rawform) in the construction of mid and high end pans. The portion of skirt that remains provides all the hoop stress necessary to ensure good mechanical stability of the instrument.

6) A Non-transposing Musical Instrument

(a) The steelpan is a ***non-transposing*** musical instrument from which it follows that *panists* and *musical conductors*, when talking to different sections of a *steel orchestra*, can easily refer to a particular pitch in an unambiguous manner. The steelpan shares this property with the piano.

(b) A *transposing instrument i*s a musical instrument for which *written notes* are *read* at a pitch different from concert pitch. Instruments that transpose at the octave are not playing in a different key from concert pitch instruments, but sound an octave *higher* or *lower* than <u>written</u>. Generally speaking, *transposing* means moving a melody from one key, or tonality, to another. Examples of transposing instruments are the clarinet, trumpet, horn, trombone, and saxophone, among others. While steelpans are members or *species* of a family of instruments of the same *genus* that differ mainly in their musical ranges, they don't all have the same note arrangement on the pan face. The pan family can be likened to a fractured piano keyboard where each pan member is represented by one of the fractured parts with overlap. A player adjusts his ***stick action*** to suit each instrument in the family. As a result it is not necessary to transpose these instruments on the basis of their ranges.

7) **Resident Octave and Resident Twelfth**
   Because tuners may use the tuning option provided by sympathetic vibration, when discussing the *Marshall Pairs*, two *octaves* appear; one found on the physical note containing the *key-note* and the other found on the other (higher) member of the pair. Reference to these two octaves can sometimes be confusing. To avoid this problem, I shall adopt the following terminology: using the example of the {G_4: G_5} pair, the *key-note* is contained on the physical note labeled G_4. On this same physical note is found an octave which will be called the '*Resident Octave*' — it *resides* on the same physical note as the key-note. The other member of the pair, a physically separate note, the G_5, is an octave of the key-note G_4. The simple title of '*Octave*' will be used for this (G_5) note. In the standard tuning arrangement there also exists a *Twelfth* on each note. To avoid confusion, the term '**Resident Twelfth**' may also be used.

8) The **Adopted Musical Scale**
   The *de facto* Standard System of tuning for the *key-notes* on the pan is the ***Western 12-Tone Equal Temperament (12-TET) system***.

9) The **Tuned State of a note**
   The word '*tune*' means 'to bring to a state corresponding to a set frequency on the musical scale.' There are of course the exceptions to this definition when one is tuning the higher partials; in this case one tunes by *compressing* or *stretching* the octave or twelfth.

   Pans above the Bass are tuned in the ***Key-note-Octave-Twelfth Format***. In Pan circles, the *Twelfth* is referred to as the *Fifth* (*the fifth above the octave*). Some tuners may apply this format to the Bass but the most appropriate setting is found in the ***Key-note-Octave-Third Format*** where *third* refers to *the third above the octave*. This has certain advantages that we shall come to later.

10) The ***Compressing and Stretching Rule***,

    (a) This rule, first demonstrated for the steelpan by Achong (1996b) reads:

- *While all key-notes must be tuned in agreement with the 12-TET system, all **partials** above the key-notes must be tuned by **compressing** or **stretching** with respect to the corresponding harmonics of the key-note frequencies. This is referred to as '**detuning**.'*

(b) Therefore, in practice, the higher partials of a note on the steelpan *do not* follow the 12-TET system. However, the instruments remain *perfectly tuned* in this manner. There is only one exception to this Rule where one finds both the key-note and the *twelfth* in agreement with the 12-TET scale; it occurs when the detuning parameter for the *twelfth* is set to the value $\sigma_2 = 2.9966 - 3 = -0.0034 \equiv -1.963$ cents. This Rule and why it applies will be explained in discussions to follow.

(c) The **Compressing/Stretching Rule** in definition 4(b) clearly indicates that the higher partials on a steelpan are not formed (tuned) on the basis of harmonics as classically (traditionally) stated. The expression 'tuning the harmonics,' in the strict sense, *cannot* be applied to the pan.

(d) In more precise terms, the Compressing/Stretching Rule applies to the relationship between (i) the key-note and the resident octave and (ii) key-note and resident twelfth. If the second and/or third partial for a given key-note is generated by the second note of a sympathetic pair, and the coupling is *strong* — a **strong Marshall Pair** — then the Compressing/Stretching Rule requires that the two notes be tuned *dependently*. If on the other hand, the coupling is *weak* — a **weak Marshall Pair** — then the two notes in the weak pair can be tuned with each member *independently* obeying the Compressing/Stretching Rule.

11) ***Amplitude Modulation*** (**AM**) on the tones of a sounding steelpan note refers to the *natural* variations in the amplitude of the velocity and displacement of the note surface. These modulations are natural in the sense that that they are produced by the note dynamics and are therefore *intrinsic*

properties of the note. On a properly tuned note all partials with the exception of the *Third* on the bass (see Section 14.26) are subject to AM. Intrinsic AM must be distinguished from *Tremolo*.

12) ***Tremolo*** is a rapid repetition of tone achieved by rapid stick-note impacts such as in the '***Roll***' (see Section 13.34). Tremolo is produced by the action of the panist.

13) ***Frequency Modulation*** (**FM**) on the tones of a sounding steelpan note refers to the *natural variations* in the frequency (or pitch) of the note. FM is produced by the note dynamics and is an intrinsic property of the note. All partials with the exception of the *Third* on the bass (See Section 14.26) on a properly tuned note are subject to frequency modulations. I*ntrinsic* FM must be distinguished from *Vibrato*.

14) ***Vibrato and Pitch Inflection: Vibrato*** in musical usage refers to small fluctuations in pitch used by the player of a musical instrument as an expressive device to intensify (or give emphasis to) a sound — you can say it is *ornamental*, but some musicians may object! Since vibrato must be induced by the player, for a panist *this is practically impossible*. The panist cannot alter the frequency of a note by using the pair of sticks. *The fundamental reason comes from the fact that the stick is in contact with the note for only a <u>fraction of the period of vibration</u> of the note (of the order of a millisecond) — too short for any pitch control. Vibrato is only possible when control lasts for a time of the order of the <u>tone duration</u> (of the order of a second — which is a thousand times longer). Any attempt to prolong stick-note contact will foil tone production.*

A related term is '***Pitch Inflection***' which refers to small '*dips*' and '*rises*' on a note to ornament the melody. A good example of this technique is found in the playing of the Japanese ***Koto*** — a long wooden thirteen stringed instrument with *movable frets* played by plucking the strings. Pitch Inflection is also *not* a practical possibility for the panist.

Comment: Do not be fooled into thinking that body antics and attractive hand actions by the panist are done to achieve pitch inflection. The panist uses these actions to achieve one or a combination of the following (i) drawing the attention of the audience to himself, (ii) moving in step with the rhythm or in response to it (a natural action because he is both player and listener), (iii) nuances of his stick action (varies with the music), (iv) particularly with the younger player, to copy another player's 'style,' (v) to achieve the tonal characteristics that depend on *strength* of stick impact such as levels of amplitude and/or frequency modulation of the sounding note (do not confuse 'frequency modulation' with 'pitch inflection').

15) A collection of steelpans of different types into Sections, with their attending players, is called a **Steel Orchestra** or **Steelband**. In context, these Steelbands may be referred to as **Bands**.

16) Within the Steel Orchestra it is customary to refer to the pan *Types* — Bass, Cello, Guitars, and Tenors — as the voices. More precisely however, these *Types* form the **Sections** of the orchestra. The instruments within a Section are the **Voices**. The number of Sections and the number of Voices allocated to each Section defines the **Structure** of a band.

17) The steelpan player is called a **Panist**.

18) The instruments are made by a **Pan Maker** and tuned by a **Tuner**. A Pan Maker may also double as a Tuner. An entire Orchestra or a Section is tuned by a **Blender**. The process of *Blending* requires greater sophistication so not all Tuners are Blenders. Some Pan Makers are Tuners and Blenders. Some Pan Makers, by their high level of instrumentation skills are referred to as **Master Pan Makers**. There is a similar designation for the **Master Tuner/Blender**. *A Master is a craftsman who is recognized by his peers as a person skilled and knowledgeable in all areas of the craft.*

19) **Sticks**: The instrument is played with a *pair of rubber-tipped sticks* although early versions, having a few notes on the low end of the musical scale, were played with a single stick. Special sticks are made for each pan *Type*; generally, exchanging sticks among pans of different type is not musically feasible.

20) **Standardization:** There is no official Standard Pan, Standard Bass or Standard Tenor so that one should really write 'Standard' Pan or 'Standard' Tenor. However, for simplicity and convenience in this work, the quotation marks will be dropped. The note layouts shown in the diagrams in this Section and elsewhere in this work are, by default, the *de facto* Standard Layouts. These layouts are taken from the author's own investigation of pans produced in Trinidad and Tobago and are consistent, for the most part, with the note placements recommended by Pan Trinbago (2009). In later Sections of this work, I shall refer to the Steelpan in its standard form as the Standard Pan or S-Pan. This will be used to distinguish the Steelpan from the newer invention, the G-Pan (see Chapter 17). There is need for this distinction as will be shown in Chapter 17.

14.3 Definitions II

To put the process of pan tuning in proper perspective I first briefly define and compare three tuning systems — *Pythagorean Intonation, Just Intonation* and *Equal Temperament*. I will not be fully comprehensive in discussing these systems so the reader desirous of more information can search the musical literature for these and other systems of musical tuning. My goal is to set the stage for our discussion on *Pan Tuning* which adopts for its key-notes, the *Western 12-Tone Equal Temperament (12-TET)* system *while the higher partials are made to deviate somewhat from this standard.*

14.3.1 Pythagorean Intonation

In music, the word *interval* is used to describe a particular ratio between the frequencies of two notes. The *Pythagorean Scale* is the pure *diatonic scale* in which the frequencies are in simple ratios, which underlie harmonies that are pleasing to the ear (it is this subjective 'pleasing aspect' that makes us select 'particular' ratios for a musical scale). In musical terms, diatonic refers to music based on the seven tones of a major or minor scale; such music center closely around a key-note and its related harmonies. A list of

Pythagorean frequency ratios obeying the *exact-integer-ratio law* is presented in the Table 14.1.

The relations shown in Table 14.1 hold for *perfectly harmonic intervals* or *pure intervals*. There are many other ratios, for example, the frequency ratios 1:2:3 are given by the *key-note, octave* and *twelfth*. The twelfth consists *of* an octave and a *fifth*, not by addition but by *multiplication — 2 x 1.5 = 3*. It is characteristic of our sense of hearing to recognize ratios, not differences or sums of frequencies. In *musical intervals*, the intervals are compounded (multiplied), not added. The ratios 2:3:4 are the key-note, fifth and octave as can be found by *dividing* by 2. Similarly, 3:4:5 is the same as 1:4/3:5/3 or key-note, *fourth* and *major sixth*. All these *chords*, as the simultaneous sounding of more than two notes is called, are harmonic (and there is much more in the theory of chords, but this will suffice here). Another example, 5:2 is 2.500 or 2 x 1.250, an octave and a *major third*.

Table 14.1

Name	Ratio
Key-note or Unison	1:1 = 1.000
Minor Third	6:5 = 1.200
Major Third	5:4 = 1.250
Fourth	4:3 = 1.333
Fifth	3:2 = 1.500
Minor Sixth	8:5 = 1.600
Major Sixth	5:3 = 1.667
Octave	2:1 = 2.000
Twelfth	3:1 = 3.000

14.3.2 Just Intonation

Just intonation is any musical tuning in which the frequencies of notes are related by ratios of small whole numbers. Any interval tuned in this way is called a *just interval*. With the restriction to small whole numbers (small integers), arbitrary frequency ratios such as 936:662 are not generally said to be justly tuned even though 936/662 = 1.4139 is a better approximation to 1.4142 than

7/5 = 1.4 for the *Tritone* (see Table 14.2). Two notes in any just interval are members of the same harmonic series.

14.3.3 Equal Temperament

First, the meaning of the musical term Octave; the musical term **Octave** means the eighth tone of a *diatonic* scale (as from *doh'* to *doh'*) or a tone seven *degrees* above or below a given tone.

The *Equal Tempered Scale* is a compromise between Pythagorean purity of harmony and the facility of having easy key changes. The equal tempered scale is the common musical scale presently used for the tuning of pianos and other instruments of relatively fixed scale. By definition, in equal temperament:

a) all notes are defined as multiples of the same basic interval,
b) the octave is divided into 12 equal *semitones*.

To satisfy the two requirements, the basic interval has to be $\sqrt[12]{2}$ — the 12th root of 2 (see Table 14.2). The integer 2 under the root symbol ($\sqrt{}$) refers to the ratio of the octave to the key-note (a 2:1 ratio). The basic interval or *semitone* is the smallest distance between two notes. A *tone* consists of two semitones. The *unison* (key-note) is assigned the value $\left(\sqrt[12]{2}\right)^0 = 1.0000$, the semitone one half step above is assigned the value $\left(\sqrt[12]{2}\right)^1 = 1.0595$, the whole tone two semitones above unison is assigned the value $\left(\sqrt[12]{2}\right)^2 = 1.1225$ etc. Two notes separated by the same number of steps always have exactly the same frequency ratio. However, except for doubled frequencies or octaves, all other intervals are not ratios of small integers instead they are irrationals. Lists of frequency ratios in the three systems are given in Table 14.2.

Do a careful study of Table 14.2 and observe the essential differences and similarities of the three scales. It is best to compare the scales using the 'Cents' columns. Observe that perfect agreement occurs only on Unison and the Octave. Very close agreement is seen on the Major Second, Perfect Fourth and the Perfect Fifth.

TABLE 14.2

Name	Semitones	Equal Temperament		Pure Intervals		Just Intonation	
		Value in 12-TET	Cents	Ratio	Cents	Ratio	Cents
Unison		$\left(\sqrt[12]{2}\right)^0 = 1.0000$	0	1.0000 = 1:1	0	1.0000 = 1:1	0
Minor Second	a semitone (half step)	$\left(\sqrt[12]{2}\right)^1 = 1.0595$	100	1.0909 = 12:11	150.62	1.0667 = 16:15	111.73
Major Second	a whole tone (whole step)	$\left(\sqrt[12]{2}\right)^2 = 1.1225$	200	1.1250 = 9:8	203.91	1.1250 = 9:8	203.91
Minor Third	3 semitones	$\left(\sqrt[12]{2}\right)^3 = 1.1892$	300	1.2000 = 6:5	315.64	1.200 = 6:5	315.64
Major Third	4 semitones	$\left(\sqrt[12]{2}\right)^4 = 1.2599$	400	1.2500 = 5:4	386.31	1.2500 = 5:4	386.31
Perfect Fourth	5 semitones	$\left(\sqrt[12]{2}\right)^5 = 1.3348$	500	1.3333 = 4:3	498.00	1.3333 = 4:3	498.00
Tritone* = Augmented Fourth ≡ Diminished Fifth	6 semitones	$\left(\sqrt[12]{2}\right)^6 = 1.4142$	600	1.4000 = 7:5	582.51	1.4000 = 7:5	582.51
Perfect Fifth	7 semitones	$\left(\sqrt[12]{2}\right)^7 = 1.4983$	700	1.500 = 3:2	701.96	1.500 = 3:2	701.96
Minor Sixth	8 semitones	$\left(\sqrt[12]{2}\right)^8 = 1.5874$	800	1.6000 = 8:5	813.69	1.6000 = 8:5	813.69
Major Sixth	9 semitones	$\left(\sqrt[12]{2}\right)^9 = 1.6818$	900	1.6667 = 5:3	884.39	1.6667 = 5:3	884.39
Minor Seventh	10 semitones	$\left(\sqrt[12]{2}\right)^{10} = 1.7818$	1000	1.7500 = 7:4	968.83	1.7500 = 7:4	968.83
Major Seventh	11 semitones	$\left(\sqrt[12]{2}\right)^{11} = 1.8897$	1100	1.8333 = 11:6	1049.3	1.8750 = 15:8	1088.27
Octave	12 semitones	$\left(\sqrt[12]{2}\right)^{12} = 2.0000$	1200	2.0000 = 2:1	1200	2.0000 = 2:1	1200

* The symbol = should be read 'the same as' while ≡ should be read as 'enharmonic to'.

It is common practice to state musical intervals in *cents*, where 100 cents is defined as one equal tempered semitone, giving the octave a total of 12 x 100 = 1200 cents. The cents notation provides a useful way to compare intervals in different temperaments and to decide whether those differences are musically significant. For the purpose of comparison, a useful parameter is the *'just noticeable difference in pitch'* which corresponds to about ±5 cents. These differences can be obtained from Table 14.2 where one observes that apart from the unison and octave, where there must be perfect agreement, one finds close agreement (within ±5 cents) among the three tuning systems at the major 2nd, perfect 4th and perfect 5th.

To express the interval in *cents* between two notes of frequency f_1 and f_2, use the formula

$$c = 1200 \times 3.321928095 \times \log\left(\frac{f_1}{f_2}\right) \text{ cents,}$$

where the logarithm (*log*) is to base 10; this function is available on most hand-held calculators. One of the advantages of the equal tempered scale is that it is the same in any musical 'key', so that musical compositions may be freely transposed up or down without changing the musical intervals.

The term *chromatic scale* or *chromatic*ity refers to the *twelve-tone* scale, including all the semitones of the octave in contrast to the *diatonic scale* based on the *seven* tones of a major or minor scale The word *chromatic* means colorful and notice that in the chromatic scale all the steps or semitones are included. There are other subtle rules on the relationship between notes and we shall go into some of them next.

When referring to the pitch of a note, instead of talking about frequency, musicians prefer to use letter names: **A, B, C, D, E, F,** and **G**. These seven letters name the **natural notes** (symbol ♮). When they get to the eighth natural note, they start the next octave on another **A**. The remaining five notes in the 12-note octave are filled by **sharps** and **flats**. Symbols known as *accidentals* are used to alter the pitch of a written note. In standard notation, the sharp symbol **#** *raises* the pitch of a note by *one semitone*; the flat symbol ♭ *lowers it by one semitone*; the *natural* symbol ♮ *restores* the note to its original pitch.

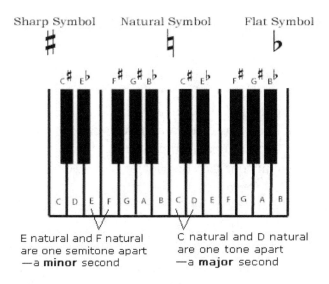

Fig. 14.1. The natural notes name the white keys on this *fractional* keyboard. The *full* keyboard found on a piano or organ, consists of a number of these fractional keyboards. The black notes are sharps and flats.

Some of the natural notes are only one semitone (half step) apart, but most of them are one tone (a whole step) apart as shown on the fractional keyboard in Figure 14.1. When they are one tone apart, the note in between them can be named using a *flat* or a *sharp*. For example between **D** and **E** there is **E**♭ (pronounced 'E-flat'). **E**♭ is the same as **D**♯ (D-sharp); **E**♭ is said to be *enharmonic* to **D**♯ — *in the same key they sound the same*. **E**♯ (pronounced 'E-sharp') is enharmonic to **F**♮ (F natural). **B**♯ is enharmonic to **C**♮ (C natural). Which of the names *flat* or *sharp* is used, depends on the scale and key in which a flat or a sharp appears.

When two letters specify an interval such as **C** to **D**, the interval is a *second*. From **C** to **E** there are three letters (**C**, **D**, **E**). This is an interval of a *third*. This Law also applies to *fourth, fifth, sixth* and *seventh*. Furthermore, when the two notes that form an interval belong to the same scale the interval is said to be **diatonic**. The diatonic interval of a tone such as **C** to **D** is called a **major** second, while the diatonic interval of a semitone such as **B** to **C** is called a **minor** second. There are no majors or minors on the *perfect fourth* or *perfect fifth*. The *tritone* is an interval that spans three whole tones. The tritone is the same as an *augmented* fourth and is enharmonic to the *diminished* fifth.

These definitions will assist readers in the interpretation of the note names given in Table 14.1, Table 14.2 and throughout this book. Going beyond these rudiments will lead us into the *theory of music* which is outside the scope of this work.

The Internationally accepted *Standard Frequency of Reference* in the Western 12-Tone Equal Temperament System is the natural $A_4 \equiv 440$ Hz. From this one gets the natural $A_3 \equiv 220$ Hz, the natural $A_5 \equiv 880$ Hz and all the other derived frequencies including the flats and sharps (the black notes on a keyboard). To obtain these frequencies, observe in Table 14.2 that an interval of n semitones is expressed by the ratio $\left(\sqrt[12]{2}\right)^n$. When the interval extends *downward* in frequency, n is a *negative* integer while n is a *positive* integer for intervals extending *upward* in frequency. Measured from A_4, one gets

$$\text{Note Frequency} = 440 \times \left(\sqrt[12]{2}\right)^n \text{ Hz,}$$

where it is usual practice to express the frequency rounded to the second decimal place. For example, measured from A_4, the E_4 note is five semitones down giving n = -5 and a note frequency of 440 x $\left(\sqrt[12]{2}\right)^{-5}$ = 329.38 Hz. Similarly G_5 is ten semitones above A_4 giving G_5 a frequency of 440 x $\left(\sqrt[12]{2}\right)^{10}$ = 783.99 Hz. The frequencies of all musical notes are obtained by this procedure. The reader should use Figure 14.2 to count the n values for a few other notes including the flats and sharps and then verify their frequencies.

14.3.4 The Fifth and Third above the Octave

Next to the key-note and octave, the musical note of special interest on the pan is the *twelfth* or the *fifth above the octave*. On the 12-TET system this note is 19 semitones above unison (the key-note) i.e. 12 semitones from key-note to the octave and 7 semitones from the octave to the fifth. The corresponding 12-TET value is:

Fifth above the octave;

$$\left(\sqrt[12]{2}\right)^{19} = \left(\sqrt[12]{2}\right)^{12} \times \left(\sqrt[12]{2}\right)^{7} = 2 \times 1.4983 = 2.9966.$$

Notice immediately that the *twelfth* in the 12-TET system is *not* equal to the third harmonic of the key-note given by:

Third Harmonic; $2 \times 1.5 = 3$,

the difference between them is 1.963 cents.

Another note of importance on the pan is the *third* above the octave which, on the 12-TET system is 16 semitones above unison. On the 12-TET system this corresponds to the value:

Third above the octave;

$$\left(\sqrt[12]{2}\right)^{16} = \left(\sqrt[12]{2}\right)^{12} \times \left(\sqrt[12]{2}\right)^{4} = 2 \times 1.2599 = 2.5198.$$

These numerical observations will be used in Sections 14.25.7 and 14.26 when describing the tuning procedures for pan notes.

14.4 The Frequency Range of Pans

Figure 14.2 shows the frequency range of each type of pan and compares them with the ranges for a number of other musical instruments. The highest note on the 'High D Tenor' steelpan the $F^{\#}_6$ corresponds to the highest notes normally played on the Clarinet, the Oboe and the Mandolin. The lowest note on the 'Nine Bass' pan, the A_1, sits above the lowest notes on the Bass Tuba and the Bass Viol. The overlap of the musical ranges found on the pan instruments is similar to that found among wind instruments and string instruments. Despite the overlap, the tones are distinctly diverse in character due to instrument size, size of the notes, size of the sticks used in playing each type and tuning characteristics that vary from the high-end instruments to the low-end bass. The diversity in types and tonality is essential as it allows the tuner and blender to create the overall scope and color required in the production of a full orchestral sound using just a set of percussion instruments in which all members are of the same basic construction.

The tonal resources of these instruments when played in the combinations found in ensembles and steel orchestras are immense. In these combinations, special conducting skills (only lightly touched upon in this book) are needed in order to obtain a proper mix. The conductor chooses (arranges) his tonal color combinations by grouping pans from different sections (of the orchestra) and orchestrating with deft manipulations in their timing and intensity. Since the duration of a pan note excited by a single impact is just around one second, and the panist must make repeated impacts in order to sustain the sound for a longer time, much of the control depends on the skills of the panists.

In the early days the human voice served as a model for steelpan builders and players as they sought to duplicate its beauty, expressiveness and particularly its vibrato. It is not that the builders and players were themselves poor singers and saw the new instrument as a replacement or substitute for their own 'poor voice,' far from it. They realized that the new instrument could give greater expressiveness than its precursor, the 'bamboo tamboo,' and used their own voice because it was close at hand. Many early tuners tuned their instruments by singing the musical scale 'Doh, Ray, Me, ...'. That's how I tuned my 'Dew Drops' as a boy! Other instruments, particularly the string instruments such as the guitar, bass and the cello were voices that they also 'copied.' In this development they discovered the rich diversity of the steelpan types as the instruments evolved.

Pan makers discovered that the tonal resources of the instrument they invented were immense. Along with this came the remarkable variety of technical resources of the panist. It is certainly true to say that pan makers, tuners and panists all share in the musical development of the instrument (which comprises both pan and sticks).

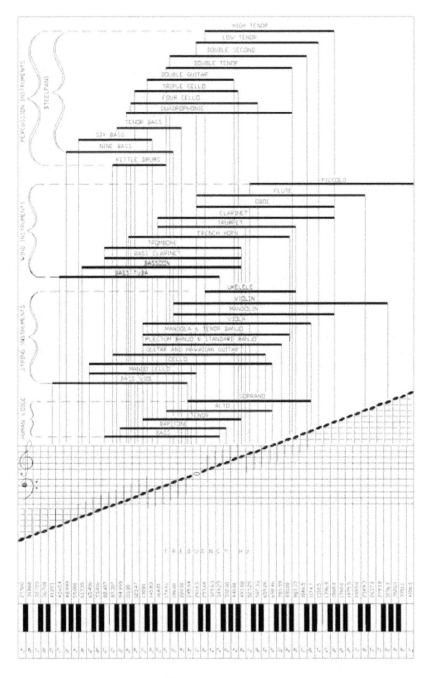

Fig. 14.2. Note frequencies on the piano, musical ranges for other instruments and the ranges of different pan types. Note frequencies follow the Western 12-Tone Equal Temperament—12-TET.

14.5 Standard Note Layout on the Pan

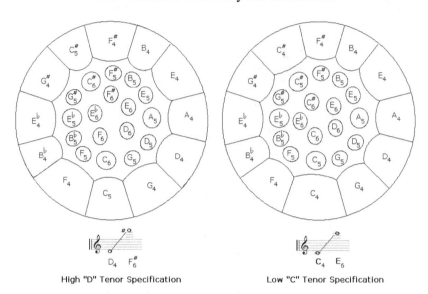

Fig. 14.3. Specifications for the High 'D' Tenor and the Low 'C' Tenor. Configuration: Fourths and Fifths. Skirt length ≈ 8¾ inches, Pan face Depth ≈ 8 to 8½ inches.

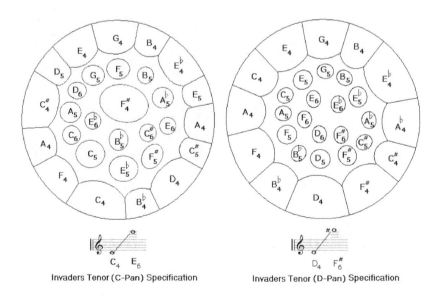

Fig. 14.4. Specification for the Invaders C-Pan and D-Pan Tenors (Configuration: Non-Standard). Total of 29 notes; C-Pan, C_4 to E_6: D-Pan, D_4 to $F^{\#}_6$. Skirt length ≈ 8¾ inches, Pan face Depth ≈ 8 to 8½ inches.

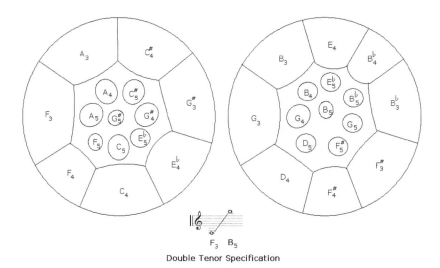

Fig. 14.5. Double Tenor Specification. Configuration: Mixed (Whole Tone +). Usually configured with double grooves between notes. Total of 31 notes from F_3 to B_5. Skirt length ≈ 7¾ inches, Pan face Depth ≈ 6¾ to 7¼ inches.

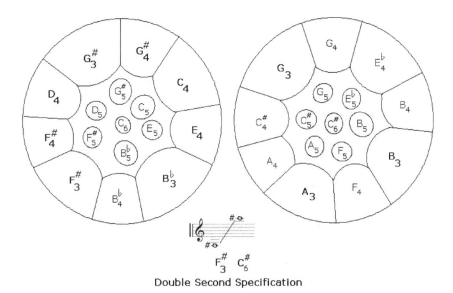

Fig. 14.6. Double Second Specification. Configuration: Mixed (4 Whole Tones + 2 Pairs per pan). Total of 32 notes from $F^\#_3$ to $C^\#_6$. Skirt length ≈ 9 inches, Pan face Depth ≈ 6½ to 7¼ inches.

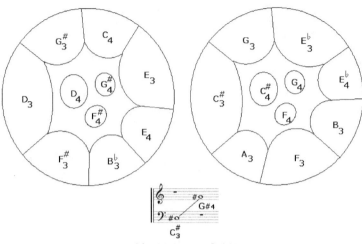

Double Guitar Specification

Fig. 14.7. Specification for the Double Guitar. Configuration: Mixed (4 Pairs + 2 Singles per pan). Total of 20 notes from $C^\#_3$ to $G^\#_4$. Skirt length ≈ 17 inches, Pan face Depth ≈ 5½ to 7 inches.

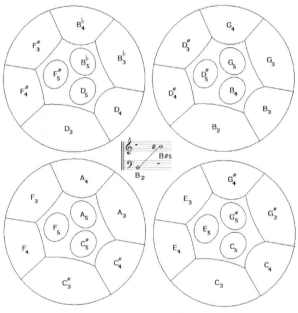

Quadraphonic Specification

Fig. 14.8. Specification for the Quadraphonic. Configuration: Whole Tone. Total of 20 notes from $C^\#_3$ to $G^\#_4$. Skirt length ≈ 17 inches, Pan face Depth ≈ 5½ to 7 inches.

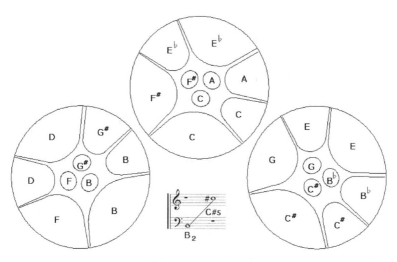

Three Cello Specification

Fig. 14.9. Specification for the Three Cello. Cinfiguration: Mixed (1 Whole Tone + 3 Pairs per pan). Total of 27 notes from B_2 to $C^{\#}_5$. Skirt length ≈ 19 inches, Pan face Depth ≈ 6 to 6½ inches.

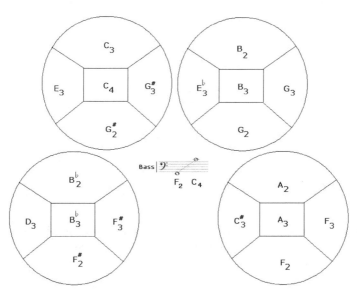

Tenor/High Bass Specification

Fig. 14.10. Specification for the Tenor/High Bass. Configuration: Mixed (2 Pairs + 1 Single per pan). Total of 20 notes from F_2 to C_4. Skirt length = 28 inches, Pan face Depth ≈ 5 to 5½ inches.

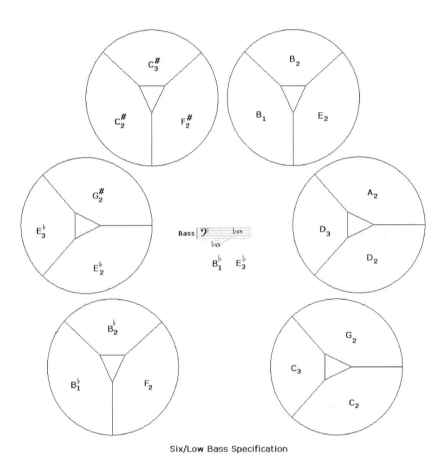

Six/Low Bass Specification

Fig. 14.11. Specification for the Six/Low Bass. Configuration: Mixed (1 Pair + 1 Single per Pan). Total of 18 notes from $B_1^\flat$ to $E_3^\flat$. Skirt length = 34 inches, Pan face Depth ≈ 4½ inches.

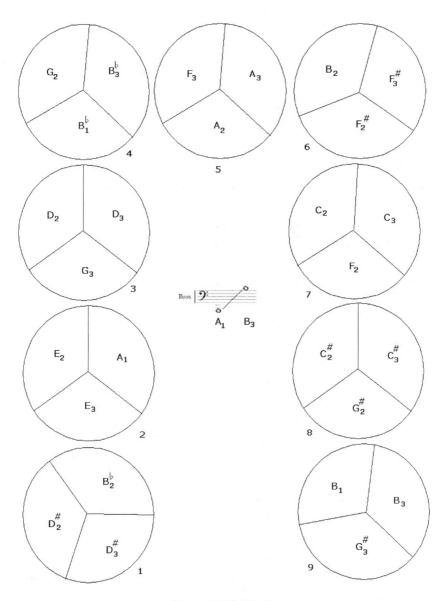

Nine Bass Specification

Fig. 14.12. Specification for the Nine Bass. Configuration: Mixed (1 Single + 1 Pair per pan except on pans #4 and #9 with Key-note-second octave combination). Total of 27 notes from A_1 to B_3. Skirt length − 34 inches, Pan face Depth ≈ 4½ inches.

14.6 Musical Range and the Distribution of Notes: Singles, Pairs and Triples on the Standard Pans

TABLE 14.3

Pan Type	Musical Range†	Musical Function	Singles s	Pairs Total P	Pairs Outer Notes Only	Triples ‡ t	Total N= 2p + s − t
Invaders C-Pan‡	$C_4 - F_6$	M	14 (22)	8 (4)	0	1	29
Invaders D-Pan	$D_4 - F^{\#}_6$	M	0	17	0	5	29
High 'D' Tenor	$D_4 - F^{\#}_6$	M	0	17	0	5	29
Low 'C' Tenor	$C_4 - E_6$	M	0	17	0	5	29
Double Tenor	$F_3 - B_5$	M, CM	0	19	3	7	31
Double Second	$F^{\#}_3 - C^{\#}_6$	M, CM, H	0	20	6	8	32
Quadraphonic	$B_2 - B^{\flat}_5$	M. CM, H	0	24	12	12	36
Three Cello	$B_2 - C^{\#}_5$	H	0	15	6	3	27
Double Guitar	$C^{\#}_3 - G^{\#}_4$	H	4	8	2	0	20
Tenor/High Bass	$F_2 - C_4$	RB, B	4	8	4	0	20
Six/Low Bass	$B^{\flat}_1 - E^{\flat}_3$	B	6	6	6	0	18
Nine Bass	$A_1 - B_3$	B	9	7 + 2*	9	0	27

M — Melody; CM — Counter Melody; H — Harmony; RB — Reinforce the Bass lines; B — Bass.

† There exists no official standard for the musical ranges; for example some Quadraphonics contain 40 notes while the High Tenor may extend to G_6.

‡ By definition for our purposes here, Triple ≡ Whole Tone (three contiguous notes for example, $\{C_3, C_4, C_5\}$).

‡ The definition of a Pair is somewhat extended on the Invaders C-Pan to include a note and its octave that are physically close, not necessarily adjacent but with no intervening note(s) along the shortest path between the two. If strict adjacency is applied as on the standard tenor, then the bracketed numbers (22) and (4) apply.

* On the Nine Bass, the pairs identified by the asterisk consists of $\{B_1:B_3\}$—a *key-note and second octave* combination found on the number 9 pan, and $\{B^\flat{}_1:B^\flat{}_3\}$—a *key-note and second octave* combination found on the number 4 pan. One may wonder if there can be any interaction between the members of these pairs. We discuss the $\{B_1:B_3\}$ pair with the same being applicable to the $\{B^\flat{}_1:B^\flat{}_3\}$ pair. Readers ought to recall that whenever any note (or any arbitrary point on the pan) is impacted, energy is transmitted away from the impact point to all areas of the pan but the direct excitation that follows has nothing to do with the interaction between notes (B_1 and B_3 in the present case). Excitation of B_3 through its interaction with B_1 when B_1 is played comes as a result of an internal resonance formed with B_3 by a two-step (non-linear) interaction; (i) the key-note on B_1 interacts with itself (yes I did say 'with itself')† to excite its *resident octave* {mode1 · mode1→mode2 (resident octave)}, (ii) the resident octave in turn interacts with itself to excite the *second octave* B_3 {mode2 · mode2→ mode4 (B_3)}. The fourth mode 'mode4 (B_3)' is really the first mode found on the B_3 note. It is also possible in another two-step process (the first step being the generation of the *resident twelfth* by the key-note and *resident octave*) for the key-note on B_1 to interact with the *resident twelfth* thereby exciting the B_3 note by note-note coupling {mode1 · mode3→mode4 (B_3)}. There are also the reverse interactions that transfer energy from B_3 back to the B_1 note. Although weakly excited, the entire surface of the true note on B_3 will vibrate in-phase. These pairs represent a clever combination and as we see from being a two-step process, it does not add an unduly intense fourth partial (second octave) to the B_1 bass note or the $B^\flat{}_1$ bass note when either is sounding.

† To those of us with musical taste, these crazy things like a mode 'interacting with itself' are the rather fine ingredients that go into the making of those pleasant 'tasting' cocktails of tones that radiate from the pan. They give the 'fizz' and the 'pop' to the 'champagne' of musical instruments.

Table 14.3 gives an overview of the tuning arrangement on each pan type. I took the liberty here of introducing my own notation — *Singles, Pairs* and *Triples* — in order to properly discuss the tuning arrangement and note distribution found on these instruments. The term 'Triple' used here refers to the set of three contiguous *physical notes* (a *whole note*), for example $\{B_1:B_2:B_3\}$, placed on the same pan face. The term *Triple* used here, must not be confused with the 'Triplet' notation found in written music. *Singles* are those notes placed on the pan face without an associated octave or second octave note — for example on the Double Guitar one finds the **C** and **B**$^\flat$ on the left pan and the **A** and **B** on the right pan. The Pairs are Marshall Pairs. See Sections 14.38 and 14.39 respectively, for specifications on Marshall Pairs and Triples. Observe that each Triple consists of two contiguous Marshall Pairs. The formula relating the number of Singles, Pairs and Triples to the total number N of notes found on the instrument is expressed as

$$N = 2p + s - t.$$

This formula for N comes from adding Singles (s) to twice the number of Pairs (2p) but since two pairs are to be found in each Triple, Triples (t) have been added twice so we must subtract the number of Triples.

Was it to be expected that a formula should be found that draws a connection among notes of different types? Did the pan makers have this in mind? What is the moral to be drawn from this?

To see what it means we must inspect the Table, maybe we can see a little of what is in the pan maker's mind. From Table 14.3 one quickly observes that the pans can be divided into two categories

(i) those with Triples and zero singles, and
(ii) those with singles and zero Triples.

Basically (i) include the high-end pans while (ii) include the low-end pans where a division occurs at the Three Cello-Double Guitar transition point. The Double Guitar, in its initial introduction to the list of pan instruments, was meant for strumming (harmony) so the assigned note distribution fits this purpose. Strumming can also be done on the Cello. *The Invaders C-Pan Tenor is an exception.* Can you spot a rule, if any, that it follows?

The choice of musical range and note distribution (into Singles, Pairs and Triples) on each instrument depends on the musical needs and requirements seen by the pan makers. Over the years as the repertoire of the panists broadened into classical and modern music newer instruments were introduced while respecting the 'voices' necessary for orchestral application of the steelpan. It must always be kept in mind that steelpans all operate under the same set of physical principles with each pan type covering a distinct range with overlap on the musical scale. Pan types must complement each other and each must present a distinctive voice. Pan makers design their pans with this firmly in their minds and it is for this reason that the peculiar features of the note distribution appear on the Table. An exception occurs here with the Low Tenor and the High Tenor where one tone (the interval C_4 to D_4) separates them on the low end of the range. As shown in Section 13.27.4, there are upper limits placed on pan notes that are playable by the manual application of impacts using rubber tipped sticks. For the type of sticks used on the tenor to accommodate the tenor range (top to bottom) and by the manner of hand action employed by the panist, this upper limit on the tenor is around $G^{\#}_6$. This means that for the production of well defined, clear and crisp notes of usable acoustical strength, that are almost free of *stick-noise* or *stick-note clap* (see Section 13.28), the $G^{\#}_6$ which sits two tones above the $F^{\#}_6$ at the top of the High 'D' Tenor is at the practical limit. Unless a special small tip stick is used on the notes above E_6, not much can be heard but using such sticks will cause the tone on the C_4 and D_4 to suffer—by producing unacceptable 'ping-ping' thin sounding tones. This problem (*Problem of the Marginal Notes*), as it relates to all pans and sticks, is thoroughly dealt with in Section 13.17 and Section 13.27.

14.7 Musical Range and the Distribution of Notes: Singles, Pairs and Triples on the Invaders C-Pan Tenor

In Table 14.3, the distribution of notes on the Invaders C-Pan is quite different from the Standard Tenor Singles, resembling more the Low–end Standard Pans. In fact greater use is made of Single notes (14 (22) out of a total of 29 notes), less reliance on Pairs (8 (4)) and only one appearance of a Triple (the **C** notes). With less reliance on Pairs and Triples, when compared to the Standard Tenors, it is clear that the Invaders C-Pan is designed for more mellow tones without the 'ringing' associated with the Standard Tenors. The expression $N = 2p + s - t$ is still followed but it appears that on the basis of note distribution (Singles, Pairs and Triples) the Invaders C-Pan Tenor looks more like a bass in this respect. On the bass, the notes are spatially separated over nine pans, on the Invaders C-Pan they are spread over a single pan. There are other early pans for which distribution counts show similarities to the Invaders C-Pan — they are of the same genre. The Invaders C-Pan has survived because of its attachment to the Invaders Steelband and for its distinguishing tonal qualities. To me, it appears to carry the tones of the earlier tenor pans with improved tuning—something akin to what Felix Röhner did on his Pang range of pans where ringing tones are suppressed by reducing the strengths of the higher partials through the combined action of reduced modal coupling and the use of a soft tipped stick. More on the Invaders pan is to come later.

14.8 Going beyond $E^b{}_7$ — Dream or Reality

Question: *How far can we enlarge the tonal compass of the pan?*

In Section 13.27 it was shown that with well prepared sticks, the highest note that can be ***directly excited*** on the pan by manually applied stick impact is the $E^b{}_7$. In practice as pan makers attempt to go higher in frequency, the $E^b{}_7$ will turn out to be unreachable. This answers our first question and shows that anything above $E^b{}_7$ with pan as we know it is a dream, but read on. As the panist plays notes in the range E_6 to G_6, the fall-off in sound intensity grows rapidly in comparison with the other notes on the pan. The same occurs on the G-Pan in the range E_6 to B_6. Neither the High Tenor nor the G-Pan tenor can beat the limitation imposed by *Frequency Band Limiting*. But not knowing that there is a physical limit at the top is like trying to scale a mountain peak covered in thick fog. The limitation is not on the part of the pan maker (or the climber), it is a physical limitation that comes with the *pan-stick* instrument itself (the mountain peak itself). But unlike the fog covered peak, *we know* where the upper limits are for each pan-stick combination (see Section 13.27). Using a pan face of a different size (smaller or larger) will not remove this limit (which can be seen as a problem!). It is a frequency related problem which will not go away by using larger notes (like the *G-Pan*) to increase acoustical output or a smaller pan (like the *Sopranino pan, not to be confused with the high Saxophone by the same name*) dedicated to higher pitch notes.

The constraint imposed by *Wavelength Band-Limiting* (see Sections 13.30 – 13.32) which has to do with stick tip size and *Contact-Width,* does not come into effect with the typical tenor sticks when playing notes in the E_6 to G_6 range. It does however enter on the higher modes on these notes or when much larger tips are used to play these notes, the effects of which are well known to all players. Wavelength-Band-Limiting forces the player to use larger sticks as the note frequency decreases or (*and this is important*) as note size is increased.

Frequency band-limiting however, *will always be present with all sticks and all sizes of notes.* The only way for the player to effectively use notes of high pitch (G_6 and above) is by using a very swift hand action that shortens the duration (*contact-time*) of the stick impact (see Section 13.11). Reducing the contact-time becomes increasingly difficult for any panist and it has the negative effect of drastically decreasing the energy imparted to the note and as a consequence the acoustical output falls while the relative strength of *stick noise (Stick-Note Clap)* increases (see Section 13.28*).* Stick noise is always a problem with these inner notes on the tenor. (*Try this, take a bass stick and play a Marginal inner note on a tenor. All you get is stick noise! Hopefully you did not use the butt end of the stick. But in case you wanted to try that, I will give you a chance to do something more drastic in the next paragraph.*)

The upper limits that arise from wavelength band-limiting and frequency band-limiting should *not* be seen as a 'defect' of the instrument. Without these limits, pan as we know it would not have been possible. Pan is a successful instrument precisely because of these upper frequency limits. All pans operate as *band-limited instruments* (see Section 13.27). Unknowingly, we use these limits in our stick selection and we adjust our hand action to suit them because our playing actions are conditioned by these limits. Believe it or not! But I prefer that you believe it not because I said it but because the pans and sticks have been 'saying' that all along. We choose particular sticks for certain pans based on their '*responsiveness'*. If you thumb the pages of this book over to Section 13.27 you will find the plots for the force spectra generated for a number of stick-note impacts. These plots are in fact similar to the responses of low-pass frequency filters — *they discriminate against high frequencies.* What actually happens during a stick note impact is that the high frequency contact forces (those that excite high frequency vibrations), are filtered out. If they were not filtered out, the following will occur:

The following is a 'Thought Experiment'. <u>Do not</u> perform on real pans! Take a 4-inch nail (I am serious) or a 6-inch nail (more serious) if that is all you can find, then play the notes of your tenor (or your friend's tenor, it does not matter to me). Like the sound? Well consider a steel orchestra that forgot its sticks and were forced to play with 6-inch nails. The result is a grand 'engine room'; they play like that all the time in the engine room. No harm in joining them, was there? Sorry for what I made you do to your tenor pan but as you probably guessed from reading this work, I am very concerned about the welfare of tuners and there is always a tuner in need of some work!

So for a particular range of notes we choose a stick that gives us the required filtering action that removes the unwanted high frequency stuff. It gets harder to do this properly as the frequency of the note increases. Eventually, the finest of sticks and the fastest of hands cannot take the instrument above a certain frequency limit while delivering crisp, well sounding tones unless of course one finds comfort in 6-inch nails, for with them we can go right up to the audible frequency limit (20 kHz).

We learn also from this analysis that one cannot arbitrarily extend the range of a pan, up or down the scale simply because the musical scale is there to exploit! If the range is extended too far then the instrument cannot be played effectively across its musical range with a single pair of sticks. Since switching sticks during play, holding four sticks or using double-tipped sticks is rather impractical as it can seriously affect one's stick action, we can rule these out as really practical and effective options (*although they have been tried!*). *The double-tipped sticks require a cowboy's double-shooter action, of spinning the guns around the trigger guard; may look fancy but can't be taken seriously—to the conductor it is a distraction and to the panist it upsets the timing. Wait until you try to return the guns to their holster with the butt end in first, that's when you get the tips mixed up or shoot yourself as the case may be — same result!* With over extension on the range, tonality will suffer on the Marginal and bottom ends. *The number of Sections that make up a complete and effective steel orchestra cannot therefore be reduced by the substitution of pans having extended ranges.* It is not only ineffective as we have just seen but more importantly, music as an unsurpassed form of human expression should not be cramped or hindered by poor tonality on the top and bottom of the range covered by the instruments — if you are interested in having a good Steel Orchestra, you wouldn't destroy the *Chorus Effect*, would you?

The moral in all this (and I could have been mathematical in my explanation but it sounds so much better this way) is that the men who gave us the Pan (and sticks) did the right things, chose the correct methods and were very responsive to the sounds they heard coming out of the instrument. Like the sculptor who sees hidden in a chunk of stone a pristine figure of beauty, so is the pan maker with a hammer and a steel drum.

Remark: E^b_7 *is the upper limit for pan notes that can be* <u>directly excited</u> *by stick impact. However, for practical purposes, as an acoustic musical instrument, the true upper limit is much lower; see Section 13.27.*

14.9 More on the Singles, Pairs and Triples

The placing of four Singles and the absence of Triples on the Double Guitar are to guarantee mellow tones suitable for strumming. On the bass, Singles can be tolerated while Triples are banned — if Table (14.3) is to speak for itself. Despite the oxymoron 'Tenor Bass,' on this pan the notes do not 'ring out'. As you move upward on the Table, pass the Three Cello, you find the extravagance of the Quadraphonic — the brainchild of Rudolph Charles and Bertie Marshall — 36 notes in total, 24 Marshall Pairs (12 of which are formed from outer notes), 12 Triples and not a Single to confuse matters — a pan that always call for a panist with matching musical temperament and skill.

Pairs dominate the pan face because they are required on all pans to counter the inefficiency of the *resident octave* as an acoustical radiator (see Chapter 12 on acoustic radiation and Sections 14.38 – 14.42 on note specification). Pairs provide the reinforcement for the second partial as spoken of by Marshall. For this reason, on the high end standard pans (Cello and higher) no Single notes appear. While on the top half of the high-end range the pairs are mainly formed by pairing an inner note and an outer note, as one descends downward to the bass, one finds an increasing use of the pairing combination using outer notes entirely. On the Six and Nine Basses there are no inner notes, making the pairs on these pans potentially more efficient than those on the high-end pans.

14.10 Note Distributions on the Standard Tenor and the Invaders C-Pan Tenor

The two designs that we now focus on are the products of two of the most famous pan makers in history. In no particular order:

1) The Standard Tenor with intervals of 'Fourths and Fifths' by Anthony Williams;
2) The Invaders (C-Pan) Tenor (or the $F^{\#}$ tenor) by Elliot 'Ellie' Mannette .

These instruments provide us with good examples of the type of innovative thinking and design that has produced the wonderful instrument, Pan. The standard, ordered arrangement of 'Fourths and Fifths' is seen on both the outer and inner rings of notes of the more common Standard Tenor. With reference to Figure 14.3 (right panel), at the bottom of the 'Low **C**-Tenor' one finds the key of **C** Major. Starting from there and going anticlockwise by ascending *fifths,* one finds the key of **G**, the key of **D** and so on, completing the circle of 12 tones of the *chromatic scale*. Similarly, by going clockwise from **C** Major at the bottom, in descending fifths one finds the key of **F**, the key of **B**♭ and so on. Reversing this 'circle' of fifths gives the 'circle' of fourths.

The arrangement of 'Fourths and Fifths' is not applied on the Invaders Tenor. To the eyes accustomed to seeing and hands trained to knowing the places for the notes on the standard tenor, the Invaders Tenor at first seems disordered. But order is restored when your eyes and hands are retrained to seeing and feeling *musical order in another form.* If you look closely at the Invaders Tenor you begin to see pairs, yes Marshall Pairs, not that Ellie borrowed the idea from Bertie (well, to be sure, I don't know), nor were they known by that name at the time, in fact it looks more like Ellie found his *own* through the odd arrangement of notes. In fact the placing of the $\mathbf{F}^{\#}_4$ note in the inner section of the pan face shows the retention, at least in this single case, of an aspect of the 'older pan structure' where some of the lower notes were placed in the middle. This teaches an important lesson, for while the standard pan follows the 'Fourths and Fifths' arrangement, *other criteria can be applied.*

As an aid in the description that follows, the $\{\mathbf{C}_4:\mathbf{C}_5\}$ Marshall Pair will be used as the example (any other pair may be substituted). First we note that on the standard tenor the pairs are always adjacent to each other. This makes for more peening work by the tuner in order to mechanically isolate the pairs. On the standard tenor the tuning of notes as *weak* or *strong Marshall Pairs* is done by combining the effects of blocking and the effects of shaping. Blocking and shaping are achieved through hammer peening. Blocking by peening (sometimes with the assistance of grooves or bores (see Section 14.12.2 – 14.12.3)) mechanically isolates the members of a pair in spite of their close spacing. Shaping sets the strengths of the resident octave and the resident twelfth. When blocking is near perfect (for it can never be absolutely perfect) the two members of a pair $\{\mathbf{C}_4:\mathbf{C}_5\}$ can then be tuned as a *weak-pair* combination which, when the lower member $\{\mathbf{C}_4\}$ is played, results in the generation of the higher partials by the corresponding resident octave and resident twelfth (both detuned). These combinations have the tonal characteristics of single notes with only weak reinforcement from the member of higher pitch $\{\mathbf{C}_5\}$. On the other hand, when the blocking between members is purposely set to be less than perfect to a greater degree, the coupling is greater and the combination is a *strong Marshall Pair*. Now, when the lower note $\{\mathbf{C}_4\}$ is played, the higher partials are generated mainly by the member of the pair of higher pitch $\{\mathbf{C}_5\}$. But this requires that the key-note and resident octave on the higher note $\{\mathbf{C}_5\}$ be detuned with respect to the key-note on the lower note $\{\mathbf{C}_4\}$. By including pairs of intermediate levels of coupling one sees that *the standard tenor can display a wide range of sonority, with characteristics conditioned by the physical closeness of members of the pair.*

On the Invaders Tenor, isolation between members of a pair is obtained firstly, by the usual method of blocking, assisted by grooves. Secondly, by increasing the *spatial separation* between a note and its octave, sometimes by separating them right across the middle section of the pan face. By increasing the spatial separation of pair members, one generates very weak Marshall Pairs (or removes the pairing entirely) which results in negligible reinforcement but with the full array of single note modulations available to the tuner (see Section 14.30 on Tuning Scenarios). These modulations are available on the standard' tenor and the Invaders Tenor but the tuning can be easier when the pair members are better isolated. Having stood at the front of the Invaders Steelband in action, just to listen to their much talked about tenor, checking that I was indeed close to the '$F^{\#}$' tenor, I was very impressed with the tenors and the entire band; the sonority of the tenors was clearly distinct, the players, it seemed, were massaging every tone out of them. The players and I were obviously hearing the same thing. My descriptions are not quite good enough so you are urged to listen to an assortment of good tenors tuned to both criteria; when properly tuned and in the hands of the right panist, they are all astonishingly magnificent.

In order to fully study and understand these pans and any other design, we must first look at the action of mechanical filters on the pan face. The discussion on the Tenors will be continued in Section 14.16.

14.11 Mechanical Filters on the Pan face — The Network or Plexus Concept

14.11.1 Filter Definition

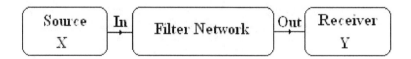

A filter consists essentially of a network of frequency dependent units (*elements*) that provide some form of impedance mismatch or impedance matching when a disturbance (signal or vibration) propagates from one end (the *Source*) of the network to the other end (the *Receiver*). *Attenuation filters* may be designed to *remove* or *attenuate* signals at a prescribed frequency (*a notch filter*), a band of frequencies (*band filter*), a range of frequencies extending from a given maximum down to zero (*high-pass filter*) or a range of frequencies extending upward from a given minimum upwards to infinity (*low-pass filter*). *Transmission filters* are designed to *pass* signals rather than remove them while rejecting others. Filter elements may also be *lossy* or *resistive*.

On the pan, these elements are sections of the internote, each with a characteristic frequency (or a set of frequencies) and the notes, each with their characteristic frequencies (modes of vibration). Both of these elements can act as *resonant absorbers*. For example the G_4 note on a tenor pan will act as a resonant absorber for vibrations (waves) incident on it at the frequency of the G_4 note. These waves could originate from the stick impact on the G_4 note or elsewhere on the pan. All mechanical filters on the pan whether formed from notes or the internote are lossy or resistive. The characteristic frequencies need not be equal to the frequencies of the source and receiver (X and Y respectively) located at the input and output of the network. The path along the internote is itself a distributed element along which vibrational energy is lost as the disturbance propagates from source (X) to receiver (Y). *On the pan, the source (X) and receiver (Y) are <u>not</u> generally interchangeable* — **you cannot, for example, switch the positions of two notes (by re-tuning) without altering their performance and that of the pan generally.**

14.11.2 The Filter Network on the Pan

In the 1980s I worked on the physics of the steelpan as a system of connected oscillatory domains (*notes*) linked by a network of mechanical filters (the *internote*). Most of the early ideas were reported in my seminal paper delivered in 1992 (Achong 1992). In that work, I laid down a number of basic principles that must be incorporated into any correct theory of the steelpan. These served as the guiding principles for the rest of my work that followed.

In Chapter 12, the concept of mechanical impedance was discussed in the context of note vibration and the resulting acoustical radiation. We now extend this concept to the pan face as a whole. This is necessary because the pan face (and skirt) consists of connected domains (see Chapter 5) each of which responds with displacements and velocities that are dependent on the driving frequencies, magnitude and phases of the applied forces (see Section 13.9). For connected domains, there are mutual forces between domains sharing common boundaries that have their origin in the initially applied contact-force at the point of stick-note impact. When a note is played the impact generates a *spectrum of forces* (the *primary forces,* see Section 13.25) — the magnitude of each force component being dependent on frequency — this initiates the first motion in the sounding note. These forces are propagated as waves spreading out from the point of contact.

While the internote as a system behaves linearly, the domains (notes) that are connected through the internote are non-linear systems. When for example a note (represented by X in the above sketch) is excited, signals (waves) corresponding to the key-note and the resident octave are generated. These two signals are generated by two coupled modes within the note X. However, these two signals (you can add the third signal corresponding to the resident twelfth at X) propagate independently through the filter. They experience different degrees of attenuation along the path from X to Y because the impedances comprising the filter network depend on the frequency. It is the linear independence of these signals that allows us to treat the internote as a system of independent mechanical filters.

In addition to the *primary forces* originating directly from the *initial impact* there are *secondary forces* generated by the vibrating notes and internote. These secondary forces are propagated across the pan face (with the speed of sound characteristic of the metal pan face). The disturbances spread away from the impact point and their effect generally diminishes with distance. When the propagating disturbance arrives at a domain (or *element*) whose resonant frequency corresponds to the frequency of a force component in the disturbance, that domain responds resonantly by vibrating with amplitude that is proportional to the magnitude of the component of force. When the frequency of forcing differs from the resonant frequency of the domain, the forced response can be much lower than the resonant response. The *mechanical impedance* Z_m is a measure of how the domain resists this motion when acted upon by a force. The notes themselves resist motion when they are played for the simple reason that the notes prefer (to put it simple) to remain at rest (zero motion); when left alone; that is what they do naturally.

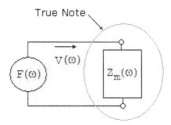

Fig. 14.13. A single note having mechanical impedance $Z_m(\omega)$ is driven by a contact force component $F(\omega)$ to produce a velocity response $V(\omega)$.

Note: *A more complete description of the non-linear processes within the note using the impedance representation will be given later in Section 14.29.*

When a perfectly isolated (blocked) note — an *element* of the system — of mechanical impedance $Z_m(\omega)$ is acted upon by a contact force component $F(\omega)$ at frequency ω, the note responds with a velocity $V(\omega)$ which 'flows' through the system as shown in Figure 14.13. The relationship between these three variables is given by

$$F(\omega) = V(\omega)Z_m(\omega).$$

This is the *elemental equation* relating these three quantities. The mechanical impedance varies with frequency and depends on the mechanical and geometrical characteristics of the note and its supports at the note (the *true note*) boundary. At the frequency of resonance the mechanical impedance is low, being reduced to just its resistive component (see Section 8.11). This means that at resonance, less force is required for the note to move with a given velocity. For the sake of clarity and meaning in this '*lumped parameter*' model of the note-internote system, one can add that the force $F(\omega)$ is defined as an '*across variable*' because it is applied *across* elements in the model, while the velocity $V(\omega)$ is a '*through variable.*' As a through variable, the velocity is considered in the manner of a current that flows *through* the element.

For the isolated note, the velocity response is given by

$$V(\omega) = \frac{F(\omega)}{Z_m(\omega)}.$$

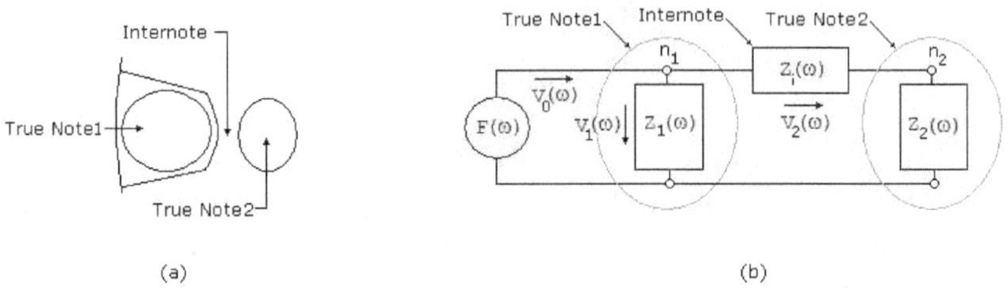

Fig. 14.14. (a) A two-note system (a Marshall Pair) connected by a section of the internote. (b) System representation as two connected velocity loops,

However, since blocking is never perfect, the impacted note, the surrounding internote and nearby notes will also respond to energy transmitted across the pan face from the point of impact. For two nearby notes such as a Marshall Pair (see Figure 14.14(a)), an idealized representation of the two connected velocity loop system is shown in Figure 14.14(b). Every bit of pan face between the two true notes is considered to be part of the internote, including the grooves and bore holes if there are any. [*Some readers may ask, 'how could holes be considered to be part of something?' As you will see in Section 14.12 (Unlocking the Secrets of Blocking), these bore holes possess physical properties that affect the propagation of vibrational waves across the traditional note boundary. These properties make these holes part of the internote.*]

The system in Figure 14.14 is idealized because following the impact, there are multiple paths for the transmitted disturbance and their reflections (*do not* at this point think about transmission by acoustical radiation, transmission is all along the pan face material). The new system is therefore simply an isolated two-note system with a single connection path along the internote; but it is useful, despite the simplifications. The extension to multiple paths is straightforward.

The impact force $F(\omega)$ produces a velocity *'flow'* $V_0(\omega)$ into the system which *'divides'* into two velocity 'flows' $V_1(\omega)$ and $V_2(\omega)$ at the *node* (or *branch point*) n_1 (refer to Figure 14.14(b)). Observe now that the velocity response of the impacted note (true note1) $V_1(\omega)$ is given by the *difference*

$$V_1(\omega) = V_0(\omega) - V_2(\omega),$$

where $V_0(\omega)$ is *related to* the velocity response of the stick tip. At the node or branch point n_1, the velocity divides into two branches, one containing $Z_1(\omega)$ and the other $Z_i(\omega)$ and $Z_2(\omega)$ in series. For the isolated (single) note in Figure 14.14(a) the velocity response $V_0(\omega)$ is always the same as the velocity response of the impacted note. However, when the coupling to a nearby note (the second note) is taken into account, they are generally different by virtue of $V_2(\omega)$ which is the response of the second note and the connecting internote section. The velocity response of the first note is given by

$$V_1(\omega) = \frac{F(\omega)}{Z_1(\omega)}.$$

The total impedance of the note, internote and second note as a sub-system (of the *stick-note system*) seen at the impact point — the *point impedance* — is given by

$$Z_n(\omega) = \frac{Z_1(\omega)[Z_i(\omega)+Z_2(\omega)]}{Z_1(\omega)+Z_2(\omega)+Z_i(\omega)}.$$

With this we get the sub-system response as

$$V_0(\omega) = \frac{F(\omega)}{Z_n(\omega)},$$

from which we get the velocity response of the second note as

$$V_2(\omega) = \frac{F(\omega)}{Z_n(\omega)} - \frac{F(\omega)}{Z_1(\omega)}$$

$$= F(\omega) \left\{ \frac{Z_1(\omega) + Z_2(\omega) + Z_i(\omega)}{Z_1(\omega)[Z_i(\omega) + Z_2(\omega)]} - \frac{1}{Z_1(\omega)} \right\}.$$

This expression can be simplified but I leave it in this form since it shows explicitly (by the negative sign within the curly { } brackets), the division of the velocity response at the node n_1. In this way I can emphasize the 'division of responses' principle and keep it for later use when the number of nodes increases. The factor in curly brackets tends to zero (the terms cancel out) as $Z_i(\omega)$ gets much larger than $Z_1(\omega)$. Therefore we can make the response of the second note as small as we like by simply increasing the internote impedance $Z_i(\omega)$. **The tuner or pan maker must therefore *stiffen* the internote beyond that of the notes themselves by hammer peening (work hardening) the internote area and with the help of grooves if necessary.**

*Note: It is informative at this point to relate this procedure to the note forming process. In forming the notes, the section of pan face on which a note is required — the traditional note area — is forced upward only partially from the underside. The completed forming must be done by peening ('hammering down') the borders of the note from the top side. The dome-shaped notes are **erected** by peening the traditional note boundary downward. In this way the note area does not receive any additional work hardening but the surrounding internote is further work hardened and stiffened by the additional peening it receives. In the end, the note surface is convex upwards, and the surrounding internote areas are stiffened as required. For completeness I should add that the compressive stresses induced along the note boundary by hammer peening, act on the true note hereby reducing the stiffness of the true note. Therefore the surrounding internote appears stiffer than the enclosed note.*

14.11.3 Extending the Concepts to the Stick-Note Impact

To find the velocity response of the stick tip, we introduce a stick-tip impedance $Z_s(\omega)$ and make use of Figure 14.15 which shows the stick-note interaction on impact. At the

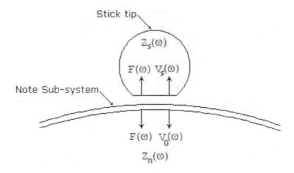

Fig. 14.15. Stick tip of impedance $Z_s(\omega)$ on impact with the note attached to the internote and coupled second note having a total impedance $Z_n(\omega)$. Note and distorted tip shown separated for clarity.

impact point, the stick tip and the note sub-system experiences the same contact force $F(\omega)$ but oppositely directed. The response velocities are also oppositely directed; one producing a compression of the tip, the other a 'downward' displacement of the note surface. Using the elemental equation, and taking the contact-force acting on the note as positive, one gets the relation

$$F(\omega) = V_0(\omega)Z_n(\omega) = -V_s(\omega)Z_s(\omega),$$

giving the stick-tip velocity response

$$V_s(\omega) = -\frac{V_0(\omega)Z_n(\omega)}{Z_s(\omega)}.$$

where the negative sign indicates that $V_s(\omega)$ and $V_0(\omega)$ are in opposite directions. For soft rubber tips and hard steel notes on rigid supports one generally has $Z_s(\omega) \ll Z_n(\omega)$ ensuring that $|V_s(\omega)| \gg |V_0(\omega)|$ and that the tip is more greatly compressed than the note on impact (see Section 13.9.6).

Question: When a note is played, can the panist be aware of or feel the effects of the nearby note(s)?

Answer: We have just shown that the nearby note and internote can affect the stick's response. But can the panist feel this change? Since this is a practical matter and depends on the sensitivity of the player, it is answered with the help of a simple experiment. The following experiment is best performed on the bass where one gets much larger note displacements and the contact-time is longer giving the hand a better chance of 'feeling' the change. Take a good bass stick and play a low bass note (call this the first note; there should be two other notes on your bass pan). Play in the normal fashion and with the same force each time. Do it a few times to get a 'feel' for the sticks response to the impact. Now place sandbags on the other two notes of the pan (two to enhance the effect) or ask a friend to hold down the two notes. The idea is to mute those two notes. Now play the first note in the same manner as you did before. Did you feel the difference in hand-stick sensation? If you did not because you forgot what it felt like the first time, then try this: Close your eyes (for mental concentration) and ask your friend to alternately mute and free the two notes while you play the first note. Got it? (It will work better with good ear plugs to reduce your awareness of the changes in sound sensation.) I can't help you to feel these changes so you are on your own.

I hope that I wasn't too abrupt with that last remark but if you were still unable to detect the presence of the nearby notes, just consider that the stick forms a simple extension of the hand. By this there must be yet another impedance to consider, that of the hand, which is connected to the stick impedance. The hand will therefore experience a response (a velocity) which you will be aware of. If you play cricket or baseball and you are a batsman or batter, when the ball is struck, this is the way in which you can tell if the ball is soft or hard.

14.12 Unlocking the Secret behind the Process of Blocking

14.12.1 Setting the Characteristic Impedance of the Internote in the Neighborhood of the Note

In the answer to the question on feeling the effects of nearby notes, the impedances of the two notes change when the sandbags are added. The extent to which it makes a difference on the stick or on the first note depends on the coupling provided by the internote i.e. on the impedance $Z_i(\omega)$. Muting the two notes effectively 'clamps' them with the result that the first note appears to be attached to a clamped (or more rigid) support. On impact, this difference can be detected by the hand through the stick. Of course the true picture is a bit more complicated because the impedance of the first note (determined by its frequency, hence my call for ear plugs) will change somewhat when the nearby surfaces are held firmly by hand or sandbags (this has to do with the de-localization of the stresses, see Section 8.18).

Before we discuss the role of the tuner in all this, let us see what else we can learn from Figure 14.14(b). We should first work out another expression for the velocity response of the second note. This is given by (the now simpler expression)

$$V_2(\omega) = \frac{F(\omega)}{Z_i(\omega)+Z_2(\omega)},$$

or

$$\frac{V_2(\omega)}{V_1(\omega)} = \frac{Z_1(\omega)}{Z_i(\omega)+Z_2(\omega)}.$$

This last equation is very important (it is consistent with the equation given earlier for $V_2(\omega)$).

- *It tells us that the ratio of the velocity response of the second note (think of the octave in a Marshall Pair) to the velocity response of the first note (the key-note in the pair) can be made very small <u>by making the impedance $Z_i(\omega)$ of the internote large in comparison with the impedance of the first</u>*

note, $Z_1(\omega)$. Here, all impedances are measured at the frequency of the signal transmitted from note 1 to note 2.

The Underlying Principle of 'Locking' or 'Tightening' a note

- *What we have just done is to unlock the secret (or discover the underlying principle) of blocking which, in pan maker's parlance is 'locking the note' or 'tightening the note.' Always remember the example I gave elsewhere; 'tightening' on the pan means the same as in 'tightening security' i.e. to 'contain' the vibrational energy within the area (domain) designated as a note (true note).*

In order to properly block the notes on a pan, as we have just seen, the internote areas must be made dynamically stiffer (at the frequency of the transmitted signal) than the *contained* resonant area forming the true note. We already found that at the resonant frequency of the note the impedance is low, becoming equal to its resistive component only. In Section 12.13, the mechanical impedance of the mass loaded (coated), acoustically radiating note was shown to be

$$Z_m(\omega) = R_m + R_c + R_r + j\left[\omega(m_n + m_c + m_r) - \frac{S_{eff}}{\omega}\right].$$

At the frequency of resonance (ω_0) of the note, the imaginary part (containing j) cancels out giving the resonance frequency

$$\omega_0 = \sqrt{\frac{S_{eff}}{m_n + m_c + m_r}},$$

or in units of Hz

$$f_0 = \frac{1}{2\pi}\sqrt{\frac{S_{eff}}{m_n + m_c + m_r}},$$

and the part that remains is purely resistive

$$Z_m(\omega_0) = R_m + R_c + R_r.$$

If a note is perfectly blocked, then the application of a driving force at the resonant frequency ω_0 will cause the note to respond with a velocity given by

$$V_0(\omega_0) = \frac{F(\omega_0)}{Z_m(\omega_0)} = \frac{F(\omega_0)}{R_m + R_c + R_r}.$$

In order to improve the velocity response (*and hence the loudness*) of the note, the resistance in the denominator on the right side of this equation must be reduced. The resistance can be reduced by the following methods:

1. Do not coat the note or pan face by powder coating, chroming, or nickel plating. If you follow this advice by not powder coating or painting, this will set R_c to zero. Furthermore, chroming and nickel plating introduces a layer of nickel unto both faces of the notes; its elimination will reduce R_m because nickel has a greater magnetomechanical damping capacity than low-carbon steel. This could be a hard decision to make because customers prefer the coating and chroming for the aesthetics and rust proofing they provide. It is hard to reverse a trend! I believe however that many musicians may prefer the louder tones! I would because if I were a panist it would give me greater dynamic range in which to perform! *My advice to pan makers is that they should exercise tight control on the thickness of the nickel plating applied to their pans — they ought to properly advise the Chroming Plant.*
2. Ensure the choice of good material, proper work hardening (sinking) and burning (tempering) in order to reduce R_m. Recall (see Section 9.7.2) that pan material resistive losses are mainly magnetomechanical so that the introduction of inclusions (carbon or nitrides) and defects, to restrict the movement of the magnetic domains, reduce losses. ***Too low a carbon content or nitrogen content (in nitrided steel)***

increases the damping capacity. The same negative effect is produced by too high a tempering temperature or too long a tempering (burning) time.
3. Because acoustic radiation (the goal of pan making) is really a loss effect in the note dynamics, this is a case where you want to maximize R_r (see Sections 12.15 – 12.18).

The section of internote adjacent to the note is deemed to be *stiff* when it shows very little response to an applied force at the resonant frequency (ω_0) of the note. *This is why the Chladni pattern traces out the boundary of the true note — a locus of points of equal dynamic stiffness on the pan face.* For this reason, the pan maker/tuner can be seen to concentrate the peening action on the areas around the true note, listening to its characteristic frequencies and by his ear alone, judged by the response he gets, decides when blocking is adequate. I should be a bit clearer here in explaining the actions of the tuner. When peening the note boundary in the way described here the tuner does not listen to 'individual sound frequencies' instead he listens to the total sound of the hammer impact (the *aural input*) and 'feels' the stiffness of the boundary by the hammer-note and hammer-internote contact sensations communicated to his hand through the hammer. In time, with experience, these two or rather three inputs (including the *visual input*), all work together in a coordinated way. This is what the tuner means when he says 'I know *how* to tune a pan!' **This is the scientifically correct way to do it. Nothing is inferior about the techniques that the pan makers and tuners have developed over the years. Contrary to commercial advertising hype, fancy and expensive tuning equipment do not necessarily guarantee the production of high quality pans. It is not simply a matter of setting a correct set of frequencies on the notes.**

While working on a note, the tuner may find that the note is a bit 'too stiff' and difficulties arise in trying to reduce the frequency to the desired value. This can happen particularly on the outer notes when, with 'over peening' (excessive sinking), the outer region on the higher pans in particular, have been unduly stiffened or work hardened. Sometimes, on a new pan in preparation, the tuner has no other choice but to re-temper the pan by taking it through a short second-burning. This will reduce the effects of work hardening and make the note areas more amenable to tuning.

Too much Carbon

- *Earlier we saw that too little carbon in the steel results in an increase in damping capacity. In the case of too much carbon, work hardening that results from sinking, forming and tuning will result in too hard a material. Difficulties then arise because the note and internote are too close in stiffness. The internote must always be stiffer than the enclosed note. The tuner's freedom in setting the note parameters become very restricted when carbon content is too high. Pan makers would hardly encounter this problem when using commercial steel drums but if they decide to manufacture their own, they can easily test run some sample sheets by indenting the material. If the carbon content is too high then during the sinking (indenting) process, the pan face will work-harden prematurely or long before the proper depth is reached which will provide sufficient surface area on which to form all the notes. The sinker can easily detect the 'saturation' that accompanies early work hardening.*

14.12.2 Employing Grooves

What we have learnt from all this is that *impedance mismatching* plays a crucial role in isolating (blocking) the notes on the pan. Stated in terms of the impedances themselves, the tuner strives to ensure the blocking requirement:

$$\text{Blocking Requirement: } Z_i(\omega) \gg Z_m(\omega)$$

which is realized when the internote is stiff in comparison with the adjacent (or enclosed) note. To assist the pan maker in achieving this he has devised the method of grooving which works in the following way: First, the high curvature of the grooves gives that area an increase in bending stiffness over neighboring areas. This increase in stiffness leads directly to an increase in the internote impedance Z_i. Second, the abrupt change in curvature of the pan face at the grooves induces high levels of stress. Third, consider the transverse vibration (perpendicular to the note surface) of waves propagated away from the note through the section of the adjacent internote towards the groove (refer to the sketch in Figure 14.16). Because of the sharp changes in curvature at the groove, the transverse vibrations are partly transformed (by *mode conversion*) into longitudinal vibrations in the plane of the note surface at the grooves. The result is an attenuated transverse vibration transmitted across the groove. Mode conversion always robs transverse vibrations of its energy at edges, folds and sharp corners.

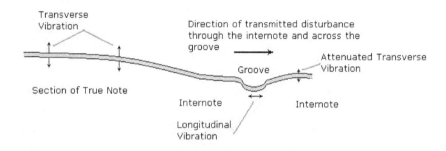

Fig. 14.16. The conversion of transverse vibration into longitudinal vibration at the groove. This results in attenuation of the transmitted transverse vibration.

Mode conversion also operates at the chime to assist in the blocking of transverse vibrational energy to the skirt. Mode conversion also occurs at the bottom edge of the skirt (the free end). But all these conversion processes depends on how the system is excited. If you take a straight metal rod (of steel, brass etc) say a meter long and you strike it along its length, transverse waves are generated, which you can hear by their excitation of the surrounding air. But when these waves travel down the length of the rod they reach the ends of the rod where they are partly converted to longitudinal waves that run up and down the length of the rod. These waves are generally of higher frequencies and are responsible for the ringing sound. Test this out by holding the rod vertically above a hard surface (concrete floor) then allow the rod to slide between your fingers impacting the floor. The high pitched longitudinal waves that run up and down the length of the rod can then be more clearly heard.

On the pan, the longitudinal vibrations are poorly radiated acoustically so that the grooves appear to function as absorbers of transverse vibrational energy transmitted through the internote and across the grooves. In practice the pan maker/tuner may partially flatten out the grooves on the higher pans and rely mostly on the *stress concentrations* that the grooved area provides (rather than its curved geometry) to produce the needed attenuation. The stress concentrations at the grooves scatter the waves incident upon the grooves (see Section 14.12.4). This reduces the propagation of vibrational energy from the excited note to the rest of the pan. In other words it isolates or blocks the note.

In section 17.24 Item 23, the principle by which the grooves act as stiffeners on the internote is explained.

14.12.3 Employing Bore Holes

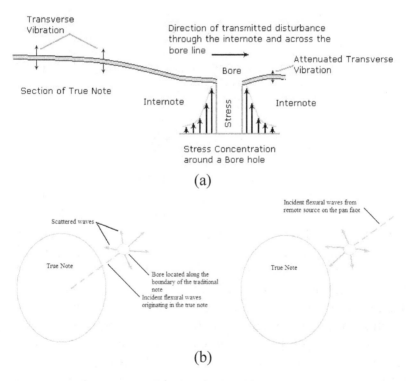

Fig. 14.17. Stress concentration at the bore holes (a) provides additional attenuation by wave scattering (b) of transverse vibration along the bore line on the internote.

Grooves provide similar blocking effects as the bore holes (courtesy of Denzil 'Dimes' Fernandez) (see Figure 14.17) where stress concentrations around the holes produce *wave scattering* on the transmissions across the internote. The effect of a bore hole is of a *localized character*. When vibrational waves propagating through the internote encounters a hole, the waves come upon an area surrounding the hole where the stress is highly concentrated (see Section 2.19). As the waves approach the bore holes they are *scattered* by the intense stress field at the hole location. Since the bore holes outline the boundary of the traditional note, by using these holes, and the wave scattering they produce, one can improve the isolation (blocking) of the true note from the rest of the pan face.

Other Benefits on the Bore Pan: At a 2009 Pan Seminar hosted by Pan Trinbago, with the author as speaker, and attended by pan makers and tuners the author heard from Denzil Fernandez that when he introduced the method of boring holes along the (traditional) note boundary he wasn't quite sure of all its benefits — a mild response from an equally mild mannered gentleman. But it was a stroke of genius because the bore holes introduced areas of compressive stress concentrations along the traditional note boundary exactly where compressive stress is required in order to tune the notes and ensure good isolation of the true note. In addition to providing scattering centers for the waves being transmitted through the internote to the surrounding areas of the pan face (see Figure 14.17(b)), the bores provide significant increase in compressive stress along the boundary that lowers the frequency of the note (see Section 3.12.4). It is therefore possible to significantly reduce the size of the note (traditional note and true note) in order to raise the frequency back to the required value. This means that these smaller notes can be spaced further apart to further reduce note-note coupling as may be desired. Pan makers have observed this size reduction effect. Yet another benefit which always comes with good note isolation and proper energy confinement is the increased acoustical output from these notes. The enhanced isolation provided by the bores allow for good confinement of the vibrational energy which results in an increase in the magnitude of the vibrational velocity on each mode; the acoustical power output, which is proportional to the square of the velocity of vibration, is thereby significantly increased (see Section 12.14). This increase in power output is also observed by pan makers and players.

14.12.4 Effect of Bore Holes and Grooves on Note-Note Coupling

In areas of stress-concentrations (see Section 2.19) as obtained at the bore holes and grooves, it is difficult for the magnetic domains in the material to be rotated. As a result, magnetomechanical damping is reduced in the immediate neighborhood of the holes and grooves. However, since the stress concentrations are confined only to those areas close to the holes or grooves, there will be essentially no resulting reduction in damping for the true note itself. However, the high stress field that grooves and bores produce around the notes will serve as scattering sites (particularly at the holes) for waves travelling through the note material and away from the sounding note (see Figure 14.17 (b), left panel). Unlike the holes which act as *scattering centers* the grooves operate as *barriers* with similar results. This scattering will result in a reduction in the coupling between the sounding note and other notes on the pan face. In addition, the bore holes or grooves surrounding a note will shield the note from waves approaching it from the 'outside.' These approaching waves will be scattered away from the enclosed note (see Figure 14.17 (b), right panel). Bore holes and grooves therefore increases the isolation of notes on the pan by reducing note-note coupling. The immediate and most noticeable effect is an increased loudness of the pan. The increase is more noticeable on the bore pans because of the high stress concentration (x 3) offered by the holes.

14.12.5 Impedance Requirement for Blocking on the Internote — The Blocking Condition

One can consider the internote section adjacent to a note as having a characteristic impedance consisting of a reactive component (by virtue of its *self resonance* observed when 'played') and a resistive component arising from magnetomechanical losses of the material, stress scattering and *mode conversion* (from transverse to longitudinal motion at the groove) to give an expression

$$Z_i(\omega) = R_m + R_{sg} + j\left[\omega m_i - \frac{S_i}{\omega}\right],$$

where R_m is the magnetomechanical resistance, R_{sg} is the effective resistance due to losses caused by stress scattering and mode conversion at the groove, m_i is the *equivalent mass* of the section of internote and S_i is the *effective stiffness* of the internote section. In this equation, acoustical radiation from the internote (which is minor or negligible on a good pan) is neglected. The resonant frequency of the section of internote adjacent to the true note is given by

$$\omega_i = \sqrt{\frac{S_i}{m_i}}.$$

(*Perhaps it would be wise to include acoustic radiation in order to deal with situations where pan face preparation is bad and excessive vibrations take place on the internote. In this case a radiation mass m_{ir} must be added to m_i and a radiation resistance R_{ir} must be added to to $R_m + R_{sg}$.*) It is important to set the resonant frequency of the internote *higher* than that of the note, by making S_i sufficiently larger than S_{eff} on the note, to give the

$$\text{blocking condition;} \quad \frac{S_i}{m_i} > \frac{S_{eff}}{m_n + m_c + m_r}$$

or

$$\text{blocking condition;} \quad \omega_i > \omega_0.$$

At the resonant frequency of the note (set lower than that for the section of internote) the impedance of the internote can be made larger (sometimes much larger) than the impedance of the note which is now very low (being equal only to its resistive part) which is the condition required for blocking. Hammer peening work hardens the internote, which increases its stiffness — *that's what all the hammering is all about as the pan maker/tuner tunes the notes on a pan.* This has to be tied in with the *saturation* (see Section 2.8) attained during sinking. Saturation is part of the microstructural control (see Section 9.8) offered by hammer peening. Saturation is important in order to establish the *blocking condition* $\omega_i > \omega_0$. (*Observe here that with the inclusion of radiation losses from the internote, where m_i is replaced by $m_i + m_{ir}$, with the lowering of the internote resonance frequency ω_i, the two conditions above, are <u>more difficult</u> to achieve. The lesson to be learnt here is that poor pan face preparation results in poor blocking.*)

A good example of the application of this blocking condition is shown in Figure 3.2 where *Advanced Tuning* (as developed by Randolph Leroy Thomas) is employed. In the examples of Figure 3.2, the inner internote area of the $C^\#_4$ note is tuned to $G^\#_5$, the inner internote of the $F^\#_4$ note is tuned to $C^\#_5$, etc. In each case the internote is tuned to a frequency higher than the adjacent note. I have seen this technique working very effectively on the 'very loud' pans made by Randolph Thomas. See the discussion in Section 14.43.1.

The effective stiffness S_{eff} is dependent on the compressive stress applied along the note boundary. Since the pan face, chime and skirt exist in static equilibrium, the compressive stresses over the pan face will be in equilibrium with the hoop stress along the chime and skirt (see *Sections 2.16 and 17.20*).

The present analysis provides us with a definition for the process of blocking which we now state:

- **Blocking** is the introduction of *mechanical impedance mismatch* between the true notes and the internote area by hammer peening and with the assistance of grooves or bores. In this mismatch, the impedance of the internote is made higher than the impedance of the adjacent note by increasing the effective stiffness of the internote relative to that of the note.

14.12.6 Mass Loading on the Internote — not recommended. Mass Loading acceptable on the Skirt.

From the expression $\omega_i = \sqrt{(S_i/m_i)}$ one sees that if the choice is made to use mass loading (see Chapter 11) on the internote, this has the effect of lowering the resonant frequency of that section of the internote containing the attached mass. It is therefore likely to conflict with the requirement $\omega_i > \omega_0$. (The same thing happens when the pan face preparation is poor and excessive internote vibrations occur as discussed earlier.) For this reason it is *not advisable* that mass loading be used as a method for blocking. ***If a section of internote located remotely from the note in question is found to vibrate sympathetically with a sounding note it is the result of poor preparation and faulty tuning***. (For a special exception to this see *Advanced Tuning* in Section 14.43.1.) While mass loading can bring relief in such a case, problems may arise when the instrument has to be re-tuned at a later date as surely it must. During the re-tuning exercise the mass loading may require readjustment (upward or downward in mass as well as changes in position of the attached mass). Mass loading on the internote is really a method for achieving a temporary 'fix.' *It cannot stand as a recommended procedure.*

The situation on the skirt is quite different. In Chapter 5, it was shown that note-skirt problems can arise when the skirt spectrum contains a resonant mode close to the frequency of a note on the pan face. Mass loading applied to the skirt was recommended as a permanent cure. This works fine because future adjustments to the attached mass will not be required. (I made this recommendation to pan makers in 1999 with the suggestion that auto wheel-balancing weights be used. I am aware that a number of pan makers have adopted this technique.)

14.12.7 Blocking Problems on Completely Press-formed Pan Face plus Notes

It is not a policy of the present author to highlight erroneous claims made by inventors and writers on the steelpan. However, where such claims have been highly publicized and by reason of the eagerness of pan enthusiasts to 'grab' at all information presented to them, I sometimes must make an exception. Chapter 17 deals in detail with such a case. In the present Section I mention, but do not identify with any reference, the claim made in one patent application for a pan forming process that includes not only the indentation of the pan face by a forming process but also the simultaneous formation of notes with geometrical forms 'copied' from pans tuned by well established pan makers! I am only concerned with the technical aspects of this claim.

Using the information in Sections 14.12.1 – 6 one can clearly see the reason for the pan maker's adoption of a note-forming process in which the boundaries defining the traditional notes (the grooves, if used) are hammer peened 'downward' on the 'top-side' of the pan face, causing the note to 'rise' from the indented pan face. The notes are never formed by peening from the underside; that is to say 'by knocking the notes out from the bottom-side.' To press-form a pan face complete with notes, the mold must be built with shapes that would cause the notes to be pushed 'upward' relative to the pan face being depressed. Sure enough you end up with what looks like a fully formed pan face complete with note but the big question is, *what is inside*?

Something that looks like a pan is not necessarily a pan! I call these things 'dummies' and I would not dare even to call them 'dummy pans'! These 'dummies' do not possess the required increased stiffness on the internote nor the necessary stress distributions relative to the 'notes' — *blocking conditions will be difficult if not impossible to establish*. To bring some functional semblance to a 'pan' the tuner would have to completely rework these dummies (I would personally advise that they not be used at all!).

- *It is clear that 'copying' note shapes is a waste of time.*
- *Press forming panface plus notes will not produce anything close to the desired state of 'tuned notes' in fact it burdens the tuner with more work. 'Detailing' has been ignored.*
- *Anyone planning to introduce a new pan making technique that involves press forming both the pan face and the notes using single or multiple die must take note of the statements immediately above!*

If it is the intention of the manufacturer of these 'dummies,' to use them only for sale at "tourist attractions' then such activity could inflict much damage on those industries featuring high-grade pan instruments. I am not being too harsh here neither would I be if I were to recommend that these 'dummies' be labeled for what they really are!

14.13 **Vibration Processes at the Chime**

As already noted, at the chime, the transverse vibrations arriving from an outer note is partially converted to in-plane longitudinal vibration. The mode conversion is depicted in Figure 14.18. The partially reflected vibrations consist of a mixture of transverse and weaker longitudinal modes. The transmitted component reaching the skirt also consists of a mixture of modes.

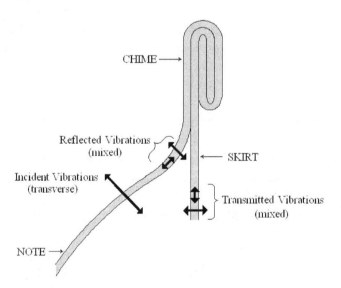

Fig. 14.18. Transverse vibrations from an outer note, incident on the chime is partially reflected as a mixture of transverse and longitudinal modes and partially transmitted as a mixture of these two modes. Amplitudes not to scale.

Because the chime itself will vibrate to some degree in mixed modes, the chime does not represent a perfect node, and the reflected transverse component is not exactly in anti-phase with the incident vibrations. Similarly, the transmitted transverse component is not exactly in phase with the incident vibrations. The shifts in phase are a result of the mode conversion process and absorption (losses) that take place at the chime. Because the in-plane longitudinal components of vibration are inefficient acoustical radiators the mode conversion process at the chime represents an energy loss. If the chime is partially open near a particular outer note (see Sections 2.10 and 2.11), considerable energy can be transferred from the note to the loose vibrating section of chime. But equally important is the transverse component of vibration transmitted from the loose chime, back to the note. This can be sufficiently strong to drive the sounding note to a different frequency of vibration. When this happens, *the affected note(s) cannot be tuned.* (See Chapter 5 for similar effects).

When notes affected in this way by a faulty chime are played, the response is usually one that begins close to the note frequency then changes to the driving frequency of the nearby vibrating loose section of the chime. The mechanical impedance of the note cannot then be uniquely defined because of the compound nature of the note-chime system.

Pan makers must pay special attention to the chime (see Chapter 2) to ensure the rigidity and soundness of this component of the pan.

14.14 Note Placements and Note-Note Coupling across the Pan Face

14.14.1 Transmission across the Pan face

When considering two notes (source and receiver) situated right across the pan face, one may have reasons to consider multiple paths. The result is that a number of different signals may reach the receiving note having traveled different paths from the source. At the receiving note, each of these signals will have its own amplitude and phase. The receiver's response can then be determined by summing the responses over these different signals. We now focus on one of these paths and assume that it is the most important one, possibly the most direct and shortest path. We ignore the contributions from any other longer path but a similar analytical treatment applies to each of them. With reference to Figure 14.19, the source is the true note labeled X while the receiver note is labeled Y (their impedances $Z_m(\omega)$ are different). There are internote sections having impedances $Z_i(\omega)$ (not necessarily all the same) and connecting notes having impedances $Z_m(\omega)$ (all different).

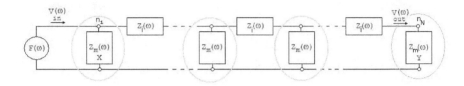

Fig. 14.19. Typical filter path between the driven note X and the receiving note Y. Sections of the internote are represented by the lumped parameter $Z(\omega)$.

At the impact point on note X the system response velocity $V_{in}(\omega)$ divides at the first node n_1, a process that continues at all the intermediate nodes until one reaches the final N^{th} note Y where the response velocity is $V_{out}(\omega)$. Since the response divides (and therefore diminishes) at each of the N-1 nodes, the output response at Y can be very small depending on the impedances seen at each node. In this fashion, the path along the pan face functions as a *'velocity divider'* or *'splitter'* at each of the N-1 nodes. The force on the far-away note Y is given by

$$F_Y(\omega) = V_{out}(\omega)Z_{m,Y}(\omega),$$

this can be very small because of the low response at Y. What we are primarily interested in is the division of the response at successive nodes. It tells us that the longer the path, and the more intermediate notes and internote sections there lie between X and Y, the greater is the isolation between Y and X.

In this simple configuration, the note Y can function as the source and the note X as the receiver. While running in the X→Y mode, the note X will transfer energy to Y preferably at its resonant frequency after it is excited by the force $F(\omega)$. But in order to do this effectively, the driving force frequency must be equal to or be within the bandwidth of the resonant frequency of X (see Sections 13.25 to 13.27 on *Contact Force Spectrum*). A similar thing holds for the excitation of Y if it were to transfer energy to X. But seeing that the resonant frequencies of X and Y may be different, the process of energy transfer via these long paths is not very effective. For a Marshall Pair for example $\{B_4:B_5\}$ with wide separation of its members (say across the pan face) and with X as B_4, Y as B_5, the transfer of energy between the resident octave on B_4 to the B_5 (the octave) is greatly diminished by the division of responses at nodes along the path and the absorption of energies by the resistive components of the impedances along the path. The reverse transfer from B_5 to the resident octave on B_4 is similarly diminished.

Our analysis has shown that if the tuner chooses to reduce or avoid sympathetic vibration on the pan, it is safe to 'hide' the second note from the first by placing it at the far end of a long path across the pan face. This 'hiding' effect is more efficient when there are intermediate notes along the connecting path(s); for *at each note there will be a velocity dividing node.*

14.14.2 'Hiding' as a Mechanism for Isolating Notes

The Invaders Tenor and un-named pans of similar design

An obvious 'oddity' on the Invaders Tenor is the $F^\#$ note near the middle of the pan, in fact the pan itself is also known as the $F^\#$ pan. My first feeling on watching this pan was the temptation to 'try out' that 'attention drawing' $F^\#$ note in the middle of the pan. You can't resist the temptation! But it is not just this note that makes this tenor different; it is the wide variation in the note positions (see Figure 14.20). A careful study of these positions shows that with few exceptions, Mannette was attempting to isolate the octaves from their key-notes as much as possible — *on the Invaders Tenor, octaves always seem to be hiding behind other notes.* In the early 1960s Herman Johnson and others did precisely the same thing. On the pan, this is an effective way to isolate notes because the *internote* acts as a more effective mechanical filter when the path between two notes is filled with notes of different frequencies. These intervening notes and sections of the internote distributed along the path linking a pair of notes (see Figure 14.21) identified by their frequencies act as *resonant absorbers*. Since a note is tuned to a definite set of frequencies, the notes that are not played but are arranged along a connecting path, act as resonant absorbers with maximum effect at their tuned frequencies. It is not necessary for the resonant frequencies of these absorbers to match the frequency of X or Y but their presence modifies the mechanical impedance (which measures the resistance of the structure to motion when acted upon by an applied force, see Section 14.11) along the path. It is important however, that the resonant frequencies of these absorbers *do not* match that of either X or Y — this may occur during the early stages of tuning but is removed as the tuning progresses.

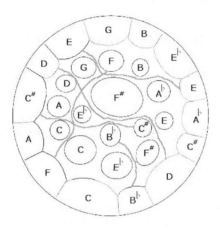

Fig. 14.20. Some long paths along the internote connecting pairs (**B♭:B♭**}, {**D:D**}, {**E:E**}, {**F:F**}. In reality there are multipath connections between any pair of notes.

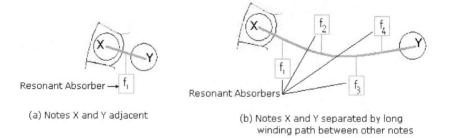

Fig. 14.21. Mechanical filters arranged as a network of elements along the internote linking two notes X and Y. The path itself (━━━) consists of distributed elements. Sections of the internote and other notes along the path act as resonant absorbers. (a) Adjacent notes, (b) widely separated notes.

When the two notes are adjacent (juxtaposed) as in the case of the Standard Tenor and in some instances on the Invaders Tenor, the situation is depicted in Figure 14.21(a) where the internote separating the two notes (to be more precise, the true notes) alone acts as the filter. On a properly prepared pan it is hardly likely for any resonance with f_1 to occur on the internote, unless the preparation is poor (see Section 2.5 for discussions on *Sinking*). If resonances occur at other locations, severe absorption of the note vibrational energy may occur at those locations. The internote in (a) is always subjected to intense peening in order to block the notes. In addition, grooves or bores may be found within the internote. As we saw earlier, grooves do something *similar* to bores by introducing areas of increased stress concentrations. ***It is therefore not necessary to use both grooves and bores together.*** (*In fact take the recommendation and **do not groove your bore pan**; if you do, you could present yourself with the problems of stress fractures and corrosion along the groove connecting the holes* starting from the underside (see Sections 2.18 – 2.21). Blocking is the introduction of *mechanical impedance mismatch* between the true notes and the internote area by hammer peening and with the assistance of grooves or bores.

In the case of long paths as in Figure 14.21(b) on the Invaders Tenor, one finds a number of distributed absorbers — it is 'behind' these absorbers that the notes are 'hiding'. There will be much attenuation of the vibrations transmitted along the path between X and Y thus ensuring good isolation of the notes. But 'hiding' is not a feature found only on the Invaders Tenor, other pans make effective use of it, sometimes in subtle ways. This brings us to the Nine Bass.

The Nine Bass

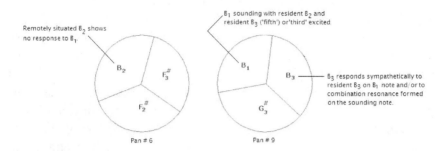

Fig. 14.22. The B_2 note is located remotely on pan #6 of the Nine Bass while the B_1 and B_3 are on the #9 pan. This arrangement allows for an interesting effect when the B_1 is played (see text).

On the standard *Nine Bass* (see Figures 14.12 and 14.22), the B_1 note is found on the No. 9 pan while the octave B_2 is hidden all the way over on the No. 6 pan! These two notes operate independently because the connecting path between them is through the air medium which, in this case, will be ineffective as a means of coupling the two pans. When B_1 is played, the adjacent B_3 responds in sympathy with (i) the resident twelfth (itself a weak B_3 mode) on the same area as the B_1 note and (ii) the combination resonance of B_1 and the weak resident octave on the same area as the B_1 note. The ear of the listener (more precisely the listener's *brain*) must now insert its own 'missing' B_2 tone to complete the whole tone (B_1, B_2, B_3) — this is what I mean by 'Subtle is the Pan.' This is a purely psychoacoustic effect which adds greater *perceived depth* to the bass tone. If the resident twelfth (or the tuner's 'fifth') is not used and the 'third' is used instead (see Section 14.26) then the sympathetic vibration of B_3 in response to B_1 is due to method (ii) given earlier. Another example is found on pan No. 4 of the Nine Bass with the $B^\flat_1$ and $B^\flat_3$ notes; in fact there is no $B^\flat_2$ note on any of the pans forming the Nine Bass — the $B^\flat_2$ is hidden to the point where no one can find it! It must be noted however, that the extent to which these 'missing octaves' are perceived psycho-acoustically, depends on the listener.

It is also possible to find that the very well experienced bass tuner may not perceive these 'missing octaves' at all! This comes about by training where over the years a tuner develops a very selective sense of hearing which allows him to hear the individual components of the tone — a necessary requirement for tuning. This acuteness actually prevents the tuner from hearing these *perceived* tones. The only octave heard by this tuner is the weak resident octave on the $\mathbf{B}_1$ (or $\mathbf{B}^\flat{}_1$) note. This is the price a good tuner must pay in order to develop his skill but he ought not to feel too bad about it because the same thing happens to Bell tuners who can't even hear the low modulated tones of a sounding bell that we all so much enjoy! I should also point out that two persons standing close to any one of these notes (the $\mathbf{B}_1$ or the $\mathbf{B}^\flat{}_1$) as it is played on the Nine Bass could perceive different sounds. You must take this seriously because these same two persons may comment differently on these notes; one may give high praise while the other might say 'well ....' The second person who obviously (to us that is) did not perceive the 'missing octave' knows that something is missing but he doesn't know what! A third person with the gift of aural perception, who hears everything (!), may say that for a bass note he finds the octave and twelfth (he really means the $\mathbf{B}_3$) are too strong! If you were the player, would you change your bass sticks because of the last comment? If your answer is 'why should I, the notes sound just right to me' then I commend you because you have responded correctly!

Back to Hiding

*Because of the great utility in the concept of the 'hiding' arrangement, I take this opportunity to introduce this new term '**Hiding**' into the list of pan production terms such as '**Burning**', '**Sinking**', '**Stretching**' and '**Blocking**' used to describe other important processes.*

With this new term in our Pan vocabulary, our understanding of note placements can be much clearer and with it, the mystery of the Invaders Tenor is solved.

14.15 More on Blocking

At this point, some readers (*not including the one that races ahead of me*), might be asking themselves the question 'what about interaction between the notes by acoustical radiation transmitted through the air medium?' This is a very good question because some readers may have already developed mental pictures of this going on 'above' the pan face. It does 'go on' but let us see at what level. The acoustical radiation exists and we can readily confirm it because that is what the pan is all about, we can hear the instrument whenever it is played. But when a note of frequency f_a (the source) is sounding, the acoustical pressure generated in the air above a second note (the receiver) of a different frequency f_b can only cause an excitation (at a level that is of immediate concern to us) if the frequencies f_a and f_b overlap by virtue of their frequency bandwidths. We also consider the following two cases:

(i) On a single pan, there are *no* two notes with the same key-note frequency, however, acoustical coupling may exist between the key-notes and higher modes of related notes (such as on Pairs and Triples) — for example between the resident octave on the B_4 note and the key-note on the B_5 note. Between nearby but separate pans, feeble secondary excitations may occur between notes of similar frequency but this is not our concern here (it is natural to expect this but it is not of any musical use even in a large steel orchestra). In these cases the coupling is linear. But more importantly, using the example, the resident octave on the B_4 note (with its anti-phase motion of the note surface) is not an efficient acoustical radiator and in addition, the acoustical impedance mismatch between the air medium and the B_5 note results in very low acoustical excitation of B_5. The excitation of the B_5 note by the B_4 note by transmission along the internote separating the two notes on the pan face is *more efficient*, despite blocking. In fact that's how the Marshall Pairs operate and I must emphasize here that sympathetic motion between Marshall Pairs *do not* work by acoustical radiation coupling.

Note: *Strictly speaking this result applies to the far-field acoustical radiation. In Section 12.11.3 it was shown that the crossover between the near field region and the far field R_{ff} satisfies the condition*

$$1.4cm \lesssim R_{ff} \lesssim 3cm.$$

This range of distances is readily exceeded by the distance separating the apex of notes found on all pans. It is therefore safe to use the far field approximation in the above discussion.

(ii) At the level of normal pan note excitation by stick impact, it is even more unlikely for excitation to occur non-linearly through the medium of acoustical radiation. In our example, the key-note of the **B**$_5$ note experiences very feeble acoustical excitation at its resonance frequency from the key-note on the **B**$_4$ — where **B**$_4$ is somewhat of a sub-harmonic of **B**$_5$ (neglecting detuning). This relates to the case of non-linear excitation of a system by a sub-harmonic (generally with detuning), which, to be effective on the pan will require greater levels of forcing than what is available through acoustical coupling of notes.

*(Despite this I have often been told by players that they have found that by playing the **B**$_5$ note they can hear and even feel the **B**$_4$ note vibrating. This is always the case where the direct transference of impact energy from the point of impact to the neighboring notes has taken place across the pan face. It is not a note-note interaction. Remember that the **B** note is just an example, you can replace it with **C**, **D**, **E** etc.)*

14.16 Return to the Tenors — Note Placement Rule

What then are the criteria for note placement and distribution? I believe that even as I write, there is someone working on some new distribution. Certainly, merely rotating the pan does not create anything new. No one that I know will even say that a new tenor has been created if you rearrange a note or two slightly (even swapping them) on the Invaders Tenor — *cosmetic changes do not count* —

although the two pans will be just that slightly different. The two major procedures for placing and isolating notes have been incorporated in the Standard Tenor — the use of the *Circle of Fifths* and *internote filters,* and on the Invaders Tenor — *Hiding* with enhanced *internote filters* using notes along the path. The use of grooves and bores are part of internote filtering. Development on the Standard Tenor concept is much easier than on the Invaders Tenor concept. It is much easier to work out a new placement of notes using the former idea than to attempt the same with the latter idea.

Most of what I wish to discuss in the following paragraphs hinges on whether or not I can find (or there exists) *a consistent note placement rule* for the Invaders Tenor so I must come clean. *I must admit my failure to come up with a placement rule that the Invaders Tenor follows* i.e. a rule which when applied tells you exactly where a new note or pair of notes should be placed. (*Perhaps our racing reader may claim to have found one! Let's see!*) Of course there is a placement rule for all the notes identified on the Invaders Tenor taken together, it simply says: 'Place the identified notes in the positions drawn on the plan shown in Figure 14.4, left panel'. But since this amounts to the same thing as saying that the pan is unique, by itself, it is not really helpful. The reason for my failure stems from the fact that *the Invaders arrangement is one among others (in fact, many others, if you have the patience to find them) that function just as effectively.* Its 'uniqueness' runs only so far as the fact that it is the only design with that particular note placement — not unique in its functionality or mode of operation when compared with similar pans in the genre. If, for example, we were to increase the size of the pan face on the Invaders Tenor to place an extra note and its octave, can we say for certainty where they should be placed or are there a number of possibilities? If the arrangements in the set of possibilities are equally favorable then choosing one can be done randomly. But notice that note placements are not done randomly. In fact, on the Invaders Tenor, a set of different procedures are followed. Take for example the *Triple* (or *whole note*) $\{C_4:C_5:C_6\}$, the pairs $\{C_4:C_5\}$ and $\{C_5:C_6\}$ are arranged adjacently, same for $\{D_4:D_5\}$ and a few others, but there is a larger number of pairs with their members much displaced — each member of a 'distant pair' forming two single notes. No consistent rule follows from the notes arrayed on the Invaders Tenor. Is one necessary?

This all depends on what a rule is expected to represent, what set of instructions it is intended to convey. The only rule that can be consistently applied is the *General Rule* which says that 'notes of well defined frequencies must be *isolated* from each other'. All pans follow this rule. How it is implemented depends on the pan maker. (*Now the reader who keeps racing ahead of me will certainly not see where I am headed.*) It is therefore the pan maker who sets his own pattern of notes as clearly shown by the many note arrangements that have been devised over the years and will continue as man maintains his inventiveness.

Of course readers may ask 'what is the optimum arrangement?' (*The racing reader may have already provided an answer.*) But, *musical criteria of this sort are always subjective, being dependent upon what musical standpoint one adheres to.* As a result **there is no definitive answer**! We must accept the fact that many arrangements are practicable and one can safely say, *equally effective.* This explains my failure (and quite possibly yours) of finding a consistent placement rule for the Invaders Tenor (C-Pan).

Note: *Arguments of the type just presented, easily lend themselves to subjectivity. But to be safe, I clearly set my purpose which was to find any possible rule that applies on a consistent basis to the placement of notes on the pan face of the Invaders Tenor. If I had included some definition of 'effectiveness' then I would have placed myself in some trouble. It is hard to maintain an objective position in this case because in musical matters, each reader has his/her own preference (or prejudice if you like). It is therefore left to the individual reader to insert his/her meaning to the expression 'equally effective'. Having read the text to this point if you now go back to the preceding paragraphs with your prejudices, you may find that you now hold a different position on 'equally effective' but this will not lead you closer to finding an optimum arrangement to which all readers (armed with their individual prejudices) can agree to. Is there an 'open minded' position? I believe there is and that it consists of holding a position that allows us to accept both the Standard Pan format, that of the Invaders Tenor and any other* *format that shows some degree of promise. This is the position that I hope we maintain. It is the closest that we can get to 'objectivity'.*

14.17 On New Pan Types

I believe a pan maker sees the need for a new pan type, not for the purpose of having his name attached to the instrument, but from what he discovers while observing the orchestral performance of the instruments. New pans are always designed from the need to fill 'musical holes' in a steel orchestra or to extend the reaches of existing instruments. However, there are restrictions on the latter and they are purely physical: (i) A player has only two hands to hold one stick each (*the holding of an extra stick between the fingers of a player, as originally introduced in a serious manner by Bertie Marshall, has now been reduced to merely an act for 'show' as revealed to me by a renown panist (not Bertie). I did indicate in the beginning, that this book is about unlocking secrets!* (ii) Extending the musical range on a pan, up or down, poses problems with the stick-note interaction (see Chapter 13). The limits placed on the musical range of a pan of a given type arise precisely because of the dynamics of stick-note impacts. There are rules, in fact laws governing the choice of sticks in relation to the frequencies of the notes to be played (see Chapter 13).

14.18 The Development of Tones that Define the Pan

On the islands of Trinidad and Tobago, the development of the steelpan from the 1930s to the 1980s was intimately bound up with the parallel evolution of calypso music. During this development, steelpan music was specially written with the calypso beat. The pan was then adapted to classical music and more lately, has been used in jazz. The input provided by calypso in particular, makes it difficult to determine whether pan music directed the pan makers or pan makers directed the musicians. The late Calypsonian, Aldwyn Roberts, better known as 'Lord Kitchener', arguably the greatest of all composers of pan music, would have admitted (the author believes), that it was the latter. The form, both physical and musical, given to the pan over the decades, remains the standard by which present-day pans are made.

The sound of the present-day steelpan is best described by the expression *'pan is beautiful.'* Although such a description contains subjective qualities, these qualities can be correlated with objective, physical quantities. These objective quantities (or *parameters*) which give pan tones their character are to be found on all pan types, from the tenor at the high end to the bass at the low end. In this Section on Tuning, the main parameter— the *detuning parameter*—is given special attention.

One must assume that the instrument to be analyzed has the fundamental (key-note) on each note properly tuned to correspond in frequency to the notes on the musical scale. The higher partials on each note are then tuned in a manner that brings them into a close *but not exact* harmonic relationship with the fundamental. This author, in previous publications, has unraveled the 'mystery' behind the tonal structure of steelpan notes by showing that the higher partials are never tuned into exact harmonicity. Despite this observation, pan makers and tuners refer to the process of tuning the higher partials as *'tuning the harmonics' — a contradiction of terms.* The partials are tuned slightly higher or lower than the harmonic frequency but the differences are so small, that taken alone cannot always be detected even by the trained musical ear of the tuner or on most frequency meters used by the tuners. What the tuner/maker detects are the resulting audible changes in the amplitude and frequency modulation structures. But I know for a fact that at the time of writing, both Anthony Williams and Bertie Marshall could decide on the correctness of a note to within *one cent*!

Unlike a Stradivarius, there is no special wood or varnish, no special steel, no special brass or aluminum (the most recent materials introduced at the experimental level), but like the Stradivarius, there is something special in the dynamics. **The secret is in the dynamics.** If one can prepare two notes of different material (metals) but executing identical dynamical motions, the tonal structure of the direct sound from these notes will be indistinguishable. The choice of material will however, influence the damping rate and limit the strength of the stick impact both of which can be used in a series of runs to differentiate the type of material used in the construction.

If the reader is puzzled by these statements, consider the following: Recorded sounds are played back using loud speakers. During playback, the stored information (on magnetic tape or disks, CD's or DVD's) are transformed into electrical signals then to mechanical vibrations of the loudspeaker cones (usually paper cones) and finally to acoustical radiations into the air medium. If it were pan music, then we could clearly identify the sound of each instrument and recognize these sounds as true steelpans. But these sounds are produced (or reproduced) by paper cones not the metal surfaces of real pan notes. Yet we recognize them as 'genuine' pan sounds! The explanation is simple; the paper cones were driven to execute dynamical motions that mimic that on the real pan note — or more precisely the audio sound generated from the real notes as picked up by the recording microphone. You cannot identify the type of paper used to make the paper cones or the cellulose of which the paper is composed. In like manner, in the sound of the real steelpan, you cannot determine or hear the carbon content, not even the iron itself in the note material. I have to make these points because I know that there are those who believe that the sound of the steelpan comes by virtue of the material composition or content. In this book whenever the opportunity presents itself I clear up misconceptions of this sort (see Achong 2000b).

14.19 Gradation of Tones

14.19.1 Introduction

To introduce this Section I now write the only two pieces of music that will appear in this book. The first is the opening notes of Beethoven's *Symphony No. 5 in C Minor*, which we can, most surely, sing out without accompaniment;

Now I ask, how should these opening notes be played by a Steel Orchestra?

An *equally enchanting* and familiar opening is the clarinet *trill* followed by the 17-note *legato* (smooth, closely connected tones) rising diatonic scale (the *gliss*) in George Gershwin's *Rhapsody in Blue*;

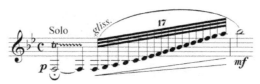

p — *piano (soft), mf* — *mezzo-forte (moderately strong)*

Readers should listen to the masterly execution of this opening by Clarinetist Ricardo Morales of the New York Philharmonic Orchestra (2011 production). The discrete tones on the steelpan may not allow the panist to execute a smooth glide through the 17 notes even when the notes are played in the familiar roll. The breaks between notes will be clearly audible. It will however, be interesting to see (hear) how closely a select group of panists playing sequentially with overlap, could get to rendering an acceptable opening to this Rhapsody. I may be asking too much on this one seeing that this clarinet glissando opening has become standard performance practice for the work. I am certainly not underestimating the artistry of our panists, just throwing out a challenge!

As a boy, listening to orchestral music on our home 5-tube General Electric radio or on one of my own home-built radios (we had no TV in those days!), I would conjure up mental pictures of the great composers writing their music. In my mind, by the mental pictures conveyed to me by the music, I would see Beethoven 'painting' with a large brush using wide curving sweeps, lifting the brush at the end of each sweep then bringing it down swiftly and forcefully. Mozart would appear with a small brush, artfully dabbing on the 'paint' here and there as a beautiful 'picture' grows out of the dabs as if he had the entire composition in all its detail all at once in his head for he never missed a stroke. The mental pictures, for me, depicted the style of the composer!.But always, it came across to me, as pleasurable excitement and joy. There were mental images for Chopin and Mozart as my eldest sister Andrea played the piano and for Bach and Beethoven as my elder brother

Dave played the violin (he mastered all the instruments in our home including the clarinet and the steelpan). I can still hear Andrea's renditions of *Chopin - Nocturne in E Flat Major* and *Mozart – The Piano Sonata No. 16 in C Major,* and the adroit Dave on his renditions of *Leonard Bernstein – Tonight, from Westside Story, Beethoven – Minuet in G* and that other minuet, *Bach - Minuet in G Major*! Whenever I hear *Chopin – Étude Op. 10, No. 3 in E Major*, I remember my father, Anthony Zachariah Cosma Achong, who, as the feeling moved him, would go to the piano and play the opening and first line of this, perhaps Chopin's loveliest of compositions — my dad never went beyond the first line! I was an unusual listener, visualizing the music as my brother or sister played their instruments. One of my most favored pieces was *Liszt – Liebestraum Nocturne No. 3* (you should listen to the more recent renditions by *Lang Lang* and by the young *Evgeny Kissin*). This piece always caught my attention and I would have to stop to listen at home or even outdoors when it was played on a neighbor's radio for in those days, Trinidadians loved to turn up the volume on their radios. There was always a continuous sound of music in our home; Roland, my eldest brother on the guitar or even me, alone in some secluded area, strumming out on the cuatro, some chords I copied from my brothers. I couldn't handle the strings of Roland's mandolin or his banjo!

So what's your answer to the question on Symphony No. 5? To play the *opening* of Beethoven's Symphony No. 5 on a single instrument (say violins only) is to swap brushes between Beethoven and Mozart! To Beethoven, you give a narrow brush where he naturally prefers a broad brush to cover as much of the *musical space* as possible in a fast, lively (*Allegro*) and vigorous (*Brio*) action. Remember that the broad brush can dab just as well as in the first three repeated notes (listen to it or sing it carefully). Then comes the longer broader sweep with the last note. You can, with pleasure, interpret it differently. To announce with depth and forcefulness what is to follow in the Fifth Symphony, I would play these opening notes using almost all the instruments in the orchestra. So how are we to do this in a Steel Orchestra with percussive pans only? We need a *broad brush of pans*! Oops! Did I say a 'broad brush of pans'? That's my way of describing the musical voicing of multiple pan tones simultaneously in one sweep.

Listen carefully to the cellos when this phrase is sounded! In meaning and interpretation it is almost an entire sentence! I can hear the cellos so I hope you can! Pan cellos are wonderful for this type of thing especially when paired with a complement of two or more quadraphonic pans.

To achieve the effect of different instruments with pans there has to be a number of sections in the steel orchestra; with a smooth *gradation of tones* from tenor to bass. *Gradation of tones* must not be confused with *musical range*. It is what I call the *'whole sound'* or *'characteristic sound'* of the instruments which involves *musical range*, *tonal color* and the *nuances* associated with the panist's touch. **How can we vary the instrumental timbres or tonal colors of an orchestra while beating only a set of percussion surfaces with no string or wind for variety?** One of the absolutely marvelous achievements of the pan makers is their invention of a wide range of pan types from Tenor to Bass. On the standard pan (S-Pan) there are some ten types of instruments. But, as it should be, the characteristic sound of the individual instrument depends on the panist; **the panist must make his pan speak with categorical eloquence**, for without this the guitar pan may sound like a continuation of the tenor or an introduction to the bass! **The setting of tones on each category of pan (tenor, seconds, guitar, cello etc) is first the responsibility of the maker/tuner and second, it is the responsibility of the panist to 'voice' his sticks to suit the pan and where it is always critical, even the musical score.**

Since we are dealing with one type of instrument (the Steelpan) and would like to produce different tonal textures on its different forms — tenors, guitars, cellos etc — we must examine the tonal structures that are possible on this instrument. This takes us back to the theoretical analysis where we examine the possible amplitude and frequency modulations possible and their dependence on the frequency relations (detuning) of the partials.

So as we leave Bach, Beethoven, Chopin, Gershwin, Liszt, members of my family and their music, prepare yourself for a long walk with me through the avenues of Pan Tuning, it is an exciting walk.

14.19.2 **Energy Loss and Detuning**

The quality factor Q of pan note resonances typically range from 20 to 100 with lower values on the bass and higher values on the tenor (see Section 9.6). The Q-factor measures the degree of sharpness (or *width*) of the mechanical resonance, and Q is *inversely proportional to the energy loss per cycle of oscillation*. The greater the loss through acoustical radiation, transmission across the note boundary and material damping, the lower the Q. Pan notes with lower Q are generally easier to tune because of the broadness of the resonance peak. If damping increases while all other parameters that determine the frequency remain constant, then the resonant frequency of the note decreases. In the process of tuning a note, as the steel pan face is peened and shaped, the losses are continually changing, settling finally to some value at the end of the process. The tuner therefore sets both the resonance frequency and the width of resonance. In Chapter 6 it is shown that the degree of damping, more precisely, the damping coefficient, is approximately the same for the first few modes (those that are musically important) on a given note on a pan.

One sees that the dynamical system involves an *energy-loss* process (damping) that shifts the resonance frequency and broadens the width of resonance. There is another process on the steelpan, the non-linear interactions of the tuned modes on the vibrating note that also affect the frequencies. These interactions, since they represent *transfer of energy* at frequencies determined by the resonance frequencies and the width of these resonances, result in further modifications to the frequency and resonance profile of each mode. In other words, compared to the linear system of non-interacting vibrators found on the majority of musical instruments, the vibrators in the non-linear steelpan system are *naturally detuned*.

There is a third and perhaps the most important source of detuning, *the tuner himself*. Because this source is external (to the pan) and *fully controllable*, detuning of the modal frequencies is, for the most part, in the hands of the tuner.

Caution: While the term detuning has already been used in earlier Sections of this book I feel compelled to issue a word of caution here because there is the possibility that some readers, especially among those who race ahead by skipping Sections, to form the misconceived notion that detuning means that the notes are untuned. Far from it! All key-notes on a pan can be correctly and accurately set according to the musical scale (12-TET). The higher partials however must be detuned so that they do not coincide with the exact harmonics of the key-note. The instrument is properly tuned in this way. Tuning the notes with the higher partials set to the harmonics, creates a dud(!), with all notes generating the unpleasant Pung tone.

14.19.3 Detuning Parameters

For more details on the topic of detuning parameters, see Chapters 4, 5 and 6. For the sake of simplicity, it is sufficient to limit the present discussions to just the first three interacting modes on a note and to assume only quadratic non-linearity for the note system. The main excitation process for the third mode (the musical twelfth) is by quadratic interaction between mode1 and mode2. By ignoring the smaller effects of cubic non-linearity the results obtained in the simulations of the third mode, though acceptable, will be inexact only from a mathematical viewpoint. In order to determine the possible interactions, the modal frequencies and their *detuning* are specified as follows:

$$\omega_2 = 2\omega_1 + \sigma_1, \quad \omega_3 = \omega_1 + \omega_2 + \sigma_2,$$

where ω_n ($n = 1, 2, 3$) are the normalized radian frequencies, and σ_j ($j = 1, 2$) are the detuning parameters. In practice and in theoretical simulations, for good tonal quality the modulus of these two detuning parameters fall within the intervals

$$0.001 \lesssim |\sigma_1| \lesssim 0.01,$$
$$0.002 \lesssim |\sigma_2| \lesssim 0.02.$$

In this specification, the first mode ($n = 1$) is the *key-note* (tonic), the second mode (n = 2) is the *octave,* and the third mode ($n = 3$) is the *twelfth*. Because of the quadratic interaction between mode1 and mode2, ω_3 is written as the sum of the modal frequencies ω_1 and ω_2

(plus a small detuning parameter σ_2). Since one expects the detuning parameters on a properly tuned pan to be small, one has the musically correct tuning arrangement, $\omega_2 \approx 2\omega_1$, $\omega_3 \approx 3\omega_1$. *These approximations cannot however be converted to equalities for use in the analytical procedures since that would completely remove the amplitude and frequency modulations present in pan tones.*

Where cubic interactions and domain interactions are negligible, and the instrument is played at the Tuning Temperature, the transverse modal displacements u_n for the first three coupled modes on a note are given by

$$\ddot{u}_n + \omega_n^2 u_n + \mu_n \dot{u}_n + \sum_{j=1}^{3}\sum_{k=1}^{3} \alpha_{jkn} u_j u_k = f(t), \quad n = 1, 2, 3$$

where μ_n are the damping coefficients, α_{jkn} are the quadratic coupling coefficients and $f(t)$ represents the force imparted to the note by stick impact. The techniques developed in this work for determining the α–parameters are given in Chapter 6 while this equation can be solved by the methods in Chapter 4.

14.19.4 Summary of Factors that Determine Pitch and Timbre

Form the work covered in preceding Sections, we now give a summary of the factors that determine the *pitch* and *timbre* of a steelpan note. Readers must refer to the relevant Sections for greater detail:

Pitch;

1) Geometrical Factors: True note size and aspect ratio a/b specified by the semi-axes a and b. Note material *thickness* h. Rise-factor H/h. Shape or *form* of the note surface specified by the *shaping function q(x)* and *shape function Q(x)* or more generally, $q(x,y,z)$ and $Q(x,y,z)$.
2) Material and Elastic properties: *Young's modulus E, Poisson's ratio* ν, and *Density* ρ.
3) Thermal Properties: *Operating Temperature T* and *Tuning Temperature* T_t. *Coefficient of thermal Expansion* α_T. For

greater details on these and other thermal parameters refer to Chapter 9.
4) Residual Stress: The *compressive stress distribution* σ_c along the note boundary.
5) The mechanical boundary conditions specified by the translational and rotational *spring constants* K and C respectively. In blocking the notes, the pan maker/tuner attempts to make these parameters constant along the note boundary and as large as possible. When both K and C are sufficiently large, near perfect blocking and isolation from the rest of the pan face is expected. Perfect mechanical blocking is not necessary however.
6) The *detuning parameters*.
7) The *material* and *acoustic damping parameters*.

Timbre:

1) The *pitch* of each partial as determined above.
2) The *modal coupling parameters* $\alpha_{jk,n}$ $(j,k,n) = 1,2,3,4$ as determined by the number of tuned modes and all permutations of j, k, n. These coupling parameters determine the relative strengths of the partials
3) The *acoustical radiation characteristics* of the notes and skirt as functions of the vibration frequency.

It should be noted that pitch and timbre are not absolutely fixed by these parameters because both pitch and timbre are dynamic properties of the vibrating system influenced by the non-linear interactions of the modes. The additional factor in the note dynamics is external. This external influence comes from the player who makes use of this non-linear behavior by varying the strength and details of the stick impact to vary in subtle ways both pitch and timbre (Chapter 13 deals extensively with these matters).

14.19.5 Pitch Setting Rules: Stretching and Compressing the Octave and Twelfth on Single Notes

The following rules apply to the tuning of the key-note and higher partials on a single note. The tuning of sympathetic notes follows an extended set of rules. These rules apply to the setting of frequency or pitch and are inserted at this point in the text, somewhat ahead of time, so that the more musically minded will gain a better appreciation of the empirical and theoretical reasons for them. Also for the more mathematically minded it serves as a good introduction to the tuning practices employed on the steelpan. Of course these practices have been given greater clarity and precision in this book than can be found anywhere else. As we shall see, the tuning and blending of pans go beyond the mere setting of pitch.

As an example in the setting of pitch, in musical terminology, if the A_4 note, an outer note on the tenor pan is to be tuned, the tuner is required to set this note on the musical scale as accurately as possible to within ±5 cents of 440 Hz. For accurate tuning of this and *all* other *key-notes* on the pan, the limit ±5 cents must be followed by the use of a good ear and/or with the aid of an accurate tuning meter. The trained tuner and good musician can judge a note to better than ±5 cents (some can achieve ±1 cent) but in our discussion, ±5 cents will serve as a *maximum limit*. I use this maximum limit so that tuning from the beginner to the professional can be accommodated. With this matter clarified I am saved from having to apologize to the master tuner whenever I use the ±5 cents limit. On the A_4 note, the tuner must also *simultaneously* tune the required higher partials consisting of the octave and the twelfth (the pan tuner's *fifth*). Both of these partials must however be detuned with respect to the corresponding harmonic by *stretching* (an *upward shift* in pitch) or by *compressing* (a *downward shift* in pitch). Therefore the octave on the A_4 (440 Hz) note cannot be tuned to A_5 (880 Hz) but *must* be *shifted up or down*. For example:

(a) If the tuner sets the A_4 key-note to precisely 440 Hz, instead of Octave = 2 x 440 Hz, one might have Octave = (2 ± 0.002) x 440 Hz. This gives a shift (detuning) on the octave of ±0.002 x 440 Hz = ±0.88 Hz ≡ ±1.73 cents. To get a *stretched octave* in this case one sets the partial to A_5 + 1.73 cents and to get a *compressed octave* one sets the partial to A_5 – 1.73 cents.

(b) If the tuner can only get the key-note to A_4 + 5.1 cents = 441.3 Hz then he cannot tune the octave to A_5 + 5.1 cents =

2 x 441.3 Hz but must tune *up* or *down* from A_5 + 5.1 cents; so by example, he can tune the note with Octave = (2 ± 0.002) x 441.3 Hz ≡ A_5 + 6.83 cents (*tuning up, stretching the octave*) or A_5 + 3.37 cents (*tuning down, compressing the octave*). The octave can also be tuned to A_5 = 880 Hz which, for this particular key-note tuned to 441.3 Hz, is a *compressed* octave *despite* being correct on the musical scale.

Please read (a) and (b) a second time because it can be a bit confusing especially to those who are accustomed to having all partials tuned exactly to the musical scale.

It should be carefully noted that the matter of stretching and compressing the octave refers to the octave of the *tuned* or *actual* key-note, NOT to the corresponding musical name (A_5 in our example). For example notice that tuning the Octave to A_5 + 3.37 cents is a *compressed octave* because it lies *below* A_5 + 5.1 cents (the true octave of the tuned key-note). Likewise A_5 + 6.83 cents is a *stretched octave* because it lies *above* A_5 + 5.1 cents.

Similar tuning procedures apply to the twelfth (the third partial or the *fifth* above the octave) and the *second octave* (the fourth partial). In example (a) above, since the key-note is set exactly on 440 Hz, the third partial cannot be tuned to (3 x 440) Hz = 1320 Hz which is the third harmonic. This partial can be tuned exactly to E_6 at 1318.5 Hz or detuned by compressing or stretching while avoiding the third harmonic at 1320 Hz. If the tuner is sufficiently skilled and can tune the second octave, since the key-note is exactly on A_4 (440 Hz) he must detune this fourth partial by stretching or compressing while avoiding the fourth harmonic at 4 x 440 Hz.

The detuning of ± 0.002 is a typical example; the range of values for σ_1 given earlier is $0.001 \lesssim |\sigma_1| \lesssim 0.01$, while the corresponding range for σ_2 was given as $0.002 \lesssim |\sigma_2| \lesssim 0.02$. Observe in the examples given here, *the delicate nature of the procedure for tuning the higher partials on the pan.*

14.20 Experimental and Simulation Results

14.20.1 Sample Note and its Simulation

The reader must be made aware that the tonal characteristics shown by the notes used in the examples are those of the individual notes tested and chosen for discussion here and that these characteristics will vary from pan to pan and note to note. They are however, typical examples of notes found on the instrument. Do not expect the notes on the pan in your possession to show *exactly* the same amplitude and frequency profiles as the notes used in these examples but they could be similar. To further clarify the point, you will see the sample $\mathbf{E}_4^\flat$ note used here displaying a particular amplitude profile (time-history) do not take it to mean that all $\mathbf{E}_4^\flat$ notes possess this profile or that this profile is what distinguishes an $\mathbf{E}_4^\flat$ note from other notes. Having said that, it is still perfectly possible and relatively simple in theory, but with much greater effort in practice, to create a tenor pan with all the notes possessing the same amplitude profile as the $\mathbf{E}_4^\flat$ sample note. These notes will then differ only in their time durations and, in the pitches of the key-notes and higher partials. As a reminder, keep in mind that the profiles will always depend on the contact force imparted to the note by the stick (see Chapter 4).

Perhaps it will be most informative to take from a real pan, a sample note with good tonal qualities (depth of modulation, duration and intensity) and to analyze its modal components then to simulate this note numerically using the system equations. Having obtained a close simulation, the detuning parameters alone are then varied to determine what effect these parameters have on tonal structure.

In order to simplify the subject matter dealt with in this Section, simulation is started at the instant the first mode attains maximum amplitude. This occurs after the stick has broken contact with the note so that matters relating to the dynamics during the time that the stick is in contact with the note are avoided here. The full treatment of the dynamics during stick impact can be found in Chapter 13.

14.20.2 The Sampled E_4^b on a Real Pan and its Simulation

The left-hand panels of Figure 14.23 show the data for the real (experimental) note E_4^b (311.1 Hz) played *forte*, while the right-hand panels of Figure 14.23 show the numerical (theoretical) simulations. The experimental data were analyzed using Short Time Fourier Transform (STFT) techniques as they provide direct correspondence with the numerical data: $S_1 \Leftrightarrow a_1$, $S_2 \Leftrightarrow a_2$ and $S_3 \Leftrightarrow a_3$, where S_n are the modal amplitudes obtained from the experimental data and a_n are the theoretical amplitudes. In Figure 14.23, amplitude, phase (ϕ_n) and frequency modulations for the first and second modes are properly reproduced by the theory. Tone duration is also good in simulation.

The parameter set for the simulations in Figure 14.23 consists of:

Detuning Parameters: $\sigma_1 = 0.002$, $\sigma_2 = 0.0048$.
Damping Coefficients: $\mu_1 = \mu_2 = \mu_3 = 0.00085$.
Coupling Parameters: $\alpha_{121} = \alpha_{211} = 0.047$, $\alpha_{231} = \alpha_{321} = 0.006$,
$\alpha_{112} = 0.019$, $\alpha_{312} = \alpha_{132} = 0.0009$,
$\alpha_{123} = \alpha_{213} = 0.007$

The detuning parameters used here correspond to the following modal frequencies;

Key-note: $f_1 = 311.1$ Hz $\equiv E_4^b - 0.167$ cents,
Stretched Octave: $f_2 = 311.1 \times (2 + 0.002)$ Hz $= 622.2 + 0.62$ Hz
$\equiv E_5^b + 1.669$ cents,
Stretched Twelfth: $f_3 = 311.1 \times (1 + 2 + 0.002 + 0.0048)$ Hz $=$
$311.1 \times (3 + 0.0068)$ Hz
$= 933.3 + 2.12$ Hz $\equiv A_5^\# + 5.728$ cents,

where (on the 12-TET scale) $E_4^b \equiv 311.13$ Hz, $E_5^b \equiv 622.25$ Hz and $A_5^\# \equiv 932.33$ Hz.

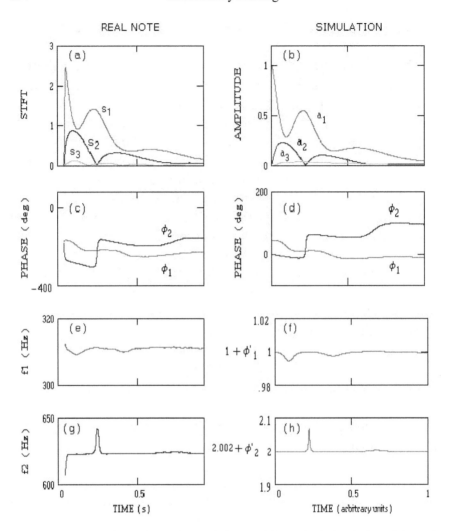

Fig. 14.23. Comparison of experimental data and theoretical simulation of the $E_4^{\flat}$ note. Left panels (a), (c), (e) and (f) show displacement STFT, phase and frequency time histories respectively. The right panels (b), (d), (f) and (h) show the corresponding theoretical simulations. In (f) the frequency modulations are seen around normalized first mode frequency $\omega_1 = 1$ while for (h) the frequency modulations take place around normalized second mode frequency $\omega_2 = 2.002$.

With some additional fine-tuning of the simulation parameters it is possible to achieve even closer matching of the amplitude modulations in Figure 14.23 panel (a) and panel (b) for all the modes. For instance if the detuning on mode3 is increased from $\sigma_2 = 0.0048$ to twice that value while increasing the values of coupling parameters α_{3kj}, α_{j3k}, α_{jk3} (j,k = 1,2), the modulation on mode3 in simulation will closely match the amplitude profile of this mode on the real note. The increase in coupling to mode3 is required in order to offset the effects of the greater frequency separation between mode3 and the excited (mode1 x mode2) parametric mode when detuning is increased. In order to teach this lesson, I purposely left the simulation for mode3 in this 'unfinished' state.

14.20.3 Varying the magnitude of the detuning parameter

Having obtained precise simulations for the E_4^b note (Figure 14.23), the detuning parameters σ_1 and σ_2 were then set to values above and below those for the matching simulation in order to cover the entire span of detuning values normally found on actual steelpan notes. All other parameters remained unchanged.

The results are shown in Figure 14.24. The simulation in Figure 14.24 left panel, were done with smaller values for the detuning parameters (σ_1 = 0.001, σ_2 = 0.002). Compared with the experimental data and precise simulation in Figure 14.23, the modulation times are now longer with hardly a third amplitude peak developing on the first mode as occurred in the results of Figure 14.23. This simulated note represents the case where the amplitude modulations (AM) attain maximum values while the frequency modulations (FM) attain minimum values.

The simulations in Figure 14.24 right panel, were done with larger values for the detuning parameters (σ_1 = 0.01, σ_2 = 0.02). This simulated note represents the case where the frequency modulations (FM) attain maximum values while the amplitude modulations (AM), attain minimum (but not zero) values. Now *the modulations are seen to be more rapid* — a direct result of the large detuning (stretching) of the octave. There are no deep amplitude modulations although the first mode frequency is seen to drift upward in frequency (Figure 14.24 (b) right panel) as it goes through a series of modulations. The drift in frequency is an example of *pitch glide*. Notice the reduction in the level of second mode excitation in Figure 14.24 (a) right panel, when the detuning is large. This is expected because the further the second mode frequency ω_2 is set from $2\omega_1$, the lower is the energy transferred from mode1 to mode2 by internal resonance. The complexity of the mode1 frequency modulation seen on Figure 14.24 (b) right panel is caused by the rapid phase changes occurring on both mode2 and mode3.

For the simulations in Figure 14.24 right panel, the detuning parameters correspond to modal frequencies;

Key-note: $f_1 = 311.1$ Hz $\equiv \mathbf{E_4}^\flat - 0.167$ cents,

Stretched Octave: $f_2 = 311.1 \times (2 + 0.01)$ Hz $= 622.2 + 3.11$ Hz $\equiv \mathbf{E_5}^\flat + 8.493$ cents,

Stretched Twelfth: $f_3 = 311.1 \times (1 + 2 + 0.01 + 0.02)$ Hz $= 311.1 \times (3 + 0.03)$ Hz
$= 933.3 + 9.33$ Hz $\equiv \mathbf{A_5}^\sharp + 19.02$ cents,

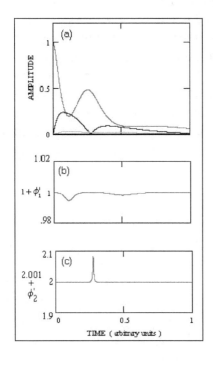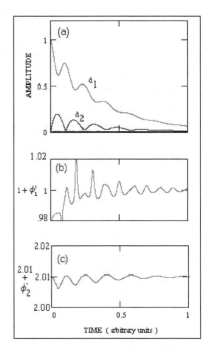

Fig. 14.24. Left panel: Simulation with $\sigma_1 = 0.001$, $\sigma_2 = 0.002$. Right panel: Simulation with $\sigma_1 = 0.01$, $\sigma_2 = 0.02$; (a) Amplitude Modulations on all three modes, (b) Frequency Modulations on the Keynote, (c) Frequency Modulations on the Octave.

14.21 The Image Note

Next we investigate the effects that the *sign* of the detuning parameter has on the amplitude and frequency profiles.

14.21.1 Note and Image, Example 1 — AM and FM Profiles

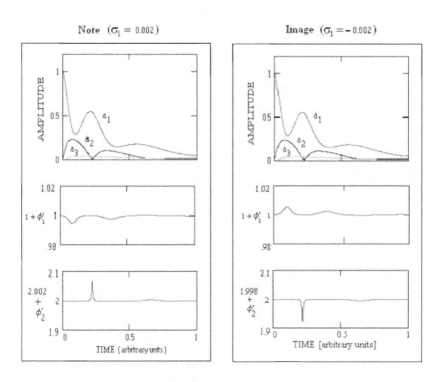

Fig. 14.25. Theoretical simulation of the $E_4{}^\flat$ note (left panel) and its *image* (right panel) using similar coupling parameters for the note in the left pane), but with negative detuning parameters, $\sigma_1 = -0.002$, $\sigma_2 = -0.0048$; AM and FM data.

A negative detuning parameter shifts the modal frequency to the *lower side* of the harmonic (***compressed octave***) while a positive value produces a shift to the *higher side* of the harmonic (***stretched octave***). The results obtained for the same set of parameter values in Section 14.20.2 except for a change in the sign of the detuning parameters to $\sigma_1 = -0.002$, $\sigma_2 = -0.0048$ are shown in Figure 14.25 right panel. When compared with Figure 14.23 or Figure 14.25 left panel, the amplitude modulations are seen to be identical. The only change is the reversal in direction of the frequency modulation on the two modes. This is expected from the fact that the phase angle changes sign as the frequency of the second mode approaches resonance at $\omega_2 \approx 2\omega_1$ from below (σ_1 negative) and proceeds above this resonance (σ_1 positive). The change in sign of the detuning parameter is reflected in changes to the frequency modulations on both modes because these modulations involve *products* of the *displacement vectors* u_1, u_2 and u_3.

14.21.2 Note and Image, Example 2 — With Trill and Pitch Glides or Glissando

Another example is taken from the $\mathbf{F}^{\#}_4$ note on a tenor shown in Figure 14.26. The first mode on this note was tuned to $f_1 = 367.3$ Hz which is 13 cents *below* the musical scale value of $\mathbf{F}^{\#}_4$ (= 369.99 Hz), while the second mode was tuned to $f_2 = 743.2$ Hz which is 7 cents *above* $\mathbf{F}^{\#}_5$ (= 739.99 Hz). This represents significant detuning (purposely introduced by the author on this note to serve as the example here) which can be modeled with a positive detuning parameter $\sigma_1 = 0.01$. Observe carefully, that this 'significant detuning' *does not* refer to the 13 cents lowering of the key-note from the correct $\mathbf{F}^{\#}_4$ frequency which, by itself, represents a '*mistuning*,' but arises from the overall 20 cents *stretching* of the octave above the harmonic at 2 x 367.3 Hz = 734.6 Hz. Neither the correct $\mathbf{F}^{\#}_4$ at 369.99 Hz nor the harmonic at 734.6 Hz are generated or heard on this sample note. Notice the low-level second mode (S_2) in Figure 14.26 (a) that characterizes the case of large detuning. Observe the strong frequency modulation that accompanies the weak amplitude modulation. This rapid modulation is similar to a *Trill* — a rapid alternation between two tones. This note and others like it is musically pleasing mainly because of the frequency modulation and pitch glide — *gliss* or *glissando*.

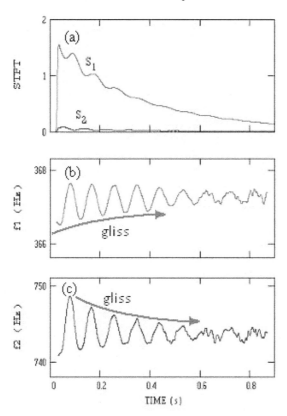

Fig. 14.26. Experimental Amplitude and Frequency Modulation (AM and FM) results for the $F^\#_4$ note on a tenor with large detuning. The solid curves with arrow heads trace the directions of the pitch glides — 'gliss' or 'glissando'..

The amplitude modulations and the frequency modulations of the simulated $F^\#_4$ note ($\sigma_1 = 0.01$) and its *image* ($\sigma_1 = -0.01$) are shown in Figure 14.27. Comparing the first mode frequency modulations on Figure 14.27 (c) and Figure 14.27 (d) one sees an inversion of the modulation and that the pitch glides downward in (c) but upward in (d). The second mode frequency modulations in Figure 14.27 (e) and Figure 14.27 (f) display similar reversals.

In practice, a tuner can never exactly produce a note and its image on a repeatable basis because the tuning process also involves making geometrical and stress changes that alter modal coupling parameters (in-plane stresses affect the coupling parameters indirectly through the mode shapes). Nevertheless, a high degree of reproducibility, sufficient for musical purposes, is possible from an experienced tuner.

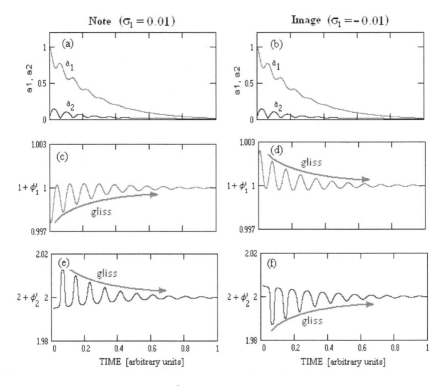

Fig. 14.27. Simulation of the $\mathbf{F}^{\#}_4$ note and its image. The amplitude profiles (a) and (b) are identical while the frequency modulations (d) and (f) are inverted 'images' of (c) and (e) respectively. The solid curves with arrow heads trace the directions of the pitch glides (gliss).

14.22 Definition and Tuning Possibilities with the Image Note

14.22.1 Definition

- The author defines the note with the sign of the detuning parameters reversed as the *Image Note.*
- *The images are just as much 'notes' as are the notes that they are the 'images' of.*
- To each steelpan note, there is an image note set to the *same* key-note frequency on the musical scale.

- The higher partials for the note and its image lie on either side of the corresponding exact harmonic.
- A note and its image have *identical* amplitude profiles but the frequency modulations are *reversed*.
- A note and its image do not appear together on the same pan for the simple reason that two notes of the same key-note frequency are never produced on the same pan. The paired combination of a note and its image can however produce tonal effects similar to the multiple stringed notes found on the piano.
- The image note has its second and third (possibly fourth) modes tuned exactly above (below) the corresponding harmonic as the note is tuned below (above) the harmonic.
- Either the note or its image can be used on the pan to produce similar musical sounds.

14.22.2 Tuning Possibilities

(i) In a 2-mode '*note* and *image*' pair, one member contains a *compressed octave* while the other contains a *stretched octave*. If one is designated as 'the note' then the other is 'the image'.

(ii) In a 3-mode '*note* and *image*' pair, the *twelfth* on one of the members is compressed while the twelfth on the other member is stretched. A mixture of stretching and compressing is possible. For example one can have the following tuning combinations:

    (a) note: compressed octave and compressed twelfth, image: stretched octave stretched twelfth,
    (b) a complete reversal of (a) but this is redundant because the terms *note* and *image* are interchangeable,
    (c) note: compressed octave with stretched twelfth image: stretched octave with compressed twelfth. However, this mixture will result in a weak twelfth because the combination resonance of the key-note and octave with the twelfth will itself be weak. This follows from the fact that in this case the combination frequency $\omega_1 + \omega_2$

will be too far from the frequency ω_3 of the twelfth to allow significant energy transfer by the non-linearly excited parametric mode at frequency $\omega_1 + \omega_2$. This tuning combination stated thus, is **not** a good one if a strong third partial is desired

(iii) If it is possible to tune the second octave (approximate ratio 4:1) then the rules in (ii) apply with the twelfth replaced by the second octave. But this mode being approximately four times the frequency of the key-note is difficult to tune accurately. The difficulty arises because on a note, all modes are tuned simultaneously* so it is not possible, in practice, to single out one of the modes for tuning while leaving the other modes untouched. Since this mode like the twelfth is weak, its interaction with the lower modes will not be greatly affected by the detuning of this second octave. Some tuners leave this second octave, when it can be heard, in a somewhat untuned state, using it mainly for the ringing sound it generates. Attempts to tune it sometimes result in its disappearance.

Do not take this to mean that all partials arrive at the tuned state at once. However, in the tuning process, to varying degrees, each partial is affected by the peening action of the tuner on each stroke of the hammer. The extent of the changes to each partial depends on the point of application of the hammer action on the note surface.

(iv) As a general practice, whenever possible, higher *untuned* modes that can be heard should be removed. Tuning experience will help the reader (now turned tuner) to identify the correct point on the note surface to apply a small tap with the hammer that removes the offending mode. This point may correspond to the location of an antinode for that particular mode.

14.22.3 A New Pan Combination — The Tenor-Pair

Having seen that a note can be tuned either as a 'note' or its 'image' it is possible to tune a pair of tenor pans with 'notes' on one pan and with the corresponding 'images' on the other pan. Although technically challenging, this tuning arrangement will allow for a greater depth in tonality when the pair is played in unison. It will also be a useful (but challenging) tuning arrangement to adopt when the tenor section of a steel orchestra is *voiced* or *blended*. This tuning arrangement will make interesting *Chorus Effects* (see Chapter 15) as the two sets of voices in the tenor section are played in unison then with the melody exchanged between instruments with the *notes,* and instruments with the *images*. Exchanges of this type should be wonderful to hear with a vigorous and powerful melody — better make that *'fast and cheerful' (Allegro form)* with *chordal modulations!* I am trying not to get carried away by all this but I can't apologize, *it must be my Trini blood!*

14.24 The 'Pung tone'

14.24.1 Introduction

Attention is now focused on the case where the detuning parameters are set exactly to zero ($\sigma_1 = 0$, $\sigma_2 = 0$). With the modes exactly harmonically related, one can generate, with respect to the key-note, a *true octave* and an *'almost true'* twelfth*. This state, although dynamically interesting, is not found on a properly tuned steelpan! This may come as a surprise to the reader and even to the tuners, who might easily consider the obvious harmonic tuning scheme $\omega_2 = 2\omega_1$, $\omega_3 = 3\omega_1$ or in musical terms, tuning the key-note and all partials in a precise harmonic arrangement, as being optimum. **It is not!** On the steelpan, tuning the higher mode to an exact octave results in a poorly sounding tone, what the author has called the 'pung tone' (Achong 2000f). The pung tone should be considered a transitional state through which a note may pass during the tuning process. **The pung tone must never be taken as the final tuned state.**

* *On 12-TET the twelfth is 19 semitones above unison which places it 1.963 cents below the third harmonic. See Section 14.3.4. The* 'twelfth' on a Pung Tone, which is tuned on the harmonic, is therefore set 1.963 cents above the 'true twelfth'.

14.24.2 A Typical Pung Tone on a Real Pan and some Simulations

A typical case for the pung tone on the real pan is shown in Figure 14.28 (a) and (b) obtained on a $C^{\#}_5$ tenor note *specially tuned* by the author for this purpose and simulated numerically using the same set of parameters as in Figure 14.27 except for the changes $\alpha_{121} = 0.01$, $\alpha_{112} = 0.004$. From the higher time resolution panel Figure 14.28 (b), it is obvious that the first mode dominates and that higher modes are at low levels, consistent with the numerical simulation Figure 14.28 (c). Figures 14.28 (a) and (c) show similar monotonic decay of the first mode component. It is the lack of structure, short duration and weakened higher modes that relegate the pung tone to the 'poor' category.

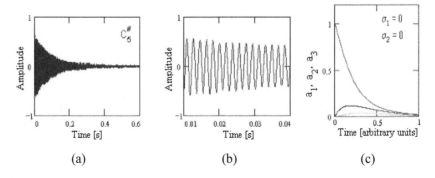

Fig. 14.28. A typical 'pung tone' where the fundamental always dominates. (a) 'pung tone' generated on a specially tuned $C^{\#}_5$ note on a tenor pan, (b) high time-resolution plot of the tone in (a), (c) numerical simulation of the $C^{\#}_5$ tone amplitude profile.

The author digresses here a bit in order to clarify once again this important matter. The present author has always insisted and tried to convey to the scientific community and to the pan makers themselves that the terminology '*harmonics*' and '*tuning the harmonics*' are incorrect when applied to the modes on the steelpan. In the first case in point, the normal modes on a note are *not* natural harmonics. Modal frequencies can take on a wide range of values as determined by a wide range of parameters. The harmonic frequency ratios (1: 2: 3: 4: ....) are quite simply, not natural on the pan. In the second case, pan makers and some researchers have been using the terminology 'tuning the harmonics' rather loosely and incorrectly. The pan makers can be excused.

Why are the modes on steelpan notes *not tuned to exact harmonics*? Prior to 1996, when the exclusion of harmonics was first demonstrated (Achong 1996b), even p*an makers were not aware of this fact*! At the 1999 Two-Day Steelpan Seminar, Port of Spain, Trinidad hosted by Pan Trinbago with the author as speaker, and at the International Conference on the Science and Technology of the Steelpan (ICSTS) 2000, Port of Spain, Trinidad, hosted jointly by Pan Trinbago and NIHERST, the misconceptions surrounding harmonics were thoroughly dealt with by the author. Pan makers cannot be faulted for their lack of knowledge in the dynamics of the notes. Their lack of scientific knowledge in this area is compensated for by their vast knowledge in the art of tuning, thanks to well-developed hearing, good musical sense and trained hands.

In the process of tuning, as the second mode in particular approaches twice the first mode frequency, one hears a developing series of modulations. If the key-note (fundamental) is set correctly on the musical scale, the note begins to take on a tuned and correct character at the discretion and ear of the tuner. However, if fine-tuning continues, the note may suddenly change tonal character and sound like a short-duration, truncated 'pung!' The note sounds *'tight'* and *'corky'*. What is the cause of this effect?

Simulated tone profiles with $\sigma_1 = 0$, $\sigma_2 = 0$, are shown in Figure 14.29 for a 3-mode note (key-note, octave and twelfth) and a 2-mode note (key-note and octave). To remove mode3 (the twelfth) in the 2-mode simulation one sets to zero the coupling to this mode by making $\alpha_{123} = 0$, $\alpha_{132} = 0$, $\alpha_{231} = 0$.

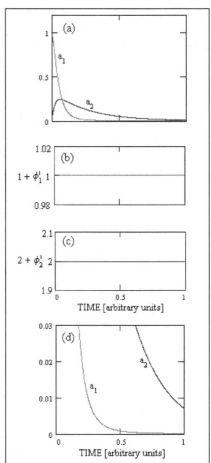

$\alpha_{112} = 0.011$, $\alpha_{121} = 0.025$, $\alpha_{123} = 0.01$, $\alpha_{231} = 0.007$, $\alpha_{132} = 0.0009$, $\mu_1 = \mu_2 = \mu_3 = 0.0006$.

$\alpha_{112} = 0.011$, $\alpha_{121} = 0.025$, $\alpha_{123} = 0$, $\alpha_{231} = 0$, $\alpha_{132} = 0$, $\mu_1 = \mu_2 = \mu_3 = 0.0006$.

Fig. 14.29. Simulated tonal characteristics for detuning parameters set to zero ($\sigma_1 = 0$, $\sigma_2 = 0$). Left panel: Three-mode simulation. Right Panel: Two-mode simulation. (a) Modal amplitudes. (b) and (c) Frequency modulations. (d) Modal amplitudes shown with greater amplitude resolution.

(i) In the 3-mode simulation, the first mode decays rapidly to near zero while the amplitudes of the second and third modes initially rise then fall slowly (Figure 14.29 (a), left panel). This is the result of energy transfers by quadratic interactions; *mode1· mode1* → *mode2* (controlled by α_{112}) and *mode1· mode2*→ *mode3* (controlled by α_{123}). The interaction *mode3 · mode2*→*Mode1* (controlled by α_{321}) produces a very small rise in amplitude of mode1 (see Figure 14.29 (d) left panel) at around 0.4 time units and is accompanied by a modulation in the frequency of mode1 (see Figure 14.29 (b) left panel). This modulation will not be heard on a real note because of the extremely low-level of the sound intensity at this stage in the tone history. Mode2 and mode3 decay steadily in amplitude while displaying no modulations in the frequencies. Throughout the tone duration mode1 dominates.

(ii) For the 2-mode simulation the amplitude modulations are almost similar to the 3-mode case except that in this case mode1 decays monotonically. The modal frequencies remain constant throughout the tone (see Figures 14.29 (b) and 14.29 (c), right panel).

(iii) For both cases, 2-mode and 3-mode, the amplitude profiles (mainly the short duration of mode1) and the frequency spectra, are consistent with the short-duration truncated 'pung tone' sound heard for notes entering this *transitional stage of the tuning process*. The pan maker/tuner will always continue to tune this note, taking the system away from this state. This is the reason why one can hardly find a pan made by an experienced pan maker with a note tuned in this 'unpleasant sounding' state. In this way, exact harmonics are avoided.

(iv) The 2-mode case is an example of *mode locking* (see Chapter 10). There is no AM because the detuning is zero and no FM because the modes are locked — no phase changes

(v) The 3-mode case does not preserve lock between mode1 and mode2 because of the interaction with mode3 (to be regarded in this case, as a *disturbance* or *perturbation*).

Notice in Figure 14.29 (b) and 14.29 (c), left panel, that the mode2 frequency is not always twice the mode1 frequency.

14.24.3 Definition of the Pung Tone

Definition: *The pung tone is its own image.*
Properties:

- *The pung tone, which has all its higher modes (partials) tuned to exact harmonicity, lacks the modulation and duration that characterizes a good steelpan note. The detuning is exactly zero.*
- It should now be perfectly clear to the reader that if, in tuning the pan, one follows to the letter the practice described by the terminology *'tuning the harmonics'* then one produces a pan with all its notes set to generate pung tones—*a very undesirable tuning arrangement.*

Recommendation and Advice:

- It is for the reason given above, that we should not encourage the use of the terminology 'tuning the harmonics' just as we *ought not* to give support to the use of the name 'drum' to describe the steelpan — both are inappropriate. Just as the pung tone irritates the ears of the author and tuners this word 'drum' irritates our feelings for the instrument and conflicts with our knowledge.

Our inquisitive reader asks:
What happens if the octave is detuned but the twelfth is tuned to the third harmonic of the key-note? Is the tone almost pung-like?

This is a good question which, because of the non-linearity of the system, requires some simulations for a complete answer. However, a perfectly acceptable descriptive answer can be given. We know that the outcome depends on the extent of the detuning of the octave and the relative coupling between the octave and the twelfth to the key-note. We also know that the *twelfth* cannot remain mode-locked to the key-note because the octave acts as a perturbation which continuously modulates the frequency of the key-note ensuring that the required 1:3 frequency ratio between the key-note and the *twelfth* is not maintained. Dynamically (i.e. when the note is played) the *twelfth* will show very low-level frequency modulation and weak amplitude modulation. When this note is played, to the extent that these weak modulations are audible, the sound of the *twelfth* component of the tone is not pung-like. The ringing tone of the *twelfth* (the *fifth* above the octave) sounds much better when it is set into stronger modulations that are audible. The experienced tuner will almost always apply some detuning to the twelfth to produce the desired modulations. When he '*gets it right*' it's because the *twelfth* (along with the octave) is detuned.

14.25 The Fundamental Law of the Steelpan, the Steelpan Law of Ratios and the $5/4^{ths}$-Law — the Wonderful Magic of Pan Tuning

A Personal Note on Bertie Marshall:

Today, the day on which this note is inserted in the manuscript, Wednesday, October 24, 2012, marks one week since the passing of Master Tuner Bertie Marshall, a dear friend, greatly missed. For this reason, I have returned to this (completed) Section to insert a note in remembrance of my dear friend. His death has caused me to reflect somewhat deeper on his struggles to understand and to develop the steelpan. For some time now, the entire manuscript for the present book had been completed and attempts made to secure a publisher — all unsuccessful. I had very much wanted three special persons to read this book, Randolph Thomas, Pat Bishop, and the Master himself, Bertie Marshall. I have no plans to introduce anything new in the manuscripts, but with the manuscripts still in my hand, I have returned to this Section which would still remain essentially unchanged, to add this small but significant note on the work of Bertie.

Bertie, as he explained to me in a 2000 interview, had worked unceasingly both mentally and physically to accomplished the task of '*elongating*' the pan note. Bertie had seen something that no one else at the time knew was possible. But more than that, it was something necessary. While the 'custom' at the time was to use 'circular' or 'rounded' notes, Bertie found that the tones which he sought, the '*overtones*' as he called them, came out much clearer when the notes were 'elongated.' Too much elongation and the notes were once again noisy. Some may say that Bertie was working ahead of his time but on the contrary I would say that Bertie was '*changing the times*'! Things around him in the musical world of pan were changing too slowly for him. Bertie continued his revolution in pan with 'gusto' by placing octaves and twelfths (fifths) on the notes in his band, *Highlanders*! Bertie's high-pitched tenor pans were given the 'teasing' name, the 'Chinese Pans!'

As we shall soon see, a circular planform constrains the vibrating note so that while it may produce a clearly defined key-note, the higher partials are ill defined. This is what drove Bertie Marshall to elongation! However, at the time when Bertie was working on the elongation problem to get his overtones correct, there were other notable pan makers around, Anthony Williams in particular, who were also searching for improved tonality; so historically I glean that there were others in the elongation race. What is quite clear however is that Bertie led the way (the Highlanders band and the teasing name 'the Chinese Pans' come readily to mind here) so, for this reason, as in all ' hundred meter sprints,' where there is always a winner (rarely a tie), I must pin the 'elongation medal' on Bertie.

Just thinking about Bertie has stimulated some good memories. I first met Bertie in person, in the year 2000 (twelve years ago) when I interviewed him for the production of the conference paper (Achong 2000d) which is based on his life and exploits on the pan. Whenever we met, Bertie and I would discuss the finer points of the instrument; on each of these points we always were in full agreement. We never disagreed on anything touching the pan. Usually our discussions were all about what tuners were now doing as against what they ought to be doing with the pan. Today, on reflection, I find it somewhat strange, yet consoling, that the only two pan makers with whom I have held private discussions on pan, the late Randolph Leroy Thomas and Bertie Marshall, apart from the common love we shared for the instrument, in our boyhood days the three of us independently, while growing up in different areas on the Island of Trinidad, shared a love for electronics and built ourselves crystal radios! During the past two weeks, my grandson

Zachary (now ten), whose comments brought the closure of these manuscripts (see the Preface) has been building himself a crystal set (radio) for his school science project! It works but I cannot guarantee that he would attach himself to the steelpan as the three of us did, although he has indicated his desire to complete this book if I should fail to do so.

Today just let me say *adios* to a good friend and fellow researcher in pan whose tune of choice would always be '*Every Valley Shall Be Exalted*' (from Handel's Messiah). I only wished I had seen Bertie more often in the short time for which I knew him. I only caught one fleeting glimpse of him during the last five years of his life. Adios!

This Section (*Section 14.25*) deals with the final resolution of the *elongation problem* and the laws and rules related to the shaping of the true note. The full resolution of the 'elongation problem' however, could not come without the introduction of the notion of the '*true note*' as distinct from the '*traditional note*' that all pan makers, including Bertie, were considering at the time and up to 1996. In 1996, the 'true note' notion was first introduced (to the scientific community) as an 'area of mode and energy confinement' on a tuned steelpan note. The latter is a proper and precise definition of the 'true note' but back then (around 1996) before I discussed the concept with the 'steelpan community' — the tuners — it became clear that to get the concept across properly, a name was needed that would 'resonate' with the tuners, so came the introduction of the name 'true note' which in fact is also a correct and proper name (terminology) for the notion. This notion defines real areas or '*domains*' on the pan, areas that clearly define the *tuned state* of the instrument. In the Pan world, most people think in terms of the 'traditional note.'

The musical tones of a tuned pan, in the strict meaning and interpretation of pan note dynamics, are *not* defined by the 'traditional notes,' those clearly visible features of the instrument usually bordered by grooves. The ambiguities in defining the contours of the traditional notes have led to a large assortment of shapes and sizes (some even patented!) that while defining the areas *within* which one finds the 'true notes,' give no means by which the shape, size, orientation or properties of the true notes can be determined. All this, while the true notes on the pan remain the most significant domains on the pan face and in which all the sound producing mechanisms for tone generation can be found.

14.25.1 The Identity of the True Note and The Fundamental Law of the Steelpan

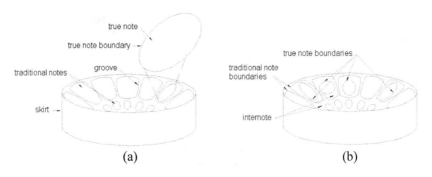

Fig. 14.30. (a) Diagram of a tenor pan showing a true note projected enlarged above the pan face and its location in relation to the associated traditional note in which it is contained. (b) More examples of true notes showing their arbitrary orientations within the traditional notes. In these diagrams, grooves define the boundaries of the traditional notes. On most pans, the outer traditional notes share common boundaries (grooves); they are shown separated here for visual clarity. Observe very carefully in (b) the areas defined as the '*internote*.' Grooves and bores are parts of the internote.

As an introduction to this Section I give a description of the Pan that should be of help to the reader. This description is necessary because it is important for the reader to *change* his/her focus on the steelpan *away* from the 'traditional notes' to the 'true notes.' For an identification of the parts of the pan ('traditional note,' 'true note,' grooves etc) described in this Section, refer to Figure 14.30. The 'traditional note' is defined by grooves and/or bores but in the case of the grooveless pan, unless bores are used, the boundary is only defined as a curved band surrounding the traditional note, that has been subjected to more intense peening without the use of grooves. It is more difficult to observe the boundaries of the traditional notes on a grooveless pan because this boundary is strictly and more precisely defined in terms of the distribution of relatively high internal stresses than by the changes in pan face curvature associated with it. The grooves or bores are features that are clearly visible and that clearly exist *irrespective* of whether the note is *tuned* or *untuned*. In other words the mere appearance of grooves and bores as some form of 'border' *does not* indicate the *musical state* of a note (as being tuned or untuned). *This is the source of the ambiguity mentioned earlier with respect to the elongation problem.* The 'traditional notes' and their boundaries are not associated with the dynamical equations that so precisely describe the system of tuned 'notes' on the steelpan. Instead, these dynamical equations relate directly to the 'true notes.' Because of the vague definition that the traditional note carries (which can be seen from the arbitrary shapes and sizes with which they may be formed) no proper dynamical equations can be used to describe them as active, musically tuned domains on the pan. Clearly, they cannot be used to describe the *sharply defined musical notes,* with all their associated partials, that are found on the instrument.

In a nutshell, the musically tuned system found on a steelpan is the system of tuned 'true notes' and *not* a system of 'traditional notes' to which strictly speaking, in the case of the latter and in the musical context, 'tuning' does not apply.

Many 'traditional notes' on a pan can have similar borders and most of them even *share* borders. The grooves and/or bores that form the borders of the 'traditional note' are what might best be described as an *'outer border'* for the area that contains the 'true note' (refer to Figure 14.30). The actual border or boundary of the 'true note' is fully contained *within the area enclosed by this 'outer border.'* The area enclosed between the 'true note' boundary and the grooves or 'outer border' form part of the *internote;* with *the grooves themselves forming part of the internote* (see Figure 14.30(b)). For this reason, the *'internote'* is defined as *all areas of the pan face <u>exclusive</u> of the 'true notes.'* Though the descriptions I have given so far, with some repetition, seem a bit 'long-winded' it is important that I 'spell it all out' because one must clearly define and distinguish between the 'true note and its boundary' and the 'traditional note and its boundary.'

The grooves/bores perform the useful function of isolating the 'true note' from other areas of the pan face and skirt (see Section 14.12). On the other hand, the 'true note' and its boundary are defined *dynamically* and *depend* on the *musical state* of the *partials assigned* to the true note *by the tuner*. The 'true note' is *always* found *within* the area of the 'traditional note.' *By definition and function, there is no ambiguity associated with the 'true note.'* In fact, when properly tuned (the key-note and its associated higher partials, at least two in the *key-note-octave-twelfth/third* format), the true notes are the most precisely defined areas on the pan face. Generally, the area of the true note is smaller than the area of the traditional note that contains it. In the case of the inner notes on the tenor however, it is possible, because of space restrictions, to find the boundary of a true note, wholly or partially, coinciding with the boundary of the traditional note. This is not the ideal situation so, for this reason, the traditional notes *must not* be made too small. In particular for those inner tenor notes where the two types of boundaries may coincide, because of the small size, one must be careful not to apply very deep grooves, too many bores, or excessive peening that would result in high compressive stresses along the boundary. When these errors are made, the note will be hard to tune.

Contrary to custom and common expression used in respect of this instrument, tuned partials *are not* defined by the 'traditional notes!' One finds the following common expression being used when referring to one of the 'traditional note,' where one says, for example, 'this is the C' when one should really be directing attention to the 'true note' with that musical property. This is not a mere quibble and cannot be glossed over with the comment that 'well, you know what I mean.' The fact is, 'I don't know what you mean?' This is a technical book and if I were to do these things (that is, involve myself in 'loose expressions' or 'sloppiness') there would be utter confusion. It is easy for someone to confuse the 'outer border' formed by the grooves with the 'true note boundary' for while the grooves and the border they form are clearly visible, the boundary of the true note can only be determined dynamically, for example by the use of a Chladni (pronounced '*kladni*') pattern (Chladni 1789; see McLaughlin 1998 for a more recent use of this method and, for some history, see Stöckmann 2007), (see Section 14.25.3). This means of identification still holds true even for those inner tenor notes where the two types of boundaries may coincide.

A Short Biographical and Historical note: *Ernst Florens Friedrich Chladni (1756-1827), born in Germany, is regarded as the 'Father of Acoustics' and the 'Father of Meteoritics.' The powder or sand method of determining the nodal contours of vibrating objects that* *is accredited to Chladni was first discovered in the year 1680 by Robert Hooke of Oxford University (Hooke is famous for the law in elasticity that carries his name).*

Whereas it is possible for 'traditional notes' to share common boundaries, **no two (or more) 'true notes' can share the same boundary**. The exclusion of this possibility rests on the following two facts:

(i) **The boundary of a 'true note' is a locus of equal dynamic stiffness** for *all* the partials of the set (musical set) defining the particular true note.
Note carefully here that this is a dynamical property dependent on the well defined frequencies of the corresponding partials.
(ii) **No two notes on a given pan are identical.**

Fact (i) is clearly a dynamical property which implies that *the true note and its boundary only exist while the note is sounding.* Readers, who continue to focus on the traditional note which is clearly visible even when the instrument is just standing there in silence, may not grasp this concept. This is why it is important to focus on the notion of the 'true note' for which the full answer to the question 'where is it?' can only be given while the note is sounding. Once you have found it by means of the Chladni method, you know where it will appear the next time you play the note; unless the note has been re-tuned or the instrument is damaged say by dropping it. Fact (ii) hardly needs any explanation! None will be given because even to the non-musician, it is 'self-evident!'

All 'true notes' defined by their specific sets of partials, tuned to specific notes on the musical scale (12-TET) *must* be spatially separated on the pan face. (I could add much more to this requirement because 'separation' here is not just spatial but I have dealt with this issue sufficiently in Sections 14.14 - 14.16.) This requirement ties in with the need for ensuring that the traditional notes are not made too small. What has already been said about the 'traditional note' and the 'true note' should make this requirement clear. Since the note dynamics relate to the true note and not to the traditional note, merging the boundaries of adjacent traditional notes will not affect 'true note' dynamics. However if there are two adjoining (juxtaposed) traditional notes (sharing a common boundary) and one attempts to tune the two 'true notes' to which these adjoining traditional notes are related, and furthermore if in doing so one tries to place these true notes too close to each other physically (equivalent in a mechanical sense, to touching) one will surely find that these two 'true notes' cannot be tuned. Because Blocking or Tightening is never perfect, the mechanical coupling between these two 'true notes' would preclude perfect tuning (see Section 5.3.2 on note-note coupling). The tuner, who believes that he is 'good enough' to do it and claims to do it on his pans, would not find his instruments to be much in demand! I can assure you of that!

We can now draw some important conclusions and state an important Law. We begin with the Law:

- **_'True notes' on the steelpan, do not share boundaries!_** I call this **_'The Fundamental Law of the Steelpan.'_**
- It is the duty of the tuner to reduce, as much as possible (or as necessary to allow for the case of Marshall Pairs) the level of 'cross-border talks' or coupling among the true notes; a process tuners call *'tightening.'* I have said elsewhere in this book that *'tightening'* should be understood in the sense of *'tightening security', not* in the sense of *'applying tension.'* Now, with our improved understanding, it is possible to add to that meaning, *'tightening security across the borders.'*
- *If two true notes are set up so close to each other that mechanically (because of the cross border coupling) their boundaries can be regarded as 'touching,' the tuned states of these notes are destroyed. This happens when one acts on the other and the other acts back on the one!*
- *Therefore, in accordance with the Fundamental Law, it is not possible to tune two adjacent true notes with <u>intersecting</u> boundaries.* **It should also be re-emphasized here that, on the contrary, it is perfectly possible to merge and intersect boundaries on the traditional notes.**

Comments: *In this book I have stated many laws and rules on the operation and tuning of the steelpan without the words 'law' and 'rule' attached to them; however, I will not go on a 'Law or Rule naming* spree' by arranging these laws/rules in a numerical order such as 'The First Law of the Steelpan,' 'The Second Law ...' etc. This is unnecessary. The 'Fundamental Law' deserves its name because of its fundamental importance in the structure and operation of the steelpan. The laws should not be arranged numerically since this may give rise to an artificial 'order of importance.' It would be unwise to give the reader this impression. Instead, where it is important to attach to a name the word 'law' or 'rule' the name will be written in a manner that clearly identifies the nature of the law or rule.

But why have I waited so long into this book to define the Fundamental Law of the Steelpan? Why was this not done very early in the book? The reason is simple. While the Law is simple to state, it has a deep meaning and the whole stable dynamics of the tuned notes rest upon it. Before the reader can understand this law properly however, it is necessary to define 'unambiguously' the true note. But one may say, in order to have a true note, the boundary must be defined and in that definition, the Fundamental Law must first be stated! I have reversed the order because it makes more sense to do so. We ought also to remember that both the true note and its boundary are defined <u>together</u> by the note dynamics.

Historically, I discovered the existence of the 'true note' and the Fundamental Law that governs its boundary almost simultaneously in 1986. In the subsequent development of these ideas and concepts I came to the realization that the true note (or the 'area of mode confinement,' the name that I used back then) and the law governing its boundary are two parts of a single picture.

A picture that really makes sense and one that conveys a deep meaning can be viewed any side up! This book is all about this picture of the Steelpan.

I can still see myself, the boy in the Preface, staring at the raised notes on the Ping Pong, wondering 'how does it work?' I got a large part of the answer in 1986!

14.25.2 Introducing the Five-Fourths $5/4^{ths}$-Law of the Steelpan

The law, which I have named *the Five-Fourths $5/4^{ths}$- Law of the Steelpan*, gets its first 'public' appearance right here and can also be called the *Four-Fifth's (4/5^{ths}) Law*, implying the inverse ratio. Despite its importance, it was first introduced 'unceremoniously' without the name in caption in a 1999 paper by the author (Achong 1999b) as an empirical (experimental) value for the ratio (the *aspect ratio*) of the semi-axes of the true notes on the steelpan. Empirically one has the aspect ratio $a/b = 1.27 \pm 0.08$ defining the ratio of the semi-major axis a to the semi-minor axis b of the elliptical boundary of the true note, applicable to all notes on the pan tuned in the standard *key-note-octave-twelfth* fashion. In terms of small integers, the aspect ratio given by $5/4 = 1.25$ falls within the experimental limits of the empirical value for a/b. Variations in this ratio, obtained on real pan notes, can be attributed to compensations, made during tuning, for note shape distortions away from a perfect ellipsoidal shape, non-uniformity in internal stresses, elastic support variations along the true note boundary and to *mistuning* especially on the mode that functions as the twelfth (the *fifth* above the octave). (***The reader must not confuse the term 'mistuning' with the term 'detuning' they carry different meanings.***) The elastic constants and density of the note material and the thickness remain essentially constant over the note surface and on a well-prepared pan, are not the sources of the deviations (the ± 0.08 error or 'spread') found in the experimental value for the ratio a/b.

We can state some basic properties of the true note and the Law related to it:

- The true note boundary is formed dynamically as it defines the locus of points on the note surface having equal dynamical stiffness and it is the same (boundary) for *all* the tuned modes on a given note. For notes *properly tuned* in the standard *key-note-octave-twelfth* fashion or in the *key-note-octave-third* fashion (for the bass), the planform or boundary of the true notes *always* take the shape of an *ellipse.*
- *There is a different law in fact a Rule related to the bass using the key-note-octave-third tuning method that we shall come to later.*
- *The Five-Fourths Law on the aspect ratio of the true note is independent of the size of the note and makes no reference to the area or shape of the traditional note defined by the grooves (for all notes) and chime (for outer notes).*

This Law also, by implication, makes no reference to the templates used in marking the notes. However, as we shall see, its use is recommended in designing the templates for the inner notes on the high-end pans. A 'simple' derivation of this law is now given from which its importance and relevance to tuning the octave and twelfth can be easily grasped. This demonstration is presented in a simplified form but its basis lies deep in the theory of thin ellipsoidal shell vibration. Although not the most rigorous route to the $5/4^{ths}$-Law (for reasons that we shall soon see), I have made every effort to present the arguments in a manner that highlights the underlying reasons for the Law. Application of the Law will enhance the pan tuning practices of pan makers and tuners and I am sure they will be delighted to hear this reference to them. The demonstration runs as follows:

(Please read the following demonstration completely and carefully because it contains important information on the tuning process).

14.25.3 Following a Path consistent with the actions of the Good Pan Maker

First, the observation made by pan makers: It is well known among pan makers and tuners that when circular templates are used for the inner notes (as seen on the early tenors) the octaves on these notes are difficult to tune, being restricted by the circular grooved boundary. To tune them properly the circular planform defined by the grooved boundary has to be reshaped to an elliptical planform. The obvious solution is to start the process with templates having elliptical shapes for the inner notes as is presently done on modern pans. This problem has an easy explanation in the theory of vibrating shells and plates. As we are going to see, the perfect geometry of the circular planform together with uniformity in the note thickness, material and elastic properties and boundary conditions, *forbids* the setting up of a tuned note having musically tuned partials beyond the key-note. These shape and boundary conditions will allow only those modes that are symmetrical about the center to be defined unambiguously. **The circular grooves of the inner notes on the pan face constrain the note dynamics to this**

particular type of motion. The frequencies of these symmetrical modes above the key-note will not correspond to the musically correct octave or twelfth and they will remain discordant. We must therefore look to the modes that show anti-phase motion about a nodal line running along a diameter of the circle.

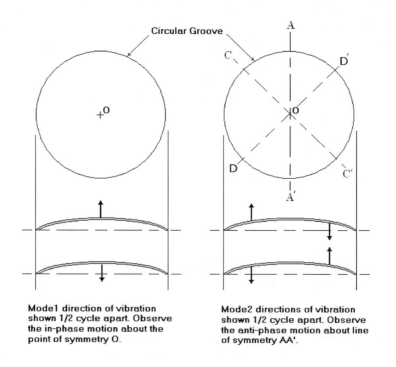

Mode1 direction of vibration shown 1/2 cycle apart. Observe the in-phase motion about the point of symmetry O.

Mode2 directions of vibration shown 1/2 cycle apart. Observe the anti-phase motion about line of symmetry AA'.

Fig. 14.31. Plan view (top) of a note formed on a circular planform. Arrows on the cross-sectional view (bottom), indicate the direction of motion of the vibrating note.

Reference is made to the note having circular planform shown in the sketches of Figure 14.31. While mode1 (the key-note) corresponds to the in-phase transverse vibration of the entire note surface with the point of symmetry at O, the next higher mode (mode2) consists of the anti-phase vibrations of the two halves of the surface with a nodal line running diametrically through the center such as AA'. The motion is *antisymmetric about the line* AA' (antisymmetric because of the anti-phase motion). But two problems arise here.

- First, the frequency of mode2 is not naturally found to be in the ratio 2:1 with mode1 and not necessarily close to 2:1 either, making it difficult for the tuner to form an octave on the circular note (circular planform).
- Second, in mode2, the circular note must find a definite diameter about which to vibrate but, on a circular planform, there is no preferred direction in space for this diameter! This gives rise to an infinite number of diameters satisfying the condition for a mode2 nodal line (for example AA', CC' and DD' in Figure 14.31 and you can fill in as many as you wish like the spokes on a bicycle wheel), and none of these directions (diameters) is favored over any of the others, making all these possible modes *degenerate* — different modes having the same frequency and same state of energy. In fact the circular note is subject to *infinite degrees of freedom* — an infinite number of these diameters can be drawn with none favored over the others as a nodal line, a totally undesirable situation!

The question is which one of this infinite number of modes will form mode2? If, in practice, it is found that a particular mode2 is excited, with a straight nodal line through O, then it can be attributed, to *pure chance*. The symmetry about the point O has been broken *randomly* (the knowledgeable reader may refer to this as *spontaneous symmetry breaking;* where the initially circularly symmetrical state has settled down into a state with smaller, or no symmetry) or it can be attributed to some small *lack of symmetry on the physical note itself* due to imperfect geometry, uneven thickness and/or to variations in boundary conditions around the note. This *broken symmetry* will play itself out as a difference in frequency — different from the other possible mode2 frequencies and different from mode1. So when the circular planform is used there can be some uncertainty, or ambiguity, as to what mode2 will sound like each time the note is played, hence the stated problem and this is not what we, the panists, or the tuners want!

If we want mode2 (the 'octave') to be consistent and predictable each time the note is played, we can *purposely break the symmetry* by shaping the inner notes into *ellipsoidal* shells on elliptical planforms (see the sketches in Figure 14.32 with major axis $2a$ and minor axis $2b$). It is clear that the symmetry is broken by having the ratio $a/b \neq 1$ *(for a circular planform (the symmetrical case), $a/b = 1$)*. In this case the key-note (mode1) still corresponds to the in-phase transverse vibration of the entire ellipsoidal note surface, but mode2 now consists of the anti-phase vibrations of the two halves of the surface with a nodal line running through the minor axis BB' as shown in Figure 14.32 (left panel). Mode2 can now be tuned as a well defined octave by varying the length $2a$ of the major axis while mode1 can be tuned by varying the lengths of *both* axes. *If these lengths are increased the frequencies decrease and when they are decreased the frequencies increase.*

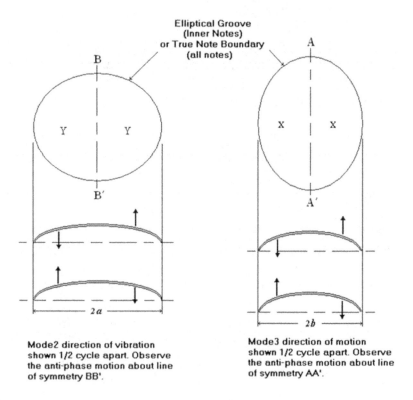

Mode2 direction of vibration shown 1/2 cycle apart. Observe the anti-phase motion about line of symmetry BB'.

Mode3 direction of motion shown 1/2 cycle apart. Observe the anti-phase motion about line of symmetry AA'.

Fig. 14.32. Note formed on an elliptical planform. Arrows indicate the direction of motion of the vibrating note. These notes are not drawn to scale.

The possibility now exists for a *third mode*, mode3 having its nodal line along the major axis AA' (see Figure 14.32, right panel) and for this mode to be tuned to the higher frequency corresponding to the *twelfth* by varying the length of the minor axis *2b*. **Observe that this is not possible on a circular planform.**

Mode Designation: In designating the modes of vibration relevant to the steelpan, the following notation will be used: Since the modes of interest correspond first to the key-note which has no radial (or axial) nodal lines, this mode is defined as the [0, 0] mode. Both the second mode (octave) and the third mode (twelfth) correspond to modes of vibration in which, for each mode, there exists a single axial nodal line. To identify these modes by their nodal lines we shall use the notation [m, n] where m = 0 or 1 represents the number of nodal lines along the major axis and n = 0 or 1, represents the number of nodal lines along the minor axis. The octave is therefore written as [0, 1] while the twelfth is written as [1, 0]. In the case of circular planforms where there are no defined radial axes, the mode [0, 1] is equivalent to the mode [1, 0] (the system being degenerate). To avoid confusion we shall, in addition, employ a subscript 'c' or 'e' to differentiate between the 'circular' and the 'elliptical' planform respectively.

Comments: *Tuners who claim the ability to tune the second and third partials correctly while using circular notes are making reference to the 'traditional notes' which in these cases are defined by circular grooves. As readers are aware, this book and its author make a clear distinction between the 'traditional note' and the 'true note.' Wherever the word 'note' is used in this book, standing by itself, it refers to the 'true note.' The traditional note does not define, unambiguously, the domain (or area) of the vibrating system. The true note does this. I also feel compelled to point out that while patents in the past have made claims to particular geometrical shapes for the notes these were all made with respect to the 'traditional notes.' With all the ambiguity hanging over these traditional notes and their shapes, the patent claims become equally ambiguous. Personally, I have never taken these patents seriously! Readers must appreciate the fact that just as the decals on a racing car does not increase its speed or stability, cosmetics do not add to a pan's performance: very often they detract!*

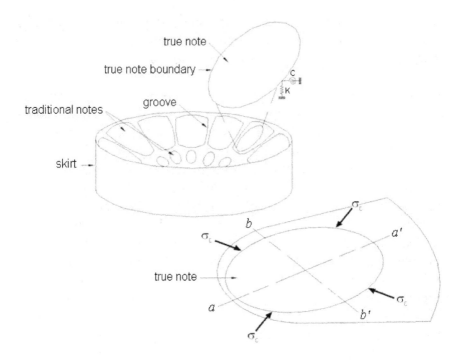

Fig. 14.33. Composite diagram showing true note location on a tenor pan face with the associated spring supports K and C and compressive stress σ_c applied at all points along the boundary.

Now these three modes must be tuned. With reference to Figure 14.33, tuning all three modes entails adjusting the note shape and rise-factor as well as peening along the note boundary to set the compressive stress distribution σ_c and spring constants K and C (see Chapter 3 for more details). In order to properly define a domain on the pan face as a *tuned note,* it is important for the tuner to set up the boundary conditions as uniformly as possible. The true note boundary only exists dynamically because, with the note at rest, one cannot observe the curved line defining the boundary. The following are possible:

a. If the tuner assigns clearly defined constant values to K, C and σ_c along the note boundary and sets the note shape then *there exists a tuned note* with well defined modal frequencies *but not necessarily in agreement with the standard musical scale.*

b. If the tuner assigns no specific values to K, C and σ_c at points along the boundary, then the note domain will be ill defined by the random values attached to these parameters. In this case *a tuned note does not exist*.

c. Of course more is required because these parameters, K, C and σ_c and all the other elastic, geometric and material parameters must be set to values *that allow the frequencies to come into close agreement with the musical scale (12-TET) to the satisfaction of the tuner. In the specification of the musically tuned state, it is necessary to include the musical reference scale (12-TET)*.

Because it is possible to set up a wide range of conditions on the pan face, most of which are unsuitable for the generation of *musical tones*, we need to define those conditions that are suitable and that allow for reproducible behavior each time the notes are played. We can discuss these conditions entirely within the framework of the theoretical methods and formulations developed in this work (see Chapter 3) but because this Section will have great appeal to the more musically minded, the tuner and the apprentice tuner, a more heuristic approach is chosen. We wisely follow the lead of the pan maker/tuner. Once again we sit beside the tuner, listening intently while focusing on his peening actions.

Assuming the proper preparations relating to sinking, forming and burning have already been carried out (a job usually done by other workers), the tuner peens and forms, to his satisfaction, the notes to the approximate heights, sizes, and shapes. In accordance with the boundary condition requirements stated earlier, the tuner ensures that the note surface, with its ellipsoidal form, is smooth (small hammer marks can be tolerated) and peening is evenly applied around the elliptical planform. This planform is not marked unto the surface but the tuner watches the note and develops a good mental picture of its location. As we watch, we too must be as observant as he is, and develop our picture to match his. As the tuning continues, the required pitches can be heard on the key-note and the next two higher partials. When the tuner is satisfied, what he has produced on the pan face are a set of domains with special properties. We show honesty if he asks for our opinion, without pretending that our ears can discern musical correctness as good as his. If you think a partial is too flat or too sharp let him know, he could have done that purposely to test you! Maybe you do have keener ears than the tuner! The point I wish to make is that tuning pan notes is a skill to be developed and one that is continually being refined by the professional tuner.

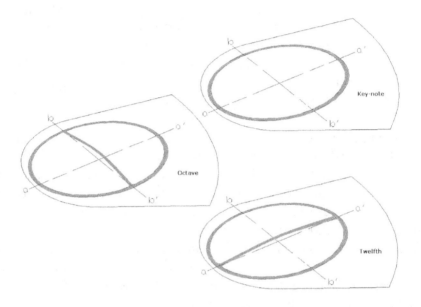

Fig. 14.34. Chladni patterns for the Key-note $[0, 0]_e$, Octave $[0, 1]_e$ and Twelfth $[1, 0]_e$ for the note sketched in Figure 14.33. On the Key-note, all parts of the ellipsoidal cap vibrate in-phase (stretch out one hand with palm horizontal and move it up and down to simulate the motion). On the Octave and Twelfth, the pair of half-ellipsoids in each case, vibrates in anti-phase (use both hands, side by side with the narrow space separating your hands lined up with bb' or aa', then move one hand up and the other down repeatedly to simulate these motions).

What is special about each domain or note, so formed, is the unique set of frequencies to which each note has been tuned consistent with the musical scale and the tuning requirements for steelpan notes. When tested by the classical Chladni powder pattern technique (see Figure 14.34) or by laser holographic interferometric technique the results always indicate well defined nodal boundaries. The holographic technique gives, in addition, a pattern of iso-deflection contour lines. For the fundamental mode corresponding to the key-note, these contour lines are a set of concentric ellipses centered about the apex of the ellipsoidal shell forming the note.

The near perfect form of these ellipses indicates that the nodal line formed by the outermost ellipse, or the single ellipse for the Chladni pattern (see the key-note in Figure 14.34), represents a boundary along which the spring supports (K and C) and compressive stress distribution (σ_c) are fairly uniformly distributed. For a given note, these boundary conditions apply to all the *tuned* modes of the note. In order for these patterns to show such uniformity it is necessary for the note material to be of constant density and fairly constant thickness over the entire note. In addition the form or shape of the note surface should be without large distortions (indentations or humps). These conditions are almost always satisfied.

When all the notes on the pan have been perfectly tuned, pan maker, tuner, panist and the listener can all agree that when each note is played in the correct manner with an appropriate stick, only the tuned modes can be heard from each note. The odd occasion where an untuned mode is generated can be dealt with by tracking down the location of the source followed by a gentle application of the hammer.

Some tuners have begun to use the Chladni technique regularly in their tuning. When this method is being used, there is no need to use any form of excitation other than stick impact. To achieve a good pattern for the key-note, the note should be played in the normal way with the right stick, making impacts to the sweetspot (the apex of the ellipsoidal shell, which on the planform corresponds to the intersection of the axes *aa'* and *bb'*). Since the nodal lines for the octave and the twelfth intersect at this point, neither the octave nor the twelfth are *initially* excited by stick impacts made at this point. While both the octave and twelfth will be excited by non-linear coupling to the key-note in the course of the time-development of the tone, their nodal lines still do not appear on the Chladni patterns formed by stick impact at the sweetspot because of the larger amplitude of the vibrations corresponding to the key-note. What the tuner will observe is the pattern seen in Figure 14.34 for the key-note. This single pattern provides all the information he needs because the location and shape of the planform will be clearly defined by the elliptical pattern while the nodal lines for the octave and twelfth are just the two perpendicular axes of this ellipse.

Note: One can make some special comments on tuning the octave and twelfth by noting the locations of the nodal lines along the axis *aa'* (for the twelfth) and along *bb'* (for the octave). In tuning the octave without affecting the twelfth, peen along the axis *aa'* (from above to lower the frequency or from below to raise it). To tune the twelfth without affecting the octave, peen along the axis *bb'*. Bear in mind however, that the key-note will always be affected by peening action applied anywhere on the note surface. All these changes in modal frequencies are brought about by changes in note shape (geometrical form) made locally in the neighborhood of the point of hammer contact. Peening along the note boundary will affect all modal frequencies by the alterations made to the boundary conditions. Peening just inside the note boundary alters the planform shape thereby affecting the modal frequencies and their ratios. In fine tuning the note the regions just inside the note boundary are good places to peen, especially at either ends of the axis *aa'* for the octave or at either ends of the axis *bb'* for the twelfth. Always check the key-note during these operations.

14.25.4 A Simple Rotation Device for Deriving the 5/4^{ths}-Law — Symmetry Considerations

We are now in a position to derive the 5/4^{ths}-Law. In mathematics, an expression or formula is said to be a *closed-form expression (closed-form formula)* if it can be expressed analytically in terms of a bounded (finite) number of 'well-known' elementary functions — such as constants, usually one variable like x, elementary arithmetic operations ($+ - \times \div$), n^{th} roots, exponents, logarithms, trigonometric functions and inverse trigonometric functions. While there are closed-form solutions for the fundamental frequency of axisymmetrical vibration for shallow spherical thin shells on circular planforms, there exist only numerical solutions for finding the corresponding frequencies for shallow ellipsoidal thin shells on elliptical planforms. For the corresponding problems involving the vibrations about the nodal lines along aa' and bb', there exists no closed-form solutions. However, approximate solutions can be found using various perturbation techniques.

My real aim is to find the *ratio* of the modal frequency of mode3 (f_3) to the modal frequency of mode2 (f_2): i.e. I seek only the ratio, or *quotient*, f_3/f_2 as a function of the *aspect ratio* a/b of the true note planform. We shall see that exact, closed-form frequency equations are not required in the derivation. The reader is therefore spared a considerable amount of hard work! Skilled mathematicians and mathematical physicists know how to reduce tedious calculations by using a variety of devices — acquired through experience. I shall develop one of these 'devices' specially crafted for our purposes on our work on the steelpan.

Observe from Figure 14.34, that mode2 (the octave) and mode3 (the twelfth) are formed by the anti-phase vibrations of *two halves of the same ellipsoidal shell* (notice the emphasis on the word '*same*'). *This observation is the key that makes a simple proof of the $5/4^{ths}$-Law possible.* This observation tells us that for these two vibrational states, *all, except one of the frequency determining parameters for mode2 and mode3 are the same. Only the nodal lines are different*; for one mode, *mode3*, the nodal line lies along AA' and for the other, *mode2*, the nodal line lies along BB' (or the equivalent lines aa' and bb' of Figures 14.33 and 14.34).

- Now comes a truly amazing insight; when it first came to my mind some years ago, for some time, days, weeks maybe, I was beside myself, somewhat in shock, all because of its simplicity and depth! During that time I felt unable to write anything on the pan! Instead I would go fishing! I now describe the whole concept which came to my mind in an instant as a complete set of ideas. I do so in *point form* followed by explanations and clarifications.
- ***By this observation — 'same ellipsoid' — we know that the frequency equations for mode2 and mode3 must be identical in form (mathematical form).***
- ***This statement (a mathematical statement), is true even though we may not know how to write down the exact equations for the frequencies of these two modes.***
- ***This mathematical form must be such that an interchange or swapping of a and b in the frequency equation switches between mode2 and mode3.*** To write this interchange as a mathematical operation I introduce two new notations, either

of which can be used to indicate the *interchange* or *swapping* of the variables *a* and *b*;

inchg[a, b] and *swap[a, b]*

The *interchange operator inchg[a, b]* interchanges the *values* of the semi-major axis *a* and the semi-minor axis *b*.

This *interchange* produces a 90° rotation of the nodal line from aa' to bb' or bb' to aa' — *it 'rotates' mode2 into mode3 or mode3 into mode2*. Refer to Figure 14.35 for a representation of this rotation. Applying the interchange twice in succession will rotate a mode2 or mode3 onto itself.

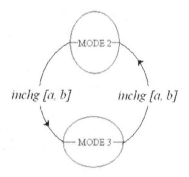

Fig. 14.35 Rotating mode2 into mode 3 or vice versa using the operation *inchg[a, b]*.

Clarification: This rotation is purely mathematical and is performed only on the frequency equations for the second and third partials. It must not be viewed as a physical rotation of the true note on the surface of the pan face. The interchange of *a* and *b* described here is *not* a mere switching of labels either. A switching of labels in the representation of semi-major axis and semi-major axis in both the diagram representing the true note and in the equations produces no dynamical changes whatsoever. By definition, *b always* represents the semi-minor axis while *a always* represents the semi-major axis. In addition the aspect ratio is *always* represented by $\frac{a}{b}$. The swapping operation is carried out only on the frequency equations. Given any one of these equations, for the second or third partial of the pan note, performing the operation *inchg[a, b]* on this equation, switches the *answer* given by this equation from the value of the octave frequency to the *value* for the frequency of the twelfth and vice-versa.

To illustrate these rotations on the modes (or tuned states) $[0, 1]_e$ and $[1, 0]_e$ one can write the operational equations

$$inchg[a, b] [0, 1]_e = [1, 0]_e,$$

$$inchg[a, b] [1, 0]_e = [0, 1]_e.$$

These operations switch the mode description from the octave to the twelfth or the twelfth to the octave. For these rotations to take place on the ellipsoidal shell *it is necessary for*

(i) the tuner to establish constant boundary conditions along the contour of the true note,
(ii) the true note to be of constant thickness and
(iii) *the density of the note material (steel or steel plus coating) to be constant over the area defining the true note.*

As a result of these conditions, we point out the following:

- On a properly prepared, tuned note, these conditions are obtained to good approximation. But what exactly do I then mean when I say in the previous paragraph that '*it is necessary for (i) the tuner to establish constant boundary conditions along the contour of the true note, (ii) the true note to be of constant thickness and (iii) the density of the note material (steel or steel plus coating) to be constant over the area defining the true note* '? Is it necessary (in an absolute sense) for these things to be constant or just *approximately* so? This requires careful explanation and clarification. If you are a pan researcher (scientist) and you are not aware of the '*detailing*' that goes into the production of a good pan for the generation of good notes you are likely to run into serious trouble with your experiments if the details discussed under the topic of '*Detailing*' are ignored. To be frank, I have seen this problem appear '*between the lines*' on the pages of reported work on the pan and I am being honest here. What exactly is '*detailing*'? For a discussion on all this, I shunt you over to Section 14.48 but before you go there I would prefer that you complete this Section and the following Sections that takes you on to Section 14.48.

How is Detailing related to the requirements (i), (ii) and (iii)? In the symmetry considerations of the vibrating pan note, one has the antisymmetric vibrations about the minor-axis of the true note that generates the octave, accompanied by the antisymmetric vibration about the major axis generating the twelfth. In each case the axis represents a nodal line for the corresponding mode. It is the *antisymmetric nature* of these vibrations that unambiguously defines these two modes. It must be recalled that there are clearly defined 'geometrical' mode shapes (ψ_n) for each of these modes. For the proper physical (physics) and mathematical description of these modes, it is necessary to assume uniformity of the boundary conditions along the contour of the *true* note. In addition, over the surface of the note both the mass density and the thickness of the material must remain constant. Hidden from our eyes are the local internal stress distributions over the notes. Stresses play a major role in the note vibration; as we have seen, areas on a note that are subject to strong localized compressive stress can buckle (flap). It is necessary therefore to avoid large changes in stress levels (large stress gradients) over small areas of the note. Detailing addresses all these concerns by ensuring that *within sufficiently tight limits* these requirements are met.

The good pan maker assisted by his 'Sinker,' sets the limits appropriate for each pan type and note location on the pan face. As a general rule, the tighter he sets his limits, the better are his pans.

- Since the boundary of the true note is established dynamically, it is the dynamics that completes this process. This may seem a bit confusing but it becomes clear if you include on the list of *methods* or *mechanisms* for tuning the note, the *mode-confinement mechanism* (see Chapter 4)

which establishes the domain for the interacting modes — key-note-octave-twelfth.
- What this means is that *the key-note frequency or the pitch heard aurally corresponds to the vibration of that ellipsoidal area of note surface bounded by an elliptical nodal line along which the dynamical stiffness is constant.*

Using the *rotation device* one can state quite generally, that so long as (i) the boundary conditions are uniform along the true note boundary and (ii) the note material is of constant density and thickness over the note surface;

- *the interval (in the musical sense) represented by the ratio of the frequency of mode3 (the third partial) to the frequency of mode2 (the second partial) depends only on the ratio $\frac{a}{b}$ (or equivalently, its inverse $\frac{b}{a}$).*

The interval cannot be related exclusively to the *product ab* because, when the interchange of *a* and *b* is made, *ab* becomes *ba* and by the commutative property of the product, *ab = ba; which does not rotate one mode into the other.* In fact for the shallow shell notes on the steelpan, the product *ab* (multiplied by π) defines the area of the note surface which remains the same for both modes.

- *Since the area of the note depends upon the product of the two semi-axes (ab), whereas the aspect ratio depends upon the ratio of these two semi-axes (a/b), it is possible to specify the area and the aspect ratio independently of each other.* In addition to being a true mathematical statement, as we shall soon see, this is of great practical importance since it allows the tuner to *independently set* two things (i) the *frequencies* of the partials through their dependence on *both* note area and the aspect ratio, and (ii) the *interval* between the second partial and the third partial which depends *only* on the aspect ratio.

Formally and for completeness I should add that the above arguments that led us to the '*rotation device*' are the '*symmetry considerations*' of the present problem. When properly used, symmetry arguments are very powerful analytical tools. These symmetry ideas, in my opinion, provides us with an excellent understanding of the tuned state of a note for which a more exact, perhaps less symmetrical (when non-ellipsoidal or ovoid notes are considered) but deeper underlying theory yields solutions that cannot be expressed in closed form.

The nice thing about the present approach is that we do not have to know anything detailed about the frequency equation itself i.e. we do not need the full and complete equation for the modal frequencies of the higher partials which will be very complicated (they will not be in closed form anyway). We need only to know that such an equation or a good approximation for it exists even in principle. (If you are not used to thinking abstractly, this could be a bit difficult to 'swallow' but press on with the proof anyway and the difficulties will soon clear themselves! Throughout this book I have been 'training' my readers to think abstractly.)

14.25.5 Setting up a Perturbational Framework that solves the Problem

Having clarified the problem, we now use *three* versions of the *Perturbation Method* to determine the quotient f_3/f_2. Basically, a perturbation method takes one of the parameters describing a system and by varying this single parameter slightly away from some fixed value (an operation defined as the '*perturbation*'), the system is 'perturbed.' (In general there are perturbational methods involving the variation of more than one parameter.) The changes made to the system in response to this perturbation are then examined to determine the dependence of the 'new' (perturbed) system on the *perturbation parameter*. In each of the methods given below, a spherical cap (or shell) is perturbed (distorted) into an ellipsoidal shell. In each case we measure this distortion by examining the *planform* (or boundary) of the shell. In each case, the planform corresponds to the boundary of the true note. To make sure that the perturbation runs properly the rise-factor (H_0/h) of the shell is kept constant.

Method 1: The first method begins with a shallow shell, on circular planform of radius r_c to be determined (see Section 3.16 for a definition of r_c). The planform is then perturbed into an ellipse with aspect ratio $\frac{a}{b}$ where a and b are the semi-major and semi-minor axes respectively of the resulting elliptical planform. The method uses a simple perturbative approach that is linear in the small *perturbation parameter* ε, which is defined as $\varepsilon \doteq \left(\frac{a}{b} - 1\right) \ll 1$. This small parameter ε is called the *ellipticity parameter* of the elliptic planform; note that the *eccentricity*, a different term, is defined as $\sqrt{[1 - (b/a)^2]}$. When $a = b$, there is no perturbation, $\varepsilon = 0$. If the shell on circular planform vibrates in the asymmetrical mode about a diameter with frequency f_c, one gets the first-order perturbation formula for the frequencies of the perturbed shell on elliptical planform corresponding to two distinct (orthogonal) modes — one higher in frequency the other lower in frequency than the corresponding mode on the circular planform. One can write the higher mode frequency as

$$f_3 = f_c(1 + \varepsilon) = f_c \frac{a}{b}.$$

Then, by using the rotation device *inchg[a, b]* on this expression, one gets the lower mode frequency

$$f_2 = f_c \frac{b}{a},$$

which results in

$$\frac{f_3}{f_2} = \left(\frac{a}{b}\right)^2.$$

(*Consistency Check*: In Method 3 (to be dealt with shortly). one finds to first order in ε, the more accurate frequency factor $(1 + 2\varepsilon)^{\frac{1}{2}}$ but for $\varepsilon \ll 1$, $(1 + 2\varepsilon)^{\frac{1}{2}} = (1 + \varepsilon)$ which is used here in Method 1. If the reader should argue that the square root (power ½) in $(1 + 2\varepsilon)^{\frac{1}{2}}$ makes this non-linear in ε, I should add that in the complete frequency analysis, one normally works with the *frequency parameter* which is proportional to the square of the frequency or, equivalently, to $(1+2\varepsilon)$ which, in the problem at hand, is to first order in ε.)

Method 2: For thin elliptical plates (see Section 3.16 and Achong 1995) on elliptical planforms with the aspect ratio $\frac{a}{b}$ close to unity (small ellipticity parameter), the fundamental frequency f_e for axisymmetric vibrations with clamped boundaries in terms of the corresponding frequency f_c on circular ($a = b$) planform is, to good approximation

$$f_e = f_c \left[\frac{a}{2b}\left(1+\left(\frac{a}{b}\right)^2\right)\right]^{\frac{1}{2}}.$$

If we assume that this relation also holds for thin, shallow ellipsoidal shells on elliptical planforms and further assume that a similar relationship holds for the vibration about minor and major axes as nodal diameters, then, by using the rotation device *inchg[a, b]*, we get for the ratio

$$\frac{f_3}{f_2} = \frac{\left[\frac{a}{2b}\left(1+\left(\frac{a}{b}\right)^2\right)\right]^{\frac{1}{2}}}{\left[\frac{b}{2a}\left(1+\left(\frac{b}{a}\right)^2\right)\right]^{\frac{1}{2}}}.$$

where *inchg[a, b]* was employed to obtain the denominator on the right side. This expression reduces to

$$\frac{f_3}{f_2} = \left(\frac{a}{b}\right)^2.$$

There are a number of approximate solutions for the fundamental mode vibration of the elliptical plate that can be found in the literature, all of which, when adapted to the present problem under Method 2, gives the same result as obtained here. For example using the expression given by Mazumdar (1971), $f_e = f_c\left[\left(3+2\left(\frac{a}{b}\right)^2+3\left(\frac{a}{b}\right)^4\right)/8\right]^{\frac{1}{2}}$ and assuming that we can apply it to the modes with a radial nodal line (which is a bit of a stretch here), we get the same result $f_3/f_2 = (a/b)^2$.

The formulas obtained by Methods 1 and 2 are in agreement and are consistent with our earlier findings that the quotient f_3/f_2 should depend only on the aspect ratio a/b. However, Method 2, which strictly applies to flat plates, is rather crude so we need to improve our technique.

Method 3: To simplify the discussion in Method 3, I shall adopt a subscripted notation that uses c to denote *spherical shell on 'circular' planform* and e to denote *perturbed or ellipsoidal shell on 'elliptical' planform*. We previously used a solution for the $[0, 0]_e$ mode (without a nodal 'diameter') for the flat plate into the problem for the $[0, 1]_e$ and $[1, 0]_e$ modes with nodal lines along the axes, now we try to improve this procedure by using the solution given in equation (3.51) for the elliptical shell. There are mathematical deficiencies with this approach because the $[0, 0]_e$ mode and the $[0, 1]_e$, $[1, 0]_e$ modes are physically different. Unfortunately there are no exact solutions for the latter modes with nodal 'diameters' that employ the aspect ratio as the variable.

While I do not want to get mired in the details, major difficulties arise in the general solution to this problem because the system (an ellipsoidal shell) is three dimensional with varying curvature over its surface. In obtaining the frequency formula for the elliptical shell by applying perturbation to a spherical shell, we were able to 'get away' in the approximate formulation of the $[0, 0]_e$ mode because of the simpler mode shape encountered on the fundamental $[0, 0]_c$ mode (without a nodal diameter). The mathematics involving the modes with nodal diameters, although it follows a similar procedure, is more difficult. But if we were to assume that ellipticity produces a *simple translation* of the frequency spectrum from the circular to the elliptical planform, then we can apply the factor $(1 + 2\varepsilon + 4\varepsilon^2)^{\frac{1}{2}}$ found in equation (3.49) to the $[0, 1]_e$ problem.

- Here, *Simple Translation* means that all the frequencies in the circular case are shifted upward by the same factor to obtain the corresponding frequencies in the elliptical case.

However, this use of *'simple translation'* of frequency, by itself, does not allow us to deal with the fact that the $[0, 1]_c$ and $[1, 0]_c$ modes are identical and have the same frequency while the $[0, 1]_e$ and $[1, 0]_e$ are of different frequencies. To resolve this degeneracy problem, we must make use of the 'rotation device' found earlier. By swapping a and b on one of the modal equations and requiring that $a \neq b$, the degeneracy is removed, giving us two distinct frequencies; one shifted above, the other shifted below the $[0, 1]_c$ frequency. Since our goal is to find the ratio of frequencies i.e. the quotient f_3/f_2, we *do not* have to know the frequency of the $[0, 1]_c$ mode (refer to Methods 1 and 2 where the actual value of f_c was not required). The $[0, 1]_c$ mode serves only as an *intermediary*.

- **Comment:** For a similar reason, in tuning the note, *what initial spherical shell we start off with does not matter. It should now be quite clear that <u>one need not even start with a spherical shell at all</u>!* This is the gist of my earlier comment that the choice of a spherical shell at the commencement of the tuning exercise is for mathematical convenience only (see Section 3.4.1).

We may still have some justifiable concerns for the accuracy of the coefficient in the quadratic term (the value 4) in the series expansion $(1 + 2\varepsilon + 4\varepsilon^2)$ when applied to the $[0, 1]_e$ and $[1, 0]_e$ modes because the ellipticity is expected to have greater effect on the higher modes (this is said in respect to our assumption of *simple translation* of the frequency spectrum) but this is about as best as we can get in the present approximation. Remember that there is no exact closed-form solution for this problem. Any perturbational method will generate subsidiary, mode-dependent, equations at various stages of the procedure. These equations that arise at various stages of the analysis can only be solved numerically (with the substitution of a numerical value for a/b) and they will generate numerical values for the necessary coefficients in the series determined through the application of the appropriate boundary conditions (or *constraints*). As the order of approximation increases (that is to say, as further corrections are made), *the aspect ratio a/b gets lost* in the numerical computations involved in the *constraint equations*. We already saw this type of thing occurring in the solution for the flat elliptical plate in Section 3.16. One sees a complicated non-polynomial structure (containing Bessel functions) emerging rather than the sought after polynomial series expansion. As already noted in Section 3.16, the coefficient for the first order term in ε takes the value 2 and is quite robust but at the second order level, only an approximate value for the coefficient can be obtained. Beyond this point, further corrections are not possible or too difficult. In particular we note that due to the asymptotic nature of the procedures the resulting series might be divergent. However, this problem is minimized and the accuracy improved as ε approaches zero (becomes very small). The boundaries of the true notes on the steelpan satisfy the latter condition; this is so because the notes are tuned to a (musical) scale with partials that are related (to good approximation) by the small integers (1, 2, 3).

For readers who want to think deeper into this problem, observe that the approximate solution we are seeking here is to be written in the form $f_e = f_c \times (function\ of\ \epsilon)$. The *function* we seek is a polynomial (more precisely a *series* with integer powers) in the ellipticity parameter ε. This polynomial requirement places severe restrictions on the mathematics. At some point we must either give up ('cop-out') or settle for the best possible. The rotation device is very clever, but to use it properly, requires a lot of preparation. This type of thing is not uncommon in mathematical physics or mathematics itself.

In case we have gone so far ahead that some readers have forgotten what we want to achieve, recall that the empirical (experimental) result shows that when the pan note is tuned in the *key-note-octave-twelfth* format, the aspect ratio a/b of the true note is equal to 1.27 ± 0.08. We can live quite comfortably by simply accepting this result to define, *empirically*, the 5/4[ths]-Law since 5/4 is equal to 1.25 which falls nicely within the experimental range for the value of the aspect ratio a/b. If I were to take this *correct and easy* route, two things will happen: (1) I would be going against my own approach to physics (which I will surely regret all the rest of my life) and consider myself 'short-changing' my readers in this wonderful story about the pan, (2) we will fail to understand this Law and lose the opportunity of finding the rule to apply when the bass notes are tuned in a *different format*, namely the *key-note-octave-third* format. I cannot deny my readers, who have been very patient in reading all this way into my book, the opportunity of witnessing the unfolding of this important *'wonderful magic'* of steelpan tuning! As hard as the goal is to achieve, it is too important for me to 'cop-out!' That is just not my style!

Writing $(1 + 2\varepsilon + 4\varepsilon^2)^{\frac{1}{2}}$ in terms of a/b gives $\left(3 - 6\frac{a}{b} + 4\left(\frac{a}{b}\right)^2\right)^{\frac{1}{2}}$ from which one gets for the frequency of the *third partial* (the twelfth)

$$f_3 = f_c \left(3 - 6\frac{a}{b} + 4\left(\frac{a}{b}\right)^2\right)^{\frac{1}{2}}.$$

Applying the interchange operation *inchg[a, b]* (the rotation device), one gets for the frequency of the *second partial* (the octave)

$$f_2 = f_c \left(3 - 6\frac{b}{a} + 4\left(\frac{b}{a}\right)^2\right)^{\frac{1}{2}}.$$

One then gets for the quotient f_3/f_2, the following *quartic (fourth order) equation* in a/b

$$\frac{f_3}{f_2} = \left(\frac{3 - 6\frac{a}{b} + 4\left(\frac{a}{b}\right)^2}{3 - 6\frac{b}{a} + 4\left(\frac{b}{a}\right)^2}\right)^{\frac{1}{2}}.$$

This can be expressed more clearly as

$$\frac{frequency\ of\ the\ twelfth}{frequency\ of\ the\ octave} = \left(\frac{3 - 6\frac{a}{b} + 4\left(\frac{a}{b}\right)^2}{3 - 6\frac{b}{a} + 4\left(\frac{b}{a}\right)^2}\right)^{\frac{1}{2}}.$$

The quartic nature (containing a variable raised to the highest *power of four*) of these expressions is more easily seen by writing $x = a/b$ to give

$$\left(\frac{f_3}{f_2}\right)^2 = \frac{4x^4 - 6x^3 + 3x^2}{3x^2 - 6x + 4}.$$

Since the equation is a quartic in x (having four roots, two of them a complex conjugate pair, the third positive real and the fourth negative real), the aspect ratio required to produce a desired frequency ratio (musical interval) must be determined by solving the quartic and taking the *positive real root*. This is a relatively simple task (I recommend that readers try out some numerical exercises using Mathcad©).

Using this equation, frequency ratios (or intervals) can be easily calculated for given values of the aspect ratio a/b. For example, with $a = 1$ (unit of length) and $b = 0.8$, aspect ratio $= 1.25$, the modal frequency f_3 is shifted *upward* by a factor *1.323* while f_2 is shifted *downward* by a factor *0.872* with respect to the $[0, 1]_c$ modal frequency of the unperturbed spherical shell on circular planform of radius $r_c = 0.892$ (see Section 3.16 for details). This gives a quotient $f_3/f_2 = 1.517$. The shells are on clamped planforms and the *rise-factor* H_0/h is the same for both the unperturbed shell and the perturbed shell. When allowances are made for the normal detuning of the twelfth and octave on the pan, the ratio of these two partials is close to 1.5 which is also close to the value 1.517 obtained in this example. The result of this example tells us that in tuning the pan in the key-note-octave-twelfth format, the aspect ratio to be used on the notes is pretty close to 1.25.

14.25.6 The Steelpan Law of Ratios

For the purposes of the discussions to follow, we will make use of the simpler formula $f_3/f_2 = (a/b)^2$ then use the quartic to provide a better numerical result. When $a = b$, as in the case of the circular planform, the two modal frequencies are equal — the degenerate case. On an elliptical planform the modal frequencies are necessarily different; mode3 (the higher mode) is assigned the role of the *resident twelfth* (the *fifth* above the octave) while mode2 (the lower mode) is the designated *octave* (the *resident octave*). Therefore, using these results we obtain the simple expression

$$\frac{Frequency\ of\ the\ twelfth}{Frequency\ of\ the\ octave} = \left(\frac{a}{b}\right)^2.$$

Inverting this expression gives

$$\frac{a}{b} = \sqrt{\frac{Frequency\ of\ the\ twelfth}{Frequency\ of\ the\ octave}}.$$

In either form, we have a **Steelpan Law** which I shall call '*The Steelpan Law of Ratios*' that relates the frequency ratio of the third and second partials to the aspect ratio of a note:

- *A simple relationship has now been found between the aspect ratio $\frac{a}{b}$ and the frequency ratio of the third partial to the second partial (in musical terminology this is the 'interval'); this relationship, elevated to a law — **The Steelpan Law of Ratios** — reads:*
  The frequency ratio or the musical interval between the third and second partial is equal to the square of the aspect ratio of the true note.
- *A purely musical quantity, the interval between the twelfth and the octave is now related, in a simple way, to the geometry or shape of the true note; this shape being defined by the aspect ratio of the true note. Things couldn't be simpler!*
- *In the same way that the ear can hear this interval, the eye can see the reason for it. Recall that the human ear is sensitive to frequency ratios (see Section 14.3.1). Since the tuner employs unison tuning (see Section 14.1), his ears are therefore made sensitive to the aspect ratio of the note, because, as we have discovered, the aspect ratio is related to the musical interval between the second and third partials of the steelpan note. This is good for the pan maker and tuner because it makes tuning by shaping a rather simple exercise (at least in theory).* **So the little boy in the Preface who, while staring at the notes on the Ping Pong and thinking about 'shape vibration,' was right after all!**

- *With all the complexities of the note dynamics that we have seen in this book it is indeed pleasing (certainly refreshing) to see this display of simplicity that the instrument presents to us. Subtlety indeed!*
- *In practice, what it means is that as the note is tuned, the tuner will hear the key-note accompanied by two higher partials whose frequency ratio (the distance between them) will be equal to the square of the aspect ratio $\frac{a}{b}$.*
- *The aspect ratio of the true note therefore plays a central role in tuning the partials. However it must be remembered that this special relation between the aspect ratio and the interval between the twelfth and the octave applies when certain conditions (such as the uniformity of the boundary conditions along the true note boundary) are satisfied. The good tuner almost always tunes in a manner that satisfies these conditions.*
- *Do not take it to mean that a note is tuned once the Law of Ratios is satisfied. To be correctly tuned, the key-note must agree with the musical scale (12-TET) and the higher partials detuned in the manner prescribed for stretching and compressing*
- *It was shown in Section 9.4, that **the Steelpan Law of Ratios is unaffected by changes in temperature of the musical instrument.** This means that as the temperature of the instrument changes, the frequencies of all the partials will change but the interval between the second and third partials will be unaffected. This conclusion was drawn from the fact that (i) the aspect ratio is independent of temperature and (ii) the musical interval between the second and third partials depend only on the aspect ratio. In Section 9.4 it was also argued that the ubiquitous Pan Jumbie (the distribution of internal stresses on the steelpan) which depends on temperature may, for sufficiently large temperature changes, alter the stress distribution on the pan face to the extent that the boundary conditions along the true note boundary (uniformity along the boundary) may change in such a manner that the conditions for the Steelpan Law of Ratios are no longer valid. For any reasonable changes in*

ambient temperature to which this musical instrument (in its finished, tuned state) would be subjected, such a drastic change in boundary conditions is unlikely to occur. The data of Section 9.5 can be shown to be in agreement with this conclusion.

- As pointed out earlier (Section 14.25.4), 'the area of the note depends upon the product of the two semi-axes (ab), whereas the aspect ratio depends upon the quotient of these two semi-axes (a/b), it is therefore possible to specify the area and the aspect ratio <u>independently</u> of each other.' When taken together with the Steelpan Law of Ratios, **this makes it possible for the tuner to tune all the partials on a note and to <u>independently</u> set the interval between the octave and the twelfth.** This can be interpreted as the (theoretical) proof that it is possible to tune the notes on a pan in the standard format as a set of musical intervals (of course we are already aware of the practical proof through the physical existence of tuned pans).

14.25.7 Our Goal — The 5/4^{ths}-Law

Now, to the extent that we can set aside the small detuning corrections for a note tuned in the *key-note-octave-twelfth* format, using the 12-TET value 2.9966 for the ratio of the twelfth to the key-note (see Section 14.3.4), the frequency ratio of the twelfth to the octave is 2.9966: 2, which gives

$$\left(\frac{a}{b}\right)^2 = \frac{2.9966}{2},$$

which leads to

$$\frac{a}{b} = \sqrt{\frac{2.9966}{2}} = 1.224.$$

Using the more accurate quartic formula one gets

$$\frac{a}{b} = 1.241$$

and by using *small integers* to either results gives the **5/4ths-Law**,

$$\frac{a}{b} = \frac{5}{4}, \quad \text{Quod erat demonstrandum (Q.E.D.)!}$$

With $\frac{5}{4} = 1.25$ this law explains the empirical value of 1.27 ± 0.08 for the aspect ratio of the true notes produced dynamically by a sounding note tuned in the *key-note-octave-twelfth* format.

When detuning is included one gets for the aspect ratio

$$\frac{a}{b} = \sqrt{\frac{3 \pm \sigma_2}{2 \pm \sigma_1}},$$

where σ_1 and σ_2 are the detuning parameters on the octave and twelfth respectively as these two partials are compressed (using the − sign) or stretched (by using the + sign). *However, this level of precision is not necessarily achieved on the note by making changes to the lengths of the major and minor axes since it can also be achieved by making small changes to the overall shape of the note surface (changing the shaping function Q) or by 'stretching' using much obliquity on the hammer which modifies localized stresses as the surface yields by plastic deformation. (I had to be a little technical here because these tuning procedures are not generally known or are usually misunderstood.)*

For the tuner who wishes to tune only the key-note and octave (although I can see no good reason for doing this on any pan other than the bass), the 5/4ths-Law should still be applied while the *twelfth* can be suppressed (the ringing component of the tone muted) by reducing the coupling of mode3 to the first two modes. Except you are tuning the low bass notes, DO NOT remove the twelfth by changing the aspect ratio a/b drastically i.e. keep it at, or close to, 5/4. To do this efficiently, tune the key-note, octave and twelfth normally (using the 5/4ths-Law) then by using the hammer to lightly tap the points (one or both) marked by X's on the sketch in Figure 14.32, shift slightly the frequency of mode3 away from the position of the twelfth on the frequency scale. Tap only lightly because while the octave frequency will hardly be affected (the tapping being made along its nodal line), the key-note may shift frequency. Some extra peening from the underside may be necessary. If the aspect ratio is changed drastically and arbitrarily, mode3 will still be heard at some arbitrary frequency and may produce some dissonance. If you wish to adjust the octave without affecting the twelfth, tap lightly from below (to raise), or on the top face (to lower) at the points marked Y in Figure 14.32. Remember that tapping the hammer anywhere on the true note surface always affects the key-note. Tuning the low bass notes without the *twelfth* is discussed later.

14.25.8 The Connection between the $5/4^{ths}$-Law and Mode-Localization or Energy Confinement — the Theory of the Pan in a Nutshell

It is important to establish the connection between the $5/4^{ths}$-Law and *Mode-Localization* or *Energy Confinement* as it explains the phenomenon readily observed during the tuning process where at the instant the note is properly tuned and all the partials are properly arranged *chromatically*, the note bursts out in a loud resonance when played. Before this point is reached, the note sounds soft, somewhat muffled. The explanation is as follows; using the form of the law when the partials are tuned in the $1:2\pm\sigma_1:3\pm\sigma_2$ ratio, the ratio a/b is equal to $\sqrt{((3\pm\sigma_2)/(2\pm\sigma_1))}$. Once established, this state allows for maximum coupling and energy transfers among these three tuned modes — key-note, octave and twelfth. The total transverse vibrational energy imparted to the note by stick impact, is therefore wholly *contained* in these three modes or *localized* within the true note area defining the modes. The expressions that best describe the coupled relationship among these three modes is given in Section 6.2, where it is shown that the weighted sum of the squares of the amplitudes of these modes is equal (up to a constant of proportionality) to the total kinetic energy of the vibrating note. These relationships are expressed by the *mirror functions* of Section 6.3.3. In fact when the detuning is zero and the modes are *locked*, energy confinement is as perfect as mechanically possible. However, one cannot like the sound produced by this state because the rate of energy transfer from the key-note to the higher modes is then too great resulting in the short duration *pung tone*.

Of course, for musical purposes, the modes must be detuned to avoid the pung sound. The detuning, when properly applied *does not* destroy the mode-localization or confinement aspects of the system.

Once the state of confinement is attained, energy is continually exchanged among the three modes while the only losses from the confinement area are by the processes of internal damping, acoustical radiation and transmission through the imperfect note boundary. At this point in the tuning process, when the note is played, the modal vibrations are at their maximum. In fact optimum tuning can be decided by the large acoustical output obtained at this point in the tuning process. Of course, accuracy of tuning must be determined by reference to the 12-TET scale.

Let us now combine this result with the Fundamental Law of the Steelpan.

- Because mode-localization and the associated energy confinement are possible on the notes of the pan, when combined with the Fundamental Law of the Steelpan according to which true notes *do not* share borders, **many tuned notes can be placed on the *same* pan face.**
- **Energy confinement and mode-localization together with the Fundamental Law constitute the *physical principles* whereby a number of well defined tuned domains can exist simultaneously on the same pan face.**

One can choose to describe the mode-localized state in terms of the frequency ratio 1:2:3 (*with corrections for detuning*) or in terms of the equivalent $5/4^{ths}$-Law for the aspect ratio. One now has a clear demonstration of the connection between these physical principles and the $5/4^{ths}$-Law and by inference the connection between the law and the very structure of the pan as a system of connected domains. *The $5/4^{ths}$-Law together with Detuning and the physical principles of Mode Localization, Confinement and the Fundamental law, are the governing principles by which the steelpan becomes a viable musical instrument.*

This, in a 'nutshell' tells us how the steelpan works and justifies the use of the term *Law* rather than *Rule* in the $5/4^{ths}$-Law. This Law, like the *physical principles and detuning,* is not a law imposed on the pan makers and tuners to guide them, but a law that a working steelpan follows. Any attempt to force the instrument to function otherwise, subdues its operation and stifles its tones

14.25.9 Some Important Questions and Comments

(i) Someone (perhaps the author himself, playing *devil's advocate*) may offer the counter argument that a note can be tuned by '*simple tuning*' in which the key-note and at most the octave are tuned, excluding the fifth, thereby circumventing the $5/4^{ths}$-Law. This tuning proposal, which is a throwback to the early days of pan making, is not satisfactory and leads to *trouble*! We shall soon see exactly what this trouble is! It was Marshall, led by the sound of his harmonica, who, by his introduction of 'complex tuning', took the pan and its sound out of the 'noisy instrument' era into its present day clean and refreshing tones (recall the '*fizz*' and the '*pop*').

The first problem with the proposal is that whatever shape is given to the true note, defined for simplicity by the ratio a/b, there will always exist at least one mode of vibration higher than the octave. This mode *must* be 'tuned' to a non-dissonant (consonant) frequency (dissonance is the reason for the noise on early pans). For the mode above the octave, the choice is limited to the fifth or the third. This means that when properly tuned either the $5/4^{ths}$-Law or the $9/8^{ths}$-Rule (see the next Section) applies. If the law is circumvented there can be audible dissonance depending on the strengths of the higher modes.

The second problem with simple tuning is that the key-note together with the octave, interact to generate a parametric mode (the result of the interaction between mode1 and mode2) of frequency equal to or close to the fifth (see Chapter 5). When mode3 is not 'tuned' or the mode made absent by having $a/b \neq 5/4$ *(or not sufficiently close),* the energy of this parametric mode which normally drives the fifth, is now wasted; resulting in a reduction in acoustical output from the key-note and octave. If the tuning is so simple (so bad really) that only the key-note is tuned (pre-Marshall days) then the situation is even worse, for so long as the notes are raised sections of the pan face, the parametric modes generated by mode1 will still exist — there being no tuned octave, this represents wasted energy. There is always a price to pay for breaking a law! That's the trouble!

(ii) It is possible to circumvent the $5/4^{ths}$-Law by the use of some special contrivance. For example one can machine an ellipsoidal note on the pan face having thickness that varies as one move away from the apex towards the note boundary. For the standard pan the note thickness is fairly constant on a given note. In this contrived case, the note thickness $h = h(r, \theta, \phi)$ becomes a new variable over the note surface. With this new variable, the note shapes and the boundary of the true note can be custom designed. There is no advantage to having such a system save that of proving the existence of a way to circumvent a law applicable to the standard method of pan making. The disadvantage will of course be the problem of maintaining the desired thickness distribution while peening the note in the tuning and re-tuning processes. To apply this method to all the notes on a pan involves unnecessary labour and complication not to mention the problems the higher untuned modes may pose. It's not worth the trouble! Obey the law and live a simple, happy life!

(iv) One may well ask, '*must tuners follow the $5/4^{ths}$-Law exactly?* The experimental data provides an answer; the spread in the empirical result $a/b = 1.27 \pm 0.08$ provided by the ± 0.08 value, shows that they don't follow the law *exactly* (not that they knew that there was a law to follow). But this represents a spread of just ± 6% showing that they follow the law *very closely*. (We have embarked on a very important discussion here on what the tuner does and the keen-eyed reader, remembering what I said before, may interrupt by saying that when it comes to the true note boundary, it is the note dynamics that assigns the final shape not the tuner. We can entertain all this but let us face reality one step at a time.) In most cases the major source of the deviations can be traced to the tuning of the third partial. In these cases, while the key-note and the octave are tuned to perfection with the aid of a tuning meter, the third partial is often tuned fully by ear because it is somewhat time-consuming to tune all the higher partials with a tuning meter. However, when the notes are properly formed (speaking of true notes) the instrument is much easier to tune. So what one finds is that well prepared pans tuned by a good tuner with an equally good pair of ears, may carry notes having aspect ratios falling well within the 1.27 ± 0.08 range. All this is *not* meant to show that the tuning meter is indispensable! I hope that most of my readers can tune a pan without a tuning meter! Or at least can tell when a note is 'off.'

One may also ask, as a follow up question, *'is the spread in aspect ratio values a result of detuning of the two higher partials?'* A definitive answer is possible here. One can take the maximum detuning on the twelfth ($\sigma_2 = \pm 0.02$) and the maximum detuning on the octave ($\sigma_1 = \pm 0.01$) to obtain the maximum and minimum *frequency ratios* $f_3/f_2 = 1.5176$ and 1.4826 respectively, which give a spread of *relative* frequency ratios of ± 0.0175 or $\pm 1.167\%$. If this detuning is achieved exclusively by adjusting the aspect ratio, then our formula $f_3/f_2 = (a/b)^2$ gives a corresponding spread in the aspect ratio of only $\pm 0.58\%$ which is ten times *smaller* than the $\pm 6\%$ spread obtained empirically (the more exact quartic formula will not significantly change these numbers). This shows that the 'spread' is not the result of detuning! It is also quite clear that the tuner, in his final actions of tuning a note, to obtain the amplitude and frequency modulations he desires, hardly makes any adjustment to the aspect ratio (as stated earlier in Section 14.25.7) but instead adjusts the note *surface shape* and *internal stresses* with a peening action that involves much *obliquity* (or *stretching*) (see Section 2.6). I urge readers to look carefully at the tuning actions of the good tuner at this stage of the tuning process. If you are a good tuner you would probably say to me 'well I know that already, but thanks!' Well just like our good tuner, I also had to learn these things the hard way but in addition as is *my way*, I had to prove it both practically and theoretically as I just demonstrated. This allows me to make the declaration that the methodology followed by the good pan maker is appropriate for the tuning of this instrument.

14.26 The $9/8^{ths}$-Rule — Using the Third on the Bass Notes

To avoid generating high frequency ringing tones on the bass the coupling to the *fifth* should be reduced by slight alterations to the note shape by peening at the points marked X Figure 14.32. The strength of this partial can thereby be reduced to a level acceptable on the bass. An alternative approach is that the *fifth* be replaced by the *third* (above the octave) as suggested to me, first by the late Randolph Leroy Thomas and later by Bertram 'Bertie' Marshall (private communications in both cases). Other tuners of the bass instrument also use the *third*.

Since the *third* sits at 2.5198 times the key-note frequency (see Section 14.3.4), the aspect ratio for the notes tuned with the *key-note, octave* and *third* by our formula $f_3/f_2 = (a/b)^2$ is

$$\frac{a}{b} = \sqrt{\frac{2.5198}{2}} = 1.122.$$

The more accurate quartic formula gives

$$\frac{a}{b} = 1.1251$$

By using small integers, this ratio can be written in the form:

$$\frac{a}{b} = \frac{9}{8},$$

where $\frac{9}{8} = 1.125$. This rule which applies to the aspect ratio when the *third* replaces the *fifth* will be called the **$9/8^{ths}$-Rule for Steelpan Bass**.

Anyone with sufficient experience in tuning the bass would have made the observation that using the *third*, as the $9/8^{ths}$-Rule implies, produces notes with a more rounded ('fatter') shape than the slender ('thinner') geometries obtained with the *fifth*. The extent to which this is noticeable depends on the rise-factor or 'height' of the notes being compared. Bass notes with larger rise-factor values can be made physically larger in area.

Unlike the case for the aspect ratio 5/4 which has been raised to the level of a law, the $9/8^{ths}$-Rule cannot be similarly elevated for the following reason. The $5/4^{ths}$-Law deserves its classification because it relates to the tuning arrangement that allows all three modes, *key-note, octave* and *fifth*, to be tightly localized within the true note area. In the case of the $9/8^{ths}$-Rule, only the *key-note* and *octave* are localized by non-linear mode coupling while the *third* is not. The energy of the parametric mode generated at frequency close to the absent fifth, as mentioned earlier in the defense of the $5/4^{ths}$-Law, is lost (there being no mode tuned to the *fifth* to make use of this energy through the agency of internal resonance). The small vibrational motion of this parametric mode can be detected by careful measurements of the note surface displacement or velocity (see Section 9.5). However, these low level vibrations do not by themselves produce audible effects unless they drive, and resonate with, a tuned mode at the *fifth*. Because we are dealing with modes of vibration having widely different frequencies well outside their individual bandwidths, energy coupling between them can only occur non-linearly. This means that only the modes that are tuned close to *integer multiples* of the key-note frequency can interact with the key-note in this way. The ratio 2.5198 of the *third* to the *key-note* is not close enough to an integer (neither 2 nor 3) for energy transfers to occur.

As it stands, using the *third* for mode3 results in a note where the key-note and the octave are mode-localized while *mode3 vibrates independently and can only be excited during the initial stick impact*. From the work on contact force spectra and band limiting (Sections 13.27 – 13.32) one finds that notes played on the bass with the bass stick are all frequency and wavelength band-limited with weak contact force components at the octave level and higher. *Direct excitation* during impact is therefore weak at the octave and weaker at the *third*. In order for the octave to be heard on the bass notes using the bass sticks, modal coupling with the key-note is necessary. While the octave will be enhanced by mode coupling, the *third* will not: it remains weak as all high partials on the bass ought to be. In addition, the *third* will *not* be amplitude or frequency modulated. Hence the inclusion of the *third* on the bass notes is done only to provide some ringing, or to be more precise, some *tonal color*, but not at such a high frequency as the *fifth*.

The $9/8^{ths}$-Rule remains just that, a rule, for implementing the option of using the *third* to replace the *fifth* as the third partial.

Note: In Section 4.11 it was shown that when a note is played more intensely, a greater fraction of the total energy is transferred to the octave (the resident octave) and to the higher partials generally. This causes problems on the bass where strong higher partials are not desired. With greater energy spilling over to the higher partials by mode coupling, the key-notes on the bass notes lose energy to these higher frequency components. Since the third is not coupled non-linearly to the key-note, its use on the bass note will not allow this spillover of energy to the third partial. The third will only receive energy directly from the initial stick impact and remain relatively weak. In addition by using the $9/8^{ths}$-Rule, the true note can be made physically larger (in surface area) thereby increasing the acoustical radiating power of the key-note. This increase in area is not immediately obvious. To see this we take into account the fact that there is always an upper limit to the size of a note that can be placed on a bass pan. It is therefore the longer of the two dimensions, a or b, that will be subjected to this restriction. By definition, the longer dimension is a. As a result, the pan maker must take a (or 2a) as the <u>principal dimension</u> in setting the size of the note. For a given a, by choosing the third, one gets $b = (8/9)a$ for a total note surface area of $A = (8/9)\pi a^2 = 2.793a^2$. Compare this with $A = (4/5)\pi a^2 = 2.513a^2$ when the twelfth is used. Using the third gives an 11% increase in surface area. If all other acoustic parameters remain the same, from equation (12.22), an 11% increase in note surface area produces a 22% increase in acoustic intensity of the key-note at a given point in the air medium. Because acoustic intensity also depends on note surface velocity and frequency, this gain may not be fully realized in practice. Overall, it is better to use the third in place of the twelfth on the bass. **These are interesting and important observations that bass makers can capitalize on.**

14.27 Marking and Forming the Notes

14.27.1 Non-Ellipsoidal (Ovoid) Note Shapes

Throughout this book I have been referring to *'spherical'* and *'ellipsoidal'* note shapes but in fact there is an infinite assortment of shapes that the tuner or pan maker can give to the note surface. The term 'note shape' here refers to the 3-Dimensional surface of the true note. These shapes include ellipsoids and ovoids (see Figure 14.36). The note surface is really a *section* or *'cap'* formed from one of these 3-D surfaces. The planform on which an ellipsoidal true note is attached to the traditional note, along the true note boundary, is elliptical in shape. But for ovoids, the planforms are ovals. For spherical notes (spherical caps really) the planforms are circular. Geometrically, no two manually produced notes are exactly alike. Stamping out notes to precisely the same shape with a specially shaped die in a press-forming process, only determines the shape of the traditional note (this method of pan manufacture has been dealt with in Sections 9.8 and 12.19 *with a warning*). On each re-tuning, a given note takes up a different shape so it is not necessary or important to produce notes with the same shape anyway.

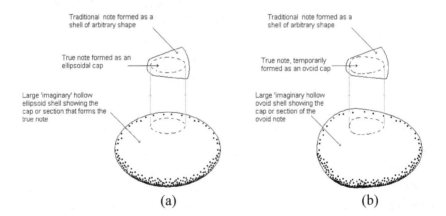

Fig. 14.36. (a) A perfectly tuned true note as an ellipsoidal cap on and arbitrarily shaped traditional note. The 'imaginary' ellipsoidal shell that forms this cap is also shown. (b) A note shown in the process of being tuned where the ovoid shape is temporarily set up. The 'egg' shaped ovoid note shown here, depending on the extent of its departure from the ellipsoidal shape, may ''arguably' produce a less than perfect set of partials.

What distinguishes the 'sphere' from the 'ellipsoid' and the 'non-ellipsoidal ovoid'? This is a knotty issue but for us we need not be too mathematical about this question or the answer! You can picture the ovoid as being 'egg shaped' with just one axis of symmetry, the long axis. But there are ovoids that are not egg shaped so I am using the 'egg shape' as an example here. The ellipsoid would have two axes of symmetry perpendicular to each other. That should be enough on the math. Remember that a note is just a 'cap' taken off one of these shapes and not the entire ellipsoid or ovoid (the entire ellipsoid or ovoid is an imaginary surface, only the caps are real, see Figure 14.36). Let us see what happens in practice and to guide our understanding we set up a thought experiment in which a note, call it the G_4 tenor note, is to be tuned by shaping and during this exercise we sprinkle some powder on the surface to view the Chladni patterns. There are many ways of running this experiment but for the present discussion let us say we begin by giving the note a spherical shape as in Figure 3.4. This shape will allow us to tune just the key-note or first partial, G_4. The Chladni pattern will form a circle outlining the true note boundary. By shaping the note further to introduce the octave G_5, the spherical shape is distorted into an ellipsoid or ovoid. While we cannot see the true shape of the note surface, as a guide, we use the Chladni pattern which has now changed into an ellipse or oval. At this point in the exercise all the higher modes on the note are untuned (in the musical sense).

There are many different shapes possible that will produce an acceptably tuned G_4 key-note and a G_5 octave (many different ellipsoids and ovoids and many different Chladni ellipses and ovals). By continuing our experiment, we can easily check this by retuning the same note to the same key-note and octave and viewing the new Chladni pattern. On viewing the pattern by eye, we cannot easily tell the difference between an ellipse and an oval so let us do something that is quite common on many a pan note. Put a 'dent' on the surface, sufficient to make it visible but not to destroy the 'note.' Now, retune the two partials (G_4 and G_5). Once more you would find that the Chladni pattern is an ellipse or an oval somewhat different from what you had before. Now what we are really concerned about is the shape of the note surface itself. With the dent still visible, the note surface is clearly neither ellipsoidal nor ovoid

— our 'dent' has seen to this. Now it does matter where you placed the dent. If you placed the dent close to the apex (the top) of the note and you had the means of exciting the octave only (say with an attached electromagnetic vibrator or a closely placed active loud speaker operating at the frequency of the octave) you will observe that the axial nodal line through the apex, as seen on the Chladni pattern, which is normally straight (see Figure 14.34), is now distorted by the dent. This distortion of the nodal line on the second partial (the octave) is necessary in order for the vibrating note to compensate for the greater dynamical stiffness of the note material in the area of the dent.

Now let us consider the dent. The dent we placed on the note surface has altered the geometry (or shape) of the surface in a small area of the note with sufficient depth to be noticeable. Now let us imagine that we smooth out this area somewhat by spreading the dent over a larger area while reducing its depth. You can imagine this happening in many different ways, even spreading the dent over the entire surface of the true note! This spreading or 'reshaping' of the dent is equivalent to converting one ellipsoid into another or an ellipsoid into an ovoid or vice versa. In each case the true note can be brought to a tuned state (within reasonable limits) with the corresponding set of partials G_4 and G_5. Looking deeper into this thought experiment we see that when the dent was localized close to the apex it modified the axial nodal line but when spread over the surface at reduced depth, the nodal line is hardly affected. This tells us the following; so far we have placed only the first two partials on our note, if we wish to add the third partial (the twelfth) *we need to be very careful about that 'dent.'* We need to be careful about the depth of the dent, its area and its location! Since the dent can modify the nodal line for the octave, it can do the same for the nodal line on the twelfth. Since nodal lines define the domains on a note corresponding to the partials, this 'dent' of ours, can make it very difficult to tune all partials correctly depending on the conditions set by the dent. So the introduction of a third partial will *further restrict* how the note must be shaped. The main restrictions, apart from the avoidance of severe dents, are covered by the $5/4^{ths}$-Law and the $9/8^{ths}$-Rule. But I don't want to stray from our main concern with the ovoids.

Notice how it is possible to make note shape changes of the 'gentle kind' (mild changes, such as spreading a dent to cover the entire note with reduced depth in many different ways) while still retaining the ability to tune the partials on a note. This means that the geometrical differences between the 'ellipsoid' and the 'non-ellipsoid ovoid' can, in practical terms, be made sufficiently small to allow both the tuner and the research analyst to treat all properly prepared, tuned notes having at least three partials, as ellipsoids. To see this more clearly let us try another experiment, this time let us go through the reshaping by looking at the state of the note after each application of the hammer beginning with the tuned ellipsoidal state. Let us say that while the initially tuned state was 'Good,' you as the tuner wish to make it 'Better.' If you are *recognized by your peers* as a good tuner, you never deviate very far from the '*Good State*' as you steer the note towards the '*Better State.*' The 'Better State' is first stored in your mind! The apprentice tuner sitting beside you don't know where you are going until you get there! He might even look a bit confused because the note already sounds good but you persist in hammering the note further! After each hammer application the note is probably still tuned and may be acceptable to most tuners (I know that some tuners would sit back and wonder at this statement but I did not label you as a good tuner, they, your very peers, did that!). The sequence of states taken up by your note (its history) immediately after each hammer application may look somewhat like *mine* which looked like this:

(tuned ellipsoid, 'Good) → *(tuned ovoid)* → *(tuned ovoid)* → *(tuned ellipsoid)* →…… *(tuned ovoid)* → *(tuned ellipsoid, 'Better')*

where the 'continuation dots' (…) represent other intermediate states in the sequence. Just as the tonal differences between the notes at each stage in the sequence are quite small so are the differences in the geometry of the note throughout its short history from 'Good' to 'Better.' This shows that we can treat all the note shapes in the sequence as if they were ellipsoids thereby avoiding the 'knotty' problem of distinguishing mathematically between ellipsoids and ovoids. This means that the 'Better State' could have ended up being an ovoid but its departure from a true ellipsoid is much too small to change the dynamics in a musically detectable way! Notice that at each stage in *my sequence* the note remained 'tuned' this occurred because I *borrowed* your title of 'Good Tuner!' While holding this title I had the ability to discern that the ovoid shapes did not give me the twelfth I had in mind so I made the necessary reshaping to the final ellipsoid that produced the 'better' note, *the one I had in mind*! I know this may sound crazy but they used to refer to Bertie as the 'mad' man so I am in good company!

Now in all our shaping and hammering we were looking at the shape given to the note by the tuner. But the pan dynamics has something to 'say' about this in relation to the true note (this is our second step in facing reality). Recall that the true note boundary is set up dynamically it is for this reason, in my note history above, as judged by the Chladni pattern, the note shape for the 'Good' and the 'Better' states were both ellipsoidal. What this teaches us is that you must always tune the notes with the elliptical shape of the true note boundary *in mind*.

14.27.2 Ellipsoidal Note Shapes on Elliptical Planforms

In the case of the inner notes on the high end pans, the true note boundary and the traditional note boundary may coincide (see Section 14.25.1). Where such coincidence or overlap occurs, the Pan makers can do well by using the $5/4^{ths}$-Law to form their templates for these inner notes. He may also do well to consciously peen within the traditional note area on all notes with this law in mind. With experience, as it is with auto driving and the road code, the application of laws of this type or these 'tricks of the trade' can become a habit or 'second nature.'

When the *key-note*, *octave* and *fifth* are used, the shape of the templates for the inner notes or the desired area within the traditional note where peening may be concentrated to define the true note, is given in Figure 14.37 (a). It must be remembered however, that the final location of the true note boundary is determined by the note dynamics. On the bass, if the *third* replaces the *fifth*, use Figure 14.37 (b) to define the true note boundary. On the high-end pans, *do not* use the shape in Figure 14.37 (b) for the inner note templates or the true note boundaries on the outer notes.

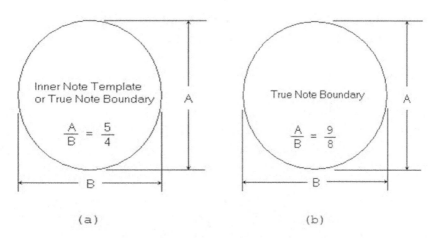

Fig. 14.37. (a) Inner note template or true note boundary using the fifth. (b) True note boundary on the bass using the third.

By applying the Law and the Rule, note-shaping and template-designing are no longer hit and miss activities but are now dressed in the fashion of exact science.

Note; *(1) The $5/4^{ths}$–Law and the $9/8^{ths}$-Rule deal with ratios of lengths — the ratio of the major axis to the minor axis of the true note. These ratios are dimensionless quantities. <u>There is no law that specifies the length or size that must be obeyed by each note that you form and tune</u>. This results from the fact that there are many parameters that determine the pitch (frequency) of a note; size is just one of them. For this reason steelpans, note templates and notes can be made in a wide range of sizes.*

(2) I should also point out that the orientation and position of the true note within the area of the traditional note is a practical matter to be decided by the tuner in the shaping and peening process. There are no 'hard and fast' rules for this because the traditional note is not defined dynamically.

14.28 Tuning the Key-note, Octave and the Fifth or Third; Using the Pan Maker's Formula

In Section 9.11 under Engineering Designs, some pan notes were designed for you. Now we are interested in seeing how this is done in practice on the real pan. We follow a procedure very similar to that used by the pan maker and, in addition, make use of the formula for the linear frequency of a steelpan note, given in equations (3.51) and (9.21b) — The *Pan Maker's Formula* — reproduced below:

$$f = \frac{1}{2\pi}\left(\frac{\alpha_0(1-s)E}{\rho(1-\upsilon^2)}\right)^{\frac{1}{2}} \frac{h}{ab}\left(3 - 6\frac{a}{b} + 4\left(\frac{a}{b}\right)^2\right)^{\frac{1}{2}}.$$

A version of this formula, by the same name, first appeared in my 1999 Pan Maker's Handbook. For easy reference the expressions for s and α_0 given by equations (8.20a) and (8.20b) are reproduced below

$$s = (\check{N}_c + \check{N}_T)\frac{M_4}{\alpha_0},$$

$$\alpha_0 = \frac{1}{12}M_1 + 8(1+\nu)\left(\frac{H_0}{h}\right)^2\left(M_2 - \frac{1}{2}(1+\nu)M_3\right).$$

In this linear expression for the frequency, the effect of damping has been ignored. To correct this (deficiency), the effect of mechanical damping (the major contributor to damping) can be included to give for the damped frequency f_d

$$f_d = f\sqrt{1 - R_m^2/8\pi^2 f^2},$$

where R_m is the mechanical resistance expressed in units of s^{-1} (see Section 8.11). The actual note frequency heard for low levels of excitation (with very small frequency modulation) corresponds to f_d.

Now I re-write the Pan Maker's Formula in the form

$$f = \frac{1}{2\pi} \left(\frac{\alpha_0(1-s)Eh^3}{m_n(1-v^2)ab} \left(3 - 6\frac{a}{b} + 4\left(\frac{a}{b}\right)^2 \right) \right)^{\frac{1}{2}}$$

$$= \frac{1}{2\pi} \sqrt{\frac{note\ stiffness}{note\ mass}},$$

where I have defined the *note stiffness* (at the key-note frequency) as

$$note\ stiffness = \frac{\alpha_0(1-s)Eh^3}{(1-v^2)ab} \left[3 - 6\frac{a}{b} + 4\left(\frac{a}{b}\right)^2 \right],$$

(although in Section 8.4, the term *stiffness parameter* was used to describe α_1, which is related to the note stiffness), and where the mass of the note (uncoated) to very good approximation is given by

$$note\ mass;\ m_n = \rho\pi abh.$$

In this way, one can readily understand why the stiffness of a note of a given surface area πab increases as the rise H_0 (contained in α_0), increases. This is particularly noticeable on the small inner notes of the tenor, but applies to all notes. We observe the following

(i) The note stiffness can be *reduced* by increasing the surface area (πab) (for example the low stiffness of the bass notes). The note stiffness can be *increased* by reducing the surface area (for example the high stiffness of the inner tenor notes).
(ii) Stiffness is increased by increasing the thickness h of the material (observe the strong dependence, to the third power of the thickness).
(iii) The Poisson's ratio v is determined by the choice of note material but hardly varies with the choice of low-carbon steel (see Chapter 9).
(iv) Note stiffness increases with the Young's modulus E.
(v) Note stiffness increases with the aspect ratio a/b.
(vi) Note stiffness decreases with increasing buckling parameter s, where s depends directly on the residual compressive

stress and on the thermal stress brought on by an increase in temperature. This means that note stiffness decreases with temperature (see Chapter 9).

(vii) Note stiffness increases with the Rise Factor H_0/h. It is recommended that stiffness be increased by increasing the rise H_0 rather than decreasing h for two reasons (1) stiffness also increases (rapidly) by increasing h (as in(ii)), (2) for stability and to avoid excessive 'boiing' sounds on the bass, the material must not be too thin. Stability matters are dealt with elsewhere in this book.

(viii) The overall geometrical note shape and the mode shape of the fundamental mode determine the parameters M_j. By combining the effects of temperature and mode shape, one sees that the note stiffness (and as a result, note frequency) is partly set by factors that are not directly under the control of the tuner.

We now expand our discussions on these points by combining them with a view from the tuner's perspective..

The roles played by the rise-factor H_0/h and the compressive/thermal stresses expressed in terms of $\check{N}_c$ and $\check{N}_T$ respectively, in determining the keynote frequency can be seen in these expressions. Let us deal with these first. The tuner adjusts the compressive stress parameter $\check{N}_c$ by adjusting the amount of 'stretching' and the degree of 'tightening' applied to the note by hammer peening. 'Tightening' is also used in 'blocking' the note but in this case we are interested in its use to 'tune' the note. When $\check{N}_c$ is increased, the buckling parameter s increases. This will decrease the value of $(1-s)$ which results in a lowering of the keynote frequency (along with the frequencies of the higher partials). As a reminder, the buckling parameter must not be allowed to reach the value $s = 1$ because this makes $(1-s) = 0$, which in turn makes the frequency $f = 0$ and the entire note will buckle or exhibit the phenomenon of 'flapping.' In practice, peening is never carried to this extreme on the entire note; at most, a small area on the note may be subjected to this highly compressive stress condition. While the tuner never allows an entire note to flap, excessive peening can set up the 'Wobbly Effect' (see Section 9.11.3). The thermal stress component $\check{N}_T$ plays the same role as the compressive stress component $\check{N}_c$ but at room temperature it produces smaller changes in frequency (see Chapter 9).

The M_j (j = 1, 2, 3, 4) coefficients depend on the shape of the note surface and the mode shape which in turn depends on the *unknown* spring constants K and C along the note boundary. This means that the exact frequency for a given note cannot be calculated because of the unknown boundary conditions — spring constants and compressive/thermal stresses. For simplicity one can assume as I have done that the notes are perfectly blocked which means that the boundary is effectively clamped.

To restate the previous paragraph more precisely, as in Section 3.4.2 the true note domain can be represented by N and the boundary by ∂N. The properties of the domain N are defined by the elastic constants E and v, the mass density ρ, the rise H_0, the thickness h, and the shape function Q. The elliptical boundary ∂N is defined as a locus of points on the note surface having equal dynamical stiffness. This boundary is a nodal line (elliptical in shape) for all the tuned modes or partials. It is along ∂N that the spring constants and compressive stresses are set by hammer peening. When tuning a note, the tuner may find that the intensity of the tone is weak or the partials inadequately defined. He will say 'the note needs tightening' which means that note is not properly 'blocked.' Life will be much easier for him and for us if the note was perfectly blocked. We take it therefore for analytical purposes, that the tuner has achieved his aim of perfect blocking which is equivalent to having a clamped boundary.

We learn from the Pan Maker's Formula that the frequency of the key-note increases with the Young's modulus E of the material and decreases with the mass density ρ. The Young's modulus is dependent on carbon content, sinking (through work hardening and modification of grain structure and grain size), tempering (burning) and to a lesser extent on temperature (see Chapter 9 for details). The density is unaffected by these processes and Poisson's ratio can be assumed to remain fairly constant as well (but see Chapter 9 for further details). If one increases the area of the note, given to good approximation by πab, the frequency decreases. (For the mathematically minded, the true surface area of the note, defined as an ellipsoidal cap, can be expressed in terms of an elliptic integral.

But this detail is not necessary here and the expression πab is sufficiently accurate.) If the thickness h is increased, the frequency increases. If the aspect ratio $\frac{a}{b}$ is increased by shaping, the keynote frequency will increase but we can use the $5/4^{ths}$-Law or the $9/8^{ths}$-Rule to decide the interval between the second and third partials. These higher partials are the octave and twelfth (or third in the case of the bass) respectively. In shaping the dome we must look to the equation for α_0 which teaches us that by increasing the rise-factor H_0/h (increasing the rise of the dome), the key-note frequency increases.

The tuner must tune all the partials together because any changes made to the note geometry (shape) or to the internal stress field, affects all the partials to varying degrees. We now discuss the steps in point form.

(1) The pan maker may decide to use grooves or bores to assist in blocking the note (see Section 14.12).

(2) Hammer peening along the general area that contains the true note boundary has two main effects; (a) the basic shape of the note, defined by the semi-major axis a and the semi-minor axis b is set. This sets up the initial values for the frequencies of the partials. If the third partial must be set as a Fifth above the octave (say for a tenor note) then the aspect ratio must take the value $a/b = 5/4$. For a Third above the octave (say on a bass note), take $a/b = 9/8$. Look at the places where a and b appear in the frequency formula. (b) The initial values for the compressive stress distribution along the note boundary is set. This sets the value for the buckling (flapping) parameter s. Increasing the compressive stress reduces the frequencies of all the partials not only that of the key-note.

(3) The 3-dimensional shaping of the note that involves the rise (H_0) of the note, adjusts the stiffness parameter α_0. Increasing the rise, increases the frequencies of all the partials. The peening involved in shaping the surface of the note also affects s and the frequencies of all the partials.

(4) The overall shape given to the note surface sets the shape function Q, which determines the frequencies of all the partials, Refer to the terms M_2 and M_3 associated with equation (8.14).

(5) Setting the frequencies of the partials is not the whole story; the relative magnitudes of the partials must also be set in order to obtain the desired timbre. This will take us on to Section 14.30 but before we get to that, there are other important effects to explain.

14.29 Energy Exchanges, Frequency Pulling, Reflected Impedances and Modulations — another Journey into the Deep Mysteries of the Pan

Note: The theory and dynamical equations that describe the mechanisms in this Section can be found in Chapters 3 – 8.

14.29.1 Energy Exchanges

The tuner with a good pair of ears, who pays close attention to the response of the notes to small alterations made near to the *tuned state* (more precisely, the '*target state*' set by the tuner) can detect the *frequency 'pulling'* by the octave on the key-note (fundamental) and the reverse effect of the key-note *pulling* the octave. One should be careful when trying to observe this effect however, because the frequencies of *all* modes will change whenever the hammer is applied to a note during the tuning exercise. The reason for these changes to *all* modal frequencies comes from the fact that hammer peening applied to a note alters the note shape, stress fields and the support conditions (boundary conditions) for all vibrational modes. There is however a *subtle effect* that the very experienced (master) tuner would surely have noticed when the partials on a given note have been brought very close to the *tuned state*. This *tuned state* we shall take as being the 'musical one' set in accordance with the musical scale (12-TET) although the '***Pulling Effect***' can take place whether or not the note is close to the '*musically tuned state*', provided that the key-note-octave-twelfth are set in a *close* 1:2:3 interval. Of course, on the pan, we do not want exact 1:2:3 intervals!

As a 'tuner' myself (a title I 'borrowed' from you in Section 14.27.1 and see a '*Thoughtful Moment*' at the end of Section

14.29.3) I am aware that tuners always think of note frequencies (pitches) in relation to the musical scale but as I indicated elsewhere, the dynamics of the pan instrument are not set by the musical scale — the musical scale is arbitrary. There are musical scales other than '12-TET' to which we can tune the instrument. I point this out to make sure that readers *do not* form the idea that 'pulling' has something to do with the musical scale. It does not; it is a purely physical effect that does not pay attention to the musical scale. Let us see how it works, but to do so we need to improve our understanding of the process of 'Energy Exchanges' on a vibrating note.

In 1999, during my 2-Day Seminar (an Open Seminar sponsored by Pan Trinbago) for Pan Tuners and Pan Makers of Trinidad and Tobago, I explained the deeply wonderful mechanism of energy exchanges that occurs on the sounding note of a steelpan. The mechanism and process were all explained in my earlier publications on the Pan but at the Seminar, without the use of Power Point Graphics for my presentation (Power Point was too costly a software for me to afford!), I used the 'more effective', 'live' adaptation of the *head* (yes the head that rest upon neck and shoulder) of Pan Trinbago's President Patrick Arnold to 'model' the 'key-note' and the heads of two other ranking Pan Trinbago Officials who stood beside Arnold, as the 'physical models' for the octave and twelfth of a vibrating pan note! After striking the 'bald' head of Arnold (with all respect, and in honor of Pan, 'handsomely bald') to excite the key-note that his head represented, I proceeded to demonstrate the exchange of energies among the three modes on the note. Since these exchanges represented mutual coupling of the modes. I asked my three volunteers to 'hold hands,' thereby showing the 'coupling' that exists among the modes. Now, by 'holding hands' they would 'stay together' and this demonstrated the *confinement* of the vibrational energy to the region defined as the 'true note' of the pan. I have often referred to this 'event' whenever I meet with Pan Tuners to discuss this concept, in fact more than a concept this 'beautiful phenomenon' that occurs each and every time a tuned steelpan note is played.

Since the full treatment of the note dynamics, modal coupling coefficients (quadratic and cubic) and energy exchanges (and confinement) are well discussed in earlier Chapters, at this stage we can enjoy the luxury of a simplified explanation of the energy exchanges among the vibrational modes on a tuned pan note. This explanation is best suited for "public' discourses on the pan using animated 'Power Point' presentations as I did at the *Steelfestt, 2012, Inaugural Trinidad and Tobago International Conference on the Steelpan,* May 6 – 9, 2012, while speaking on the topic 'The *Pan Jumbie Confronts the G-Pan Patent.*' Assuming the note has been tuned in the *key-note-octave-twelfth* format (with *'twelfth'* ≡ *'fif*th above the octave' in pan tuners' terminology), the tuned modes, key-note, octave and twelfth can be unambiguously identified by 'modal numbers' 1, 2 and 3 respectively. Refer to Figure 14.38 for details.

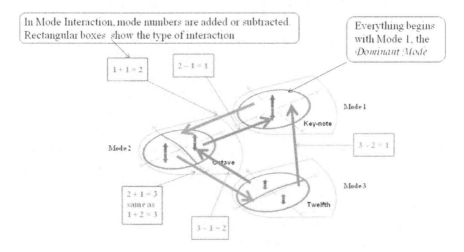

Fig. 14.38. Energy exchanges among the three modes of a tuned note. In the rectangular boxes with, $a + b = c$, this means that mode a interacts with mode b to *transfer* energy to mode c. In the boxes with, $a - b = c$, this means a interacts with b to *return* energy to c. It is easy to get the 'hang' of it by following the directions of the heavy arrows and the content of the boxes. All modes are on the same physical note surface but shown separated for clarity.

The process begins with the excitation of mode1, the key-note, by stick-note impact made at the sweetspot for this mode (situated at the apex of the note surface). Mode1 is the *dominant mode*. With mode1 excited, mode1 interacts (quadratically) *with itself* to transfer energy to mode2 (the octave). This interaction, depicted in Figure 14.38 and the energy transfer (heavy arrow) from mode1 to mode2 takes place at the frequency of the octave — shown in one of the boxes in Figure 14.38 as [1 + 1 = 2]. Now with mode1 and mode2 excited, mode2 interacts with mode1 to *return* energy (at the key-note frequency) to mode1 — this is shown in the box with [2 - 1 =1]. Mode1 and mode2 also interact in a [1 + 2 = 3] interaction to transfer energy to mode3 (the twelfth). Energy is returned to mode2 via a [3 − 1 = 2] interaction while energy is returned to mode1 via a [3 − 2 = 1] interaction. These energy transfers among the tuned modes are responsible for the *energy confinement* and *mode localization* within the domain defined as the true note. These energy transfers occur continuously throughout the lifetime of the tone (approximately 1 second) and produce the frequency and amplitude modulations of the sounding tone. These are the effects that are responsible for the *beautiful tones* on the steelpan.

14. 29.2 Frequency Pulling and Reflected (or Coupled) Impedances

There is another way to look at this process which requires a bit deeper physical insight on the dynamics of the pan. Earlier, in Section 14.11 we saw that a pan note can be represented by its *equivalent mechanical impedance $Z(\omega)$*. Sufficient for that Section, we took the note to be of single frequency an SDOF (Single Degree Of Freedom) system, having impedance which is dependent *only* on the local note parameters, the mass loading and the acoustic loading. Now if there are three tuned modes on the note (an MDOF (Multi Degree Of Freedom) system, we get a more complex (or more complicated) impedance network within the note itself. To make matters 'worse' (from a mathematical viewpoint only) the system is also non-linear! But this is no trouble for us because we have already developed the non-linear theory in earlier Chapters that can easily handle this situation. We need to go a bit further into the theory of coupled non-linear systems so I beg the indulgence of the reader. Remember we are taking an 'inside view' of the pan and I wouldn't allow you to get lost.

When the key-note (mode1) interacts non-linearly with the octave (mode2) the coupling coefficient involved here is α_{112}. The octave also interacts with the key-note using the coupling coefficient α_{121}. On the pan, one finds the condition $\alpha_{112} > \alpha_{121}$. These are the coupling parameters involved in the energy transfers we just discussed. **But something else happens on the note, something *equally subtle and interestingly beautiful*.** If you had the patience and endurance to remain with me and not skip ahead you would now be richly rewarded on this journey. **Yes, it is a journey into the deep mysteries of the pan**.

Case 1: First we consider the coupling of the octave to the key-note via the coupling coefficient α_{121} (same as α_{211}). The impedance of the key-note is not simply $Z(\omega)$ determined by local conditions alone (as in Section 14.11). Another impedance appears in *parallel* with $Z(\omega)$ and it comes about as an impedance **reflected** from the coupled second mode, the octave (resident octave). To 'picture' all of this in your mind, imagine *yourself* to be the key-note on the $E_4{}^b$ note of a tenor. If you are 'into' pan and into music you should have no problems doing this, I do things like this all the time! Having worked so long and hard on the steelpan, I have developed many mental pictures of the complex dynamics and mechanisms that are active within a sounding note! In this short digression I share with you the fact that I have discovered many interesting things about the pan using these mental pictures which are then searched for later among the complex mathematical equations describing the notes. It's fruitful and it works! Now imagine further that on this note the *'resident octave'* ($E_5{}^b$) (a *'friend'* of yours 'living' on the same note) is interacting with you (you have no choice in this matter) so you have to respond. What you now 'see' as the octave (your friend) that interacts with you, represents the *reflected (or coupled) impedance*! By using an appropriate transformation, the combined reflected *parallel* impedance and the note impedance can be replaced by an equivalent combination of two *series* impedances. I choose the series impedance representation shown in Figure 14.39 because it simplifies the discussion to follow.

Note: I have chosen the terminology 'reflected impedance' over the other terminology 'coupled impedance' although the word 'coupled' would remind readers of the modal coupling that gives rise to this effect. This choice is just a matter of personal preference. It may, perhaps, also reflect my lifelong use of 'reflected impedance' in electronics and electrical circuit theory. There was also the need to avoid a conflict that could have arisen with the use of the subscript 'c' for 'coupled' and for 'coating.'

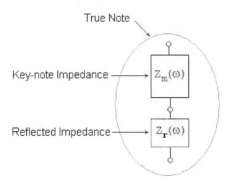

Fig. 14.39. Compare with Figure 14.13. A single note having mechanical impedance $Z_m(\omega)$ is driven by an externally applied contact force to produce a non-linearly induced series impedance $Z_r(\omega)$) reflected from the octave.

Let us take an uncoated note for simplicity, with key-note mechanical impedance given by (see Section 14.11)

$$Z_m(\omega) = R_m + R_r + j\left[\omega(m_m + m_r) - \frac{S_{eff}}{\omega}\right].$$

When the octave interacts with the key-note it presents a *reflected series impedance*

$$Z_r(\omega) = R_{mr} + R_{rr} + j\left[\omega(m_{mr} + m_{rr}) - \frac{S_{r,eff}}{\omega}\right]$$

seen by the key-note (the stiffness, resistance and mass components of the reflected impedance are identified by the extra 'r' subscript). Since the quadratic coupling between the key-note and octave only occurs when mode2 is *close* to the true octave of mode1, the reflected impedance $Z_r(\omega)$ must vanish (go to zero) very rapidly as the modal frequencies (key-note and octave) move away from the 1:2 frequency ratio. For this to happen, the reflected resistances R_{mr} and R_{rr}, must be very small (much smaller than R_m and R_r on the key-note). It will turn out in practice that this condition is satisfied otherwise the pan notes will not operate properly (as a musical instrument). The resulting impedance given by the sum of these two impedances contains a lot of information and is given by

$$Z(\omega) = (R_m + R_{mr}) + (R_r * R_{rr}) + j\left[\omega(m_m + m_{mr} + m_r + m_{rr}) - \frac{S_{eff} + S_{r,eff}}{\omega}\right].$$

Notice a number of things

(i) The key-note frequency is now given by $\omega = \sqrt{\frac{S_{eff} + S_{r,eff}}{(m_m + m_{mr} + m_r + m_{rr})}}$, being now dependent on the components of the reflected impedance of the octave. *This dependence of the key-note on the octave will be observed as a 'pulling' by the octave on the frequency of the key-note.*

(ii) The effective stiffness of the key-note increases to $S_{eff} + S_{r,eff}$. This increase in stiffness does not immediately translate into an increase in key-note frequency because the effective mass of the key-note has also increased to the new value $m_m + m_{mr} + m_r + m_{rr}$. This increase in *'mass loading'* applied to the key-note will tend to *reduce* the frequency of the key-note. Whether the key-note frequency is pulled *downward* or *upward* by the octave depends on the frequency of the parametric excitation that drives this energy exchange process. It therefore depends on the detuning of the octave (whether the octave is *stretched* or *compressed*, see for example Section 14.19.5). A *stretched octave* tends to pull the key-note *upward* while a *compressed octave* tends to pull the key-note downward. The magnitude of the frequency shift depends on the Q-factors of the key-note and octave, the magnitude and sign of the detuning and the coupling coefficient α_{121}. For the low-Q notes ($Q \lesssim 40$) found on the bass, pulling can be masked by the broad frequency response of the notes. On the high-Q notes ($Q \gtrsim 80$) found on the tenor the small frequency shift caused by pulling can more readily be resolved.

For there to be any energy transfer from one mode to another it is necessary for the spectral peak of the mode receiving the energy to overlap the spectral peak of the parametric excitation that is transferring the energy. The spectral plots in Figure 14.40 show these overlapping peaks for the key-note and the octave. We simplify our present discussion by ignoring the twelfth; we lose nothing by doing this here.

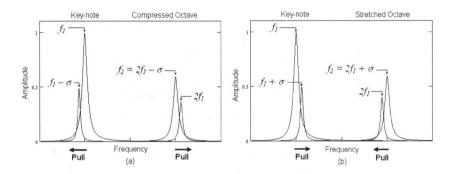

Fig. 14.40. Overlapping peaks in the spectra of Key-note, Octave and accompanying Parametric Excitations (with amplitudes scaled slightly upwards for clarity) for a note tuned with (a) a Compressed Octave and (b) a Stretched Octave. Frequency pulling on key-note and octave are directed *towards* the interacting parametric excitation. Key-note appears at frequency f_1 while the octaves appear at frequencies $2f_i \pm \sigma$. Parametric excitations appear at frequencies $2f_1$ and $f_1 \pm \sigma$.

The spectra sketched in Figure 14.40 will help the reader to better understand how the small pitch changes produced by pulling, depend on the detuning of the octave (*stretched* and *compressed*). When the key-note of frequency f_1 interacts with the octave of frequency f_2, two parametric modes are generated (see Section 4.5 and Chapter 7); a lower parametric mode of frequency $f_2 - f_1$ which returns energy to the key-note and an upper parametric mode of frequency $f_2 + f_1$ which transfers energy to the twelfth. Since we are not considering the twelfth in this discussion we shall set aside the upper parametric mode.

In Figure 14.40(a) the octave (mode2) is *compressed* with frequency given by $f_2 = 2f_1 - \sigma$ where f_1 is the frequency of the key-note (mode1) and σ is the detuning. Now the lower frequency *parametric excitation* produced by the interaction of mode1 and mode2 appears at a frequency $f_1-\sigma$ and is shown in Figure 14.40(a) located to the left of the peak representing the key-note. The transfer of energy from this parametric excitation lying in the neighborhood of the key-note, to the key-note, represents an *'internal resonance'* (see Section 3.3). When this occurs, the key-note is *'pulled'* slightly lower in frequency towards the parametric mode. This is why I have often mentioned a *'small detuning'* that occurs dynamically when writing about these interactions (see for example Section 7.6.2). When the detuning is large enough the parametric peak and the key-note peak can be resolved (see for example Figure 7.2). On the bass, because of the low Q of the notes, the spectral peaks are relatively broad making it difficult to resolve the nearby weaker parametric peaks. On a well tuned tenor pan, even with its higher Q, it is sometimes difficult (or impossible) to resolve these two peaks with the parametric peak blending into the key-note peak with a net *broadening* of the resultant peak.

When the octave is *stretched* with frequency $f_2 = 2f_1 + \sigma$ the parametric excitation with frequency $f_1 + \sigma$ now appears to the right of the key-note peak as shown in Figure 14.40(b). The resulting internal resonance pulls the key-note frequency slightly *upward* accompanied by a *broadening* of the peak.

Peak broadening in both these cases implies a lowering of the quality factor Q of the key-note which means an increase in energy losses. This is consistent with (iii) and (iv) below.

(iii) The acoustic resistance is now given by $R_r + R_{rr}$. This increase in radiation resistance comes about because some of the kinetic energy (in the vibration) of the octave having been *down-converted* to the frequency of the key-note (with some detuning) and transferred to the key-note, is now radiated acoustically (*a system energy loss*) by the key-note. Understand this correctly; part of the vibrational energy of the octave has been *down-converted* to the key-note frequency (or very close to it at $f_1 \pm \sigma$) and radiated acoustically at the key-note frequency. The overlapping of spectral peaks sees to this.

(iv) The mechanical resistance (representing *internal losses*) increases to $R_m + R_{mr}$. The penalty we pay for all these subtle activities on the pan note is a slight increase in the damping of the key-note.

Case 2: Now when we consider the energy transfer from the key-note to the octave via the coupling coefficient α_{112}, we find similar effects as in (i) to (iv) above, with an impedance reflected from the key-note unto the impedance of the octave. ***The key-note therefore 'pulls' the octave.*** The pulling effect is mutual. The directions of the 'pull' on the octave are shown in Figure 14.40 for the *Compressed* Octave and the *Stretched* Octave.

Case 3: Similar effects also occur with the *twelfth*. Both the octave and key-note are affected by pulling introduced by the twelfth. Because the twelfth is a relatively weak mode, here the pulling action is weaker still.

Note; *Because there are no internal resonances involving the third (above the octave), as used on the bass, there is no frequency pulling associated with the third. If a 'tuner' tells you he can hear 'pulling' on the third then he is 'pulling your leg!'*

The General Case: Since Cases 1, 2 and 3 occur at the same time, the impedance diagram obtained in practice (that accounts for Figure 14.38) is somewhat complicated. I have chosen to separate the three cases only for simplicity in order to get the ideas across but the total picture remains the same.

When the detuning is made sufficiently small (within the 'pull-in range') and mode2 becomes a true octave the note enters the mode-locked state (see Sections 10.4 – 10.7). In this case the 'pulling action' is strong enough to keep the key-note and octave in a 1:2 frequency ratio with no modulation on the corresponding partials. The pung tone is generated in this case.

When tuning Marshall-Pairs similar but relatively smaller levels of 'pulling' are possible between the two members of the pair. Strong Marshall-Pairs should be avoided.

I must however, again warn the reader that normal hammer peening action may mask these effects; this is why the true effects of 'pulling' can only be seen in the last stages of tuning and only by careful application of the hammer and detection by a keen ear. When 'searching' for these effects one must be careful to avoid the 'frequency-locked' mode which generates the pung tone. *The general reader is advised to seek the help of an expert tuner who can repeat these effects 'at will' during tuning for the benefit of the listener (assuming of course that the listener has a 'good ear' and can detect these minute changes in pitch).*

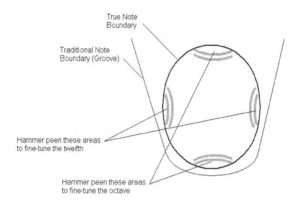

Fig. 14.41. Sketch showing areas on the true note where peening can be applied to fine-tune the octave and the twelfth. The key-note is always affected by these peening actions. Do not confuse this with 'pulling'.

Figure 14.41 shows areas on the true note where hammer peening can be applied to fine-tune the note. In all hammer peening action applied to the note, all the modes are affected to varying degrees depending on the point of application of the hammer impact, strength of impact and the *obliquity* of the impact (see Section 2.6). By increasing the obliquity, the local stress field can be modified to bring about frequency (pitch) changes. These actions applied in the final stages of the tuning process affect the frequencies of *all* partials and *must not* be confused with 'pulling'. These frequency changes are the result of alterations made to the note geometry and the local stress field.

The absence of amplitude and frequency modulations does not imply the absence of pulling! In the case of the pung tone on a note with just the tuned key-note and octave with no twelfth (or with mode3 tuned sufficiently away from the twelfth), there is no frequency modulation or amplitude modulation. This state can be achieved by tuning the octave within the *'pull-in range'* defined by equation (10.9). The octave will then be rapidly pulled until it is 'locked' to the keynote in a precise 2:1 frequency ratio. Listening to this note when played, we are not made aware that the two partials have been pulled. All we detect are the "pulled frequencies" not a 'pulling' from some initial frequency as the tone progresses from beginning to end. Acoustically this locked mode (pung tone) is a musically uninteresting and unpleasant tone but it is fascinating dynamically even though the tuner hates it. I only like to hear it when I am investigating it! When we play a note, not set to the locked state, we are also not aware of the frequency pulling.

As the tuner adjusts the pitches of the partials by ear or aided by a frequency meter, the 'pulling' action within the note operates to set the final tone correctly. It is *only* in this final tuning operation that the tuner is made aware of the frequency pulling that takes place between the two interacting modes (key-note and octave). ***He senses this because the note appears to do much more ('pitch-wise') than he intended by his hammer action!*** A good tuner can always sense when something *additional* is taking place that he was not 'directly' responsible for. Sometimes it may go in the direction he wants the note to go, at other times it goes in a contrary direction! With practice and experience, he learns to make accommodation for this natural internal pulling action of the note. In time, his method of dealing with these effects are incorporated into what he would regard as his 'normal' tuning action — he then tunes without 'thinking' about the pulling action. *These are some of the subtleties of tuning that the apprentice tuner has to observe in order to truly master the art!*

14.29.3 Further Insight on the Frequency and Amplitude Modulations

A Question that the insightful reader may well ask: Is this *frequency pulling* related to the *frequency modulations* observed on a sounding note?
Answer: *Yes indeed*! But I must elaborate on this answer. Figure 14.42 will help us.

In the impedance representation of the note dynamics the frequency modulation and amplitude modulation observed in the sounding tone can be understood by including the driving forces and the velocity responses in the impedance diagram. In the *two-loop* (two *velocity loops*) representation given in Figure 14.42(a), the note is driven by a stick impact with force component $F(\omega)$ at the key-note frequency ω. $F_r(\omega)$ is the force component, also at frequency ω (or close to it depending on the detuning), driving the parametric excitation (see Section 4.5 and Chapter 7) that transfers energy from the octave to the key-note. Observe in Figure 14.42 that the force $F_r(\omega)$ appears *across* the reflected impedance. The force $F_r(\omega)$ is proportional to the *product* of the displacement of the key-note and the displacement of the octave. In the dynamical equation (3.30) describing the mechanical vibration of a note surface, this force, expressed in units of force per unit mass corresponds to the term $\alpha_{12,1} w_1 w_2$ where w_1 and w_2 are the time-dependent displacements of the key-note and the octave modes respectively. The force $F_r(\omega)$ therefore exists only when there is a tuned octave and so long as both the key-note and the octave are excited. After impact (when the contact force $F(\omega)$ goes to zero) the note executes free vibration as shown in Figure 14.42(b). The note response velocity $V(\omega)$, is modulated by the velocity response $V_r(\omega)$ driven by $F_r(\omega)$. Associated with this velocity modulation is the amplitude (displacement) modulation and the related frequency modulation observed in the tone of the *sounding* note. The picture is completed by drawing (i) a figure (not shown) similar to Figure 14.42 that shows the impedance representation of the octave and the series connected reflected impedance of the key-note (in this case the reflected driving force per unit mass will be given by $\alpha_{11,2} w_1^2$) (ii) a figure containing the third partial and the associated reflected impedances. The complete picture must therefore be represented by a network of velocity loops corresponding to the energy transfers shown in Figure 14.38.

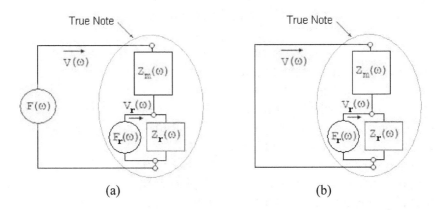

Fig. 14.42. The two-loop representation of the key-note, having mechanical impedance $Z_m(\omega)$, driven by an external contact force component $F(\omega)$ to produce a velocity response $V(\omega)$ and a non-linearly induced reflected response $F_r(\omega)$ and $V_r(\omega)$) from the octave; (a) Forced response during stick impact, (b) free vibration after impact. All responses F, F_r, V, and V_r, are vectors and functions of frequency and time.

All driving forces and velocity responses in Figure 14.42 are vector quantities having amplitude and phase that vary with time as the note is excited, vibrates and radiates acoustic energy, coming finally to rest when all the energy is dissipated.

A Thoughtful Moment: On May 12, 2012 while addressing members of the *Pan Tuners Guild of Trinidad and Tobago*, as I explained the interaction of the tuned modes on the pan notes discussed above, *Master Tuner Tony Slater* interjected by saying '*you would make a good tuner!*' Having been so long in the pan business but never proclaiming myself to be anything(!), neither tuner nor panist, I took the remark quietly. On these matters I respect the voices of the many excellent tuners in my homeland, and among these voices, one that I identify with clarity and correctness is that of Tony Slater — a fine and knowledgeable gentleman cast in the mold of the great Bertie Marshall.

14.30 Typical Tuning Scenarios in Musical Space: The Amplitude and Frequency Profiles of the Pan

14.30.1 Typical Tuning Scenarios

Anyone who has sat beside a master pan maker as he tunes a pan must be fascinated by the sequence of tonal alterations that notes undergo as the *target tone* set by the maker is approached and finally attained. To the casual observer it seems all a mystery. Using the pan theory developed in this work, one can explain and create exactly, the sequence of changes that a typical note undergoes in the tuning process.

When tuning a note for the first time the modal frequencies are initially at arbitrary values. The tuner then peens the note while listening to the tones and steers the note towards the desired pitch. This may require repeated reshaping or forming of the note shape. Since all the other audible untuned modes on the note are at arbitrary frequencies we are not able to specify them all so we ignore them (as the tuner does—in fact the very experienced tuner does not hear them*) while tuning continues and the desired key-note becomes clearer and begins to dominate. At this point the tuner listens for the octave and must shape the note in the general region that will form the true note.

(* This is an important point. When the casual observer listens to the sound of the note being tuned, he/she listens to 'everything', even the noise of the hammer impact as distinct from the tones it generates and confusion results. By training the ear to listen only to the important tones, the tuner quickly gets to the desired key-note and octave while all the other undesired tones fall by the wayside and fade away.)

In order to study the complex changes on the pan face as the tuner alters the 3-D shape of the note, varies the in-plane stresses and modifies the note dynamics that follow when the note is played, we must re-create exactly, the stick-note system mathematically and follow the note's response to a stick impact. We have available to us the means to do this in the equations of Chapter 13, but for our present purposes we focus our attention not on the effects of varying all the 30 stick-note parameters for a note tuned with key-note, octave and twelfth (three modes) but the simpler case of a note on which only the detuning parameters σ_1 and σ_2 for the octave and twelfth respectively are varied. In practice, the tuner is unable to select just these two parameters (out of the 30) to vary because hammer peening can vary up to 16 parameters in one or a few hammer strikes. We have the advantage of changing any number while keeping the rest constant.

Note: *These 30 parameters are not arbitrary. The material parameters such as density, Young's modulus etc for the pan face material and stick tip can be obtained from tables of physical constants for the materials while the coupling parameters can be calculated. In the examples treated in this Section, these procedures are by-passed.*

The coupled dynamical equations describing a selected note (according to the fixed values assigned to the remaining 28 parameters) are solved to produce the amplitude profiles for the surface displacements of the three modes. As a practical matter, the 28 parameters are absorbed into a few quantities representing modal frequencies (ω_n), modal coupling coefficients ($\alpha_{jk,n}$), damping coefficients (μ_n) and the contact force $f(t)$. We now turn to the *tuning scenarios* obtained by solving these equations.

We shall not be concerned here with the stick tip parameters, the stick-note contact parameters or the effect of the impact force. For this reason, in the profiles presented below we consider only the free phase beginning at the instant that the note amplitude maximizes and ignore the initial impact phase.

A typical tuning scenario is shown in Figure 14.43. The panels show the profiles defined by the author as the *Amplitude Profiles* of the Steelpan tones. The complements to these Amplitude Profiles are the *Frequency Profiles* (not shown in Figure 14.43 but are scattered throughout this work in a number of figures) that together, fully complete the description of a pan note. (One of these will be illustrated later, complete with the frequency profiles for the key-note, resident octave and resident twelfth). The coupling parameters are the same as in the example shown in Figure 14.29 (left panel) except that the detuning parameters are changed in each panel.

In Figure 14.43, t*he categorization from Poor to Excellent is based on levels of modulation not on tonal quality.* The categorization according to tonal quality of the sound is a subjective matter — each tuner, panist or listener has his/her own interpretation and preferences. However, I believe *all will agree on what is a poor sounding note*! It is because we can and do disagree on what sounds are 'excellent' that a whole 'assortment' of good pans can be produced by tuners. I believe that we ought to keep it that way.

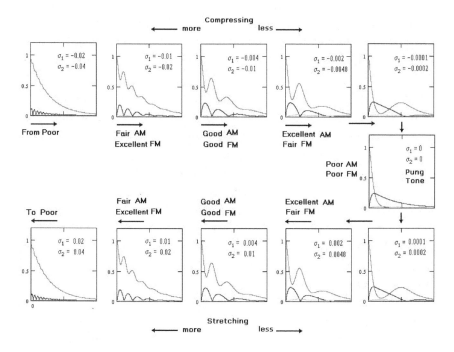

Fig. 14.43. The Amplitude Profiles—A typical tuning scenario of tones (at the *forte* level)that can be produced by a trained tuner. The notes on the lower panels are images of the notes on the upper panels. The pung tone is its own image. The labels good, excellent etc depend on whether AM or FM is the desired quality.

The scene begins at the panel in the upper left corner of Figure 14.43, with the second mode frequency ω_2 below $2\omega_1$ and the third mode frequency ω_3 below $3\omega_1$ i.e. initially the detuning parameters on the note are negative — *the Octave and Twelfth are compressed*. At first, in the Tuning Scenario of Figure 14.43, the note generates a poor sound (poor timbre and very under-modulated) even if the first mode (key-note) frequency ω_1 is musically correct. As the tuner peens and shapes and the detuning parameters become less negative (*compression of the upper partials reduced*) the tone, by the changes made to its amplitude modulation, progresses through the sequence **poor** → **fair** → **good** → **excellent** → **good** → **fair** →

poor. The labels good, excellent etc apply depending on whether AM or FM is the desired quality.

At the end of this sequence (far right and middle panel of Figure 14.43) the detuning parameters are at zero value and the modes are set to exact harmonicity ($\sigma_1 = 0$, $\sigma_2 = 0$). The sound of the note at this point is what the present author describes as the short-duration **pung tone**. It can often be heard during tuning and has been specially generated on steelpans by the author, in order to determine its cause.

If tuning is continued beyond this point, with the same direction of frequency changes, as the detuning parameters increase positively —*the Octave and Twelfth are stretched*—, the sequence is reversed; **poor** → **fair** → **good** → **excellent** → **good** → **fair** → **poor**.

It is also possible to run the scenario in reverse order by starting at the panel in the lower left corner of Figure 14.43 until the scene at the panel in the upper left corner of Figure 14.43 is reached.

If it is in the tuner's preference to have FM as the desired tonal quality then the tuner stops around the upper or lower left corner of Figure 14.43 where FM is strongest. In this case the designation shifts from **fair** or **good** to **excellent**.

The actual amplitude and frequency modulations on a particular note on another pan may differ from those in Figure 14.43 because of differences in the coupling parameters that characterize the note. Although negative and positive sets of detuning parameters produce identical amplitude modulations, the frequency modulations possess *opposite phases*. The tuning sequence of Figure 14.43 is therefore not symmetrical but it is reversible — *a note can be distinguished from its image using phase information.*

14.30.2 Musical Space and Flavor

- *Notice that excellence in FM and excellence in AM are not achieved simultaneously! This is a fundamental aspect of steelpan note dynamics. This aspect of the dynamics is good for the instrument since it adds greater dimension to the* **musical space**. *One tuner can go for more FM, another can go for more AM still another can mix it up in a lot of different ways. I feel tempted to call this the '***flavor***' in pan tuning. 'A little bit of this' and 'a little bit of that' as in* *cooking to give the food the required flavor. I am speaking here from experience; my grandfather on my father's side was born in Canton China so cooking is in the family! My grandfather on my mother's side was of Spanish stock, so a lot of spice is expected!*

- *The individual tuner decides where to place his notes in this 'musical space'; this is why a Bertie Marshall tenor can be aurally distinguished from an Anthony Williams tenor and a Bertram Kellman tenor (or my tenor if you care to ask!). Musical Space is expansive but every tuner in the development of his skills eventually settles into a region (or regions, one for each type of pan) of this space that he takes as his own; all good tuners are accorded this **right of occupancy**. Of course this right or the exercising of it, must still meet the approval of the panists and listeners for after all, they are the ones to accept or reject his instruments.*

- *It is not the expanse of musical space a tuner occupies that determines his claim to fame; instead it is the **quality of the space** that he occupies. Very few are those that occupy the space at the pinnacle of excellence! The names of three men occupying these spaces were given above — Marshall, Williams and Kellman but I should add Herman Guppy, Lloyd Gay and Tony Slater.*

14.30.3 A 'Busy Note' — Good AM and FM

The reader will undoubtedly ask if the note and image classification also works when the octave is stretched (compressed) while the twelfth is compressed (stretched). This possibility was stated earlier but its demonstration is given at this point where its importance to tuning can be better appreciated by the reader.

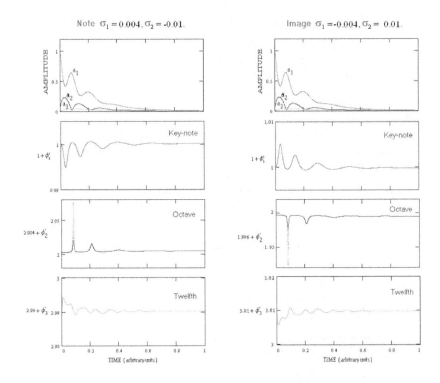

Fig. 14.44. Simulation of a note and its image played the equivalent to *forte* having good ratings in both amplitude modulation (Top panels) and normalized frequency modulation (Lower three pairs of panels). Time t = 0 begins the moment the note amplitude maximizes after impact. Impact phase not shown.

To demonstrate that this is in fact true, the tuning arrangement in Figure 14.43 classified as Good in both FM and AM is reproduced in Figure 14.44 with modification in the signs of the detuning parameters. The note in Figure 14.44 is simulated for the case of a *stretched octave* and a *compressed twelfth* using the detuning parameters $\sigma_1 = 0.004$, $\sigma_2 = -0.01$. The image is simulated with the signs reversed, $\sigma_1 = -0.004$, $\sigma_2 = 0.01$ representing a *compressed octave* and a *stretched twelfth*. In both cases the normalized amplitude profiles obtained here are identical to those in Figure 14.43 for the corresponding (Good AM - Good FM) cases. In addition, Figure 14.44 shows why this tuning arrangement and the similar cases in Figure 14.43 received a good rating for both AM and FM. This follows from the production of strong amplitude modulation and great depth of frequency modulation for this choice of detuning parameter values.

Comment: *Some tuners (or players) may not like the note (or image) that appears in Figure 14.44 because 'too much' seems to be happening — a 'busy note' — when the note (or image) is sounding. But, to be fair, we must cater for those who like much icing on the cake!*

In Figure 14.44, normalized frequencies and normalized time are employed. In order to give the reader a better understanding, the frequency modulation results in real time are presented in Figure 14.45 for the same note in Figure 14.44 with the key-note tuned to A_4 (= 440 Hz). In Figure 14.45 the reader should focus first on the frequency modulations on the key-note.

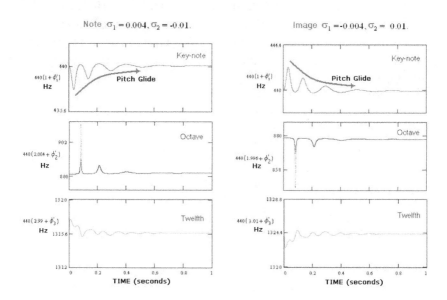

Fig. 14.45. Simulation of a note and its image played the equivalent to *forte* as in Figure 7b showing only the frequency modulations on a note tuned to A_4 (= 440 Hz). Solid curves with arrow heads show directions of pitch glide.

When the note is played the frequency does not remain fixed on A_4 (440 Hz) instead it begins to show frequency modulation (a series of rising and falling of the pitch). Observe that the modulation on the note is opposite to that on the image. Both of these modulations are audible but because of the rapid changes it will be very difficult for the untrained ear of the casual listener to detect the difference between the sound of the image and that of the note. Observe the details here: on the note the key-note glides upward in pitch while the image glides downward in pitch. Frequency modulations are also seen on the octave and twelfth (notice the opposite sense of the modulations on the note compared to what takes place on the image). Notice that even on the twelfth, one does not hear an even tone but a frequency modulated (FM) tone — what one normally associate with a 'ringing' sound. Did you see the glides on the twelfth? These are some of the subtle things that the inattentive apprentice tuner may fail to hear. Hearing them and appreciating them comes more easily as the ear is developed. In teaching myself about the pan I had to develop a discerning ear while finding the physical meaning of what I was hearing by analyzing the information mentally. Why mentally? Because I did a lot of my 'ear training' standing in the pan yards of Trinidad. But to be truly honest, it is very difficult to describe these mental processes (which goes beyond psychoacoustics) in words (English or otherwise).

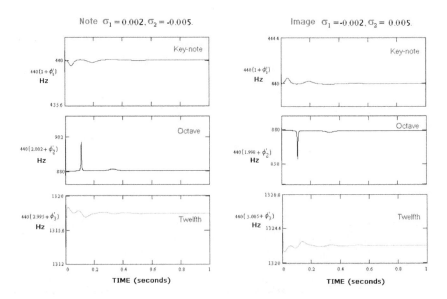

Fig. 14.46. Simulation of a note and its image played the equivalent to *forte* as in Figure 14.45 but with different detuning. Only the frequency modulations on the note tuned to A_4 (= 440 Hz) are shown here.

For those who find the note (and image) in Figure 14.45 too 'busy' for their liking we can re-tune the note with less detuning to make it more acceptable. Figure 14.46 shows the modulations on a note and its image with smaller detuning than the note in Figure 14.45. Observe the smaller range of the frequency modulations when compared with the note in Figure 14.45. As the detuning is reduced to zero the modulations disappear altogether to produce the pung tone. Notice how small changes in the detuning parameters produce large variations in the frequency modulations (and in the AM as well). This explains the difficulty experienced by tuners in fine tuning this instrument — a skill that requires years of training to bring to perfection.

Note: *There is no idealized set of detuning parameter values that fits all notes. Each note must be individually tuned with its own set of parameters. In practice, if a given note is to be re-tuned then an entirely new set of parameters will be necessary in order to bring the tone to match the previous setting or tonality.*

14.31 Four Types of Note Settings

Finally, to emphasize the uniqueness of this musical instrument and the importance of detuning, using the example in Figure 14.44, the intervals (frequency ratios) of key-note, octave and twelfth while set by the tuner to

$$1:2.004:2.99 \quad (\textit{Tuner's Setting; an example}),$$

will show variations throughout the duration of the sounding tone when played by stick impact and be represented by

$$1 + \phi_1': 2.004 + \phi_2': 2.99 + \phi_3'$$
(*Dynamical Values; determined by the Panist*).

Compare these with the classical setting,

$$1:2:3 \quad (\textit{Classical Harmonic Setting})$$

or one, fixed to the musical scale,

$$1:2:2.9966 \ (Fixed\ to\ 12\text{-}TET).$$

If the Classical Setting (no detuning) is strictly applied on the pan then it generates the unpleasant pung tones which, *as a result of mode locking, cannot be modified by the player's stick actions.* Since the key-note and octave dominate the tone acoustically, *even the setting fixed to 12-TET will sound like the pung tone.*

- *If the notes on a pan are tuned the Classical (Harmonic) way, the pung tones it generates sound the same way no matter who plays the notes. You are left with a frustratingly stubborn instrument; No 'pop' no 'fizz' just plain 'corky' dullness!*
- Ever tasted an old wine that was left lying on its side for a long time and got the taste of the cork? You want to spit it out! That's what I mean!
- *The moral of this story is that if you ignore detuning by relying entirely on the tuning meter (no matter what brand) and you believe in 'tuning the harmonics,' the classical way, then expect a dull, boring pan. As for taste, 'insipid' is a fitting description!*

The Tuner's Setting lies close to the Dynamical Values which are dependent on the player's stick action. Now, with this ability to dynamically alter a tone, accomplished panists can make a note sound much better than most tuners can! Tuners are always delighted by this as music writers are of their performing artists. The author recalls watching a televised performance where Stevie Wonder performed the Burt Bacharach, Grammy winning tune 'Alfie' on the harmonica. A truly brilliant performance to which the present author stood up to listen and which brought tears to the eyes of Burt. Brilliant form! Marvelous! Good music, good instrument and genius! I believe Burt saw that Stevie had achieved in Alfie, his (Burt's) musical aims for the piece better than he himself might have imagined. This is the power of music.

The observant reader may ask the question:

How can the Tuner's setting be different from the Dynamical Values seeing that the tuner himself must play the notes?

This is a good question that requires the following detailed answer:

One can never know what the setting of a given note is until the note is played. This information is bound up in the many geometrical, elastic, material and stress parameters that are stored in the note. Not all of these parameters are directly accessible without exciting the note in some way. The Tuner's setting forms the basis for all degrees of excitations that panists may execute on the notes. As the basis, it correctly refers to the setting that corresponds to weak excitations by stick impacts. For these weak excitations the frequency modulations produced by the ϕ'_n (the rate of change of phase or the frequency modulation) are negligible. This implies that the Dynamical Values reduce to the Tuner's setting when the modulations are negligible as clearly is the case. Normal and intense playing action will always add to the Tuner's setting and to the frequency modulations that gives the pan tones their richness. The experienced tuner will carefully excite each tuned note with a range of stick impacts made at a number of different points on the note surface while aurally checking the tonal responses. Sometimes this may call for the use of the butt end of the stick as well. In this way he ensures the fidelity of his notes, an attribute most desired by the panist.

One surely finds that a good panist is always consciously aware of the capabilities of the instrument s/he is playing. The good panist will always equip herself/himself with a fine instrument.

14.32 Setting the Timbre by altering the α-parameters

As spice is to a good meal, so is *tonal color* or *timbre* to music. Without it the sounds are dry, without taste to the palate. Excuse the mixture of the auditory and the savory but there is much in common between music and the culinary arts for the pleasure we all derive from them both.

The quadratic coupling parameters or α-parameters are due to curvature of the note surface. Refer to Chapters 3 and 8 for details on the dependence of the α-parameters on curvature and compressive stress. Since these parameters determine the strengths of the higher partials, they are directly responsible for the *timbre* of the sounding note.

As the tuner varies the obliquity of the hammer peening strokes applied to the top surface of the note, the curvature is altered by indenting (using low obliquity) or the compressive stress altered by stretching (using high obliquity). Tuning by the process of hammer peening alters all α-parameters without exception. Therefore, only in a limited way is it possible to investigate experimentally the effects of individual α-parameters on tonal structure with the real steelpan. With the present theory and numerical methods, this investigation is fully possible and easily implemented. The two main α-parameters α_{112} and α_{121} are selected for this study. The former controls the coupling of mode1 to mode2 while the latter allows for the reverse coupling.

Figures 14.47 and 14.48 show the progression of changes to the tonal structure as the α_{112} parameter is reduced by one order of magnitude from the value 0.019 down to 0.001. From a state of strong coupling (α_{112} = 0.019) with well modulated modal amplitudes of the type that produces excellent tones excited at the *forte* level, the note is reduced to a state of low coupling (α_{112} = 0.001) with a tonal structure that somewhat resembles that of a note excited at the piano level but with very weak higher modes. These modal simulations demonstrate the importance of the coupling coefficient α_{112} to the generation of the second mode (the octave).

Figures 14.49 and 14.50 show the progression in the tonal structure as the α_{121} parameter is reduced from the value 0.047 down to 0.01. From a state of strong coupling (α_{121} = 0.047) with well modulated modal amplitudes of the type that produces excellent tones excited at the forte level, the note is reduced to a state where the octave dominates the tone for approximately 25% of the tone duration. The parameter α_{121} determines the amount of energy that mode2 returns to mode1. By keeping α_{112} high while reducing α_{121}, a point is reached when mode2 will dominate the note dynamics for an appreciable fraction of the tone duration as seen in Figure 14.50, right panel.

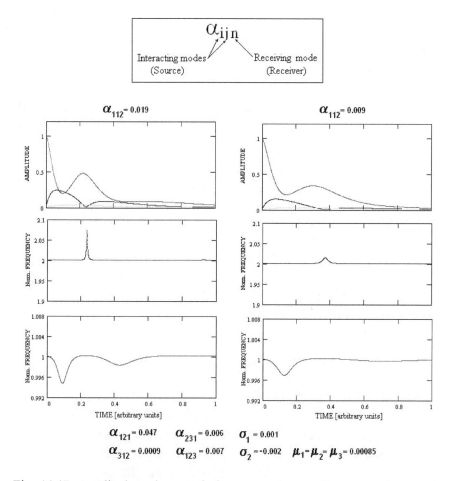

Fig. 14.47. Amplitude and spectral changes as the coupling parameter α_{112} is reduced from 0.019 to 0.009. AM and FM on the Key-note and Octave are shown. FM on the Twelfth not shown.

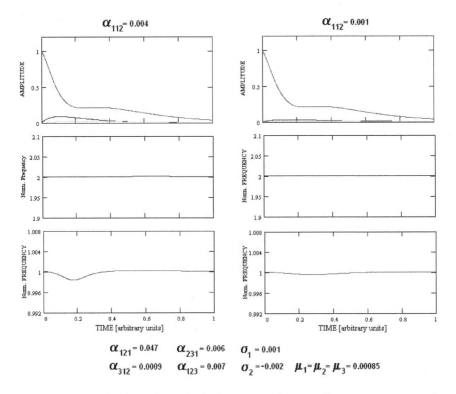

Fig. 14.48. Amplitude and spectral changes as the coupling parameter α_{112} is reduced from 0.004 to 0.001. AM and FM on the Key-note and Octave are shown. FM on the Twelfth not shown.

There are three important aspects to be emphasized:

(i) The excitation of the octave (mode 2) depends on the quadratic interaction of mode1 with itself (a parametric excitation set by the value of α_{112}) generating an internal resonance that transfers energy from mode1 to mode2.
(ii) In order to ensure that all tuned modes are properly excited the couplings that are responsible for energy transfers to and from each mode should be set to optimum levels consistent with the desired tonal structure. At the same time, it is important for the fundamental (mode1) to dominate throughout the duration of the tone. When mode1 couples too strongly to mode2 without sufficient reverse coupling back to mode1, the result is a rapid drop in tone intensity even when mode2 dominates. This happens

because mode2 with its phase-anti-phase mode of vibration over equal halves of the note surface area is not an efficient acoustical radiator (see Chapter 12).

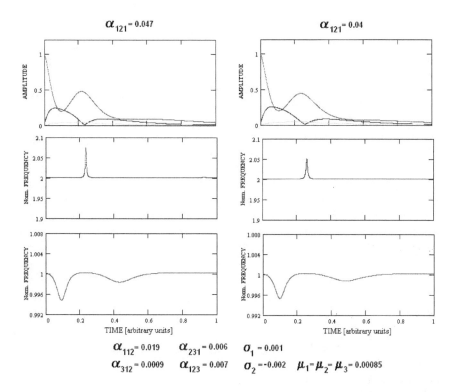

Fig. 14.49. Amplitude and spectral changes as the coupling parameter α_{121} is reduced from 0.047 to 0.04. AM and FM on the Key-note and Octave are shown. FM on the Twelfth not shown.

(iii) Simply setting the fundamental and the octave (and twelfth or second octave if needed) to the correct frequencies (stretched or compressed) **does not** guarantee a good tone. In the present simulation the detuning parameters are quite small ($\sigma 1 = .001$, $\sigma 2 = -.002$) ensuring close but not exact agreement with the musical scale. Despite this, one sees that the tone suffers when particular coupling parameters are too small. It is important for the coupling parameters to be properly set as well as the frequencies. ***For this reason, steelpans cannot be tuned using electronic frequency meters as the only detection device. Ear discrimination***

(the human factor) is a necessary requirement for good tonality.

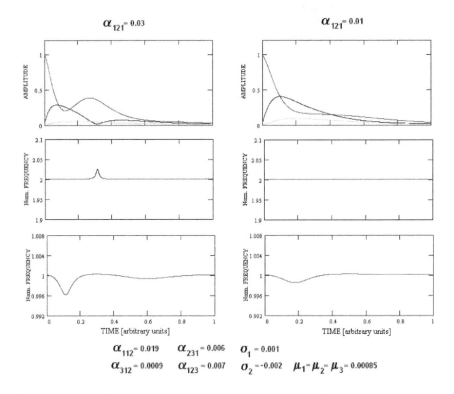

Fig. 14.50. Amplitude and spectral changes as the coupling parameter α_{121} is reduced from 0.03 to 0.01. Observe that the frequency modulation on mode 2 disappears when its amplitude decreases monotonically as it does when $\alpha_{121} = 0.01$. AM and FM on the Key-note and Octave are shown. FM on the Twelfth not shown.

14.33 Tuning to Produce Strong Octave and Twelfth

For a given level of stick impact, the strengths of the octave and the twelfth are dependent on the quadratic coupling α-parameters. In the dynamical equations for note vibrations the quadratic terms appear because of the curvature of the note surface. In Chapter 3 it is shown that the coupling parameters $\alpha_{11,2}$ and $\alpha^*_{jk,n}$ are expressed as

$$\alpha_{11,2} = 2(1+v)\left(\frac{H_0}{h}\right)\left\{\overline{Y}_2(\psi'_1, Q\psi'_1) + \frac{1}{2}\overline{M}_2(Q\psi'^2_1) - \frac{1}{2}\overline{S}_2(\psi'^2_1, Q) - \overline{V}_2(Q\psi_1\psi'_1)\right\},$$

$$\alpha^*_{jkn} = 2(1+v)\left(\frac{H_0}{h}\right)\{\overline{Y}_n(\psi'_j, Q\psi'_k) + \overline{Y}_n(\psi'_k, Q\psi'_j) + \overline{M}_n(Q\psi'_j, \psi'_k)$$
$$- \overline{S}_n(\psi'_j \psi'_k, Q) - \overline{V}_n(Q\psi_j, \psi'_k) - \overline{V}_n(Q\psi_k, \psi'_j)\}, \quad (j \neq k).$$

I wish to insert here this short piece with the hope that it will bring some comfort to the many non-mathematicians who read this book. I know your unease whenever I put up a formula like the ones above but you are not alone because some mathematically minded readers may also struggle with them! Let me place a piece of music next to one of these formulas

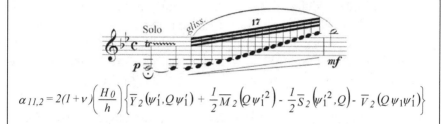

$$\alpha_{11,2} = 2(1+v)\left(\frac{H_0}{h}\right)\{\overline{Y}_2(\psi'_1, Q\psi'_1) + \frac{1}{2}\overline{M}_2(Q\psi'^2_1) - \frac{1}{2}\overline{S}_2(\psi'^2_1, Q) - \overline{V}_2(Q\psi_1\psi'_1)\}$$

If you are a musician, the first of these 'makes sense,' while the second would 'make sense' to a mathematician. If you are neither musically nor mathematically minded they both appear as mysterious objects composed of unknown signs and symbols. These objects are meant to be read not 'gazed' upon. But 'how' you read these objects depend on the level of your musical or mathematical skill. A good musician would read the first object as a single (but complex) idea. A good mathematician reads the second object in much the same way. The more complex the idea, the more detailed is the object. Both objects are coded in symbols that one has to learn in meaning and in use. Both objects are also written in a compact form which can be expanded out to reveal the coded information. In one case musical notes are the basic units while in the other, numbers are the basic units! If I were writing a music book for pan it would contain much of the former, but I am not! But in writing this book I usually listen to pan music for inspiration. The first object can be brought to life on a pan (or a set of pans) while the second object (believe it or not) *always* comes to 'life' on a sounding pan note! Both objects 'bring music to my ear!' I hope that as you read through this book you would be able to say the same.

On relative importance: just as the above musical object is indelibly marked as the opening for *Rhapsody in Blue*, there would be *no Octave* on the pan note without the mathematical object given above!

I would hope that non-mathematical readers do not skip this Section because of the daunting appearance of these formulas; continue reading because what I wish to say about them is not very mathematical, really. Those who are highly mathematical would have no difficulty with the expressions but to be fair to everyone I had better see to it that I explain the physical aspects of these expressions, particularly how those daunting terms and symbols in the formulas relate to what the tuner does.

The rise (H_0) to thickness (h) ratio H_0/h is a simple term that is set by the tuner. The thickness h refers to the *final thickness* of the tuned note and is determined by the initial gauge of steel material chosen for the pan face and the subsequent hammer peening applied (this includes sinking, smoothing, stretching etc). The rise H_0 measured at the apex of the note surface is determined by note forming and tuning. If you make $H_0 = 0$, then you have a flat plate with $\alpha_{11,2} = 0$; $\alpha_{11,2}$ vanishes and so does the octave because the parametric excitation that drives the octave no longer exists. On a flat plate the corresponding mode is NOT related to the fundamental note in a manner that allows it to function as an octave. This is what I meant in the table insert above when I said '*there would be no Octave on the pan note without the mathematical object given above!*'

The Poisson's ratio v, is an Elastic constant of the note material (steel) that is fairly constant having a value around 0.3 for steel. Even when the pan is 'chromed' the Poisson's ratio is still essentially constant around 0.3. However, one ought not to make the suggestion that if a material with larger Poisson's ratio were used in making the pan then the octave would be stronger. While on the face of it that seems to be true, using such a material will produce a number of other effects because Poisson's ratio is found in many other terms in the note dynamics. In any case the maximum value for v is 0.5, obtained to good approximation for soft rubber, which is unsuitable material for making a pan, so there is not a whole lot to be gained by this.

But what about all those '*smart stuff*' like $\overline{Y}_n(\psi'_j, Q\psi'_k)$ for example? What do these have to do with the tuner? Well first of all when you see 'smart stuff' like $\overline{Y}_n(\psi'_j, Q\psi'_k)$, the $\overline{Y}_n$ describes a mathematical operation to be performed on the quantities within the brackets ( ); in this case the operation $\overline{Y}_n$ is performed on ψ'_j and on the product $Q\psi'_k$. Similar explanations apply to the other 'smart stuff' terms.

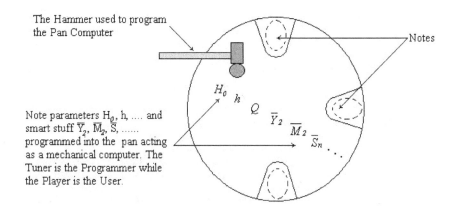

Fig. 14.51. The author's concept of the Tuning Process as the programming of the Pan represented as a mechanical computer with the Tuner acting as the Programmer and the Player as the User. The programming is of a global kind where the *Smart Stuff* is set as a group not as individual components.

Here is a deep revelation, one that I have held back until this time and place in this book because it requires a clear head for its full understanding. I highlight it with a 'bullet' and describe it in Figure 14.51;

❖ *Using a hammer, the tuner sets up on each individual note that he tunes, a mechanical system that computes each and every term in the 'smart stuff' that appears in the dynamical and statical equations describing these notes. Viewed as a mechanical computer, the pan is programmed to perform specific sets of functions, one set for each note. Once 'programmed,' the notes require mechanical energy in order to operate and once excited it will run through the operations defined by the tuner-programmer and completes its task in a time of 1 second. If the program, stored within the note as the set of note parameters, is modified in any way — a process called re-tuning — the excited note will perform the new set of operations defined by the new program. The stick not only acts as the switch that turns on this mechanical computer, but in the hand of the panist, it supplies the mechanical energy that powers the system. In addition and most importantly, as the player supplies the energy through the stick-note impact, he also encodes this burst of energy with information transferred from his brain, to his hands, then to the stick-tip and finally the note. Over the span of several stick impacts, this information is as complex as the music itself and carries with it the personality, nuances and feelings of the panist.*

Becoming a Good Tuner

Now you can understand why Chapter 13 occupied so much of my time and why it is so long! That Chapter deals with the encoding and decoding of the information transferred by impact to the sounding note on the pan. Every stick impact must encode a musical tone! The panist must be able to trust his instrument to perform this function repeatedly and in precisely the way he has defined it. He must therefore trust the tuner in his capacity as a pan programmer! This is the relationship between the Tuner and the Smart Stuff. From my perspective the information encoded in each impact is simple enough to be described by relatively simple mathematical operations. But, the information encoded in time as a sequence of impacts made by the panist shows the complexity of the music.

Do I really believe that the tuned notes on a pan actually perform these Smart Stuff operations? I certainly do! This is why you need to have a 'clear head' in order to understand and appreciate this concept.

To the reader who complains that all this programming stuff is still over his head my words of comfort are to try your best to understand the pan in a practical way and try to win the friendship of a good tuner who would allow you to become an apprentice or an understudy. I never had the opportunity to be an apprentice tuner under any of the tuners or master tuners who became my friends but I was a Trade Apprentice at the Texaco Oil Refinery at Pointe-a-Pierre, Trinidad in my boyhood days and together with my earlier schooling at the San Fernando Technical Institute (the old school originally at

Les Effort West, San Fernando) I acquired much of the technical skills that you see played out in the pages of this book. It is a pity that today, Technical Education in my country is no longer what it used to be in my days! I chose those places of learning for a reason; I had a 'plan!'

Be patient because there is much to be learnt, many skills to acquire, and many days of frustration to overcome in tuning a difficult pan. So not having the 'clear head' which I asked for could place you at a disadvantage. You see your head is clear when you have not allowed yourself or your mind really, to be filled with wrong notions about this instrument. One of the inhibiting factors to understanding the pan and learning to tune it properly is to become drawn to the wrong notion or concept that the pan is just a drum and just as easy to tune. From my experience, having lectured to dozens of professional tuners at a time (all from my homeland, where the very best reside), I can say that wrong notions and improperly developed skills (manual and aural) are the two major inhibiting factors to becoming a good tuner. Be open-minded and learn from each and every mistake you make in tuning a pan. You make a leap forward on each success! Watch the masters very carefully. Sit with them. Don't become 'swell headed' into thinking that you are as good as they are because you are in their company. Let them know that you are there to learn. One day others would be learning from you. Listen to their pans. Learn to develop notes mentally in your head; with and without all the partials. In other words, program your mind to the tuning of a pan. Now, with the 'clear head' you have developed, transfer that program onto the next pan you tune.

Returning to the 'easy stuff,' the shape function Q is determined by the shape which the tuner gives to the surface of the note. *No two notes have exactly the same shape* therefore Q is unique for a particular note. However, a good tuner is quite proficient and he can closely reproduce the shapes that make his notes easier to tune and which also satisfies his tonal requirements. The term ψ is the mode shape of the vibrating note therefore it only '*exists*' when a note is played; it depends on *how* the note is played and on the conditions set up by the tuner for the particular note. Since ψ depends on many parameters, the tuner cannot exercise full control on this term. However, the dynamics of the pan is such that all the ψs fall into a well defined class of functions which guarantees that these functions are reproduced each time a note is played. This is the reason why a note and the instrument generally, sounds the same way each time it is played (unless of course something destructive has occurred, like carelessly hammering the instrument, dropping the instrument or sitting on it). So the 'smart stuff' in the formulas really describes those dynamical operations that take place within the material forming the note while the note is sounding. We continue with the '*easy stuff*' but they are just as 'smart!'

Immediately one observes from these expressions that the α-parameters are directly proportional to the rise-factor H_0/h, which means that by increasing the rise H_0 of the note (by raising the dome of the note), greater amounts of energy can be transferred from mode1 to mode2. This increases the '*strength*' of the octave. The same can be achieved by decreasing the thickness h of the note. It will be unwise to recommend decreasing the thickness however, because, as shown in Chapter 2, thicker notes are generally more stable. Modal frequencies also depend on H_0 and h, so that there is always some compromise to be made. But when the process is carried out with a well-prepared pan (i.e. proper indenting, forming and annealing) it is always possible to produce good notes with a strong octave on a repeatable basis. The same holds for the twelfth ($\approx 3\omega_1$) and the second octave ($\approx 4\omega_1$) if the tuner is sufficiently skilled and possesses a good ear. The twelfth depends on the parameter $\alpha_{12,3}$ while the second octave depends on $\alpha_{22,4}$.

The full expressions for $\alpha_{11,2}$ and $\alpha^*_{jk,n}$ also show that the α-parameters depend on the *shape* of the note surface through the *shape function* Q. It is not unusual to see the tuner making soft hammer impacts to the note surface not so much to alter the frequency (which will change) but to enhance (or mute) a particular mode. It is the shaping function q(x) on which Q depends, that is being altered with these soft impacts.

While the tuner can modify the α-parameters with the hammer he cannot make modifications individually to any given α-parameter, in fact he modifies them all at once to varying degrees.

Don't take this restriction as a fault of the hammer (being a heavy metal object) for while better control is possible with a light (small) hammer, a small hammer is still subject to this restriction. In a way it is like breathing; although it is the oxygen we want from the air, when we breath we take into our nostrils and lungs everything that is present before our nose, nitrogen, oxygen, carbon dioxide, water vapor even dust and smoke.

So the question arises:

Question: *Since all the α-parameters are modified with each application of the hammer, how can the tuner gain control of these parameters which are so important in determining the relative strengths of the partials — the key-note, the octave and the twelfth?*

Answer: *There will be a repetition of some of the points made earlier but they are made wherever necessary in order to re-emphasize their importance.* We have partially answered this question already but first let us see what further details we can 'dig out' of the expressions. They tell us immediately that the degree of coupling among the key-note, octave and twelfth depends directly on the rise-factor H_0/h. If we make $H_0/h = 0$, a geometrically flat note, all the α-parameters will be identically zero. This will not work because we will not have a 'pan note' it will not sound like one! In order to generate the required higher partials, a pan note must consist of a raised surface on the pan face! So the first control afforded to the tuner from these equations is control on the strengths of the two partials (octave and twelfth). Increasing H_0/h increases all α-parameters. In the expressions, <u>the physical mechanisms</u> related to the terms within the curly brackets { } <u>cannot</u> be disentangled by the tuner in order to selectively alter a particular mode of vibration (we are only interested in mode1, mode2 and mode3). But we are not at a loss in controlling what the pan does with these modes.

Now read the following lines very carefully for here is another aspect of the subtle nature of the pan; Observe the mode shape functions ψ_j (the subscripts are sometimes written as k and these take the values 1, 2 3). These functions describe the shape and relative magnitude of the vibrating modes (ψ_1 for mode1 (the key-note), ψ_2 for mode2 (the octave) and ψ_3 for mode3 (the twelfth)). Now, the tuner cannot directly modify the mode shapes ψ because <u>mode shapes are dynamical in nature</u>. The mode shapes only exist while the note is vibrating. However, they depend on the following, with the most important one first then the others in random order: (1) **mode frequency**, (2) the **shape** that the tuner gives to the note surface, (3) the **boundary conditions** set by hammer peening, (4) **blocking** (which may incorporate grooves or bores), (5) **sinking** and (6) the **annealing process**. So it goes right back through all the processes of pan preparation —foul up any one and you ruin the pan —what you put on the pan is what you get.!

Now for the really subtle part: it is really a repeat of 'what you put on the pan is what you get'. Remember what I said, that the normal modes on a pan note are <u>not natural harmonics</u>. I have tried repeatedly in this work to 'drum' this misconception out of the mind of the reader and I hope that by now I have succeeded. If not, you may have trouble with what follows. Don't fear it's simple. It is my fear that because it is so simple that you may miss it so I am building up our approach to it with expectancy in the hope that you don't miss it. I write it in point form for emphasis. Here it is;

- *You need a key-note of <u>well defined frequency</u>, so tune the note with the hammer to establish one (say G_4), make sure that in the end it is correctly placed on the musical scale (12-TET). Tuning involves setting the right note boundary (not the traditional note boundary) and the approximate height of the note at the apex. This establishes the correct mode shape for ψ_1 as the note surface vibrates. This mode will need correcting as you move along to the other modes.*
- *You need an octave on the same physical note, the resident octave, (say a detuned G_5, compressed or stretched to your liking) so use the hammer to establish one that is correctly set at a detuned frequency relative to the harmonic of the key-note. This establishes the correct mode shape ψ_2 as the note surface vibrates. This automatically sets the α-parameters, $\alpha_{11,2}$ and $\alpha_{12,1}$. These will change because tuning is not yet complete.*
- *You need a twelfth, a resident twelfth (or fifth as 'we' tuners call it, I am happy for the promotion), but if you are tuning a bass you may prefer the third. Decide now! You decide on a twelfth (a detuned G_6) so establish this mode (use the $5/4^{ths}$-*

Law, by now this has become second nature). This establishes the correct mode shape ψ_3 and will automatically set the α-parameters, $\alpha_{12,3}$ (same as $\alpha_{21,3}$), $\alpha_{31,2}$ (same as $\alpha_{13,2}$) and $\alpha_{23,1}$ (same as $\alpha_{32,1}$). This alters $\alpha_{11,2}$ and $\alpha_{12,1}$ but that is all part of the process. You must check both the key-note and resident octave making any fine adjustments as required — it's all your choice. If you were on the bass and chose to use the third, just go ahead and establish the third (use the $9/8^{ths}$-Rule) <u>there are no α-parameters involved with the third</u> *but establishing the third alters $\alpha_{11,2}$ and $\alpha_{12,1}$ so re-check the key-note and resident octave.*

- *Second nature comes with much practice. You will get it wrong many times even the best of us do, especially when we are under the weather. Now it seems as if we must tune the octave before the twelfth. Strictly speaking this is not really so. In fact we tune them both simultaneously along with the key-note. This order of key-note, octave, and twelfth is only for writing purposes because with the hammer (as opposed to the pen) everything changes as the note is impacted (peened).*

- *Depending on the pan being tuned, you may be using the $5/4^{ths}$-Law or the $9/8^{ths}$-Rule in either case you have to apply some fine tuning to the two higher partials. You will prefer, certainly, to do this without affecting greatly the key-note. You can make small adjustments to the aspect ratio by lightly tapping around the points A and/or A′ (see Figure 14.32) to adjust the octave and at B and/or B′ to adjust the fifth or third as the case may be.*

- *Always listen to the modes (**all of them**) as you tune, correcting the key-note or octave as you move along. This is the way in which the tuner can hone in on the correct values for the parameters that we are concerned with. As you listen to the modes, if a strange, discordant tone pops out, remove it by correcting the changes made by the last hammer strike.*

- *Notice that it appears as if I have said nothing different about tuning a note here. Well that is just the point, it couldn't have been more subtle! It is the note, not you, not the tuner or panist that operates according to the dynamical equations so that as you follow the guide above,* <u>the note sets itself up</u> *and* *establishes these complicated relations and interactions between the modes. The dynamics of the note ensure these things while the note is sounding. But since <u>the dynamics run independently of the musical scale</u> (the notes never met the great man Pythagoras and they know nothing about Just or 12-TET) and it is the human preference to use 12-TET on the steelpan, so <u>it is you</u>, the tuner, that must enter this frequency (pitch) information that comes with the musical scale, into the pan (this is what 'programming' means).*

- *Remember this; it is the physical mechanisms that are adjustable with the hammer. Tuning the pan is not just a matter of getting the frequencies right. With practice and lots of patience, not to mention keen eyes and ears, eventually the apprentice tuner learns to shape the note surface to achieve the right modal couplings while setting the modal frequencies.*

The cubic coupling parameters play only minor roles in the note dynamics because they are very small numerically. However, under very intense excitations the cubic terms cannot be ignored. Since the steelpan as a musical instrument is never played in this fashion, the cubic couplings can be ignored in the tuning process.

14.34 **Tuning by Altering the Compressive Stresses**

The effect of the residual compressive stress on modal frequency has been dealt with extensively in Chapters 3 and 8. It remains for us to discuss how it is used in tuning the notes. Excessive peening can develop large compressive stresses in small localized areas of the note surface with the likelihood of flapping or buckling. The usual remedy is to peen with much obliquity (stretching) just outside the flapping region. This action flattens out the surface and redistributes the residual stresses acting on the note because taken over the entire pan face, chime and skirt the stresses (hoop, tensile and compressive) must exist in a state of equilibrium. This is the reason why striking anywhere on the pan with a hammer alters the tuned state of the notes. Since flapping tells us that the frequency of the affected area has been *reduced* to zero, this knowledge can be applied in the tuning process to alter the frequency of the modes on the note being tuned. There are two ways to do this:

(1) **By Peening**: All hammer peening actions on the pan modifies the compressive stress distribution on the pan face. Peening along the true note boundary modifies the compressive stress boundary condition and changes the frequency of all modes on the note.

(2) **By Heating**: In this procedure, which is used as a method of fine tuning, the note is placed under low heat by a torch in order to thermally reduce the residual compressive stresses on the treated note. On cooling, this results in an *increase* in frequency of the partials. This method cannot be used to decrease the frequency *unless* the temperature of the note is raised *excessively* to soften the work hardened steel. This extreme treatment is *not recommended*. Some tuners have also tried what I would refer to as '*spot quenching*' where an area of the note is heated with the torch and quenched by dropping water on the hot material. These techniques are mere '*stop gap*' procedures applied to improperly prepared notes and pan faces. A good pan maker should not have to rely on them!

Note: *By heating to those high temperatures accessible with a torch, all modal frequencies and couplings are affected in an unpredictable way so* **the author does not recommend the torch method for high quality steelpans**.

14.35 Setting the Boundary Conditions — The Spring Supports

The true note boundary (see Figures 14.33 and 14.34), is a shared boundary for all the tuned modes; it defines the locus of points of equal stiffness for each tuned mode. It is important to understand that on a given note all the tuned modes share this common boundary. To define this boundary, the traditional note must be hammer-peened in the area defining the true note boundary and in the process the boundary conditions consisting of the spring supports (K and C) and compressive stresses are defined. For best results, the tuner must work evenly around the note. Modal frequencies are however only partly defined by the spring supports.

Because it is not possible to completely define the modal frequencies for the shallow shell notes in this way, the pan notes cannot be tuned by peening on the boundary alone. The shape of the note surface must also be adjusted in order to establish good coupling among the tuned modes.

Researchers Muthukumaran et al. (1999) showed that for flat rectangular plates, spring supports (K and C) can be found for which the modal frequencies of the plate are all set into a harmonic relation. Contrary to the claim by these researchers who applied these flat plate (2-D) results to the steelpan where one finds shells or dome-shaped (3-D) notes, *boundary conditioning alone cannot account for the frequencies of the tuned notes found on the steelpan.* In the first place, in Muthukumaran et al., only the spring supports (K and C) along the flat plate boundary are set. In addition, again contrary to the claim, the frequencies of the partials on the steelpan notes do not fall automatically into a harmonic relationship when boundary conditions are set. The 3-D structure of the notes on the steelpan along with the in-plane stresses (a factor not included in the Muthukumaran et al. work) present a much greater range of parameters that determine the frequencies of the system. Apart from the fact that modal frequencies on the steelpan are not fully defined by the boundary conditions, merely assigning a nearly harmonic set of frequencies to the tuned modes will not suffice. The octaves must be tuned as *pseudo-octaves* (stretched or compressed) while the third and higher partials (if accessible) must be stretched or compressed relative to the corresponding harmonic. *Harmonic tuning is not employed on the steelpan.*

14.36 Forming and Tuning Grooveless Notes

Early in the development of my work on the steelpan, I made the observation that on the basis of mode-localization and energy confinement, grooves were not necessary. Pan maker Randolph Leroy Thomas, with whom the author had many discussions on the instrument, pursued the experimental work and developed it to perfection (see Achong 1996b). My input was an idea backed by theoretical work the rest was Thomas' practical work. Thomas' procedure was to scribe lines defining the traditional notes and to shape the notes by hammer peening only, no use of the punch. The areas that ultimately define the true note boundary are specially peened with much stretching (much obliquity in the peening action) in order to create a uniform, compressively stressed boundary. Without the help of the grooves along the traditional note boundary, mechanical blocking rested entirely on the peening applied to the pan face (a task requiring the hands of an experienced pan maker). Development of the Grooveless Pan was quickly achieved and Thomas deserves the credit for its invention and development. This pan incorporates two major aspects of pan note construction and the production of truly good notes; (1) the setting of good boundary conditions by hammer peening in the internote area between the true note boundary and the traditional note boundary; (2) strong mode-mode quadratic coupling on the tuned notes to enhance energy confinement. Thomas turned the grooveless tenor into one of his standard pans. He also applied the same procedure to his bore tenors. The tenor in the author's personal possession, by choice, is an unchromed, unpainted grooveless tenor, made and tuned by Thomas.

Tuning the notes on the grooveless pan follows the same procedure as described here for the normal pan.

14.37 Forming and Tuning the Low-End Pans

The notes on the low-end pans — cellos and the basses — because of their low frequencies and the restricted pan face area especially on the bass, require the use of high compressive stresses along the boundaries. In Section 8.18, where notes were designed as an engineering exercise, it was shown that on the bass notes in particular, because of their large physical size, problems associated with low mechanical bias could develop. The maximum contact force that could safely be applied to any note is determined by the mechanical bias. The greater the mechanical bias, the greater the maximum contact force that can be applied with the stick before the tone begins to show distortion. This is just the opposite of what is obtained on notes of the high-end pans which are physically smaller and where the mechanical bias is more than adequate to prevent distortion for all conceivable manually applied stick impacts.

Note: Designers of pans with larger than normal pan faces and notes should take note of this problem. The same problems that bass players experience when attempting to play the bass with strong stick impacts may afflict the larger notes on these pans.

Mechanical bias F_0 is directly proportional to the product of in-plane compressive stress σ_c along the note boundary, the Rise H_0 and the note thickness h, $F_0 = -4\pi\sigma_c H_0 h M_8$ (see Section 8.18). The compressive in-plane stress along the note boundary and hence the mechanical bias can be increased by hammer peening. For the bass and cello notes, this requires a lot of work along the boundaries — a task that many pan makers and tuners leave to the professional bass makers. Large compressive stress is also required in order to lower the note frequency. *In fact the low bass note frequencies cannot be attained without compressive stresses along the boundary.* When tuning these lower notes, apply the $9/8^{ths}$-Rule to keep the true notes as large as possible. The smaller the physical size of the bass note the greater must be the compressive stress along the boundary. This means that it is harder (more peening required) to tune the low bass notes if there is size or space restriction. The alert reader will observe that there is a compromise to be made here between having a large note with lower compressive stress and a smaller note with greater compressive stress. My recommendation is to ensure that the largest compressive stress possible is set up on the note without worrying about the size of the note. In this way, the player can afford to play the finished note with much vigor without generating unwanted audio distortions. While this recommendation seems to be in perfect order, if the area allocated to the note is too small, then the Wobbly Effect may set in, leading to other problems (see the 'Wobbly Effect' in Section 9.11.3).

Use a large rise-factor (H_0/h) on these notes in order to generate resident octaves of adequate strength. In this way mode-localization and energy confinement of the key-note and octave can be well established thereby generating a strong or loud sounding bass. Do not try to increase H_0/h by using a thin (high numbered gauge) material. This lowers the mechanical bias causing your bass notes to generate the annoying 'boiing' sound. Of course it is assumed here that all prior preparations of the pan were properly carried out and that heavy gauge steel materials having good specifications were used to make the pan face and skirt.

Some of the higher notes on the bass cannot be adequately excited with the bass sticks (see Chapter 13) but they are used to reinforce the octaves on the lower notes — together they form weak Marshall Pairs. This combination is useful only if both notes are placed on the same pan face (as most of them in fact are, with some notable exceptions on the nine-bass). The higher notes are not difficult to tune but this ought to be done in the same manner as in tuning weak Marshall Pairs.

14.38 Tuning Marshall Pairs on the Tenor and Medium Range Pans: Weak and Strong Marshall Pairs

Marshall Pairs were introduced by Bertie Marshall to reinforce the resident octave on the first member (the lower member) of the pair. We use the $\{C_4:C_5\}$ pair on the tenor as an example to explain the pair operation. When the C_4 note is played, the *resident octave* on C_4 vibrates with each half of the true note executing a phase-anti-phase motion. Because each half of the note radiates acoustically and in anti-phase, the far-field acoustic vibrations effectively cancel out. Apart from the radiation from the weakly excited skirt (in particular), very little by way of a second partial can be heard at a far distance from the resident octave. To reinforce the second partial, the second member of the pair, C_5, is coupled to C_4 through the internote separating C_4 and C_5. This path allows the resident octave on C_4 to interact linearly with the key-note on C_5 and for the key-note on C_4 to interact non-linearly (quadratic non-linearity) with the key-note on C_5. The result is the sympathetic vibration of C_5—the octave—with the entire surface of the true note on C_5 vibrating in phase. There is now no cancellation of the far field for the acoustic radiation emanating from C_5 (save that which occurs for the resident octave (now a second octave) on C_5). By making use of the coupled octave in this way, the Marshall Pair has an *acoustical advantage* over the single note. A stronger second partial is now generated. The amplitude and frequency modulations produced by the sympathetic octave differ from that obtained on the resident octave of C_4 (see Chapter 5).

Marshall Pairs provide an alternative tonal structure that is very useful in providing additional 'amplitude' (amplitude characteristics) and 'color' (frequency characteristics) to the sound produced by a group of pans played in unison (simultaneously). Although they were introduced as a tuning option to reinforce the *resident octave* on the outer notes of the tenor pan, excessive coupling between the pair can severely reduce the intensity of the key-notes on the outer notes. When Marshall Pairs are used exclusively on the outer notes of a tenor, the instrument has to be played at moderate to low levels because for a pair to operate properly the two notes *cannot be fully blocked*. Applied to all the pairs on the instrument, this means that stick impact energy is lost from the played note to all parts (domains) of the instrument not only to the other note in the pair. When these notes are played in rapid succession the instrument sounds 'noisy'. This problem can severely limit the strength of the stick impact for acceptable tonal quality. The author has listened to a bore tenor pan tuned entirely with strong Marshall Pairs, a case of excessive pairing, and judged it as a disaster.

To varying degrees, all the outer notes on a tenor are paired to an inner note so the term 'Marshall Pair' applies to them all in the *weak* sense. In the *strong* class of 'Marshall Pair', the note-note coupling between members of a pair must be sufficiently strong for the dynamics of the outer note to be restricted to an essentially monochromatic (single-frequency) mode with the inner note alone providing the octave component. On a good high-end pan, most of the notes are weak Marshall Pairs and each member can be tuned independently. Some are Triples such as $\{G_4: G_5: G_6\}$ but the G_6 does not contribute any appreciable acoustic energy to the Triple when the G_4 note is played. High level sinusoidal excitation of the G_4 note from an external sinusoidal source is required to observe this Triple (and similar Triples) in sympathetic vibration.

The two notes in a strong Marshall Pair cannot be tuned independently. For example take the $\{G_4:G_5\}$ pair, if one were to place a small sandbag or magnet (to act as a *mute*) on the inner G_5 note, then tune the G_4 note and follow this with the sandbag on the G_4 note while tuning the G_5, the resulting pair cannot be guaranteed to produce an acceptable tone. The reason is that because of non-linear and linear coupling between the pair, the G_4 and G_5 when played independently (with a sandbag on one note or the other) the frequencies *are different* from the corresponding frequencies when played as a pair. Whenever notes or modes interact there is always some amount of detuning. In fact when used as a pair and the G_4 note is played the frequency of the sympathetic G_5 note is not the same as when the G_5 note is played (no sandbags used). These are small but important differences in frequencies that determine the amplitude and frequency modulations (amplitude and color) of the tone.

The tuning of weak Marshall Pairs is straightforward since each member can be tuned independently—the procedure for single notes is followed.

14.39 Tuning the Triples (Whole Notes) on the Three Cello

The *Three Cello* is a wonderfully crafted instrument containing a total of 27 notes—9 notes per pan. On each pan face one finds a Triple of notes — $\{B_2, B_3, B_4\}$, $\{C_2, C_3, C_4\}$ and $\{C^{\#}_3, C^{\#}_4, C^{\#}_5\}$ — and a number of weak Marshall Pairs some of which are formed from the outer notes. One can always split a Triple into two Marshall Pairs to give a total of six (6) pairs formed entirely of outer notes (2 per pan) and nine (9) pairs (3 per pan) formed from a combination of outer and inner notes. The notes on this pan are tuned by the methods for weak Marshall Pairs and Triples.

14.40 Tuning weak Marshall Pairs on the Bass

Marshall Pairs are found on all the lower pans down to the bass. On the bass in particular, the author recommends their use only as *weak* Marshall Pairs. These weak Marshall pairs can be tuned with the same caution as obtained for the high-end pans. For their large physical sizes, the acoustical output of the bass pans is notoriously low (see Chapter 12). Tuning the notes on the bass as *strong* Marshall Pairs only serves to worsen the situation because the octave formed by the adjacent note, robs the key-note of much of its energy. It is much better for the tuner to strengthen the *resident octave* and allow mode-localization and confinement to control the note dynamics. With a stronger resident octave, sufficient energy will be transferred to the adjacent octave to make use of the acoustical advantage that pairing offers. Tuners who depend more heavily on the adjacent octave rather than the resident octave are relying on a much greater energy transfer across the note boundaries to excite the octave. There is little control on energy losses from the key-note when this is done. *Save some of that energy for acoustical radiation instead.* Acoustical radiation is what a musical instrument should be designed to produce. But being loud is not the story about pan!

Using the *fifth* here will rob the key-note and *resident octave* of some energy but this energy will be subject to confinement. Using the option of the *third* will not rob the key-note or *resident octave* of any energy. Work hard at peening the note boundary (*don't ignore the area adjacent to the chime or rim*) because (i) blocking is very important on the bass and (ii) large compressive stresses are needed to set up a high mechanical bias on each note (see Chapter 8). On the bass this will require a punch so a grooveless bass (one formed without a punch) is extremely difficult to produce unless you have the guts. Always use heavy gauge steel on your basses, remember 'Easy Come, Easy Go.' Pay attention to the rise-factor or 'height' (*don't attempt to increase the rise-factor by using a thin pan face*), use the $9/8^{ths}$-Rule, and use a small but non-zero detuning for the *resident octave* to ensure good modulation and confinement. Always ensure that the chime is tightly fitted and welded if possible (see Chapter 2). Ensure that the skirt is of heavy gauge steel and that there are at least two circumferential stiffeners (stringers or rolling hoop to use the original name). Never use the attractive looking but 'weaker' and poorly performing straight skirt without the rolling hoops, you will be sorry if you do.

These are the secrets to getting a truly loud bass but chief among them is containment. Follow the advice given here to obtain good mode localization.

14.41 Summary of Tuning Rules and Practice: Single Notes and Marshall Pairs

Aided by the above, we can now summarize the rules and procedures for tuning the steelpan:

Note: *This shortlist cannot be expected to be complete. For this reason I try to avoid listing rules in numerical order.*

1) Remember tuning a pan is next to impossible without proper preparation — proper sinking, forming and burning.
2) At the outset, the $5/4^{ths}$-Law should be applied to the marking and forming of the inner notes. To avoid 'fishing around' for a suitable shape for the note surface within the

area of the traditional note, hammer peening should be applied in accordance with the law.

3) When using the option of tuning the *third* on the bass notes, the $9/8^{ths}$-Rule applies.

4) Assuming all the notes have been formed (raised), begin by tuning the key-note with peening applied within the area intended as the true note. Peening both from the top and bottom will establish the initial rise-factor (H_0/h) and form-factor (Q). With practice and by playing the note with the tip and butt ends of the stick the general area of the true note can be found. Peening with much obliquity (stretching) along the boundary of the true note will modify the stress distribution thereby raising or lowering the pitch. The tuner who is new to the art may find it useful to sprinkle some talcum powder on the note surface to identify the true note boundary as it establishes itself.

5) The tuner usually begins on the note which best serves him/her as the reference for the other notes up and down the scale. This first note is brought close but not exactly to the desired state because it must be re-tuned after the next few notes receive their first tuning. This procedure of returning to previously tuned notes continues until all the notes receive their first tuning. If the pan has already been coated (powder or chrome) then final tuning should not commence for at least 24 hours. If the pan has not yet received its required coating, final tuning should begin afterwards. The reason for the delay or 'rest period' is to allow the residual stress distribution to relax. Stress relaxation is important in order to bring the pan to a stable state on completion of the final tuning (see Chapter 9). The tuner will observe the notes to 'run sharp' during this period of stress relaxation. Final 'touch up' can be done a few days after final tuning. Never be in a hurry if you want a truly good pan. The frequency stability of the pan at this point depends critically on the quality of the *sinking* and the *burning* (tempering) processes to which it was subjected. In keeping with the findings of this work it is recommended that tuners record the temperature at which the pan was tuned and to make this information available to the owner or player of the instrument. *This is not the present practice, but a sticker*

on the inner surface of the skirt should be used to record this information.

6) Two concepts fundamental to tuning are those of *frequency ratio* on which much has already been said, and of *consonance* and *dissonance*. As the notes are tuned in succession (sometimes with the aid of reference tones) the technique of playing one note then another while listening for consonance or dissonance, guides the tuner towards the correct setting. The same technique is used in piano tuning, knowledge of which was gained by the author who grew up in a home with a piano and has spent his adult life as the owner of one of these grand instruments, which, believe it or not, he can tune!

7) The experienced tuner, a person with a 'musical ear,' relies on his/her in-built reference tones stored in the brain, with which to compare a sounding tone for consonance or dissonance. Or simply put, to decide on the accuracy of a sounding note.

14.42 Specifications for the Tuned State of a Note

We are aware, by the very existence of the pan as a musical instrument, that while there can exist a vast number of possible untuned states for notes on the pan face, there are sets, call them the *Musical Sets*, or the *Musically Tuned Sets*, to which one associate places on the musical scale (12-TET). While the *Musically Tuned Sets* are special I must re-emphasize the fact that:

The fundamental principles under which the steelpan operates under excitation by stick impacts are independent of the musical scale.

At first it may be difficult for some readers to grasp this fact, being accustomed to the idea that a pan as a musical instrument only works when it is tuned to the musical scale (12-TET). The musically tuned state does hold a special position over the musically untuned states. We can easily recognize this difference aurally but we may never have bothered to really understand what makes the difference. 'Well it sounds tuned' is hardly the answer. But seeing that the full answer lies in psychoacoustics, another book must be devoted to this topic. For our present purposes we rely on the good judgment of the expert tuner to bring the note to the state we recognize as tuned and musically pleasing to the ear. But there are many, infinitely many, states that obey the principles of mode-localization and confinement, and also follow the $5/4^{ths}$-Law or the $9/8^{ths}$-Rule but lie outside the musical scale. This is what I mean when I say that the operation of the pan is independent of the musical scale. It is the tuner who brings the notes in line (or almost in line) with the musical scale. The *Musically Tuned State* is a '*desired state.*' If I say that the state *must* be formed within the 12-TET scale then I am being prejudicial — I am sounding *Westernized*! Other 'societies' or people of other cultures may prefer their own musical scales within which their musical instruments, even pans, have to function!

14.43 Notes of Quality for a 'Competition Grade' Pan

14.43.1 Complex Tuning and Advanced Tuning

The concepts of *Complex Tuning* and *Advanced Tuning* were introduced in Section 3.2.2. As described in Section 14.25.8, Complex Tuning was introduced by Bertie Marshall and it has been adapted as standard practice today. In Complex Tuning, a note is tuned with its key-note set at the required frequency on the 12-TET scale (the adopted reference) while the higher partials, are tuned to the octave and twelfth. In rare circumstances one may also find a weak second octave. The *Detuning Rules* as I have outlined, with respect to compressing and stretching the higher partials also must apply.

Advanced Tuning, a new term introduced here for the first time, gives a name to a tuning procedure that can find good use in the hands of the master tuner. The notes are tuned in the manner indicated by the example shown in Figure 3.2 (see also Figure 2 of Achong (1999b)). In this procedure domain interaction is deliberately incorporated into the note dynamics. This tuning procedure (without a name) was used by pan maker Randolph Thomas from whom I became acquainted with the technique. This *advanced form of tuning* is in fact superior to the straightforward *Simple Tuning* (key-note only) and *Complex Tuning* (key-note, octave and twelfth) for the following reasons: In Advanced Tuning, one takes a note tuned to the complex tuning format and subjects the internote areas adjacent to the note to further hammer peening. The objective is to tune these internote areas to the frequency of the octave of the adjacent note (refer to Figure 3.2 and keep a marker on that page in order to follow the description given here). For example the 'front' of the $C^{\#}_4$ note is tuned to $G^{\#}_5$. It must be recalled that adjacent notes on the steelpan, while positioned close in ordinary 3-Dimensional space, are in fact greatly separated in musical space. Tuning the internote at the front of the $C^{\#}_4$ note to $G^{\#}_5$ introduces an area of relatively high mechanical impedance (see Section 14.11) which offers enhanced blocking for the $C^{\#}_4$ note. Any vibrational energy acquired by the internote area tuned to $G^{\#}_5$ by direct transmission following stick impact may partly be communicated to the inner $G^{\#}_5$ note. The low-level acoustical radiation from the weakly excited $G^{\#}_5$ note will be concordant or harmonious with the sounding $C^{\#}_4$. But the advantage of Advanced Tuning is the improved blocking and the resulting increase in acoustical output it provides for the notes. From the dynamical perspective, tuning the nearby section of internote to a higher 'pitch' than the note, gives the internote a greater dynamical stiffness than the note itself, a procedure that increases blocking and satisfies the blocking condition given in Section 14.12.5. Advance Tuning works best on grooveless pans (a Thomas invention) and requires much more precise peening.

Since Advanced Tuning involves tuning the section of internote that partially adjoins the true note, the boundary conditions on the true note, set during the Complex Tuning phase, will be modified somewhat. It is therefore necessary to tune or re-tune the note as a whole during the internote tuning phase of Advanced Tuning. Since this tuning procedure comes at the end of the tuning process the changes to note frequencies (all partials) are small — the process is a form of fine tuning with the objective of increasing acoustic output and putting a 'finishing touch' to the tone. You will find the tones to be audibly brighter.

Note: The pitch of the tuned internote area used in Advance Tuning is best determined by striking the area with the butt end of the stick while tuning — <u>all decisions being made by ear</u>; don't use a frequency meter for this subtle aspect of tuning. If you are totally dependent on frequency meters, Advanced Tuning is not for you!

A *Competition Grade* Pan is best described by its sound. It incorporates all that is good in pan making and some extra input from the pan maker/tuner. Each Master Tuner produces his 'own' Competition Grade pan which resides in a special place in musical space with its distinctive sound. When properly carried out, Advanced Tuning as described here or with subtle alterations can raise a good pan to the level of 'Competition Grade.' But there are other requirements for Quality that goes into a Competition Grade pan so we attend to these in the next Section.

14.43.2 Maximizing the Accuracy of Partials and Attaining Quality

Maximizing the Accuracy of Partials

I will now carefully discuss the issue of frequency accuracy but the essential physics have already been developed in earlier Sections and Chapters. On this instrument, where the note dynamics is entirely non-linear, the accuracy of the frequencies of all the tuned partials are inextricably linked to the frequency of the lowest partial or the fundamental mode (mode1 or the key-note). This arises from the fact that the excitation of all the tuned partials above the key-note is a direct result of the parametric driving forces generated by mode1. Maximum accuracy is therefore derived only when the key-note has been properly set with respect to the reference musical scale (12-TET).

If the mode1 frequency is given by f_1, then the excited mode2 (the octave) acquires a frequency $2f_1 + \sigma_1$, where σ_1 is the detuning of mode2 measured in Hertz (σ_1 *can be positive (stretched octave) or negative (compressed octave))*. The frequency of the (sinusoidal) parametric driving force which induces this parametric resonance described as the octave is $2f_1$. Any error in setting f_1 is therefore *doubled* in the octave frequency. Tuners may not have observed this effect during tuning because it requires careful frequency measurements to be made close to the optimized setting. The tuner simply 'zeroes' in on the correct setting as indicated by the loudness of the octave (true parametric resonance), the desired tonality, and overall pitch accuracy; he does not observe the fine details contained in the *numerical* values of the frequencies. The detuning

σ_l does not contribute to the 'error' of the octave frequency. The detuning determines the AM and FM aspects of the octave and is *not* a source of error. There is a smaller contribution to the set frequency of the octave which comes from the interaction with the third partial (mode3 or the twelfth) but this appears only in the form of a frequency modulation that is weaker than that caused by the mode1 x mode1 interaction. Recall that it is mode1 interacting *with itself* that generates the driving force that excites mode2.

The parametric excitation that drives the third partial (twelfth), is produced by the mode1 x mode2 interaction at frequency $f_1 + f_2$ where f_2 is the frequency of the octave. There is a weaker cubic excitation which we can ignore here. The frequency of the 'driven' third partial is now set at $f_1 + f_2 + \sigma_2 = 3f_1 + \sigma_1 + \sigma_2$ where $\sigma_1 + \sigma_2$ is the detuning of the twelfth (compressed or stretched). In interpreting the detuning of the third partial, recall that 'detuning' is measured with respect to the corresponding harmonic frequency of the key-note ($3f_1$ in this case). (*Having mentioned the harmonic frequency here, please remember that only the parametric excitations appear as harmonics of the key-note and that these excitations are not sufficiently strong to be audible. Tuners DO NOT tune the note to these frequencies.*) The error in the third partial set into parametric resonance with mode1 and mode2 is now *triple* the error in the key-note. Any attempt to tune the third partial independently of the lower two partials will result in greater error and a weaker third partial.

The overall accuracy of the tuned partials is therefore dependent on the accuracy of the key-note.

When the *third* (above the octave) is used as the third partial, its frequency can be set independently of the lower two partials because parametric resonances are absent. As we have already shown the third is used only on the bass.

Attaining Quality

- In the following, a *note of quality* is defined as one which is tuned with its key-note *precisely* on the musical scale (12-TET to be precise) and its higher partials set in accordance with the detuning rules (stretching and compressing) that the notes must obey.

- If this fundamental requirement stated above is not obeyed by a note or pan then all other factors that determine quality such as tonality which in turn depends on the relative strengths of the partials, are of no effect.

This definition is necessary because in the following paragraphs, statements are to be made on the frequencies of the partials on the pan in relation to an *independent* system, namely the fixed 12-TET Musical Scale. If there is an error in the frequency of the key-note then technically the 12-TET system is not strictly followed.

The musically tuned state of a pan note of *quality* is specified by the following attributes:

Note: Readers should pay close attention to these details in the specifications for the resident octave, the resident twelfth and the third.

In all cases the term 'harmonic' refers to integer multiples of the frequency of the key-note. The use of this term should not be taken to mean that the normal modes of the notes are harmonics, for they are not.

1) **Single Notes**:

   a. The **Key-note**: This vibrational mode of a sounding note identifies (labels) the note by agreement in frequency with one of the assigned standard values on the musical scale (12-TET). These labels we call $B_n^\flat$, $F_n^\#$, E_n etc., where n defines the position of the note on the register (on the pan, n = 1, 2, 3, 4, 5, 6). The correctness of this frequency assignment is not left to the discretion of the tuner. The tuner is bound by the accepted standard. In practice, small 'errors' or 'deviations' from the standard frequencies are expected in the tuning process. Deviations may also be caused by natural 'elements' such as changes in temperature (see Chapter 9). However, these small deviations do not change the label assigned to a particular note. Of course these things degrade the *quality* of the note.

   b. The **Octave—the Resident Octave**: On the pan, this is identified as the mode lying *approximately* 12 semitones above the key-note and *residing* on the same physical note as the key-note. It carries no label but is identified only with respect to the key-note. On the 12-TET scale, 12 semitones above unison is an exact second harmonic. Therefore, to avoid the pung tone the resident octave must be detuned from its standard position on the musical scale — indeed, it cannot be set exactly 12 semitones above the key-note. The detuning is at the discretion of the tuner who must choose the amount by which to **compress** or **stretch** the octave. The necessary avoidance of the pung tone forces him to do this each time the note is tuned.

c. The *Twelfth*—the **Resident Twelfth** or *Fifth above the octave* in tuner's parlance: This is identified as the mode which in the tuned state generally sits *approximately* 19 semitones above the key-note (or *approximately* 7 semitones above the octave). This mode *resides* on the same physical note as the key-note. Like the resident octave, it carries no label but is identified with respect to the key-note. **The twelfth must *always* be detuned**. Observe that on the 12-TET scale, 19 semitones above unison is 1.963 cents *below* the third harmonic, therefore, with the key-note accurately set, by tuning the twelfth precisely on the musical scale the mode is set in a *detuned, compressed* state. Therefore, unlike the octave, the twelfth can be tuned precisely on the musical scale. Since detuning is at the discretion of the tuner he may choose other settings that *compresses* or *stretches* the twelfth while avoiding the third harmonic frequency.

d. The *Third*: This appears on the bass when the option of choosing the *third* (above the octave) in place of the *fifth* is adopted. It is identified as the mode lying 16 semitones above the key-note. Like the *fifth*, it carries no label but is identified with respect to the key-note. But unlike the *fifth*, the *third does not* require detuning from its standard position on the musical scale — **however, it should, by recommendation, be tuned exactly 16 semitones above the key-note.**

Note: The terms 'weak' and 'strong' used here to classify Marshall Pairs refer to the degree of coupling between members of the pair not to the intensity of the sounding note A weak Marshall Pair is one where the coupling between the two members across the pan face is weak. A strong Marshall Pair is one with strong coupling.

2) **Strong Marshall Pairs**: In the case of strong Marshall Pairs, two labels are required for example {G_4: G_5}. The first label (G_4) indentifies the *key-note* of the pair while the second label (G_5) identifies the *octave*.

   a. The **Key-note**: The key-note in the pair must be tuned accurately and in accordance with the 12-TET scale.
   b. The **resident Octave**: This carries no label but is identified relative to the key-note on the same physical note (G_4). The resident octave on a strong Marshall Pair is generally very weak. Since, in the case of strong Marshall Pairs, the tuner relies on the adjacent octave note for the second partial it is difficult to tune the weak resident octave.
   c. The **Octave**: The octave, for dynamical reasons previously stated, *must* be detuned with respect to the second harmonic of the key-note—stretched or compressed. Since the octave, (G_5 in our example), must, in its own right, function as a single note when it is played, this note will be somewhat displaced on the musical scale. As explained earlier, the frequency of the played octave (G_5 in our example) is slightly different from the frequency sounded sympathetically by this note when the key-note (G_4) is played.
   d. The resident **Twelfth**: On a strong Marshall Pair, in the absence of a strong resident octave, the resident twelfth is very weak and once again, this makes it difficult to tune.

Because of the higher level of tuning difficulty presented by these strongly coupled pair of notes, some compromise must always be made in the tuning options with a strong Marshall Pair. Pans tuned exclusively with strong Marshall Pairs are generally noisy. The reason for this should be made clear. When relying on the octave note (the higher member of the pair) for the second partial, a strong *resident octave* is not available to interact with the key-note to produce a parametric mode of reasonable strength to drive the resident twelfth. The interaction of the key-note and the resident *octave* (**key-note · octave → twelfth**) in the pair, is generally weak and cannot be relied upon to assist the resident twelfth on a consistent (reproducible) basis. As a result some modes above the key-note are left untuned. When these are excited the pan sounds noisy. *Recommendation*: Unless you have the time and patience for long periods of tuning, avoid the use of strong Marshall Pairs. It was not Bertie's intention that they be used this way. The pairs were originally intended to be used as 'reinforcement,' as in the manner of Weak Marshall Pairs.

3) **Weak Marshall Pairs:**

   a. The **Key-note, resident Octave** and **resident Twelfth**: Only the *key-note* is given a label, $B_n^{\flat}$, $F_n^{\#}$ etc. The key-note, resident octave and resident twelfth must be tuned in the manner of a S*ingle note*.

   b. The **Octave**: The octave and higher modes on the second member of the pair only plays a supporting role in the pair and must be tuned accurately to the musical scale in the manner of a S*ingle note*. This allows the octave to function properly as a single note when played. In this specification there is no conflict with the detuning rule (between key-note and octave) because weak Marshall Pairs rely on the natural detuning of the octave when it responds sympathetically to the key-note (non-linearly) and resident octave (linearly).

   Comments: (i) *Between the two extreme classes, Strong Marshall Pair and Weak Marshall Pair there is a wide range of coupling possible between the pairs. The time spent by the tuner who needs reinforcement for his notes is mostly devoted to trying to get the detuning just right. Unless this is done* *properly the combined notes do not produce an agreeable sound.*

(ii) *When the pan face has not been properly prepared, say by lousy sinking and/or careless burning (tempering), areas may exist on the pan face where note-note coupling is unacceptably high. Blocking is next to impossible. The tuner is forced into tuning pairs with a wide variation in coupling between the members. Immense tuning problems arise in the process of transforming these shoddy 'things' into pans! Tuners usually return these 'things' to their source or dump them in a specially prepared bin!*

4) **Triple (Whole Note):** A *Triple* consists of two contiguous Marshall Pairs. For example, $\{C_3^\#:C_4^\#\} + \{C_4^\#:C_5^\#\} \rightarrow \{C_3^\#:C_4^\#:C_5^\#\}$. While three notes identify a Triple, only when the first is played ($C_3^\#$ in the example) can there be sympathetic response from the other two notes. Each note in a Triple must function as a note in its own right (i.e. it has a place on the musical scale) therefore it must be tuned as a *single note*. Each constituent pair can then function as a weak Marshall Pair (to the extent determined by the tuner). Detuning of the octave ($C_4^\#$) relative to the key-note ($C_3^\#$), and ($C_5^\#$) relative to ($C_4^\#$) is achieved naturally (dynamically) when the members respond sympathetically. Of course, since each note is tuned as a *single note*, detuning of the *resident octave* and *resident twelfth* is expected. If the tuner demands more acoustical output on the second partial of the sounding low note in the Triple (the $C_3^\#$), then he must strengthen the coupling between $C_3^\#$ and $C_4^\#$. This allows for better use of the *acoustical advantage* (see Section 12.11.2) that the $C_4^\#$ note offers over the resident octave on the $C_3^\#$ note. But the more you increase this coupling the greater the difficulty in tuning the pair correctly. (*Readers should pay attention to these fine points.*) The same holds for all Pairs and Triples not only the $C^\#$

which is serving as the example here. Triples do not appear on the bass.

When specifications (1a), (1b) and (1c) are met, the note geometry follows the $5/4^{ths}$-Law. When (1a), (1b) and (1d) are met the $9/8^{ths}$-Rule is followed. These specifications were written with guidance from the non-linear theory developed in Chapters 3 and 4 and are in full agreement with experimental data on the operation of the instrument. It should be recalled that the theory on note dynamics indicates that when tuning is done with the *key-note* and *resident octave* arrangement or with the *key-note, resident octave* and *fifth* arrangement, all the tuned modes are mutually coupled — mode-localized. Because of mutual coupling, the modes are not independent and must be tuned as a dependent set. The use of the *third* in place of the *fifth*, introduces an independent mode, uncoupled from the other tuned modes and it follows from this that detuning is not required on the *third*.

14.44 Excitation of the Steelpan by an External Agency and the role played by Blocking

Excitation of a steelpan note by a player is normally achieved *impulsively* with the use of a pair of sticks. We have dealt extensively with this form of excitation by stick impact in Chapter 13. In experimental work it is sometimes necessary to excite the notes *continuously* by means of an externally applied sinusoidal source of variable frequency. This is usually done by one of four methods; (1) acoustical excitation by placing an electrically driven loudspeaker above or below the pan, (2) by attaching an electromagnetic vibrator at a remote spot on the skirt, (3) mechanically attaching the electromagnetic vibrator to a 'remote' spot on the pan face (easier done on the bore pan), or (4) using a small section (or area) of the steel surface of the pan as part of a magnetic loop (magnetic flux circuit).

Method 1: In this method, the loudspeaker is driven by a sinusoidal electrical signal of frequency equal to that at which excitation is needed. A preferred speaker location is under the pan. If one is interested in interferometric work, one must exercise care in the interpretation of the responses recorded photographically (whether stored as hardcopy or as a computer file); it will not be possible to accurately compare levels of excitation at different domains on the pan face because of the variations in the incident acoustic field intensity over the panface and the dependence on localized acoustic coupling.

Method 2: In this method the vibrator is driven at the desired excitation frequency and is useful for exciting vibrations on the skirt as well as the notes.

Method 3: This method is useful for note excitations especially on the bore pan.

Method 4: In this case there are two different procedures; (a) if a simple electromagnet (one with zero Magnetic Bias) is employed to drive the surface of a note, since maximum note displacement occurs twice per cycle of the driving frequency, the electrical signal fed to the electromagnet must be set to one-half the frequency of the note. (b) By introducing a permanent magnetic field — a Magnetic Bias — in the magnetic flux linking the electromagnet and the note surface, the signal frequency can be made equal to the note frequency. This is a more convenient arrangement.

In running these excitation experiments and in the interpretation of the recorded data it must be remembered that the notes on a properly tuned pan are blocked. This blocking is effective for vibrational energy *leaving* the notes as well as vibrational energy *entering* the notes. Blocking is effective on all the methods listed above except for Method 1. Method 1 is however, subject to the variations in acoustic drive and coupling. As a result, the data collected when using any of the four methods will not allow for the unambiguous comparison of levels of excitation on different domains of the pan face.

If the level of excitation is relatively high, it is possible for excitations to occur on multiple notes, even on the internote. For example, at a driving frequency of A_4 (440 Hz), non-linearities can induce excitations at A_5 and higher multiples of 440 Hz. Under the normal playing action of the panist, where the notes alone are directly excited, the internote behaves linearly when excited at the low levels expected from these by stick-note impacts, but when driven strongly by any of the above methods they may display non-linear responses thereby producing excitations at different areas of the pan face. The full picture is somewhat more complicated than this, especially when

Advanced Tuning (see Section 14.43.1) is used, but the operation of the instrument is saved by the blocking mechanism that operates on all the notes of a properly tuned pan. Complications may arise for example, again with external sinusoidal excitation, because the blocking mechanism itself relies on the tuning of the internote surrounding a given note to a frequency higher than the enclosed note. It is always possible for the frequency of an area on the internote to be 'tuned' close to the frequency of a note situated some distance away. The analysis in Sections 14.11 to 14.15 can be applied to cases like these to show that the excitation of a remote domain (one in 'Hiding') can be made quite small. This is part of the tuning procedure and is particularly linked to the 'Tightening' or Blocking of the notes.

14.45 Voicing

14.45.1 Symptoms of a Pan-Stick Combination in need of Voicing

A list of symptoms:

(i) 'Ringing' or 'Pinging' sound in pan tones.
(ii) The pan is excessively bright or harsh sounding.
(iii) Excessively mellow or soft tone.
(iv) Inconsistent volume or tonal quality from note to note.
(v) Excessive Stick-Note Clap or Stick Noise.

In the case of (i) this may be caused by high modes of vibration (tuned or untuned) above the third partial but on a properly tuned pan, may be the result of using a hard stick tip or a single-layer tip, With the latter, the 'proximity effect' of the shaft dominates the impact (see Sections 13.20 and 13.21).

With (ii) there is a close relationship to (i) but with (ii) the problem is usually with the stick. Too hard a tip, too small a tip radius or both. This problem arises when a mid-range or lower pan is played with a stick too small for the musical range.

In the case of (iii) the tip is likely to be too soft, resulting from aging or wrong choice of tip material. This problem can arise on all pans when trying to use excessively soft stick tips. Soft tips of the wrapped variety (see Section 13.14 for details) can be corrected by re-wrapping with the same material using increased wrapping tension or by using a new length of rubber band.

In the case of (iv) if the problem originates from the stick then it may, most likely, be the result of choosing a stick more suited for playing at one end (either end) of the musical range for the particular pan type. Notes over the musical range for the instrument cannot then be equally excited by impact with this stick. One should also check each member of the pair of sticks for dynamic balance. *Always use a pair of matched sticks.* If the problem originates from the pan then take the instrument to your trusted tuner for balancing. If you are a knowledgeable musician you should remain at the tuner's instrumentation room during the exercise to ensure your notes attain the pan-like tonal quality of your liking with even progression of tone throughout the musical span of your instrument.

In (v), where excessive Stick Noise or Clap is the problem, the stick tip is very likely overused and lossy. If it is a wrapped stick check for loose wraps. Re-wrap with new rubber and with adequate tension (see Section 13.14). Sticks that generate excessive clap on the inner notes may not show the same problem on the outer notes. In this case, if the problem is on a top-end pan, change to a smaller tip with low-loss rubber material such as silicone rubber. Too soft a tip on the bass stick can generate annoying clap. Another aspect of the annoyance comes as the 'clap' (the sound of it) is made on each contact with the notes, thereby keeping the rhythm. *It is annoying if you have to listen to noise in synchrony with the desired musical tones.* Change to a firmer, balanced pair of tips. See Section 13.28 for further details.

Readers should check Chapter 13 for full details on Stick-Note impact for information that leads to the resolution of any problems related to the quality of sound generated when playing the instrument.

14.45.2 Voicing the Sticks

Each type of pan calls for a special set of sticks. While the bass sticks normally come prepared as a rubber or sponge ball or half-ball, the middle and higher sticks are usually prepared by the players. In each steelband one can always find a few specialist stick makers on whom the less experienced players may rely for their stick preparation. The experienced player usually develops the skill of good stick making and may be quite proficient in wrapping the middle and high-end sticks. It is necessary however, to go a step or two further into the art and science of *voicing the stick.*

- ***To be fully effective one must voice both the pan and the pair of sticks as complementary parts of a whole instrument.*** A properly voiced pan, fresh from the tuner requires, at all times, sticks that are specially voiced for the instrument in order to bring out beautiful tones each time you step up to play.
  - *A properly voiced stick is not so much what it looks like as what it plays like.*

Voicing of the high-end wrapped sticks is a skilled art, and unfortunately, many players never take the time or commit the expenses to ensure that their sticks and pan receive the voicing care they deserve. If you use the same pair of sticks repeatedly, the pan's tone will change as the stick tips age. As the tips wear, and the rubber oxidizes, the tone often becomes too soft, robbing you of the ability to produce a sweet sound. In addition as a panist, you lose control over volume and tone. On all pan types, these effects are most noticeable in quiet playing where delicate pianissimo passages become very difficult if not impossible to play. In the worse case some notes may not sound at all if played lightly with these aged sticks.

In Section 13.22 it was shown that stick tips having COR values in the range $0.5 \leq \varepsilon_r \leq 0.75$ provide the panist the best impact control. I recommend that the reader make repeated references to the relevant parts of Chapter 13 while reading this section on voicing.

The following are some 'tips' that are useful in voicing the sticks:

1. ALWAYS voice sticks in pairs!
2. A voicing technician (professional, amateur, or apprentice) MUST be a musician.
3. Don't pride yourself as a voicing technician if all you do is inspect the stick, squeeze it, re-wrap it, squeeze it again and return it to the player as a 'voiced stick.' Worse yet, don't just look at it, return it and say 'that looks good!'

4. You can custom design your stick tips by varying the wrapping tension from the inner-most layers to the outer layers. If you want to create on the tenor for example a bright tone you can increase the tension on the last few layers. This will increase the pre-stress on the outer layers (see Section 13.14) giving the tip the property of variable effective stiffness depending on the depth of compression on impact. The same effect is possible by using a narrower rubber band. If a softer response is desired, the outer layers can be wrapped with reduced tension and wider rubber bands. This method is useful on the wrapped guitar and cello sticks.
5. Another good procedure is to change the rubber in the wrap. For example you can choose to begin the wrap with a hard rubber for the first few layers and complete the wrap with a softer rubber. This will produce a soft response. You can also begin with a soft rubber and use a harder rubber on the outer layers for a brighter response. This technique can be used together with tension variations in (4) to produce a range of responses suited specially to your musical needs.
6. A brighter response is almost always possible by using a hollow shank (see Section 13.12) because solid shanks generally display greater losses than hollow shanks. Some stick makers use hollow aluminum tubes others may use bamboo. My preference is the bamboo (see Section 13.12) but you are free to experiment with other natural and man-made materials to suit your liking. Bamboo will be superior to the man-made product, carbon fiber, in its usual commercial form. So you can avoid experimenting with this relatively costly product. I can foresee commercial producers using the attractive properties of this relatively new material to lure players into purchasing carbon fiber sticks so readers be wise and careful in making your choices if you intend to purchase sticks. The sound of the pan is not in the stick shanks! You already know that so don't let anyone make you forget!
7. The size of the stick head or tip must be chosen in accordance with the information supplied in Chapter 13, depending on the pan type. Use the information relating contact-time and contact-area to tip radius if you plan to

design your sticks. If you have been making sticks 'for years' then the information will improve your knowledge and understanding and make you a better 'more professional' stick maker. Your product can only improve and you will not go wrong!
8. NEVER voice a pair of sticks on a 'practice pan' when its final destination if for use on a Competition Grade Pan!

14.45.3 Accent

Among the Giants of Section 1.5 we first single out Ellie Mannette for the early introduction of the *indented panface* (concave downward), a crucial step in the development of the pan as a system of statically stable notes. The introduction of *Fourths and Fifths* as a tuning arrangement of notes by the Giant, Tony Williams, improved the stability of the instrument and enhanced the definition of its tones. And of course, Giant, Bertie Marshall, who, by introducing *complex tuning* and the *Marshall Pairs,* zeroed in on the truly defining aspects of note dynamic stability and tonal definition. Despite these major developments, or perhaps, because of them, the tonality of the steelpan defies explicit classification. I have struggled hard with this classification problem!

Why go into all this trouble? The main reason is that the instruments in a steel orchestra are all of one type — an unusual structure for any orchestra. In this structure one finds a number of sections. Is it musical range alone that determines the instruments within a section or are there other characteristics of the instrument by which the sound of a section can be distinguished? What word can we use to collectively describe the features that determine the makeup of these sections? The reader must appreciate the limitations of using the English language to express musical concepts. Often, in music, when writing in English for example, Italian words are used when such deficiencies exist. In defining tonality of one musical instrument when compared with another, one often uses the word 'timbre' to express the differences in the partials that constitute the tone or the differences in one instrument compared with another. The unique feature of steelpan tones is the appearance of frequency and amplitude modulations arising from the coupling between the modes that generate the partials. For this reason a word of broader meaning than *'timbre'* must be found for pan tones in order for the AM and FM aspects to be included. To this end I suggest the English word *'accent'*.

Unfortunately, the word *accent* comes with its own baggage from common usage and its use also as a musical term with the following meaning; *'The emphasis on a beat resulting in that beat's being louder or longer than another in a measure or a mark representing this.'* But I will be using it not only to differentiate the pan instruments or *sections (or pan types)* within an *orchestra* but also to differentiate the *voices* within a section.

I find the word 'accent' to be very appropriate with support given by 'The American Heritage Dictionary', 1976 edition, publishers, Houghton Mifflin Company, where the following meaning is given;

> 'The relative prominence of a particular syllable of a word by greater intensity (*stress accent*), or by variation or modulation of pitch or tone (*pitch accent*).'

The musician is already familiar with the word 'accent' when used to give special stress to a musical note in a phrase. The word *'accent'* in our context, includes what is commonly meant, in the musical vocabulary, by the word *'timbre'* which describes the quality of a musical note perceived through its spectrum and envelope. An expert tuner will impart the *basis* of a distinctive *'stress accent'* by emphasizing certain partials and give further character to his notes by the frequency modulations he makes possible to achieve in the tone (*pitch accent*). Of course in actual play, it is the panist that must take this 'basis' and construct by cleverness of his stick impact, the wide variations made possible by the tuner's work. A Bertie Marshall tenor has a distinctive *'accent'* by which his work can be identified in the same manner as the well known Frenchman, President Charles De Gaulle had a distinctive French accent even when he spoke English! No matter who plays a Marshall tenor, one knows it is Marshall's! If you somehow remove the AM and FM not even Marshall will be capable of recognizing his tenor! In fact steelpan tones are so special that if you remove these two types of modulations even when the frequency components (partials) are musically correct, the result is a *pung tone* with its 'corky' sound! I dare say, that 'because of the *mutual interactions* among the partials, *key-note, octave* and *twelfth,* the tones of the steelpan are *'more alive'* than the tones found on other instruments!'

I shall have more to say on 'accent' when dealing with the orchestra playing in full glory.

14.46 Balancing

14.46.1 Definition I, for the Individual Pan

'Balancing' is the process by which the tonal qualities of notes on a pan are brought to a high degree of similarity.

There will always remain some subjectivity in the term 'degree of similarity' so my choice of definition is 'as coming from the same musical instrument (same physical pan)'. In each definition there will always be a subjective word, now it is the word 'same'. This type of thing is natural and it occurs quite often. So I beg the readers' patience and hope that we have not too different a meaning attached to these words and phrases.

When an experienced tuner is teaching his apprentice (an assistant perhaps) and during the tuning process he asks 'Did you hear that?' the apprentice is likely to respond with 'heard what?' Sounds like that heard by the tuner which last for a fleeting moment cannot be easily reproduced for the benefit of the inattentive apprentice. But those sounds are important in understanding what changes are taking place on the note being tuned. But we are not now interested in those transient sounds we are interested in the reproducible sounds. But then, what are we required to hear from each note on a pan in order to deem them 'similar'? It is sometimes difficult to put in words what one hears in music — the printed page can only go so far in conveying these things. But are we listening to music when we check the notes on a pan for 'similarity' or are we just comparing tones? Is it enough to run up and down the scale? My answer — it is all of these, music, scale, tones even loudness, the often forgotten attribute. Musical taste aside, we can all agree, by loudness across the array of notes, on whether the pan, in this respect, is balanced or unbalanced.

Now consider this: Four good tuners A, B, C and D, are selected at random and asked to tune a new set of Quadraphonic pans, one pan of the 4-pan set to each tuner. They are placed in isolated rooms. During the tuning process we assemble a hundred panists, twenty five of whom get their pans from A; twenty five get theirs from B; etc. At the end of the tuning process the tuners are assembled and introduced to the panists. The pans are then placed before the panists as a set and tested for balance. There are no distinguishing marks to associate pans with tuners. If the four groups of panists, seated at random, can correctly judge which pan was tuned by whom, is the Quadraphonic balanced? If the pans are distinguishable, then they cannot be balanced as a set. But each pan sounds good! 'Sounding good' is not a criterion in balancing! Or is it?

Sounding good is a criterion for tonal acceptability not for balance. Interestingly, if the hundred panists *could not* identify their respective tuner's pan we could not use this (negative) result to establish balance. The hundred panists must agree to something for the result to be usable. If the cause of the panists' uncertainty in identifying the respective tuner lies in the similarity in the tones of the four pans, then they can agree, they must agree on that similarity. There are other outcomes but the only one that points towards balance is agreement on similarity. I am not trying to develop a rigorous 'test of hypothesis' here so we will not bring in a fifth unknown tuner who can be used to randomly replace one of the four tuners in the room. If we did, this fifth tuner must remain unknown throughout the test. I believe that we have sufficiently explored the problem of deciding whether or not it is possible to determine similarity of tuning or balance.

Our *thought experiment* just concluded, teaches us that tuners do impart to the pan their own preferred tonal attributes. In addition, balance can only be possible if across *each* pan there is tonal similarity. If tuners A, B, C and D could not achieve this on their individual pans, we could hardly rate them as 'good tuners' in the first place — they would then have given us four unbalanced pans. If you are a logician you may wish to examine the question 'if four pans, each having unbalanced notes, are arranged as a set, is the set unbalanced?' What is similar among these four pans? If there is similarity (there is, since each pan consists of unbalanced notes) then why is the set not balanced?

But why must a pan be balanced in the first place? Let the panist answer! He has been waiting throughout this work for an opportunity to express himself with so much already being said about the pan maker and the tuner. The panist, with full sincerity and forcefulness will say: 'On the pan, we panists desire most of all, a balance of timbre and correctness in pitch, to allow for our individual interpretation of written musical works with all the nuances and subtleties with which we express our musical thoughts and feelings. But we do have our own 'tuners of choice.' We can add much more to this but the rest we express with our sticks when we play the pan, great joy awaits the listener!'

The tonal attribute we look for in balancing the pan is something more than *timbre* — *it is the 'accent.'* To be balanced, all members of the quadraphonic set of pans must speak with the same accent. How would a quartet of four singers, singing an English song, sound if they are all 'heavy' in their native dialects French, Chinese, Hindi and Celtic when they were not allowed the opportunity of practicing together before their performance? 'Practicing together' allows the singers to adjust and 'balance' their voices on each word or note.

Because of the qualitative and subjective nature of balancing the individual pan, our discussion is still open for input from readers; that's how we enjoy music!

Remember this, a good panist can compensate for some imbalances on a tuned pan. Having gained familiarity with a pan, the panist can correct, dynamically, any idiosyncrasies of a pan (within reasonable limits of course). A tuner however, should not leave it to the panist to correct his mistakes while playing; this takes away some freedom from the panist. An observant listener especially one viewing the playing actions of the panist will surely become aware that something is wrong. Don't be surprised, especially if that observer is an adjudicator or judge, when he steps up on the stage after the performance to play the offending note (or notes).

14.46.2 **Definition II for the Steel Orchestra**

Now there are subtle differences between the terms *Balancing* and *Blending* when applied to the whole steel orchestra. They cannot be discussed, one without the other. To see where the differences lie (in this subjective world of music) we first define the terms (or try to);

Blending *is the process where the tonal qualities of the pan instruments comprising the orchestra or ensemble are brought to a level of fine-tuning that allows the different voices to play their supportive roles or to independently express their own musical interpretation while allowing the cohesiveness that characterizes pan music.*

Balancing *a steel orchestra is the process of removing 'musical holes' in the total sound by ensuring that the different sections are all present and that they can equally express themselves in tonality and volume (acoustical output).*

Observe here, that these definitions do not imply that the voices, or the instruments comprising these sections, must sound alike.

*While we cannot quantify these terms, the blender can easily emphasize one quality over another, or weigh them all to his liking, to give his **signature** to a blended, balanced orchestra.* This prompts the following questions:

Have you ever stood outside the confines of the North Stand and the Main (South) Stand at the Port of Spain Savannah on the night of a Panorama Final perhaps because of the crowd or for lack of tickets? You were far enough to hear the bands but not the voice of the announcer. While there, were you able to identify the bands by the sound of the instruments alone? Most fans of steelband competitions may answer in the affirmative. Certainly the judges of the competition must be able to do this; if they are good judges! If you are like most fans then you are able to recognize the musical signature of the respective blenders of the bands — you did this by your ability to identify *blended tones.*

But this is not all, for certainly the players are involved. So I ask another question, 'Who can best play the pans of the Desperadoes Steel orchestra so that they, as a band, can be recognized as Desperadoes?' Certainly it must be the players of that band, for they 'alone' can make the pans 'speak' or 'play' in the true Desper's accent! There is always the panist's input. Now that we have reached the level of the orchestra we can hear that 'accent' and know that it is something dynamic, not belonging to the pans alone but the product of pans and players.

Have you ever (sure you have!) listened to a steelband and felt like the bass was too weak or the 'engine room' (don't ever forget them) was too loud? These are examples of 'imbalance' in the band. They can arise from 'beating the pan' instead of 'playing the pan', 'too many or too few instruments in a Section', or in the case of musical holes, just a set of 'weak pans' with low acoustic output. In the latter case these 'weak pans' if they are played too intensely to overcome their deficiencies, produce distorted sounds (see Section 8.18). The reader may have heard these distorted tones generated by 'weak basses' (most likely with thin gauge steel on the pan face) when struck intensely (in an effort to create the effect of a naturally louder bass). If you are able to recognize these imbalances whenever they appear, you did this by your ability to identify the lack of balance.

Along with loudness and timbre, what are the other qualities that enter into the processes of *Tuning, Balancing and Blending*? By what tonal attributes can two pans of the same type be judged as similar?

14.47 Blending

When a professional tuner tunes a pan, in addition to setting the modes on each note to the correct frequencies he adds an *accent*. This new term in pan's musical vocabulary is commonly used in connection with the human voice. In the same way that one can recognize someone speaking by his accent so too one can recognize a pan tuned by a professional tuner when the pan is sounding. We understand this by the Bertie Marshall example given earlier. The same is true of a Bertram Kellman pan. It is the *accent* that puts the tuner's *signature* to a pan. When the blender applies this (his) treatment to all the pans in an orchestra, his signature goes everywhere. *But he is careful (subtle) in stamping his signature because each voice must carry a variation of it, giving a subtle change in accent.* To understand this idea I will say that some pans receive just his *initials* while others receive his *full signature*, As an artist, he is not bound to dotting his i's or crossing his t's, because on the pan he has given a different meaning to these letters from which he constructs the phrases of his notes. We know that the partials he sets must differ from the pitches on the 12-TET system so he is free to detune them to his personal taste. So the G_4 resident octave on the G_3 Second Tenor note being different from the 12-TET scale allows it to be set differently (with its own modulations and strength) from the G_4 note on the Tenor. The better he is at doing this, the more sought after he is as a blender or tuner.

Pans are blended strictly according to purpose. It is an extension of the tuning process applied to an entire Steel Orchestra, a Section or a small Ensemble. The process requires the tuning of each individual instrument in a way that allows for the desired coordination of the voices to achieve the best *Chorus Effect*. Discussions on the Chorus Effect can be found in Chapter 15.

Blending ought not to begin and end with the Blender. For maximum results, the Blender should work together with the Arranger/Conductor who must present the *written* music, a single piece or a multi-course menu. Together they work out the details for the total sound they wish the instruments and their players to present. There is a full range of tonal choices on the menu (see the Section 14.30 on Tuning Scenarios). The idea is for the pans to complement the music like food and good wine. In the author's own experience he can think of no better example of this selection, combination of musical skills and fine tuning than that which came from the combined work* of Clive Bradley, Bertram 'Bertie' Marshall (assisted by Tony Slater), Rudolph 'Hammer' Charles and the Desperadoes Steel Orchestra. To work at its best, there must be a matching of skills from the conductor, the tuner/blender and the panists. Preparing for a Panorama Final requires from them a meticulousness bordering on obsession. However, all the potential of the pan as discussed throughout this work is of no value if the instruments are set aside to lay dormant only to be joined by the written music on the unopened music sheets. When the pages are opened and the instruments are excited they give life to any music with unmatched vibrancy and life!

It is not the number of examples of type that I give in this work but their quality that counts most.

The arranger/conductor must choose carefully how he intends to convey the music and its meaning to the listener. He cannot do this without knowledge of what the instruments are capable of. He must know the range and quality, the acoustic output, of all the voices set before him.

For the listener, live music is not something that can be returned to and be heard again, far less to modify, yet each voiced expression must build upon the expressions that preceded it. The players and the conductor cannot call them back! It is not just craftsmanship — to know the notes and having the technical skill to play the notes with ease — but to possess also a thorough knowledge of the musical piece set for interpretation by the steel orchestra and the individual player. Many a skilled panist have learned the craft but ignored the equally important ability to read and interpret the music for himself. All this does not lead us away from the topic of blending instead it keeps us on track. We must fully understand its purpose.

The blender gives to the players, instruments with which to interpret the music. He must therefore be a knowledgeable musician himself. Unlike a symphonic orchestra with its string and wind sections, with the steel orchestra all the instruments belong to one family — pan. The symphonic conductor can call on the very varied voices from the array of instruments to give full interpretation of the music. The pan conductor has to have some preparatory work done with the pans in order to create the same effects. On the pan, we cannot get the range equivalent to the piccolo (see Figure 14.2) so the arranger must try something else. But the instruments so chosen must possess the tonal qualities that best create the effect. Arrangers should not leave it entirely to the blender to set the voices he must check that it is done to his liking.

Blending combines tuning and balancing.

14.48 Detailing

I have placed this topic at the end of this very long Chapter because it encompasses all of the above. Let me first point out that *'detailing' on the pan, is not about making the instrument look presentable or beautiful!*

Detailing is an all encompassing term involving all the important aspects of pan preparation and note tuning. The term 'Detailing' is not found in past work on the steelpan or in the spoken language of pan makers and tuners nor have I myself, used the term before in my published work. Like so many things that I have worked on and researched in my life, even some that form entire research papers yet to appear in print, 'Detailing' is one of those that I keep 'in the back of my head.' Things like these are usually 'dislodged' from their 'hiding places' in my brain by a casual walk along the beach, while driving, or while fishing! To write fully on 'Detailing' I would have to draw on the material covered in all areas of this book but I wish to avoid doing that so I concentrate on those aspects placed on the pan by the tuner that are hard or impossible to observe visually and for completeness include some that are easily seen.

You cannot take your finished pan, or one you bought, to the Master Tuner for detailing! You can do that on your car where the car will receive vacuuming, wash up and polishing, all superficial (which do not make your car any faster or stop it from smoking)! Detailing is not a single 'one-shot' process in pan making or something 'tacked on' at the end of a tuning process but rather a series of coupled (linked) processes that begins early, even as the pan face is being indented. All these processes except that of 'Burning' (Low-Temperature Stress Anneal) are carried out with the hammer. Since these processes are all thoroughly described in various parts of this book, I will not repeat them here. Instead I list their 'names' and their locations. As I cautioned earlier, do not expect a 'blow-by-blow commentary'; so unless you are a tuner (professional or non-professional) you are asked to seek the assistance of a knowledgeable tuner for the fine practical details on hammer peening. It is hard to teach these things from a book because some readers are 'heavy handed' while others are 'easy on the touch.' Some aspects of detailing are best demonstrated 'live' or on well explained recorded video movie with 'close-ups' (I am not aware of the existence of any such videos). Here is a short-list: (i) Sinking, Section 2.5 ; (ii) Burning, Section 2.23 ; (iii) Smoothing, Sections 2.5 - 2.8 ; (iv) Grooving, Sections 14.12.2 – 14.12.4 ; (v) Boring, Sections 14.12.3 and 14.12.4 ; (vi) Forming (Shaping and Raising the notes), Sections 14.11.2 (see the Note recorded there on erecting the notes) ; (vii) Blocking (Tightening), Sections 14.12.5, 14.12.7, 14.12.15, 14.44 ; (viii) Tuning (First Tuning, 'Resting', Final Tuning), Sections 3.2.2, 3.13, 9.1.1, 9.10, 17.10 and Chapter 14., (ix) Coating, Sections 2.24, 2.25, 12.21; (x) Blending, Section 14.47; (xi) Balancing, Section 14.46. Rawform selection and preparation (nitriding for example, if used) precedes all these processes.

One might argue that I should have reserved the term *'detailing'* for the final work done by the professional tuner on instruments submitted to him by a less capable tuner or pan owner. On the contrary, for I know only too well the problems that the professional could experience with instruments that were not properly prepared in the first place. The professional, despite his name, fame and title, cannot return the instrument to the earlier stages of sinking, smoothing, burning etc to correct any deficiencies introduced there. There are aspects of detailing to be carried out *at each* processing stage of pan making. When we hear finished instruments prepared by the professional we may well say that he is a musical genius who performs 'magic' with the instruments but he *cannot* undo a 'mess'!

CHAPTER 15

The Chorus Effect in Steel Orchestras

15.1 Introduction

The *Chorus Effect* or *Ensemble Effect* occurs when a group of musicians play the same melody, such as in a string section of an orchestra or sing together, such as the tenor section of a choir. We will however, focus our attention on musical instruments, in particular, the steelpan. The mixed sound of an ensemble or choir is not just the sum of exactly identical sounds, which is simply a louder version of the individual sound, but a mixture of *time-delayed* 'almost' identical sounds producing a new timbre with a rich and complex spectrum. This is caused by slight differences of pitch, time delay and, amplitude among individual sounds, producing uncorrelated beatings of the partials. The timbre of orchestral music is rich and complex, distinguished from the 'thin' sound of a single musical instrument. The Chorus Effect adds *thickness* to the sound, and gives it that feature or flavor that is often described as 'lush' or 'rich'.

A particularly good chorus effect is obtained when a number of guitars are strumming; the effect is somewhat similar to the sound of marching soldiers. This effect can be created when the voices in the steelpan guitar section all strum together with each player impacting the notes on their individual pans with just that small time difference expected from player-to-player and the differences in *transit-times* from the pans to your ear. If I could spell out the sound one will hear, it should sound like 'd-d-d-r-r-u-u-u-mm' repeated a few times. You will have to roll your tongue to get the effect right. Try it! Got it? If you didn't get it then it's because you were spelling the word and not trying to pronounce it. Try it again! If you failed then try thinking of the 'Little Drummer Boy' striking the drum with his pair of sticks in rapid fire! Now try it again.

Time delays at the listener location, is a combination of the *lack of perfect synchrony* among the musicians and differences in *transit-times* from individual players to the listener. *Differences in pitch* are partly instrumental and are related to detuning of the individual instrument as well as the action of the player. This detuning may exist on the key-note and on the set of related partials comprising the individual tones. On the steelpan, since the octave and higher partials are stretched or compressed, detuning is a natural feature. Steelpans, *tuned* or *blended* (***voiced***) to play in a section, *do not* receive such critical or precise tuning that makes them all *exactly alike* in frequency. As a result each instrument in a section will display unique frequency- and amplitude-modulation patterns for each note. This is good, especially as these modulations can be put to the players' advantage in producing *context-sensitive* variations as the music demands or as the *mood* of the music demands. This is possible because these modulations are dependent on the contact force delivered to the notes. Contact force will vary among pan players playing the same melody together as a section. Even when the instruments in a section are played in unison, the sounding partials will be uncorrelated (*incoherent*—in the sense defined in Section 12.7).

15.2 **The Parameters**

The following are the parameters that control the chorus effect in steel orchestras:

1. Number of Sections N_s
2. Number of Voices (players) (N_v) in each Section
3. Maximum detuning of each note
4. AM and FM Modulations
5. Tremolo, Trill (and Vibrato)

6. Spread in Delay Time (measured in milliseconds, ms)
7. Spectral magnitude of key-note and higher partials

15.2.1 Number of Sections N_s

For clarity and emphasis, I state with some repetition from Section 14.2, that within the steel orchestra (steelband), it is customary to refer to the pan types — Bass, Cello, Guitars, and Tenors — as the voices. More precisely however, these *types* form the *Sections* of the orchestra. The instruments within a Section are the *Voices*. The number of Sections N_s defines the *Structure* of a band. Each Section is capable of producing its own distinctive Chorus Effect. It is the musical arranger or orchestral conductor who must maximize these effects by indicating the change of dynamics or volume for each section with expressive, readable body and hand movements, baton at the finger tips! In my homeland I have seen a number of excellent authoritative conductors, each with their own panache, temperament and personality — Guillermo Antonio Prospect and (Arranger, Conductor) Clive Bradley were prominent among them. If I may indulge myself on this topic a little longer, these two named conductors were great orchestrators because they both possessed a thorough knowledge of the capabilities of all the pan instruments. To my knowledge they had no understudy so the young conductors today should meet with the older players who fell under the authority of these masters to learn something about their skills and techniques and become for themselves, *masters of the baton*!

Again, in my homeland, panists play from memory, without score sheets; *the conductors and their players have the music in their heads and not their heads in the music*! I believe this allows quick responses from all players in a section to the cues from the conductor.

It will be incomplete for me merely to say that the number N_s is important without saying why. The role of the conductor in the orchestration given above partly answers why but it is the combined sound of these sections, the mix and the choral sound that fully explains the reason why. The shadings and nuances conveyed to these sections by the conductor, shapes the dynamics of the complete performance. It is not number for numbers sake but purpose and the availability of many sections each with their own tonality and range so that they can be called upon as the music demands. This total sound depends on the Chorus Effect produced by each section and on the number of sections.

15.2.2 Number (N_v) of Voices in a Section

The number of Voices N_v allocated to each Section also defines the *Structure* of a band. The right conditions exist for the chorus effect when the number of voices within a Section is sufficiently large ($N_v \gtrsim 5$). Such numbers can be found in the medium and large band categories. A small band, equipped with electronic sound amplification and/or with pans having larger notes, to raise the sound intensity to the level of a medium sized band *will not*, by these methods, replicate the chorus effect that is possible on the medium sized band. Similarly, a medium sized band cannot, by means of these methods, replicate a large well structured band in full brilliance.

15.2.3 Maximum detuning

Individual Notes on a pan:-The key-notes on a pan can readily be tuned to within ± 6 cents or a frequency ratio of 1.00347 to 0.99654 of the frequencies on the musical scale. Because stretched or compressed octaves must be used for the second mode on all notes, detuning the octaves results in a greater spread of frequencies. Relative to the key-note, the true octave is, by ratio, 2.00000 ($\equiv$ 1200 cents) while, on the pan, the *upper bound* of the *stretched octave* is around 2.01 ($\equiv$ 1208.6346 cents, a difference of +8.6346 cents) and the *lower bound* on the *compressed octave* is around 1.98 ($\equiv$ 1191.3221 cents, a difference of -8.6779 cents). When sympathetic vibration between the outer and inner notes is employed, the inner note, serving as the octave, must be detuned by stretching or compressing the frequency. In such cases the inner member of the sympathetic pair will always be detuned with respect to the musical scale. Since sympathetic pairing, on a good instrument, is never the dominant mode-mode interaction (which requires over-coupling pairs of notes with disastrous consequences caused by transmission losses) the detuning on the inner note must be kept within reasonable bounds.

(a) ***The Voices in a Section***:- From pan to pan within a Section, it is possible for the key-notes to show somewhat greater detuning than notes on a single pan (or voice) either as a result of using *different tuners, blender's choice* or some *technical problem*. One can however accept a range of ± 6 cents as acceptable especially if the blender has the chorus effect in mind and provides among the voices in each Section, an even distribution over this (or larger) range. But one can equally argue that in view of the frequency modulation (see below) of the partials one can tune the voices by first dividing them into two sets, then one set is detuned positively and the other set detuned negatively. *In this way one can incorporate a **note** and its **image*** (see Sections 14.21 and 14.22) on a ***Tenor-Pair***. Of course this is a great technical feat for the tuner/blender but it can certainly be done for the tenor section. When this method is adopted, tenors in a section can then be paired, with each member of a pair being played by a single player.

- *Tenor panists, even in orchestral music, have a tendency to be 'soloists' so it will take some additional training to play these Tenor-Pairs (not to be confused with the double tenors) with the two panists playing in unison without the added individual 'flair.' Of course a good pair of panists can always be allowed the occasional 'run' on the pan face!*
- *When this procedure, or any one of its many variants, is followed consistently by the tuner/blender of a given band (players, arranger and conductor), the characteristics of the chorus effect become associated with that band or tuner. This is one of the ways in which a steelband develops a tonal depth and character by which that steelband can be readily identified even from recorded music.*

There exists therefore, a wide range of possibilities for the blender/tuner. The frequency spread for the octaves and higher partials can also equal or exceed the ± 17.3 cents found on the individual pan. This is where the beats generated by mixing of these uncorrelated partials impart to the Tenor Section particularly, that *shimmering metallic ring for which the steel orchestra (the steelband) is well known.*

From pan-to-pan in the high end section one can therefore expect detuning values up to 12 cents (from +6 cents to -6 cents) for the key-note and up to 17 cents (from +8.6346 cents to -8.6779 cents) for the octave. Instruments falling well outside these maximum ranges must be treated as untuned. Of course, a good musician will work well within these ranges and deem an instrument as untuned before these maximum values are reached. *However the spread of detuning values from the high end section is to be expected and in fact required in order to enhance the chorus effect. I encourage steelbands to experiment with the detuning within a section.*

(b) ***The Voices in the Bass Section***: - On the bass, the absolute value of the detuning (in Hz) on the key-notes must be kept small otherwise the individual notes will sound out-of-tune. Although when the notes are played in unison with other bass voices in the section they may not sound out-of-tune, because of the low frequencies on the bass and the greater distance between notes (spread over a number of pans) and the distance between voices in the section, one should depend on *time-delays* for the generation of the chorus effect. This means that the chorus effect produced by the key-notes (the first partials) on the bass is *not* mainly dependent on detuning.

There are some technical problems with the bass pans which makes it necessary to retain the higher notes on these instruments despite the problem of actually playing them with the bass stick (see Chapter 13). In resolving these problems, the higher notes are used as the octave in sympathetic pairs. If the note-note coupling is sufficiently strong in these pairs they can be tuned with smaller detuning so as to allow for AM domination or with much detuning if

FM modulation is desired (see Section 14.30). Since these 'octaves' for higher notes on the bass are not really playable* as key-notes because of the large stick size, their detuning do not pose a problem for solo playing or in the Chorus Effect.

* Surely I am being very restrictive here because these notes are still played nevertheless. Despite their reduced acoustic output it is necessary for the bassist to play them in order to 'keep up' with the rest of the band.

15.2.4 AM and FM Modulations

The steelpan holds a unique position among melodic musical instruments by reason of its non-linear generation of *Frequency Modulation* (FM) and *Amplitude Modulation* (AM) on all the partials in its tones. For this, it holds the position of being the only melodic instrument that depends almost exclusively on non-linear interaction for the generation and dynamical behavior of the modes responsible for its partials. The incorporation of FM, a distinctive feature of the instrument, provides for the introduction of an *instrument-related parameter* into the chorus effect.

Because the mechanisms generating the two types of modulations found on the pan are related, these two effects must be taken together. In Chapters 4 and 5, the relationship between AM and FM is fully developed. Briefly, a pan tone that is FM dominated shows weaker AM while a note that is AM dominated shows weaker FM. In tones with strong octaves, AM dominates because in order to generate and maintain a strong octave the mode-mode quadratic coupling between the fundamental and octave must be relatively strong. These AM dominated tones display a slow modulation rate of about 4 – 15 Hz. These rates should not be interpreted as being sub-sonic and inaudible. They represent slow modulations of the amplitude envelope of the vibrations taking place at the tonal frequency (440 Hz for the A_4 note, 369.99 Hz for the $F^\#_4$ note etc). This makes them audible. FM dominated tones show modulation rates, typically around 20 $Hz \cdot s^{-1}$ on the key-note and up to 100 $Hz \cdot s^{-1}$ on the octave. Here also, these modulation rates in units of $Hz \cdot s^{-1}$ must be properly interpreted.

One must multiply the time duration of the FM by the rate in $Hz \cdot s^{-1}$ in order to obtain the frequency change in Hz.

The two modulation parameters involved in the Chorus Effect in steel orchestras are:

a) **Frequency Modulation rate** $(Hz \cdot s^{-1})$:- The FM in the spectrum of a sounding tone. FM can be *slow, fast, wide* or *narrow*.
b) **Amplitude Modulation rate** *(Hz):-* The AM within the amplitude envelope of a sounding tone. AM can range from *weak* to *intense* or *deep*.

AM and FM while being intrinsic to the particular sounding note depend on the intensity with which the note is played. Deeper modulations occur at the higher intensities.

The lower-frequency member of a sympathetic pair usually shows relatively fast AM and FM rates but of reduced range because the detuning and note-note coupling are kept small in order for the inner note (the octave) to be more precisely tuned as a keynote in its own right.

15.2.5 Tremolo, Trill (and Vibrato)

In Section 14.2, AM, FM, Tremolo (and Vibrato) on the steelpan were clearly defined. *Tremolo* and *Trill* are aspects of a sounding note or notes that are determined by the panist in combination with the characteristics of the steelpan being played. Very often one can find the panist executing rapid repetitions of a tone — *Tremolo* — by a quick up-and-down movement of the sticks on the same note. Similar to this is the *Trill*, a rapid alternation between a tone and one musically adjacent to it (a half or whole note apart). The tremolo and the trill create a fluttering or tremulous sound but the trill is more of a *warble*. The parameters here are:

a) the rapidity and
b) the strengths of the impact,
c) the tonality of the individual note(s) and
d) within a section of the orchestra, the variations in these characteristics among the pans and panists.

The combined effect (the Chorus Effect) of all these tones produced by say ten tenor pans plus panists contains more depth and excitement than any one of the components acting alone — this is the meaning of the Chorus Effect.

Vibrato is a player-controlled modulation in pitch. On a string instrument, this throbbing effect is achieved by rapid wrist-and-finger movement on the string that slightly alters the pitch. Vibrato which is a 'controlled pitch variation' is practically impossible on the steelpan because the player cannot selectively alter the pitch by using a pair of sticks (see Section 14.2). Pitch variations produced by a sounding pan note are all classified under 'Frequency Modulation' which is intrinsic to the dynamics of the note being played. While the player can vary the strength of the stick impacts, this produces variations in both AM and FM. Independent pitch alteration is not possible. *This is the reason why 'Vibrato' was bracketed in the sub-title above.*

I issue a caution to the reader *not* to confuse *vibrato* with *FM* found on a steelpan that is tuned to maximize FM (whether slow, fast, wide or narrow)! The struck note produces frequency modulation by the non-linear mechanism intrinsic to the played note. The panist cannot produce vibrato on the notes of a pan by using a pair of sticks. What the panist can produce is tremolo and trill. In jazz music where vibrato is used extensively, the panist finds that he must depend on the intrinsic variations available to him through AM and FM and that he must rely on his own impartation of tremolo and trill. He must also select a pan with the tonality that best suits his style of play.

15.2.6 **Spread in Delay Time** (milliseconds, ms)

The spread in delay time is about 5 to 100 *ms*. This spread covers the various arrival times at the listener and results from the spatial separation of the instruments on the stage. This delay is proportional to the number of players since a larger number of players will occupy a larger space on-stage and arises from a combination of (i) location of the listener, (ii) separation of the voices (or individual pans), (iii) the distance between notes on the pan face and (iv) the players reaction time. The bass pans, as previously noted, must depend on delay time for adding musical depth through the chorus effect. The upper end on the time delay range (100 *ms*) applies mainly to the bass section. The band leader or conductor should therefore select optimum positions for the bass voices consistent with the hall acoustical characteristics or open-air conditions and distance to the audience. In a concert hall there will therefore be seating locations where the chorus effect is enhanced, and as a result, the knowledgeable ('seasoned') listener may prefer these locations from among other seating positions. The lower end of the time delay range (*5 ms*) apply mainly to the high end voices in the tenor section.

Listeners may have observed that the tenor section in a steel orchestra is arranged compactly while the bass section may be spread around the other sections of the band. *The compact arrangement for the tenors is ideal if their natural AM and FM characteristics are to be fully utilized.* Spreading the tenors around the band will introduce large delay times that reduce the effectiveness of these modulations or completely destroy the chorus effect for the tenor section. If the tenor section of the band contains at least three T*enor-P*airs then the Chorus Effect can be generated by the use of the AM-FM modulations with small time delays resulting mainly from the players reaction times. Under these conditions, the upward and downward pitch glides produced on the pairs will create sounds of amazing beauty.

15.2.7 Spectral magnitude of key-note and higher partials

As pointed out in Chapter 14. the natural vibration modes of the untuned notes on the pan take up arbitrary frequencies. On each note, the tuner must tune each mode individually beginning with the key-note and the octave. These two partials must be tuned simultaneously because of the quadratic coupling between them. The third mode or twelfth must also be tuned along with the key-note and octave because the first three modes are linked by quadratic coupling while the first mode is linked to the third mode with the help of the second mode, also by quadratic coupling. A weak *second octave* which is quadratically coupled to the octave may also appear in the frequency spectrum of a tuned note. All other higher frequency modes are outside the direct control of the tuner but if they appear in the spectrum and can be detected aurally, **they should be and usually are suppressed** by careful hammer peening. These points have been made in earlier Sections of this book but are repeated here for emphasis because of what is to follow:

The higher modes can lead to a successful and pleasing chorus effect or a total disaster (see Chapter 16 for the reason why)! First of all, whether the sound of music is pleasing or annoying (harsh) depends on the psychoacoustic effects it induces. <u>*The chorus effect is not something developed on the instruments or in the sound medium (air)*</u>*.* <u>*The effect is developed in the ear and the brain of the listener!*</u> *As such, each listener hears his/her own version of the effect.* **The players in the tenor section of the orchestra or those in the bass section do not hear the effects they create in the ears of the listening audience!**

The piano, where each hammer may strike a multiple of strings, the 12-string guitar and some synthesizers can meet some of these requirements for producing the chorus effect. As it turns out, the tonal characteristics of the notes on the steelpan are just right for the generation of very distinctive and pronounced chorus effects when the instruments are played in sections of a steel orchestra. In the author's experience, at live steelpan orchestra performances of Handel's *Hallelujah Chorus* from *Messiah*, the effect is well pronounced even more so as the percussive nature of the instrument is well suited for this piece of music.

Of all the Steelbands I have listened to, I will say, based on the sheer brilliance of its pans and panists, the frontline pans (tenors and double tenors) of the *Trinidad All Stars Steel Orchestra* takes my prize for the best produced Chorus Effect. They, almost always, put the Chorus Effect to maximum use when they play. As the saying goes, 'I take my hat off to them.' The players in this band, I cannot say if it is by tradition or by training, are consistent in their presentation of well orchestrated sounds, produced with a high level of skill. Style of play perhaps! To reconfirm in my mind that what I have held to be true of this band is true indeed, as I write I am listening and watching Trinidad All Stars playing *'Curry Tabanca'* arranged by Leon 'Smooth' Edwards. I know what I am hearing in the background as I write and the reconfirmation is clear. Readers should get the sound and video for this performance. Microphone placements, while good for the frontline pans, do not allow a fair assessment of the chorus effect on the bass with this recording. I therefore recommend that readers listen to the bass in this band's 1980 rendition of Scrunter's *Woman on the Bass* arranged also by none else but 'Smooth.' However, I must warn readers that there are other recordings of All Stars playing this tune where microphone placements are not as good. You must listen to the 'official' recording done for the 1980 Panorama Final. All Stars played these two tunes *Curry Tabanca* and *Woman on the Bass* with much fire — *con fuoco*! All Stars is for me, the official 'Sailors Band' many, I am sure, will agree, just listen to these panists sailing smoothly over rough waters in their 1984 rendition of Sparrow's *'Doh Back Back.'* I am sure Dr. Francisco 'Sparrow' Slinger (Birdie) takes a few steps backward whenever he hears this recording!

CHAPTER 16

Harshness Produced by Orchestral Steelpan Tones

16.1 Introduction

Depending on the performing orchestra, listeners to steelpan music may be subjected to annoying noise generated during the performance. This noise goes beyond the incidentals of stick impact noise, the jostling of players' feet and creaky pan supports. Poorly prepared pans can ruin an otherwise good musical arrangement. Because pans are meant for music and music is to be appreciated only by listening, the perception of tones by the human ear cannot be ignored in the tuning process. This Chapter examines this problem as it applies specifically to the myriad of tones (tuned and untuned) capable of being generated by the sounding notes in a pan orchestra.

When an individual steelpan is played, barring acoustical problems that arise due to the environment, the sound of the instrument is normally clear and the tones distinct. When a performance is delivered by a modern day steelband of some 100 players, each pan, with its own diversity of tonal resources, range of dynamics, and tonal color, can result in a beautiful sound of music or a disaster in noise.

In its country of origin, Trinidad and Tobago, the steelpan is often played with much vigor in order to carry the excitement of a

Panorama competition and to produce the acoustic power that the listeners crave. With an orchestra composed entirely of one type of musical instrument, the Pan, similarity in tone and high 'decibels' form a recipe for the perception of harshness or 'noise' (the common expression) in the ear of the listener.

The sound of music, as subjective as that might be, is the goal but occasionally, poorly produced instruments creates an annoying harshness that needs investigating. The origin of this harshness is due to a combination of poorly positioned modal frequencies on the instruments and the perception of pure tones by the human ear. It is also the observation of the present author, that the degree of harshness is very dependent on the listener even to the extent that two nearby listeners may disagree on whether or not the performance is 'noisy.' This is a good indication that the effect is one caused by the perception of tones by the ear.

This chapter addresses the problem by first looking at how the human auditory system perceives pure tones and then looks at the tuning practices of pan makers and tuners in setting the frequencies of the partials on the steelpan.

16.2 The Human Auditory System — The Ear

When the level of acoustical disturbance in the air is low, the human ear responds linearly and allow the listener to discern pure tones provided that they are sufficiently separated in frequency space. When a Steelband is performing with some 100 players, the sound levels can be extremely high while the tones produced by the individual instruments compete for the same frequency space. In the psychophysics of tone perception, one is therefore concerned with the ability of the listener to process tones affected by superposition. There are two types of superposition effects, depending on where the processing is taking place in the listener's auditory system:

(a) *First-order superposition effects*: in these cases the processing is mechanical, and takes place in the cochlear fluid and along the basilar membrane of the inner ear (see Figure 16.1).
(b) *Second-order superposition effects*: these are much more difficult to detect, describe and measure unambiguously.

The discussion focuses only on the first order effects.

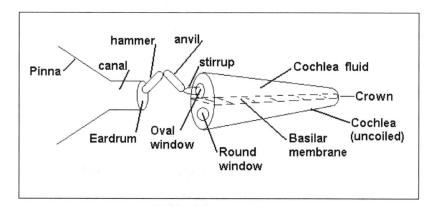

Fig. 16.1. The human auditory system; the outer ear on the left and the inner ear on the right. The cochlea is shown uncoiled for clarity. A typical cochlea measures about 2.5 cm (roughly 1 inch).

When a sound disturbance enters the *pinna* or *outer ear*, it undergoes a series of amplification steps (for a total amplification factor of approximately 900) till it reaches the *oval window*. If the disturbance is a low-amplitude pure-tone sinusoidal wave, a travelling wave moves down the *cochlea fluid* producing a well defined resonance region on the *basilar membrane*. Low frequencies are detected towards the *crown* of the cochlear while high frequencies are resolved closer to the *round window*.

Figure 16.2 shows the case for two low-amplitude tones of distinct frequencies that are well separated both in the frequency domain and along the basilar membrane. When the two tones of frequencies f_1 and f_2 are closely spaced, they may not be properly resolved along the basilar membrane as illustrated in Figure 16.3. The audible result is that a *fused tone* of frequency $\frac{1}{2}(f_1 + f_2)$ is heard together with the expected beats at $|f_1 - f_2|$. Beats are however heard only when the frequency difference $|f_1 - f_2|$ does not exceed around 15 Hertz. This applies to all tonal frequencies and corresponds to the Region 1 in Figure (4). In Region 1 the sound is modulated by beats. In order for the tones to be heard at clearly discernible pitches, the frequency difference $|f_1 - f_2|$ must exceed the *Limit of Frequency Discrimination* Δf_d.

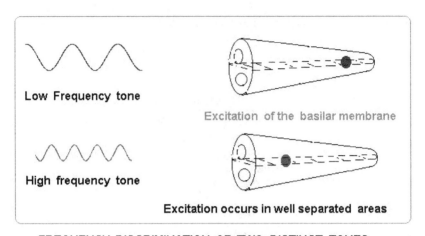

Fig. 16.2. Two tones, well separated in frequency space are well resolved along the basilar membrane.

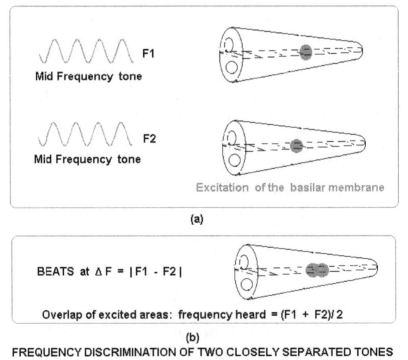

Fig. 16.3 Two closely separated tones excite areas on the basilar membrane producing overlap. In addition to the expected beats, the fused tone frequency is heard.

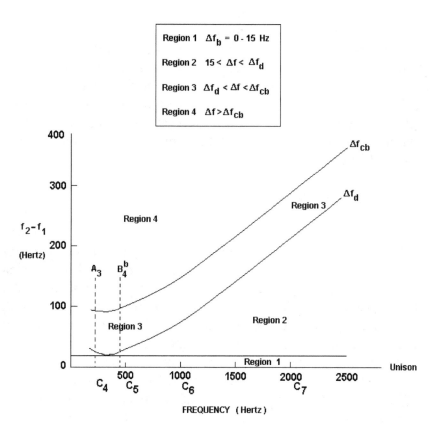

Fig. 16.4. The perception of two tones beginning with the case of unison where the frequencies are equal through Region 1 where beats are heard, Region 2 where the fused tone is harsh, Region 3 where the sound is rough and the tones are distinct, finally to Region 4 where the tones are smooth and separated.

In the frequency range 15 Hz < $|f_1 - f_2|$ < Δf_d (Region 2) the sound is still that of the fused tone but it is perceived with *harshness* and without beats. In Region 3, which extends up to the *Critical Band* Δf_{cb} the tones are resolved but the sound is *rough*. Beyond the critical band the sound is smooth and the tones are distinct. These limits are almost independent of the intensity of the tones.

Inspection of Figure 16.4 shows that the limits of pitch discrimination Δf_d exceeds one semi-tone throughout the frequency range and exceeds a whole tone on the low and high frequency ends of the range. It is no wonder that tuners often refuse to tune a pan in the midst of 'practicing' players. While the tuner can detect minute changes on a single sounding note he may not be able to do the same for two notes played simultaneously.

As an example of these effects, two notes tuned close to C_6 (1046.5 Hz) played simultaneously create a harsh tone if they differ by 15 Hz to 75 Hz (see Figure 4). The range for harshness is even smaller for the C_5 note. In fact for most notes on the pans (see Figure 16.4 for the range A_3 to B_4^b) problems of beats, harshness or roughness may easily arise. But what tuning practices could lead to these problems?

16.3. Steelpan Spectra

The experienced tuner is more careful and selective when tuning (*Blending*) the instruments for a steelband as against tuning pans for solo performances. Since tuning is normally confined to the first three (possibly four) partials on the higher pans (tenors, seconds etc) the higher modes could be left untuned. On the lower pans (bass), tuning is rarely extended beyond the second mode or partial so that most of the higher modes are left untuned. It is to the tuners' advantage that untuned modes (those not following closely to the harmonic progression) are usually of low intensity when the pan is played. This is because the tuned modes derive a great deal of their energies from mode coupling, which requires tuning closely to the harmonic progression. The 'random' scatter of these higher modes on pans used for orchestral purposes can pose serious problems for the reasons outlined in the previous section on tone discrimination. To illustrate the problem 'typical' plots of note spectra with the potential for 'noise' production are shown in Figure 16.5.

In Figure 16.5, the four spectra show frequency differences on nearly all modes. If these four E_4^b notes are played simultaneously, one hears beats, fused tones and roughness produced in the ear by the superposition of the corresponding partials. The blending of these tenors require first, the selection of a desired timbre (one that characterizes the sound of the particular orchestra), then the tuning of all the pans in conformity with that selection. What about the lower pans on the register?

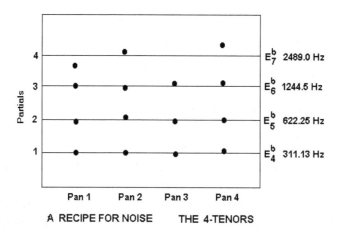

Fig. 16.5. A recipe for harshness and rough sounds in a set of four tenors with unequal partials.

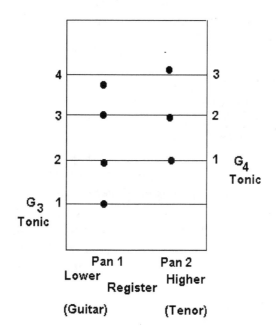

Fig. 16.6. Two pans competing for the same frequency space. Mode1 on the tenor corresponds to mode2 on the guitar, mode2 on the tenor corresponds to mode3 on the guitar and so on.

Figure 6 show notes selected from a Guitar Pan and a Tenor Pan. The G_4 mode on the tenor now corresponds to the second octave (second mode) of the G_3 note on the guitar. The higher modes can similarly be paired off. If these two notes on these instruments are played simultaneously, then, because the notes have not been properly blended, the harshness problem turns up. A first step in remedying this problem is to remove the third mode on the guitar.

16.4. Combination Tones and Aural Harmonics

When two intense tones are heard simultaneously, the non-linear response of the cochlea produces additional pitch sensations. These pitches are not present in the sound incident on the ear. These tones are of two types: (a) aural harmonics at frequencies $2f$, $3f$, etc that accompany an incident tone of frequency f when the intensity is above 75 dB, and (b) combination tones of frequency ($mf_1 \pm nf_2$) where *m* and *n* are small integers produced by two tones of frequencies f_1 and f_2. Thus, when a *pure musical fifth* of frequency $f_2 = \frac{3}{2} f_1$ is played loudly together with the note of frequency f_1, the first combination tone is $\frac{3}{2} f_1 - f_1 = \frac{1}{2} f_1$ which is the sub-harmonic of the tone at f_1 (an octave below f_1). There are many other combination tones that are produced. *The aural harmonics that accompany intense tones are generated in the ear of the listener and are perceived as additional pitches.*

These effects add a great deal of complexity to the perceived sounds from the orchestra when the instruments are played at high levels. These problems are usually worsened by the use of poor quality sound amplifiers and speakers to boost the sound level of the orchestra. These audio (Public Address — PA) systems are usually run under overload conditions where the operation is non-linear with the result that unwanted harmonics and combination tones are generated.

16.5. Chapter Summary

The solution to the harshness problem in steelpan orchestras is the proper and precise blending of all instruments. The *Blender* must decide which partial (higher modes) to remove from a set of instruments in order to reduce the possibility for problems. Excessive sound amplification should be avoided whenever tonal correctness and quality are essential (as they should always be).

CHAPTER 17

The G-Pan — My Critical View in Defense of the Steelpan

This Critique is all about the disproof of fallacies in the G-Pan Patent and restoring the status of the Steelpan. For a short version of this critique which focuses mainly on the definition of the G-Pan as a '*steelpan drum*' and the use of *tension*, refer to Achong (2012).

The G-Pan patent is founded on a remarkable *non causa pro causa*. In its treatment of the patented instrument, it purports that the Steelpan is a Drum from the circumstance that the *substance* of the patent is the 'Steelpan Drum.' Categorically, the Steelpan is a member of the class, *Idiophone* while the Drum is a member of the class, *Membranophone*. There is no connection between the two objects found in these two *different* classes contrary to what is implied in the writer's creation 'Steelpan Drum.' The patent enters into a state of confusion when, in passing, it correctly states that the Steelpan is an idiophone. It is therefore expedient for me to point out that there is a 'time honored' classification of musical instruments, well respected by musicians, instrument makers and composers; *Aerophones, Chordophones, Idiophones* and *Membranophones*. The created instrument 'Steelpan Drum' cannot be found, exclusively, in any one of these classes although, as the G-Pan, it is patented in the class *'Drums.'* These observations will explain the process of enquiry adopted in the following Critique.

17.1 The G-Pan Patent Abstract

My assessment of the G-Pan that follows is based on the Patent Document — PCT Application Ser. No. PCT/TT2007/000001 titled *'G-Pan Musical Instrument'*— by *Inventor*: Brian R. Copeland, *Assignees*: Republic of Trinidad and Tobago, IPC8 Class: AG10D1302FI, USPC Class: 84411 R. Class name: Drums. Patent application by Grossman, Tucker, Perreault and Pfleger, PLLC. Patent application in class Drums.

The second 'reformatted' application (a continuation of PCT/TT2007/000001) identified by Patent No. US 7,750,220 B2, Dated: July 6, 2010 contains a change of Assignee. The new Assignee is the Government of the Republic of Trinidad and Tobago, Port of Spain (TT).

Because all items mentioned in the *Abstract* to the G-Pan Patent (both applications) will come under scrutiny in this Critique, the abstract is quoted in its entirety; it reads:

'An ensemble of acoustic steelpan musical instruments, being an innovation which significantly improves upon traditional acoustic steelpan prior art. Said improvements include an extension of note range across the assemblage of G-Pans, a substantial reduction in the number of steelpans required to effectively cover the steelpan musical range, the use of a compound design whereby individual component parts of the instrument, specifically the playing surface, chime, rear attachment, or skirt and the playing stick or mallet, are optimized for their specific function, the application of a variety of techniques for eliminating or reducing, non-musical sympathetic vibrations and the inclusion of a variety of mechanical and acoustic resonator designs, to enhance optimally, the sound projection of the aforementioned instrument.'

Of the G-Pan there are four types — *Soprano* ($C_4 - B_6$), *Second* (36 contiguous notes upward from B_2), *Mid* ($A_2 - A^\flat_5$) and *Bass* ($G_1 - C_4^\#$), The diameter of these pans is $26^1/_2$ inches compared to the $22^1/_2$ inches on the Standard Pan (S-Pan). The musical range on each pan is $2^1/_2$ to 3 octaves compared to $2^8/_{12}$ octaves found on the Quadraphonic and $2^5/_{12}$ octaves on the Tenor S-Pan. Among the claims is the musical compass of G_1 to B_6 over the entire four-pan set.

I shall make use of the term S-Pan along with the term B-Pan (Bore Pan) only in this Chapter for easy comparison with the G-Pan. In no way should the term S-Pan be taken as a re-naming of the Steelpan. In this 'contracted name' S-Pan, 'S' stands for 'Standard' not 'Steel.' There being no official Standard Pan (none is needed), the traditional steelpans are taken as representing the de facto Standard Pan. This is a safe position to take in my opinion.

17.2 Preamble

Prior to 2010 the talk within pan circles that fell on my ears convinced me that something was very wrong with the G-Pan. I knew what the likely causes of the problems were even without making contact with the instrument or its makers. As late as July 2010, I had no plans whatsoever of including the G-Pan in this book because I heard through the 'thin walls' that surrounded the instrument in my homeland, Trinidad, that the instrument was being patented as a drum; this meant that there was no need to include it because drums were not a topic in this book. However, just prior to August 09, 2010, I received a telephone call and a series of emails from an interested party which aroused my curiosity. The following Critique was written by the present author after having seen and read the patent application PCT/TT2007/000001, for the first time on August 09, 2010. After browsing through the document my curiosity changed to dismay! My first reaction was to disregard the document by continuing to leave it out of this book and to take my comments directly to pan makers in Trinidad when I return home later that year. But I asked myself 'then who would defend the Steelpan?'

The G-Pan patent contains a large number of technical, scientific and historical errors and failed to recognize the remarkable processes that underpin the careful and meticulous development of the steelpan by the traditional pan makers.

- *To 'significantly improve' on these developments a patent must 'come good' in fact, 'very good.' The G-Pan patent has not done this.*

I therefore write this Critique in defense of the Steelpan. Of course I could have taken the 'easy road' and left it to time, for surely, in time all truth will be revealed — the victories of truth are slow but sure! But on matters concerning the Steelpan, that 'easy road' is not the road I travel.

Other claims heard publicly and made outside of the patent will only be addressed where those claims have a direct bearing on the potential use of the G-Pan. Since the patent document was not written with the precision and format of a scientific paper, a number of scientifically incorrect statements in the patent document will not be addressed but I shall have cause to make a few exceptions. In dealing with these exceptions however, the same rigor that characterizes the analyses in this book will be applied.

- *I cannot afford to lower my aim or my sights on matters concerning the Steelpan.*

Included in the list of topics for discussion is the application of the patented G-Pan to Steel Orchestral use which will be dealt with as a fundamental issue.

The second 'reformatted' application filed; July 11, 2008 (a continuation of PCT/TT2007/000001) identified by Patent No. US 7,750,220 B2, Dated: July 6, 2010, was brought to my attention on May 18, 2011 at a meeting of *The Steelpan Tuners Guild of Trinidad and Tobago*. As a member of the Guild, I used that occasion with my advisory function, to address the meeting on musical and technical issues related to the patented G-Pan.

I take it that the *Owner* of the patent is the Assignee. The Assignee, who owns intellectual property rights to the patent, is *The Government of the Republic of Trinidad and Tobago*. If the original Assignees, *The Republic of Trinidad and Tobago,* had been retained, the implication would have been that the Citizens of the *Republic* are the Owners. Having dedicated a large part of my scientific researches to the steelpan, I write this critique from my position as a *physicist* and with the dedication of a *Citizen of the Republic*.

For referencing purposes, all claims and details that are referred to in this critique will be prefaced by its claim or detail number for example number '[0006]' just as they appear in the original Patent

Document PCT/TT2007/000001. For referencing from the second application filed: July 11, 2008, the corresponding Page and Line Number on that document will follow the '[00xx]' number in the form {Page No.; Line No/s}.

Consistent with the class Drums in which the Patent was sought, the writer of the patent has chosen a description of the Pan operation which cannot be considered to be even a simplified version of the correct operation of the Pan. For the most part, the *modus operandi* in the patent is one appropriate for an acoustical drum which under the general category of 'Percussion Instruments' falls under the sub-category of 'Membranophone.' The Pan or Steelpan is not a Drum (see Section 14.2). The description in the patent, especially with reference to the exclusive use of *Tension*, is simply wrong. This has led to numerous errors many of which would have gone into the design and construction of the G-Pan if the G-Pan makers believed the contents of the patent to be true and I cannot see them doing otherwise. Merely re-applying for the patent in the correct category will not solve the problems. The drum concepts are deeply embedded in the patent.

It should be noted that:
1. *The claims of a patent should be verifiable otherwise there will be no way of defending the patent against intrusion, use of, or attack by a competitor.*
2. *In this critique I make a clear distinction between the patented G-Pan and a working G-Pan. The two are not equivalent! In this work, the term 'G-Pan' standing by itself refers to the 'patented G-Pan.'*

It cannot be claimed that at the time of patent writing, the contents of this book were unavailable to the patent writer, hence the reliance on the drum mechanisms by default. This is not a way out of the problem. The main mechanisms of shell vibrations as they relate to the steelpan were given in my publications over fifteen years ago (by 2010 reckoning) and were certainly available to the patent writer. Over these years, the present author has presented the theory and principles of operation of the steelpan at seminars and conferences (internationally and locally in Trinidad and in Tobago) with pan makers and tuners in attendance. I shall give to the inventor and owner, a simple test by which their claim on the use of *tension* on the G-Pan can be verified or refuted. It is reasonably simple and will incur no additional production or research costs.

One can be decidedly sloppy about the scientific niceties of the Steelpan which in my opinion is disgraceful to the *National Instrument of Trinidad and Tobago*, or one can preserve, even enhance, the pride of this instrument by having it treated, even in patents, with thorough scientific correctness. Let me go on to declare:

- In this critique the present author makes a clear distinction between the Steelpan (the *Standard Pan* or *S-Pan*) and the G-Pan.
- It will not be assumed *a priori* that the S-Pan and the G-Pan are *operationally* the same, nor will it be assumed that when one speaks of the G-Pan, one is speaking of a Steelpan. The latter is a harsher line to take but it is brought about by the patent itself.
- ***The substance of a patent is known by its classification.***

The inventor and/or writer of the G-Pan Patent have made the following claims (highlighted in **bold letters** for emphasis and identification) that cannot be applied to the Steelpan (or S-Pan):

(i) By applying for a patent in the class *Drums*, the G-Pan, by choice of its inventor, has been categorized as a Drum. ***The claim; the G-Pan is a Drum.*** **The specific name given to the object of the patent is the '*steelpan drum*'** (see [0003], {1; 17, 18}). In this claim, the word 'steelpan' is used to describe the type of drum being patented; in like manner one refers to a 'snare drum,' a 'tabla drum' or a pair of 'bongo drums.' 'Steelpan drum' however, is a strange and incongruous mixture of instrument types.

(ii) By repeatedly employing *tension* and *areal density* (mass per unit area) as the means by which modal frequencies are adjusted on the G-Pan, the writer, in a consistent way, has followed the methodologies of the Drum. ***The claim; as in the case of drums and***

(iii) *string instruments, tuning by tension applies to the G-Pan*
Skirts or rear attachments on the G-Pan are removable for the purposes of tuning, ease of transportation and change of acoustical radiation characteristics. ***The claim; skirts on the G-Pan are removable.***

Other claims that are inconsistent with the Steelpan can be found in the discussions that follow. But before we get there I must caution the reader that it is wrong to say that 'a G-Pan is a steelpan with removable skirt.' If you take a *Competition Grade* steelpan and remove its skirt it fails to function with the skirt removed. It also fails when the skirt is re-attached!

I know that some readers may say 'but the G-Pan is something new, a new invention, so these things are allowed.' Sure: by themselves they are allowed, but not when placed alongside the well established 'Steelpan' as if the patented instrument belongs to the Class in which one finds the Steelpan. The patent addresses something different, a 'steelpan drum' which does not belong to the same Class as the Steelpan! I also know that there are those who may say 'but I should know what instrument the inventor is referring to!' This idea is even worse because it is the inventor and him alone who must clearly define the invention and according to the patent it is the 'steelpan drum!'

- *'Steelpan drum,' with 'steelpan' as a noun, is a deliberate contradiction, an oxymoron, designed either to confuse or to cause, by repeated use, to become an accepted expression or name!*
- *If in 'steelpan drum,' 'steelpan' is merely an adjective, the term is still oxymoronic, but in addition 'steelpan' then describes the <u>type of drum</u> to which the patent speaks!*
- *I must ask the patent writer the following question: Since the patented instrument — the 'steelpan drum' — is, by the writer's definition, a drum, why was the instrument not called by the more appropriate name, the 'G-Drum?'*

This is not a mere play on words. One must pay attention to the patent details to determine the nature of the thing! The patent in its *Abstract* claims that it supersedes the traditional art so it must be read very carefully to see if it lives up to this claim. To those readers who may think that I am just making heavy weather of all this, I must give a statutory warning that I shall be pressing these points very hard in this critique. **The *identity* and *good name* of the Steelpan are at stake!**

17.3 On Patents

For those readers troubled by patents that put claim to note shapes and sizes, such claims are made with respect to the *traditional notes* not the *true notes*. Traditional note shapes and sizes specified in a patent claim are in reality only specifications for a set of templates. Anyone with paper and scissors can make 'cut-outs,' label them with the symbols of the musical scale and call them 'note templates' but they bear no physical relationship to the true notes or to steelpan note dynamics. Therefore any formula relating the dimensions of traditional notes to note frequency is, to use the mathematicians' term, 'general nonsense;' (for more on this topic see Section 17.11). Those patents specifying shapes and sizes are therefore made on style and appearance and are not worth the costs of litigations because they are *cosmetic*. Likewise they are not worth the cost of the patents because the exclusive rights that the patents purport to give the inventors protect nothing that affects the working of the instrument. What about patenting the musical selection of notes on an individual pan? Well, the *de facto* scale *adopted* by contemporary pan makers is that found in Western Music but one is *free* to depart from this custom. The selection and placement of a set of notes found on any musical scale, on a single instrument, to be played in any order as the player wishes, cannot be considered a novelty. This selection and placement is *common practice* found on steelpans built in all manner of shapes and sizes every day. Anyone with plans for pan *cosmetics* should take note of this. However, this does not remove one's right to cosmetize. The *scalloped pan skirt* is an example of this right, indeed a bad example, for it can introduce untuned, unwanted, high frequency vibrational modes to the skirt that should function mainly as a non-resonant passive radiator.

17.4 Traditional Prior Art

Is the claim in the Abstract *'significantly improves upon traditional acoustic steelpan prior art'* genuine? As far as I know, this claim has not been established, but before answers are given, take note of the following:

As a caution to the readers, one should not see 'traditional' as being of an inferior kind; to do so will amount to a downgrading of one's own improvements to it. The steelpan traditional art is well developed and scientifically sound. As I have repeatedly said in my seminars and public lectures, the traditional pan makers are first-class engineers in their own right; I deeply respect them and their work and have proven their methods and their products to be of high standard and quality even when subjected to very rigorous scientific scrutiny.

Contrary to the above is patent claim/description [0006], {1; 31-39}:

'[0006], {1; 31-39} *The heretofore mentioned instrument is played in percussive mode and was first invented in the island of Trinidad in the Republic of Trinidad and Tobago, some time in the late 1930s. The exact date of invention is unknown as the origins of the instrument are steeped in folklore, having been first fashioned by individuals who were mostly working class and generally technically illiterate. However, the first published report of the instrument was printed in the Trinidad Guardian newspaper on Feb. 6, 1940.'*

This description raises some serious questions, answerable only by the patent writer. *By whom have these 'individuals' been judged?* Remember, the patent is a technical document available in the public domain (worldwide). *'Working class'* and *'technically illiterate'* together form a very heavy burden for these *'individuals'* to bear, all in one claim! Is that also part of the *'folklore'* or is it an established fact? Is the description on illiteracy which begun, as is claimed, in the 1930s, still applicable today? If not, then when and why did it cease?

What is the meaning of *folklore*?

The American Heritage Dictionary of the English Language, 1976 Edition, William Morris Editor, Houghton Mifflin Co., gives for the meaning of folklore:

'(1) The traditional beliefs, practices, legends and tales of the common, uneducated people, transmitted orally;
(2) The comparative study of folk knowledge and culture;
(3) A body of widely accepted but specious notions about a place, group, or institution.'

I should inform readers and the patent writer:

In the Republic of Trinidad and Tobago, the Steelpan is an ever-present fixture of community life; it is an 'Institution.'

I must enquire of the patent writer:

Is the traditional steelpan an Institution whose origins, according to the patent, are 'steeped in folklore,' now to be brought out of its legendary past and cleansed of its specious notions by the 'modern scientific methods' of the G-Pan Patent? For what other reason is claim [0006] in the patent? One should first ask, are the 'modern scientific methods' in the G-Pan Patent correct? Can they be applied to the Institution? We shall soon see!

If the claim 'working class technical illiterate' is truly a part of history then we may examine its relative historical importance by means of the counterfactual — 'What if these 1930s pan inventors were professors of science and engineering?' This is counterfactual even without reference to the claim of the patent but one can hardly expect the timeline of development of the Steelpan to be any different and it would still have been banned as a 'noisy instrument' by the government and law authorities of the day. If the instruments were not banned then the authorities would have shown greater respect for the status of the inventors than for the invention itself! Today, learned men of science and engineering still continue to misunderstand this instrument. The results of the counterfactual which in themselves are just the byproducts are not the major points of the present critique.

The patent Owner is entitled to and should defend the contents of the patent. As it turns out, I cannot abandon my rights as a citizen of Trinidad and Tobago and it is indeed my Government, on the behalf of me and my fellow citizens that owns the Patent. I therefore inform readers that I do not subscribe to claim [0006], {1; 31-39} either in its wording or in its connotations.

- In this Critique *I shall prove (in Items 9 – 13 of Section 17.23) and establish on behalf of all the un-named pan inventors in [0006], using their 'legends' and in their own idiom, that the steelpan <u>does not</u> operate as a drum under tension.* If their invention, Pan, is not a drum it has no place among drum patents. If the G-Pan is different it can go wherever the inventor sees fit. In which case, **the Steelpan will be better served by having the word 'Pan' removed from the name 'G-Pan.'**

17.5 My Critical View

- It should be pointed out again, that *a <u>working G-Pan</u> is not equivalent to the G-Pan of the patent*. A 'working G-Pan' is not a drum! A 'G-Pan' is a drum by patent rights and description. This distinction will become clear as the analysis develops. In all these discussions, unless the name G-Pan is prefaced by the word 'working,' G-Pan refers to the patented G-Pan.

The principles and theory of operation of a <u>working G-Pan</u> and its sticks are identical to those of the S-Pan and its sticks and both Pans are subject to *wavelength* and *frequency band-limiting* in the same way (see Chapter 13). However, with the increased musical range and increase in note size on the working G-Pan, these band-limiting restrictions pose greater problems — there will be conflicting requirements for the stick tips on the top and bottom ends of the range on each working G-Pan type. The problem is more severe on top-end instruments and is exacerbated when the range of these instruments are extended downward (without a compensating lowering of the top). If the lower notes are not extended downward (on the musical scale) but are increased in physical size (compared with 'traditional art') then these notes must be played with a larger stick tip which is in conflict with the requirements for the notes on the upper end which has been extended upward on the scale. Larger note size can also introduce greater difficulty in producing notes with adequate mechanical bias (the *Bass problem*, see Section 9.7); this will increase instability and reduce the maximum stick-note contact force that can be applied to the notes before distortion sets in (see Section 8.18). This limitation can however be countered by playing softer and by making use of the increased *acoustical efficiency* (*not* a claim in the patent, but will be discussed later) of the larger notes to provide the compensation. But then the main benefit of the increase in size is reduced if not lost altogether.

It is commonly said that the 'G' stands for Genesis meaning that it marks a new era — 'Genesis' — in Pan. Also, what seems to be a common claim is that these instruments, by their 'loudness' should replace the existing pans in the premier event in pan music — the Panorama Steelband Competition. The sources of these two claims are unknown to the author and therefore they cannot be thoroughly discussed here especially since being louder cannot be the criterion for exclusivity and the start of a new generation! I can hardly bring myself to reconcile this odd concept. But there is a hitch, the large pans that pre-date the G-Pan means that the G-Pan is denied some of its novelty; it is not the first in the line of large pans nor will it be the last. The art of assembly of pan face and skirt by use of a chime is common practice; welding along the chime (see Chapter 2) and pre-forming are well known and adopted in the earlier but still up-to-date Felix Röhner Pans of the Pang and Ping families of instruments. But closer to 'home,' the steelband from South Trinidad, *Broadway Syncopators* welded their pans prior to 1960 possibly as early as the late 1940s — my research tells me that the welding shop was located in the vicinity of Kings Wharf, San Fernando (the town of my birth).

With increased loudness and musical range, the argument continues, *fewer pans will be required by the bands in orchestras*. Sounds like good economics but what does economics have to do with music? Choirs and orchestras are made up of large numbers of voices *not for the purpose of being loud*! The division in the

Panorama Competition between Large Bands and Medium Bands is not based on loudness. The *Bore Pan* (B-Pan) can easily be made louder than the S-Pan yet there is no call to replace all the high-end S-Pans with B-Pans. There are strengths and weaknesses with the B-Pan as surely there are with the working G-Pan. With greater number of notes on each pan, the G-Pan covers a larger musical compass than the S-Pan. What is missing? What is different?

Note: *In the acoustic radiation process, the area that defines a note is the area of the true (ellipsoidal) note. If the area defined by the 'traditional note' is used, this gives an overestimate of the radiation power of the vibrating note. The area outside the true note and bounded by the curve describing the traditional note (technically a part of the internote) does not contribute to the acoustic radiation field. Therefore, a pan having large traditional notes may not necessarily have an acoustical advantage over a pan of similar type having smaller traditional notes. If areas on the pan face outside the true note contribute significantly to the acoustic output then the note is not properly blocked, is lossy and inefficient. There are other parameters apart from area that determine the acoustical output of a pan (see Chapter 12).*

17.6 Musical Range — Stick-Note Problem

Let us first look at musical range with the piano as a reference. The four (4) pan types that constitute the G-Pan present us with a set of four fractional parts of the piano with overlap. This concept is also found on the S-Pan but its compass is built using 10 pan types—10 fractional parts of the piano with overlap. If the musical range on a pan is too large (for example the G_1 - $C_4^\#$ on the G-Pan Bass), then as earlier noted, serious stick-note problems arise (see Section 13.32). The reader should take note of the fact that:

- ***These stick-note limitations on the steelpan are of a fundamental nature and cannot be removed.*** *They can only be accommodated by wise choice of sticks for each pan with suitably limited musical range. Playing notes in the Marginal Zone (see Section 13.27) is an art in stick action to be acquired by the player and perfected by the expert panist;*

it is not one that can be made easy for the novice by stick selection alone.

In fact the piano uses a set of individual hammers, one designed for each note. The patent makes the claim in the abstract that this problem is solved by some sort of 'optimization'. Because all musicians possess individual points of view and musical appreciation (all subjective), one must be very careful when using the words 'optimum' and 'optimization' in connection with musical instruments. The Patent merely says in the Abstract, *'optimized for their specific function'* in a broad manner, obviously, so we do not know how the many issues are addressed. I do not believe this ambiguity is intentionally inserted in order to preserve *trade secrets* for the simple reason that the limitations are fundamental and cannot be removed. *There can be no 'trade secrets' that can do it.* However, I see insurmountable problems with any optimization procedure for the G-Pan sticks — the problem having been made worse by the extended range (span) of the instruments and the use of 'covers.' That is the nature of a 'fundamental limitation.' Chapter 13 deals with these matters. The next Section deals with an issue that clearly demonstrates that optimization of the G-Pan sticks was not achieved; in defense one may claim that the G-Pan is a *'Work in Progress'* but if the patent is any guide, the future looks pretty gloomy!

17.7 G-Pan Note Covers

The G-Pan addresses the stick-note limitations by using (felt-like) *Note Covers* on the outer notes of the G-Soprano. These covers are mentioned in various places on the patent; Claim 1, [Table US-00001 item 1c], {11; item 1c}, [0156], [34; 18 – 23}. These note covers are similar to the 'mat' discussed in Section 13.14.6. But in Section 13.14.6, the use of this 'mat' was not recommended because as a lossy sub-system, it will negatively affect tonality. The mat was used in Section 13.14.6 for experimental 'proof of principle' purposes only. By making all the covered notes *lossy stick-note systems* during impact, the freedom of the panist in executing his/her full range (repertoire) of stick actions will be seriously diminished. Why must all the covered notes suffer? *Making a musical instrument lossy is not 'optimization'!* In Section 13.32, I proved that losses in stick-note interactions <u>cannot</u> be used to optimize stick-note impact. *This is a very high price to pay in order to add more notes on the top!* But to repeat myself, this is the nature of a fundamental problem! You solve it with something stupid; which is not a solution at all!

On the S-Pan and B-Pan, the 'optimization' has been cleverly found by restricting the number of notes per pan (musical range) with the realization that a player has only two hands. The pan makers for the S- and B-Pans were unaware that the stick-note limitations were of a fundamental nature; they merely improved on their sticks while keeping the musical range in check and <u>not restricting the panists' stick action</u> — a perfectly scientific approach in my opinion — *one that survives or lives within the confines of the fundamental limitations.*

I wish to state as points of clarification:

- *The basic function of the pan-stick combination is musical in nature. As a direct consequence, any optimization of function on its component parts must be consistent with this more basic function. That the G-Pan optimizes this function significantly above that seen (or heard) on the S-Pan is a subjective issue, depending upon what musical standpoint one adheres to.*
- *The stick tips on the Rohner Pang and Ping instruments were covered with a layer of soft felt-like material to muffle the high pitched tones. As Rohner explained to me privately in 2000, this was done because the Swiss players found these high-pitched tones annoying. This is an example of the subjective nature of the present problem.*

17.8 Coupling on the Pan Face

The patent criticizes the S-Pan (for example in [0162], {35; 1 – 11}) for the coupling between pairs of notes on the tenor and suggests its own *2-bowl* solution. This note-note coupling, as readers are well aware, is made through the internote and makes the Marshall Pairs possible. This note-note coupling only becomes a problem on badly prepared pan faces. Labeling this coupling as a problem, when in fact it is not, easily draws one into a situation where the 'recommended' solution, if applied, only serves to create a real problem!

Before I deal further with [0162] I must mention some problems that I have with [0160], {34; 54 – 65} and [0163], (35; 12 – 22}. In [0160], I don't know how chemical treatment and increased residual tensions can produce an '*improved medium*' for note creation when in fact chemical treatment together with tension is the perfect recipe for SCC (Stress Corrosion Cracking)! I shall have more to say on this later. For [0163] the best I can do right now is to refer the readers to Sections 14.11 to 14.15 to see how I should respond to all the 'acoustic wave reflections' and 'echoing' that are said (by the patent) to be taking place on the pan face of the S-Pan. I also refer readers to Section 14.44 for what my reaction will be to the 'interferometric measurements.' Since no references are given in the patent I cannot comment fully on the claim but those interferometric reports that I have seen do not supply any information on relative levels of excitation and in any event the Blocking Mechanism is ignored. *One cannot rely on processed photographic images to indicate levels of excitation.* In fact the last sentence in [0163] gives support to the traditional pan makers' practice of Blocking or Tightening the notes (not to be confused with the tightening of guitar strings mentioned in [0160]). Remember that as a musical instrument the notes are excited by stick impact and NOT in the continuous manner that Interferometry demands. ***One cannot separate the response of a system from the mode of excitation — a system's output response is a function of the input.*** I will be more alarmed if by continuous external excitation, as required for Interferometry, the notes were to be greatly excited. But then these '*higher vibration levels*' found on areas other than the notes as reported in the patent (and in the unspecified interferometric studies) can only point to one or all of the following: (i) poor preparation (poor blocking), (ii) an incomplete pan, (iii) excessively strong excitation of the pan system in order to excite weak modes on the internote and to allow good photography of the interferometric patterns.

Now, we return to [0162]. To remove the pan makers' ability to couple the inner and outer notes, or inner and central notes, as done on the G-Soprano with its *2-bowl soft-tape isolator* structure and note covers will cramp the style of G-Pan making (well pan makers may have to pay for a license to make this instrument anyway). The G-Pan makers may reply that the pairs can still be formed by coupling through acoustical radiation; it is a mistaken notion to associate Marshall Pairs with acoustic coupling through the air medium. The coupling between the members of a pair is through the internote. If this coupling is seriously restricted then even Weak Marshall Pairs will not be possible (see the *Invaders Tenor* in Chapter 14). The excited outer note (or inner note) then has to rely on the *inefficient* resident octave and *inefficient* resident twelfth for the acoustical radiation that produces the second and third partials— there being no *reinforcement* coming from the *more efficient* higher member of the Marshall Pair. Since the G-Pan makers see internote coupling as a bad aspect of the S-Pan and tries to reduce it further, Marshall Pairs cannot be incorporated (at least on the inner bowl of the 2-bowl Soprano). The inventor must consider carefully the consequences of criticizing well established principles of pan making! Having found fault with the S-Pan and its coupling one cannot expect note-note coupling or Marshall Pairs in particular to be found on a G-Pan!! If these pairs are found then it adds to the many other contradictions found in the patent! In fact I have found this very contradiction in the patent; it appears on Sheet 9 of the patent but more on that later!

There is an important and well known fact, proven analytically in Chapter 13 that a tenor pan cannot be played with a bass stick. Already, on the S-Pan tenor, one cannot seriously hope to get anything from its lowest note, the C_4, using a standard bass stick. It is true that this same note, the C_4, is found on the S-Pan bass, its highest note, but as explained in Chapter 14, this note, and some lower notes, is on the bass mainly to function as the higher member of a weak Marshall Pair. They are not useful on the bass as notes to be played (seriously). For what purpose then, is the even higher $C^{\#}_4$ note on the G-Pan bass? Is it to be played with a pair of sticks that must also extend its reach downward to G_1 (lower still than the S-Pan bass)? By the introduction of 'note covers' any note on any of the G-Pans may be covered including the low bass notes in order to allow the higher notes (the $C^{\#}_4$) to be played with a smaller tipped bass stick. If this is contemplated or actually used on the G-Pan

Bass then woe be unto those pans and players. The bass tones suffer the most compared to the tenor tones when propagated to distant listeners (see Chapter 12). The lossy covers and smaller tips will further aggravate this problem. But returning to the rejection of coupling, how are the higher notes on the working G-Bass used in relation to the lower notes if not by note-note coupling? It should be made clear that all working G-Pans (G-Soprano to G-Bass) work on exactly the same set of principles.

Claim [0162] links coupling of the inner notes on the S-Pan to stiffness and relates this stiffness to tension. The reasoning in claim [0162] is <u>*completely wrong*</u> so I must write in **bold letters** that **tension is not used on the inner notes of the standard steelpan (S-Pan) in order to increase stiffness and generate the high pitches**. Quite the opposite is the case; compressive stresses are used on the pan face of the S-Pan. Compressive stress reduces the note stiffness and the pitch. To achieve high stiffness on the inner notes the middle and central areas of the pan face must be properly <u>work hardened</u> by indenting to (relatively) great depths; take a look at a fully prepared tenor pan. This reminds me of Bertie Marshall's attempt at tuning a super-large tenor (twice the normal size) supplied to him by someone unknown to me. When Bertie showed me the tenor, I was just as amazed at its size as by the fact that the pan face appeared somewhat 'shallow!' He was unable to tune the inner notes because the pan face needed 'deeper sinking.' The material at the central regions of the pan face was simply too soft and flexible! Only on the *patented G-Pan* is tension used to obtain increased stiffness and to achieve high pitches; but in practice, on the real instrument, the *working G-Pan* (if it exists), <u>this is a technological and scientific impossibility</u>! In the *tuned state* of the instrument described in the patent, **tension cannot be set up and maintained in the manner and in the places where the patent requires it!** Neither can it be done on the tuned steelpan. <u>***The G-Pan cannot work as claimed in the patent***</u> and ***the S-Pan does not work as [0162] claims***! All this confusion can be traced back to the adopted drum concepts. I should therefore state that by merely naming the invention a 'steelpan drum' does not make it a drum!! The pan face is not a stretched membrane under tension!! Since this misconception crops up over and over in the patent, I had better explain this matter thoroughly in the following paragraph.

In order to form the pan face, the original flat pan face is either indented by hammer peening (the traditional way) or by press forming, hydro-forming etc. In all cases the material is stretched by the application of tension (tensile loading, or tensile stress) from an <u>external agency</u>. This external agency can be a machine in the case of press forming, a manually operated pneumatic impactor or manually operated hand-held hammer. In the absence of the external agency, the tensile loading is zero. After each application of the hammer to the pan face, <u>the tensile loading returns to zero</u>. It should also be clear to the reader that in order to press-form a flat plate, the outer edges must be clamped. In the case of hammer peening using the traditional steel drum as the rawform, the pan face is secured around the rim (or chime) by the skirt (see Chapter 2 for details). If the material is simply <u>stretched elastically</u>, when the tensile loading is removed, <u>the material will return to its original shape.</u> This happens if you tap the pan face very lightly with the hammer. However, to permanently shape the pan face and the notes, the material must be <u>stretched beyond its yield point</u> which means that the material must undergo <u>plastic flow</u> (plastification, see Section 2.9). This puts the material that has yielded under compression. When the externally applied tension is removed, <u>the yielded material does not return to its original shape</u>. Therefore to form the pan face and notes, which are permanent shapes, the material must yield and be placed under compression. Refer to Section 2.5.

The patent writer makes the mistake of retaining the tension used to form and shape the pan face and notes long after the tensile loading has been reduced to zero i.e. even after the external agency has been removed! *If sinking is done manually then the G-pan maker has to keep hammering the notes for the rest of the G-pan's life or his life whichever is shorter!*

All the tensioning of the notes and the guitar string analogy of [0160] are totally irrelevant and misleading but they certainly are consistent with the drum mechanism which employs an elastically stretched membrane (held under permanent but adjustable tension) and which forms the basis of the patent.

17.9 **Tuning, Blending and the Gradation of Tone**

This brings us to the second aspect: There is an often forgotten aspect of pan tuning that the pan maker and blender always keep close to their heart. Each pan type (Tenor, Seconds, Guitar Cello .....) must have a *distinctive* voice—*with an accent* (see Chapter 14). The tuner/blender is the *'accent maker'* — he decides the aspects and components of a tone to be *emphasized* or *de-emphasized* (see Chapter 14). *(Remember that emphasis and de-emphasis can only be effective if the panist is allowed full freedom to exercise his/her repertoire of stick actions.)* On the G-Pan there can only be four voices (technically, four *Sections*) in an orchestra; while, with the S-Pan there can be as many as ten. (***I am using the term 'voices' in the manner commonly used by players but the more precise meaning is given in Chapter 14.***) One has to be very careful when blending, that the Guitar does not sound like the Tenor or the lower notes of an extended Tenor. This is crucial because when a Guitar (pan) note is played, its higher partials must not appear or sound like they are coming from the Tenor. On the S-Pan, to effectively differentiate the Low 'C' Tenor from the High 'D' Tenor, the skilled tuner can increase the relative strengths of the octave (*resident octave* and the *octave* formed by the higher member in the pairs) and the twelfth, to give the High Tenor a stronger 'ringing' tone —a *higher pitched accent*. (I often hear these distinctive tones on the Desperadoes and All Stars tenors). A 'ringing tone' contains high-pitched *modulated* components.

These subtleties of pan tuning and preparation are aspects of the **Gradation of Tone** *(see Chapter 14) found on the instruments comprising a steel orchestra.* Pan makers strove towards this goal not because it is easy but because it is hard and the rewards are great. This difficulty (made relatively easy by the expert pan maker) should not be seen as a defect of the 10-pan system, as patent claim or detail [0042], {6; 28 – 33} wants it, but as an opportunity for musical effectiveness—to attain that *'captivating' feature* (I shall have more to say on this later).

To be effective, the changes in accent on the working G-Pan has to be strong because there are only 4 voices. *I make use of the term 'accent' on the working G-Pan with the assumption that these pans are tuned in a manner similar to the S-Pan.* (To appreciate the concept, one can compare a person with a strong French accent with another having a strong Chinese accent when both are speaking or singing in English). Keep in mind the overlap in musical range of these four voices — for example the top of the working G-Pan Second instrument must not sound like the mid-to-lower Soprano. Any way this change in accent between the Soprano and Second is achieved, whether by differences in sticks or tuning of the partials, or a combination of both, the result must be strong. Just like the conductor who prefers not to ask for two *identical* 'Piano + Pianist' because to the audience it's the same thing each time no matter which one plays. But he may call for two 'Piano + Pianist' with different timbre. Even so, he is only just coming to grips with the problem. He needs two (to start with) but of *very different* kinds! That is why the accent changes on just four voices on the working G-Pan has to be 'strong.' On the ten S-Pans there can be a more gradual change in accent but the overall changes on the range of pans between Tenor and Guitar can be deep. Among the S-pans designated for harmony (Guitar, Cello, Quadraphonic) there can be subtle accent changes that when played together **colorizes the harmony with varying hues** as the melody progresses. **This aspect is lost on the working G-Pan —certainly the hues are missing**! Do lossy note covers added to this make matters better or worse?

17.10 Orchestral use of the G-Pan

The third aspect, the most serious in my view, is the way in which the <u>***Chorus Effect***</u> (see Chapter 15) ***of the whole orchestra will suffer with the working G-Pan***. One should also include the possibility that there could be fewer players per section in the G-Pan orchestra. Readers are asked to analyze the 4-member working G-Pan for themselves using the contents of Chapter 15. I have thrown this in their laps so that they can be free to exercise their own musical preferences (prejudices).

But I must seriously ask;

- *What is Pan Music without the dialogue between the youthful and merry pronouncements of the Tenors and the wise, sobering answers of the Cellos with the*

Quadraphonics patiently anticipating the pauses to fill them with their sweetness while the Guitars perform their balancing act to support the overall tonal structure? And what is the pounding I hear, is it my heart beating to the rhythm, or is it the deep sound of the Basses combining with and deepening the line of the Cellos to gain thematic supremacy over the rest of the orchestra?

- *For a good example of this 'dialogue' return to Section 15.2.7 for a description of the beautiful performance by steel orchestra Trinidad All Stars in their 1980 rendition of Scrunter's 'Woman on the Bass.' Time has not changed the quality of this performance; I met All Stars arranger Leon 'Smooth Edwards in 2012 and discussed the importance of musical dialogue with him specially mentioning the 'Woman on the Bass.'*

One readily forms a quartet with four singers or four instrumentalists, but a choir or orchestra requires many more performers and instruments. An orchestra is not an enlarged (louder) quartet of instrumentalists nor is a choir a collection of quartets. That's where, along with the soprano one finds the contralto with truly deep often dark hues and the mezzo-soprano occupying nearly the soprano and contralto registers. The tenors, the baritones (of which there are subtle flavors) and basses. Similarly the sections and voices of a symphonic orchestra are many. This has been the pattern for the standard steel orchestra, which, despite the use of instruments of the single genus — Pan — there are sections (6 to 10) and voices with ranges and 'accents' to make available to the conductor the palette of colors that allows him/her and the orchestra **to form all the imaginative objects of the music.**

With the G-Pan orchestra how are the transitions between voices to take place smoothly — how can the players capture the roaring tempest of the sea and the transition — *the bridge* — to slow wavy calmness? To the listeners, will it be jerky? After all, many of us are quite sensitive to these things! Where is the color spectrum of instruments among four? If a musical sentence is repeated must it sound the same way each time? What if the second time was to 'wake up!' a sleeping audience? It is the shifting of tonality as a potential problem when performed by a G-Pan orchestra that worries me — a family of four is just not big enough. The standard pan, with its wealth of voices, affords the opportunity to move smoothly from one tonality to another and the players execute it well.

I can certainly say that *the 4-member working G-Pan describes a different texture in instrumentation.* But having said that, being of a different texture does not mean it is a *'significant improvement.'* There are many significantly good attributes on the S-Pan that are lacking on the patented G-Pan. These have not been replaced by the extension of musical range for example. In fact things have gotten worse. As I see it, the working G-Pans should be played over more restricted ranges than in the patent specifications. This can be set by the musical arranger. But then where is the G-Pan as patented?

Let us return to Handel's *Hallelujah Chorus* which was mentioned in Section 15.2.6. Throughout the Chorus, Handel varies the texture of the music from *homophony* (texture with principal melody and accompanying harmony), to *monophony* (melody without accompaniment) to *polyphony* (two or more melodic lines combined into a multi-voiced texture). When played by a full complement of players and pans in the Standard Steel Orchestra, there are adequate instruments available — high tenor, low tenor, double tenor, double second and quadraphonic — for producing the polyphonic fabric of the chorus — a woven fabric, formed as an overlapping mixture of voices and melodies from all the instruments (basses to tenors). I love to hear these performances. But where do we stand with a 4-Section G-Pan Orchestra? *Okay* for the monophony, *reasonable but dull* for the homophony parts and *greatly lacking* in the important polyphonic parts of the Chorus!

The criticism leveled by the patent in [0042], {6; 28 – 33} against the standard steelpan orchestra for its 'clutter' of musical instruments is therefore seen to be <u>highly misplaced</u>. Also, contrary to [0042] the instruments <u>did not</u> evolve in a *'generally ad hoc manner.'* The evolution of the standard pans showed purpose both in their musical function and by their efficacy. You must view these instruments with a 'musical eye' (my readers can grasp this concept) in order to 'see' their purpose. It is not until the steel orchestra performs the complex and diverse musical structures found in the work of world renown composers does the necessity for all the specially crafted instruments found in the Standard Steel Orchestra become apparent.

17.11 **Some Major Technical Errors and Difficulties**

For the sake of my readers who may read the patent application for the G-Pan, I must correct some of the major errors and misrepresentation on the patent document. For example, in the construction steps it states, in part, under 'Background of the Invention':

'[0016], {2; 59 – 67}, (3; 1-4} *Note bearing areas may now be demarcated, often by engraving grooves or channels between note areas with a punch. This step is not absolutely necessary and serves only as a means for pannists [sic] to easily identify note areas. What is more important is the degree of separation and isolation between the notes; this is essential to a good sounding instrument as it provides an acoustic barrier which reduces the transmission of vibration energy between notes thus improving the accuracy of the instrument:....* '

Dealing first with what is considered to be more important 'the degree of separation and isolation', while this is generally true, physical separation does not always achieve this unless other measures are put in place (see the discussions on 'Hiding' in Chapter 14). Grooving and boring are two of these measures. The patent writer did not recognize the grooves as a means of achieving '*what is more important,*' the '*isolation between notes;*' grooves were seen as having only *cosmetic value.*

The Grooveless Pan by Randolph Leroy Thomas (see Chapter 4 and Section 14.36) clearly shows that '*this step is not absolutely necessary*' but what follows '*and serves only as a means for pannists [sic] to easily identify note areas*' (emphasis with the underline is mine) **is totally incorrect. This is a clear denial of function**. In fact, operationally, grooves are not demarcations or a means of identification at all — **grooves are dynamically functional in the Blocking process**. Item [0016] gives the grooves only a passive or *cosmetic* role. If the claims in [0016] were true one might just as well simply paint on the grooves! Don't be misled by visual appearances! When I collaborated with Randolph Thomas, among many other things, we did exploratory work on *cryogenically treated steelpans* but my input to the Grooveless Pan was theoretical and motivational. Thomas succeeded in the practical development of this instrument which remains, in my assessment, the loudest of the tenors that I have ever heard. He deserves full credit for its invention. As discussed in Section 14.36, this pan incorporates two major aspects of pan note construction; (1) the setting of good boundary conditions by hammer peening in the internote area between the true note boundary and the traditional note boundary; (2) strong mode-mode quadratic coupling on the tuned notes to enhance energy confinement. <u>These two characteristics cannot be attained on a drum</u>!

Claim/detail [0016] cannot be allowed to take away from the traditional pan makers the achievement represented here by their 'Blocking Mechanism' that goes under the name of 'Grooves.' To me it is equivalent to Goodyear's introduction of sulfur to natural rubber when he invented the process of 'Vulcanization.' It wasn't for the purpose of changing the color of the rubber (a cosmetic change) but to impart better mechanical (wear resistant) properties to the rubber which today we use to make tires. In the same manner we use grooves as a blocking mechanism in the making of Pans.

There are statical and dynamical reasons for the placing of grooves (and bores) on the pan: the grooves are no 'window dressing,' not just 'cosmetic markings,' not mere 'border lining' for *'pannists [sic] to easily identify note areas.'* A player may see them that way if he chooses but a pan maker, an inventor or pan researcher should not! When grooves and bores are not used, <u>something else must replace them</u> (see Section 14.12) and not some cosmetic, superficial markings. *But not having seen or understood the real purpose of grooves, the G-Pan inventor may not have seen the need to replace them with anything else!* Since the early pan makers hammered in grooves for a reason (a genuinely scientific reason), I cannot see how this important aspect of pan making *and the underlying reasons for grooves or its equivalent, can be missed by the researcher(s)* who undertook the job of designing and constructing the G-Pan! **This alone can explain why the patented G-Pan is not equivalent to a working G-Pan.** By its careful wording, it cannot be a slip of the pen!

If it is, then I can now understand the possible reason for the other errors—'slip of the pen'! But seriously, since the G-Pan is patented and here to stay, this matter (and others) has left me with some amount of discomfort because it projects to me and the readers (if I may speak for them, having read this far into my book), that <u>all may not be well with the G-Pan</u>.

I wish to place on record an additional criticism; this time, to a remark made against the Steelpan. This is in reference to the following under 'Background to the Invention:'

'[0052], {7; 55 – 58}: *Regrettably, traditional acoustic steelpans do not allow for the easy removal and replacement of the skirt to facilitate maintenance, transportation, or change in instrument sound radiation characteristics.*'

Indeed it is regrettable that these comments were ever made! The patent writer cannot be serious! However, I must step in to defend the Steelpan and its Makers. *How do they take all this?* This suggestion is on par with asking that a Steinway Grand Piano, which for its size, in order to be portable should have been made to be easily disassembled! *How would Henry Steinway have taken that?* Consider the pianist nervously watching the on-stage re-assembly as keyboard, pedals, soundboard, hammers and all the assorted pieces are fitted back together! Then comes the '*what if*!' What if it comes apart in the middle of the performance? What if the finely 'voiced' hammers were squashed by the hands of a careless technician? Is the steelpan a less delicate instrument or has the patent writer taken its finely tuned state for granted? Detail [0052] shows a lack of appreciation for '*voicing,*' a subtle ingredient on all musical instruments.

I must express my dismay and annoyance with this statement of regret. Each time I return to this section of my work to check and refine my comments on [0052] I am forced to leave my computer with my head shaking for a sip of lemonade in order to regain my composure — seriously! Detail [0052] is truly unbelievable!

The comments in '[0052]' 'easy removal and replacement to facilitate' (a) 'maintenance', (b) 'transportation' or (c) 'change in instrument sound radiation characteristics' *clearly show a misunderstanding of this musical instrument.* The steelpan makers knew better than to try this! Some of them in their early scientific investigations must have done so, only to abandon it for its futility! Pan makers, whom I regard as engineers in their own right, are quite capable of challenging statement [0052]. I need only refer the readers to Chapter 2, where the role of the skirt is discussed. In [0052] there are three comments merged into one but first I give my general criticism; steelpans that are dismantled in the manner suggested whether for *maintenance, transportation* or to *change its radiation characteristics* MUST be re-tuned, blended and voiced after reassembly before they can be put into use. One may also find that reassembly is impossible (from a musical standpoint). There is no 'easy' way!

On *'maintenance'* presumably this means re-tuning or fine tuning. Any use of detachable skirts will seriously affect the hoop stress distribution on the skirt, produce deformation of chime and pan face and ultimately modify the frequencies of the notes. After re-assembly the instrument will require re-tuning. The writer of the patent document should know that one cannot attach such detachable skirts loosely for very obvious reasons (like rattling sounds etc). Gaskets and other isolators cannot come to the rescue here! But if they are attached firmly when needed then the points or areas of attachment will modify the stress distribution and the note frequencies. Buckling (do not look for a total collapse) may also result when the skirt is removed (see Chapter 2). The role of the skirt is both of a statical and a dynamical nature. This type of *'denial of function'* also appeared in [0016] and I ask 'does it show a proper understanding of the stresses on this musical instrument?' In fact such 'detachable skirts' on the G-Pan are what I refer to as 'window dressing' and 'cosmetic,' both of which, pan can do without as the fully successful S-Pan has been showing us for years.

On *'change in instrument sound radiation characteristics'* the readers of Chapter 12 can easily deal with this. But I can offer them some help. It is clearly unknown to the writer of the patent document the degree to which the sound radiation is intimately coupled to the note dynamics. If you make such changes to the sound radiation characteristics that are sufficiently audible and useful, then the radiation impedance and the equivalent radiation mass will change and through the coupling with the note dynamics, even the note modal frequencies and tonal characteristics will be altered. But despite this, the claim is that the skirt can be changed (being attached with bolts or clamp) to alter the sound radiating characteristics. **Well it certainly would, but in unpredictable ways**! Therefore one ought not to think that one can select an assortment of skirts (rear attachments) that are interchangeable and provide desired changes to the sound radiating characteristics of the instrument — that being all it will produce on the instrument!

- *A panist must know the characteristics of the instrument he plays. If it is variable or unpredictable because of the cosmetic aspect of disassembly-reassembly it is a disaster in the making. This can cause the worse form of 'stage fright' that a performer (panist) can have!*

One can easily find fault with the following patent detail:

[0124], {30; 32 – 39} ' ... *The need to allocate notes to multiple drums is determined by the physics of the instrument design which dictates that notes on the lower register must be larger in size than notes in the higher register. It is believed that the frequency is inversely proportional to the longest dimension of the note area to the power 3/2. As technology develops and allows for a reduction in note size, it will become possible for the lower registers to be placed on a single drum.*'

First of all I must make a general comment to an error in expression that I find occurring much too often in printed work on the Steelpan even in pan specifications compiled by Pan Trinbago! When a steelpan consists of *multiple pans* for example the Six Bass, the careless writer describes the instrument as made up of 'six drums.' Writers must refrain from this 'bad habit' and instead, use the correct expression '*six pans*' for the example used here. Even though the 'Six Bass' is considered a single instrument, it is made up of six parts, **each part being a 'pan' in its own right**. [0124] should refer to 'multiple pans' and 'single pan' but one is already aware that in the patent there is no such distinction! Of course one can attempt to get away with the lame excuse that one is referring to the rawform and not the finished instrument! It's lame because there are no notes (musical notes) on the rawform!

Continuing with [0124], physics does not *dictate* that *'notes on the lower register must be larger in size than notes in the higher register.'* By proper use of compressive stress on the boundaries of a note (assisted by grooves or bores if you wish), the physical size of a low note can be reduced. **Physics tells us that!** Real life experience with the pan bears it out also! Bore pan makers are well aware of the note size reduction afforded by the bores. **One can easily cross registers with notes of the same size.** While one will surely find that low notes are generally made larger than high notes one must be careful with the use of the word 'note'. The word 'note' in the patent refers to the traditional note. Properly interpreted, the boundaries of the traditional notes (usually bounded by grooves) refer to the boundaries of the *templates* used in marking out the notes. Except in the case of the inner notes on the tenor pan and other high-end pans, the template outline may not coincide with the true note. The disparity is greatest on the outer notes. Even on the inner notes the true note boundary can be found within the template outline.

If one tries to form a functional relationship (an equation) relating note size to frequency and uses *'the longest dimension of the note'* (remember that 'note' in the patent refers to the traditional note) the relationship so formed is essentially between template dimensions and the note frequencies stamped on the templates! Problems!

> (1) Physics dictates no universal template for traditional notes so anyone, including a child, can draw and cut out templates of any size and shape then stamp frequencies on them.
>
> (2) The information on the templates cannot establish a relationship between size and frequency since this <u>will not involve the properties and dynamics of the steelpan notes</u>. In fact ***it does not involve the real steelpan notes at all***! Even the templates used successfully over many years by a pan maker bear no physical relationship to the note frequencies. Neither do these same templates improve with age! What improves with age is the pan maker's ability to tune the 'true notes' corresponding to these familiar traditional notes to the desired frequencies. Their repeated use will not cause this physical relationship ever to be established. If this were

possible then a pan built with templates to mark out the notes is *ipso facto* a tuned pan!!

(3) The general observation that lower notes are larger in size cannot be used to establish a mathematical relationship between longest (traditional) note dimension and frequency. In mathematics, 'relationships' of this type are referred to as *'general nonsense.'*

(4) The 3/2-power law (*three halves power law*) referred to in [0124] is a result based on general nonsense. In fact as one increases the number of notes used in the data set from which this 'power law' was determined, the degree of scatter increases. Eventually, by adding more and more unbiased data, this 'power law' will lose statistical significance. In science there is the physically reliable principle, that when the data set is expanded the correctness of a physically true hypothesis stands out more and more. This does not happen in the case of this 3/2-power law. I do not recommend that this power law be taken with any degree of seriousness. *Worst of all don't be fooled by some future patent which makes the claim that a certain numerical value for the power works best!*

Try the following experiment. Here, and only here, in order to conform to the patent I shall temporarily use the term 'note' to mean the traditional note. Select a tuned set of four pans (from tenor to bass) along with their frequency stamped templates and four independent assistants. The assistants must be sequestered so that their individual data remain confidential during the experiment. Assistants #1, #2, and #3 are not allowed access to the templates. Assistant #1 must measure the longest dimension of the notes on the pans and take as the note frequencies, the values listed on the musical scale. Assistant #2 must measure the longest dimension of the notes on the pans but must use an accurate frequency meter to measure the actual frequencies of the notes on the pans. Before introducing assistant #3 to the pans, take a hammer and retune (or mistune) all the notes. Now allow assistant #3 to take size measurements and to measure the note frequencies. Assistant #4 works entirely with the templates and is not allowed access to the pans. As a precaution, choose #4 as someone with no knowledge whatsoever about steelpans and who resides in a foreign country then have the templates mailed to him! By now, all my readers are pan scientists and they can easily see that when the assistants plot graphs of *frequency versus longest note size*, #1 and #4 graphs will agree despite the fact that #1 never saw the templates while #4 never saw the pans! Assistants #2 and #3 saw the pans and measured the frequencies for notes having the same sizes but between them, their results are different and their results do not agree with either #1 or #4. This is nonsense!

If, for completeness, you want further test of this nonsense, choose another four *independent, sequestered assistants; supply each of them with identical copies of a long* list of note frequencies taken from the musical scale. Next ask each of them to design note templates for each frequency on the list, with size and shapes of their own choosing. Let them send you their templates from which you take measurements of note sizes. Finally you plot the graphs and fit a power law to each graph. You will surely find a wide range of powers. One may even be close to 3/2 = 1.5. A clever assistant who reads the instructions I have given here and knows what you are about can even set his note sizes to ensure that you get the value pi/2 (that is (3.141593)/2 =1.570796) for the power law! Another clever reader of this book uses his computer to generate the sizes that will give you a power exactly equal to e/2 where e is the base of the natural logarithm (that is (2.718282)/2 =1.359141). Nothing wrong with designing note templates on a computer! The thing is, all these sets of templates are useable and to deepen the plot (no pun intended), you can shuffle around all the templates in a box then, with your eyes closed, randomly pick out a set to construct your pan! I can guarantee you that if you are a skilled traditional tuner you will get your pan to work! The odd assortment of note shapes and sizes does not matter neither does the numerical value of the power that fits the frequency versus dimension graph for these randomly selected templates.

I asked for only four assistants but if you have the time, increase the number to a few hundred and choose them from around the world to see if the improved statistics or geographical location makes a difference. Among these assistants, there is likely to be many smart ones like the little Australian lad who, using his 'down-under' computer, supplies you with the set of templates for which the power is $\sqrt{2}$ (the positive square root of 2). If you trip and spill all these thousands of templates on the floor, it still will not matter, just gather them up and use any random set to make your pan.

In science and physics in particular when something does not work out or produces inconsistent results (call all that 'nonsense'), it's a 'sure bet' that a wrong assumption was made at some earlier stage. In the present case *it is wrong to assume that there exists a well defined mathematical relationship between note frequency and the longest dimension (or any dimension) defining the traditional note. There is no consistent 'power law' that applies in the present case as the above experiments clearly show.* Just in case a reader makes the objection that the two clever assistants and the little Australian 'cheated' in their designs, one must ask 'what did the others do?' If it is that they left it all to chance or with some thought figured out that a note of 'this frequency' should be about 'this or that size' then they were all guessing. This is precisely what goes on in practice because **there is no universal power law like the one suggested in the patent**, that we all must follow, or the notes themselves follow! In these experiments everyone is allowed to guess! In a guessing game no one can cheat!

That future technology will allow the size of notes to be reduced to the point where the low registers can be accommodated on a single pan (or *single drum* as the patent prefers) is beyond wishful thinking. If future technology makes the bass notes so small, what will be the size of a high tenor note? If the low notes are reduced to such small sizes, acoustical radiation will suffer. This is unavoidable. A bass with small notes will be so acoustically inefficient that the instrument will be found unsuitable for orchestral even personal use. If acoustics is included in this 'developed technology' it surely will not lead to a small bass. I hope we are still talking about acoustic pans played with sticks! If we are not then there is a strong element of confusion here! In this state of confusion one may ask for an acoustic steelpan on the tip of a needle!! The patent writer should read what this book has to say about 'generalized wavelengths' and how it applies to all notes on the steelpan, including the bass notes. Readers who have properly grasped the concept of generalized wavelengths and wavelength band-limiting can very easily dispose of the claim that some future technology would reduce the size of notes as claimed in [0124].

The whole of [0124] is confusing because it begins with 'physics dictating' and it ends with future 'technology' saying something else, something that contradicts what 'physics says' at the beginning!! In the middle there is the erroneous belief surrounding a 3/2 power law on which neither physics nor technology has anything to say except that it is totally wrong!!!! Readers please forgive me for spending so much time with this bizarre set of statements but I have seen this 3/2 power law used before (see Rossing et al., 1996 and Rossing and Hansen 2000) and commented on it then (Achong 2000b), so it is time to have the matter laid to rest. *Do we need the 'little Aussie' to tell us that?*

17.12 **Resonators and the non-existent 'Plague' reported in the patent**

In criticism of the S-Pan skirt, in {0143}, {32; 26 – 34} the patent speaks of sympathetic resonances on the skirt and labels it a 'plague.' If such a plague existed, pan would be dead long ago!! This claim, [0143], is incorrect as the patent writer has greatly overstated the case for these skirt resonances. As seen in Chapters 5 and 14 these resonances are rare and can always be dealt with (as I showed in my 1999 lectures to pan makers on the material covered in my *Pan Makers' Handbook*). **As a general rule, the skirt should not be used in resonance with any of the note frequencies** (see Chapters 5 and 14). Later in the patent, the writer then turns around and makes the mistake — a *'goof'* — of implementing in one of the designs, [0215], {41; 17 – 26}, the very sympathetic resonances it criticized(!) — *the G-Pan contacted the 'plague'* — but more on that later. The skirt should only be used as a *passive soundboard*. If an active (resonant) soundboard is to be used, then the modal density must be high with sufficient damping to allow for an almost smooth frequency response across the audible range. The cylindrical skirt (with or without rolling hoops) does not function in this manner; in fact there are clearly defined natural resonances over its spectral response. You make the skirt work as a passive soundboard only by avoiding resonances.

On '*acoustic resonator designs*' (taken from the *Abstract* and body of the patent document) this must be taken to mean the acoustic resonance of the air cavity formed between the pan face and the skirt. At the low-end frequencies of the bass where such resonances may be possible, it will be unwise to use these resonances for musical purposes. The modal density of these resonances is extremely sparse; which means that only a few resonances (if any at all) can be found. These resonances may not coincide with the note frequencies on the low end. If one does coincide and such a resonance is excited for the particular note then whenever that note is played, a loud booming sound will be heard. This will be in stark contrast to the sound of the other notes — very undesirable. The shorter skirts of the other S-Pans do not allow this air cavity to function as a resonator because in simple language 'the air is not really trapped beneath the pan' (see Section 12.1) To make use of resonators, versions of the G-Pan are equipped with *multi-tube rear attachments* each tube tuned to the note above it. While this is not the first use of resonators on the pan, its application will prolong the tones in a manner unsuitable for some musical applications as a replacement for the pan. The G-Pan borrows this idea from the Xylophone and Marimba which are percussive instruments with tube resonators placed below the active notes.

I must express my skepticism about these tube resonators (and 'reeds') combined with the removable skirt (or resonator) idea (see Sections 12.1 and 12.22). Consider the following: To tune this pan the resonant tubes must be removed to gain access to the underside of the notes. After the notes are tuned, two things happen on reassembly of the resonant tubes: (1) stress redistribution appears on the chime and pan face with possible shape distortion, (2) changes in the acoustic coupling to the notes (the tube resonators couple differently to the notes than the *free air* during tuning). Both of these effects will change the frequencies and tonality of the notes. The G-Pan inventor must be informed that for these resonators to be as acoustically effective as intended in the patent there must be acoustic coupling (which, because one is dealing with *standing waves*, involve energy transfers both ways) between notes and resonators. These couplings influence the note frequencies and tonality. ***This means that the notes cannot be tuned with the resonators removed! To make matters worse, the notes cannot be tuned with the resonators in place at the undersides of the notes!*** Just in case the reader is concerned about the Marimba and Xylophone I should add that the resonant elements or notes on these instruments are free (or relatively free) vibrators. These vibrators can be removed if they need replacing but they hardly go off-tune anyway. *The notes on the pan are permanently affixed to and form part of the pan face and must be tuned in-situ.*

17.13 **The Confusion**

In the patent application one can find numerous use of the description 'steelpan drum.' The confusion begins in the 'Background of the Invention' with:

[0003], {1; 17, 18} *'This application relates to musical instruments and, in particular, to steelpan drums.'*

It is quite clear in [0003] that the particular musical instrument to which the patent application relates is the 'steelpan drum.' The designation 'steelpan drum' is no different from 'steel drum,' (refer to Section 14.2).

Patent Application PCT/TT2007/000001, filed on Jul. 13, 2007, ends with the information
'Patent applications by Grossman, Tucker, Perreault and Pfleger, PLLC
Patent applications in class Drums.'

Having labeled the instrument in the patent as the 'steelpan drum' the patent writer selected the category of 'Drums,' in which to make the G-Pan patent application.

More confusion arises with the following detail:

'[0088], {12; 17-25} *Steelpan: a definite pitch percussion instrument in the idiophone class, traditionally made from a cylindrical steel drum or steel container although they may now be made from other materials ... . The cylindrical portion of the drum from which the traditional steelpan is made is usually retained to act as resonator and to provide physical support for the playing surface.'*

It is understood that the word 'drum' used in [0088] refers to the rawform and not to the finished instrument. However the G-Pan is patented as a Drum instrument and given the name 'steelpan drum' so it must be carefully pointed out that <u>Idiophones and Drums belong to different categories of instruments</u>! *Is it that the patent writer does not view the 'G-Pan' and the 'Steelpan' as belonging to the same category?* This is the only mention of the class 'Idiophones' in the patent and no use is made of it in respect to the G-Pan having sought the patent under the class of 'Drums' and remained consistent throughout the document with the drum methods of operation. The 'drum concepts' are deeply embedded in the patent document. This shows confusion in the patent! The only resolution is that in the patent, **the G-Pan is not regarded as a Steelpan**! The patent brings this upon itself; by choice not by omission or lack of clarity.

Detail [0088] oversimplifies the role of the '*cylindrical portion of the drum*' as a means of support for the playing surface. It is much more than that; *it is an integral part of the playing surface* as we shall soon demonstrate (see Section 17.19).

[0088] is in error when it states that '*The cylindrical portion of the drum from which the traditional steelpan is made is usually retained to act as resonator....*' **The truth is that the skirt (the cylindrical portion referred to) on the Steelpan is NEVER used as a resonator**. Resonance between notes and skirt is totally avoided on the Pan. Neither is the air within the skirt set into resonance with the vibrating notes. Note-Skirt resonance makes it impossible to tune the participating note (see Chapter 5 on the Note-Skirt interactions). Experienced pan makers and tuners are fully aware of this.

I have observed in the patent some incorrect use of the term 'resonance' so some explanation is in order. First of all, a vibrating object is not necessarily in a state of '*resonance*' acting as a '*resonator*' nor is it necessarily executing '*sympathetic*' vibration. Now for simplicity we restrict our discussion to linear systems only. If an object A (such as a tuning fork) having a well defined natural frequency is set into vibration, and then put in contact with an object B, the object B will be driven or forced into oscillation at the frequency of A; this is called '*forced oscillation.*' It is only if B has a *normal mode* (or *natural mode*) of vibration corresponding to the frequency of A (or the modal frequencies overlap within the range defined by the bandwidths of the interacting modes), will B be set in *resonance* with A or will B function as a *resonator*. On the steelpan, the skirt is <u>never</u> designed to perform this 'resonance' function. In the case of the pan, the vibrating note is the driving source that *forces* the skirt into oscillation — a case of *forced 'non-resonant' oscillation*. Only on rare occasions (*a rare occasion does not signal a plague*) by pure coincidence will the skirt possess a natural mode that resonates with a note (see Chapter 5) and when it does, the problem is either corrected or ignored if the effect on the note is sufficiently small.

17.14 What is a Drum?

In as much as it is not necessary for me to define wind or string instruments in this work on the Steelpan — an Idiophone in the sub-category of Shells — I thought it unnecessary until now to define a Drum — a Membranophone. We need only its categorization among musical instruments and a clear and concise description of it *modus operandi*. Under the general category of Percussion Instruments is the category Membranophone and under which one finds the sub-category Drums. Briefly, a Drum consists of a flat, membrane (skin) held under tension (stretched). This membrane forms the drumhead. Some drums employ uniform membranes others may use membranes with thicknesses that vary over the surface. The vibrational modes and frequencies are determined by *tension*, *mass per unit area* of the membrane, *area* and *shape* of the playing (2-Dimensional) surface. Technically, the drum is an <u>unpitched musical instrument.</u>

The drum is played by hand or with the use of a mallet. Using the fingers or palm of the hand, localized forces can be applied to alter the excited modes, their frequencies and temporal structure during play. In some versions that make use of animal skins, such as the *Tassa*, the drum is preheated to remove moisture from the membrane and by the resulting skin contraction, increase the applied tension. When the membrane or playing surface is displaced, the *restoring force due to stiffness is negligible* in comparison with that due to tension. Tension provides the restoring force for the vibrating membrane. Some drums may employ a closed space behind the drumhead so that pressure changes may act upon the membrane and influence its vibration. *The tension that keeps the drumhead taut cannot be replaced by compressive forces because the stiffness of the drumhead is essentially zero. Without stiffness, the drum membrane (the drumhead) cannot support compression.*

- *You can at times, hear the expression, 'the membrane is <u>stiff</u> because of the tension!' Technically, this is incorrect. The correct expression is 'the membrane is <u>taut</u> because of the tension.' Stiffness as a technical term is associated with bending. An ideal membrane offers no opposition to bending, it is perfectly pliable. In practice all membranes will offer some small opposition to bending.*
- *Any application of the principles of the drum to the G-Pan must, **of necessity**, discard compressive stresses — the patent ran headlong into this trap!* ***Compressive stresses are nowhere mentioned in the patent!***

17.15 **The Correct Historical Setting of the Steelpan**

The single use of the term 'shell' throughout the entire patent occurred in detail [0038], {5; 60 – 65} where it states

'[0038]……. Until its [the steelpan] invention in Trinidad and Tobago in the 1940s, musical instruments made from steel shells and steel plates were relegated for use only as rhythmic instruments such as gongs, cymbals and bells.'

This claim is **historically incorrect**! The claim is also ***factually incorrect***! The *Carillon*, a musical instrument consisting of an ordered collection of musically tuned bells, shows that bells are <u>not</u> relegated for use only as rhythmic instruments. *The Carillon pre-dates the steelpan!* The Carillon can be heard playing full musical scores at churches, cathedrals and even historical sites. One of the most breathtaking experiences I have had with the Carillon occurred in Atlanta, Georgia, at a lake site (Stone Mountain Lake). For me, the best location to listen to the wonderful music was sitting among the trees as the sound of the bells flowed through the trees and across the lake.

There are other tuned 'shell' instruments of oriental origin used for playing melodiously, such as the Chinese *Bianzhong (Zhong)* and the *Gongs* found in the *Gamelan ensemble* of Java and Bali. *Some of these instruments are dated in antiquity. I have shown*

(Achong, 1994) that the Zhong and Gamelan Gongs share some important operational aspects with the Pan.

- *I say therefore, that the steelpan is not the first tuned melodious shell instrument. The steelpan is however, the first tuned melodious shell instrument with all the notes placed on a single larger shell (the pan face). This is made possible by non-linear mode localization that confines the vibrational energy to finite domains designated as notes. Tuning according to the $5/4^{ths}$-Law that applies to the standard key-note-octave-twelfth arrangement optimizes energy confinement to the designated note areas.*

17.16 My Further Views

The use of other materials beside low-carbon steel is not novel; the use of brass and aluminum (refer to the works by the Murr group) have been accompanied by tuning problems. With aluminum in particular, on the Murr aluminum pan the inner notes could not be tuned. I have studied these problems and arrived at the conclusion that with these soft metals it will be extremely difficult to obtain the right material properties and boundary conditions for the inner notes by indenting (sinking) and peening. All notes must be blocked (tightened). Tightening is problematic on soft metals (see Section 8.24). The nitrided-steel used by Felix Röhner is in fact the best alternative material used to date. A number of ideas in the G-Pan patent can be seen on the earlier Pang and Hang family of pans built by Felix Röhner — for example the larger diameter pan face and skirt, the spherical pre-forming of the pan face from flat blanks, affixing the pan face to a skirt rolled from flat sheet metal, and welding of the seam. The semi-enclosed chamber (replacing the open-ended skirt) found on the Hang is similar to the G-Pan design shown in Figure 11, Sheet 11, of the Patent US 7,750,220 B2.

The patent listed a wide range of metals and alloys (a wide net) some of which will make very poor steelpans! Nitrided-steel and gold are not among them but there are *gold plated* tenor pans! Neither is the use of large notes or large diameter pans novel ideas (see the example displayed in Chapter13, Figure 13.87). As the overlap of musical ranges on the standard pan clearly shows, one can easily form individual notes of larger (or smaller) sizes on the S-Pan. Because the B-Pan allows you to shrink the size of a note (see Section 14.12.3) this can be used to 'pad up' more notes per pan. But I don't like this idea and will not suggest it because you will be 'back to square one' having thereby lost, by some measure, the other advantages of having the bores. We see by these suggestions, that there is some room to maneuver even on the S-Pan and B-Pan.

The G-Pan with its greater diameter, in my opinion, should only be used to increase the size of the notes to capitalize on the increased *acoustic radiation efficiency* (I seem to have missed this aspect on reading the patent document, so I read it a second time). *Acoustic radiation efficiency* is not among the claims but then it is not expected to be there because this effect is already in use on the S-Pan and B-Pan. I should point this out very clearly and with some emphasis, lest it be used as a novelty. On the S-Pan, the C_4 on the bass is acoustically more efficient than the C_4 on the tenor, but in comparing them they must both be played with tenor sticks or better, a special tenor-like stick for the larger note on the bass. It is possible though for the tenor C_4 to be better isolated than the bass C_4, this will affect the results somewhat.

Note: *Do not confuse acoustic radiation efficiency with loudness. Something can be loud without being acoustically efficient.*

A cautionary advice with respect to stick tip size is that it is impossible to entirely remove the band-limiting problems by adjusting tip size, material or construction — the optimization of sticks has limitations.

- *For the sake of tonality, all pans <u>must</u> operate as frequency band-limited and wavelength band-limited instruments (see Sections 13.27 through 13.32). If the musical range of a pan is set too wide, problems exist on both ends of the range in attempting to satisfy these requirements with a single pair of sticks. It must be emphasized that there is no optimal criterion for stick setting that satisfies all situations.*

As shown in Section 13.27, the *absolute upper limit* for notes on the pan is E^b_7 (the *practical limit* is lower at $G^\#_6$) and all notes above E^b_6 fall in the Marginal Zone. This places the B_6 note of the G-Pan further into the Marginal Zone where attenuation is more severe than the G_6 of the S-Pan High Tenor, (for a numerical assessment on these Marginal Notes, refer to Section 13.27).

To accommodate the *Wavelength Band-Limited* restriction, once the notes are made physically larger, for a given frequency, *stick tip size must increase* otherwise unwanted untuned high frequency modes may be excited. The stick tip when chosen properly will suppress these modes for a range of frequencies and note sizes. On the other hand, *Frequency Band-Limiting* is dependent on the contact time so it is a matter to be dealt with by the panist. Generally, there are limitations on the smallness of the contact time set by the tip material and by the stick action of the panist. The smaller the contact time, the higher is the playable frequency of the note. We see therefore that there are limits placed at the top and at the bottom of the musical range for any pan played with a given set of sticks.

17.17 Claims on the use of Tension — while Compressive Stress is totally ignored

The matter of '*significant improvement*' (see the Patent Abstract) is of great concern here because the patent, having cast aside the fundamental importance of grooves on the S-pan by casting its role as being cosmetic in nature, the role played by *compressive stresses* (***not mentioned at all in the patent***) that grooves (and bores on the B-Pan) provide (see Sections 14.12.2 and 14.12.3), is similarly cast aside by **denial of function**. The term '*tension*' (*the opposite of 'compression'*) has been used at least five times in the patent application (not a typographical error or oversight, seeing that it was correctly used in claim or detail [0199], {39: 28 – 33} for piano strings). Contrary to the statements in claims or details [0023], [0134], [0160] and [0162] (corresponding to the following entries in the reformatted application {3; 56 – 62}, {31; 36- 42}, {34; 54 – 65} and {35; 1 – 11} respectively) where tension is shown to be 'put to use' on the G-Pan, *one must take note of the fact that tension is not used on the S-Pan as a means of increasing the frequency of the inner notes on the tenor (or any note on the S-Pan or B-Pan) nor is it used to adjust internote frequency or coupling on these pans.*

- The only reason I can come up with, on why compressive stresses are totally ignored in the patent, is to maintain consistency with the drum theory. Introduce compressive stresses into the patent and the whole deck or cards literally crumble.
- The notion that 'tension' is a means of tuning these instruments is inappropriate.

The Test mentioned in the Preamble: *The claim in the G-Pan patent that the G-Pan makes use of tension in setting the frequencies of notes can be put to the test by the G-Pan makers themselves in the following way. If the test confirms that their pan operates under tension then I suggest they take out a new patent for their method of maintaining tension on the G-pan face because it will be worth more than the weight of all the G-pans in gold. It will be very profitable because it will provide a novel way to pressure-test containers without the need for expensive pressurizing equipment. Using the next fresh batch of G-Pans that have just received first tuning, measure the note frequencies accurately with a frequency meter (to within a fraction of a Hertz) then safely set them aside for 24 hours. It will be preferred that this be done in a temperature stable air conditioned room to ensure that temperature plays no part in the test. Overnight, the residual 'tensional' stresses will have time to relax and be reduced. The next day, 24 hours later, measure the frequencies of all the notes again and compare them with the earlier measurements. If the notes are found to run flat after the 24-hour stress relaxation, then you have tensional stresses on your G-pan and a profitable patent awaits you. If the notes run sharp however, don't be disappointed because that's how it is supposed to work anyway with compressive stresses, no new patent but you will have to make changes to your first patent.*

Tension or more precisely, tensile stress, is 'bad news' on these steel instruments for **whereas compressive stresses suppress corrosion, tensile stress assists in rapid corrosion and crack propagation (SCC)** (see Sections 2.18 and 2.19). Is this what really 'goes on' on the G-Pan? The S-Pan makers have the clever method of using hoop stress at the chime and skirt to achieve a statical balance with the compressive stresses on the pan face. The patent claims that on the secondary bowl (see their Figure 6) tension is used to achieve the high frequencies on the notes (see [0160], {34; 54 – 65}).

Mass loading (see Section 14.12.4), a term used in the patent (refer to [0174], {36; 18 – 27} of the patent), is not a replacement for the application of beneficial hammer peening on the internote. In the *Pan Maker's Handbook* (1999) (distributed by Pan Trinbago) and in the *Lecture Series* that accompanied its publication, I clearly indicated the role of mass loading in the suppression of unwanted vibrations. If the G-Pan uses mass loading to alter the frequency characteristics of the internote (as the patent claims) then on each tuning (or re-tuning) exercise, the mass distribution over the internote must be re-adjusted. This will involve changing not only the magnitude of the added masses but their positions on the pan face as well. Consider having to do this after reattaching the removable skirt! I do not see this as a practical exercise for any tuner or pan maker! This situation will arise on each re-tuning exercise unless the patent writer expects the behavior of the offending area on the pan face to remain unchanged — a very unlikely expectation.

- *For the benefit of the readers I should point out the following special characteristics of Mass Loading: When point or distributed masses are added to a vibratory system, (see Chapter 11) the first noticeable effect is the reduction in the vibrational frequencies of the modified modes. Both the magnitude and position of the added mass along with the modal characteristics of the vibrator determine the extent of the shifts in frequency. Mass loading cannot be used to increase the frequency. If, as the patent claims, mass loading is used on the pan face of the G-Pan to reduce annoying vibrations then the following problems may arise but first a comment; **only on a pan with shoddy preparation will annoying vibrations be produced on the pan face, in which case the use of mass loading is a poor remedy.** The first problem relates to coupling and the propagation of vibrational stress energy across the pan face through mass-loaded areas. As the analysis of Section 14.12.4 shows, it is wise to stiffen the* *internote thus increasing the local modal frequency. This is achieved by hammer peening. Mass loading takes the affected region of the internote in the opposite direction. The second problem has to do with the re-tuning and fine tuning. These operations modify the behavior of the internote so that a reliance on mass loading will require a redistribution of the added masses. This is a lengthy, tedious and rather unwise set of operations for any tuner to undertake for each note.*

Why should the G-Pan require the use of commercial dampers such as *Dynamat* [0175], {36; 28 -33} to absorb energy (this vital commodity)? Is it because there are serious vibrational problems on the G-Pan face? Pan face sound is not a problem on the traditional pans and they do not require such extreme treatment. A musical instrument outfitted with Dynamat or *Dynamat Xtreme* (both are energy absorbing materials), is an inefficient instrument, that's the bottom line! **Since mass loading and Dynamat are used to get rid of vibration problems on the G-Pan face, why not solve the vibration problem outright by using the well developed methods of hammer peening used in the construction of the traditional pans?**

With respect to prior art, the patent does not lay claim to any special annealing process that improves upon traditional methods; it merely mentions a nominal temperature of 300 °C (somewhat lower than the minimum annealing temperature set for pans in Chapter 2). Readers should refer to Section 2.23 for the annealing 'burning' process.

17.18 Ring of Bolts and All That

With bolt fasteners securely installed on the mated chime and flange, the effectiveness of the vibration absorbing gaskets (see claim [0200], {39: 36 – 40}) will be lost. If these gaskets are meant to silence any noise caused by the differential motion of the mated parts then *these joints become absorbers of vibrational energy* which reduces the efficiency of the instrument. This wasting of energy occurs whether or not the vibrations are discordant. When the bolts are tightened and the combined system made mechanically sound, the two fastened members cannot be said to be isolated from each other. If it is intended to use rubber isolators on the bolts then this increases the degree of freedom of the bolted structure, introduces additional vibrational modes and motions and greatly complicates the dynamics. ***With all these additional vibrational modes, this is not a Pan any more, a G-Pan yes, by definition***! (This could be one of the reasons for the use of Dynamat.) These gaskets under compression by the tightened nuts and bolts, will only serve to compensate for mismatch of the two surfaces to be bolted together. The extent to which these two mating surfaces require the gasket to compensate for their dissimilarities determines the torque to be applied to the bolts and the consequent distortion that will result in the attempt to mate these two surfaces. These removable rear pieces (skirts) and 'matching' mate must therefore be fabricated to very high precision or selectively chosen for mating and identified to avoid confusion with similar looking mates in attempts to effect a *'change in instrument sound radiation characteristics'* (another claim in the patent). These complications will make the G-Pan an extremely expensive instrument costing much more than the 'gold plated tenor.' The reason why all this is thought to be 'easy' with gaskets (as the patent implies), is because the stresses on bolted members have been ignored.

- *Unlike many other metal instruments the steelpan is a musical instrument whose tones depend on the internal stresses and force distributions (fields) within the structure. The steelpan cannot be treated as other non-musical metal structures which can be assembled with nuts and bolts and be disassembled for purposes of convenience (transportation). When re-assembled the G-Pan will be in need of proper re-tuning (and redistribution of the mass loading).*

The distortions produced by bolting (or clamping) together the mating members will produce stress changes on the pan face and note shape distortions that will together result in frequency and tonal changes. Once assembled and tuned, the G-Pan should not be disassembled unless a tuner is available on re-assembly. Even so the tuner may not always be able to re-tune the G-pan!! This is not an aspect of *'significant improvement'* to traditional art!

In [0199], {39: 28 – 33} of the patent the writer stated:

'[0199]…*heat treated to relieve the internal stresses created by the rolling process. The reduction in internal stresses will also tend to reduce the modal frequencies set up by said stresses, in like fashion to the reduction of pitch that occurs with the reduction in string tension in pianos or guitars.*'

There is some confusion here because internal stresses are of two kinds and they have opposite effects on the modal frequencies. In [0199], this frequency reduction applies when tensile stresses are reduced. Even here the compressive stresses that result from rolling are ignored. All stresses in the patent appear as tensile stresses.

Let me explain for the readers' sake. Take a penny; drop it on a hard surface such as a thick sheet of steel or hard concrete and listen to the 'tinkling' sound it makes. Now lay the penny down on this hard flat surface. With a ball peen hammer (I assume you have one nearby for your pan tuning), strike the center of the penny boldly with the ball or peening tip of the hammer. If you were too timid the first time, strike it again, harder this time, it's only a penny! Observe that the penny curls upward. This is because of the compressive stresses produced on the top face of the penny by the *yielding* (*plastic flow*) of the top side of the penny in the neighborhood of the impact. This is like curling up the fingers of your hand to compress a sponge ball. Drop the penny again unto the hard surface and listen to the sound it makes, 'barely a tinkle' more of a dead sound. The sound frequencies that the penny makes are now *lower*. If you hit the penny again, it curls up some more. Try dropping it onto the surface again and listen! This happens in rolling and also when the note material is struck with the hammer during sinking or tuning. But something more happens on the carbon steel of the notes, it is also work hardened. If you are wondering about the balance of forces on the penny after the hammer blow, the whole penny is in equilibrium under the compressive forces on the top face and the tension on the bottom face produced when the penny curls up thereby stretching the lower face. But the area of the penny that was struck, the part now experiencing the residual compressive stresses, has *yielded* so the penny remains curled up. If you heat the penny some of the residual compressive stresses are relieved and the penny uncurls a little. With some uncurling, the bottom face is not stretched that much so the tension on the bottom side is reduced.

I should proceed further to clarify the role of the stresses on the pan. With reference to the work covered in Section 9.7, where engineering note designs were studied, we saw that as the physical size of the note is increased there was greater difficulty in applying the required compressive stresses along the note boundary that sufficiently increases the mechanical bias to the level that ensures dynamic stability. This is the reason why poorly prepared basses produce that annoying '*boiing*' sound when played intensely.

- *Although pan makers in their idiom use the term 'Tightening' one should not use the 'string instrument' idea and think of this as applying tension. On the steelpan, 'Tightening' or 'Blocking' means the application of compressive stress concentrations by hammer peening and additional work hardening to the internote areas around the note being tuned. 'Tightening' here means 'to contain' or 'block.' It's like 'tightening security!'*

This is an important consideration and as discussed more fully in Section 8.18, when a pan is fully tuned, each note is characterized by a distribution of forces acting along the outward normal to the note surface at each point. The net outward force is the *Mechanical Bias*. The mechanical bias characterizes the *Quiescent Point* or *Quiescent State* about which the note will vibrate when excited by stick impact. The mechanical bias sets the magnitude range for contact forces that can be applied by the stick before distortion sets in. The larger the mechanical bias, the 'harder' the notes can be played. **If the role of the lowly grooves on the tenor pan in the setting up of this condition is denied then the role of the larger grooves on the bass has not been fully understood!** Removable skirts will affect the mechanical bias and the quiescent points. But this does not seem to matter because on the G-Pan there is no need for mechanical bias (it is not mentioned or deemed necessary in the patent which describes a system operating strictly under tension).

Note: *On the stretched membrane of a drum there is* no *mechanical bias. If one therefore assumes that the instrument is a drum one will see no need for mechanically biasing the note or setting its quiescent point.* Grooves therefore lose their function!

- *The use of tension on the G-Pan turns everything around by increasing instability both dynamically and statically. The mechanical bias is wrong! The quiescent point is 'ill defined' if at all! It's like reversing the polarity of your car battery! Does it work? Does it start the car?* **Don't try it, please! If you do and you find that the rectifiers in the car alternator are burnt out and the car computer (Powertrain Control Module) is fried, I am not responsible!** *(I once posed this same question jokingly to a group of auto mechanics. While all except one said 'no!' there was this sharp response from the odd one out; 'Yes it will start but you can only drive in reverse and it puts gas back in your tank!!' Well as you know this is not possible but I hope you got the point.)*

17.19 The Ubiquitous Pan Jumbie — Structural Engineering in Traditional Art

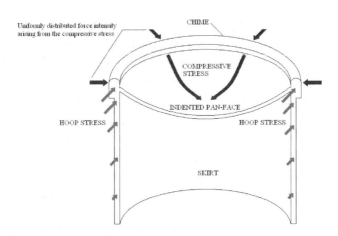

Fig. 17.1. The Pan Maker's Pan Jumbie — a cut-away view of the S-Pan showing compressive stresses on the indented pan face in equilibrium with the hoop stress in the chime and skirt. The detailed distribution of stresses on the pan face made complex by the notes and internote are not shown here. Not drawn to scale.

The G-Pan patent met it first public and scientific challenge in May 2012, at the *'Inaugural International Conference on the Steelpan'* — *Steelfestt, May 6 – 9, 2012'*, Port of Spain, Trinidad where I presented a paper *'The Pan Jumbie Confronts the G-Pan*

*Pa*tent.' Today, December 11, 2012, as I review this Section prior to publication, the proceedings of this conference have not yet been published so the general public is still somewhat 'in the dark' on the problems facing the G-Pan. The paper did however make the inventor and Patent Owner aware of some of the very troubling problems which the invention faces.

I have already written much about what is good about the traditional art of Steelpan making and of the Steelpan itself. The patent has seen it to be deficient and in need of significant improvement. The engineering success of the Steelpan is a remarkable fact — a clear demonstration of the skill, *technical know-how* and *intellectual competence* of these pan makers. From the 1930s' onward, the early pan makers, these *workers of class*, have displayed the technical know-how that matched the product — from the simple (single note) pans to the highly intricate (multi-note) structures.

- *Do not let the visual appearance of a steelpan mislead you for within that steel structure one can find the hidden secrets of the pan.*

It takes a *technical literate* to conceive and construct even the simplest of these steelpan instruments — for the simple reason that *it works* — *an engineering requirement*. To summarize their achievements in bringing mechanical stability to a complex structure (an exercise in *structural engineering*) one must refer to Figure 17.1. In the original draft of the manuscript for this book, this figure was situated in Chapter 2 where compressive stresses and hoop stress are discussed. Its relocation to this Section was deemed appropriate because of its importance in demonstrating the stability of the S-Pan design and the problems that will arise if modifications such as those contained in the G-Pan patent are made to the structure.

Clarification:

- *On the Internet one finds a host of sites using the term 'Pan Jumbie.' None of these are of concern to us in our present*

discussion. They have all borrowed the term and attached their own meaning to it.
- *This Section deals with the 'original' or 'true' Pan Jumbie. A concept or **notion** formed and used by the traditional makers of pan and couched in the idiom of the people of Trinidad from the period of birth and through the incubation and growth of Pan.*
- *In the idiom of the local pan makers of Trinidad and Tobago, particularly in the idiom of the early pan makers, Figure 17.1 depicts the 'Pan Jumbie.' It is a common mistake even among learned scientists to dismiss ideas phrased in the 'common language' or idiom of a people; some consider the vocabulary too limited to convey mathematical and scientific concepts. There are examples of this in the history of Science and Mathematics. For example consider the case of Nikolai Ivanovich Lobachevsky, one of the fist mathematicians to give to the world a non-Euclidian geometry; his original work was written in Russian, a language once considered too crude for mathematical expressions. This work first appeared in 1826 but it was not until 1840 when the French version appeared was the work given credibility and Lobachevsky began to receive the recognition he deserved. Perhaps under the name 'Pan Jumbie,' the steelpan makers' concepts and their acceptance suffered. However, I want to take the idiomatic expressions of the traditional pan makers as far as possible because I believe there is much clarity to be derived from them. Those of us who use them can very easily make the transition (a translation actually) from the Pan Jumbie to the Stress Fields of Figure 17.1.*
- *If I were to take it that the Pan Jumbie was 'folklore,' 'superstition' or as we say in Trinidad, just plain 'ole talk,' I would be in ignorance of one of the most revealing scientific concepts that govern the steelpan.*
- *However, with musical instruments in particular, **experience is a better teacher than precept**. One should take seriously, in fact, very seriously, the ideas of the instrument maker developed through years of experience. As a result, the concept of the pan makers' Pan Jumbie warrants serious*

*consideration. In these matters **one should always pay more attention to notion rather than notation** (see Items 15 - 19 of Section 17.23 for further discussions on this topic).*
- *In Section 8.14 I 'proudly' referred to the Pan Jumbie as the agent affecting the note shape whenever the tuner alters the buckling (flapping) parameter. By doing so, the rigor of my analysis and description has not been diminished one iota!*
- **Pan Jumbie — The Notion**: *There exists some hidden or unseen force or <u>entity</u> that, in addition to the conditions set by the pan maker and tuner, controls the tuned state of the pan. This entity has a strange ubiquitous nature.*
- **The Notation**: *This force or entity in the Pan Makers' idiom is the **Pan Jumbie**. The equivalent scientific term is 'Internal Stresses' or 'Stress Fields.' In the mathematical representation one uses symbolic notations to express this concept or notion.*
- *In order to incorporate skirt removal and replacement in its design, the **G**-Pan cannot tolerate the Pan Jumbie or in scientific terms, it cannot allow the stress fields depicted in Figure 17.1.*

As described in Chapter 2, the sinking (indenting) process by hammer peening produces plastic strain in the pan face material thereby inducing compressive stresses. Plastic strain is also induced if the pan face is pressed-formed. With reference to Figure 17.1, the indented pan face tends to curl itself inward under the action of compressive stresses produced *during and after* the sinking process. To prevent the structure from buckling (collapsing inward) the chime and skirt provide the necessary hoop stress that keeps the entire structure in equilibrium. In Figure 17.1 the compressive stresses produce a fairly uniformly distributed force intensity at all points around the chime while the hoop stresses act in opposition to the compressive stresses (see Chapter 2 for details). Notice that the hoop stress maximizes at the chime and drops to zero at the bottom of the skirt. For a long skirt, the hoop stress can be considered to be essentially zero at some depth below the chime before the end of the skirt is reached. One can therefore cut the skirt to that length while maintaining statical equilibrium but for acoustical purposes, as a musical instrument, doing so may not always be wise. The S-Pan makers are well aware of these facts having learnt from experience—*they are experimental scientists*. Not being theoretical scientists they need not have gone into stress analysis and that sort of thing. The fact is they got it right, through the scientific procedure of experimentation.

On the 'working G-Pan' (not the G-Pan described in the patent), when the pan face is pressed-formed, the hoop stress that balances the compressive stresses induced by the press-forming action is provided by the machine clamps (flange) attached to the outer edge of the sheet metal blank. After press-forming, when the machine clamps are removed, the hoop stress they provided is removed causing the bowl shaped pan face to curl further inward. When the outer edge of the bowl is cut to size to allow for seaming and/or welding, there is further inward curling. The rear attachment clamped to the outer edge of the bowl must provide the hoop stress that will surely arise when the notes are formed and tuned. If the notes are formed without a rear piece or skirt the free edge of the pan face will surely suffer distortion. Finally, when the working G-Pan is finished and tuned, the rear attachment or skirt cannot be removed. Removal will take away the hoop stress causing the pan face and notes to be distorted. <u>Re-attaching the skirt will not restore the working G-Pan to its original state.</u>

***Note**: I was careful to use the 'working G-Pan' in the above description because on the 'patented G-Pan' something else seems to take place which allows the skirt to be removed and re-attached at the owner's choosing! It is easy to see that this is possible only if there are no compressive stresses! But the patent states that the notes are kept under' tension!' So is it then possible, with this 'tension' to remove and replace the skirt at will? The answer is simple. Since it is physically impossible to keep the notes under tension as the patent requires, the question is without merit!*

Figure 17.1, for simplicity, does not show the notes but here is where the collective genius of these Steelpan makers is revealed; they do not complete this stable pan face in isolation—***they erect the notes***. *Erect* is the operative word here because after marking the boundaries of the (traditional) notes they add the grooves (if required) then peen along the marks so as to further indent those areas. During this process as the marked areas are indented the notes are seen to rise out of the pan face. This is the correct method both practically and theoretically because this allows the internote areas to be further work hardened while the note areas remain relatively more ductile and of lower stiffness. *Since hammer-peening work-hardens the material, the note areas are surrounded (bounded) by the stiffer internote.* We need not go through the whole process which is covered in other sections of this work. **This is good structural engineering put into practice by the traditional pan makers**. For this they score high on my *'technical literacy'* chart!

After the entire process, the pan maker has produced a pan face with tuned notes under compression from the surrounding internote areas (assisted by the grooves or bores if used). This sub-system, kept under a compressive stress distribution (field), is still being held in check by the hoop stress provided by the chime and skirt. Aspects of the Pan Jumbie on the notes were discussed in Section 3.11.

Note: Using tension in the manner described in the claims and details of the patent, it is impossible to construct, for the G-Pan, a consistent stress diagram corresponding to Figure 17.1.

17.20 The Pan Jumbie and Non-local Effects on the Pan Face

On a tuned pan with its notes properly blocked, except in the case of Marshall pairs, the excitations on a sounding note are well localized or confined to the area of the true note. In the case of the Marshall Pairs, each Pair must be treated as a single, blocked system. However, as explained in Section 17.19 and earlier Sections of this book, distorting or cutting the skirt will produce changes to the stress fields depicted in Figure 17.1 which results in distortions to the surfaces of the notes, changes in note frequencies and changes in tonality. This means that the state of a note is subject not only to the conditions set up locally by shaping and tuning of that particular note but is dependent also on the activities (stress changes) occurring non-locally or remotely. When for example, the pan is being tuned, the tuner must return repeatedly to retune notes already brought close to the tuned state when remote notes on the same pan face are being tuned. The Pan Jumbie or Stress Fields shown in Figure 17.1 allow remote areas on the pan (notes, internote, chime and skirt) to become linked. While pan makers and tuners of the instrument are aware of this non-local effect, especially during tuning, the Pan Jumbie is permanent and it continues to control the static state and the dynamic performance of the pan after tuning and throughout the life of the instrument. This is the ubiquitous nature of the Pan Jumbie. <u>It is this *entrenched* characteristic of the Stress Fields that gave me cause to re-name the 'Pan Jumbie', the 'Ubiquitous Pan Jumbie' — it never seems to go away, it 'possesses' the pan.</u> These stress fields are influenced by changes in temperature and respond to externally applied loading or distortions made to any part of the instrument.

17.21 Removing the Skirt is Folly

Take a look at Figure 17.1 and you will see that **if the skirt is removed** (as [0052], {7; 55 - 58} would like to have it), **the skirt takes with it all the hoop stress it provided**! The shape of the skirt, chime and pan face will immediately be altered. This is what buckling is all about (see Section 2.17). If you have an old tenor to spare try cutting off the skirt! Do not start by cutting from the bottom of the skirt, along the length of the skirt then up to the chime. Do all the cutting right around the top of the skirt where it meets the chime. (*Do not use a pair of shears for this, use a rotary cutting tool. The 'shearing' action of the pair of shears will introduce distortions of its own.*) Then place the pan face with chime to rest on a flat surface, chime facing downward. Do the same with the skirt, chime end facing downward. You will find that neither of these sections rest with all points touching the flat surface. If you now try to fit the pan face and chime back unto the skirt, they don't match! This is the problem on the G-Pan with removable skirt where the skirt is not cut off, it is unbolted or unclamped!

If the skirt on the finished pan is cut in any way the hoop stress distribution is modified and the notes are shifted in frequency. If the cut-off is severe the system may buckle. Our pan makers knowing this would never have conceived the idea of taking off the skirt for reassembly later! ***They are scientists yes but not mad scientists***!

To repeat my earlier caution (see Section 17.2), 'it is wrong to say that a G-Pan is a steelpan with removable skirt.' **A steelpan**

with removable skirt does not exist. Each time a G-Pan has its skirt removed, the notes are transformed into a set of notes with new frequencies! Don't think for a moment that on the G-Pan, if you tighten the clamps the second time the same way you did the first time, the notes would automatically be back in tune. In pan maker's idiom, the Pan Jumbie does not operate that way. When the skirt is replaced, and the clamps tightened, the 'new instrument' is not the same as the 'original instrument' and it now has a 'New Pan Jumbie' or new and different stress fields. This series of transformations will cause the instrument, described as a 'tuned instrument,' to lose this defining characteristic. That the *patented* G-Pan can do this while remaining tuned is a mystery to me and science. *The Pan Jumbie has a ready scientific explanation but this 'skirt changing idea' has none.* Readers can now fully understand why I said that the G-Pan of the patent is not a Steelpan. It should now be equally clear why a *working* G-Pan is not equivalent to the patented G-Pan. **In addition a working G-Pan can only be one with a fixed skirt! But then we have made a full circle, back to the traditional S-Pan!**

17.22 A Host of Pan Jumbies

One counter argument I expect to come from the G-Pan camp is that the G-Pan has no Pan Jumbie; they would say that this Pan Jumbie is just 'old hat,' 'folklore' and 'mumbo jumbo!' I shall argue my case in the pan makers' idiom without making any reference to 'internal stresses.'

The fact is that dismantling and reassembling the skirt on the G-Pan for whatever reason generates a host of Pan Jumbies, all different. Barring the impossibility of building anything that is fully consistent with the patent requirements, readers would find the following experiment very exciting. If the reader wishes to test or search for the ubiquitous Pan Jumbie which according to the G-Pan camp (I am assuming) is really the 'elusive' Pan Jumbie, the best approach is to use a G-Pan with removable skirt. Or you can perform a 'one shot' experiment by removing the skirt on your traditional pan. If on a G-Pan, there are no Pan Jumbies or the *same* Pan Jumbie always occupy a given pair of pan face and skirt whether in the assembled or disassembled state then once tuned in the assembled state, the G-Pan with its skirt removed can still be played with all the notes remaining musically correct as they were before skirt removal. However, if there is a Pan Jumbie on a tuned, assembled G-Pan and the skirt is removed, all the notes would go off-tune. The *new* Pan Jumbie will see to this! When the G-Pan is reassembled these notes will still be off-tune but not as they were on the disassembled instrument and certainly different from the originally tuned state. A *third* Pan Jumbie has replaced the earlier ones! Only on the G-Pan can one find a host of Pan Jumbies if Pan Jumbies exist. If Pan Jumbies do not exist then G-Pan owners can play their G-Pans without the extra weight of the skirt in practice as well as in concert! G-Pan owners can easily perform these experiments but rather than agreeing with me that the Pan Jumbie does in fact exist, they more likely would say that their beloved 'tension' has changed with the skirt removal and replacement and if they do, then they would be contradicting the patent which requires that no such changes occur!

By replacing the notation 'Pan Jumbie' with the scientific notation 'Stress Field,' the reader, from any camp, can get an equivalent and equally true description in the *science lingo*.

17.23 A Victim of its Own Complexity

In attempting to include in the patent *'everything under the Sun'* the G-Pan has been made *a victim of its own complexity*. Some patent writers try to do this in order to cover as many possible designs as possible. This is risky business because some or all of the designs may be impossible to implement. How can these G-Pans with multi-tube skirts, dismantled or not, be easier to transport than the S-Pan? In the dismantled form, 'top' and 'skirt,' each G-pan has to be reassembled with its exact mate (with new gaskets) and bolted together with the torque specified for each bolt spaced 5 cm all around the perimeter of the pan (see [0200], {39: 36 – 40}) or, with some form of metal strap acting as a 'belt' to keep the skirt from falling off! All this, with a tuner nearby! Even with the tuner, how will tuning be possible with the multi-tube rear already bolted up?

On the *'secondary notes'* or *'side notes'* (both are my terminologies) described in [0215], {41; 17 – 26} and Sheet 9 of the patent, how are they expected to work? These 'secondary notes' are formed on the skirt or rear attachment. The type of note-skirt interaction that this arrangement involves received full treatment in my original 1997 paper and in Chapter 5 of this book. By purposely putting tuned elements, 'notes' or 'reeds,' on the skirt, the dynamics of the *primary notes* on the pan face are destroyed. When reeds are used, the higher natural modes of the reeds will be excited producing complex discordant tones. These 'secondary notes' cannot be properly blocked. They serve first to rob the primary notes of vibrational energy then, by controlling their dynamics cause the primary notes to vibrate at the frequencies of the poorly tuned secondary notes! *I don't believe the inventor actually tried these attachments! Experience, that good teacher, teaches us the lesson that these things don't work on a musical instrument; certainly not on a tuned instrument of class!* To further complicate matters Sheet 9 shows these side notes formed on one of those 'ill fated' removable skirt (rear attachment) designs that are subjected to stress variations by the mounting-un-mounting or clamp-tightening procedures! These side notes cannot remain tuned! But it doesn't matter anyway!

If the G-Pan was named differently, not containing the word 'Pan,' say for example the 'G-Drum,' then there would be no need for me to go into any discussion on it here — for clearly, its dependence on tension and its classification as some form of a drum, really makes it something else. I ask its Owner, is it?

Before I leave this subject, I should emphasize the following (the list is long but it could have been longer if I had touched on each and every error and misrepresentation of the Steelpan made in the patent document):

1) The Steelpan is a musical instrument so any truly significant improvement on the Pan must express itself in the sound it produces — after all, that is what we get from it. **The claim 'significant improvement' to the traditional art is the linchpin of the entire G-Pan concept.** If the working G-Pan has been successful then, by now, it should be a 'rush to see' or rather, 'rush to hear' attraction. I work at home so I am not always aware of the clamor out there!

2) What comments have I received? Well there have been a number of not-too-complimentary remarks made but as in all matters concerning Pan, I prefer that you, the readers, hear only from the experts or the masters. I heard the following brief comments from two reputable tuners: (i) there are problems with the preparation for tuning on the G-Soprano and Second-pan; (ii) the only good G-Pan is the G-Bass! Although these comments are in full agreement with my own expectations, based on the patent information, I prefer not to add to the views of these two tuners; as coming from the masters, I am inclined to agree! But if readers insist that I comment on these views, please refer to '*shoddy preparation*' in Section 17.17 and the comparison I made between 'press forming' and the traditional 'hammer peening' method in Sections 9.8 and 12.19, all in this book.

3) My criticism of the G-Pan is based on the patent but it is hard to see how the real test which is practical and musical can be performed because **the G-Pan cannot work as patented**. What will be tested is something not covered by the patent. **One cannot build a G-Pan that works (in the manner of a Steelpan) by following <u>to a rule</u>, the prescription(s) in the patent! Therefore one may rightly ask; 'exactly what is really protected by the G-Pan Patent?'** <u>The patent Owner must take this seriously because of copyright implications.</u>

4) With pipe resonators included, the sound of the G-Pan moves closer to that of the Xylophone or Marimba making it unsuitable as a direct substitute for the S-Pan. With the Marimba-like or Xylophone-like construction in circular form as specified in the patent, the G-Pan <u>cannot</u> carry the 'originality' and 'uniqueness' that the Steelpan enjoys. The Steelpan is the National Instrument of Trinidad and Tobago, totally indigenous, <u>with nothing borrowed</u>. *As a point of interest the Marimba is the National Instrument of Guatemala — merging the two instruments seems to me to be a step towards some sort of confederation!*

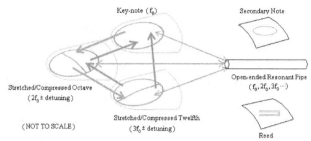

Fig. 17.2. Energy exchanges on a pan note (the Primary Note) fitted with a pipe resonator. Compare with Figure 14.38. Also shown are other skirt attachments, Secondary Note and Reed. These attachments couple linearly to the primary note.

But why do I find it hard to recommend pipe resonators on the pan? Take a look at Figure 17.2 which shows a pan note working in combination with a nearby open-ended resonant pipe. Compare this Figure to Figure 14.38. Observe the energy exchanges taking place among the key-note, octave, twelfth and the pipe. As required, the octave and twelfth are stretched or compressed so that they do not correspond to harmonics of the key-note. With fundamental f_0 as on the key-note, the upper resonant frequencies of the pipe are harmonically related, $2f_0$, $3f_0$, etc. To maintain standing waves in the pipe at these frequencies, energy must be exchanged with the corresponding partials on the primary note. If the coupling is weak, the note frequencies are only mildly affected, but then the pipe serves no purpose other than to function as a sink for energy loss from the tuned partials. If the coupling is sufficiently strong to make the pipe effective then in addition to having the frequencies of the upper partials $2f_0 \pm detuning$ and $3f_0 \pm detuning$ <u>pulled towards</u> $2f_0$ and $3f_0$ respectively, the natural process of *mode confinement of the tuned partials on the note is negatively affected*. Using multiple pipes on each note is not a solution. All in all, tonality (frequency and amplitude modulations) and tone duration will suffer because the controlling primary key-note must share its energy with the attached pipe thereby robbing the higher pan note partials of energy. If there is any persistence it will be due to the air resonating in the

pipe without the true pan-like tonal characteristics and at pitches different to the true detuned partials. The tones will start with those formed by the true note, enter into a mixed state with pipe resonances and end with pipe resonances. **On the Pan, non-linear mode confinement is sacrosanct!**
Note: I should point out that the attached pipe functions in the same manner as secondary notes formed on the skirt or the attached reeds mentioned in the patent. **To this list one can add a loose chime; they all impact negatively on tonality.**

5) With all the claims of tension and tensile stresses used in accomplishing the workings of the G-Pan, this instrument has to be strongly susceptible to Stress Corrosion Cracking (SCC) and other negative effects (see Sections 2.18 to 2.21). A vulnerable section is the inner bowl of the soprano which, according to patent claims, is chemically treated and under tension (see [0160]). This is the right prescription for SCC, although I cannot see how these tensile stresses are applied and maintained.

6) Now, in defense of the panists I have this to say: The use of note covers in combination with stick tips of smaller than normal tip radius or formed from harder material, does not provide the required *wavelength band-limiting* demanded by the outer notes. It is not sufficient to look only at the contact-time. The conditions to be satisfied by the *generalized wavelengths* must also be addressed. This information was readily available to the patent writer as far back as 1996 and 2000 in references contained in the *Proceedings of the First International Conference on the Science and Technology of the Steelpan (2000).*

A technique sometimes used on the Bass Drum (in Italian, the *cassa grande*) is to cover the drum head thereby muffling it to create a mysterious sound. This is not the purpose of the note covers on the G-Pan but it certainly introduces some amount of muffling.

The sacrifice that the covered notes on the G-Pan must make in order to claim an extension of range further into the Marginal Zone is not worth it. Also sacrificed along with the covered notes is the freedom of the panists by having their hand action so seriously restricted.

- It is a serious handicap to play a covered then an uncovered note with the rapidity, precision and especially the finesse required by the tenor (soprano) panists.
- *This could kill the **nuances of touch!***
- How can the G-Pan makers ignore the endless shades and nuances that lie between piano level and forte level for it is here that the art of the panist is distinguished! Note covers, like a mute, adversely affect this range.
- With the lossy note covers in use, it cannot be said that the stick tip is fashioned to '*optimize the tones*' — a panist has to take a good pair of sticks and accomplish his optimization *dynamically*. **A pair of sticks does not a panist make!!**

7) With all the difficulties that I see with the G-Pan in the form described in the patent, I cannot go along with the forceful claim '*significantly improves upon traditional acoustic steelpan prior art.*'

8) ***If a working G-Pan is in existence then it does not conform to the claims of the patent! Technically, it is not a G-Pan for the simple reason that the G-Pan cannot work as patented!***

9) I expect to find among my readers, those who may say that I have gone too far with the Pan Jumbie and that the pan makers could never have conceived anything as deep as Figure 17.1 — ***that's the 'illiteracy' mind-set.*** But which is deeper, the Pan Jumbie or Figure 17.1? Readers may well divide themselves on this question but as they do, I must inform them that among traditional pan makers, Master Tuner and Pan Maker Bertie Marshall got the closest to discovering the forces depicted in Figure 17.1. I hold all pan makers and tuners in Bertie's echelon, the few that there are, in very high regard.

- *The 'traditional pan makers' have tried in their idiom, to express important physical concepts which* may not have been couched antiseptically in the precise language of modern science but their very expressions have added richness to their ideas. ***It is the notion not the notation that should concern us.***

10) It is hard to see how they could have made progress without agreeing that the pan appears to be endowed with an unseen but certainly observed ability to control the structure even to change the settings which they, as pan makers, try to impose upon the instrument. They communicated this notion through the concept of the Pan Jumbie; *communication is the key to progress.* Anyone with good pan making experience can certainly vouch for the pan in this regard. (The precise physical and mathematical description for this as it applies specifically to the notes, is given in Chapter 3).

- ***The pan makers' Pan Jumbie <u>proves</u> that the Pan is not a drum!***

11) No one should disparage the Steelpan makers for their colloquialism which in most cases, I find more to the point. For example, their word 'flapping' better describes the localized compression-induced 'buckling' (the technical term) observed during the tuning process! The pan makers' word 'flapping' describes the phenomenon that occurs when compressive stresses have reduced the stiffness of the affected area on the note to zero so it flaps around with the slightest touch. It is fascinating to watch! Every student of Pan should get the opportunity to observe this phenomenon. If you see it and still remain unconvinced then; Hello! Knock! Knock! Are you there? A piece of solid steel has been reduced to flapping like the pages of the book in your hand!! From this one can see that the terminology 'flapping' for this direct physical manifestation of compressive stresses on the steelpan is indeed apposite.

12) As an advice to the G-Pan patent Owner, **the notion that tension reigns supreme on the G-Pan (or Pan in general) must be abandoned. The occurrence of**

flapping (a term found in the pan makers' idiom), a phenomenon induced by compressive stresses (an aspect of the Pan Jumbie in pan makers' idiom), proves this notion wrong. At the stage of sophistication that we have arrived at now with the Steelpan, where we have correctly identified the nature of the forces and stresses on the instrument, this change should not be difficult. In the 1990s I made this known to the scientific community and pan makers especially. If the typist employed to write the patent document were to claim that the word-processor 'find-replace' operation was intended to be used locally on the words 'compression' and 'tension' and by accident the operation was performed globally, one could not buy that because of the context.

13) *In more prosaic terms, one must abandon the 'common-sense' notion that since stretching (tension) increases the frequencies of strings it can be imported 'lock, stock and barrel' into the workings of the steelpan. This same error of a surface under tension having been similarly imported from the acoustic drum into the workings of the steelpan has led to the erroneous conclusion that the steelpan is a drum! This 'Pro-Drum' movement or concept has no factual basis, is a terrible irritation, and if left in place will do great harm to the musical acceptance of the steelpan. It leads students of Pan in the wrong direction.*

14) In Items (9 – 13) I have used the common language, the idiom, of the pan maker to show that the steelpan is not a drum nor does it operate under tension. I take no credit for this. All credit goes to the pan makers from the 1930s onward. They knew it! That is the reason why they gave the instrument a name that distinguishes it from all other musical instruments — the Steelpan.

15) Even after all the 'Rum and Coca-Cola' of the 1940s to early 60s some (particularly in the USA) still continue with the 'steel drum' (now re-named 'steelpan drum') description started by the American tourists; *at least the Rum should have worn off by now*!! **I believe there is a more sober position to be taken!**

16) In the patent there are numerous instances where the oxymoron 'steelpan drum' is used and just as often one sees the use of the principles of the drum applied to the notes. For example there is much confusion in detail [0104], {27; 56 – 59} where despite the fact that with the steelpan notes the frequency increases with note thickness, the opposite seems to be assumed. The problem clearly arises from the use of *'mass per unit area'*, a quantity appropriate for the description of the drum membrane (skin) as the detail explicitly states:

'[0104].... the use of thicker blanks facilitates the suppression [of] high pitched overtones due to the higher mass per unit area. The latter also tends to minimize note frequency modulation incurred by structural flexure of the entire drum.'

For a given note on the pan, if all parameters remain constant while the thickness of the material increases, the frequency of the vibrating note increases. I believe the patent writer, expecting the drum concepts to work on the pan, has been misled by the misinterpretation of two facts; (1) on the Steelpan tenor for example, the pan face is thinner in the middle where the higher notes are located than at the outer areas where the lower notes are located; (2) the pan face on the tuned bass with its low notes is thicker than the tenor pan face with its higher notes. This may appear to contradict my opening statement on the relationship between frequency and thickness for the pan but it seems consistent with the drum. Again, if one uses drum ideas one will make wrong conclusions. But let me explain to the reader from the pan perspective.

On the Steelpan, the sinking process on the high-end pans is one that produces a middle area that is stiffer (by more work hardening) than the outer area — higher stiffness relates directly to higher note frequencies. To achieve this, the middle area is indented to greater depth by extra hammer peening resulting in a smaller thickness — not so much to be thinner as to be stiffer. Let me dispel any notion of tension here (as the patent would have you believe), this increase stiffness is not due to tensional stress imposed on the material. Tension is used or applied only during hammer impacts to put the material into a state of plastification in order for it to retain the indented shape. Once shaped you don't have to keep striking the indented material with the hammer (that is apply tension) to keep it in shape (readers know this). The extra work hardening of the middle section is good for the notes located there because the damping capacity is reduced (see Section 14.12). In the 'burning' process that follows, the pan maker must be careful not to overheat the middle section thereby removing the beneficial effects of work hardening (see Chapter 2). If this mistake is made the middle notes cannot be tuned! On the bass there is less sinking resulting in a thicker finished material after peening. But the Pan makers are smart. They know that they can get low notes easily on the bass with thinner material (some lazy ones do take this easier route), but ECEG, *Easy Come Easy Go*; when played by stick impacts these thin notes do not last long in the tuned state and very readily produce distorted sounds when played intensely, as all bass must be played at times. By this we see that there are good reasons why things are done as they are on the pan; quite the opposite to what one should expect for a drum. In all this, my opening statement in the previous paragraph still remains valid.

With the drum membrane, as the 'mass per unit area' increases, the membrane frequency decreases. The patent writer wants this to happen on the pan especially on the bass with its thicker notes! *This is a gross error. That 'higher mass per unit area' (or higher areal density) minimizes flexure is also in error as it stands.* This is inexcusable. What the writer is looking for with respect to the flexure of the drum are geometrical ratios for example the ratio of the diameter of the cylindrical drum to the thickness of the material. If he/she is concerned with flexure under its own weight then both the mass density of the material and the geometric ratios are needed. For example consider our soda can models of Section 2.13, which are quite rigid in their normal sizes. Try scaling this up to a large can x100 in diameter and length while keeping the thickness constant. The areal density of the material is constant but the super large can will be very flimsy and wobbly! We need to resist flexure, so following the patent we decide to increase the areal density (mass per unit area) by making the super-can out of lead! This will not resist flexure as the patent claims: in fact the whole lead super-can may buckle under its own weight(!) 'mass per unit area' is not it!

What does 'mass per unit area' really represent on the membrane of a drum or on the thin sheets of steel that goes into forming a pan note? For an area A of membrane or sheet steel of thickness h and density ρ, the mass is $\rho A h$. Dividing by the area A gives the 'mass per unit area' ρh. Now, for the steel material forming a pan note the density ρ is essentially the same for all pans and all notes so by speaking of differences in 'mass per unit area' one is really speaking about differences in thickness h. Rather than focusing only on thickness the patent writer switches over to 'mass per unit area' with the claim that *'higher mass per unit area' minimizes flexure*. By doing this the writer has opened up a 'can of worms' all in an attempt to make use of the drum (membrane) ideas. This is unfortunate.

- Again I give another of my simple tests for the readers. Take a sheet of quarto size paper (approx. $8.5'' \times 11''$). Hold it along one of the shorter edges and try to set it horizontally, in air, without it bending over. It's hard, almost impossible; you will have to curl the sheet around to make it work. Now fold the sheet over and over to form ½-inch pleats running along the length of the paper. Now try setting the pleated sheet horizontally by holding it along the short edge. It's easy. But it is not so easy if you hold it along the long edge; it bends over! What you have verified is that structural rigidity (against flexure) depends on geometrical structure. You will also discover that the pleated (corrugated) sheet possesses two degrees of bending stiffness (one high, the other low) measured at right angles to each other. Now the 'mass per unit area' remained constant in all your tests up to now, so get a heavier sheet of paper (greater mass per unit area) and a lighter sheet like 'tracing paper' (smaller mass per unit area), both of quarto size. Repeat the tests. You will find <u>the same difficulty</u> keeping the (new) flat sheets horizontal but you also find that it works when pleated. Draw your final conclusions.

- o This is the principle under which corrugated galvanize sheets used as a roofing material, acquire their flexural rigidity.
- o This is the principle under which the rolling hoops on the drums used as the rawform for steelpans impart flexural rigidity to the pan skirts.
- o ***This is also the principle by which the grooves act as stiffeners on the internote — in this case, a single line of corrugation along the boundary of the traditional note..***

17) In the 'drum' viewpoint, there is no place or use for grooves. Grooves of the type formed on the pan face can support compressive stresses, the drum membrane cannot.

- Here is another simple experiment for the reader it's as low-cost as you can get: You ought to be wearing either a shirt or a blouse made of a material (cloth) which has the properties of a membrane; it can be easily laid flat and be stretched. Now, with both hands grab your shirt or blouse then put it under tension by stretching it. It stretches just fine. Now without releasing your shirt or blouse, try to compress it by reversing the direction of the forces exerted by your hands. Did it compress or did it just become loose and all crumpled up? Becoming loose or crumpled up means that your shirt or blouse cannot support compression. The same is true for the drum skin. In the drum viewpoint, the grooves are mere markings, cosmetic markings, like the color designs or patterns on your shirt or blouse; they do not provide or support compressive stresses! It is easy to see how one can be misled in the framework of the drum and to dismiss the grooves as done in the patent.

18) **The drum is NOT a simplified version of a steelpan to any level of approximation whatsoever.**

19) **The idea of removable skirts should also be abandoned entirely.** This of course will leave the G-Pan in a 'stripped-down' form but as I see it anyway, this 'changing skirt' idea is just bad cosmetics, not as fashionable as one might have thought. If one makes removable, light skirt endings that do not interfere with the hoop stress and acoustic coupling with the notes then these are not just cosmetic, they are literally 'frills.' On the other hand, if they are acoustically effective they become an integral part of the note dynamics in which case their removal and replacement <u>destroys</u> the note setting — a non-viable proposition for a musical instrument. Just in case one should try to compare this idea to the use of a removable mute by a trumpeter (or violinist), it should be pointed out that a trumpeter (or violinist) can compensate by changing the pitch of his tones '*ex tempore*' or '*on the fly*,' a panist cannot!

20) The outer bowl (with the middle cutout, see [0156], {34; 18 -23}) of the 2-bowl structure used on the pan face of the soprano G-Pan with removable rear attachment **is structurally unsound**. The pan face of the soprano G-Pan is subject more so than the S-Pan tenor to flexural-torsional-buckling (see Chapter 2 on 'Tin-Can experiments on a budget'). The use of 'high quality' steel or other metals and alloys will not resolve this type of structural problem (in Section 2.13 the reader has already tested this out by using aluminum and steel cans). The soprano G-Pan is very fragile as a result of this poor design. This fragility will play itself out in the inability of the soprano (with cutout) to remain in the tuned state. There will be greater risks of buckling on this pan during

handling and transportation especially when the rear attachment is removed. The inner bowl and outer bowl are held together with <u>double-sided tape(!)</u> (see [0156]) which can hardly be relied upon to improve rigidity. On the face of it, it does appear to be a wobbly structure. With the buckling possibility looming, the 2-bowl design therefore defeats the goal of easy transportation by skirt removal. *This is a classic case of over-design without the required 'engineering requirement' of <u>model testing</u> being performed for a wide range of situations to which the real G-Pan will be subjected in practice* (see 'Conclusion' at the end of this Section).

21) There is a serious dynamical problem that the inventor has overlooked in the use of this 2-bowl structure. The inner edges of the outer bowl and the outer edge of the inner bowl are *free edges*. At these free edges the transverse vibrations transmitted through the bowl from the note will be partially converted to longitudinal vibration (mode conversion, see Section 14.12.2). The double sided sticky tape will not significantly damp these longitudinal vibrations. These longitudinal modes are of high frequency and would produce annoying 'cymbal-like' tones. I know that Dynamat (by dissipating energy) can reduce this problem but why create the problem in the first place?

22) The very same torsional modes of vibration that the inventor appears to fear in a number of claims (claim #7), {48; 21 – 25} and details ([0036], {5; 33 – 46} and [0037], {5; 47 – 55}) for example have been unwittingly introduced (another 'goof') on the G-Pan by the 2-bowl cutout design. This does not make good sense and certainly does not represent good engineering.

It must be pointed out that in [0037], the claim;

'The consequent fluctuating shape distortion of the playing surface on the traditional steelpan drum due to the torsion mode of vibration is largely responsible for the changes in note pitch frequency [which] at times occur, particularly on the notes closest to the edge of the playing surface, and therefore negatively affects note clarity and accuracy'

is completely wrong.

The terminology 'traditional steelpan drum' used only in the patent, is new, so the 'drum instrument' in question cannot be 'traditional'! The torsional modes of skirt and pan face vibration require considerable energy for their excitation. To induce torsional modes on the skirt and chime that will result in 'twisting' pan face distortions will require the action of an externally applied torque of considerable magnitude applied to the pan-face-chime-skirt system for a short period of time. **Pan stick impacts applied to the notes are not capable of doing this! This suggestion is very unphysical and erroneous!** Stick impacts can however excite low-level transverse (non-torsional) skirt vibrations that may produce, in turn, low level modulations on the note (see Chapter 5). The claim in [0037] is inconsistent with theoretical and good, reliable, experimental data; it represents a misidentification of the causes of frequency (and amplitude) modulations that are naturally produced on the steelpan. The mechanisms that are largely responsible for changes or modulations in note pitch are the non-linear modal interactions. These modulations do not *'negatively affect note clarity and accuracy'* but are sought after by tuners, panists and listeners and are the underlying properties that give steelpan tones their beauty and identity. *It is a pity that the G-Pan patent writer sees otherwise! But did I not say that the G-Pan is not a Steelpan?*

23) Readers should take a look at the drawing in Figure 1 on Sheet 1 of the patent. Observe the twelve relatively slender notes at the center. The $5/4^{ths}$- Law tells us that it would be impossible to tune these notes. One would find the boundaries of these slender 'traditional notes' too restrictive for the setting up of the right conditions for tuning in the *key-note-octave-twelfth* format. Has anyone claimed success in tuning these notes? It is much harder than walking on water!! At least with water (without the faith) one can wait for it to freeze over!

24) It is physically impossible for the inner bowl with its free outer edge to be in a state of tension so the first requirement of the patent cannot be met. If you will permit me to use the same piano or guitar string employed in the patent to introduce, by analogy, tension on the G-Pan then the inner bowl with its free outer edge is like the string lying flat on a table with both its ends free! These two free systems are <u>not</u> under tension! So let us place the inner bowl (which is easily detached from the sticky tape) of the soprano on the same table as the string and try to play them! Nothing comes out from the string, which is not surprising, but when played with a stick by striking anywhere on the surface, the bowl sounds like a cymbal or gong or any one of the other idiophones found in the '*engine room*' of the traditional steelband. *In the engine room one finds the cymbals, gongs, scratchers and the 'iron', all idiophones.* Therefore, the G-Soprano in its patent design state, must settle for something less than what we normally associate with the Steelpan!

25) On a musical instrument there are a number of modalities for energy loss — acoustical radiation is just one of them. *The note covers used on the G-Pan do not freely levitate themselves over the outer notes. Any part of the note covers resting on the vibrating notes, that takes part in the vibration (induced by contact) will be a source of damping and will introduce random mass loading of the note.* Therefore, if additional losses are introduced such as through the use of note covers which act as dampers during the stick impact and while the note is sounding, the overall efficiency of the instrument as a source of acoustical radiation is reduced. *Note covers take away energy from the acoustical radiation, that's the bottom line!*

26) How are we to interpret [0165], {35; 34 – 40}? It appears to read like physics but it is not!

'[0165], {35; 34 – 40} The use of thinner material to form the secondary bowl ... facilitates a modest increase in note size as the mass of the note on the traditional instrument can now be distributed over a larger area. On

this basis of mass conservation, a reduction in thickness by a factor k, would require an increase in area on the secondary bowl ... by the same factor k and a corresponding increase by $\sqrt{k}$ in any note dimension.'

There is a fallacy here! The disproof of this fallacy is almost as brief as the fallacy itself but for the sake of the readers I am obliged to explain this matter very thoroughly. By referencing the '*note on the traditional instrument*' and using the definite statement '*would require,*' the implication is that something on the traditional note other than mass is to be preserved. This can only be the frequency (although the word 'frequency' was not used) otherwise there would be no connection with what follows a few lines later about this [0165] facilitating '*the creation of a full octave of notes on the G-Soprano*' (see [0167], {35, 45 – 51}). What else does '*a full octave of notes*' mean other than notes of well defined frequencies? If frequency (pitch) was not on the agenda then [0165] is left hanging; doing nothing else than conserving mass without a purpose as far as the notes are concerned and in which case it serves no real purpose on the instrument.

It cannot be physics (or engineering) that is used here at all! First of all, on the traditional instrument, the frequency (f) of a note is directly proportional to the note thickness (h) and inversely proportional to the note area (A) and I am using the true note here not the 'traditional note' as used throughout the patent. Thus one has the simple relation $f \propto h/A$ (the symbol $\propto$ means 'proportional to'); so if as in [0165] the thickness is <u>reduced</u> by a factor k and the area is <u>increased</u> by the same factor k, then, contrary to what [0165] implies, the frequency is <u>reduced</u> by a factor k^2. The mass of the true note which is proportional to the product hA remains unchanged but this 'conservation' <u>has nothing to do with the note frequency</u> as shown by the very fact that the frequency is <u>reduced</u>. [0165] gets this wrong! No 'funny' math can be used to show that mass conservation is operative in note tuning! If the type of 'math' used in [0165] is used in the engineering designs of the G-Pan then I can only feel sorry for those involved! By the careful wording of [0165] one cannot use the excuse of a misplaced 'k' or square root sign $\sqrt{\ }$.

In [0165] one sees a misapplication of *the physics principle of mass conservation* to the tuning of notes. Let me state categorically: **The principle of conservation of mass plays no role (or 'basis') in the tuning of steelpan notes.** If it were applicable, as the patent claims, then the larger the area of the note for a given frequency, the thinner it must be in order to keep the mass constant (conserved). So the large notes on the G-Pan must be very thin indeed! This is what happens when you misapply a physical law. **One cannot take a law or principle and apply it willy-nilly!** *Is this principle applied in tuning all the notes on a G-Pan?*

For the reader's sake I must thoroughly clear up this 'mass conservation' matter so that it does not arise in the future. There are just three cases to consider:

- *Consider a pan which we label as 'P.' If P, having a certain mass, is initially in an 'untuned state' (with no notes corresponding to the musical scale), then, provided we do not drill holes, cut off or add material (by mass loading) or coat the pan, this mass will remain the same (is conserved) while P is being tuned and at the end, when it has been fully tuned. Therefore this 'mass conservation' has nothing to do with the musical state of the pan; it is just as irrelevant to tuning as the weight of the tuner!!*
- *In the patent, the word 'note' refers to the 'traditional note.' so one can also correctly say that the mass of each traditional note on P is independent of its state of tuning. Even if two traditional notes on the pan P require re-tuning and this is undertaken by a tuner different from the first and he decides to switch the positions of these two notes — which is permissible (see 'note placement' in Chapter 14) but much to the annoyance of the player or owner of the instrument — the mass of each re-tuned*

traditional note still remains unchanged (conserved) even though it is now set to a different pitch. From this it is clear that mass conservation plays no role in the tuning of a traditional note.

- To be precise, we must consider the 'true note' whenever we are addressing issues on tuning. **In the 'untuned state' there is no domain within the traditional note that can be defined as a 'true note.' This is what 'untuned' in the musical sense really means.** To illustrate this, take the following example; within an untuned traditional note there is no domain or true note defined as an $F_4^\sharp$, a G_3 or any other note on the scale. With this understanding we see that the mass of the 'true note' within an untuned 'traditional note' cannot be defined (**it does not exist**) — can one ask, what is the mass of the $F_4^\sharp$ note in the previous example where there is no $F_4^\sharp$ note? When that note is tuned to $F_4^\sharp$ however, the true note for $F_4^\sharp$ or its defining domain then exists (dynamically) with a mass well defined within that particular traditional note on that pan. If this note requires re-tuning and this is carried out by the same tuner or someone else, in the new tuned state, because of the large number of parameters involved, the domain defining the true note will very likely be different from the first and so will be the mass. The mass gained or lost is simply exchanged between the true note and the remainder of the traditional note. Even if the mass of the true note remained constant (an unlikely occurrence) during the re-tuning process, the domain could have shifted and changed shape within the traditional note area. Clearly, mass conservation plays no role in deciding the tuned state of a true note.

27) If the patented G-Pan is different and for that reason it is patented under the sub-class, Drums, and carries the name '*steelpan drum*,' then its full categorization is under the general category of (Unpitched) Percussion Instruments,

under the sub-category Membranophone, and as a sub-class, Drum;

(Unpitched) Percussion Instrument
Membranophone
Drum → **G-Pan, the Steelpan Drum** (patented)

What is very strange about this categorization is that the drum is an <u>unpitched percussion instrument</u> yet the G-Pan is said to be melodically tuned! This is the present categorization of the patented G-Pan, in which case, the use of 'Pan' in the name 'G-Pan' is inappropriate.

Meanwhile, the Steelpan or Pan, the National Instrument of the Republic of Trinidad and Tobago continues to fall in the general category of Pitched Percussion Instruments, under the sub-category of Idiophones, and as a sub-class, Shells;

Pitched Percussion Instrument
Idiophone
Shells → **Steelpan** (unpatented but in common use)

28) Patenting the G-Pan as a drum (steelpan drum) is certainly within the prerogative of the inventor. However, if one treats the Steelpan (not to be confused with the G-Pan) as a drum it would represent bad science and poor musical judgment. In the case before us, the G-Pan is defined and patented as a Drum. This choice has been questioned! The risk we face is that a defense for the patent can be set up by using the many types and variations of designs in the patent to transmogrify the G-Pan whenever the patent or a G-Pan type is criticized. This is not a workable way out because each type, defined in the patent, has its own set of problems.

29) While the patent speaks to an instrument, defined in the patent as the 'steelpan drum' some readers of the patent may fall into the trap of applying this grotesque depiction to the Steelpan. It will be disastrous for any reader of the patent to take the drawings on Sheet 9 (see [0215], (41;

17 – 26}), showing 'secondary notes' on a removable skirt as representing some new *'improvement on the traditional art'* of the Steelpan. In fact the design on Sheet 9 is in double jeopardy with its secondary notes on a removable skirt! The 'reeds' (see [0215]) that may be substituted for the 'secondary notes' on this G-Pan design will be found to be ***more problematic and destructive to tonality than a loose chime!*** I have simulated the design on Sheet 9 using tone generating techniques not discussed in this book by replacing skirt resonances first with 'secondary notes' and then, with 'reeds' even though I knew what to expect. The sounds were awful to put it lightly! Having said so much about the Pan Jumbie, if I were not so well informed, I should be afraid, literally scared out of my wits, to meet the real 'steelpan drum,' depicted on Sheet 9, at night! Fear will arise not from its 'manifestation' but from its 'voice!'

30) Having said all of the above, do I have any curative instructions for the patent writer or inventor? This is difficult to answer because ***it is not at all clear in the patent (certainly not to my mind) exactly what the inventor wants to invent!*** I say this because there are many designs in the patent; in them one can find contradictory details. For example, for fear of dissonance, statements are made against torsional oscillations but this is followed up by the inclusion of 2-bowl designs with their propensity for this mode of oscillation. In the patent, the resonant skirt vibrations which are said to plague the traditional Steelpan are first rejected but this rejection is closely followed by the total inclusion of the secondary resonant skirt notes in the design on Sheet 9. *Contradictions* are self destructive because one rejects what one accepts; like *circularities* (*'argumentum in circulo'*) where one assumes what one wants to prove, there is no cure. So what if the inventor has a change of mind and is now prepared to accept resonances and sympathetic vibrations on the skirt, will that make the design on Sheet 9 acceptable? Not at all: acceptability here is not a state of mind! The voice of the device on

Sheet 9 is not altered by one's state of mind although one's state of mind might be altered by the voice(!) (see Item (29) above); this voice is frighteningly non-musical! That's a fact! The reader is asked to look again at Section 5.5.5 where the note-skirt coupling on the $F_3^{\#}$ note on a particular double-second pan is discussed.

31) I have not discussed the errors in the order in which they appear in the patent nor have I selected only the worse.

Conclusion

Was it optimism that propelled this patent with all its errors into the public domain? *Optimism is an occupational hazard in scientific research.* As it stands, from a technical viewpoint based on all the issues in the patent including those not taken up in this critique, the patented device, by its description, is unworkable. From a musical viewpoint, I cannot see the described device being acceptable in any of the well defined categories of percussion instruments. I fail to see how it fell into the drum (membranophone) category!

The patented G-Pan has failed the 'fit checks' carried out in this Critique. To restore confidence to the program the Patent Owner should undertake a rigid program of computer and solid modeling to accurately represent the general and the most intricate design details of the patent. As part of this program, all that is incorrect must be discarded. I should hope that funding for the original program is still available but if the G-Pan is 'out of money,' I, being an 'out-of-pocket' pan researcher can only provide the help that comes from the pages of this book. *A wrong move here on any future program could put the Republic at risk by allowing our Pan superiority to atrophy to the point where it inflicts great harm on our traditional force of Pan Makers and Tuners. There is no doubt that the Republic has always been at the forefront of Pan Production and Innovation; we should keep it that way.*

1) **Writing strictly as a Citizen of the Republic, my last comments in defense of the Steelpan are addressed especially to the *People of the Republic of Trinidad and Tobago* and to the Patent *Assignee*.**

2) *If the G-Pan patent is intended to cover the Steelpan, the National Instrument, then we must ask ourselves the following questions; they are hard questions, maybe somewhat harsh, but they must be asked and answered:*
    - *(i) **Is this G-Pan patent, the best that we, the originators of the Steelpan, can come up with?***
    - *(ii) More seriously, why have we gone so far as to patent these wrong ideas and concepts on what others will certainly call our National Instrument?*
3) **It is not possible to improve something that is wrong! Nothing substantial can be built on wrong concepts — especially those that 'slip and slide' like the contradictions in the patent! I have read the following comment (paraphrased somewhat) made by someone with an interest in the patent: 'there is enough in there to cover the steelpan as well!' If this idea is widely held and one were to pretend that all is well because the Pan now seems to be covered by a patent, then I fear for the future of the instrument. I am more afraid of this than I am of the instrument on 'Sheet 9!'**
4) *The Nation must ensure that its children — in '**Pan in the Classroom**' or elsewhere — are properly and correctly instructed on the principles of operation and the categorization of their National Instrument.*
5) **The Steelpan, that Institution of Civic Pride and Accomplishment, symbolizes the ingenuity of a people who have done exceedingly well to give to the world a unique instrument, one of superb musical beauty.**
6) *The Steelpan — the National Instrument of the Republic of Trinidad and Tobago, the Institution, the national symbol of civic pride — demands the corrections to all incorrect references to it and its makers including the use of its name, that 'good name,' where it does not apply.*
7) **The Pan is to us, the People of the Republic of Trinidad and Tobago, no lesser a symbol of our status than the Belfries of Belgium and France are to Belgians and French.**

CHAPTER 18

EXOTIC EFFECTS ON THE STEELPAN — Jump Phenomenon, Hopf Bifurcation and Chaos

18.1 Excitation of the Non-Linear Steelpan Note System

I saved this Chapter on Exotic Effects for last because I expect that most readers will be primarily interested in the musical aspects of the Steelpan. While the final lines of the previous Chapter contain the words that are suitable for bringing a book of this kind to a fitting conclusion, at least for pan enthusiasts, I have to be fair to the Steelpan by giving it a chance to *'show itself off'* by demonstrating how superb an instrument it is. It 'shows off' each time it appears on stage but now it wants to *'go solo'* and to show what it is capable of when it is *'pushed'* to the limit.

This final Chapter presupposes a higher degree of mathematical maturity on the part of the reader than is required elsewhere in this book. If this Chapter were omitted from this book, then a very important aspect of the full dynamics of this remarkable instrument would be kept from the readers. It is my desire to share with my readers all that I know about this instrument so omission is not on the table!

Up to now we have been concerned only with the musical aspects of the steelpan. However, there was one exception found in Chapter 10 where Mode Locking was the subject — a sounding note makes only fleetingly short passages through this locked mode when conditions are right. But even there, in Chapter 10, we maintained the same means of excitation used in playing the instrument — stick impact. We have seen the richness of the note dynamics that results from the non-linear coupling of the tuned vibrational modes. In order to produce those sounds which we describe as musical, it is necessary to confine the surface displacements of the vibrating notes to relatively small amplitudes. The normal levels of stick excitation and the inherent losses of the excited note (which includes the acoustic radiation that we so desire) guarantee the proper operation expected of a percussion musical instrument. The short duration stick-note impacts produce tones that last for a short time around 1 second. All these stick-note excitations take place around a quiescent point (more generally, the *Quiescent State,* see Section 8.15.3) set by the tuner. This Quiescent State is a *stable state* consistent with the note surface at rest. To the panist, tuner and pan maker, the '*preferred*' quiescent state is known as the '*tuned state.*' The quiescent state is however subject to changes if the temperature of the instrument changes. These changes (see Chapter 9) are regarded as 'normal' and are usually acceptable if the temperature varies by just a few degrees. Now we ask the question; what happens when the note is excited continuously by an external harmonic (sinusoidal) force? Furthermore, we may also ask, what happens when the external forcing is great and the forcing frequency is varied around the resonant frequency of the note?

The answers to these questions take us into the realm of *Exotic Effects*! The underlying requirement for these effects to be observable is for the system to display non-linear dynamics. The steelpan is well endowed with these non-linearities. As discussed in Chapter 3 and elsewhere in this work, the non-linear coupling that exists between substructures on the instrument is the driving mechanism for *sympathetic pairs* (pairs consisting of key-note and octave, such as $F^{\#}_4$ - $F^{\#}_5$). We have also seen how non-linear mode coupling allows the partials to be frequency and amplitude modulated. But these are all *stable* excitations and are not the exotic effects we seek. We must go further by looking at the *unstable behavior* of the vibrating notes.

In this Chapter the *quasi-periodic* and *chaotic* dynamics of the thin, shallow, domed-shaped notes on the steelpan are investigated on the real steel instrument and by implementing the notes on (patented) electronic circuits. Some numerical experiments are also performed on a reduced form of these equations. The non-linear behavior of these mechanical structures has been discussed in the earlier Sections of this work. It is indeed remarkable that this musical instrument makes very effective use of the quadratic and cubic non-linearities of shells in the generation of its musical tones when excited by impact with a stick.

In Chapter 4, the vibration of the notes on the steelpan was reduced to the solution of a system of ordinary differential equations containing quadratic and cubic non-linear terms. The quadratic non-linearity together with internal (2:1) resonances have been shown by the present author in Achong (1996b) to be responsible for the *Jump phenomenon* and *Hopf bifurcations* observed on steelpan notes driven harmonically. These effects and the *Chaos* (Achong 1999c) that results from extreme forcing are the exotic effects that we now examine.

18.2 System Equations

For convenience, reference will be made to the existing equations of motion for the excited steelpan notes given in equation (4.2). In the main analysis to follow, only quadratic non-linearities are retained in these equations. An additional analysis involving both quadratic and (the weaker) cubic non-linearities will be included. Following the lead of the pan maker who tunes the frequencies of the normal modes in an 'almost harmonic' relation (for musical reasons), close (not necessarily exact) harmonicity $\omega_n \approx n\omega_1$ is assumed in the dynamical equations. Close harmonicity produces *internal resonances* and ensures energy coupling between modes. For regular, periodic vibrations, exact harmonicity produces the unpleasant pung tone.

18.2.1 Analysis of 2-Mode Systems (with 2:1 Resonances)

The notes on the properly tuned steelpan show strong or moderately strong quadratic coupling and much weaker cubic non-linearities. Whereas the musical aspects of the steelpan notes were previously studied under stick impact excitation, these notes are now studied under harmonic excitations of the form $f_1 \cos(\Omega \tau)$ with the forcing frequency Ω close to the natural frequency ω_1 of model. By neglecting the cubic terms, and introducing an order parameter ε, the 2-mode form of equation (4.2) can be analyzed using the method of multiple time-scales to yield the following set of equations (see Chapter 4 for details)

$$a_1' = -\mu_1 a_1 + (\alpha_{121}^*/4\omega_1)a_1 a_2 \sin\gamma_1 + f_1 \sin\gamma_2,$$

$$a_2' = -\mu_2 a_2 - (\alpha_{112}/4\omega_2)a_1^2 \sin\gamma_1,$$

$$\phi_1' = -(\alpha_{121}^*/4\omega_1)a_2 \cos\gamma_1 - \frac{f_1}{a_1}\cos\gamma_2,$$

$$\phi_2' = -(\alpha_{112}/4\omega_2)\frac{a_1^2}{a_2}\cos\gamma_1, \qquad (18.1\text{a-d})$$

$$\gamma_1 = \varepsilon\sigma_1\tau + \phi_2 - 2\phi_1, \quad \gamma_2 = \varepsilon\sigma_2\tau - \phi_1, \qquad (18.2\text{a, b})$$

where a_i (i = 1, 2) represent the amplitudes of the modal vibrations, ϕ_i (i = 1, 2) are the relative phases, f_1 is a normalized force magnitude, $\alpha^*_{12.1}$ (= $\alpha_{12,1} + \alpha_{21,1}$), σ_1 and σ_2 are detuning parameters defined according to

$$\omega_2 = 2\omega_1 + \varepsilon\sigma_1, \quad \Omega = \omega_1 + \varepsilon\sigma_2 \qquad (18.3\text{a,b})$$

with the prime (') denoting differentiation with respect to the 'slow time' $\tau_1 = \varepsilon\tau$.

In previous Chapters we have studied these equations strictly within the context of musical sounds generated by stick impacts on the pan notes. Now it is appropriate to show the scope of applicability of these equations on the steelpan and to understand the full structure of the instrument that is encoded in these equations.

- *Just as the sound of the musical instrument is beautiful, the structure encoded in the system equations is one of remarkable elegance. After all, the equations into which the structure is encoded are the defining equations of the Steelpan!*

18.3 Steady-State Periodic Orbits

Definitions:

Data on a vibrating pan note are usually acquired as velocity or displacement measurements. These data are normally converted from the raw continuous form into a sequence of 'points' or discrete values by sampling and digitizing for computer storage. The data to be analyzed are therefore in the form of *discrete-time series*. In order to make quantitative statements on these real data sets, a variety of analytical tools need to be introduced and a number of terms are required in our description of the vibrating note so we define these terms now.

> ***Orbit, Trajectory and Phase Space***: For a time series, the sequence of points (u_0, u_1, u_2, ...) is called the *orbit* or *trajectory*. The orbit is 'viewed' in *phase-space*. For example, if you tie a string to a ball and whirl it around in a circle the continuous path taken by the ball is its orbit or trajectory. In this example the orbit is viewed in ordinary space. In this case the phase-space is just the familiar ordinary 3-D space plus one more for the time dimension. You can, in our 'whirling ball' example also include other coordinates such as velocity and acceleration which are time-derivatives of the spatial coordinates. In general we can construct other systems, even purely mathematical ones or physical systems such as the vibrating note on a steelpan, where the 'motion' takes place in a real or in an abstract space which we call the phase-space. Phase Space is generally multi-dimensional even infinitely dimensional. A purely random process 'lives' in a phase space of infinite dimensions.

Flow: This is the trajectory drawn out in phase-space by the evolving system. It is the 'picture' represented in phase-space. The term 'flow' is also used to represent the evolution equation (the system equation) itself.

Limit Cycle: (i) A limit cycle is an *orbit* defined for all time t that is a closed loop. (ii) A limit cycle is an *attracting set* to which orbits or trajectories converge and upon which trajectories are *periodic*. For example consider the rings of the planet Saturn. These rings are limit cycles to which the circulating 'particles' converge to form regular ring patterns that have existed for millions of years.

Periodic Orbit: (i) An *orbit* is a limit cycle if and only if its solutions are *periodic*. (ii) *For a vector field G, G(t) is a periodic orbit if G(t +T) = G(t) for some smallest T > 0 called the primitive period of G.* For a time series (or map) f, u is a periodic point of f with primitive period p if $f_p(u) = u$ but $f_k(u) \neq u$ for k = 1, 2, …, p-1. For example the period of Earth's orbit around the Sun is 1 year because Earth returns to the same position (more or less) in space after one year — stated mathematically as E(t +1 year) = E(t). I said 'more or less' for two reasons; (i) the period is not exactly one year but we allow the 'error' to accumulate then make a correction every four years by adding an extra day to form a leap year. (ii) The Earth's trajectory is more complicated than just the regular orbits around the Sun. Earth is part of the Solar System that moves through our Milky Way Galaxy. The Milky Way, in turn, has its own motion among the Local Cluster of galaxies and the Local Cluster moves within the Universe as a whole. We live second by second, hour by hour without taking notice of all this complicated motion taking place. This example should make you aware of the fact that we do quite a lot of 'moving around' in our lifetime! Enjoy the ride!

Continuing with our description from Section 18.2.1, the closeness of the periodic excitation frequency Ω to the primary mode (mode1) of frequency ω_1 is measured by the detuning parameter σ_2 in (18.3b). The detuning of mode2 is measured by σ_1 in (18.3a). In the analysis, σ_2 is a variable frequency with σ_1 taking the role of a parameter. For a musical instrument such as the steelpan, one is usually interested in dynamics that are periodic (having some well defined frequency to which we associate the pitch of a note) but more general trajectories, even non-periodic ones are possible on the steelpan. Using (18.2a, b), (18.1a-d) can be written as

$$a_1' = -\mu_1 a_1 + \frac{\alpha_{121}^* a_1 a_2}{4\omega_1}\sin\gamma_1 + f_1 \sin\gamma_2,$$

$$a_2' = -\mu_2 a_2 - \frac{\alpha_{112} a_1^2}{4\omega_2}\sin\gamma_1,$$

$$\gamma_1' = \sigma_1 + \left(\frac{\alpha_{121}^* a_2}{2\omega_1} - \frac{\alpha_{112} a_1^2}{4\omega_2 a_2}\right)\cos\gamma_1 + \frac{2f_1}{a_1}\cos\gamma_2,$$

$$\gamma_2' = \sigma_2 + \frac{\alpha_{121}^* a_2}{4\omega_1}\cos\gamma_1 + \frac{f_1}{a_1}\cos\gamma_2. \qquad (18.4\text{a-d})$$

The system of n (= 4) first-order ordinary differential equations in (18.4) is of the general *Pfaffian form* (a differential form of degree 1), where the *2n-dimensional space* consisting of the possible values of $(a_1, a_1', a_2, a_2', \gamma_1, \gamma_1', \gamma_2, \gamma_2')$ is its *phase-space*.

One can seek periodic solutions corresponding to the steady state of (18.4) by *setting* $a_1' = 0 = a_2'$, $\gamma_1' = 0 = \gamma_2'$. From (18.5c) and (18.5d) one gets

$$\gamma_1' - 2\gamma_2' = (\sigma_1 - 2\sigma_2) - \frac{\alpha_{112} a_1^2}{4\omega_2 a_2}\cos\gamma_1,$$

which, on using $\gamma_1' = 0 = \gamma_2'$ gives

$$\cos \gamma_1 = -\frac{4\omega_2 v_2 a_2}{\alpha_{112} a_1^2}, \qquad (18.5)$$

where $v_2 = 2\sigma_2 - \sigma_1$. Setting $a'_2 = 0$ in (18.4b) gives

$$\sin \gamma_1 = -\frac{4\omega_2 \mu_2 a_2}{\alpha_{112} a_1^2}. \qquad (18.6)$$

From (18.5) and (18.6) one gets

$$\tan \gamma_1 = \frac{\mu_2}{v_2}. \qquad (18.7)$$

Since the amplitude a_2 must be positive, it follows from (18.5) and (18.6) that as long as v_2 remains positive, the angle γ_1 must satisfy $\pi \leq \gamma_1 \leq 3\pi/2$ (the 3rd quadrant) as shown in the sketch below. For v_2 negative, γ_1 is found in the 4th quadrant but since the sign of v_2 will take care of the switching of quadrants, we can use the sketch below to obtain all the required trigonometric relations.

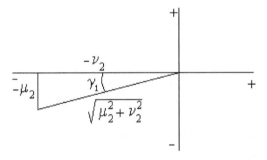

Using either (18.5) or (18.6) and the angle γ_1 defined in the sketch, one gets

$$a_2 = \frac{\alpha_{112} a_1^2}{4\omega_2 (\mu_2^2 + v_2^2)^{\frac{1}{2}}}. \qquad (18.8)$$

Setting $\gamma_2' = 0$ in (18.4d) and taking $\cos\gamma_1 = -v_2/\sqrt{\mu_2^2 + v_2^2}$ gives

$$\cos\gamma_2 = -\frac{\sigma_2}{f_1}a_1 + \frac{\alpha_{121}^* v_2}{4\omega_1 f_1(\mu_2^2 + v_2^2)^{\frac{1}{2}}} a_1 a_2. \tag{18.9}$$

In (18.4a), by setting $a_1' = 0$, taking $\sin\gamma_1 = -\mu_2/\sqrt{\mu_2^2 + v_2^2}$, using (18.9) to eliminate $\sin\gamma_2$ and using (18.8) to express a_2 in terms of a_1, gives

$$\delta^2 a_1^6 + 2\delta(\mu_1\mu_2 - v_1 v_2)a_1^4 + (\mu_1^2 + v_1^2)(\mu_2^2 + v_2^2)a_1^2 = f_1^2(\mu_2^2 + v_2^2), \tag{18.10}$$

where $v_1 = \sigma_2$, $\delta = \alpha_{121}^* \alpha_{112}/16\omega_1\omega_2$.

18.4 Bifurcation

Frequency response curves for the two modes can be generated by plotting (18.8) and (18.10) with the detuning σ_2 of the external driving frequency as the variable, and σ_1, μ_1, μ_2, δ and f_1 as system parameters. Mode1 at normal mode frequency ω_1 is externally driven at Ω while mode2 at normal mode frequency ω_2 is parametrically driven at 2Ω (see Chapter 7). For stable orbits the phases ϕ_1 and ϕ_2 for mode1 (period $2\pi/\Omega$) and mode2 (period $2\pi/2\Omega$) respectively, grow linearly with time because $\phi_1' = \sigma_2$ and $\phi_2' = 2\sigma_2 - \sigma_1$.

The system equations in (18.4) may be written formally as

$$\mathbf{u}' = \mathbf{F}(\mathbf{u}, \sigma), \tag{18.11}$$

where $\mathbf{u} = (u_1, u_2, ...)$ is a *state vector*, $\mathbf{F}$ is an *analytic state function* (a *holomorphic* function — infinitely differentiable at all points and can be expanded as a power series (Taylor series) at all points in its domain) and σ is a real-valued system parameter (or bifurcation parameter). Varying the parameter σ corresponds to changing the driving frequency Ω.

18.5 Linear Stability Analysis

Assume $u_0(\tau)$ is the orbit one wants to check for stability. It is *asymptotically stable* (see Section 8.12) if any infinitesimally small perturbation δu decays. Thus, make the *ansatz* (or *starting equation*) $u = u_0 + \delta u$, put it into the dynamical equations and drop quadratic and higher order terms in δu. One gets

$$\delta u' = \mathbf{J}_{u_0} F(u) \delta u, \qquad (18.12)$$

where $\mathbf{J}_{u_0} F(u)$ is the *Jacobian*, otherwise called the *Jacobian matrix* $\left\{ \dfrac{\partial F}{\partial u} \right\}_{u_0}$ evaluated at u_0. This *linearized* equation of motion is justified as long as the orbit doesn't go too far away from u_0. For *fixed points* (see Section 8.12), the fundamental solutions are of the form $e^{\lambda_s \tau} \delta u$. The *eigenvalues* λ_s ($s = 1, 2, ..., n$) are the roots of the *characteristic equation*

$$det \left| \mathbf{J}_{u_0} F(u) + \lambda \mathbf{I} \right| = 0, \qquad (18.13)$$

where *det* is the *determinant of matrices* and $\mathbf{I}$ is an *(n x n) identity matrix*. In the present case, $n = 4$. One can evaluate the eigenvalues λ_s to determine the stability of the system.

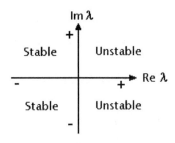

Fig. 18.1. The domains of stability and instability in the complex plane.

The fixed point u_0 is asymptotically stable if all eigenvalues λ_s are inside a stability area of the complex plane as shown in Figure 18.1. In the time-continuous case, this stability area is the half-plane left of the imaginary axis where $\text{Re}(\lambda)$ is negative. If at least one eigenvalue is outside the stability area (on the right of the imaginary axis where $\text{Re}(\lambda)$ is positive) the corresponding fundamental solution will increase exponentially and. the fixed point will be unstable. If an eigenvalue is just on the border of stability, one cannot decide by linear stability analysis whether the fixed point is unstable, asymptotically or marginally stable.

For a time-continuous system, the questions on stability can be answered without explicitly calculating the eigenvalues by making use of the theorem of Routh and Hurwitz (Routh 1877, Hurwitz 1895: see also the more recent references; Hurwitz 1964 (an English translation of the 1895 paper), Ho et al. 1998, Gradshteyn and Ryzhik 2000, Dorf and Bishop 2007). This theorem says that *the real parts of all roots of a polynomial are negative if and only if certain conditions are fulfilled which can be easily calculated.* The calculation can be easily done using the *Routh array* which is a tabular method (the *Routh Tableau*) that allows one to establish the stability of a system using only the coefficients of the characteristic equation.

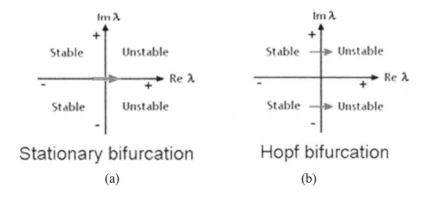

Fig. 18.2. Crossing the imaginary axis for (a) Stationary bifurcation and (b) Hopf bifurcation.

When an eigenvalue crosses the imaginary axis along the real axis, i.e. one eigenvalue passes through zero, $\lambda_1 = 0$ the instability is a *stationary bifurcation* (see Figure 18.2(a)) and corresponds to the *Jump Phenomenon*. This jump from one amplitude to another, takes place at points of vertical tangencies on the amplitude-frequency response curves (see Section 8.11.6). The Jump Phenomenon has been observed on the steelpan and was first reported by the author in 1996 (Achong 1996b).

Stability is lost when a pair of complex conjugate eigenvalues $\lambda_2, \bar{\lambda}_2$ of the Jacobian crosses the imaginary axis in the complex λ-plane with *positive speed* (meaning that they cross from the LHS of the complex plane to the RHS of the complex plane) (see Figure 18.2(b)). The trivial state $\boldsymbol{u} = \boldsymbol{0}$ (a solution of $F(u,\sigma)=0$), loses stability as the parameter σ is increased (or decreased, if approached from above) past a critical point σ_H — *the Hopf bifurcation point* (Marsden and McCraken 1976). The resulting state is marked by *limit-cycle oscillations* with $\boldsymbol{u}$ becoming aperiodic or *amplitude modulated* (Hale 1963). *Hopf bifurcation* may exist for a range of system and excitation parameters and have been observed on the steelpan (Achong 1996b). Other good reading sources on this bifurcation are: Nayfeh and Balachandran 1995 and Nayfeh and Mook 1979.

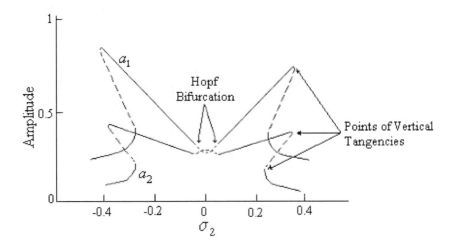

Fig. 18.3. Sketch of response curves for small orbit motions: —, stable; - - -, unstable.

A typical plot of (18.10) is shown in Figure 18.3 where stable branches are depicted as solid lines while unstable branches are shown as dotted lines. Along the outer edges of the two wings of the curves for each mode (a_1 and a_2) the unstable responses (dotted lines) meet the stable responses (solid lines) at points of vertical tangencies corresponding to *tangent (fold) bifurcations*. These points are also known as *tipping points* (for somewhat obvious reasons). The system will respond with an upward or downward jump at these points — the *Jump Phenomenon*. On the steelpan, this will produce a fast audible change in the sound intensity that is detectable as a step up or step down in loudness.

Differentiating (18.10) with respect to σ_2, one finds that at the points of *vertical tangencies* where $da_1/d\sigma_2 \to \infty$, $\sigma_2 \to \sigma_{2,cr}$ (the *critical detuning frequency*) the following condition is satisfied

$$\left(\mu_1^2 + v_1^2\right)\left(\mu_2^2 + v_2^2\right) + 4\delta(\mu_1\mu_2 - v_1v_2)a_1^2 + 3\delta^2 a_1^4 = 0. \qquad (18.14)$$

Condition (18.14) corresponds to the vanishing of the eigenvalue λ_1. It is clear that for (18.14) to be satisfied, one must have the weaker condition

$$\begin{aligned} v_1 v_2 &> \mu_1 \mu_2 \\ \sigma_2(2\sigma_2 - \sigma_1) &> \mu_1 \mu_2. \end{aligned} \qquad (18.15)$$

The dependence of the jump condition (18.14) on the driving force f_1 is implied by the dependence of a_1 on f_1 given in (18.10). For a given force magnitude f_1, if the damping coefficients (μ_1, μ_2) are large enough, the jump condition may not be satisfied. As (18.15) shows, for a given detuning set (σ_1, σ_2), in order for the jump condition to be satisfied, the damping coefficients (μ_1, μ_2) cannot be too large. But even when the weaker condition (18.15) is satisfied, (18.14) must still be satisfied for the Jump phenomenon to occur. These considerations illustrate why the Jump phenomenon may not be observed under heavy damping. In addition it should be noted that the detuning parameters σ_1 and σ_2 can take on positive or negative values (as in the case of *stretched octave* and *compressed octave* respectively).

Applying (18.13) to the dynamical system (18.4), where u_0 is the steady state obtained by setting $a'_1 = 0 = a'_2$, $\gamma'_1 = 0 = \gamma'_2$, one finds after some (relatively long) algebra, that the eigenvalues λ_s are the roots of the *characteristic polynomial*

$$J_4\lambda^4 + J_3\lambda^3 + J_2\lambda^2 + J_1\lambda + J_0 = 0, \qquad (18.16)$$

where

$$J_0 = J_4\left[(\mu_1^2 + v_1^2)J_4 + 4\delta(\mu_1\mu_2 - v_1v_2)a_1^2 + 3\delta^2 a_1^4\right],$$
$$J_1 = 2J_4\left(J_4\mu_1 + \mu_2(v_1^2 + \mu_1^2)\right) + 4J_4(\mu_1 + \mu_2)\delta a_1^2 - 2\mu_2\delta^2 a_1^4,$$
$$J_2 = J_4\left[J_4 + 4\mu_1\mu_2 + \mu_1^2 + v_1^2\right] + 4\delta J_4 a_1^2 - \delta^2 a_1^4,$$
$$J_3 = 2(\mu_1 + \mu_2)J_4,$$
$$J_4 = \mu_2^2 + v_2^2. \qquad (18.17\text{a-e})$$

Using $\mu_1 = \mu_2 = \mu$ (the equal damping condition) which is applicable on the pan notes (see Section 6.7), one gets the slightly simplified version of (18.17a-e)

$$J_0 = J_4\left[(\mu^2 + v_1^2)J_4 + 4\delta(\mu^2 - v_1v_2)a_1^2 + 3\delta^2 a_1^4\right],$$
$$J_1 = 2\mu\left[J_4(2\mu^2 + v_1^2 + v_2^2) + 4\delta J_4 a_1^2 - \delta^2 a_1^4\right],$$
$$J_2 = J_4(6\mu^2 + v_1^2 + v_2^2) + 4\delta J_4 a_1^2 - \delta^2 a_1^4,$$
$$J_3 = 4\mu J_4,$$
$$J_4 = \mu^2 + v_2^2.$$

From (18.16) it is clear that one eigenvalue is zero — *a necessary condition for the jump phenomenon* — when $J_0 = 0$ (the Stationary bifurcation, see Figure 18.2(a)), which gives, from (18.17a)

$$(\mu_1^2 + v_1^2)J_4 + 4\delta(\mu_1\mu_2 - v_1v_2)a_1^2 + 3\delta^2 a_1^4 = 0,$$

which is identical to (18.14). In addition, by applying the Routh–Hurwitz criterion to the polynomial in (18.16), one finds that the conditions

$J_1 > 0$, $J_2 > 0$, and $J_2J_3 > J_1J_4$, (18.18a-c)

guarantee that the other three eigenvalues all have *negative* real parts. Some simple algebra performed on (18.18a-c) in their fully expanded form, shows that if (18.18a), $J_1 > 0$, is satisfied, then since J_4 is the sum of squares and therefore *positive-definite*, the other two conditions (18.18b) and (18.18c) are automatically satisfied. From this observation we find that (18.14) and (18.18a) provide the necessary conditions for the jump instability.

The necessary and sufficient condition for Hopf bifurcation and limit cycle oscillations to occur is for a pair of *complex* eigenvalues to cross the imaginary axis with positive speed (see Figure 18.2(b)). For this crossing to occur, the system must have a simple pair of purely imaginary (Re(λ) = 0) eigenvalues $\lambda_{1,2} = \pm i\omega_0$, $\omega_0 > 0$. By substituting these two eigenvalues into (18.16) one can readily show that this condition is satisfied if

$$J_1(J_1J_4 - J_2J_3) + J_0J_3^2 = 0.$$ (18.19)

The critical frequencies at which Hopf bifurcation occurs on the response curve can be determined by the intersection of (18.10) and (18.19).

18.6 Numerical Results: Jump and Hopf Instabilities

The solutions for (18.10) when the detuning parameter is set to $\sigma_1 = -0.2$ and $\sigma_1 = 0.2$, are shown in Figure 18.4a and Figure 18.4b respectively. While the jump phenomenon is seen in Figures 18.4a and 18.4b, the driving force $f_1 = 0.08$ is too small for Hopf bifurcation to occur. This means that (18.14) and (18.18) are satisfied while (18.19) is not. Since $\sigma_1 = -0.2$ in Figure 18.4a, the wings of the response curve are asymmetrical about the axis $\sigma_2 = 0$ with a shift to the left giving a '*rightward leaning*' appearance. However, with $\sigma_1 = 0.2$, observe in Figure 18.4b both the shift to the right of the response curve and the asymmetry in the amplitude of the response with the '*leftward leaning*' appearance.

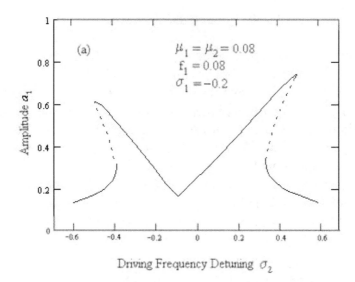

Fig. 18.4a. Rightward leaning response curves for a system driven by low-level sinusoidal force $f_1 = 0.08$, $\delta = 1$. Asymmetrical branches for $\sigma_1 = -0.2$. For the parameter values used here, Hopf bifurcations do not occur at this low level of forcing.

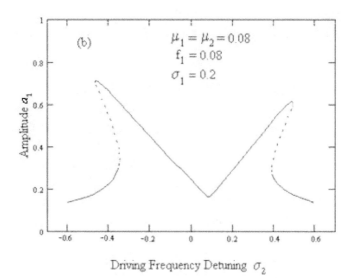

Fig. 18.4b. Leftward leaning response curves for a system driven by low-level sinusoidal force $f_1 = 0.08$, $\delta = 1$. Asymmetrical branches for $\sigma_1 = 0.2$. For the parameter values used here, Hopf bifurcations do not occur at this low level of forcing.

The forcing is now increased with $f_1 = 1$. The preceding discussions and Figure 18.5a show that for perfect tuning $\sigma_1 = 0$, the left and right branches of the system response described by (18.10) remain symmetrical about $\sigma_2 = 0$. For sufficiently large damping ($\mu_1 = \mu_2 = 0.7$) in Figure 18.5a, the response is stable at all frequencies showing that (18.14), (18.18) and (18.19) are not satisfied.

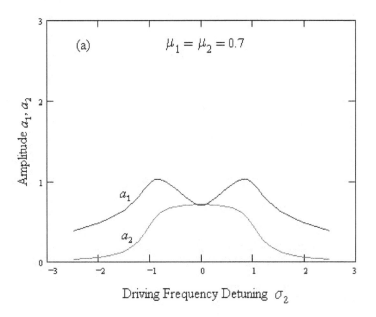

Fig. 18.5a. Stable response curves for the system with $\sigma_1 = 0$, $f_1 = 1$, $\delta = 1$, $\alpha_{112}/4\omega_2 = 1$. The branches are symmetrical about $\sigma_2 = 0$ because $\sigma_1 = 0$. Stable responses are obtained under strong damping.

As the damping is reduced ($\mu_1 = \mu_2 = 0.3$), the jump and Hopf instabilities appear as in Figure 18.5b. The system in Figure 18.5b satisfies the condition (18.15) with jump instabilities occurring provided $|\sigma_2| > 0.212$. Observe here that the system bifurcates into two types of behavior expected for non-linear springs with the left wing showing the characteristics of a *softening spring* (see Section 8.11.6) while the right wing displays the *hardening effect*. The Hopf Bifurcation region exists for σ_2 in the range $-0.279 \leq \sigma_2 \leq +0.279$.

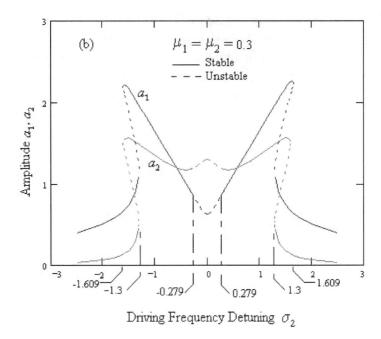

Fig. 18.5b. Response curves of the system with $\sigma_1 = 0$, $f_1 = 1$, $\delta = 1$, $\alpha_{112}/4\omega_2 = 1$. The branches are symmetrical about $\sigma_2 = 0$ because $\sigma_1 = 0$. Stable and unstable responses are obtained under weaker damping. The critical frequencies are identified on these curves.

18.7 Real Pan Results

In this section we examine the experimental results for a real tenor pan. The motion of an excited note is sampled at regular intervals with a sampling frequency of $f_s = 11$ KHz or 22 KHz, depending on the note frequency and the desired time resolution. Sampling produces data in the form of a time series $u(t) = (u(0), u(\tau_s), u(2\tau_s), \ldots u(N\tau_s))$ where τ_s is the sampling interval and $N+1$ is the total number of data points. The continuous time signal is therefore converted into a discrete time signal.

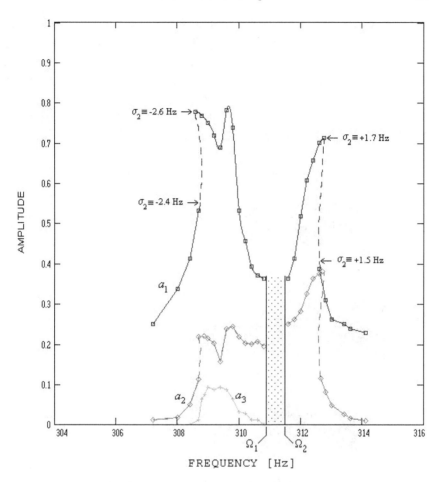

Fig. 18.6. E_4^b bifurcation diagram: —, Stable response; - - -, Unstable response; [⋯], Hopf bifurcation. Critical frequencies for Hopf bifurcation: $\Omega_1 = 310.85$ Hz, $\Omega_2 = 311.5$ Hz.

The E_4^b (311.1 Hz) note on a bore tenor pan was first analyzed by the methods of Chapters 4 and 6 to obtain the note parameters: $f_1 = 311.1$ Hz, $f_2 = 624.0$ Hz, and $f_3 = 930.6$ Hz. Under normal low-level excitation the primary mode at frequency f_1 displayed a *Quality Factor Q* of 93. *This high Q means that all the internal resonances that accompany the jump and bifurcation phenomena will take place over a narrow range of frequencies.* From the values for f_1 and f_2, the second mode detuning (σ_1) is +1.8 Hz (a *stretched octave*). Since the detuning is non-zero and positive, an asymmetrical bifurcation diagram leaning to the left is expected in the system response to sinusoidal excitation. The note was then subjected to sinusoidal excitation at driving frequencies around the first mode resonance. Figure 18.6 shows the observed bifurcation diagrams with the expected leftward leaning shape. On the left and right branches, the unstable regions (broken lines), the limits of which are marked by Jump phenomena, are observed clearly for modes 1 and 2.

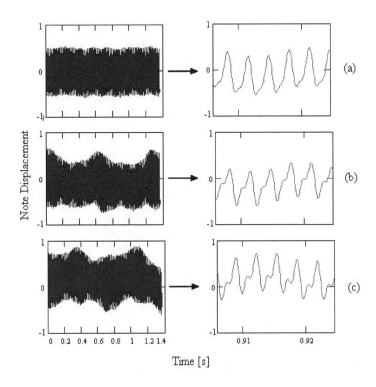

Fig. 18.7. E_4^b response to the sinusoidal excitation in the Hopf bifurcation region; low time-resolution on the left panels and high time-resolution on the right panels: (a) $\Omega = 310.8$ Hz. (b) $\Omega = 310.9$ Hz, (c) $\Omega = 311.2$ Hz.

The left branches on modes 1 and 2 are partially split due to the occurrence of the combination resonance with mode 3 (the tuned musical *twelfth*), which peaks at around $\Omega = 309$ Hz. This internal resonance (mode1 x mode2 → mode3) which is a normal occurrence on the pan notes, adds this additional feature to the response curve. Corresponding to this internal resonance, 'dips' appear on the frequency response because energy is transferred from both mode1 and mode2 to mode3 (the twelfth). If mode3 was left untuned (and well away in frequency from $f_1 + f_2$), the 'dips' would not have appeared. In fact the observed 'dips' and the associated modal interactions support the energy exchange mechanisms discussed in Section 14.29.1.

The critical frequencies for the Jump bifurcations are indicated on Figure 18.6 by the equivalent detuning (σ_2) of the driving frequency from the first mode frequency. We observe that because of the high Q, all the jump and bifurcation phenomena took place over the narrow span of approximately 4.5 Hz.

The second type of instability exhibiting limit-cycle oscillations occurs between the Hopf-bifurcation points, $\Omega_1 = 310.85$ Hz and $\Omega_2 = 311.5$ Hz. As the excitation frequency Ω is increased, the third mode amplitude first increased then dropped to zero before the system entered the Hopf bifurcation region. Effects of the third mode did not reappear at higher frequencies as expected. The aperiodic behavior expected for u_1 and u_2 is shown in the composite diagram of Figure 18.7 (for other systems with this non-linear behavior see for example Nayfeh and Zavodney 1988, Lee and Hsu 1994). Just before the bifurcation (at $\Omega = 310.8$ Hz) the motion is stationary (Figure 18.7a) but becomes unstable (Figure 18.7b, c) as the two modes constantly exchange energy. At very low levels of external sinusoidal excitation all instabilities disappear.

Observational note: *In 1994, during a routine resonance exercise performed in my lab on a Randolph Thomas tenor, I made my first observation of the Hopf Instability Phenomenon on the E_4^b note. I heard an unusual amplitude modulation coming from the note in response to an applied constant-amplitude excitation over a very narrow range of frequencies covering just ½ Hz centred around 311 Hz. The response was very sharp so I reduced the scanning rate and increased the scanning range only to hear additional changes in loudness as the note performed the 'jumps' in intensity that characterize the Jump Phenomenon. I found other notes that displayed this behavior, all, over very narrow frequency bands. This book and reference Achong (1996b) carry records of the first observation. After returning the pan to Thomas, some time had passed before I decided that I should purchase and keep this pan as a memento. Unfortunately the pan was sold and as I was told, its* *new owner was a visiting Canadian resident! Whoever now owns this pan is in possession of a very fine musical instrument.*

18.8 Results from Electronic Simulations

Electronic circuits were designed, built and patented to simulate the systems described by equations (18.20) (corresponding to a note with tuned first and second modes with quadratic non-linearities only) and equation (18.21) which describes a note with *simple tuning* (only the first mode is tuned) with quadratic and cubic non-linearities.

$$\frac{d^2 w_n}{d\tau^2} + \mu_n \frac{dw_n}{d\tau} + \omega_n^2 w_n + \sum_{i,j=1}^{2} \alpha_{ijn} w_i w_j = f_0 + f_i(\tau), \quad (18.20)$$

$$\frac{d^2 w_1}{d\tau^2} + \mu_1 \frac{dw_1}{d\tau} + \omega_{10}^2(1-s)w_1 + \alpha_1 w_1^2 + \beta_1 w_1^3 = f_0 + f_1(\tau), \quad (18.21)$$

where $f_1(\tau) = F\cos(\Omega\tau)$ with the driving frequency Ω close to ω_{10}. In these equations $\alpha_1 = \alpha_{11,2}$, $\beta_1 = \beta_{111,3}$, f_0 is a thermally/compressively induced static loading, and s is a buckling parameter. The stiffness $\omega_{10}^2(1-s)$ is positive when the compressive and thermal loading is weak (s < 1 for pre-buckling) and becomes negative under strong loading (s > 1 for post buckling). In practice, only a small area and not the entire note is observed to buckle under the compressive forces arising during tuning by hammer peening. Both s and f_0 are dependent on the thermal and in-plane compressive loading.

Equation (18.21) can be written as an autonomous system of 3 ODEs in the general Pfaffian form $w' = f(w)$ where $()' = d()/d\tau$

$$w' = w_2,$$
$$w_2' = -\mu_1 w_2 - \omega_{10}^2(1-s)w - \alpha_1 w^2 - \beta_1 w^3 + f_0 + F\cos(\phi),$$
$$\phi' = \Omega,$$

(18.22a-c)

where w is the note surface displacement and w_2 is the surface velocity.

In the circuit representations of equations (18.20) and (18.21) or (18.22a-c) the mechanical bias, f_0, takes the form of a DC input offset voltage. 'Displacement' (w) and 'velocity' ($\dot{w}$) were digitized with a sampling time of 90 µs and the data stored on a digital computer for evaluation. Amplitude and phase were monitored on an oscilloscope.

18.9 The Experimental Results

18.9.1 2-Mode system: Hopf Bifurcation and Jump Phenomena

The circuit representing equation (18.20) was set up to simulate an F_3 note (174.61 Hz on the musical scale) by tuning the first mode (key-note) to 174.5 Hz and the second mode (octave) to 350.0 Hz. *There were no tuned third partial used on this simulated note.* The coupling settings and damping were adjusted with the system under pulse excitation until the combined signals $w_1 + w_2$ produced an audible sound (monitored on an amplifier/loudspeaker system) with tonal qualities expected of a properly tuned F_3 note on the real steelpan. This procedure guaranteed equivalent performance and dynamics to that of a real note having relatively strong quadratic non-linearities. From the author's experience with the steelpan, it is extremely difficult to come across two notes (even similar on the musical scale) having nearly identical sets of parameters. For this reason no matching of parameters between the simulated note and a real note was attempted. However, this can be done by following the procedures in Chapter 6. The only criterion adopted was that of similarity in performance (musical and dynamical).

Figure 18.8 shows the experimentally determined frequency-response curves when the excitation frequency is close to the first natural frequency of 174.5 Hz. The initial detuning was set to $\omega_2 - 2\omega_1 = 2\pi$ rad/s ($\equiv$ 1.0 Hz) while the amplitude of the external excitation was set at 490 mV. For external excitations below 220 mV, Hopf bifurcation was absent. (Only the relative magnitudes of voltages given here are of real importance). The coupling and damping parameters of this system are best represented in non-dimensional form when the frequencies are normalized according to $\omega_1 = 1$, $\omega_2 = 2.006$. They are: $\mu_1 = 0.0041$, $\mu_2 = 0.0049$, $\alpha_{112} = 0.071$, $\alpha_{121} = \alpha_{211} = 0.092$. *The level of damping used here corresponds to a note with a very low Quality Factor of approximately Q = 12.* A low Q was chosen in order to broaden the frequency response sufficiently for the bifurcation diagram to be clearly resolved as seen in Figure 18.8. The reader can appreciate this by noting that the bifurcations shown in Figure 18.6 for the real note with a Q = 93, all occur over a narrow frequency band of 4.5 Hz while the corresponding band for the model note in Figure 18.8 is much wider at approximately 35 Hz.

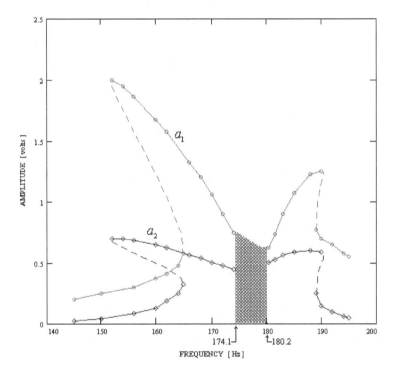

Fig. 18.8. Experimental response curves for the electronic steelpan note for excitation frequencies close to the first natural frequency of 174.5 Hz. The full lines represent stable responses while the dotted lines show the unstable responses. The shaded area represents the region of Hopf bifurcation.

In Figure 18.8, the lower and upper Hopf bifurcation points that mark the transitions from periodic to almost periodic responses are at 174.1 Hz and 180.2 Hz respectively. On these response curves, jump responses will occur at points with vertical tangents located at the extreme ends (at the folds) of the dotted lines on Figure 18.8. These response curves and the almost periodic oscillations shown in Figure 18.9 are qualitatively in agreement with those found for real steelpan notes excited harmonically. Compare Figure 18.6 and Figure 18.8 ignoring the effects of the third mode in Figure 18.6.

Notice in Figure 18.9 how dependent is the system response on frequency — observe differences on the modal responses for a frequency change of just 1 Hz. On the real note responses in Figures 18.6 and 18.7, similar changes are possible for a frequency change of only 0.1 Hz, all because of the much higher Q-factor on the real instrument.

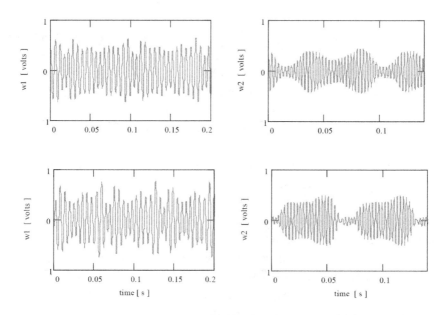

Fig. 18.9. Amplitude modulations in the Hopf bifurcation region for excitation frequency at 177.0 Hz (top) and at 178.0 Hz (bottom). Mode1, left panel: Mode2, right panel.

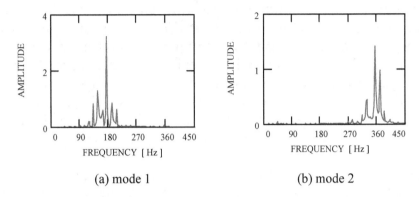

(a) mode 1 (b) mode 2

Fig. 18.10. Frequency spectra for almost-periodic oscillations within the Hopf bifurcation region for a driving frequency of 178.0 Hz.

One observes from Figure 18.10 that in the frequency spectrum for each of the two modes there is one dominant frequency component. The dominant frequency varies with the driving frequency. The frequency sidebands on the spectra in Figure 18.10 are the result of the amplitude modulations associated with the quasi-periodicity of the Hopf instability as seen in Figure 18.9.

The combined response (w1 + w2) shown in Figure 18.11 can be compared with the note displacement on the real pan obtained during Hopf bifurcation in Figure 18.7.

Figure 18.12 shows the points of instability on the system response of this 2-mode system. To best understand what happens here, follow the route taken by the system when the driving frequency is slowly increased starting from 145 Hz on the left of the diagram. Throughout this whole exercise the amplitude of the external forcing signal was kept constant. The following explanation applies to both mode1 and mode2 in Figure 18.12.

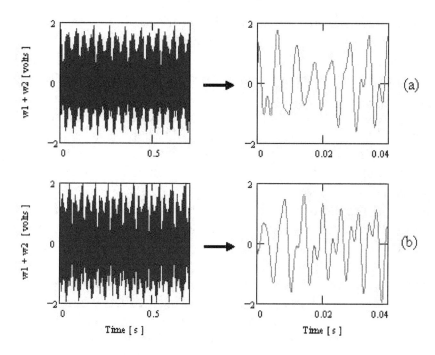

Fig. 18.11. Combined response (w1 + w2) similar to note displacement in Figure 18.7. Driving frequency (a) 177 Hz, (b) 178 Hz.

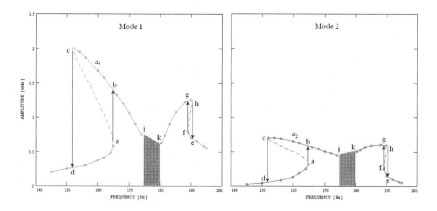

Fig. 18.12. Points of instability on the two modes of the 2-mode system. Arrows indicate the directions of the jumps.

Starting from the left, as the frequency is increased, the system response slowly increases to the point 'a' where a sudden *upward* jump in amplitude a→b takes the system to the point 'b'. Now let us slowly decrease the frequency. The response increases up to the point 'c' when a sudden downward jump c→d takes the response to the point 'd'. If this procedure is repeated the path 'abcd' can be retraced. Corresponding jumps on mode1 and mode2 occur simultaneously. If on reaching the point 'b', after the a→b jump, the frequency is increased, the response decreases to the point 'j' where the Hopf bifurcation begins. This instability continues as the driving frequency is increased until the point 'k' is reached where the Hopf bifurcation ceases. As the frequency increases, the response increases to the point 'h' when a sudden *downward* jump h→e occurs. As the frequency is further increased, the system returns to 'normal' oscillations on both modes. If, on reaching 'e' the frequency is reduced, the system encounters a jump at 'f' which takes it up to the point 'g.' The path 'efgh' can be retraced by increasing and decreasing the frequency at the appropriate times. This can be done repeatedly. If the driving frequency begins at 195 Hz (on the right) and the frequency is decreased monotonically to 145 Hz, the route taken is 'efgkjbcd'. Reversing the change in frequency i.e. from 145 Hz to 195 Hz takes the system through 'dabjkghe'. Because of the jumps, the paths are *not* reversible. The unstable paths shown as dashed lines in Figure 18.12 are *never* traversed by the system. A similar description holds for the real pan response in Figure 18.6.

Note: *The reader may ask; what type of solution is obtained for the system equation in the unstable regions shown as dotted lines in Figures 18.8 and 18.12? The real system made of metal (the steelpan note) or silicon (the electronic system) never enter these regions. The mathematical solutions yield complex numbers (having real and imaginary parts) for amplitudes and velocities showing that they cannot be realized or observed in practice. In numerical solutions performed on the dynamical equations the transition points can be determined as the frequency values where the solutions switch from being purely real to complex. The transitions are (numerically) very sharp and can be calculated very accurately.*

18.10 Chaos

18.10.1 Analytical Methods

We have been successful in earlier Chapters with Fourier Transform (FT) and Short Time Fourier Transform (STFT) in analyzing the steelpan dynamical behavior under stick impact. For a wider range of excitation however, the time series representing displacement or velocity of this non-linear dynamical system may contain information that is hard to capture using any form of Fourier analysis. A Fourier spectrum provides useful information if the signal is generated by a linear source. However, for signals generated by a non-linear source, the Fourier spectrum will typically reveal a wide-band (infinite dimensional) structure even though the dynamical system exists in a finite dimensional space. Hence, additional methods are required for the characterization of such time series.

These 'additional' methods can be classified as *metric, dynamical,* and *topological.* The metric approach depends on the computation of distances on the system's attractor, and it includes Grassberger-Procaccia *Correlation Dimension* (D_{cor}). The dynamical approach deals with computing the way nearby orbits diverge (or converge) by means of *Lyapunov exponents.* Topological methods are characterized by the study of the organization of the *strange attractor*, and they include *close returns plots* and *recurrence plots*. Since the general reader may not be familiar with these terms I must now see to relieving their stress by providing the following definitions:

18.10.2 Definitions

Readers should consult the following references on chaos and attractors: Grassberger and Procaccia 1983a, 1983b and 1984, Eckmann and Ruelle 1985, Ott (1993), Ott et al. 1994, Strogatz 1994.

Basin of Attraction: The set of points in the space of system variables such that initial conditions chosen in this set dynamically evolve to a particular *attractor*.

An **Attractor** is a set of states (points in the phase-space), invariant under the dynamics, towards which neighboring states in a given basin of attraction asymptotically approach in the course of dynamic evolution. An attractor is defined as the smallest unit which cannot be itself decomposed into two or more attractors with distinct basins of attraction. This restriction is necessary since a dynamical system may have multiple attractors, each with its own basin of attraction. Conservative systems do not have attractors, since the motion is periodic. For dissipative dynamical systems however, volumes shrink exponentially so attractors have zero volume in n-dimensional phase-space.

Strange Attractors are bounded regions of phase-space (corresponding to positive Lyapunov characteristic exponents) having *zero measure* in the embedding phase-space and a *fractal* (fractional) dimension. Trajectories within a strange attractor appear to move around randomly. (The terms *measure* and *zero measure* have very precise meanings in Measure Theory but it would suffice to say that 'zero measure' refers to a set of points capable of being enclosed in intervals whose total length is arbitrarily small.)

Poincaré Map: In the vicinity of a limit cycle the Poincaré map P is defined as the *Poincaré section S*, a plane intersecting the limit cycle transversely (see Figure 18.13). For a point u_0, the point $P(u_0)$ is defined as the next intersection of the orbit through u_0 with S. Instead of considering the orbit of the vector field, one can now study the orbit of the point u_0 under the iteration of P.

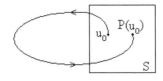

Fig. 18.13. Representation of a limit cycle, Poincaré map P and Poincaré section S.

Lyapunov exponents: A non-linear system can be described using a *state-space* model with a number of observable output *states*. The time evolution of these observables in the state-space constitutes a trajectory. *Lyapunov exponents* associated with a trajectory provide a quantitative measure of average rates of convergence and divergence of neighboring trajectories. For a given dynamical system, there exists a whole spectrum of Lyapunov exponents, the number being equal to the dimension of the phase-space. These exponents are an important invariant characterization of the underlying dynamical system and may be zero, positive or negative. Zero exponents indicate that the system is a flow (having a regular trajectory such as a hula-hoop whirling around your waist). Negative exponents indicate that trajectories will be drawn in towards a basin of attraction. Positive exponents (at least one) indicate that the system is *chaotic*. One exponent in the spectrum must be zero since a perturbation along the path results in no divergence. Lyapunov exponents are therefore a good measure to distinguish between fixed points, periodic, quasi-periodic and chaotic motions.

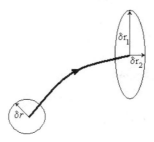

Fig. 18.14. Trajectory of an evolving system in phase space.

To understand the meaning of the Lyapunov spectrum, imagine an infinitesimal small ball with radius δr sitting on the initial state of a trajectory (refer to the sketch in Figure 18.14). The flow will deform this ball into an ellipsoid (see Figure 18.14). That is, after a finite time t all orbits that have started in that ball will be in the ellipsoid. Notice that if there were negative exponents and at least one positive exponent no matter how small, after a sufficiently long time the ellipsoid collapses in all dimensions except for the dimension containing the positive exponent. The long-term behavior of the system is therefore controlled by the single positive exponent and the system will be chaotic. One sees from this that the sensitivity of the dynamical system to initial conditions is quantified by the Lyapunov exponents. Chaotic systems have the property of sensitive dependence on initial conditions. This means that two infinitely close vectors in state space gives rise, in the evolution, to two trajectories that separate exponentially fast.

The larger the positive exponent, the more chaotic is the system i.e. the shorter is the time scale of the system's predictability. The sum of positive Lyapunov exponents is called the *entropy* H; a measure for the rate at which information about the state of the system is lost in the course of time. Its reciprocal $H^{-1} \sim T_{av}$, is roughly the average time into the future for which knowledge of the state of the system can be used to predict its evolution. For a regular trajectory, $H = 0$ making $T_{av} = \infty$, while for a purely random system, $H = \infty$ giving $T_{av} = 0$. The reader's intuition will allow these points to 'make sense', for one can clearly see that for a random system, no prediction can be made into the future i.e. the predictability time is zero. The evolution of a regular system on the other hand can be followed without limit into the future.

Since the Lyapunov exponent λ_L is a measure of the rate at which nearby trajectories in phase-space diverge, if two nearby trajectories start off with a separation δr at time $t = 0$, then the trajectories diverge so that their separation at time t, $\delta r(t)$, satisfies the expression: $\delta r(t) = \delta r e^{\lambda_L t}$. By taking logarithms, the ith Lyapunov exponent for an n-dimensional system is defined by the limit

Continuous time: $$\lambda_{Li} = \lim_{t \to \infty} \frac{1}{t} ln\left(\frac{\delta r_i(t)}{\delta r}\right), \quad (18.23)$$

Discrete time: $$\lambda_{Li} = \lim_{n \to \infty} \frac{1}{n} ln \sum_{k=1}^{\infty}\left(\frac{\delta r_i(k)}{\delta r}\right), \quad (18.24)$$

where $\delta r_i(t)$ (continuous case) or $\delta r_i(k)$ (discrete case) is the radius of the ellipsoid along its ith principal axis. For an n-dimensional system with $\lambda_{L1} > \lambda_{L2} > ... > \lambda_{Ln}$, the largest exponent will dominate making these limits (18.23) and (18.24) useful only for the largest exponent. Readers may consult the following references on Lyapunov exponents: Sano and Sawada 1985, Rosenstein et al 1993, Kantz 1994 and Kantz and Schreiber 1997.

Reconstructed Phase-Space: In our present study, the dynamical information for our system, the steelpan note, is available on a univariate (single variable) time series *u* (velocity or displacement) which is part of a larger n-dimensional (possibly deterministic) system. The system behavior can be graphically displayed by plotting one variable (for example, velocity) against another variable (displacement). *Takens theorem* (Takens 1981) shows that we can recreate a topologically equivalent picture of the original multidimensional system behavior by using the time series of a *single* observable variable, by means of the method of time delays. This pseudo phase-space is called the *Reconstructed Phase-Space* (RPS). This method takes a scalar signal *u* and turns it into a vector signal; at each scalar u_i on the time series one constructs the *embedding vector* $u_i^{\{m\}} = (u_i, u_{i+d}, ..., u_{i+(m-1)d})$ where *m* is the *embedding dimension* and *d* is the *delay*. The operation therefore involves sliding a window of length *m* through the data to form a new series of vectors. This operation does not create any new information, it only reorganizes the information. However, the sequence of embedded vectors is useful only if parameters *m* and *d* are properly chosen.

Self Similarity: In mathematics, an object (physical or purely mathematical) is said to be self-similar if it looks "roughly" the same on any scale. The 'object' of interest here is the attractor generated by the non-linear dynamics of the harmonically driven steelpan note. Self-similar objects with parameters *M(r)* and *r* are described by a power law such as $M(r) \propto r^D$ where *D* is the "dimension" of the scaling law, known as the Hausdorff dimension (Hausdorff 1919 see also Harris and Stocker 1998, Ott 1993, Schroeder 1991), Self-similarity is a typical property of fractals (objects having fractional dimension). *Scale invariance* is an exact form of self-similarity where at any magnification there is a smaller piece of the object that is similar to the whole. The non-trivial similarity evident in fractals is distinguished by their fine structure or detail on arbitrarily small scales. On the other hand, any portion of a straight line may resemble the whole, but no further detail is revealed by magnification because a straight line is one dimensional.

In fractal geometry one normally refers to the *Minkowski–Bouligand dimension*, also known as *Minkowski dimension* or *box-counting dimension* (see for example Falconer. 1990). In box-counting, one counts the number of *nearest neighbors* (neighboring points in phase-space) in a *box* of size r. The box-counting dimension is defined in the limit as the size of the box tends to zero (limit r →0). If this limit does not exist then one refers to the upper box dimension or the lower box dimension (corresponding to the upper and lower bound respectively). Both the upper and lower box dimensions are related to the Hausdorff dimension. The generalized dimensions D_q or *Renyi dimensions* (Renyi, 1971) parameterized by q, differ in the way regions of different densities in the object are weighted. One can see the need for this because we would like to give greater weight to the regions that are more often visited within the attractor as the system evolves. D_0 (for $q = 0$) is equivalent to the *capacity dimension*, D_1 is *the information dimension*, while D_2, is the *Correlation dimension* which is related to the *Correlation sum* (for $q =2$) which we now define.

Correlation Sum: Correlation analysis can be used to determine the minimum embedding dimension of a time series. The *Correlation dimension* provides information on the minimum number of dynamic variables needed to model a system by placing a lower bound on the number of possible degrees of freedom. The *Correlation sum* $C(r,m)$ measures the probability that a pair of points in the attractor are within a distance r of one another. The correlation analysis calculates the *correlation dimension* as a function of the embedding dimension by using the Correlation sum (Grassberger and Procaccia 1983).

$$C(r,m) = \frac{1}{N_{pairs}} \sum_{i=m}^{N} \sum_{j<i-w} H(r-||u_i^{\{m\}} - u_j^{\{m\}}||) \quad (18.25)$$

where $N_{pairs} = (N-m+1)(N-m-w+1)/2$, $||\cdot||$ is a norm (e.g. Euclidian norm; for the scalar set $x = (x_1, x_2, \cdots x_n)$, $||x|| \doteq \sqrt{x_1^2 + \cdots + x_n^2}$),

w is the *Theiler window* (Theiler 1987), (chosen to exclude temporally correlated points from the pair counting) and H is the *Heaviside step function* defined as

$$H(x) = \begin{cases} 0 & x \leq 0 \\ 1 & x > 0 \end{cases}. \tag{18.26}$$

The Theiler window should be at least half a period for almost periodic patterns, but is best chosen much larger since typically not much statistics is lost as long as the window remains smaller than about 10% of the data set size. The Heaviside function is used to assess the probability.

Correlation Dimension: On sufficiently small distance scales the correlation sum is related to the correlation dimension D_{cor} by $C(r,m) \propto r^{D_{cor}}$ so one can write

$$D_{cor} = \lim_{r,r' \to 0^+} \frac{\ln\left(\frac{C(r,m)}{C(r',m)}\right)}{\ln\left(\frac{r}{r'}\right)}. \tag{18.27}$$

If an attractor exists, then an estimate of D_{cor} saturates above some m given by the *fractal Whitney embedding prevalence theorem*

$$m \geq 2D_{cor} + 1. \tag{18.28}$$

Although Whitney (1936) did not have time series or fractals in mind and D had to be an integer, Takens (1981) and later, Sauer et al. (1991), Sauer and Yorke (1993) with some technical specifications, were able to generalize the theorem. When the correlation dimension saturates the attractor is unfolded for the specific embedding dimension (m). The implication is that a maximum of m independent variables is required to construct a model to simulate the behavior of the time series. This saturation can be identified by plotting the local slopes of C(r, m) versus the distance r. A 'plateau' should appear if self-similarity exists and the plateau will also define the scaling range.

18.11 Route to Chaos

We can a look at the quasi-periodicity of the Hopf bifurcation as a route to chaos. In this dynamical state, a stable fixed point turns into a limit cycle via a Hopf bifurcation described on a torus (a 1-torus). The limit cycle then goes through a second Hopf bifurcation described on a two frequency torus or 2-tori. Under further changes in the control parameter the torus becomes unstable and may either develop into 3-tori or into a chaotic attractor with the two frequencies dominating the chaotic motion. This is the route to chaos via *quasi-periodicity*.

The dynamical system describing the steelpan notes may also follow the *Feigenbaum Scenario* route to chaos; a period-doubling cascade, *Periodic → Period-Doubling → Chaos*.

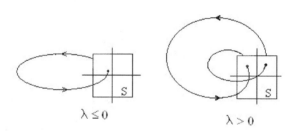

Fig. 18.15. Poincaré sections for period-1 orbit ($\lambda \leq 0$) and period-2 (period-doubling) attractor $\lambda > 0$.

The diagrams in Figure 18.15 on the Poincaré section S (a plane in the phase space of the dynamical system) show the points for a period-1 orbit with $\lambda \leq 0$ (left panel) and a period-2 attractor $\lambda > 0$ (right panel). Points on the section for the period-2 (period-doubling) attractor jump back and forth across the vertical and horizontal axes of the plane.

The period-doubling limit cycle is in fact the boundary of a Möbius strip. The Möbius strip (after August Ferdinand Möbius 1790–1868) which has only *one side* and *one edge* is an example of a *non-orientable space*. To make a Möbius strip all you need to do is take a rectangular strip of paper rotate one end 180° (half a turn) and glue it to the other end. A continuous *one-sided surface* is formed as sketched in Figure 18.16. As you can easily check, it takes *two revolutions* around the strip until you return to the starting position when starting at the point '*a*' in the sketch. Run your finger along the edge to verify for yourself that there is only one edge.

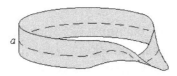

Fig. 18.16. A Möbius strip or band.

The *Poincaré-Bendixson theorem* (Poincaré 1892, Bendixson 1901) states that for a pair of first order differential equations (2D system), only fixed points and periodic orbits (limit cycles) can occur. Furthermore, we can state this theorem as the trichotomy: *If a trajectory in a plane is bounded, then the trajectory must (i) be a closed orbit, (ii) approach a closed orbit or (iii) approach an equilibrium point as $t \to \infty$.* The implication of the Poincaré-Bendixson theorem is that if we can find a *trapping region* for a dynamical system which does not contain an equilibrium point then there must be at least one limit cycle within the region. If a stationary system has only two dimensions, then it cannot be non-periodic because its *attractor* will be confined to a single plane. These trajectories cannot cross each other, because this will imply that the system behaves differently for exactly the same conditions (as obtained at the point of intersection on the plane). The trajectories must therefore either be attracted to a fixed point, spiral outward indefinitely (non-stationary), or follow a single repeating (periodic) path. This means that *there can be no chaos in 2D flows*. For the system $w' = f(w)$ to be chaotic, the system must be **at least** 3-dimensional. This condition is satisfied for the system in (18.22) as well as in (18.20) as seen from its representation as 4 ODEs in (18.4).

The non-linearity requirement is also satisfied. **It is therefore possible for the steelpan note to be driven into chaos!**

18.12 Chaotic Behavior of the 2-Mode System

The experimental results reported here on the 2-mode system appeared in the paper Achong (1999c) but an expanded and more refined presentation is given here. A low level 60 Hz (AC contamination) noise signal was filtered from the original data recorded on the mode1 channel. No contamination was observed on the mode2 channel. Filtering was done by interpolating between the adjacent unaffected frequency bins in the FT. The Inverse Fourier Transform (IFT) then provided the constructed filtered signal. The attractor was found to be only marginally affected by this weak contamination. One may think of using an electronic notch filter centered on 60Hz in the data acquisition circuit to accomplish this filtering action but there are two undesirable features in this procedure: (i) 60Hz is quite a low frequency so a practical high–Q notch with a 'flat' response outside the notch, would be difficult, (ii) a good electronic filter invariably employs feedback which, introduces an additional degree of freedom. We want to be sure at all times that we do not introduce artifacts of the filtering process.

Without any changes to the parameters of the system described in Section 18.9, the amplitude and frequency of the external excitation were varied within the Hopf bifurcation region in a search for conditions that may give rise to chaotic behavior. At a frequency of 178.0 Hz, the system response moved through a series of Hopf bifurcations to chaotic behavior as the drive amplitude was increased. The chaotic response to a forcing signal of amplitude 2.4 volts is shown in Figure 18.17

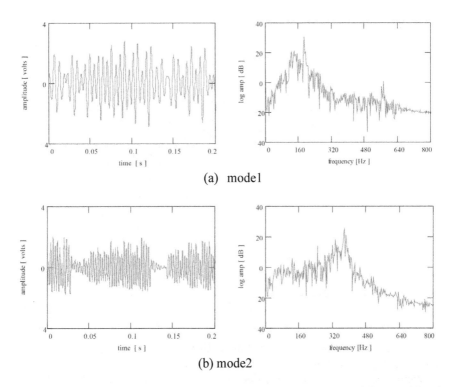

Fig. 18.17. Time histories (left panels) and frequency spectra (right panels) of chaotic responses for the 2-mode system excited at 178.0 Hz with a drive amplitude of 2.4 volts.

On close inspection of the time-histories, the differences between the *chaotic* of Figure 18.17 and the *almost-periodic* (quasi-periodic) oscillations of Figure 18.11 can be seen. The audible difference in the output sound is more dramatic however, becoming noise-like in the chaotic mode. Compare the spectra in Figure 18.10 with those in Figure 18.17; the change in the spectra from discrete in appearance (Figure 18.10) to almost continuous (Figure 18.17) indicates a change in the nature of the response. This change signifies the *quasi-periodicity* → *chaotic* transition. Period-doubling spectra with their characteristic sharp spikes at the 'sub-harmonics' are not observed here (refer to Figure 18.22 for a comparison).

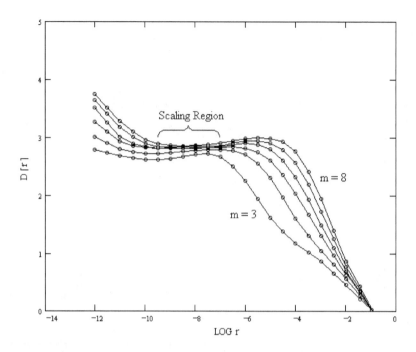

Fig. 18.18. (Model Filtered data, Log is to base 2.). Local slopes D(r) of the correlation sum for the flow data filtered to remove a low level 60 Hz contamination. Embedding dimensions $m = 3, 4, 5, 6, 7, 8$ counted from below. A scaling region identified by the plateau, extends from log (r) ≈ -9.5 to log (r) ≈ -7 is established. The attractor dimension is just below 3. For $r < 2^{-12}$, effects of the grid set by the 12-bit resolution and unfiltered experimental noise distort the plots.

Correlation dimensions were estimated from the time-series for the first and second modes over a duration corresponding to 16384 data points. To determine whether the response is chaotic, the data must be searched for a region of self-similarity that characterizes this type of behavior. The local slopes of the correlation sum (these slopes represent the local D(r) values) were plotted against the distance r to search for a plateau signifying a convergence to the correlation dimension of the attractor. Figure 18.18 shows the plots of the model filtered data and a plateau over the range log(r) ≈ -9.5 to log (r) ≈ -7. The log-log plots of the correlation integral $C(r, m)$ versus the distance r for embedding dimensions $m = 3, 4 \ldots 8$ are shown in Figure 18.19.

We are looking for a power law $C(r, m) \propto r^{D_{corr}}$ to give us the straight lines on the log-log plots of Figure 18.19. When searching for the characteristics of chaotic behavior, two points should be kept in mind (i) noise removal can extent the scale of the linearity on the log-log plot, (ii).when using sampled data, the regularity of discretization in phase space is equivalent to a grid for which the dimension is necessarily zero. Discretization therefore makes the effective scaling exponent D go to zero when looked at on scales smaller than the resolution. With the 12-bit resolution employed on the system data, this distortion is effective below log (r) = -12 One can reduce the effect of the grid by introducing a low level white noise component to knock the points randomly off the grid. The results of these experiments with added noise are not reported here. One needs to keep in mind also that the dimension of 'white noise' is infinite so D would tend to 'run off' to large values at scales where the noise dominates.

The estimates over the dimensions $m = 6, 7, 8$ give
for *mode1*: $D_{corr} = 2.90 \pm 0.07$,
for *mode2*: $D_{corr} = 2.66 \pm 0.08$.
For mode1, filtered data, over $m= 7, 8$: $D_{corr} = 2.86 \pm 0.03$.

On the inset in Figure 18.19, observe the saturation for $m > 6$ on the plots of the correlation dimension (D_{corr}) versus embedding dimension (m). The saturation occurs on mode1 for $m \geq 2(2.9) +1$ $(= 6.8)$ and $m \geq 2(2.66) +1$ $(= 6.32)$ for mode2, in agreement with the fractal Whitney embedding prevalence theorem.

It is important to first observe the plateau on the linear-log plot of the local correlation slope D(r) versus Log r before using the Log-Log plot of Log C versus Log r because of the compression obtained on the Log-Log plot (where curved lines appear as straight lines). In Figure 18.19 for example, the straight line one is looking for seems to extend over a greater range on this Log-Log plot than the Scaling Range on Figure 18.18. The plateau is the key indicator of self- similarity.

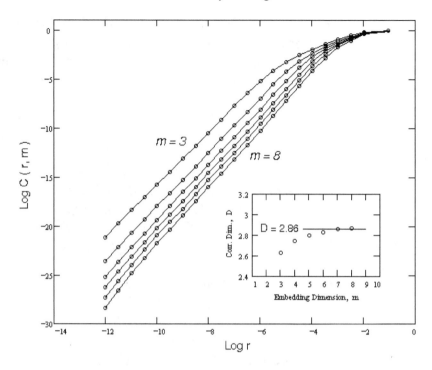

Fig. 18.19. (Model Filtered data, Log is to base 2.). Log-log plot of the correlation integral $C(r, m)$ vs r for embedding dimensions $m = 3, 4, 5, 6, 7, 8$. Inset: the convergence to D_{corr} with increasing m. $D_{corr} = 2.86 \pm 0.03$. estimated over m = 7 and m = 8.

The maximal Lyapunov exponent for each of the two time series was estimated using equation (18.24), producing the values:

mode1: $\lambda = 0.064 \pm 0.005$ per sample interval

and

mode2: $\lambda = 0.087 \pm 0.009$ per sample interval.

The positive values for the Lyapunov exponents and the estimated correlation dimensions show the response to be chaotic.

18.13 Simulated Partially Tuned Note (Single Mode — Simple Tuning)

18.13.1 Numerical Experiments and Results

Without damping and external forcing the Hamiltonian $H = K + V$ for equation (18.21) has kinetic energy $K = w_1'^2/2$ and potential energy

$$V = \omega_{10}^2(1-s)\,w_1^2/2 + \alpha_1 w_1^3/3 + \beta_1 w_1^4/4 - f_0 w_1. \qquad (18.29)$$

The potential function (18.29) is asymmetric for $(\alpha_1, f_0) \neq 0$. Figure 18.20 shows the potential well for a model note approximated by a shallow spherical cap on a circular planform, having a rise–to–thickness ratio (H_0:h) of 2:1, a rise-to-radius ratio (H_0:a) of 1:40, clamped at its edges and subject to in-plane compressive loading (see Chapter 8 for analytical details). The primary well for $s = 0$ (zero compressive load) is located at the point of zero displacement.

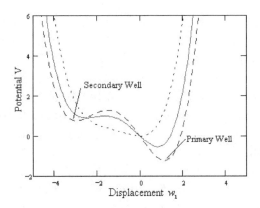

Fig. 18.20. Potential well for the model note: $s = 0$ (dotted line), $s = 0.8$ (solid line), s = 1.2 (dashed line), w_1 in units of shell thickness. $\omega_{10} = 1$, $\alpha_1 = 0.9773$, $\beta_1 = 0.2953$, $f_0 = 1.2464s$.

In Figure 18.20, as s is increased from zero, a secondary well appears while the trough of the primary well shifts in the direction of positive displacement (upwards on the pan face, to the right in the figure). Under normal stick excitation, the note vibrates in the primary well with displacements typically under one note thickness, $w_1 < h$. Interesting and exotic behavior will be observed on this note when $w_1 \sim 4h$ or greater allowing the motion to span both the primary and secondary wells.

The static problem of equation (18.29) for $w_1 = Q$ is governed by

$$\partial V / \partial Q = \omega_{10}^2 (1-s) Q + \alpha_1 Q^2 + \beta_1 Q^3 - f_0 = 0. \quad (18.30)$$

The real roots of (18.30) (with the same parameters as that of Figure 18.20) are shown in Figure 18.21. Two roots emerge and are joined at the critical value $s^* = 0.61947$ (the creation of the secondary well). Q_1 describes the minimum of the primary well. Q_2 corresponds to the saddle point (corresponding to the upside-down equilibrium position in Figure 18.20) while Q_3 describes the minimum of the secondary well. An external driving force converts the static equilibrium points Q_1 and Q_3 to limit cycles. In common language one says that the note surface, initially at rest, is driven into oscillation (vibration).

On the real steelpan notes, Q_1 traces out the path of the bottom of the primary well (physically, the rest position of the apex of the note surface) in which the normal oscillations that gives rise to the musical sound takes place. This path evolves during the tuning process as the in-plane stresses vary with hammer peening. The final position of this well depends on the final *s-value* given to the note. If the peening and other production processes produce a large enough *s-value* (corresponding to large residual compressive stresses), another well develops as traced out by Q_3 in which oscillations can also take place. The critical s value s^* depends on the note geometry. Vibrations around Q_1 (in the primary well) will produce distinctively different tones to those produced by vibrations around Q_3 (in the secondary well). When played excessively hard, a note (more likely a bass note of thin material) can execute a mixture of both types of vibrations (this is the annoying 'boiing' sound heard when the bass note is played excessively hard).

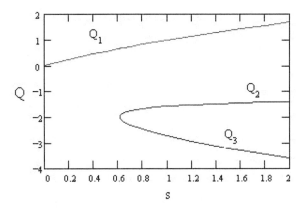

Fig. 18.21. Figure showing the trough of the potential energy surface from the real roots of equation (18.29). The bifurcation point (critical point where Q_2 and Q_3 emerge) occurs at $s = s^* = 0.61497$.

Inspection of the potential well in Figure 18.20 reveals that in order to observe the dynamics of the single mode note over the primary and secondary wells, displacements greater than four shell thicknesses ($4h$ or in our sample note, $w_1 > 2$ mm) are required. This range of excitation is extremely difficult to produce and maintain on the steel shell structures found on the pan. One can get some idea of the difficulty by comparing the displacements on the paper cone of a large loudspeaker driven by a power amplifier supplying 100 watts or more of audio power. In this case the displacements of the speaker cone are clearly noticeable but there are a few things to remember (i) one can easily displace the speaker cone manually with the hand, even with the finger but not so for the pan notes (ii) the inner and outer speaker cone suspensions are very flexible (usually made of rubber or paper) compared with the very rigid steel suspension on the pan note (in fact the boundary of the pan note is assumed to be fixed). I have driven pan notes on the more easily excited bass (the tenor notes are more rigid by comparison) using an electromagnetic exciter driven by a 200 watt audio power amplifier running 'flat out' only to find after the exercise that the notes were shifted downward in frequency. Driving the notes with such large forces approaches the conditions set up by the driving forces one obtains with hammer impacts during tuning.

To study these dynamics, (18.21) was solved numerically using an 8th order Runge-Kutta scheme. In order to ensure that the bifurcations and chaotic motions appearing in the numerical results were real and not '*ghost solutions*' (see for example, Brezzi et al. 1984, Iserles 1987 and Prüfer 1985) the results were checked using an independent 8th order Finite Difference method. The parameters were the same as used in Figures 18.20 and 18.21 for the model note: $\alpha_1 = 0.9773$, $\beta_1 = 0.2953$, $f_0 = 1.2464s$, with $\mu_1 = 0.295$, $\omega_{10} = 1$, $\Omega = 0.9$, s = 0, 0.8, 1.2.

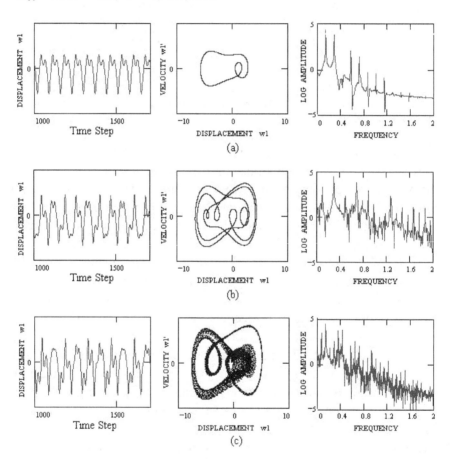

Fig. 18.22. Displacement plots (left panels), phase portraits (middle panels) and frequency spectra (right panels) of equation (18.26) responses. (a) *s = 0.8, f = 5* (period doubling, Period-2); (b) *s = 0.8, f = 10*, (period doubling, Period-8); (c) *s = 0.8, f = 15* (Chaotic).

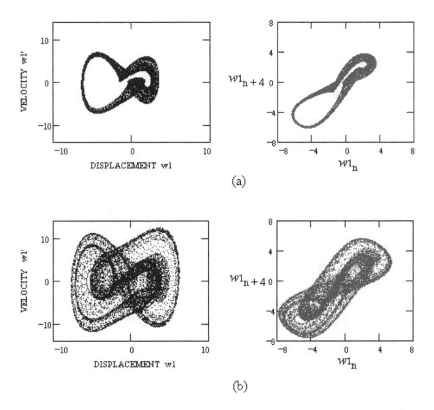

Fig. 18.23. Phase portraits showing strange attractors for our steelpan model, equation (18.21). Left panel shows velocity versus displacement; Right panel shows displacement delay vectors in the Reconstructed Phase-Space. (a) $s = 0$, $f = 10$ and (b) $s = 1.2$, $f = 15.2$

Since truly interesting motions occur on the steelpan only for sufficiently large driving forces that ensures trajectories enter both potential wells only those are represented here. Displays of some of the numerical solutions are given in Figures 18.22 and 18.23. To visualize the attractors we use a *velocity-displacement subspace* unto which the attractors are projected as seen in Figure 18.22 (middle panels). For a driving force magnitude of $f = 5$, the phase plot shows periodic motion about both equilibrium points in Figure 18.20. The frequency spectrum (Figure 18.22(a)) is discrete in this case. Observe the double loop in the trajectory on Figure 18.22(a), middle panel. This means that the system has undergone a period-doubling bifurcation, which is clearly observed on the spectra in Figure 18.22(a), right panel. As the driving amplitude is increased, this system passes through a series of period-doubling bifurcations (Figure 18.22(b)) leading to chaos around $f = 15$ (Figure 18.22(c)). For larger values of f, the system returns to period-doubling responses.

As shown in Figure 18.23 one can observe increased complexity in the trajectories for the post-buckling case $s = 1.2$ when compared with the pre-buckling case with $s = 0$ (zero compressive stress on the note edges). In all observed cases, the route to chaos was via the Feigenbaum scenario: periodic $\rightarrow$ period-doubling $\rightarrow$ chaos.

The steelpan attractors in Figure 18.23 are used to demonstrate Takens theorem by showing that topologically equivalent pictures of the original multidimensional system behavior can be obtained by using the time series of a single observable (displacement $w1$) in time-delay plots. Visual inspection of the left and right panels in Figure 18.23 reveals that the original structure of the system attractor in the velocity ($w1'$)-displacement ($w1$) phase-space is preserved in the reconstructed (time-delay) phase-space.

18.13.2 Experimental Results for the Electronically Simulated Partially Tuned Note

The simulations of equation (18.21) on the electronic circuit presented technical problems not encountered in the numerical experiments. The active devices in the electronic simulator had to be operated within their linear range (maximum output voltage swing ± 14 volts) and overloading avoided. To ensure this, the maximum input/output swings on all devices were limited to ± 5 volts. These considerations also resulted in restrictions on the coupling parameters. This was especially true of the cubic coefficient β_1 as the term $\beta_1 w_1^3$ can easily generate voltages that exceed the required limits.

The experimental results reported here on the single-mode system also appeared in the paper Achong (1999c) with a minimum of details. Low level 60 Hz AC noise that sometimes contaminates the signal of an electrically operated system, despite taking the necessary precautions, and an even lower level 180 Hz harmonic (contained in a single bin of the FT) were filtered from the original data. As in the 2-mode case, filtering was done by interpolating between the adjacent unaffected frequency bins in the FT then taking the IFT to construct the filtered signal.

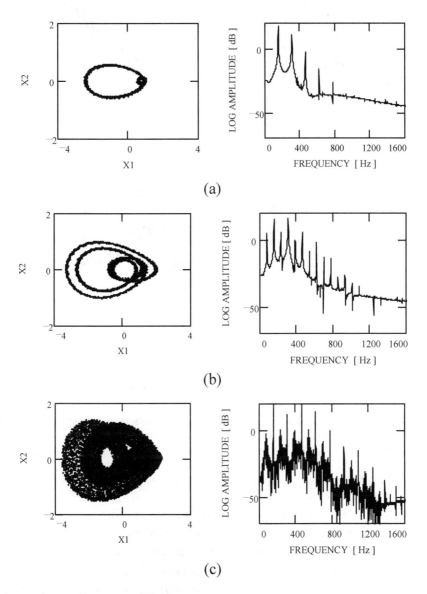

Fig. 18.24. Phase portraits and spectra ($X1 = w_1$, $X2 = w_1'$) with $X1$ and $X2$ in volts. (a) $\alpha_1 = 0.25$, Period-2 (16384 data points), (b) $\alpha_1 = 0.31$, Period-4 (16384 data points), (c) $\alpha_1 = 0.42$, Chaotic (32768 data points). Driving amplitude 1.0 volt and driving frequency 155 Hz.

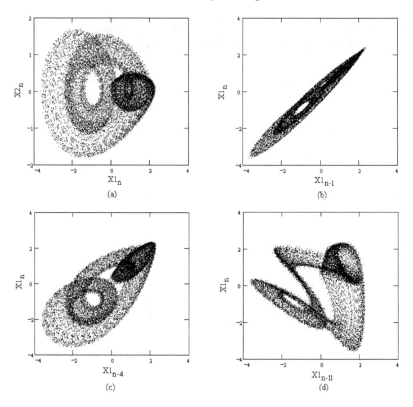

Fig. 18.25. Phase portrait and Delay representations of the data for the single mode system with $\alpha_1 = 0.42$. (a) Phase portrait; 'Velocity' ($X2 = w_1'$) vs 'Displacement' ($X1 = w_1$) with $X1$ and $X2$ in volts. (b) Delay representation of the displacement data with delay = 1; all the data are close to the diagonal since consecutive values are similar. (c) With delay = 4 (corresponding to ¼ the period of the autocorrelation of the squared X1 data corresponding to the quadratic term in equation (18.21)), the features are similar to those revealed in (a). (d) With delay = 11 (corresponding to the first zero of the autocorrelation function of the X1 data) the features of the attractor are well unfolded.

In order to maintain operation within the limits set for the electronic system the experimental values for the coupling coefficients were set lower than the values in the numerical model. The parameters were set at the normalized values: $f_0 = 0$ *(initial value)*, $\beta_1 = 0.19$, $\mu_1 = 0.038$ with ω normalized to unity. To tune the system initially set to 523 Hz (C_5) as a linear, damped oscillator with buckling parameter $s = 0$, the frequency was first reduced to 220 Hz (A_3) by applying the electrical equivalent of compressive stress; analytically equivalent to raising the buckling parameter s.

The non-linear components were then introduced and the buckling parameter further increased to $s \approx 0.7$ to reduce the frequency to E^b_3 = 155.56 Hz. The driving frequency was set to 155 Hz (close to E^b_3 to which the system was tuned) with amplitude of 1.0 volt. To take the system through a series of bifurcations the quadratic coefficient α_1 was increased continuously from 0.2 up to 0.5. The plots in Figure 18.24 show the development after the appearance of an initial *kink* in a periodic orbit to a period-2 mode (Figure 18.24(a)). As the coupling parameter α_1 was further increased, period doubling continued to a period-4 mode (Figure 18.24(b)) and eventually to chaos (Figure 18.24(c)).

Using the methods described in Section 18.12, the attractor dimension and maximal Lyapunov exponent were found to be:

$$D_{corr} = 2.91 \pm 0.04, \lambda = 0.042 \pm 0.002 \text{ per sample interval.}$$

The filtered data viewed in delay coordinates are shown in Figure 18.25 together with a phase portrait of the 'velocity' $X2 = w_1'$ versus the 'displacement' $X1 = w_1$. In Figure 18.25(b) for delay = 1, all data are close to the diagonal because consecutive values are similar. In Figure 18.25(c), with delay = 4 (corresponding to ¼ the period of the autocorrelation of the squared X1 data representing the quadratic term in equation (18.21)), the features of the phase portrait in Figure 18.25(a) are clearly reconstructed. In Figure 18.25(d), with delay = 11 (corresponding to the first zero of the autocorrelation function of the X1 data) the features of the attractor are well unfolded. The ancillary details given here should give the reader some insight into the way that one may search the data for information useful in unraveling the complex dynamical structure of an evolving non-linear system.

The velocity data w_1' were recorded directly as an output signal of the simulator as were the displacement data w_1. It is possible to obtain the velocity data from the displacement time series data using the derivative coordinates

$$w_1'(t) = (w_1(t + \Delta t) - w_1(t - \Delta t))/2\Delta t,$$

where Δt is the sampling interval. Since the derivative coordinates (velocities) are just linear combinations of the displacement coordinates one can deduce from this that the reconstructed state space in derivative coordinates should be the same as in displacement coordinates. This explains the similarity between Figure 18.25(c) and Figure 18.25(a). The problem that arises here when derivative coordinates are *derived* from the displacement is one of noise. If the displacement time series contains noise then the derivative coordinates computed from it will contain a higher level of noise.

BIBLIOGRAPHY

Abramowitz, M. and Stegun, I. A. (eds.). Handbook of Mathematical Functions with Formulas, Graphs, and Mathematical Tables, 9th printing. New York: Dover, 1972.

Achong, A. 1992 The Physics of the Steelpan (presented at *The 3rd Caribbean Conference in Physics*. UWI, St. Augustine, Trinidad).

Achong, A., Achong, T. D. A. and Achong, C. M. A. 1993 *Trinidad and Tobago Patent* **No.39**. Tunable Steelpans - method and device.

Achong, A. 1994 (*Unpublished*). The Steelpan, the Zhong and the Gamelan Gong — some operational similarities.

Achong, A 1995 *Journal of Sound and Vibration*, **183**(1), 157-168. Vibrational analysis of circular and elliptical plates carrying point and ring masses and with edges elastically restrained.

Achong, A. 1996a *Journal of Sound and Vibration*, **191**, 207-217. Vibrational analysis of mass loaded plates and shells by the receptance method with application to the steelpan.

Achong, A. 1996b *Journal of Sound and Vibration*, **197**, 471-487. The Steelpan as a system of non-linear mode-localized oscillators, Part I: Theory, Simulations, Experiments and Bifurcations.

Achong, A. 1997 The Steelpan: Theory of Operation, NIHERST *Sci-TechKnoFest 97*.

(NIHERST, National Institute of Higher Education Science and Technology).

Achong, A. and Sinanansingh, K. A. 1997 *Journal of Sound and Vibration*, **203**, 547-561. The Steelpan as a system of non-linear mode-localized oscillators, Part II: Coupled sub-systems, simulations and experiments.

Achong, A. 1998 *Journal of Sound and Vibration*, **212**, 623-635. The Steelpan as a system of non-linear mode-localized oscillators, Part III: The inverse problem — parameter estimation.

Achong, A 1999a *The Pan Makers' Handbook*. Department of Physics, University of the West Indies.

Achong, A. 1999b Journal of Sound and Vibration, **222**, 597-620. Non-linear analysis of compressively/thermally stressed elastic structures on the steelpan and the underlying theory of the tuning process.

Achong, A. 1999c Non-linear behaviour and chaos in an electronically simulated steelpan note, in: M. Ding, W. L. Ditto, L. M. Pecora, M. L. Spano (eds.), Proceedings of the Fifth Experimental Chaos Conference, World Scientific, Singapore, pp. 133-140.

Achong, A. 2000a Steelpan excitation: the stick properties and the impact phase. Part 1 — the impact phase, in: A. Achong (ed.) Proceedings of the First International Conference on the Science and Technology of the Steelpan, TT Government Printery, Trinidad, pp. 137-145.

Achong, A. 2000b The Theory of the Steelpan, in: A. Achong (ed.) Proceedings of the First International Conference on the Science and Technology of the Steelpan, TT Government Printery, Trinidad, pp. 1-16.

Achong, A. 2000c Note-Note coupling and sympathetic pairs on the steelpan: the Good, the Bad and the Ugly, in: A. Achong (ed.) Proceedings of the First International Conference on the Science and Technology of the Steelpan, TT Government Printery, Trinidad, pp. 245-252.

Achong, A. 2000d Bertie Marshall: The Life and Work of an Extraordinary Pan Pioneer, in: A. Achong (ed.) Proceedings of the First International Conference on the Science and Technology of the Steelpan, TT Government Printery, Trinidad, pp. 211-214.

Achong, A. 2000e Steelpan Excitation: The stick properties and the impact phase, Part I: Theory, in: A. Achong (ed.) Proceedings of the First International Conference on the Science and

Technology of the Steelpan, TT Government Printery, Trinidad, pp. 137-145.

Achong, A. 2000f Detuning and tonal structure of steelpan notes, in: A. Achong (ed.) Proceedings of the First International Conference on the Science and Technology of the Steelpan, TT Government Printery, Trinidad, pp. 41-52.

Achong, A. and Rosemin, C. 2000 Steelpan Excitation: The stick properties and the impact phase, Part II: Experiments, in: A. Achong (ed.) Proceedings of the First International Conference on the Science and Technology of the Steelpan, TT Government Printery, Trinidad, pp. 146-155.

Achong, A. 2003 *Journal of Sound and Vibration.* **266**, 193- 197. Mode locking on the non-linear notes of the steelpan.

Achong, A. 2012 *The Pan Jumbie confronts the G-Pan Patent*, delivered at The Inaugural International Conference on the Steelpan, Steelfestt, May 6-9, 2012, Port of Spain, Trinidad.

Acton, F. S. Numerical Methods That Work, 2nd printing. Washington, DC: Math. Assoc. Amer., p. 103, 1990.

Allen, J.B. and Rabiner, L.R. 1977 *Proceedings of the IEEE*, **65**, 1558-1564. A unified approach to short-time Fourier analysis and synthesis.

ANSI 1997, *American National Standard For Steel Drums and Pails*, ANSI MH2-1997, American National Standards Institution.

Arfken, G. Mathematical Methods for Physicists, 3rd ed. Orlando, FL: Academic Press, pp. 492-493, 1985.

Azimi, S. 1988a *Journal of Sound and Vibration* **120**(1), 19-35. Free vibration of circular plates with elastic edge supports using the receptance method.

Azimi, S. 1988b *Journal of Sound and Vibration* **127**(2), 391-393. Free vibration of a circular plate carrying a concentrated mass at its center.

Azimi, S., Hamilton, J. F. and Soedel, W. 1984 *Journal of Sound and Vibration* **93**(1), 9-29. The receptance method applied to the free vibration of continuous rectangular plates.

Barenblatt, G. I. 1962 *.Advances in Applied Mechanics*, vol. 7, pp. 55-129, Academic Press Inc., New York.

Barrows, S. E.; Eberlein, T. H. 2005 "Understanding Rotation about a C=C Double Bond". J. Chem. Educ. 82: 1329.

Bastiaans, M. J. 1980, *Proceedings of the IEEE*, **68**, 538-539. Gabor's expansion of a signal into Gaussian elementary signals.

Bendixson, Ivar 1901, "Sur les courbes définies par des équations différentielles", *Acta Mathematica* (Springer Netherlands) **24** (1): 1–88.

Bishop, R. E. D. and Johnson, D. C. 1960 *The Mechanics of Vibration*. London: Cambridge University Press.

Blades, J. 1975 *Percussion Instruments and their History.* Faber and Faber, London.

Bracewell, R. 1999 "The Fourier Transform and Its Applications," 3rd ed. New York: McGraw-Hill.

Brezzi, F., Ushikj, S., & Fujii, H. 1984 Real and ghost bifurcation dynamics in difference schemes for ODEs. In: *Numerical Methods for Bifurcation Problems* (T. Kupper, H. D. Mittlemann & H. Weber, Eds). Birkhauser, Basle.

Bucco, D. and Mazumdar, J. 1983 *Computers & Structures* **17**(3), 441-447. Estimation of the fundamental frequencies of shallow shells by a finite element isodeflection contour method.

Callister, W. Materials Science and Engineering. John Wiley and Sons, New York 1994.

Cartwright, J. H. E. and Piro, O. "The Dynamics of Runge-Kutta Methods." Int. J. Bifurcations Chaos 2, 427-449, 1992.

Chladni, E. F. F., 1789 *Entdeckungen über die Theorie des Klanges* ("Discoveries in the Theory of Sound"). Leipzig.

Cochardt, A.W., 1953, "The origin of damping high strength ferromagnetic alloys", Journal of Applied Mechanics, v.20, pp.196-200.

Connor, J. Jr. 1962 *NASA TH B1510*, 623-642. Nonlinear transverse axisymmetric vibrations of shallow spherical shells.

Copeland, B. R., Morrison, A., Rossing, T. D. 2001 "Sound Radiation from Caribbean Steelpans" 142nd ASA Meeting, Fort Lauderdale, FL.

Coronel, V.F. and Beshers, D.N., 1988, "Magnetomechanical damping in iron", Journal of Applied Physics, vol.64, pp.2006-2015.

Dorf, R. C. and Bishop, R. H., 2007, Modern Control Systems, 11th ed., Prentice Hall.

Eckmann, J. P. and Ruelle, D. "Ergodic Theory of Chaos and Strange Attractors," *Reviews of Modern Physics,* vol. 57, pp. 617-656, July 1985.

Evensen, D. A. 1963, *American Institute of Aeronautics Astronautics Journal* **1**, 2857-2858. Some observations on the nonlinear vibration of thin cylindrical shells.

Ewing, J.A. 1895, Experimental research in magnetism. *Philosophical Transactions of the Royal Society of London,* 176, II.

Falconer, K. 1990 *Fractal geometry: mathematical foundations and applications.* Chichester, John Wiley.

Ferreyra, E., Maldonado, J. G., Murr, L. E., Pappu, S., Trillo, E. A., Kennedy, C., Posada, M., De Alba, J., Christie, R. and. Russell, D. P 1999, *J. Mater. Sci.* **34**, 981.

Fletcher, H and Munson, W. A. 1933 "Loudness, its definition, measurement and calculation" J. Acoust. Soc Am.5, 82–108.

Fletcher, N. H. and Rossing, T. D. 1991 *The Physics of Musical Instruments.* Springer – Verlag, New York.

Frank, R. C., Schroeder, C. W., Johnson, B. G., and Swanson, P. A. 1969 "Magnetomechanical Damping in the Temperature Range of 78°—300°K", J. Appl. Phys. 40, 1088.

Fukuhara, M. and Sanpel, A. 1993, Elastic Steels Moduli and Internal Friction as a Function of Temperature of Low Carbon and Stainless. ISIJ International, Vol. 33, No, 4, pp. 508-512.

Gabor, D. 1946, *Journal of the Institute of Electrical Engineers,* **93**, 429-457. Theory of communication.

Gardner, F. M. 1979 *Phaselock Techniques.* New York: Wiley-Interscience.

Gladwell, G. M. L. 1986 *Applied Mechanics Review,* **39**, 1013-1018. Inverse problems in vibration.

Gladwell, G. M. L. 1996 *Applied Mechanics Review,* **49**, S25- S34. Inverse problems in vibration – II.

Goel, R. P. 1975 *Journal of Sound and Vibration* **41**, 85-91. Axisymmetrical vibration of a circular plate having an elastic edge beam and a central mass.

Gradshteyn, I. S. and Ryzhik, I. M., 2000, Routh-Hurwitz Theorem, §15.715 in Tables of Integrals, Series, and Products, 6th ed. San Diego, CA: Academic Press.

Grassberger, P. and Procaccia, I. 1983a. Estimation of the Kolmogorov entropy from a chaotic signal. *Phys. Rev. A*, 28(4):2591.

Grassberger, P. and Procaccia, I. 1983b Measuring the strangeness of strange attractors. *Physica*, 9D:189.

Grassberger, P. and Procaccia, I. 1984 Dimensions and entropies of strange attractors from a fluctuating dynamics approach. *Physica*, 13D:34.

Griffith, A.A. 1962 *Trans. Roy. Soc. (London), Ser. A*, vol. 221, pp. 163-198.

Grossi, R. O., Laura, P. A. A. and Narita, Y. 1986 *Journal of Sound and Vibration* **106**(2), 181-186. A note on vibrating polar orthotropic circular plates carrying concentrated masses.

Grossman, P. L., Koplik, B. and Yu, Y. -Y. 1969 *Transactions of the American Society of Mechanical Engineers Journal of Applied Mechanics* **39E**, 451-458. Nonlinear vibrations of shallow spherical shells.

Haas, H. (1951). "Uber den Einfluss eines Einfachechos auf die Horsamkeit von Sprache," Acustica, 1, 49–58.

Haas, H. 1972, JAES Volume 20 Issue 2; 146-159,"The Influence of a Single Echo on the Audibility of Speech"

Hale, K. K. 1963 Oscillations in Nonlinear Systems. New York: McGraw-Hill.

Hansen, U. J. 1995 *Journal of the Acoustical Society of America*. **98**(5), Pt.2, 2975. Modal analysis and materials considerations in Caribbean steelpans. (Presented at the 130th Meeting: Acoustical Society of America)

Hansen, U. J., Rossing, T. D., Mannette, E. and George, K. 1995 *MRS Bulletin* **20**(3), 44-46, "The Caribbean steel pan: Tuning and mode studies".

Harris, C. M. ed. 1987 Shock and Vibration Handbook. McGraw-Hill

Harris, J. W. and Stocker, H. 1998 "Hausdorff Dimension." in Handbook of Mathematics and Computational Science. New York: Springer-Verlag, pp. 113-114,

Hausdorff, F. "Dimension und äußeres Maß." Math. Ann. 79, 157-179, 1919.

Helstrom, C. W. 1966, *IEEE Transactions on Information Theory*, **IT-12**, 81-82. An expansion of a signal in Gaussian elementary signals.

Herschfeld, A. 1935 "On Infinite Radicals." Amer. Math. Monthly 42, 419-429.

Hertz, H., 1882, Über die Berührung fester elastischer Körper, Journal für die reine und angewandte Mathematik (Crelle), 92, 156-171.

Hertzberg, R. Deformation and Fracture Mechanics of Engineering Materials. John Wiley and Sons, New York 1996.

Hlawatsch, F. and Boudreaux-Bartels, G.F.1992, *IEEE Signal Processing Magazine*, **9**, 21-67. Linear and quadratic time-frequency signal representations.

Ho, M.T., Datta, A., Bhattacharyya, S.P., 1998, An elementary derivation of the Routh Hurwitz Criterion, IEEE Trans. Automatic Control 43 (3) 405–409.

Hodges, C. H. 1982 *Journal of Sound and Vibration*, **82**, 411-424. Confinement of vibration by structural irregularity.

Hurwitz, A., 1895, Über die Bedingungen, unter welchen eine Gleichung nurWurzeln mit negativen reellen Teilen besitzt, Math. Ann. 46, 273–284.

Hurwitz, A. 1964, On the conditions under which an equation has only roots with negative real parts, Selected Papers on Mathematical Trends in Control Theory. (An English translation of the 1895 paper).

Iserles, A. 1987 Dynamical systems and nonlinear stability theory for numerical ODEs. In: *Numerical Treatment of Differential Equations, Halle 1987* (K. Strehmel, Ed.). Teubner, Berlin.

Jeffreys, H. and Jeffreys, B. S. "The Adams-Bashforth Method." §9.11 in Methods of Mathematical Physics, 3rd ed. Cambridge, England: Cambridge University Press, pp. 292-293, 1988.

Johnson, W. 1982 *Mechanics of Solids* (eds. H. G. Hopkins and M. J. Sewell, Pergamon Press, Oxford), 303-356. The mechanics of some industrial pressing, rolling, and forging processes.

Jones, D. J. 1995 "Continued Powers and a Sufficient Condition for Their Convergence." Math. Mag. 68, 387-392.

Kalker, J. J., 1990, Three-dimensional elastic bodies in rolling contact, Kluwer Academic Publishers.

Kantz, H, and Schreiber, T. 1997 *Nonlinear Time Series Analysis*. Cambridge: Cambridge University Press.

Kantz, H. (1994). A robust method to estimate the maximal Lyapunov exponent in a time series. *Phys. Lett. A*. **185**, 77.

Kevorkian, J. 1987 *Society for Industrial and Applied Mathematics Review*, **29**, 391-462. Perturbation techniques for oscillatory systems with slowly varying coefficients.

King, M. E. and Vakakis, A. F. 1995 *International Journal of Solids and Structures*, **32**, 1161-1177. Asymptotic analysis of nonlinear mode localization in a class of coupled continuous structures.

Koster, W. and Metallk, Z. 1948 Die Temperaturabhängigkeit des Elastizitätsmoduls reiner Metalle. Vol 39, pp. 1-9.

Lancaster, P. and Maroulas, J. 1987 *Journal of Mathematical Analysis and Applications*, **123**, 238-261. Inverse eigenvalue problems for damped vibrating systems.

Lawergren, B. 1980 *Acustica* **44**, 194-206. On the motion of bowed violin strings.

Lee, W. K. and Hsu, C. S. 1994 Journal of Sound and Vibration **171**,335-359. A global analysis of an harmonically excited spring-pendulum system with internal resonance.

Liew, K. M. 1992 *Journal of Sound and Vibration* **156**(1), 99-107. Vibration of eccentric ring and line supported circular plates carrying concentrated masses.

Lim, C. W. and Liew, K. M. 1994 *Journal of Sound and Vibration* **173**(3), 343-375. A pb-2 Ritz formulation for flexural vibration of shallow cylindrical shells of rectangular planform.

Marsden, J. E. and McCraken, M. 1976 The Hopf Bifurcation and Its Applications, Springer-Verlag, New-York.

Masubichi, K., 1980, Analysis of Welded Structures, Oxford, New York, Pergamon Press.

Mazumdar, J., 1971, *Journal of Sound and Vibration* **18**, 147-155. Transverse vibration of elastic plates by the method of constant deflection lines.

McIntyre, M. E. and Woodhouse, J. 1979 *Acustica* **43**, 93-108. On the fundamentals of bowed-string dynamics.

McIntyre, M. E., Schumacher, R. T. and Woodhouse, J. 1983 *Journal of the Acoustical Society of America*, **74**, 1325-1345. On the oscillations of musical instruments.

McLaughlin, J. 1998 "Good Vibrations", American Scientist, v. 86, No.4, pp. 342.

Mickens, R. E. 1981 *Introduction to Nonlinear Oscillations*. Cambridge; Cambridge University Press.

Morse, P. M. and Feshbach, H. Methods of Theoretical Physics, Part I. New York: McGraw-Hill, pp. 464-465, 1953.

Moss, G. P.; Smith, P. A. S. 1995. "Glossary of Class Names of Organic Compounds and Reactive Intermediates Based on Structure (IUPAC Recommendations 1995)". Pure and Applied Chemistry 67: 1307–1375.

Mottershead, J. E. and Friswell, M. I. 1993 *Journal of Sound and Vibration*, **167**, 347-375. Model updating in structural dynamics: A survey.

Muddeen, F and Copeland, B, 2000 Polar Results of a Tenor Steelpan, in: A. Achong (ed.) Proceedings of the First International Conference on the Science and Technology of the Steelpan, TT Government Printery, Trinidad, pp. 115-127.

Murr, L. E., Ferreyra, E., Maldonado, J. G., Trillo, E. A., Pappu, S., Kennedy, C., De Alba, J., Posada, M., Russell, D. P. and White, J. L. 1999 *J. Mater. Sci.* **34**, 967.

Murr, L. E., Gaytan, S. M., Lopez, M, I., Bujanda, D. E., Martinez, E. Y., Whitmyre, G. and Price, H. 2008 Metallurgical and acoustical characterization of a hydroformed, 304 stainless steel, Caribbean-style musical pan. Materials Characterization, Vol. 59, Issue 3, 321-328.

Murr, L. E., Esquivel, E. V., Bujanda, A. A., Martinez, N. E., Soto, K. F., Tapia, A. S., Lair, S., Somasekharan, A. C., Imbert, C. A. C., Kerns, R., Irvine, S. and Lawrie, S. 2004 Metallurgical and acoustical comparisons for a brass pan with a Caribbean steel pan standard. ***Journal of Materials Science Volume 39, Number 13*** 4139-4155

Murr, L.E., Esquivel, E.V., Lawrie, S.C., Lopez, M.I., Lair, S.L., Soto, K.F., Gaytan, S.M., Bujanda, D., Kerns, R.G., Guerrero, P.A. and Flores, J.A. 2006, *Materials Characterization* Vol. 57, Issues 4-5, pp 232-243. Fabrication of an aluminum, Caribbean-style, musical pan: Metallurgical and acoustical characterization.

Muthukumaran, P., Bhat, R. B. and Stiharu, I. 1999 *Journal of Sound and Vibration*, **220**, 847-859, Boundary conditioning technique for structural tuning.

National Physical Laboratory: "Stress Corrosion Cracking" (Guides to Good Practice in Corrosion Control), Middlesex (UK), 2000.

Nayfeh, A. H. 1973 *Perturbation Methods*, New York, Wiley and Sons.

Nayfeh, A. H. and Balachandran, B. *Applied Nonlinear Dynamics*, Wiley Interscience, New York, New York, USA, 1995.

Nayfeh, A. H. and Mook, D. T. 1979 *Nonlinear Oscillations*. New York: Wiley-Interscience.

Nayfeh, A. H. and Zavodney, L. D. 1988 *ASME Journal of Applied Mechanics*, **55**, 706-710. Experimental observation of amplitude- and phase-modulated responses of two internally coupled oscillators to a harmonic excitation.

Newman, R. C and Procter, R. P.M. 1990 Stress Corrosion Cracking: 1965-1990, British Corrosion Journal, vol. 25, no. 4, pp. 259-269.

Newman, R.C. 1995 Stress Corrosion Cracking Mechanisms. Corrosion Mechanisms in Theory and Practice, eds P. Marcus and J. Oudar, 2nd ed, pp 399-450, Marcel Dekker.

Niku-Lari, A. 1981 First *International Conference on Shot Peening* (ed. A. Niku-Lari, Pergamon Press, Oxford), 1-21. Shot peening.

Okrouhlik, M. (Ed.) 1994 "Mechanics of Contact Impact", Appl. Mech. Rev., vol. 47 (2).

Ott, E., 1993 *Chaos in Dynamical Systems*, Cambridge University Press.

Ott, E., Sauer, T. Yorke, J. A. , 1994 *Coping with chaos*, Wiley Interscience, New York, New York, USA.

Papoulis, A. 1974, *Journal of the Optical Society of America* **64**, 779-788. Ambiguity function in Fourier optics.

Parkins, **R.N**. 2000. "Stress Corrosion Cracking", in Uhlig's Corrosion Handbook 2nd Edition (R.W. Revie Ed.), Wiley, New York.

Peekna, A. and Rossing, T. D. 2000 Measuring Residual Stresses in a Steelpan, in: A. Achong (ed.) Proceedings of the First International Conference on the Science and Technology of the Steelpan, TT Government Printery, Trinidad, pp. 203-210.

Pierre, C. and Dowell, E. H. 1987 *Journal of Sound and Vibration*, **114**, 549-564. Localization of vibrations by structural irregularity.

Poincaré, H. 1892, "Sur les courbes définies par une équation différentielle", *Oeuvres*, **1**, Paris.

Press, W. H.; Flannery, B. P.; Teukolsky, S. A.; and Vetterling, W. T. "Multistep, Multivalue, and Predictor-Corrector Methods."

§16.7 in Numerical Recipes in FORTRAN: The Art of Scientific Computing, 2nd ed. Cambridge, England: Cambridge University Press, pp. 740-744, 1992.

Press, W. H., Flannery, B. P., Teukolsky, S. A. and Vetterling, W. T. "Convolution and Deconvolution Using the FFT." §13.1 in Numerical Recipes in FORTRAN: The Art of Scientific Computing, 2nd ed. Cambridge, England: Cambridge University Press, pp. 531-537, 1992.

Prüfer, M. 1985 Turbulence in multistep methods for initial value problems. *SIAM J. Appl. Math.* **45**, 32-69.

Rabiner, L. R. and Schafer, R. W. 1978 *Digital Processing of Speech Signals*, Englewood Cliffs, NJ: Prentice-Hall Signal Processing Series.

Rayleigh, J. W. S. "The Theory of Sound," vol. 2, 2nd ed., 1896, reprinted by Dover, New York, 1945, sec. 278.

Rekach, V. G. 1978 *Static Theory of Thin-walled Space Structures* (translated from the Russian by A. Petrosyan). Moscow: Mir. See pp. 13 and 146.

Renyi, A. 1971 *Probability Theory*, North Holland, Amsterdam.

Robinson, D. W. and Dodson, R. S. 1956 "A re-determination of the equal-loudness relations for pure tones" Br. J. Appl. Phys. 7, 166-181.

Rohner, F. and Schärer, S. 2000 The Pang Instruments, in: A. Achong (ed.) Proceedings of the First International Conference on the Science and Technology of the Steelpan, TT Government Printery, Trinidad, pp. 197-201.

Rosenstein, M. T., Collins, J. J. and De Luca, C. J. 1993 A practical method for calculating largest Lyapunov exponents from small data sets. *Physica D*, **65**, 117.

Rossing, T. D., Hampton, D. S. and Hansen, U. J. 1995 *Journal of the Acoustical Society of America.* **98**(5), Pt.2, 2975. Acoustics of steelpans. (Presented at the 130th Meeting: Acoustical Society of America).

Rossing, T. D., Hampton, D. S. and Hansen, U. J. 1996 *Physics Today*, March, 24-29. Music from oil drums: The acoustics of the steel pan.

Rossing, T. D., Hansen, U. J. and Hampton, D. S. 2000 "Modes of Vibration in Tenor and Double Second Pans" in: A. Achong (ed.) Proceedings of the First International Conference on the

Science and Technology of the Steelpan, TT Government Printery, Trinidad, pp. 83-95.

Routh, E. J. (1877). A Treatise on the Stability of a Given State of Motion: Particularly Steady Motion. London, Macmillan and Company.

Sano, M. and Sawada, Y. "Measurement of the Lyapunov Spectrum from a Chaotic Time Series," *Physical Review Letters*, vol. 55, pp. 1082-1085, 1985.

Sauer, T, and Yorke, J. A. 1993. How many delay coordinates do you need? *Int. J. Bifurcation and Chaos*, **3**, 737.

Sauer, T., Yorke, J. A. and Casdagli, M. 1991. Embedology. *J. Stat. Phys.*, **65**, 579.

Saunders, W. H. 1964. Patai, S. (ed). The Chemistry of Alkenes. Wiley Interscience. pp. 149–150.

Schafer, R.W. and Rabiner, L.R. 1973, *IEEE Transactions on Audio Electroacoustics*, **AU-21**, 165-174. Design and simulation of a speech analysis-synthesis system based on short-time Fourier analysis.

Schärer, S. and Rohner, F. 2000 Hardening Steel by Nitriding, in: A. Achong (ed.) Proceedings of the First International Conference on the Science and Technology of the Steelpan, TT Government Printery, Trinidad, pp. 179-188.

Schärer, S., Rohner, F. and Schober, P. 2000 The Technology of a New Rawform, in: A. Achong (ed.) Proceedings of the First International Conference on the Science and Technology of the Steelpan, TT Government Printery, Trinidad, pp. 189-195.

Schroeder, M. 1991 Fractals, Chaos, Power Laws: Minutes from an Infinite Paradise. New York: W. H. Freeman, pp. 41-45.

Shampine, L. F., and Gordon, M. K., Computer Solution of Ordinary Differential Equations: The Initial Value Problem. San Francisco:, Freeman, 1975.

Shampine, L. F.. Numerical Solution of Ordinary Differential Equations. New York: Chapman and Hall, 1994.

Sharma, C. B. 1974 *Journal of Sound and Vibration* **35**, 55-76. Calculation of natural frequencies of fixed-free circular cylindrical shells.

Smith, G.W. and Birchak, J.R., 1968, "Effect of internal stress distribution on magnetomechanical damping", Journal of Applied Physics, vol.39, pp.2311-2316.

Smith, G.W. and Birchak, J.R., 1969, "Internal stress distribution theory of magnetomechanical hysteresis - An extension to include effects of magnetic field and applied stress", Journal of Applied Physics, vol.40, pp.5174-5178.

Soedel, W. 1980 *Journal of Sound and Vibration* **70**, 309-317. A new frequency formula for closed circular cylindrical shells for a large variety of boundary conditions.

Sonemblum, M., Gil, E., Laura, P. A. A., Filipich, C. P., Bergman, A., and Sanzi, H. C. 1989 *Applied Acoustics* **28**, 1-7. A note on vibrations of elliptical plates carrying concentric, concentrated mass.

Starek, L. and Inman, D. J. 1992 *Transactions of the American Society of Mechanical Engineers, Journal of Vibration and Acoustics*, **114**, 564-568. A symmetric inverse vibration problem.

Starek, L. and Inman, D. J. 1995 *Journal of Sound and Vibration*, **181**, 893-903. A symmetric inverse vibration problem with overdamped modes.

Steuermann, E., 1939, On Hertz Theory of local deformations of compressed bodies, Computes Rendus (Doklady) de l'Academie des Sciences de l'URSS, 25, 359.

Stöckmann, H. –J. 2007 "Chladni meets Napoleon" Eur. Phys. J. Special Topics 145, 15 – 23. Springer-Verlag.

Strogatz, S, H. 1994. *Nonlinear Dynamics and Chaos*. Addison Wesley publishing company.

Tada, H., Paris, P. C. and Irwin, G. R. 2000 *The Stress Analysis of Cracks Handbook*, American Society of Mechanical Engineers; 3rd edition.

Takens, F. 1981 Detecting strange attractors in turbulence. In: Dynamical systems and Turbulence- Lecture Notes in Mathematics, vol. 898, Rand D.A., Young L.S., eds, Springer-Verlag, Berlin.

Theiler, J. 1987, Efficient Algorithm for Estimating the Correlation Dimension from a Set of Discrete Points, Physical Review A, Vol 36, No 9, pp 4456-4462.

Timoshenko, S. P. and Goodier, J. N., 1970 Theory of Elasticity, 3rd. ed. New York: McGraw-Hill.

Vakakis, A. F. and Cetinkaya, C. 1993 *SIAM Journal of Applied Mathematics*, **53**, 265-282. Mode Localization in a class of multidegree-of-freedom nonlinear systems with cyclic symmetry.

Vakakis, A. F., Nayfeh, T. and King, M. E. 1993 *ASME Journal of Applied Mechanics*, **60**, 388-397. A multiple-scales analysis of nonlinear, localized modes in a cyclic periodic system.

Wade, L.G. (Sixth Ed., 2006). Organic Chemistry. Pearson Prentice Hall. pp. 279.

Wallach, H., Newman, E. B., and Rosenzweig, M. R. (1949) *The American Journal of Psychology*, 62, 315–336. The precedence effect in sound localization.

Wei, S. T. and Pierre, C. 1988a *ASME Journal of Vibration, Acoustics, Stress, and Reliability in Design*, **110**, 429-438. Localization phenomena in mistuned assemblies with cyclic symmetry, Part I: Free vibrations.

Wei, S. T. and Pierre, C. 1988b *ASME Journal of Vibration, Acoustics, Stress, and Reliability in Design*, **110**, 439-449. Localization phenomena in mistuned assemblies with cyclic symmetry, Part II: Forced vibrations.

Whitney, H. 1936 Differentiable manifolds, Ann. Math., **37**, 645.

Wilken, I. D. and Soedel, W. 1976a *Journal of Sound and Vibration* **44**(4), 563-576. The receptance method applied to ring-stiffened cylindrical shells: analysis of modal characteristics.

Wilken, I. D. and Soedel, W. 1976b *Journal of Sound and Vibration* **44**(4), 577-589. Simplified prediction of the modal characteristics of ring-stiffened cylindrical shells.

Wu T. W. and Seybert A. F., 2000 "Case study evaluation of the Rayleigh integral method (A)" J. Acoust. Soc. Am. Volume 108, Issue 5, pp. 2451-245.

Yu, Y. -Y. 1963 *Journal of Applied Mechanics* **30**, 79-86. Application of variational equation of motion to the non-linear vibration analysis of homogeneous and layered plates and shells.

Zweifel, G. S., Nantz, M. H. 2007. Modern Organic Synthesis: An Introduction. New York: W. H. Freeman & Co.. pp. 322–339.

INDEX

A

Abrasion, 87, 104, 106, 480, 486, 490
Absorption (shank), 566, 588, 589, 590, 605, 622, 626, 655, 662,673
Absorption mats, 627, 628, 664, 754
Accent. 46, 739, 740, 781, 1010, 1014, 1016, 1060
Acoustic Efficiency, 436, 459, 460,476, 477, 481
Acoustic Impedance, 436, 460, 462,515, 567
Acoustic mass, 463, 469, 475, 480
Acoustic Radiation Power, 436,
Acoustical Pressure, 436, 440, 856
Acoustical Radiation 196, 199, 230, 365, 377, 379, 432, 435, 440, 731, 762, 857, 1057
Acoustical reaction force, 436, 460,
Acoustical Resistance 478
Acoustics, 422
Acquisition mode, 396, 399, 402, 403
Advanced tuning, 112, 187, 845, 995 – 997
Advanced stick retrieval, 616 – 617,620
Air column, 422 - 423
Aluminum, 57, 184, 186, 277 – 279, 577 – 581, 1009, 1109
Amorphous, 489,
Amplitude Modulation 153, 161 – 180, 204, 207 – 215, 402 – 403, 438, 756, 797, 875 – 879, 956, 1027, 1139

Amplitude Profiles 116, 880, 887, 960-964
Analytical methods, 147, 1147
Analytic state function, 1127
Analyzing frequency ,42, 164, 168, 232, 244
Anechoic chamber, 426
Anneal, 54, 59-60, 70, 92, 95, 97-103, 133, 270, 318, 753
Annealing, 54, 59-60, 70, 92, 95, 97-103, 133, 270, 318, 753
ANSI, 53
Ansatz, 158, 1128
Anthony Williams, 824, 861, 890, 963
Antinode, 570, 685, 698, 763, 882
Anvil, 53, 65
Area of Confinement, 181
Aspect ratio 114, 117, 131, 144-150, 364-365, 370, 411, 868, 898, 910, 913, 915-941
Asymptotically stable, 298, 300, 1128, 1129
Attachment (rear attachment), 264, 329, 330, 381, 1042, 1068, 1092, 1097, 1099, 1108
Attractor, 1147, 1148, 1151-1158, 1166-1169
Augmented Fourth, 803, 806
Aural Harmonics, 1040
Aural Perception, 855
Austenite, 98, 99

B

Baffle, 436-439, 440, 446, 447
Balancing, 250, 672, 1007, 1012-1016, 1019, 1062
Band-limiting, 620, 646, 725, 737-743, 744-747, 763, 768-771, 779-780, 821, 1051, 1080, 1100
basilar membrane, 1034-1036
Basin of attraction, 1147-1149
Bass, 34, 35, 44, 48, 111, 114, 145, 159, 170, 179, 193-194, 208-217, 492, 511, 642-645, 653-654, 738, 989, 991-993, 1000, 1026-1032
Bass Loss Problem, 427-429
Baton, 1023
Beats, 790, 1026, 1035-1038
Bells, 33, 1078
Bertie Marshall, 50, 51, 85, 172, 186, 190, 272, 823, 860-861, 889-890, 963, 995, 1011, 1017, 1101
Bessel function, 39, 261, 405, 448, 706, 765, 919,
Bifurcation, 115, 120, 296, 297, 302, 314, 316,-322, 395, 1119, 1127-1166
Blender (definition), 799, 807, 1015, 1025, 1060,
Blending, 799, 870, 953, 1014, 1015, 1016-1019, 1038, 1060
Blocking, 36, 90, 114, 149, 150, 186, 260, 279, 316, 328, 377-378, 445, 465, 472, 753, 791, 825, 835-845, 846, 853, 856, 869, 943, 982, 992, 996, 1003-1006, 1019, 1064, 1087,
Blocking Condition, 844-847
Blowtorch, 141, 142
'boiing' sound, 303, 307, 329, 331, 942, 988, 1087, 1162,
Bond (attachment), 97, 359, 361, 485-487
Bore Holes, 87-89, 378, 381, 830, 841-843
Bore Pan, 35, 87, 88-92, 378, 381, 842, 843, 853, 1043, 1053, 1069,
Boundary Conditions, 44, 112, 120, 125, 135, 142, 147, 153, 258, 315, 419, 421, 514, 869, 899, 904, 907, 913, 985-987, 1065

Bowl 1055, 1057, 1108, 1111, 1116,
B-Pan, 1043, 1053, 1055, 1060, 1080
Branch point, 831
Brass, 57, 87, 184, 277-279, 317-326, 333-341, 481, 1079,
Bridge 740, 1062
Buckling, 59, 75-86, 112, 142-143, 267-271, 300-329, 390, 479, 912, 984, 1067, 1091, 1094, 1108,
Buckling parameter, 271, 273, 276, 298, 300, 318, 320, 323, 941-942, 1140
Burning ,54, 85, 92, 97-102, 316, 382, 837-839, 993, 1003, 1019, 1105
Busy note, 963, 965

C

Caoutchouc, 485
Carbon Content, 60, 99, 862, 943
Carbon Steel, 55, 56, 57, 86, 93, 95, 97-100, 104, 105, 279, 358-361, 381, 465, 839, 1086
Carburizing, 57, 98, 106,
Carillon, 1078,
Case hardening, 105
Cementite, 98-99
Cello, 35, 45, 111, 281, 323, 372-376, 553, 642-646, 651, 737-747, 793, 813, 865, 987-988, 991,1009
Chaos 1119, 1121, 1147-1170
Chaotic behaviour, 1147-1170
Characteristic equation, 1128, 1129,
Characteristic impedance, 57, 441, 568-569, 570, 580, 581, 835, 843
Characteristic polynomial, 1132
Chemical treatment, 87, 1056
Chime, 53-55, 63-86, 82-88, 368, 840, 848-849, 1052, 1082, 1091, 1116,
Chime Rotation, 72, 85
Chladni pattern, 181, 247, 316, 419, 838, 894-895, 906-907, 935, 936
Chorus Effect, 429, 439, 457, 883, 1017, 1021-1032, 1061
Chromatic scale, 781, 804, 824, 926,
Chrome-Plated Notes, 34, 103, 104, 477, 481, 482, 762, 976,
Chroming, 57, 60, 92, 93, 103, 104, 106, 478, 481, 837

Circle of Fifths, 781
Clarinet, 44, 152, 795, 807, 863, 864
Classical Setting, 967, 968
Classification of Sticks, 786
Coated notes (, 103, 104-105, 414-417, 458, 459, 460, 468, 476-478, 480, 762, 837, 1019
Cochlea, 1034, 1035, 1040
Coefficient of Restitution (COR), 539, 546, 582-584, 585-595, 626-627, 654-678
Coherence (coherent), 429, 430, 438, 439, 443,
Cold-work (Cold Working), 87, 95, 97, 100, 381, 382,
Combination Resonances, 139, 183, 191, 197, 204, 215, 256, 257, 404, 854, 1138,
Combinatorics, 184
Compatibility, 65, 70, 119, 407, 520
Competition Grade pan, 42, 661, 795, 995, 997, 1010, 1047
Complex conjugate, 158, 921, 1130
complex mechanical impedance, 287,
complex tuning, 114, 928, 995, 996, 1010
Compliance, 67, 413, 415, 458, 466, 494- 496, 535, 536,
Compound Zone, 105
Compressing/Stretching Rule, 797
Compression, 62, 65, 80, 109, 110, 122, 273, 323, 494, 517, 586,
Compression Formula, 622-626, 628, 656,
Compression phase, 494, 495, 496,
Compression-Restitution, 495-499, 509, 526, 530, 585, 683
Compressive Stress, 58, 89-92, 112, 122, 141, 270-277, 315-330, 338, 384, 388, 390-394, 832, 842, 912, 984, 1089-1098, 1102-1103
Computational Methods, 166, 198
Conductor (masters of the baton), 675, 795, 808, 822, 1017-1018, 1023, 1030, 1062
Confinement, 38-40, 114, 181-182, 230, 246, 791, 794, 926-927, 986-995,
1099, 1100
Conservation of mass, 1113
Constitutive Laws, 65, 66, 70
Contact area, 120, 153, 154, 492, 493, 549, 574-575, 607, 651
Contact force, 330, 515, 540, 590, 607, 665. 677. 761, 717, 744
Contact force spectrum, 701-717, 730-744
Contact pressure, 501, 601-604, 679-685, 691-692
Contact time, 121, 167, 179, 534-539, 553, 554-576
Contact width, 349, 493, 547, 821
Contact-force time history, 526, 541-542, 618, 646-649
Contact-width Band-limiting, 646, 763, 768, 821
Control of SCC, 92
Convolution, 710, 713
COR equation, 585, 658
Corky, 885, 968, 1011
Correlation Dimension, 1147, 1152, 1153, 1158-1160
Correlation sum, 1152, 1158
Corrosion, 58, 86-93, 1082
Counter Melody, 816
Coupling coefficient (parameter), 108, 137-139, 372, 383
Coupled impedance, 948-949
Coupling Strength, 380
Covalent, 361, 486
Cracking, 86-93, 487, 489, 1082
Cracks, 58, 61, 88-92, 380-381, 486, 1082
Crisscross Wrap, 603
Critical Band, 1037
Critical Points, 297-304
Critical detuning frequency, 1131
Crystal imperfection, 381
Crystallographic structure, 93-97, 381
Cubic Coupling, 139, 161, 204, 984
Cubic dependence, 380
Curvature, 124-125, 276, 284, 333
Cut-off Frequency, 617, 619, 647/ 649, 708, 720, 722
Cutout, 78, 81, 1108, 1109

Cymbals, 33, 1078, 1109, 1111

D

Damping, 94, 104, 122, 245, 246, 353, 375-377, 378, 380-383, 866
Damping capacity, 102, 104, 375-378, 382-383, 837-839
Damping Capacity Coefficient, 376-377
Dashpot, 519-520
Dead Sticks, 704, 710-716, 723-739, 780
Decibel (db), 424, 425, 427
De-emphasis, 693-695
Defects, 95, 379, 382, 837
Degrees of Freedom, 81, 135, 686, 901, 1152
Delay time, 1023, 1029-1030
Delayed stick retrieval, 614-617
De-localization, 324, 328-329, 794
Density — (brass, steel, air), 57
(air, wood, bamboo, rubber), 570
Determinant, 407, 1127
Detuning, 137, 159, 202, 257, 366, 797, 866-867, 869, 880, 883, 888, 967, 995-1004, 1024
Diatonic, 800-805
Diene, 486
Diffusion Zone, 106
Diminished Fifth, 803, 806
Directivity function, 452, 455
Discretization, 233, 566, 1159
Discrete time series, 783, 1123
Dislocation, 95-97, 381-382
Displacement, 81, 117, 126, 129, 130, 134, 140, 166, 171-188, 280
Displacement Controlled Oscillator (DCO), 398
Displacement-time profile, 554, 557,
Dissipation, 378-380, 481, 536-540
Distribution function, 121, 684, 698
Distribution of notes (table), 816, 819
Domain, 113, 184-188, 196-210, 230, 379, 1079, 1114
Domain walls, 379-383
Double Bonds, 486, 487
Double Guitar, 793, 812, 816, 818

Double Peaks, 255, 373, 374
Double Second, 36, 102, 111, 213-217, 793, 811, 816
Double Tenor, 793, 811
Drift, 252-253, 415, 875
Driving force, 137, 154, 285, 600, 700-753
Drum, 53-72, 792, 888, 1041, 1045-1047, 1051, 1075, 1077
Dynamic stiffness, 112, 271, 274, 375, 377, 637, 895
Dynamical Analysis, 509,
Dynamical Equations, 108, 122, 125, 134-135, 260, 689, 754-761

E

Ear (the human ear), 423, 425-432, 1033-1040
Effective COR (eCOR), 594, 627, 676,
Effective stiffness, 458, 466, 604, 637, 845, 951,
Eigenmodes, 438, 443
Eigenvalue, 78, 409, 1128-1133
Elastic, 56, 58, 62, 82, 107, 110
Elastic Deformation, 110
Elastomer, 488
Electromagnetic vibrator, 121, 417, 464, 1004
Elliot "Ellie" Mannette, 50, 51, 824, 851, 1010,
Ellipsoidal Notes, 41-42, 143-147, 356, 391, 407, 411-412, 902-906, 908-909, 911-916, 934-937, 938-943
Elliptical planform, 114, 131, 143-148, 388, 903, 917, 921, 938
Elliptical plate, 40, 146, 153, 407-412
Embedding dimension, 1151-1153, 1158-1160
Emphasis (mode), 693
Energy balance, 585-588
Energy Balance Method, 589, 593, 654-659
Energy Exchanges, 39, 196, 778, 945, 1099
Energy loss, 104, 378, 379, 459, 460, 478, 482, 588, 662, 866, 953, 1111,

Engineering Designs, 353, 386, 940, 1112
Engineering Formulas
— the Major Sound, 754, 756
— the Minor Sound, 761
Enharmonic, 803, 805, 806
Ensemble Effect — see Chorus Effect
Entropy, 488, 1150
Equal-loudness contours, 426, 427, 432
Equal-loudness curves, 426, 427
Equal Temperament, 796, 800, 802-803
Equilibrium, 61, 62, 65, 70, 155, 271, 297, 298-302, 323, 1091
Equivalent Electrical Circuit, 466, 467
Equivalent radiation mass, 458, 463, 1067
Error displacement, 398, 400
Euler Load, 323,
Eutectoid Reaction, 97, 98
Eutectoid temperature, 98, 100, 101
Exact-integer-ratio law, 801
Exotic effects, 1119, 1120, 1121
Expansion, 56, 57, 363,
Exponential law, 229

F

Far-field, 440, 441, 443, 449, 450-454, 989
Fatigue, 58, 74, 90, 106, 279, 486,
Feedback— Aural, 615, 674-677
—Tactile, 566, 574, 582, 606, 615, 674-677
—Visual, 674
Feel, 534, 574, 604, 677
Feigenbaum scenario, 1154, 1166,
Ferrite, 98, 100, 106
Fifth, 365, 796, 801, 803-806, 854, 931, 938, 940, 992, 1000, 1040
Fillet weld, 73, 74, 85, 86, 90
Filter, 826-827
Filter network, 827-828
Fine tuning, 141, 254, 908, 967, 985, 996, 1015
Finishing touch, 996

First Tuning, 103, 132, 383, 384, 993, 1019,
Five-Fourths (5/4ths) Law, 42, 117, 131, 144, 365-366, 889, 897-899, 908-932, 939, 992, 1079, 1110
Fixed point, 296-298, 633, 1128, 1129, 1155
Flapping, 59, 112, 143, 267-271, 282, 942, 984, 1091, 1102, 1103,
Flat (musical definition), 252, 804-806
Flat radiator, 440-443, 454,
Flavor, 962, 963, 1021, 1062
Flexural/torsional buckle, 75-79, 1108
Flexure, 1104, 1105-1106
Flexural rigidity, 120, 1107
Flow—analogy, 64, 66, 829-831,
—in phase space, 228, 1124, 1149
—plastic, 62, 1059, 1086
Force Distribution, 64, 82, 129, 326-329, 758, 1085
Force Profiles, 527, 544, 649, 718, 736
Forced Oscillations, 120, 1076
Force-fitted, 595
Force-Time history, 121, 530, 717
Forge, 105
Forming, 53, 54, 56, 60, 62, 85, 89, 124, 185, 832, 847, 934, 986, 1019
Forte (definition), 170, 172, 179, 208
Fourier expansion, 702, 703
Fourier Transform, 42, 163, 164, 198, 231, 442, 703-714, 768, 1156
Fractal, 1148, 1151-1159
Free Phase, 157, 403, 523, 755-761, 783, 960
Free Vibration, 154, 161, 188, 515, 523
Frequency band-limiting, 154, 493, 620, 737-742, 744, 746, 763-779, 820-821, 1051, 1081
Frequency Discrimination, 1035
Frequency domain, 164, 439, 703
Frequency doubling, 157
Frequency Modulation, 161, 175-178, 209-212, 252, 400, 439, 798, 875, 1085
Frequency meters, 861, 973, 996
Frequency Profiles, 872, 877, 959-960
Frequency pulling, 945, 948-956

Frequency Shifts, 112, 114, 159, 252, 274-276, 354-365, 367, 415, 951
Frequency Splitting, 257
Frequency-Amplitude Dependence, 231, 252
Frobenius Method, 512
Functionals, 127, 267
Fully band-limited, 743, 745
Fundamental Law of the Steelpan, 889, 892-897, 927
Fundamental mode, 108, 151, 366, 410, 416, 454
Furnace, 99, 102, 106
Fused tone, 1035-1038

G

Galerkin average, 127, 128, 265, 690
Gamelan, 345, 1078, 1079
G-Bass, 1058, 1098
General nonsense, 1048, 1070
Generalized Wavelength, 105, 493, 763-770, 774, 1072, 1100
Glassy, 489
Gliss (Glissando), 863, 878-880
Gong, 345, 1078
Good Stick, 648, 661, 711, 716, 723-725, 779
G-Pan, 1041
Gradation of Tones, 862
Grain size, 95-96, 943
Grain boundaries, 95-96, 943
Grayness, 96
Grassberger-Procaccia (see Correlation Dimension)
Green's function, 441
Grooveless Notes, 46, 90, 103, 186, 986-987, 996
Grooves, 79, 87-90, 114, 151, 378, 439-440, 794, 839-841, 843, 1107,
G-Soprano, 1054, 1098, 1111
Guiding Principles, 771, 779, 827
Guitar, 47, 111, 219, 223, 489, 619, 651, 784, 793, 812, 816, 865, 1060

H

Half-Sine Force Function, 121, 169, 649

Hammer, 50, 60-62
Hammer marks, 327, 332, 905
Hammer Peening, 54, 57-59, 60-62, 95, 96, 111-112, 270, 293, 382, 832, 844-847, 955, 977, 1059
Hand Action, 484, 525, 528, 609, 614, 645, 717
Hand Control, 523, 676
Handel's Hallelujah Chorus, 891, 1031, 1063
Hard Note, 525, 582
Hardening Springs, 258, 293, 294, 295-297, 349, 1135
Hardsurfacing, 490
Harmonic (definition of), 126, 159, 172, 202
Harmonics, 115, 253, 257, 366, 380, 399, 404, 797, 861, 867-877
Harmonic Balance Method (HBM), 250
Harmonic loading, 120, 121
Harmony, 802, 816, 1061, 1063
Harshness, 717, 1033
Hass effect, 455
Heat treatment, 57, 59, 60, 96, 97, 99, 101, 279, 382
Heating, 141, 142, 382, 985
Heaviside step function, 616, 1153
Hertzian impact, 499, 560
Heterodyning, 253, 256
Hiding, 851-858
Holomorphic, 1127
Homogeneous, 34, 119, 340, 573
Homophony, 1063
Hooke's Law, 110, 494, 520
Hoop stress, 62, 82-86, 366, 795, 1067, 1082, 1088-1092, 1094
Hopf bifurcation, 115, 1119-1146
Horns, 365, 482
Humps, 332, 600-603
Hydrogenation, 486
Hysteresis, 228, 297, 488, 494-497, 522, 539, 562, 564, 612, 640
Hysteretic Losses, 585-587, 655
Hysteretic tip, 590

I

Identity matrix, 1128

Idiophone, 33, 792, 1041, 1076, 1077, 1111, 1115
Image Note, 877-883
Impact Abrasion, 490
Impact Dynamics, 515, 609, 679
Impact Equations, 689
Impact force spectrum, 719, 737-739,
Impact Phase, 153, 483, 492, 522, 683, 755, 757, 783,
Impactor, 58, 499-508
Impact speed (velocity), 121, 660, 771
Impedance, 57, 287, 436, 441, 457-459, 460, 568, 581, 826-839, 843-853, 945, 948
Impulse, 151, 156
Impulsive loading, 153, 492
Impulsive Sine, 706
Inclusions, 381, 837
Incoherent sources, 429-430
Indentations, 58, 332, 503
Inflection point, 337, 339-340
Initial contact force, 540-544, 747
Initial Mode Excitation, 771, 777
In-plane loading, 122, 124, 267, 370
Instantaneous frequency, 400
Intensity, 81, 91, 203, 209, 286, 390, 425, 426, 428, 431, 449-454, 464-468, 472, 636, 677, 731
Internal Damping, 122, 228, 379, 400, 927
Internal Forces, 280, 282-284, 330, 510
Internal Resonance, 108, 115, 122, 138, 139, 156, 183, 191, 197, 254, 257, 282, 349, 953, 954, 1121
Internal Stresses, 73, 80, 112, 129, 132, 248, 353, 892, 923, 1085, 1091
Internote, 112, 184, 186, 279, 325, 329, 390, 436, 440, 791, 794, 827, 828-834, 835, 839-850, 887-897, 1055
Interval (musical), 365, 366, 800-806, 913, 922-924, 945, 967,
Invaders C & D-Pan Tenor, 810, 816, 818, 819
Inverse Problem, 108, 227, 231
Inverse Square Law, 427, 428, 449,
Isophones, 426

Isoprene, 485, 486
Isotropic, 340, 363, 454
Iteration, 137, 628, 636, 1148

J

Jacobian (matrix), 1128, 1130
Jump Phenomenon, 115, 296, 297, 309, 1119, 1121-1141

K

Key-note, 39, 135, 161, 308, 322, 388, 393, 790, 796, 797, 940, 947, 1002

L

Latex, 485
Law of Ratios, 366, 889, 921, 922-924
Limit cycle, 1124, 1130, 1148, 1154
Linear Approximation, 510, 511, 533, 535, 552
Linear Expansion Coefficient, 57
Linear expansion/contraction, 57, 363
Linear Internal Forces, 282, 285, 294, 295, 306, 307
Linear stability, 1128,
Linearize, 78, 156, 188, 305, 307, 509, 510, 528, 1128,
Load Analysis, 63, 68
Loading ratio, 410
Loading-unloading cycles, 494-498
Load participation factor, 688
Localized Stresses, 85, 87, 588, 925
Lock, 395, 396, 399-401
Locked modes, 396, 397, 403
Locking condition, 400-403
Longitudinal modes (vibration), 119, 154, 378, 840, 841, 848, 1109
Lorentzian, 710
Loss, 76, 105, 375-379, 427, 437, 459, 465, 476, 481, 531-546, 627, 662, 711, 728, 747, 761
Lossy overlay, 605, 628, 662, 754, 774
Loudness, 390, 426 428, 468, 843, 1053, 1080
Loudness problem (bass), 390

Low carbon steel, 55-57, 86, 95, 99-100, 279, 360, 481,
Low Temperature Stress Relief Anneal, 96-102, 318, 1019,
Lumped parameter, 187, 829, 850
Lyapunov exponents, 1147, 1148-1150, 1160, 1169

M

Magnetic Anisotropy, 381
Magnetic Domain (walls), 379, 380, 837, 843
Magnetization, 95, 379, 381
Magnetomechanical Damping (MMD), 97, 230, 247, 377, 379, 457, 459, 465, 477, 481, 843
Magnetomechanical Energy, 380, 381,
Magnetostriction, 104, 381
Major, 800
Major [Second, Third etc), 801-803, 805, 824,
Malleability, 97, 934, 992
Mannette, Ellie (see Elliot Mannette)
Marginal Notes, 648-650, 725, 727-742
Marginal Zone, 650, 725, 727-742
Marginally stable, 1129
Marimba, 1074, 1098
Marking, 111
Marshall, Bertie (see Bertie Marshall)
Marshall Pairs, 190, 196, 794, 796, 818, 954, 989- 992, 1001-1003, 1057
Martensite, 99,
Mass conservation (see conservation of mass)
Mass loading, 104, 213, 225, 405-421, 457, 463, 475, 481, 846, 951, 1083, 1084, 1111
Master Pan Maker, 25, 85, 103, 799
Master Tuner, 35, 36, 272, 323, 472, 799, 889, 985
Master Blender, 799
Maximum Detuning, 930, 1022, 1024
MDOF, 126, 135, 259, 294, 684, 689
Mechanical Bias, 324, 328-331, 387, 388-393, 755, 987, 988, 1052, 1087
Mechanical computer, 977

Mechanical Failure, 61, 90
Mechanical Filters, 183, 186, 826-828, 851, 852
Mechanical impedance, 287, 457-459, 827-836, 845, 849, 853, 948-958
Mechanical resistance, 104, 287, 289, 375, 376, 459, 476, 480, 521, 605, 662, 701, 714, 747,
Mechanical work, 585, 587
Melody, 740, 795, 798, 816, 883, 1021, 1061
Membranophone, 972, 1041, 1045, 1077, 1115
Microphone, 418, 429, 431, 1032
Microstructural Control, 353, 381, 382, 845
Minimization, 233
Mini-Pans, 76-81
Minor (Scale, Second etc), 800-805
Mirror Functions, 232-246
Mistuning, 159, 878
Möbius strip, 1154
Modal Amplitudes, 161, 220, 230, 246, 397, 970
Modal Equivalent Mass, 687, 688
Modal Frequencies, 140, 173, 217, 284, 375, 415, 438, 690, 775, 908, 921, 945, 960, 984, 985, 1086
Mode Confinement, 38, 41, 152, 215, 246, 987, 1009, 1100
Mode conversion, 359, 378, 840, 844, 848, 1109
Mode coupling, 115, 281, 397, 932, 1038, 1120
Mode Localization, 111, 114, 151-152, 230, 246, 791, 794, 926, 988, 1079
Mode locking (see Lock)
Model stick, 499, 518
Monomer, 485
Monophony, 1063
Multi Time-scale Analysis, 157, 189
Musical range, 34, 111, 293, 745, 746, 807, 809, 816, 819, 1042, 1053
Musical Scales — Pythagorean, 800
— Just Intonation, 801
— Equal Temperament (12-TET), 802

Musically tuned state, 905, 945, 994, 995, 999
Musical space, 959, 962, 997

N

Natural (musical definition), 804-806
Near-field, 450, 857
Nested Radical, 628, 630-633
Nickel-Plated Notes, 57, 92, 103, 104, 477, 481, 482, 762, 837
Nine bass, 793, 807, 815
Nine-Eights (9/8ths) Rule, 117, 365, 366, 393, 931-939, 988, 992, 1004
Nipple, 343, 345, 348, 349
Nitriding, 105
Non-linear Internal Forces, 282
Non-linear Springs, 1135,
Note Geometries, 280, 397
Non-Linearity, 108, 139, 156, 395, 494, 822, 1156
Non-resonant oscillation, 466, 708, 752, 753, 1048, 1077
Non-transposing, 795
Note covers, 1054
Note Distributions, 817-819, 824
Note Placements, 810, 824, 849, 857,
Note Shape, 44, 130, 134, 262, 272, 277, 311, 333-350, 472, 847, 904, 934, 937
Note stiffness, 269, 273, 341, 354, 384, 941-942
Note Types (singles, pairs, triple), 816-818
Note-note coupling, 100, 199, 202, 205, 812, 843, 849, 1003, 1026, 1028, 1055
Note-Skirt Interactions, 183, 187, 193, 198, 208, 213, 224, 435, 744, 1076, 1097
Nuances (of touch), 660, 661, 799, 865, 1014, 1023, 1101
Number of players — multiple voices, 1029,
Numerical Modeling, 139, 169, 172, 178, 179, 207, 641

Numerical Solution, 144, 147, 169, 235-256, 309, 333, 469, 540, 755, 1161

O

Obliquity, 59
Octave, 39, 155, 159, 161, 201, 225, 308, 395, 785, 796, 802, 940, 974
Optimizing, 244
Optimization, 131, 321, 322, 339, 342, 472, 1054, 1055, 1080, 1101
Orbit, 298, 300, 1123, 1148, 1154,
Closed orbit, 298, 1124
Orchestra, 35-37, 49, 450, 646, 740, 795, 799
Ordinary Differential Equation (ODE), 136, 265, 782, 1121, 1125
Oxidation, 486-490
Oxygen, 486-490
Ozone, 486-490

P

Panist, 693, 799
Pan Face, 817, 826, 846, 847, 849, 892, 904, 927, 1003, 1055, 1084, 1088, 1093
Pan Jumbie, 131, 1088-1091, 1093, 1095, 1101, 1102, 1103
Pan maker, 799, 899
Pan Maker's Formula, 143, 149, 150, 940
Pan types, 793, 799, 809, 860
Pang, 342, 348
Parametric Excitations, 156, 201, 248-257
Partially Opened Skirts, 217, 25, 423
Partially tuned note, 248, 1161, 1166
Partials, 139, 144, 159, 322, 756, 796, 797, 798, 800, 867, 869-872, 882, 895, 910, 913, 922-924
Pascal, 318
Patents, 1041, 1048
Pearlite, 98, 99

Peening (see hammer peening)
Perceived Depth (tonal), 854
Percussion, 185, 278, 395, 742, 792, 865, 1077, 1114-1115
Perfect Fifth, 802-805
Perfect Fourth, 802-805
Period, 1123-1123
Period-Doubling, 1154, 1157, 1166
Periodicity, 1123-1124
Periodic orbit, 298, 1123, 1124, 1155
Perturbation, 146-148, 272, 914
Phase ambiguity, 165
Phase Flow, 228, 1124
Phase portrait, 1164-1169
Phase space, 230, 298, 355, 1123-1125, 1148, 1151
Phasor, 440, 442, 448
Phons, 427, 428
Piano, 179, 180, 208, 211, 802
P-index, 489, 495-498, 509, 683
Ping-Pong, 26, 30, 50, 793
Pinning sites, 97, 381, 383,
Pipes, 365, 581, 1098, 1099-1100
Pitch, 426, 771, 795, 798, 804, 868-872, 1011
Pitch flattening, 152
Pitch Glide, 872, 878-880, 965
Pitch inflection, 798, 799
Pitch-matching, 790
Planform, 114, 117, 131, 143-147
Plastic Flow (deformation), 62, 90, 92, 96, 99, 110, 1059, 1086,
Plasticity, 97
Plastic strain, 1091
Player's Action, 27, 692
Playing the Roll, 781
Plexus, 183, 230, 791, 826
Poincaré-Bendixson theorem, 1155
Poincaré Map, 1148
Poincaré section, 1148, 1154
Point Impedance, 831
Poisson's ratio, 56, 57, 110
Polar radiation pattern, 452, 456
Polymer, 104, 485, 486-489
Polyphony, 1063
Potential Energy, 78, 280, 299-304, 585, 587, 673, 1161, 1163

Potential Wells, 204, 258, 280, 297, 299, 314
Powder Coating, 104, 414, 457, 468, 478, 480, 762, 837
Power law, 257, 495, 499, 522, 683, 1070-1073, 1151, 1158,
Power Relations, 289
Precedence Effect, 455-457
Prefinishing, 106
Preload, 67, 71
Preparation, 36, 52, 92, 100, 111, 247, 382, 391, 472, 753, 844-846, 982, 992, 1018, 1056, 1083, 1098
Pressure distribution, 503, 608, 679, 680, 684
Pre-stress, 65, 324, 608, 609, 620, 637, 660, 777
Primary forces, 701, 708
Process Control Schedule, 59-60
Product Rule, 138
Protective chemicals, 489,
Proximity effect, 574, 664, 672, 687, 1006
Psychoacoustic, 423, 456, 457, 854, 1031, 1034
Pulling, 945-956
Pulling Effect, 945
Pull-in range, 401, 954, 956
Pumping action, 215
Pung tone, 159, 347, 403, 430, 867, 883-884, 887, 954-968, 1000, 1011
Pure tones, 426, 1034, 1035

Q

Quadraphonic, 740, 793, 812, 816, 823, 1042
Quadratic Coupling, 115, 137, 160, 200- 207, 295, 351, 868, 950, 969, 974, 1030
Quadratic non-linearity, 115, 139, 156, 867
Quality Factor, Q, 258, 291-293, 375, 418, 437, 703, 866, 953, 1137, 1142
Quasi-periodic, 164, 172, 1120, 1144, 1154, 1157
Quiescent point, 155, 315, 325, 332, 339, 349, 386, 391, 654, 690, 755

Quiescent State, 129, 130, 139, 156, 302, 308, 314, 315, 336, 716, 1087, 1120

R

Radiation directivity, 436, 452, 454
Radiation mass (see equivalent radiation mass)
Radiation pattern, 432-435, 451-456,
Radiation pressure (see Acoustical pressure)
Raman waves, 152
Rawform, 52-106, 278
Rayleigh Integral Method, 439, 440-466
Receptance Method, 405-421
Reconstructed phase space, 1151, 1165, 1170
Recovery, 97, 99
Recrystallization, 97, 99
Recurrence formula (relation), 628-635
Recurrence plots, 1147
Reflected Impedance, 945-957
Reinforcement, 190, 434, 823, 825, 1002, 1057
Resident Octave, 201, 202, 395, 443-444, 785, 796-797, 817, 823, 921, 949, 982-983, 988-1004
Resident Twelfth, 395, 443-444, 796-797, 817, 921, 982-983, 988-1004
Residual compression, 497, 539, 585-587, 612, 627, 657, 662-663
Residual Stress, 34, 58, 60-62, 73, 75, 85-87, 90, 91, 133, 247, 271, 274 354, 869, 984, 993
Resistance (see Mechanical Resistance)
Resistive force, 542-547, 716, 717, 751,
Resonance, 115, 122, 138, 156, 191-197, 218, 224-226, 267, 289- 296
Resonance Curve, 289, 291, 296
Resonant Absorber, 827, 851-852
Resonator, 365, 1073, 1074-1076, 1099
Response, 284, 285, 463
Responsiveness, 604, 641, 662, 736, 821
Restitution, 497-499, 509, 582-890

Restitution Formula, 611-614, 622-628
Restitution phase, 494-496, 427, 530, 544, 617
Restoring Forces, 64, 156, 251, 603, 605
Return plots (see Recurrence plots), 1147
Rhythm, 44, 675, 784, 793, 799
Rigid vibrators, 33, 395
Rise, 44, 116-117
Rise factor, 117
Roots, 218, 261
Roughness, 1038
Routh array (tableau), 1129
Routh-Hurwitz criterion (theorem), 1129, 1132
Rubber, 27, 35, 57, 485-491, 496-498, 534, 570

S

Sampling, 165, 168, 233, 706, 1123, 1136
Saturation, 60-61, 839, 845,
Scale invariance, 1151
SDOF, 249, 258-267, 174, 312, 458, 509, 517, 522, 524, 683, 686, 702, 747, 760, 948,
Seam (see Chime)
Second octave, 161, 185, 187, 202, 817, 871, 882, 973, 995, 1030
Secondary notes (side notes), 1096, 1096, 1099
Secondary Well, 302, 303-308, 314-322, 1161--62,
Secular terms, 159-160
Self Similarity, 380, 1151, 1154, 1158
Semitone, 802, 803-806
Shallow shell, 111, 117, 118, 148, 405, 792-794, 913,
Shank, 487
Shank absorption (losses), 573, 588, 622, 626, 627, 655, 662, 674, 699
Shape Function, 124-139, 868
Shaping, 34, 42, 104, 124, 309, 959, 1019

Shaping Function, 124, 264, 312, 335, 339, 472, 868
Sharp (musical definition), 112, 804-805
Shells, 33, 34, 41, 84, 85, 107-120, 405
Short Time Fourier Transform, 163, 198, 231, 873, 1147
Signal Processing, 163, 232
Silicone, 487, 673, 711, 1007
Simple piston, 445-447, 457
Simulation, 151, 183, 234, 239, 243, 872, 873, 884, 1140
Sinking, 54, 57, 59, 60, 63, 68, 332, 382, 472, 839, 845, 855, 982, 1003, 1019, 1091
Skirt, 34, 53, 75, 193, 194, 198, 217, 221, 224
Slater, Tony, 958, 963, 1017
Slip and stick, 152
Slow time, 158, 189, 232, 396
Softening effect, 258, 294, 296, 638
Softening Springs, 293
Solvability Equations, 160, 191, 195
Sonority, 825, 826
Sopranino pan, 820
Sound (definition of), 423
Sound Intensity, 425-426
Sound Intensity Level, 425-426
Sound Level, 431-433
Sound Level meter, 431
Sound Pressure Level (SPL), 424-431
S-Pan, 800, 865, 1043, 1046
Spatial coherence, 438, 443
Spatial Fourier Transform, 442, 768
Spatial frequency, 442
Spectra (spectrum), 108, 126, 170-172, 200-214, 255, 367
Spectral Distribution of Contact Forces, 719-744 932
Spectral Magnitude, 1023, 1030
Spectral peaks, 254, 366, 368, 372-385
Speed (Velocity) of Sound, 57, 425, 438,
Spring Supports, 904, 907, 985, 986
Stability, 53, 58, 75, 78, 84, 85-86, 102, 275, 303-308, 330, 336, 795, 942, 993, 1010, 1052, 1086
Stable state, 76, 302, 993, 1120

Stainless steel, 56
Standard Frequency of Reference, 806
Standard Pan (Standardization), 826, 819, 859, 1042, 1043
Standing waves, 422, 482, 1074, 1099
Static and Dimensional Stability, 75
Static force, 62, 65, 129, 130, 132, 136, 325-327, 329, 330
Static State, 127, 129, 133, 139, 259, 267, 271
Statical Analysis, 107, 499
Stationary point, 297, 298
Stationary bifurcation, 1129-1132
Steady state, 250, 285, 286, 458, 1123
Steel Gauges, 55
Steelband (Steel Orchestra, Ensemble or Band), see orchestra
Steelpan (Pan) (definition), 791
Steelpan Cut-Off Frequency, 722
Steelpan Law, 922
Steelpan Law of Ratios, 366, 889, 921-924
Stick, 27, 35, 485
Stick aging, 485
Stick compliance, 494, 496
Stick compression, 494, 497, 522,
Stick Compression Formula, 624-626, 628, 629, 656,
Stick Contact Noise (SCN), 747, 749-753, 759, 761, 819, 821, 1006
Stick dissipation (losses), 536, 548, 755, 774, 780, 1055
Stick Impact, 43, 120, 153, 179, 330, 387, 388, 390, 517, 646-654, 746, 758, 772
Stick-Note Interaction, 120, 481, 610, 773, 933, 1055,
Stick-Note Clap (SNC) see SCN
Stick Restitution, 628, 647, 655, 683
Stick Restitution Formula, 626-627, 656
Stick retrieval (advanced & delayed), 454, 614-620, 622, 644-645, 648, 645
Stick Retrieval Force, 616, 617, 644-649, 653, 718
Stick tip, 549, 553, 565, 576, 595, 605, 637, 674

Stick-Note Impact Function, 692, 693-704, 769
Stick-Note System, 499, 509
Stick-print technique, 553
Stiffeners, 85, 194, 218, 223, 224, 841, 992, 1107
Stiffness, 66,67, 77, 112, 120, 269, 338, 339, 637, 839, 941
Stiffness matrix, 433
Strain, 109
Strain hardening, 58, 97
Strange attractor, 1147, 1148, 1165
Stress, 109
Stress Concentration, 61, 82, 89, 90, 841-843, 1087
Stress Corrosion Cracking (SCC), 86-93, 1056, 1100
Stress Loading, 81, 301-305
Stress Relaxation, 61, 112, 279, 384, 385, 993
Stress Relief (stress relief anneal), 59, 60, 90, 92, 97-102, 133, 143, 270, 279, 293, 329, 382
Stretch-fitted (stick tip), 595
Strong Marshall Pair, 797, 825, 954, 989, 1001
Structural defects, 379
Structural engineering, 1088, 1093
Strumming, 47, 784, 818, 823, 1021
Sub-harmonic, 202, 857, 1040
Superposition, 250, 457, 753, 1034
Sweetspot, 121, 170, 196, 315, 693, 694, 698
Swinging stick method, 665-672
Swinging stick COR formula, 669
Symmetry, 901, 908, 913-914
    broken symmetry, 901
Sympathetic Pairs, 107, 190, 742, 784, 1120
Sympathetic Vibration, 190, 196, 225, 436, 744, 785, 796, 851, 854, 989, 1024, 1042(read 1076),
Synchronous mode, 399, 402
Synthetic rubber, 486, 595
System Stability, 307, 336

T

Tactile (feedback), 566, 573, 574, 615, 674-677, 684
Tangent (fold) bifurcation, 1131
Technical errors, 1064
Temperature Effects, 123, 124, 341
Template, 60, 390, 899, 938, 939, 1048, 1069-1072
Tenor, 34, 35, 103, 111, 185, 219, 236, 367, 643, 644, 645, 721740
Tenor-Pair, 883
Tension, 109, 1007-1009, 1041, 1045-1047, 1051, 1056-1059, 1077, 1078, 1081, 1082, 1087
Tensional Stress, 109, 1082, 1085
Theiler window, 1153
Thermal Energy, 383
Thermal Stress, 108, 114,122, 123, 129, 132- 135, 139, 142, 264, 273, 275, 276, 325, 330, 338, 353
Third (key-note-octave-third), 796
Time-continuous system, 1139
Tight, 52, 65
Tight (as in 'Corky'), 885
Tightening (see Blocking), 149, 279, 333, 472, 836, 896, 942
Timbre, 366, 368, 371, 615, 773, 781, 865, 868, 869, 961, 969, 1010, 1011, 1014, 1038
Time-dependent Contact Pressure Distribution, 680
Time Domain, 153, 171, 250, 704, 710
Time-History, 116, 121, 153, 173, 182, 200, 214, 492, 706
Time-weighting, 432
Tin-Can experiments, 76
Tip Compression, 505, 624, 626, 786
Tip displacement, 494, 554, 646
Tipping point, 1131
Tip stiffness, 489, 536, 637, 673, 757
Tonal color, 808, 865, 969, 1053
Tonal Structure, 861, 865, 970, 989, 1063
Tonality, 48, 104, 136, 142, 159, 268, 310, 369, 390, 395, 481, 540, 620, 661, 675-677, 974, 999

Tonic, 282, 308
Torsion, 75, 77
Torsional modes, 75-81, 119, 1108-1110, 1116
Traditional note, 39, 41, 111, 113, 114, 439, 791, 832, 891, 892
Trajectory, 1123
Transient, 151, 285-286, 588
Transition Period, 383-384
Transitional state, 883
Transition temperature, 489
Transmission, 186-188, 566-578
Transmission Losses, 186, 196, 230, 377, 378, 465
Transposing (non-transposing), 795
Tremolando, 781
Tremolo, 798, 1022, 1028,
Triple (see Note types)
Triple-Seamed Chime, 54, 72, 85
Tritone, 802, 803
True Note, 79, 114, 144, 145, 151, 181, 183, 230, 246, 377, 377, 381, 439, 687, 693, 791, 794
Tuner (definition), 790, 796, 799
Tuning, 789-1020
Tuning down, 871
Tuning up, 871
"Tuning the harmonics", 884, 885, 888, 968
Tuned State, 106, 142, 278, 308, 341, 795, 796
Tuning Rules, 992-1004
Tuning Scenarios, 789, 959-967
Tuning Temperature, 274, 330, 341, 353-354
Turning point, 297, 299, 304, 336, 526
Twelfth, 796, 797, 801, 806, 807, 817, 825, 854, 967, 869-871, 873-876, 903-908, 1000-1011

U

Unsaturation, 486,
Unstable behaviour, 1120
Untuned, 198, 246, 247, 249, 316, 357, 366
Unwrapping procedure, 165,
UV, 489,

V

Velocity (of sound) see speed of sound
Velocity method, 589, 593, 654, 656
Velocity potential, 441, 442
Velocity response, 199, 829-835, 957-958
Vertical tangencies, 1130, 1131, 1143
Vibrato, 798, 808
Voice, 46, 457, 646, 799, 818, 819, 1011, 1015- 1030, 1060-1066
Voicing — the pan, 883, 1008
—the sticks, 662, 782, 865, 1008-1010

W

Wave number (see Spatial Frequency)
Wave Scattering, 381, 565-568, 588, 841-843, 844
Wavelength, 105, 154, 332, 441, 449, 454, 493
Wavelength Band-Limiting, 646, 700, 738, 763-775, 821, 1051, 1072, 1080, 1081, 1100
Weak Marshall pair, 797, 825
Weighting network, 432
Weights, 432, 846
Weld, 54, 58, 72-86, 90, 1052
Weld run, 75
Weld toe, 73
Welded Chimes (Seams), 72, 74, 86, 1079
Whitney embedding prevalence theorem, 1153
Whole Tone, 802, 803, 811-813, 817, 851, 1037
Williams, Anthony (see Anthony Williams)
Window, 164-165
Wobbly Effect, 390-391
Work hardening, 465, 832, 837, 839, 1087. 1104, 1105
Working G-Pan, 1045, 1051, 1058, 1051
Wrapped stick, 490, 491, 495, 547, 567, 574-576, 587, 594-604

Wrapping stress, 598
Wrapping tension, 594-604

X

Xylophone, 1074, 1098

Y

Yield, 379, 386,
Young's modulus, 57, 103, 110, 358

Z

Zhong, 1078, 1079

CPSIA information can be obtained
at www.ICGtesting.com
Printed in the USA
BVHW041727190819
556131BV00004B/1/P